Notable Last Facts

Notable Last Facts

A Compendium of Endings, Conclusions, Terminations and Final Events Throughout History

Compiled by
William B. Brahms

Reference Desk Press, Inc.
Haddonfield, New Jersey

www.referencedeskpress.com

To Gina-Marie, Matthew and Giovanna

Publisher Cataloging-in-Publication Data
Brahms, William B. (1966 -)
    Notable Last Facts / by William B. Brahms.
        p.   cm.
    Includes bibliographic references and index
    ISBN 0-9765325-0-6
    1. Encyclopedias and dictionaries. I. Title
    AG5.B73   2005
    031.02—dc22   2005901194

Manufactured in the United States of America
Printed on acid-free, recycled paper
(90% recycled, 50% post consumer waste, 50% processed chlorine-free)
Reference Desk Press, Inc. supports the Green Press Initiative (GPI).

SAN: 256-4300

Reference Desk Press, Inc.
305 Briarwood Avenue
Haddonfield, NJ 08033-2907

info@referencedeskpress.com

www.referencedeskpress.com

Introduction

I started to accumulate information for *Notable Last Facts* in the early 1990s as a library student at Rutgers University. While reviewing core reference sources in a class on reference librarianship, the topic of researching famous or notable "firsts" was discussed and an excellent, encyclopedic resource was demonstrated. This prompted me to ask: Where would one go to research famous or notable "lasts?" When my question yielded nothing definitive, the idea (or rather the need) for an extensive basic reference work on "lasts" was born. I started collecting "lasts" in a file folder and then a database. This led to an organized exploration of specific subjects, searching for "lasts" for more than ten years. This first effort—a compilation of more than 16,000 "lasts"—is presented here as *Notable Last Facts*.

As a reference librarian, one of my goals in putting this material into print was to present it in the clearest, most concise way possible so that researchers can find the facts they seek quickly. Each "last" fact appears in boldface and is preceded by a bullet and the word "last" or an equivalent word, such as "end." The entry is accompanied by a brief description of the category, using the fewest words necessary to convey helpful background information for the fact seeker. An expanded table of contents provides an overview of the subject matter. And a detailed index lists the many thousands of notable last facts included in the book.

The facts came from many sources. The books, magazines, journals, atlases, almanacs, encyclopedias and other sources that provided helpful information are listed in the References (Books) section at the back of the book. Additionally, more than 5,000 web sites were consulted. Web sites that were particularly helpful were extracted and are listed in the References (Web Resources) section.

Use *Notable Last Facts* as a pathway to find more information about a subject. It will greatly aid in narrowing down a web or literature search. For example, if you want to find more about the last Confederate Civil War general in the field to surrender, you might get a half million hits if you do a web search with the words: "last," "Confederate," and "general." But *Notable Last Facts* will give you the name of that person: "General Stand Watie." By searching "Stand Watie" on the web you can reduce the hits to those that specifically mention him.

Every attempt has been made to provide the most accurate information possible. Sometimes conflicting data cropped up. In those instances, I've used what I believe was the most credible source after considerable digging and cross-checking. Despite the care with which *Notable Last Facts* has been checked and rechecked, it would be foolhardy to think no errors have crept in. When working with a huge amount of data such as this, it is very easy to introduce an error simply by brushing against the wrong key. If you spot an error, we would appreciate hearing from you at info@referencedeskpress.com or at Reference Desk Press, Inc., 305 Briarwood Avenue, Haddonfield, NJ 08033-2907. Give your sources, and we will check them out. And, if there are "lasts" you would like to see included, let us know about them, too.

Bill Brahms

Reference Desk Press, Inc.

Reference Desk Press, Inc., founded in 2004, is a publisher of books by librarians for librarians. RDP's corporate philosophy centers on the research experience of librarians to determine and produce unique reference sources that libraries especially need. RDP also works to support library advocacy, librarian recruitment and others issues related to the changing face of librarianship.

Expanded Table of Contents

Ages and Eras
(*See also* Literature; Nations; United States.)

Ages and Eras—Alexandrian Age
The Alexandrian Age was an era when Greek literature and learning were centered in Alexandria, Egypt. The Alexandrian Age began in the reign of Ptolemy I (323-285 B.C.). During that time, the great library was founded at Alexandria.
• **End of the Alexandrian Age:** c. 30 B.C. It ended when Rome became the dominant power.

Ages and Eras—Age of Aquarius, Age of Pisces, Age of Gemini, etc.
Age of Aquarius, Age of Pisces, Age of Gemini, etc., are astrological terms that refer to the procession of the equinoxes. There is no firm consensus among astrologers as to when any of these ended or will end.

Ages and Eras—Atomic Age *See* Ages and Eras—Industrial Revolution/Industrial Age.

Ages and Eras—Augustan Age
The Augustan Age was an era of peace in Rome (*pax Romana*) during which Roman literature and arts flourished. It was the period when Horace, Virgil and Ovid were working. Some scholars say it began in 31 B.C., when Octavian became Augustus Caesar, the sole ruler of the Roman Empire. Others set the beginning date at 27 B.C., when he announced his plans to restore the Roman Republic.
• **End of the Augustan Age:** 14 A.D., with the death of Augustus Caesar.

Ages and Eras—Baroque Era
The Baroque Era, or the Age of the Baroque, occurred during the 17th and part of the 18th centuries in Europe. It was a style of art, architecture or music that used elaborate ornamentation in an effort to create a dramatic effect.
• **End of the Baroque Era in art and architecture:** by the beginning of the 1700s.
• **End of the Baroque Era in music:** by 1750, the year Johann Sebastian Bach died.

Ages and Eras—Bronze Age *See* Ages and Eras—Stone Age, Bronze Age, Iron Age.

Ages and Eras—Age of Ceramics *See* Ages and Eras—Industrial Revolution/Industrial Age.

Ages and Eras—Classical Era
The Classical Era, or Classical Period, followed the Baroque Era. It was a time of restraint in literature, music, architecture and other arts. Classicism had its roots in ancient Greece and Rome and often served as a model for later classicists. It stressed order, balance, simplicity and proportion.
• **End of the Classical Era in Europe:** end of the 18th century or early in the 19th century, when it gave way to a nearly opposite period of Romanticism. In music, the ending dates often given are between 1820 and 1830.

Ages and Eras—Cold War Era *See* Wars and Battles—Cold War.

Ages and Eras—Colonial Era *See* United States—Colonial America.

Ages and Eras—Computer Age *See* Ages and Eras—Industrial Revolution/Industrial Age.

Ages and Eras—Confederation Era *See* United States—Confederation Era.

Ages and Eras—Counter-Reformation *See* Ages and Eras—Reformation/Counter-Reformation.

Ages and Eras—Dark Ages
The early centuries of the Middle Ages, beginning with the fall of the Roman Empire in the 5th century, are often referred to as the Dark Ages because when compared with other times in history, little written information has survived to describe life during that time.
• **End of the Dark Ages:** the 11th century A.D. The Dark Ages were followed by the High Middle Ages, which ended with the onset of the Renaissance.

Ages and Eras—Edwardian Age

The Edwardian Age is named for King Edward VII, who ruled the United Kingdom of Great Britain and Ireland from January 1901 until 1910. Among the upper classes, the era was a time of carefree, lighthearted behavior that marked a sharp departure from the primness and rigidity of the Victorian Age.

• **End of the Edwardian Age:** 1914, with Britain's entry into World War I; however, some historians say it ended on May 6, 1910, when Edward VII died.

Ages and Eras—Age of Enlightenment

The Enlightenment, or the Age of Reason, was a way of thinking in Europe that began in the late 1600s, picked up momentum with the death of French King Louis XIV in 1715, and peaked later in the 18th century. Many important scientific discoveries at that time produced a greater understanding of the natural world. Scientists were less superstitious and more rational in their explanations.

• **End of the Enlightenment:** the late 18th century. Some historians say it ended in 1789, with the beginning of the French Revolution. Others say it ended in 1799, when Napoleon I seized power.

Ages and Eras—Era of Good Feelings

The term Era of Good Feelings is often used to characterize the administration of U.S. President James Monroe, but that is not what it was originally intended to describe. It was coined in July 1817 after Monroe visited Boston, Massachusetts. A local newspaper used the phrase to describe the five days during which Monroe was given a glowing welcome by the city.

• **End of the Era of Good Feelings:** 1825, when James Monroe left office after his second term.

Ages and Eras—Age of Exploration

The Age of Exploration generally describes the time of European exploration and expansion that began in the 15th century.

• **End of the Age of Exploration:** 1620, 1779 or 1911. In the narrowest or traditional sense, the term Age of Exploration is applied to the period of initial exploration and conquest of the Western Hemisphere and is considered to have ended when organized settlements were established in America. Virginia settlements and the landing of the Pilgrims at Plymouth Bay in 1620 are often cited. By another definition, it ended with Captain James Cook. He was killed while exploring Hawaii in 1779. In the broadest sense, the Age of Exploration covers the entire time frame of exploration of new continents by Europeans (and later Americans) ending in 1911, when the first explorers reached the South Pole in Antarctica.

Ages and Eras—Geological Time Scale

Name	Began	Ended
Precambrian Time:		
Hadean Time	4.5 billion years ago	3.8 billion years ago
Archaean Era	3.8 billion years ago	2.5 billion years ago
Proterozoic Era	2.5 billion years ago	650 million years ago
Ventian Period	650 million years ago	544 million years ago
Paleozoic Era:		
Cambrian Period	544 million years ago	505 million years ago
Ordovician Period	505 million years ago	440 million years ago
Silurian Period	440 million years ago	410 million years ago
Devonian Period	410 million years ago	360 million years ago
Carboniferous Period:		
Mississippian Period	360 million years ago	325 million years ago
Pennsylvanian Period	325 million years ago	286 million years ago
Permian Period	286 million years ago	248 million years ago

Mesozoic Era:		
Triassic Period	248 million years ago	213 million years ago
Jurassic Period	213 million years ago	145 million years ago
Cretaceous Period	145 million years ago	65 million years ago. Mass extinction of the dinosaurs occurred at the end of this period.
Cenozoic Era:		
Tertiary Period:		
Paleocene Epoch	65 million years ago	55.5 million years ago
Eocene Epoch	55.5 million years ago	33.7 million years ago
Oligocene Epoch	33.7 million years ago	23.8 million years ago
Miocene Epoch	23.8 million years ago	5.3 million years ago
Pliocene Epoch	5.3 million years ago	1.8 million years ago
Quaternary Period:		
Pleistocene Epoch	1.8 million years ago	8,000 years ago. Ice Age ended.
Holocene Epoch	8,000 years ago	Present time

Ages and Eras—Gilded Age

The Gilded Age was an era of rapid economic, industrial, cultural and social expansion in the United States that began in 1865 at the end of the Civil War. It was a time when the pursuit of profit created corruption in business and government, a showy display of wealth and ruthless exploitation of natural resources. It took its name from the title of a novel *The Gilded Age* by Mark Twain and Charles D. Warner, published in 1873.

• **End of the Gilded Age:** Historians are divided on when the Gilded Age ended. Some place the ending at 1890, when the Progressive Era began. Others say it ended in 1900, with the end of the 19th century. Others say it ended in the first decade of the 20th century, during a monetary crisis. Still others say it ended in 1912, with the sinking of the *Titanic*.

Ages and Eras—Industrial Revolution/Industrial Age

The term Industrial Revolution originally was used to describe the technological changes that ended about midway through the 19th century as some nations moved from an agricultural to an industrial economy. However, some historians would argue that the Industrial Revolution is really a series of on-going phases. Using this view, the Industrial Age can be divided into a series of stages when specific technological changes stood out: Mechanical, Transportation and Chemical.

• **End of the Mechanical Revolution:** about 1800. The age was characterized by the development and proliferation of machines of production.

• **End of the Transportation Revolution:** around 1860. Other mechanical developments continued during this period, but the most significant changes that occurred were improvements in transportation technology, such as railroads and steamboats.

• **End of the Chemical Revolution:** about the 1970s. Mechanical and transportation developments continued during this period, but the most significant changes during this phase were represented by chemical engineering advances that led to the development of synthetic substances which were superior to and cheaper than natural substances. These products led to the decline in steel production, once the core of U.S. industry. New economic powers began to arise that lacked the natural resources to support a traditional industrial economy. Some scholars have suggested that the present stage of the Industrial Revolution could be termed the Age of Ceramics, Age of Plastics, Atomic Age, Age of Genetic Engineering, Age of the Computer, Information Age, Jet Age, Space Age and even the Post-Industrial Age. However, Ceramics, Plastics, Atomic

Energy, Genetic Engineering and Jets might all be viewed as later parts of the Transportation and Chemical Revolutions, leaving Computer and Information technology changes to forge a fourth revolution, perhaps called the Information Revolution.

Ages and Eras—Information Age *See* Ages and Eras—Industrial Revolution/ Industrial Age.

Ages and Eras—Jazz Age
The Jazz Age took its name from the syncopated improvisational music form that moved north from New Orleans, Louisiana, after World War I. The term was popularized in 1922 in *Tales of the Jazz Age*, a story by F. Scott Fitzgerald. It was a time of rebellion against the repressiveness of prewar America. Young people defied authority in their actions, arts and attire.
• **End of the Jazz Age:** 1929, with the stock market crash and the beginning of the Great Depression.

Ages and Eras—Jet Age *See* Ages and Eras—Industrial Revolution/Industrial Age.

Ages and Eras—Middle Ages
The fall of the Roman Empire at the end of the 5th century marked the end of ancient times and the beginning of the Middle Ages.
• **End of the Middle Ages:** with the beginning of the Renaissance. *See* Ages and Eras—Dark Ages; Renaissance.

Ages and Eras—Age of Plastics *See* Ages and Eras—Industrial Revolution/Industrial Age.

Ages and Eras—Progressive Era
The Progressive Era in the United States began around 1890. It was a time when a serious effort was made to reform political, economic and social problems. Reformers attacked child labor, slums, sweat shops, concentrated wealth, limited suffrage, political machines and corruption, discrimination, inequitable tax laws and other ills. The Muckrakers were active during the Progressive Era.
• **End of the Progressive Era:** Some historians say it ended in 1913. Others say it was over in 1917, when the U.S. entered World War I. Still others say it lasted until 1920, and the advent of Prohibition.

Ages and Eras—Age of Reason *See* Ages and Eras—Age of Enlightenment.

Ages and Eras—Reformation and Counter-Reformation
The Reformation was an effort by religious reformers to address a controversy over how to interpret the Christian faith. It started when Martin Luther nailed Ninety-Five Theses to the door of a church in Wittenberg, Germany, in 1517. The Counter-Reformation was a transformational movement within the Roman Catholic Church in reaction to the Reformation. It began during the pontificate of Pope Pius IV (1559-65). It was marked by a religious revival within the church that reached its peak during the first half of the 1600s.
• **End of the Reformation:** mid 16th century, with the deaths of Luther (1546) and John Calvin (1564). By then, Protestant churches had separated from the Roman Catholic church and gained political recognition.
• **End of the Counter-Reformation:** mid 17th century, with the end the Thirty Years' War (1648).

Ages and Eras—Regency
The Regency in Great Britain began in 1811 when George, Prince of Wales, assumed the office of regent, or substitute ruler. He stepped in when the sanity of his father King George III was questioned.
• **End of the Regency:** January 29, 1820, with the death of George III, and the prince acceded to the throne as King George IV.

Ages and Eras—Renaissance
The Renaissance was a revival of the classic style of art in the 15th and 16th centuries and of Italian architecture early in the 15th century. The Renaissance also was a revival of

learning and its effect on literature and society. The Renaissance had no specifically identifiable beginning or end. Historians do not agree on when it began: dates range from the late 1200s to the early 1400s, and even later farther north.

• **End of the Renaissance:** as early as the 1490s, according to some scholars. Others set the end date in the early 1600s. And others even extend it to the end of the Baroque Era in the 1700s. Some historians tie the end of the Italian Renaissance to the death of Michelangelo in 1564, while others prefer 1532, when Florence ceased to be an independent republic and became the Duchy of Tuscany.

Ages and Eras—Restoration

The Restoration was the time in British history when the Stuarts were returned to the throne. It began in 1660, when King Charles's son Charles II ascended to the throne. After he died in 1685, his brother James II succeeded him and ruled until 1688, when he was forced from power in the Glorious Revolution. James II was the last male ruler in the direct Stuart line.

• **End of the Restoration:** 1685, with the end of the reign of Charles II. Some historians say it ended in 1688, with the end of the reign of James II.

Ages and Eras—Romanticism

Romanticism was a rejection of the Classicism of the 1700s and a turn toward nature, simplicity, folklore and even the supernatural.

• **End of Romanticism in literature:** around 1850. The movement, which began around 1830, faded by the mid-19th century, as people began to crave realism in what they were reading.

• **End of Romanticism in music:** early 1900s. It gave way to Post-Romanticism toward the end of the 1800s. By the beginning of World War I, the Romantic movement had run its course.

Ages and Eras—Space Age *See* Ages and Eras—Industrial Revolution/Industrial Age.

Ages and Eras—Stone Age, Copper Age, Bronze Age, Iron Age

Archaeologists divide the prehistoric and early historic development of people into Stone, Copper, Bronze and Iron Ages.

Stone Age The Stone Age is the stage in human development when people used stone, bone, wood, ivory and other natural materials for primitive weapons and tools. The Stone Age is made up of three stages, based on the level of sophistication of the objects people made: Paleolithic (or Early), Mesolithic (or Middle) and Neolithic (or New).

Paleolithic, or Early Stone Age The Paleolithic, or Early Stone Age, began roughly 500,000 to 1,000,000 (or more) years ago with the first evidence of tools. The earliest people hunted for their food and used very primitive tools, such as chipped rocks and simple stone axes. During this time, they learned to make and control fire.

• **End of the Paleolithic Age:** around 8,000 to 10,000 years ago, with the end of the Ice Age. As the climate grew warmer, people moved around more.

Mesolithic, or Middle Stone Age The Mesolithic, or Middle Stone Age, began roughly 8,000 to 10,000 years ago. People became less dependent on hunting and more on plant gathering to feed themselves. The bow and arrow appeared during this age.

• **End of the Mesolithic Age:** when people began to settle down to domesticate animals and grow crops. This occurred at different times in different places. The end of the Middle Stone Age is tied to what humans learned to do, not when they learned to do it.

Neolithic, or New Stone Age The Neolithic, or New Stone Age, began when people began to cultivate crops such as corn and wheat. They needed to know the seasons for farming, so they developed calendars. They also began to weave and make pottery. By this time, they had learned to spin cloth from wool and other fibers.

• **End of the Neolithic Age:** at different times in different places. Historians generally consider the New Stone Age as having ended when early people began to use metal.

Copper Age Copper, gold and silver were among the earliest metals people learned to smelt. There is evidence that some people were working with these metals as early as 7,000 years ago.
• **End of the Copper Age:** at different times in different areas. The Copper Age ended with the Bronze Age, when people began adding tin to copper to produce bronze, a more durable material.

Bronze Age The Bronze Age was a time when bronze was used for weapons, utensils and tools. Some people began using bronze as early as 3500 to 4000 B.C. They continued to use bronze until sometime between 1500 and 1000 B.C., then iron, which first appeared in Asia Minor, became common.
• **End of the Bronze Age:** at different times in different areas. The traditional date for its end in Greece is about 1200 B.C. In most regions, the Bronze Age overlapped with an earlier Stone Age and a later Iron Age.

Iron Age The Iron Age started when people began to use iron as the main material for their weapons, utensils and tools. Among some Middle Eastern cultures, this was 1000 B.C. or earlier. Not all cultures went through the various metal ages and eras. For example, some early people of South America rarely used iron.
• **End of the Iron Age:** Strictly speaking, the Iron Age has not ended. However, some scholars consider the end of prehistory—the time before writing was developed—as the end of the Iron Age.

Ages and Eras—Victorian Age
The Victorian Age corresponded with the years of the reign of Victoria, Queen of the United Kingdom of Great Britain and Ireland and Empress of India. Victoria ascended to the throne in 1837 when she was 18. She ruled for 63 years, longer than any other English monarch to that time.
• **End of the Victorian Age:** January 22, 1901, with the death of Queen Victoria. Her death brought her son Edward VII to the throne and the beginning of the Edwardian Age.

Agriculture
(*See also* United States—
Agencies; Cabinet.)

Agriculture—Dust Bowl
The Dust Bowl was the result of a decade-long severe drought in the central United States that began in 1931. The lack of rain caused a devastating chain reaction of crop failure, wind erosion, dust storms and more crop failure. In 1935, the U.S. Soil Conservation Service was created and farmers began to use soil-conserving crops to save their soil.
• **End of the Dust Bowl:** around 1939, when the drought ended. A combination of abundant rain and better land management put an end to it. Today, U.S. farmers are better prepared to handle drought and blowing soil. Another Dust Bowl is possible, but not likely.

Agriculture—Horse Power—Great Britain
Until the 20th century, most farming equipment and machines were still powered by heavy work horses. These horses were slowly replaced by other power sources, save for the few that are paraded in fancy harnesses at agricultural shows.
• **Last British farm continuously powered by horse power:** Sillywrae Farm in Northumberland. The family of John Dodd has lived on Sillywrae for more than 150 years. And for all that time, horses have been the source of power.

Agriculture—Johnny Appleseed
During his lifetime, Massachusetts-born John Chapman (a.k.a. Johnny Appleseed) planted apple seeds in Indiana and Ohio that grew into orchards. He died in Fort Wayne, Indiana, on March 18, 1845, age 70.
• **Last surviving tree planted by Johnny Appleseed:** believed to be on the Harvey farm in Nova, Ohio. The tree was damaged in a storm in 1996 and no longer produces

fruit, but cuttings have been grafted to produce descendants.

Agriculture—Union Stock Yards
The Union Stock Yards were built at Halsted Street and Exchange Avenue in Chicago, Illinois, in 1864. The Armour, Swift and Wilson companies had plants there.
• **Last of the Union Stock Yards:** closed July 31, 1971. Only the gate was preserved. It was named a Chicago landmark in 1972.

Airfield, Airplanes, Aircraft, Airships
See Aviation; Disasters; War and Battles.

Alliances, Confederations, Leagues, Pacts, Treaties and Unions
(*See also* Nations; United States; Wars and Battles.)

Alliances, etc.—Achaean League
The Achaean League was a confederation of 12 cities of Achaea (Greece) formed in the 5th century B.C. It engaged in wars with Sparta, Macedon and Aeolia. The league was dissolved by Alexander the Great but reorganized around 280 B.C.
• **End of the Achaean League:** 146 B.C., when Achaean troops were defeated near Corinth and the league's leaders were killed. That portion of Greece became a Roman province.

Alliances, etc.—Arab Union
The short-lived Arab Union was formed between Jordan and Iraq in February 1958. The union was created to counter the union of Egypt and Syria as the United Arab Republic a short time earlier.
• **End of the Arab Union:** August 1958, terminated by Jordan's King Hussein after Iraq's monarchy was overthrown.

Alliances, etc.—Brazzaville Group
The Brazzaville Group was created in 1961 by the French-speaking nations of Africa that shared political, economic and military interests. They favored a gradual approach to African unity.

• **End of Brazzaville Group:** May 1963, dissolved with the creation of the Organization of African Unity. (*See also* Alliances, etc.—Casablanca Group; Monrovia Group.)

Alliances, etc.—British East Africa
British East Africa was the name given to Britain's colonial dependencies on the east coast of Africa before they gained their independence between 1961 and 1963. It was comprised of Kenya, Tanganyika, Uganda and Zanzibar.
• **End of British East Africa:** 1963, when Kenya, the last of the four colonial dependencies, gained its independence.

Alliances, etc.—British West Africa
British West Africa was the name of Great Britain's colonial dependencies on the west coast of Africa before they achieved independence. British West Africa was comprised of Nigeria, Gold Coast (including Ashanti and the Northern Territories), The Gambia, Sierra Leone, British Cameroons and British Togoland.
• **End of British West Africa:** 1965, when The Gambia, last of these colonial dependencies, achieved independence.

Alliances, etc.—Casablanca Group
The Casablanca Group was a bloc of African countries that sought the immediate unity of the nations of the African continent. It was formed in 1961 to counterbalance the Brazzaville Group. It consisted of Algeria, Ghana, Guinea, Mali and the United Arab Republic (Egypt and Syria).
• **End of the Casablanca Group:** May 1963. The group was dissolved with the creation of the Organization of African Unity. (*See also* Alliances, etc.—Brazzaville Group; Monrovia Group.)

Alliances, etc.—Central American Federation
The Central American Federation, or Central American Union, was a political confederation of the republics of Central America—Costa Rica, Guatemala, Honduras, Nicaragua and El Salvador—created in

1825. The member nations had gained their independence from Spain in 1821 and were annexed to the Mexican Empire until 1823. The Central American Federation was their first attempt at unity.
• **End of the Central American Federation:** 1838. It disintegrated over dissension, petty rivalries and nationalist loyalties within the group.
• **Last president:** Francisco Morázan, who served from 1830 to 1838. An attempt to recreate the Central American Federation from June 13, 1921, to February 7, 1922, was unsuccessful.

Alliances, etc.—Central Treaty Organization (CENTO)
The Central Treaty Organization (CENTO) was a mutual defense alliance among Turkey, Iran, Iraq, Pakistan and Great Britain. It began as the Baghdad Pact in 1955. After Iraq dropped out in 1959, headquarters were moved to Ankara, Turkey, and the alliance was renamed the Central Treaty Organization.
• **End of CENTO:** September 26, 1979, when the Middle Eastern members withdrew.

Alliances, etc.—Dominion of New England
The Dominion of New England was established in 1686 and ruled by royal governor Edmund Andros. It was a union of all the New England colonies except Connecticut. New York and New Jersey joined in 1688.
• **End of the Dominion of New England:** 1689, when the colonists learned of the Glorious Revolution in England and removed Andros from office. The rule of Andros was too autocratic.

Alliances, etc.—European Community (EC)
The European Community (EC) was a political network of European nations that comprised the European Coal and Steel Community (ECSC), European Economic Community (EEC) and European Atomic Energy Commission (EAEC).

• **End of the European Community:** December 1993, following the Maastricht Treaty, when the EC was replaced by the European Union.

Alliances, etc.—Federation of Rhodesia and Nyasaland
In September 1953, the British protectorates of Northern Rhodesia and Nyasaland joined with the self-governing British colony of Southern Rhodesia as the Federation of Rhodesia and Nyasaland.
• **End of the Federation of Rhodesia and Nyasaland:** December 31, 1963. The federation was dissolved when Nyasaland seceded to seek independence as the nation of Malawi. Meanwhile, Northern Rhodesia was making plans to become independent as Zambia, and in Southern Rhodesia, people were demanding independence as Zimbabwe.

Alliances, etc.—French Equatorial Africa
French Equatorial Africa, created in 1910, was a federation of the French overseas territories of Gabon, Middle Congo, Ubangi-Shari and Chad.
• **End of French Equatorial Africa:** 1959, when the territories opted to become self-governing republics within the French Community. The four nations received total independence in 1960. Middle Congo was renamed Republic of the Congo. Ubangi-Shari became the Central African Republic.

Alliances, etc.—French India
French India consisted of five settlements in India—Chandernagor, Pondicherry, Karikal, Yanam and Mahe. Chandernagor was restored to India in 1951.
• **End of French India:** 1954, when France agreed to turn over its last four territories to India. The treaty of transfer was signed in 1956.

Alliances, etc.—French Indochina
French Indochina was the name given to French dependencies in Southeast Asia that are today the nations of Cambodia, Laos and Vietnam.

• **End of French Indochina:** 1954, with the signing of the Geneva Agreement that ended the Indochina War of 1946-54.

Alliances, etc.—French Union
The French Union was created in 1946 by the French constitution. It was comprised of France and all of its colonies, overseas territories and protectorates.
• **End of the French Union:** 1958, when the new French constitution established the French Community.

Alliances, etc.—French West Africa
French West Africa was a federation of French dependencies in West Africa created in 1895. It consisted of Dahomey, Senegal, Mauritania, French Guinea, French Sudan, Ivory Coast, Niger and Upper Volta.
• **End of French West Africa:** 1958, when the federation was dissolved prior to decolonization and all but French Guinea voted to become self-governing republics within the French Community. French Guinea opted for immediate independence as Guinea. In 1960, the other republics gained their independence.

Alliances, etc.—German East Africa
German East Africa was organized in 1884 as a protectorate of German holdings in eastern Africa that included Tanganyika and Ruanda-Urundi.
• **End of German East Africa:** 1918, with Germany's defeat in World War I. After the war, much of German East Africa was mandated by the League of Nations to Great Britain as Tanganyika. Ruanda-Urundi was mandated to Belgium. Kionga, a small portion in the southeast, went to Portugal as part of Mozambique. Tanganyika became independent in 1961 and joined with Zanzibar in 1964 to form the nation of Tanzania. Ruanda-Urundi gained independence in 1962 as the two nations of Rwanda and Burundi.
• **Last governor of German East Africa:** Heinrich Schnee, who served from 1912 to 1918. He died in Berlin, Germany, on June 23, 1949, age 78.

Alliances, etc.—Gran Colombia (Great Colombia) Confederation
Venezuelan-born Simon Bolivar helped to liberate several South American nations from Spanish rule. He had hopes for a union of South American countries when he proclaimed the Gran Colombia Confederation (a.k.a. the Republic of Great Colombia) on December 17, 1819. The confederation was confirmed in 1821 at the Congress of Cúcuta, in Colombia, with Bolivar as its first president. At first, it was a union of Venezuela and Gran Colombia (Colombia, and Panama). Ecuador joined in 1822, after the Spanish were defeated at the Battle of Pichincha. Venezuela withdrew in January 1830, to become a separate nation, followed by Ecuador in May 1830. Bolivar, in ill health, resigned as president on May 4, 1830. He died near Santa Marta, Colombia, on December 17, 1830. The confederation had a series of presidents after Bolivar left.
• **End of the Gran Colombia Confederation:** dissolved on November 21, 1831, when Gran Colombia was officially separated into Ecuador, Venezuela and New Granada (Colombia and Panama).
• **Last president of the Gran Colombia Confederation:** Domingo Caycedo y Sanz de Santamaria, who served from May 3, 1831, to November 21, 1831.

Alliances, etc.—Hanseatic League
The Hanseatic League, a mercantile organization, was a medieval confederation of German cities, including Lübeck, Hamburg and Bremen. The league was founded in the 12th century to protect Baltic coast port cities against piracy. It reached its peak in the mid-1300s, then gradually declined. The Hanseatic League was greatly weakened by the Thirty Years' War (1618-48).
• **Last general assembly of the Hanseatic League:** 1669. The Hanseatic League was never formally dissolved.

Alliances, etc.—Kalmar, Union of
Denmark, Sweden and Norway united as the Union of Kalmar in 1397. The union was named for the town of Kalmar, where it was

formed. It was established to combat the superiority of the Hanseatic League, a German mercantile organization.

• **End of the Union of Kalmar:** 1523. Dissolved when King Christian II of Sweden was exiled and his successor, King Gustavus I, withdrew his nation.

Alliances, etc.—League of Nations

The League of Nations was established after World War I. The covenant that created the League went into force on January 10, 1920, with members from 42 nations.

• **Last meeting of the League of Nations:** April 8-18, 1946, at the United Nations in Geneva, Switzerland, when it was dissolved. All of its assets were transferred to the United Nations.

• **Last League of Nations Assembly president:** Carl Hambro of Norway, who served from 1939 to 1946.

• **Last League of Nations secretary-general:** Sean Lester of Ireland, who served from 1940 to 1946.

Alliances, etc.—Monrovia Group

The Monrovia Group was created in 1961 by African nations that opposed the Casablanca Charter, which sought the immediate unity of the African continent. It consisted of Cameroon, Central African Republic, Chad, Dahomey, Ethiopia, Gabon, Ivory Coast, Liberia, Malagasy Republic, Niger, Nigeria, People's Republic of Congo, Senegal, Sierra Leone, Somalia, Togo, Tunisia and Upper Volta. Many of the Monrovia Group nations were members of the Brazzaville Group that favored a gradual approach to African unity.

• **End of the Monrovia Group:** May 1963. It was dissolved with the creation of the Organization of African Unity. (*See also* Alliances, etc.—Brazzaville Group; Casablanca Group.)

Alliances, etc.—New England Confederation

The New England Confederation was formed in 1643 after the Pequot War by the New England colonies of Massachusetts Bay, Plymouth, New Haven and Connecticut. One of its aims was to provide military strength against their common enemies.

• **End of the New England Confederation:** 1684. The confederation lost some of its strength in the 1660s, after New Haven became part of Connecticut. It dissolved after the Massachusetts Bay Colony's charter was revoked.

Alliances, etc.—North Atlantic Treaty Organization (NATO)

The North Atlantic Treaty Organization was established in 1949 by Belgium, Canada, Denmark, France, Iceland, Italy, Luxembourg, Netherlands, Norway, Portugal, United Kingdom and the United States. Other nations have subsequently joined. NATO is a mutual defense organization. Members agree to regard an attack on one member as an attack on all.

• **Last time NATO was headquartered in Paris, France:** 1967, when it moved its headquarters to Evere, Belgium, near Brussels. The same year, the offices of the Supreme Headquarters Allied Powers Europe (SHAPE) were moved from Paris to Casteau, Belgium.

Alliances, etc.—South East Asia Treaty Organization (SEATO)

The South East Asia Treaty Organization was established in 1954 for mutual defense and economic support. The signers were Australia, France, Great Britain, New Zealand, Pakistan, the Philippines, Thailand and the United States. Pakistan withdrew in November 1972.

• **End of SEATO:** June 30, 1977, when it was disbanded by mutual consent.

Alliances, etc.—United Arab Republic (UAR)

The United Arab Republic (UAR) was created as a union of Syria and Egypt in 1958.

• **End of the United Arab Republic (Syria/Egypt):** 1961. United Arab Republic then became the official name of Egypt alone.

• **End of the United Arab Republic**

(Egypt): 1971, when Egypt changed its name to the Arab Republic of Egypt.

Alliances, etc.—United Nations (UN)

The United Nations (UN) was created after World War II. The United Nations Charter, which defines the purposes and functions of the organization, was signed in San Francisco, California, on June 26, 1945.
• **Last surviving U.S. signatory of the United Nations Charter:** Harold E. Stassen, who died in Bloomington, Minnesota, on March 4, 2001, age 93.

Alliances, etc.—Utrecht, Union of

The Union of Utrecht was a defense treaty signed in 1579 by seven northern provinces of the Netherlands when the country was controlled by Spain. The provinces were Holland, Zeeland, Utrecht, Groningen, Overijssel, Gelderland and Friesland.
• **End of the Union of Utrecht:** 1795, when the Netherlands came under the control of the French Republic.

Alliances, etc.—Warsaw Treaty Organization (Warsaw Pact)

The Warsaw Pact was signed in Warsaw, Poland, in 1955, by Albania, Bulgaria, Czechoslovakia, East Germany, Hungary, Poland, Romania and the Union of Soviet Socialist Republics. Albania withdrew in 1968. The 20-year pact was renewed in 1975.
• **Last surviving signatory of the Warsaw Pact:** Andras Hegedus of Hungary, who died on October 23, 1999, age 76.
• **End of the Warsaw Pact:** 1991. On February 25, 1991, the member nations agreed to disband. On March 31, the military arm was disbanded. And on July 1, 1991, the Warsaw Pact was officially dissolved in Prague, Czechoslovakia.

Alliances, etc.—West Indies Federation

The West Indies Federation was an alliance of British Commonwealth colonies within the West Indies archipelago in the Caribbean Sea. It went into effect on January 3, 1958. Members were: Antigua, Barbados, Domin-

ica, Grenada, Jamaica, Montserrat, Saint Christopher-Nevis-Anguilla, Saint Lucia, Saint Vincent and Trinidad and Tobago. Although the federation gave its members internal autonomy, it lasted only four years. It ended when the first of the colonies declared their independence.
• **Last of the West Indies Federation:** dissolved on May 31, 1962. Two of the federation members—Jamaica and Trinidad and Tobago—gained their independence that year.

Alphabets and Writing Systems

Alphabets and Writing Systems—Cuneiform

Cuneiform is a writing system that uses wedge-shaped signs formed by triangular marks impressed in clay. It was developed for the Sumerian language in the 3rd millennium B.C. and later adapted to Akkadian and other languages of the ancient Near East, including Elamite, Hittite and Old Persian. It began to be replaced by Phoenician script in the 7th and 6th centuries B.C.
• **Last use of cuneiform:** the 1st century A.D. The most recent remaining example dates to 75 A.D.

Alphabets and Writing Systems—Demotic Script

Demotic, a simplified form of hieroglyphics, was used in Egypt for about a thousand years. It was gradually replaced by Greek writing.
• **Latest remaining example of Demotic script:** dates from 425 A.D., in a graffito in the temple of Philae.

Alphabets and Writing Systems—Egyptian Hieroglyphs

Egyptian hieroglyphic writing is one of the oldest writing systems in the world. Over time, the symbolic hieroglyphs evolved into a cursive form of hieretic and eventually became Demotic, or a simplified written form.

• **Latest remaining hieroglyphic inscription:** 394 A.D., written on the temple walls of Philae. By then, Coptic—a Greek-based alphabet with some Demotic signs—had become the main writing system in Egypt.

Alphabets and Writing Systems— English-Language Alphabet Letters

The English-language alphabet had only 24 letters until the Middle Ages. The letter "U" came into general use by the 1500s.
• **Last addition to the English-language alphabet:** The letter "J." It did not appear in any alphabets until the 14th century. It was not until 1630 in England that "J" was finally differentiated from the letter "I."

Alphabets and Writing Systems— Germanic Black Letter Script

Germanic Black Letter Script (a.k.a. Gothic, Black Letter Script and Fraktur) was used in much of Europe from the time of Gutenberg until the 16th century, then was abandoned. Germany, however, clung to it much longer as the typeface for newspapers, books and other publications.
• **Last widespread use of Black Letter Script in German newspapers, etc:** 1941, during World War II. The Nazis determined that Fraktur was un-German and abolished it on Hitler's orders. Black Letter Script is no longer used except in a few books or as a specialty type for banners or titles, much like Old English Script is used.

Alphabets and Writing Systems— Roman Literary Cursive Script

Roman Literary Cursive Script was written on papyrus with a reed pen. It was used in the Roman Empire for business, administrative records and private letters.
• **Latest remaining example of Roman Literary Cursive Script:** Possibly 166 A.D. The exact date of a fragment discovered in Egypt and acquired by the British Museum in 1900 is uncertain, but probably dates to the 1st to 2nd centuries A.D.

American Indians, *see* Native Americans; United States; Wars and Battles.

Animals

Animals—Endangered—Bison

Bison (*Bison bison*), often called buffalo, once roamed the central and western United States in vast herds. The wholesale slaughter of the bison began in the late 1860s. More than 30 million were killed over the next dozen years. By the end of the 1870s, the bison had disappeared from the southern Great Plains. By 1890, they were almost extinct on the northern plains.
• **Last surviving herd of wild bison:** in Yellowstone Park. The herd was established with 21 bison during the Grover Cleveland administration.

Animals—Endangered— California Condor

The California condors (*Gymnogyps californianus*) are among the largest of all condors, weighing about 22 pounds. They were probably never numerous, but they began to die off as California's human population grew and their food supply was reduced.
• **Last known free-flying California condor in the wild:** California Condor AC-9, captured April 19, 1987, and placed in a breeding program in southern California. At that time, only 27 California condors were left in the world. California Condor AC-9 was re-released into the wild in May 2002. By then, the number of condors had increased to more than 200.

Animals—Endangered—Whales

The United States banned commercial whaling by U.S. citizens with the 1972 Marine Mammal Protection Act. (*See also* Ships—Whalers.)
• **Last commercial killing of whales in the U.S.:** December 18, 1971, when the permit for the four-ship Del Monte Fishing Company—the only remaining U.S. whaling fleet—expired.
• **Last active U.S. whaling station:** near Point San Pablo, California, operated by Del Monte from 1956 to 1971. Much of it was destroyed by fire in the 1990s.
• **Last active U.S. whale harpoon maker:**

Edward R. Cole, a shipsmith in Fair Haven, Massachusetts, who retired in 1934. He died in Fair Haven on February 24, 1944, age 84.
• **Last active U.S. whalebone cutter:** George Messman, who had a shop on Duane Street in New York, New York. He retired on June 1, 1920, after 56 years. The whalebone cutting business had become obsolete after the disappearance of hoopskirts and the increased use of steel in umbrellas. Messman died in Brooklyn, New York, on June 9, 1933, age 84.

Animals—Endangered—Whooping Crane
The whooping crane (*Grus americana*) is one of the rarest birds in America.
• **Last surviving flock of whooping cranes:** Aransas/Wood Buffalo flock, which had been reduced to just 15 in 1941. All current whooping cranes descend from this group of 15. They winter at the Aransas National Wildlife Refuge on the Texas coast and breed 2,600 miles away at Wood Buffalo National Park, a remote wilderness area in northern Canada. Today, numbering several hundred, the whooping cranes have been separated into three groups, and a number are held in captivity.

Animals—Endangered—Wolves
Gray wolves (*Canis lupis*) were extinct in Great Britain and Ireland by the late 18th century.
• **Last wolves in Wales:** 1166 (last mention).
• **Last wolves in England:** 1480s, during the reign of King Henry VII.
• **Last wolves in Scotland:** 1691 (documented); however, there was an undocumented report of a wolf attack in 1743.
• **Last wolves in Ireland:** mid-1700s, in County Wicklow.

Animals—Extinct—Atitlan Grebe
Birds known as Atitlan grebes (*Podilymbus gigas*) once lived around Lake Atitlan in Guatemala.
• **Last Atitlan grebes seen in the wild:** 1980s, when the total population numbered less than 80. One of the theories about why the Atitlan grebes became extinct is that a 1976 earthquake around Lake Atitlan caused the water level of the lake to drop, and the birds were unable to compete with the Pied-billed grebes that also inhabited the lake.

Animals—Extinct—Auroch
The auroch (*Bos taurus primigenius*) was a huge wild ox that once inhabited Europe. It was the urus of Caesar's time.
• **Last auroch:** died in Poland in 1627. A small herd was kept in a royal forest at Masovia in Poland. By 1564, it had dwindled to 30. By 1602, only four were left.

Animals—Extinct—California Grizzly
Cousins of the California grizzly (*Ursus horribilis*) have survived in other states, but the bear that is on the California state flag is gone.
• **Last California grizzly in captivity:** Monarch, who died in San Francisco in 1911. The bear was stuffed and put on display at the California Academy of Science.
• **Last California grizzly killed in southern California:** October 26, 1916, killed in Los Angeles County by Cornelius Johnson.
• **Last California grizzly killed in the wild:** killed in August 1922 in Tulare County, California.
• **Last California grizzly seen in the wild:** 1924, spotted in Sequoia-Kings Canyon National Park.

Animals—Extinct—Carolina Parakeet
The Carolina parakeet (*Conuropis carolinensis*) was the last of the native parrots of the United States. The once-plentiful, colorful birds began to be killed off when they became pests to farmers. Also, people hunted them for their plumage. Some killed them just for sport.
• **Last Carolina parakeet killed in the wild:** 1913, in Florida.
• **Last known pair of Carolina parakeets in captivity:** Lady Jane and Incas, who lived at the Cincinnati Zoo in Ohio for 35 years. Lady Jane died in the late summer of 1917. Incas died on February 21, 1918.

Animals—Extinct—Dodo and Solitaire

The dodo (*Raphus cucullatus*) existed only on the Mascarene Islands in the Indian Ocean. It was discovered by outsiders in 1598. The bird was big, awkward and unable to fly. Because it was both fearless and defenseless, it was extinct within less than a century. The only painting of the bird was made in 1628. The solitaire was a flightless bird closely related to the dodo.

• **Last dodo disappeared:** soon after 1680.

• **Last surviving remains of the last dodo:** the head and a claw. The rest of the dodo was destroyed in 1755 by authorities at the Ashmolean Museum in Oxford, England, because of its decrepit condition: the stuffed body had become moth-eaten. When the Ashmolean dodo was destroyed, it was the last genuine specimen. The remains are now in the university museum.

• **Last Réunion solitaire (*Raphus solitarius*):** disappeared in 1746.

• **Last Rodriguez solitaire (*Pezophaps solitaria*):** disappeared around 1791.

Animals—Extinct—Falkland Island Wolf (Warrah)

The Falkland Island wolf (*Dusicyon australis*), or warrah, had a thick brownish-red coat that made it a desirable target for fur hunters. It was hunted into extinction.

• **Last warrah killed in the wild:** 1876, at Shallow Bay, West Falkland.

Animals—Extinct—Great Auk

Auks are marine birds. The largest of them, the great auk (*Alca impennis*), resembled the penguin and was flightless. It was hunted into extinction in the 19th century.

• **Last great auks seen in the wild:** June 3, 1844, on an island off the coast of Iceland. Two great auks were killed by collectors.

Animals—Extinct—Heath Hen

The heath hen (*Tympanuchus cupido cupido*), a subspecies of the prairie chicken, lived in the eastern United States. It was a popular food source. The heath hen began to disappear in the 19th century. By 1870, it was found only on Martha's Vineyard, in Massachusetts. A fire on the island in 1916 destroyed much of the heath hen's habitat.

• **Last heath hen seen in the wild:** March 11, 1932. It is presumed to have died later that year.

Animals—Extinct—Mastodon and Mammoth

Mastodons and mammoths were both closely related to the elephant. The mammoths were larger than the mastodons and had different teeth. Both were pursued by early human hunters.

• **Last mastodons became extinct:** around 8,000 years ago, at the end of the last Ice Age.

• **Last mammoths became extinct:** Full-size mammoths disappeared about 8,000 years ago on the Great Plains of America, and about 3,000 to 4,000 years ago in Siberia. A dwarf species survived until around 2000 B.C. on an island off the coast of Siberia.

Animals—Extinct—Passenger Pigeon

The passenger pigeon (*Ectopistes migratorius*) was native to North America. It was similar to the mourning dove, but larger. Its extinction is a mystery. Passenger pigeons numbered in the billions during the 1700s, and were the most numerous bird in America in the 1870s. Several theories have been put forth about their disappearance, including disease, loss of habitat/food supply and indiscriminate killing.

• **Last passenger pigeons seen in the wild:** March 24, 1900, in Pike County, Ohio.

• **Last passenger pigeon in captivity:** Martha, who died at the Cincinnati Zoo in Ohio on September 1, 1914. Her body was sent to the National Museum of Natural History in Washington, D.C. The Passenger Pigeon Memorial in the Cincinnati Zoo displays a bronze of Martha and the body of the last passenger pigeon seen in the wild.

Animals—Extinct—Steller's Sea Cow

Steller's sea cow (*Hydrodamalis gigas*) was about 25 feet long and resembled a seal. It once lived in the Bering Sea off the coast of Alaska. The sea cow was named for Georg Wilhelm Steller, the naturalist who first de-

scribed it in 1741.
• **Last Steller's sea cow:** died in 1768, just 27 years after Steller first identified it.

Animals—Extinct—Tasmanian Tiger

The Tasmanian tiger (*Thylacinus cynocephalis*) lived in Australia and Tasmania. It was not popular with sheep ranchers. Many were killed after a bounty was placed on them in the mid-1800s. By 1910, the remaining Tasmanian tigers were eradicated by disease.
• **Last Tasmanian tiger in captivity:** Benjamin (a female), who died at the Hobart Zoo in Australia on September 7, 1936. Benjamin's death marked the end of an entire family of carnivorous marsupials that had lived for millions of years.

Antarctica
(*See also* Explorers and Explorations.)

Antarctica—Antarctic Peninsula

Antarctica is an ice-covered continent that surrounds the South Pole. The Antarctic Peninsula extends from the mainland into the Weddell Sea. It was originally named for Nathaniel Palmer, an American whaler who was the first to visit the region in 1820-21.
• **Last known as Palmer Peninsula:** 1964. That year, by international agreement, the name was changed to Antarctic Peninsula.
• **Last time Antarctica was completely ice-free:** about 14 million years ago.

Architecture
(*See also* Artists; Buildings: Entertainment–Theaters.)

Architecture—Bauhaus

The Bauhaus School of Design was Germany's seminal modernist institution before the Nazis shut it down in 1933. The teachers emigrated to the United States.
• **Last Bauhaus director:** Ludwig Mies van der Rohe, who died in Chicago, Illinois, on August 18, 1969, age 83.
• **Last Bauhaus teacher:** Anni Albers, who died in Orange, Connecticut, on May 10, 1994, age 94.

Architecture—Gothic Revival

Gothic Revival ecclesiastical architecture (c. 1750-c. 1900) is noted for its use of medieval decorative elements. Gothic Revival residential architecture first appeared in the United States in the late 18th century. Like its ecclesiastical counterpart, it was noted for its use of medieval decorative elements.
• **Last Gothic-style cathedral completed in the U.S.:** the National Cathedral (Cathedral Church of Saint Peter and Saint Paul) in Washington, D.C. The building was constructed between 1907 and 1990.
• **Last Gothic-style cathedral constructed worldwide:** St. John's Cathedral in Brisbane, Australia, designed in 1888 by John Loughborough Pearson. It is still under construction.
• **Last remaining example of residential Gothic Revival architecture in the U.S.:** Sedgely Porter's Lodge in Fairmount Park, Philadelphia, Pennsylvania, designed by architect Benjamin Latrobe in 1799 as the carriage house for the Sedgely Estate. It was used as a farmhouse for many years then served as a headquarters for the Fairmount Park police before it was abandoned in the late 1970s. The building was saved by the Fairmount Park Historic Preservation Trust and restored.

Architecture—Queen Anne Forecourt

A Queen Anne forecourt is composed of four outbuildings: a large two-story kitchen, laundry house and two L-shaped barns.
• **Last remaining Queen Anne Forecourt in the U.S.:** Shirley Plantation, in Charles City, Virginia, built in 1723.

Architecture—Zoomorphic

Zoomorphic buildings are structures built in the shape of animals.
• **Last surviving historic zoomorphic building in the U.S.:** Lucy the Elephant in Margate, New Jersey. The structure was built in 1881 to attract potential real estate buyers. Lucy is 65 feet tall and has been completely restored. She is a National Historic Landmark and is visited by thousands of tourists annually.

Architect	Last Work
Aalto, Alvar	Finnish architect/designer Hugo Alvar Henrik Aalto died in Helsinki, Finland, on May 11, 1976, age 78. • **Last building Aalto designed in the U.S.:** Mount Angel Abbey Library, St. Benedict, Oregon, in 1964-70. • **Last major project:** Finlandia Hall, Helsinki, in 1967-71; Congress Wing added, 1973-75.
Adam, Robert	Scottish-born architect/interior designer/furniture designer Robert Adam died in London, England, on March 3, 1792, age 64. • **Last project:** Design for Charlotte Square, New Town, Edinburgh, Scotland, constructed in 1791-94.
Bacon, Henry	American architect Henry Bacon died in New York, New York, on February 16, 1924, age 57. • **Last project:** Lincoln Memorial in Washington, D.C., dedicated in 1922.
Brunelleschi, Filippo	Italian architect/sculptor Filippo Brunelleschi died in Florence, Italy, in 1445, age around 69. • **Last project:** Santo Spirito (Church of the Holy Spirit) in Florence, Italy.
Bulfinch, Charles	American architect Charles Bulfinch died in Boston, Massachusetts, on April 4, 1844, age 80. • **Last project:** architect for the final stages of the Capitol Building in Washington, D.C. He was on the project until 1829. • **Last of India Wharf, Boston:** demolished in 1962. The Wharf, which was built c. 1805, was the last remaining commercial building designed by Bulfinch in Boston.
Burnham, Daniel H.	American architect Daniel Hudson Burnham died in Heidelberg, Germany on June 1, 1912, age 76. He was part of the partnership of Burnham and Root, founded in 1873. • **End of partnership with John Wellborn Root:** 1891, when Root died. • **Last major project:** a redesign of the city of Chicago, Illinois, with open spaces and a view to Lake Michigan. He submitted his report in 1909.
Esherick, Joseph	American architect Joseph Esherick died in San Francisco, California, on December 15, 1998, age 83. • **Last project:** Tenderloin Community School in San Francisco.
Fuller, R. Buckminster	American architect/educator/designer/inventor R. Buckminster Fuller died in Los Angeles, California, on July 1, 1983, age 88. He spent the last years of his life traveling the world, lecturing on ways to better use the world's resources. • **Last invention:** the Hang-It-All, based on his twenty-fifth and last patent.
Furness, Frank	American architect Frank Furness died in Media, Pennsylvania, on June 30, 1912, age 72. • **Last project:** Girard Trust Corn Exchange Bank (later known as Girard Trust Company and Girard Bank), built between 1905 and 1908 in Philadelphia, Pennsylvania. The Greek temple design is a departure from Furness's ornate Victorian Gothic style. The bank wanted a non-Furness-like design. He worked on the design anonymously.

Gaudi, Antonio	Spanish architect Antonio Gaudi died in Barcelona, Spain, in June 10, 1926, after he was hit by a streetcar. He was 74. • **Last project (unfinished):** Church at Plaça de La Sagrada Familia (Church of the Holy Family), Barcelona. Work began in 1883 and was in progress when Gaudi died. The church was finally completed in 1987. • **Last project (completed):** Casa Mila, built in Barcelona between 1906 and 1910.
Gilbert, Cass	American architect Cass Gilbert died in Brockenhurst, England, on May 17, 1934, age 74. • **Last project:** United States Supreme Court Building, Washington, D.C. Gilbert died one year before the building was completed.
Goff, Bruce	American architect Bruce Alonzo Goff died in Tyler, Texas, on August 4, 1982, age 78. • **Last house:** The "Eyeball House," Woodland Hills, California. He died soon after construction began. • **Last major project:** Pavilion for Japanese Art, Los Angeles County Museum of Art, completed in 1986.
Gropius, Walter	German architect Walter Gropius was the founder of the Bauhaus, a design school that used innovative materials to create original buildings and furniture. He died in Boston, Massachusetts, on July 5, 1969, age 86. • **Last project:** Walter Gropius School (elementary school) Berlin, Germany, completed in 1968.
Hood, Raymond	American architect Raymond Hood was known for his Art Deco designs. He died in Stamford, Connecticut, on August 14, 1934, age 53. • **Last project:** Electricity Building, 1933 Century of Progress Exhibition, Chicago, Illinois.
Horta, Victor	Belgian Art Nouveau architect/designer/decorator Victor Horta died in Brussels, Belgium, on September 8, 1947, age 86. • **Last major projects:** Halle Centrale, Main Railway Station, Brussels, Belgium, begun in 1914, completed in 1952, and the Belgian Pavilion, Exposition des Arts Decoratifs, Paris, France, completed in 1925.
Howe, George	American architect George Howe died in Cambridge, Massachusetts, on April 17, 1955, age 68. • **Last project:** Evening and Sunday Bulletin Building, Philadelphia, Pennsylvania, completed in 1954.
Hunt, Richard Morris	American architect Richard Morris Hunt designed several Vanderbilt residences, including The Breakers in Newport, Rhode Island. He died in Newport on July 31, 1895, age 67. • **Last Vanderbilt project:** Biltmore House, the George W. Vanderbilt country chateau near Asheville, North Carolina. Major construction began in 1889 and ended in 1895, the year Hunt died.
Kahn, Louis I.	Estonian-born American architect Louis I. Kahn died in New York, New York, on March 17, 1974, age 73. • **Last project:** Yale Center for British Art, New Haven, Connecticut, built between 1969 and 1974.
Latrobe, Benjamin Henry	English-born American architect Benjamin Henry Latrobe was chief architect of the U.S. Capitol in Washington, D.C. He was working on a project when he died of yellow fever in New Orleans, Louisiana, on

	September 3, 1820, age 56. • **Last public building:** Louisiana State Bank, New Orleans, Louisiana, designed in 1820, the year he died. • **Last houses designed by Latrobe:** Only three of more than 60 houses designed by him have been documented: Adena built in 1805 in Chillicothe, Ohio; Pope Villa built in 1811 in Lexington, Kentucky; and Decatur House built in 1817 in Washington, D.C.
Le Corbusier (Charles-Edouard Jeanneret-Gris)	Swiss architect Charles-Edouard Jeanneret-Gris, known professionally as Le Corbusier, died in Cap Martin-Roquebrune, France, on August 27, 1965, age 78. • **Last building designed by Le Corbusier:** Centre Le Corbusier (Heidi Weber Museum), Zurich, Switzerland, built between 1963 and 1967.
McKim, Mead and White	McKim, Mead and White, founded in 1879 in New York, New York, was one of the leading U.S. architectural firms in the late 19th and early 20th centuries. • **Last of McKim, Mead and White-designed Pennsylvania Station (New York City):** Built in 1910. Demolished in 1964. • **Last of McKim, Mead and White-designed Madison Square Garden (New York City):** Built in 1890. Demolished in 1925. The Saint-Gaudens 18-foot statue of Diana that once topped the Garden is now at the Philadelphia Museum of Art. • **Last of the firm of McKim Mead, and White:** dissolved in 1919. Charles Follen McKim died in St. James, New York, on September 9, 1909, age 62. William Rutherford Mead died in Paris, France, in June 20, 1928, age 81. Stanford White was 53 when he was murdered by Harry K. Thaw in the rooftop restaurant of Madison Square Garden on June 25, 1906.
Mies van der Rohe, Ludwig	German-born architect/furniture designer Ludwig Mies van der Rohe emigrated to the United States in 1938. He died in Chicago, Illinois, on August 18, 1969, age 83. • **Last project:** New National Gallery, Berlin, Germany, built between 1962 and 1968.
Mills, Robert	American architect/engineer Robert Mills designed the Washington Monument. Construction began in 1848 but was not completed until 1884, nearly 30 years after he died. Mills was Architect for Public Buildings in Washington, D.C., from 1836 to 1851 and worked on several major federal buildings. Mills died in Washington, D.C., on March 3, 1855, age 73. • **Last project:** supervised construction of the Smithsonian Institution from 1847 to 1855.
Mizner, Addison	American architect Addison Mizner was noted for his Mediterranean style of architecture. He died in February 1933, age 61. • **Last project:** Casa Coe da Sol, St. Petersburg, Florida, built in 1931. It is listed on the National Register of Historic Places.
Nash, John	Welsh-born British architect/municipal planner John Nash was responsible for much of the layout of Regency London. He designed Trafalgar Square, Marble Arch and Clarence House. Nash died on the Isle of Wight on May 13, 1835, age 83. • **Last project:** Transformation of Buckingham House into a royal palace.

Olmsted, Frederick Law	American landscape architect and writer Frederick Law Olmsted was the designer of the Columbian Exposition in Chicago in 1890-93. He died in Brookline, Massachusetts, on August 28, 1903, age 81. • **Last project:** Grounds for the Biltmore House, George W. Vanderbilt's country chateau near Asheville, North Carolina. Major construction began in 1889 and ended in 1895. Olmsted was in his 70s when he retired in 1895.
Palladio, Andrea	Italian architect Andrea Palladio died in Venice, Italy, in 1580, age around 72. • **Last project:** Teatro Olimpico in Venice, Italy. It was completed after his death.
Polk, Willis Jefferson	American architect Willis Jefferson Polk died in San Francisco, California, in 1924, age 57. • **Last project:** Beach Chalet at Golden Gate Park, San Francisco, built in 1925.
Pope, John Russell	American architect John Russell Pope's use of classicism in his designs earned him the title "Last of the Romans." He died in New York, New York, on August 27. 1937, age 63. • **Last project:** Jefferson Memorial in Washington, D.C. It was completed by his successors after he died.
Post, George Browne	American architect George Browne Post was known as the "father of the tall building in New York." His 22-story Saint Paul Building, completed in 1899 was the city's tallest building. Post was among the earliest designers to use elevators. He died in Bernardsville, New Jersey, on November 28, 1913, age 75. • **Last major project:** Beaux-Arts-styled Wisconsin State Capitol in Madison, built between 1906 and 1917.
Renwick, James (Jr.)	American architect James Renwick Jr. was the designer of the Smithsonian Institution Building in Washington, D.C., and Saint Patrick's Cathedral in New York, New York. He died in New York City on June 23, 1895, age 76. • **Last project:** All Saints Roman Catholic Church in Harlem, New York, built between 1882 and 1893.
Richardson, Henry Hobson	American architect Henry Hobson Richardson died in Brookline, Massachusetts, on April 2, 1886, age 47. • **Last project:** William H. Gratwick House, Buffalo, New York, built in 1886, demolished in 1919, and the Glessner House, Chicago, Illinois, completed in 1887.
Root, John Wellborn	American architect John Wellborn Root was part of the partnership of Burnham and Root, of Chicago, Illinois. • **Last project:** Monadnock Building in Chicago, Illinois. Root died in Chicago during construction on January 15, 1891, age 41. The Headquarters for Frances Willard's Woman's Christian Union, built in 1892, is also among his last major works; demolished in 1926.
Saarinen, Eero	Finnish-born architect/sculptor Eero Saarinen died in Ann Arbor, Michigan, on September 1, 1961, age 51. • **Last projects:** John Deere and Company, Moline, Illinois, completed in 1963; Lincoln Center, New York, New York, completed in 1963; and Gateway Arch, St. Louis, Missouri, completed in 1966.

Stone, Edward Durell	American architect Edward Durell Stone died in New York, New York, on August 6, 1978, age 76. • **Last project:** Standard Oil Building (a.k.a. Amoco Building), Chicago, Illinois, completed in 1973. Renamed Aon Center.
Strickland, William	American architect William Strickland was a pupil of Benjamin Latrobe. He died in Nashville, Tennessee, on April 6, 1854, age 67. • **Last project:** Tennessee State Capitol. Strickland died during the construction and is buried beneath the building. • **Last of the Strickland-designed Arch Street Theater (Philadelphia, Pennsylvania):** demolished 1936. It was built in 1828.
Sullivan, Louis H.	American architect Louis Henry Sullivan designed more than 100 buildings. He died in Chicago, Illinois, on April 14, 1924, age 67. • **Last project:** Krause Music Store, Chicago, Illinois, built in 1922. Today, it houses the Museum of Decorative Arts.
Wood, Waddy Butler	American architect Waddy Butler Wood died at his home near Warrenton, Virginia, January 25, 1944, age 74. • **Last project:** Interior Department Building, Washington, D.C., built between 1935 and 1936.
Wren, Sir Christopher	English architect Sir Christopher Wren began working on Saint Paul's Cathedral in London, England, in June 1675, when he was 43. He was 79 when the work was completed. Wren died in London on February 25, 1723, age 91. • **Last work completed on Saint Paul's Cathedral:** 1711, when Parliament declared the work was finished.
Wright, Frank Lloyd	American architect Frank Lloyd Wright was active in architecture for 70 years and completed more than 400 buildings. He died in Phoenix, Arizona, on April 9, 1959, age 88. • **Last residential commission:** The second Louis Penfield House. Wright had designed a house for Penfield, but when a highway encroached upon part of the land, Penfield commissioned a second house. The completed drawings were on Wright's drawing board when he died. • **Last projects:** Solomon R. Guggenheim Museum in New York, New York, Beth Sholom Synagogue in Elkins Park, Pennsylvania, and Kalita Humphreys Theater in Dallas, Texas, completed in 1959. • **Last commission awarded to Frank Lloyd Wright:** Post Office on the Marin County Civic Center Campus site in March 1959. Wright died a month later. • **Last of Wright's public building designs to be constructed:** Monona Terrace Convention Center in Madison, Wisconsin. Although designed in 1938, it was not completed and dedicated until 1997. • **Last of Wright-designed Midway Gardens (Chicago, Illinois):** Built in 1914. Demolished 1929. • **Last of Wright-designed Lake Geneva Inn (Lake Geneva, Wisconsin):** Built in 1911/12. Demolished 1980. • **Last of Wright-designed Larkin Building (Buffalo, New York):** Built in 1904. Demolished 1950.

Art

Art—Artist Groups—The Eight

The Eight were American artists who were united in their opposition to academic standards during the early 20th century. They

included Robert Henri, John Sloan, George Luks, Everett Shinn, William Glackens, Ernest Lawson, Maurice Prendergast and Arthur B. Davies.
• **Last joint exhibit of The Eight:** 1908, held in a gallery in New York, New York. It was also the only joint exhibit of The Eight.
• **Last surviving member of The Eight:** Everett Shinn, who died in New York on May 1, 1953, age 76.

Art—Artist Groups—Group of Seven
The Group of Seven were Canadian landscape painters who were inspired by Post-Impressionism. The group expanded and later operated under the name Canadian Group of Painters. They were active from 1910 to the 1930s. The original seven included Tom Thomson, J.E.H. MacDonald, Arthur Lismer, Frederick Varley, Frank Johnston, Franklin Carmichael and A.Y. Jackson. Lawren S. Harris joined in 1913 and Thomson died in 1917. When Frank Johnston resigned in 1926, A.J. (Alfred Joseph) Casson joined and became the youngest member of the group. Edwin Holgate and Lionel LeMoine Fitzgerald later were part of the group
• **End of the Group of Seven:** disbanded in the early 1930s after the death of Mac-Donald.
• **Last surviving member of the Group of Seven:** A.J. (Alfred Joseph) Casson, who died in Toronto, Canada, on February 19, 1992, age 93.

Art—Artist Groups—Pre-Raphaelite Brotherhood
The Pre-Raphaelite movement came along four centuries after the great Italian artist Raphael lived. It began in 1848 with the founding of the Pre-Raphaelite Brotherhood by a group of English artists who scorned contemporary art and instead chose to imitate the simplicity of Raphael and other early Italian painters.
• **End of the Pre-Raphaelite Brotherhood:** 1854, when the group divided because of different interests.
• **Last surviving member of the original Pre-Raphaelite Brotherhood:** William Michael Rossetti, who was best known for his later role as an art critic. He died on February 5, 1919, age 89.

Art—Artists
Last Works of Some Major Painters and Sculptors

Artist	Last Work
Bellini, Giovanni	Several works were completed by Giovanni Bellini shortly before he died in Venice, Italy, in 1516 in his late 80s. • **Last masterpiece:** The work often cited as his last masterpiece is the *Feast of the Gods*, an oil on canvas, undertaken around 1514 and completed by the time Bellini died. The work was commissioned by Duke Alfonso d'Este. A portion was subsequently painted over by Dosso Dossi. Titian made more changes in 1529. Today, it hangs in the National Gallery of Art in Washington, D.C.
Bernini, Giovanni Lorenzo	Giovanni Lorenzo Bernini died in Rome, Italy, on November 28, 1680, age 81. • **Last sculpture:** *Bust of the Savior* (1679-80), completed when Bernini was 80. The bust is in the Chrysler Museum of Art in Norfolk, Virginia.
Bonnard, Pierre	Pierre Bonnard died in Le Cannet, France, on January 23, 1947, age 79. • **Last completed painting:** *Almond Tree in Blossom*, oil and charcoal on canvas painted the year he died. It depicts a flowering tree that was visible from Bonnard's bedroom window. He was frail as he completed the work, so he instructed his nephew to change the grass color in the

	lower left-hand corner of the painting. Bonnard also left a number of works unfinished at the time of his death.
Botticelli, Sandro (Alessandro di Mariano Filipepi)	Sandro Botticelli died in Florence, Italy, in 1510, age around 65. His later works reflect the refuge he sought in mysticism after the death of the monk Savonarola. • **Last completed painting:** presumed to be *Mystic Nativity* (c. 1501), a tempera on canvas that is now in the National Gallery in London, England. It is the only work Botticelli signed and dated. It features an enigmatic Greek inscription alluding to the Apocalypse.
Canova, Antonio	Antonio Canova died in Venice, Italy, on October13, 1822, age 64. • **Last sculpture:** *Sleeping Nymph.* The model was completed in 1821. When Canova died a year later, the work was completed under the supervision of his brother, the Abbe Canova.
Caravaggio (Michelangelo Merisi da Caravaggio)	Caravaggio died in Tuscany, Italy, on July 18, 1610, age 36. • **Last completed painting:** unknown. *David and the Head of Goliath* (or *David and Goliath*), an oil on canvas at the Villa in Rome, Italy, is most frequently identified as Caravaggio's last work. The work has been dated as early as 1605 and as late as 1609-10. In the late 1990s, another canvas surfaced that may lay claim to being Caravaggio's last: *St. John the Baptist*, a painting of his favorite subject. The painting originally sold for a modest sum as the work of one of his followers. Some support has been gathering that *St. John the Baptist* may in fact be the work of Caravaggio and perhaps his last work.
Cassatt, Mary	Mary Cassatt's eyesight began to fail after she developed cataracts in the early 1900s. The American-born painter stopped painting in 1915. She died in France on June 14, 1926, age 82. • **Last major exhibit:** a series of paintings on women's suffrage in 1915.
Chagall, Marc	Marc Chagall died at La Colline, his home near St. Paul-de-Vence, France, on March 28, 1985, age 97. • **Last painting:** still on the easel in his studio.
Currier & Ives	The American lithography firm of Currier & Ives began production in 1835. It produced more than 1 million prints and over 7,500 different titles. Nathaniel Currier retired in 1880 and died in 1888, age 75. James Merritt Ives remained active with the firm until he died in 1895, age 70. • **Last year of firm's operation:** 1907. • **Last surviving artist who worked for the firm of Currier & Ives:** Louis Maurer, who retired in 1884. He died in New York, New York, on July 19, 1932, age 100.
Dali, Salvador	Salvador Dali died in Figueras, Spain, on January 23, 1989, age 84. • **Last painting:** *The Swallow's Tail* (1983), completed while he was living at a castle in Pubol, Spain.
Duchamp, Marcel	Marcel Duchamp died in Neuilly-sur-Siene, France, on October 1, 1968, age 81. • **Last major painting:** *You...me* (1918) a large oil and graphite on canvas, combining real and painted objects. • **Last work:** *Etant Donnés,* a multimaterial simulation of a doorway begun in 1945 but not completed until 1966; now in the Philadelphia Museum of Art.

Eakins, Thomas	Thomas Eakins died in Philadelphia, Pennsylvania, on June 25, 1916, age 71. • **Last outdoor work:** *Cowboys in the Bad Lands* (1888). Eakins devoted the rest of his years to portraiture. • **Last portrait:** *Dr. Edward Anthony Spitzka.* The painting was on Eakins' easel when the artist died. Some sources say it was painted in 1913; others state that Eakins was working on it when he died in 1916.
Gauguin, Paul	French-born painter Paul Gauguin spent most of the last 12 years of his life in the South Pacific. In 1901, he moved from Tahiti to the island of Hiva Oa in the Marquesas. He died there on May 8, 1903, age 55. • **Last painting:** landscape of Brittany, France, in winter.
Giacometti, Alberto	Alberto Giacometti died in Chur, Switzerland, on January 12, 1966, age 64. • **Last sculpture:** *Lotar* (1965), which depicts the artist's friend photographer Elie Lotar. • **Last work:** he prepared the text for *Paris san fin,* a book of lithographs of places where he had lived.
Giotto (Giotto di Bondone)	Giotto died in Florence, Italy, in 1337, age about 70. • **Last work:** presumed to be the campanile (bell tower) in Florence that Giotto was hired to design. It remained unfinished at the time of his death in 1337. From 1335 to 1336, Giotto may have worked for Prince Azzoni Visconti in Milan; however, all of the frescoes that were there have been lost. • **Last major surviving paintings:** frescoes in the Bardi and Peruzzi chapels.
Goya, Francisco	Spanish artist and printmaker Francisco Goya died in Bordeaux, France, on April 16, 1828, age 82. • **Last major printmaking project:** *Los Disparates,* created between 1815 and 1824. • **Last work:** *Bulls of Bordeaux,* a series of lithographs Goya made in 1824.
El Greco (Domenikos Theotokopoulos)	El Greco, who was born on the Greek island of Crete, died in Toledo, Spain, in April 1614, age around 73. • **Last work:** Chapel of the Hospital of St. John the Baptist, Toledo, Spain. El Greco spent the last six years of his life working on it. He painted three pictures for the altars between c. 1608 and 1614. Only one was completed: *Baptism of Christ.* Two remain unfinished: *Vision of St. John* and the *Annunciation.*
Haring, Keith	Keith Haring died in New York on February 16, 1990, age 31. • **Last work:** gold altarpiece entitled *The Life of Christ,* completed two weeks before Haring's death from AIDS. He finished the mold drawings and selected the bronze and patina for the castings; however, he never saw the work in its final cast form. The altarpiece is now in Grace Cathedral in San Francisco, California, where it is the centerpiece of the cathedral's AIDS Memorial Chapel. Another edition of the altarpiece is installed at the Cathedral of St. John the Divine in New York, New York.
Homer, Winslow	Winslow Homer died in his studio in Prout's Neck, Maine, on September 29, 1910, age 74. • **Last painting:** *Driftwood* (1909), finished shortly before his death.

Hopper, Edward	Edward Hopper died in New York, New York, on May 15, 1967, age 84. • **Last painting:** *Two Comedians* (1965), which depicts two commedia dell'arte figures dressed in white taking their bow, viewed from the orchestra pit.
Inman, Henry	Henry Inman died in New York on January 14, 1846, age 44. • **Last painting:** *An October Afternoon* (1845, showing a schoolhouse at the edge of a wooded area, with children playing.
Kahlo, Frida	Frida Kahlo died in Mexico City, Mexico, in 1954, age 47. • **Last painting:** *Joseph Stalin* (1954), an unfinished portrait.
Klee, Paul	Paul Klee died in Muralto-Locarno, Switzerland, on June 29, 1940, age 60. • **Last painting:** *Still Life* (1940).
Leonardo da Vinci	Italian-born Leonardo da Vinci spent the last few years of his life at the Château de Cloux, near Amboise, France. He arrived there in 1517 at the invitation of King Francis I of France. There is sparse documentation of what Leonardo did during these final years. He had a stroke soon after he reached Cloux, so he probably did little or no painting after that. • **Last known painting:** *St. John the Baptist*, painted between 1509 and 1516; one of three paintings in his possession when he died at Cloux on May 2, 1519, age 67. • **Last sculpture:** an equestrian statue made as a model for a larger monument for King Francis I. As well as laying possible claim to being the last sculpture of da Vinci, it may also be his last work. The bronze piece is at the Museum of Fine Arts in Budapest, Hungary, and carries the ascribed date of 1516-19.
Lorrain, Claude	Claude Lorrain died in Rome, Italy, in November 1682, age 81 or so. • **Last painting:** *Ascanius Shooting the Stag of Silvia* (1682). It depicts a hunting scene.
Manet, Edouard	Edouard Manet died in Paris, France, on April 30, 1883, age 53. • **Last painting:** *Bar at the Folies-Bergère* (1882). The painting is part of the Courtauld Institute of Art Collection in London, England.
Matisse, Henri	Henri Matisse died in Vence, France, on November 3, 1954, age 84. In his final years, he was in failing health and did more paper cut-outs and less painting. He made his last painting from his bed in 1951. • **Last completed work:** stained glass windows at the Union Church of Pocantico Hills, North Tarrytown, New York. They were created as memorials for the Rockefeller family. The windows were completed in 1954, just two days before Matisse died.
Michelangelo (Michelangelo di Buonarroti Simoni)	Michelangelo died in Rome, Italy, on February 18, 1564, age 88. • **Last work:** Saint Peter's Basilica in Rome. Michelangelo was appointed architect in 1542, and devoted the next 22 years to the project. He was working on it when he died in 1564. He left unfinished two sculptures, both Pietas: the Florence *Pieta*, which he intended for his tomb, and the Rondanini *Pieta*.
Mondrian, Piet	Dutch-born Piet Mondrian died in New York, New York, on February 1, 1944, age 71. • **Last painting:** *Victory Boogie Woogie*, unfinished. He was taken ill with pneumonia while working on it and died within a few days. The painting is now in the Gemeente Museum in The Hague, the Netherlands, which holds the largest Mondrian collection in the world.

Monet, Claude	Claude Monet died in Giverny, France, on December 5, 1926, age 86. The summer before he died, he arranged to have some 60 of his canvases destroyed. • **Last work:** *Water Lily Pond,* a series of 22 panels for the Museé de l'Orangerie in Paris, France, commemorating the victorious end of World War I. In 1919, while working on the project, Monet's eyesight began to fail. After he had glaucoma surgery in 1922, he was able to resume work.
Moses, Grandma (Anna Mary Robertson Moses)	Anna Mary Robertson Moses, who was better known as Grandma Moses, did not begin her artistic career until she was 80 years old. She died in Hoosick Falls, New York, on December 13, 1961, age 101. • **Last painting:** *The Rainbow* (1961), completed shortly before she died.
Parrish, Maxfield	Maxfield Parrish died in Plainfield, New Hampshire, on March 31, 1966, age 95. • **Last painting:** *Getting Away from It All* (1961), an uncommissioned landscape. • **Last figurative work:** "Jack Frost," for the October 24, 1936, cover of *Collier's* magazine.
Picasso, Pablo	Spanish-born Pablo Picasso continued to paint, draw and work on a series of etchings until he died in Mougins, France, on April 8, 1973, age 91. • **Last surviving pupil:** Marcel Mouly.
Pollock, Jackson	Jackson Pollock died near East Hampton, New York, on August 11, 1956, age 44. • **Last completed painting:** *Search* (1955).
Raphael (Raffaello Santi)	Raphael died in Rome, Italy, in 1520, age 37, • **Last painting:** *The Transfiguration* (c.1519-20), commissioned by Cardinal Giulio de' Medici. Raphael died before finishing the painting.
Rembrandt (Rembrandt Harmensz van Rijn)	Rembrandt died in Amsterdam, Holland, on October 4, 1669, age 63. • **Last completed painting:** *Return of the Prodigal Son* (1669). It is now in The Hermitage in Saint Petersburg, Russia. • **Last pupil:** Aert de Gelder, who died in 1727.
Renoir, Pierre Auguste	Pierre Auguste Renoir died in Cagnes-sur-Mer, near Nice, France, on December 3, 1919, age 78. • **Last major painting:** *The Bathers,* finished shortly before he died. When he painted it, he was so crippled by rheumatism that he could work only from a wheelchair with the brush strapped to his arm.
Rockwell, Norman	Norman Rockwell died in Stockbridge, Massachusetts, on November 8, 1978, age 84. • **Last *Saturday Evening Post* cover:** a painting of the late President John F. Kennedy for the December 14, 1963, issue. • **Last Boy Scout calendar:** "The Spirit of 1976" (1976).
Rubens, Peter Paul	Peter Paul Rubens died in Antwerp, Belgium, in 1640, age 63. • **Last painting:** *Perseus Liberating Andromeda,* an oil on canvas left unfinished at the time of Rubens' death. It was finished by Jacob Jordaens (1593-1678). The painting is now in the Prado (Museo del Prado) in Madrid, Spain.
Saint-Gaudens, Augustus	Irish-born American sculptor Augustus Saint-Gaudens died in Cornish, New Hampshire, age 59.

	• **Last sculpture:** *Marcus Daly* (bronze). It is now on the campus of the University of Montana.
Sargent, John Singer	American painter John Singer Sargent died in London, England, on April 15, 1925, age 69. • **Last project:** painting, sculpture and architectural elements for the interior of the newly built Museum of Fine Arts in Boston, Massachusetts. Sargent was about to return to Boston to supervise the installation of the last murals when he died in 1925. The murals were unveiled later that year. • **Last portrait:** *John D. Rockefeller* (1917), painted at the request of Rockefeller.
Seurat, Georges	Georges Seurat died in Paris, France, on March 29, 1891, age 31. • **Last painting:** *Circus* (1890). Although the painting was not finished, Seurat exhibited it at the Salon des Independents. He became ill and died before the exhibit ended.
Stuart, Gilbert	Gilbert Stuart died in Boston, Massachusetts, on July 9, 1828, age 72, • **Last painting:** sketch of Nathaniel Bowditch (1828). Stuart died before completing the painting.
Tanner, Henry Ossawa	American-born Henry Ossawa Tanner died in Paris, France, on May 25, 1937, age 77. • **Last painting:** *Return from the Crucifixion* (1936). The painting is now in the Howard University Gallery.
Titian (Tiziano Vecellio)	Titian was active as an artist until his death in Venice, Italy, in 1576 at about age 91. • **Last work:** *Pieta*, now in the Academy Museum in Venice. The work was created for Titian's tomb and was completed after his death by Palma il Giovane.
Toulouse-Lautrec, Henri de	Henri de Toulouse-Lautrec died at Chateau de Malrome, France, on September 9, 1901, age 36. • **Last painting:** *Examination Board* (1901).
Van Dyck, Anthony	Flemish-born Anthony Van Dyck died in London, England, on December 6, 1641, age 42. • **Last painting:** believed to be *The Martyrdom of St. George* altarpiece now in the Musée Bonnat in Bayonne, France.
Van Gogh, Vincent	Dutch painter Vincent Van Gogh shot himself in a field near Auvers, France, on July 27, 1890, at the scene of what many people claim was his last painting: *Wheat Field with Crows*. He died two days later, age 37. He left no information to indicate that this was actually his last work. • **Last painting:** unknown. Van Gogh worked on many canvases during the last few months of his life. In a letter he wrote just four days before he shot himself, he mentioned two new works: *Daubigny's Garden* and *Cottages with Thatched Roofs*. These are more likely to be among his last works than the often-cited *Wheat Field with Crows*. • **Last painting Van Gogh sold in his lifetime:** *Red Vineyard at Arles* in 1889. The painting is now in the Pushkin Museum in Moscow, Russia. The number of paintings sold in Van Gogh's lifetime is unknown. Estimates range from one to five.
Watteau, Antoine	Antoine Watteau died in Nogent-sur-Marne, France, on July 18, 1721, age 36.

	• **Last completed painting:** *The Halt During the Chase* (1721) when Watteau was in failing health.
Wood, Grant	Grant Wood died in Iowa City, Iowa, on February 12, 1942, age 50. • **Last completed painting:** *Spring in Town* (1941). It appeared on the cover of the *Saturday Evening Post* in 1942. The painting is now in the Swope Art Museum in Terre Haute, Indiana.

Automobiles
(*See also* Sports—Auto Racing.)

Automobiles—Designers—Porsche, Dr. Ferdinand
Bohemian-born auto designer Dr. Ferdinand Porsche died in Stuttgart, West Germany, on January 30, 1951, age 75.
• **Last car designed by Dr. Ferdinand Porsche:** 1550 Silver Spyder Porsche.

Automobiles—Designs—Jet-Powered—Chrysler Turbine Car
The Chrysler turbine car was an experimental jet-powered car built for use by the general public.
• **Last remaining example of a Chrysler turbine car:** built in 1963, and reported to be the culmination of more than 20 years of research and development. The car was completely restored in 1994-95 and is on display at the National Museum of Transport in St. Louis, Missouri.

Automobiles—Designs—Rear-Hinged Doors
Rear-hinged automobile doors were sometimes dubbed "suicide doors" because they could whip backward and accidentally open.
• **Last U.S. auto maker to use rear-hinged doors:** Lincoln-Continental. The company abandoned rear-hinged doors in 1969, when the design was found to be unsafe. The doors have reappeared but only in a modified design. The new rear-hinged doors cannot be opened unless the front doors are open.

Automobiles—Equipment—Seatbelts
The U.S. federal government set seatbelt design standards in 1963.
• **Last year U.S. cars were manufactured without seatbelts:** 1964. Front seatbelts were required in all American cars manufactured or assembled after January 1, 1965. Rear seatbelts were required for all cars made after January 1, 1968.

Automobiles—Makers—Nonunionized Workforce
The United Auto Workers union was chartered in 1935. Within two years, all but one of the top auto makers had unionized.
• **Last major U.S. auto manufacturer to unionize its work force:** Ford Motor Company. Ford resisted the first attempts to unionize workers in 1933. Ford's security staff was unionized in 1937. The Ford plant signed a contract with the UAW-CIO in June 1941.

Automobiles—Makers
Last Automobiles of Some Major Manufacturers

Automaker, Country and Years Made	Last Automobiles
Alvis (Great Britain, 1920-67)	Alvis was sold to British Leyland in 1973 and later to Unified Scientific Holdings in 1981, but they did not make passenger vehicles. • **Last Alvis model produced:** TF-21. Chassis production of this model ended in May 1967, after only 105 were made. • **Last Alvis car produced:** September 29, 1967.

American Motors Corp. (United States, 1954-87)	American Motors Corporation (AMC) was created in 1954 by a merger of Nash-Kelvinator and Hudson. In 1978, Renault began to acquire large amounts of AMC stock, and the two companies' cars were marketed together for awhile. Both were bought by Chrysler in 1987. • **Last AMC Rambler produced:** June 30, 1969. • **Last AMC Pacer produced:** December 3, 1979. • **Last AMC vehicles produced:** 4x4 Eagle, produced December 11, 1987. A few Canadian and French-built Renault models were carried over under the name Eagle.
Armstrong-Siddeley (Great Britain, 1919-60)	Armstrong-Siddeley merged with Bristol Aero Engines Ltd. in 1959, resulting in Bristol-Siddeley Engines Ltd., which was taken over by Rolls-Royce in 1967. • **Last Armstrong-Siddeley model produced:** Star Sapphire, 1960. • **Last Star Sapphire limousine produced:** September 6, 1960.
Auburn (United States, 1902-36)	Declining sales during the Depression hurt the Auburn Automobile Company, forcing E.L. Cord, the owner, to halt production in 1936. • **Last Auburn model produced:** 1937 model, of which only prototypes were manufactured.
Austin (Great Britain, 1906-89)	Austin became the Austin-Rover Group in 1982. Despite the fact that the 10 millionth Austin rolled off the assembly line in 1985, the company was out of business by 1989. It was consolidated as Rover. Herbert Austin died in 1941. • **Last Austin Maestro and Montego produced:** 1989. They became Rovers. • **Last Austin Metro produced:** 1990. It became a Rover model.
Benz (Germany, 1885-1926)	Karl Benz's car was the first gasoline-powered automobile to run successfully and lead to production. Benz died in 1929. • **Last of Benz:** merged with Mercedes on July 1, 1926, creating Mercedes-Benz, which survives.
Bugatti (Germany/ France, 1909-56)	In 1963, Bugatti was purchased by Hispano-Suiza, an aircraft engine manufacturer. The Bugatti name has been revived twice: once by a British company, and once by an Italian company that sold out to Volkswagen in 1998, which continues the name. Ettore Bugatti died in 1947. • **Last Bugatti produced:** 1952. In 1956, a Grand Prix car was produced but was never completed.
Cord (United States, 1929-37)	The Cord was made by Auburn Automobile Company, owned by E.L. Cord. He later made a fortune in uranium speculation. Cord served as a Democratic U.S. senator from Nevada in the 1950s. He died in January 1974. • **Last original Cord model produced:** 1931. The last 157 cars were called 1932 models. The Cord was launched again in 1935, but production was short-lived the second time around. • **Last Cord models sold:** 810 and 812, in 1937.
Crossley (Great Britain, 1904-37)	After Crossley stopped manufacturing passenger cars, the company continued to make buses and trolleybuses until 1956. • **Last Crossley passenger cars produced:** 1937, a few three-liter sixes styled like the Regis models that were probably made for the company's directors.
Daimler (Germany, 1886-1901)	Gottlieb Daimler's automobiles were among the earliest successfully marketed gas-powered cars. • **Last (Gottlieb) Daimler cars produced:** 1901, shortly after Daimler's

	death in 1900. The name was carried on by a British company that started in 1896. That second company continues today despite the fact that Daimler's legacy went with the Mercedes-Benz merger of 1926.
Datsun (Japan, 1914-83)	The Datsun name was given to the majority of Nissan Motor Company cars between 1933 and 1983. • **Last use of the Datsun name:** January 1, 1984. It was dropped in favor of Nissan as part of a corporate identity program.
De Dion-Bouton (France, 1883-1932)	Count Albert De Dion died in 1946; Georges Bouton died in 1938. • **Last De Dion-Bouton passenger cars produced:** 1932. The company continued producing utility vehicles such as garbage trucks until the late 1940s.
Delage (France, 1905-53)	The Delage company went into liquidation in 1935. The company was purchased by Walter Watney, and the name survived for nearly 20 more years. In 1954, Delage was absorbed into Hotchkiss along with Delahaye. Louis Delage died in 1947. • **Last Delage produced:** October 1953.
Delahaye (France, 1895-1954)	Emile Delahaye died in 1905. • **Last Delahaye produced:** June 9, 1954. Delahaye merged with Hotchkiss, and the new company became known as Societe Hotchkiss-Delahaye. All cars produced after that date carried the Hotchkiss name.
Delorean (Great Britain, 1981-82)	John Delorean's company was beset by financial mismanagement and allegations of illegal drug activity that landed the company in receivership and Delorean in jail. When Delorean failed to find financial banking, the firm was forced to declare bankruptcy. • **Last car produced by Delorean's company:** December 1982. A company purchased Delorean's inventory and produced cars during the following year.
DeSoto (United States, 1928-60)	DeSoto was a marque set up by Chrysler. Sales trailed off in the late 1950s and 1960. • **Last DeSoto models produced:** 1961. Production was halted after only about 3,000 were made.
Duesenberg (United States, 1919-37)	Duesenberg came under the ownership of E. L. Cord in 1926. • **Last Duesenberg model produced:** Model J, in 1935. The cars were sold through 1937. The Cord empire ceased in 1937, ending any possibility of further Duesenberg production. Approximately 480 Model Js were produced, and about 390 have survived. Frederick Duesenberg died in 1932; August Duesenberg died in 1955. The Duesenberg name has been revived several times, and replicas are still being made.
Durant (United States, 1921-32)	Production ceased on February 1, 1932, after Durant filed for bankruptcy. William C. Durant died in 1946. • **Last Durant models produced:** 1932 models. They were 1931 models that had been updated with some cosmetic changes.
Edsel (United States, 1957-59)	Edsel was a marque set up by the Ford Motor Company that turned into a legendary failure. Sales of the Edsel were poor. • **Last Edsel models produced:** 1960 models. Production stopped on November 19, 1959, after only 2,846 were made.
Franklin (United States, 1902-34)	Franklin was one of the early U.S. auto manufacturers. It produced wood-frame cars until 1927. • **Last Franklin produced:** 1934. Franklin was a victim of the Great Depression. In its final year, the company only sold 360 cars. The factory was

	taken over by Air Cooled Motor Corp., producers of airplane and helicopter engines, and the company later changed its name to the Franklin Engine Company. In the 1970s, the factory building was torn down to make room for a high school.
Hispano-Suiza (Spain, 1904-44)	A French branch of the company made cars from 1911 to 1938. • **Last Hispano-Suizas produced:** 1944. In 1946, the government-controlled Instituto Nacional de Industria took over the Hispano-Suiza factory. The factory later produced passenger vehicles under the name Furgoneta Hispano SA.
Hotchkiss (France, 1903-55)	• **Last Hotchkisses produced:** 1955, a year after the company merged with Delahaye. Car production stopped except for Jeeps under license from Willys-Overland. In 1956, the company was absorbed by Brandt, a manufacturer of electronic household appliances. Hotchkiss-Brandt continued to produce jeeps and military vehicles until 1971.
Hudson (United States, 1909-57)	Hudson merged with Nash to form American Motors Corp. (AMC) in 1954. • **Last Hudson Essex produced:** 1932. • **Last Hudson-Tailton produced:** 1938. • **Last Hudson Terraplane produced:** 1938. • **Last year the Hudson name appeared on cars:** 1957. • **Last Hudson model produced:** V8 Hornet.
Humber (Great Britain, 1896-1976)	In 1967, the Rootes Group, parent company of the Humber, was acquired by Chrysler. • **Last Humber model produced:** Sceptre, made until 1976.
Hupmobile (United States, 1908-40)	• **Last Hupmobile model produced:** Skylark, which reached the market in May 1940. Production ended in July 1940, after only 319 were produced. The last ones were sold in 1941 as 1941 models.
Isotta-Fraschini (Italy, 1900-48)	Isotta-Fraschini came under new ownership during World War II. Only prototypes of post-war models were built. • **Last Isotta-Fraschini produced:** 1948. The company was forced into liquidation in September 1948. Later, the company produced buses, trolley buses and some trucks. In 1993, the name was revived by Fissore.
Kaiser (United States, 1946-55)	Henry J. Kaiser died in 1967. • **Last vehicle Kaiser built in the U.S.:** four-door passenger car delivered March 1955.
Kissel Kar (United States, 1906-30)	• **Last Kissel Kar produced:** 1930. Kissel went into voluntary receivership in September 1930. The company reorganized as Kissel Industries and made outboard motors. Kissel Industries was purchased by West Bend Aluminum Company in 1944.
Lagonda (Great Britain, 1906-89)	• **Last Lagonda produced:** 1989, after about 600 were made. The wedge-shaped four-door Lagonda had been produced since 1976.
LaSalle (United States, 1927-40)	LaSalle was a marque of the Cadillac Motor Company, created and marketed as a lower-end option to a regular Cadillac. • **Last LaSalle produced:** 1940.
Locomobile (United	• **Last Locomobile produced:** March 1929. Locomobile was beaten out by its competitors. Durant, the owner, temporarily suspended production in

States, 1899-1929)	1929 to reorganize and design a new line. The stoppage proved permanent and only 328 Locomobiles were sold that year.
Martini (Switzerland, 1897-1933)	Martini decided to halt production after several years of losses. • **Last Martini model produced:** the NF. The company was liquidated in June 1934.
Maxwell (United States, 1904-25)	Maxwell came under the management of Walter P. Chrysler in the early 1920s, and he put the company into receivership. • **Last Maxwell produced:** 1925. After Chrysler renamed the company Chrysler Corp. in 1926, the Maxwell became a Chrysler, which evolved into the Plymouth in 1928.
Maybach (Germany, 1921-41)	• **Last Maybach produced:** 1941. During World War II, Maybach switched from passenger cars to the wartime production of half-tracks and tanks. After the war, the company did not return to passenger cars, but instead manufactured big diesel engines for boats and railroad cars. The company merged with Daimler-Benz in 1960, the year Karl Maybach died.
Morris (Great Britain, 1912-83)	William Morris died in 1963. • **Last Morris model produced:** the Ital in December 1983. With the end of production, the Morris name also ended. In 1984, the dies for the Ital were sold to Pakistan.
Nash (United States, 1917-57)	Charles Nash died in 1948. In 1954, the company merged with Hudson to form American Motors Corp. (AMC). • **Last year the Nash name appeared on cars:** 1957. • **Last Nash Lafayette produced:** 1939. • **Last Nash Healey produced:** 1954. • **Last Nash models produced:** Ambassador and Rambler. In 1958 they were marketed by AMC.
NSU (Germany, 1905-77)	• **Last NSU model produced:** K-70. In 1969, NSU merged with Volkswagen to form Audi NSU Auto Union AG. The Audi NSU cars were manufactured until 1977.
Oldsmobile (United States, 1897-2004)	The Olds Motor Vehicle Company, America's oldest car company, was founded by Ransom Eli Olds in 1897. The company mass-produced the first automobile in 1901 and became part of General Motors Corporation in 1908. Olds died in 1950. • **Last Oldsmobile produced:** metallic red Special Edition Olds Alero, in Lansing, Michigan, on April 29, 2004.
Packard (United States, 1899-1958)	• **Last Packard produced:** August 15, 1956, on the Detroit assembly line. The Packard name survived on Studebakers until 1958. • **Last Studebaker-designed Packard produced:** July 13, 1958.
Panhard- Levassor (France, 1890-1967)	Emil Levassor died in 1897. Louis Panhard died in 1908. Adrien Panhard died in 1955. Joseph Panhard died in 1969. In 1965, Panhard-Levassor merged with Citroen. • **Last Panhard-Levassor produced:** 24BT saloon model, July 20, 1967.
Pierce- Arrow (United States, 1901-38)	Pierce-Arrow was a pioneer American auto manufacturer. In 1921, it was the last U.S. auto maker to abandon the right-side driver's seat. • **Last Pierce-Arrow model produced:** VI2 sedan, built in the summer of 1938 for Karl Wise, who later became chief engineer at Bendix Aviation Corp. Only 17 1938-model Pierce-Arrows were manufactured, all from 1937 components. The Pierce-Arrow company assets were sold off in 1938. Rights to the VI2 engine were sold to Seagrave for use in fire engines.

Riley (Great Britain, 1898-1969)	The Riley name was discontinued by British Leyland in late 1969. • **Last Riley models produced:** four-door saloon 4/68 and 4/72, the Elf, and the Kestrel, all manufactured through 1969.
Singer (Great Britain, 1905-70)	In 1970, Chrysler took over the Rootes Group, which was then the parent company of Singer. • **Last British-built Singer Vogue produced:** March 1970. Production continued for a short time in New Zealand.
Stanley (United States, 1897-1927)	Stanley went bankrupt in 1923, and the remnants of the company were acquired by the Steam Vehicle Corp. of America in February 1924. • **Last Stanley produced:** 1927. Steam Vehicle Corp. of America was liquidated in 1929.
Studebaker (United States/ Canada, 1902-66)	• **Last new Studebaker model produced:** Avanti coupe, released in 1963. Production problems caused a low turn-out in 1963 and 1964. • **Last Studebaker Lark produced:** December 9, 1963. • **Last Studebaker truck produced:** December 1964, South Bend, Indiana. • **Last Studebaker production:** March 1966 at the Hamilton, Ontario, Studebaker plant. The Studebaker name survived in the form of Studebaker-Worthington after a 1967 merger with Wagner Electric and Worthington Corp. In 1979, this company was bought out by McGraw-Edison.
Stutz (United States, 1911-35)	Sales of Stutz models dwindled in the 1930s; only six were sold in 1934. • **Last Stutz Bearcat model produced:** 1925. • **Last Stutz model produced:** 1935, but 1935 models were probably old chassis put together and sold that year. The company continued manufacturing delivery vans for a few years but declared bankruptcy in 1937. The name was revived between 1970 to 1985, but only about 60 cars were sold.
Sunbeam (Great Britain, 1899-1937)	Sunbeam went into receivership in 1935 and ceased operation in 1937. The Rootes Group acquired the assets of Sunbeam and British Talbot. They combined these in 1938 to create the Sunbeam-Talbot line of cars. • **Last Sunbeam produced:** Sunbeam Thirty, a prototype put together for the 1936 Olympia car show.
Talbot (Great Britain, 1903-38)	• **Last Talbot models produced:** Talbot Ten and a Talbot three-liter for the 1938 model year. The following year, they were renamed Sunbeam-Talbot. A French car company by the same name produced cars from 1919 to 1959.
Tatra (Czech Republic, 1919-98)	• **Last Tatra produced:** 1998. During the final year, only seven Tatras were produced. The last one was in September 1998, after which the factory was closed.
Triumph (Great Britain, 1923-84)	• **Last Triumph model produced:** Triumph Acclaim (based on the Honda Acclaim). The last were made in June 1984.
Tucker (United States, 1946-48)	The Tucker was a short-lived but famous attempt as a start-up car company. Only 51 Tuckers were made and most have survived. Preston Tucker died in 1956. • **Last Tucker produced:** 1948.
Voisin (France, 1919-39)	Although Voisin production ended in 1939, Gabriel Voisin stayed on with the company that acquired control. Some prototypes displayed at car shows carried the Voisin name. Voisin died in 1973.

	• **Last Voisin vehicle produced:** a small six-wheeled truck shown by Voisin at the Paris Salon in 1958.
Willys (United States, 1914-63)	John North Willys died in 1935. Kaiser bought Willys-Overland in 1953 and changed the name to Willys Motor Company. Willys went out of the car business and concentrated on jeep production. • **Last Willys automobile produced:** May 1955. • **Last use of the Willys name:** 1963, when the company was renamed Kaiser-Jeep Corp. A Brazilian company, Ford Willys do Brasil, continued until 1970. An Australian company, Willys Motors Ltd., continued until 1972.
Wolseley (Great Britain, 1896-1975)	• **Last Wolseley model produced:** 18/22 series. The model was announced in March 1975 and lasted until October. Only a few thousand were manufactured. The following year, all the models in the series were renamed Princess.

Automobiles—Mass-Produced

The 1896 Duryea wagon was the first mass-produced automobile in the United States. Thirteen were made.

• **Last remaining 1896 Duryea wagon:** on display at the Henry Ford Museum at Greenfield Village, Dearborn, Michigan.

Automobiles—Models—Cadillac Eldorado

Cadillac produced the first Eldorado in 1953.

• **Last Cadillac Eldorado produced:** April 22, 2002, in Lansing, Michigan. It was donated to the Cadillac Museum.

Automobiles—Models—Chevrolet Camaro

The Chevrolet Camaro was introduced in mid-year 1966 as a 1967 model.

• **Last Chevrolet Camaro produced for public sale:** a 2002 Z28 coupe with automatic transmission, 5.7 liter V8 engine and all the extras. It was auctioned off on September 1, 2002, by Chevrolet through Kruse International for $71,500.

• **Last Chevrolet Camaro produced:** sent to the Chevrolet Museum.

Automobiles—Models—Chevrolet Corvair

Chevrolet introduced the Corvair in October 1959.

• **Last Chevrolet Corvair produced:** May 14, 1969, an Olympic gold Monza coupe made at the Willow Run assembly line in Ypsilanti, Michigan.

Automobiles—Models—Ford Model A

The Ford Model A was a successor to the Model T. Five million were manufactured by Ford Motor Company between 1927 and 1932.

• **Last Ford Model A produced:** February 28, 1932.

Automobiles—Models—Ford Model T

The mass-produced Model T—or Tin Lizzie—introduced in 1909, was a landmark in automobile manufacturing. The design remained the same during its lifetime. It was available only in black for most of its existence. When production of the Model T ended, more than 15 million had been sold.

• **Last of the all-black Ford Model Ts:** The 1925 model year. For the 1926 models, Ford announced his cars, previously all black would also be available in "deep channel green" or "rich Windsor maroon."

• **Last Ford Model T produced:** May 26, 1927, at the Ford factory in Highland Park, Michigan. As the last car rolled off the line, Henry Ford climbed into it with his son Edsel, the president of the Ford Motor Company, and drove to the Dearborn Engineering Laboratory, 14 miles away. The car was then parked next to two other historic vehicles: the first automobile that Henry Ford built in 1896, and the 1908 prototype for the Model T. In 2001, Ford announced plans to produce six Model Ts to commemorate the car's centennial.

Automobiles—Models—Ford Thunderbird

The Thunderbird was first produced in September 1954.

• **Last two-seat Ford Thunderbird produced:** December 13, 1957.

• **Last Ford Thunderbird produced:** September 4, 1997, in Lorain, Ohio.

Automobiles—Models—Reliant Robin

Reliant Robins were made for 65 years. Most of the 44,000 in use are in the United Kingdom.

• **Last Reliant Robin three-wheeled car produced:** February 14, 2001.

Automobiles—Models—Volkswagen Beetle (original)

The first Volkswagen Beetles were made in Germany in 1947. The first export models appeared in 1949. A modern updated version of the Beetle is still being made.

• **Last original Volkswagen Beetle produced in Germany:** January 19, 1978, at the Emden Volkswagen plant.

• **Last original Volkswagen Beetle sedan produced in the U.S.:** 1977.

• **Last original Volkswagen Beetle convertible produced in the U.S.:** 1979.

Automobiles—Models—Volkswagen Rabbit

The Volkswagen Rabbit was introduced in 1974. Volkswagen started producing them in Pennsylvania in 1979.

• **Last Volkswagen Rabbit produced:** July 1988, after which Volkswagen closed its New Stanton, Pennsylvania, plant.

Automobiles—Registration

The first state to register automobiles was Michigan in 1905.

• **Last U.S. state to require automobile registration:** Louisiana, in 1914.

Automobiles—Taxes—Horsepower Tax

The horsepower tax, introduced in Great Britain in the 1920s, was a method of taxing automobiles according to the horsepower of the vehicle.

• **End of the British "horsepower tax":** 1947. The tax was replaced by a flat-rate tax to allow the British cars to be more competitive in the export market.

Aviation
(*See also* Airships; Disasters; Wars and Battles.)

Aviation—Aircraft—Civil
Last Models of Civil Aircraft of Some Major Manufacturers

Model of Aircraft	Last Aircraft
Armstrong Whitworth Argosy	• **Last aircraft produced before Armstrong Whitworth was part of Hawker Siddeley Aviation:** Armstrong Whitworth Argosy, a four-engine civil and military cargo aircraft. • **Last remaining Armstrong Whitworth Argosy:** former Royal Air Force T2 XP447 that was sold to Duncan Aviation in the United States in 1976. It was retired from service with the Bureau of Land Management in Alaska in 1991. It is now at a museum at Fox Field in Lancaster, California.
Avro Avian	The Avro Avian established a number of records, including the first solo UK-Australia, UK-South Africa, and U.S. coast-to-coast flights. • **Last Avro Avian still flying:** originally sold in 1927 and used for a run to New South Wales, Australia, and for barnstorming. The plane was abandoned in Brisbane, Australia, in 1946. A man in Brisbane saved it in the 1970s and stored it under his house. In the late 1990s it was totally restored.

Beech Model 18	The Beech Model 18 was the first truly successful light twin-engine aircraft when it was produced in 1937. • **Last Beech Model 18 version produced:** Super H18, beginning in 1962. • **Last Super H18 produced:** November 26, 1969, and sold to Japan Air Lines to serve as a trainer for pilots.
Boeing 247	When the Boeing 247 was developed in 1933, it was the first modern civil airliner; 76 were built. Several were converted to C-73 trainer and transport planes during World War II, then returned to civilian service after the war. Some were still flying in the late 1960s. • **Last of the Boeing 247s:** Only two 247s have survived: one is at the Boeing Museum in Seattle, Washington; the other is at the Smithsonian's National Air and Space Museum.
Boeing 307 Stratoliner	The Boeing 307 Stratoliner was the first pressurized commercial airliner. Only 10 were produced, beginning in the late 1930s. Most went to Pan Am and TWA. Howard Hughes bought one. • **Last surviving Boeing Stratoliner:** The Clipper Flying Cloud, built in 1940. After it was retired from service by Pan Am in 1948, it went through a series of owners. The Smithsonian acquired it in the early 1970s. It completed a six-year restoration in Seattle, Washington, by retired Boeing employees in 2001, so that it could be showcased at the Smithsonian's new National Air and Space Museum. During tests in 2002, the plane had to be ditched into Elliott Bay, but sustained only minor damage. It was recovered and fully restored within the year. The Clipper Flying Cloud was flown to Washington, D.C., in October 2003, to take its place at the museum. • **Last of Howard Hughes's Stratoliner:** only the fuselage remains. It is being used as a houseboat in Fort Lauderdale, Florida.
Boeing 314 Clipper	When the Boeing Model 314 Clipper began transoceanic service for Pan American World Airways in 1939, it was the largest and most luxurious commercial aircraft ever built. Only 12 were produced. • **Last Boeing 314 Clipper produced:** Capetown Clipper (NC18612) in 1941. It was used by the U.S. Navy from 1942 to 1947 and was sunk at sea by the U.S. Coast Guard on October 14, 1947. • **Last Boeing 314 Clippers retired from commercial service:** in 1946, by Pan American World Airways. Some were purchased and used by smaller airlines until around 1950. • **Last remaining Boeing 314 Clipper:** the Anzac Clipper (NC18611), scrapped in 1951 in Baltimore, Maryland.
Boeing 707	The Boeing 707 was the first transoceanic jetliner and Boeing's first jet passenger liner. • **Last Boeing 707 produced:** a Boeing E-3D AWACS, built as a military plane in Renton, Washington, in May 1991.
Boeing 727	The Boeing 727 was designed to meet the needs of the short- to medium-range and medium-capacity market for airliners. • **Last Boeing 727 produced:** a 727-200F in September 1984, sold to Federal Express. Boeing sold 1,832 of the 727s. • **Last flight of the first Boeing 727 produced:** January 14, 1991. The plane had been in continuous service with United Air Lines since 1964. It was donated to the Museum of Flight in Seattle, Washington.
Concorde	Concorde, an Anglo-French venture, made its first commercial flight in January 1976.

	• **Last Concorde produced:** No. 16 [Concorde 216; a.k.a. G-BOAF (216)]. completed production on April 19, 1979, at Filton, England. The plane was operated by British Airways. • **Last flight of Concorde AF-4590:** July 25, 2000. The Air France flight crashed outside Paris, en route to New York, killing 113 on the plane and four on the ground. • **End of Concorde service:** Air France ended service on May 31, 2003, with a flight from New York to Paris, France. British Airways ended service on October 24, 2003, when three planes touched down at Heathrow Airport in England. Falling passenger revenue and rising aircraft maintenance costs brought the end of Concorde service, and with it the end of the era of commercial supersonic airline travel. • **Last Concorde flight:** November 26, 2003. G-BOAF (216) carrying 100 British Airways flight crew members, made a ceremonial flight over the Bay of Biscay then landed at Filton, where the Concorde was met by Great Britain's Prince Andrew. He accepted the handover of the plane and presented it to the Bristol Aviation Heritage Museum. G-BOAF (216) was both the last Concorde produced and the last to fly.
De Havilland Comet	The De Havilland Comet was the first operational jet airliner. It went into service in May 1952. • **Last De Havilland Comet model produced:** Comet 4C. • **Last De Havilland Comet produced:** XV148. Comet production ended in 1962. • **Last De Havilland Comet in use and last flight:** Dan Air, the last major airline operator of the Comet, retired its last Comet 4C on November 9, 1980. The last commercial flight departed Gatwick Airport in London, England. The last flight of any kind was on September 30, 1981, when a Dan Air crew flew a Comet to East Fortune, Scotland, for permanent display.
Douglas DC-3	The Douglas DC-3 was a standard liner and workhorse aircraft that was manufactured under several names. It was the Dakota in Canada. The Douglas C-47, the "Gooney Bird," is the military version. • **Last Douglas DC-3 produced:** delivered March 1947 to Sabena Airlines of Belgium. It crashed while landing at Heathrow, England, in March 1948. • **Last Douglas C-47 in U.S. military service:** a C-117D that was phased out by the U. S. Navy on July 12, 1976. • **Last Douglas C-47 in Canadian military service:** 1988, when the last Dakota was retired by the Royal Canadian Air Force.
Douglas DC-10	McDonnell Douglas built the Douglas DC-10 for American Airlines. The first one went into service in 1971. • **Last American Airlines DC-10 in service:** retired November 22, 2000.
Ford Trimotor 5-AT	The Ford Trimotor, or "Tin Goose," was the first American airliner to be produced in large numbers. The most popular of the series was the 5-AT. • **Last Ford Trimotor 5-AT produced:** 1933. Approximately 117 were built. About a dozen or so are known to be still flying.
Lockheed L-1011	Lockheed ended production on the L-1011 after 250 were built. • **Last Lockheed L-1011 TriStar produced:** August 19, 1983 (the 250th), at Lockheed's Palmdale, California, factory. • **Last Delta L-1011 TriStar in service:** Orlando Flight 1949, retired August 1, 2001, at Hartsfeld Atlanta International Airport; donated to The

	Flying Hospital. Delta had the largest L-1011 fleet and was the last major airline to use the aircraft.
Lockheed Constellation	The Lockheed Constellation (the "Connie") was designed in 1939 to meet TWA's need for a long-range commercial transport. • **Last Lockheed Constellation model produced:** L-1649A Starliner version of the Super Constellation. • **Last Super Lockheed Constellation produced:** delivered to Lufthansa on February 12, 1958. • **Last Lockheed Constellation in commercial service:** retired on July 16, 1975, at Le Bourget in France.
Martin 130 China Clipper	The Martin 130 China Clipper was the first trans-Pacific airliner. Three Martin clippers were produced; all eventually crashed. • **Last Martin 130 China Clipper:** destroyed in a botched landing near Port of Spain, Trinidad, in January 1945. It had logged more than 3 million miles.
Sikorsky S-42 Clipper	Sikorsky produced ten S-42 clippers. The first entered service in May 1934. • **Last Sikorsky S-42 clipper to enter service:** Pan American Clipper III, in 1937. It was destroyed in Manos, Brazil, on July 27, 1943. • **Last of the Sikorsky S-42 clippers:** Antilles Clipper, Brazilian Clipper, Columbian Clipper and Jamaica Clipper. All were used in Latin America, and all were scrapped on July 15, 1946.

Aviation—Aircraft—Biplanes

• **Last biplane in regular American airliner service:** the Curtiss Condor, last flown by American Airways in 1934.

• **Last biplane fighter produced in large numbers for the U.S. Army Air Corps:** Curtiss P-6E "Hawk" in the early 1930s. Forty-six were made.

• **Last remaining Curtiss P-6E:** at the U.S. Air Force Museum, Wright-Patterson Air Force Base, Dayton, Ohio. It was restored by the Purdue University Department of Aviation Technology in 1963.

• **Last U.S. Army Air Corps biplane fighter:** Curtiss XP-23. When the first XP-23 was delivered in April 1932, the U.S. Army Air Corps recognized the end of the biplane fighter era. Instead, they decided to use the Boeing P-26A monoplane fighter.

• **Last World War I-type biplanes ordered:** by the U.S. Navy. The order for 20 single-seat FU-1 biplanes was issued to Vought on June 30, 1926.

• **Last wooden biplane to enter British Royal Air Force service:** Gloster Gamecock in March 1926. It was last in service in 1931.

• **Last U.S. Navy biplane fighter:** Grumman F3F-3. Only 27 were ordered. The last F3F was retired from service in November 1943. Today, four are still airworthy.

Aviation—Aircraft—Propeller

• **Last propeller aircraft to score a combat victory against another propeller aircraft:** a Vought F4U-5 Corsair. A Honduran officer scored the victory during the 1969 conflict between Honduras and El Salvador.

Aviation—Aircraft—Military
Last Models of Military Aircraft of Some Major Manufacturers

Model of Aircraft	Last Aircraft
Avro Anson	The Avro Anson was the first monoplane used by the British Royal Air Force (RAF). More than 11,000 Avro Ansons were produced.

	• **Last Avro Anson produced:** May 1952. • **Last Avro Anson in RAF service:** retired June 1968.
Avro 504	The Avro 504 was the only aircraft to serve in operational duty in both World War I and World War II. Its use in World War II was limited to radar experiments on wooden aircraft. • **Last Avro 504 production version:** the 504N. • **Last Avro 504N produced:** 1933.
Boeing B-17 Flying Fortress	The Boeing B-17 Flying Fortress was the first effective heavy bomber. • **Last Boeing B-17 Flying Fortress produced:** a B-17G that was the 12,371st to roll off the Lockheed-Vega assembly line on April 9, 1945. • **Last home of the B-17D Flying Fortress nicknamed "Swoose":** Smithsonian's National Air and Space Museum. In the late 1940s, Frank Kurtz, who was the plane's captain during World War II, saved the "Swoose" from being scrapped. The plane is the only known U.S. military aircraft to have seen combat from the first day of the war until the war's end. And it was the last B-17 to be built without the large dorsal fin. • **Last Boeing B-17 lost in World War II:** aircraft 44-8640 of the 95th Bombardment Group, shot down off the coast of Suffolk, England, on May 7, 1945. Four of the 13 aboard survived. • **Last Boeing B-17 flown in the Korean War:** believed to be aircraft 43-39359. Eleven crew members were killed.
Boeing B-29 Superfortress	The Boeing B-29 Superfortress dropped the atomic bombs on Hiroshima and Nagasaki, Japan, in August 1945. • **Last Boeing B-29 Superfortress produced:** delivered on June 10, 1946 (the 3,627th). When World War II ended, orders for 5,092 B-29s were canceled; however, the B-29s that were on the production lines were eventually completed. • **Last Boeing B-29 Superfortress in service:** a B-29A (aircraft 42-94032) that made its last flight from the 307th Bombardment Wing in Okinawa, Japan, to Davis-Monthan Air Force Base in Arizona for storage on November 4, 1954. • **Last Boeing B-29 Superfortress version to be retired from the U.S. Air Force:** TB-29 (aircraft 42-65234), a radar evaluation plane removed from inventory on June 21, 1960.
Boeing B-47 Stratojet	The Boeing B-47 Stratojet was the first arrow-winged jet bomber and was the mainstay of U.S. nuclear deterrence at the time. A total of 2,041 B-47s were built. • **Last Boeing B-47 Stratojet produced:** a B-47E (aircraft 53-6244), delivered to the 100th Bomb Wing at Pease Air Force Base in New Hampshire on February 18, 1957. • **Last Boeing B-47 Stratojet in service:** retired from service on February 11, 1966. • **Last of any version of the Boeing B-47 Stratojet in service:** RB-47H (aircraft 53-4296) of the 58th Wing. Flown to Davis-Monthan Air Force Base for storage on December 29, 1967. This marked the end of B-47 service with the U.S. Air Force.
Boeing B-50 Superfortress	The Boeing B-50 Superfortress was the last propeller-driven bomber to be delivered to the U.S. Air Force. • **Last Boeing B-50 Superfortresses produced:** TB-50H trainers deliv-

	ered in March 1953. The U.S. Air Force cancelled production of the last 24 B-50Ds in 1951 and instead ordered 24 of a modified version, the TB-50H trainer (Model 345-31-26). The delivery of the last of these marked the end of B-50 production. • **Last Boeing B-50 Superfortress in service:** a B-50D (aircraft 49-330), withdrawn from the 97th Bombardment Wing at Biggs Air Force Base in Texas on October 20, 1955.
Boeing B-52 Stratofortress	The Boeing B-52 Stratofortress was a nuclear-deterrent bomber for 35 years. In all, 744 B-52s were made. • **Last Boeing B-52 Stratofortress produced:** the B-52H (Model 464-261). The 102nd and last B-52H was delivered to the 4,136th Strategic Wing at Minot Air Force Base, North Dakota, on October 26, 1962, ending Stratofortress production. • **Last Boeing B-52G Stratofortress in service:** flown to an aircraft storage facility at Davis-Monthan Air Force Base in Arizona in 1994.
Brewster Buffalo	The Brewster Buffalo was the first all-metal navy monoplane with retractable landing gear. It had the best kill ratio in World War II. • **Last Brewster Buffalo produced:** the F2A-3 (Brewster Model B-439). • **Last Brewster Buffalo F2A-3s delivered to the U.S. Navy:** 1942, in Miami, Florida, and used for training. The F2A-3s did not last long. The few remaining in service in late 1943 and early 1944 were scrapped. • **Last remaining Brewster Buffalo:** No complete planes have survived. Wreckage of a Finnish Air Force Brewster 329 that crashed in World War II has been found in a lake in Russia and awaits restoration.
Consolidated B-24 Liberator	The Consolidated B-24 Liberator was produced in greater number than any other U.S. military aircraft. More than 18,000 were built. • **Last Consolidated B-24 Liberator produced:** a YB-24N at the Ford plant on May 31, 1945, a few weeks after World War II ended in Europe. Orders for more than 5,000 B-24N-FO bombers were cancelled. The delivery of the few YB-24Ns by Ford ended Liberator production.
Consolidated PBY Catalina	The Consolidated PBY Catalina was the most important of the Allied flying boats of World War II. About 4,000 were built. • **Last Consolidated PBY Catalina produced:** delivered in September 1945. • **Last Consolidated PBY Catalina in service:** retired from the U.S. Navy in 1957. Many of the aircraft later served in forest fire fighting operations.
Convair B-58 Hustler	The Convair B-58 Hustler was the first supersonic bomber. • **Last Convair B-58 Hustler in service:** retired from the 305th Bomb Wing on January 16, 1970. The last two B-58 Hustlers retired (aircrafts 55-0662 and 61-0278) were flown to Davis-Monthan Air Force Base in Arizona for storage.
Convair F-106	The Convair F-106 completed the first fully automated cross-country flight in 1958. • **Last Convair F-106 produced:** Aircraft 59-0148 in November 1960, the 340th F-106 Convair built. It crashed in April 1969, while in service with the 318th FIS at McChord Air Force Base, Washington. • **Last Convair F-106 in service:** retired on May 17, 1991, after 32 years of continuous service and transferred to the Virginia Air and Space Center at Hampton, Virginia. Although it had been released from the U.S.

	Air Force in 1970, it later was used for developmental work at NASA's Langley Research Center and later still at Dryden Flight Research Center. It returned to Langley in 1979 where it was used for meteorological work and research.
Curtiss J4N Jenny	The Curtiss Jenny was the most famous of the U.S. World War I planes. Curtiss produced thousands for the U.S. Army between 1915 and 1927. • **Last version of the Curtiss J4N Jenny produced:** the JN-5H with a Hispano engine built by Wright. More than a thousand were built before production ended in 1927.
Curtiss P-40 Warhawk	The Curtiss P-40 Warhawk was the first mass-produced U.S. fighter. More than 13,000 were produced. • **Last Curtiss P-40 Warhawk produced:** a P-40N-40-CU that left the assembly line on November 30, 1944.
Curtiss SB2C Helldiver	The Curtiss SB2C Helldiver was the last in a line of planes developed for the U.S. Navy for dive bombing. Production amounted to about 7,200. • **Last Curtiss SB2C Helldiver produced:** 1945. Almost all of the Helldivers were scrapped. • **Last surviving airworthy Curtiss SB2C Helldiver:** an SB2C-5 (BuNo 83589) that belongs to the Commemorative Air Force in Texas. Another is now under restoration.
Douglas A-24 Dauntless/ Douglas SBD Dauntless	The Douglas A-24 was the U.S. Army's version of the Navy SBD carrier-based dive bomber. The Douglas SBD Dauntless is said to have single-handedly turned the tide of World War II in the Pacific. After the war, the few surviving A-24s were redesignated F-24s in the fighter sequence. • **Last Douglas A-24 Dauntlesses in service:** used in Mexico as trainers and for border patrol; the last of these was retired in 1959. • **Last remaining Douglas SBD Dauntless:** an SBD-6 (BuNo 54605) at the Smithsonian's National Air and Space Museum. A few A-24s still exist, but this is the only surviving authentic SBD.
Douglas A-26/ B-26 Invader	The Douglas B-26 Invader was introduced in the latter part of World War II as the A-26 attack bomber. • **Last Douglas A-26/B-26 Invader in service:** a VB-26B (aircraft 44-34610), operated by the Air National Guard. It was retired in September 1972 and donated to the Smithsonian Institution's National Air and Space Museum.
Douglas AD/A-1 Skyraider	The Douglas AD/A-1 Skyraider was the last U.S. Navy and Air Force reciprocating-engine combat aircraft. Altogether, 3,180 were produced. • **Last version of the Douglas AD/A-1 Skyraider:** the AD-7. • **Last Douglas AD/A-1 Skyraider produced:** February 18, 1957. In September 1962, all remaining Douglas AD-7 Skyraiders were redesignated A-1Js. • **Last Douglas AD/A-1 Skyraiders in service:** retired in 1972 by the U.S. Navy and Air Force.
Douglas A-4 Skyhawk	Nearly 3,000 Douglas A-4 Skyhawks were produced. • **Last Douglas A-4 Skyhawk produced:** A-4M Skyhawk (BuNo 160264), delivered to the VMA-331 Squadron at Cherry Point, North Carolina, on February 27, 1979. • **Last active-duty Marine squadron to fly the Douglas A-4 Skyhawk:** The Wake Island Avengers.

Focke-Wulf Fw-190	The Focke-Wulf Fw-190 was the last piston fighter produced by Germany during World War II and is widely regarded as Germany's best fighter. Approximately 19,500 were made. • **Last Focke-Wulf Fw-190 produced:** 1945.
Fokker Dr. I Triplane	The Fokker Dr. I Triplane became famous as the aircraft of choice for Manfred von Richthofen, the "Red Baron," beginning in 1917. Total production was about 320, and its lifespan was rather short. • **Last Fokker Dr. I Triplane produced:** May 1918. None have survived. Those seen today are replicas.
Fokker D. VII Biplane	The Fokker D. VII Biplane was perhaps the finest fighter of World War I. It was introduced in April 1918. Approximately 775 were used on the Western Front. The plane was so notorious that the Versailles Treaty specifically indicated all the front-line Fokker D.VIIs were to be handed over to the Allies. After the war, Anthony Fokker took hundreds of engines and dismantled plane parts to Holland and reassembled them. • **Last Fokker D. VIIs in service:** in the late 1920s in the Dutch East Indies.
Grumman F-14 Tomcat	The Grumman F-14 Tomcat is the U.S. Navy's standard supersonic carrier-based fighter. More than 700 were produced. • **Last version of the Grumman F-14 Tomcat produced:** the F-14D. • **Last Grumman F-14 Tomcat produced:** F-14D XV-9 (BuNo. 164604) in July 1992.
Grumman F4F Wildcat	The F4F Wildcat was Grumman's first successful monoplane fighter. • **Last Grumman F4F Wildcat produced:** August 1945. More than 7,800 were made. Less than 20 are still airworthy.
Grumman F6F Hellcat	The Grumman F6F Hellcat had the most victories of any U.S. aircraft in the Pacific during World War II. It was the Navy's main shipboard fighter during the last two years of the war. More than 12,000 were produced. • **Last Grumman F6F Hellcat produced:** November 1945. • **Last Grumman F6F Hellcat in service:** retired in 1954.
Grumman F8F Bearcat	The F8F Bearcat was the last of the Grumman piston-engine carrier-based fighters. The F8F Bearcat was flown by the Blue Angels from 1946 to 1952 and was their last propeller-driven aircraft. • **Last Grumman F8F Bearcat produced:** May 1949. In all, 1,266 were built. • **Last Grumman F8F Bearcat in service:** retired by the U.S. Navy in late 1952. The Bearcat later saw service with the French and Thai air forces.
Grumman F9F Panther	The Grumman F9F Panther was the first U.S. Navy jet in combat. Approximately 1,300 were built. In 1962, the last remaining Panthers in service with the Navy, all F9F-5KD drone directors, were redesignated DF-9Es. • **Last Grumman F9F Panther in U.S. service:** retired in the mid-1960s. • **Last Grumman F9F Panther in service anywhere:** Argentina; the last was retired in 1969. • **Last surviving airworthy Grumman F9F Panther:** an F9F-2B owned by the Cavanaugh Flight Museum, Addison, Texas.
Hawker Hurricane	The Hawker Hurricane was a staple of the British Royal Air Force during World War II and is considered one of the most versatile fighters of the

	war. More than 14,000 were built. • **Last Hawker Hurricane in service with the RAF:** January 1947. • **Last Hawker Hurricane British production version:** the Mark IV. • **Last Hawker Hurricane produced:** a Mark IIC, delivered in September 1944. The Hawker Company purchased one of the last Hurricanes produced and named it "The Last of the Many." It has been maintained in flying condition.
Lockheed F-104 Starfighter	The Lockheed F-104 Starfighter was the first plane designed for optimal flight over Mach 1. More than 2,500 were built. • **Last Lockheed F-104 Starfighter produced:** an F-104S, delivered in March 1979.
Lockheed F-117 Nighthawk	The Lockheed F-117 Nighthawk was the first operational Stealth aircraft. • **Last Lockheed F-117 Nighthawk produced:** delivered on July 12, 1991, to the U.S. Air Force at Palmdale, California.
Lockheed P-38 Lightning	The Lockheed P-38 Lightning is regarded as the first true fighter. • **Last Lockheed P-38 Lightning production version:** the P-38L. About 80 were later converted to a configuration called P-38M. The end of World War II in 1945 brought an end to production. After the war, many P-38Ls were scrapped or sold off as surplus. Those that remained in U.S. Air Force service in 1948 were re-designated F-38L.
Lockheed P-80 Shooting Star	The Lockheed P-80 Shooting Star was the first U.S. combat jet fighter and the first U.S. combat plane to exceed 500 miles per hour in level flight. • **Last Lockheed P-80 Shooting Star production version:** the P-80C. • **Last Lockheed P-80 Shooting Stars produced:** delivered to the U.S. Air Force in 1951.
Martin B-10	The Martin B-10 was the first all-metal monoplane bomber in service with the U.S. Army. • **Last Martin B-10 produced:** a Model 139WH-3 made for the export market that rolled off the Baltimore, Maryland, assembly line on May 5, 1939. • **Last surviving Martin B-10 Model 139:** an ex-Argentine plane that was returned to the United States in 1970s, refurbished and put on display at the U.S. Air Force Museum at Wright-Patterson Air Force Base in Dayton, Ohio.
Martin B-26 Marauder	The Martin B-26 Marauder was one of the most important medium bombers of World War II. More than 5,200 were built. • **Last Martin B-26 Marauder production version:** the B-26G, delivered by Martin's Baltimore facility on April 18, 1945. • **Last mission flown by Martin B-26 Marauders:** January 9, 1944, in the South Pacific.
McDonnell F-4 Phantom II	The McDonnell F-4 Phantom II was the most widely used U.S. jet in the 1960s and 1970s. In all, 522 were built between December 1966 and January 1972. • **Last McDonnell F-4 Phantom II production version for the U. S. Navy and Marine Corps:** the F-4J.
McDonnell Douglas F-15 Eagle/ F-15 Strike Eagle	The McDonnell Douglas/Boeing F-15 Eagle is the most widely used fighter in the U.S. Air Force. One version is the F-15 Strike Eagle The McDonnell Douglas F-15E Strike Eagle is the Air Force's most versatile fighter. • **Last McDonnell Douglas F-15E Strike Eagle produced:** delivered to

	the U.S. Air Force June 1994. It was the 200th. However, due to attrition, some replacements were ordered in 1997 and 1998.
Messer-schmitt Bf-109/ Me-109	The Messerschmitt Bf-109 was one of the staple fighters of the German Luftwaffe during World War II. Total production exceeded 30,000, more than any other single-engine fighter in history. • **Last Messerschmitt Bf-109 produced:** 1945. • **Last Messerschmitt Bf-109 production version:** the Bf-109K, which entered service in the fall of 1944. • **Last Messerschmitt Bf-109 in service:** with the Spanish Air Force in the 1960s.
Mitsubishi Reisen A6M Zero-Sen	The Mitsubishi Reisen A6M Zero-Sen, or "Zero," was the main Japanese fighter plane during World War II. • **Last Mitsubishi Reisen A6M Zero produced:** 1945. • **Last Mitsubishi Reisen A6M Zero production version to see combat:** the A6M6c. • **Last airworthy Zeroes:** Only 16 of more than 10,500 Zeroes produced by Mitsubishi and Nakajima have survived, and only two of them are airworthy. One is at the Planes of Fame Museum in Chino, California. The Commemorative Air Force in Texas safeguards the other. Many Zero replicas exist; some were built for movies.
North American B-25 Mitchell	The North American B-25 Mitchell was the medium bomber used on General James Doolittle's 1942 raid on Tokyo. The last version was the B-25J (NA-108). More than 9,000 were built. • **Last North American B-25 Mitchell produced:** a B-25J delivered from Kansas City, Missouri, to the U.S. Army Air Force in August 1945. The Kansas City plant closed the day after World War II ended.
North American F-86 Sabre/ FJ-4 Fury	The Korean War-era North American F-86 Sabre was the first successful swept-wing jet fighter and the last of the true gunfighters. • **Last North American F-86 Sabre produced:** the Navy's FJ-4 Fury. • **Last North American FJ-4B Fury delivered:** May 1958. • **Last North American F-86 Sabres in service:** The last Japanese F-86F made its final flight on March 15, 1982. Some sources say the last three Philippine F-86F Sabres were withdrawn from service in 1984. The last Venezuelan F-86F Sabre transferred to Bolivia was retired in 1993.
North American F-100 Super Sabre	The North American F-100 Super Sabre was the first U.S. jet to fly faster than the speed of sound in level flight. • **Last North American Super Sabre production version:** the F-100F, delivered in October 1959. Approximately 2,300 were built. • **Last North American F-100 Super Sabres in service:** retired from the Air National Guard in the late 1980s.
North American P-51 Mustang	The North American P-51 Mustang is regarded as the best fighter of World War II. More than 14,000 were built. • **Last North American P-51 Mustang production version:** the P-51H, in 1946. • **Last North American Mustang P-51 flown in combat:** a P-51 (re-designated F-51) on January 23, 1951, during the Korean War. • **Last North American P-51 Mustang in service in the U.S.:** a P-51D assigned to a tactical unit. It is on display at the Air Force Museum. It is painted as the plane flown by Col. C. L. Sluder, Commanding Officer of the 325th Fighter Group, 15th Air Force, in Italy in 1944.

	• **Last North American P-51 Mustang in service worldwide:** in the Dominican Republic. It was still in use in 1984.
North American SNJ/T-6 Texan	The North American SNJ/T-6 Texan was the most important trainer for the Allies during World War II. • **Last North American SNJ/T-6 Texan production version:** the T-6J, produced for the U.S. Air Force in the early 1950s. • **Last North American T-6 Texan in service:** used by the South African Air Force, which retired about 100 T-6 trainers in the early 1990s.
North American X-15	The North American X-15 introduced space flight and set speed and altitude records. It was the first winged aircraft to travel at Mach 4, 5 and 6 (four, five and six times the speed of sound). Only three X-15s were built and flown. • **Last North American X-15 flight:** the 199th mission, on October 24, 1968, piloted by NASA's Bill Dana, making him the last person to fly the X-15. • **Last of the North American X-15s:** No. 1 is in the Smithsonian National Air and Space Museum. No. 2, the fastest of the three, is at the Air Force Museum at Wright-Patterson Air Force Base in Dayton, Ohio. No. 3 crashed in a California desert in November 1967 when it went out of control during reentry, killing test pilot and NASA astronaut Major Michael Adams.
North American XB-70 Valkyrie	The North American XB-70 Valkyrie was designed as a high-altitude strategic bomber able to deliver nuclear weapons at speeds up to Mach 3. Only two were built. • **Last North American XB-70 Valkyrie flight:** February 4, 1969. • **Last of the North American XB-70s:** No. 1 was flown to the Air Force Museum at Wright-Patterson Air Force Base, Dayton, Ohio, on February 4, 1969. No. 2 crashed on June 8, 1966, following a mid-air collision. North American test pilot Al White ejected safely. His co-pilot, Major Carl W. Cross, was killed in the crash.
Northrop A-17A	The Northrop A-17A was the last pre-World War II single-engine attack aircraft ordered into production by the U.S. Army Air Corps. • **Last Northrop A-17A written off U.S. Army Air Forces records:** in early 1945. • **Last surviving Northrop A-17A:** aircraft 36-207, put on display at the U.S. Air Force Museum at Wright-Patterson Air Force Base in Dayton, Ohio, in 2000.
Northrop B-2A Spirit "Stealth Bomber"	The Northrop B-2A Spirit "Stealth Bomber" was the first operational flying wing with no vertical control surfaces. Six test aircraft were built before the plane went into production. • **Last test Northrop B-2A Spirit "Stealth Bomber":** the sixth, first flew on February 2, 1993.
Northrop F-5	The Northrop F-5 was sold to a number of countries through the U.S. foreign military sales program. • **Last Northrop F-5 produced:** delivered on January 16, 1987, to the U.S. Air Force. The final two F-5s off the assembly line did a fly-by at Wright-Patterson Air Force Base in Ohio.
Northrop P-61 Black Widow	The Northrop P-61 Black Widow was the first U.S. night fighter. • **Last Northrop P-61 Black Widow in service:** a P-61C that left U.S. Air Force service in 1952.

Northrop T-38 Talon	The Northrop T-38 Talon was the first supersonic trainer. Production amounted to nearly 1,200. • **Last Northrop T-38 Talon production version:** the T-38A. • **Last Northrop T-38A Talon produced:** January 1972.
Republic F-105 Thunderchief	The Republic F-105 Thunderchief was the first practical nuclear-capable long-range fighter bomber. • **Last Republic F-105 Thunderchief production version:** the F-105F. • **Last Republic F-105F Thunderchief produced:** aircraft 63-8366, delivered in January 1965. • **Last Republic F-105 Thunderchiefs in service:** a group of F-105Gs with the 128th TFW of the Georgia Air National Guard, which operated them until 1983.
Republic F-84 Thundstreak/ Thunderjet	The Republic F-84 Thunderstreak/Thunderjet was a widely used fighter and marked a successful switch from straight-wing to arrow-wing aircraft. • **Last Republic F-84 production version:** the F-84F. • **Last Republic F-84F produced:** rolled off the assembly line at Farmingdale, New York, in August 1957. • **Last Republic F-84 in U.S. service:** with the Air National Guard. The last F-84F left Air National Guard service in 1971. Some F-84s in service with Greece and Turkey remained in operation until the late 1970s.
Republic P-47 Thunderbolt	The Republic P-47 Thunderbolt was the most widely produced U.S. fighter of World War II. About 15,660 were built, and an order of 5,934 was cancelled on V-J Day in 1945. • **Last version of the Republic P-47 Thunderbolt produced in quantity:** the P-47N, a special long-range version built for service in the Pacific. The end of World War II brought production to an end in 1945. • **Last Republic P-47 Thunderbolt in service:** phased out in 1955 by the Air National Guard.
Sopwith Camel	The British-made Sopwith Camel was the leading Allied fighter plane of World War I. Total production ran to about 5,500, beginning in 1917. • **Last Sopwith Camel produced:** November 1918. • **Last surviving airworthy Sopwith Camel:** B6291, restored in the same British factory where it was originally built in 1917. The plane is now owned by a private collector.
Stearman N2S/PT-17 Kaydet	The Stearman was the basic training aircraft of U.S. and British pilots during World War II. Total production amounted to more than 10,300 between 1933 to 1945. • **Last Stearman Kaydet produced:** E-75, at Boeing's Wichita, Kansas, plant in February 1945 (aircraft 42-17794). It was the 10,346th Kaydet.
Vickers- Supermarine Spitfire	The Vickers-Supermarine Spitfire was the standard British fighter during World War II. • **Last Vickers-Supermarine Spitfire production versions:** Mks 21, 22 and 24, produced until 1947. • **Last Vickers-Supermarine Spitfire produced:** Mk 24, which rolled off the assembly line in 1947 and was delivered on February 20, 1948. • **Last Vickers-Supermarine Spitfire flown in combat:** April 1, 1954, by the British Royal Air Force against terrorists in Malaya.
Vought F4U Corsair	The Vought F4U Corsair was the best naval fighter of World War II and the last U.S. production prop fighter aircraft. Altogether, 12,571 were produced.

	• **Last Vought F4U Corsair produced:** an F4U-7, made for the French Navy and based on the F4U-4B. It rolled off the assembly line in 1952. • **Last Vought F4U Corsair in service:** 1964.
Vought F-8 Crusader	The Vought F-8 Crusader was the last U.S. fighter designed with guns as its primary weapon. It logged more than 2 million hours and more than 385,000 carrier landings. • **Last Vought F-8 Crusader in service:** RF-8G (BuNo. 146860), retired March 29, 1987. It was handed over to the National Air and Space Museum.

Aviation—Airlines—United States
Last Year of Operation of Major American Airlines by Corporate Name

Airline	Last Year Operated by That Name	Reason for Name Change
AC/EA	1968	Merged with Alaska Airlines.
Air Cal	1987	Merged with American Airlines.
Air California	1981	Renamed Air Cal.
Air Oregon	1982	Acquired by Horizon Airlines.
Air West	1970	Acquired by Howard Hughes and renamed Hughes Air West.
Alaska Air Transport	1939	Merged with Marine Airways as Alaska Coastal Airlines.
Alaska Coastal Airlines	1968	Merged with Alaska Airlines.
Alaska Star Airlines	1944	Renamed Alaska Airlines.
Alaska-Washington Airways	1932	Ceased operations.
All American Airways	1953	Renamed Allegheny Airlines.
All American Aviation	1949	Renamed All American Airways.
Allegheny Airlines	1979	Began operating as a USAir carrier.
American Airways	1934	Renamed American Airlines.
Arizona Airways	1950	Merged with Monarch Air and Challenger Airlines as Frontier Airlines.
Boeing Air Transport	1931	Merged with National Air Transport, Varney Air Lines and Pacific Air Transport as United Air Lines.
Bonanza Air Lines	1968	Merged with Pacific Air Lines and West Coast Airlines as Air West.
Bonanza Air Services	1945	Renamed Bonanza Air Lines.
Braniff Airlines	1930	Renamed Braniff Airways.
Braniff Airways	1946	Renamed Braniff International Airways.
Braniff International Airways	1992	Ceased operations. Resurrected as Braniff, Inc. (1984-89) and again as Braniff International (1991-92).
Capital Airlines	1960	Acquired by United Air Lines.
Central Airways	1967	Acquired by Frontier Airlines.
Central Vermont Airways	1940	Renamed Northwest Airlines.

Challenger Air Lines	1950	Merged with Monarch Air Lines and Challenger Airlines as Frontier Airlines.
Chicago & Southern Airlines	1953	Acquired by Delta C&S Air Lines.
Cordova Airlines	1967	Merged with Alaska Airlines.
Delta Air Corporation	1945	Renamed Delta Air Lines, Inc.
Delta Air Lines, Inc.	1953	Renamed Delta C&S Air Lines with purchase of Chicago & Southern Airlines.
Delta Air Services	1930	Renamed Delta Air Corporation.
Delta C&S Air Lines	c. 1955	Renamed Delta Air Lines.
Eastern Airlines	1991	Ceased operation.
Eastern Airlines Shuttle	1989	Renamed Trump Shuttle.
Ellis Airlines	1962	Merged with Alaska Coastal Airlines as AC/EA.
Empire Airlines	1986	Merged with Piedmont Airlines.
Federal Express	1994	Renamed FedEx.
Flying Tiger Line	1989	Acquired by Federal Express.
Frontier Airlines	1986	Acquired by Continental Airlines. In 1994, a new Frontier Airlines was established.
Hanford's Tri-State Airlines	1938	Renamed Mid-Continent Airlines.
Hughes Air West	1980	Acquired by Republic Airlines.
Inter-Island Airways Ltd.	1941	Renamed Hawaiian Airlines.
Jet America	1987	Acquired by Alaska Airlines.
Lake Central Airlines	1968	Merged with Allegheny Airlines.
MGM Grand Air	1994	Ceased operation. Acquired by Champion Air in 1995.
Mid-Continent Airlines	1952	Merged with Braniff International Airways.
Midway Airlines	1991	Ceased operation. Aircraft, gates and some employees acquired by Southwest Airlines.
Mohawk Airlines	1972	Acquired by Allegheny Airlines.
Monarch Air Lines	1950	Merged with Challenger Airlines and Arizona Airways into Frontier Airlines.
National Air Transit	1931	Merged with Boeing Air Transport, Varney Air Lines and Pacific Air Transport as United Air Lines.
National Airlines System	1937	Renamed National Airlines.
National Airlines	1981	Merged with Pan Am.
National Park Airways	1937	Acquired by Western Air Express.
New York Air	1987	Acquired by Continental Airlines.
New York Airways	1931	Acquired by Eastern Air Transport.
North Central Airlines	1979	Merged with Southern Airways; name changed to Republic.
Northern Air Transport	1934	Acquired by Northwest Airways, which then was renamed Northwest Airlines.
Northeast Airlines	1972	Merged with Delta Air Lines.
Northwest Airlines	1947	Renamed Northwest Orient Airlines. Retained that name until 1988.

Northwest Airways	1934	Renamed Northwest Airlines.
Northwest Orient Airlines	1988	Dropped "Orient." Resumed former name: Northwest Airlines.
Ozark Air Lines	1986	Merged with Trans World Airlines.
Pacific Air Lines	1968	Acquired by Air West along with Bonanza and West Coast airlines.
Pacific Air Transport	1931	Merged with Boeing Air Transport, Varney Air Lines and National Air Transport as United Air Lines.
Pacific Alaska Airways	1975	Ceased operations.
Pacific Northern Airways	1947	Renamed Pacific Northern Airlines.
Pacific Northern Airlines	1967	Merged with Western Airlines.
Pacific Southwest Airlines	1988	Acquired by USAir.
Pan American World Airways (Pan Am)	1991	Ceased operations. In 1996, a new Pan Am operated briefly, then went bankrupt. The Pan Am name was purchased by another company.
Pan-American Grace Airways	1967	Acquired by Braniff International Airways.
Pennsylvania-Central Airlines	1948	Renamed Capital Airlines.
People Express	1987	Acquired by Continental Airlines.
Piedmont	1989	Merged with USAir.
Pitcairn Aviation	1930	Renamed Eastern Air Transport, Inc.
Reno Air	1998	Acquired by American Airlines.
Republic Airlines	1986	Acquired by Northwest Orient Airlines.
Resort Air, Inc.	1989	Renamed Trans States Airlines, Inc.
Robinson Airlines	1952	Renamed Mohawk Airlines.
Southern Airways	1979	Merged with North Central Airlines; name changed to Republic Airlines.
Southwest Airways	1958	Renamed Pacific Air Lines.
Southwest Pacific Airlines	1988	Merged with USAir.
Star Air Service	1937	Renamed Star Airlines.
Star Airlines	1942	Renamed Alaska Star Airlines.
Texas International Airways	1982	Merged with Continental Airlines.
Trans America	1986	Ceased operations.
Trans-Caribbean Airways	1970	Acquired by American Airlines.
Transcontinental & Western Air	1950	Renamed Trans World Airlines.
Trans International Airways	1976	Renamed Trans America.
Transwestern Airlines	1983	Acquired by Horizon Airlines.
Trans World Airlines (TWA)	2001	Ceased operations. Sold to American Airlines.
Trump Shuttle	1992	Renamed USAir Shuttle.
Turner Airlines	1951	Renamed Lake Central Airlines.
USAir	1997	Renamed US Airways.
ValuJet	1997	Merged with Air Tran Airways.
Varney Air Lines	1931	Merged with National Air Transport, Boeing Air Transport and Pacific Air Transport as United Air Lines.

West Coast Airlines	1968	Merged with Bonanza and Pacific Air Lines as Air West.
Western Air Express	1941	Renamed Western Airlines.
Western Airlines	1987	Merged with Delta Air Lines.
Wisconsin Central Airlines	1952	Renamed North Central Airlines.
Woodley Airways	1945	Renamed Pacific Northern Airways.

Aviation—Airports and Airfields

Aviation—Airports and Airfields—Chicago Midway Airport (Illinois)
Opened as Chicago Municipal Airport in 1927.
• **Last known as Chicago Municipal Airport:** 1949. Renamed Chicago Midway Airport to honor participants of the World War II Battle of Midway.

Aviation—Airports and Airfields—Chicago O'Hare International Airport (Illinois)
Some of the land on which O'Hare stands held a Douglas aircraft factory and airfield during World War II. The city of Chicago purchased the land after the war and acquired 7,000 additional acres for a new airport.
• **Last known as Chicago Orchard Airport:** 1949. Renamed Chicago O'Hare International Airport in honor of Lieutenant Edward O'Hare, a Navy pilot who was killed in World War II.

Aviation—Airports and Airfields—Fort Worth Meacham International Airport (Texas)
Opened as Fort Worth Municipal Airport in 1925.
• **Last known as Fort Worth Municipal Airport:** 1927. Renamed Meacham Field, in honor of former Fort Worth Mayor H. C. Meacham.
• **Last known as Meacham Field:** 1985. Renamed Fort Worth Meacham Airport.
• **Last known as Fort Worth Meacham Airport:** 1995. Renamed Fort Worth Meacham International Airport.

Aviation—Airports and Airfields—General Mitchell International Airport (Wisconsin)
• **Last known as Milwaukee County Airport:** 1941. Renamed General Mitchell Field to honor Milwaukee native and aviation activist General William ("Billy") Mitchell who argued for a strong air force. He died in 1936.
• **Last known as General Mitchell Field:** 1986. Renamed General Mitchell International Airport.

Aviation—Airports and Airfields—John F. Kennedy International Airport (New York)
Opened as New York International Airport at Idlewild in Queens, New York, in 1948.
• **Last known as New York International Airport:** 1963. Renamed John F. Kennedy International Airport shortly after the assassination of President John F. Kennedy.

Aviation—Airports and Airfields—LaGuardia Airport (New York)
Dedicated October 1939 as New York City Municipal Airport.
• **Last known as New York City Municipal Airport:** November 1939. Renamed New York Municipal Airport-LaGuardia Field.
• **Last known as New York Municipal Airport-LaGuardia Field:** 1947. Renamed LaGuardia Airport to honor New York City Mayor Fiorello LaGuardia who died in 1947.

Aviation—Airports and Airfields—Logan International Airport (Massachusetts)
Opened as Boston Airport in 1923.
• **Last known as Boston Airport:** 1956. Renamed Logan International Airport to honor Boston native Lieutenant General Edward Lawrence Logan.

Aviation—Airports and Airfields— Louis Armstrong New Orleans International Airport (Louisiana)

Opened in the mid-1940s as Moisant Field, named for French-Canadian aviator John B. Moisant, who was killed in a plane crash in 1910.

• **Last known as Moisant Field:** 1962. Renamed New Orleans International Airport.

• **Last known as New Orleans International Airport:** 2001. Renamed Louis Armstrong New Orleans International Airport to honor the great jazz trumpeter, singer and entertainer during the celebration of the centennial of Armstrong's birth.

Aviation—Airports and Airfields— Nashville International Airport (Tennessee)

Opened as Berry Field in 1937.

• **Last known as Berry Field:** 1988. Renamed Nashville International Airport.

Aviation—Airports and Airfields— Newark Liberty International Airport (New Jersey)

Opened as a municipal airport in 1928.

• **Last known as Newark International Airport:** 2002. Renamed Newark Liberty International Airport to honor those who died in the 9/11 terrorist attacks.

Aviation—Airports and Airfields— Norfolk International Airport (Virginia)

Opened as Norfolk Municipal Airport in 1938.

• **Last known as Norfolk Municipal Airport:** 1968. Renamed Norfolk Regional Airport.

• **Last known as Norfolk Regional Airport:** 1976. Renamed Norfolk International Airport.

Aviation—Airports and Airfields— Orlando Executive Airport (Florida)

Opened in 1928 as Orlando Municipal Airport.

• **Last known as Orlando Municipal Airport:** 1940. Renamed Orlando Air Base, when the U.S. Army took over the airport for military training.

• **Last known as Orlando Air Base:** 1962. Renamed Herndon Airport.

• **Last known as Herndon Airport:** 1982. Renamed Orlando Executive Airport.

Aviation—Airports and Airfields— Rick Husband Amarillo International Airport (Texas)

Opened in 1929 as English Field.

• **Last known as English Field:** 1952. Renamed Amarillo Air Terminal.

• **Last known as Amarillo Air Terminal:** 1976. Renamed Amarillo International Airport.

• **Last known as Amarillo International Airport:** 2003. Renamed Rick Husband Amarillo International Airport to honor native son and commander of the space shuttle *Columbia* that disintegrated over Texas in February 2003.

Aviation—Airports and Airfields— Ronald Reagan Washington National Airport (Washington, D.C.)

Opened in 1941 as Washington National Airport.

• **Last known as Washington National Airport:** 1998. Renamed Ronald Reagan Washington National Airport to honor the former president.

Aviation—Airports and Airfields— Saint Louis Downtown-Parks Airport (Missouri)

Opened in 1929 as Curtiss-Steinberg Airport.

• **Last known as Curtiss-Steinberg Airport:** 1940. Renamed Curtiss-Parks Airport.

• **Last known as Curtiss-Parks Airport:** Mid 1940s. Renamed Parks Metropolitan Airport after World War II.

• **Last known as Parks Metropolitan Airport:** 1965. Renamed Bi-State Parks Airport. The airport was reopened after being closed for six years.

• **Last known as Bi-States Parks Airport:** 1984. Renamed Saint Louis Downtown-Parks Airport.

Aviation—Airports and Airfields—
Salt Lake International Airport (Utah)
Opened in 1920 as Woodward Field, named for local pilot John P. Woodward.
- **Last known as Woodward Field:** 1930. Renamed Salt Lake City Municipal Airport.
- **Last known as Salt Lake City Municipal Airport:** 1968. Renamed Salt Lake International Airport.

Aviation—Airports and Airfields—
San Francisco International Airport (California)
Opened in 1927 as Mills Field Municipal Airport.
- **Last known as Mills Field Municipal Airport:** 1931. Renamed San Francisco Airport.
- **Last known as San Francisco Airport:** 1948. Renamed San Francisco International Airport.

Aviation—Airports and Airfields—
Ted Stevens Anchorage International Airport (Alaska)
Opened in 1951 as Anchorage International Airport.
- **Last known as Anchorage International Airport:** 2002. Renamed Ted Stevens Anchorage International Airport to honor Alaskan U.S. Senator Ted Stevens.

Aviation—Airports and Airfields—
Tweed-New Haven Airport (Connecticut)
Opened in 1931 as New Haven Municipal Airport.
- **Last known as New Haven Municipal Airport:** 1961. Renamed Tweed-New Haven Airport for Jack Tweed, manager of the airport, who died that year.

Aviation—Air Races—All-Women's Transcontinental Air Race
The first All-Women's Transcontinental Air Race in 1929 ran from Santa Monica, California, to Cleveland, Ohio, and was dubbed the "Powder Puff Derby" by humorist/actor Will Rogers. Nineteen women participated in the 2,759-mile race.
- **Last surviving participant in the first**

All-Women's Transcontinental Air Race:
pilot Evelyn Trout, who died in La Jolla, California, in February 2003, age 97.

Aviation—Airships
(*See also* Disasters—Airships.)

Aviation—Airships—United States
The rigid airship program in the United States got started after World War I, with the help of British and German technology. The U.S. Naval Air Station opened in Lakehurst, New Jersey, in 1921 with a hanger large enough to hold an airship.
- **Last U.S. rigid airship to use hydrogen:** *Roma,* which crashed in 1922.
- **Last of the U.S. rigid airship program:** ended after the *Macon* disaster in 1935.

Aviation—Airships—United States—
USS *Los Angeles*
The USS *Los Angeles* was partially funded by World War I reparations and was to be used only for civilian purposes. She was completed as LZ 126 at Friedrichshafen, Germany, in August 1924 and was commissioned in the United States in November 1924 as ZR 3. During her flying days, she made more than 300 flights, earning for her the reputation of being the most successful of the Navy's rigid airships.
- **Last of the USS *Los Angeles*:** decommissioned on June 30, 1932, and stored at the Lakehurst airship hanger in New Jersey. She was used for three years in non-flying experiments such as mooring. *Los Angeles* left the hanger for the last time in November 1937. In October 1939, she was stricken from the Navy List and scrapped.

Aviation—Airships—Zeppelins—
Hindenburg
The *Hindenburg* (LZ 129), a sister ship of the *Graf Zeppelin II,* was launched in March 1936, and traveled between Friedrichshafen, Germany, and the Naval Air Station at Lakehurst, New Jersey. On May 6, 1937, while landing at Lakehurst, the *Hindenburg* burst into flames and burned within seconds. Thirty-six of the 97 passengers and crew

were killed at the time or died later from burns. A commission concluded the explosion was caused by several factors, including a spark of static electricity near a hydrogen gas leak. Some people believed the crash was an anti-Nazi act of sabotage. Later theorists have implicated the formula for making the dope—the oil-based sealer mixed with aluminum used on the outer canvas covering the ship—as the probable cause of the disaster. The dope had recently been changed by the Zeppelin Company.

• **End of the Age of the Airship:** The *Hin-* *denburg* crash was the culmination of a long series of airship disasters, and it hastened the end of the Age of the Airship. Tragedies such as the *Akron, Dixmude, Macon, Roma* and *Hindenburg* had claimed more than 300 lives. In Germany, the *Graf Zeppelin I* was retired from service after the *Hindenburg* crash and stored in a hanger until 1940, when Herman Goering ordered its destruction so that its materials could be used in the war. The *Graf Zeppelin II*, an airship identical to the *Hindenburg*, was also scrapped in 1940 for its materials.

Aviation—Airships—Germany
Last of Some of the German Airships of World War I

Note: LZ stands for Luftshiffbau Zeppelin, one of the two German factories that produced the rigid airships (luft = air; shiff = ship; bau = built). The number represents the sequence in which the ships were produced. SL stands for the Schütte-Lanz Company, Germany's other dirigible maker.

Airship	Description
LZ 2	Destroyed in a gale during its second flight, January 18, 1906.
LZ 4	Destroyed by fire, August 5, 1908.
LZ 5	Destroyed after a forced landing, May 10, 1910.
LZ 14	Crashed into the North Sea, September 9, 1913.
LZ 18 (L2)	Exploded while airborne, September 17, 1913.
LZ 22 (Z-VII)	Shot down, August 23, 1914.
LZ 23 (Z-VIII)	Shot down, August 23, 1914.
LZ 24 (L3)	Stranded and destroyed on the coast of Jutland, Denmark, during a gale, February 17, 1915.
LZ 25 (Z-IX)	Destroyed in a shed in Dusseldorf, Germany, when it was bombed by the Royal Naval Air Service, October 8, 1914.
LZ 27 (L4)	Stranded and destroyed on the coast of Jutland, Denmark, during a gale, February 17, 1915.
LZ 29 (Z-X)	Dismantled, August 16, 1915, after being hit by gunfire during a raid over Russia.
LZ 31 (L6)	Destroyed in its shed in Fühlsbüttel, Germany, September 16, 1916. It caught fire while being inflated. LZ 36 was also destroyed in the fire.
LZ 32 (L7)	Shot down by the cruisers *Phaeton* and *Galatea*; destroyed by the British submarine E31 on May 4, 1916.
LZ 33 (L8)	Shot down near Ostend, Belgium, March 5, 1915.
LZ 36 (L9)	Destroyed in its shed in Fühlsbüttel, Germany, September 16, 1916. It burned in the same fire that destroyed LZ 31.
LZ 37	Destroyed by the Royal Naval Air Service at Ghent, Belgium, June 6-7, 1915.
LZ 38	Destroyed in its shed at Evere, near Brussels, Belgium, on June 7, 1915. LZ 38 was the first German airship to bomb London, England, killing seven people and injuring 35 on May 31, 1915.

LZ 39	Destroyed during a forced landing following a raid, October 14, 1916.
LZ 40	Destroyed by lightning, September 3, 1915.
LZ 46 (L14)	LZ 46 (L14) and five other German Navy Zeppelins were wrecked by their crews at Nordholz, Germany, on June 23, 1919, to prevent being handed over to the Allies, as ordered by the Versailles Peace Treaty.
LZ 47	Burned during a raid, February 21, 1916.
LZ 48 (L15)	Shot down off the English coast, April 1, 1916.
LZ 50 (L16)	Dismantled October 19, 1917, after being wrecked on landing.
LZ 52 (L18)	Burned in its shed at Toska, Germany, November 17, 1915.
LZ 53 (L17)	Caught fire and was destroyed in its shed at Tondern, Germany, December 28, 1916. The LZ 69 (L24) was also destroyed when it ignited.
LZ 54 (L19)	Shot down over the North Sea by British aircraft after a raid on England, February 2, 1916.
LZ 61 (L21)	Shot down off Lowestoft, England, by British fighters, November 28, 1916.
LZ 64 (L22)	Shot down over England by a British flying boat, May 28, 1916.
LZ 66 (L23)	Shot down near Jutland, Denmark, August 21, 1917.
LZ 69 (L24)	Burned in its shed at Tondern, Germany, when the LZ 53 (L17) caught fire, December 28, 1916.
LZ 72 (L31)	Shot down by British aircraft over Potters Bar, England, October 1916.
LZ 74 (L32)	Caught fire in raid over England. Fell at Great Burstead, September 23-24, 1916.
LZ 76 (L33)	Forced to land in England after being badly damaged by anti-aircraft fire, September 23-24, 1916.
LZ 78 (L34)	Shot down off Hartlepool, England, November 27, 1916.
LZ 79 (L41)	LZ 79 (L41) and five other German Navy Zeppelins were wrecked by their crews at Nordholz, Germany, on June 23, 1919, to prevent being handed over to the Allies, as ordered by the Versailles Peace Treaty.
LZ 82 (L36)	Destroyed during forced landing in a fog, February 7, 1917.
LZ 84 (L38)	Forced to land in Russia, December 29, 1916.
LZ 85 (L45)	Forced to land behind enemy lines in France. The airship was destroyed by the crew, October 20, 1917.
LZ 86 (L39)	Shot down by anti-aircraft guns over France, March 17, 1917.
LZ 87 (L47)	Destroyed in an explosion at the sheds in Ahlhorn, Germany, with four other German airships, January 5, 1918.
LZ 89 (L50)	LZ 89 (L50) and five other German Navy Zeppelins were wrecked by their crews at Nordholz, Germany, on June 23, 1919, to prevent being handed over to the Allies, as ordered by the Versailles Peace Treaty.`
LZ 92 (L43)	Shot down over the North Sea by British planes, June 14, 1917.
LZ 93 (L44)	Shot down by anti-aircraft fire over France, October 20, 1917.
LZ 94 (L46)	Destroyed with four other German airships in an explosion at the sheds in Ahlhorn, Germany, January 5, 1918.
LZ 95 (L48)	Shot down over Suffolk, England, by British planes, June 17, 1917.
LZ 96 (L49)	Forced to land behind enemy lines in France, where it was captured on October 20, 1917.
LZ 97 (L54)	Destroyed with four other German airships in an explosion at the sheds in Ahlhorn, Germany, January 5, 1918.
LZ 99 (L54)	Destroyed by aircraft flown from the HMS *Furious,* July 19, 1918.
LZ 100 (L53)	Shot down, August 11, 1918.

LZ 101 (L55)	Wrecked during a forced landing, October 20, 1917. Ship was dismantled.
LZ 102 (L57)	Exploded while entering its shed at Jüterbog, Germany, October 8, 1917.
LZ 103 (L56)	LZ 103 (L56) and five other German Navy Zeppelins were wrecked by their crews at Nordholz, Germany, on June 23, 1919, to prevent being handed over to the Allies, as ordered by the Versailles Peace Treaty.
LZ 104 (L59)	Burned while airborne, April 7, 1918. Known as the African ship.
LZ 105 (L58)	Destroyed in an explosion at the Ahlhorn sheds with four other German airships, January 5, 1918.
LZ 108 (L60)	Destroyed by British aircraft from HMS *Furious,* July 19, 1918.
LZ 110 (L63)	LZ 110 (L63) and five other German Navy Zeppelins were wrecked by their crews at Nordholz on June 23, 1919, to prevent being handed over to the Allies, as ordered by the Versailles Peace Treaty.
LZ 111 (L65)	LZ 111 (L65) and five other German Navy Zeppelins were wrecked by their crews at Nordholz on June 23, 1919, to prevent being handed over to the Allies, as ordered by the Versailles Peace Treaty.
LZ 112 (L70)	Shot down off the coast of Norfolk, England, August 5-6, 1918. The LZ 112 (L70) was the last airship to be used as a strategic bomber during World War I.
LZ 113 (L71)	Germany's last airship built during World War I. Surrendered to the British in June 1920. The engines were reused in Britain's R 36 airship.
LZ 126	*See* Aviation—Airships—United States—USS *Los Angeles.*
LZ 127 (*Graf Zeppelin I*)	*Graf Zeppelin I* was broken up in its shed at Frankfurt, Germany, in March 1940.
LZ 129	*See* Aviation—Airships—Zeppelins—*Hindenburg.*
LZ 130 (*Graf Zeppelin II*)	*Graf Zeppelin II* was broken up in its shed at Frankfurt, Germany, in March 1940.
SL 2	Wrecked in a storm, January 10, 1916.
SL 11	Shot down over London, England, August 2-3, 1916.
SL 20	Destroyed with four other German airships in an explosion at the sheds in Ahlhorn, Germany, January 5, 1918.

Aviation—Airships—Zeppelins—ZMC-2

The ZMC-2 (Zeppelin Metal-Clad 2), made for the U.S. Navy by Aircraft Development Corporation in Detroit, Michigan, in 1929 was the only operational metal-clad airship ever built. It was decommissioned in 1941.

• **Last surviving member of the team that built the ZMC-2:** Vladimir H. Pavlecka, who later was chief of research at Northrop. Pavlecka died in Tustin, California, on June 29, 1980, age 79.

Aviation—Balloonists—Blanchard, Jean-Pierre

Pioneer hot air balloonist Jean-Pierre Blanchard of France made the first balloon ascent in the United States in January 1793, from Philadelphia, Pennsylvania, to Gloucester County, New Jersey.

• **Blanchard's last flight:** February 1809. He had a heart attack while traveling over The Hague in the Netherlands, during his 60th balloon ascension. Blanchard died on March, 1809, age 55.

Aviation—Balloonists—Montgolfier Brothers

The Montgolfier brothers, Joseph Michael and Jacques Etienne, of France invented the hot air balloon. They sent animals aloft at Versailles in September 1783 and later that year sent the first humans—two French noblemen—aloft in their balloon.

• **Last flight of Joseph Montgolfier:** January 19, 1784, in Lyon, France. It was his only recorded flight. Joseph Montgolfier died in Balaruc-les-Bains, France, on June 26, 1810, age 69. Jacques Etienne Mont-golfier died in Serrieres, France, on August 2, 1799, age 54.

Aviation—Balloonists—Wise, John
In July 1859, John Wise set a long-distance balloon flight record that stood for more than a half century and is still considered one of the greatest ever made. He traveled from Saint Louis, Missouri, to Henderson, New York, in about 20 hours.
• **Wise's last balloon flight:** September 29, 1879. His balloon fell into Lake Michigan and he was never seen again. Wise was 71.

Aviation—Designers and Manufacturers —Curtiss, Glenn
Glenn Curtiss is considered the Father of Naval Aviation.
• **Last flight of Curtiss as a pilot:** May 1930, in a Curtiss Condor transport plane that he flew from Albany, New York, to New York City. Curtiss died in Buffalo, New York, on July 23, 1930, age 52.

Aviation—Designers and Manufacturers —Fokker, Anthony Herman
Anthony Herman Fokker opened his first factory in Berlin, Germany, in 1912. He built planes for the German army during World War I, including the popular fighters DR. I and D. VII. After the war, he opened a factory in Amsterdam, Holland.
• **Last aircraft designed by Anthony Herman Fokker for Germany:** Fokker D. VII monoplane in 1918, designed for the German war effort in World War I. Fokker died in New York on December 23, 1939.
• **Last plane to carry the Fokker name:** the Fokker 50, which rolled off the assembly line at Amsterdam Airport Schiphol in May 1997. The last Fokker 50 was delivered to Ethiopian Airlines. The Fokker company declared bankruptcy in March 1996.

Aviation—Designers and Manufacturers —Hughes, Howard
When Howard Hughes' Spruce Goose (Hughes HK-1 "Hercules" NX37602) took to the air in 1947, it was the largest plane ever flown at that time.

• **Last (and only) flight of Hughes HK-1 "Hercules":** November 2, 1947. The plane flew little more than a mile at an altitude of 70 feet over Los Angeles Harbor in California. After Hughes died, the plane was placed in a special hanger, alongside the ocean liner *Queen Mary*, in Long Beach, California. In 1993, it was moved to McMinnville, Oregon, where it is now on display at the Evergreen Aviation Museum.

Aviation—Designers and Manufacturers —Lear, William P., Sr.
William Powell Lear Sr. pioneered the small passenger jet with the Learjet in 1959.
• **Last aircraft designed by William P. Lear, Sr.:** Lear Fan Model 2100. It made its first flight on January 1, 1981. The plane is now in the Museum of Flight in Seattle, Washington. Lear died in Reno, Nevada, on May 14, 1978, age 75.

Aviation—Designers and Manufacturers —Wright Brothers
Wright Flyer I ("Kitty Hawk") was the aircraft used in the first sustainable controlled powered flight.
• **Last surviving person to work on Wright Flyer I:** Charles E. Taylor, bicycle mechanic for the Wright Brothers. He was their only employee and is credited with building the Wright brothers' plane engines from their designs. Taylor died on January 30, 1956, age 88.
• **Last journey of Wright Flyer I:** 1948. After their successful flight experiments at Kill Devil Hill on the North Carolina seacoast on December 17, 1903, Orville and Wilbur Wright never flew the Wright Flyer I again. It fell apart after the flights. The brothers packed it up and shipped it back to their Dayton, Ohio, home. Wright Flyer I was later reassembled and displayed a few times in New York and once at the Massachusetts Institute of Technology in Cambridge. But mostly it remained stored in a shed in Dayton. The Smithsonian Institution initially considered Wright Flyer I to be the first power-propelled plane to fly successfully. But later it chose a plane by Samuel

Langley. The Wright plane was sent to the Science Museum in London in 1928. In 1943, after years of controversy over whether it was the first successful airplane, the Smithsonian decided it was and asked for the plane. The plane was returned to the United States in 1948. It was refurbished and placed on display on December 17, 1948. It is now in the Milestones of Flight Gallery at the Smithsonian Institution's National Air and Space Museum in Washington, D.C.

• **Last flight of Wright Flyer II:** December 9, 1904, near Dayton, Ohio. It was the plane's 105th flight. Wright Flyer II was then placed in storage for the winter. The following spring, the Wright brothers used the engine, propellers and hardware from Flyer II to build Wright Flyer III.

• **Last flight of Wright Flyer III:** September 17, 1908, at Fort Myer, Virginia, in a test for the U.S. government. Wright Flyer III, piloted by Orville Wright, crashed. Later, his passenger, U.S. Army Lieutenant Thomas Selfridge, died of injuries sustained in the crash. Wright Flyer III was later rebuilt and restored under the supervision of Orville. It is now on display at Carillon Park and Museum in Dayton, Ohio.

• **Last flight of the Wright Brothers together:** May 25, 1910, at Huffman Prairie Flying Field, near Dayton, Ohio. Orville piloted. It was also the only time the Wright brothers flew together.

• **Last flight of Wilbur Wright as pilot:** May 21, 1910, at Huffman Prairie. Wilbur Wright died of typhoid fever in Dayton, Ohio, on May 30, 1912, age 45.

• **Last flight of Orville Wright as pilot:** May 13, 1918. Orville Wright flew frequently until 1915, the year he sold his interest in the Wright Company.

• **Last plane Orville Wright designed:** OW-1 Aerial Coupe in 1919. Orville Wright died in Dayton, Ohio, on January 30, 1948, age 77.

Aviation—Helicopters

Helicopter	Description
Bell 47/H-13 Sioux	The Bell 47/H-13 was one of the most popular light-utility helicopters ever built. Production amounted to about 5,000. • **Last Bell 47/H-13 Sioux produced in the U.S.:** 1973. • **Last Bell 47/H-13 Sioux produced in other countries:** 1976. • **Last version acquired by the U.S. Army:** the TH-13T.
Bell AH-1 Cobra	The Bell AH-1 Cobra was the first dedicated attack helicopter and was deployed for nearly every U.S. combat operation from Vietnam until 1999. • **Last Bell AH-1 Cobra flight by an active duty U.S. Army unit:** Schofield Barracks in Oahu, Hawaii, on March 15, 1999.
Cierva C.8W Autogiro	The Autogiro was the predecessor to the helicopter. The word "Autogiro" was coined by Juan de la Cierva. One of the pioneering Autogiros was the Cierva C.8 Mk.IV (or C.8W). • **Last Cierva C.8W Autogiro flight:** July 22, 1931, when Pitcairn aviation test pilot Jim Ray completed a flight from Willow Grove, Pennsylvania, to the Smithsonian Institution in Washington, D.C., where it was accepted into the national collection.
Sikorsky S-61/ SH-3 Sea King	The Sikorsky S-61/SH-3 Sea King is the classic search-and-rescue helicopter and the most widely used heliliner. • **Last Sikorsky S-61 produced:** delivered June 19, 1980. During its production run, more than 1,100 of all versions of the S-61 were produced.

Aviation—Pilots—Earhart, Amelia

American aviator Amelia Earhart was the first woman to fly solo across the Atlantic Ocean in 1932. In 1937, she attempted the first round-the-world flight near the Equator. She and navigator Captain Frederick J. Noonan started their 27,000-mile journey from Miami, Florida, on June 1st.

• **Last time Earhart and Noonan were seen:** July 1, 1937, in Lae, New Guinea, as they began the most difficult leg of their trip, the 2,556-mile flight to Howland Island in the Pacific Ocean.

• **Last confirmed radio contact with Earhart and Noonan:** July 2, 1937. A message from Earhart to the U.S. Coast Guard, gave their direction of flight but nothing else: "We are on a line position 157/337. Will repeat this message on 6210 kilocycles. … We are running North and South."

• **End of the search for Earhart and Noonan:** July 18, 1937, when they were given up for dead after an extensive Navy search of the area. Their fate is unknown.

Aviation—Pilots—Early Birds of Aviation

Membership in the Early Birds of Aviation, founded in 1928, required a pilot to provide evidence that the person had soloed in an aerial craft prior to December 17, 1916.

• **Last surviving member of the Early Birds of Aviation:** George Debaun Grundy Jr., who died in Leesburg, Florida, on May 19, 1998, age 99.

Aviation—Pilots—Kingsford-Smith, Charles Edward

Sir Charles Edward Kingsford-Smith made the first airplane crossing of the Pacific Ocean from Oakland, California, to Australia in June-July 1928. He set off on November 6, 1935, with navigator and mechanic Tommy Pethybridge in an attempt to make another record flight, from the United Kingdom to Australia.

• **Last sighting of Kingsford-Smith's plane:** November 8, 1935, over the Andaman Sea (part of the Bay of Bengal). On November 9, 1935—the expected comple-

tion day for one of the legs of the flight—the two failed to arrive in Singapore. After Kingsford-Smith and Pethybridge left Burma, they apparently met with bad weather over the Bay of Bengal. On July 7, 1937, part of the aircraft's undercarriage washed up on an island along the coast of Burma (now Myanmar). But no trace of the plane's passengers was found.

Aviation—Pilots—Lindbergh, Charles

On May 20-21, 1927, Charles A. Lindbergh became the first person to fly solo nonstop across the Atlantic Ocean. He was also the first to fly from New York to Paris, France, in a heavier-than-air craft. He made the trip in a Ryan NYP he called "Spirit of St. Louis."

• **Last flight of the "Spirit of St. Louis":** April 30, 1928, from Lambert Field in Saint Louis, Missouri, to Bolling Field, Washington, D.C. Lindbergh delivered the "Spirit of St. Louis" to the Smithsonian Institution, where it was placed on exhibit in the Arts and Industries Building. The plane is now in the Milestones of Flight Gallery at the Smithsonian's National Air and Space Museum.

• **Last plane flight of Lindbergh:** August 1974, from New York to Honolulu, Hawaii, after he left a New York hospital, where he had been treated for cancer. Lindbergh was flown to his home in Hana, Maui, Hawaii, where he died on August 26, 1974, age 72.

Aviation—Pilots—Post, Wiley

American aviator Wiley Post made flights around the world in 1931 and 1933. American humorist Will Rogers was an aviation enthusiast.

• **Last flight of Wiley Post and Will Rogers:** August 15, 1935, when the plane Post was piloting crashed in a fog near Point Barrow, Alaska. Post and his passenger Will Rogers were killed. Rogers was 55. Post was 36.

Aviation—Pilots—1919 Trans-Atlantic Flight

In 1919, eight years before Lindbergh made

his historic flight, a six-man crew flew a U.S. Navy seaplane across the Atlantic.

• **Last surviving crew member of the 1919 Trans-Atlantic Flight**: Walter Hinton, who also made the first flight from New York to Rio de Janeiro, and piloted an aerial mapping expedition into uncharted parts of the Amazon River valley in the 1920s. Hinton died in Pompano Beach, Florida, on October 28, 1981, age 92.

Banking and Finance

Banking and Finance—Banks—Bank of Amsterdam

The Bank of Amsterdam in the Netherlands was established by city ordinance in 1609 and became one of the most important exchange banks in Europe. The bank was forced to close in the wake of a report that showed the city of Amsterdam was largely indebted to it.

• **Last of the Bank of Amsterdam:** 1820. It shut down soon after the debt was paid off.

Banking and Finance—Banks—Bank of Hamburg

The Bank of Hamburg, in Germany, was established in 1619 and was one of the largest and longest surviving exchange banks in Europe.

• **Last of the Bank of Hamburg:** February 15, 1873. It was formally closed by an act of the German parliament that removed local silver coins—much of the bank's means of exchange—and replaced them with a national gold standard.

Banking and Finance—Banks—Bank of North America

The Bank of North America, chartered by the Continental Congress in 1781, was America's first true commercial banking institution.

• **Last of the Bank of North America:** 1929, when it was absorbed by a competing institution, the Pennsylvania Company for Banking and Trusts.

Banking and Finance—Banks—First Bank of the United States

The First Bank of the United States, chartered in 1791, was America's first nationally chartered bank under the U.S. Constitution.

• **Last of the First Bank of the United States:** 1811. That year its charter came up for renewal, but it was defeated in Congress by a single vote. The bank was liquidated by U.S. Secretary of the Treasury Albert Gallatin, and its branches were sold off to various state banks.

Banking and Finance—Banks—Postal Savings Banks

Postal Savings Banks, set up in 1910, were select post offices that were authorized to take deposits and pay interest. The banks' strength was in their government backing. They began to be outmoded when Federal Deposit Insurance Corporation (FDIC) and Federal Savings and Loan Insurance Corporation (FSLIC) programs were introduced in the 1930s.

• **Last of the Postal Savings Banks:** abolished by the U.S. Congress on July 1, 1967.

Banking and Finance—Banks—Second Bank of the United States

The Second Bank of the United States was chartered in April 1816. It helped to stabilize the money system in the United States, but it had many enemies, including President Andrew Jackson, who did not have confidence in it. He vetoed its recharter in 1832. The following year, he ordered all federal money to be withdrawn and placed in state banks.

• **Last of the Second Bank of the United States:** 1836, when its original 20-year charter expired. Nicholas Biddle, the bank's owner, converted it to a state bank with a charter from Pennsylvania. That bank lasted until 1841, when it was forced into bankruptcy by an economic downturn.

Banking and Finance—Stock Exchanges—American Stock Exchange

The American Stock Exchange was established as the New York Curb Exchange in 1842.

• **Last known as the New York Curb Exchange:** 1921, when it was renamed the New York Curb Market Association.
• **Last known as the New York Curb Market Association:** 1953, when it was renamed the American Stock Exchange.

Banking and Finance—Stock Exchanges —New York Stock Exchange

The New York Stock Exchange was established as the New York Stock and Exchange Board in 1817.
• **Last known as the New York Stock and Exchange Board:** 1863, when it was renamed New York Stock Exchange. At that time, it moved to Wall Street.
• **Last time one person was able to command sufficient financial resources to change the course of an unfavorable market:** October 1907, when John Pierpont Morgan organized a group of major banks to subscribe more than $25 million to support the market. A run on the banks had caused the market to fall.

Banking and Finance—Stock Exchanges —Securities Pricing Format

Fractional pricing gives price increments of 1/8 or 1/16 of a dollar.
• **Last time fractions were used by the U.S. securities industry:** August 28, 2000, when the industry changed its pricing format to decimals. The new format gave price increments of two decimal points, such as $0.05 or $0.10. Most foreign markets already used decimal pricing.
• **Last time fractions were used by U.S. stock exchanges:** January 29, 2001, when the New York Stock Exchange and the American Stock Exchange switched to decimals. The National Association of Securities Dealers Automated Quotations (NASDAQ) made the switch in April.

Books
(*See also* Libraries; Literature.)
Books—Almanacs—Banneker, Benjamin
Benjamin Banneker, of Maryland, was a self-taught mathematician and astronomer.

In 1791, he compiled the first in a series of almanacs that included the ephemeris (astronomical calculation of the celestial placement of planets and stars).
• **Last known issue of Benjamin Banneker's Almanac:** for the year 1797; however, he did continue to compile his astronomical calculations until 1804. Banneker died in Ellicott Mills, Maryland, on October 9, 1806, age 74.

Books—Almanacs—*Poor Richard's Almanack*

Benjamin Franklin began publishing *Poor Richard's Almanack* in 1732. He wrote the many maxims and adages that appeared in the almanac under the pen name Richard Saunders. Franklin died in Philadelphia, Pennsylvania, on April 17, 1790, age 84.
• **Last issue of *Poor Richard's Almanack*:** Signed July 7, 1757, before Franklin went to England to represent Pennsylvania colonists in a case against the Proprietors.

Books—Dictionaries—*Oxford English Dictionary*

The *Oxford English Dictionary* (OED) took more than 40 years to publish. It was published in fascicles (separate installments) under the name *A New English Dictionary on Historical Principles*.
• **Last OED fascicle published:** April 1928.
• **Last supplement to the original edition of OED published:** 1986. The supplements were later integrated into a single set that became the second edition.
• **Last surviving original OED lexicographer:** Charles T. Onions, who joined the staff in 1895, when he was 22. He died in 1965, age 91.

Books—Dictionaries—*Webster's Dictionary*

Noah Webster worked approximately 20 years on *An American Dictionary of the English Language*.
• **Last of Webster's 70,000 definitions completed:** 1828. The dictionary was published in November of that year.
• **Last work by Webster on the revised**

edition: 1840. The revised dictionary was published in March 1841.

• **Last publication by Webster:** a collection of papers, published in May 1843. Webster died in New Haven, Connecticut, on May 28, 1843, age 84. After his death, his family sold the right to publish his dictionary to G&C Merriam and Company.

Books—Diderot's *Encyclopédie*

French encyclopedist/author Denis Diderot worked more than 20 years compiling his 28-volume *Encyclopédie.* It included 17 volumes of text and 11 volumes of illustration.

• **Last volume of Diderot's *Encyclopédie* published:** 1772. Diderot died in Paris, France, on July 31, 1784, age 70.

Books—*Index of Forbidden Books*

The *Index of Forbidden Books* (*Index Librorum Prohibitorum*) is a list of several thousand publications that Roman Catholics were forbidden to own or read without permission. Most of the works were concerned with matters of theology. The rest were books that attacked the Roman Catholic religion, were obscene, or dealt with taboo subjects such as suicide, heresy and superstitious practices.

• **Last edition of the *Index of Forbidden Books*:** 1948.

• **Last of the *Index of Forbidden Books*:** abolished in 1966, by the Congregation for the Doctrine of the Faith.

Buildings
(*See also* Architecture;
Crime—Terrorism—September 11, 2001;
Engineering—Seven Wonders
of the Ancient World;
Entertainment—Theaters;
Hotels; Lighthouses; Sports.)

Buildings—Churches—Saint Paul's Cathedral

Saint Paul's Cathedral in London, England, was designed by Sir Christopher Wren and built on a site where a church has stood since the 11th century.

• **Last construction work on Saint Paul's Cathedral:** 1710, when the last block was set in place by Wren. He had set the first block in place 35 years earlier. Although Saint Paul's Cathedral suffered some damage from German bombs during World War II, it was rebuilt according to Wren's original plans. (*See also* Architects.)

Buildings—Churches—Saint Peter's Basilica

Saint Peter's Basilica in Vatican City, Rome, Italy, was built on the site of the crucifixion of Saint Peter and on grounds that once housed Nero's Circus. A church has stood on the site since the 4th century. Construction on Saint Peter's Basilica began in 1445 and took more than 180 years to complete.

• **Last major construction on Saint Peter's Basilica:** 1626. That year, Pope Urban VIII formally dedicated the completed church.

Buildings—Parthenon

Construction on the Parthenon in Athens, Greece, began in 447 B.C. The building was built as a sacred temple to the goddess Athena. It became a church in the 5th century A.D. and a mosque in the 15th century.

• **Last construction work on the Parthenon:** 432 B.C.

• **Last year the Parthenon was intact:** 1687. That year, a Venetian cannonball hit gunpowder that the Turks had stored in the building. The resulting explosion killed 300 people and did considerable damage to the building. Lord Elgin took a large section of the frieze back to England in 1801.

Buildings—Seashell-shaped Shell Oil Gas Station

In 1930, the owners of Quality Oil Company built eight seashell-shaped Shell stations to promote sales at their Shell Oil Gas Stations. The stations were constructed using wire forms plastered with concrete.

• **Last remaining seashell-shaped Shell Oil Gas Station:** at the corner of Sprague and

Peachtree streets in Winston-Salem, North Carolina. The station is no longer used, but it has the distinction of being the first individual gas station to be included on the National Register of Historic Places.

Buildings—Skyscrapers Without Steel Frame Construction
Before architects began to use steel-frame construction for tall buildings, the structures were usually supported by thick masonry walls.
• **Last building of substantial height built without steel-frame construction:** the 16-story Monadnock Building in Chicago, Illinois, designed by Daniel Burnham and John Wellborn Root and completed in 1891. The structure is supported by six-foot-thick brick walls and is possibly the tallest masonry-wall-bearing building in the world.

Buildings—Winchester Mystery House
The Winchester Mystery House was built by Sarah Pardee Wirt Winchester, widow of an heir to the Winchester Rifle fortune. She started building the house after a psychic told her the deaths of her husband and daughter were revenge for people killed by Winchester rifles, and her only chance to achieve eternal life was to buy a house out west and continually build and expand it. Mrs. Winchester purchased a house in San Jose, California, and constantly built, demolished and added onto it for 38 years.
• **Last construction on the Winchester House:** ended with the death of Sarah Winchester in San Jose, California, on September 4, 1922, age 83. Altogether, she added 160 rooms and a confusing maze of stairways and dead ends. Today, the house is a tourist attraction.

Buildings—Construction—Tallest

Building	Location	Completed	Last Year It Was the Tallest Building
Petronas Towers II	Kuala Lumpur, Malaysia	2000	Present
Sears Tower	Chicago, Illinois, USA	1974	2000
One World Trade Center	New York, New York, USA	1972	1974
Empire State Building	New York, New York, USA	1931	1972
Chrysler Building	New York, New York, USA	1930	1931

Business and Industry

Business and Industry—Companies—AT&T
The American Telephone and Telegraph Company was sued by the Justice Department in 1974 for trying to monopolize the phone industry. An agreement was reached whereby AT&T would divest itself of its 22 local companies.
• **End of AT&T control of local phone companies:** January 1, 1984, when AT&T divested them.

Business and Industry—Companies—Burma-Shave Company
Burma Shave signs—clustered in groups of four, five or six and containing rhyming advertising, safety tips, humor and folk wisdom—were familiar sights along American roadways beginning in the late 1920s.
• **Last Burma Shave road sign message:** *Our Fortune Is... Your Shaven Face... It's Our Best... Advertising Space.* It appeared in 1963 and was the last of more than 7,000 signs. In 1963, the Odell family sold the Burma-Shave Company to Gillette (later

part of Philip Morris, Inc.), and a decision was made that television would advertise the product better.

Business and Industry—Companies—Christie's Auction House

Founded in 1766, Christie's is the oldest fine arts auction house in the world.

• **Last member of Christie family to be associated with the firm:** James Christie IV, who retired in 1889.

Business and Industry—Companies—Ford Motor Company

For the first 52 years of its existence, the Ford Motor Company was owned completely by family members, making it the world's largest family-owned industrial empire.

• **Last time Ford was owned only by family:** January 1956. In November 1955, the company announced it would make stock available to the public on that date. (*See also* Automobiles.)

Business and Industry—Companies—Merrill Lynch

The investment brokerage group Merrill Lynch was founded as Merrill Lynch & Company in 1915. It became Merrill Lynch, Pierce, Fenner & Beane in 1941. The name was changed to Merrill Lynch, Pierce, Fenner & Smith in 1958.

• **Last surviving Merrill Lynch founding member:** Edward Allen Pierce, who died on in New York, New York, December 16, 1974, age 100.

Business and Industry—Companies—Standard Oil Company

The breakup of John D. Rockefeller's Standard Oil Company of New Jersey was the seminal case of anti-trust litigation in the early 20th century.

• **Last Standard Oil trust-breaking decision handed down:** May 15, 1911. A six-month deadline for the dissolution was set. Rockefeller died in Ormond, Florida, on May 23, 1937, age 97.

Business and Industry—Companies—Closings—East India Companies

British East India Company
The British East India Company was chartered on December 31, 1600, by Queen Elizabeth I to control trade in the Eastern Hemisphere. The British Parliament ended the company's monopoly with laws enacted in 1813 and 1833. In 1858, after the Sepoy Mutiny in India, the British Crown took control of the East India Company's operation.   • **End of the East India Company:** dissolved by the British Crown in 1874.
Dutch East India Company
The Dutch East India Company, chartered in 1602, became almost insolvent by the end of the 18th century.   • **End of the Dutch East India Company:** 1798.
French East India Company
The French East India Company was chartered in 1664.   • **End of the French East India Company:** 1769, when it ran into financial problems and was dissolved.
Swedish East India Company
The Swedish East India Company was chartered in 1731.   • **End of the Swedish East India Company:** 1813, when the company ceased operations after more than 82 years and 132 voyages to Asia.

Business and Industry—Companies—Closings—Chain Stores

Store Chain Name	Closed or Last Operated by that Name
Alexander's	1992
Ames	2002
Best Stores	1997
Bradlees	2001
Builders Square	1999
Bullock's	1996
Caldor	1999
Clover	1996

Fannie May and Fannie Farmer	2004
Fedco	1999
G.C. Murphy's	2002
GEM (a.k.a. GEX)	1973
Gimbel's	1987
Globe	1992
Hechinger	1999
Hills	1999
HQ	1999
Jamesway	1995
Jefferson Ward	1985
J.J. Newberry's	1996
J.M. Fields	1978
John Wanamaker	1995
Jordan Marsh	1996
King's	1986
Korvettes	1980
Kress Stores	1994
Lechmere	1997
Lit Brothers	1977
Lucky Stores	1999
McCrory	2001
Montgomery Ward	2000
Rich's	1997
Service Merchan-	2002

dise	
Stuarts	1995
Two Guys	1980
Venture	1998
White Front	1973
Woolco	1983
Woolworth	1997
W.T. Grant	1976
Zayre	1989

Business and Industry—Companies—Closings—Enron

Texas-based energy giant Enron was once the seventh largest corporation in the United States and the 16th largest worldwide. It had pioneered methods of trading in energy and was looked upon as a corporate leader. In October 2001, Enron officials admitted the company had hidden huge debts and heavy losses and was worth billions less than it had shown on its balance sheets.

• **Last of Enron:** December 2, 2001, when Enron declared bankruptcy. It was the largest bankruptcy in corporate history. Thousands of employees lost their jobs and thousands of investors (many of whom were employees) lost billions of dollars.

Business and Industry—Companies—Name Changes
(*See also* Aviation—Airlines—United States.)

Old Name	Last Used Old Name	New Name
American Arithmometer Company	1905	Burroughs Adding Machine Company
American District Telegraph Company	1980s	ADT
American Family Corporation	1992	AFLAC, Inc.
Armstrong Cork Company	1980	Armstrong World Industries Inc.
Associated Tide Water Oil Company	1966	Getty Oil Company
Boston Wire Stitcher Company	1948	Bostitch
Burroughs Adding Machine Company	1953	Burroughs Corporation
California Perfume Company	1929	Avon (Avon Products after 1939)
Cities Service Company	1965	Citgo
Computer-Tabulating-Recording Company	1924	International Business Machines Corporation (IBM)
Consolidated Rubber Tire Company	1914	Kelly-Springfield Tire Company
Consolidated Talking Machine Company	1901	Victor Talking Machine Company
Cooper Engineering Company	1946	Sunbeam Corporation

Federal Express	1994	FedEx
First National City Corporation	1976	Citicorp NA
G. & C. Merriam Company	1982	Merriam-Webster Incorporated
G. Binswanger and Company	1886	General Electric Apparatus Company
Geophysical Service, Incorporated	1951	Texas Instruments Inc.
Hygrade Sylvania Corporation	1942	Sylvania Electric Products, Inc.
Johns-Manville Corporation	1981	Manville Corporation
Kelly Girl Service, Inc.	1966	Kelly Service, Inc.
Kentucky Fried Chicken	1991	KFC
Liberty Coast Wagon Company	1987	Radio Flyer
Minnesota Mining & Manufacturing Company	2002	3M Company
Mistake Out Company	1968	Liquid Paper Corporation
Monsanto	2000	Pharmacia
Mosaic Communications Corporation	1994	Netscape Communications Corporation
National Cash Register Corporation	1974	NCR Corporation
Phillip Best Company	1889	Pabst Brewing Company
Pittsburgh Aluminum Company	1907	Aluminum Company of America (Alcoa)
Radio Corporation of America	1965	RCA Corporation
Relational Software Inc.	1983	Oracle Corporation
Remington Rand	1955	Sperry Rand
Retail Credit Company	1976	Equifax Inc.
Rolscreen Company	1992	Pella Corporation
S.S. Kresge Company	1977	Kmart Corporation
Smith & Heminway Company	1966	Red Devil Tools
Sperry Rand	1978	Sperry Corporation
Suzuki Loom Works	1954	Suzuki Motor Co., Ltd.
The Howdy Corporation	1936	The Seven-Up Company
The Precision Optical Research Laboratory	1947	Canon Camera Company
The Texas Company	1959	Texaco Inc.
Tokyo Telecommunications Engineering Corporation	1958	Sony Corp.
United Telecommunication Inc.	1992	Sprint Corporation
Victor Talking Machine Company	1929	Radio-Victor Division of Radio Corporation of America. Later known as RCA-Victor.

Business and Industry—Schemes, Scams and Speculations—Law's Mississippi Bubble

John Law of Scotland came up with a plan for debt-ridden France that would liquidate the country's national debt and make him rich. In 1717, he was appointed France's controller of finance. A bank was opened, trading companies were started, and Law sold hundreds of thousands of shares in French-held land in Louisiana and along the banks of the Mississippi River in North America.

• **Last of Law's Mississippi Bubble:** collapsed in 1720. As people began selling their shares, the value of the stock plummeted and investors were ruined. France was left with a debt of $340 million, and Law fled the country. He died in Vienna, Austria, in 1729. One positive outcome of Law's Mississippi Bubble was that it spurred the settlement of New Orleans, Louisiana.

Business and Industry—Schemes, Scams and Speculations—South Sea Bubble

The South Sea Bubble was afloat at the same time as Law's Mississippi Bubble. Law's scheme affected France. This one involved England. The South Sea Company, a joint-stock company, was formed in 1711 to take over the national debt of England. In return, the company was given the exclusive privilege of carrying on trade in South America and the Pacific islands. The price of stock in the company rose sharply. As stock prices soared, people scrambled to get in on the action.

• **Last of the South Sea Bubble:** September 1720, when the bottom fell out of the market. Several fraudulent companies that had tried to cash in on the project collapsed. When the South Sea Bubble burst, a financial panic ensued. The affair led to legislation in England banning similar unincorporated joint stock ventures.

Business and Industry—Schemes, Scams and Speculations—Tulip Mania

Tulip mania is the name given to the wild speculation in tulip bulbs from 1634 to 1637. After the flowers were introduced in western Europe from Turkey, the Dutch developed a fascination for them to the point that even the poorest people got involved in the tulip trade. As more buyers sought tulip bulbs, the prices rose. Some people were willing to pay exorbitant prices for them, including several thousand dollars for the *Semper Augustus* bulb.

• **End of tulip mania:** 1637. Some speculators were reduced to poverty and many noble families saw their fortunes disappear. It would take many years for the Dutch economy to recover.

Cartoons—Animated
Last Theatrical Release of Some Major Cartoon Series

"Cartoons" here generally refer to animated film shorts released by the major studios during the theatrical-release era, also known as "the Golden Age" of cartoons: the 1930s to the 1960s. Most early cartoons were created as theatrical releases that later had a second life on television. The dates provided here are for the last theatrical release of shorts of major cartoon series. If the cartoon was created specifically for a TV audience it is noted: (TV). Feature-length films are not included, and cameo appearances in feature length films are excluded.

Cartoon Character	Title of Last Cartoon	Studio	Date of Release
Andy Panda	*Scrappy Birthday*	Universal Studios	February 11, 1949
Baby Huey	*Pest Pupil*	Famous Studios	January 25, 1957
Bosko	*Little Ol' Bosko in Baghdad*	MGM	January 1, 1938
Bugs Bunny	*False Hare*	Warner Brothers	July 16, 1964
Casper the Friendly Ghost	*Casper's Birthday Party*	Paramount (Famous Studios)	July 31, 1959
Chip n' Dale (Last in Donald Duck feature.) **Chip n' Dale** (Last in Chip n' Dale series.)	*Chips Ahoy* *The Lone Chipmunks*	Walt Disney	February 24, 1956 April 7, 1954
Daffy Duck	*See Ya Later Gladiator*	Warner Brothers	June 29, 1968

Droopy Dog	*Droopy Leprechaun*	MGM	July 4, 1958
Elmer Fudd	*What's My Lion?*	Warner Brothers	October 21, 1961
Felix the Cat (Silent)	*The Last Life*	Pat Sullivan Studio	August 5, 1928
Felix the Cat (Sound)	*Bold King Cole*	Van Bueren Studio	May 29, 1936
Felix the Cat (TV)		Trans-Lux	May 6, 1960
Flintstones, The (TV)	*My Fair Freddy* (Episode 165)	Hanna-Barbera Studio	March 25, 1966
Foghorn Leghorn	*Banty Raids*	Warner Brothers	June 29, 1962
Fritz the Cat	*The Nine Lives of Fritz the Cat*	Steve Krantz Productions	June 24, 1974
Goofy	*Goofy's Freeway Trouble*	Walt Disney	September 22, 1965
Heckle & Jeckle	*Messed-Up Movie Makers*	Terrytoons	March 1966
Hippety Hopper	*Freudy Cat*	Warner Brothers	March 14, 1964
Koko the Clown (Silent)	*Chemical Ko-Ko*	Max Fleischer	July 26, 1929
Little Audrey	*Dawn Gawn*	Famous Studios	December 14, 1958
Marvin the Martian	*Mad as a Mars Hare*	Warner Brothers	October 19, 1963
Mr. Magoo	*Terror Faces Magoo*	United Productions of America	July 9, 1959
Porky Pig	*Corn on the Cop*	Warner Brothers	July 24, 1965
Ruff & Reddy (TV)	Series	Hanna-Barbera Studio	1964
Silly Symphonies	*The Ugly Duckling*	Walt Disney	April 7, 1939
Speedy Gonzalez	*See Ya Later Gladiator*	Warner Brothers	June 29, 1968
Spike & Tyke	*Scat Cats*	MGM	July 26, 1957
Sylvester Pussycat	*Cats & Bruises*	Warner Brothers	January 30, 1965
Tom & Jerry	*Purr Chance to Dream*	MGM	1967
Tom & Jerry (TV)	Series	Hanna-Barbera Studio	1977
Tweety & Sylvester	*Hawaiian Aye Aye*	Warner Brothers	June 27, 1964
Wile E. Coyote & Road Runner	*Sugar and Spies*	Warner Brothers	November 5, 1966
Wile E. Coyote & Road Runner (Last directed by Chuck Jones.)	*War & Pieces*	Warner Brothers	June 6, 1964
Woody Woodpecker	*Bye Bye Blackboard*	Walter Lantz (Universal)	1972
Yosemite Sam	*Pancho's Hideaway*	Warner Brothers	October 24, 1964

Cartoons—Animated—Golden Era
The Golden Era in animated film shorts began in the 1930s and lasted until the 1960s.
• **Last Golden-Era cartoon studio to close:** Walter Lantz (Universal). The studio produced cartoons until 1972. Back then, it took ten years for a cartoon to earn back its cost, and 72-year-old Lantz decided not to work

for rewards that far in the future.
• **Last Lantz cartoon:** Woody Woodpecker in *Bye Bye Blackboard* (1972).

Cartoons—Animated—Studios—Walt Disney

Walt Disney Studio was founded in the 1920s. Mickey Mouse first appeared in 1928.
• **Last Golden Era Mickey Mouse cartoon:** *The Simple Things,* released on April 18, 1953. It was the last classic Mickey Mouse and the last Mickey Mouse theatrical cartoon short made during Walt Disney's lifetime. Mickey did not appear again in a theatrical feature or short until *Mickey's Christmas Carol* in 1983, some 30 years later.
• **Last Disney (and Mickey Mouse) theatrical cartoon using black-and-white film:** *Mickey's Kangaroo,* released on April 13, 1935.
• **Last Silly Symphony theatrical cartoon short using black-and-white film:** *Bugs in Love,* released October 1, 1932.

Cartoons—Animated—Studios—Warner Brothers

Warner Brothers Studio was founded in 1923 by four brothers. It became a leader in animated short subjects.
• **Last Golden Era theatrical cartoon short produced at Warner Brothers:** *Senorella and the Glass Huarache,* released August 1, 1964. It was directed by Hawley Pratt, with a story by John Dunn and animated by Gerry Chiniquy, Virgil Ross, Bob Matz and Lee Halpern. Warner Brothers returned to making theatrical shorts in 1987.
• **Last Warner Brothers theatrical cartoon short directed by Arthur Davis:** *Quackodile Tears* (1962).
• **Last Warner Brothers theatrical cartoon short directed by Robert Clampett:** *The Big Snooze* (1946).
• **Last Warner Brothers (and Looney Tunes) theatrical cartoon short using black-and-white film:** *Puss n' Booty,* released on December 11, 1943. It was directed by Frank Tashlin, with a story by

Warren Foster and animated by Cal Dalton.
• **Last cartoon to feature the voice of Mel Blanc:** *Night of the Living Duck,* a Daffy Duck theatrical short that premiered at the New York Film Festival on September 23, 1988. It was directed by Greg Ford and Terry Lennon and featured Mel Tormé voicing Daffy's singing in a nightclub. Mel Blanc died in Los Angeles, California, on July 10, 1989, age 81.

Cartoonists—Editorial/Political

Cartoonists—Editorial/Political—Block, Herbert L. (Herblock)

Herbert L. Block (Herblock) had a career as an editorial and political cartoonist that spanned more than 72 years under 13 U.S. presidents. Most of his career was spent at the *Washington Post,* where he won four Pulitzer Prizes. He died in Washington, D.C., on October 7, 2001, age 91.
• **Last Herblock political cartoon:** published August 26, 2001.

Cartoonists—Editorial/Political—Hirschfeld, Al

Albert ("Al") Hirschfeld began contributing celebrity caricatures to the *New York Times* in the 1920s.
• **Last Hirschfeld cartoon:** a commission of the Marx brothers. Hirschfeld was working on it two days before he died in New York, New York, on January 20, 2003, age 99.

Cartoonists—Editorial/Political—Marcus, Edwin

Edwin Marcus had a career as a political and editorial cartoonist with the *New York Times* that spanned more than 50 years.
• **Last Marcus political cartoon:** published on January 5, 1958. He died in 1961.

Cartoonists—Editorial/Political—Nast, Thomas

German-born American cartoonist Thomas Nast helped to create such political icons as the Democratic donkey, Republican elephant and Uncle Sam. His drawings of Santa Claus in *Harper's Weekly* gave the public the image of the jolly, fat, bearded Santa Claus that is popular today. His *Harper's Weekly* political cartoons are credited with helping to bring about the defeat of presidential candidate Horace Greeley in the 1872 campaign. Nast died of yellow fever in Guayaquil, Ecuador, on December 7, 1902, age 62, while serving as U.S. Consul-General.

• **Last Nast engravings in *Harper's Weekly*:** 1886, in the Christmas issue.

Civil Rights
(*See also* Education; Elections; Slavery; Sports; United States.)

Civil Rights—Big Four
The Big Four leaders of the civil rights movement of the 1960s were Dr. Martin Luther King Jr., Whitney Young, Roy Wilkins and James Farmer.

• **Last surviving Big Four member:** James Farmer, who helped found the Congress of Racial Equality in 1942. He was awarded the Presidential Medal of Freedom in 1998. Farmer died in Fredericksburg, Virginia, on July 9, 1999, age 79.

Civil Rights—Birmingham Demonstrations
On April 2, 1963, Dr. Martin Luther King Jr. began a series of marches and sit-ins in Birmingham, Alabama, to protest discrimination in stores, restaurants and jobs. In May, Birmingham firefighters used high-pressure hoses, and police used dogs to break up the demonstrations. Photos of the violence against African Americans were shown worldwide and drew attention to their cause.

• **End of the Birmingham demonstrations:** May 9, 1963, after Dr. King and other black leaders worked out a tentative agreement with local business people. The federal government stationed 3,000 troops nearby to keep the peace.

Civil Rights—King, Dr. Martin Luther (Jr.)
In April 1968, civil rights leader the Rev. Dr. Martin Luther King Jr. was in Memphis,

Tennessee, supporting striking sanitation workers.

• **Last sermon of Dr. King:** "I've Been to the Mountaintop," delivered April 3, 1968, at the Mason Temple in Memphis. The following day, as he stood on the balcony outside his room at the Lorraine Motel, he was shot and killed by a sniper. He was 39.

Civil Rights—March to Montgomery, Alabama (Voting Rights)
The march to seek voting rights for disenfranchised black Americans began in Selma, Alabama, on March 21, 1965, with 3,200 marchers, led by the Rev. Dr. Martin Luther King Jr. They were joined along the way by thousands of people of all races, ages and religions. By the time they reached the State Capitol Building in Montgomery, 25,000 people had joined the march. They were guarded along the way by several thousand troops sent by President Lyndon B. Johnson.

• **End of the March to Montgomery:** March 25, 1965. The 54-mile route of the marchers from Selma to Montgomery is now a National Historic Trail.

Civil Rights—Racial Segregation—Buses
The movement to desegregate buses in he United States began when Rosa Parks, a black woman, refused to give up her bus seat to a white man in Montgomery, Alabama, on December 1, 1955.

• **End of the Montgomery bus boycott:** December 21, 1956, when Dr. Martin Luther King Jr. and Rev. Glen Smiley, a white minister, sat together in the front of a public bus. The bus boycott by Montgomery's black residents lasted 381 days.

• **End of racial segregation on buses:** Alabama's bus segregation was declared unconstitutional by a federal court. The ruling was upheld by the U.S. Supreme Court and on December 20, 1956, federal injunctions were served on the bus company and the city of Montgomery forcing officials to obey the court order.

Civil Rights—Racial Segregation— Government-funded Public Places

Until the mid-1950s, many Americans were banned from using government-funded public places such as golf courses, parks and playgrounds because of their race.

• **End of racial segregation in government-funded parks, playgrounds, golf courses and other places supported by public funds:** November 7, 1955, in two unanimous decisions of the United States Supreme Court.

Civil Rights—Racial Segregation— Marriage

By 1945, more than half of the states had antimiscegenation statutes. In 1948, California was the first state to strike down the statute that banned the marriage of whites to persons of "Negro, Mongolian or Malayan" blood. The statute was voided by the California Supreme Court in a ruling that held it violated the U.S. Constitution.

• **End of the ban on interracial marriage:** July 1967, when the U.S. Supreme Court struck down a Virginia law banning interracial marriages. During the next two decades, all the states except one removed the interracial marriage ban from their constitutions,

• **Last state with an interracial marriage ban in its constitution:** Alabama.

Civil Rights—Racial Segregation— Public Housing

As recently as the early 1960s, some Americans were banned from living in public housing because of their race.

• **End of racial segregation in public housing:** 1962, when President John F. Kennedy signed an order banning segregation in housing owned or insured by the federal government.

Civil Rights—Racial Segregation— Public Schools

The movement to desegregate schools gained momentum in the late 1940s, when several class-action suits were combined as *Brown v. Board of Education of Topeka, Kansas.*

• **End of racial segregation in public**

schools: May 17, 1954, in *Brown v. Board of Education of Topeka, Kansas,* when the U.S. Supreme Court unanimously overturned the "separate, but equal" doctrine that had allowed states to segregate students based on race. The Supreme Court declared racially segregated schools were unconstitutional because they are a denial of the equal protection clause in the 14th Amendment. Desegregation did not happen immediately or peacefully. Stormy confrontations occurred in places such as Little Rock, Arkansas, and Alabama before the Court's ruling on *Brown* was fully implemented.

• **Last surviving member of the *Brown* v. *Board of Education* plaintiff group:** Annie Gibson, who died on March 6, 2001, age 90. She was part of a group of South Carolina plaintiffs who sued to end racial segregation in public schools in the late 1940s. The case—*Briggs* v. *Elliot*— brought by Eliza and Harry Briggs and 18 other black Clarendon County residents, including Annie Gibson, was merged with other lawsuits into *Brown* v. *Board of Education.*

Civil Rights—Scottsboro Case

The Scottsboro case was a series of trials that began in 1931, involving nine young black men who were charged with the rape of two young white women in Scottsboro, Alabama. The fourth trial in 1937 led to the conviction of five of the men; charges were dropped against the remaining four. The convicted five were turned down for parole three times. In the 1940s, four were paroled. In 1948, the fifth man escaped and fled to Detroit, Michigan.

• **Last known surviving Scottsdale defendant:** Clarence Norris, who was paroled in 1946. He fought for years to clear his name. In 1976, he was officially declared not guilty and granted a full pardon by Governor George Wallace of Alabama. Norris died on January 23, 1989, age 75.

Civil Rights—Women's Rights— Anthony, Susan B.

Women's rights advocate Susan B. Anthony died in Rochester, New York, on March 3,

1906, age 86.

• **Last public appearance of Susan B. Anthony:** February 15, 1906, at a celebration of her 86th birthday, held at the Universalist Church in Washington, D.C. She ended her speech with "Failure is impossible," a phrase that would become the rallying cry for the women's rights movement.

Civil Rights—Women's Rights—Mott, Lucretia

Women's rights advocate Lucretia Mott died near Philadelphia, Pennsylvania, on November 11, 1880, age 87.

• **Last public appearance of Lucretia Mott:** April 1880, at the Philadelphia Yearly Meeting of the Society of Friends.

Comic Strips and Comic Books
Last Day of Issue of Some Major Comic Strips and Comic Books

The "last" shown here is the last day of the Sunday or daily newspaper strip, whichever ended later, or the last issue of a comic-book series. Comic-book characters are often brought back years after their last appearance, or they may cross over into other series, so a firm "last" is considerably more difficult. Most major comic-book characters are not included here; however, some finite series are.

Comic Strip Name	Creator	Date of Last Issue	Artist for Last Issue
Abbie & Slats	Al Capp and Raeburn van Buren	1971	Raeburn van Buren
Ain't It a Grand and Glorious Feelin'?	Claire Briggs	January 3, 1930*	Claire Briggs
And Her Name Was Maud	Frederick B. Opper	August 14, 1932****	Frederick B. Opper
Barnaby	Crockett Johnson	February 2, 1952	Crockett Johnson
Bib and Bub	May Gibbs	September 1967	May Gibbs
Bloom County	Berke Breathed	August 6, 1989	Berke Breathed
Boner's Ark	Mort Walker (a.k.a. Addison)	May 27, 2000	Frank B. Johnson
Boob McNutt	Rube Goldberg	September 30, 1934	Rube Goldberg
Boots and Her Buddies	Edgar Martin	October 15, 1960	Les Carroll
Brick Bradford	Clarence Gray	May 10, 1987	Paul Norris
Bringing Up Father	George McManus	May 28, 2002	Frank B. Johnson
Bruce Gentry	Ray Bailey	January 6, 1951	Ray Bailey
Buck Rogers in the 25th Century	Philip F. Nowlan and Richard Calkin	Fall 1983	Jack Sparling
Buck Ryan	Jack Monk and Don Freeman	July 31, 1962	Jack Monk
Bungle Family, The	Harry Tuthill	June 2, 1945	Harry Tuthill
Buster Brown	R.F. Outcault	August 15, 1920	R.F. Outcault
Buz Sawyer	Roy Crane	1989	Joe Kubert
Calvin and Hobbes	Bill Watterson	December 31, 1995	Bill Watterson
Captain and the Kids	Rudolph Dirks	1979	John Dirks
Casey Court	J. S. Baker	September 12, 1953	Charlie Pease
Crime & Punishment	Lev Gleason (publisher)	August 1955	Lev Gleason (publisher)

Crime Does Not Pay	Charles Biro and Bob Wood/ Lev Gleason (publisher)	July, 1955 Issue #147	Charles Biro and Bob Wood/Lev Gleason (publisher)
Dickie Dare	Milton Caniff	October 1957	Coulton Waugh
Dingbat Family, The	George Herriman	January 5, 1916	George Herriman
Don Dixon and the Hidden Empire	Bob Moore and Carl Pfeufer	July 6, 1941	Bob Moore and Carl Pfeufer
Don Winslow of the Navy	Frank V. Martinek and Leon A Beroth	July 30, 1955	Al Levin
Dondi	Gus Edson and Irwin Hasen	June 8, 1986	Bob Oksner and Irwin Hasen
Drago	Burne Hogarth	November 10, 1946	Burne Hogarth
Foxy Grandpa	Charles E. ("Bunny") Schultze	1929	Charles E. ("Bunny") Schultze
Freckles & His Friends	Merrill Blosser	1971	Henry Formhals
Friday Foster	Jim Lawrence and Jorge Lonagron	May 1974	Jim Lawrence and Gray Morrow
Fritz the Cat	Robert Crumb	*People's Comics,* 1972***	Robert Crumb
Funnies, The	George Delacorte, New Fiction Co.	October 16, 1930, Issue # 36	George Delacorte, New Fiction Co.
Gordo	Gus Arriola	March 1985	Gus Arriola
Gumps, The	Sidney Smith	October 17, 1959	Gus Edson
Hairbreadth Harry	C.W.Kahles	1940	F.O. Alexander
Half Hitch	Hank Ketcham	1975	Hank Ketcham
Happy Hooligan	Frederick B. Opper	August 14, 1932	Frederick B. Opper.
Harold Teen	Carl Ed	October 10, 1959	Carl Ed
Haunt of Fear, The	Bill Gaines (publisher); Al Feldstein (editor)	November-December 1954 Issue #28	Graham Ingels, Bernie Krigstein, Jack Kamen and Jack Davis
Heart of Juliet Jones	Elliot Caplin and Stan Drake	January 1, 2000	Frank Bolle
Jane	Norman Pett	October 10, 1959	Michael Hubbard
Joe and Asbestos	Ken Kling	1966	Ken Kling
Joe Palooka	Ham Fisher	November 4, 1984	Tony DiPetra
Johnny Hazard	Frank Robbins	August 1977	Frank Robbins
Jungle Jim	Don Moore (writer), Alex Raymond (artist)	August 8, 1954	Various
Just Kids	Ad Carter	June 26, 1957*	Ad Carter
King of the Royal Mounted	Allen Dean	March 1954	Charles Flanders and Jim Gary
Krazy Kat	George Herriman	April 25, 1944*	George Herriman
Li'l Abner	Al Capp	November 13, 1977	Al Capp
Little Iodine	Jimmy Hatlo	1986	Bob Dunn and Hy Eisman
Little Jimmy	James Swinnerton	April 27, 1958	James Swinnerton
Little King, The	Otto Soglow	June 20, 1975	Otto Soglow

Little Lulu	Marge Henderson (Marjorie Henderson Buell)	1967 (Strip) April 1984 (Book)	Various
Little Nemo in Slumberland	Windsor McCay	1947	Robert McCay
Mary Perkins On Stage	Leonard Starr	September 9, 1979	Leonard Starr
Mickey Finn	Lank Leonard	July 31, 1976	Morris Weiss
Moon Mullins	Frank Willard	June 1991	Ferd Johnson
Mutt and Jeff	H. C. ("Bud") Fisher	November 1983	George Breisacher
Mystery in Space		September 1966, Issue #110	
Nebbs, The	Sol Hess and W. A. Carlson	1946	Stanley Baer
Nize Baby	Milt Gross	February 17, 1929	Milt Gross
Oaky Doaks	Ralph Briggs Fuller	1961	Ralph Briggs Fuller
Old Doc Yak	Sidney Smith	December 8, 1935*	Sidney Smith
Our Boarding House	Gene Ahern	December 1984	Les Carroll
Out Our Way	J. R. Williams	1977	Ed Sullivan
Peanuts	Charles M. Schulz	January 3, 2000 (daily); February 13, 2000 (Sunday)	Charles M. Schulz
Pete the Tramp	C. D. Russell	December 12, 1963	C.D. Russell
Pip, Squeak, and Wilfred	Bertram Lamb and A. B. Payne	March 9, 1955	Hugh McClelland
Pogo Possum	Walt Kelly	1983	Walt Kelly
Polly and Her Pals	Cliff Sterrett	June 15, 1958	Paul Fung
Red Ryder	Fred Harman	1964	Bob McLeod
Rip Kirby	Ward Greene and Fred Dickenson	June 26, 1999	John Prentice
Rusty Riley	Frank Godwin	Summer 1959	Frank Godwin
Secret Agent X-9	Alex Raymond and Dashiell Hammett	February 10, 1996	George Evans
Short Ribs	Frank O'Neal	May 1982	Frank Hill
Skippy	Percy Crosby	December 8, 1945	Percy Crosby
Smilin' Jack	Zack Mosley	April 1, 1973	Zack Mosley
Smitty	Walter Berndt	1973	Walter Berndt
Smokey Stover	Bill Holman	1973	Bill Holman
Spirit, The	Will Eisner	September 28, 1952	Wally Wood
Steve Canyon	Milton Caniff	June 4, 1988	Richard Rockwell
Strange World of Mr. Mum, The	Irving Phillips	1974	Irving Phillips
Tales from the Crypt	Bill Gaines (publisher) and Al Feldstein (editor)	February-March 1955, Issue #46	Bill Gaines (publisher) and Al Feldstein (editor)
Tillie the Toiler	Russ Westover	March 1959	Bob Gustafson
Tim Tyler's Luck	Lyman Young	February 12, 1984*	Lyman Young
Toonerville Folks	Fontaine Fox	February 9, 1955	Fontaine Fox
Toots and Casper	Jim Murphy	1958	Jim Murphy

Treasure Chest	George A. Pflaum (publisher)	July 1972	George A. Pflaum (publisher)
Vault of Horror	EC Comics	December– January 1954–55, Issue #40	EC Comics
Vic Jordan	Payne Wexler	April 30, 1945	Bernard Bailey
Wash Tubbs	Roy Crane	1988	Jim Lawrence and Bill Crooks
Watchmen	Alan Moore and Dave Gibbons	October 1987	Alan Moore and Dave Gibbons
Weary Willie and Tired Tim	Tom Browne	September 12, 1953	Percy Cocking
Wee Willie Winkie's World	Lyonel Feininger	January 20, 1907	Lyonel Feininger
Winnie Winkle	Martin Branner	July 28, 1996	Frank Bolle
Yellow Kid	R.F. Outcault	February 6, 1898**	R.F. Outcault
Young Romance	Joe Simon and Jack Kirby	November/ December 1975, Issue #208	
Adventure Comics (*New Comics; New Adventure Comics*)	Wheeler-Nicholson	September 1983, Issue #503	Wheeler-Nicholson
The Funnies (II)	Dell	March 1962, Issue #288	Dell

* Strip ended with creator's death.
** Day creator moved to a different publisher, causing strip to end.
*** Strip brought back after absence, just to kill off main character.
**** Date of last episode carried by most newspapers.

Comics—Classic (Golden) Age
The Classic, or Golden Age of comics began in the late 1930s and lasted until the early 1950s.
• **Last of the important "Golden Age" comics titles to debut:** *Superboy* in *More Fun Comics* Issue #101 in 1945. He was granted his own title by *Adventure Comics* in 1949.

Comics—Companies—Charlton Comics
Charlton Comics began producing comic books in 1946.
• **Last of Charlton Comics:** operated until the 1980s. Charlton Comics sold its popular 1960s-era superheroes to DC Comics in 1983, and the company's other properties and assets were sold at auction a few years later, in 1986. In 1999, the building that had once housed Charlton Comics was demolished, along with the then-antiquated printing equipment.

Comics—Companies—Dell Comics
Dell Comics started with *The Funnies* in 1929. It was the first American publication to specialize in comics that were not newspaper reprints.
• **Last of Dell Comics:** ceased publishing comic books in 1973.

Comics—Companies—Gold Key Comics
Western Printing and Lithographing Company began producing comics under the Gold Key logo in 1962.
• **Last of the Gold Key logo:** 1981, after which Western Printing and Lithographing Company released the comics under the Whitman logo. The company voluntarily allowed many of the licenses to lapse, and they were completely out of the comic book business by 1984.

Comics—Companies—King Features Syndicate
The King Features Syndicate, owned and operated by publishing magnate William Randolph Hearst, is credited with being the main driving force behind early American

comic strips. Hearst died on August 14, 1951, age 88.
• **Last comic strip personally approved by Hearst:** *Beetle Bailey,* created by Mort Walker in 1950

Comics—Strips—Full-Color, Full-Page Story

When comic strips were first introduced, they were often an entire page and were in full color. But as newspaper space became more valuable, the large comic strips began to disappear.
• **Last major comic feature created as a full-page, full-color story strip:** *Prince Valiant,* created by Harold ("Hal") Foster in 1937.

Controlled Substances

Controlled Substances—Cocaine—

Cocaine is derived from the leaves of the coca plant. It was first used as a local anesthetic in the late 19th century. The recreational use of cocaine became popular in the 20th century.
• **Last year cocaine production and sale were not federally regulated in the U.S.:** 1914. That year, the Harrison Act banned the importation and nonmedical use of cocaine.

Controlled Substances—Heroin

Heroin was first developed from morphine in 1898. It was used in medicine but was found to be highly addictive.
• **Last year heroin manufacture was permitted in the U.S.:** 1924. That year, the Heroin Act banned the manufacture, possession and use of heroin.

Controlled Substances—LSD

The hallucinogenic drug LSD (lysergic acid diethylamide) gained popularity in the 1960s.
• **Last time LSD was legally marketed in the U.S.:** April 1966, when it was removed from sale by its only authorized U.S. distributor, Sandoz Pharmaceuticals, after pub-

lic concern over alarming reports of its effects, especially on young people. The use of LSD is banned in the U.S. except for limited controlled research situations.

Controlled Substances—Marijuana

Marijuana comes from a plant in the hemp family. When the dried leaves and flowering tops are smoked, they create an intoxicating effect.
• **Last time possession of marijuana in the U.S. was not a crime:** 1937. That year, the Marijuana Tax Act declared the possession and sale of marijuana were criminal acts.

Controlled Substances—Opiates

Opiates such as morphine were readily available in patent medicines in the U.S. until the early 20th century.
• **End of the unregulated use of opiates in the U.S.:** 1905, by the U.S. Congress. The import of opium was banned except for medical purposes in 1909. The Harrison Narcotics Act of 1914 ended the use of opium and its derivatives in patent medicines and for any purpose except medicinal.

Crime

Crime—Crime Fighters—Earp, Wyatt

The events surrounding the shootout at the O.K. Corral in Tombstone, Arizona, in 1881 and the feud between the Earp brothers and members of the Clanton gang made Wyatt Berry Stapp Earp a legend. In the months after the gunfight, Wyatt's brother Virgil Earp was injured and brother Morgan Earp was killed. Wyatt and his posse tracked down and killed three suspects in Morgan's shooting.
• **Last of Earp's vengeance killings:** Curly Bill Brocius on March 24, 1882. Earp may also have tracked down and killed John Ringo, the last of the Clanton leaders in July 1882.
• **Last of Earp's law-enforcement jobs:** aiding Luke Short as a member of the Dodge City Peace Commission in 1883. During the 1920s, Earp publicized his adventures and

worked in Hollywood as a technical consultant on the western movies of Tom Mix and William S. Hart. Earp died in Los Angeles, California, on January 13, 1929, age 80.

Crime—Crime Fighters—Garrett, Pat
Patrick Floyd Garrett gained legendary status on July 14, 1881, when he shot and killed Billy the Kid (William H. Bonney) at Fort Sumner, New Mexico. (*See also* Crime—Robbery—Billy the Kid.)
• **Last of Garrett's law-enforcement jobs:** territorial detective in New Mexico, searching for the murderers of Albert J. Fountain and Fountain's son in 1896. Garrett spent his final years on his ranch near Las Cruces, New Mexico. He was murdered there by a feuding neighbor on February 29, 1908, age 57 or 58.

Crime—Crime Fighters—Holliday, Doc
John Henry ("Doc") Holliday was a Georgia dentist who moved west after being diagnosed with tuberculosis. His friendship with Wyatt Earp led to his involvement with taking on members of the Clanton gang at the O.K. Corral in 1881. Holliday had a number of run-ins that ended in gunfire.
• **Last of Holliday's gunfights:** in Leadville, Colorado, on August 19, 1884, when he shot a bartender named Billy Allen, to whom he owed money. He was acquitted. Holliday died in Glenwood Springs, Colorado, on November 8, 1887, age 35 or 36.

Crime—Crime Fighters—Scotland Yard
Scotland Yard is the name used to describe the headquarters of the metropolitan police in London, England. Scotland Yard's first home was at 4 Whitehall Place, beginning in 1829.
• **Last time Scotland Yard was at Whitehall:** 1890, when police headquarters were moved to a brick building on the Thames Embankment that became known as New Scotland Yard.
• **Last time New Scotland Yard headquarters were at the Thames Embankment:** 1967, when they were relocated to a 20-story building on Victoria Street. They are still called New Scotland Yard.

Crime—Crime Fighters—Tilghman, Bill
William ("Bill") Tilghman's most famous exploit was capturing Bill Doolin singlehandedly in Arkansas in 1896. Later, he held the offices of sheriff and state senator. He resigned as a senator to take his last major law enforcement position, as police chief of Oklahoma City, Oklahoma, from which he resigned in 1913.
• **Last of Tilghman's law enforcement jobs:** Tilghman accepted a job in law enforcement in the crime-ridden oil boom town of Cromwell, Oklahoma. He was 70 when he was shot and killed there on November 1, 1924, in a struggle with a prohibition agent named Wiley Lynn. Tilghman is considered the last of the great western lawman to die on the job.

Crime—Crime Fighters—Untouchables, The
Federal agent Eliot Ness worked with a group of U.S Treasury agents—G-men—known as "The Untouchables."
• **Last surviving member of The Untouchables:** Albert H. Wolff (a.k.a. "Wallpaper Wolff"), who served as a technical consultant during the filming of the 1987 movie *The Untouchables*. Wolff died in Mason, Ohio, in May 1998, age 95.

Crime—Feuds—Hatfields and McCoys
The feud between the Hatfield and McCoy families began in the late 1860s in Pike County, Kentucky. By the time it ended on March 21, 1891, more than a dozen family members had been killed. The feud ended when the governments of West Virginia and Kentucky intervened and arrested many of the leading clan members.
• **Last surviving member of the original feuding McCoy clan:** Jasper McCoy, who died in Zebulon, Kentucky, on August 16, 1951, age 84.

Crime—Fraud—Weil, Joseph ("Yellow Kid")
Joseph ("Yellow Kid") Weil was a world-class con man who reformed around the age of 70, after serving jail time on a bond

scheme. During his later years, he dictated his memoirs to Chicago, Illinois, journalist W.T. Brannon.

• **Last con of Weil:** selling the movie rights to his life to both Brannon and a movie studio, who then had to fight over possession of them. Weil died in 1976, shortly after celebrating his 100th birthday with a big party. Some evidence now suggests that he was only 99 and lied about his aged—so perhaps this was his last con. Although he may have scammed more than $12 million in his life, he died penniless and was buried in a potter's field in Chicago.

Crime—Murder—Boston Strangler

A string of murders of women in Boston, Massachusetts, from 1962 to 1964 confounded experts and earned for the perpetrator the name "the Boston Strangler."

• **Last murder victim of the Boston Strangler:** believed to be 19-year-old Mary Sullivan, who was raped and strangled on January 4, 1964, in her Boston apartment. She was the 13th victim of the Boston Strangler.

• **Last of the Boston Strangler:** Unknown. After Albert DeSalvo was arrested for rape, he confessed that he was the Boston Strangler. However, with no evidence to substantiate his confession, he was not charged with the crimes. He stood trial for other crimes and was sent to prison for life in 1967. DeSalvo was found murdered in his cell on November 26, 1973.

Crime—Murder—Jack the Ripper

From August to November 1888, a murderer prowled the East End of London, England, targeting prostitutes. He brutally slashed and killed his victims. Letters believed to have been written by him earned him the name Jack the Ripper. Five murders have been confirmed as his. He may have committed others. He was never caught. Many theories abound as to his identity. His crimes have spawned books, plays and movies.

• **Last known murder victim of Jack the Ripper:** Mary Jane Kelly, who was found murdered in her room at 13 Miller's Court, on November 9, 1888.

Crime—Murder—Sacco and Vanzetti

Nicola Sacco and Bartolomeo Vanzetti were charged in Boston, Massachusetts, in connection with the 1920 killing of a shoe factory employee. Although they were being tried only for the murder, their radical political views remained a focus of their trial. They were found guilty and convicted in 1921. For the next six years, a campaign was waged to overturn the conviction, based on a lack of conclusive evidence and allegations that Sacco and Vanzetti had been unfairly treated. The case created worldwide attention but in the end, the campaign to free them failed. The case inspired the play *Winterset* by Maxwell Anderson and Harold Hickerson, and the book *The Never Ending Wrong* by Katherine Anne Porter. It has also been the subject of several movies.

• **Last surviving member of the Sacco and Vanzetti jury:** Harry E. King.

• **Last of Sacco and Vanzetti:** executed in Boston on August 23, 1927. Sacco was 36. Vanzetti was 39.

• **Last ruling on Sacco and Vanzetti:** The controversial guilty verdict was repudiated on July 19, 1977—a half-century after Nicola Sacco and Bartolomeo Vanzetti were executed—when they were vindicated by proclamation of Massachusetts Governor Michael Dukakis.

Crime—Organized Crime—Capone, Al

Alphonse ("Al") Capone, also known as "Scarface," had a string of arrests in his lifetime.

• **Last arrest of Capone:** October 1931, for income tax evasion. Capone was fined and sent to a federal penitentiary in Atlanta, Georgia. In 1934, he was transferred to Alcatraz, in San Francisco, California. He left there in January 1939 and was transferred to a correctional institution at San Pedro, California.

• **Last imprisonment of Capone:** Capone left San Pedro in October 1939 and was taken to the federal prison in Lewisburg, Pennsylvania, where he was discharged on November 16, 1939, and placed in the custody of his wife and brother. Capone had untreated syphilis that had destroyed his central nervous system and developed into paresis of the brain. Family members took him to Baltimore, Maryland, where he became a patient in Union Memorial Hospital. He was then taken to Miami, Florida. Capone died in Miami Beach on January 25, 1947, age 48.

Crime—Piracy and Privateering

Piracy is robbery on the high seas. Privateering is the practice of licensing privately owned ships to seize and plunder vessels of a hostile power.

• **End of privateering:** abolished in 1856, by the Declaration of Paris. The United States did not sign the declaration, as it would have required amending Article One of the Constitution; however, the United States accepted the declaration in practice. Privateering in the U.S. died out after the Civil War.

• **Last American hanged for piracy:** Captain Nathaniel Gordon, who was executed in Tombs Prison in New York, New York, on February 21, 1862. Gordon had smuggled almost 900 Africans on his ship the *Erie* and was planning to sell them into slavery in Cuba. Conditions were so bad aboard ship that about one third of the Africans died en route. Gordon was charged with piracy, found guilty and sentenced to death.

Crime—Prisons—Australia— Penal Colonies

Britain began to send its petty criminals to Australia in the 1780s, after the American Revolution put an end to shipping them to North America.

• **Last convict ship from Ireland:** the *Phoebe Dunbar,* which sailed from Kingstown near Dublin and reached Australia on August 30, 1853.

• **Last convict ship from Great Britain:** the *Hougoumont,* which arrived in Australia on January 9, 1868, carrying 269 convicts.

• **Last remaining convict ship:** the *Edwin Fox*, built by William Henry Foster on the River Hooghly near Calcutta, India, in 1853. It served as a convict transport to Australia

in 1858. It also holds several other "lasts" claims including: last surviving Indian-built East Indiaman; last surviving Crimean War troop ship; and last wooden immigrant ship to New Zealand. The ship is now moored in Picton, New Zealand.

Crime—Prisons—France—Bastille, *see* Wars and Battles—French Revolution.

Crime—Prisons—France— Devil's Island

The French penal colony at French Guiana in South America was established in 1852, when Emperor Napoleon III closed two prisons in France and sent the prisoners there. It was made up of scattered camps on the mainland and on three nearby islands, one of which was Ile du Diable—Devil's Island. The entire colony—mainland and islands—came to be called Devil's Island. French officer Alfred Dreyfus was probably the island's most famous prisoner.

• **End of Dreyfus's confinement:** June 1899. He returned to France after more than four years of confinement for treason.

• **Last prisoner sent to Devil's Island:** 1938.

• **Last prisoners left Devil's Island:** August 22, 1953. After World War II, the prisoners were gradually phased out. However, when Devil's Island was abandoned in 1953, one prisoner refused to be repatriated. His name is unknown.

Crime—Prisons—Germany—Spandau

After World War II, Spandau Prison in Berlin, East Germany, was used to house Nazi war criminals.

• **Last prisoner in Spandau:** high-ranking German Nazi Rudolf Hess. From 1966 until his death, he was the sole prisoner at Spandau. He died on August 17, 1987, age 93.

• **Last of Spandau Prison:** demolished shortly after Hess died.

Crime—Prisons—Great Britain— Fleet Prison

The notorious Fleet Prison, built in London, England, in 1189, was destroyed three times.

The first was during the Peasants' Revolt in 1381. It was destroyed again after the Great Fire of 1666. It burned again in 1780, during the Gordon riots. By the mid-1700s, Fleet Prison was used mostly for debtors and people who were bankrupt. Charles Dickens mentioned the prison in *Pickwick Papers*.

• **Last of the Fleet marriages:** abolished with the 1753 Marriage Act. Fleet marriages were secret unions performed in the prison by debtor clergy for payments ranging from gin to money.

• **Last time Fleet Prison was used:** 1842. It was then permanently closed. It was demolished in 1845-46.

Crime—Prisons—Great Britain—
Millbank Penitentiary
Millbank Penitentiary, built on the banks of the Thames in London, England, was completed in 1821. The prison used the solitary system that had come into use in Pennsylvania in the early 19th century: prisoners were confined to separate cells and had no contact with one another.

• **Last time Millbank was used as prison:** May 1886. Millbank was closed November 1890 and demolished. Beginning in 1897, the National Gallery of British Art (later Tate Gallery) occupied the site.

Crime—Prisons—Great Britain—
Newgate Prison
Newgate Prison was on the site of an ancient gatehouse in London, England, where a jail had stood since the 13th century. A second jail was destroyed in London's Great Fire of 1666. A third prison was built between 1778 and 1780 but was partially destroyed soon afterward during riots. Conditions at Newgate were so dismal that after the Prison Act of 1877, the prison was used only for people awaiting trial or execution.

• **Last time Newgate Prison was used:** May 1902, when it was permanently closed. It was torn down in 1902-03.

Crime—Prisons—Great Britain—
Tower of London
The Tower of London, on the Thames in

southeastern London, England, dates from the 11th century. The central part, known as the White Tower, was built by William the Conqueror.

• **Last English monarch who used the Tower as a royal residence:** James I.

• **Last traitor beheaded at the Tower:** Robert Devereux, Earl of Essex.

• **Last prisoner confined at the Tower:** Hitler's deputy Rudolf Hess. After he parachuted near Glasgow, Scotland, in 1940, Hess was imprisoned in the Tower for the duration of World War II. At the Nuremberg War Crimes trials, Hess was sentenced to life for war crimes and was transferred to Spandau Prison in Berlin. (*See also* Crime—Prisons—Germany.)

• **Last execution at the Tower of London:** Josef Jakobs, a German spy, who was shot by a firing squad on August 4, 1941. He had parachuted into England on January 31, 1941, and was captured as he landed. He was taken to Waterloo Barracks at the Tower. Unable to stand, Jakobs was seated for his execution. The chair remains in the Tower but is not on public display.

Crime—Prisons—India—
Black Hole of Calcutta
The Black Hole of Calcutta, India, was a small airless room into which 145 Englishmen and one woman were confined at musket point on the hot summer night of June 21, 1756. According to stories about the event, 123 of the prisoners died during the next ten hours. But the story is full of inconsistencies, so it is difficult to ascertain what is true.

• **Last purported survivor of the Calcutta Black Hole incident:** John Mills. His 1811 epitaph in the Saint Pancras churchyard in London, England, reads: "John Mills, the last survivor of the few Persons who came out of the Black Hole of Calcutta Bengal in the year 1756."

Crime—Prisons—United States—
Alcatraz
Alcatraz, an island in San Francisco Bay in California, was used by the United States

Army as disciplinary barracks from 1859 to 1909 and later as a military prison. In 1934, it became a federal prison and was set up to have the highest level of security. Known as the "Rock," Alcatraz was thought to be escape-proof. Numerous escape attempts failed.

• **Last escape attempt from Alcatraz:** December 16, 1962. John Paul Scott and Daryl Parker, both bank robbers, slipped through the bars of a window in the prison kitchen and reached the water before the manhunt picked up their trail. Parker made it about 100 yards before giving up on a outcropping of rocks known as Little Alcatraz. Scott was captured at the base of a retaining wall at Fort Point near the Golden Gate Bridge.

• **Last time prisoners were confined at Alcatraz:** May 15, 1963. The last 27 federal prisoners were removed from Alcatraz in leg irons and chains.

• **Last prisoner to leave Alcatraz:** Frank Weatherman. He was the last of a group of 27 to leave the island. As he boarded the boat, he remarked to the crowd of reporters and photographers, "Alcatraz was never no good for nobody."

• **Last Alcatraz warden:** Olin G. Blackwell, who held the position from 1961 to 1963.

• **End of the Native American Indian occupancy of Alcatraz:** June 11, 1971. Alcatraz had been occupied by the Native American Indians of All Tribes for 19 months, beginning on November 20, 1969. In the fall of 1973, Alcatraz was opened to visitors as part of the United States National Park Service.

Crime—Prisons—United States— Andersonville *See* Wars and Battles— Civil War.

Crime—Prisons—United States— Eastern State Penitentiary
When Eastern State Penitentiary opened in Philadelphia, Pennsylvania, in 1829, it was the first prison to use a solitary system in which prisoners were confined to separate cells and had no contact with one another.

The extreme isolation, known as the "Pennsylvania System," did not have the calming effect the planners had intended. Some prisoners went mad and others committed suicide. When Charles Dickens visited the prison in 1842, he found the Pennsylvania System cruel and wrong.

• **End of the Pennsylvania System of confinement at Eastern State Penitentiary:** officially abandoned in 1913.

• **Last time prisoners were held at Eastern State Penitentiary:** 1971. Most prisoners were removed in January 1970. The city of Philadelphia used it briefly as a city prison. It closed permanently the following year. The massive fortress-like structure with its 12-foot high stone walls is an architectural wonder and is now a National Historic Landmark.

Crime—Prisons—United States— Moyamensing
The Gothic-style Moyamensing Prison in Philadelphia, Pennsylvania, was built in the early 1830s. It was used to hold Confederate prisoners of war during the Civil War.

• **Last of Moyamensing Prison:** closed on November 13, 1963; demolished in 1968.

Crime—Punishment—Corporal Punishment—Flogging, Caning, Spanking
• **End of corporal punishment of children in schools and at home:** Sweden was the first to ban it in 1979. Other nations followed, including: Austria (1989), Croatia (1999), Cyprus (1994), Denmark (1997), Finland (1983), Germany (2000), Israel (2000), Italy (1996), Latvia (1998), Norway (1987), Zambia (2000) and Zimbabwe (1999).

• **End of spanking of students in Great Britain:** 1986, in state-run schools; 1998, in private schools. In almost half of the states in the United States, it is still legal for a school teacher to spank a student.

• **End of flogging in the U.S. Army:** abolished August 5, 1861.

• **End of flogging in the U.S. Navy:** abolished September 28, 1850.

• **Last state to abolish the flogging of con-**

victed felons: Delaware in 1952.

• **End of flogging in Great Britain:** the flogging of sailors was abolished in 1957 and of prisoners in 1967. Flogging was abolished in Britain as a form of sentenced punishment in 1948.

Crime—Punishment—Cruel and Unusual Punishment—United States
• **End of cruel and unusual punishment:** December 15, 1791, with ratification of the 8th Amendment to the U.S. Constitution. The amendment ended extreme punishments such as imprisoning a person for many years for stealing a loaf of bread and cruel punishment such as amputating a limb or other forms of torture. The amendment also put an end to excessive bail.

Crime—Punishment—Execution—Australia
• **Last man hanged in Australia:** Ronald Ryan on February 3, 1967, for shooting a prison warden while attempting to escape from Pentridge Prison near Melbourne.
• **Last woman hanged in Australia:** Jean Lee, who was executed on February 19, 1951, in Pentridge Prison for the murder of 73-year-old William ("Pop") Kent. Two male companions were also hanged for the crime.

Crime—Punishment—Execution—Canada
• **Last men hanged in Canada:** Ronald Turpin and Arthur Lucas on December 11, 1962. Both men were executed for killing police officers.
• **Last woman hanged in Canada:** Marguerite Pitre, at Montreal's Bordeaux Prison in 1953 for her part in a 1949 airplane explosion that killed 23 people.

Crime—Punishment—Execution—Crucifixion
Crucifixion was a common form of punishment used by the Romans on slaves and people whom they had conquered. It was not used to execute Roman citizens.
• **Last use of crucifixion in the Roman**

Empire: abolished by the Roman Emperor Constantine in 337 A.D.
• **End of execution by crucifixion in France:** abolished in 1127.

Crime—Punishment—Execution—France
France abolished capital punishment in 1981.
• **Last public execution by guillotine in France:** Eugene Weidmann, six-time murderer, on June 15, 1939. When pictures of the event were published in newspapers, they created an outage, demanding an end to public executions.
• **Last execution by guillotine in France:** Convicted murderer Hamida Djandoubi, a Tunisian immigrant, on September 10, 1977.

Crime—Punishment—Execution—Great Britain
Although the death penalty was abolished for murder and other serious crimes in Great Britain in 1965, it is technically still available for convicted traitors. All the gallows in Britain were dismantled, but one set of gallows inside the Wandsworth Prison in South London was retained.
• **Last execution by beheading with an axe in Great Britain:** Scottish nobleman Simon Fraser, Lord Lovat, on April 9, 1747, at the block on Tower Hill in London. He was 80 years old. The axe used to kill him is at the Tower of London.
• **Last execution by beheading after hanging in Great Britain:** May 1, 1820, outside Newgate Prison in London, England, when the Cato Street conspirators were hanged, cut down and then beheaded by a masked executioner using a large surgeon's knife. The conspirators had planned to assassinate key members of the British government.
• **Last execution by burning at the stake in Great Britain:** Phoebe Harrius, in 1786, in front of Newgate Prison in London. She had been convicted of "coining" (counterfeiting) money, a crime that was considered high treason at the time.
• **Last execution for forgery in Great**

Britain: Thomas Maynard on December 31, 1829, at Newgate Prison. In 1832, forgery was reclassified as a noncapital crime.

• **Last execution of a woman by hanging then burning in Great Britain:** Christian Murphy (a.k.a. Bowman) on March 18, 1789. She had been convicted of "coining." In 1790, the execution law was changed so that women were condemned only to hanging for their crimes.

• **Last execution of a woman by hanging in Great Britain:** Ruth Ellis, who was executed on July 13, 1955, at Holloway Prison in London for the murder of David Blakely.

• **Last execution by hanging in Scotland:** Henry John Burnett on July 25, 1963, in Aberdeen for the murder of Thomas Guyan.

• **Last execution by hanging in Great Britain:** Peter Anthony Allen and Gwynne Owen Evans (a.k.a. John Robson Welby) were executed on August 13, 1964, at two different prisons: Allen in Manchester, Evans in Liverpool.

• **Last use of the Maiden in Great Britain:** in 1685 to behead the Earl of Argyll. The Maiden is a Scottish guillotine-like instrument of torture.

• **Last public execution of a man in Great Britain:** Michael Barrett, a Fenian, on May 26, 1868, before the gates of Newgate Prison. Subsequent executions were private.

• **Last public execution of a woman in Great Britain:** Francis Turner Kidder, on April 2, 1868. She was hanged outside Maidstone Prison

• **Last royal execution for treason in Great Britain:** James, Duke of Monmouth (a.k.a. James Fitzroy and James Crofts), the oldest illegitimate son of Charles II. He was beheaded at the Tower of London on July 15, 1685, for leading a rebellion against his uncle, King James II.

• **Last execution at Tyburn Tree:** John Austen, hanged on November 7, 1783. Tyburn, a few miles from the city walls of London, was noted for English executions. Originally, those sentenced were hanged from trees in the area. The trees were eventually replaced by a gallows known as Tyburn Tree. When the area around Tyburn became a fashionable neighborhood, complaints brought an end to the hangings. Newgate Prison in London became the new public execution spot. The city of York also had a spot called Tyburn Tree that was used for executions. The gallows outside that city was last used in 1801.

• **Last execution from a yardarm in the British Navy:** Marine Private John Dalliger, on the HMS *Leven*, in the Yangtze River in China on July 13, 1860. He was executed for attempted murder.

Crime—Punishment—Execution— Impalement

Impalement was an ancient form of execution that was intended to intensify the suffering of the person being put to death. It consisted of a long "pale" or wooden spike that was hammered through the victim's body (lengthwise) then was stuck into the ground until the victim died a slow death.

• **Last recorded instance of state-sanctioned impalement:** 1907, in Romania, when Romanian royal law dictated its use to punish the leaders of a peasant' uprising.

Crime—Punishment—Execution— Ireland

• **Last execution of a man by hanging in Ireland:** Michael Manning of Limerick on April 20, 1954, for the murder of a nurse.

• **Last execution of a woman by hanging in Ireland:** Annie Walsh, May 8, 1925, in Dublin, for the murder of her husband.

Crime—Punishment—Execution— United States

• **Last execution by bludgeoning in the United States:** Bartellemy Pichon, a soldier, in Michigan on November 7, 1707.

• **Last execution in the United States by break-on-wheel:** 1754, when four men were executed in Louisiana for murder. One of the men was a courier named Baudrot.

• **Last U.S. military execution:** U.S. Army Private Eddie Slovik, age 24, who was executed for the crime of desertion on January 31, 1945, during World War II. He was shot by his unit in the French town of Ste. Marie aux Mines by order of General Dwight D. Eisenhower. Slovik was buried in a secret location where other executed soldiers were interred. Slovik's wife tried for many years to have his body returned to the U.S., but she did not live long enough to see it happen. She died in 1979. In 1987, his body was brought to the U.S., and he was buried next to her.

• **Last state to retain the electric chair as the primary means of execution:** Nebraska. The United States is the last nation to use electrocution as a method of execution.

• **Last electric chair execution survivor in the United States:** Willie Francis, a 16-year-old black youth who was convicted of murder in 1944 by an all-white jury in Saint Martinsville, Louisiana. On May 3, 1946, the portable electric chair was set up at the Saint Martinsville Parish Court House. After Francis was strapped in, he was jolted with electric current but did not die. Francis's lawyers filed an appeal on the grounds that a repeated attempt would constitute cruel and unusual punishment. The U.S. Supreme Court did not agree. The court ruled in a 5-4 decision that it was not "cruel and unusual" to finish carrying out the sentence since the state acted in good faith in the first attempt. Francis was finally executed on May 9, 1947.

• **Last states to authorize execution by hanging:** Delaware, New Hampshire and Washington. These three states also authorize another method of execution, and it is doubtful whether hanging would ever be employed again.

• **Last U.S. Navy executions for mutiny:** December 1, 1842. Three sailors— Midshipman Philip Spencer, Boatswain Samuel Cromwell and Seaman Elisha Small—were hanged aboard the USS *Somers* for plotting a mutiny. Spencer was the son of U.S. Secretary of War John C. Spencer.

• **Last execution by pressing in the United States:** Giles Corey in Salem, Massachusetts, on September 16, 1692.

• **Last public execution in the United States:** Rainey Bethea, on August 14, 1936,

in Owensboro, Kentucky. About 20,000 people witnessed the execution. Bethea, a young man, was hanged for raping and killing an elderly woman.

• **Last scaffold reprieve in the U.S.:** Will Purvis, on February 7, 1894, in Columbia, Mississippi. He had been convicted of the murder of Will Buckley and was sentenced to be hanged. As Purvis went through the trap, the noose loosened and he fell to the ground. Among those attending the execution was a doctor who examined the rope and refused to hand it over to the executioners for a second try. A minister asked the crowd if anyone thought Purvis should be hanged again. No one answered. Purvis was sent back to his cell and his sentence was later commuted to life imprisonment. In December 1898, he received a full pardon. In 1917, Joe Beard, a Mississippi farmer, confessed to the murder of Will Buckley and implicated another man. The Mississippi legislature awarded Purvis $3,000 in compensation for his false imprisonment and for rope-burn injury.

Crime—Punishment—Execution— United States—Last Meal

The last meal for Death Row inmates is an American death-penalty ritual.

John Wayne Gacy had fried chicken, fried shrimp, French fries and strawberries.

Ted Bundy had steak, eggs, hash browns and coffee.

Gary Gilmore had hamburgers, eggs, potatoes and coffee.

Timothy McVeigh had mint chocolate chip ice cream.

Crime—Punishment—Execution— United States—Moratorium

The United States had a moratorium on capital punishment for several years. No civilian prisoner was executed between 1967 and 1977. The U.S. Supreme Court ruled in 1972 that the death penalty was cruel and unusual punishment. However, in 1976, the U.S. Supreme Court upheld the death penalty for murder, ruling that capital punishment was not inherently cruel or unusual.

• **End of the U.S. moratorium on capital punishment:** January 17, 1977, with the execution of Gary Gilmore in Utah.

Crime—Punishment—Imprisonment for Debt—United States

• **End of imprisonment for debt (except for fraud or refusal to pay):**
Alabama: abolished in 1839.
Connecticut: abolished in 1842.
Kentucky: abolished in 1821.
Maine: abolished in 1834 for debts less than $30.
Massachusetts: abolished in 1834 for debts less than $30; in 1857 for all but cases of fraud.
Michigan: abolished in 1838.
New Hampshire: abolished in 1834 for debts less than $30; in 1840 for all but cases of fraud.
New York: abolished in 1831.
Ohio: abolished in 1838.
Pennsylvania: abolished in 1842.
South Carolina: abolished in 1834 for debts less than $30.
Tennessee: abolished in 1840.
Vermont: abolished in 1838.
By 1869, every state had abolished imprisonment for debt except for fraud or refusal to pay.

Crime—Punishment—Imprisonment for Debt—Various Nations

• **End of imprisonment for debt (except for fraud or refusal to pay):**
Belgium: abolished in 1871.
Britain: abolished in 1869.
France: abolished in 1867.
Ireland: abolished in 1872.
Italy: abolished in 1877.
Norway: abolished in 1874.
Scotland: abolished in 1880.
Switzerland: abolished in 1874.

Crime—Punishment—Pillory

The pillory, an old instrument of punishment, consisted of a wooden frame with holes for the head and hands of the wrongdoer, who was then at the mercy of the mob.

• **Last use of the pillory in Great Britain:** abolished except for perjury in 1816. The pillory was finally abolished in 1837.
• **Last man to be pilloried in England:** Peter Bossey, who was sentenced in June 1830.
• **Last state to use the pillory in the United States:** Delaware, which abandoned the pillory in 1905.

Crime—Punishment—Public Dunking

The ducking stool was used mostly to punish women. A woman was fastened to the chair that was attached to a beam. The chair was dunked in water like a seesaw.

• **Last use of the ducking stool in England:** Jenny Pipes (a.k.a. Jane Corran) in 1809, at Leominster, Herefordshire. She was paraded through the streets on the ducking stool before the punishment was administered. In 1817, Sarah Leeke, also of that town, was sentenced to the ducking stool. However, when the procession reached the river's edge, it was determined that the water level was too low.

Crime—Punishment—Torture

Torture as a means of punishment involved devices such as the rack, thumbscrew, boot, and red-hot pincers.

• **Last use of torture as punishment in England:** 1638. It was never recognized by English law, but it was used by royal prerogative until this year, then it was declared illegal.

Crime—Punishment—Treadwheel

Punishment by treadwheel, or treadmill, in British prisons was introduced in the early 1800s. The practice became so unpopular by the 1890s that steps were taken to abolish the devices.

• **Last use of the treadwheel in Great Britain:** 1902.

Crime—Punishment—Whipping Post

• **Last state in the United States to allow punishment by whipping:** Delaware.
• **Last legal whipping post in the United**

States: "Red Hannah" in Delaware.
• **Last public whipping in Delaware:** 1952.
• **End of the whipping post in Delaware:** abolished on July 6, 1972.

Crime—Robbery—Barker Gang

Arizona Donnie Clark Barker (a.k.a. Ma Barker) planned the bank robberies and kidnappings committed by her four sons (Arthur, Fred, Herman and Lloyd).
• **Last of Ma Barker:** died in a shootout with FBI agents in Florida on January 16, 1935. She was never arrested for a crime during her lifetime.
• **Last of the Barkers:** Fred Barker, Ma Barker's son, was killed with her in 1935. Arthur ("Doc") Barker died while trying to escape from Alcatraz in June 1939. Herman Barker committed suicide in 1927. Lloyd Barker was killed by his wife in 1949.
• **Last surviving member of the Barker Gang:** Alvin ("Old Creepy") Karpis. He was arrested by J. Edgar Hoover and sent to Alcatraz, where he spent more time on the Rock than anyone in history—26 years. He was finally paroled in 1969 and deported to Canada. In Toronto, he wrote his memoirs, gave lectures on his life on the Rock, and starred in beer commercials. He committed suicide in 1979 during a visit to Spain.

Crime—Robbery—Billy the Kid

Henry McCarty (a.k.a. William H. Bonney; Kid Antrim; and later Billy the Kid) became a legend of the Old West for his murders and robberies.
• **Last crime and last prison break by Billy the Kid:** April 28, 1881, when he killed two prison guards while escaping from the Lincoln County, New Mexico, courthouse. On July 14, 1881, Billy the Kid was killed by Sheriff Pat Garrett at the ranch of Pete Maxwell near Fort Sumner, New Mexico.

Crime—Robbery—Black Bart

Charles E. Boles (a.k.a. Charles Bolton), later known as Black Bart, was the most famous of the California highwaymen who robbed the Wells Fargo stagecoaches in the Old West.
• **Last holdup of Black Bart:** November 3, 1882, the Sonora-to-Milton stage. He left behind a handkerchief. A distinctive laundry mark traced the handkerchief back to a Charles Bolton in San Francisco, and Black Bart was finally arrested.

Crime—Robbery—Bonnie and Clyde

Bonnie Parker and Clyde Barrow were ruthless killers who murdered for the thrill of killing. They were shot to death in a police ambush near Gibsland, Louisiana, on May 23, 1934.
• **Last surviving member of Bonnie and Clyde's gang:** Ralph Smith Fults, who died on March 15, 1993, age 82.
• **Last surviving member of the group that killed Bonnie and Clyde:** Ted C. Hinton, a Dallas County, Texas, deputy who was one of six members of a law enforcement posse that ambushed the pair near Gibsland, Louisiana. Hinton died in Dallas, Texas, in October 1977, age 73.

Crime—Robbery—Butch Cassidy, The Sundance Kid and The Wild Bunch

Robert LeRoy Parker (a.k.a. Butch Cassidy) and Harry Alonzo Longabaugh (a.k.a. The Sundance Kid) belonged to a loose-knit gang known as "The Train Robbers' Syndicate," "The Hole-in-the-Wall Gang" and "The Wild Bunch." They robbed banks, trains and mine payrolls in the Rocky Mountain West from the late 1880s to early 1900s.
• **Last heist of Butch Cassidy and The Sundance Kid:** robbing the Aramayo Mine payroll at Tupiza, Bolivia, November 4, 1908. No one knows for sure what happened to Butch Cassidy and Sundance after that. Most accounts say they were killed by soldiers in San Vicente, Bolivia, a few days later. However, Cassidy's sister Lula claimed he visited the family in Utah in 1925 and died around 1937 in Nevada, where he was buried. The Pinkerton detectives, lacking definitive proof of Cassidy

and Sundance's death, never called off their search for them.

• **Last heist by a Wild Bunch member:** attributed to Ben Kilpatrick, who was killed in an attempt to rob the Galveston, Harrisburg & San Antonio Railroad's passenger train at Baxter's Curve, in Terrell County, Texas, on March 13, 1912.

• **Last Wild Bunch members:** the last surviving member who participated in at least one robbery was Walt Punteney, who died in 1948. The last member who did not participate in a robbery was convicted counterfeiter Laura Bullion (a.k.a. Della Rose), female companion of Kilpatrick. She settled in Nashville, Tennessee, where she was known as Mrs. Maurice Lincoln, widow. She worked as a seamstress and dressmaker and died in Nashville in 1961.

Crime—Robbery—Dalton Gang

The Dalton Gang was one of the last great outlaw gangs of the Old West. The Dalton family had ten sons and five daughters. Many of them worked on one side of the law or the other—some worked on both.

• **Last crime by the Dalton Gang:** May 23, 1894, at the Longview, Texas, bank.

• **Last surviving Dalton brother:** Emmett Dalton, who was sentenced to life in prison but was pardoned in 1907. Afterward, he married and had a successful career as a building contractor, real estate agent and movie consultant. He spent much of his later years as a vigorous anti-crime crusader. Emmett Dalton died on July 13, 1937.

Crime—Robbery—Dillinger, John

John Dillinger and his gang terrorized the Midwest from September 1933 to July 1934, killing ten men, wounding seven others, robbing banks and police arsenals, and staging three jail breaks. Dillinger's downfall began when he stole a sheriff's car and drove across the Indiana-Illinois state line during a jail break, thus violating federal law. That allowed the FBI to become actively involved in his pursuit.

• **Last robbery by the Dillinger Gang:** Merchants National Bank in South Bend, Indiana, June 30, 1934. The gang also included Baby Face Nelson, Homer Van Meter and John Paul Chase. Dillinger was shot to death by federal agents on July 22, 1934, outside Chicago's Biograph movie theater.

• **Last surviving member of the group that killed John Dillinger:** Thomas J. Connor, a lawman, lawyer and baseball player. He died in Southbury, Connecticut, on April 14, 1997, age 91.

Crime—Robbery—Doolin Gang

Bill Doolin and his gang made a name for themselves with their robberies throughout the Old West.

• **Last heist of the Doolin Gang:** April 3, 1895, when they robbed a train at Dover, Oklahoma Territory. Afterward, the gang made their way westward, unaware that a posse was closing in on them. The gang members were killed off gradually. Doolin was killed on August 24, 1896. Remaining gang members Little Dick West and Dynamite Dick Clifton headed south into the Creek Nation. They robbed a number of stores before Clifton was killed in a shootout with Heck Thomas that November.

• **Last surviving member of the Doolin Gang:** Little Dick West, who was killed on April 8, 1898, by Deputy Bill Fossett and Sheriff Frank Rinehart, members of the Heck Thomas posse.

Crime—Robbery—Highwaymen

During the 17th and 18th centuries, masked pistol-carrying horsemen known as highwaymen prowled the roads of England, robbing travelers and gaining a reputation for their elusiveness, bravado and charm.

• **Last documented highwayman in Britain:** George Cutterman, who robbed travelers on the Great North Road in North Yorkshire. He also worked as landlord of the King's Head in Kirklington. Cutterman was finally tracked down in 1824, after a reward was posted for his capture. On his way to York for trial, he escaped from the top of the coach that was transporting him and was never seen again.

Crime—Robbery—James-Younger Gang

Frank and Jesse James teamed up with the Younger brothers (Cole, Jim, John and Bob) to form the James-Younger Gang, who robbed banks, stores, stagecoaches and trains during the 1860s and 1870s.

• **Last holdup of the James-Younger Gang:** near Glendale, Missouri, on September 7, 1881. That night, the last active incarnation of the James Gang—Jesse, Frank, Dick Liddil, the Hite brothers (Wood and Clarence) and newcomer Charlie Ford—stopped a Chicago & Alton Railroad train, then boarded and robbed the express car and more than 100 passengers.

• **Last surviving James brother:** Frank James, who surrendered to Missouri Governor Thomas T. Crittenden on October 4, 1882. Through a series of trials and legal maneuvers, Frank James was acquitted. He lived 30 more years, working county fairs and traveling shows and as a theater doorman. In 1903, he and Cole Younger became partners in the *James-Younger Wild West Show*. James died at his family's Missouri farmstead on February 18, 1915, age 72.

• **Last surviving Younger brother:** Cole Younger, who sold tombstones and insurance after he was paroled in 1901. For a time, he was involved in the *James-Younger Wild West Show* venture with Frank James. His last job was with the lecture circuit. Younger died in Lee's Summit, Missouri, on March 21, 1916, age 71.

Crime—Robbery—Newton Gang

The Newton Gang is often credited with being the last of the daring American bank and train robbing gangs. By their own accounts, gang members robbed more than 80 banks and six trains. They stole more money than all of the famous Old West outlaw gangs combined.

• **Last train robbery of the Newton Gang:** the Chicago, Milwaukee & St. Paul mail train near Rondout, Illinois, on June 24, 1924. They stole $3 million, which put hundreds of lawmen on their trail. The Newtons were finally caught.

• **Last bank robbery of the Newton Gang:** Dock Newton attempted to rob a bank when he was 76 and living in a nursing home. He was indicted for bank robbery and tried in 1968. Because of his age and deteriorating health, he was sentenced to two years in the penitentiary. Dock Newton died in 1974.

• **Last surviving Newton Gang member:** Joe Newton, who died in 1989, age 88.

Crime—Robbery—Stagecoaches

Stagecoaches began to disappear in the late 19th century as railroads were built in the West. But a few were still running in the early 20th century.

• **Last recorded U.S. stagecoach robbery:** December 15, 1916, near Jarbridge, Nevada. Ben Kuhl and Ed Beck stole $3,000.

Crime—Terrorism—Oklahoma City Bombing

The nine-story Alfred P. Murrah Federal Building in Oklahoma City, Oklahoma, was destroyed in a bombing by Timothy McVeigh and accomplice Terry Nichols on April 19, 1995.

• **Last survivor taken from the Murrah Building:** 15-year-old Brandy Liggins.

• **Last day of the search for victims:** May 4, 1995.

• **Last bodies removed from the Murrah Building:** those of Christi Rosas, Virginia Thompson and Alvin Justes, who were in the building's Credit Union. Their bodies were in unstable rubble and were removed on May 29, 1995, after the rest of the building was demolished on May 23, 1995. The death toll was finalized at 168. Timothy McVeigh was executed on June 11, 2001. Terry Nichols was sentenced to life without chance of parole.

Crime—Terrorism—1972 Olympics—Munich Olympic Village

In September 1972, eight members of Black September, a Palestinian terrorist group, attacked and killed two members of the Israeli Olympic team at the Olympic Village in Munich, West Germany. Five of the terrorists were killed in a shoot-out with police.

Two of the three original surviving terrorists were later killed by Israeli assassination squads.

• **Last surviving member of the 1972 Olympics terrorist group:** Jamal Al Gashey, who came out of hiding for the film *One Day in September* (1999). He is believed to be in hiding in Africa with family.

Crime—Terrorism—1996 Olympics—Centennial Park

The 1996 Summer Olympics were held in Atlanta, Georgia. At 1:20 a.m. on July 27, Atlanta's crowded Centennial Park was rocked by an explosion that killed one person and injured at least 65 others. Following the bombing, the FBI relentlessly pursued security guard Richard Jewell as the main suspect. Jewell was innocent.

• **Last day Richard Jewell was held as a suspect:** October 26, 1996, at which time he was finally cleared by the FBI. Later, Eric Robert Rudolph was indicted for the Olympics bombing, as well the bombing of a clinic in Birmingham, Alabama, that performed abortions.

• **End of the search for Eric Robert Rudolph:** arrested on May 31, 2003, in Murphy, North Carolina, after a five-year manhunt.

Crime—Terrorism—September 11, 2001

On the morning of September 11, 2001, Muslim extremists hijacked four American planes. They launched two suicide attacks on the World Trade Center in New York, New York, and one on the Pentagon near Washington, D.C. The fourth plane crashed in a field near Somerset, Pennsylvania.

• **Last of American Airlines Flight 11:** hit between the 94th and 98th floors of Number One World Trade Center (North Tower) at 8:46 a.m. Flight 11 was en route from Boston, Massachusetts, to Los Angeles, California, with 92 people aboard.

• **Last of United Air Lines Flight 175:** hit between the 78th and 84th floors of Two World Trade Center (South Tower) at 9:02 a.m. Flight 175 was en route from Boston to Los Angeles, with 65 people aboard. The last transmission was at 8:42 a.m.

• **Last of American Airlines Flight 77:** hit E Section on the west side of the Pentagon, between the first and second floors, at 9:38 a.m. Flight 77 was en route from Washington, D.C., to Los Angeles with 64 people aboard. At the Pentagon, 125 people were killed in the attack.

• **Last of American Airlines Flight 93:** crashed near Somerset, Pennsylvania, about 10:06 a.m. Sources differ on the precise crash time, ranging from 10:00 to 10:10 a.m. A U.S. Army seismic study shows the crash time to be 10:06:05 a.m. A cell phone call made by a passenger on Flight 93 at 9:58 a.m. was the last call made by any passengers on any of the hijacked planes. The passenger, calling from the plane's washroom, told a 911 emergency dispatcher the plane was being hijacked. The caller was not identified at the time of the crash. Later, investigators said they believe he was Edward Felt, the only passenger not accounted for on cell phones. Flight 93 was en route from Newark, New Jersey, to San Francisco, California, with 45 people aboard.

• **Last of Two World Trade Center (South Tower):** collapsed at 9:59 a.m. on September 11, 2001.

• **Last of One World Trade Center (North Tower):** collapsed at 10:28 a.m. on September 11, 2001. Five and Six World Trade Center were severely damaged.

• **Last of Seven World Trade Center:** collapsed at 5:20 p.m. on September 11, 2001. The 47-story building had been evacuated.

• **Last World Trade Center survivors found:** September 12, 2001, the day following the attacks. The final death total (as of January 2004): 2,749, Remains of more than 1,100 victims have been identified.

• **Last of cleanup and recovery effort at Ground Zero (World Trade Center):** ended officially Thursday, May 30, 2002, eight months and 19 days after the attack. The last 50-ton steel column removed was from the southeast corner of the South Tower.

Crime—Terrorism—Unabomber

In the late 1970s, Theodore J. ("Ted")

Kaczynski began a campaign against technological progress by sending bombs to his victims. Before he was apprehended in 1996, he killed three people and injured nearly two dozen others with letter bombs sent to his victims through the mail. Kaczynski, nicknamed the "Unabomber," pleaded guilty and was sentenced in 1998 to life in prison without parole.

• **Last person killed by the Unabomber:** Gilbert Murray, president of the California Forestry Association, in Sacramento, California, on April 24, 1995.

Crime—Witchcraft—Colonial America

Between 1684 and 1693, more than 100 women were convicted of being witches in America. Many were hanged. Massachusetts Governor William Phipps established special courts for witchcraft trials. The worst trial was in 1692. Hysteria led to the hanging of 19 people between May and September.

• **Last execution of Salem witches:** September 22, 1692, when eight were put to death. Five weeks later, the court that condemned them was dissolved, ending the witchcraft hysteria in Salem. In 1711, the Massachusetts legislature annulled the convictions and made reparation to the heirs of the victims. In 1957, the state of Massachusetts formally issued an apology.

Crime—Witchcraft—Continental Europe

• **Last execution for witchcraft in France:** Louis Debaraz, a priest, at Lyons in 1745.

• **Last person burned as a witch in continental Europe:** Maria Renata Sänger, in Würzburg, Germany, in 1749. She was condemned and burned in the marketplace.

• **Last person executed as a witch in continental Europe:** Anna Maria Schwagel of Germany. She was beheaded on April 11, 1775.

Crime—Witchcraft—Great Britain

In Great Britain, witchcraft was recognized as a crime punishable by death until 1736. The accused were burned at the stake or decapitated by an axe. Perhaps as many as 30,000 people were executed for witchcraft. The abuses reached a peak during the reign of King James I (1603-25).

• **End of witchcraft as a crime in Great Britain:** 1736, with the Witchcraft Act. Parliament retained the penalty of one year's imprisonment for "telling fortunes or pretending to locate stolen or lost property." The 1736 Witchcraft Act was repealed by the Fraudulent Mediums Act of 1951.

• **Last mass witchcraft execution in England:** August 18, 1682, when three women—Susannah Edwards, Mary Trembles and Temperance Lloyd of Bideford—were hanged at Exeter upon a sentence imposed by Judge Sir Francis North.

• **Last person sentenced to death as a witch in England:** Jane Wenham, who was convicted and sentenced to death in 1712 but was pardoned soon after sentencing. She died of natural causes in 1730.

• **Last person convicted of witchcraft in England:** Helen Duncan in 1944. Duncan, a medium, claimed to have psychic powers. She traveled around Great Britain holding séances at which spirits of the dead were said to materialize. She was found guilty of offenses under the Witchcraft Act and was jailed for nine months. The act had not been used for more than a century. Winston Churchill, angered that Witchcraft Act had been used in a modern court of justice, demanded a report on why it happened. Duncan died on December 6, 1956, age 59.

• **Last execution for witchcraft in Scotland:** 1722, an old woman in Dornoch who was accused of bewitching her neighbors' cows and pigs. The death statute was repealed in Scotland in 1736, the same year as in England. Future punishment of those who practiced magic and witchcraft would be whipping, pillory or imprisonment.

Customs and Traditions

Customs and Traditions—Tontine

Tontines were originally financial arrangements by which subscribers paid into a fund

and received yearly payments. As the subscribers died off, the annual payments of individuals grew larger. Sometimes the last survivor received everything. Other times, the program would be stopped at a certain time and the money would be divided among the surviving members. The first tontine was started in 1689 when King Louis XIV of France set a fund with 1.4 million subscriptions.
• **Last survivor of the first tontine:** Charlotte Barbier. When she died in 1726 at age 96, she was receiving an annual income worth 245 times what she invested.

Disappearances

Disappearances—Arnold, Dorothy
Dorothy Harriet Camille Arnold was the niece of a justice of the U.S. Supreme Court. Her disappearance attracted a great deal of publicity because she was from a prominent family.
• **Last time Dorothy Arnold was seen:** December 12, 1910, outside Brentano's Bookshop in New York City. She vanished without a trace. Tips about her whereabouts were reported for many years.

Disappearances—Bierce, Ambrose
Ohio-born short-story writer Ambrose Bierce gained a reputation for his biting, satiric wit.
• **Last time Ambrose Bierce was heard from:** 1913, while covering the Mexican Revolution as a newspaper correspondent. In his last letter, dated December 26, 1913, from Chihuahua City, he said he was going to see the fighting in Ojinaga. He was never seen or heard from again. Speculation about his disappearance continued for many years. Bierce was 71 when he disappeared.

Disappearances—Boggs, Hale, and Nick Begich
On October 16, 1972, U.S. House of Representatives Democratic leader Hale Boggs of Louisiana and Alaska's Representative Nick

Begich boarded a Cessna 310 to carry them from Anchorage to Juneau, Alaska, on a political junket. With them were Begich's aide Russ Brown and pilot Don Jonz.
• **Last time the Boggs/Begich plane was heard from:** October 16, 1972, as the plane was approaching the Chugach Mountain range in southeastern Alaska. The plane's disappearance launched the most massive air search in history, but no trace of the plane or its passengers was found.

Disappearances—Cooper, D.B.
On November 24, 1971, a Northwest Airlines Boeing 727 was hijacked over Portland, Oregon, by a man identified only as D.B. Cooper, who threatened to blow up the plane. Cooper was given $200,000 ransom and four parachutes when the plane landed at Seattle, Washington, and 36 passengers were allowed to leave.
• **Last time D. B. Cooper was seen:** en route from Seattle to Reno, Nevada. Cooper parachuted out of the plane and vanished. In 1980, $5,880 in decaying bills were found along the Columbia River. The money matched ransom bills given to Cooper.
• **Last of the plane Cooper hijacked:** the Boeing 727 was sold to Piedmont Airlines sometime before 1982, then acquired by Key Airlines in 1985. WorldCorp. acquired the plane in 1993. It was scrapped in 1993.

Disappearances—Crater, Judge Joseph
Judge Joseph Crater was 41 years old and a justice of the New York Supreme Court when he disappeared.
• **Last time Judge Crater was seen:** August 6, 1930, after he dined with friends at a restaurant in New York, New York. He hailed a cab on West 45th Street, waved goodbye to them, and was never seen again.

Disappearances—Diesel, Rudolf
German engineer Rudolf Diesel invented the internal combustion engine that bears his name.
• **Last time Rudolf Diesel was seen:** September 30, 1913, on a steamer crossing the

English Channel from England to Belgium. Diesel was 55.

Disappearances—Hoffa, Jimmy
Former Teamsters Union President Jimmy Hoffa was 62 when he disappeared.
• **Last time Jimmy Hoffa was seen:** July 30, 1975, in the parking lot of the Machus Red Fox Restaurant in West Bloomfield, near Detroit, Michigan. He was on his way to a meeting with two reputed mobsters. Neither of them showed up. Hoffa was officially declared dead in 1983.

Disappearances—Howard, Leslie
British actor/director Leslie Howard was 50 when he disappeared during World War II.
• **Last time Leslie Howard was seen:** June 1, 1943, when the plane in which he was a passenger left Lisbon, Portugal, for London, England. It was shot down over the English Channel by German aircraft and all passengers were presumed lost.

Disappearances—Hudson, Henry
English navigator Henry Hudson was on his fourth voyage of discovery when he reached the bay that now bears his name. His ship, the *Discovery,* became trapped in ice during the winter. Many of the crew died. Hudson wanted to continue his search for the Northwest Passage, but members of his crew wanted to return to England.
• **Last time Henry Hudson was seen:** June 23, 1611, when Hudson and eight others on the *Discovery* were set adrift by mutineers.

Disappearances—Hyde, Glen and Bessie
In November 1929, honeymooners Glen and Bessie Hyde set off on a rafting trip through the Grand Canyon in a homemade raft. If they had succeeded, Bessie Hyde would become the first woman to raft the treacherous Colorado River.
• **Last time the Hydes were seen:** November 18, 1929, rafting on the Colorado River. In December, their raft was found in calm water, still loaded with supplies. The Hydes were never found.

Disappearances—Lafitte, Jean
French-born pirate Jean Lafitte headed a band of privateers and smugglers who operated in the Caribbean. He was active in New Orleans, Louisiana, prior to the War of 1812 and helped Andrew Jackson during the final battle of the war. Later, Lafitte moved to Galveston Island, Texas.
• **Last time Jean Lafitte was seen:** 1821, when he burned his base of operations in Galveston and sailed away after a U.S. expeditionary force came looking for him. No one knows what happened to him, but as late as 1825, people claimed they saw him on the Yucatan Peninsula. Rumors persist that some of his loot is buried either in New Orleans or in Galveston.

Disappearances—Morgan, William
In 1826, William Morgan of Batavia, New York, announced that he planned to publish a pamphlet revealing the secret work of the Masons.
• **Last time William Morgan was seen:** 1826, in upstate New York. His disappearance created much speculation. Some people claimed he was murdered. Others said he was paid to change his identity and leave the country.

Disappearances—Miller, Glenn, *see* Music—Pop Performers.

Disappearances—Wallenberg, Raoul
Swedish diplomat Raoul Wallenberg is credited with saving many thousands of Jews from Nazi concentration camps during World War II.
• **Last time Raoul Wallenberg was seen:** January 1945 in Budapest, Hungary, when he was arrested, taken to the Soviet Union and accused of spying. In December 2000, Russian officials acknowledged that Wallenberg had been imprisoned in a KGB prison for two-and-a-half years until he died. They also reported that Wallenberg's driver, Witmos Langfelder, was arrested with him and died at the same time. How or where they died was not revealed.

Ship Name and Last Contact Date	Details of Disappearance
Carroll A. Deering January 29, 1921	Left Rio de Janeiro, bound for Norfolk, Virginia. She passed Cape Hatteras, North Carolina, on January 29, 1921, then was caught in a gale and stranded at Diamond Shoals. *Carroll A. Deering* was located on January 31st, but there was no sign of the crew of 11. Only the ship's cat was on board.
City of Boston January 28, 1870	Inman Line steamer *City of Boston* vanished between New York and Liverpool, England, with 177 aboard. The ship left New York on January 15, 1870, and was last seen near Halifax, Nova Scotia, on January 28, 1870. The ship may have been caught in a storm.
City of Glasgow March 1854	Liverpool and Philadelphia Steam Ship Company (Inman Line) steamer *City of Glasgow* vanished in March 1854 between Glasgow, Scotland, and Philadelphia, Pennsylvania, with 480 aboard.
Conestoga March 25, 1920	*Conestoga* was first operated as a tug and salvage vessel. The U.S. Navy took her over in 1917. USS *Conestoga* was ordered to go to Samoa in the South Pacific in 1920, with a crew of 56 officers and men. She left Mare Island, California, on March 25, 1920, and was never heard from again. The Navy declared the ship lost on June 30, 1921.
Cyclops March 4, 1918	The collier USS *Cyclops* sailed from Rio de Janeiro, Brazil, en route to Baltimore, Maryland, on February 16, 1918, with 306 crew and passengers. After the ship left Barbados on March 4, 1918, she was never heard from again.
Joyita October 3, 1955	*Joyita* left Apia, Western Samoa, on October 3, 1955, with 25 aboard bound for Tokelau Island, 270 miles to the north. For 36 days, no word was heard from the crew. On November 10, 1955, *Joyita* was found drifting north of Vanua Leva. She was deserted and waterlogged. *Joyita* returned to the sea again in 1956 but was grounded. She was refitted in 1958 then hit a reef, ending her sailing days.
Kobenhavn December 22, 1928	*Kobenhavn,* a five-masted training ship with a crew of 75, including 45 boy cadets, left Montevideo Harbor, Uruguay, for Melbourne, Australia, on December 14, 1928. The last radio contact with the ship was on December 22, 1928. *Kobenhavn* is the largest sailing ship to vanish.
Marine Sulphur Queen February 3, 1963	*Marine Sulphur Queen* left Beaumont, Texas, for Norfolk, Virginia, on February 2, 1963, carrying bulk sulfur. A radio message on February 3 put her position south of Pensacola, Florida. She was reported missing on February 6, 1963. A few lifejackets, a life ring and minor debris were found off the coast of Key West, Florida, but no trace has been found of the *Marine Sulphur Queen* or the 39 aboard.
Mary Celeste November 25, 1872	The fate of the passengers of the brigantine *Mary Celeste* is one of the great mysteries of the sea. The ship left New York for Genoa, Italy, on November 7, 1872, with the captain, two officers, a steward, the ship's four-man crew and the captain's wife and daughter. The last log entry was made on November 25, 1872. The *Mary Celeste* was recovered on

	December 4, 1872, by the *Dei Gratia,* a British ship, about 600 miles off the coast of Gibraltar, between the Azores and Portugal. Everyone aboard ship had vanished. After the *Mary Celeste* was found in December 1872, the ship was taken to Gibraltar for a few months then released and sailed to Genoa. Following that fateful 1872 voyage, the ship had several owners. In 1885, she sank after she hit the Rochelois Reef off the coast of Haiti. Divers located the wreckage of the *Mary Celeste* in 2001 and photographed it for a documentary.
Naronic February 11, 1893	The White Star Line ship *Naronic* left Liverpool, England, for New York with 74 passengers on February 11, 1893, and was never seen again. About a month later, two of the ship's lifeboats were spotted off the coast of Nova Scotia. Four bottles with messages from passengers washed up on beaches in New York and Virginia. Two of the messages said the ship hit an iceberg. A court of inquiry doubted the truth of the messages as no ice had been spotted in the vicinity.
Poet October 24, 1980	The SS *Poet* with 34 aboard, vanished en route from Cape Henlopen, Delaware, to Port Said, Egypt, with a load of grain on October 24, 1980.
Samir March 9, 1997	The Egyptian-owned cargo ship *Samir* vanished in the Mediterranean Sea without a trace en route from Alexandria, Egypt, to Trapani, Sicily, on March 7, 1997. The last contact with *Samir* was on March 9, 1997, when she checked in with *Mediterranean Queen* and revised her time of arrival to March 11. She sent no distress signal. No trace has been found of the 12 crew members or the ship—no wood, oil slick or debris.
Waratah July 26, 1909	The British steamer *Waratah* left Durban, South Africa, on July 26, 1909, bound for London, England, carrying 211 crew and passengers. She was scheduled to stop at Cape Town, South Africa. *Waratah* was last seen the following day by the SS *Clan MacIntyre* at Port St. Johns, South Africa, where the two ships exchanged signals.

Disasters—Airships
(*See also* Aviation—Airships.)

Name and Date of Disaster	Details of Disaster or Last Flight
Akron **(ZRS-4)** April 4, 1933	The U.S. airship *Akron* (ZRS-4) was made by the Goodyear-Zeppelin Company of Akron, Ohio. It was touted as the largest Navy dirigible when it was christened in 1931. The *Akron* crashed during a storm and fell into the sea off Barnegat, New Jersey, on April 4, 1933. Aviation chief Rear Admiral William A. Moffett and 72 were lost in the crash.
Dixmude December 21, 1923	The French airship *Dixmude* disappeared over the Mediterranean Sea on December 21, 1923; 52 people were lost. The ship may have been struck by lightning.
Hindenburg May 6, 1937	*See* Aviation—Airships—Zeppelins—*Hindenburg.*

Macon (ZRS-5) February 12, 1935	The U.S. Navy's $3.5-million airship *Macon* (ZRS-5) sank in the Pacific Ocean off Point Sur, California, on February 12, 1935; all the crew were rescued except for two. With the *Macon* disaster coming after the loss of *Akron* and *Shenandoah*, the Navy had lost all but one of it rigid airships, the *Los Angeles*, which was out of service.
Roma February 21, 1922	The *Roma*, built in Italy for the United States, exploded when it hit electrical wires on February 21, 1922, and crashed near Hampton Roads, Virginia; 34 of its 45 passengers died. *Roma* was the last American airship to use hydrogen, a highly combustible gas.
R1 (*Mayfly*) September 24, 1911	Great Britain's first rigid airship, the R1, also known as *Mayfly*, was destroyed in an accident on September 24, 1911, as it was preparing to make its first flight.
R38 (ZR-2) August 24, 1921	The R38 (ZR-2 in the U.S.) was the largest dirigible ever built. The U.S. Navy had planned to buy it from England. The British airship crumpled in the middle, burst into flames, dropped and exploded on a trial flight near Hull, England, on August 24, 1921. All but 5 of its 49 crew and passengers were drowned or burned.
R101 October 5, 1930	When the British $5-million dirigible R101 was built in 1929, it was the largest airship in the world. On October 5, 1930, en route from England to India, R101 hit a wooded hillside in France, crashed, exploded and burned; all 47 aboard were killed. Great Britain sold its R100 airship for scrap in 1931, after the R101 disaster. The crash of the R101 halted airship development for many years in Britain, ending a dream of a lighter-than-air domination of the skies.
Shenandoah (ZR-1) September 3, 1925	The U.S. Navy rigid airship *Shenandoah* (ZR-1) left Lakehurst, New Jersey, for Saint Paul, Minnesota, on September 2, 1925. It was torn to pieces in a thunderstorm over Ava, Ohio, the following day, killing 14.

Disasters—Dams

Name and Date Dam Last Stood	Description
Bouzey Dam 1895	The Bouzey Dam on the Moselle River in France was built in 1881. The dam's poor construction caused a large piece to break off in 1884. The dam stood for the last time in 1895. That year, a larger piece broke off, resulting in the loss of 155 lives.
Buffalo Creek Dam February 26, 1972	When the Buffalo Creek Dam collapsed in West Virginia, 125 people were killed and 4,000 lost their homes. The dam failure led to the National Dam Inspection Act of 1972.
Dale Dyke Dam March 11, 1864	The Dale Dyke Dam in Sheffield, England, was built in 1858 to supply water to Sheffield. When the dam collapsed, 250 people were killed and more than 4,000 houses were damaged.
Kelly Barnes Dam November 6, 1977	The Kelly Barnes Dam on Toccoa Creek in Georgia ruptured after a torrential rainfall. Most of the 39 people killed were college students. Property damages were estimated at $2.8 million.

Laurel Run Dam July 19-20, 1977	The Laurel Run Dam in Cambria County, Pennsylvania, failed during the night of July 19-20, 1977, killing more than 40 people in the valley below.
Malpasset Dam December 1959	The Malpasset Dam, built on the Argens River in Frejus, France, from 1952 to 1954, collapsed, killing more than 300 people.
Marib Dam (Yemen Dam) c. 580 A.D.	The Marib Dam, also known as the Yemen Dam, was built in Saba, Yemen, in the fifth century B.C., and was one of the great ancient irrigation dams. It stood for a thousand years before it was washed away around 580 A.D.
Saint Francis Dam March 12, 1928	The Saint Francis Dam was built to provide a backup supply of water for Santa Paula, California, about 50 miles north of Los Angeles. When it ruptured just before midnight on March 12, 1928, it created a 78-foot wall of water that destroyed everything in its path. At least 470 were killed and Santa Paula was buried in 25 feet of mud in what was at that time California's second worst disaster.
South Fork Dam (Johnstown Dam) May 1889	The South Fork Dam built in 1839 in Johnstown, Pennsylvania, was one of the earliest dams in the United States. It was abandoned in 1857 and was used for fishing and later to provide water to locomotive boilers. In 1875, it was taken over by a hunting and fishing club that made some alterations. The Johnstown Flood occurred on May 31, 1889, when the South Fork Dam collapsed, killing 2,209 people. The last Johnstown Flood survivor was Frank Shomo, who was only a few months old at the time of the tragedy. He died on March 20, 1997, age 108. The second to last Johnstown survivor was Elsie Frum, who died in 1991.
Teton River Dam June 5, 1976	Eleven people were killed and an estimated 30,000 were made homeless when the Teton River Dam collapsed, sending 80 billion gallons of water into the Upper Snake River Valley in eastern Idaho. Damage costs were put in the hundreds of millions of dollars. The newly constructed dam was being filled for the first time. The project was controversial from the beginning. Long before construction began in 1971, geologists and environmentalists had argued the site was not suitable.
Vaiont (Vajont) Dam October 9, 1963	The Vaiont Dam, built in 1961, crossed the reservoir on the Piave River in northern Italy. When the dam gave way, a wall of water destroyed seven towns and killed 2,000 people. It is considered the largest dam disaster in the world, caused by ignorance and a failure to pay attention to geology.

Disasters—Fire—Chicago, Illinois—1871

The cause of the devastating 1871 fire in Chicago, Illinois, is unknown, but some people claim it started in the cow barn of the O'Leary house on DeKoven Street on the west side of the city around 9 p.m. on Sunday, October 8, 1871.

• **End of the Chicago fire:** extinguished by Tuesday noon October 10, 1871, helped by a rainfall that began on Monday evening. An estimated 300 people were killed and 90,000 people were left homeless. About one third of the city was destroyed in the blaze.

• **Last surviving reporter of the Chicago fire:** Michael Ahern, a police reporter for the *Chicago Republican* who disputed the authenticity of the claim that Mrs. O'Leary's cow started the fire. In 1921, Ahern wrote that the cow story had been concocted by two reporters, John English and Jim Haynie. Ahern believed the fire was caused by the spontaneous combustion of hay stored in O'Leary barn. Ahern died in Chicago, Illinois, on February 19, 1927.

Disasters—Fire—Iroquois Theater

The Iroquois Theater fire in Chicago, Illinois, was the city's most deadly fire. It occurred on December 30, 1903, just a month after the fireproof theater opened. The building was packed with 1,900 people, mostly women and children, watching a holiday performance of the musical *Mr. Blue Beard Jr.* Of the 566 people who died, all but one were audience members. Only one of the several hundred performers and backstage personnel was killed. The greatest casualties were not burn victims; they were audience members who were trampled to death while trying to escape.

• **Last of the Iroquois Theater:** After the fire, the largely undamaged building was renovated and reopened as the Colonial Theater. It was torn down in 1925.

Disasters—Fire—Triangle Shirtwaist Company

The Triangle Shirtwaist Company was a sweatshop in New York, New York, that had blocked exit doors and only one fire escape. The fire on March 25, 1911, killed 146 people, mostly women factory workers.

The disaster led to the passage of some of the first worker safety laws in the United States.

• **Last survivor of the Triangle Shirtwaist Company fire:** Rose Freedman, who died in Beverly Hills, California, on February 15, 2001, age 107. Bessie Gabrilowich Cohen, who died in Los Angeles, California, on February 21, 1999, age 107, also survived the fire.

Disasters—Nuclear—Chernobyl

Chernobyl Nuclear Power Plant, near Kiev, Ukraine, experienced the worst civil nuclear disaster in history on April 26, 1986, when the cooling system for Reactor No. 4 failed and the reactor's core overheated and melted down. Released radioactive material spread over part of the Soviet Union, Eastern Europe, Scandinavia and Western Europe. The reactor was encased in a concrete "sarcophagus." Reactor No. 2 was shut down in 1991 after a fire. Reactor No. 1 was shut down in 1996, after its lifespan had expired.

• **Last Chernobyl Nuclear Power Plant reactor to be shut down:** No. 3 on December 15, 2000.

Disasters—Marine
Last Voyages of Some Major Ships and Submarines
(*See also* Disappearances—Marine.)

Name of Vessel and Date of Disaster	Details of Last Voyage and Fate of Vessel
Andrea Doria July 25, 1956	The Italian ocean liner *Andrea Doria* was making her 51st crossing from Genoa to New York, when she was rammed broadside by the *Stockholm* in a fog bank near Nantucket, Massachusetts, on July 25, 1956, and sank. Both ships had radar. The *Andrea Doria* was only three years old and considered unsinkable. Within four hours, the *Ile de France*, *Cape Ann* and *Private William H. Thomas* arrived and rescued 1,118 survivors in one of the greatest sea rescues of all time. The 51 casualties were from injuries sustained by the impact when the two ships collided. The *Stockholm* returned to service and is still in use. She has been renamed several times. Her most recent name: *Caribe*. • **Last song played on board the *Andrea Doria*:** "Arrividerci Roma." • **Last person to leave the *Andrea Doria*:** Robert Hudson, who slept through the collision and evacuation and woke at 4:30 a.m. to find the ship empty. Hudson had been injured on another ship and

	was transferred to the *Andrea Doria* for passage home. He had fallen into a heavily sedated sleep and awoke to find the ship listing heavily. He was able to reach the ship's stern, where a lifeboat searching for survivors spotted him.
Atlantic March 1873	• **Last of the *Atlantic*:** The White Star Line steamship *Atlantic* got caught in a gale-force storm en route from Liverpool, England, to New York in March 1873, and ran aground east of Halifax Harbor in Nova Scotia. Stormy seas split open the hull and swept the lifeboats overboard. Crew members swam ashore with a line that enabled 250 crew and passengers to be ferried to safety. But not one woman and only one child survived. Casualty estimates range from 450 to 585.
Bismarck May 27, 1941	The German battleship *Bismarck* saw only one combat mission. On May 24, 1941, during World War II, it blew up the British battle cruiser *Hood,* the largest warship afloat. • **Last of the *Bismarck*:** Three days later, the *Bismarck* sank in the Atlantic Ocean off the coast of France, during a British naval air attack. The British cruiser *Dorsetshire* and the destroyer *Maori* rescued 115 survivors, but 1,977 crew members went down with the *Bismarck*. Marine geologist Dr. Robert Ballard located the *Bismarck* wreckage in 1989.
Britannic November 21, 1916	The passenger ship *Britannic* was originally to be called *Gigantic,* but was renamed after the *Titanic* sinking. *Britannic* made her maiden voyage on December 23, 1915. She was a hospital ship during World War I. • **Last of the *Britannic*:** struck a mine on November 21, 1916, and sank in the Aegean Sea. French undersea explorer Jacques Cousteau found the wreck in 1975. In 1995, the ship was documented by Dr. Robert Ballard.
City of Benares September 17, 1940	SS *City of Benares* left Liverpool, England, for Canada on September 13, 1940, during World War II. • **Last of the *City of Benares*:** torpedoed by a German submarine in the north Atlantic on September 17, 1940. The ship was carrying 406 passengers and crew, including 90 children who were evacuating England; 258 were killed, including 77 of the children. The disaster put an end to the British policy of evacuating children overseas during the war.
Eastland July 24, 1915	The Great Lakes excursion steamer SS *Eastland* overturned while it was still tied to the dock on the Chicago River, in Chicago, Illinois, on July 24, 1915. The ship was carrying 2,500 picnickers. The *Eastland* tragedy that claimed 844 lives is one of the greatest U.S. marine disasters. • **Last of the *Eastland*:** Immediately after the disaster, *Eastland* was righted. The U.S. Navy purchased the ship in 1917 and converted her to a training gunboat renamed USS *Wilimette*. The ship saw service on the Great Lakes until 1945, then scrapped in 1947.
Edmund Fitzgerald November 10, 1975	• **Last of the *Edmund Fitzgerald*:** On November 10, 1975, the Great Lakes ore boat sank during a violent storm with no survivors. All 29 of the crew were lost. The disaster was later immortalized in Gordon Lightfoot's ballad "Wreck of the Edmund Fitzgerald." The

	ship's bell was recovered in 1995 and taken to the Great Lakes Shipwreck Museum in Whitefish Point, Michigan.
Empress of Ireland May 29, 1914	• **Last of the *Empress of Ireland*:** The Canadian Pacific's RMS *Empress of Ireland* was hit by the Norwegian collier *Storstad* in heavy fog on May 29, 1914, en route from Quebec to England. The ship sank in just 14 minutes. Only 465 of about 1,500 passengers and crew survived. • **Last survivor of the *Empress of Ireland*:** Grace Hanagan Martyn, who died on May 15, 1995.
Estonia September 28, 1994	• **Last of the *Estonia*:** Estonian Steamship Line's vehicle/passenger ferry *Estonia* was lost in the Baltic Sea while crossing from Tallinn, Estonia, to Stockholm, Sweden, on September 28, 1994. More than 850 passengers and crew were lost when *Estonia* capsized and sank in the stormy sea about 25 miles off the coast of Finland; 144 survived. The *Estonia* tragedy was one of the worst marine disasters of all time and caused three nations—Finland, Sweden and Estonia—to declare national mourning.
General Slocum June 15, 1904	The steamboat *General Slocum* was headed for a Long Island, New York, beach on June 15, 1904, carrying more than a thousand residents of Manhattan's Lower East Side to their annual church outing. The ship caught fire on the East River and was burning out of control before it was noticed. The official death count was 1,020. James Joyce mentioned the *General Slocum* disaster in *Ulysses.* • **Last of the *General Slocum*:** converted to a barge and renamed the *Maryland.* She sank in March 1908, while carrying an oversized load of bricks. The *Maryland* was raised and finally went down in stormy weather near the Atlantic Ocean in December 1911. • **Last survivor of the *General Slocum*:** believed to be Adella Martha Liebenow Wotherspoon, who died in Berkeley, New Jersey, on January 26, 2004, age 100. She was six months old at the time of the sinking. Her parents survived, but she lost other relatives, including two sisters.
H.L. Hunley February 17, 1864	• **Last of the CSS *H.L. Hunley*:** the Confederate Civil War submarine sank the *Housatonic* in Charleston (South Carolina) Harbor in 1864, then was lost. Nine men went down with the submarine. In 1995, the *Hunley* was found in 30 feet of water in the harbor, and in 2000, the sub was raised and opened by archaeologists.
Kiangya December 3, 1948	• **Last of the *Kiangya*:** *Kiangya,* a Chinese refugee ship, was carrying 3,450 passengers and crew when it hit a Japanese mine on December 3, 1948. About 1,000 are believed to have died.
L'Atlantique January 4, 1933	When *L'Atlantique,* a French ocean liner, made her maiden voyage September 1930, she was the 12th largest ship afloat. • **Last of *L'Atlantique*:** wrecked by fire in the English Channel on January 4, 1933. No passengers were aboard; just crew. The ship was never used again. She was scrapped in Port Glasgow, Scotland, in 1936.
La Bourgogne July 4, 1898	• **Last of *La Bourgogne*:** the French Line steamer collided with the British ship *Cromartyshire* on July 4, 1898, and sank 60 miles south of Sable Island, Nova Scotia; 560 of the 725 passengers and crew aboard drowned.

Lady of the Lake May 11, 1833	• **Last of the *Lady of the Lake*:** struck an iceberg while sailing from England to Quebec, Canada, on May 11, 1833, killing 215 of the crew and passengers.
Lusitania May 7, 1915	• **Last of the *Lusitania*:** the British Cunard ship was sailing from New York to Liverpool, England, when she was torpedoed and sunk by a German submarine off the coast of Kinsale, Ireland, on May 7, 1915. The disaster claimed 1,201 lives, including 124 Americans. • **Last to leave the *Lusitania*:** Captain William Thomas Turner. He died on June 23, 1933. His son Percy was killed during World War II, when his ship was torpedoed just a mile from where the *Lusitania* went down. • **Last survivor of the *Lusitania*:** Mrs. Yvonne Marichal Pugh, who was six years old when the ship went down. She died in Hereford, England, on September 15, 2001, age 92.
Morro Castle September 8, 1934	• **Last of the *Morro Castle*:** was en route from Havana, Cuba, to New York, when she caught fire off the coast of Asbury Park, New Jersey, on September 8, 1934, killing 134 people. The captain had died the previous day and command of the ship had passed to his first officer. Those in charge of evacuating the ship were convicted of negligence, but the conviction was overturned on appeal.
Moselle April 25, 1838	• **Last of the *Moselle*:** the steamer was en route from Cincinnati, Ohio, to Saint Louis, Missouri, on April 25, 1838, with 150 to 200 passengers and crew, when she exploded on the Ohio River near Cincinnati, killing 100 people.
Noronic September 17, 1949	• **Last of the *Noronic*:** the Canadian pleasure cruiser/Great Lakes passenger steamer was swept by fire at a Toronto dock on September 17, 1949. In all, 104 people were killed, and 14 were missing. Soon after the fire, the ship was broken up for scrap.
Principe de Asturias March 5, 1912	• **Last of the *Principe de Asturias*:** the Spanish steamer struck a rock off Sebastian Point, Spain, on March 5, 1912; 500 drowned.
Principessa *Mafalda* October 26, 1927	• **Last of the *Principessa Mafalda*:** the Italian liner was carrying 1,259 passengers and crew when she sank 90 miles off the coast of Brazil on October 26, 1927, after a boiler explosion; 326 were lost. The rest of the passengers and crew were rescued by ships that rushed to the rescue.
Pulaski June 14, 1838	• **Last of the *Pulaski*:** the steamer was en route from Charleston, South Carolina, to Baltimore, Maryland, when she exploded off the coast of North Carolina on June 14, 1838, killing 140 people. The *Pulaski* tragedy occurred just six weeks after the *Moselle* disaster.
Queen Elizabeth (I) January 9-10, 1972	The British passenger liner *Queen Elizabeth (I)* was built for Cunard and launched in 1938 as a companion to the *Queen Mary*. She was used as a troop ship in World War II. The ship's first commercial trip was October 16, 1946. She was sold in 1968 to an American company. After plans to convert the ship to a convention center fell through, the *Queen Elizabeth (I)* was sold to a Taiwanese shipping tycoon. In 1970, she sailed from Florida to Hong Kong Harbor, where she was to be converted to a floating campus for Chapman College of Orange, California. • **Last of the *Queen Elizabeth (I)*:** capsized in Hong Kong Harbor

	after a spectacular fire on January 9-10, 1972. The ship was later cut up for scrap.
St. Philibert June 14, 1931	• **Last of the St. Philibert**: the French excursion steamer overturned in a gale off St. Nazaire. More than 450 died.
Salem Express December 14, 1991	• **Last of the Salem Express**: the Egyptian ferry was carrying 650 passengers and crew and many vehicles when she hit a reef in the Red Sea off the coast of Safaga on December 14, 1991. The official death toll was set at 470.
Scandinavian Star April 7, 1990	• **Last of the Scandinavian Star**: the North Sea ferry was carrying 482 passengers and crew from Oslo, Norway, and Fredrikshavn, Denmark, when she was hit by a fire on April 6, 1990. The fire claimed 158 lives.
Scorpion May 22, 1968	• **Last of the USS Scorpion**: the nuclear submarine failed to surface near Norfolk, Virginia, after a voyage from the Mediterranean with 99 men on board. She was last heard from on May 22, 1968. On June 5, the *Scorpion* was presumed lost. In October 1968, parts of the hull were found in 10,000 feet of water southwest of the Azores.
Squalus May 23, 1939	On May 23, 1939, the submarine USS *Squalus* sank with 59 men aboard during a routine diving cruise five miles east of Portsmouth, New Hampshire; 33 were rescued by a diving bell. The rest drowned in a flooded compartment. • **Last of the USS Squalus**: raised in August 1939 and towed to the Portsmouth Navy Yard where she was renamed USS *Sailfish*. The *Sailfish* saw action during World War II in the Pacific and was sold for scrap in 1948.
Sultana April 27, 1865	• **Last of the Sultana**: the steamboat was destroyed on April 27, 1865, when three of her four boilers exploded on the Mississippi River a few miles above Memphis, Tennessee, killing 1,547, including 1,100 veterans returning from the Civil War. The actual number is unknown, it could be as high as 2,000. Only a few hundred people survived. The *Sultana* catastrophe was the worst steamboat explosion on the Mississippi and one of the worst marine disasters ever, with more casualties than the *Titanic*. • **Last Sultana survivor**: Charles M. Eldridge of Tennessee, who had been a prisoner of war in Alabama. He died in 1941, age 96.
10th of Ramadan May 25, 1983	• **Last of the 10th of Ramadan**: an estimated 375 people were killed on May 25, 1983, when the Nile River steamer caught fire and sank in Lake Nasser, Egypt.
Thresher April 10, 1963	• **Last of the USS Thresher**: the nuclear-powered submarine sank in the Atlantic Ocean about 220 miles east of Boston, Massachusetts, on April 10, 1963, with 129 crew members aboard.
Titanic April 14, 1912	See description below table.
Turner January 3, 1944	• **Last of the USS Turner**: the destroyer exploded in New York Bay on January 3, 1944, killing 15 officers and 123 crew members.
Yarmouth Castle November 13, 1965	The passenger cruise ship *Yarmouth Castle* left Miami, Florida, on November 12, 1965, for a 12-hour cruise to Nassau, Bahamas. • **Last of the Yarmouth Castle**: the 38-year-old ship burned and

sank northeast of Nassau killing 90 people; 456 were saved. The *Yarmouth Castle* disaster led to passage of the Safety at Sea Act of 1966. Subsequently, no wood could be used in the construction of any vessel flying the U.S. flag if the ship carried 50 passengers or more on an overnight or longer passage.

Disasters—Ships—*Titanic*

The Royal Mail Steamer *Titanic* left Southampton, England, for New York on her maiden voyage on April 10, 1912. The ship hit an iceberg at 11:40 p.m. Sunday, April 14 and began to sink. She disappeared into the sea 2 hours and 40 minutes later. The *Carpathia* arrived on the scene around 4:30 a.m. and picked up 712 survivors, but more than 1,500 passengers and crew were lost. In 1985, remains of the *Titanic* were found by a French-American expedition led by Dr. Robert Ballard. In 1986, the ship was documented on film by another expedition. Subsequent expeditions have gathered many artifacts from the *Titanic*.

• **Last voyage of the *Carpathia***: July 17, 1918, during World War I. The *Carpathia* was traveling to Boston, Massachusetts, in a convoy when she was torpedoed and sank, 120 miles west of Ireland. Five crew were killed. The rest of the crew and passengers were rescued by the HMS *Snowdrop*.

• **Last life boat/last person to leave the *Titanic***: Mrs. Martin Luther Ball (Ada E. Hall), 36, who was escorted into a lifeboat by her brother-in-law, Rev. Robert James Bateman. She later recalled that he forced her into the last boat, saying he would follow her later. As the boat was lowered Bateman took off his necktie and gave it to her as a keepsake.

• **Last music played on board the *Titanic***: The ship's band played most of the time the *Titanic* was sinking. They played ragtime for a while. The hymn "Nearer My God to Thee" has often been suggested as the last tune played by the musicians on the *Titanic*. Some historians contend that— based on the recollections of survivor Harold Sydney Bride—the last music the band played was the hymn "Autumn."

• **Last person taken from a lifeboat:** *Ti-tanic* Second Officer, Charles Herbert Lightoller, who was put on board the *Carpathia*.

• **Last survivor who could remember the *Titanic* sinking:** Eva Hart. In her autobiography, she recalled being awakened by her father. He wrapped her in a blanket, carried her outside to her mother. She never saw her father again, but from her lifeboat, she did see the luxury liner slip below the surface. Hart later was critical of the White Star Line for not providing enough lifeboats to save her father and the rest of the ship's passengers who perished. She also criticized the commercial venture to raise the *Titanic*'s sunken hull and salvage its artifacts, comparing it to grave robbing. Hart died on February 14, 1996, age 91.

• **Last surviving Belgian passenger on the *Titanic*:** Julius Sap, who died on December 15, 1966.

• **Last surviving first-class passenger on the *Titanic*:** Marjorie Newell (later Mrs. Floyd Robb), who died in Fall River, Massachusetts, on June 11, 1992, age 103.

• **Last surviving first-class ticket for the *Titanic*:** dated April 10, 1912, and issued to Rev. John Stuart Holden. He had intended to sail on the ill-fated ship but cancelled at the last moment because his wife was ill. He saved the ticket and framed it. It is now in the Merseyside Maritime Museum in Liverpool, England.

• **Last surviving Irish passenger on the *Titanic*:** Ellen Natalia Shine (later Callaghan), who died on March 5, 1993, age 101.

• **Last surviving male passenger on the *Titanic*:** Michel Navratil, who was three years old when the *Titanic* sank. He died in Montpellier, France, on January 31, 2001 age 92.

• **Last surviving *Titanic* crewman:** Sidney

E. Daniels, who died on May 25, 1983, age 89.

• **Last surviving *Titanic* officer:** Commander Joseph Groves Boxhall. He was the fourth officer, and the only officer on watch that night who survived the *Titanic*. He died on April 20, 1967, age 83. His ashes were scattered in the Atlantic Ocean at approximately where the *Titanic* sank. Every year, on April 20th, Cunard vessels fly the White Star Burgee to commemorate the death of the last surviving officer of the *Titanic*.

Disasters—Weather—Donner Party

The Donner party, a group of 87 people led by George Donner, left the Midwest bound for California in the late spring of 1846. In the Sierras of Utah they reached a pass blocked by snow and were forced to stay there throughout the winter. Forty-six members of the original group survived the ordeal and made it to California in 1847.

• **Last survivor of the Donner Party:** Margaret Isabella Breen (later Mrs. Thomas McMahon), who was an infant when she went to California in the Donner Party with her parents and six siblings. She died in Hollister, California, on March 25, 1935, about age 90.

Dueling and Duels

Dueling is ritualized combat between two people using lethal weapons and fought according to a strict code of honor in the presence of witnesses. Duels were most numerous in France, but they occurred in Great Britain and the United States, as well. American duels were more common in the South than elsewhere, especially in the 1830s and 1840s, and few states banned the practice. Dueling died out not because of legislation but because of popular opinion. The practice was scorned by the public and widely criticized in the press. Today, most countries have laws that ban dueling.

• **Last documented duel in the United States:** August 10, 1889, between John R. Williamson and Patrick Calhoun in Cedar Bluff, Alabama. Shots were fired, but no one was hurt. The combatants shook hands.

• **Last publicly fought duel in England:** July 1, 1843, between two army officers, Lieutenant Colonel Fawcett and Lieutenant Munroe. Munroe was killed. His death caused a public outcry against dueling and an anti-dueling association was formed. The following year, dueling among army officers was made a punishable offense. Fawcett was later tried and convicted of manslaughter. After the Fawcett-Munroe duel, a few more were staged in England, but they were held in secret.

• **Last documented duel in England:** Frederick Cournet, who was killed in 1852 by a Monsieur Bartholmy in the village of Egham, near Windsor. Both men were from France. Bartholmy was later arrested, tried and hanged for murder. The duel fought between Percy Clinton Sydney Smythe (Lord Strangford), and Colonel Frederick Romilly in Weybridge in 1852 is also listed as the last duel fought in England.

• **Last documented duel in Scotland:** fought in August 1826, at Cardenbarns Farm, between George Morgan, a banker with the Bank of Scotland in Kirkcaldy and David Landale. Morgan had disclosed that Landale was in financial difficulty. Morgan was fatally wounded in the duel. Landale was acquitted in a trial in the High Court in Edinburgh.

• **Last documented duel in Australia:** 1851. Stuart Donaldson fought surveyor-general Sir Thomas Mitchell. Three shots were fired, and a draw was called with no one injured. However, Donaldson's hat was reputedly shot off.

Education

Education—Colonial Colleges
Nine colleges were founded by royal decree in colonial America: Brown, Columbia, Dartmouth, Harvard, Pennsylvania, Princeton, Rutgers, William and Mary and Yale.

• **Last of the colonial colleges founded by royal decree:** Dartmouth College in 1769.

Education—Ivy League Schools

Ivy League is a term used to describe a group of older East Coast private colleges: Yale, Harvard, Princeton, Columbia, Dartmouth, Cornell, University of Pennsylvania and Brown.

• **Last Ivy League school to be established:** Cornell in 1865.

• **Last all-male college in the Ivy League:** Columbia University. Women were admitted in 1983.

Education—Military Schools

The United States service academies are United States Air Force Academy, United States Coast Guard Academy, United States Merchant Marine Academy, United States Military Academy and United States Naval Academy.

• **Last all-male enrollment at the U.S. service academies:** 1976. That year, President Gerald Ford signed Public Law 94-104, which required the United States service academies to open their enrollment to women. Females were admitted for the first time in the fall of 1976. The service academies graduated their last all-male classes in 1979.

• **Last all-male publicly funded schools in the U.S.:** Virginia Military Institute (VMI). In 1996, the U.S. Supreme Court ruled that VMI would have to admit women if it wished to remain a public institution. The Class of 2000 was VMI's last all-male class.

Education—Nursing Schools

• **End of all-female enrollment in state-operated nursing schools:** July 1, 1982, with the U.S. Supreme Court's 5-4 ruling that state-operated nursing schools cannot constitutionally exclude males.

Education—Rhodes Scholars

The Rhodes Scholars program started in 1904 at Oxford University in England, after Cecil Rhodes left part of his fortune to support Oxford scholarships for male students in British colonies and the United States.

• **Last year Rhodes Scholars candidates were males only:** 1975. That year, the British Sex Discrimination Act gave trustees of the will of Rhodes permission to change the men-only provision. Women were admitted as Rhodes Scholars the following year.

Education— American Colleges and Universities—Name Changes

Alabama State University

• **Last known as Alabama Colored People's University:** 1889.

• **Last known as Normal School for Colored Students:** 1929.

• **Last known as State Teacher's College:** 1948.

• **Last known as Alabama State College for Negroes:** 1954.

• **Last known as Alabama State College:** 1969.

Albion College

• **Last known as Albion Female Collegiate Institute:** 1857.

• **Last known as Wesleyan Seminary and Female College at Albion:** 1861.

Alcorn State University

• **Last known as Alcorn University:** 1878.

• **Last known as Alcorn Agricultural and Mechanical College:** 1974.

Alfred University

• **Last known as Select School:** 1843.

• **Last known as Alfred Academy:** 1857.

Arcadia University

• **Last known as Beaver Female Seminary:** 1872.

• **Last known as Beaver College and Musical Institute:** 1907.

• **Last known as Beaver College:** 2001.

Auburn University

• **Last known as East Alabama Male College:** 1872.

• **Last known as Alabama Agricultural and Mechanical College:** 1899.

• **Last known as Auburn Polytechnic Institute:** 1960.

Baltimore International College
• **Last known as Community College of Baltimore:** 1976.
• **Last known as Baltimore Culinary Institute:** 1997.

Bard College
• **Last known as Saint Stephen's College:** 1934.

Bates College
• **Last known as Maine State Seminary:** 1864.

Bloomsburg University of Pennsylvania
• **Last known as Bloomsburg Literary Institute:** 1869.
• **Last known as Bloomsburg Literary Institute and State Normal School:** 1916.
• **Last known as Bloomsburg State Normal School:** 1927.
• **Last known as Bloomsburg State Teachers College:** 1960.
• **Last known as Bloomsburg State College:** 1983.

Bowie State University
• **Last known as Industrial School for Colored Youth:** 1908.
• **Last known as Normal School No. 3:** 1925.
• **Last known as Bowie Normal and Industrial School for the Training of Colored Youth:** 1935.
• **Last known as Maryland State Teachers College:** 1963.
• **Last known as Bowie State College:** 1988.

Bradley University
• **Last known as Bradley Polytechnic Institute:** 1946.

Brown University
• **Last known as Rhode Island College:** 1804. That year it was renamed for Nicholas Brown, son of one of the school's founders.

Bucknell University
• **Last known as University of Lewisburg:**

1886, when the college was renamed to honor benefactor William Bucknell.

California Institute of Technology
• **Last known as Throop University:** 1892.
• **Last known as Throop Polytechnic Institute:** 1912.
• **Last known as Throop College of Technology:** 1920.

Carnegie Mellon University
• **Last known as Carnegie Technical Schools:** 1912.
• **Last known as Carnegie Institute of Technology:** 1967, when Carnegie merged with Mellon Institute.

Case Western Reserve University
• **Western Reserve University last known as Western Reserve College:** 1884.
• **Case Institute of Technology last known as Case School of Applied Science:** 1947.
• **Last known as Western Reserve University and Case Institute of Technology:** 1967, when the two schools federated as Case Western Reserve University.

Chestnut Hill College
• **Last known as Mount Saint Joseph College:** 1938.

Cheyney University of Pennsylvania
• **Last known as The Institute for Colored Youth:** 1914.
• **Last known as Cheyney Training School for Teachers:** 1951.
• **Last known as Cheyney State Teachers College:** 1959.
• **Last known as Cheyney State College:** 1983.

Citadel, The (The Military College of South Carolina)
• **Last known as South Carolina Military Academy:** 1919.

Clemson University
• **Last known as Clemson Agricultural College of South Carolina** (a.k.a. **Clemson A&M; Clemson College**): 1964.

Colgate University
• **Last known as Hamilton Literary and Theological Institution:** 1846.
• **Last known as Madison University:** 1890, when it was renamed to honor benefactors, the Colgate family, soap manufacturer.

College of New Jersey, The
• **Last known as New Jersey State Normal and Model Schools:** 1908.
• **Last known as New Jersey State Normal School in Trenton:** 1929.
• **Last known as New Jersey State Teachers College and State Normal School at Trenton:** 1937.
• **Last known as New Jersey State Teachers College at Trenton:** 1958.
• **Last known as Trenton State College:** 1996.

Columbia University
• **Last known as King's College:** 1784. Classes were suspended during the American Revolution. In 1784, the New York legislature revived King's College as Columbia College.
• **Last known as Columbia College:** 1896.

Connecticut, University of
• **Last known as Storrs Agricultural School:** 1893.
• **Last known as Storrs Agricultural College:** 1899.
• **Last known as Connecticut Agricultural College:** 1933.
• **Last known as Connecticut State College:** 1939.

Delaware, University of
• **Last known as Newark Academy:** 1833.
• **Last known as Newark College:** 1843. The school was closed from 1859 to 1870. It reopened as a land-grant school.
• **Last known as Delaware College:** 1921.

Denison University
• **Last known as Granville Literary and Theological Institution:** 1845.
• **Last known as Granville College:** 1854.

Renamed to honor benefactor William S. Denison.

DePaul University
• **Last known as Saint Vincent College:** 1907.

Dominican University (Illinois)
• **Last known as Saint Clara Academy:** 1901.
• **Last known as Saint Clara College:** 1918, when the school was renamed Rosary College and the campus moved from Wisconsin to Illinois.
• **Last known as Rosary College:** 1997.

Drexel University
• **Last known as Drexel Institute of Art, Science and Industry:** 1936.
• **Last known as Drexel Institute of Technology:** 1970.

Duke University
• **Last known as Brown's Schoolhouse:** 1839.
• **Last known as Union Institute:** 1851.
• **Last known as Normal College:** 1859.
• **Last known as Trinity College:** 1924, when the school was renamed Duke University to receive a multi-million-dollar trust fund from the Duke family.

Duquesne University of the Holy Ghost
• **Last known as Pittsburgh Catholic College of the Holy Ghost:** 1910.
• **Last known as University of the Holy Ghost:** 1911, when the name was changed to Duquesne University of the Holy Ghost. It was shortened to Duquesne University in 1935, but restored to Duquesne University of the Holy Ghost in 1960.

Emerson College
• **Last known as Boston Conservatory of Elocution, Oratory, and Dramatic Art**: 1881.
• **Last known as Monroe Conservatory of Oratory:** 1890.
• **Last known as Emerson College of Oratory** : 1939.

Fordham University
• Last known as Saint John's College: 1907.

Franklin and Marshall College
• Last known as Marshall College and Franklin College: 1853, when the two schools were merged.

Gallaudet College
• Last known as National Deaf-Mute College: 1894, when the college was renamed to honor the president's father, Thomas Hopkins Gallaudet.

George Washington University
• Last known as Columbian College: 1873.
• Last known as Columbian University: 1904.

Georgia Institute of Technology
• Last known as Georgia School of Technology: 1948.

Gettysburg College
• Last known as Pennsylvania College: 1921.

Goucher College
• Last known as Woman's College of Baltimore City: 1890.
• Last known as Woman's College of Baltimore: 1910, when the school was renamed to honor benefactors Dr. and Mrs. John Franklin Goucher.

Haverford College
• Last known as Haverford School: 1856, when school began granting degrees.

Hawaii, University of
• Last known as College of Agriculture and Mechanic Arts: 1911.
• Last known as College of Hawaii: 1920.

Hood College
• Last known as Woman's College of Frederick: 1913.

Houston, University of
• Last known as Houston Junior College: 1934.

Hunter College of the City of New York
• Last known as Daily Normal and High School for Females: 1869.
• Last known as Female Normal and High School: 1870.
• Last known as Normal College of the City of New York: 1914, when the name was changed to honor the school's first president, Thomas Hunter.

Idaho State University
• Last known as Academy of Idaho: 1915.
• Last known as Idaho Technical Institute: 1927.
• Last known as Southern Branch of the University of Idaho: 1947.
• Last known as Idaho State College: 1963.

Illinois, University of
• Last known as Illinois Industrial University: 1885.

Indiana State University
• Last known as Indiana State Normal School: 1929.
• Last known as Indiana State Teachers College: 1960.
• Last known as Indiana State College: 1965.

Indiana University
• Last known as Indiana State Seminary: 1828.
• Last known as Indiana College: 1838.

Iowa, University of
• Last known as the State University of Iowa: 1962.

Iowa State University of Science and Technology
• Last known as Iowa State Agricultural College and Model Farm: 1959.

Juniata College
• Last known as Huntingdon Normal School: 1878.
• Last known as Brethren's Normal School and Collegiate Institute: 1896.

Kansas State University of Agriculture and Applied Science
• Last known as Kansas State Agricultural College: 1931.
• Last known as Kansas State College of Agriculture and Applied Science: 1959.

Kentucky, University of
• Last known as Agricultural and Mechanical College of Kentucky University: 1878.
• Last known as Agricultural and Mechanical College of Kentucky: 1908.
• Last known as State University, Lexington, Kentucky: 1916.

Knox College
• Last known as Prairie College: 1837.
• Last known as Knox Manual Labor College: 1857.

Lincoln University
• Last known as Ashmun Institute: 1866.

Loyola University (Chicago)
• Last known as Saint Ignatius College: 1909.

Marshall University (West Virginia)
• Last known as Marshall Academy: 1858.
• Last known as Marshall College: 1961.

Massachusetts, University of
• Last known as Massachusetts Agricultural College: 1931.
• Last known as Massachusetts State College: 1947.

Morehouse College
• Last known as Augusta Institute: 1879.
• Last known as Atlanta Baptist Seminary: 1897.
• Last known as Atlanta Baptist College: 1913. Renamed for Rev. Henry L. Morehouse.

Morgan State University
• Last known as Centenary Bible Institute: 1890, when it was renamed for benefactor Dr. Lyttleton F. Morgan.
• Last known as Morgan College: 1939.
• Last known as Morgan State College: 1975.

Muhlenberg College
• Last known as Allentown Seminary: 1867.
• Last known as Allentown Collegiate Institute and Military Academy: 1867.

New Hampshire, University of
• Last known as the New Hampshire College of Agriculture and Mechanical Arts: 1923.

New York City College of Technology
• Last known as New York State Institute of Applied Arts and Sciences: 1953.
• Last known as New York City Community College: 1980.
• Last known as New York City Technical College: 2002.

North Carolina State University at Raleigh
• Last known as North Carolina College of Agriculture and Mechanical Arts: 1965.

Oberlin College
• Last known as Oberlin Collegiate Institute: 1850.

Ohio State University
• Last known as Ohio Agricultural and Mechanical College: 1878.

Pennsylvania, University of
• Last known as College and Academy of Philadelphia: 1779.
• Last known as University of the State of Pennsylvania: 1791.

Pennsylvania State University
• Last known as Agricultural College of Pennsylvania: 1874.
• Last known as Pennsylvania State College: 1953.

Philadelphia University
• Last known as Philadelphia Textile School of the Pennsylvania Museum of Art: 1941.
• Last known as Philadelphia Textile Institute of the Philadelphia Museum of Art: 1960.
• Last known as Philadelphia College of Textiles and Science: 1999.

Princeton University
• **Last known as College of New Jersey:** 1896.
• **Last in located in Newark, New Jersey:** 1756, when the college moved to Princeton, New Jersey.

Radcliffe College
• **Last known as Harvard Annex:** 1882.
• **Last known as Society for the Collegiate Instruction of Women:** 1894, when it was renamed to honor Ann Radcliffe, who established the first scholarship at Harvard College in 1643.

Rensselaer Polytechnic Institute
• **Last known as Rensselaer School:** 1832.
• **Last known as Rensselaer Institute:** 1851.

Rhodes College
• **Last known as Clarksville Academy:** 1848.
• **Last known as Masonic University of Tennessee:** 1850.
• **Last known as Montgomery Masonic College:** 1855.
• **Last known as Stewart College:** 1875.
• **Last known Southwestern Presbyterian University:** 1925, when the college moved to Memphis and changed its name to Southwestern University.
• **Last known as Southwestern University:** 1945.
• **Last known as Southwestern at Memphis:** 1984, when the name was changed to Rhodes College to honor President Peyton Nalle Rhodes.

Rice University (William Marsh Rice University)
• **Last known as Rice Institute:** 1960, when it was renamed William Marsh Rice University.

Rider University
• **Last known as Trenton Business College:** 1897.
• **Last known as Rider Business College:** 1901.
• **Last known as Rider-Moore and Steward School of Business:** 1921.

• **Last known as Rider College:** 1994.
Roanoke College
• **Last known as Virginia Collegiate Institute:** 1853.

Rowan University
• **Last known as Glassboro Normal School:** 1937.
• **Last known as the New Jersey State Teachers College at Glassboro:** 1958.
• **Last known as Glassboro State College:** 1992, when it was renamed Rowan College of New Jersey for benefactors Henry and Betty Rowan who gave a $100 million gift to the school.
• **Last known as Rowan College of New Jersey:** 1997.

Rutgers, The State University of New Jersey
• **Last known as Queen's College:** 1825, when it was renamed for benefactor Henry Rutgers.
• **Last known as Rutgers College:** 1917.
• **Last known as Rutgers College and the State University of New Jersey:** 1956.
• **Last time Douglass College was known as New Jersey College for Women:** 1955, when it was renamed for Mabel Smith Douglass, the college's first dean.
• **Last time Rutgers-Camden campus was known as College of South Jersey:** 1950.

Saint Louis University
• **Last known as Saint Louis Academy:** 1820.
• **Last known as Saint Louis College:** 1832.

Saint Mary's College of Maryland
• **Last known as Saint Mary's Female Seminary:** 1949.
• **Last known as Saint Mary's Seminary and Junior College:** 1959.
• **Last known as Saint Mary's Junior College:** 1964.

Seton Hall University
• **Last known as Seton Hall College:** 1950.

South Carolina State University
• **Last known as Colored Normal Industrial, Agricultural and Mechanical Col-**

lege of South Carolina: 1954.
• Last known as South Carolina State College: 1992.

South Dakota State University
• Last known as Dakota Agricultural College: 1907.
• Last known as South Dakota State College of Agriculture and Mechanical Arts: 1964.

Southern Illinois University
• Last known as Southern Illinois Normal University: 1947.

Southern Mississippi, University of
• Last known as Mississippi Normal College: 1924.
• Last known as Mississippi State Teachers College: 1940.
• Last known as Mississippi Southern College: 1962.

Stillman College
• Last known as Tuscaloosa Institute: 1898, when it was renamed for benefactor founder Rev. Charles A. Stillman.
• Last known as Stillman Institute: 1948.

Tennessee, University of
• Last known as Blount College: 1807.
• Last known as East Tennessee College: 1840.
• Last known as East Tennessee University: 1879.

Towson University
• Last known as Maryland State Normal School: 1934.
• Last known as Maryland State Teachers College at Towson: 1963.
• Last known as Towson State College: 1976.
• Last known as Towson State University: 1997.

Trinity College (Connecticut)
• Last known as Washington College: 1845.

Tufts University
• Last known as Tufts College: 1955.

Tulane University
• Last known as University of Louisiana: 1884, when it was renamed for benefactor Paul Tulane.

United States Naval Academy
• Last known as the Naval School: 1850.

University of the Arts
• Last known as The Pennsylvania Museum & School of Industrial Art: 1939.
• Last known as Philadelphia Museum School of Industrial Art: 1949.
• Last known as Philadelphia Museum School of Art: 1959.
• Last known as Philadelphia Museum College of Art: 1964.
• Last known as Philadelphia College of Art: 1985.
• Last known as Philadelphia Colleges of the Arts: 1987.

University of the Sciences in Philadelphia
• Last known as Philadelphia School of Apothecaries: 1822.
• Last known as Philadelphia College of Pharmacy: 1921.
• Last known as Philadelphia College of Pharmacy and Science: 1997.

Utah State University
• Last known as Agricultural College of Utah: 1929.
• Last known as Utah State Agricultural College: 1957, when the school became Utah State University of Agriculture and Applied Science.

Vassar College
• Last known as Vassar Female College: 1867.

Virginia Polytechnic and State University
• Last known as Virginia Agricultural and Mechanical College: 1896.
• Last known as Virginia Agricultural and Mechanical College and Polytechnic Institute: 1944.

• Last known as Virginia Polytechnic Institute: 1970.

Wake Forest University
• Last known as Wake Forest Manual Labor Institute: 1838.
• Last known as Wake Forest College: 1967.

Washington and Jefferson College
• Washington College last known as Washington Academy: 1806.
• Jefferson College last known as The Canonsburg Academy and Library Company: 1802.
• Last year Washington and Jefferson Colleges were separate institutions: 1865.

Washington and Lee University
• Last known as Augusta Academy: 1776.
• Last known as Liberty Hall: 1782.
• Last known as Liberty Hall Academy: 1798.
• Last known as Washington Academy: 1813.
• Last known as Washington College: 1871.

Washington University in Saint Louis
• Last known as Eliot Seminary: 1854.
• Last known as Washington Institute of Saint Louis: 1857.
• Last known as Washington University: 1976.

Wesleyan College
• Last known as Georgia Female College: 1843.
• Last known as Wesleyan Female College: 1919.

West Virginia State College
• Last known as West Virginia Colored Institute: 1915.
• Last known as West Virginia Collegiate Institute: 1929.

Western Illinois University
• Last known as Western Illinois Normal School: 1921.

• Last known as Western Illinois State Teachers College: 1957.

Western Kentucky University
• Last known as Western Kentucky State Normal School: 1922.
• Last known as Western Kentucky State Normal School and Teachers College: 1930.
• Last known as Western Kentucky State Teachers College: 1948.
• Last known as Western Kentucky State College: 1966.

Western Michigan University
• Last known as Western State Normal School: 1927.
• Last known as Western State Teachers College: 1941.
• Last known as Western Michigan College of Education: 1955.
• Last known as Western Michigan College: 1957.

Widener University
• Last known as Bullock School: 1846.
• Last known as Alsop School: 1853.
• Last known as Hyatt's Select School for Boys: 1859.
• Last known as Delaware Military Academy: 1862.
• Last known as Pennsylvania Military Academy: 1892.
• Last known as Pennsylvania Military College: 1966.
• Last known as PMC Colleges (Pennsylvania Military College and Penn Morton College): 1972.
• Last known as Widener College: 1979.

Yale University
• Last known as Collegiate College: 1716, when the school moved from Saybrook to New Haven, Connecticut, and was renamed for benefactor Elihu Yale.
• Last known as Yale College: 1887.

Education—Public Schools
(*See also* Civil Rights—
Racial Segregation.)

Education—Public Schools—Compulsory Education

The first state to enact compulsory education was Massachusetts in 1852.
• **Last state to require compulsory education:** Mississippi in 1918.

Education—Public Schools—Evolution

On July 24, 1925, biology teacher John T. Scopes was found guilty of teaching evolution in a Tennessee high school. He was fined $100 and court costs. Scopes's conviction was reversed on January 10, 1927, on the ground that only a jury could impose a fine of more than $50, but the Tennessee Supreme Court upheld the state's anti-evolution ("Monkey") law.
• **Last of Tennessee's Monkey law:** repealed May 1967.
• **Last anti-evolution law in U.S.:** struck down in Louisiana by the U.S. Supreme Court in a 7-2 decision on June 19, 1987. The Court ruled that the state law which required the teaching of "creation science" in the public schools whenever evolution was taught had a "religious purpose," and thus violated the separation of church and state required by the First Amendment to the U.S. Constitution.

Education—Public Schools—Religious Education

• **End of religious education in public schools:** March 8, 1948, when the U.S. Supreme Court ruled in *McCollum* v. *Board of Education* that "religious education conducted in public schools which promoted particular religious views" violates the First Amendment to the U.S. Constitution.
• **End of state-sponsored prayer in public schools:** 1962, in *Engel* v. *Vitale,* when the U.S. Supreme Court ruled that state-sponsored prayer as part of instruction in the public schools was unconstitutional. Schools cannot require students to pray. In 1963, the U.S. Supreme Court ruled in *Abington School District* v. *Schempp* that reading the Bible over the school intercom was unconstitutional. In 1992, in *Lee* v. *Weisman,* the Court ruled that prayers at public school graduation ceremonies violate the First Amendment.

Elections and Voting (U.S.)
(*See also* Political Parties—U.S.)

Elections and Voting—Age

For many years, the minimum age for being drafted to serve in the military was 18, but the minimum age for voting in most states was 21. This became a point of contention especially during the Vietnam War era of the late 1960s.
• **Last year the voting age was 21:** 1970. President Richard Nixon signed a bill on June 22, 1970, lowering the voting age to 18 in national elections. The voting age was lowered from 21 to 18 with ratification of the 26th Amendment to the U.S. Constitution on July 1, 1971.

Elections and Voting—Congressional Nominating Caucus

Until 1824, the selection of candidates for the office of U.S. president and for state offices was made by caucus. But the method proved to be unsatisfactory.
• **Last congressional nominating caucus:** convened in February 1824 and nominated William H. Crawford of Georgia for president. Only 66 of 216 members attended the caucus to vote. In August 1824, the first nominating convention was held in Utica, New York. And for the first time, electors of nominees for office were chosen by popular vote.

Elections and Voting—Electoral College —President and Vice President

The Electoral College was established in Article II of the U.S. Constitution. It explains how the president and vice president are to be elected.
• **Last time the Electoral College chose only the president:** 1800. That year, members of the Electoral College voted for two people without specifying president and vice president; the person with the highest votes

was to be president. But there was no "highest" vote in the first balloting. Both candidates, Thomas Jefferson and Aaron Burr, received the same number of electoral votes: 73. It took 36 ballots in the House of Representative before Jefferson was chosen over Burr. The 12th Amendment to the U.S. Constitution, ratified in 1804, changed Article II, Section 1, Clause 3—the method of electing the president. Henceforth, electors would vote separately for president and vice president.

Elections and Voting—Electoral College —Washington D.C.

When the Constitution was written, Article II specified that "each state" shall appoint electors to choose the president. But it did not mention the District of Columbia. People who lived in the nation's capital could not vote for president or vice president.
• **Last year Washington, D.C., was not represented in the Electoral College:** 1961. The 23rd Amendment ratified on March 29, 1961, gave the District of Columbia authority to appoint electors.
• **Last presidential election in which Washington, D.C., residents did not have the right to vote:** 1960, in the election that placed John F. Kennedy in the White House.

Elections and Voting—Grandfather Clauses

After the Civil War, Southern states wrote provisions into their constitutions in an attempt to disenfranchise ex-slaves. Known as grandfather clauses, they tried to limit the right to vote to those who could meet the following conditions: be able to read and write any article of the U.S. Constitution; be employed during most of the year prior to registering to vote; and own property worth $300 on which they paid the taxes. The only exceptions were the descendants of men who had voted before January 1, 1867.
• **End of the grandfather clauses:** 1915, when the U.S. Supreme Court declared them unconstitutional. They violated the 15th Amendment.

Elections and Voting—Hayes-Tilden Election Dispute

In the 1876 presidential election, Rutherford B. Hayes had the majority of the popular vote, but neither he nor his opponent Samuel J. Tilden had the requisite number of electoral votes. Tilden was one vote short of the needed 185. Hayes had 165. Twenty votes were in doubt.
• **End of the Hayes-Tilden election dispute:** resolved March 2, 1877, when an electoral commission appointed by the U.S. Congress voted eight to seven in favor of Hayes. His critics charged that a deal was struck between the Republicans and Southern Democrats to end Reconstruction.

Elections and Voting—Literacy and Other Tests

The Voting Rights Act signed on August 6, 1965, prohibited the use of any test or device to deprive citizens of their right to vote in federal, state and local elections.
• **Last time literacy tests were a requirement for voter registration:** August 6, 1975, when they were permanently abolished by the U.S. Congress.

Elections and Voting—Native Americans

The Snyder Act (Indian Citizenship Act), passed on June 2, 1924, gave full citizenship and the right to vote in federal elections to American Indians born in the United States. However, some of the states continued to disenfranchise Native Americans. State opposition began to crumble in 1948, when the Arizona Supreme Court struck down a provision of its constitution that barred Native Americans from voting.
• **Last state to end the ban on granting Native Americans the right to vote in state elections:** New Mexico in 1962.

Elections and Voting—Poll Tax

A poll tax, also known as a head tax, was assessed against a person rather than against his or her property. Some states would impose a charge of $1 or more as a provision for voting.
• **End of the poll tax:** The 24th Amendment to the U.S. Constitution, ratified on January

23, 1964, banned the use of a poll tax or any other tax to qualify people to vote in primaries or presidential elections.

• **Last state to have a poll tax:** Mississippi. The U.S. Justice Department filed an action to abolish the poll tax as prerequisite for voting in Mississippi on August 7, 1965. The Mississippi poll tax was outlawed by a federal court in Jackson on April 8, 1966.

Elections and Voting—Race, Color, Previous Condition of Servitude

• **Last time African-American males were denied the right to vote:** 1870. The 15th Amendment to the U.S. Constitution, ratified on February 3, 1870, banned discrimination on the basis of "race, color or previous condition of servitude." Women and Native Americans, however, continued to be excluded from voting.

Elections and Voting—Senators, U.S.

Article 1, Section 3 of the U.S. Constitution specified that senators were to be chosen by the legislature of each state.

• **Last time U.S. senators were chosen by state legislatures:** prior to April 8, 1913. The 17th Amendment, ratified on that date, modified the Constitution by providing that United States senators were to be elected directly by the people.

Elections and Voting—Women's Suffrage —Canada

Although Canada granted women the right to vote in federal elections by 1920, some provinces restricted women from voting in local province elections.

• **Last Canadian province to allow women the right to vote in all elections:** Quebec in 1940.

Elections and Voting—Women's Suffrage —United States

The 19th Amendment to the U.S. Constitution states: "The right of citizens of the United States to vote shall not be denied or abridged by the United States or by any State on account of sex." It was sent to the states for ratification on June 4, 1919.

• **Last of the required states to ratify the**

19th Amendment: Tennessee, on August 18, 1920, provided the 36th and last needed vote to reach the three-fourths margin. The amendment passed by one vote. With the vote tied at 48 to 48, Harry Burn—a 24-year-old Republican legislator who previously voted against suffrage—cast the deciding last vote because his mother admonished him to do so. The 19th Amendment was signed into law by Secretary of State Bainbridge Colby on August 26, 1920.

• **Last state to ratify the 19th Amendment:** Mississippi on March 22, 1984. Mississippi had previously rejected the amendment on March 29, 1920.

Elections and Voting—Women's Suffrage —United States—State Elections

Some states granted women voting rights for state elections prior to passage of the 19th Amendment to the U.S. Constitution in 1920. Listed in the table are the dates women became enfranchised to vote in state elections in those states.

State	Right to Vote
Arkansas	1917
Alaska	1913
Arizona	1912
California	1911
Colorado	1893
Idaho	1896
Illinois	1913
Indiana	1917
Kansas	1912
Michigan	1917
Montana	1914
Nebraska	1917
Nevada	1914
New York	1917
North Dakota	1917
Oregon	1912
Oklahoma	1918
Rhode Island	1917
South Dakota	1918
Utah	1895
Washington	1910
Wyoming (territory)	1869
Wyoming (state)	1890

• **Last presidential election in which women nationwide did not have the right to vote:** the Campaign of 1916, that re-elected Woodrow Wilson president.

Elections and Voting—Women's Suffrage—Worldwide

Most of the nations of the world include provisions in their constitutions that grant women the right to vote. And in most of these nations, women gained the right to vote in the 20th century.

• **Last nation in which women, but not men, are denied the right to vote:** Kuwait. However, steps were taken by the government in 2004 to grant women the right to vote. In the Vatican, voting is conducted only by the all-male College of Cardinals. In the United Arab Emirates, neither men nor women have the right to vote.

Elections and Voting—Women's Suffrage—Worldwide

Women gained the right to vote in different countries at different times. In some nations (including the United States), women were permitted to run for public office before they had the right to vote. In other countries, the right to vote was granted first. In most countries, both rights were granted at the same time. The following table lists the last time women were denied these rights. Some entries have multiple years separated by slashes. The first date indicates that certain restrictions were applied when rights were granted to women. The subsequent date(s) reflect the removal of some or all of these restrictions. The table indicates federal or national elections. In many countries, women were allowed to take part in local elections much earlier.

Nation	Last Year Right to Vote Denied	Last Year Right to Stand for Election Denied
Afghanistan	1963 (later revoked) reinstated in 2001	1963 (later revoked) reinstated in 2001
Albania	1920	1920
Algeria	1962	1962
Andorra	1970	1973
Angola	1975	1975
Antigua and Barbuda	1951	1951
Argentina	1947	1947
Armenia	1921	1921
Australia (whites)	1902	1902
Australia (aborigines)	1962	1962
Austria	1918	1918
Azerbaijan	1921	1921
Bahamas	1961/1964	1961/1964
Bahrain	1973	1973
Bangladesh	1972	1972
Barbados	1950	1950
Belarus	1919	1919
Belgium	1919/1948	1921/1948
Belize	1954	1954
Benin	1956	1956
Bhutan	1953	1953
Bolivia	1938	1952
Bosnia and Herzegovina	1949	1949

Botswana	1965	1965
Brazil	1934	1934
Bulgaria	1944	1944
Burkina Faso	1958	1958
Burundi	1961	1961
Cambodia	1955	1955
Cameroon	1946	1946
Canada (military)	1917	1920/1960
Canada (some provinces)	1918	
Canada (all provinces)	1920	
Cape Verde	1975	1975
Central African Republic	1986	1986
Chad	1958	1958
Chile	1931/1949	1931/1949
China	1949	1949
Colombia	1954	1954
Comoros	1956	1956
Congo	1963	1963
Congo, Democratic Republic of the	1967	1970
Costa Rica	1949	1949
Côte d'Ivoire	1952	1952
Croatia	1945	1945
Cuba	1934	1934
Cyprus	1960	1960
Czech Republic	1920	1920
Denmark	1915	1915
Djibouti	1946	1986
Dominica	1951	1951
Dominican Republic	1942	1942
Ecuador	1929/1967/1946	1929/1967/1946
Egypt	1956	1956
El Salvador	1939	1961
Equatorial Guinea	1963	1963
Eritrea	1955	1955
Estonia	1918	1918
Fiji	1963	1963
Finland	1906	1906
France	1944	1944
Gabon	1956	1956
Gambia	1960	1960
Georgia	1918/1921	1918/1921
Germany	1918	1918
Ghana	1954	1954
Greece	1952	1952
Grenada	1951	1951
Guatemala	1946	1946
Guinea	1958	1958
Guinea-Bissau	1977	1977

Guyana	1953	1945
Haiti	1950	1950
Honduras	1955	1955
Hungary	1918	1918
Iceland	1915/1920	1915/1920
India	1950	1950
Indonesia	1945	1945
Iran	1963	1963
Iraq	1980	1980
Ireland (women over 30)	1918	1918
Ireland (women over 21)	1928	1928
Israel	1948	1948
Italy	1945	1945
Jamaica	1944	1944
Japan	1945/1947	1945/1947
Jordan	1974	1974
Kazakhstan	1924/1993	1993
Kenya	1963	1963
Kiribati	1967	1967
Korea (North)	1946	1946
Korea (South)	1948	1948
Kyrgyzstan	1918	1918
Laos	1958	1958
Latvia	1918	1918
Lebanon	1952	1952
Lesotho	1965	1965
Liberia	1946	1946
Libya	1964	1964
Liechtenstein	1984	1984
Lithuania	1918	1918
Luxembourg	1919	1919
Madagascar	1959	1959
Malawi	1961	1961
Malaysia	1957	1957
Maldives	1932	1932
Mali	1956	1956
Malta	1947	1947
Marshall Islands	1979	1979
Mauritania	1961	1961
Mauritius	1956	1956
Mexico	1947	1953
Micronesia	1979	1979
Moldova	1978/1993	1978/1993
Monaco	1962	1962
Mongolia	1924	1924
Morocco	1963	1963
Mozambique	1975	1975
Myanmar	1935	1946

Namibia	1989	1989
Nauru	1968	1968
Nepal	1951	1951
Netherlands	1919	1917
New Zealand	1893	1919
Nicaragua	1955	1955
Niger	1948	1948
Nigeria (north)	1978	1978
Nigeria (south)	1958	1958
Norway	1913	1907
Pakistan	1947	1947
Palau	1979	1979
Panama	1941/1946	1946
Papua New Guinea	1964	1975
Paraguay	1961	1961
Peru	1955	1955
Philippines	1937	1937
Poland	1918	1918
Portugal	1931/1934/1976	1931/1934/1976
Moldova	1978/1993	1978/1993
Romania	1929/1945	1929/1945
Russia	1918	1918
Rwanda	1961	1961
Saint Kitts and Nevis	1951	1951
Saint Lucia	1924	1924
Saint Vincent and the Grenadines	1951	1951
Samoa	1990	1990
San Marino	1959	1973
São Tomé and Príncipe	1975	1975
Senegal	1945	1945
Seychelles	1948	1948
Sierra Leone	1961	1961
Singapore	1947	1947
Slovakia	1920	1920
Slovenia	1945	1945
Solomon Islands	1974	1974
Somalia	1956	1956
South Africa (whites)	1930	1930
South Africa (non-whites)	1984/1994	1984/1994
Spain	1931 (later revoked) reinstated in 1976	1931 (later revoked) reinstated in 1976
Sri Lanka	1931	1931
Suriname	1948	1948
Swaziland	1968	1968
Sweden	1919/1921	1919/1921
Switzerland	1971	1971
Syria	1949/1953	1953
Tajikistan	1924	1924

Notable Last Facts

Tanzania	1959	1959
Thailand	1932	1932
Togo	1945	1945
Tonga	1960	1960
Trinidad and Tobago	1946	1946
Tunisia	1959	1959
Turkey	1930	1934
Turkmenistan	1927	1927
Uganda	1962	1962
Ukraine	1919	1919
United Kingdom (women over 30)	1918	1918
United Kingdom (women over 21)	1928	1928
United States	1920	1788
Uruguay	1932	1932
Uzbekistan	1938	1938
Vanuatu	1975/1980	1975/1980
Venezuela	1946	1946
Vietnam	1946	1946
Yemen (Arab Republic)	1970	1970
Yemen (PDR)	1967	1967
Yugoslavia	1946	1946
Zambia	1962	1962
Zimbabwe	1957	1978

Electronics

Electronics—Companies—Texas Instruments

Texas Instruments (also known as TI) was founded in 1930 as Geophysical Service. In 1951, it was renamed Texas Instruments Incorporated.

• **Last surviving founder of Texas Instruments:** Cecil Howard Green, who died in La Jolla, California, on April 12, 2003, age 102.

Electronics—Computers—Cray

Seymour Cray was the first computer designer to use integrated circuit technology and was the Father of the Supercomputer. He died in Colorado Springs, Colorado, on October 5, 1996, age 71.

• **Last computer designed by Cray:** Cray 4. It was abandoned in 1994 before reaching the marketplace.

Electronics—Computers—First Generation

The earliest commercially exploited computers are known as first-generation computers.

• **Last remaining intact first-generation computer:** CSIRAC (previously known as CSIR Mk 1 computer), a room-sized computer, completed in 1949 and officially unveiled in 1951. It was Australia's first computer and the fifth electronic stored-program computer in the world. CSIRAC was built by a research group led by Maston Beard and Trevor Pearcey at the Sydney-based Radiophysics Laboratory of the Council for Scientific and Industrial Research. The computer is now housed at the Museum of Victoria, at Carlton Gardens, Melbourne, Australia.

Electronics—Computers—Personal Computers—Scelbi

In 1973, Scelbi (Scientific, Electronic and Biological) Computer Consulting Company offered the first computer kit in the United States using a microprocessor.

• **Last Scelbi sold:** December 1974. The

company discontinued production of the computer to concentrate on software.

Electronics—Transistors

The transistor was invented in 1947 at Bell Labs in Murray Hill, New Jersey, and resulted in the 1956 Nobel Prize in Physics for its creators.

• **Last surviving member of group that invented the transistor:** John Bardeen, who won another Nobel Prize in 1972. He died in Boston, Massachusetts, on January 30, 1991, age 82.

Electronics—Videorecording Equipment —Betamax

Sony introduced the first Betamax video cassette recorders (VCRs) in the United States in February 1976.

• **Last Betamax VCR produced:** Model SL-200D, produced until the end of 2002 by Sony Tokyo.

• **Last Betamax produced for the U.S. market:** SL-HF2000, introduced in 1993.

Empires and Kingdoms

Empires and Kingdoms—Assyrian Empire

The Assyrian Empire dominated the Middle East for nearly six centuries. It began its rise to power around 1200 B.C. At its peak in the 700s B.C., during the reign of King Sargon II, it extended from the Mediterranean to the Caspian seas and from the Red Sea to the Persian Gulf. The empire was constantly threatened by wars and revolts, which eventually led to its demise.

• **Last great Assyrian king:** Assurbanipal, who ruled from c. 669 to 633 B.C.

• **End of Nineveh, the capital:** destroyed in 612 B.C.

• **End of the Assyrian Empire:** collapsed sometime around 610 B.C., when it was overrun by the Medes.

Empires and Kingdoms— Austro-Hungarian Empire, see Nations— Austria; Hungary.

Empires and Kingdoms—Aztec Empire

The Aztecs arrived in the Valley of Mexico in the late 1100s A.D. They built the city of Tenochtitlan and established a powerful empire. The Spanish, led by Hernan Cortes, arrived in 1519. By 1521, they had captured and imprisoned the Aztec leader Montezuma. When Montezuma died, his nephew Cuauhtémoc was elected ruler. He was a tougher foe than Montezuma and forced Cortez out of Tenochtitlan (now Mexico City). Cortes and his men laid siege to the city for 80 days.

• **End of the Aztec Empire:** August 13, 1521, when Tenochtitlan surrendered.

• **Last independent Aztec ruler:** Cuauhtémoc, who was executed by Cortes in 1525.

Empires and Kingdoms—Babylonian Empire

Babylon grew from a small town to a large city between the 1800s and the 1500s B.C. It became so powerful that much of Mesopotamia became known as Babylonia. Through rivalries and invasions, the empire gradually weakened.

• **Last king of Babylon:** Nabonidus.

• **End of the Babylonian Empire:** 538 B.C., when it was conquered by Cyrus of Persia.

• **End of the Babylonian Captivity:** 538 B.C., after the Persian conquest of the city. The captivity of the Jews of Babylon, which was carried out by King Nebuchadnezzar, began in 597 B.C.

Empires and Kingdoms—Byzantine Empire

The Byzantine Empire began when administration of the eastern part of the Roman Empire was transferred from Rome to the city of Byzantium in 330 A.D. by the Emperor Constantine I. The city was renamed Constantinople, the city of Constantine. The Byzantine Empire began to decline when it was taken over by Crusaders in the 13th century.

• **End of the Byzantine Empire:** 1453, when it fell to the Ottoman Turks.

• **Last Byzantine emperor:** Constantine XI Palaeologus, who died defending the city of Constantinople against the Ottoman Turks on May 29, 1453. With his death, Constantinople passed to the Muslims and the Byzantine Empire ended.

Empires and Kingdoms—China

The Shang was the first of China's great historical dynasties to leave written records. It began around 1766 B.C. and lasted more than five centuries.

• **Last of the Shang dynasty:** Some scholars believe it ended around 1050 B.C., when the Chou dynasty overthrew the last Shang ruler. Others put the end of the Shang at 1122 B.C. The Chou rulers who succeeded the Shang unified China for the first time in its long history. During their rule, they introduced a feudal system in which the ruler gave land to vassals who were then obliged to provide military service, pay tribute to their ruler and obey his orders. The great Chinese philosopher Confucius (551-479 B.C.) lived during the Chou dynasty

• **Last of the Chou dynasty:** 256 B.C., when it was destroyed by the Ch'in. During the next 35 years, the Ch'in wiped out the rest of their rivals and established themselves as rulers of China. The Ch'in (or Ts'in) dynasty, which began in 221 B.C. gave China its name. The Ch'in dynasty marked the end of feudalism in China. Shih Huang-ti, the first Ch'in emperor, built much of the Great Wall. He also tried to simplify the written language. When he died in 210, his son Hu Hai succeeded him but proved to be incompetent.

• **Last of the Ch'in dynasty:** Ch'in rule ended with the murder of Hu Hai in 207 B.C. The Han dynasty began in 202 B.C. It took its name from the Han River (Heavenly River). The four centuries of Han rule were a time of political and cultural centralization in China. Rebellions in the early 3rd century A.D. brought about the downfall of the Han.

• **Last of the Han dynasty:** 220 A.D., when the last Han emperor was deposed. His successor created the Wei dynasty in northern China. By then, China had become fragmented into a number of rival kingdoms. Beginning in 265 A.D., the Tsin (Chin) dynasty brought temporary unity. During this time Buddhism began to have an impact.

• **Last of the Tsin (Chin) dynasty:** 420 A.D. By then, China had been divided again into several northern and southern dynasties. A few short-lived dynasties ruled in southern China from 420 to 581. The north saw invasions by Mongols and Tibetans. The fragmentation of China ended c. 589, when the Sui dynasty gained control. Yang Chien, the first Sui emperor, reunited China for the first time in four centuries. During the Sui dynasty, the Great Wall was strengthened and the Grand Canal—a network of rivers and steams—was built, linking the north with the Yangtze Valley. The Sui established excellent communications and administration systems within China. Yang Chien was killed in 604 by his son Yang Kuang.

• **Last of the Sui dynasty:** 618, with the death of Yang Kuang by Li Yüan, founder of the T'ang dynasty. During the nearly three centuries of the T'ang dynasty, China rose to new artistic heights. Toward the end of the Sui dynasty, trouble along China's borders, coupled with mismanagement led to the downfall of the T'ang.

• **Last of the T'ang dynasty:** 906 A.D., After the murder of the last T'ang emperor, China lacked order for the next half century in what would be its last period of political fragmentation. The time was marked by fighting among rival Chinese states. The Sung dynasty began in 960 when Chao K'uang-yin (Kao Tsu) consolidated several of the warring states and seized control of China. The Sungs moved the capital to Hangchow in southern China. During this time, Genghis Khan conquered much of northern China.

• **Last of the Sung dynasty:** c. 1279, when Kublai Khan, the grandson of Genghis Khan, conquered southern China and overthrew the Sungs. The Mongols ruled China until 1368 as the Yüan dynasty. The capital was established at Cambaluc (Beijing). Marco Polo visited China during this time. Eventually, the Mongols found China was too difficult to control. Their problems were compounded by bad weather conditions that affected farming and sparked revolts among the Chinese peasants.

• **Last of the Yüan dynasty:** 1368, when the Chinese began expelling the Mongols. Chu Yüan-chang (Hung Wu) established the Ming dynasty. During this time, China became a sea power. Europeans began arriving in China. The Ming dynasty began to disintegrate from within during the 1500s as the emperors sought shelter inside the palace and allowed others to run the country. A flawed administration and natural disasters caused the peasants to rebel, leading to the collapse of the dynasty.

• **Last of the Ming dynasty:** 1644, when it was overthrown by the Manchus of Manchuria. (*See also* Nations—China, People's Republic of.)

Empires and Kingdoms—Egypt

The Fatimid caliphate was founded in Tunisia in 909 A.D. The caliph claimed to be a direct descendant of Fatima, daughter of the prophet Muhammad. By 969, the center of the Fatimid caliphate was in Cairo, Egypt.

• **Last Fatimid caliph:** al-Adid, who ruled until 1171. With his death, his nephew Saladin (Salah-el-Din) assumed power and founded the Ayyubid Sultanate. The Ayyubid sultanate was founded by Saladin after al-Adid, the last Fatimid caliph, died in 1171. By 1187, the Ayyubid sultanate governed Egypt, Syria, Palestine and Upper Mesopotamia (Iraq).

• **Last of the Ayyubid sultanate:** 1250, after the Mamluks (or Mamelukes)—Turkish soldiers who were former slaves—staged a coup and ended Ayyubid control. Al-Saleh, the last Ayyubid sultan of Egypt, was murdered and replaced by a Mamluk general. In 1517, when the Ottoman Turks seized control, the Mamluks survived and gain a degree of power. Some became governors of Egypt.

• **Last of the Mamluks:** 1811, when Muhammad Ali was appointed Ottoman governor of Egypt. Seeing the Mamluks as a threat, he had them annihilated. (*See also* Empires and Kingdoms—Ottoman Empire; Nations—Egypt.)

Empires and Kingdoms—Etruria, Kingdom of

Napoleon I formed the Kingdom of Etruria from the Grand Duchy of Tuscany in 1801. Louis, Duke of Parma ruled as King Louis I.

• **End of the Kingdom of Etruria:** 1808, when Napoleon abolished it and incorporated the lands and people into the French Empire.

Empires and Kingdoms—Holy Roman Empire

The Holy Roman Empire had its beginning in 800 A.D., when Charlemagne was crowned emperor of Rome by Pope Leo III.

• **Last Salian Emperor of the Holy Roman Empire:** King Henry V of Germany. When he died in May 1125, he left no children. The crown passed to Lothair, Duke of Saxony.

• **Last Holy Roman Emperor:** Francis II, of the House of Hapsburg, who was forced to abdicate in 1806. He was the last to use the title. As Francis I, he reigned as Emperor of Austria from 1804 until 1835.

• **End of the Holy Roman Empire:** formally dissolved on August 6, 1806, by Francis II, after he proclaimed himself hereditary emperor of Austria.

• **Last surviving monarchy of the Holy Roman Empire:** Liechtenstein.

Empires and Kingdoms—Inca Empire

The Inca Empire extended along the western coast of South America from the southern tip of Colombia to central Chile. It flourished from around the 13th century A.D. until 1533, after the Spanish conquistadors arrived. The Inca Empire was incorporated into the Viceroyalty of Peru.

• **Last Inca emperor who ruled before the Spanish conquest:** Atahualpa, who was captured at Cuzco (Peru) on November 16, 1532, by the Spanish, led by Francisco Pizarro. He was put to death at Cajamarca on August 29, 1533. With his death, the Inca Empire began to fall apart. It was unable to withstand the Spanish military organization.

• **Last Inca leader:** Tupac Amaru, who was executed by the Spanish in 1572. His death marked the end of the Inca attempt to regain control.

Empires and Kingdoms—Mali, Empire of

The Empire of Mali flourished in West Africa in the 14th century. It grew powerful by controlling and trading gold and salt. It was the site of Timbuktu, an important trade center. The empire reached its peak during the reign of Mansa Musa, from about 1312 to 1337. After his death, competition from outside groups and internal revolts weakened the Mali people.

• **Last of the Empire of Mali:** ended during the 15th century, when the Songhai Empire rose in power.

Empires and Kingdoms—Mongol Empire

The Mongols of Central Asia, led by Genghis Khan, began their conquests in the late 12th century. Over the next two centuries, they conquered much of present-day China, Korea, Tibet, Mongolia and parts of Russia, Siberia and Eastern Europe.

• **Last of the great Mongol conquerors:** Tamerlane, a descendant of Genghis Khan, who seized much of the Middle East in the late 14th century.

• **End of the Mongol Empire:** 1405, with the death of Tamerlane.

Empires and Kingdoms—Moors

The term Moors once referred to the people of Mauritania and later to those who lived in Africa north of the Sahara. Still later, it was the name given to the people of Morocco who occupied southern Spain beginning in 1237. From 1492, Moors (or Moriscos) in Spain who refused to give up their Islamic religion were persecuted and were targets of the Spanish Inquisition.

• **Last of the Moors in Spain:** 1614, during the reign of King Philip III. About a half million Moors, or Moriscos, were driven from Spain from 1609 to 1614. Moorish influence in the arts, literature, medicine, science and learning ended when they were expelled from Spain.

Empires and Kingdoms—Mycenaean Civilization

The Mycenaeans began to flourish around 2000 B.C. on the island of Crete off the coast of Greece. Around 1400 B.C., they conquered Knossos and ruled for about three centuries. Homer's epic poems the *Iliad* and the *Odyssey* deal with events that occurred in the Mycenaean period.

• **Last of the Mycenaeans:** around 1100 B.C., when the Dorians began to rule Greece and many of the islands of the Aegean. Knossos was destroyed around this time. Some scholars believe the Dorians were responsible for the destruction.

Empires and Kingdoms—Ottoman Empire

The Ottoman Empire was formed when the Ottoman Turks, led by Osman, declared their independence from the Seljuk Turks toward end of the 13th century. The Turks gained control over Byzantine-ruled lands in Asia Minor. In 1453, they captured Constantinople and ended the Byzantine Empire. The Janissary—formed in the 14th century—were the standing army of the Ottoman Turks. In their early years, they were highly disciplined and loyal. But by the 19th century, the one-time elite organization became inefficient and unruly.

• **Last of the Janissary:** June 1826, when Sultan Mahmud II realized they were a detriment to the empire. He ordered their massacre and had the artillery open fire on their barracks.

• **Last of the Ottoman Empire:** defeated by the Allied Powers in World War I. The Ottoman Empire had begun its decline in the 1800s. It officially ceased to exist after the war, when it was broken up by the 1920 Treaty of Sevres. *See also* Nations—Turkey.

Empires and Kingdoms—Persian Empire

The first great leader of the Persian Empire was Cyrus who ruled from c. 550 to 529 B.C. He conquered much of the Middle East and brought it under Persian control. Under Darius the Great, who ruled from 521 to 486 B.C., the empire expanded until it extended into India, Greece and Egypt. The Persian Empire declined under later rulers.

• **End of the Persian Empire:** around 330 B.C., when it was finally conquered by the armies of Alexander the Great.

• **Last Persian emperor:** Darius III, who ruled from 336 to 330 B.C. He was the last ruler of the Achaemenid dynasty.

Empires and Kingdoms—Roman Republic and Empire

The Romans emerged as a distinct culture around 750 B.C. By the 500s B.C., they began expanding and conquering neighboring lands. By c. 31 B.C., the Roman Republic covered all of Italy and other lands along the Adriatic Sea, much of Spain, Portugal and Greece, and parts of north Africa and Turkey.

• **End of the Roman Republic:** 31 B.C., with the Battle of Actium and the suicides of Antony and Cleopatra. Octavian emerged as leader of the Roman world. He became first ruler of the Roman Empire.

• **End of the Bacchanalia:** 186 B.C., when it was banned by Roman law. The Bacchanalia was a rite that honored the god Bacchus. It started out as a religious ceremony but became noted for its debauchery and drunkenness. The excesses became so great that the Bacchanalia was outlawed.

• **End of Pax Romana (Roman Peace):** 180 A.D., with the death of Marcus Aurelius. Pax Romana is the name given to the two centuries of peace and stability that began when Octavian became emperor in 27 B.C. After the death of Marcus Aurelius, a series of corrupt and incompetent emperors weakened the Roman Empire over the next century or so.

• **End of the Praetorian Guards:** disbanded after they lost a battle against Constantine the Great in 312 A.D. The Praetorian Guards were originally the bodyguards of Roman generals when they were formed in the 2nd century B.C. In 27 B.C., they became the bodyguards of the Roman emperors. During their existence, they gained so much power that they were able to elect and depose the emperor.

• **Last Roman emperor of the West:** Romulus Augustulus. In 476 A.D., Odoacer, a German chieftain, overthrew him and became king of Italy.

• **End of the Western Roman Empire:** When Romulus Augustulus was deposed in 476 A.D., the western half of Europe ceased to acknowledge an empire and the Western Roman Empire ceased to exist.

Empires and Kingdoms— Saracens/ Kingdom of Granada

The Saracens were the earliest and most ardent converts to Islam. In the 7th century A.D., they conquered Arabia, North Africa and part of Asia. In 711, they conquered Spain. The caliphate at Cordova was established in 756. It lasted until 1031, when it was divided into smaller governments. The last of those was the Kingdom of Granada.

• **End of the Kingdom of Granada:** 1492, when it succumbed to Ferdinand of Spain.

• **Last king of the Kingdom of Granada:** Abu Abdullah Mohammed (Spanish name: Boabdil), who ruled as Mohammed XI in 1482-83 and 1486-92. He was overthrown and fled to Morocco.

Empires and Kingdoms—Scythians

The Scythians lived in southeastern Europe, north of the Black Sea from the Carpathian Mountains to the River Don. They conquered land from the Cimmerians around the 7th century B.C.

• **End of the Scythians:** around 200 B.C., when they were driven from their lands by the Sarmatians who came from what is now Iran.

Empires and Kingdoms—Songhai, Empire of

The Empire of Songhai in West Africa reached the peak of its power under Askia Mohammad, who ruled from 1493 to 1528. He extended the empire and controlled the gold and salt trade. In 1591, Songhai's main cities were overrun by a Moroccan army.

• **End of the Empire of Songhai:** gone by 1618, when the Moroccans left the region.

Empires and Kingdoms—Vandals

The Vandals were one of the Germanic peoples who overthrew the Roman Empire. In 406 A.D., they crossed the Rhine and invaded Gaul (France), then they entered

Spain. They invaded Roman Africa in 429 and established a kingdom there. In 455, they captured and plundered Rome.

• **End of the Vandal Kingdom:** 533, when the Vandal kingdom in Africa was overthrown by Belisarius, Byzantine Emperor Justinian I's general.

Energy

Energy—Oil—Embargo of 1973-74

The Arab oil embargo began in October 1973, when nine OPEC nations retaliated against the United States and other Western nations that supported Israel during the Yom Kippur War by banning oil deliveries to them.

• **End of the Arab oil embargo against the U.S.:** March 18, 1974.

Energy—Oil—First Oil Well

The first oil well was drilled in Titusville, Pennsylvania, and struck oil on August 17, 1859. The derrick burned down two weeks later.

• **Last surviving witness to the first oil well strike:** Pete Hoffman. He was featured in *Frontier Times Magazine* in 1932.

Energy—Oil—Pipelines—Big Inch

Before World War II, 95 percent of the crude oil that reached refineries on the East Coast of the United States arrived there on tanker ships. But shipping became risky when war was declared and German submarines posed a threat. The solution was the Big Inch, a 24-inch oil pipeline that extended from Longview, Texas, to Phoenix-ville, Pennsylvania, with 20-inch branches to New Jersey and Philadelphia. Construction of the ditch four feet deep, three feet wide and 1,254 miles long began on August 3, 1942.

• **Last Big Inch construction:** August 14, 1943. In 1947, after the war ended, the pipeline was converted to carry natural gas.

Energy—Oil—Pipelines—Trans-Alaska

In 1968, when oil was found at Prudhoe Bay, Alaska, above the Arctic Circle, it was the greatest oil deposit ever discovered in the United States. Gaining access to it meant a massive pipeline construction project through land frozen much of the year. The job was tackled by a consortium of major petroleum companies. Work began on the Trans-Alaska Pipeline on April 29, 1974.

• **Last Trans-Alaska pipeline section competed:** June 20, 1977, at a cost of approximately $8 billion. It was the largest privately funded construction project undertaken to that time.

Engineering

Engineering—Aqueducts

The Romans built 11 major aqueducts in Europe beginning in 312 B.C.

• **Last of the early Roman aqueducts to be constructed:** Aqua Alexandrine, built in 226 A.D. by Emperor Alexander Severus. By then, many of the earlier Roman aqueducts had fallen into disrepair or disuse. Later, some of the ancient structures were restored.

Engineering—Bridge Engineers
Last Bridges of Some Major Bridge Builders

Engineer	Last Bridge and Location	Description
Brunel, Isambard Kingdom	Clifton Suspension Bridge (Bristol, England)	Completed in 1864. Brunel died on September 15, 1859, age 53. • **Last railway bridge:** Royal Albert over Tamar River near Plymouth, England. It was completed in April 1859.

Buck, Leffert Lefferts	East River Suspension Bridge (a.k.a. Williamsburg Suspension Bridge, New York)	Completed in 1903 with a span of 1,600 feet. Buck's last bridge was the first all-metal suspension bridge of its kind and the largest in the world at that time. Buck died on July 17, 1909, age 72.
Eads, James Buchanan	Eads Bridge (across Mississippi River at Saint Louis, Missouri)	Completed in 1874. Construction began in 1867. • **Last major engineering project:** removed silt and mud from the mouth of the Mississippi; project completed in 1879. Eads died in Nassau, Bahamas, on March 8, 1887, age 66.
Roebling, John Augustus	Brooklyn Bridge (Brooklyn, New York)	While Roebling and his son Washington were surveying near the Fulton Ferry, a ferry-boat crushed one of his feet, and he sustained serious head injuries. Roebling died of lockjaw 16 days later, on July 22, 1869, age 63. The Brooklyn Bridge was completed by his son, Washington.
Roebling, Washington Augustus	Brooklyn Bridge (Brooklyn, New York)	In 1872, Roebling contracted the bends while working in one of the compressed air caissons used in the construction of the bridge. His health was severely affected, and he took no further active part in professional engineering work after the Brooklyn Bridge was completed in 1883. He died in Trenton, New Jersey, on July 21, 1926, age 89.

Engineering—Bridges—Covered— United States

Perhaps as many as 10,000 covered bridges were built in the United States in the 19th century. Today, only about 875 remain. Most states that once boasted having hundreds of historic covered bridges now have less than a dozen. Several states have just one bridge remaining.

• **Last major U.S. city with a historic covered bridge:** Philadelphia, Pennsylvania.

• **Last remaining historic covered bridge in Alaska:** Chickaloon River Bridge built in 1917, in the borough of Matanuska-Susitna. A modern covered bridge also stands near Anchorage.

• **Last remaining historic covered bridge in Minnesota:** Zumbrota Bridge, built in 1869. It was moved from its original location in Zumbrota to a campground in 1970. It remained there until it was moved back to the Zumbro River in 1997, soon after which it was restored. A few modern covered bridges also stand in Minnesota.

• **Last remaining historic covered bridge in New Jersey:** Green Sergeant's Bridge built in 1872 across the Wickecheoke Creek near Flemington in Hunterdon County. A modern covered bridge also stands in Cherry Hill, Camden County, New Jersey.

• **Last remaining historic covered bridge in Rhode Island:** none. However, Rhode Island does have a replica of a 19th-century covered bridge, the Swamp Meadow Covered Bridge in Foster. The replica was built in 1994 by volunteers using locally cut lumber. The bridge was torched by an arsonist that same year and rebuilt in 1996.

• **Last remaining historic covered bridge in South Carolina:** Campbell Bridge built in 1909, near Gowensville. It is now closed to traffic.

• **Last remaining historic covered bridge in Wisconsin:** Cedarburg Bridge, built in 1876 near Cedarburg, about 20 miles north of Milwaukee. Wisconsin also has several modern covered bridges.

Engineering—Bridges—Famous and Still in Use—Benjamin Franklin Bridge

The cable suspension bridge that spans the Delaware River and links Philadelphia, Pennsylvania, and Camden, New Jersey, was known as the Delaware River Bridge when it opened in July 1926. At 1,750 feet, it was the longest suspension bridge in the United States at that time.

• **Last known as the Delaware River Bridge:** July 20, 1955, when it was renamed Benjamin Franklin Bridge in anticipation of the upcoming 250th birthday celebration of one of the city's most important historic residents.

• **Last held the title as the longest U.S. suspension bridge:** 1929, when the Delaware River Bridge was outranked by the Ambassador Bridge (1,850 feet), linking Detroit, Michigan, and Windsor, Canada.

Engineering—Bridges—Famous and Still in Use—Brooklyn Bridge

The 1,595-foot Brooklyn Bridge connects Manhattan and Brooklyn in New York. It was opened on May 24, 1883, by President James A. Garfield and the governor of New York. It cost $15.5 million and was the longest suspension bridge then in existence.

• **Last wire strung across the river:** October 5, 1878.

• **Last trolley crossed the Brooklyn Bridge:** March 6, 1950.

• **Last held the title as the longest U.S. suspension bridge:** 1903, when the Williamsburg Bridge (1,600 ft.) opened in New York, New York.

Engineering—Bridges—Famous and Still in Use—Golden Gate Bridge

The Golden Gate Bridge (4,200 feet) was under construction from 1933 to 1937. Eleven lives were lost while the bridge was being built, 10 in one day.

• **Last rivet driven:** May 27, 1937.

• **Last held title as the longest U.S. suspension bridge:** 1964. That year the Golden Gate Bridge was surpassed by the Verrazano-Narrows Bridge (4,260 feet) in New York Harbor.

Engineering—Bridges—Famous and Still in Use—London Bridges

• **Last of the Old London Bridge:** 1832. It was demolished after New London Bridge was completed. Old London Bridge was built by Peter of Colechurch, a monk, beginning in 1176. It was finished in 1209, after his death.

• **Last of New London Bridge in London:** 1968-69. New London Bridge was built by John Rennie and completed in 1831. When engineers discovered the bridge was sinking into the Thames and cracks were appearing, a decision was made to replace it. Construction began on a third London Bridge in 1967. In 1968, New London Bridge was sold to the McCulloch Oil Corporation, developers of Lake Havasu City, Arizona. Thousands of tons of carefully numbered granite blocks were removed, shipped to Lake Havasu and reassembled between 1969 and 1971.

Engineering—Bridges—Famous and Still in Use—Verrazano-Narrows Bridge

The Verrazano-Narrows Bridge crosses the Verrazano Narrows in New York Harbor, between Staten Island and Brooklyn. It was designed by Othmar Ammann, who died on September 22, 1965, age 86.

• **Last construction completed:** 1964. The Verrazano-Narrows Bridge opened on November 21, 1964.

• **Last held title as the longest suspension bridge worldwide:** 1981, when the Verrazano-Narrows Bridge was surpassed by the Humber River Bridge in England. It is still holds the record in America.

Engineering—Bridges—Famous and Still Standing But Not in Use—Casselman River Bridge

Casselman River Bridge was built in Grantsville, Maryland, in 1813-14, and was the largest stone-arch bridge in the United States at the time. It was part of the National Road project that linked Cumberland, Maryland, with the Ohio River. It is now part of a state park and is closed to vehicular traffic.

• **Last year Casselman River Bridge was open for traffic:** 1953. The bridge was restored by the State of Maryland in 1964.

Engineering—Bridges—Famous and Still Standing But Not in Use— Kinzua Viaduct

When the Kinzua Viaduct was built by Octave Chanute in Kushequa, Pennsylvania, in 1882, it was the highest and longest railroad bridge in the world (302 feet high; 2,052 feet long). It was built to carry the Erie Railroad across the Kinzua Creek Valley.
• **Last regular train across the Kinzua Viaduct:** June 21, 1959. It is still the fourth-tallest railroad bridge in the United States and is on the National Register of Historic Places and on the National Register of Historic Civil Engineering Landmarks. The bridge is in Kinzua Bridge State Park. The ravages of time, weather and rust have caused the bridge to be placed off limits to pedestrians as engineers try to find a way to shore it up.

Engineering—Bridges
Longest Suspension Bridges Worldwide

Bridge	Location	Last Held Record
Akashi Kaikyo Bridge	Japan, completed 1998	Present
Great Belt Link	Denmark, completed 1996	1998
Humber River Bridge	England, completed 1981	1996
Verrazano-Narrows Bridge	New York, completed 1964	1981
Golden Gate Bridge	San Francisco, completed 1937	1964
George Washington Bridge	New York, completed 1931	1937
Ambassador International Bridge	Detroit/Canada, completed 1929	1931
Benjamin Franklin Bridge	Philadelphia, completed 1926	1929

Engineering—Bridges—Metal Railroad
• **Last surviving intact all-metal railroad bridge in the United States:** Reading-Hills Station Bridge in Muncy, Pennsylvania. The bridge was built in 1846 for the Reading Railroad tracks in Muncy, Pennsylvania. Although the bridge has been rebuilt over the years, it remains in its original location.

Engineering—Bridges—Truss Railroad— Bollman Truss Bridge

Wendell Bollman designed a bridge that became the standard for the Baltimore & Ohio Railroad for many years. Bollman's design used wrought-iron suspended trusses.
• **Last surviving Bollman Truss Bridge:** across the Little Patuxent River in Savage, Maryland. The bridge was built c. 1887, when a spur of the B&O Railroad was laid out to the Savage Mill factory. In 1966, the bridge became the first to be recognized as a National Historic Civil Engineering Landmark by the American Society of Civil Engineers. The Bollman Truss Bridge is also on the National Register of Historic Places.

Engineering—Bridges—Truss Railroad— Fink Truss Bridge

German designer Albert Fink designed a bridge known as a through truss because traffic passed through the structure of the bridge. His bridges were also used by the Baltimore & Ohio Railroad.
• **Last surviving Fink through truss bridge:** Zoarville Station Bridge in Zoarville, Ohio. The bridge was built in 1868 by Smith, Latrobe and Company of Baltimore, Maryland, as part of a locomotive span in Dover, Ohio. In 1905, after it became obsolete, it was moved to its present location across Conotton Creek. A nearby highway was abandoned in the 1940s, and the bridge was left to decay. In 1997, the bridge was acquired by the Camp Tuscazoar Foundation that is working on a restoration plan.

Engineering—Bridges—Truss Railroad—Haupt Truss Bridges

Herman Haupt was a West Point instructor and a chief engineer and general in the Civil War. He designed an iron truss bridge that was used exclusively by the Pennsylvania Railroad between 1851 and 1861.

• **Last iron Haupt truss bridges:** two have survived. Both were built in 1854 for the Pennsylvania Railroad. One, now disassembled, is at the Railroaders' Memorial Museum in Altoona, Pennsylvania. The other bridge is still standing in Ardmore, Pennsylvania.

• **Last wooden Haupt truss bridge:** Bunker Hill Covered Bridge, across Lyles Creek near Claremont, North Carolina. It was built in 1895.

Engineering—Bridges—Torn Down or Destroyed
Last Year Some Important Bridges Were Standing

Bridge and Location	Last Stood	Cause of Failure or Reason for Demolition
Ashtabula Bridge Ashtabula, Ohio	1876	Fatigue crack. A train on the Lake Shore & Michigan Southern Railway broke through the bridge on the evening of December 26, 1876, and crashed, killing more than 85 of the 156 aboard and injuring the rest.
Colossus Bridge (Upper Ferry Bridge) Schuylkill River, Philadelphia, Pennsylvania	1838	Destroyed by fire. When it was built by Lewis Wernwag in 1812, it was believed to be the longest bridge ever constructed of wood or stone.
Danube Canal Bridge Vienna, Austria	1885	Torn down. When built in 1830 by Ignaz von Mitis it was the first bridge to use steel in its construction. In 1860, it was replaced by a stronger railroad suspension bridge that was replaced a second time in 1885.
Falls View Suspension Bridge (No. 1) Niagara Falls, New York	1889	Brought down by gale-force winds. Remnants of the bridge remain submerged in 150 feet of water. • **Last person to cross Falls View Suspension Bridge (No. 1):** Doctor J.W. Hodge, who was answering a sick call on January 10, 1889, the night of the storm.
Falls View Suspension Bridge (No. 2) Niagara Falls, New York	1898	Torn down. Replaced with a heavyweight bridge that could support modern transportation. The dismantled suspension bridge was moved and became Queenston-Lewiston Suspension Bridge No. 2.
Falls View Bridge "Honeymoon Bridge" (Upper Steel Arch) Niagara Falls, New York	1938	Unstable foundation was crumpled by an ice jam on January 27, 1938. The bridge had been closed because of an inevitable collapse. The rest of the bridge collapsed on April 12-13, 1938.
I-5 Arroyo Pasajero Twin Bridges Coalinga, California	1995	Rapidly moving water weakened the foundation and caused it to collapse. Seven people were killed on March 10, 1995, when the bridge fell.
Grand Pont Suspendu Sarine River, Fribourg, Switzerland	1923	Torn down. When built in 1834 by Joseph Chaley, it was the longest suspension bridge in the world. Chaley was the first bridge designer to use bundled cables and aerial spinning.

Jacobs Creek Bridge Uniontown, Pennsylvania	1833	Demolished. When built in 1801 by James Finley, it was the longest suspension bridge in the world and the first in the United States.
King Street Bridge Yarra River, Melbourne, Australia	1962	Brittle fracture, design flaw, poor steel selection caused one span to collapse.
McCall's Ferry Timber Arch Bridge Susquehanna River, Pennsylvania	1817	Destroyed by ice when it was only two years old. When it was built in 1815, it was the longest single-span timber bridge in the world.
Mianus River Bridge Mianus River, Connecticut	1983	Pin failure and inadequate inspection caused collapse, killing three.
Michigan Central Railway Cantilever Bridge Niagara Falls, New York	1925	Torn down. Built in 1883. Stood for more than 40 years. Replaced by a more heavyweight bridge.
Million Dollar Bridge Casco Bay, Portland, Maine	1997	Torn down. Built in 1916. Replaced by a new bridge that was dedicated in 1997.
Mostar Bridge (original) Neretva River, Bosnia-Herzegovina	1993	Originally built in 1556. Destroyed by Croatian Nationalists during the 1992-95 conflict. The historic bridge was reconstructed. It reopened in July 2004.
Neuilly Bridge Paris, France	1932	Torn down to provide better navigation in the Seine. Built in 1772.
Niagara Falls Suspension Bridge (No. 1) Niagara Falls, New York	1855	Torn down. When built in 1848, it was the first bridge over the Niagara River. Replaced by a heavier bridge.
Niagara Falls Suspension Bridge (No. 2) Niagara Falls, New York	1896	Torn down. Originally built in 1855 and rebuilt in 1886. Replaced by a heavier bridge.
Peace River Bridge Alcan Highway, British Columbia	1957	Collapsed in October 1957. The footings had been built on unstable soil. The north end shifted and created a gap, giving advance warning that a collapse was imminent. Camera crews were present to record the event.
Permanent Bridge Schuylkill River, Philadelphia, Pennsylvania	1875	Destroyed by fire. Originally built 1805; rebuilt and widened in the 1850s.
Point Pleasant or Silver Bridge Point Pleasant, West Virginia, and Kanauga, Ohio	1967	Collapsed into Ohio River, killing 46 and injuring nine. A series of fractures caused a chain to snap. When the bridge could no longer support its weight, it collapsed into the river.
Queenston-Lewiston Suspension Bridge (No. 1) Queenston, Canada	1854	Destroyed by gale-force winds. The bridge was four years old. In 1899, it was replaced by a second Queenston-Lewiston suspension bridge.
Queenston-Lewiston Suspension Bridge (No. 2) Queenston, Canada	1962	Moved from Niagara Falls in 1899. Sold and dismantled between December 1962 and March 1963. Replaced with heavyweight third Queenston-Lewiston (steel arch) bridge.
Sando Arch Sando, Sweden	1939	Collapsed into Aangermann River, killing 32.

Schaffhausen Bridge Rhine River, Switzerland	1799	Burned by Napoleon's troops. The bridge was built in 1757 and had two spans.
Schoharie Creek Bridge Schoharie Creek, New York	1987	Collapsed, killing eight. The five-span New York Thruway bridge was built in 1956. It collapsed when soil beneath one of the piers washed away, causing the foundation to crack.
Second Narrows Bridge Vancouver, British Columbia	1958	A large part of the bridge collapsed on June 17, 1958, killing 18 workers. At the time, a new bridge was under construction alongside the older bridge that was built in 1925.
Tacoma-Narrows Bridge ("Galloping Gertie") Tacoma Narrows, Washington	1940	Design flaw. The bridge collapsed four months after it was completed. Wind forces caused pronounced swaying. The collapse was captured on film. A dog was killed when a car fell into the Narrows. There were no human fatalities. A new bridge was built in 1950. The last person on the Tacoma-Narrows Bridge was photographer Howard Clifford.
Tay Bridge Firth of Tay Dundee, Scotland	1879	A great storm on December 28, 1879, brought winds of 70 miles per hour that caused the bridge to collapse, killing 75 passengers aboard the Edinburgh train. A new bridge was built alongside the old piers.

Engineering—Canals and Waterways—Canada—Saint Lawrence Seaway

The Saint Lawrence Seaway opened on June 26, 1959. Its 2,300-mile-long, 27-feet-deep channel for ocean-going vessels through the Great Lakes and St. Lawrence to the sea made it the biggest waterway project since the Panama Canal.

• **Last major Saint Lawrence Seaway construction completed:** April 25, 1959.

Engineering—Canals and Waterways—Egypt—Suez Canal

The Suez Canal, in Egypt, connects the Red Sea with the Mediterranean. Construction began in 1859, under French engineer, Ferdinand de Lesseps. He left the project in 1863.

• **Last Suez Canal construction:** 1869. On November 17, 1869, the Suez Canal was open to navigation. The British took control of the canal in 1875, after they bought out the Egyptian ruler's interest.

• **End of British control:** June 13, 1956, during the Suez Canal crisis. A month later, the waterway was nationalized by Egyptian President Gamal Abdel Nasser.

• **End of the Arab-Israeli War Suez Canal shutdown:** reopened June 5, 1975. The canal had closed on June 5, 1967, during the Arab-Israeli War. It reopened eight years later.

Engineering—Canals and Waterways
Last Commercial Use of Some Major U.S. Canals

Canal and Location	Last Commercial Use	Description
Chesapeake and Delaware Canal Chesapeake City,	1919 (private use)	Completed in 1829. In 1919, the canal was sold to the U.S. government and designated "Intra-Coastal Waterway, Delaware River to Chesapeake Bay, Delaware

Maryland, and Delaware City, Delaware		and Maryland." It reopened in 1927.
Chesapeake and Ohio Canal Cumberland, Maryland to Washington, D.C.	1924	The 184-mile canal began operation in 1828, primarily to transport coal to market from western Maryland. It was acquired by the National Park Service in 1938. In 1971, it was designated the Chesapeake and Ohio Canal National Park.
Delaware Canal Easton to Bristol, Pennsylvania	1931	Completed in 1830 and operated by the Lehigh Coal and Navigation Company. The canal has retained almost all of its original structures and today is preserved as Delaware Canal State Park. The last Delaware Canal coal boat, No. 181, delivered its last load on October 17, 1931.
Delaware and Hudson Canal Honesdale, Pennsylvania, to Kingston, New York	1891	Completed in 1828 and deepened and expanded through the 1840s and 1850s. The canal hit its peak transporting coal in 1872, but competition from the railroads led to its closing within 20 years. The canal was sold in January 1899. The last Delaware and Hudson Canal coal boat delivered its last load on November 5, 1891.
Delaware and Raritan Canal New Brunswick, New Jersey to Delaware River near Trenton	1932	Completed in 1834, the canal linked the Delaware River and Raritan Bay. Today, the canal is both a recreational facility as the Delaware and Raritan Canal State Park and a major source of water for central New Jersey.
Illinois and Michigan Canal Chicago to LaSalle, Illinois	1933	Completed in 1848. When the Sanitary and Ship Canal opened in 1906, the Illinois and Michigan Canal lost much of its traffic. It finally closed to navigation in 1933. The canal was designated a National Historic Corridor in 1984. The old towpath is now a biking and hiking trail.
Illinois and Mississippi Canal (Hennepin Canal) Rock River, Illinois, to Mississippi River	1951	When it began operation in 1907, the canal provided a direct link between Chicago, Illinois, and the Mississippi River. Today, the canal is part of Hennepin Canal Parkway State Park and is on the National Register of Historic Places.
Lehigh Coal and Navigation Company Canal Mauch Chunk to Easton to Philadelphia, Pennsylvania	1942	When the canal ceased full-scale operations in 1932, it was the last fully functioning towpath canal in North America. Portions were used to transport coal silt until 1942, when a flood ended towpath navigation. In 1962, most of the canal was sold to public and private organizations for recreational use. Today, a portion of the canal is within Hugh Moore Park. The last Lehigh Coal and Navigation Company boat captain was Alan Strohl, who transported coal silt to the New Jersey Zinc Company in Palmerton.
Miami and Erie Canal Cincinnati to Toledo, Ohio	1929	The canal connected Lake Erie with the Ohio River. The first section opened in 1829; the last, in 1845. A major flood ended canal traffic in 1913, but the canal did not officially close until 1929.

Middlesex Canal Charlestown to Lowell, Massachusetts	1853	Completed 1803, it was one of the earliest U.S. canal projects. It transported goods between Lowell and Boston. Competition from the railroads drove the Middlesex Canal out of business in 1853.
Morris Canal Easton, Pennsylvania, to Jersey City, New Jersey	1915	Completed from Easton to Newark in 1831 and to Jersey City in 1836. Commercial traffic ceased in 1915. The state of New Jersey took over the canal in 1924 and decided to abandon it. By 1929, the canal was mostly destroyed.
Pennsylvania Canal Union Canal to Juniata River, to Pittsburgh to the Kiskiminetas River	1857	The canal lasted only 23 years. It fell victim to the railroad, which was faster and did not shut down in the winter. Many of the canal's rights-of-ways were converted to rail lines.
Portage Canal Keweenaw Bay to Lake Superior	1951	Opened in 1873. Commercial operations shut down on July 7, 1951. The U.S. government owned the canal until 1961, when ownership was transferred to the state of Wisconsin. Today, the canal is on the National Register of Historic Places.
Santee Canal Charleston to Columbia, South Carolina	1850	Opened in 1800. Santee was the first U.S canal to be completed. Business dwindled when a railroad line opened in the 1840s. Today, Old Santee Canal Park occupies the southern part of the canal.
Susquehanna and Tidewater Canal Wrightville, Pennsylvania, to Havre de Grace, Maryland	1901	Completed in 1836. The canal was busy until 1889, when railroad competition and a flood forced it to close.
Union Canal Schuylkill River to Susquehanna River, Pennsylvania	1885	Completed in 1828. The Union Canal was for a time the only commercial link between eastern and western Pennsylvania. In 1862, flooding wiped out one of the canal's dams. By then, rail transportation was cheaper. The canal was not rebuilt.
Wabash and Erie Canal Miami and Maumee Canal to Terre Haute, Indiana	1876	The first section opened in 1835. Extensions opened over the next 20 years. When completed in 1853, it was the longest canal in the Western Hemisphere. The south part was abandoned in 1860, a victim of railroads that could transport goods faster and cheaper. The last Wabash and Erie Canal boat carried cargo in 1874. By 1876, the entire canal was abandoned.

Engineering—Canals and Waterways— Panama—Panama Canal

The first attempt to build a canal across the Isthmus of Panama was made by Ferdinand de Lesseps and the French Panama Canal Company in 1882.

• **Last work by the French Panama Canal Company:** 1891. The project was abandoned when the company went bankrupt.

The U.S. purchased the incomplete waterway from de Lesseps' successors for $40 million in 1904 and finished it.

• **Last major construction completed on the Panama Canal:** by August 15, 1914, when the canal opened for traffic. The official opening was July 12, 1920.

• **Last administered by the U.S.:** December 31, 1999. In 1978, the U.S. Senate voted to turn the canal over to Panama in 1999.

• **Last surviving Panama Canal construction worker:** Alexander Bernard Heron, who was 16 years old in 1908 when he arrived in the Isthmus from Colombia with his father, looking for job opportunities. He worked on the most difficult phase, the Culebra Cut, a stretch that took seven years to excavate. In 1998, at age 104, Heron was featured in the documentary *The Panama Canal: Eighth Wonder of the World.*

Engineering—Dams

Engineering—Dams—Aswan High Dam
Construction of the Aswan High Dam began in January 1960. When the dam was completed, it inundated some 300 miles of the Nile Valley. However, it greatly increased the amount of arable land and boosted the energy potential for Egypt. Two massive stone temples at Abu Simbel were endangered by flooding from the dam. They dated from the time of Ramses II, c. 1250 B.C. The temples were rescued through the efforts of an international operation sponsored by UNESCO and supported by more than 50 nations.

• **End of the Abu Simbel rescue:** 1966. Moving the two temples took two years.

• **End of Aswan High Dam construction:** July 1970.

Engineering—Dams—Bear Valley Dam
The first Bear Valley Dam was built in the San Bernardino Mountains in California in 1884. It was designed by F.E. Brown and was the first arch dam built in the United States. The need for more water resulted in the construction of a larger structure, the Big Bear Valley Dam in 1911.

• **Last use of Old Bear Valley Dam:** 1911. It was submerged after the new dam was completed. It now is covered by Big Bear Lake, the reservoir created by the new dam.

Engineering—Dams—Croton Dam
The old Croton Dam on the Croton River in New York, New York, was completed in 1842 by John B. Jervis. The dam provided one of the earliest successful systems for bringing water to New York City. Increasing demands led to the building of the New Croton Dam between 1892 and 1906, farther downstream.

• **Last use of Old Croton Dam:** 1906, the year the New Croton Dam was finished. The old dam now lies under the reservoir created by the new dam.

Engineering—Dams—Hoover Dam
Hoover Dam straddles the lower Colorado River on the Arizona-Nevada border near Boulder City, Nevada. It is the highest concrete arch dam in the United States. Construction began in 1931.

• **Last batch of concrete poured on the dam:** May 29, 1935. The dam was dedicated by President Franklin D. Roosevelt on September 30, 1935.

• **End of dam construction:** March 1, 1936.

• **Last known as Boulder Dam:** April 30, 1947. During the planning stages, the dam was known as the Boulder Canyon Project. During construction, the site was called both Hoover Dam and Boulder Canyon Dam. When it was completed in 1935, the name was formally designated Boulder Dam. In 1947, the U.S. Congress officially renamed it Hoover Dam for former President Herbert Hoover, who was Secretary of Commerce when the project was planned.

Engineering—Great Wall of China
The first parts of the Great Wall of China were built around the 700s to 800s B.C. by small states to keep out warlike nomadic tribes. The walls were connected during the reign of Emperor Ch'in Shih Hüang Ti (c. 246-210 B.C.). Today, the wall is about 4,187 miles (6,700 kilometers) long, 50 feet high, 26 feet at the base and 16 feet at the top.

• **Last major construction on the Great Wall:** during the Ming dynasty (1368-1644), when it underwent major repairs and extensions.

Engineering—Land Reclamation—Lago Fucino (Lake Fucinus)

The Lake Fucinus Emissarium in central Italy, built from 41 to 52 A.D., was an early Roman land reclamation project. It was a drainage tunnel than ran from Lake Fucinus to the River Liri. However, when it was completed, it failed to work properly. As a result, Lake Fucinus (Lago de Celano) remained a lake.

• **Last time Lake Fucinus was a lake:** 1875, when it was finally successfully drained by Italian and Swiss engineers. The project allowed Prince Alessandro Torlonia to add nearly 40,000 acres to his estate. In 1950, the Italian government expropriated most of the land and divided it among several thousand families of settlers.

Engineering—Machines—Barker's Turbine Engine

Barker's turbine was invented as a laboratory curiosity at the end of the 17th century and was the earliest practical reaction type engine. Water jetting from brass nozzles at the ends of arms caused the arm-and-shaft assembly to rotate.

• **Last remaining Barker turbine:** Hacienda Buena Vista, Puerto Rico; owned by the Puerto Rico Conservation Trust. It was built by the West Point Foundry in Cold Spring, New York, in 1853. It can produce about 6 horsepower at 22 revolutions per minute.

Engineering—Machines—Roebling Wire Rope Machine

The famed large suspension bridges and other engineering landmarks of the Roebling Company required heavy metal rope. Large machines twisted strands of metal cable into the heavy metal rope in a process known as closing.

• **Last remaining Roebling wire rope machine:** at the Historical Industrial Complex in Trenton, New Jersey. The 80-ton machine was designed by Charles G. Roebling, president of the Roebling Company. When it was built in 1893, it was the largest wire-rope closing machine.

Engineering—Seven Wonders of the Ancient World

A list of "Seven Wonders" was mentioned by the Greek historian Herodotus in the 5th century B.C. and later by Alexandrian librarian Callimachus of Cyrene, in the 3rd century B.C. The Seven Wonders listed here are the most widely accepted ones, finalized in Europe in the Middle Ages.

• **Last remaining wonder of the Seven Wonders of the Ancient World:** Great Pyramid of Giza, built around 2560 B.C. during the reign of Khufu as his tomb. It is the largest of the pyramids and covers nearly 13 acres. Some of the facing stone and top stone have been stolen. At one time, it reached a height of 481 feet. At the base, each of its four sides measures about 755 feet. It was the tallest structure in the world for more than 4,000 years.

Engineering—Seven Wonders— Colossus of Rhodes

The Colossus of Rhodes was a massive bronze statue of the sun god Helios, completed in 280 B.C. The 120-foot statue stood on a promontory at the entrance to a harbor on the Isle of Rhodes in the Aegean Sea.

• **Last of the Colossus of Rhodes:** destroyed by an earthquake around 226 B.C. The ruins remained on the ground almost 900 years. Around 654 A.D., outsiders invaded the area and sold the pieces of the statue for scrap metal.

Engineering—Seven Wonders— Temple of Diana (or Artemis)

The Temple of Diana at Ephesus in Ionia (now Turkey) was built in the 6th century B.C. for Croesus, King of Lydia. The building was made of marble and contained 127 columns.

• **Last of the Temple of Diana (or Artemis):** destroyed by fire around 356 B.C. but rebuilt. It was burned a second time by the Goths c. 262 A.D. The temple last stood in 401 A.D. That year it was torn down by Christians. English archaeologist John T. Wood unearthed fragments of the original columns in the 1870s. They are in the British Museum. Some of the statuary is at the New Hofburg Museum in Vienna.

Engineering—Seven Wonders—Hanging Gardens of Babylon
The Hanging Gardens of Babylon were about 30 miles south of Baghdad (Iraq). They lasted a very short time and were not well documented.
• **Last of the Hanging Gardens of Babylon:** The gardens were most likely destroyed within a century after they were built by King Nebuchadnezzar II in the 6th century B.C. (Some researchers suggest the gardens were built a century earlier by Sennacherib.) Xerxes destroyed Babylon in 480s B.C. When Pliny visited Babylon in 79 A.D., the gardens had been leveled and nothing remained. In the early 20th century, German archaeologist Robert Koldewey excavated the area where the foundation of the Gardens once was located. Today, some crumbling mud bricks are all that remain.

Engineering—Seven Wonders—Statue of Zeus at Olympia
The statue of the Olympian Zeus at the Temple of Zeus in Greece was created by the Greek sculptor Phidias after 450 B.C. It stood more than 40 feet tall and had a robe covered in gold. The statue survived a failed attempted move by Caligula in the first century A.D. and a fire that destroyed the temple in the fifth century A.D. After the fire, wealthy Greeks moved the statue to a palace in Constantinople.
• **Last of the Statue of Zeus at Olympia:** destroyed by another fire in Constantinople in 462 A.D. Nothing remains of the statue but fragments of the pedestal. Only rocks, debris and fallen columns are left from the temple.

Engineering—Seven Wonders—Mausoleum of Halicarnassus
The Mausoleum of Halicarnassus (Tomb of King Mausolus) in present-day Bodrum, Turkey, was built in 352 B.C. by Artemisia, the wife of Mausolus for her recently departed husband. The tomb, which gave the

world the word *mausoleum,* was made of white marble and alabaster and decorated with gold. Massive statues adorned the structure.
• **Last of the Mausoleum of Halicarnassus:** destroyed in 1496, when stones were taken from the building by the Knights of Saint John to fortify a castle in the region. That castle still stands. Nothing remains of the mausoleum. In 1857, English archaeologist Charles Newton excavated the area and found fragments at the ruins of the mausoleum. Some of the statues are now in the British Museum. Others are in the Bodrum Museum and the Istanbul Museum. A single column in a marshy field in Bodrum marks the spot where the mausoleum once stood.

Engineering—Seven Wonders—Lighthouse at Alexandria
The Lighthouse of Alexandria (Pharos of Alexandria)—a white marble lighthouse on an island off the coast of Alexandria, Egypt—was the last of the Seven Wonders to be built. It was completed sometime around 280 B.C. It rose 400 feet and was illuminated by a flame whose glow was intensified by large metal mirrors. The light could be seen 30 or more miles at sea.
• **Last of the Lighthouse of Alexandria:** destroyed by a series of earthquakes. It was finally toppled by one in 1323. In 1480, a sultan built a fortress on the site. That land is now underwater.

Engineering—Tunnels

Engineering—Tunnels—LaSalle Street Tunnel
The LaSalle Street Tunnel designed by William Bryson and built in 1871, was the second traffic tunnel constructed in Chicago, Illinois.
• **Last time the LaSalle Street Tunnel was used:** November 1939, when the tunnel was closed during the construction of the Dearborn Street Subway.

Engineering—Tunnels—Rove Tunnel
The Rove Tunnel was part of the Marseilles-

Rhone Canal in Arles, France. The tunnel was constructed in 1927 and was the largest canal tunnel in the world.
• **Last time the Rove Tunnel was opened to traffic:** 1963. It was closed that year after a section of the tunnel collapsed.

Engineering—Tunnels—Washington Street Tunnel
The Washington Street Tunnel, under the Chicago River, was constructed by J.K. Lake and built in 1869. It was the first traffic tunnel constructed in Chicago, Illinois.
• **Last time the Washington Street Tunnel was used:** 1953.

Entertainers
(*See also* Movies, Music, Radio, Television.)

Entertainers—Comedy Teams—Marx Brothers
The Marx Brothers were Chico (Leonard), Groucho (Julius Henry), Gummo (Milton), Harpo (Adolph Arthur) and Zeppo (Herbert).
• **Last surviving Marx Brothers member:** Zeppo Marx, who died in Palm Springs, California, on November 30, 1979, age 78.

Entertainers—Comedy Teams—Ritz Brothers
The Ritz Brothers were the three Joachim brothers: Al, Harry and Jimmy.
• **Last surviving Ritz Brothers member:** Harry Ritz, who died in San Diego, California, on March 29, 1986, age 78. Harry died four months after his brother Jimmy.

Entertainers—Comedy Teams—Seven Little Foys
The Seven Little Foys were a singing, dancing and comedy vaudeville team of siblings. They were the children of vaudeville performer Edward Fitzgerald, who worked professionally as Eddie Foy. The family was the subject of the movie *The Seven Little Foys.*
• **Last surviving member of the Seven Little Foys:** Irving Foy, who died in Albuquerque, New Mexico, on April 20, 2003, age 94. He was also the youngest of the group.

Entertainers—Comedy Teams—Three Stooges
The original Three Stooges were Larry Fine (Louis Feinberg), Moe Howard (Moses Horwitz) and Shemp Howard (Samuel Horwitz). When Shemp left, his brother Curly (Jerome Lester Horwitz) joined the trio. When Curly became ill, Shemp returned to the act. Shemp died in Hollywood, California, on November 25, 1955, age 60. After his death, Joe Besser took his place. When Besser left, he was replaced by Joe DeRita.
• **Last surviving Three Stooges member (original cast):** Moe Howard, who died in Los Angeles, California, on May 5, 1975, age 78. Moe died four months after Larry Fine.
• **Last surviving Three Stooges member (all casts):** Joe DeRita (real name Joseph Wardell) who died in Woodland Hills, California, on July 3, 1993, age 83.
• **Last Three Stooges feature movie**: *The Outlaws is Coming* (1965), starring Larry Fine, Moe Howard and Joe DeRita.

Entertainers—Dancers, Choreographers and Dance Directors
Last Production or Performance of Some Major
Dancers, Choreographers and Dance Directors
(*See also* Movies—Performers.)

Dancer/ Director/ Choreographer	Description
Ashton, Sir Frederick	Ecuadorian-born British choreographer Sir Frederick Ashton died in Sussex, England, on August 18, 1988, age 83.

	• **Last ballet choreographed for Margot Fonteyn:** *Marguerite and Armand* (1963). • **Last ballet choreographed:** *The Creatures of Prometheus,* June 6, 1970, Bonn, West Germany. • **End of association with Great Britain's Royal Ballet:** retired at the end of the 1969/70 season. Curtain Call performance July 24, 1970, at the Royal Opera House, London, England.
Atkins, Charles ("Cholly")	American dancer/teacher/Broadway and Motown choreographer Charles Atkins died in Las Vegas, Nevada, April 19, 2003, age 89. • **Last Broadway appearance as a dancer:** September 15, 1952, *Gentlemen Prefer Blondes,* at the Ziegfeld Theater. • **Last Broadway appearance as a choreographer:** January 20, 1991, *Black and Blue* at the Minskoff Theater. The show ran for 829 performances and earned Atkins a Tony Award. • **Last danced with partner Charles ("Honi") Coles:** 1959.
Balanchine, George	Russian-born American choreographer George Balanchine died in New York, New York, on April 30, 1983, age 79, shortly after working on a revival of *On Your Toes.* • **Last major works:** choreographed a new version of *Mozartiana* (1981) and ballets for *On Your Toes* revival (1983). • **Last movie:** *Baryshnikov at the White House* (TV, 1979).
Castle, Vernon and Irene	English-born dancer Vernon Castle was a World War I pilot. He was killed in a plane crash in Texas, on February 15, 1918, age 30. His wife, American dancer Irene Castle, died in Lake Forest, Illinois, on January 25, 1969, age 75. • **Last movie of Vernon Castle:** *Whirl of Life* (1915, his only film). • **Last movie of Irene Castle:** *Broadway After Dark* (1924). • **Last dance creation of Irene Castle:** *The World's Fair Hop* for the 1939 World's Fair.
Champion, Gower	American director/performer/choreographer Gower Champion died on August 25, 1980, age 59, before *42nd Street,* his last work, opened. • **Last Broadway musical (director, choreographer):** *42nd Street,* opened August 25, 1980. It ran for 3,486 performances and earned for Champion the 1981 Tony Award for Best Choreography and a nomination for best Direction of a Musical. • **Last movie (choreographer):** *The Girl Most Likely* (1957). • **Last movie (actor):** *Sharon, Portrait of a Mistress* (TV, 1977). • **Last film (director):** *Bank Shot* (1974). • **Last film with Marge Champion:** *Three for the Show* (1955).
Coles, Charles ("Honi")	American choreographer/dancer/creative consultant Charles ("Honi") Coles taught dance and dance history at Yale, Cornell, Duke and George Washington University in the 1980s. He died in New York, New York, on November 12, 1992. • **Last choreographic contributions:** 1992, for *Tommy Tune Tonite!* • **Last Broadway performance:** March 3, 1985, *My One and Only,* for which he won the Tony Award as Best Featured Actor in a Musical. The show ran for 767 performances. • **Last danced with partner Charles ("Cholly") Atkins:** 1959.
Danilova, Alexandra	Russian ballerina/teacher/choreographer Alexandra Danilova died in New York, New York, on July 13, 1997, age 93.

	• **Last performance:** December 30, 1951, opposite Frederic Franklin in *Gaîté Parisienne* at the Music Hall in Houston, Texas.
De Mille, Agnes	American choreographer/director Agnes De Mille died in New York, New York, on October 6, 1993, age 88. • **Last choreography for a Broadway musical:** 1980 revival of *Brigadoon.* She also did the musical staging. • **Last Broadway musical as director:** *Come Summer* (1969).
Denishawn Dancers	The Denishawn dance troupe was founded by American dancers Ruth St. Denis and Ted Shawn. St. Denis died in Hollywood, California, on July 21, 1968, age 90. Shawn died in Orlando, Florida, on January 9, 1972, age 80. • **Last choreography by St. Denis for a Broadway show:** *The Light of Asia,* which opened October 9, 1928, at Hampden's Theater. It ran for 23 performances. • **Last surviving member of the original Denishawn company:** Jane Sherman, who toured Asia with Denishawn in 1926. • **Last choreography by Shawn for a Broadway show:** *Doodle Dandy of the U.S.A.,* which opened December 26, 1942, at the Belasco Theater.
Diaghilev, Sergei	Russian ballet impresario Sergei Diaghilev organized the Ballets Russes in 1911. He died in Venice, Italy, on August 19, 1929, age 57. • **Last of Les Ballets Russes de Diaghilev:** disbanded in 1929 with Diaghilev's death. Some of the group reassembled in 1931 as Ballets Russes de Colonel Wassily de Basil. Others in the group emerged as the Ballets Russes de Monte Carlo. The de Basil group disbanded in 1952, a year after the colonel died. Ballets Russes de Monte Carlo lasted until 1962.
Duncan, Isadora	American dancer Isadora Duncan greatly influenced modern dance by emphasizing natural movements and freedom of expression. • **Last performance:** Theatre Mogador in Paris, France, July 1927. Two months later, while in Nice, France, Duncan was strangled when the scarf she was wearing caught in the wheel of her car. She was 50 years old.
Fonteyn, Dame Margot	English prima ballerina Dame Margot Fonteyn died in Panama City, Panama, on February 21, 1991, age 71. • **Last Broadway performance:** November 29, 1975, *Fonteyn & Nureyev on Broadway* at the Uris Theater. • **Last performance of *Marguerite and Armand* with Rudolf Nureyev:** 1977, when Fonteyn was 58.
Fosse, Bob	American director/choreographer/writer Bob Fosse was rehearsing the touring company of *Sweet Charity* when he died on September 23, 1987, age 60. • **Last Broadway production:** *Sweet Charity*, March 15, 1987, at the Minskoff Theater. • **Last Broadway award:** 1986 Tony Award for Best Choreography for *Big Deal*.
Graham, Martha	American choreographer/dancer Martha Graham died on April 1, 1991, age 96. • **Last performance as a dancer:** *Cortege of Eagles* (1970), when she was 76.

	• **Last choreography:** *Maple Leaf Rag* (1990). She was choreographing *The Eye of the Goddess* for the Olympics in Barcelona when she died.
Massine, Léonide	Russian choreographer/dancer/artistic director Léonide Massine died in Cologne, West Germany, on March 15, 1979, age 83. • **Last with Ballets Russes de Monte Carlo:** 1943. • **Last company for whom he choreographed:** Oakland Ballet (California).
Nicholas Brothers	American dancing brothers Harold and Fayard Nicholas dazzled audiences with their breathtaking leaps and sophisticated routines. • **Last Broadway performance together:** *Sammy,* May 4, 1974, at the Uris Theater. • **Last movie together:** *Janet Jackson: The Rhythm Nation Compilation* (1990). • **Last surviving Nicholas Brother:** Fayard. Harold Nicholas died in New York, New York, on July 3, 2000, age 79.
Nijinsky, Vaslav	Russian dancer Vaslav Nijinsky ended his professional ballet career when he was 28. He spent much of the rest of his life in treatment for schizophrenia. He died in England on April 8, 1950, age 60 (or 62). • **Last danced with Diaghilev and Ballets Russes:** September 26, 1917, in Buenos Aires, Argentina. • **Last public performance as a dancer:** 1919, at a benefit before an invited audience at Festsaal in Suvretta-Haus, a hotel in Saint Moritz, Switzerland. His accompanist was pianist Bertha Asseo.
Nureyev, Rudolf	Russian dancer/actor Rudolf Nureyev died in Paris, France, on January 6, 1993, age 54. • **Last Broadway performance:** *Boston Ballet Company*, September 1980, at the Uris Theater. • **Last ballet production:** *The Bayadère,* October 1992, at the Paris Opera. • **Last movie as an actor:** *Exposed* (1983).
Pan, Hermes	American dancer/choreographer Hermes Pan (Panagiotopulos) died in Beverly Hills, California, on September 19, 1990, age 80. He worked on more than 75 films as dance director or choreographer, including all the Astaire-Rogers movies of the 1930s. • **Last movie choreographed for Astaire:** *Finian's Rainbow* (1968). • **Last movie as a choreographer:** *Help Me Dream* (1981).
Pavlova, Anna	Russian dancer Anna Pavlova died in The Hague, Netherlands, on January 23, 1931, age 48. • **Last performance in Russia:** partnered with Anatoly Obuknov, 1914. • **Last performance:** December 1930 at Golder's Green Hippodrome in London. She was scheduled to perform *The Dying Swan* in The Netherlands but died six weeks after her London performance.
Robbins, Jerome	American producer/director/choreographer/performer Jerome Robbins died in New York, New York, on July 29, 1998, age 79. • **Last award for an original Broadway musical:** *Jerome Robbins' Broadway,* which ran from February 1989 to September 1990. He won the 1989 Tony Award for Best Direction of a Musical. • **Last ballet choreographed:** *Brandenburg,* premiered by the New York City Ballet, January 12, 1997.
Step Brothers	The original Step Brothers who formed in 1927 as a tap dance trio were Maceo Anderson, Al Williams and Red Walker. Two years later

	they became a quartet with Sherman Robertson. • **Last surviving original Step Brother:** Maceo Anderson, who died on July 4, 2001, age 90. • **Last surviving Step Brother:** Prince Spencer, who performed with the group for 39 years.
Tudor, Anthony	English dancer/choreographer/teacher Anthony Tudor died on April 16, 1987, age 78. • **Last ballet choreographed for a British company:** *Knight Errant.* • **Last performance:** *Nimbus* (1950).

Entertainers—Theater Performers
Last Performances of Some Major Theatrical Performers
(See also Movies—Performers.)

Performer	Description
Adams, Maude	American actress Maude Adams retired in 1918 but made comebacks in 1931 and 1934. She was chair of the drama department at Stephens College from 1937 to 1943. Adams died in Tannersville, New York, on July 17, 1953, age 80. • **Last Broadway performance:** 1917, *A Kiss for Cinderella* at the Empire Theater. • **Last theatrical performance:** 1934, as Maria in *Twelfth Night.*
Barrymore Family	Actor Maurice Barrymore was born in India as Herbert Blythe. He moved to the U.S. and married Georgiana Emma Drew in 1876. (*See below,* Drew Family.) They were the parents of American actors Lionel, Ethel and John Barrymore. Maurice Barrymore died in Amityville, New York, on March 26, 1905, age 57. • **Last Broadway performance of Maurice Barrymore:** *Becky Sharp,* at the Fifth Avenue Theater. Opened September 12, 1899. • **Last Broadway performance of Ethel Barrymore:** January 13, 1945, *Embezzled Heaven* at the National Theater. • **Last Broadway performance of John Barrymore:** May 18, 1940, *My Dear Children* at the Belasco Theater. • **Last Broadway performance of Lionel Barrymore:** 1925, *Man or Devil,* at the Broadhurst Theater. • **Last theatrical performance of Lionel and John Barrymore together:** February 20, 1920, revival of *The Jest* at the Plymouth Theater.
Bayes, Nora	American actress/singer Nora Bayes died in Brooklyn, New York, on March 19, 1928, age 48. • **Last Broadway performance:** November 11, 1922, *Queen O' Hearts* at George M. Cohan's Theater. She continued to perform in vaudeville until shortly before her death.
Bernhardt, Sarah	French actress Sarah Bernhardt died in Paris, France, on March 26, 1923, age 78. • **Last Broadway performance:** September 15, 1917, *Du Thèâtre au champ d'honneur* at the Knickerbocker Theater. • **Last theatrical performance:** 1922, *La Gloire.* • **Last movie:** *La Voyante* in 1923. Bernhardt was so ill at the time that her hotel room was converted to a film studio so that she could appear. She died before the movie was completed.

Booth Family	English-born American actor Junius Brutus Booth Sr. was the father of ten children, three of whom became popular American actors: Junius Brutus Jr., Edwin and John Wilkes Booth, the assassin of Abraham Lincoln. • **Last theatrical tour of Junius Brutus Booth Sr.:** 1852, to California, where he performed with his sons Edwin and Junius Brutus Jr. He had planned to retire at the end of the tour but fell ill in New Orleans, Louisiana. Booth died on a steamboat en route to an engagement in Cincinnati, Ohio, on November 30, 1852, age 56. • **Last theatrical performances of Junius Brutus Booth Sr.:** November 1852, as Sir Edward Mortimer and John Lump at the Saint Charles Theater in New Orleans. • **Last theatrical performance of Edwin Booth:** April 4, 1891, *Hamlet* at the Brooklyn Academy of Music in New York. He died on June 7 1893, age 59. • **Last Broadway performance of Junius Brutus Booth Jr.:** *Julius Caesar* (1864), a benefit performance at the Winter Garden Theater. Booth was more involved in the theater as a manager than an actor. He died in Manchester, Massachusetts, on September 16, 1883, age 62. • **Last Broadway performance of John Wilkes Booth:** *Julius Caesar* at the Winter Garden . Opened November 25, 1864. • **Last theatrical performance of John Wilkes Booth:** Duke Pescara in *The Apostate* at Ford's in Washington, D.C., on March 18, 1865, just four weeks before he killed President Lincoln. Booth died near Bowling Green, Virginia, while fleeing on April 26, 1865, age 26. (*See also* United States—Presidents.)
Brougham, John	Irish-born American actor John Brougham was also the author of nearly 100 plays. He died in New York, New York, on June 7, 1880, age 66. • **Last theatrical performance:** 1879, *Rescued* at Booth's , New York.
Cushman, Charlotte	American actress Charlotte Saunders Cushman died in Boston, Massachusetts, on February 18, 1876, age 59. Cushman made many farewell performances, beginning in the 1850s. • **Last theatrical tour ended:** November 7, 1874, *Macbeth* at Booth's in New York, New York. • **Last theatrical performance:** May 15, 1875, *Macbeth* at the Globe in Boston. • **Last appearance:** June 2, 1875, as a reader in Easton, Pennsylvania.
Davenport, Fanny	English-born actress Fanny Davenport, who had an American father, grew up in Boston, Massachusetts. She died in South Duxbury, Massachusetts, on September 26, 1898, age 48. • **Last Broadway performance:** 1883, *Fedora,* at the 14th Street . • **Last theatrical performance:** March 1898, *A Soldier of France* at Chicago's Grand Opera House. She died six months later.
Drew Family	Irish actor John Drew married English actress Louisa Lane in 1850. Their children Georgiana and John Drew Jr. were also in the theater. Georgiana Drew married Maurice Barrymore and was the mother of Lionel, Ethel and John. (*See above,* Barrymore Family.) • **Last theatrical performance of John Drew Sr.:** May 9, 1862. He died in Philadelphia, Pennsylvania, on May 21, 1862, age 45. • **Last theatrical performance of Louise Lane Drew:** January 1897, in *The Sporting Duchess.* She died in Larchmont, New York, on August 31,

	1897, age 77. • **Last Broadway performance of John Drew Jr.:** 1927, *Trelawny of the Wells* at the New Amsterdam . Opened January 31, 1927. Closed after 56 performances. He died in San Francisco, California, on July 9, 1927, age 73. • **Last theatrical performance of Georgiana Drew Barrymore:** February 1892 in New York City. She died in Santa Barbara, California, on July 2, 1893, age 38.
Duse, Eleanora	Italian actress Eleanora Duse fell ill with pneumonia while on tour and died in Pittsburgh, Pennsylvania, on April 23, 1924, age 65. • **Last Broadway performance:** December 1923, *Lady from the Sea* at the Metropolitan Opera House. • **Last performance:** April 1924, at the Syrian Mosque in Pittsburgh, Pennsylvania. She became ill while performing and died a few days later.
Fontanne, Lynn and Lunt, Alfred	English-born actress Lynn Fontanne and American actor Alfred Lunt were married in 1922. Over the next half century, they performed in 27 theatrical productions together. Lunt died in Milwaukee, Wisconsin, on August 3, 1977, age 83. Fontanne died in Genesee Depot, Wisconsin, on July 30, 1983, age 95. • **Last theatrical performance together:** November 29, 1958, *The Visit* at the Morosco , New York, New York. • **Last TV performance together:** 1972, *The Magnificent Yankee.*
Forrest, Edwin	American actor Edwin Forrest died in Philadelphia, Pennsylvania, on December 12, 1872, age 66. • **Last Broadway performance:** 1849, *Macbeth* at the Broadway . • **Last theatrical performance:** April 1-2, 1872, *Richelieu* at the Globe , Boston, Massachusetts. Later, in failing health, he attempted to give Shakespearean readings. • **Last reading:** at Tremont Temple, Boston, December 7, 1872. A stroke ended his life within the week.
Gielgud, Sir John	English actor Sir John Gielgud acted on the stage until he was in his 80s. He died in Buckinghamshire, England, on May 21, 2000, age 96. • **Last theatrical performance:** 1988, *Best of Friends* by Hugh Whitemore.
Hayes, Helen	American actress Helen Hayes died in Nyack, New York, on March 17, 1993, age 93. • **Last Broadway performance:** May 2, 1970, *Harvey* at the ANTA Playhouse. • **Last theatrical performance:** 1971, *Long Day's Journey Into Night* in Washington, D.C.
Jefferson, Joseph, III	American actor Joseph Jefferson III died in Palm Beach, Florida, on April 23, 1905, age 76. He was famous for his portrayal of Rip Van Winkle. • **Last film performance as *Rip Van Winkle*:** 1903, a silent, black-and-white movie. He is believed to be the earliest American actor to make a film. • **Last theatrical performance:** May 1904.
Kean, Edmund	English actor Edmund Kean's son was performing with him the night Kean collapsed on stage. He died two months later on May 15, 1833, age 56. • **Last theatrical performance:** March 1833, *Othello* at Covent Garden, London, England.

King, Dennis	Actor/singer Dennis King died in New York, New York, on May 21, 1971, age 73. • **Last Broadway performance in a musical:** June 1956, *Shangri-la* at the Winter Garden . • **Last Broadway performance:** 1969, *A Patriot for Me* at the Imperial .
Lawrence, Gertrude	English actress Gertrude Lawrence died in New York, New York, on September 6, 1952, age 54. • **Last theatrical performance:** 1952, as Anna in *The King and I* at the St. James , New York, New York. She died shortly after she withdrew from the cast because of ill health.
Macready, George	English actor George Macready died in Cheltenham, England, on April 27, 1873, age 80. • **Last performance in U.S. (Astor Place Riot):** May 10, 1849. Macready was appearing at the Astor Place Opera House in New York, New York, before an audience of Edwin Forrest fans. A riot outside the theater, spurred on by Forrest followers, caused the death of 23 people and seriously injured many others. Forrest blamed the magistrates. The poor blamed the rich, the Yankees blamed the Irish, and the newspapers blamed one another. Macready hastily returned to England and never again appeared in the U.S. Macready retired two years later. • **Last theatrical performance:** 1851.
Menken, Adah Isaacs	American actress Adah Isaacs Menken died in Paris, France, August 10, 1868, age 33. • **Last Broadway performance:** 1859, *The French Spy* at Purdy's New National .
Modjeska, Helena	Polish-born actress Helena Modjeska died in East Newport, California, on April 8, 1909, age 68. • **Last Broadway performance:** 1900, *Twelfth Night* at the Fifth Avenue . • **Last theatrical performance:** 1909, *Macbeth* at a benefit in Los Angeles, California for Sicilian earthquake victims, shortly before she died.
Russell, Lillian	American actress/singer Lillian Russell died in Pittsburgh, Pennsylvania, on June 5, 1922, age 60. • **Last Broadway performance:** 1912, *Hokey-Pokey* at the Broadway . She continued to perform in vaudeville until shortly before she died.
Stone, Fred	American actor Fred Stone had a stage career that spanned a half century. He was also a movie actor. • **Last Broadway performance:** 1938, *Lightnin'* at the John Golden Theater. • **Last theatrical performance:** 1945 revival, *You Can't Take It With You.*
Taylor, Laurette	American actress Laurette Taylor died in New York, New York, on December 7, 1946, age 62. • **Last Broadway performance:** August 3, 1946, *The Glass Menagerie* at the Royale Theater.
Terry, Dame Ellen	English actress Dame Ellen Terry died in Kent, England, on July 22, 1928, age 81. • **Last Broadway performance:** 1907, *Captain Brassbound's Conversion* at the Empire Theater. • **Last theatrical performance:** June 1919, *Romeo and Juliet* at the Lyric Theatre in London.

Entertainers—Wild West Showmen—
Cody, William ("Buffalo Bill")

William Frederick ("Buffalo Bill") Cody was a buffalo hunter, Pony Express rider, frontiersman, Union scout during the Civil War, Indian fighter, Congressional Medal of Honor winner, writer and showman.

• **Last official Army duty of Cody:** Indian fighter with the U.S. Army's Fifth Cavalry under Major General Wesley Merritt in July 1876. During that assignment, Cody killed and scalped Cheyenne chief Yellow Hair. Pictures of Cody holding up that scalp and announcing that it was for Custer became one of the classic images of the Old West. Cody spent the last 40 years of his life in show business. He spent 25 of those years with his *Wild West Show.*

• **Last performance of Cody's** *Wild West Show:* July 21, 1913, when it was closed in Denver, Colorado, to pay off Cody's debts. He worked briefly in movies and with a circus before ending his career with *Miller and Arlington's Wild West Show.*

• **Last performance of Cody:** November 4, 1916, in *Miller and Arlington's Wild West Show* at Portsmouth, Virginia. He became ill and left the show. Cody died in Denver, Colorado, two months later, on January 10, 1917, age 71.

• **Last ruling on Cody's Congressional Medal of Honor:** After Cody's death, the Congressional Medal of Honor he had been awarded in 1872 was revoked. The revocation occurred because he was a not a regular member of the armed forces when the award was made. In 1989, the rules were rewritten to allow the Congressional Medal of Honor to be restored to Cody posthumously.

• **Last appearance of Sitting Bull with Buffalo Bill's** *Wild West Show:* 1885. It was also his only appearance. Sitting Bull, a chief of the Hunkpapa Sioux, died in North Dakota on December 15, 1890, age c. 56.

Entertainment—Amusement Parks
Last of Some Major American Amusement Parks

Park Name(s) and Location	Last Used	Description
Atlantic Beach Amusement Park (Bay View Park; Joyland Park) Atlantic Highlands, New Jersey	1940	Opened 1914. Closed at the end of the 1940 season. Sold to an investment company. Now the site of single-family homes.
Bay Shore Park Baltimore County, Maryland	1947	Built in 1906 by the United Railways and Electric Company. Land is now occupied by North Point State Park.
Brandywine Springs Amusement Park Faulkland, Delaware	1923	Opened in 1886 near Wilmington, Delaware. Now a suburban neighborhood.
Buckroe Beach Amusement Park Hampton, Virginia	1985	Opened in 1897. The park's carousel, made by the Philadelphia Toboggan Company, was purchased by the city of Hampton and is now a Virginia Historic Landmark.
Busch Gardens Van Nuys, California	1978	Opened 1966 as a tropical theme park and bird preserve near the Anheuser-Busch brewery. Closed to make room for brewery expansion.
Celoron Amusement Park Jamestown, New York	1962	Opened in 1893. The Greyhound roller coaster and Ferris wheel were damaged in a tornado in 1959.
Dogpatch USA Dogpatch (Marble Falls), Arkansas	1993	Opened in 1968. Based on the *Li'l Abner* comic strip. The town of Dogpatch changed its name back to Marble Falls in 1997.

Dreamland Park Coney Island, New York	1911	Opened in 1904. The Dreamland Tower, a popular attraction, was 375 feet and covered with 100,000 electric lights. The park and the tower were destroyed in a fire in May 1911 just before opening day.
Euclid Beach Park on the shore of Lake Erie, Cleveland, Ohio	1969	Incorporated in 1895. The only remaining park feature: carved archway entrance. It was declared a Cleveland historic landmark in 1973.
Freedomland Bronx, New York	1964	Opened 1960. Depicted New York in the late 19th century. Reenacted Chicago Fire, San Francisco in 1906. Torn down. Apartment complex built on the site.
Glendale Park **(Woodstock Park)** Nashville, Tennessee	1932	Opened in 1887 as Woodstock Park. Name changed to Glendale Park in 1890. Closed during the Great Depression.
Idora Park **(Terminal Park)** Youngstown, Ohio	1984	Opened in 1898. Closed after a fire destroyed several rides. Most of the rides that remained have gradually disappeared. The ballroom burned in 2001.
Legend City Phoenix, Arizona	1983	Opened in 1963. Land sold to Salt River Project for an office park.
Luna Park Coney Island, New York	1944	Opened in 1903. Fire destroyed the roller coaster before the 1944 season began. Another fire on August 12, 1944, destroyed much of the rest of the park. The land was sold in 1946. A housing development now occupies the site.
Marineland Palos Verdes, California	1987	Opened in 1954. Sold to the owners of Sea World. The animals were placed in Sea World parks.
Oakwood Park **(Lake View Park; Casino Park)** Kalamazoo, Michigan	1925	Opened in 1893 as Lake View Park. Renamed Casino Park in 1904. Renamed Oakwood Park after it was torn down and rebuilt in 1907. Park property was sold and subdivided into a residential neighborhood named Parkdale.
Ocean Park Million Dollar Pier Santa Monica, California	1912	Opened in 1911. Destroyed by fire on September 4, 1912.
Ocean View Park Norfolk, Virginia	1978	Opened in 1929. Demolition of the park was shown in the movie *Death of Ocean View Park* (1979). The Rocket roller coaster was featured in the movie *Rollercoaster* (1977).
Olentangy Park **(Villa Park)** Columbus Ohio	1937	Opened in 1893 as Villa Park. Renamed Olentangy Park in 1896. Land was sold in 1938 and became Olentangy Village, an apartment complex. Only the park's swimming pool remains in the Village.
Pacific Ocean Park Santa Monica, California	1967	Opened in 1958 by CBS and the Los Angeles Turf Club at the Ocean Park Pier. Changed ownership several times. Bankrupt in 1967. Hit by several fires. Demolished in 1973-74.

Palisades Amusement Park Cliffside Park, New Jersey	1971	Opened in 1898. Torn down to make room for condominiums. Many of the rides were sold to other parks.
Riverside Park Hutchinson, Kansas	1930s	Opened in 1888. The land is now part of Carey Park.
Riverview Beach Amusement Park (Riverview Beach) Pennsville, New Jersey	1967	Opened in the late 19th century as Silver Grove picnic ground. Became Riverview Beach in 1914, and Riverview Beach Amusement Park in 1922. Roller coaster and Old Mill destroyed by fire in 1966. Rides were removed at end of the 1967 season. A picnic area remains.
Riverview Park Chicago, Illinois	1967	Opened in 1904. Increased operating expenses plus the high value of the land led to its closing. The park was sold to a developer.
Rockaway's Playland Rockaway Beach, New York	1986	Opened in 1901 as Thompson's Amusement Park. High insurance premiums and a changing neighborhood led to its closure in 1986. The park was bulldozed in 1987.
Steeplechase Park Coney Island, New York	1964	Opened in 1897. Closed permanently on October 20, 1964. Steeplechase was the last of Coney Island's three large amusement parks to close. (Luna and Dreamland were destroyed by fire.)
Whitney's Playland-at-the-Beach San Francisco, California	1972	Opened in 1928. Park was demolished. Condominiums now occupy the site.
Willow Grove Park Willow Grove, Pennsylvania	1976	Opened in 1896. Music Pavilion where Sousa once played was demolished in 1956. Six Gun Territory operated at the park in the 1970s. It closed in 1976. A mall now occupies the site.

Entertainment—Amusement Parks—Disneyland

Disneyland opened in Anaheim, near Los Angeles, California, in July 1955. The park was the fulfillment of the dream of its creator, Walt Disney.

• **Last surviving original employee:** Bob Penfield, who retired on July 31, 1997, after 42 years of service. He began working at Disneyland as a ride operator on the King Arthur Carousel in Fantasyland, four days before the park opened. He retired as construction field superintendent. A Main Street Store window was inscribed with his name at retirement.

Entertainment—Amusements Parks—Rides—Over-the-Jumps

The motion of the Over-the-Jumps is similar to today's Himalaya rides, in which wooden horses and chariots travel over an undulating track.

• **Last remaining Over-the-Jumps ride in the U.S.:** Little Rock, Arkansas. It was manufactured in mid-1920s by Spillman Engineering of North Tononwanda, New York. It operated originally as a traveling carnival attraction before being placed at Little Rock's War Memorial in 1942. Friends of the Carousel was formed in 1991 to purchase the ride, restore it and place it back into operation.

Entertainment—Amusement Parks—Rides—Roller Coasters

John A. Miller was famous for his innovative roller coaster designs. He died on June 24, 1941, age 66, while in Houston, Texas, designing a roller coaster for that city.

• **Last remaining "Twister-style" ride in**

the U.S. designed by John Miller: The Thunderbolt at Coney Island, shut down in 1983. It was torn down by the city of New York on November 17, 2000.

• **Last remaining Prior & Church "Bobs-style" ride in the U.S.:** The Giant Dipper at Belmont Park/Mission Beach in San Diego, California, that opened on July 4, 1925. The park closed in 1976. The Giant Dipper was later restored and reopened to the public in 1990.

• **Last remaining Side-Friction Figure Eight ride in the U.S.:** Leap-The-Dips roller coaster at Lakemont Park, Pennsylvania. It is also the oldest standing roller coaster in the world. Leap-The-Dips was built in 1902 by E. Joy Morris to replace the Gravity Railroad that burned down in 1901.

Entertainment—Amusement Parks—Side Shows—Banner Artist

Side Show Banners are the large, succinctly worded, boldly colored, exaggerated streamers that aim to lure fair-goers into spending money to see a side-show attraction. Sideshow banner painting is now a dying art.

• **Last master practitioner of side-show banner painting:** Johnny Meah, of Connecticut. He also augments his income sideshow lecturing, fire eating and sword swallowing.

Entertainment—Amusement Parks—Side Shows—10-in-1

The 10-in-1 Side Show is an attraction that features ten acts, one after another.

• **Last remaining 10-in-1 side show:** Sideshows by the Seashore, which was opened in 1985 by Coney Island USA, of Brooklyn, New York. The attraction is billed as the only "10-in-1" side show operating in North America.

Entertainment—Amusement Parks—Signs—"Fun Face"

The Tilyou-style Fun Face image got its start in 1897 with Coney Island's Steeplechase Park and became synonymous with it. The Coney Island Fun Faces were all destroyed, but the style endures in one place.

• **Last remaining Tilyou-style Fun Face:**

"Tillie," which once adorned the wall of the Palace Amusements building in Asbury Park, New Jersey. It is now awaiting installation as part of a hotel that will occupy the same site.

Entertainment—Beauty Pageants—Miss America

The first Miss America pageant was held in Atlantic City, New Jersey, after Labor Day in 1921. It was staged by local businessmen to attract visitors to the resort city after the summer vacation season ended.

• **Last surviving member of the original 1921 Miss America pageant committee:** Harry L. Godshall.

• **Last year married women and women with children competed in the pageant:** 1923. Pageant officials never intended to allow married women or women with children to compete; however, in 1923, three married women entered the pageant, one with an infant child. Rules were amended to specifically state "no one married, or having been married, and no one having a child" would be eligible for the competition. Future married contestants who slipped into the pageant, such as 1933's Miss Arkansas were disqualified.

• **Last year Miss America could marry during her reign as Miss America:** 1949, during the reign of Jacque Mercer. The rules were amended so that Miss America could not longer remain Miss America if she married during the year she held the title.

• **Last year Miss America could hold the title more than once:** 1923. That year Mary Katherine Campbell won for the second year in a row. The rules were amended so that no one could hold the title more than once.

• **Last year the pageant was held without a talent competition:** 1934. The talent portion was begun in 1935 at the insistence of Executive Director Lenora Slaughter.

• **Last year the winner was not officially known as "Miss America":** 1939. Although the term Miss America was unofficially coined in 1921 by Herb Test—an *Atlantic City Daily Press* reporter who was hired to do publicity for the original contest—it was not officially adopted by pageant officials until 1940. The original official name for the contest was the National Beauty Tournament.

• **Last Miss America crowned in the Atlantic City Boardwalk's Steel Pier Marine Ballroom:** Patricia Donnelly in 1939. In 1940, the pageant moved to the Atlantic City Convention Center. During World War II, the U.S. Army used the Convention Center, and the pageant was moved elsewhere. Jo-Carroll Dennison, the winner in 1942, was crowned in New York City, the last and only winner crowned outside Atlantic City. The remaining wartime pageants were held at the Warner Theater in Atlantic City.

• **Last year Miss America was not a scholarship competition:** 1944. The first scholarship ($5,000) was awarded to Bess Myerson in 1945. Ironically, Myerson was the first college graduate to win the crown.

• **Last Miss America who represented a city rather than a state:** Miss Memphis, Barbara Jo Walker, who won the Miss America crown in 1947. She was also the last winner who was crowned while wearing a swimsuit.

• **Last winner not crowned on TV:** Evelyn Ay in 1954. Since 1955, the pageant has been televised. Lee Meriwether, in 1955, was the first Miss America to be crowned on TV.

• **Last year the Miss America contest was not telecast in color:** 1965.

• **Last year Miss Congeniality award was given out:** 1974. The award, which featured a $1,000 scholarship and was voted on by the contestants, was cancelled because pageant officials thought the prize was turning into a popularity contest.

• **Last year Bert Parks hosted the Miss America Pageant:** 1979. The following year, Parks was replaced by Ron Ely, who last hosted the pageant in 1982. Bert Parks died in La Jolla, California, on February 2, 1992, age 87.

• **Last year Miss America contestants did not have to support a social platform:** 1988. In 1989, platform programs were instituted to focus on the achievements of the contestants.

Entertainment—Beauty Pageants—Miss Canada

Women's groups in Canada succeeded in bringing about the elimination of the Miss Canada Pageant after 1991, by protesting because it was degrading to women.

• **Last Miss Canada:** Nicole Dunsdon, who completed her reign in October 1992.

Entertainment—Circuses—Big Top

The circus tent has been a common feature of circuses since the early 19th century. None was more memorable than the Big Top of Ringling Brothers and Barnum & Bailey Circus.

• **Last use of the Big Top by Ringling Brothers and Barnum & Bailey Circus:** July 16, 1956, while performing in Pittsburgh, Pennsylvania. The circus took down its Big Top for the last time and cut short its summer tour. The circus had been sold and the new owner decided to limit shows to indoor arenas.

Entertainment—Circuses—Jumbo

Circus owner P.T. Barnum purchased the gigantic elephant Jumbo from London's Royal Zoological Gardens to perform in his circus. Jumbo arrived in the United States in 1882 and gave the English language a new word for *big*.

• **End of Jumbo's circus career:** September 16, 1885, when he was killed by a freight train on the Grand Trunk Railway in St. Thomas, Ontario, Canada, as he was being led across the tracks. P.T. Barnum had Jumbo stuffed. His skeleton was sent to the American Museum of Natural History. His heart went to Cornell University. Jumbo's mounted stuffed hide went to Barnum Hall, Tufts University, Medford, Massachusetts.

• **Last of stuffed Jumbo:** April 14, 1975, when a fire in Barnum Hall destroyed Jumbo's remains. After the fire, a Tufts employee collected some of Jumbo's ashes in a peanut butter jar. It now is in the athletic department, where it has become a good luck symbol for Tufts athletes who rub the jar before games.

Entertainment—Theater—Broadway Performances
Last Performance of Long-running Shows
(1,500+ performances, original production.)

Title	Opened	Last Performance	Number of Performances
Abie's Irish Rose	May 23, 1922	October 1, 1927	2,327
Ain't Misbehavin'	May 9, 1978	February 21, 1982	1,565
Annie	April 21, 1977	January 2, 1983	2,377
Barefoot in the Park	October 23, 1963	June 25, 1967	1,530
Best Little Whorehouse in Texas, The	June 19, 1978	March 27, 1982	1,629
Born Yesterday	February 4, 1946	December 31, 1949	1,642
Cats	October 7, 1982	September 10, 2000	7,485
Chorus Line, A	July 25, 1975	April 28, 1990	6,137
Crazy For You	February 19, 1992	January 7, 1996	1,622
Dancin'	March 27, 1978	June 27, 1982	1,774
Deathtrap	February 26, 1978	June 13, 1982	1,793
Dream Girls	December 20, 1981	August 11, 1985	1,522
Evita	September 25, 1979	June 26, 1983	1,568
Fantastiks, The	May 3, 1960	January 13, 2002	17,172
Fiddler on the Roof	September 22, 1964	July 2, 1972	3,242
42nd Street	August 25, 1980	January 8, 1989	3,486
Gemini	May 21, 1977	September 6, 1981	1,819
Grease	February 14, 1972	April 13, 1980	3,388
Hair	April 29, 1968	July 1, 1972	1,750
Harvey	November 1, 1944	January 15, 1949	1,775
Hello, Dolly!	January 16, 1964	December 27, 1970	2,844
Jekyll & Hyde	April 28, 1997	January 7, 2001	1,543
La Cage aux Folles	August 21,1983	November 15, 1987	1,761
Les Misérables	March 12, 1987	May 18, 2003	6,680
Life with Father	November 8, 1939	July 12, 1947	3,224
Magic Show, The	May 28, 1974	December 31, 1978	1,920
Mame	May 24, 1966	January 3, 1970	1,508
Man of La Mancha	November 22, 1965	June 26, 1971	2,328
Mary, Mary	March 8, 1961	December 12, 1964	1,572
Miss Saigon	April 11, 1991	January 28, 2001	4,092
My Fair Lady	March 15, 1956	September 29, 1962	2,717
Oh! Calcutta!	September 24, 1976	August 6, 1989	5,959
Oklahoma!	March 31, 1943	May 29, 1948	2,212
Pippin	October 23, 1972	June 12, 1977	1,944
Smokey Joe's Café	March 2, 1995	January 16, 2000	2,036
South Pacific	April 7, 1949	January 16, 1954	1,925
Tobacco Road	December 4, 1933	May 31, 1941	3,182
Voice of the Turtle, The	December 8, 1943	January 3, 1948	1,557
Wiz, The	January 5, 1975	January 28, 1979	1,672

Notable Last Facts

Entertainment—
Theaters—London, England

Entertainment—Theaters—London—Blackfriars Theatre

Two theaters named Blackfriars Theatre used the old Dominican Black Friars' monastery between Ludgate Hill and the Thames in London, England. The first Blackfriars Theatre was used between 1576 and 1584. The second theater operated on the site from 1596 to 1642.
• **Last of the second Blackfriars Theatre:** dismantled in 1655. The site was later occupied by the *London Times*.

Entertainment—Theaters—London—Drury Lane Theaters

Several old theaters have occupied Drury Lane in London, England. The first, known as Theatre Royal, opened in 1663.
• **Last of Theatre Royal (Drury Lane):** destroyed by fire in 1672; replaced in 1674 by a building designed by Christopher Wren.
• **Last of Wren's theater:** demolished in 1791. A third building opened in 1794 and burned down in 1809. A new Drury Lane Theatre was built in 1812. This building, the fourth to occupy the site since 1663, is still standing.

Entertainment—Theaters—London—Globe Theatre

When the Globe Theatre was built in 1599 just outside London, it was England's first permanent playhouse. Many of Shakespeare's plays were first performed there.
• **Last of the original Globe Theatre:** destroyed by fire on June 29, 1613, during a performance of Shakespeare's *King Henry the Eighth*. The theater was rebuilt but torn down in 1644 by the owners of the land on which it stood. Houses were built on the site. A new Globe Theatre opened on the South Bank on August 21, 1996. It is a replica of the earlier Globe.

Entertainment—Theaters—London—Theatre Royal Covent Garden

Theatre Royal opened in London, England, in 1732. Before the site held a theater, it was the garden of the Abbey of Saint Peter, Westminster.
• **Last of the original Theatre Royal:** damaged by fire in 1808. The theater was rebuilt the following year. The building was destroyed by a second fire in 1856. The third theater was built on the site two years later, in 1858. In 1892, it was renamed Covent Garden—the Royal Opera House. (Covent is a contraction of the word "convent.")

Entertainment—Theaters—New York, New York,
Last of Some Major Theaters
(Note: Theaters are listed by their original names.)

Theater Name and Address	Last Stood	Description
Abbey's Theater 1396 Broadway (38th Street)	1930	Built in 1893. Renamed Knickerbocker Theater (1896). Demolished to make room for buildings in the garment district.
Academy of Music 126 East 14th Street	1926	Built in 1854. Burned in 1866, then rebuilt. Demolished to make room for the ConEd building.
Astor Place Opera House Broadway	1852 (theater) 1890 (building)	Built in 1847. Scene of Macready-Forrest riot in 1849. Opera house closed 1852. Building renamed Clinton Hall. Became home of Mercantile Library of New York in 1854. Demolished in 1890. New Clinton Hall built on site. Library moved to East 47th Street in 1932.

Astor Theater Broadway at 45th Street	1982	Built in 1906. Demolished along with the Helen Hayes, Victoria (Gaiety), Bijou and Morosco theaters to make room for the Marriott Marquis Hotel.
Banyard's Museum 1211 Broadway	1920	Opened in 1867. Renamed Wood's Museum (1868), Metropolitan Theater (c. 1870), Broadway Theater (1876) and Daly's Theater (1879). Demolished.
Bijou Theater 209 West 45th Street	1982	Built 1917. Closed 1936-43 and 1959-62. Renamed D. W. Griffith Theater (1962), Toho Cinema (1963) and Bijou (1965). Demolished along with Morosco, Astor, Victoria (Gaiety) and Helen Hayes theaters to make room for the Marriott Marquis Hotel.
Bryant Theater 223 West 42nd Street	1996	Built in 1910. Renamed Apollo (1920), New Apollo (1978); and Academy Theater (1983). Demolished along with Lyric Theater to clear space for Ford Center for the Performing Arts.
Casino Theater Broadway at 39th Street	1930	Built in 1882. Damaged by fire and rebuilt in 1905. Demolished to make room for buildings in the garment district.
Central Theater 1567 Broadway (47th Street)	1998	Built in 1918. Renamed Columbia Theater (1934), Central Theater (1934), Gotham Theater (1944), Holiday Theater (1951), Odeon Theater (1958), Forum Theater (1965), Forum 47th Street Theater (1975) and Movieland (1980). Demolished.
Comedy Theater 108 West 41st Street	1942	Built in 1909. Renamed Mercury Theater (1937) and Artef (1940). Demolished.
Earl Carroll Theater 753 Seventh Avenue	1930 1990	Built in 1922. Demolished 1930. New building opened as New Earl Carroll Theater in 1931. Renamed Casino Theater (1932) by Ziegfeld. Changed to a cabaret and renamed French Casino (1933). Renamed Casa Manana (1936) by Billy Rose. Building closed in 1939 and converted to a Woolworth store. Demolished 1990.
Edyth Totten Theater 247 West 48th Street	1988	Built in 1926. Renamed President (1929), Hindenburg (1932), Caruso Cinema (1933), Midget Theater (1933), President (1934), Artef Theater (1934), Acme Theater (1937), American Show Shop (1937), Show Shop (1938), 48th Street Theater (1938), President (1943) and Erwin Piscator's Dramatic Workshop (1953). Closed in 1956. Building sold to Mamma Leone's (restaurant) and demolished.
Empire Theater Broadway at 40th Street	1953	Built in 1893. Demolished.
Fifth Avenue Opera House 24th Street (5th and Madison Avenues)	1873	Built in 1865 and used by Christy Minstrels. Renamed Brougham's Theater (1868) and Daly's Fifth Avenue Theater (1869). Burned in 1873.

Folies Bergere 210 West 46th Street	1982	Built in 1911. Closed a few months later. Re-opened as Fulton Theater. Renamed Helen Hayes Theater (1955). Demolished along with the Astor, Victoria (Gaiety), Bijou and Morosco theaters to make room for Marriott Marquis Hotel. When the Helen Hayes Theater was demolished, the Little Theater on West 44th Street was renamed for her.
Forty-Eighth Street Theater 157 West 48th Street	1955	Built in 1912. Became a movie house as the Windsor (1937). Renamed 48th Street Theater (1943). Demolished after building sustained heavy damage when a water tower on the roof broke.
Forty-Ninth Street Theater 235 West 49th Street	1940	Built in 1921. Closed in 1938. Reopened as Cinema 49. Demolished.
Gaiety Theater Broadway at 46th Street	1982	Built in 1908. Renamed Victoria (1942) and Embassy Five (1982). Demolished along with the Astor, Bijou, Helen Hayes and Morosco theaters to make room for Marriott Marquis Hotel.
George M. Cohan's Theater Broadway at 43rd Street	1938	Built in 1911. Demolished. Retail stores built on site.
Hammerstein's Lyric Theater Between 44th and 45th Streets	1935	Built in 1895. Renamed Criterion (1899), Vitagraph (1914) and back to Criterion (1916). Demolished.
Hammerstein's Victoria Theater Broadway and 44th Street	1935	Opened in 1895. Closed in 1915. Demolished.
Hippodrome Sixth Avenue between 43rd and 44th Streets	1939	Built in 1905 with a seating capacity of 5,200 people. Took up an entire city block and at one time was the largest theater in New York. Famous for staging spectacular events with animals, many performers and opulent sets. Purchased by RKO (1925). Vacant for five years after RKO sold the property in 1929. Closed permanently in 1936 after presenting Billy Rose's *Jumbo*. Demolished three years later.
Klaw Theater 251 West 45th Street	1954	Built in 1921. Renamed the Avon (1928) and CBS Radio Playhouse No. 2 (1934). Demolished.
Lew M. Fields Theater 254 West 42nd Street	1997	Built in 1904 by Oscar Hammerstein I and Lew Fields. Renamed The Harris (1911), Frazee (1920), Wallack's (1924) and Anco Cinema (1940). Demolished.
Lyceum Theater Fourth Avenue between 23rd and 24th Streets	1902	Built in 1885. The Lyceum was the first theater to use electric lighting throughout the building. Thomas Edison supervised the installation. Demolished to make room for Met Life building.
Lyric Theater 213 West 42th Street	1996	Built in 1903. Demolished along with Academy Theater to clear space for Ford Center for the Performing Arts. Façade remains intact.
Madison Square Garden	1968	Built in 1925. Demolished.

Eighth Avenue at 50th Street		
Madison Square Roof Garden 22 East 27th Street	1925	Built in 1890. Demolished. New York Life Insurance Company erected a skyscraper on the site.
Majestic Theater 5 Columbus Circle	1954	Built in 1903. Renamed Park Theater (1911), Minsky's Park Music Hall (1922), Cosmopolitan Theater (1923), Theater of Young America (1934), Park Theater (1935), International Theater (1944), Columbus Circle (1945) and International Theater (1945). Used by NBC as a television studio (1949-54). Demolished.
Maxine Elliott's Theater 109 West 39th Street	1960	Built in 1908. Used in the 1940s by CBS as a radio and television studio. Demolished. A skyscraper was built on the site.
Metropolitan Opera House Broadway at 39th Street	1966	Opened 1883 as the New Opera House. Renamed Metropolitan Opera House (1890). Auditorium destroyed by fire on August 27, 1892, and rebuilt. In 1966, the Metropolitan Opera moved to the Lincoln Center complex. The old building was demolished. • **Last performance:** gala concert, April 16, 1966.
Morosco Theater 217 West 45th Street	1982	Built in 1917. Demolished along with the Astor, Bijou, Victoria (Gaiety) and Helen Hayes theaters to make way for the Marriott Marquis Hotel.
Niblo's Garden and Theater Broadway and Prince Street	1895	Built in 1827. Destroyed in fires in 1846 and 1872 and rebuilt. Demolished and replaced with an office building.
Norworth Theater 125 West 48th Street	1951	Built in 1918. Renamed Belmont Theater (1918), Theatre Parisien (1919) and Belmont Theater again (1920). Demolished.
Olympia Theater Roof Garden 1514 Broadway (44th Street)	1935	Built in 1895 as part of Hammerstein's entertainment complex. Also known as Winter Garden Theater. Renamed Cherry Blossom Grove (1900), New York Roof (1905) and Jardin de Paris (1907). Demolished.
Playhouse Theater 137 West 48th Street	1969	Built in 1911. Used as ABC Studios (1949-52). Demolished. McGraw-Hill Building is now on the site.
Punch & Judy Theater 153 West 49th Street	1987	Built in 1914. Renamed Charles Hopkins Theater (1926), Westminster Cinema (1934), World Theater (1935) and Embassy 49th Street Theater (1982). Demolished.
RKO Roxy Theater Sixth Avenue and 49th Street	1954	Built in 1932. Renamed RKO Center (1933) and Center Theater (1934). Used as NBC studios (1950-54). Demolished to make room for an office building.
Roxy Theater Seventh Avenue and 50th Street	1961	Built in 1927. One of the city's largest theaters, with seating for more than 6,000. Demolished. Office building now on the site.
Tripler Hall 624 Broadway	1867	Built in 1850. Renamed Jenny Lind Hall (1850) and Metropolitan Hall (1851). Burned in 1854.

		Rebuilt as Laura Keene's Variety House. Renamed Burton's New Theater (1856) and Winter Garden Theater (1859). Burned again in 1867. Demolished.
Union Square Theater 58 East 14th Street	1936	Built in 1870. Burned in 1888 and rebuilt. Renamed Acme Theater (1921). Demolished.
Vanderbilt Theater 148 West 43rd Street	1954	Built in 1918. Used as radio studio by NBC and ABC (1939-52). Demolished to make room for parking garage.
Victoria Theater Seventh Avenue and 42nd Street	1935	Built 1899. Renamed Rialto Theater (1916). Demolished. A complex of offices, stores and a theater was built on the site..
Waldorf Theater 116 West 50th Street	1968	Built in 1926. Demolished to make room for the Exxon Building at Rockefeller Center.
Weber & Fields' Music Hall 216 West 44th Street	1945	Built in 1912. Renamed Forty-Fourth Street Theater (1913). Demolished to make room for Times Building.
Ziegfeld Theater Sixth Avenue at 54th Street.	1966	Built in 1927. Used as NBC television studio (1955-63). Demolished to make room for a skyscraper.

Environment

Environment—Adrin and Dieldrin
The Environmental Protection Agency ordered a halt to the production of the pesticides Adrin and Dieldrin because they posed a hazard of cancer and other illnesses.
• **Last production of Adrin and Dieldrin:** August 1974.

Environment—DDT
DDT was first used during World War II as an insecticide to control mosquitoes and lice that carry malaria and typhus. It was widely used after the war. Meanwhile, evidence accumulated showing DDT was harmful to the environment and to humans. In November 1969, the U.S. Secretary of Health, Education and Welfare announced the federal government would phase out DDT over the next two years.
• **Last widespread use of DDT in the U.S.:** December 31, 1972, when the Environmental Protection Agency put a near-total ban it. The only crops the pesticide was used on after the ban date were onions, green peppers and sweet potatoes. DDT is still used elsewhere in the world.

Environment—Fluorocarbon Propellants
In 1977, the FDA announced it would require warning labels on aerosol containers using fluorocarbon as a first step toward the eventual elimination of the non-essential use of such propellants.
• **Last use of nonessential fluorocarbon-propelled aerosols in the United States:** banned as of October 15, 1978.

Environment—Gasoline, Leaded
The lead that was added to gasoline to enhance its performance was found to be a source of air pollution. Beginning in 1975, cars were produced with catalytic converters that required lead-free fuel.
• **Last use of leaded gasoline in the U.S.:** January 1, 1996, when leaded gasoline was banned by the Clean Air Act. By then only a small amount of lead was still being used.

Environment—Ocean Dumping of Hazardous Materials
Pollution of the ocean and its impact on humans, marine life and the environment led to federal legislation.
• **Last time ocean dumping of hazardous materials was allowed:** 1972. That year the

Marine Protection, Research and Sanctuaries Act banned the dumping of biological, chemical and radiological warfare agents and high-level radioactive wastes.

Environment—*Rainbow Warrior* (original)

The ship *Rainbow Warrior* was owned by Greenpeace, an international environmental and antinuclear organization.
- **Last of the original *Rainbow Warrior*:** sustained heavy damage on July 10, 1985, while anchored in Auckland, New Zealand. The ship was in the region to protest French nuclear tests in the South Pacific. French agents were blamed for two explosions. A photographer was killed in the second blast. The ship was so badly damaged it could not be repaired. It was scuttled at sea. A new *Rainbow Warrior* was launched in 1987.

Explorers and Expeditions

Explorers and Expeditions—Amundsen, Nobile and the *Italia*

General Umberto Nobile's airship *Italia* reached the North Pole on May 24, 1928, with a crew of 16. On the way back to Spitsbergen, Norway, the *Italia* crashed. The gondola, carrying six crew members, separated and drifted away. Nobile was rescued on June 23. Eight other survivors were rescued by a search party in July.
- **Last contact with Amundsen:** Norwegian polar explorer Roald Amundsen headed a rescue party to search for Nobile and his crew. Amundsen was last seen on June 18, 1928, the day his plane left Tromso, Norway. The search for Amundsen was called off in August. He was 56.
- **Last survivor of the *Italia* expedition:** Guilio Bich, who was a member of the search party sent to find Nobile. Bich, who later worked as an alpine guide, died in Cervinia, Italy, in February 2003, age 95.

Explorers and Expeditions—Andrée, Salomon August

Swedish explorer Salomon August Andrée and two companions left Spitsbergen, Norway, in a hot air balloon on July 11, 1897, headed for the North Pole. They were never seen again alive.
- **Last word received from Andrée:** July 13, 1897, a message delivered by carrier pigeon to a ship near Spitsbergen.
- **Last of the Andrée expedition:** On August 6, 1930, the remains of Andrée and one of his companions were found on White Island. Andrée's diary found beside him indicated they died after October 2, 1897.

Explorers and Expeditions—Byrd, Admiral Richard E.

American polar explorer Admiral Richard E. Byrd was the first man to fly over the South Pole.
- **Last expedition by Byrd to Antarctica:** in 1955-56. It was his fifth expedition. Byrd died in Boston, Massachusetts, on March 11, 1957, age 69.
- **Last survivor of the 1928-30 Byrd expedition:** Norman Vaughn, who was lead dog driver. Vaughan was interviewed in 2002, when he was 96 and living in Alaska.

Explorers and Expeditions—*Challenger* Oceanographic Expedition

The steamship HMS *Challenger* left England in December 1872. It circumnavigated the world and covered more than 68,000 nautical miles. The expedition was the first conducted primarily to study the ocean for scientific purposes. Its findings filled 50 volumes, published between 1886 and 1895.
- **End of the *Challenger* expedition:** May 1876, when the ship returned to England.

Explorers and Expeditions—Columbus, Christopher

Christopher Columbus made four voyages to the Western Hemisphere, beginning in 1492.
- **Last voyage of Columbus:** his fourth, which began in 1502 and ended on November 7, 1504. Columbus made the journey with four ships and 150 men. He believed that if he sailed farther west this time, he would reach Asia. He explored the coasts of what are today the nations of Honduras,

Nicaragua, Costa Rica and Panama. Until his death, Columbus was convinced he had reached the Far East. When he died in Valladolid, Spain, on May 20, 1506, at around age 55, he was a poor, forgotten man whose exploits were largely unknown by his contemporaries. The significance of his voyages would not be recognized until many years after his death.

• **Last of the *Niña, Pinta* and *Santa Maria***: *Niña* accompanied Columbus on his first two voyages. In June 1495, on the second voyage, she was the only one of his ships to survive a hurricane in the Caribbean. After *Niña* returned to Spain in 1496, she was captured by pirates then recaptured. In 1498, she sailed to Hispaniola as advance guard for Columbus's third voyage. The last written record of *Niña* was in 1501, along the Pearl Coast (Panama). Nothing is known of her history after that time.

Pinta was the smallest of the three ships Columbus used on his first voyage to the Western Hemisphere. *Pinta* left with *Niña* to return to Spain in 1493, but the two ships were separated in a storm. *Pinta* made the voyage back across the Atlantic safely and arrived in Spain just a few hours after the *Niña,* which was carrying Columbus. Nothing is known of her fate after that.

Santa Maria, Columbus's flagship, was wrecked when she was grounded on a coral reef off the coast of Hispaniola on Christmas Day in 1492. The crew salvaged everything they could, including the timber, which they used to built a fort.

Explorers and Expeditions—Cook, James

British naval officer and explorer James Cook's third voyage of exploration was his last. He left England in July 1776 for the Pacific.

• **Last major discovery of Cook:** Hawaiian Islands in January 1778. Cook named them the Sandwich Islands. He later sailed along the Pacific coast of North America, searching for the Northwest Passage, a water route between the Atlantic and Pacific oceans via the Arctic. Cook returned to Hawaii later in the year.

• **Last of Cook:** killed on February 14, 1779, by natives in a dispute over the theft of a boat at Kealakekua Bay on the west coast of the island of Hawaii. He was buried at sea by his men.

Explorers and Expeditions—De Long Expedition

American naval officer Lieutenant Commander George Washington De Long and his expedition left San Francisco, California, for the North Pole in July 1879 on the steamer *Jeannette*. In September, the ship became trapped in an ice pack and remained there until June 1881, when it was crushed. The crew set out for the coast of Siberia on three of the ship's boats. They probably reached the mouth of the Lena River around October 1881.

• **Last of the De Long expedition:** a search party found the bodies of De Long and the others and their records in the Siberian tundra on March 23, 1882. The bodies of De Long and his 11 companions were brought to New York, where they were buried in February 1884. Remains of the *Jeannette* were discovered near Julianehaab along the southwestern coast of Greenland in 1884.

• **Last entry in De Long's journal:** October 30, 1881.

Explorers and Expeditions—De Soto, Hernando

Spanish explorer Hernando DeSoto arrived in Florida in 1539 to begin his exploration of what would someday be the southwestern United States. He became ill while he and his men were exploring the Mississippi River. They encamped along the river in Louisiana.

• **Last resting place of DeSoto:** the Mississippi River. The ailing De Soto asked his men to select a new leader. He died the next day, May 21, 1542, and his body was buried at the main entrance to the camp. His men feared the local natives might try to dig up and desecrate his body, so they disinterred his casket and placed it in the middle of the river.

Explorers and Expeditions—Drake, Francis

English navigator Sir Francis Drake made many voyages for his country. In 1577-80, he became the first English explorer to circumnavigate the world. For his accomplishment, he was knighted by Queen Elizabeth I aboard his ship the *Golden Hind*.

• **Last voyage of Drake:** to the West Indies. He died of dysentery aboard ship on January 28, 1596, and was buried at sea off the coast of Portobello (Panama).

Explorers and Expeditions—Franklin Expedition

In May 1845, British explorer John Franklin set out to find the Northwest Passage. His two ships were carrying 129 people and a three-year supply of food when they left England.

• **Last contact with the Franklin Expedition:** seen by two whaling ships entering Lancaster Sound, northwest of Baffin Island in late July 1845. When Franklin was not heard from for three years, several expeditions searched for him with no success. In 1858, a search party funded by Franklin's wife discovered skeletons and a written record on the northwest shore of King Williams Land. It revealed that Franklin's two ship had gotten trapped in ice east of Victoria Island and that Franklin had died on June 11, 1847. Other members of his expedition died while trying to reach safety.

Explorers and Expeditions—Gama, Vasco da

Portuguese navigator Vasco da Gama was the first European to travel by sea to India in 1497-99. He made his second voyage to India in 1502-03.

• **Last voyage of da Gama to India:** 1524, when the king of Portugal appointed da Gama a viceroy, and he returned to India a third time. He died in Cochin, India, on December 24, 1524, at about the age of 64.

Explorers and Expeditions—Greely Expedition

U.S. Army officer Adolphus Washington Greely and 24 others set out on an Arctic expedition in 1881. The expedition was to represent the United States in the first Circumpolar Year (1882-83). A relief ship failed to reach them in 1883.

• **Last of the Greely expedition:** When a rescue party reached the expedition on June 22 1884, only seven members had survived. Greely was one of them. He died in Washington, D.C., on October 20, 1935, age 91.

• **Last survivor of the Greely expedition:** Brigadier General David L. Brainard, who died in Washington, D.C., on March 22, 1946, age 89.

Explorers and Expeditions—Heyerdahl, Thor

Norwegian anthropologist Thor Heyerdahl made several voyages to show the role of sea travel in the migration of early people.

Kon-Tiki Heyerdahl and five Scandinavian scientists sailed the balsa raft *Kon-Tiki* 4,300 miles from Callao, Peru, to the Raroia Reef in the South Pacific to demonstrate that Polynesians could have been descendants of Peruvian Incas. The raft left Peru on April 28, 1947.

• **End of the *Kon-Tiki* voyage:** reached the Raroia Reef on August 7, 1947. Today, *Kon-Tiki* is in the Kon-Tiki Museum in Oslo, Norway.

Ra I The *Ra I* voyage sailed from Morocco on May 25, 1969, to prove Heyerdahl's theory that ancient Egyptians could have reached Central America.

• **End of the *Ra I* voyage:** July 18, 1969, when Heyerdahl and his six-man crew abandoned the 50-foot papyrus reed boat several hundred miles short of its destination.

Ra II On May 17, 1970, Heyerdahl and a crew of seven sailed from Safi, Morocco, in *Ra II,* in his second attempt to prove ancient Egyptians could have reached Central America.

• **End of the *Ra II* voyage:** July 12, 1970. After a 57-day voyage, the craft sailed into Bridgetown Harbor, Barbados. Today *Ra II* is in the Kon-Tiki Museum in Oslo, Norway.

Tigris The *Tigris* expedition was the last of Heyerdahl's trans-oceanic voyages. He and a crew of 11 began a five-month journey on the 60-foot reed boat in December 1977. They started at the Tigris River in Iraq, sailed down the Persian Gulf to the Red Sea and then to Pakistan. The *Tigris* then journeyed back across the Indian Ocean to the Horn of Africa. Heyerdahl was endeavoring to show that ancient Sumerians might have taken a similar route.

• **End of the *Tigris* voyage:** April 3, 1978 when Heyerdahl burned the *Tigris* in Djibouti, after the ship completed a 4,200-mile journey. His action was a protest against the wars being waged in the region. Heyerdahl died on April 18, 2002, age 87.

Explorers and Expeditions—Kane Expedition

Elisha Kent Kane's expedition sailed from New York in May 1853 to find British explorer Sir John Franklin. When Kane's ship became icebound, he and his party set out in open boats. After 1,300 miles and 83 days, they reached a Danish settlement in Greenland.

• **End of the Kane Expedition:** October 11, 1855, when Kane's party returned to New York.

• **Last surviving officer of the Kane Expedition:** Henry Brooks, who was Kane's First Officer in the expedition. He died at the Brooklyn Navy Yard on June 29, 1858, age 45. Elisha Kent Kane died in Havana, Cuba, on February 16, 1857, age 37.

Explorers and Expeditions—Karluk Expedition (a.k.a. Canadian Arctic Expedition of 1913)

In 1913, HMCS *Karluk* set sail from British Columbia on an ill-prepared Arctic expedition. The ship became trapped in ice and the crew was abandoned by its leader. The ship was later carried into the Arctic Ocean where it sank on January 11, 1914.

• **Last of the *Karluk* Expedition:** September 1914, when a rescue ship reached Wrangel Island. The ordeal had taken the lives of 16 members of crew of 25. The expedition generated much controversy about whether its leader, Viljhalmur Stefansson,

deliberately or unintentionally abandoned his crew.

• **Last Inuit survivor of the *Karluk* Expedition:** Mugpi, the young daughter of an Inuit hunter who was three years old when she accompanied her father on the journey.

• **Last non-Inuit survivor of the *Karluk* Expedition:** William Laird McKinlay, a meteorologist/magnetician who was 24 years old when he joined the scientific staff. McKinlay's account of the expedition was published in 1976, when he was 88.

Explorers and Expeditions—La Pérouse Expedition

In August 1785, French navigator Jean François de Galoup, Conte de La Pérouse, set out with two ships on an expedition to find the Northwest Passage. He reached Alaska in July 1786. From there, he traveled to Hawaii, Macao, the Philippines and Japan.

• **Last time La Pérouse was seen:** 1788, when he reached Botany Bay, Australia. The hilt of his sword was found on Vanikoro, New Hebrides (now Vanuatu), in 1826. Two years later, a French search party found the wreckage of his ships on Vanikoro.

Explorers and Expeditions—Lewis and Clark Expedition

In 1804, the Lewis and Clark expedition set out from Saint Louis, Missouri, to chart a vast portion of the northwestern United States, much of which had recently been acquired with the Louisiana Purchase.

• **End of the Lewis and Clark Expedition:** September 23, 1808, when they returned to Saint Louis.

• **Last surviving Lewis and Clark Expedition member:** Sergeant Patrick Gass, who died in April 1870, age 99. He kept a journal of the expedition that included events not recorded elsewhere.

• **Last of Lewis and Clark:** Meriwether Lewis was 35 when he died at an inn along the Natchez Trace in Tennessee on October 11, 1809, while traveling to Washington, D.C. Whether he shot himself or was murdered is a matter of dispute. William Clark died in Saint Louis on September 1, 1838, age 68. At the time of his death, he was superintendent of Indian affairs in Saint Louis.

Explorers and Expeditions—Magellan, Ferdinand

Ferdinand Magellan is often credited with being the first to circumnavigate the globe. But he never got farther than the South Pacific. Magellan left Spain in September 1519 with five ships and a crew of about 260 men. He was killed by a group of natives in the Philippines in April 1521.

• **Magellan's last ship:** *Victoria,* the only one of Magellan's five ships to complete the journey. She arrived back in Spain in September 1522. Only 18 men survived the first voyage around the world.

Explorers and Expeditions—Old-time Arctic Explorers

• **Last of the old-time Arctic explorers:** Admiral Donald Baxter MacMillan, an explorer and scholar who made 29 voyages to the Arctic from 1908 to 1954. MacMillan made 26 of his Arctic voyages in the ship *Bowdoin.* He died in Provincetown Massachusetts, on September 7, 1970, age 95.

Explorers and Expeditions—Peary, Robert E.

American explorer Robert E. Peary made eight expeditions to the Arctic, beginning in 1886.

• **Last Peary expedition to the North Pole:** began March 1, 1909, from Cape Columbia on Ellesmere Island, the northernmost point in Canada. On April 6, Peary and his party were the first to reach the North Pole. They were back at their base in Cape Columbia on April 23. In the years following this expedition, Peary's accomplishment was clouded by controversy. Dr. Frederick A. Cook claimed he had reached the pole first. However, the U.S. Congress recognized Peary as the rightful claimant in 1911. Peary died in Washington, D.C., on February 20, 1920, age 63.

• **Last expedition of Henson with Peary:** 1909. Matthew Alexander Henson accompanied Robert E. Peary on most of his eight expeditions to the Arctic. He died in New York, New York, on March 9, 1955, age 88.

• **Last Inuit survivor of the Peary expeditions:** Ootah (Odaq), a member of the April 1909 expedition. He died near Thule, Greenland, in May 1955, age 80. He was one of four Inuits who reached the North Pole with Peary.

• **Last Peary expedition survivor:** Donald Baxter MacMillan, who was part of Peary's 1909 expedition to the North Pole.

Explorers and Expeditions—Polo Family

Brothers Niccolo and Matteo Polo of Venice, Italy, set out in 1260 to trade in Constantinople. Their route was blocked by a civil war. Their detour ultimately took them to the court of Kublai Khan in Cambaluc, China.

• **End of the first Polo journey:** 1269. Their total journey took them nine years. In 1271, the Polo brothers set out on a second journey to China, this time with Niccolo's 17-year-old son Marco.

• **End of the second Polo journey:** the winter of 1295. The journey lasted 24 years. Marco Polo kept a detailed record of all the things his family saw and did. His account of the journey was later published as a book. During the Renaissance, Marco Polo's book was the primary source of information about Asia for Westerners.

Explorers and Expeditions—Ponce de Leon, Juan

In 1513, Spanish explorer Juan Ponce de Leon was the first European explorer to reach Florida. He returned a second time in 1521.

• **Last expedition of Ponce de Leon:** 1521. He was seriously injured by a native while trying to land along the west coast of Florida. He was taken to Havana, Cuba, where he died in February 1521, age 61. He was buried in Havana. Later, his body was taken to San Juan, Puerto Rico.

Explorers and Expeditions—Scott, Robert Falcon

English explorer Robert Falcon Scott made two expeditions to the South Pole. The first was in 1901-04 on the HMS *Discovery.*

• **Last surviving member of Scott's 1901-04 Antarctic Expedition:** Frank Plumley, who was 25 when he joined the expedition in 1901. He died in Newport, Isle of Wight, in 1971, age 95. In 2001, Sotheby's auctioned off a number of items that Plumley had saved from the expedition.

• **Last of the HMS *Discovery*:** Scott's ship *Discovery* returned to England. It remained in London until March 1986, then it was moved to the Discovery Point Antarctic Museum in Dundee, Scotland.

Scott's second expedition, which began in 1910, was a race against Norwegian polar explorer Roald Amundsen. When Scott and his men reached the South Pole on January 18, 1912, they found Amundsen had already beaten them there.

• **Last of Scott and his crew:** died returning from the South Pole. They ran out of food and fuel and froze to death in a tent on the Ross Ice Shelf in late March 1912. On November 12, 1912, the bodies of Scott and two others were found. They were only 11 miles from a supply depot.

• **Last diary entry made by Scott:** March 29, 1912. Scott's diary was later published.

Explorers and Expeditions—Shackleton and the *Endurance*

The *Endurance* was the ship used by British explorer Ernest Shackleton on his expedition to Antarctica in 1914. The rescue of the crew of the *Endurance* is one of the great maritime survival success stories.

• **Last of the *Endurance*:** sank in late 1915. The ship had become locked in ice. For months the crew tried unsuccessfully to free the ship. They were able to save three small boats from the *Endurance*. By April, they had made their way to Elephant Island, about 180 miles away. From there, Shackleton and five volunteers set off for a whaling station on South Georgia Island, 800 miles away. They reached the island and were able to get help for the others.

• **Last of the Shackleton expedition:** August 25, 1916, when the 22 stranded men on Elephant Island were finally rescued.

• **Last survivor of the Shackleton expedition:** Lionel Greenstreet, first officer of the *Endurance,* who died in England on January 13, 1979, age 89.

• **Last surviving relic from the *Endurance*:** a spar (timber) that was donated by William Byrne to the Scott Polar Research Institute at Cambridge University in England in 1997.

• **Last Antarctic trip of Shackleton:** 1921-22. When he returned to the Antarctic, Shackleton had a heart attack. He died aboard a ship off South Georgia Island on January 5, 1922, age 48. He was buried atop a mountain on the island.

Expositions and World's Fairs

Expositions and World's Fairs— Centennial Exposition (Philadelphia)

The Centennial Exposition was held in Philadelphia, Pennsylvania, in 1876 to commemorate the 100th anniversary of the signing of the Declaration of Independence. About 200 buildings were constructed in the city's Fairmount Park. Almost 10 million people visited the exposition that opened on May 19, 1876.

• **Last day of the Centennial Exposition:** November 10, 1876. Later, the Arts and Industries Building (part of the Smithsonian Institution in Washington, D.C.) was built to showcase many of the materials displayed at the Centennial Exposition. It opened in 1881.

• **Last surviving exposition buildings still in Philadelphia:** Memorial Hall and Ohio House. Both are in Fairmount Park, site of the exposition. Memorial Hall is the last surviving main exhibition building. It was the home of the Philadelphia Museum of Art until the 1920s. It is used today for many functions. Ohio House, the official building of the state of Ohio, later housed the Fairmount Park police.

• **Last of the Corliss Engine:** scrapped in 1910 and sold as junk. The gigantic 70-foot-tall Corliss Engine furnished the power to operate the 14 acres of machinery in the exposition's Machinery Hall. Emperor Dom Pedro of Brazil and U.S. President Ulysses S. Grant started the Corliss Engine on the opening day. On the closing day, Grant stopped the engine using a telegraph signal at the Judge's Hall on the Centennial grounds. Afterward, the engine was sold to industrialist George Pullman and shipped to Chicago, Illinois. It powered his sleeping car plant for 30 years.

Expositions and World's Fairs—Century of Progress International Exposition (Chicago)

The Century of Progress International Exposition was held for two years. It opened in Chicago, Illinois, on May 27, 1933, and closed on November 12, 1933. It reopened the following year on May 26, 1934.
• **Last day of the Century of Progress International Exposition:** October 31, 1934.
• **Last remaining exposition object at its original site:** Balbo's Column, a gift from Italy. It now stands near Soldier Field on South Lake Shore Drive. The column came from ruins of a Roman temple in Ostia, Italy. The column commemorates Italian aviator General Italo Balbo's flight to Chicago in 1933.

Expositions and World's Fairs—Crystal Palace (London)

The Crystal Palace was built in Hyde Park in London, England, for the Great Exhibition of 1851. Three years later, the iron, glass and wood structure, which covered 19 acres, was moved to Sydenham, where it served as a museum and was used for concerts, including the Handel festivals.
• **Last of the Crystal Palace:** a transept at the north end that formed a palm house burned down in 1866. The rest was destroyed by fire on November 30, 1936. The ruins were torn down in 1941 when they were found to be a landmark for German planes during the air raids on Britain.

Expositions and World's Fairs—Crystal Palace (New York)

The Crystal Palace was built in Reservoir Square (later known as Bryant Park) in New York, New York. In 1853-54, it was the site of a world's fair known as the Exhibition of the Industry of All Nations.
• **Last of the Crystal Palace:** destroyed by fire on October 5, 1858.

Expositions and World's Fairs— Louisiana Purchase Exposition (Saint Louis)

The Louisiana Purchase Exposition (a.k.a. Universal Exposition of Saint Louis) commemorated the centennial of the Louisiana Purchase. It opened in Saint Louis, Missouri, on April 20, 1904.
• **Last day of the Louisiana Purchase Exposition:** December 1, 1904. Among the expo buildings that have survived is the Palace of Fine Art, now the Saint Louis Art Museum.
• **Last home of the great pipe organ:** now in Philadelphia, Pennsylvania. A massive pipe organ was built especially for the Louisiana Purchase Exposition by the Los Angeles Art Organ Company. After the expo, it was purchased by merchant John Wanamaker for the Grand Court of his new department store in Philadelphia, Pennsylvania. The store is no longer owned by the Wanamaker family. But the organ is still part of the building's Grand Court and is a National Historic Landmark.

Expositions and World's Fairs—New York World's Fair 1939-40

Two World's Fairs were held in Flushing Meadows, New York, on what was once the old Corona Ash Dump. The first commemorated the 150th anniversary of George Washington's inaugural as U.S. president. It opened April 30, 1939, and closed October 31, 1939. The following year, it opened on May 11.
• **Last day of the 1939-40 New York World's Fair:** October 27, 1940. Among the surviving buildings and items from the fair are the New York Building (now the Queens Museum of Art), the AmphiTheater and the Art Deco flagpoles near the Unisphere.

Expositions and World's Fairs—New York World's Fair 1964-65

The 1964-65 New York World's Fair commemorated the 300th anniversary of the British gaining control of New Amsterdam from the Dutch. The first year of the fair began on April 22, 1964, and ran until October 18, 1964. The second year opened on April 21, 1965.

• **Last day of the 1964-65 New York World's Fair:** October 17, 1965. Among the last surviving structures of the fair are the stainless steel Unisphere, New York State Pavilion and the Hall of Science. The Unisphere is 140 feet tall and 120 feet in diameter. It is the focal point of Corona Park. Time capsules were created for both the 1939-40 and the 1964-65 fairs. They are buried under a granite marker near the Unisphere.

Expositions and World's Fairs—Pan American Exposition (Buffalo)

The Pan American Exposition opened in Buffalo, New York, on May 1, 1901. It celebrated a century of scientific and cultural progress in the Western Hemisphere. The expo was held on the Rumsey farm. The lease stipulated that all the land was to return to its natural state when the expo ended.

• **Last day of the Pan American Exposition:** November 2, 1901. Demolition began soon after the fair ended and was completed by March 1902.

• **Last remaining Pan American Exposition structure:** the New York State Pavilion, which now houses the Buffalo and Erie County Historical Society. It is the only building that was planned to be permanent.

• **Last appearance of U.S. President William McKinley:** September 6, 1901. He was shot by an anarchist while he attended a reception in the Exposition's Hall of Music. McKinley died on September 14th after his wound became infected. He was 58.

Expositions and World's Fairs—World's Columbian Exposition (Chicago)

The World's Columbian Exposition officially opened in Chicago, Illinois, on May 1, 1893. It commemorated (a year late) the 400th anniversary of Columbus's landing in America.

• **Last day of the World's Columbian Exposition:** October 31, 1893.

• **Last of the Viking ship:** sank in the Chicago River on September 5, 1894, during a storm. It was later raised and given to the Field Museum in Chicago.

• **Last remaining World's Columbian Exposition building:** Palace of Fine Arts. After extensive renovations, it reopened in the 1930s as the Museum of Science and Industry. Most of the exposition buildings were deliberately set on fire on July 5, 1894, during the Pullman strike. Among those destroyed were the six great buildings surrounding the Court of Honor, as well as the Terminal building.

• **Last of the Ferris Wheel:** sold for scrap in 1906. The huge Ferris Wheel was a major attraction on the Midway at the Columbian Exposition. It was 264 feet high, 250 feet in diameter and could carry 2,160 passengers in its 36 cars. The wheel was named for its creator, Pennsylvania bridge builder George W. Ferris. The wheel was disassembled in 1894 after the exposition and used again in 1904 at the Louisiana Purchase Exposition in Saint Louis, Missouri.

Fashion

Fashion—Clothing—Knee Breeches

Knee breeches became fashionable for men in Europe and elsewhere in the late 1700s. They gradually went out of style in the early 1800s.

• **Last United States president to wear knee britches to his inauguration:** James Monroe, fifth president of the United States, who was inaugurated for the first time in 1817. He also wore a powdered wig tied into a queue. And along with the knee britches, Monroe wore long white stockings, buckled shoes and a black tailcoat. Monroe served as president until March 4, 1825

• **Last time members of the United States diplomatic service were permitted to wear** knee breeches: 1853. That year, the U.S. Secretary of State warned that they would no longer be tolerated.

Fashion—Hair—Full Wigs
Wigs have been the symbol of office for judges and lawyers in Great Britain since the 17th century and are still worn. In the United States, the practice of wearing a wig while in court began to be discarded after the American Revolution.
• **Last American jurist to wear the full wig of an English judge:** Associate Justice of the U.S. Supreme Court William Cushing, who died in Scituate, Massachusetts, on September 13, 1810, age 78.

Foods

Foods—Beechnut Company—Circus Bus
The Beechnut Foods Company of Canajoharie, New York, used circus buses during the 1930s to promote their products.
• **Last remaining Beechnut Circus Bus:** at the New York State Museum. It is the last of six.

Foods—Candy and Snack Food—
Good Humor Company Trucks
The first Good Humor trucks were put on the streets in the early 1920s to provide Harry Burt with a venue to sell his novelty—ice cream on a stick.
• **Last of the company-owned Good Humor ice cream trucks:** phased out in 1976 when the company abandoned the direct-selling business in favor of grocery stores and free-standing freezer cabinets. Some Good Humor trucks are still on the road, but they are owned by ice cream distributors and private individuals, not by Good Humor.

Foods—Candy and Snack Food—
Hershey Bar
When Hershey bars were marketed in 1908, they weighed 9/16ths of an ounce and cost 2¢. The first 5¢ Hershey bars were introduced in 1921 and weighed 1 ounce.
• **Last 5¢ Hershey bar:** 1968. The final 5¢ bars weighed 3/4 oz.

Foods—Candy and Snack Food—
Lance Nickel Packs
From the time the Lance Company was founded in 1913 until 1964, the company's individually packaged items sold for a nickel. The 10¢ cracker sandwich six packs were introduced in 1964.
• **Last of Lance's nickel merchandise:** manufactured on March 6, 1970. That year, the company switched to the larger 10¢ packages.

Foods—Candy and Snack Food—
Planters Peanuts—Stores
Planters Peanuts was founded in 1906. Mr. Peanut, the popular Planters icon, was created in 1916. By the 1930s, there were hundreds of Planters Peanut shops throughout the U.S. In 1961, the company became part of Standard Brands. Planters began selling off its stores in the 1960s.
• **Last Planters Peanut store:** closed in 1980. It was on the Boardwalk at Virginia Avenue, across from Steel Pier in Atlantic City, New Jersey.

Foods—Food and Drugs
Concern over contaminated food and patent medicine frauds led the U.S. Congress to pass legislation in the early 20th century to protect the public.
• **Last unregulated sales of foods and drugs:** June 30, 1906, when the Pure Food and Drug Act was enacted to prohibit the manufacture and interstate shipment of adulterated or misbranded foods and drugs. The Food, Drug and Cosmetic Act of 1938 imposed tighter controls.

Foods—Oleomargarine
Oleomargarine was introduced as a butter substitute in the United States in 1874. The competition from oleo caused the dairy industry to appeal to the government for protection. The dairy states imposed taxes on oleomargarine and most other states followed. In 1886, the U.S. Congress placed a federal tax on oleomargarine. A dairy shortage during World War II swayed some public opinion to the side of eliminating the oleo tax, and in the 1948 election, it became a

major campaign issue.
• **Last of the oleo tax:** 1950.
• **Last state to lift the ban on yellow oleo:** Wisconsin, in 1967. In its original state, oleomargarine is white. When it was first marketed, by law it could not be sold colored. The white oleo was sold with a separate yellow coloring packet. The consumer had to do the mixing. After World War II, states began to repeal the law banning the sale of colored oleomargarine. By 1955, only two holdouts remained: Minnesota and Wisconsin, both major dairy states.

Games and Toys

Games and Toys—Chess—Morphy, Paul
American-born chess genius Paul Charles Morphy was considered one of the greatest players of his era. He was the national chess champion when he was 20.
• **Morphy's last games:** 1859, when he was 22. After that, he give up competing and studied law. He died in New Orleans, Louisiana, on July 10, 1884, age 47.

Game and Toys—Lawn Darts (Jarts)
Lawn Darts (Jarts), a popular outdoor game, consisted of large dart-shaped objects with pointed tips that were thrown underhand at a target. When misused, the darts could puncture a human skull. The darts resulting in 700 injuries in one year and in the death of three children before they were banned.
• **Last time Lawn Darts were sold in the U.S.:** December 19, 1988, banned by the United States Consumer Product Safety Commission. Lawn darts with metal tips were banned in Canada in 1989.

Games and Toys—Mr. Potato Head
Mr. Potato Head, the popular children's toy, was introduced in 1952 as a set of accessories to be used with a real potato.
• **Last time Mr. Potato Head was sold for use with a real potato:** 1964.
• **Last time Mr. Potato Head was sold with a pipe:** 1987. The pipe was eliminated under pressure by Surgeon General C. Everett Coop. Mr. Potato Head handed his pipe over to Dr. Coop at a press conference for the Great American Smokeout.

Glass, Pottery, Porcelain and Ceramics
Last of Some Major American
Glass, Pottery, Porcelain and Ceramics Manufacturers

Company	Ceased Operation	Description
Amelung Glass (New Bremen Glass Manufactory)	1795	Established in 1784 by German glassmaker John Frederick Amelung as the New Bremen Glass Manufactory near Frederick, Maryland. He employed glassmakers from Bohemia and Germany. Among the company's products were bowls, bottles and goblets. Amelung died in 1798.
American Art China Company	1894	Established in 1891 by John C. Rittenhouse and George Evans in Trenton, New Jersey. It remained in business just three years. The company made exceptionally fine Belleek ware.
American China Manufactory (Bonnin and Morris)	1772	Established in 1770 in Philadelphia, Pennsylvania, by Gousse Bonnin and Anthony Morris. They were the first major American manufacturers of porcelain. Morris left the business in 1771, and Bonnin went to England in 1772. A month later, the kilns, buildings and equipment were put up for sale at public auction. There were no buyers.

American Flint Glass Manufactory (Stiegel Glass)	1780	Established in 1763 as the American Flint Glass Manufactory in Manheim, Pennsylvania, by German immigrant Henry William Stiegel. After he left the factory in 1774, several attempts were made to keep it open. It finally shut down in 1780.
American Porcelain Manufacturing Company (Charles Cartlidge and Company)	1856	Established in 1848 in the Greenpoint section of Brooklyn, New York, as Charles Cartlidge and Company. The company made porcelain dinnerware, buttons, doorplates, door knobs, drawer pulls and other household items. It hit hard times in 1854 and was dissolved. It was reorganized as the American Porcelain Manufacturing Company. The new company lasted less than two years.
American Terra Cotta Company (Spring Valley Tile Works) (American Terra Cotta and Tile Company)	1966	Established in 1881 in Terra Cotta, Illinois, as Spring Valley Tile Works. Renamed American Terra Cotta and Tile Company in 1887. It specialized in pale silvery-green pottery. Teco pottery was made from 1902 to c.1923. The company was sold in 1930 and renamed American Terra Cotta Company. It closed in 1966.
Arequipa Pottery	1918	Established in 1911 for women tuberculosis patients at Arequipa Sanitarium in Marin County, California.
Avon Faience Pottery Company (Tiltonsville Pottery)	1903	Established in Tiltonsville, Ohio, and originally named Tiltonsville Pottery Company. It was sold in 1903 and operated for two years as a division of the Wheeling Pottery Company.
Bennett (Edwin) Pottery Company (E. Bennett Chinaware Factory)	1936	Established as the E. Bennett Chinaware Factory in 1844 in Baltimore, Maryland. It was the first pottery in that city. It also operated as E & W. Bennett (1847-56); Edwin Bennett Pottery (1856-90); and Edwin Bennett Pottery Company, Inc. (1890-1936). The company—which made many kinds of wares, including porcelain, majolica, Rockingham, yellowware, whiteware and graniteware—went bankrupt in 1936.
Boston and Sandwich Glass Company	1888	Established in 1825 in Sandwich, Massachusetts, by Deming Jarvis. The company pioneered pressed glass. Jarvis left in 1858 and founded Cape Cod Glass Works. Boston and Sandwich closed when it could not compete with producers that made cheaper glass.
Brush Pottery Company (Brush-McCoy Pottery)	1982	Established in 1906 in Zanesville, Ohio, by George S. Brush. After the plant burned down in 1908, Brush went to work for J.W. McCoy Pottery Company. Brush and McCoy merged in 1911. The McCoy name was dropped in 1925. The company continued as Brush Pottery until it closed in 1982. The building that housed Brush Pottery was destroyed by a fire on July 15, 1999.
Camark Pottery (Camden Art Tile and Pottery Company)	1983	Established in 1926 in Camden, Arkansas. Production began the following year. The company was sold in the 1960s. After that, production was limited until 1983, when it halted altogether and the company closed.
Cambridge Glass Company	1958	Established in 1901 in Cambridge, Ohio. Cambridge was sold to National Glass Company in 1907. When National

		Glass Company was sold in 1954, the plant was briefly closed, but reopened the following year. It closed for the last time in 1958. In 1960, Imperial Glass Company, Bellaire, Ohio, acquired the molds and equipment. After Imperial went bankrupt in 1984, National Cambridge Collectors acquired many of the molds and other Cambridge assets. The Cambridge Glass factory was torn down in 1989.
Cape Cod Glass Works	c. 1869	Established in 1858, after Deming Jarvis left Boston and Sandwich Glass Company. The business ended shortly after Jarvis died in 1869.
Ceramic Art Company	1906	Established in 1886 in Trenton, New Jersey, by Walter Scott Lenox and Jonathan Coxon Sr., two former associates of Ott and Brewer. In 1906, Lenox gained sole control of the company and incorporated it under his name. Lenox Incorporated is still in business.
Cook Pottery Company	1929	Established in Trenton, New Jersey, when Charles H. Cook purchased the pottery of Ott and Brewer after it went into receivership in 1893. Cook produced Belleek ware and Delftware.
Dallas Pottery	1882	Established in 1865 in Cincinnati, Ohio, by Frederick Dallas. Maria Longworth Nichols, one of the women who used his kilns, later established the Rookwood Pottery. Dallas died in 1881. His company closed soon afterward.
Dedham Pottery (Chelsea Pottery) (Chelsea Keramic Art Works)	1943	Established in 1866 as Chelsea Pottery by Alexander Robertson in Chelsea, Massachusetts. When his brother Hugh joined the company around 1868, the firm operated as A.W.H.C. Robertson. From 1875 until the company went bankrupt in 1889, it operated as Chelsea Keramic Art Works. In 1891, Hugh Robertson started up a pottery again. In 1895, the company moved to Dedham, Massachusetts, where it produced as Dedham Pottery. Robertson's son and grandson ran the business until it closed in 1943.
Durand Glass	1931	Established in 1924 by Victor Durand Jr. after he bought his father's share of Vineland Flint Glass in New Jersey and added other glass factories. The glass division became famous for its Quezal designs in items such as lamps and vases. The company closed after Durand was killed in an automobile accident in April 1931.
Fostoria Glass Company	1986	Established in 1887 in Fostoria, Ohio. Moved to Moundville, West Virginia, in 1891. Lancaster Colony Corporation of Lancaster, Ohio, purchased the company in 1983 and closed the Fostoria factory in 1986. Fostoria introduced its popular "American" pattern in 1915. Lancaster Colony took over its manufacture.
Fulper Pottery Company (Samuel Hill Pottery)	1935	Established in 1815 as the Samuel Hill Pottery in Flemington, New Jersey. In 1899, it was reincorporated as Fulper Pottery Company. In the 1920s, Fulper and Stangl shared a logo. After Fulper's Plant No. 1 was hit by a devastating fire in 1929, Stangl Pottery bought out the business and dropped the Fulper name. Fulper's Plant No. 2 in Flemington ceased manufacturing in 1935 and was converted to a retail outlet.

Glasgow Pottery	c. 1905	Established around 1863 by John Moses in Trenton, New Jersey. Known for its white graniteware and cream-colored earthenware. Closed after Moses died in 1902.
Greenwood Pottery	1933	Established in Trenton, New Jersey, in 1861 as the firm of William Tams, James P. Stephens and Charles Brearley. Renamed Greenwood Pottery Company in 1868. Greenwood began producing its art porcelain Ne Plus Ultra ware in 1884. It discontinued the line in the early 1890s but continued to make white granite hotel ware until it closed in 1933.
Grueby Faience Company	1920	Established in 1897 in Boston, Massachusetts, by William H. Grueby. The company made ceramic pots, tiles and statuary. It filed for bankruptcy in 1909. After that, production was limited until the company closed.
Hampshire Pottery	1923	Established in 1871 by James Taft in Keene, New Hampshire. The company, known for its matte green glaze, was sold in 1916. It closed the following year but reopened in 1918, then closed permanently in 1923.
Heisey, A. H., Company	1957	Established in 1895 by Augustus H. Heisey in Newark, Ohio. Faced with competition from foreign markets and rising production costs, the company closed in 1957. Its molds were sold to Imperial Glass Corporation of Bellaire, Ohio. Imperial used the Heisey trademark until 1968.
Holt-Howard Company	1990	Established in 1948 by John and Robert Howard and A. Grant Holt in Stamford, Connecticut. The company was known for its Pixieware, manufactured from 1958 until the early 1960s. It also made planters, lamps and other home décor items. The company was sold to General Housewares Corporation in the early 1970s and relocated to Massachusetts. Production ceased in 1990.
Hull, A.E., Pottery	1985	Established in 1905 in Zanesville, Ohio. The company started with stoneware, then made tiles after 1931. It specialized in art pottery in the 1940s. The plant was destroyed by a flood and fire in 1950 and then was rebuilt. By the 1970s, it made mostly dinnerware and floral ware.
Imperial Glass Corporation (Imperial Glass Company	1984	Established in 1904 in Bellaire, Ohio, as Imperial Glass Company. Reincorporated in 1931 as Imperial Glass Corporation. The company made bottles, jars, art glass and several lines of tableware. Imperial went through several changes of ownership in its final years. It closed in 1984.
Knowles, Taylor and Knowles	1929	Established in 1854 by Isaac Knowles in East Liverpool, Ohio. When his son and son-in-law entered the firm in 1870, it became Knowles, Taylor and Knowles. The company made whiteware, hotel china, Belleek and art ware. A fire in 1889 destroyed the factory. After it was rebuilt, the company made a special line of art bone china called Lotus Ware from 1890 to around 1897. The product was discontinued when it proved to be too costly to produce.
Mercer Pottery	1939	Established in 1869 in Trenton, New Jersey, by James Moses, whose brother operated the Glasgow Pottery. The company specialized in pottery dinnerware and decorative pieces.

Nelson McCoy Pottery Company (Nelson McCoy Sanitary and Stoneware)	1990	Established in 1910 in Roseville, Ohio, as Nelson McCoy Sanitary and Stoneware. During the Depression, the company joined several others as American Clay Products. It did not work out, so in 1933, McCoy became the Nelson McCoy Pottery Company. It specialized in cookie jars. The company was sold to Mount Clemens Pottery Company in 1967, then to Lancaster Colony Corporation in 1974. In 1985, Designer Accents took over the company. After McCoy ceased production in 1990, some of the molds were sold. Part of the pottery burned in 1991.
New England Glass Company (New England Glassworks)	c. 1878	Established in 1818 in Cambridge, Massachusetts. The company fell on hard times in the 1870s and put the building and materials up for sale. The business was leased to William Libbey in 1878 as New England Glassworks. The company was later named William Libbey & Son. The original New England Glass Company property was sold in 1889. The factory chimney was torn down in 1921.
Norton Pottery (Norton Stoneware Company)	1894	Established in 1793 by John Norton in Bennington, Vermont. The pottery was active for many years making jugs, crocks, brown-glazed pottery, yellowware and whiteware as the Norton Stoneware Company. After Norton retired in 1823, the company was renamed several times as different Norton descendants entered the business. Pottery production ceased in 1894. The company continued operation as a wholesaler until 1911.
Onondaga Pottery (Empire Pottery)	1966	Established in 1841, with the pottery of W. H. Farrar that made such items as jugs, crocks and clay animals. It became the Empire Pottery in 1855 and added whiteware. In 1871, the company was reorganized and renamed Onondaga Pottery. It became part of Syracuse China Company in 1966.
Ott and Brewer (Etruria Pottery)	1893	Established in 1863 in Trenton, New Jersey, as Etruria Pottery. It was renamed Ott and Brewer in 1871. The company was among the larger American pottery firms. In addition to hotel china and Belleek ware, it made parian art objects. The company went into receivership and ceased production in 1893. The company was then reorganized as Cook Pottery.
Rookwood Pottery	1961	Established in 1880 in Cincinnati, Ohio. It took its name from the family estate of founder Maria Longworth Nichols. When Rookwood Pottery closed in 1961, the molds were sold to a company that produced a few pieces. The molds were sold again in 1983. The new owner does limited firings. The original Rookwood factory was converted into a restaurant.
Roseville Pottery Company	1954	Established in 1890 in Roseville, Ohio. It expanded to Zanesville, Ohio, in 1898, and purchased two factories from a competitor. The company closed its Roseville plant in 1910. The Zanesville plants closed in 1954.
Shawnee Pottery	1961	Established in 1937 in Zanesville, Ohio. The company made a wide variety of items, including dinnerware, vases,

		novelty ware, figurines and cookie jars. As was the case with many American potters after World War II, Shawnee could not compete with cheaper foreign imports.
Stanger's Glass House	1781	Established in 1779 in what later became Glassboro, New Jersey. Earlier, Stanger had worked for Caspar Wistar and left to start his own business. Stanger was forced to shut down in 1781, a victim of the American Revolution. His factory was purchased in 1786 and became the Heston-Carpenter Glassworks. That company was succeeded by several others, the most recent of which was Owens-Illinois Glass Company.
Stangl Pottery Company	1978	Johann Stangl, who headed Fulper Pottery, added the Stangl name to the company logo in the 1920s. After one of Fulper's factories in Flemington, New Jersey, burned in September 1929, Stangl bought out the business and dropped the Fulper name. Stangl Pottery Company was sold to Wheaton Glass in 1972. Stangl dinnerware was made until 1978, when Pfaltzgraff Pottery purchased the trademark. Royal Cumberland took over many of the Stangl bird molds.
Steubenville Pottery Company	1959	Established in 1879 in Steubenville, Ohio, by a group of Steubenville residents. The popular Russell Wright designs, including American Modern, were made by Steubenville from 1939 to 1959. The plant closed in December 1959, and the buildings were sold. The pottery's molds were purchased by Canonsburg Pottery in Pennsylvania. Items were made under the Steubenville name until 1965.
Stockton Terra Cotta Company	1902	Established in 1891 in Stockton, California. The company made Rekston art pottery after 1897. After a fire shut down the business in 1902, the Stockton pottery never reopened.
Tiffany Glass Company (Tiffany Glass & Decorating Company) (Tiffany Furnaces) (Louis C. Tiffany Furnaces)	1928	Established in 1885, when Louis Comfort Tiffany began making lamps. He introduced his Fabrile ware in 1892, then changed the spelling to Favrile in 1894. He worked under several corporate names: Tiffany Glass Company (1885-92); Tiffany Glass & Decorating Company (1892-1902); Tiffany Furnaces (1902-20) and Louis C. Tiffany Furnaces (1920-28). Tiffany died in New York, New York, on January 17, 1933, age 84. Laurelton Hall, his home on Long Island was destroyed by fire in 1957.
Tiffin Crystal (A.J. Beatty Glass Company)	1980	Established in 1879 as the A.J. Beatty Glass Company in Steubenville, Ohio. The company relocated to Tiffin, Ohio, in 1888. When it merged with United States Glass Company in 1892, it became one of 19 corporate factories and was known as Factory R. After United States Glass went bankrupt, employees purchased the plant and ran it from 1963 to 1966 as Tiffin Art Glass Company. In 1966, it was sold to Continental Can Company and once again was known as Tiffin Glass Company. It was sold again in 1968 but retained its name. In 1979, it was sold to Towle Silversmiths and operated as Tiffin Crystal. The Tiffin furnaces shut down in May 1980.

Tucker Porcelain Company (Tucker and Hulme) (Joseph Hemphill Porcelain Company) (Tucker and Hemphill)	1837	Established in 1826 in Philadelphia, Pennsylvania, as the Tucker Porcelain Company by William Ellis Tucker. He took John Hulme as his partner in 1828. The partnership lasted only a few months, but many pieces of porcelain carry the name Tucker and Hulme. In 1831, Joseph Hemphill purchased a partnership in the business. When Tucker died in 1832, Hemphill became the sole owner of the company. The firm of Tucker and Hemphill (or Joseph Hemphill Porcelain Company) lasted until 1837. That year, Hemphill retired and sold out his share of the business.
Uhl Pottery	1944	Established around 1849 in Evansville, Indiana. Uhl moved to Huntingburg, Indiana, in 1908. The company made a wide variety of stoneware and glazed pottery items, including jugs, miniatures, garden ware and crocks.
Union Porcelain Works (Union Porcelain Company) (William Boch and Brothers)	c. 1922	Established sometime before 1844 as William Boch and Brothers in Greenpoint, Brooklyn, New York. Thomas C. Smith took over the Boch company and changed the name to Union Porcelain Company in 1858. He renamed it Union Porcelain Works around 1863. The company made porcelain dinnerware, shaving mugs and house trimmings. It produced the first American porcelain that could compare favorably with French fine china. The company shut down after the death of its owner.
United States Pottery Company (Fenton's Works)	1858	Established in the mid-1840s by Christopher W. Fenton in Bennington, Vermont as Fenton's Works. When a partner joined the firm in 1849, the name was changed to United States Pottery Company. The company, which was famous for its parian marble items, experienced financial problems in the mid-1850s and closed in 1858. After the company went out of business, Fenton moved to Peoria, Illinois, where he founded the American Pottery Company.
Vernon Potteries (Vernon Kilns)	1958	Established in 1931 in Vernon, California, as Vernon Potteries. By 1948, it was operating as Vernon Kilns. After the company ceased operation in 1958, Metlox purchased the molds and equipment and continued to market Vernon shapes and patterns as Vernonware until 1989.
Warwick China Company	1951	Established in 1887 in Wheeling, West Virginia. Warwick made semi-porcelain dinnerware, platters, shaving mugs and hand-painted portrait items. In 1912, the company added restaurant and railroad china. It began producing bone china around 1940.
Watt Pottery Company	1965	Established in 1922 in Crooksville, Ohio, when William J. Watt and his sons purchased the Globe Stoneware Company and renamed it. The popular Apple series was introduced in 1952. Production ceased when a fire destroyed the factory and warehouse in 1965.
Weller Pottery Company	1948	Established in 1872 by Samuel A. Weller in Fultonham, Ohio. The company moved to Zanesville, Ohio, in 1888. Weller began making portraitware after the move. The

		company introduced the Hudson line in 1917. Prior to World War I, Weller was the world's largest producer of art pottery.
William Young and Company (William Young's Sons)	1879	Established in 1853 in Trenton, New Jersey. The firm operated as William Young and Sons (1860-71) and as William Young's Sons (1871-79). It specialized in earthenware and porcelain trimmings such as doorknobs and door plates. It also made dinnerware. The company was the first Trenton potter to make whiteware.
Wistar Glass (Wistarburgh)	1780	Established c. 1740 by Caspar Wistar at Alloway Creek, near Salem, New Jersey. The main products were bottles and window glass. After Wistar died in 1752, his son Richard took over production.
Zanesville Art Pottery	1962	Established in 1900 in Zanesville, Ohio. The company made faience umbrella stands, pedestals and jardinieres. In 1920, the company was sold to Weller Pottery.

Gold
(See also Money—United States.)

Gold—Gold Bullion
The ban on the private possession of gold bullion began in 1933 with an executive order issued by President Franklin D. Roosevelt.
• **Last time Americans were not permitted to own gold bullion:** December 31, 1974, when the U.S. Congress restored the right of Americans to own gold in bullion form.

Gold—Gold Rushes—California
The California Gold Rush began after word spread that James Marshall found gold at John Sutter's sawmill in Coloma, California, on January 24, 1848.
• **End of the California Gold Rush:** There is no precise date for the end of the California Gold Rush. But by the end of 1852, all the rivers had been prospected and most of the big strikes had been made. Stragglers kept coming to California until 1859, the year the Comstock lode was discovered in what is now Nevada. Many of the miners packed up and moved there.

Gold—Gold Rushes—Klondike
The Klondike Gold Rush began in 1897 as soon as news of the August 1896 discovery of gold along Bonanza Creek in the Yukon

Territory of northwestern Canada reached the outside world. As thousands of gold seekers rushed to Canada, the town of Dawson sprang up and a railroad was built from Scagway.
• **End of the Klondike Gold Rush:** There is no precise date for the end of the Klondike Gold Rush, but it began to decline around 1900 when gold seekers found they were too late to stake claims. The peak gold rush years were 1897-99. Within a few years, the mining population plummeted from 27,000 to less than 9,000 in 1911 and half that number by 1921.

Gold—Mines—Reed Gold Mine
The Little Meadow Creek on Reed's Farm in Concord, North Carolina, was the first gold mine in the United States. Gold was discovered there in 1799 but organized mining did not begin until 1831. So much gold was discovered there that the government opened a mint in Charlotte in 1837.
• **Last underground mining at the Reed Gold Mine:** 1912. Since 1971, Reed's Farm has been owned by the state of North Carolina and is open to the public. It attracts 100,000 visitors a year. Tourist mining goes on there, but the ore is brought in from the Cotton Patch Gold Mine in Stanley County, North Carolina.

Health and Medicine

Health and Medicine—Epidemics—AIDS
Acquired Immune Deficiency Syndrome (AIDS) was first reported in the United States in June 1981. Within two years, 2,500 cases had been reported.
• **Last state to have a confirmed case of AIDS:** North Dakota in 1985.

Health and Medicine—Epidemics— Bubonic Plague
Bubonic plague is spread to human beings by the bite of a flea from an infected rat. There have been several major outbreaks, including Europe and Asia from 540 to 590 A.D., the Black Death from 1347 to 1351 and the Great Plague of London in 1665-66. The bacillus that causes bubonic plague was identified in 1894. Treatment with antibiotics has greatly reduced fatalities.
• **Last major bubonic plague outbreak worldwide:** 1910, when 60,000 people died in eastern Siberia within seven months. The same epidemic hit India and China and lasted until 1913. The exact death toll is unknown but may have reached 12 million.
• **Last significant bubonic plague outbreak in the United States:** Los Angeles, California, in 1924-25.

Health and Medicine—Epidemics— Bubonic Plague—Black Death
Black Death is the name given to the bubonic plague epidemic that swept Europe in the 14th century. It earned its name from the black spots its victims developed on their skin. The plague was carried to southern Italy in 1347 by rats on ships arriving from the Middle East. The Black Death was the worst epidemic in human history. The lack of detailed records makes it impossible to give an accurate number of plague fatalities, but estimates suggest from one fourth to one third of all Europeans died of the Black Death during these years. Italy was especially hard-hit.
• **End of the Black Death epidemic in western Europe:** began to disappear by 1351. The peak years were 1348-50.

Health and Medicine—Epidemics— Poliomyelitis
Poliomyelitis—commonly known as polio and in the past as infantile paralysis—has been controlled with vaccines since the 1950s. But prior to that, polio epidemics were a cause for great alarm. The Salk vaccine arrived first, followed by the Sabin. Poliomyelitis is now rare.
• **Last case of polio in the United States due to natural infection:** 1979.
• **Last case of polio in the Western Hemisphere due to natural infection:** a three-year-old boy in Peru in 1991.

Health and Medicine—Epidemics— Smallpox
Smallpox is a highly contagious, often fatal disease that leaves a deep rash on the skin. It is caused by a virus.
• **Last smallpox case diagnosed in the United States:** 1947.
• **Last routine smallpox vaccinations in the United States:** 1972.
• **Last routine smallpox vaccinations worldwide:** 1980. In 1979, the World Health Organization announced smallpox had been eradicated. The following year the announcement was accepted as official.
• **Last case of smallpox due to natural infection:** Ali Maow Maalin, a young man in Somalia on October 26, 1977. He survived.
• **Last lab death from smallpox:** September 1978. Janet Parker, an English medical photographer, was exposed to smallpox as the result of a laboratory accident. She died of the exposure.

Health and Medicine—Epidemics— Spanish Influenza
The Spanish influenza epidemic of 1918 claimed as many victims in four months as World War I did in four years. The exact number of deaths is unknown, but estimates range from 21 to 40 million deaths in the outbreak that raced throughout the U.S., Europe, and much of Asia. It was called Spanish influenza because a much milder flu outbreak hit Spain earlier that year. The best evidence suggests the Spanish influenza

epidemic started at Fort Riley, Kansas, in March 1918. Two months later, soldiers carried the virus to Europe, where it spread rapidly and became a full-blown epidemic.

• **End of the Spanish influenza epidemic:** by December 1918, the worst part of the epidemic was over. Some isolated cases were reported in 1919 and 1920, but by then Spanish influenza had run its course.

Health and Medicine—Epidemics— Swine Flu Immunization Program

The swine flu immunization program was an attempt by the U.S. government to prevent a serious flu epidemic. When the first vaccinations were given in September 1976, 56 people died and 600 were hospitalized.

• **Last of the swine flu immunization program:** December 16, 1976, when federal officials halted the nationwide swine flu immunization shots because of concern over possible links to reported cases of paralysis.

Health and Medicine—Epidemics— Typhoid Fever—Typhoid Mary

Mary Mallon worked as a cook in at least five New York-area households between 1897 and 1906. In each house, one or more people fell ill with typhoid fever while she was working there. She was tracked down and placed in an isolation ward, where doctors determined that although she was healthy, she was a carrier of the deadly microorganism that causes the fever. In 1907, she was placed on North Brother Island in the East River in New York City. When she promised to take special precautions, she was released in 1910. But within five years, she contaminated more people.

• **Last of Typhoid Mary:** On October 27, 1915, Mallon was returned to North Brother Island, where she spent the rest of her life. She died there on November 11, 1938, age 68. At least 35 cases of typhoid fever and three deaths were attributed to Typhoid Mary.

Health and Medicine—Epidemics— Yellow Fever—Philadelphia

The yellow fever epidemic that started in the summer of 1793 in Philadelphia, Pennsylva-nia, was the largest ever to hit the United States. The disease entered the city through cargo from the West Indies. From August to November there were 4,044 deaths. Philadelphia was then the nation's capital. The U.S. government suspended operations and federal officials fled the city.

• **End of the Philadelphia yellow fever epidemic:** late autumn 1793. Philadelphia had two additional serious yellow fever epidemics in 1794 and 1796-97, but not as serious as the one in 1793.

Health and Medicine—Epidemics— Yellow Fever—Reed Experiment

In 1900, U.S. Army Major Walter Reed began his experiment to determine the cause and transmission of yellow fever. He conducted his tests in Quemados, near Havana, Cuba, using Spanish and American volunteers. The experiment, which ended on January 31, 1901, demonstrated that the highly infectious disease was spread by mosquitoes.

• **Last survivor of Reed's Yellow Fever Experiment:** Gustaf E. Lambert, who died in Chicago, Illinois, on August 1962, age 87. Reed died in Washington, D.C., on November 23, 1902, age 51.

Health and Medicine—Health Hazards— Asbestos

When fibers from asbestos are released in the air and inhaled, they pose a serious risk of cancer of the lungs and chest lining.

• **Last use of asbestos in spackling compounds and other wall-patching mixtures in the U.S.:** 1978, when the Consumer Product Safety Commission banned its use. Asbestos in imitation logs and ash used in gas fireplaces were also banned.

Health and Medicine—Health Hazards— Fen-Phen

Two diet drugs, Pondimin (fenfluramine) and Redux (dexfenfluramine), were often used together to fight obesity and are known as Fen-Phen.

• **Last marketing of Fen-Phen in the United States:** September 1997. The two drugs were withdrawn from the market by their manufacturers at the request of the U.S. Food and Drug Administration (FDA) when evidence indicted they likely caused heart valve problems.

Health and Medicine—Health Hazards—Oraflex

The arthritis drug Oraflex reportedly caused serious liver and kidney damage and resulted in the deaths of 61 people in Great Britain and nine in the United States.

• **Last use of Oraflex in the United States:** August 1982.

Health and Medicine—Health Hazards—Phenformin

Phenformin, a drug used by many diabetics, was found to be a public health hazard.

• **Last use of Phenformin in the United States:** July 1977.

Health and Medicine—Health Hazards—Radium

A group of young women who worked at the Radium Dial Company in Ottawa, Illinois, in the 1920s developed radium poisoning that eventually led to their death. They were given the name The Society of the Living Dead. The women had used their lips to moisten their paintbrushes when they applied radium to the watch dials. The radium made the dials glow in the dark.

• **Last member of the Society of the Living Dead:** Mrs. Cecil Williams, who died in 1954.

Health and Medicine—Health Hazards—Radium Water

Radium water was produced in the 1920s and sold as Radithor. It was supposed to cure mental illness and retardation. Each bottle contained a microgram of radium and a microgram of esothorium. Pittsburgh steel tycoon Ebeen Beyers began taking Radithor when he was 51. He died two years later, on March 30, 1932, after consuming 1,400 bottles.

• **Last of the radium water cure in the United States:** 1932, when news of the cause of Beyers' death was publicized in newspapers.

Health and Medicine—Health Hazards—Red Dye No. 2

Red Dye No. 2 was the most widely used food coloring until it was found to be a possible cancer-causing agent.

• **Last use of Red Dye No. 2 in the United States:** January 1976, when it was banned by the FDA.

Health and Medicine—Health Hazards—Shoe-fitting Fluoroscopes

In the 1930s and 1940s, fluoroscope machines for fitting shoes were often found in stores where shoes were sold. When customers placed their feet in the machines, the fluoroscope produced an image of the bones of the feet and the outline of the shoes. By 1950, it was determined that shoe-fitting fluoroscopes posed a radiation hazard. By 1970, the machines had been banned in 33 states, and the remaining states had such stringent laws about their operation that using them became impractical.

• **Last shoe-fitting fluoroscope in use in the United States:** in a Madison, West Virginia, store in 1981. When the store managers learned West Virginia law prohibited operating the device, they donated it to the U.S. Food and Drug Administration.

Health and Medicine—Health Hazards—Smoking—Advertising

Cigarettes were once widely advertised on television. Cigarette ads were banned in the United Kingdom after July 31, 1965. The ads were banned in the United States after January 1, 1971.

• **Last TV cigarette commercial aired in the United Kingdom:** July 31, 1965, for Rothman International.

• **Last TV cigarette commercial aired in the United States:** 11:59 p.m., January 1, 1971, for Virginia Slims on the *Tonight Show Starring Johnny Carson*. The actress/model in the commercial was Veronica Hamel.

Health and Medicine—Health Hazards—Smoking—Airlines

• **End of smoking on commercial airline flights within the United States:** October

1989. This augmented the 1987 ruling banning smoking on flights of two hours or less, which represented about 80 percent of all flights.

Health and Medicine—Health Hazards—Smoking—California
• **Last time smoking was allowed in the workplace in California:** December 31, 1994. The law that became effective January 1, 1995, banned smoking of tobacco products in an enclosed space at a place of employment.
• **End of smoking in California bars and restaurants:** December 31, 1997.

Health and Medicine—Health Hazards—Smoking—New York, New York
• **End of smoking in New York, New York, bars and restaurants:** March 30, 2003.

Health and Medicine—Health Hazards—Thalidomide
Thalidomide was developed to prevent vomiting and was often prescribed for pregnant women.
• **Last use of Thalidomide for pregnant women:** early 1960s. Thalidomide was found to cause a wide range of birth defects. More than 10,000 babies born between 1959 and 1962 in Europe were affected before it was withdrawn. Thalidomide had not been given FDA approval and was not marketed in the U.S. In 1998, the drug was approved by the FDA for other uses, including leprosy symptoms.

Health and Medicine—Iron Lungs
Iron lungs—about 7 feet long and weighing 750 pounds—were once used by people who sustained lung damage from polio and needed assistance in breathing. With the virtual eradication of polio in the 1950s and 1960s and the invention of portable ventilators, the iron lung ostensibly became obsolete. It is estimated that only about 75 to 100 Americans still use irons lungs today. The equipment is no longer manufactured.
• **Last iron lungs manufactured:** 1992. Five portable iron lungs, called the Spencer-DHB iron lung, were produced under special arrangement in 1992 in Great Britain.

Health and Medicine—Medical Organizations—American College of Surgeons
The American College of Surgeons was founded in 1913 to improve the quality of care for surgical patients.
• **Last surviving founding member:** Dr. Fayette Clay Ewing, who died in Pineville, Louisiana, on April 15, 1956, age 94.

Health and Medicine—Medical Organizations—American Diabetes Association
The American Diabetes Association was founded in 1940. It is the nation's leading voluntary health organization supporting diabetes research, information and advocacy.
• **Last surviving founding member:** Dr. Charles Brook Flint Gibbs, who died in Rochester, New York, on August 4, 2000, age 105.

Health and Medicine—Medical Organizations—American Psychological Association
The American Psychological Association was founded in 1892 for the advancement of psychology as a science. The association was incorporated in 1925 in Washington, D.C.
• **Last surviving founding member:** Lightner Witmer, who died on July 19, 1956.

Health and Medicine—Medical Organizations—American Society for Clinical Pathology
The American Society for Clinical Pathology was founded by a group of pathologists in 1922.
• **Last surviving founding member:** Willis Pollard Butler, who died in Tennessee in 1991, age 103.

Health and Medicine—Medical Organizations—College of Physicians of Philadelphia
The College of Physicians of Philadelphia

(Pennsylvania) was founded in 1787 to promote a greater understanding of medicine and the role of the physician.
• **Last surviving founding member:** Dr. Thomas Parke. He was president of the College of Physicians from 1818 until his death in Philadelphia, on January 9, 1835, age 85.

Health and Medicine—Medical Studies—Plutonium and Uranium
In 1946, the U.S. government conducted a radiation experiment on people in a New York hospital to study how they would react to an atomic bombing. The victims were unaware they were being injected with uranium and plutonium.
• **Last surviving participant in the U.S. government's secret uranium and plutonium tests:** Mary Jean Connell. In 1996, Energy Secretary Hazel R. O'Leary personally apologized for the experiment.

Health and Medicine—Medical Studies—Syphilis
The "Tuskegee Study of Untreated Syphilis in the Negro Male" was a federally funded program carried out in Alabama from 1932 to 1972, involving more than 600 black men. The U.S. Public Health Service wanted to learn more about syphilis and the need for treatment programs. Because the study denied treatment to part of the group, about 400 men with syphilis went untreated for many years. In 1997, President Bill Clinton issued a formal apology to the participants.
• **Last survivor of the Tuskegee Syphilis Study:** Ernest Hendon, who died in Opelika, Alabama, on January 19, 2004, age 96.

Holidays

Holidays—Armistice Day
November 11, 1918, was the day the Armistice was signed, ending World War I. In the United States, Armistice Day was proclaimed a holiday in 1919.
• **Last U.S. celebration of Armistice Day:** 1953. The following year, Armistice Day was renamed Veterans Day, to honor all the troops who have served in the U.S. armed forces. (*See also* Holidays—Veterans Day.)

Holidays—Feast of Fools
The Feast of Fools had its origins in France in the 12th century. It was an occasion for people to poke fun at religious rituals by having lesser clergy take on the roles of higher officials. It started on January 1 and lasted several days. The holiday was most popular in France, Spain, England and Germany.
• **Last celebration of the Feast of Fools:** 1435. Celebration of the event got so out of hand that the Roman Catholic Church abolished it at the Great Council of Basel. The event then went underground and was celebrated secretly well into the 16th century.

Holidays—Veterans Day
In 1968, the U.S. Congress changed the national day for commemorating Veterans Day from November 11 to the fourth Monday in October. It was not a popular choice.
• **Last time Veterans Day was officially celebrated on the fourth Monday in October:** 1978. Many people felt the November 11th date had significance that was being lost with the change to October. (*See also* Holidays—Armistice Day.)

Hotels
Last of Some Major United States Hotels
(Note: Hotels are listed by their original names; subsequent names are in parentheses.)

Hotel and Location	Last Used	Description
Adirondack Lodge Clear Lake, New York	1903	Built in 1878-79. Destroyed during a forest fire.

Alvarado Hotel Albuquerque, New Mexico	1970	Built in 1902. The largest of the Harvey Houses was a historic landmark when it was demolished.
Astor House New York, New York	1913	Opened in 1836. Designed by Isaiah Rodgers. Demolished.
Astor Hotel New York, New York	1967	Built in 1902-04 for William Waldorf Astor. Designed by Clinton & Russell. Demolished to make room for an office building.
Bella Union Hotel **(Clarendon Hotel)** **(St. Charles Hotel)** Los Angeles, California	1940	Built in 1835 as a store and residence. Served as the last capitol of Alta California under Governor Pio Pico in 1845-46. Converted to Bella Union Hotel in the 1850s, the first hotel in Los Angeles. Name changed to Clarendon Hotel in 1873 and to St. Charles Hotel in 1875. Demolished. Site now occupied by a mall.
Broadway Central Hotel **(University Hotel)** New York, New York	1973	Built in 1867. Later renamed University Hotel. Scene of the murder of financier Jim Fisk in 1872. Building collapsed in 1973, killing four people.
Capital Hotel Johnstown, Pennsylvania	1960	Built in 1860. The only hotel that survived the 1889 flood. Demolished and replaced by a parking lot.
Charleston Hotel Charleston, South Carolina	1960	Built in 1839. The Greek Revival building was demolished.
Chicago Hotel **(Great Northern Hotel)** Chicago, Illinois	1940	Designed in 1890-92 by Burnham and Company. Later renamed Great Northern Hotel. Demolished.
Dunes Hotel and Casino Las Vegas, Nevada	1993	Opened in 1955. Implosion in 1993 was witnessed by more than 200,000 spectators. Site cleared to make room for Bellagio hotel/casino.
El Rancho Vegas **Hotel-Casino** Las Vegas, Nevada	1960	Built in 1941. One of the early hotel-casinos in Las Vegas. Destroyed by fire.
Fifth Avenue Hotel New York, New York	1908	Opened in 1859. Designed by William Washburn. It was the first hotel to have an elevator. Once New York's most exclusive hotel, its popularity waned as the area became more commercial. Demolished.
Garden of Allah Los Angeles, California	1959	Built in 1928 on the estate of movie star Alia Nazimova on Hollywood's Sunset Strip. The hotel and bungalow complex was a gathering place for movie celebrities. It was torn down after the property was sold to a building and loan association.
Grand Union Hotel Saratoga, New York	1953	Built in 1802. Once a popular vacation hotel for the wealthy during the Gilded Age. Torn down.
Hotel Del Monte Monterey, California	1924	Built in 1880. Burned down in 1887. Rebuilt and burned down again in 1924. The hotel was rebuilt in 1926, and was later taken over by the U.S. Navy. It is now the home of the Naval Postgraduate School.
Lake Geneva Inn Lake Geneva, Wisconsin	1970	Built in 1911-12. Designed by Frank Lloyd Wright. Demolished.
LaSalle Hotel Chicago, Illinois	1976	Built in 1909. A fire in 1946 killed 61 people. The damage was repaired and the hotel continued to oper-

		ate until 1976, when it was demolished. The site is now occupied by Two North LaSalle.
Lexington Hotel Chicago, Illinois	1995	Built in 1892. Designed by Clinton Warren. Occupied by Al Capone from 1928 to 1931. Demolished.
Maxwell House Nashville, Tennessee	1961	Built in 1859. One of the last hotels designed by Isaiah Rogers. The hotel gave its name to a brand of coffee. Destroyed by fire.
Mount Vernon Hotel Cape May, New Jersey	1856	Opened in 1853. The gas-illuminated Mount Vernon advertised that it was the largest hotel in the world. It was destroyed by fire in September 1856.
Mountain Park Hotel Hot Springs, North Carolina	1920	Built in 1886. Destroyed by fire.
New Yorker Hotel Miami, Florida	1981	Built in 1939. The Art Deco hotel was considered the greatest design of Henry Hohauser. Its demolition led to local laws protecting other buildings in the Miami Architectural Historic District.
Nueces Hotel Corpus Christi, Texas	1971	Opened in 1913. It was the tallest building south of San Antonio. Famed for its Tropical Garden and Sun Parlor. Converted to a retirement home. Demolished.
Park Avenue Hotel New York, New York	1927	Opened in 1878. Designed by John Kellum. Demolished. Original owner, A. T. Stewart planned it as a hotel for working women but died before it was completed. Room rates were so high that Stewart's philanthropic plan was abandoned and it opened as a luxury hotel.
Ritz-Carlton Hotel New York, New York	1951	Built in 1910. Designed by Warren and Wetmore. Demolished to make room for an office building.
Ryan Hotel Saint Paul, Minnesota	1962	Built in 1882. Demolished. The Minnesota Mutual Life building was constructed on the site in 1981.
Saint Charles Hotel **(Exchange Hotel)** **(Sheraton St. Charles)** New Orleans, Louisiana	1974	Three Saint Charles Hotels occupied the same site from the late 1830s to 1974. The first, also known as Exchange Hotel, was destroyed by fire in 1851. The second, built two years later, burned down in 1894. The third opened in 1896 and was later known as the Sheraton St. Charles. Despite protests from preservationists, it was demolished by its owner, who later admitted it was his biggest mistake.
Sands, The Las Vegas, Nevada	1996	Built in 1952. The circular hotel-casino was once the playground of the Rat Pack. It was demolished to make room for a hotel-casino with a Venetian theme.
Senator Hotel Miami Beach, Florida	1988	Designed in 1939 by L. Murray Dixon. Demolition of the hotel led to the strengthening of Miami Beach preservation laws.
Shamrock Hotel Houston, Texas	1985	Opened in 1949. Built by oil wildcatter Glenn McCarthy. Hilton bought the hotel in 1955. It remained a luxury hotel until 1985, when it was purchased by the Texas Medical Center. Demolished two years later.
Traymore Hotel Atlantic City, New Jersey	1972	Built in the 1870s. Started as a cottage near the Boardwalk. By 1915, it was 14 stories tall and had rooms for 600 people. Demolished in 1972.

Tremont House Galveston, Texas	1928	Built in 1839. Destroyed by fire in 1865. A second Tremont House opened in 1872. It was demolished in 1928. A new Tremont was built near the original one in 1985.
Waldorf Astoria Hotel New York, New York	1931	Built in 1893. It was demolished to make room for the Empire State Building. A new, much larger Waldorf-Astoria opened in 1931.
Willard Hotel Washington, D.C.	1968	Built in the 1830s at 14th and Pennsylvania Avenues as Fuller's City Hotel. Sold to Willard in 1850 and rebuilt. The original hotel building was torn down in 1901 and a larger structure went up in its place.

Human Body

Human Body—Cannibalism

Cannibalism was practiced in Fiji and the Marquesas Islands of the South Pacific until near the end of the 19th century.

• **Last documented instance of cannibalism in Fiji:** 1867, when the Rev. Thomas Baker, a British missionary, was eaten after he accidentally touched the chief's head. His boot—believed to have been boiled while he was cooked—is on display in the Fiji Museum in Suva. In 2003, the village whose ancestors killed and ate Baker extended an apology to descendants of Baker.

• **Last recorded instance of ceremonial cannibalism:** 1887, during a ceremony in the Puamau Valley on the island Fatu-Hiva. The practice of cannibalism had been outlawed in 1879.

• **Last man in Marquesas Islands who ate human flesh:** Tei Tetua, a former chief of four tribes. In 1936, Thor Heyerdahl visited Fatu-Hiva and encountered him in the Ouia Valley.

Human Body—Eunuchs

Eunuchs were castrated men who worked in women's quarters in palaces. They were used in imperial China and in the palaces of the Byzantine and later Ottoman emperors. Some rose to positions of power and held high offices. The custom of using eunuchs in choirs began among the Ottomans in Constantinople in the 16th century. It spread to Europe and gave rise to the castrati singers in the papal choirs and in opera. (*See also*

Music— Performers, Classical—Castrati.)

• **Last use of eunuchs in China:** 1912, with the collapse of the Manchu dynasty.

• **Last eunuch of the Chinese emperor:** Sun Yaoting, who died in Beijing, China, in December 1996 at age 93. Shortly after he was castrated in 1911, the Manchu Dynasty came to an end, and with it the end of the eunuch system.

• **Last use of eunuchs in the Ottoman Empire:** 1922, when the Ottoman Turkish sultanate ended.

• **Last use of eunuchs in India:** 1955, when both eunuchs and harems were outlawed.

Human Body—Foot Binding of Females

The practice of foot binding may have started in T'ang dynasty in China. When young girls were around five years old, their feet were bound with long strips of fabric to halt growth.

• **End of foot binding of females in China:** 1949, when it was officially banned by the Communist government. The practice had begun to die out when China had contact with Western cultures. It generally fell out of practice by 1911, except for isolated cases.

Labor

(*See also* Slavery and Involuntary Servitude)

Labor—Child Labor

Child labor was once a serious problem in the United States. As many as 2 million children between the ages of 10 and 15 were working in factories, mills and mines when the 1910 federal census was taken.

• **Last time child laborers were not protected by law:** 1938. The Fair Labor Standards Act (a.k.a. Wages and Hours Act) passed by the U.S. Congress that year limits the age of working children to 16 or older and to 18 if the job is hazardous. Children under 16 are permitted to work under certain conditions. The law also requires employers to pay children at least the minimum wage.

Labor—Feudalism
Feudalism was a political and socioeconomic system in which wealthy landowners made grants of fiefs (feudal estates) to vassals (feudal tenants) in exchange for the promise of military or political service. It existed mainly in Europe, China, Japan and some parts of Africa. The rise of nationalism in the 18th century played a major role in ending European feudalism.

• **End of feudalism in France:** August 4, 1789, when feudalism was legally abolished by the National Assembly.

• **End of feudalism in Austria:** legally abolished in 1848, at the Vienna Reichstag. Earlier that year, Emperor Ferdinand promised to free the peasants of all dues tied to the land, effective January 1, 1849.

• **End of feudalism in Japan:** legally abolished in 1871, when the fiefs were divided into prefectures by imperial decree. In 1869, many of the daimyos (feudal lords) voluntarily surrendered their feudal rights.

Labor—Indentured Servants
Indentured, or bonded, servants were a major source of labor in colonial America in the 17th and early 18th century. They came mainly from England and Germany and fit into three groups: (1) redemptioners, who arranged to serve for a specific number of years; (2) people who were forced into servitude for religious or economic reasons or were kidnapped; and (3) convicts. In 19th-century America, the practice of using indentured servants was continued with Chinese laborers known as "coolies."

• **Last of the imported indentured servants:** The practice of using indentured servants was outlawed by the Alien Contract Act of 1885. It banned companies or people from bringing foreigners to the United States under contract to work here except under special conditions, such as domestic help or skilled workers.

Labor—Luddites
From 1811 to 1816, a group of rioters known as Luddites in Yorkshire, Lancashire and Nottinghamshire, England, went about breaking factory machinery in the belief that such labor-saving devices were causing the nation's high unemployment and low wages. The protestors took their name from Ned Lud, a mentally challenged man who was chased into a factory by tormenters. In frustration, he wrecked some knitting frames that were in the building.

• **Last of the Luddites:** 1817. In 1812, several Luddites and an employer were killed, causing the British Parliament to enact a strict law against their activities. The Frame Breaking Act passed in 1812 called for the death penalty for anyone who broke machines. Sporadic acts of violence continued after the Frame Breaking law was passed, but within five years Luddite activity had ended.

Labor—Molly Maguires
A secret miner's organization known as The Molly Maguires was active in the coal region of Pennsylvania from the 1860s to 1880. In 1875, a mine official was murdered, setting off an investigation. After an employee of the Pinkerton Detective Agency infiltrated the Molly Maguires, several members were indicted and convicted of murder. By 1880, 19 had been hanged and many more were imprisoned. The convictions put an end to the terrorism of the Molly Maguires.

• **Last of the Molly Maguires to be put to death:** John ("Black Jack") Kehoe, who had been tried and found guilty of murder. He was executed before a large crowd in Pottsville, Pennsylvania, on December 18, 1878, even though the governor of Pennsylvania did not believe Kehoe was guilty. In 1979, more than a century later, Kehoe received a full pardon from Pennsylvania Governor Milton J. Shapp.

Labor—Strikes—General Motors/United Auto Workers Sit-Down Strike

The first major labor dispute in the U.S. automobile industry occurred when members of the United Auto Workers of America, working with the Congress of Industrial Organizations (CIO), organized a sit-down strike in December 1936 to protest working conditions at General Motors (GM).

• **Last day of the UAW/CIO GM strike:** February 11, 1937. General Motors agreed to an additional pay increase and to union recognition. The striking workers evacuated the building and operations resumed the following Monday.

Labor—Strikes—Grape War

The Grape War began in 1966 after California grape workers had been on strike nearly a year with no sign of a resolution. Cesar Chavez—head of the AFL-CIO United Farm Workers Organizing Committee—asked the public to support the strikers by boycotting table grapes. His nonviolent strategy paid off. He attracted millions of supporters to the cause of the grape workers.

• **End of the Grape War:** July 29, 1970, when Chavez signed a contract with 26 major table grape growers in Delano, California. The strike had lasted five years. Chavez later earned the Presidential Medal of Freedom. He died on April 23, 1993, age 66.

Labor—Strikes—Great Anthracite Coal Strike

The Great Anthracite Coal Strike in Pennsylvania was the first major labor confrontation of the 20th century. The strike began in May 1902, and estimates of its cost ran close to $150 million.

• **Last day of the Great Anthracite Coal Strike:** October 16, 1902, after more than 160 days, when the White House issued an official statement indicating that a commission would mediate the differences.

Labor—Strikes—Homestead Steel Strike

On July 1, 1892, 3,800 men employed at the Carnegie Steel Company in Homestead, Pennsylvania, were locked out in a wage dispute. They were members of the Amalgamated Association of Iron, Steel and Tin Workers. On July 6, 1892, about 300 strikebreakers were brought in, supplied by the Pinkerton Detective Agency. During the resulting fighting, 10 people were killed. The National Guard was called in and remained on duty at the plant until October 1, 1892.

• **Last day of the Homestead Steel Strike:** November 20, 1892. The steel workers at the plant were unable to form unions until 1937.

Labor—Strikes—Ludlow Coal Strike and Massacre

In September 1913, several thousand workers began a strike at the Rockefeller-owned Colorado Fuel and Iron Works in Ludlow, Colorado. During the negotiations, strikers and their families lived in nearby tent colonies.

• **Last day of the Ludlow Coal Strike:** April 20, 1914, when the National Guard fired on one of the tent colonies and killed two women, 11 children and several of the strikers. The killings became known as the Ludlow Massacre.

Labor—Strikes—Pullman Strike

The Pullman strike began in May 1894, in south Chicago, Illinois, after the Pullman Palace Car Company cut wages to workers and refused arbitration. The American Railway Union (ARU) forbid members to work on the Pullman cars. The strike spread to 27 states. After mob violence in July, U.S. President Grover Cleveland ordered federal troops to Chicago, the scene of the worst activity. As the violence continued, two men were killed and several were injured when U.S. marshals fired on the strikers on July 6, 1894.

• **Last day of the Pullman strike:** August 2, 1894, after a court injunction was placed against the ARU. The ARU's leader Eugene V. Debs was arrested and sentenced to six months in jail. In July, during the violence, many of Chicago's Columbian Exposition buildings were set on fire and destroyed.

Labor—Unions—AFL and CIO

When the American Federation of Labor (AFL) and the Congress of Industrial Organizations (CIO) decided to merge, they were the two largest labor unions in the United States, with a combined membership of 16 million.

• **Last time the AFL and CIO were separate organizations:** December 5, 1955. The two unions merged as the AFL-CIO. Merger negotiations had been worked on during the year and were agreed upon at a convention in New York, New York, that December. George Meany, AFL president, became president of both unions. He served until 1980. Walter Reuther, president of the CIO, became vice-president.

Labor—Unions—International Federation of Trade Unions (IFTU)

The International Federation of Trade Unions (IFTU) was formed 1913, replacing an earlier union that was formed in 1901.

• **Last of the IFTU:** 1946, when it dissolved. Earlier, in October 1945, the World Federation of Trade Unions was formed.

Labor—Unions—Knights of Labor

The Knights of Labor were created in 1869. By the late 1870s, their membership numbered 700,000.

• **Last of the Knights of Labor:** just about gone by 1900. The public blamed the Knights for the 1886 Haymarket riot. The American Federation of Labor (AFL) launched an attack to lure away Knights members. Thousands made the switch to the AFL. The greatly weakened Knights gradually faded away in the late 1890s.

Labor—Unions—Knights of Saint Crispin

The Knights of Saint Crispin was a secret union of boot and shoe workers, established in 1867 in Wisconsin. It was formed at a time when shoemaking was becoming industrialized. The union directed much of its energies toward preventing the mechanization of the craft. The Knights of Saint Crispin spread to other states where shoes were manufactured. It had some success in strikes during its early years but suffered a series of defeats during the Panic of 1873.

• **Last of the Knights of Saint Crispin:** late 1874. Many of its members later joined the Knights of Labor.

Labor—Unions—Knights of the Golden Circle/Order of American Knights/Order of the Sons of Liberty

The Knights of the Golden Circle were a pre-Civil War secret society of Northern-based Southern sympathizers who were pro-slavery and pro-secessionist. They came together in the 1850s. The group reorganized during the Civil War as the Order of American Knights. In 1864, the name was changed to the Order of the Sons of Liberty.

• **Last of the Knights of the Golden Circle/Sons of Liberty:** 1865, as the Civil War drew to an end. When it was apparent that the North would be victorious, the group dissolved. Activities of a few splinter factions were reported briefly after the war, but the original group had ceased to exist.

Labor—Unions—National Labor Union (NLU)

The National Labor Union (NLU) was established in Baltimore, Maryland, in 1866, when several unions joined together to seek reform through political action. The NLU was the first major national union in the United States. It sought to expand the currency with greenbacks unsupported by gold. It also wanted to end the convict-labor system and establish an eight-hour workday. The NLU began to disintegrate in 1871 when several unions withdrew support. The Knights of Labor drew away membership.

• **Last of the NLU:** ceased operation after the Panic of 1873.

Labor—Wages

The Wages and Hours Act, the national minimum wage law, was enacted June 25, 1938, under the Fair Labor Standards Act. It set the minimum wage at 25¢ an hour.

Minimum Wage in the United States

Old Rate	Last Year at Old Rate	New Rate
25¢/hr.	1939	30¢/hr.
30¢/hr.	1944	40¢/hr.
40¢/hr.	1949	75¢/hr.
75¢/hr.	1955	$1.00/hr.
$1.00/hr.	1960	$1.15/hr.
$1.15/hr.	1962	$1.25/hr.
$1.25/hr.	1966	$1.40/hr.
$1.40/hr.	1967	$1.60/hr.
$1.60/hr.	1973	$2.00/hr.
$2.00/hr.	1974	$2.10/hr.
$2.10/hr.	1975	$2.30/hr.
$2.30/hr.	1977	$2.65/hr.
$2.65/hr.	1978	$2.90/hr.
$2.90/hr.	1979	$3.10/hr.
$3.10/hr.	1980	$3.35/hr.
$3.35/hr.	1989	$3.80/hr.
$3.80/hr.	1990	$4.25/hr.
$4.25/hr.	1996	$4.75/hr.
$4.75/hr.	1997	$5.15/hr.

Labor—Worker's Compensation Insurance

The first worker's compensation insurance law was enacted in Maryland in 1902.
• **Last state to require worker's compensation:** Mississippi, in 1948.

Languages— Extinct Languages

The following "lasts" are documented last native speakers of languages worldwide that have become extinct or at one time were extinct. It does not include Native American languages. For those lasts, *see* Native Americans—Languages.

Languages—Extinct—Aasáx (Tanzania)

A victim of German colonialism, power struggles, economics and other factors, the Aasáx language spoken in Tanzania moved toward extinction in the 20th century as many native speakers died off and others shifted to another language.

• **Last remaining native Aasáx speaker:** died in 1976. The Aasáx have survived as an ethnic group; however, their language has disappeared.

Languages—Extinct—Ainu (Japan)

Karafuto Ainu, a dialect of the Ainu people of South Sakhalin, was spoken occasionally among the elderly Karafuto Ainu who relocated to Hokkaido after World War II.
• **Last speaker of Karafuto dialect of Ainu:** Asai Take, who died on April 30, 1994, age 92.
• **Last speaker of Shizunai dialect of Ainu:** Sute Orita, who worked with a linguist in Hokkaido in the 1980s.

Languages—Extinct—Bare (Brazil and Venezuela)

The Bare language was once spoken by thousands of Indians who lived along the Upper Rio Negre in Brazil and Venezuela.
• **Last fluent speaker of Bare in Brazil:** Candeláno de Silva, who worked with a linguist in 1991. His death left only a few Bare speakers in Venezuela.

Languages—Extinct—Cornish (England)

Cornish, a Celtic language, was spoken by the early people of Cornwall, Devon and West Somerset, England. Its use began to decline in the 17th century with the introduction of the English language in books and in commerce.
• **Last traditional Cornish speakers:** Some linguists claim Cornish lost its last traditional speaker in 1777, when Dolly Pentreath died. William Bodinar, who died in 1789, also has been identified as one of the last to have spoken the language fluently. And more recently John Davey, who died in 1891, was claimed to be the last fluent speaker of the Cornish language. However, other linguists argue that the language never died out. Today, Cornish has 2,000 speakers and many people are studying the language.

Languages—Extinct—Dalmatian (Croatia)

Dalmatian, a Romance language, was spoken along the Adriatic shores of Croatia and on the nearby islands. It may have been in

use since Roman colonists settled the region in the last centuries of the pre-Christian era.
• **Last speaker of Dalmatian:** Antonio Udina (Tuone Udaina), who died in 1898.

Languages—Extinct—Dutch Creole (Caribbean islands)
Dutch Creole was once spoken in the U.S. Virgin Islands, the Leeward Islands and Puerto Rico.
• **Last fluent Dutch Creole speaker:** died in 1987.

Languages—Extinct—Gagadju (Australia)
The Gagadju (or Kakadu) language was once widespread in the Kakadu National Park region in the Northern Territory of Australia.
• **Last speaker of Gagadju (Kakadu):** Big Bill Neidjie, who died in July 2002.

Languages—Extinct—Jiwarli (Australia)
Jiwarli, an Aboriginal language, was once spoken in western Australia.
• **Last native speaker of Jiwarli:** Jack Butler, who died in April 1986.

Languages—Extinct—Kalkadoon (Australia)
Kalkadoon, an Aboriginal language, was spoken in western Queensland, Australia.
• **Last fluent speaker of Kalkadoon language:** Lardie Moonlight, an Aboriginal woman of the town of Boulia, in western Queensland, who died in the 1980s.

Languages—Extinct—Manx (Isle of Man)
The Manx language is related to Gaelic. It was spoken into the 19th century on the Isle of Man, then its use waned. In recent years, Manx is again being taught in schools.
• **Last original native speaker of Manx:** Edward ("Ned") Madrell, who died on the Isle of Man in 1974.

Languages—Extinct—Martuthunira (Australia)
Martuthunira is a language of the Pilbara Region of western Australia.
• **Last fluent speaker of Martuthunira:** Algy Paterson, who died on August 6, 1995.

Languages—Extinct—Moksela (Indonesia)
Moksela was once spoken in central Maluku (Moluccas), Indonesia.
• **Last native speaker of Moksela:** died in 1974.

Languages—Extinct—Moriori (New Zealand)
The Moriori language was spoken on the Chatham Islands, east of the New Zealand archipelago.
• **Last full-blooded Moriori:** Tommy Solomon (Moriori name: Tama Horomona Rehi), who died on March 19, 1933.
• **Last surviving person with direct knowledge of the Moriori language:** Johann Friedrich Wilhelm Baucke, a linguist, ethnologist, journalist and interpreter who died in Otorohanga, New Zealand, on June 6, 1931, age 82.

Languages—Extinct—N|u (South Africa)
N|u is the last of the !Ui languages of the Kalahari region of South Africa.
• **Last fluent N|u speaker:** Elsie Vaalbooi, a great-grandmother in her late 90s, who lives in a village on the southern edge of the Kalahari Desert.

Languages—Extinct—Nyulnuyl (Australia)
Nyulnuyl, an Aboriginal language spoken in western Australia, is moving toward extinction.
• **Last fluent speakers of Nyulnuyl:** author Magdalene Williams of Beagle Bay, who died in 1995, and Mary Carmel Charles. About ten people have some fluency in the language.

Languages—Extinct—Old Sirinek Language (Siberia)
Old Sirinek, a language of northern Russia, is part of the Eskimo family. Its speakers lived in eastern Chukotka. By the 1990s, only four people remained who still could speak it.
• **Last speaker of Old Sirinek:** Valentina Wye, who died in 1997.

Languages—Extinct—Omurano (Peru)
Omurano is one of 14 extinct languages

among the 106 indigenous ones of Peru.
• **Last native speaker of Omurano:** died in 1958.

Languages—Extinct—Ubykh (Turkey)
Ubykh was once spoken in the northern Caucasus.
• **Last fluent speaker of Ubykh:** Tefvik Escenc, a farmer from the Turkish village of Haci Osman, who died in 1992. Attempts are being made to revive the language.

Languages—Extinct—Waka Waka (Australia)
Waka Waka was spoken among Aboriginal Australians of southeastern Queensland.
• **Last fluent speaker of Waka Waka:** Willie Mackenzie (Geerbo or Gaiarabau), who died in 1968. Mackenzie was a full-blood Aboriginal and the last member of the Darwarbadam tribe.

Languages—Extinct—Warrungu (Australia)
Warrungu is an Aboriginal language of the Upper Herbert River area of northern Queensland.
• **Last original native speaker of Warrungu:** Alf Palmer (Jinbilnggay). In the 1970s, he helped to document his Aboriginal language for future generations.

Languages—Extinct—Yavitero (Venezuela)
Yavitero was one of the indigenous languages of the Orinoco region of Venezuela.
• **Last native speaker of Yavitero:** died in 1984.

Law and Order

Law and Order—Courts—Court of Appeals in Cases of Capture (United States)
The Court of Appeals in Cases of Capture was created in the United States in 1780 to replace a standing committee that heard cases from the states.
• **Last of the Court of Appeals in Cases of Capture:** abolished in 1787, when the Supreme Court of the United States was established.

Law and Order—Courts—Court of High Commission (England)
The English Court of High Commission was established in 1561 to handle ecclesiastical matters. It enforced prescribed forms of worship and halted heresy. It was originally abolished by Parliament in July 1641 but reestablished in 1686 by James II.
• **Last of the Court of High Commission:** permanently abolished in 1688, during the Glorious Revolution.

Law and Order—Courts—Court of the Star Chamber (England)
The Star Chamber started out as the English monarch's council in judicial matters. Originally, it served a useful purpose in that it curbed nobles who were beyond ordinary law. In 1487, the chamber was illegally changed into a separate judicial body by Henry VIII, and its powers were extended by his successors.
• **Last of the Star Chamber:** abolished by Parliament in 1641, after it became abusive in dealing with matters unfettered by the rule of law or by juries.

Law and Order—Courts—U.S. Supreme Court
The U.S. Constitution created the Supreme Court, but Congress determines the number of justices.
• **Last time the court had five, six, seven, eight and ten members:** The Judiciary Act of 1789 set the number of Supreme Court members at six: a chief justice and five associate justices. The Judiciary Act of 1801 lowered the number of justices to **five**. That number was raised again to **six** the following year with the Judiciary Act of 1802. In 1807, the act creating the 7th Circuit raised the number of justices to **seven**. The number of justices increased to nine with the establishment of the 8th and 9th Circuits in 1837. The court reached **ten**, its highest number, in 1863 with the establishment of the 10th Circuit. In 1866, during the Andrew Johnson administration, the number was cut to **eight** to prevent him from appointing a justice during the remainder of his term. The current membership of **nine** was established

three years later, with the Judiciary Act of 1869.

• **Last time the U.S. Supreme Court met in Philadelphia, Pennsylvania:** August 15, 1800, in a building now known as Old City Hall, near Independence Hall. The nation's capital then moved to a new site along the Potomac between Virginia and Maryland.

• **Last time U.S. Supreme Court justices were required to ride circuit:** 1891. For 101 years, except for a brief time in the early years of the 19th century, the justices of the U.S. Supreme Court were required to travel to each of the judicial districts and hold court twice a year. The practice was abolished with the creation of the U.S. Circuit Courts of Appeals, to which circuit judges were assigned.

• **Last time the U.S. Supreme Court was all-male:** 1981, when Sandra Day O'Connor became the first woman appointed to the Court. She took her seat on September 25, 1981.

• **Last time the U.S. Supreme Court was all-white:** 1967, when Thurgood Marshall became the first African American to be appointed to the Court. He took his seat on October 2, 1967.

Law and Order—Laws—Alcohol— Minimum Drinking Age

Today, the minimum drinking age is 21 in all states and the District of Columbia. Back in the early 1970s, many states had lowered the legal age to 18, the age at which people could be required to serve in the armed forces. In the early 1980s, MADD (Mothers Against Drunk Driving) lobbied to have the drinking age raised to 21 for all states to cut down on alcohol-related driving deaths among young people.

• **Last time the U.S. had no federal minimum drinking age:** 1984. The National Minimum Drinking Age Act signed into law on July 17, 1984, by President Ronald Reagan set the minimum age at 21. The act tied minimum-drinking-age compliance to federal highway funding to states. Funding would be withheld from those states that failed to raise the minimum age to 21.

Law and Order—Laws—Alcohol— Prohibition

The 18th Amendment to the U.S. Constitution was ratified on January 16, 1919, and became effective one year later. It banned the manufacture, sale or transportation of alcohol within the United States or between the United States and other nations. In 1919, Congress passed the Volstead Act, which gave federal law officers the power to enforce it.

• **Last state to ratify the 18th Amendment:** New Jersey on March 9, 1922. The amendment had already became law with ratification by the 36th state, Nebraska, on January 16, 1919. Two states did not ratify the amendment: Connecticut and Rhode Island. The Volstead Act, which reinforced the amendment, went into effect on January 17, 1920.

• **End of Prohibition:** December 5, 1933, when Utah became the 36th state to ratify the 21st Amendment to the U.S. Constitution.

• **End of Prohibition in Oklahoma:** April 7, 1959, when Oklahoma voters opted to repeal the state's prohibition law that had been in effect since 1907. That left Mississippi as the last dry state.

• **Last state to abandon Prohibition:** Mississippi, on May 21, 1966, when the state legislature adopted a local-option liquor law. Mississippi's prohibition law had been in effect since 1908.

Law and Order—Laws—Benefit of Clergy

In early times in England, members of the clergy were exempt from the jurisdiction of the secular courts. Later, the exemption privilege was expanded to include laymen who could read and write.

• **Last benefit-of-clergy exemption in England:** 1827. Abuses of the benefit-of-clergy exemption had become so excessive in Great Britain that the privilege was abolished by the Criminal Law Act of 1827.

• **Last benefit-of-clergy exemption in the U.S.:** abolished in federal courts April 30, 1790, when the U.S. Congress ruled there should be no benefit-of-clergy privilege for any capital crime against the United States. The exemption disappeared from state courts by around 1850.

Law and Order—Laws—Draco's Laws

Draco was a lawgiver who, according to tradition, wrote down the first code of laws in Athens, Greece, around the 620s B.C. His code is noted for its severity. Draco called for the death penalty for most crimes, even offenses as minor as stealing fruit. The word "Draconian" has become synonymous with harshness or extreme severity.

• **Last of Draco's laws:** 594 B.C., when all of Draco's laws, except those on homicide, were abolished by Solon.

Law and Order—Laws—Property— Entail

Entail is a principle of law that governs the inheritance of property. It dates back to Europe in the Middle Ages. When the owner of an estate dies, the entire estate is bequeathed to his heir (usually a son) and from that heir to a set line of direct descendants. This system of land ownership was practiced in colonial America but was viewed by some of the enlightened colonists as undemocratic.

• **End of entail in the United States:** banned first in Virginia in 1776 on motion of Thomas Jefferson. By the time Jefferson finished his term as U.S. president in 1809, the practice of entail had just about disappeared in the United States.

Law and Order—Laws—Property— Primogeniture

Primogeniture is a legal principle that all of a parent's property descends intact to the oldest son, to the exclusion of all other children in the family.

• **End of primogeniture in the United States:** Virginia abolished primogeniture in 1785. By the end of the 18th century, it had been abolished throughout the United States for intestate estates. Rhode Island was the last state to abolish primogeniture in 1798.

• **End of primogeniture in Great Britain:** abolished for all but members of the royal family in 1925. In Europe, the practice ended gradually as feudalism ended.

Law and Order—Laws—Quakers' Great Law (Quaker Code of 1682)

The Society of Friends (Quakers) were a major force in prison reform in the American colonies. The Great Law of the Quakers (Quaker Code of 1682) established a set of more humane laws of punishment in Pennsylvania. Hard labor replaced death for serious crimes, and capital punishment was eliminated altogether from the original codes. Later, only premeditated murder was punishable by death. The Quakers' Great Law also did away with religious offenses and dealt only with secular criminal jurisprudence, a departure from other colonial and European codes.

• **End of the Quaker Code of 1682:** July 31, 1718, when the code was repealed one day after the death of Pennsylvania's proprietor, William Penn. The Quaker Code was replaced by the Anglican Code of England that restored harsh punishments and more extensive capital punishment.

Law and Order—Lawyers—Advertising

Although the advertising of legal services was common in the 19th century, in 1908, the American Bar Association banned advertising by lawyers in the United States by equating it to an unethical activity.

• **End of the ban on advertising legal services:** 1977, when the U.S. Supreme Court handed down the Bates decision, which said states did not have the right to bar legal advertising through blanket prohibitions. Subsequent decisions expanded the rights of lawyers to communicate their services and limited the rights of states to bar or otherwise regulate them. In 1982 and 1985, the U.S. Supreme Court held that a state cannot prohibit advertising or marketing that is not false, deceptive or misleading.

Libraries

Libraries—Alexandrian Library

The Alexandrian Library, built during the

reign of Ptolemy I (323-285 B.C.), made Alexandria, Egypt, the intellectual center of the Hellenistic world. It is said to have contained some 700,000 volumes. The library was damaged by a fire in 47 B.C. It sustained more damage during a civil war in the late 200s A.D.

• **Last of the original Alexandrian Library:** 391 A.D., when it was destroyed by order of Byzantine Emperor Theodosius. A new library was accumulated, but it was burned by outsiders around 641 A.D. In the late 20th century, steps were taken to begin rebuilding the Alexandrian Library.

Libraries—Library of Congress

The Library of Congress was in the Capitol Building in Washington, D.C., from its founding until 1897.

• **Last of the original U.S. Library of Congress:** 1814, when the British set fire to the Capitol during the War of 1812. The Library of Congress was restored in 1815 and restocked with more than 6,400 books purchased from the personal library of Thomas Jefferson.

• **Last of many of Jefferson's books:** destroyed in 1851, when another fire in the Capitol Building destroyed 35,000 of the 55,000 books in the Library of Congress. About two thirds of the books purchased from Jefferson were lost in the fire.

Libraries—Library of Congress—Card Catalogs

The Library of Congress began selling duplicates of its 3-by-5-inch catalog cards to libraries around the world in 1902. The peak year for the cards was 1968, when 78 million were sold. By 1996, annual sales had dropped to less than 580,000. Most libraries began converting to online public access catalogs (OPACs) in the 1980s and 1990s. By the late 1990s, with the dwindling number of card catalogs in use, the Library of Congress decided to suspend production of its catalog cards.

• **Last day libraries could order catalog cards from the Library of Congress:** February 28, 1997. Some commercial vendors still produce the cards to support the remaining card catalogs.

Lighthouses
Last of Some American Lighthouses

Name and Location of Lighthouse	Last Used	Description
Avery Rock Machias Bay, Machias, Maine	1946	Built in 1875 on Avery Rock, about three miles from the mainland. The station was automated and the keeper was removed after a violent storm in 1926. Demolished in a storm in 1946. • **Last keeper:** Edward Pettigrew.
Back River Hampton, Virginia	1936	Built in 1829. Deactivated in 1936. Fell into disrepair. Destroyed in a hurricane.
Ballast Point San Diego, California	1961	Built as a harbor light in 1890. Torn down to make room for U.S. Navy base expansion. The fog bell is now in the San Diego Maritime Museum. • **Last keeper:** Radford Franke.
Bayou Bonfouca Northern Lake Ponchartrain, Louisiana	1862	Built in 1848. Destroyed during the Civil War when it was burned by Confederate troops after Union forces captured New Orleans.
Bergen Point Newark Bay, near Bayonne, New Jersey	1949	Built in 1849. Rebuilt in 1857-59. Deactivated in 1949. Torn down two years later and replaced by a skeleton tower.

Billingsgate Billingsgate Island, Cape Cod Bay, Massachusetts	1922	Built in 1822. Rebuilt in 1858. Deactivated in 1922. The island on which the station stood eroded to the point that it had disappeared by 1942.
Bishops and Clerks Hyannis (Barnstable), Nantucket Sound, Massachusetts	1928	Built in 1858. Deactivated in 1928. By 1952, the tower was in such bad condition that the U.S. Coast Guard made the decision to demolish it. A large crowd watched the destruction on September 11, 1952.
Blakistone Island (a.k.a. **Blackistone Island**) Potomac River, St. Marys, Maryland	1932	Built in 1851. Deactivated in 1932. Destroyed by fire in July 1956.
Bombay Hook (a.k.a. **Smyrna River**), near Wilmington, Delaware	1912	Built in 1831. Deactivated in 1912. The lighthouse was demolished in 1974 when it became a hazard after years of vandalism.
Brazos Santiago Gulf of Mexico, near Port Isabel, Texas	1940	Built in 1853. Destroyed by fire in 1940.
Bullock's Point Providence River, Providence, Rhode Island	1938	Portable beacon installed in 1872 was replaced with a permanent lighthouse in 1876. Lighthouse and pier were seriously damaged in a 1938 hurricane. Station deactivated soon afterward and torn down a few years later. • **Last keeper:** Andrew Zuius, who was keeper from 1927 to 1938.
Cape Henlopen Delaware Bay, Cape Henlopen, Delaware	1924	Built in 1767. The second oldest lighthouse in the U.S. Deactivated in 1924. The 7-story octagonal stone tower collapsed from erosion in April 1926.
Cherrystone Bar Cape Charles Harbor, Virginia	1919	Built in 1858. Deactivated in 1919 and moved in 1920 to Maryland to become the Choptank River Light. Dismantled in 1964 and replaced with an automatic flashing beacon.
Cohansey Cohansey River, Delaware Bay, near Greenwich, New Jersey	1933	Built in 1838, possibly on the site of an earlier lighthouse. It was heavily damaged by October 1879 storm. New lighthouse completed by 1883. Destroyed by fire on July 21, 1933.
Corpus Christi Corpus Christi Harbor, Texas	mid 1870s	Built in 1859. Heavily damaged by Confederate forces in 1863 during the Civil War when a Union invasion seemed imminent. Lighthouse was repaired and used until the mid-1870s, then fell into disrepair. It was declared a dangerous public nuisance and demolished in 1878.
Coxsackie Rattle Snake Island, Hudson River, near Coxsackie, New York	1939	Lit in 1830. Deactivated in 1939. Torn down. Replaced by a skeleton tower.
Cross Ledge Delaware Bay, near Downe, New Jersey	1910	Completed in 1875. Deactivated in 1910, when its granite foundation began to crumble. Burned down by the U.S. Coast Guard in 1962. All that remains is the foundation, known to local residents as the "Rock pile."

Crabtree Ledge Frenchman's Bay near Hancock, Maine	1930	Completed in 1889. Built in sparkplug style, a popular method of lighthouse construction, so called because the structure resembled a large sparkplug. Deactivated in 1930 and sold. Toppled and destroyed in a winter storm.
Craney Island Elizabeth River, near Norfolk, Virginia	1936	In 1859, a lighthouse replaced a lightship that was stationed there since 1820. The building was replaced in 1884 by hexagon screwpile-style structure. Deactivated in 1936 and replaced by an automated light.
Deep Water Shoals James River, near Fort Eustis, Virginia	1936	Built in 1855. Destroyed by ice in 1867. Replaced the following year. Deactivated in 1936. Demolished in 1966. Replaced by automated steel tower.
Dog Island Gulf of Mexico, near Apalachicola, Florida	1873	Began operating in February 1839. Damaged in a hurricane in 1842. Erosion caused tower to lean in 1872. In 1873, the station was destroyed in a hurricane.
Egg Island Point Delaware Bay, near Heislerville, New Jersey	1935	Built in 1838. Another structure was built in 1856. Deactivated in 1938. The lighthouse was destroyed by fire on August 20, 1950.
Egg Rock Nahant Bay, north of Boston Harbor, Massachusetts	1922	Built in 1856. Burned in 1897. Replaced by square tower attached to keeper's quarters. Deactivated in 1922 and put up for sale. While the buyer was moving the building, it fell into the bay. The tower was destroyed in 1927 and all remaining wooden structures were burned. The island is now a bird sanctuary.
Galveston Jetty Galveston Bay, Texas	1972	Lit in 1918. Deactivated in 1972 and replaced by an automated light on a skeleton tower. The lighthouse was to have been moved to a state park, but it was toppled by a storm and destroyed in May 2000.
Gould's Island Narragansett Bay, near Jamestown, Rhode Island	1947	Built in 1889. Deactivated in 1947 and replaced by a skeleton tower. Demolished in 1960.
Gull Rocks North entrance to Newport Harbor, near Newport, Rhode Island	1928	Built in 1887. Deactivated in 1928. A skeleton tower replaced the red and white lantern lights. The station and tower were removed in 1970. Only the oil house remains on the island.
Greenbury Point Shoal Entrance to Severn River and Annapolis Harbor, near Annapolis, Maryland	1934	Built in 1891. The cottage screwpile-style lighthouse was badly damaged by ice in 1918. Replaced by automated light on a skeleton tower in 1934.
Humboldt Harbor Humboldt Bay, near Eureka, California	1892	Lit in 1856. Damaged in an earthquake in 1877 and in a cyclone in 1885. Deactivated in 1892. The tower collapsed in 1933. The cupola and a piece of the tower are at the Humboldt Bay Maritime Museum.
Kalamazoo (a.k.a. **Saugatuck Light**) Kalamazoo River on Lake Michigan, near Saugatuck, Michigan	1915	Lit in 1839. First building washed away by erosion. Replaced in 1859. Deactivated in 1915. Destroyed by a tornado in 1956. • **Last keeper:** George Sheridan, who was keeper from 1909 to 1915.

Lake Maxinkuckee North shore, near Culver, Indiana	1913	Completed in 1900. Partly blown down in a storm in 1913.
Lamberts Point Elizabeth River, near Norfolk, Virginia	1911	Completed in 1872. Deactivated in 1892. Used for ten years as a fog signal station, beginning in 1901. Collapsed in 1911.
Mare Island North shore San Pablo Bay at entrance to Carquinez Strait, Vallejo, California	1917	Lit in 1873. Station was abandoned in 1917 and demolished in the 1930s. • **Last keeper:** Kate McDougal, who retired in 1916, when the fog signal was automated.
Mispillion Mispillion River, Delaware Bay, near Milford, Delaware	1929	Three lighthouses occupied the site. The first was built in 1831. The second was built in 1839. The third lighthouse was built in 1873. It was deactivated in 1929 and replaced by an automated skeleton tower. In 1932, the government sold the property at auction. It was privately owned when it was struck by lightning and heavily damaged in 2002. Building was dismantled and removed.
Mussel Island (a.k.a. **Muscle Shoal**) Channel between Narragansett Bay and Mount Hope Bay, near Portsmouth, Rhode Island	1938	Lit in 1873. Replaced in 1879. Second building sustained ice damage and was replaced by a third one. In 1938, in danger of collapsing, building was deactivated and replaced by a steel skeleton tower. It was demolished in 1939.
Narrows (a.k.a. **Bug Light**) Outer Boston Harbor, near Boston, Massachusetts	1929	Lit in 1856. Rebuilt in 1867. Keeper's house and tower burned down accidentally by a keeper using a blow torch in June 1929. Pilings are visible at low tide.
Natchez Mississippi River, near Natchez, Mississippi	1840	Lit in 1828. Destroyed in the tornado that devastated Natchez on May 8, 1840.
Northwest Passage Gulf of Mexico, near Key West, Florida	1921	Lit in 1855. Replaced in 1879. Automated in 1913. Deactivated in June 1921. Destroyed by fire in August 1971. Pieces of the iron frame remain.
Pascagoula River East bank of Pascagoula River, near Mississippi	1906	Built in 1854. Destroyed in a violent storm in September 1906. Keeper and family rescued shortly before the building collapsed.
Passaic Newark Bay, near Passaic, New Jersey	1914	Lit in 1849. Rebuilt in 1859. Lighthouse deactivated in 1914. May have been torn down in the 1930s. • **Last keeper:** Eliza MacCashin who was keeper from 1903 to 1914.
Point Adams Entrance to Columbia River, near Astoria, Oregon	1899	Lit in 1875. Deactivated in 1899. Demolished in 1912. The lighthouse was built in the stick style that was popular in the late 19th century.
Point Aux Herbes South shore of Lake Pontchartrain, near Point Aux Herbes, Louisiana	c. 1945	Lit in 1875. Deactivated around 1945, at the end of World War II. The screwpile-style lighthouse was burned down by vandals in the 1950s.
Proctorsville Lake Borgne, Louisiana	1860	Lit in 1848. The screwpile-style lighthouse was destroyed by a hurricane in 1860.

Pungoteague River Chesapeake Bay, near Pungoteague Creek, Virginia	1856	Lit in 1854. The first screwpile-style lighthouse on Chesapeake Bay. Destroyed by moving ice in February 1856.
Racine Reef Near Racine Harbor entrance, Racine, Wisconsin	1961	Lit in 1906. The Victorian-style building was demolished in 1961. By then, advances in radar and radio navigation made the light obsolete.
Ragged Point Chesapeake Bay, entrance to Potomac River, near Coles Point, Virginia	1962	Lit in 1910. The hexagon-shaped screwpile-style building was the last lighthouse built in Chesapeake Bay. It was dismantled in 1962 and replaced with a flashing light on a tower.
Rebecca Shoal East of Garden Key, Dry Tortugas, Florida	1953	First lighthouse begun in 1854. Destroyed in a storm in 1858 before it was finished. Second building completed in 1886 after many delays. Destroyed in a hurricane in 1953.
Redfish Bar Galveston Bay, Gulf of Mexico, near Galveston, Texas	1936	Lit in 1854. The screwpile-style building was burned during the Civil War, then rebuilt in 1868. A new building was placed in service in 1900. It was dismantled and replaced by channel lights on pilings in 1936.
Rockland Lake Hudson River, near Rockland Lake Landing, New York	1923	Soon after it opened in 1893, the sparkplug-style tower began to lean. Despite its tilt, it remained in use until 1923, when it was decommissioned, demolished and replaced by a skeleton tower.
Round Island Pascagoula Harbor, Gulf of Mexico, near Pascagoula, Mississippi	c. 1949	Built in 1833 and replaced by a brick structure in 1859. It was deactivated c. 1949 and destroyed by Hurricane Georges on September 27, 1998. The Round Island Lighthouse Preservation Society is now working to rebuild it, using as much of the original tower as possible.
Sabin Point Providence River, near Providence, Rhode Island	1968	Lit in 1872. Deactivated and demolished in 1968, prior to the widening and deepening of the channel.
Saint Croix River Saint Croix Island (a.k.a. **Dochet's Island**), near Calais, Maine	1976	Built in 1857. Rebuilt in 1901. The keeper was removed when the light was automated in 1957. Accidentally destroyed by fire in 1976.
Saluria Saluria Bayou, Gulf of Mexico, near Saluria, Texas	1862	Built in 1852. Confederate troops dismantled the lighthouse in 1862 during the Civil War when a Union invasion seemed imminent.
Santa Barbara Santa Barbara Channel, near Santa Barbara, California	1925	Built in 1856. The Cape Cod-style building was destroyed in a magnitude 6.3 earthquake on June 29, 1925.
Scotch Cap Unimak Island, Alaska	1946	Built in 1903. The first lighthouse on Alaska's outer coast. A second structure, built in 1940, was destroyed on April 1, 1946, in a tsunami following two major earthquakes. Five keepers were killed. Temporary light stood until 1950, then was replaced by an automated light on a skeleton tower.

Shinnecock Bay (a.k.a. **Great West Bay Light**; **Ponquoque Light**) Ponquogue Point, Shinnecock Bay, Long Island, New York	1931	Lit in 1858. Discontinued in 1931. Replaced by beacon on steel tower. Demolished by the U.S. Coast Guard in December 1948.
Stuyvesant Hudson River, near Stuyvesant, New York	1933	Built in 1829. Destroyed by ice in 1832, killing four members of the keeper's family. Rebuilt in 1838 and 1868. Deactivated in 1933 and demolished a short time later. Replaced by skeleton tower. Some of the foundation stones were used for a porch base for the Stuyvesant Falls Post Office.
Tucker Island Little Egg Inlet near Tuckerton, New Jersey	1927	Built in 1868. Swept out to sea in 1927. A replica of the lighthouse is in Tuckerton Seaport, a museum complex in Tuckerton, New Jersey.
Watts Island Chesapeake Bay, between Tangier Island and the Eastern Shore of Virginia.	1944	Built in 1833. Tower built in 1867. Keeper's house built in 1891. Automated in 1923. The tower and keeper's house were demolished in a storm in 1944. Erosion has claimed the entire island.
Whale Rock Narragansett Bay, near Jamestown, Rhode Island	1938	Built in 1882. Demolished in a hurricane in September 1938. An assistant keeper was killed. A steel tower has replaced the light.
Wickford Harbor Narragansett Bay, near North Kingstown, Rhode Island	1930	Built in 1882. Deactivated in 1930 and torn down. The light was replaced by an automated beacon. • **Last keeper:** Edmund Andrews, who was keeper from 1893 to 1930.
Willapa Bay (a.k.a. **Shoalwater Bay Lighthouse**) Willapa Bay, near North Cove, Washington	1938	Lit in 1858. Known originally as Shoalwater Bay Lighthouse. Name changed in the 1890s. Deactivated in 1938. On December 26, 1940, the Cape Cod-style lighthouse was destroyed when it fell off the side of a cliff.
Wolf Island South entrance to Doboy Sound, near Darien, Georgia	1899	Lit in 1822. Destroyed by Confederate troops during the Civil War. Rebuilt in 1868. Deactivated in 1899 and torn down.

Literature

Literature—Literary Movements and Groups—Bloomsbury Group

The Bloomsbury Group was a circle of radical British writers, intellectuals and artists who hung out in Bloomsbury—a section of London near the British Museum—in the 1920s and 1930s. The group included writers Virginia Woolf and E.M. Forster, economist John Maynard Keynes, art critic Roger Fry, painters Duncan Grant and Dora Carrington, among others.
• **Last surviving member of Bloomsbury Group:** Frances Marshall Partridge, who died in London on February 5, 2004, age 103. Her husband Ralph Partridge was also part of the group.

Literature—Literary Movements and Groups—Harlem Renaissance

The Harlem Renaissance was a movement marked by a literary and artistic revival of interest in African-American heritage. It began at the end of World War I and lasted until around 1929. Some historians place the end in the 1930s.
• **Last surviving member of the Harlem Renaissance:** Louise Thompson Patterson, a longtime associate of poet/playwright Lang-

ston Hughes. She formed a salon called *Vanguard* that attracted Harlem artists with concerts, dances and discussions of Marxist theory. She also co-founded the Harlem Suitcase Theater with Hughes. She died in New York on August 27, 1999, age 97.

Literature—Literary Movements and Groups—Imagists

The Imagists were a group of American and English poets, active from 1908 to around 1916, who followed the lead of philosopher T.E. Hulme and writer Ezra Pound in their precise, disciplined approach to poetry. They rejected the florid styles of the Romantics and instead created poetry that was expressed in the language of common speech. They were influenced by the brevity of haiku (Japanese poetry) and often wrote short poems that were only a few lines in length.

• **End of Imagism:** died out soon after publication of the last Imagists' anthology in 1917.

Literature—Literary Movements and Groups—Inklings

The Inklings were a group of 20th-century Christian writers associated with Oxford University in England. They included J.R.R. Tolkien and C.S. Lewis.

• **Last meeting of the Inklings:** a supper on October 20, 1949.

Literature—Literary Movements and Groups—Irish Literary Renaissance

When Standish O'Grady's *History of Ireland: Heroic Period* was published in 1878, it set off a burst of nationalism among Irish writers. They swept aside British influences and developed their own style, turning to their folklore, traditions and legends for inspiration. During the Irish Literary Renaissance, Ireland developed a national theater, and the Gaelic League was founded to restore Gaelic as the national language.

• **End of the Irish Literary Renaissance:** Some sources say it ended in 1922, the year the Irish Free State was created. Others say it lasted until the 1940s.

Literature—Literary Movements and Groups—Parnassians

The Parnassians were a group of mid-19th-century poets who reacted to the emotionalism of the Romantic movement by using restraint, objectivity and precision in their works. The group took their name from *Parnasse contemporain*, the title of a journal that published their anthologies in 1866, 1871 and 1876. The Parnassians limited their subject matter to concrete areas such as marble statues, porcelains and gems and avoided such topics as contemporary social or moral issues.

• **End of the Parnassians:** faded after publication of the third series of their anthology *Parnasse contemporain* in 1876.

Literature
Last Works of Some Major Authors

Author	Description
Abe, Kobo	Japanese novelist/poet Kimifusa (Kobo) Abe died in Tokyo, Japan, on January 22, 1993, age 68. • **Last works:** *Tobu Otoka* (*Flying Man;* not translated), *Kangaru Noto* (*Kangaroo Notebook*, translated in 1997).
Agee, James	American author Rufus James Agee died in New York, New York, on May 16, 1955, age 45. • **Last novel:** *A Death in the Family* (published posthumously in 1958).
Alcott, Louisa May	American author Louisa May Alcott died in Boston, Massachusetts, on March 6, 1888, age 55. • **Last book:** *A Garland for Girls* (1888).

	• **Last completed work:** "Lu Sing" (short story; published posthumously in *St. Nicholas* magazine in 1902).
Aleichem, Sholom	Russian-born Yiddish short-story writer Sholom Aleichem (Solomon Yakov Rabinowitz) died in New York, New York, on May 13, 1916, age 57. • **Last book:** *A Great Fair* (autobiography). He was working on it at the time of his death.
Amis, Sir Kingsley	English author/critic/teacher Sir Kingsley Amis died on October 22, 1995, age 73. • **Last completed novel:** *The Biographer's Moustache.* • **Last unfinished novel:** *The Oldest Devil.*
Andersen, Hans Christian	Danish author Hans Christian Andersen died in Copenhagen, Denmark, on August 4, 1875, age 70. • **Last novel:** *Lucky Peer* (1870). • **Last series of *Fairy Tales*:** 1872. The first fairy tales appeared in 1835. The rest appeared at regular intervals.
Anderson, Maxwell	American playwright James Maxwell Anderson died in Stamford, Connecticut, on February 28, 1959, age 70. • **Last play:** *The Bad Seed* (1954).
Anderson, Sherwood	American novelist/playwright/short-story writer Sherwood Anderson died in Colon, Panama, on March 8, 1941, age 64. • **Last book published in Anderson's lifetime:** *Home Town* (1940).
Asimov, Isaac	Russian-born American author/science fiction writer Isaac Asimov died in New York, New York, on April 6, 1992, age 72. • **Last science fiction anthology:** *Gold* (published in 1991). • **Last *Foundation* novel:** *Forward the Foundation* (published posthumously in 1993). • **Last autobiographical work:** *Asimov: A Memoir* (published posthumously in 1993).
Austen, Jane	English novelist Jane Austen died in Winchester, England, on July 18, 1817, age 41. • **Last completed novel:** *Persuasion* (published posthumously in 1818). During her last few months, she worked on *Sanditon.*
Baldwin, James	American author/playwright/essayist James Baldwin died in Saint-Paul-de-Vence, France, on December 1, 1987, age 63. • **Last work:** *The Evidence of Things Not Seen* (1985). • **Last essay:** "Whose Harlem is This Anyway?" (drafted for *Essence* magazine; unfinished when he died).
Balzac, Honoré de	French novelist Honoré de Balzac died in Paris, France, on August 18, 1850, age 51. • **Last novel:** *Le Cousin Pons* (1847).
Barrie, Sir James M.	Scottish novelist/playwright Sir James M. Barrie died in London, England, on June 19, 1937, age 77. • **Last novel:** *Farewell Miss Julie Logan* (1932). • **Last play:** *The Boy David* (1936). • **Last work published in Barrie's lifetime:** *The Greenwood Hat* (1937; a collection of articles he had written earlier).
Barry, Philip	American playwright Philip Barry died in New York, New York, on December 3, 1949, age 53.

	• **Last play:** *Second Threshold* (unfinished; completed by Robert Emmet Sherwood and produced in 1951).
Baum, L. Frank	American author and playwright L(yman) Frank Baum died in Hollywood, California, on May 5, 1919, age 62. Baum wrote 14 Wizard of Oz books, beginning with the *Wonderful Wizard of Oz* in 1900. • **Last *Oz* book:** *Glinda of Oz* (published posthumously in 1920).
Beauvoir, Simone de	French author/philosopher Simone de Beauvoir died in Paris, France, on April 14, 1986, age 78. • **Last work:** *Adieux: A Farewell to Sartre* (1981).
Beckett, Samuel	Irish playwright/poet Samuel Barclay Beckett died in Paris, France, on December 22, 1989, age 83. • **Last poem:** "What is a Word" (1986). • **Last play:** *L'Image* (1988).
Bellamy, Edward	American author Edward Bellamy died in Chicopee Falls, Massachusetts, on May 22, 1898, age 48. • **Last work:** *Equality* (1897; sequel to *Looking Back*).
Belloc, Hilaire	French-born English author (Joseph) Hilaire (Pierre) Belloc died in Guildford, Surrey, England, on July 16, 1953, age 82. • **Last published work:** *The Last Rally* (1939). He suffered a stroke in 1942 and spent the rest of his life in retirement.
Biggers, Earl Derr	American mystery writer Earl Derr Biggers died in Pasadena, California, on April 5, 1933, age 48. • **Last *Chan* novel:** *Keeper of the Keys* (1932), his sixth book featuring Chinese detective Charlie Chan.
Borges, Jorge Luis	Argentinean poet/short-story writer/essayist Jorge Luis Borges died in Geneva, Switzerland, on June 14, 1986, age 86. • **Last major work published in Borges' lifetime:** account of his travels to different parts of the world (1984). He wrote the text. Maria Kodama, whom he married in 1986, took the photographs.
Boswell, James	Scottish lawyer/biographer James Boswell died in London, England, on May 19, 1795, age 55. • **Last work:** *The Life of Johnson* (1791).
Bowen, Catherine Drinker	American biographer Catherine Drinker Bowen died in Haverford, Pennsylvania, on November 1, 1973, age 76. • **Last work:** *The Most Dangerous Man in America: Scenes from the Life of Benjamin Franklin* (1974).
Brontë, Anne	English novelist Anne Brontë died in Scarborough, England, on May 28, 1849, age 29. • **Last novel:** *Tenant of Wildfell Hall* (1848).
Brontë, Charlotte	English novelist Charlotte Brontë died in Haworth, England, on March 31, 1855, age 38. • **Last novel:** *Villette* (1853).
Brontë, Emily	English novelist Emily Brontë died in Haworth, England, on December 19, 1848, age 30. • **Last novel:** *Wuthering Heights* (1847; her only novel).
Browning, Elizabeth Barrett	English poet Elizabeth Barrett Browning died in Florence, Italy, on June 29, 1861, age 55. • **Last work:** *Last Poems* (published posthumously in 1862).

Browning, Robert	English poet Robert Browning died in Venice, Italy, on December 12. 1889, age 77. • **Last work:** *Asolando* (published the day he died).
Bryant, William Cullen	American poet/newspaper editor William Cullen Bryant died in New York, New York, on June 12, 1878, age 83. • **Last public appearance:** delivered an address at the unveiling of the statue of Italian patriot Giuseppe Mazzini in Central Park, New York City, on May 29, 1878. He fell after the ceremony and died two weeks later. • **Last poem:** "The Twenty-second of February," written in 1878 to commemorate the birthday of George Washington.
Buck, Pearl S.	American author Pearl S(ydenstricker) Buck died in Danby, Vermont, on March 6, 1973, age 80. • **Last novel:** *The Rainbow* (published posthumously in 1974). • **Last of Buck's novels made into a movie in her lifetime:** *Satan Never Sleeps* (1962; the last of five).
Burgess, Anthony	English novelist/composer/critic John Anthony Burgess Wilson died in London, England, on November 26, 1993, age 76. • **Last novel:** *Byrne* (completed shortly before he died).
Burke, Edmund	British statesman/author Edmund Burke died in Beaconfield, England, on July 9, 1797, age 68. • **Last work:** *Letters on a Regicide Peace* (1796-97).
Burns, Robert	Scottish poet Robert Burns died in Dumfries, Scotland, on July 21, 1796, age 37. • **Last songs:** Burns wrote 51 songs during his last three years, including "Comin' Thro the Rye" (published posthumously in 1796-1803).
Burroughs, Edgar Rice	American novelist Edgar Rice Burroughs died in Los Angeles, California, on March 19, 1950, age 74. • **Last *Tarzan* novel published in Burroughs' lifetime:** *Tarzan and the Foreign Legion* (1947). He wrote it while in Hawaii in 1944.
Byron, Lord (George Gordon)	English poet George Gordon, Lord Byron died at Missolonghi, Greece, on April 19, 1824, age 36. • **Last verses:** lines to celebrate his birthday: "On this Day I complete my thirty-sixth year," written on January 22, 1824, at Missolonghi, while fighting for Greek independence.
Camus, Albert	French novelist/journalist/dramatist Albert Camus died in an auto accident near Sens, France, on January 4, 1960, age 46. • **Last novel:** *The First Man* (unfinished). The manuscript was found in his briefcase near the wreckage of the car in which he died.
Capek, Karel	Czech novelist/dramatist/short-story writer Karel Capek died in Prague, Czechoslovakia, on December 25, 1938, age 48. • **Last play:** *The Mother* (1938).
Capote, Truman	American author Truman Capote died in Los Angeles, California, on August 25, 1984, age 59. • **Last book published in Capote's lifetime:** *Music for Chameleons* (1980). • **Last unfinished book:** *Answered Prayers*. After Capote died, only three chapters were found. They had already been published in *Esquire* magazine in 1975 and 1976.

Carlyle, Thomas	Scottish historian/essayist Thomas Carlyle died in London, England, on February 5, 1881, age 85. • **Last work:** *Early Kings of Norway* (1875).
Carroll, Lewis	English mathematician/author Charles Lutwidge Dodgson wrote mathematical treatises under his own name and children's books under the pseudonym Lewis Carroll. He died in Guildford, Surrey, England, on January 14, 1898, age 65. He • **Last mathematical work:** *Symbolic Logic, Part I* (1896). • **Last novel:** *Sylvie and Bruno* (two volumes; 1889-93).
Cather, Willa	American novelist/short-story writer Willa Cather died in New York, New York, on April 24, 1947, age 73. • **Last novel:** *Sapphira and the Slave Girl* (1940).
Cervantes, Miguel de	Spanish author Miguel de Cervantes Saavedra died in Madrid, Spain, on April 23, 1616, age 68. • **Last work:** *The Exploits of Persiles and Sigismunda.* Cervantes wrote the last lines of the dedication just before his death. The book was published posthumously the following year.
Chandler, Raymond	American mystery writer/screenwriter Raymond Chandler died in La Jolla, California, on March 26, 1959, age 70. • **Last completed *Philip Marlowe* novel:** *Playback* (1958). His unfinished novel *Poodle Spring* was completed by Robert B. Parker in 1959.
Chaucer, Geoffrey	English poet Geoffrey Chaucer died in London, England, on October 25, 1400, around age 60. • **Last major work:** *The Canterbury Tales,* begun in 1387, unfinished. • **Last *Canterbury* tale:** "The Parson's Tale." • **Last work:** "The Complaint of Chaucer to His Purse" (1400).
Cheever, John	American author John Cheever died in Ossining, New York, on June 18, 1982, age 70. • **Last novel:** *Oh What a Paradise It Seems* (1982).
Chekhov, Anton	Russian dramatist/short-story writer Anton Pavlovich Chekhov died at Badenweiler, a German health resort, on July 14, 1904, age 44. • **Last story:** *The Betrothed* (1903). • **Last play:** *The Cherry Orchard*, written and produced during his last year. He died a few months after seeing a performance of it.
Chesterton, G. K.	English author G(ilbert) K(eith) Chesterton died in Beaconsfield, England, on June 14, 1936, age 62. • **Last *Father Brown* detective story:** *The Scandal of Father Brown* (1935).
Christie, Dame Agatha	English mystery writer/playwright Dame Agatha Mary Clarissa Miller Christie died in Wallingford, England, on January 12, 1976, age 85. • **Last *Miss Marple* novel written by Christie:** *Nemesis* (1971). • **Last *Miss Marple* novel published:** *Sleeping Murder*, written during World War II and published in 1976 after Christie's death. • **Last *Hercule Poirot* novel:** *Curtain: Poirot's Last Case* (1975; written nearly 30 years earlier). • **Last *Tuppence and Tommy Beresford* novel:** *Postern of Fate* (1973; the last novel Christie wrote).
Coleridge, Samuel Taylor	English author/critic Samuel Taylor Coleridge died in Highgate, near London, England, on July 25, 1834, age 61. • **Last work published in Coleridge's lifetime:** *Constitution of the*

	Church and State (1830). Works published posthumously include *Literary Remains* (1836), *Confessions of an Inquiring Spirit* (1840) and *Theory of Life* (1848).
Colette	French novelist Sidonie Gabrielle Claudine Colette died in Paris, France, on August 3, 1954, age 81. • **Last full-length novel:** *Julie de Carneilhan* (1941). • **Last work published in Colette's lifetime:** *Chéri* (play; 1952).
Collins, Wilkie	English novelist/short-story writer/playwright Wilkie Collins died in London, England, on September 23, 1889, age 65. • **Last novel:** *Blind Love* (unfinished; completed by Walter Besant and published in 1890).
Congreve, William	English author/playwright William Congreve died in London, England, on January 19, 1729, age 58. • **Last play:** *The Way of the World* (1700).
Conrad, Joseph	Ukrainian-born English author Joseph Conrad (Jozef Teodor Konrad Korzeniowski) died in Kent, England, on August 3, 1924, age 66. • **Last novels:** *The Rover* (1923); *The Nature of Crime* (1924; with Ford Madox Ford). • **Last nonfiction work:** *Last Essays* (published posthumously in 1926).
Cooper, James Fenimore	American author James Fenimore Cooper died in Cooperstown, New York, on September 14, 1851, age 61. • **Last *Leatherstocking* novel:** *The Deerslayer* (1841). • **Last works:** *The Ways of the Hour,* a murder mystery, and *Upside Down; or Philosophy in Petticoats,* his only play, produced in New York in 1850.
Coward, Sir Noel	English playwright/actor/composer Sir Noel Pierce Coward died in Jamaica on March 26, 1974, age 73. • **Last play:** *Suite in Three Keys* (produced in 1966): "Song at Twilight," "Shadows of the Evening," "Come Into the Garden, Maude." • **Last major theatrical project:** directed Beatrice Lillie in *High Spirits* (1964).
Cowper, William	English poet William Cowper died in East Derenham, England, on April 25, 1800, age 68. • **Last poem:** "The Castaway" (1799).
Crane, Hart	American poet Harold Hart Crane died at sea, traveling from Mexico on April 27, 1932, age 33. • **Last poem:** "The Broken Tower" (1931).
Crane, Stephen	American author Stephen Townly Crane died in Germany on June 5, 1900, age 28. • **Last novel:** *Active Service.* Crane was working on the novel *The O'Ruddy* when he died. Several of his last works were published posthumously, including: *Whilomville Stories* (1900), released for publication in *Harper's New Monthly Magazine* just before he died.
Cullen, Countee	American poet/author Countee Porter Cullen died in New York, New York, on January 9, 1946, age 42. • **Last work:** script for the play *St. Louis Woman.* He died a few months before the play opened on Broadway. • **Last novel:** *One Way to Heaven* (1932; his only novel).
cummings, e. e.	American poet E(dward) E(stlin) Cummings died in North Conway, New Hampshire, on September 3, 1962, age 67.

	• **Last work:** *Adventures in Value* (1962). *73 Poems* were published posthumously in 1963.
Dante Alighieri	Italian poet Dante Alighieri died in Ravenna, Italy, on September 13 (or 14), 1321, age 56. • **Last work:** *Quaestio de aqua et de terra* (1320).
Defoe, Daniel	English novelist/journalist Daniel Defoe died in London, England, on April 24, 1731, age 71. • **Last major fiction work:** *Roxana* (1724). After that, he wrote mostly travel books and memoirs. • **Last major nonfiction works:** *History of the Pyrates* (1728) and *Robert Drury's Journal* (1729).
Dickens, Charles	English author Charles Dickens died in Kent, England, on June 9, 1870, age 58. • **Last completed novel:** *Our Mutual Friend,* published in monthly installments in 1864-65. • **Last novel:** *The Mystery of Edwin Drood,* unfinished. He had completed about half of it when he had a stroke and died. • **Last visit to the United States:** November 19, 1867, to April 22, 1868. It was his second visit. He also visited the U.S. in 1842.
Dickey, James	American poet/novelist/essayist James Lafayette Dickey died in Columbia, South Carolina, on January 19, 1997, age 73. • **Last novel:** *To the White Sea* (1993). • **Last work published in Dickey's lifetime:** *Striking In: The Early Notebooks of James Dickey* (1996). • **Last class taught at University of South Carolina:** January 14, 1997. He died five days later.
Dickinson, Emily	American poet Emily Dickinson died at her family's home in Amherst, Massachusetts, on May 15, 1886, age 55. She wrote nearly 1,800 poems, but only a few were published (anonymously) during her lifetime. Most were published after she died. • **Last of Dickinson's poems to be published for the first time:** *Bolts of Melody: New Poems of Emily Dickinson* (1945).
Dinesen, Isak	Isak Dinesen is the pseudonym of Danish author Baroness Karen Christence Blixen, who died in Rungsted, Denmark, on September 7, 1962, age 77. • **Last major work:** *Albondocani,* unfinished. Parts appeared in *Last Tales* (1957).
Donne, John	English poet/preacher John Donne died in London, England, on March 31, 1631, age 59. • **Last sermon:** "Death's Duell," delivered at St. Paul's Cathedral a month before he died. His last poems show a preoccupation with his pending death. Donne's poems were not published until after he died.
Doolittle, Hilda	American poet Hilda Doolittle, who wrote under the pen name H.D., died in Zurich, Switzerland, on September 27, 1961, age 75. • **Last work:** *Helen in Egypt* (written in 1961).
Dr. Seuss	Dr. Seuss is the pseudonym of American author/illustrator Theodor Seuss Geisel, who died in La Jolla, California, on September 24, 1991, age 87. • **Last books:** *Daisy-Head Maysie* (published posthumously in 1994); *Hooray for Diffendoofer Day* (published posthumously in 1998).

Dos Passos, John	American novelist/historian John Dos Passos died in Baltimore, Maryland, on September 28, 1970, age 74. • **Last novel:** *Century's Ebb: The Thirteenth Chronicle* (unfinished; published posthumously in 1974. *Easter Island* (travel book) and *The Fourteenth Chronicle: Letters and Diaries of John Dos Passos* were also published posthumously.
Dostoyevsky, Feodor Mikhailovich	Russian author Feodor Mikhailovich Dostoyevsky died in St. Petersburg, Russia, on January 29 (Old Style), February 9 (New Style), 1881, age 59. • **Last novel:** *Brothers Karamazov* (1880).
Doyle, Sir Arthur Conan	English physician/mystery writer Sir Arthur Conan Doyle died in Windlesham, Sussex, England, on July 7, 1930, age 71. • **Last *Sherlock Holmes* story:** *The Adventures of Shoscombe Old Place* (1927). Doyle wrote four full-length Sherlock Holmes novels and 56 short stories. They were published in five volumes. The fifth and last volume, *The Casebook of Sherlock Holmes,* was published in 1927. • **Last work:** *The Edge of the Unknown* (1930).
Dreiser, Theodore	American author Theodore Dreiser died in Hollywood, California, on December 28, 1945, age 74. • **Last work published in Dreiser's lifetime:** *America is Worth Saving* (1941). • **Last novels:** *The Bulwark* (1946) and *The Stoic* (1947), the last two volumes of a trilogy, published posthumously.
Dryden, John	English poet/dramatist/critic John Dryden died in London, England, in May 1700, age 68. • **Last major work:** *Fables, Ancient and Modern* (1700).
Dumas, Alexandre (father)	French author Alexandre Dumas (Dumas pere; the father) died at Puys, near Dieppe, France, on December 5, 1870, age 68. • **Last novel:** *The Prussian Terror* (1867). • **Last play:** *The Whites and the Blues* (premiered in 1869). • **Last major work:** *Le Grand Dictionnaire de Cuisine.* Dumas spent his last years working on it (published posthumously in 1873).
Dumas, Alexandre (son)	French playwright/novelist Alexandre Dumas (Dumas fils; the son) died at Marly-le-Roi, France, on November 27, 1895, age 71. • **Last play:** *The Return from Thebes* (unfinished).
Du Maurier, Daphne	English author Daphne du Maurier died in Cornwall, England, on April 19, 1989, age 82. • **Last novel:** *Rule Britannia* (1972). • **Last biography:** *The Winding Stair* (1976). • **Last short stories:** *The Rendezvous and Other Stories* (1980).
Dunbar, Paul Laurence	American poet/novelist Paul Laurence Dunbar died in Dayton, Ohio, on February 9, 1906, age 33. • **Last novel:** *The Sport of the Gods* (1902).
Eliot, George	George Eliot is the pseudonym of English novelist Mary Ann Evans, who died in London, England, on December 22, 1880, age 61. • **Last novel:** *Daniel Deronda* (1876).
Eliot, T.S.	American-born British poet/dramatist T(homas) S(tearns) Eliot died in London, England, on January 4, 1965, age 76. • **Last major poetry:** *Four Quartets* (1936-42). • **Last play:** *The Elder Statesman* (1958).

Ellison, Ralph	American author Ralph Waldo Ellison died in New York, New York, on April 16, 1994, age 80. • **Last work:** *Juneteenth* (unfinished; published posthumously in 1999).
Emerson, Ralph Waldo	American poet/essayist/philosopher Ralph Waldo Emerson died in Concord, Massachusetts, on April 27, 1882, age 78. • **Last public address:** 100th anniversary of the Battle at Concord on April 19, 1875, when Daniel C. French's statue of the Minute Man was unveiled. Emerson wrote little after that. • **Last public appearance:** February 1881, when he read a paper at the Massachusetts Historical Society on the death of Carlyle.
Faulkner, William	American author William Faulkner died in Oxford, Mississippi, on July 6, 1962, age 64. • **Last *Snopes* novel:** *The Mansion* (1959). Faulkner wrote three novels about the Snopes family. • **Last novel:** *The Reivers: A Reminiscence* (1962).
Ferber, Edna	American novelist/short-story writer/playwright Edna Ferber died in New York, New York, on April 16, 1968, age 80. • **Last novel:** *Ice Palace* (1958).
Fielding, Henry	English author Henry Fielding died in Lisbon, Portugal, on October 8, 1754, age 47. He had gone there hoping to restore his failing health. • **Last novel:** *Amelia* (1751). • **Last nonfiction work:** *The Journal of a Voyage to Lisbon* (published posthumously in 1755).
Fitzgerald, F. Scott	American author F(rancis) Scott Key Fitzgerald died in Hollywood, California, on December 21, 1940, age 44. • **Last completed novel:** *Tender is the Night* (1934). • **Last novel:** *The Last Tycoon*. Fitzgerald was working on it when he died. *The Last Tycoon: An Unfinished Novel* was published posthumously in 1941.
Flaubert, Gustave	French novelist Gustave Flaubert died near Rouen, France, on May 8, 1880, age 58. • **Last novel:** *Bouvard et Pécuchet* (published posthumously in 1881). Flaubert was working on the final chapter when he died.
Fleming, Ian	English author Ian Fleming died in Sandwich, England, on August 12, 1964, age 56. • **Last *James Bond* novel completed by Fleming:** *You Only Live Twice* (1962). Fleming worked on *The Man with the Golden Gun* but did not complete it.
Forster, E.M.	English author E(dward) M(organ) Forster died in Coventry, England, on June 7, 1970, age 91. • **Last novel:** *A Passage to India* (1924), his fifth novel. Despite their success, Forster made the decision when he was 45 that he would write no more novels.
France, Anatole	Anatole France is the pseudonym of French novelist/poet/critic Jacques Anatole François Thibault, who died near Tours, France, on October 12, 1924, age 80. • **Last work:** *La vie en fleur* (1922). It completed the cycle he started in *Le Livre de Mon Ami* (1885).
Franklin Benjamin	American statesman/scientist/philosopher/author Benjamin Franklin died in Philadelphia, Pennsylvania, on April 17, 1790, age 84.

	• **Last work:** *Autobiography*, begun in 1771. Franklin continued working on it until 1788. (*See also* Books—Almanacs.) • **Last writing published in Franklin's lifetime:** Letter to the Editor of the *Federal Gazette,* March 23, 1790, less than a month before he died. In it, he lampooned the pro-slavery view of a U.S. senator from Georgia. He signed the letter "Historicus." • **Last public political act:** signed a memorial against slavery as president of the Abolition Society in 1789. It was presented before the U.S. House of Representatives, then meeting in Philadelphia.
Frost, Robert	American poet Robert Frost died in Boston, Massachusetts, on January 29, 1963, age 88. • **Last poetry collection published in Frost's lifetime:** *In the Clearing* (1962).
***Fun with Dick and Jane* series**	*Fun with Dick and Jane* was a reading series published by Scott, Foresman. At the height of its popularity, about 80 percent of American school children read the books. • **Last surviving author of the *Fun with Dick and Jane* books:** Dr. A. Sterl Artley, a professor of education at the University of Missouri, who was hired by Scott, Foresman in the late 1940s to revise the series. Artley died in Overland Park, Kansas, on July 7, 1998, age 91.
Galsworthy, John	English author John Galsworthy died in Hampstead, England, on January 31, 1933, age 65. • **Last novel:** *One More River* (1933).
García Lorca, Federico	Spanish poet/dramatist Federico García Lorca was shot to death near Granada, Spain, on August 19, 1936, during Spain's Civil War, age 38. • **Last work:** *The House of Bernard Alba* (published posthumously in 1945). He finished the first draft two months before he was killed.
Gardner, Erle Stanley	American mystery writer Erle Stanley Gardner died in Temecula, California, on March 11, 1970, age 80. • **Last *Perry Mason* novel published in Gardner's lifetime:** *The Case of the Murderous Bride* (1969). His final five Perry Mason novels were published after his death. • **Last *Perry Mason* novel:** *The Case of the Postponed Murder* (1973). • **Last *A.A. Fair* novel:** *All Grass Isn't Green* (1970). Gardner wrote 29 Bertha Cool and Donald Lam novels under the pseudonym A.A. Fair. • **Last *Doug Selby* novel:** *The D.A. Breaks an Egg* (1949). • **Last nonfiction work:** *Cops on Campus and Crime in the Streets* (1970). • **Last *Perry Mason* TV episode:** "The Case of the Final Fade Out," May 22, 1966. Gardner appeared as a judge.
Gibbon, Edward	English historian Edward Gibbon died in London, England, on January 16, 1794, age 56. • **Last work:** *Miscellaneous Works of Edward Gibbon* (two volumes; published posthumously in 1796).
Gibran, Kahlil	Lebanese-born American poet/philosopher Kahlil Gibran died in New York, New York, on April 10, 1931, age 48. • **Last work published in Gibran's lifetime:** *The Earth Gods* (1931).
Gide, André	French author André Paul Guillaume Gide died in Paris, France, on February 19, 1951, age 81. • **Last work:** *Theseus* (1946).

Goethe, Johann Wolfgang von	German poet/playwright/novelist Johann Wolfgang von Goethe died in Weimar (Germany) on March 22, 1832, age 82. • **Last novel:** *Wilhelm Meister's Journeyman Years* (1828). • **Last major work:** *Faust,* his masterpiece. Goethe worked on it two different times, a half century apart: the first in 1770, the second in 1831, a few months before he died.
Gogol, Nikolai	Russian novelist/playwright Nikolai Vasilevich Gogol died in Moscow, Russia, on March 4, 1852, age 42. • **Last major work:** *Selected Passages from Correspondence with Friends* (1847). Shortly before he died, Gogol destroyed his manuscript for a sequel to *Dead Souls.*
Goldsmith, Oliver	Irish-born English poet/playwright/novelist Oliver Goldsmith died in London, England, on April 4, 1774, age 45. • **Last novel:** *The Vicar of Wakefield* (1766; his only novel). • **Last work:** *The Retaliation* (1774).
Gorky, Maxim	Maxim Gorky is the pseudonym of Russian author Aleksei Maximovich Peshkov, who died near Moscow, Russia, on June 18, 1936, age 68. • **Last work:** *The Life of Klim Samgin* (four volumes, 1929-36; unfinished).
Gray, Spalding	American playwright/screenwriter/raconteur/actor Spalding Gray died in New York, New York, around January 10, 2004, age 62. • **Last movie of a Gray screenplay:** *Gray's Anatomy* (1996). • **Last movie as an actor:** *Kate and Leopold* (2001). • **Last Broadway production as a writer:** *Morning, Noon and Night.* Last performance, January 10, 2000, at the Vivian Beaumont Theater, New York, New York.
Gray, Thomas	English poet Thomas Gray died in Cambridge, England, on July 30, 1771, age 54. He was buried at Stoke Poges in the churchyard he made famous in *Elegy Written in a Country Churchyard.* • **Last poetic work:** *Ode for Music* (1769).
Greene, Graham	English author Henry Graham Greene died in Vevey, Switzerland, on April 3, 1991, age 86. • **Last novel:** *The Captain and the Enemy* (1988). • **Last work:** *A World of My Own* (published posthumously in 1994).
Hammett, Dashiell	American novelist/screenwriter Samuel Dashiell Hammett died in New York, New York, on January 10, 1961, age 66. • **Last novel:** *The Thin Man* (1934).
Hardy, Thomas	English author Thomas Hardy died in Dorchester, England, on January 11, 1928, age 87. • **Last novel:** *Jude the Obscure* (1897). • **Last work published in Hardy's lifetime:** *Human Shows, Far Phantasies, Songs and Trifles* (1925). • **Last work:** *Winter Words in Various Moods and Metres,* a book of poems (published posthumously in 1928). Hardy was working on it when he died.
Harris, Joel Chandler	American author Joel Chandler Harris died in Atlanta, Georgia, on July 3, 1908, age 59. • **Last *Uncle Remus* book published in Harris's lifetime:** *Uncle Remus and Brer Rabbit* (1907).

Hawthorne, Nathaniel	American author Nathaniel Hawthorne died in Plymouth, New Hampshire, on May 19, 1864, age 59. He was visiting the White Mountains with his friend, former president Franklin Pierce. • **Last novel published in Hawthorne's lifetime:** *The Marble Faun* completed in England and published in 1859. • **Last novels:** During the last few years of his life, Hawthorne started several novels that remained unfinished. They were published posthumously: *Septimius Felton* (1871), *The Dolliver Romance* (1876), *Dr. Grimshawe's Secret* (1883) and *The Ancestral Footstep* (1883).
Heinlein, Robert A.	American science-fiction writer Robert A. Heinlein died in Carmel, California, on May 8, 1988, age 80. • **Last novel:** *To Sail Beyond the Sunset* (1987). • **Last work:** *Grumbles from the Grave* (a collection of letters published posthumously in 1989).
Heller, Joseph	American author Joseph Heller died on Long Island, New York, on December 12, 1999, age 76. • **Last novel published in Heller's lifetime:** *Closing Time* (1994, a sequel to *Catch-22*). • **Last novel:** *Portrait of the Artist As an Old Man* (published posthumously in 2000).
Hellman, Lillian	American author/playwright Lillian Hellman died on Martha's Vineyard, Massachusetts, on June 30, 1984, age 79. • **Last novel:** *Maybe* (1980). • **Last work for the stage:** *Toys in the Attic* (1960). • **Last work:** *Eating Together: Recipes and Recollections* (1984).
Hemingway, Ernest	American author Ernest Hemingway died at his home in Ketchum, Idaho, on July 2, 1961, age 61. • **Last works published in Hemingway's lifetime:** *Old Man and the Sea* (novel, 1952)*, The Dangerous Summer* (published in three installments in *Life* magazine, 1960). Hemingway left many works that have been published posthumously, including *A Moveable Feast* (1964), *Islands in the Stream* (1970) and *True at First Light* (1999; edited by his son Patrick). • **Last dated document:** Letter written in June 1961, to cheer up the nine-year-old son of his physician. Hemingway wrote it just days before he shot himself.
Henry, O.	O. Henry is the pseudonym of American short-story writer William Sidney Porter, who died in New York, New York, on June 5, 1910, age 47. • **Last short story written as W. S. Porter:** *Miracle of Lava Canyon* (1897). • **Last short story:** *The Dream* (1910; unfinished).
Herbert, Frank	American science-fiction writer Frank Herbert died in Madison, Wisconsin, on February 11, 1986, age 65. • **Last *Dune* book:** *Charterhouse:Dune* (1985; last in a series of six). • **Last novel:** *Man of Two Worlds* (with son Brian).
Hersey, John	American journalist/novelist John Hersey died in Key West, Florida, on March 24, 1993, age 78. • **Last novel:** *Antonietta* (1991). • **Last work:** *Key West Tales* (1993).

Hesse, Herman	German-born Swiss novelist Herman Hesse died in Montagnola, Switzerland, on August 9, 1962, age 85. • **Last novel:** *The Glass Bead Game* (1943).
Hilton, James	English novelist/screenwriter James Hilton died in Long Beach, California, on December 20, 1954, age 54. • **Last novel:** *Time and Time Again* (1953). • **Last movie as a screenwriter:** *So Well Remembered* (1947; he also served as the film's narrator).
Holmes, Oliver Wendell	American physician/writer Oliver Wendell Holmes died in Boston, Massachusetts, on October 7, 1894, age 85. • **Last work:** *Over the Teacups* (1890).
Housman, A.E.	English poet/classical scholar A(lfred) E(dward) Housman died on April 30, 1936, in Cambridge, England, age 77. • **Last work:** *More Poems* (published posthumously in 1936).
Howells, William Dean	American author/editor/critic William Dean Howells died in New York, New York, on May 11, 1920, age 83. • **Last novel:** *The Vacation of the Kelwyns, an Idol of the Middle Eighteen Seventies* (published posthumously in 1920).
Hughes, Langston	American poet James Langston Hughes died in New York, New York, on May 22, 1967, age 65. • **Last book:** *The Panther and the Lash: Poems of Our Time* (published posthumously in 1967).
Hugo, Victor	French novelist/poet/playwright Victor Marie Hugo died in Paris, France, on May 22, 1885, age 83. • **Last novel:** *Ninety-Three* (1874). • **Last drama:** *Torquemada* (1882).
Huxley, Aldous	English novelist Aldous Leonard Huxley died in Los Angeles, California, on November 22, 1963, age 69. • **Last essay:** "Shakespeare and Religion, written as he was dying (published posthumously in *Show Magazine,* 1964). • **Last novel:** *Island* (1962).
Ibsen, Henrik	Norwegian playwright/poet Henrik Ibsen died in Christiania (now Oslo), Norway, on May 23, 1906, age 78. • **Last play:** *When We Dead Awaken* (1899).
Inge, William	American playwright William Motter Inge died in Los Angeles, California, on June 10, 1973, age 60. • **Last play:** *The Last Pad* (1970). • **Last novel:** *My Son is a Splendid Driver* (1971).
Ionesco, Eugene	Romanian-born French playwright Eugene Ionesco died in Paris, France, on March 28, 1994, age 81. • **Last play:** *Journeys Among the Dead* (1980).
Irving, Washington	American author Washington Irving died at Sunnyside, near Tarrytown, New York, on November 28, 1859, age 76. • **Last work of fiction:** *Tales of a Traveller* (1824). • **Last work:** five-volume *The Life of Washington*, completed in 1859.
Jackson, Shirley	American novelist/short-story writer Shirley Jackson died in North Bennington, Vermont, on August 8, 1965, age 48. • **Last completed novel:** *We Have Always Lived in the Castle* (1963). • **Last novel:** *Come Along with Me* (unfinished; published posthumously in 1968 along with a collection of her short stories).

James, Henry	American novelist/critic Henry James died in London, England, on February 28, 1916, age 72. • **Last completed novel:** *The Outcry* (1911). • **Last unfinished novels:** *The Ivory Tower; The Sense of the Past* (both published posthumously in 1917). • **Last nonfiction works published in James's lifetime:** *Notes of a Son and Brother* (1914); *Notes on Novelists* (1914). James spent his last six years working on his autobiography but completed only two of the planned five volumes. *The Middle Years*, the second part, was published posthumously in 1917.
Jeffers, Robinson	American poet John Robinson Jeffers died in Carmel, California, on January 20, 1962, age 75. • **Last works:** *Hungerfield and Other Poems* (1954). *The Beginning and the End and Other Poems*, a collection of his works, was published posthumously in 1963.
Johnson, James Weldon	American author/poet/critic/educator James Weldon Johnson was killed in an automobile accident in Maine on June 26, 1938, age 67. • **Last book of poems:** *St. Peter Relates an Incident of the Resurrection* (1930). • **Last nonfiction work:** *Negro Americans, What Now?* (collection of lectures published in 1934).
Johnson, Samuel	English poet/essayist/lexicographer Samuel Johnson (Dr. Johnson) died in London, England, on December 13, 1784, age 75. • **Last major work:** *Lives of the Poets* (10 volumes, 1779-81). • **Last work:** "List of the Authors of the Universal History" (published in *The Gentleman's Magazine,* December 1784).
Jones, James	American novelist James Jones died on Long Island, New York, on May 9, 1977, age 55. • **Last work:** *Whistle* (last of his war trilogy; unfinished; completed by friend Willie Morris, using his notes; published posthumously in 1978).
Jonson, Ben	English playwright Ben Jonson was stricken with paralysis in 1628 and eventually was confined to bed. He produced little after that. He died in London on August 6, 1637, age 65. • **Last play:** *The Sad Shepherd's Tale* (unfinished; published posthumously in 1641).
Joyce, James	Irish novelist/poet James Augustine Aloysius Joyce died in Zurich, Switzerland, on January 13, 1941, age 58. • **Last work:** *Finnegan's Wake.* Joyce spent 17 years on it and completed it 1939.
Kafka, Franz	Austrian author Franz Kafka died of tuberculosis in a sanatorium near Vienna, Austria, on June 3, 1924, age 40. • **Last novel:** *The Castle* (unfinished). Only a few of Kafka's short stories were published during his lifetime. He ordered his manuscripts to be destroyed after his death, but his friend Max Brod recognized the value of his work and ignored his wishes. Brod arranged to have *The Castle* (1925), *The Trial* (1926) and *Amerika* (1927) published.
Kane, Joseph Nathan	American researcher/author Joseph Nathan Kane died in West Palm Beach, Florida, on September 22, 2002, age 103. • **Last book:** *Necessity's Child: The Story of Walter Hunt, America's Forgotten Inventor* (1997).

Kantor, MacKinlay	American novelist/screenwriter MacKinlay Kantor died in Sarasota, Florida, on October 11, 1977, age 73. • **Last novel:** *Valley Forge* (1975).
Kawabata, Yasunari	Japanese novelist Yasunari Kawabata died in Tokyo, Japan, on April 16, 1972, age 72. • **Last work:** *Gleanings from Snow Country,* (a reduction of his earlier work *Snow Country*).
Keats, John	English poet John Keats died in Rome, Italy, on February 23, 1821, age 25. • **Last works published in Keats's lifetime:** *Lamia, Isabella, The Eve of St. Agnes and Other Poems* (July 1820). • **Last known letter:** written November 30, 1820, to Charles Brown, his closest friend. • **Last poem:** *Hyperion* (begun in 1818; unfinished).
Kerouac, Jack	American novelist/poet Jean-Louis ("Jack") Kerouac died in St. Petersburg, Florida, on October 21, 1969, age 47. • **Last work published in Kerouac's lifetime:** *Vanity of Duluoz.* (1968).
Kipling, Rudyard	English author Rudyard Kipling died in London, England, on January 18, 1936, age 70. • **Last novel:** *Kim* (1901). • **Last work:** *Something of Myself—For My Friends Known and Unknown* (autobiography; published posthumously in 1937).
La Fontaine, Jean de	French author Jean de la Fontaine died in Paris, France, on April 13, 1695, age 73. • **Last fables:** written in 1694, shortly before he died. La Fontaine spent 20 years writing his *Fables*. Altogether, he wrote 238, published in 12 books.
Lamb, Charles	English author Charles Lamb, who used the pen name Elia, died in London, England, on December 27, 1834, age 59. • **Last work published in Lamb's lifetime:** *The Last Essays of Elia,* published in book form in 1833. They had been published earlier in *London Magazine* (1820-25).
Lardner, Ring	American author Ringgold Wilmer Lardner died in East Hampton, New York, on September 25, 1933, age 48. • **Last work published in Lardner's lifetime:** *Lose with a Smile* (1933; short stories written for the *Saturday Evening Post* in 1932).
Lawrence, D.H.	English novelist/essayist/poet D(avid) H(erbert) Lawrence died in Vence, France, on March 2, 1930, age 44. • **Last completed novel:** *Lady Chatterley's Lover* (1928). • **Last work:** *Apocalypse* (published posthumously in 1931). Lawrence was working on it when he died.
Lewis, C.S.	English author/professor/critic C(live) S(taples) Lewis died in Oxford, England, on November 22, 1963, age 64. • **Last novel:** *Till we Have Faces* (1956). • **Last *Chronicles of Narnia* story:** *The Last Battle* (seventh in series). • **Last book:** *Letters to Malcolm: Chiefly on Prayer* (published posthumously in 1964). • **Last writing:** "We Have No 'Right to Happiness'" (article for *Saturday Evening Post* Christmas issue, 1963).

Lewis, Sinclair	American novelist/playwright/social critic Harry Sinclair Lewis died in Rome, Italy, on January 10, 1951, age 66. • **Last novel:** *World So Wide* (published posthumously in 1951).
London, Jack	American author John Griffith ("Jack") London died at his ranch in Glen Ellen, California, on November 22, 1916, age 40. • **Last short story:** *The Water Baby,* completed a month before London died. • **Last book published in London's lifetime:** *The Little Lady of the Big House* (1916).
Longfellow, Henry Wadsworth	American poet Henry Wadsworth Longfellow died at his home in Cambridge, Massachusetts, on March 24, 1882, age 75. • **Last poem:** "The Bells of San Blas," written 10 days before he died. It was included in his last collection of verse, *In the Harbor* (1882).
Lowell, Amy	American author Amy Lowell died in Brookline, Massachusetts, on May 12, 1925 age 51. • **Last works:** two-volume biography of John Keats and a book of poetry, *What's O'Clock*, published the year she died.
Lowell, James Russell	American author James Russell Lowell died in Cambridge, Massachusetts, on August 12, 1891, age 72. • **Last book of poetry:** *Heartsease and Rue* (1888). • **Last poem published in Lowell's lifetime:** "My Book," which appeared in the *New York Ledger* in December 1890.
Lowell, Robert	American poet Robert Traill Spence Lowell Jr. died in New York, New York, on September 12, 1977, age 60. • **Last work:** *Day By Day* (published shortly before he died).
Macaulay, Thomas Babington	English author/historian Thomas Babington Macaulay died in London, England, on December 28, 1859, age 59. • **Last completed work:** the fifth volume of his *History of England* (published posthumously in 1861).
Malamud, Bernard	American novelist/short-story writer Bernard Malamud died in New York, New York, on March 18, 1986, age 71. • **Last novel published in Malamud's lifetime:** *God's Grace* (1982). • **Last short story:** "A Lost Grave" (published in *Esquire,* 1985).
Mann, Thomas	German author Thomas Mann died in Zurich, Switzerland, on August 12, 1955, age 80. • **Last novel:** *The Confessions of Felix Krull, Confidence Man* (1954; unfinished).
Marquand, John P.	American author John P(hillips) Marquand died in Newburyport, Massachusetts, on July 16, 1960, age 67. • **Last novel:** *Timothy Dexter Revisited*, published posthumously in 1960). • **Last *Mr. Moto* book:** *Right You Are, Mr. Moto* (1957; also called *Stopover Tokyo* and *The Last of Mr. Moto*).
Maugham, W. Somerset	English author W(illiam) Somerset Maugham died in St.-Jean-Cap-Ferrat, France, on December 16, 1965, age 91. • **Last novel:** *Catalina* (1948). • **Last play:** *Sheppy* (1933).
Maupassant, Guy de	French author Henri Rene Albert Guy de Maupassant died in Paris, France, on July 6, 1893, age 42. • **Last novel:** *Notre Coeur* (*Our Heart;* 1890; unfinished).

McCullers, Carson	American novelist Lulu Carson Smith, who used name Carson McCullers professionally, died in Nyack, New York, on September 29, 1967, age 50. • **Last work:** *Illumination and Night Glare* (unfinished autobiography; published posthumously in 1999). She worked on it during her final months.
McKay, Claude	Jamaican-born American author/poet Claude McKay died in Chicago, Illinois, on May 22, 1948, age 58. • **Last novel:** *Banana Bottom* (1933). • **Last poem published in McKay's lifetime:** "The Middle Ages" (1946). • **Last nonfiction book:** *Harlem: Negro Metropolis* (1940; a sociological study).
Melville, Herman	American author Herman Melville died in New York, New York, on September 28, 1891, age 72. • **Last novel published in Melville's lifetime:** *The Confidence Man: His Masquerade* (1857). • **Last novel:** *Billy Budd, Foretopman,* written between 1885 and 1891 but not published until 1924, 33 years after his death. The unfinished manuscript was found in his desk after he died.
Meredith, George	English poet/novelist George Meredith died in Surrey, England, on May 18, 1909, age 81. • **Last novel:** *The Amazing Marriage* (1896). • **Last poetry collection:** *A Reading of Life and Other Poems* (1901).
Michener, James	American author James Michener died in Austin, Texas, on October 16, 1997, age 90. • **Last novel:** *Recessional* (published in 1994) • **Last work:** *A Century of Sonnets* (published on his 90th birthday).
Millay, Edna St. Vincent	American poet Edna St. Vincent Millay died in Austerlitz, New York, on October 19, 1950, age 58. • **Last book of poems:** *Collected Poems* (published posthumously in 1956. Contains her last poem, "Mine is the Harvest").
Milne, A.A.	English author A(lan) A(lexander) Milne did no further writing after he had a stroke in 1952. He died in Hartfield, Sussex, on January 31, 1956, age 74. • **Last *Winnie the Pooh* book:** *The House at Pooh Corner* (1928). • **Last book published in Milne's lifetime:** *Year In, Year Out* (1952).
Milton, John	English poet/author John Milton died in London, England, on November 8, 1674, age 65. • **Last major work published in Milton's lifetime:** *Samson Agonistes* (1671). • **Last work:** *Of True Religion, Heresy, Schism Toleration and What Best Means May be Used Against the Growth of Popery* (1673). • **Last surviving house of Milton:** "Milton's Cottage," Deanway, Chalfont St. Giles, Buckinghamshire, England. Milton lived there in 1665 while he completed *Paradise Lost.*
Mishima, Yukio	Yukio Mishima is the pseudonym of Japanese novelist Hiraoka Kimitake, who died in Tokyo, Japan, on November 25, 1970, age 45. • **Last novel:** *The Decay of the Angel* (fourth volume of his tetralogy *The Sea of Fertility,* 1969-70).

Mitchell, Margaret	American author Margaret Mitchell was hit by a car while crossing a street in Atlanta, Georgia, and died on August 16, 1949, age 48. • **Last novel:** *Gone With the Wind* (1936; her only novel).
Molière	Molière was the stage name of French actor/dramatist Jean Baptiste Poquelin, who died in Paris, France, on February 17, 1673, age 51. • **Last play:** *The Imaginary Invalid* (1673); premiered a week before Molière died.
Murdoch, Dame Iris	Irish-born English author/lecturer/novelist Dame Jean Iris Murdoch died in Oxford, England, on February 8, 1999, age 79. • **Last novel:** *Jackson's Dilemma* (1995).
Nabokov, Vladimir	Russian-born author Vladimir Vladimirovich Nabokov died in Lausanne, Switzerland, on July 2, 1977, age 78. • **Last completed novel:** *Look at the Harlequins!* (1974).
Nash, Ogden	American poet Ogden Nash died in Baltimore, Maryland, on May 19, 1971, age 68. • **Last work published in Nash's lifetime:** *Bed Riddance* (1970). • **Last work:** *The Old Dog Barks Backward* (published posthumously in 1972).
Neruda, Pablo	Pablo Neruda is the pseudonym of Chilean poet Neftalí Ricardo Reyes Basoalto, who died in Santiago, Chile, on September 23, 1973, age 69. • **Last work:** *The Book of Questions,* in which Neruda used a new poetic form: a series of unanswerable questions presented as two-line stanzas (written 1973; published posthumously in 1974).
Norris, Kathleen	American author Kathleen Thompson Norris died in San Francisco, California, on January 18, 1966, age 85. • **Last novel:** *A Family Gathering* (1959).
O'Casey, Sean	Irish-born dramatist John Casey, who used Sean O'Cathasaigh (the Gaelic form of his name) and was also known professionally as Sean O'Casey, died in Torquay, England, on September 18, 1964, age 84. • **Last play:** *Behind the Green Curtain* (1961).
O'Connor, Flannery	American author Flannery O'Connor died in Milledgeville, Georgia, on August 3, 1964, age 39. • **Last novel published in O'Connor's lifetime:** *The Violent Bear It Away* (1960). • **Last short story:** *Parker's Back* (1964, shortly before she died).
Odets, Clifford	American playwright/screenwriter/director Clifford Odets died in Los Angeles, California, on August 14, 1963, age 57. • **Last completed play:** *The Flowering Peach* (1954). • **Last play televised in Odets's lifetime:** *Golden Boy* (1962).
O'Hara, John	American author/screenwriter John Henry O'Hara died in Princeton, New Jersey, on April 11, 1970, age 65. • **Last novel:** *The Ewings* (published posthumously in 1972). Two short-story collections—*The Time Element and Other Stories* (1972) and *Good Samaritan and Other Stories* (1973)—were also published posthumously.
O'Neill, Eugene	During his last 10 years, American playwright Eugene Gladstone O'Neill suffered from a debilitating disease that ended his writing. He died in Boston, Massachusetts, on November 27, 1953, age 65. • **Last play produced on Broadway in O'Neill's lifetime:** *The Iceman*

	Cometh (September 4, 1946). • **Last play published in O'Neill's lifetime:** *A Moon for the Misbegotten* (1952). O'Neill left several plays in manuscript form, including *A Touch of the Poet* and *More Stately Mansions*. His masterpiece, *Long Day's Journey Into Night* was produced on Broadway in 1956.
Orwell, George	George Orwell is the pseudonym of English novelist Eric Arthur Blair, who died in London, England, on January 21, 1950, age 47. • **Last novel:** *Nineteen Eighty-Four* (written in 1948-49).
Pasternak, Boris	Russian novelist/poet Boris Leonidovich Pasternak died in Peredelkino, Russia, on May 30, 1960, age 70. • **Last book of poetry:** *When the Weather Clears* (written in the 1950s, published in 1960). • **End of ban on *Dr. Zhivago* in the Soviet Union:** 1988. Pasternak's book was banned in the USSR in 1957.
Pepys, Samuel	English diarist Samuel Pepys died in London, England, on May 26, 1703, age 70. Pepys started keeping his diary on January 1, 1660, and had to stop when his eyesight began to fail. After his death, the diary was bequeathed to Magdalene College, Cambridge. • **Last diary entry:** May 31, 1669, in his 36th year, the year his wife died. He wrote the last entry in a shorthand code.
Pirandello, Luigi	Italian novelist/playwright Luigi Pirandello died in Rome, Italy, on December 10, 1936, age 69. • **Last play:** *The Mountain Giants* (unfinished). On his deathbed, he gave notes to his son on how he wanted it finished. It was later completed and produced.
Plath, Sylvia	American-born author/poet Sylvia Plath died in London, England, on February 11, 1963, age 30. • **Last poem:** "Edge," written just before she died.
Poe, Edgar Allan	American mystery writer/poet Edgar Allan Poe died in Baltimore, Maryland, on October 7, 1849, age 40. • **Last major poem:** "Annabel Lee" (1849). • **Last tale:** *To the Light-House* (1849; unfinished). Poe wrote only seven or eight stories during his last few years. • **Last book:** *Eureka* (1848).
Pope, Alexander	English poet Alexander Pope died in Twickenham, Middlesex, England, on May 30, 1744, age 56. • **Last works:** *The Dunciad in Four Books* (1743). Pope completed the work in three volumes in 1728 but revised it the year before he died. • **Last major work:** *Imitations of Horace* (1733-39).
Porter, Katherine Anne	American author Callie Russell (Katherine Anne) Porter died in Silver Spring, Maryland, on September 18, 1980, age 90. • **Last work:** *The Never Ending Wrong* (1977; the Sacco-Vanzetti case). • **Last novel:** *Ship of Fools* (1962; her only novel).
Potok, Chaim	American author Herman Harold (Chaim) Potok died in Merion, Pennsylvania, on July 23, 2002, age 73. • **Last novel:** *Old Men at Midnight* (2001).
Priestley, J.B.	English author J(ohn) B(oynton) Priestley died in Warwickshire, England, on August 14, 1984, age 89. • **Last nonfiction work:** *Instead of the Trees* (1977; autobiography).

Proust, Marcel	French novelist Marcel Proust died on November 18, 1922, age 51. Proust spent much of his life writing recollections of his past. His *Remembrance of Things Past* is in seven parts. The last three parts were published posthumously between 1923 and 1927. • **Last "Remembrance":** *Time Regained* (1927).
Pushkin, Alexander Sergeyevich	Russian author Alexander Sergeyevich Pushkin died on February 10 (New Style), January 29 (Old Style), 1837, age 37. • **Last novel:** *The Captain's Daughter* (1836). • **Last scholarly work:** *History of the Pugachev Rebellion* (1834).
Rand, Ayn	Ayn Rand is the pseudonym of Russian-born American novelist Alissa Zinovievna Rosenbaum, who died in New York, New York, on March 6, 1982, age 77. • **Last novel:** *Atlas Shrugged* (1957). • **Last public speech:** "The Sanction of the Victims," presented before the National Committee for Monetary Reform, New Orleans, Louisiana, November 1981. • **Last issue of** *The Ayn Rand Letter*: January-February 1976.
Rawlings, Marjorie Kinnan	American novelist Marjorie Kinnan Rawlings died in St. Augustine, Florida, on December 14, 1953, age 57. • **Last novel:** *Sojourner* (1952).
Remarque, Erich Maria	Erich Maria Remarque is the pseudonym of German-born author Erich Paul Remark (family name Kramer in reverse), who died in Locarno, Switzerland, on September 25, 1970 age 72. • **Last novel published in Remarque's lifetime:** *The Night in Lisbon* (1962). • **Last novel:** *Shadows in Paradise* (published posthumously in 1971).
Rice, Elmer	Elmer Rice is the pseudonym of American playwright Elmer Leopold Reizenstein, who died in England, on May 8, 1967, age 74. • **Last play:** *Court of Last Resort* (published in 1965).
Rilke, Rainer Maria	Czech-born German poet/author Rainer Maria Rilke (Rene Karl Wilhelm Joseph Maria Rilke) died in Valmont, Switzerland, on December 26, 1926, age 51. • **Last major works published in Rilke's lifetime:** *Duino Elegies; Sonnets to Orpheus* (1923).
Rinehart, Mary Roberts	American author Mary Roberts Rinehart died in New York, New York, on September 22, 1958, age 82. • **Last novel:** *The Swimming Pool* (1952).
Robinson, Edwin Arlington	American poet Edwin Arlington Robinson died in New York, New York, on April 6, 1935, age 65. • **Last book:** *King Jasper* (published posthumously in 1935). Robinson worked on the galley proofs while he was dying in a New York hospital.
Rohmer, Sax	Sax Rohmer is the pseudonym of English mystery writer Arthur Henry Sarsfield Ward, who died in London, England, on June 1, 1959, age 75. • **Last novel:** *Emperor Fu Manchu* (1959).
Rousseau, Jean Jacques	Swiss philosopher/author Jean Jacques Rousseau died near Paris, France, on July 2, 1778, age 66. • **Last work:** *The Reveries of a Solitary Stroller* (written the year he died; published posthumously).
Runyon, Damon	American short-story writer Alfred Damon Runyon died in New York, New York, on December 10, 1946, age 62.

	• **Last short story:** *Death Pays a Social Call.* • **Last movie made of one of Runyon's stories during his lifetime:** *It Ain't Hay* (1943), based on *Princess O'Hara.*
Ruskin, John	English author/art critic John Ruskin died in Coniston, England, on January 20, 1900, age 80. • **Last work:** *Praeterita* (unfinished; published intermittently 1885-89.)
Saki	Saki is the pseudonym of Burmese-born British short-story writer Hector Hugh Munro, who was killed in action in France on November 14, 1916, during World War I, age 45. • **Last novel:** *When William Came* (1914). Many of his works were published posthumously.
Sand, George	George Sand is the pseudonym of French author Amandine Aurore Lucile Dupin, Baroness Dudevant, who died at Nohant, France, on June 8, 1876, age 72. • **Last work:** *The Tower of Percemont* (1876).
Sandburg, Carl	American poet/historian/novelist Carl August Sandburg died in Flat Rock, North Carolina, on July 22, 1967, age 89. • **Last book of poems:** *Honey and Salt* (1963). • **Last work:** *Always The Young Stranger* (1952; autobiography).
Saroyan, William	American author/playwright William Saroyan died in Fresno, California, on May 18, 1981, age 72. • **Last work published in Saroyan's lifetime:** *Obituaries* (1979). He left a number of unpublished manuscripts.
Sayers, Dorothy L.	English novelist/medieval scholar Dorothy L(eigh) Sayers died in Witham, Essex, England, on December 17, 1957, age 64. • **Last *Lord Peter Wimsey* story:** *Thrones, Domination* (unfinished, 1938; completed by Jill Paton Walsh, published 1998). • **Last scholarly work:** *Further Papers on Dante* (1957).
Schiller, Friedrich von	German poet/dramatist/historian/philosopher Johann Christoph Friedrich von Schiller died in Weimar, Germany, on May 9, 1805, age 46. • **Last completed play:** *William Tell* (premiered in 1804). • **Last work:** *Demetrius,* unfinished; fragment published posthumously in 1815).
Scott, Sir Walter	Scottish poet/novelist Sir Walter Scott died at Abbotsford, his home in Scotland, on September 21, 1832, age 61. • **Last major poem:** "The Lord of the Isles" (1815). • **Last works:** *Count Robert of Paris* and *Castle Dangerous* (1832).
Shakespeare, William	English playwright/poet William Shakespeare died in Stratford, England, on April 23, 1616, age 52. • **Last work:** uncertain. Some scholars believe it was *Henry VIII.* Others consider *The Tempest* his last work. Shakespeare's life is not well documented; however, it is known that in either 1612 or 1613 he retired as the leading playwright of the King's Men, a group of court entertainers who performed at court during the reign on James I. *Henry VIII* was written during his tenure with the group. • **Last direct descendant:** granddaughter Elizabeth Hall Nash Barnard, Lady Barnard (1608-70), daughter of Susanna Shakespeare and John Hall.
Shaw, George Bernard	Irish-born English playwright/social critic George Bernard Shaw died in Hertfordshire, England, on November 2, 1950, age 94.

	• **Last play:** *Why She Would Not* (1950; written to celebrate his 94th birthday). • **Last works:** worked on the movie *Caesar and Cleopatra* when he was 90, finished *Buoyant Billions* at age 91 and wrote the play *Farfetched Fables* when he was 93. His autobiographical *Sixteen Self Sketches* were also published that year.
Shelley, Mary Wollstonecraft	English author Mary Wollstonecraft Godwin Shelley died in London, England, on February 1, 1851, age 53. • **Last gothic novel:** *The Last Man* (1826). • **Last book:** *Rambles in Germany and Italy, 1840, 1842 and 1843* (published in 1844).
Shelley, Percy Bysshe	English poet Percy Bysshe Shelly drowned in a storm in Italy on July 8, 1822, age 30. He was last seen off the coast of Reggio. • **Last poem:** "The Triumph of Life" (1822; unfinished). He wrote it while staying at a house on the bay of Spezia, near where he died.
Sheridan, Richard Brinsley	Irish-born English dramatist Richard Brinsley Sheridan died in London, England, on July 7, 1816, age 64. • **Last play:** *The Critic* (1779). Sheridan also worked on an adaptation of an English translation of *The Spanish in Peru* (produced in 1799 as *Pizarro*).
Shirer, William L.	American author/World War II historian William L(awrence) Shirer died in Boston, Massachusetts, on December 28, 1993, age 89. • **Last work:** *Love and Hatred: The Troubled Marriage of Leo and Sonya Tolstoy* (published posthumously in 1994).
Shute, Nevil	English author/aeronautical engineer Nevil Shute Norway died in Melbourne, Australia, on January 12, 1960, age 61. • **Last novel:** *Trustee from the Tool Room* (published posthumously in 1960).
Simenon, Georges	Belgian-born author Georges Jacques Christian Simenon died in Lausanne, Switzerland, on September 4, 1989, age 86. He created Inspector Jules Maigret and put the crime fighter in more than 100 novels and short stories, as well as a popular television series in the 1950s and 1960s. • **Last *Maigret* story:** *Maigret et Monsieur Charles* (1972). After that, he wrote only nonfiction. • **Last work:** *Intimate Memoirs* (1981).
Sinclair, Upton	American author/novelist/playwright Upton Beall Sinclair died in Bound Brook, New Jersey, on November 25, 1968, age 90. • **Last play:** *The Enemy Had It Too* (1950). • **Last *Lanny Budd* story:** *The Return of Lanny Budd* (1953).
Spenser, Edmund	English poet Edmund Spenser died in London, England, on January 16, 1599, at about the age of 47. • **Last major works published in Spenser's lifetime:** *A Viewe of the Present State of Irelande* (1597?). Two shorter works were published in 1596: *Fowre Hymnes; Prothalamion*.
Stein, Gertrude	American author Gertrude Stein died in Paris, France, on February 27, 1946, age 72. • **Last book:** *Brewsie and Willie* (1946).
Steinbeck, John	American author/screenwriter John Ernst Steinbeck died in New York, New York, on December 20, 1968, age 66.

	• **Last major works:** *The Winter of Our Discontent* (novel; 1961); *Travels with Charley in Search of America* (autobiography, 1962); *America and Americans* (essays on U.S. travel, 1966).
Stendhal	Stendhal is the pseudonym of French author Marie Henri Beyle, who died in Paris, France, on March 23, 1842, age 59. • **Last major work published in Stendhal's lifetime:** *The Charterhouse of Parma* (1839. He left several unfinished works that were published posthumously.
Sterne, Laurence	English clergyman/novelist Laurence Sterne died in London, England, on March 18, 1768, age 54. • **Last work:** *Sentimental Journey Through France and Italy* (1768. He completed only two of four planned volumes.)
Stevenson, Robert Louis	Scottish author Robert Louis Stevenson died in Samoa on December 3, 1894, age 44. • **Last completed work:** *Prayers Written at Vailima.* • **Last unfinished works:** *The Weir of Hermiston* (novel, published posthumously in 1896); *St. Ives,* an adventure story (completed by Arthur Quiller-Couch; published in 1897).
Stoker, Bram	Irish-born English author Abraham (Bram) Stoker died in London, England, on April 20, 1912, age 64. • **Last novel:** *The Lair of the White Worm* (1911). • **Last nonfiction work:** *Famous Imposters* (1910).
Stout, Rex	American mystery writer Rex Todhunter Stout died in Danbury, Connecticut, on October 27, 1975, age 88. He introduced Nero Wolfe, the fat detective who could solve crimes without ever leaving his home, in *Fer-de-Lance* in 1934. • **Last *Nero Wolfe* novel published in Stout's lifetime:** *A Family Affair* (1975). • **Last *Nero Wolfe* novel by Stout:** *An Officer and a Lady* (published posthumously in 1985). • **Last *Nero Wolfe* novel by Goldsborough:** *Silver Spire* (1994). Robert Goldsborough took over the series in the 1980s.
Stowe, Harriet Beecher	American author Harriet Beecher Stowe died in Hartford, Connecticut, on July 1, 1896, age 85. • **Last novel:** *Poganuc People* (1878).
Stratemeyer, Edward	American author/entrepreneur Edward L. Stratemeyer died in Newark, New Jersey, on May 10, 1930, age 68. He created, produced and/or wrote many children's classics in the late 19th and early 20th century. Stratemeyer's syndicate was responsible for the Rover Boys, Bobbsey Twins, Tom Swift, the Hardy Boys and Nancy Drew, among others. • **Last original *Bobbsey Twins* book:** *The Bobbsey Twins: The Coral Turtle Mystery*, 72nd in the series. The original Bobbsey Twins books appeared under the pseudonym Laura Lee Hope and were published by Grosset and Dunlap between 1904 and 1979. • **Last 1980-86 series *Bobbsey Twins* book:** *Grinning Gargoyle Mystery* (14th in the series), published by Simon and Schuster. • **Last 1987-92 series *Bobbsey Twins* book:** *The Mystery of the Mixed-up Mail*, 30th in the series. • **Last *Hardy Boys Casefiles* book:** *Dead in the Water* (1998). • **Last *Rover Boys* book:** *Winning a Fortune*, 30th in the series pub-

	lished between 1899 and 1926 under the pseudonym Arthur M. Winfield. • **Last first-series _Tom Swift_ book:** _Planet Stone_, 38th in the first series that ran from 1910 to 1935. Tom Swift appeared in four series under the pseudonyms Victor Appleton and Victor Appleton II. • **Last _Tom Swift Junior_ book:** _Tom Swift and the Galaxy Ghosts_, 33rd in the series published between 1954 and 1978. • **Last _Tom Swift_ (Wanderer):** _Planet of Nightmares,_ 11th in the series published between 1981 and 1984. • **Last _Tom Swift_ (Archway edition):** _Quantum Force_, 13th in the series published between 1991 and 1993.
Strindberg, August	Swedish playwright/novelist August Strindberg died in Stockholm, Sweden, on May 14, 1912, age 63. • **Last play:** _The Great Highway_ (1909).
Swift, Jonathan	Irish clergyman/author/satirist Jonathan Swift published his satire _Gulliver's Travels_ in 1726. After that, he spent much of his time doing church work. He suffered from mental illness in his later years. In 1742, he was placed in the care of guardians. He died in Dublin, Ireland, on October 19, 1745, age 78. • **Last major work:** _The Legion Club_ (1736).
Synge, John Millington	Irish playwright John Millington Synge died in Dublin, Ireland, on March 24, 1909, age 38. • **Last plays:** _Deirdre of the Sorrows_ (unfinished; produced in 1910). _The Tinker's Wedding_ (produced in 1911).
Tagore, Rabindranath	Bengali poet/novelist/educator Rabindranath Tagore died in Calcutta, India, on August 7, 1941, age 80. • **Last poems:** _Rabindranath Tagore: Final Poems_, written during his last year. He dictated his last poem just hours before he died.
Tarkington, Booth	American novelist/playwright Newton Booth Tarkington died in Indianapolis, Indiana, on May 19, 1946, age 76. • **Last novel:** _The Show Piece_ (1947).
Tennyson, Alfred Lord	English poet Alfred Lord Tennyson died in Surrey, England, on October 6, 1892, the age of 83. • **Last major collection of verse:** _The Death of Oenone, Akbar's Dream, and Other Poems_ (1892).
Thackeray, William Makepeace	English novelist William Makepeace Thackeray died in London, England, on December 24, 1863, age 52. • **Last completed novel:** _The Adventures of Philip on His Way Through the World_ (last of his Arthur Pendennis trilogy; published in _Cornhill_ magazine, 1861-62). • **Last unfinished novel:** _Denis Duval_ (published in _Cornhill_ magazine, 1864).
Thomas, Dylan	Welsh poet/author Dylan Marlais Thomas died in New York, New York, on November 9, 1953, age 39. Thomas has been described as Great Britain's last Romantic poet. • **Last completed poem:** "In the White Giant's Thigh." • **Last novel:** _Adventures in the Skin Trade_ (unfinished; published posthumously in 1954). • **Last work:** _Under Milk Wood: A Play for Voices_ (1953). He died while he was in New York to direct a production of the play.

Thoreau, Henry David	American author Henry David Thoreau died in Concord, Massachusetts, on May 6, 1862, age 44. • **Last of the Walden experiment:** September 1847. It began on March 1845. An account of his experience, *Walden, or Life in the Woods*, was published in 1854. • **Last book published in Thoreau's lifetime:** *Walden, or Life in the Woods* (1854). Only two of Thoreau's books were published during his lifetime. The other was *A Week on the Concord and Merrimack Rivers* published in 1849. Thoreau's 14-volume *Journal*, which covers his life from 1837 until his death, was not published until 1906.
Thurber, James	American humorist/cartoonist James Grover Thurber died in New York, New York, on November 2, 1961, age 66. • **Last fairy tale for adults:** *The Wonderful O* (1957). • **Last work:** *Lanterns and Lances* (collection of stories; published posthumously in December 1961).
Tolkien, J.R.R.	English scholar/author J(ohn) R(onald) R(euel) Tolkien died in Bournemouth, England, on September 2, 1973, age 81. • **Last of the *Lord of the Rings* trilogy:** Part III, *The Return of the King* (1955). Tolkien's son Christopher edited *Silmarillon* and published it in 1977. He also published his father's incomplete works in 1980 as *Unfinished Tales of Numenor and Middle Earth*.
Tolstoy, Leo	Russian novelist Leo Nikolayevich Tolstoy died in Astapovo, Russia, on November 7, 1910, age 82. • **Last novel published in Tolstoy's lifetime:** *Resurrection* (1899). • **Last writings:** "I Can Not Be Silent," a protest against the execution of a revolutionary (1908); "Last message to mankind" written for an international peace congress in Stockholm, Sweden (1909).
Trollope, Anthony	English novelist Anthony Trollope died in Hastings, Sussex, England, on December 6, 1882, age 67. • **Last works:** three novels published posthumously: *Mr. Scarborough's Family* (1883); *The Landleaguers* (1883); and *An Old Man's Love* (1884). Trollope's *Autobiography*, written in 1875-76, was published the year after he died.
Trumbo, Dalton	American novelist/screenwriter Dalton Trumbo died in Los Angeles, California, on September 10, 1976, age 70. • **Last novel:** *Night of the Aurochs* (unfinished; published posthumously in 1979). • **Last screen play:** *Ishi, the Last of His Tribe* (1978). The screen play was finished by his son Christopher.
Tuchman, Barbara	American author/historian Barbara Wertheim Tuchman died in Greenwich, Connecticut, on February 6, 1989, age 77. • **Last work:** *The First Salute* (1988).
Turgenev, Ivan	Russian author Ivan Sergeyevich Turgenev died in near Paris, France, on September 3, 1883, age 64. • **Last major novel:** *Virgin Soil* (1877). • **Last work published in Turgenev's lifetime:** *Poems in Prose* (written 1878-82; published in 1883).
Twain, Mark	Mark Twain is the pseudonym of American author/humorist Samuel Langhorne Clemens, who died in Redding, Connecticut, on April 21, 1910, age 74.

	• **Last work published in Twain's lifetime:** *Extract from Captain Stormfield's Visit to Heaven* (1909). Twain spent his last six years writing his autobiography. It was published 14 years after his death. Some of his last essays were published for the first time in 1962 in *Letters from the Earth*. • **Last Tom Sawyer book:** *Tom Sawyer, Detective* (1896). Tom Sawyer also appeared in *The Adventures of Tom Sawyer* (1876); *Adventures of Huckleberry Finn* (1884); and *Tom Sawyer Abroad* (1894).
Undset, Sigrid	Norwegian author Sigrid Undset died in Lillehammer, Norway, on June 10, 1949, age 67. • **Last novel:** *Madame Dorothea* (1939). • **Last book:** *Happy Times in Norway* (1942).
Verne, Jules	French novelist Jules Verne died in Amiens, France, on March 24, 1905, age 77. • **Last novel published in Verne's lifetime:** *The Invasion of the Sea* (1905). Another novel, *Lighthouse at the End of the World* (attributed to his son Michel), was being published when he died.
Voltaire	Voltaire is the pseudonym of French author/philosopher François Marie Arouet, who died in Paris, France, on May 30, 1778, age 84. • **Last play:** *Irene,* written when he was 83. He lived long enough to see it produced at the National Theatre in Paris.
Warren, Robert Penn	American novelist/poet Robert Penn Warren died in Stratton, Vermont, on September 15, 1989, age 84. • **Last work:** *New and Selected Essays 1923-1985* (1989).
Waugh, Evelyn	English novelist Evelyn Arthur St. John Waugh died in Somerset, England, on April 10, 1966, age 62. • **Last work:** *A Little Learning* (1964), the first volume of his three-volume autobiography. • **Last travel book:** *A Tourist in Africa* (1960).
Wells, H.G.	English novelist H(erbert) G(eorge) Wells died in London, England, on August 13, 1946, age 79. • **Last novel:** *You Can't Be Too Careful* (1941). • **Last works:** *Mind at the End of Its Tether* (1945). The year before he died, Wells submitted his doctoral thesis to London University: "The Quality of Illusion in the Continuity of Individual Life."
Welty, Eudora	American author/photographer Eudora Welty died in Jackson, Mississippi, on July 23, 2001, age 92. • **Last novel:** *The Optimist's Daughter* (1972). • **Last work:** *Country Churchyards* (photographs; 2000).
West, Morris	Australian novelist Morris Langlo West died in Sydney, Australia, on October 9, 1999, age 83. • **Last work:** *The Last Confession* (finished shortly before he died).
West, Nathanael	Nathanael West is the pseudonym of American novelist/screenwriter Nathan Weinstein, who died in a car crash near El Centro, California, on December 22, 1940, age 37. • **Last novel:** *Day of the Locust* (1939). • **Last screenplay:** *Let's Make Music* (1940).
West, Dame Rebecca	Dame Rebecca West is the pseudonym of English novelist/ journalist/critic Cicily Isabel Fairfield Andrews, who died in London, England,

	on March 15, 1983, age 90. • **Last novel:** *The Birds Fall Down* (1966).
Wharton, Edith	American novelist Edith Newbold Jones Wharton died in St. Brice-sous-Forêt, France, on August 11, 1937, age 75. • **Last novel:** *The Buccaneers* (unfinished; completed by Marian Mainwaring and published in 1938).
White, E.B.	American children's author/essayist E(lwyn) B(rooks) White died in North Brooklin, Maine, on October 1, 1985, age 86. • **Last book for children:** *The Trumpet of the Swan* (1970).
Whitman, Walt	American poet Walt Whitman died in Camden, New Jersey, on March 26, 1892, age 72. • **Last work:** The "Deathbed" edition of *Leaves of Grass* (1891-92), which concludes with "A Backward Glance O'er Travel'd Roads," written shortly before he died.
Whittier, John Greenleaf	American author/abolitionist John Greenleaf Whittier died in Hampton Falls, New Hampshire, on September 7, 1892, age 84. • **Last poems:** *At Sundown* (1890).
Wilde, Oscar	Irish-born English author/playwright Oscar Fingal O'Flahertie Wills Wilde died in Paris, France, on November 30, 1900, age 46. • **Last novel:** *The Picture of Dorian Gray* (1890; his only novel). • **Last play:** *The Importance of Being Earnest* (1895). • **Last work:** *The Ballad of Reading Gaol* (1898).
Wilder, Laura Ingalls	American author Laura Ingalls Wilder was the last surviving member of the pioneering Ingalls family. She began writing the novels based on her childhood experiences when she was 65. She died at her home near Mansfield, Missouri, on February 10, 1957, age 90. • **Last *Little House* book:** *These Happy Golden Years* (1943). • **Last book:** *West from Home* (published posthumously in 1974).
Wilder, Thornton	American playwright/novelist Thornton Niven Wilder died in Hamden, Connecticut, on December 7, 1975, age 78. • **Last novel:** *Theopilus North* (1973). • **Last play:** *Infancy* (1960).
Williams, Tennessee	American playwright Thomas Lanier ("Tennessee") Williams died in New York, New York, on February 25, 1983, age 71. • **Last plays:** *Clothes for a Summer Hotel* (1980); *A House Not Meant to Stand* (1982; originally one act; expanded to full play).
Williams, William Carlos	American author/poet/pediatrician William Carlos Williams died in Rutherford, New Jersey on March 4, 1963, age 79. • **Last poems published in Williams' lifetime:** *Pictures from Brueghel and Other Poems* (1962), which won him a posthumous Pulitzer Prize.
Wodehouse, P.G.	English humorist/author P(elham) G(renville) Wodehouse died in Southampton, New York, on February 14, 1975 age 93. Wodehouse introduced Bertie Wooster and his valet Jeeves in a short story *The Man with Two Left Feet* in 1917. • **Last *Jeeves and Wooster* story:** "Aunts Aren't Gentlemen" (1974).
Wolfe, Thomas	American author Thomas Wolfe died in Baltimore, Maryland, on September 15, 1939, age 37. • **Last novel published in Wolfe's lifetime:** *Of Time and the River* (1935. Several of his works were published posthumously, including

	The Web and the Rock (1939); *You Can't Go Home Again* (1940) and *The Hills Beyond* (1941).
Woolf, Virginia	English author Adeline Virginia Stephen Woolf died in Lewes, Sussex, England, on March 28, 1941, age 59. • **Last novel:** *Between the Acts* (1941). Several of her works were published after her death, including *A Writer's Diary* (1953) and *Letters* (1956.)
Wordsworth, William	English poet William Wordsworth died in Westmoreland, England, on April 23, 1850, age 80. • **Last major poem:** "Extempore Effusion Upon the Death of James Hogg" (1835).
Wright, Richard	American author Richard Nathaniel Wright died in Paris, France, on November 28, 1960, age 52. • **Last works:** *The Long Dream* (1958; unfinished); *Island of Hallucination* (unfinished). Just before he died, Wright became interested in haiku poetry and wrote many poems during his final days.
Yeats, William Butler	Irish poet/playwright William Butler Yeats died in Menton, France, on January 28, 1939, age 73. • **Last play:** *The Death of Cuchulain,* completed a few days before he died. • **Last work:** *Last Poems* (published posthumously in 1940).
Zola, Emile	French novelist Emile Zola died in Paris, France, on September 29, 1902, age 62. • **Last major work:** *Les Quatre Evangiles* (*Four Gospels*), began in 1899. At the time of his death, he had completed three of the four parts: *Fruitfulness* (1899), *Work* (1901) and *Truth* (1903). Left unfinished: *Justice.*

Magazines and Periodicals
Last Issue of Some Major American Magazines and Periodicals

Title	Last Issue	Description
American Magazine	August 1956	A continuation of *Frank Leslie's Popular Monthly Magazine*. Merged with *American Magazine* in 1905.
Atkinson's Casket	1840	Founded in 1826 as *Atkinson's Casket, Gems of Literature, Wit and Sentiment*. Merged with *Burton's Gentleman's Magazine* as *Graham's Lady's and Gentleman's Magazine*.
Bowling	July 2002	Founded in 1934. Magazine of the American Bowling Congress.
B. Smith Style	Winter 2000	Founded in 1999 by African-American restaurant owner/cookbook author/former model Barbara Smith.
Burton's Gentleman's Magazine	1840	Founded in 1837. Merged with *Atkinson's Casket* as *Graham's Lady's and Gentleman's Magazine*.
Byte	July 1998	Founded in 1975. Computer magazine.
Collier's	January 4, 1957	Founded in 1888 as *Collier's Once a Week*. Renamed *Collier's the National Weekly* in 1895.
Compute!	September 1994	Founded in 1979. Monthly computer magazine.

Creative Computing	December 1985	Founded in 1974. First personal computing magazine.
Etude Magazine	May/June 1957	Founded in 1883 by Theodore Presser Company. A major music magazine.
Everybody's Magazine	March 1929	Founded in 1899. One of America's most popular magazines in the early 20th century.
Flair	January 1951	Founded in 1950 by Fleur Cowles. Sophisticated general-interest magazine.
Frank Leslie's Popular Monthly	1905	Founded in 1876 by Frank Leslie Publishing House. Merged with *American Magazine*.
George	February/ March 2001	Founded in 1995 by John F. Kennedy Jr. as a blend of politics and culture. Final issue was tribute to Kennedy who was killed in a plane crash on July 16, 1999, age 38.
Godey's Lady's Book	1898	Women's magazine; took that name around 1837, when two publications were merged. In 1877, Louis Godey sold the magazine and long-time editor Sara Josepha Hale retired at age 90. The magazine went through a series of owners and eventually folded.
Graham's Magazine	1858	Founded in 1841. Renamed *Graham's Magazine of Literature and Art* (1844); *Graham's American Monthly Magazine of Literature and Art* (1848); *Graham's Illustrated Magazine of Literature, Romance, Art, and Fashion* (1856). Edgar Allan Poe was an editor and contributor.
Hampton's	1912	Founded in 1907 to provide readers with information on controversial political issues. Owner was forced to close after publishing a controversial piece about a railroad.
Harper's Weekly	May 13, 1916	Founded in 1857 by Harper & Brothers. Published works of Herman Melville, Theodore Dreiser, Jack London, Booth Tarkington, Mark Twain, William Dean Howells, Horace Greeley and political cartoons of Thomas Nast.
Hearst's Magazine	February 1925	Founded in 1901 as *World Today*. Renamed when Hearst took over in 1912. Merged with *Cosmopolitan* in March 1925.
I.F. Stone's Weekly	1971	Founded in 1953. Presented political issues.
Knickerbocker, The	January-June 1865	Founded in 1833 by novelist C.F. Hoffman. Added *American Monthly* to title in early 1860s. Last issue dropped name *Knickerbocker* and appeared as *American Monthly*. Published works of Washington Irving.
Lear's	April 1994	Founded in 1989 by Frances Lear for the sophisticated, mature woman.
Liberty	1950	Founded in 1924. Published works of Sinclair Lewis, F. Scott Fitzgerald, Erle Stanley Gardner among others.
Life	May 2000	Founded in 1936. Ceased publication (original run) on December 29, 1972. Revived then canceled in 2000. Revived aggain in 2004 as newspaper supplement.
Lippincott's Magazine	1915	Founded in 1868. Appeared as *Lippincott's Magazine of Literature, Science and Education; Lippincott's Magazine of Popular Literature and Science;* and *Lippincott's Monthly Magazine*.

Look	October 19, 1971	Founded in 1937 by Gardner Cowles.
Mademoiselle	November 2001	Founded in 1935. Fashion magazine for young women.
McCall's	March 2001	Founded as a pattern booklet: *The Queen—The Illustrated Magazine of Fashion.* Renamed for founder James McCall in 1897. Reformatted as *Rosie* magazine after *McCall's* folded. *Rosie* ceased publication in 2002.
McClure's	March 1929	Founded in 1893. Literary and political magazine that was a major forum for social reform. Carried articles by Muckrakers such as Ida Tarbell, Ray Stannard Baker and Lincoln Steffens. It also published works of Rudyard Kipling, Robert Louis Stevenson, O. Henry and others.
Mirabella	April 2000	Founded in 1989 as a *Vogue* spin off. Women's magazine.
Munsey's	1929	Founded in 1889 as *Munsey's Weekly.* Renamed *Munsey's Magazine* (1891). Format changed to all-fiction in 1921. Merged with *Argosy All-Story* in 1929.
Nation's Business	June 1999	Founded in 1907. Journal of the Chamber of Commerce of the United States.
National Observer	July 11, 1977	Founded in 1962 by Dow Jones and Company. Weekly news magazine.
Niles' Weekly Register	1849	Founded in 1811 as *The Weekly Register* by Hezekiah Niles. Renamed *Niles Weekly Register* (1814). Published articles on political issues such as anti-slavery and tariffs.
North American Review	Winter 1939/40	Founded in 1815 in Boston, Massachusetts. Moved to New York City in the 1870s. Published the works of major political and literary names, including Daniel Webster, Longfellow and Lewis Cass.
Overland Monthly	1930	Founded in 1868 in San Francisco, California, as a literary journal with Bret Harte as editor. Also known as *The Californian* and *The Californian and Overland Monthly.* Featured early works of Ambrose Bierce, Mark Twain, Jack London and others.
Penny	1845	Founded in 1832 as *The Penny Magazine of the Society for the Diffusion of Useful Knowledge.* Appeared weekly.
Puck	September 1918	Founded in 1876 by cartoonist Joseph Keppler. Named for the character in Shakespeare's *Midsummer Night's Dream.*
Punch	June 2002	Founded in 1841 in England. Circulation fell in the 1980s. Closed in 1992. An attempt to revive it in 1996 failed. *Punch* ceased publication a second time in June 2002.
Putman's Monthly	1910	Founded in 1853 as *Putnam's Monthly Magazine of American Literature, Science and Art.* Renamed *Emerson's Magazine and Putnam's Monthly* (1857). Ceased publication in 1860s, then revived as *Putnam's Magazine.* Lasted a few years. Revived a third time in 1906 as *Putman's Monthly and the Critic.*
Rosie, see McCall's		
St. Nicholas	February 1940	Founded in 1873. A major magazine for children's literature.

Saturday Review of Literature	September 1986	Founded in 1924. *Saturday Review of Literature* renamed *Saturday Review/World* (1973).
Scribner's Monthly	1929	Founded in 1870. Renamed *Century Magazine/ Scribner's Monthly* (1881); *Century Illustrated* (1882); *Century* (by 1904); and *Century Monthly* (1925). Merged with the *Forum* in 1929.
Sports Afield	June 2002	Founded in 1887. A magazine for those who sought high-end sporting pursuits such as big-game hunting.
Strand	1950	Founded in 1891 in England. Published Arthur Conan Doyle's Sherlock Holmes stories and works of H.G. Wells and P.G. Wodehouse.
'Teen	May 2002	Founded in 1957. Absorbed *Sassy Magazine* in 1994.
Woman's Home Companion	1957	Founded in 1873 as *Ladies' Home Companion*. Renamed *Woman's Home Companion* in 1895.
Women's Journal	1917	Founded in 1870 by the American Woman Suffrage Association. Replaced by *Woman Citizen* in 1917.
Working Women	September 2001	Founded in 1976. Folded after its 25th anniversary issue.

Manufacturing

Manufacturing—Silk-Weaving, Hand (England)
Although silk is still hand woven elsewhere in the world, only one factory remains in England that carries on the tradition.
• **Last surviving factory for weaving silk by hand in England:** Humphries Weaving Company, de Vere Mill in Castle Hedingham, England. Using 19th-century looms, it produces fine fabrics for palaces around the world as well as for the White House.

Manufacturing—Washers— Hand-operated
Maytag produced hand-operated wringer washers for 76 years and was the last major appliance company to make them.
• **Last Maytag wringer washer produced:** Model E, last manufactured on November 22, 1983.

Military
(*See also* United States—Military)

Military—Conscription (The Draft)
Conscription, also known as "the draft," is a government's mandatory induction of its citizens, typically young men, into the armed forces for military service to that country. Many countries still have some form of conscription, while some nations have changed to non-military civilian service. A number of nations have never had conscription since achieving independence. They include Antigua and Barbuda, Bahamas, Bahrain, Barbados, Belize, Botswana, Brunei, Dominica, The Gambia, Iceland, India, Jamaica, Kenya, Liberia, Malta, Namibia, Nepal, Nigeria, Oman, Pakistan, Qatar, Saudi Arabia, Suriname, Trinidad and Tobago, United Arab Emirates and Zambia. Listed here are only those nations that had provisions for, or practiced conscription into military service prior to abolishing it.

Military—Conscription (The Draft) End of National Conscription in Some Nations

Country	Last Year
Argentina	1994
Australia	1972
Belgium	1992
Burkina Faso	1990
Cambodia	1993

Congo Brazzaville	1969
Costa Rica*	1949
Djibouti	1994
Ethiopia	1991
France**	2002
Guyana	1980
Haiti*	1994
Japan	1945
Jordan	1992
Liechtenstein*	1868
Luxembourg	1967
Malaysia	1964
New Zealand	1973
Nicaragua	1990
Panama*	1989
Seychelles	1993
South Africa	1994
Spain	2003
Thailand	1997
United Kingdom	1960
United States	1973

* Conscription was abolished when the armed forces of that nation were disbanded.
** Conscription has been replaced by a compulsory one-day citizenship course.

Money

Money—Europe
The euro is the currency of 12 European Union countries in western Europe and is used by more than 300 million people. Both euro banknotes and euro coins are in circulation. When the euro became legal tender on January 1, 2002, it replaced the following European monetary units:

Austrian schilling
Belgian franc
Finnish markka
French franc
German mark
Greek drachma (Europe's oldest currency)
Italian lira
Irish punt
Luxembourg franc
Netherlands guilder
Portuguese escudo
Spanish posteta

Money—Union of Soviet Socialist Republics
The Union of Soviet Socialist Republics (USSR) was dissolved in December 1991.
• **Last paper money issued by the Bank of the USSR:** a 1,000 ruble note in 1992. The discontinued note featured the USSR emblem (hammer and sickle) coat of arms, and a portrait of Lenin. Later in 1992, a new series of bank notes was issued.

Money—United States—Coins

Half-Cent Coins
Several versions of the U.S. half-cent coin with different Liberty Head designs were issued, beginning in 1793.
• **Last U.S. half cent issued:** 1857. The last design was the Coronet Head with Braided Hair, first issued in 1840.

One-Cent ("Penny") Coins
Several versions of the one-cent ("penny") coin with different Liberty Head designs were issued, beginning in 1793. Originally, they were large-size coins. Large cents were abandoned in favor of small cent coins without the Liberty Head.
• **Last U.S. large one-cent coin issued:** 1857, Coronet Head with Braided Hair. Replaced by small cent with Flying Eagle in 1856. Both large and small cents were issued in 1856 and 1857. In 1868, a small number of "fantasy pieces" of the large cent were made. (Fantasy pieces were coins struck at the fancy of Mint officials.)
• **Last U.S. Flying Eagle one-cent coin issued:** 1858. Replaced by copper/nickel Indian Head cent.
• **Last U.S. copper/nickel Indian Head one-cent coin issued:** 1864. One-cent coins produced from 1859 to 1864 were copper/nickel. Replaced by 95% copper, 5% zinc/tin Indian Head cents.
• **Last U.S. Indian Head one-cent coin issued:** 1909. One-cent coins produced from 1864 to 1909 were 95% copper, 5% zinc/tin. Replaced by the Lincoln cent with the wheat-design back to commemorate the 100th anniversary of Lincoln's birth. Known as the "Wheatie."

- **Last U.S. Lincoln one-cent coin with wheat back ("Wheatie") issued:** 1958. The wheat design on the reverse side of the one-cent coin was replaced by the Lincoln Memorial in 1959 to commemorate the 150th anniversary of Lincoln's birth.
- **Last U.S. Lincoln one-cent coin with initials V.D.B. on reverse issued:** 1909, the year the coin was first issued. The initials were removed that year. In 1918, the initials of the coin's designer Victor D. Brenner were returned to the coin, but this time they were placed on the obverse under Lincoln's shoulder.
- **Last U.S. steel one-cent coin issued:** 1943. Faced with a copper shortage during World War II, the U.S. Mint made the one-cent coin from zinc-coated steel. The substitute did not work out well, so from 1944 to 1946, the Mint used a brass alloy before returning to 95% copper.
- **Last U.S. copper one-cent coin issued:** 1982. One-cent coins produced since 1864 contained 95% copper, except briefly in World War II. In 1982, the content was changed to copper-plated zinc (97.5% zinc; 2.5% copper).

Two-Cent Coins

The U.S. two-cent coin was first issued in 1864 and was about the size of a nickel. It was the first U.S. coin to bear the motto "In God We Trust."
- **Last U.S. two-cent coin issued:** 1873. Shield design.

Three-Cent Coins

U.S. three-cent coins were first issued in silver in 1851. The first nickel three-cent coins were issued in 1865 as a substitute for silver during the Civil War.
- **Last year silver three-cent coins were minted for circulation:** 1872. They were discontinued by the Mint Act of 1873. Only the nickel three-cent coin—which had been co-issued with the silver variety since 1865—remained in circulation.
- **Last U.S. silver three-cent coin issued:** 1873, only as a non-circulating proof.
- **Last U.S. nickel three-cent coin issued:** 1889, Liberty Head design.

Five-Cent ("Nickel") Coins

U.S. five-cent ("nickel") coins were first minted in 1866 with a Shield design.
- **Last U.S. Shield five-cent coin issued:** 1883. Replaced by the Liberty Head nickel.
- **Last U.S. Liberty Head five-cent coin issued:** 1913. Replaced by the Buffalo nickel.
- **Last U.S. Buffalo five-cent coin issued:** 1938. Replaced by the Jefferson nickel.
- **Last U.S. silver Jefferson five-cent coin issued:** 1945. From 1942 to 1945, silver was mixed into the composition.

Five-Cent ("Half Dime") Coins

Five-cent ("half dime") coins were first minted in 1794, based on a 1792 Liberty Head design. The Seated Liberty design replaced three earlier Liberty Head designs in 1837.
- **Last U.S. Seated Liberty five-cent coin issued:** 1873.

Ten-Cent ("Dime") Coins

U.S. ten-cent ("dime") coins were first minted in 1796. The Seated Liberty design replaced three earlier Liberty Head designs in 1837.
- **Last U.S. Seated Liberty ten-cent coin issued:** 1891. Replaced by the Barber design in 1892.
- **Last U.S. Barber ten-cent coin issued:** 1916. Named for Mint Chief Engraver Charles Edward Barber. Replaced by the Winged Victory design in 1916.
- **Last U.S. Winged Victory ten-cent coin issued:** 1945. Popularly known as the Mercury dime because some people thought Liberty wearing a winged cap was Mercury of Roman mythology. Replaced by the Roosevelt dime in 1946 in commemoration of President Franklin D. Roosevelt's death a year earlier.
- **Last U.S. silver Roosevelt ten-cent coin issued:** 1964, excluding errors and later special non-circulation silver issues. Replaced by a copper/nickel-clad composition in 1965.

Twenty-Cent Coins

U.S. twenty-cent coins were first minted in 1875 with a Seated Liberty design. They were discontinued because they were confused with quarters.

• **Last U.S. twenty-cent coins issued:** 1878. Seated Liberty design.

Twenty-Five-Cent ("Quarter") Coins

U.S. twenty-five-cent ("quarter") coins were first minted in 1796. The Seated Liberty design replaced two earlier Liberty Head designs in 1838.

• **Last U.S. Seated Liberty twenty-five-cent coin issued:** 1891. Replaced by the Barber design in 1892.

• **Last U.S. Barber twenty-five-cent coin issued:** 1916. Named for Mint Chief Engraver Charles Edward Barber. Replaced by the Standing Liberty design.

• **Last U.S. Standing Liberty twenty-five-cent coin issued:** 1930. No quarters were minted in 1931. Replaced by the Washington quarter in 1932, issued to honor the 200th anniversary of George Washington's birth.

• **Last U.S. silver Washington twenty-five-cent coin issued:** 1964, excluding later special non-circulation silver issues. Replaced by a copper/nickel-clad composition in 1965.

• **Last U.S. Bicentennial Design twenty-five-cent coin issued:** 1976. Minted in 1975 and 1976. Special three-piece silver-clad collector's Bicentennial issue was sold through the U.S. Mint until 1982.

• **Last state quarter in the State Commemorative Quarter series to be issued:** Hawaii, scheduled for release in 2008. The series began in 1999. State coins are issued in the order in which the states ratified the Constitution or were admitted into the Union.

Fifty-Cent ("Half Dollar") Coins

U.S. fifty-cent ("half dollar") coins were first minted in 1794. The first of several Seated Liberty designs was issued in 1839.

• **Last U.S. Seated Liberty fifty-cent coin issued:** 1891. Replaced by the Barber design in 1892.

• **Last U.S. Barber fifty-cent coin issued:** 1915. Named for Mint Chief Engraver Charles Edward Barber. Replaced by the

Walking Liberty design in 1916.

• **Last U.S. Walking Liberty fifty-cent coin issued:** 1947. Replaced by the Franklin design in 1948.

• **Last U.S. Franklin fifty-cent coin issued:** 1963. Replaced by the Kennedy design in 1964 in commemoration of President John F. Kennedy's death a year earlier.

• **Last U.S. 90% silver Kennedy fifty-cent coin issued:** 1964, excluding later special non-circulation silver issues. Replaced by a silver-clad composition.

• **Last U.S. 40% silver-clad Kennedy fifty-cent coin issued:** 1970, excluding later special non-circulation silver issues. Replaced by a copper/nickel-clad composition in 1971.

• **Last U.S. Bicentennial design fifty-cent coin issued:** 1976. Minted in 1975 and 1976. A special three-piece silver-clad collector's Bicentennial issue was sold through the U.S. Mint until 1982.

One Dollar ("Silver Dollar") Coins

Dollar ("silver dollar") coins were first minted in 1794. No dollar coins were made from 1805 to 1839. The Seated Liberty design replaced two earlier Liberty Head designs in 1840.

• **Last U.S. Seated Liberty dollar coin issued:** 1873. Replaced that year by the trade dollar with design of Miss Liberty seated.

• **Last U.S. trade dollar coin issued:** 1885. Trade dollars were minted only as proofs from 1879 to 1885. The last circulating trade dollar issue was 1878. It was replaced that year by the Morgan design, nicknamed for its designer George T. Morgan.

• **Last U.S. Morgan dollar coin issued:** 1921. Replaced by the Peace design in 1921. No Morgan dollars were minted between 1905 and 1920.

• **Last circulating U.S. Peace dollar coin issued:** 1935. It was the last circulating dollar coin made of silver and the last true "silver dollar." No dollar coins were minted between 1936 and 1965.

• **Last U.S. Peace dollar coin minted:** 1964 Peace dollar, minted in May 1965. All 316,076 were destroyed before they were released to the public. They were eventually replaced by the Eisenhower design in 1971. No other dollar coins were minted during that time.

• **Last U.S. Bicentennial-design dollar coin issued:** 1976. Minted in 1975 and 1976. A special three-piece silver-clad collector's Bicentennial issue was sold through the U.S. Mint until 1982.

• **Last U.S. Eisenhower dollar coin issued:** 1978. Replaced by the Susan B. Anthony dollar in 1979. The Eisenhower dollar was the last large dollar coin.

• **Last U.S. Susan B. Anthony dollar coin issued:** 1999. No dollar coins were minted from 1982 to 1998. Replaced by the gold-toned Sacagawea dollar in 2000.

One Dollar ("Gold Dollar") Coins
U.S. gold one-dollar coins were first minted in 1849 with a Liberty Head design. The Indian Princess design gold dollar coin replaced the Liberty Head design in 1854.

• **Last U.S. gold dollar coin issued:** 1889. Indian Princess design. It was the last circulating gold dollar coin.

• **Last U.S. 22-karat gold Sacagawea dollar coins issued:** 1999. Only 39 non-circulating 22-karat gold Sacagawea dollars were minted and 27 were destroyed. All were minted in West Point, New York, in 1999, and the 12 remaining coins are now stored at Fort Knox in Kentucky. All other Sacagawea dollars are golden-toned clad coins.

Two-and-a-Half-Dollar ("Quarter Eagle") Coins
U.S. gold two-and-a-half-dollar ("quarter eagle") coins were first minted in 1796 with a Liberty Head design. The Indian Head design replaced the four earlier Liberty Head designs in 1908.

• **Last U.S. gold two-and-a-half dollar coin issued:** 1929. Indian Head design.

Three-Dollar Coins
U.S. gold three-dollar coins were first minted in 1854 with an Indian Princess design.

• **Last U.S. gold three-dollar coin issued:** 1889.

Five-Dollar ("Half Eagle") Coins
U.S. gold five-dollar ("half eagle") coins were first minted in 1795 with a Liberty Head design. The Indian Head design replaced the five earlier Liberty Head designs in 1908.

• **Last U.S. gold five-dollar coin issued:** 1929. Indian Head design. No gold five-dollar coins were minted between 1916 and 1928.

Ten-Dollar ("Eagle") Coins
U.S. gold ten-dollar ("eagle") coins were first minted in 1795 with a Liberty Head design. The Indian Head design replaced the three earlier Liberty Head designs in 1907.

• **Last U.S. gold ten-dollar coin issued:** 1933. Indian Head design. Most of the coins were destroyed before leaving the Mint. No gold ten-dollar coins were minted between 1917 and 1919, 1921 and 1925, 1927 and 1929, or in 1931. Discontinued by President Franklin Roosevelt's Executive Order ending the circulation of gold coins and notes.

Twenty-Dollar ("Double Eagle") Coins
U.S. gold twenty-dollar ("double eagle") coins were first minted in 1849. Only two proofs of this date are known. Large numbers of coins with the Liberty Head design were minted beginning in 1850. The Saint-Gaudens design replaced the two earlier Liberty Head designs in 1907.

• **Last U.S. gold twenty-dollar coin issued:** 1933. Saint-Gaudens, named for its designer Augustus Saint-Gaudens. Discontinued by President Franklin Roosevelt's Executive Order ending the circulation of gold coins and notes. Almost all the coins were destroyed before leaving the U.S. Mint. Only one 1933 gold twenty-dollar coin is in private hands.

Money—United States—Coins—Foreign
• **Last time foreign coins were legally part of U.S. coinage:** February 21, 1857. The U.S. Congress passed a law removing foreign coins from circulation.

• **Last time U.S. silver coins could legally circulate in Canada:** April 15, 1870.

Money—United States—Coins—Silver

• **Last year dimes and quarters were made with 90% silver:** 1964, when the Coinage Act authorized eliminating silver from dimes and quarters.

• **Last year half dollars were made with 90% silver:** 1964. The Coinage Act reduced the silver content of half dollars from 90% to 40%. As silver coins were phased out, cupronickel-clad coins were introduced. In 1970, the remaining silver was removed from the half dollars.

• **Last of the marketable U.S. silver:** October 1970, when the federal government auctioned off 1.5 million ounces at $1.84 an ounce and formally went out of the silver business. The government retained 35 million ounces of unrefined silver, earmarked for Eisenhower dollars.

Money—United States—Currency (Paper Money)

Continental Currency

U.S. Continental currency was the money issued by the Continental Congress during the American Revolution. It was so over issued that it soon became worthless, giving rise to the expression "not worth a Continental."

• **Last issue of Continental Currency:** November 29, 1779. The bills were printed by Hall and Sellers of Philadelphia, Pennsylvania, in denominations of $1, $2, $3, $4, $5, $20, $30, $35, $40, $45, $50, $55, $60, $65, $70 and $80. They carried the date January 14, 1779.

Demand Notes

In 1861, during the Civil War, the U.S. Congress authorized the U.S. Treasury to issue paper money in the form of non-interest-bearing Treasury Notes called Demand Notes.

• **Last issue of Demand Notes:** 1862. They were all issued by April 1, 1862. The notes were later replaced by United States Notes.

Federal Reserve Bank Notes

When the U.S. Congress created the Federal Reserve System in 1913, the Federal Reserve banks were authorized to issue Federal Reserve Bank Notes. The notes first appeared in 1916. They carried the name of the Federal Reserve Bank that issued them.

• **Last issue of Federal Reserve Bank Notes:** 1933. Issuing of notes was stopped by proclamation of President Franklin Roosevelt on March 6, 1933. The notes were replaced by Federal Reserve Notes.

Fractional Currency (Postage Stamp Currency/Shinplasters)

U.S. fractional currency was first issued in 1862. It was printed in small denominations, including 3¢, 5¢, 10¢, 15¢, 25¢ and 50¢, to alleviate a shortage of coins during the Civil War. Derisively called "shinplasters," it was also known as postage stamp currency.

• **Last issue of fractional currency:** 1876. The fifth general issue of fractional currency ran from February 26, 1874, to February 15, 1876. This general issue included denominations of 10¢, 25¢ and 50¢ notes.

Gold Certificates

U.S. gold certificates were authorized in 1863 and were first issued in series in 1865.

• **Last circulating gold certificate series:** Series 1928, issued in denominations of $10, $20, $50, $100, $500, $1,000, $5,000 and $10,000. Series 1928A certificates were printed but never released to the public. They are presumed destroyed.

• **Last circulating gold certificates issued:** $100 gold certificate, discontinued in 1934. On January 17, 1934, it became illegal for private citizens to own gold certificates. On April 24, 1964, the Secretary of the Treasury removed these restrictions on acquiring or holding gold certificates.

• **Last printing of $100,000 gold certificates:** January 9, 1935; Series 1934. The $100,000 gold certificate bore the portrait of President Woodrow Wilson and was the largest denomination of U.S. currency printed by the Bureau of Engraving and Printing. The certificates were issued to the Federal Reserve System for use in official transactions among their banks. They did not circulate among the public and were the only denomination of gold certificates printed after 1934.

Large-Size Paper Money

When paper money was first issued in 1862, it measured $3^{1}/2$ by $7^{3}/8$ inches— about one third larger than it is now. Paper money remained that size for more than a half century.

• **Last issue of large-size paper money:** July 1929; Series 1923. The large bills were replaced by bills about two thirds their size: $2^{11}/16$ by $6^{5}/16$ inches, beginning in July 1929. All further bills, regardless of denomination were made the same size.

Large U.S. Currency Denominations

The Federal Reserve System's Board of Governors discontinued the printing of $500, $1,000, $5,000 and $10,000 notes, but the bills continued to be released for circulation for 24 years.

• **Last printing of circulating large denomination U.S. currency:** December 27, 1945.

• **Last circulation of large denomination U.S. currency:** January 14, 1969. The U.S. Treasury Department and the Federal Reserve Board announced they would immediately stop distributing denominations greater than $100. They withdrew denominations of $500, $1,000, $5,000 and $10,000 from circulation that year. Although officially withdrawn, many of the notes, particularly the $500 and $1,000 denominations, continue to circulate. The faces on the discontinued bills were:

$500: President William McKinley;
$1,000: President Grover Cleveland;
$5,000: President James Madison;
$10,000: Treasury Secretary Salmon P. Chase.

National Bank Notes

U.S. National Bank Notes were issued in denominations of $5, $10, $20, $50 and $100 by thousands of national banks beginning in 1863.

• **Last National Bank Notes issued:** 1935; Series 1929.

Silver Certificates

U.S. silver certificates were first issued in 1878.

• **Last silver certificates issued:**

$1 Series 1957B and 1935H (printed until 1963);
$5 Series 1953B (printed until 1963);
$10 Series 1953B (printed until 1962).

• **Last day silver certificates were redeemable in silver dollars:** March 24, 1964. As of March 25th, silver certificates were redeemable in silver bullion.

• **Last day silver certificates were backed by silver:** June 24, 1968. That day, there was a rush to cash in silver $1 certificates worth $1.70.

Treasury or Coin Notes

U.S. Treasury or Coin Notes were issues in denominations of $1, $2, $5, $10, $20, $50, $100 and $1,000, beginning in 1890. The $500 denomination was designed but not printed.

• **Last issue of Treasury or Coin Notes:** 1891 series.

Two-Dollar Bills (Jefferson; Monticello on back)

The U.S. Thomas Jefferson $2 bill with Monticello on the back first appeared in 1928.

• **Last issue of Jefferson $2 bill with Monticello on the back:** 1963A series (printed until 1966). Jefferson $2 bills with the Signing of the Declaration of Independence on the back were issued in 1976.

United States Notes

United States Notes were first issued in 1862. They were nicknamed "greenbacks" because their back was tinted with green to discourage counterfeiting.

• **Last issue of United States Notes:** $100 Series 1966A, printed until 1971and placed into circulation by the U.S. Treasury Department on January 21, 1971.

• **Last year United States Notes were redeemable in gold: United States Notes:** 1933, when the U.S. abandoned the gold standard.

Money—U.S. Savings, Defense and War Bonds

U.S. Savings Bonds first went on sale on March 1, 1935. In 1941, they became known as U.S. Defense Savings Bonds.

• **Last known as U.S. Defense Savings Bonds:** April 1942, when their name was changed to U.S. War Savings Bonds.

• **Last known as U.S. War Savings Bonds:** December 1945, soon after the war ended, when they once again became Savings Bonds.

Money—U.S. Savings Stamps

U.S. Savings Stamps were first issued in World War I to support Liberty Bonds. During World War II, they were known as War Savings Stamps. They were sold in denominations as small as 10 cents. Purchasers accumulated the stamps in booklets and exchanged them for bonds.

• **Last Day for the U.S. Savings Stamp program:** June 30, 1970.

Money—United States—Treasury Bill, Bond and Note Certificates

• **Last year Treasury Bill, Bond and Note Certificates were issued:** 1986. Since then, these issues have been available only in book-entry form. Some certificates remain in circulation.

Money—Wampum Belts

Wampum beads were made from the shells of the quahog clam. Some Native American groups east of the Mississippi River strung the beads together and used them as a medium of exchange.

• **Last known use of an authentic wampum belt:** The "Vatican Belt" made at the Lac des Deux Montagnes missionary community near Montreal, Canada, in 1831 and given to Pope Gregory XVI in Rome. It was made about 30 years after the end of the secular use of diplomatic wampum belts.

Monuments
(*See also* Engineering—
Seven Wonders of the Ancient World.)

Monuments—Eiffel Tower

The Eiffel Tower in Paris, France, was designed by architect Stephen Suavestre and constructed by noted bridge builder Alexandre Gustave Eiffel for the International Exhibition of Paris of 1889. The event commemorated the centennial of the French Revolution. Construction began on January 23, 1887.

• **Last construction on the Eiffel Tower:** March 1889. The tower was inaugurated on March 31, 1889, when Eiffel climbed the structure's 1,710 steps and placed the French flag at the top. The grand opening of the Exhibition was June 10, 1889. For many years, the 984-foot high wrought-iron tower was the world's tallest building.

• **Last time the Eiffel Tower was world's tallest building:** 1930, when it was displaced by the Chrysler Building in New York, New York.

• **Last time the Eiffel Tower was lit by gaslights:** 1900, when gas illumination was replaced by electricity. Eiffel died in Paris, France, on December 27, 1923, age 91.

Monuments—Ellis Island Immigration Center

Ellis Island in New York Bay was the main United States immigration center, beginning in 1892.

• **Last year Ellis Island was used as an immigration center:** 1943. That year, the immigration center was moved to New York City. The island was used as a detention spot for deportees until 1954. It became part of the Statue of Liberty National Monument in 1965 and reopened as a museum in 1990.

• **End of New Jersey-New York Ellis Island ownership dispute:** 1998, when the U.S. Supreme Court ruled that nearly 90 percent of Ellis Island (24.2 acres of landfill) is in New Jersey, while the original 3.3 acres are in New York.

Monuments—Lascaux Caves

The Lascaux caves, near Montignac, in southwestern France, date from c. 15,000-18,000 B.C. They were discovered in 1940 and opened to the public in 1948.

• **Last time the Lascaux caves were opened to the public:** 1963. The Lascaux caves were closed when it was discovered that humidity from tourists' breath and perspiration were causing the wall paintings to deteriorate rapidly. In 1983, Lascaux I—an exact copy of the caves—was opened nearby for visitors.

Monuments—Liberty Bell and Independence Hall

Independence Hall in Philadelphia, Pennsylvania, is unquestionably America's most historic building. It began as the Pennsylvania State House. The Pennsylvania Assembly first met there in 1735. The Liberty Bell was placed in the tower in 1753. Independence Hall was later used by the U.S. government. The Declaration of Independence, Articles of Confederation and the U.S. Constitution were drafted and adopted there. The Continental Congress and the Congress of the Confederation met there. After the nation's capital moved from Philadelphia, Independence Hall was used for a variety of purposes.

• **Last time Peale's Museum was in Independence Hall:** 1828. Artist Charles Willson Peale converted much of Independence Hall to a museum of natural history and a portrait gallery that opened in 1802. After Peale left, part of the building was used for federal offices until 1854, then city offices took over.

• **Last time Independence Hall held a dog pound:** 1851. A city ordinance was issued that year banning the use of the cellar as a "receptacle" for stray dogs

• **Last U.S. president to lie in state in Independence Hall:** Abraham Lincoln in April 1865.

• **Last time Independence Hall was used for municipal offices:** 1895, when the Philadelphia Council moved out. Soon afterward, a series of restorations began that brought the hall back to its appearance when the U.S. Congress sat there.

• **Last time the city of Philadelphia had custody of Independence Hall:** January 1, 1951, when the care and maintenance of the hall, a group of neighboring historic buildings and Independence Square were transferred to the National Park Service.

• **Last time the Liberty Bell was in Independence Hall tower:** 1852. That year, it was brought down and placed in several locations before being located near the south doorway.

• **Last time the Liberty Bell was inside Independence Hall:** December 1975. For easier viewing by the public, the Liberty Bell was moved from Independence Hall to a nearby specially built glass-and-steel pavilion just after midnight on January 1, 1976, as the Bicentennial year began. The bell was relocated once again in October 2003. The Liberty Bell was moved a short distance from the pavilion to the Liberty Bell Center, near the newly opened National Constitution Center.

• **Last time the Liberty Bell was away from Philadelphia:** 1915, when the Liberty Bell traveled by rail to the Panama-Pacific Exposition in San Francisco, California. Prior to 1915, the Liberty Bell was taken out of Philadelphia several times to be part of celebrations of fairs and exhibitions: New Orleans, Louisiana (1885), Chicago, Illinois (1893), Atlanta, Georgia (1895), Charleston, South Carolina (1902), Boston, Massachusetts (1903) and Saint Louis, Missouri (1904).

• **Last time the Liberty Bell was away from the Independence Hall area:** October 10, 1917, during World War I, when the Liberty Bell was mounted on a truck and driven through the streets of Philadelphia as part of the First Liberty Loan Parade. That was the bell's last road trip. The Liberty Bell did not leave its home inside Independence Hall again until it was moved at midnight as the Bicentennial year began in 1976.

• **Last clear sound from the Liberty Bell:** February 22, 1846. Sometime prior to 1845, the bell developed a hairline crack. It was repaired in time to commemorate Washington's birthday in 1846, But when the bell was tolled, a zigzag fracture occurred. Since that time, the bell has had a muffled sound.

Monuments—Mount Rushmore

American sculptor Gutzon Borglum began work on the Mount Rushmore National Memorial (a.k.a. Shrine of Democracy) in the Black Hills of South Dakota in 1927. The head of George Washington, the first completed figure, was dedicated on July 4, 1930. Thomas Jefferson was completed in 1936, Abraham Lincoln in 1937, and Theo-

dore Roosevelt in 1939. Gutzon Borglum died in Chicago, Illinois, on March 6, 1941, age 74.
• **Last Mount Rushmore construction:** October 1941. Borglum's son Lincoln, his chief assistant, carried on the work until then. Although the original site was dedicated by U.S. President Calvin Coolidge in 1927, the final monument was not formally dedicated until July 1991 by President George H.W. Bush.

Monuments—Statue of Liberty
On February 22, 1877, the U.S. Congress approved Bedloe's Island, in New York Harbor, as the site for the Statue of Liberty. The 12-acre island was the location suggested by the statue's designer Frederic Auguste Bartholdi. Construction work on the Statue of Liberty was completed in France in 1884. It was then dismantled and shipped to the United States. It arrived in New York in June 1885. Reassembling of the Statue of Liberty began June 12, 1886, when the first rivet was driven.
• **Last stone of the Statue of Liberty pedestal swung into place:** April 22, 1886.
• **Last rivet driven:** October 28, 1886, when U.S. President Grover Cleveland dedicated the monument. The Statue of Liberty became a national monument in 1924.
• **Last time the Statue of Liberty site was known as Bedloe's Island:** August 3, 1956, when U.S. President Dwight D. Eisenhower approved a resolution of Congress changing its name to Liberty Island.

Monuments—Stone Mountain
Three leaders of the Confederacy—Jefferson Davis, Robert E. Lee and Thomas J. ("Stonewall") Jackson—are carved on Stone Mountain in northwestern Georgia. Gutzon Borglum started the project in 1923 but left a short time later after a disagreement with the project's sponsors. Work resumed briefly in 1928, then was halted when the owners of the mountain reclaimed the land. In 1958, the Georgia legislature took steps to purchase the land. Walter Kirtland Hancock was engaged as sculptor in 1964. The monument was dedicated on May 9, 1970, but construction continued for a few more years.
• **Last Stone Mountain construction:** March 1972. The project was completed by Roy Faulkner, who worked on it for eight years.

Monuments—Washington Monument
The Washington Monument in Washington, D.C., was planned as early as 1836. It was authorized by the U.S. Congress in 1848, and the cornerstone was laid on July 4th of that year. Construction slowed down after architect Robert Mills died in 1855. It halted completely during the Civil War. Finally, construction on the Washington Monument resumed during the Centennial year 1876.
• **Last Washington Monument construction:** 1884. The monument was dedicated in February 1885 and opened to the public on October 9, 1888. Technically the monument is unfinished: Mills had designed a Greek-style rotunda, but it was never constructed.

Motorcycles—Makers
Last Motorcycles Produced by Some Major Companies

Name, Country and Years Made	Description
Ace (United States; 1919-28)	Ace began producing motorcycles in 1919. The company suffered financial difficulties in 1924, and for the next two years Ace motorcycles were made by the Michigan Motors Corporation. In 1927, Indian acquired the rights to Ace. • **Last Indian Ace produced:** 1928; however, Ace designs were the basis of Indian's four-cylinder motorcycles until 1942.

AJS (Albert John Stevens; Great Britain; 1911-67)	AJS began producing motorcycles in 1911. The company ran into difficulties in the 1930s and sold out to Matchless. AJS production continued with Matchless and later AMC (Associated Motor Cycles). Poor sales led AMC to sell out to Norton Villiers in 1967. Some AJS motorcycles were built with Norton parts but were unsuccessful, and the factory ceased production shortly afterward. The rights to the name and the manufacture of motor-cross bikes were later sold to Fluff Brown. • **Last AJS four-stroke motor-cross bike produced:** 1967; after which the company manufactured only two-stroke motor-cross bikes.
Ariel (Great Britain; 1898-1965)	Ariel began producing motorized cycles in 1898. The company was acquired by BSA (Birmingham Small Arms) in 1944. • **Last square four Ariel produced:** 1959. • **Last true Ariel produced:** 1965; a two-stroke twin introduced in 1958. The Ariel name was used until 1970 on a three-wheeled moped.
Brough Superior (Great Britain; 1920-40)	Brough began producing motorcycles in 1920. Although the Brough Superior was once dubbed the "Rolls Royce of motorcycles" by *Motor Cycle* magazine, production never restarted after World War II. • **Last Brough Superior produced:** 1940.
BSA (Birmingham Small Arms; Great Britain; 1910-73)	BSA began producing motorcycles in 1910. The company acquired Ariel in 1944 and Triumph in 1951. When BSA folded in 1973, Norton Villiers took over and dropped the BSA name. The name was revived in the late 1970s and attached to Yamaha-engine trail bikes primarily intended for the export market. • **Last BSA Bantam models produced:** 1971.
Condor (Switzerland; 1901-c.1959)	Condor began producing motorcycles in 1901 and later became the number-two motorcycle producer in Switzerland. • **Last Condor model produced:** the A250 that appeared in 1959. Although Condor stopped production, the company continued as an importer of Italian bikes.
DKW (Das Klein Wunder; Germany; 1919-70s)	DKW began producing motorcycles in 1919. By the 1930s, it was the world's largest motorcycle producer, with annual production over 300,000 by 1935. The company was involved in several mergers, including the short-lived 1966 takeover of Zweirad Union by Fichtel & Sachs, but the name continued on some exports. • **Last DKW produced:** late 1970s, when the name was used on some Hercules machines.
Douglas (Great Britain; 1907-57)	Douglas began producing motorcycles in 1907. In 1951, it acquired Vespa, the Italian scooter company. • **Last Vespa scooters produced by Douglas:** c. 1964; however, the company continued to import them into the 1980s. • **Last Douglas model launched:** The Dragonfly in 1955. • **Last Douglas motorcycles produced:** 1957.
Excelsior (Great Britain; 1896-1964)	Excelsior began producing motorcycles in 1896. In 1919, the company was taken over by R. Walker & Son, makers of the Monarch. Excelsior produced scooters until the late 1950s and Talisman motorcycles until the 1960s. In 1964, Excelsior was bought by Britax, and all Excelsior production stopped. • **Last Excelsior Talisman produced:** 1962.

Notable Last Facts

Excelsior Supply Co. (United States; 1907-31)	Excelsior Supply Co. began producing motorcycles in 1907. Schwinn bought the company in 1911, and Excelsior became the number-three motorcycle producer in the U.S., after Indian and Harley-Davidson. In 1931, during the Great Depression, Schwinn closed its motorcycle division. In the 1990s, the rights to the Excelsior and Henderson names were sold to Hanlon. • **Last Excelsior produced:** 1931.
Gilera (Italy; 1909-93)	Giuseppe Gilera began producing motorcycles in 1909. In 1969, the company was acquired by Piaggio. Piaggio closed the Gilera factory at Arcore, near Milan, Italy, in 1993. • **Last Gilera produced:** 1993.
Henderson (United States; 1912-31)	Bill and Tom Henderson began producing motorcycles in 1912. Schwinn purchased the company in 1917, and the Henderson Brothers left in 1919. Bill Henderson then established Ace. In 1931, during the Great Depression, Schwinn closed its motorcycle division. In the 1990s, the rights to the Excelsior and Henderson names were sold to Hanlon. • **Last Henderson produced:** 1931.
Hildebrand and Wolfmuller (Germany; 1894-97)	The Hildebrand brothers and Alois Wolfmuller began producing motorcycles in 1894. The company made the first two-wheeled powered production vehicle offered to the public. They also coined the word *motorrad* (motorcycle). About 1,000 or 2,000 motorcycles were made before the company stopped production. • **Last Hildebrand and Wolfmuller produced:** 1897.
Indian (United States; 1901-53)	Indian began producing motorcycles in 1901 and made the first motorcycle with an electric starter in 1914. The bulk of Indian's sales after 1920 were the Scout and the Chief. • **Last Indian Scout produced:** 1931. • **Last Indian four-cylinder produced:** 1942. • **Last Indian Chief produced:** 1953. After 1953, the name was attached to a number of lesser-quality machines and ownership of the name changed frequently without success.
James (Great Britain; 1902-66)	James began producing motorcycles in 1902. In 1951, the company was taken over by AMC (Associated Motor Cycles). The James name died with the collapse of AMC. • **Last James produced under AMC:** 1966.
Matchless (Great Britain; 1899-1969; 1987)	Matchless began producing motorcycles in 1899. In 1931, the company formed part of the basis of AMC (Associated Motor Cycles). AMC collapsed in 1966, but a resurrection as Norton Villiers kept the Matchless name alive until 1969. In 1987, a brief revival of the name occurred with a single-cylinder machine with a Rotax engine. • **Last Matchless produced:** 1969, with the exception of the 1987 brief revival.
Monark (Sweden; 1913-75)	Esse began producing motorcycles in 1913, and the Monark name was used after 1927. By the early 1950s, Monark was the largest motorcycle producer in Sweden. In 1960, Monark took over NV (Nymans-Verkstader). Monark stopped making motorcycles in 1975. • **Last Monark produced:** 1975.

Motosacoche (Switzerland; c.1898-1956)	Henri and Armand Sufaux & Cie began producing motorcycles about 1898; the Motosacoche appeared in 1905. Once the most famous Swiss marquee, the company withdrew from the motorcycle market. • **Last Motosacoche produced:** 1956.
NSU (Neckarsulum Strick-machine Union; Germany; c. 1900-69)	NSU began producing motorcycles about 1900 or 1901. Despite making more than a million Quickly mopeds in the 1950s, the company stopped producing motorcycles and mopeds to focus on automobile production. • **Last NSU motorcycle produced:** 1963. • **Last NSU moped produced:** 1965. In 1969, the company was taken over by Volkswagen.
Ossa (Spain; 1949-85)	Ossa began producing motorcycles in 1949. In 1984, the company was replaced by a workers' cooperative that lasted only one year. • **Last Ossa produced:** 1985.
Puch (Austria; 1903-87)	Johann Puch began producing motorcycles in 1903 and soon became Austria's leading producer. In 1987, Piaggio took over the name and production in Austria ended. • **Last Austrian-made Puch produced:** 1987.
Royal Enfield (Great Britain; c.1898-c.1970)	Royal Enfield began producing motorcycles about 1898. The company was sold in 1962. In 1967, the factory was closed, and production was subcontracted. The old factory machines were sent to India. In 1970, the company went into liquidation and the remaining engines were placed in Rickman chassis. • **Last Royal Enfield Interceptor produced:** 1968.
Scott (Great Britain; 1908-78)	Scott began producing motorcycles in 1908. In the 1950s, the company went under new management, and motorcycles were made in limited numbers in Birmingham. The name faded away by 1965, but some of the Squirrel model were made until the late 1970s. • **Last Scott Squirrel produced:** 1978.
Sears (United States; 1912-69)	Sears-Roebuck added motorcycles to their catalog in 1912. The motorcycles were other makes with the Sears name. The last were Gilera and Puch, sold in the 1960s. • **Last motorcycle produced with the Sears name:** 1969.
Sunbeam (Great Britain; 1912-56)	Sunbeam began producing motorcycles in 1912. In 1936, Sunbeam was purchased by AMC (Associated Motor Cycles), and in 1943 Sunbeam was sold to BSA (Birmingham Small Arms). BSA continued using the Sunbeam name on some of its motorcycles until 1956. From 1959 to 1964, the name was used on some BSA scooters; this was the last use of the Sunbeam name. • **Last true Sunbeam motorcycle produced:** 1956, 487cc shaft-driven in-line twins produced by BSA under the Sunbeam name.
Terrot (France; 1901-62)	Charles Terrot began producing motorcycles in 1901. In 1927, Terrot took over Magnat Debon and by 1930, it was the leading French producer of motorcycles. From 1954 to 1961, Peugeot took over Terrot and moved production to its Automoto factory. The 498cc models were dropped in 1958. • **Last Terrot motorcycles produced:** 1962, the 125cc and 175cc, two small two-stroke machines.

Velocette (Great Britain; 1905-71)	Cycle manufacturer Taylor-Gue began producing motorcycles in 1905, and the Velocette name appeared in 1913. The company closed in 1971. • **Last Velocette produced:** 1971.
Vincent (Great Britain; 1928-55)	Phillip C. Vincent bought the HRD trademark for his motorcycles in 1928. At one time, the company claimed the fastest production motorcycle on the market and its large speedometers were marked up to 150 mph. • **Last Vincent produced:** 1955.
Zundapp (Germany; 1921-84)	Zundapp began producing motorcycles in 1921. The company collapsed in 1984, despite a 50cc Zundapp rider taking a World Championship that year. Liquidation followed a year later. The remains of the company were sold to China. • **Last Zundapp produced:** 1984.

Motorcycles—Makers—Harley-Davidson
William S. Harley and Arthur Davidson began producing motorcycles in 1903. In 1969, AMF (American Metals Foundries) took over Harley Davidson.
• **Last time Harley-Davidson was owned by AMF:** 1981. The repurchasing of the company by Harley-Davidson in 1981 lead to major changes in quality, reliability and a new emphasis on style and heritage.

Movies
(*See also* Cartoons.)

Movies—Animation—Walt Disney
Walt Disney died in Los Angeles, California, on December 15, 1966, age 65.
• **Last animated movie personally overseen by Walt Disney:** *The Jungle Book* (1967).
• **Last animated film started while Walt Disney was alive:** *The Aristocats* (1970).
• **Last Disney animated full-length feature painted by hand:** *The Little Mermaid* (1989). The two-minute storm in the opening sequence took ten special effects artists more than a year to complete. One thousand colors were used on 1,100 backgrounds, and more than one million drawings were produced for the film.

Movies—Associations—Academy of Motion Picture Arts and Sciences

The Academy of Motion Picture Arts and Sciences (AMPAS) was founded in 1927 by 36 film professionals.
• **Last surviving AMPAS founder:** author/actor/director/producer Henry King, who died in Toluca Lake, California, on June 29, 1982, age 86.

Movies—Associations—Directors Guild of America
The Directors Guild of America was founded in 1936 by 15 of Hollywood's top directors.
• **Last surviving founding member of the Directors Guild of America:** Rouben Mamoulian, who died in Los Angeles, California, on December 4, 1987, age 90.

Movies—Associations—Screen Actors Guild
The Screen Actors Guild (SAG) was founded in 1933 by a group of 19 actors.
• **Last surviving SAG founder:** stage, screen and television actor Leon Ames, who served as its national president in 1957.

Movies—Censorship—Hays Code
The Motion Picture Association of America (MPAA) implemented the Production Code (Hays Code) in 1930 to cut crime, violence, sex and offensive language in films. Will H. Hays, who administered the code, died in Sullivan, Indiana, on March 7, 1954, age 74. In the 1960s, the Hays Code was abandoned

by the film-making industry, causing the MPAA on November 1, 1968, to implement a voluntary system using the G, PG, R and X rating system.

• **Last chief censor of MPAA:** Geoffrey M. Shurlock (1954-69). He succeeded Joseph Breen as Production Code head and stayed until the G, PG, R, X rating system was installed. Shurlock died in Woodland Hills, California, on April 26, 1976, age 81.

Movies—Serials

Serials were adventure film series shown in short weekly episodes, usually in 12 to 15 installments of less than 20 minutes each. Three studios were the major producers of serials: Republic, Columbia Pictures and Universal Studios. The Golden Age of movie serials was the late 1930s and early 1940s.

• **Last Republic serials:** 1955. *Panther Girl of the Kongo* (12 chapters) and *King of the Carnival* (12 chapters).

• **Last Columbia Pictures serial:** 1956. *Perils of the Wilderness* (15 chapters) and *Blazing the Overland Trail* (15 chapters).

• **Last Universal serials:** 1946. *The Scarlet Horsemen* (13 chapters); *Lost City of the Jungle* (13 chapters); and *The Mysterious Mr. M* (13 chapters).

• **Last serial by a studio other than the Big Three:** 1937. *Blake of Scotland Yard* (Victory Pictures, 15 chapters).

Movies—Silent Films

Warner Brothers announced in August 1928 that all of its films planned for the 1928-29 fiscal year would have sound. United Artists made the same announcement in November 1928. Twentieth-Century Fox announced in February 1929 that it had made its Last silent movie. Columbia Pictures released its last silent movie (*The Quitter*) on April 1, 1929.

• **Last major silent film made in the early years of sound film:** *Modern Times* (re-leased 1936), starring Charlie Chaplin. It was not entirely silent. Chaplin does sing and use some sound effects.

• **Last year a large number of silent films were produced:** 1929. By then, most films were being made with sound. Some film historians contend that the "Silent Era" was over when *Modern Times* was released.

• **Also considered the last films of the "Silent Era":** Charlie Chaplin's *City Lights*, begun in 1928 but released in 1931, and F.W. Murnau's *Tabu* (1931), an Academy Award winner for Best Cinematography.

• **Last major studio to convert to sound:** MGM.

• **Last silent movie by MGM:** *The Kiss*, which wrapped up filming in September 1929. *The Kiss* was also Greta Garbo's last silent movie.

• **Last surviving silent film director:** believed to be Andrew Lysander Stone, who directed the silent films *The Elegy* (1927) and *Liebensraum* (1928). Stone died in Los Angeles, California, on June 6, 1999, age 96.

• **Last silent movie to win the Academy Award for Best Picture:** *Wings* (1927).

• **Last silent movie nominated for the Academy Award for Best Picture:** *The Patriot* (1928).

• **Last silent *Our Gang* comedy:** *Saturday's Lesson* (1929).

• **Last silent *Laurel & Hardy* comedy:** *Angora Love* (1929).

• **Last country to show silent films routinely:** Thailand. The Thai film industry was disrupted during World War II and all Thai feature films made until the 1960s were shot silent on 16mm film. Sound was added in the theater by actors reading lines offstage. The practice ended in 1970 with the adoption of 35mm sound film.

• **Last silent movie produced by Hollywood:** *Legong: Dance of the Virgins* (1935). The movie was filmed in Bali and features an all-native cast. It was directed by Henri de La Falaise.

Last Movies of Some Major Film Directors
(*See also* Movies—Performers.)

Director	Last Film(s) and Last silent movie(s)	Comment
Aldrich, Robert	*All the Marbles* (1981).	Died in Los Angeles, California, December 5, 1983, age 65.
Bacon, Lloyd	*She Couldn't Say No* (1954). Last silent movie: *Honky Tonk* (1929).	Died in Burbank, California, November 15, 1955, age 65.
Borzage, Frank	*The Big Fisherman* (1959). Last silent movie: *Lucky* (1929).	Died in Hollywood, California, June 19, 1962, age 67.
Brooks, Richard	Feature film: *Fever Pitch* (1985); documentary: *Listen Up! The Lives of Quincy Jones* (1991).	Died in Beverly Hills, California, March 11, 1992, age 79.
Buñuel, Luis	*That Obscure Object of Desire* (1977). Last silent movie: *The Andalusian Dog* (1929).	Died in Mexico City, Mexico, July 29, 1983, age 83.
Capra, Frank	*Pocketful of Miracles* (1961).	Died in La Quinta, California, September 3, 1991, age 94.
Cassavetes, John	*Big Trouble* (1986). Last film as actor: *Love Streams* (1984).	Died in Los Angeles, California, February 3, 1989, age 59.
Chaplin, Sir Charles	*A Countess from Hong Kong* (1967). Last silent movie: *Modern Times* (1936).	Died in Vevey, Switzerland, December 25, 1977, age 88.
Cocteau, Jean	*The Testament of Orpheus* (1959).	Died in Ile-de-France, France, October 11, 1963, age 74.
Cukor, George	*Rich and Famous* (1981).	Died in Los Angeles, California, January 23, 1983, age 83.
Curtiz, Michael	*The Comancheros* (1961). Last silent movie: *The Gamblers* (1929).	Died in Hollywood, California, April 10, 1962, age 73.
DeMille, Cecil B.	*The Ten Commandments* (1956). Last silent movie: *The Godless Girl* (1929).	Working on a documentary of Robert Baden-Powell and the Boy Scouts when he died in Hollywood, California, January 21, 1959, age 77.
De Sica, Vittorio	*A Brief Vacation* (1973); *The Voyage* (1974).	Died near Paris, France, November 13, 1974, age 73.
Eisenstein, Sergei M.	*Ivan the Terrible* (1948). Last silent movie: *Frauennot–Frauenglück* (1929).	Died of a heart attack in Moscow, Russia, February 10, 1948, age 50, while working on the film.
Fassbinder, Rainer Werner	*Querelle* (1982).	Died in Munich, Germany, June 10, 1982, age 37.
Fellini, Federico	*Voice of the Moon* (1989).	Died in Rome, Italy, October 31, 1993, age 73.

Fleming, Victor	*Joan of Arc* (1948). Last silent movies: *Wolf Song* (1929); *Abbie's Irish Rose* (1929).	Died in Cottonwood, Arizona, January 6, 1949, age 65.
Ford, John	*7 Women* (1966). Last silent movie: *Strong Boy* (1929).	Died in Palm Desert, California, August 31, 1973, age 78.
Griffith, D. W.	*The Struggle* (1931). Last silent movie: *Lady of the Pavements* (1929). May have directed part of *One Million B.C.* (1940). Uncredited.	Died in Hollywood, California, July 23, 1948, age 73.
Hathaway, Henry	*Hangup* (1974).	Died in Hollywood, California, February 11, 1985, age 86.
Hawks, Howard	*Rio Lobo* (1970). Last silent movie: *Trent's Last Case* (1929).	Died in Palm Springs, California, December 26, 1977, age 81.
Hitchcock, Sir Alfred	*Family Plot* (1976). Last silent movie: *The Manxman* (1929).	Died in Los Angeles, California, April 29, 1980, age 80.
Hu, King	*Painted Skin* (1992).	Died in Taipei, Taiwan, January 14, 1997, age 65.
Huston, John	*The Dead* (1987).	Died in Middletown, Rhode Island, August 28, 1987, age 81.
Keaton, Buster	*Streamlined Swing* (1938). Last uncredited film: *The Railrodder* (1965). Last silent movie: *Spite Marriage* (uncredited; 1929).	Died in Woodland Hills, California, February 1, 1966, age 70.
Kieslowski, Krzysztof	*Three Colors: Red* (1994).	Died in Warsaw, Poland, March 13, 1996, age 54.
Kramer, Stanley	*The Runner Stumbles* (1979).	Died in Woodland Hills, California, February 19, 2001, age 87.
Kubrick, Stanley	*Eyes Wide Shut* (1999).	Died in Hertfordshire, England, on March 7, 1999, age 70, before the film was released.
Kurosawa, Akira	*Not Yet* (1993).	Died in Tokyo, Japan, September 6, 1998, age 88.
LaCava, Gregory	*Living in a Big* (last completed film; 1947). Last silent movie: *His First Command* (1929). Worked briefly on *One Touch of Venus* (1948).	Died in Malibu, California, March 1, 1952, age 59.
Lang, Fritz	*The Thousand Eyes of Dr. Mabuse* (1960). Last silent movie: *Woman in the Moon* (1929).	Died in Los Angeles, California, August 2, 1976, age 85.
Lean, David	*A Passage to India* (last completed film; 1984).	Working on pre-production of *Nostromo*; died in London shortly before filming, April 16, 1991, age 83.
Leone, Sergio	*Once Upon a Time in America* (1984).	Died in Rome, Italy, April 30, 1989, age 60.
LeRoy, Mervyn	*Moment to Moment* (1965).	Died in Beverly Hills, California, September 13, 1987, age 86.

Logan, Joshua	*Paint Your Wagon* (1969).	Died in New York, New York, July 12, 1988, age 79.
Lubitsch, Ernst	*That Lady in Ermine* (1948); completed by Otto Preminger. Last silent movie: *Eternal Love* (1929).	Died in Los Angeles, California, November 30, 1947, age 55, while filming *That Lady in Ermine*.
Malle, Louis	*Vanya on 42nd Street* (1994).	Died in Beverly Hills, California, November 23, 1995, age 63.
Mamoulian, Rouben	*Silk Stockings* (1957); *Cleopatra* (1963). Uncredited; replaced by Joseph L. Mankiewicz.	Died in Los Angeles, California, December 4, 1987, age 90.
Mankiewicz, Joseph L.	*Sleuth* (1972).	Died in Bedford, New York, February 5, 1993, age 83.
Mann, Anthony	*A Dandy in Aspic* (1968).	Died in Berlin, Germany, midway through filming, April 29, 1967, age 60.
Marshall, George	*Hook, Line and Sinker* (1969). Last silent movie: *The Back Trail* (1924).	Died in Los Angeles, California, February 17, 1975, age 83.
McCarey, Leo	*Satan Never Sleeps* (1962). Last silent movies: several shorts made in 1929, including *Hurdy-Gurdy*; *Wrong Again*.	Died in Santa Monica, California, July 5, 1969, age 70.
Milestone, Lewis	*Mutiny on the Bounty* (1962). Last silent movie: *Betrayal* (1929).	Died in Los Angeles, California, September 25, 1980, age 84.
Minnelli, Vincente	*A Matter of Time* (1976).	Died in Beverly Hills, California, July 25, 1986, age 76.
Mizoguchi, Kenji	*Street of Shame* (1959). Last silent movie: *The Downfall of Osen* (1935).	Died in Kyoto, Japan, August 24, 1956, age 58.
Murnau, F.W.	*Tabu: A Story of the South Seas* (also his Last silent movie; 1931).	Died in Santa Barbara, California, March 11, 1931, age 42, a few weeks before the film premiered.
Naruse, Mikio	*Scattered Clouds* (a.k.a. *Two in the Shadow*; 1967).	Died in Japan, July 2, 1969, age 63.
Ophüls, Max	*Lola Montés* (1955).	Died in Hamburg, Germany, March 25, 1957, age 54.
Ozu, Yasujiro	*An Autumn Afternoon* (1962).	Died in Tokyo, Japan, December 12, 1963, age 60.
Paradjanov, Sergei	*The Lovelorn Minstrel* (1988).	Died in Yerevan, Armenia, July 21, 1990, age 66.
Peckinpah, Sam	*The Osterman Weekend* (1983).	Died in Inglewood, California, December 28, 1984, age 59.
Powell, Michael	*The Boy Who Turned Yellow* (1972).	Died in Avening, Gloucestershire, England, February 19, 1990, age 84.
Preminger, Otto	*The Human Factor* (1980).	Died in New York, New York, April 23, 1986, age 80.

Ratoff, Gregory	*Oscar Wilde* (1959).	Died in Solothurn, Switzerland, December 14, 1960, age 63.
Ray, Satyajit	*The Stranger* (1991)	Died in Calcutta, India, April 23, 1992, age 70.
Renoir, Jean	*The Little Theater of Jean Renoir* (made for French TV; 1971). Last silent movie: *Le Bled* (1929).	Died in Beverly Hills, California, February 12, 1979, age 84.
Ritt, Martin	*Stanley and Iris* (1990).	Died in Santa Monica, California, December 8, 1990, age 70.
Ross, Herbert	*Boys on the Side* (1995).	Died in New York, New York, October 9, 2001, age 74.
Rossellini, Roberto	*The Messiah* (1978).	Died in Rome, Italy, June 3, 1977, age 71.
Rossen, Robert	*Lilith* (1964).	Died in Hollywood, California, February 18, 1966, age 57.
Sidney, George	*Half a Sixpence* (1969).	Died in Las Vegas, Nevada, May 5, 2002, age 85.
Siodmak, Robert	*The Battle for Rome* (1968).	Died in Locarno, Switzerland, March 10, 1973, age 72.
Sirk, Douglas	*Imitation of Life* (1959).	Died in Lugano, Switzerland, January 14, 1987, age 89.
Sternberg, Josef von	*The Saga of Anatahan* (1954). Last silent movie: *The Case of Lena Smith* (1929).	Died in Hollywood, California, December 22, 1969, age 75.
Stevens, George	*The Only Game in Town* (1970).	Died in Lancaster, California, March 8, 1975, age 70.
Stevenson, Robert	*The Shaggy D.A* (1976).	Died in Santa Barbara, California, November 4, 1986, age 81.
Sturges, Preston	*The French, They Are a Funny Race* (1957).	Died in New York, New York, August 6, 1959, age 60.
Tarkovsky, Andrei	*The Sacrifice* (1986).	Died in Paris, France, December 28, 1986, age 54.
Truffaut, François	*Confidentially Yours* (1983).	Died near Paris, France, October 21, 1984, age 52.
Van Dyke, Woodbridge S.	*Journey for Margaret* (1942). Last silent movie: *The Pagan* (1929).	Died in Brentwood, California, February 5, 1943, age 53.
Vidor, King	*Solomon and Sheba* (1959). Last silent movie: *Show People* (1928).	Died in Paso Robles, California, November 1, 1982, age 87.
Walsh, Raoul	*A Distant Trumpet* (1964). Last silent movies: *Sadie Thompson* (1928)*, Me, Gangster* (1928), *The Red Dance* (1928).	Died in Simi Valley, California, December 31, 1980, age 93.
Wellman, William A.	*Darby's Rangers* (1958). Last silent movie: *Chinatown Nights* (1929). One third filmed as a silent, rest had sound.	Died in Los Angeles, California, December 9, 1975, age 79.

Welles, Orson	*Filming Othello* (documentary; 1978).	Died in Los Angeles, California, October 10, 1985, age 70.
Wilder, Billy	*Buddy, Buddy* (1981).	Died in Beverly Hills, California, March 27, 2002, age 95.
Wood, Edward D. (Jr.)	*Necromania* (1971).	Died in North Hollywood, California, December 10, 1978, age 54.
Wood, Sam	*Ambush* (1949). Last silent movie: *Queen Kelly* (1929). Uncredited; film had several directors and was finally credited to Erich von Stroheim.	Died in Hollywood, California, September 22, 1949, age 66.
Wyler, William	*The Liberation of L. B. Jones* (1970). Last silent movie: *The Shakedown* (1929).	Died in Los Angeles, California, July 27, 1981, age 79.
Zinnemann, Fred	*Five Days One Summer* (1982).	Died in London, England, March 14, 1997, age 89.

Movies—Performers
(*See also* Entertainers—Theater—Performers; Movies—Directors.)

Name	Last Feature Movie(s) and Last TV Movie(s)	Comment
Abel, Walter	*The Ultimate Solution of Grace Quigley* (1984).	Died in Essex, Connecticut, March 26, 1987, age 88.
Abbott, Bud	Last "Meet" movie: *Abbott and Costello Meet the Mummy* (1955). Last movie with Lou Costello: *Dance with Me Henry* (1956).	The team of Abbott and Costello split up in 1957. Abbott died in Woodland Hills, California, April 24, 1974, age 78.
Adams, Nick	*Fever Heat* (1968).	Died in Los Angeles, California, February 7, 1968, age 36.
Akins, Claude	*Falling from Grace* (1992). Last TV movie: *Sherlock Holmes and the Incident at Victoria Falls* (1991).	Died in Altadena, California, January 27, 1994, age 71.
Albertson, Jack	*Dead and Buried* (1981). Last TV movie: *Grandpa, Will you Run with Me?* (1982).	Died in Hollywood Hills, California, November 25, 1981, age 74.
Allen, Gracie	*Two Girls and a Sailor* (1944).	Died in Hollywood, California, August 27, 1964, age 58.
Allgood, Sara	*Sierra* (1950).	Died in Woodland Hills, California, September 15, 1950, age 66.
Ameche, Don	*Corrina, Corrina* (1994).	Died in Scottsdale, Arizona, December 6, 1993, age 85, soon after completing his scenes.
Ames, Leon	*Jake Speed* (1986).	Died in Laguna Beach, California, October 12, 1993, age 91.
Anderson, Dame Judith	*Impure Thoughts* (narrator, 1986).	Died in Santa Barbara, California, January 3, 1992, age 93.

Andrews, Edward	*Gremlins* (1984).	Died in Santa Monica, California, March 8, 1985, age 70.
Angel, Heather	*Backstairs at the White House* (TV miniseries, 1979).	Died in Santa Barbara, California, December 13, 1986, age 77.
Angeli, Anna Maria Pier	*Octaman* (1971).	Died in Beverly Hills, California, September 10, 1971, age 39.
Arbuckle, Roscoe ("Fatty")	*Tomalio* (1933); *Close Relations* (1933); *How've You Bean?* (1933); *Buzzin' Around* (1933); *In the Dough* (1932); *Hey, Pop!* (1932; six short movies filmed at Coney Island.) Last silent movie: *Go West* (uncredited, 1925).	Last films as a director were made in 1932, using the name William Goodrich. He also wrote under that name until 1931. Died in New York, New York, June 29, 1933, age 46.
Arden, Eve	*Pandemonium* (1982); *Grease II* (cameo; 1982). Last TV role: *Faerie Tale Theater: Cinderella* (1984).	Died in Beverly Hills, California, November 12, 1990, age 82.
Arlen, Richard	*Won Ton Ton, the Dog Who Saved Hollywood* (1976); *A Whale of a Tale* (1976); *The Sky's the Limit* (1975).	Retired in the 1960s. Returned to make three films the year he died. Died in Hollywood, California, March 28, 1976, age 75.
Arliss, George	*Dr. Syn* (1937). Last silent movie: *Twenty Dollars a Week* (1924).	Died in London, England, February 5, 1946, age 77.
Arnaz, Desi	*The Escape Artist* (1982).	Died in Del Mar, California, December 2, 1986, age 69.
Arnold, Edward	*Miami Expose* (1956).	Died in Encino, California, April 26, 1956, age 66.
Arthur, Jean	*Shane* (1953).	Died in Carmel, California, June 19, 1991, age 85.
Astaire, Fred	*Ghost Story* (1981). Last musical film: *Finian's Rainbow* (1968). Last of ten films with Ginger Rogers: *The Barkleys of Broadway* (1949). Last silent movie: *Fanchon, The Cricket* (with sister Adele, 1915).	Died in Los Angeles, California, June 22, 1987, age 88.
Astor, Mary	*Hush, Hush...Sweet Charlotte* (1965). Last TV movie: *Hollywood* (miniseries, 1980). Last silent movie: *The Woman from Hell* (1929).	Died in Woodland Hills, California, September 25, 1987, age 81.
Atwill, Lionel	*Lost City of the Jungle* (serial, 1946).	Died in Pacific Palisades, California, April 22, 1946, age 61, while making *Lost City of the Jungle*.
Auer, Mischa	*Arrivederci, Baby!* (1966).	Died in Rome, Italy, March 5, 1967, age 61.
Axton, Hoyt	*King Cobra* (1999).	Died in Helena, Montana, October 26, 1999, age 61.
Baddeley, Hermione	*The Secret of NIMH* (voice, 1981).	Died in Los Angeles California, August 19, 1986, age 77.

Bainter, Fay	*The Children's Hour* (1962).	Died in Hollywood, California, April 16, 1968, age 74.
Ball, Lucille	*Mame* (1974).	Died in Los Angeles, California, April 26, 1989, age 77.
Balsam, Martin	*Legend of the Spirit Dog* (1997).	Died in Rome, Italy, February 13, 1996, age 76.
Bankhead, Tallulah	*Die! Die! My Darling* (1965); *The Daydreamer* (voice, 1966). Last silent movie: *His House in Order* (1928).	Died in New York, New York, December 12, 1968, age 65.
Bara, Theda	*Madame Mystery* (also her last silent movie, 1926).	Died in Los Angeles, California, April 7, 1955, age 65.
Bari, Lynn	*The Young Runaways* (1968).	Died in Santa Barbara, California, November 20, 1989, age 75.
Barrie, Wendy	*It Should Happen to You* (cameo as herself, 1954).	Died in Englewood, New Jersey, February 2, 1978, age 65.
Barrymore, Ethel	*Johnny Trouble* (1957). Last silent movie: *The Divorcee* (1919).	Died in Beverly Hills, California, June 18, 1959, age 79. Barrymore's son Samuel Colt appeared in her last film.
Barrymore, John	*World Premiere* (1941); *Playmates* (as himself, 1941). Last silent movie: *Eternal Love* (1929).	Died in Los Angeles, California, May 29, 1942, age 60.
Barrymore, Lionel	*Bannerline* (1951); *Main Street to Broadway* (cameo as himself, 1953). Last silent movie: *The Mysterious Island* (originally silent, converted to sound; 1929).	Died in Van Nuys, California, November 15, 1954, age 76.
Barthelmess, Richard	*The Mayor of 44th Street* (1942). Last silent movie: *Drag* (a.k.a. *Parasites*; 1929).	Died in Southampton, New York, August 17, 1963, age 68.
Bartholomew, Freddie	*St. Benny the Dip* (1951).	Died in Sarasota, Florida, January 23, 1992, age 67.
Barty, Billy	*I/O Error* (1998).	Died in Los Angeles, California, December 23, 2000, age 76.
Basehart, Richard	*Being There* (1979). Last TV movie: *Masada* (miniseries, 1981).	Died in Los Angeles, California, September 17, 1984, age 70, after narrating 1984 Olympics closing ceremony in Los Angeles.
Baxter, Anne	*Jane Austen in Manhattan* (1983). Last TV movie: *Sherlock Holmes and the Masks of Death* (1984).	Narrated documentary on her grandfather: *Portrait of an Artist: Architecture of Frank Lloyd Wright* (1983). Died in New York, New York, December 12, 1985, age 62.
Baxter, Warner	*State Penitentiary* (1950). Last of 10 Crime Doctor films: *Crime Doctor's Diary* (1949).	Died in Los Angeles, California, May 7, 1951, age 60.
Beavers, Louise	*The Facts of Life* (1960).	Died in Hollywood, California, October 26, 1962, age 60.
Beckett, Scotty	*Three for Jamie Dawn* (1956).	Died in Los Angeles, California, May 10, 1968, age 38.

Beery, Wallace	*Big Jack* (1949). Last silent movie: *Stairs of Sand* (1929).	Died in Beverly Hills, California, April 15, 1949, age 64.
Begley, Ed (Sr.)	*The Dunwich Horror* (1970).	Died in Hollywood, California, April 28, 1970, age 69.
Bellamy, Ralph	*Pretty Woman* (1990).	Died in Los Angeles, California, November 29, 1991, age 87.
Belushi, John	*Neighbors* (1981).	Died in West Hollywood, California, March 5, 1982, age 33.
Bendix, William	*Young Fury* (1964).	Died in Los Angeles, California, December 14, 1964, age 58. Film released after his death.
Bennett, Constance	*Madame X* (1966).	Died in Fort Dix, New Jersey, July 24, 1965, age 60, shortly after completing her scenes.
Bennett, Joan	*Suspiria* (1977). Last TV movie: *Divorce Wars: A Love Story* (1982)	Died in Scarsdale, New York, December 7, 1990, age 80.
Benny, Jack	Last feature movie: *The Horn Blows at Midnight* (1945). Last movie: *The Man* (as himself, 1972).	Died in Los Angeles, California, December 26, 1974, age 80.
Bergman, Ingrid	*Autumn Sonata* (1978). Last TV movie: *A Woman Named Golda* (miniseries, 1982).	Died in London, England, August 29, 1982, age 67.
Berkeley, Busby	Last movie as choreographer: *Billy Rose's Jumbo* (1962). Last film as director: *Annie Get Your Gun* (1950; one of three directors, credited to George Sidney). Last film as actor: *The Phynx* (as himself, 1970).	Died in Palm Springs, California, March 14, 1976, age 80.
Bickford, Charles	*A Big Hand for the Little Lady* (1966).	Died in Los Angeles, California, November 9, 1967, age 76.
Binns, Edward	*After School* (1989).	Died in Brewster, New York, December 4, 1990, age 74.
Bissell, Whit	*Casey's Shadow* (1978).	Died in Woodland Hills, California, March 5, 1996, age 86.
Blakely, Colin	*Don Camillo* (1983). Last TV movie: *Paradise Postponed* (1986).	Died in London, England, May 7, 1987, age 56.
Blondell, Joan	*The Woman Inside* (1981). Last TV movie: *The Rebels, Part 2* (miniseries, 1979).	Died in Santa Monica, California, December 25, 1979, age 70.
Blore, Eric	*Bowery to Baghdad* (1955).	Died in Hollywood, California, March 2, 1959, age 71.
Bogarde, Sir Dirk	*Daddy Nostalgia* (a.k.a. *These Foolish Things*; 1990).	Died in London, England, May 8, 1999, age 78.
Bogart, Humphrey	*The Harder They Fall* (1956). Last of four films with Lauren Bacall: *Key Largo* (1948).	Died in Los Angeles, California, January 14, 1957, age 57.

Bolger, Ray	*Just You and Me Kid* (cameo, 1979); *The Runner Stumbles* (cameo, 1979); *That's Dancin'* (as himself, 1985). Last TV movie: *Heaven Only Knows* (1979).	Last surviving lead from *The Wizard of Oz*. He appeared as himself in *The Whimsical World of Oz* (TV; 1985). Died in Los Angeles, California, January 15, 1987, age 83.
Bond, Ward	*Rio Bravo* (1959).	Died in Dallas, Texas, November 5, 1960, age 57, while making a professional appearance at the Cotton Bowl.
Bondi, Beulah	*Robin Hood* (voice; 1973). Last TV movie: *She Waits* (1971).	Died in Hollywood, California, January 11, 1981, California, age 92.
Boone, Richard	*The Bushido Blade* (1979). Last TV movie: *The Last Dinosaur* (1977).	Died in St. Augustine, Florida, January 10, 1981, age 65.
Bow, Clara	Last feature movie: *Hoopla* (1933). Last silent movie: *Three Weekends* (1928).	Retired in 1933. Appeared as herself in *The Love Goddess* (1965). Died in Los Angeles, California, September 27, 1965, age 60.
Boyd, William (Hopalong Cassidy)	Last Hopalong Cassidy feature movie: *Hopalong Cassidy: Strange Gamble* (1948). Last film as Hopalong Cassidy: *The Greatest Show on Earth* (cameo; 1952). Last film as William Boyd: *Hollywood Bronc Busters* (1955).	Died in Laguna Beach, California, September 12, 1972, age 74.
Boyer, Charles	*A Matter of Time* (1976). Last silent movie: *Captain Fracasse* (1929).	Died in Phoenix, Arizona, August 26, 1978, age 80.
Bracken, Eddie	*Baby's Day Out* (1944). Last TV movie: *The Ryan Interview* (2000).	Died in Montclair, New Jersey, November 14, 2002, age 87.
Brady, Scott	*Gremlins* (1984).	Died in Los Angeles, California, April 16, 1985, age 60.
Brand, Neville	*Evils of the Night* (1985).	Died in Sacramento, California, April 16, 1992, age 71.
Brando, Marlin	Last completed film: *The Score* (2001)	Died in Los Angeles, California, July 1, 2004, age 80.
Brennan, Walter	*Smoke in the Wind* (1971). Last TV movie: *Home for the Holidays* (1972).	Died in Oxnard, California, September 21, 1974, age 80.
Brent, George	*Born Again* (1978).	Died in Solana Beach, California, May 26, 1979, age 75.
Bressart, Felix	*Take One False Step* (1949).	Died in Los Angeles, California, while making film version of *My Friend Irma,* March 17, 1949, age 56.
Bridges, Lloyd	*Mafia!* (a.k.a. *Jane Austen's Mafia*; 1998). Last TV movies: *The Deliverance of Elaine* (1996); *Peter and the Wolf* (1996).	Died in Los Angeles, California, March 10, 1998, age 85.
Bronson, Charles	*Death Wish V: The Face of Death* (1994). Last TV movie:	Died in Los Angeles, California, August 30, 2003, age 81.

	Family of Cops III (1999). Last of 15 films with wife Jill Ireland: *Assassination* (1987).	
Brook, Clive	*The List of Adrian Messenger* (1963).	Died in London, England, November 17, 1974, age 87.
Brooks, Louise	*Overland Stage Raiders* (1938). Last silent movies: *Pandora's Box* (1929); *Diary of a Lost Girl* (1929).	Died in Rochester, New York, August 8, 1985, age 78.
Brown, Joe E.	*The Comedy of Terrors* (1964).	Died in Brentwood, California, July 6, 1973, age 80.
Brown, Johnny Mack	*Apache Uprising* (1966).	Died in Woodland Hills, California, November 14, 1974, age 70.
Bruce, Nigel	*World for Ransom* (1954). Last film as Dr. Watson: *Dressed to Kill* (1946).	Died in Santa Monica, California, October 8, 1953, age 57.
Brynner, Yul	*Lost to the Revolution* (1980, narrator). Last major films: *Futureworld* (1976); *Death Rage* (1976).	Last stage appearance in *King and I*, June 30, 1985, after more than 4,600 performances. Died of lung cancer in New York, New York, October 10, 1985, age 70. Made an anti-smoking commercial that was aired after his death.
Buchanan, Edgar	*Benji* (1974).	Died in Palm Desert, California, April 4, 1979, age 76.
Buono, Victor	*The Flight of Dragons* (voice, 1982).	Died in Apple Valley, California, January 1, 1982, age 43.
Burke, Billie	*Sergeant Rutledge* (1960); *Pepe* (cameo, 1960).	Died in Los Angeles, California, May 14, 1970, age 84.
Burns, George	*Radioland Murders* (1994).	Died in Beverly Hills, California, March 9, 1996, age 100.
Burr, Raymond	*Delirious* (1991); *Showdown at Williams Creek* (1991). Last Perry Mason TV movie: *The Case of the Killer Kiss* (1993).	Died in Sonoma, California, September 12, 1993, age 76.
Burton, Richard	*1984* (1984). Last TV movie: *Ellis Island* (miniseries, 1984). Last movie with Elizabeth Taylor: *Divorce His, Divorce Hers* (TV; 1973).	Died in Geneva, Switzerland, August 5, 1984, age 58, as he was beginning to make *Wild Geese II*. Daughter Kate Burton appeared in *Ellis Island*.
Butterworth, Charles	*Dixie Jamboree* (1944).	Died in Los Angeles, California, June 14, 1946, age 49.
Byington, Spring	*Please Don't Eat the Daisies* (1960).	Died in Hollywood, California, September 7, 1971, age 84.
Cabot, Bruce	*Diamonds are Forever* (1971).	Died in Woodland Hills, California, May 3, 1972, age 68.
Cabot, Susan	*The Wasp Woman* (1959).	Died in Encino, California, December 10, 1986, age 59.
Cagney, James	*Ragtime* (1981). Last TV movie: *Terrible Joe Moran* (1984).	Died in Stanfordville, New York, March 30, 1986, age 86.

Calhern, Louis	*Forever Darling* (1956); *High Society* (1956).	Died in Nara, Japan, May 12, 1956, age 61, while filming *Tea House of the August Moon.*
Calhoun, Rory	*Pure Country* (1992).	Died in Burbank, California, April 28, 1999, age 76.
Cambridge, Godfrey	*Scott Joplin* (1977).	Died in Los Angeles, California, November 29, 1976, age 43, while working on TV movie *Victory at Entebbe.*
Cameron, Rod	*Love and the Midnight Auto Supply* (1978).	Died in Gainesville, Georgia, December 21, 1983, age 73.
Candy, John	*Canadian Bacon* (1994).	Died in Durango, Mexico, March 4, 1994, age 43, while filming *Wagons East.* Directed *Hostage for a Day.* He also made a cameo appearance shortly before his death.
Carey, Harry (Sr.)	*Red River* (1948), *The Babe Ruth Story* (uncredited; 1948), *So Dear to My Heart* (1949). Last silent movies: *Border Patrol* (1928); *Burning Bridges* (1928); *The Trail of '98* (1928).	Died September 21, 1947, in Brentwood, California, age 69. His last three movies were released after his death. His son also appeared in *Red River.*
Carey, MacDonald	*It's Alive 3: Island of the Alive* (1987). Last TV movie: *A Message from Holly* (1992).	Last TV appearance as Tom Horton, *Days of Our Lives*: March 1994. His voice continued to be used for the introduction. Died in Beverly Hills, California, March 21, 1994, age 81.
Carlson, Richard	*The Valley of Gwangi* (1969); *Change of Habit* (1969).	Died in Encino, California, November 25, 1977, age 65.
Carney, Art	*Last Action Hero* (1993).	Died in Chester, Connecticut, November 11, 2003, age 85.
Carradine, John	*Buried Alive* (1989).	Died in Milan, Italy, November 27, 1988, age 82.
Carrillo, Leo	*The Girl from San Lorenzo* (last Cisco adventure, 1950).	Died in Santa Monica, California, September 10, 1961, age 80.
Carroll, Leo G.	*That Funny Feeling* (1965).	Died in Hollywood, California, October 16, 1972, age 79.
Carson, Jack	*King of the Roaring Twenties* (1961). Last TV movie: *Sammy the Way-Out Seal* (1962).	Died in Encino, California, January 2, 1963, age 52.
Cass, Peggy	*The Emperor's New Clothes* (1993). Last TV movie: *Zoya* (1995).	Died in New York, New York, March 8, 1999, age 74.
Cassidy, Jack	*W.C. Fields and Me* (1976). Last TV movie: *The Private Files of J. Edgar Hoover* (1977).	Died in West Hollywood, California, December 12, 1976, age 49.
Chandler, Jeff	*Merrill's Marauders* (1962).	Died in Los Angeles, California, June 17, 1961, age 42, during filming.
Chaney, Lon (Sr.)	*The Unholy Three,* his first and only talking film (1930). Last silent movie: *Thunder* (no copies sur-	Died in Hollywood, California, August 26, 1930, age 47, before *The Unholy Three* was released.

	vive; 1929). Last surviving silent film: *Where East is East* (1929).	
Chaney, Lon (Jr.)	*Dracula vs. Frankenstein* (1971).	Died in San Clemente, California, July 12, 1973, age 67.
Chaplin, Sir Charles	Last starring performance: *A King in New York* (1957). Last film: *A Countess from Hong Kong* (cameo; 1967). Last Little Tramp film: *Modern Times* (also last silent movie, 1936).	Died in Vevey, Switzerland, December 25, 1977, age 88. (*See also* Movies—Directors .)
Chase, Charles	*South of the Boudoir* (1940). Last silent movie: *Movie Night* (1929).	Died in Hollywood, California, June 20, 1940, age 45.
Chatterton, Ruth	*A Royal Divorce* (1938). Last TV performance: *Hamlet* (1953).	Died in Norwalk, Connecticut, November 24, 1961, age 67.
Chevalier, Maurice	*Monkeys, Go Home!* (1967); *The Aristocats* (voice, sang title song, 1970).	Died in Paris, France, January 1, 1972, age 83.
Ciannelli, Eduardo	*MacKenna's Gold* (1969).	Died in Rome, Italy, October 8, 1969, age 80.
Clark, Fred	*Apache Vengeance* (1970).	Died in Santa Monica, California, December 5, 1968, age 54.
Cleveland, George	*Fireman Save My Child* (1954).	Died in Burbank, California, July 15, 1957, age 70.
Clift, Montgomery	*The Defector* (1966).	Died in New York, New York, July 23, 1966, age 45, soon after completing movie. Was scheduled to be in *Reflections in a Golden Eye*.
Cobb, Lee J.	*Nick the Sting* (1976).	Died in Woodland Hills, California, February 11, 1976, age 64.
Coburn, Charles	*John Paul Jones* (1959); *Pepe* (cameo, 1960).	Died in New York, New York, August 30, 1961, age 84.
Coburn, James	*American Gun* (2002).	Died in Los Angeles, California, November 18, 2002, age 74.
Colbert, Claudette	*Parrish* (1961). Last TV movie: *The Two Mrs. Grenvilles* (1987).	Died in Bridgetown, Barbados, July 30, 1996, age 92.
Collins, Ray	*Touch of Evil* (1958).	Died in Santa Monica, California, July 11, 1965, age 75.
Colman, Ronald	*The Story of Mankind* (1957).	Died in Santa Barbara, California, May 19, 1958, age 67.
Connors, Chuck	*Salmonberries* (1991). Last TV movie: *3 Days to a Kill* (1992).	Died in Los Angeles, California, November 10, 1992, age 71. Film released after his death.
Conrad, William	*Hudson Hawk* (narrator, 1991). Last TV movie: *Vengeance* (1989).	Died in North Hollywood, California, February 11, 1994, age 73.
Conried, Hans	*Oh, God, Book 2* (1980). Last TV movie: *Tut & Tuttle* (1982).	Died in Burbank, California, January 5, 1982, age 64.
Conte, Richard	Last Hollywood movie: *The Godfather* (1972). Last European film: *Violent Rome* (1975).	Died in Los Angeles, California, April 15, 1975, age 61.

Conway, Tom	*What a Way to Go* (1964); *One Hundred and One Dalmatians* (voice; 1961). Last Falcon film: *The Falcon's Adventure* (1946).	Died in Culver City, California, April 22, 1967, age 63.
Coogan, Jackie	*The Escape Artist* (1982). Last silent movies: *Buttons* (1927); *Bugle Call* (1927); *Johnny Get Your Hair Cut* (1927).	Last portrayal of Uncle Fester: *All New Addams Family Halloween* (TV movie, 1977). Died in Santa Monica, California, March 1, 1984, age 69.
Cook, Elisha (Jr.)	*Hammett* (1982). Last TV movie: *The Man Who Broke 1,000 Chains* (1987).	Died in Big Pine, California, May 18, 1995, age 91.
Cooper, Gary	*The Naked Edge* (1961). Last silent movie: *Betrayal* (1929).	Died in Beverly Hills, California, May 13, 1961, age 60.
Cooper, Dame Gladys	*A Nice Girl Like Me* (1969).	Died in Henley-on-Thames, England, November 17, 1971, age 82.
Corby, Ellen	*Napoleon and Samantha* (1972).	Last Walton appearance (Grandma Walton): *A Walton Thanksgiving Reunion* (1993). Died in Woodland Hills, California, April 14, 1999, age 87.
Corrigan, Ray ("Crash")	*It! The Terror from Beyond Space* (1958). Last TV movie: *Sharad of Atlantis* (1966). Last Three Mesquiteers film: *New Frontier* (1939). Last Range Busters film: *Bullets and Saddles* (1943).	Died in Brookings Hollow, Oregon, August 10, 1976, age 74.
Costello, Lou	*The 30-Foot Bride of Candy Rock* (1959). Last movie with Bud Abbott: *Dance with Me Henry* (1956).	The team of Abbott and Costello broke up in 1957. Died in Los Angeles, California, March 3, 1959, age 52.
Cotton, Joseph	*Delusion* (1980); *The Survivor* (1981). Last TV movie: *Casino* (1980).	Died in Westwood, California, February 6, 1994, age 88.
Cowan, Jerome	*The Comic* (1969).	Died in Encino, California, January 24, 1972, age 74.
Crabbe, Larry ("Buster")	*The Comeback Trail* (1982). Last Billy Carson movie: *Outlaw of the Plains* (1946).	Died in Scottsdale, Arizona, April 23, 1983, age 76.
Crawford, Broderick	*Ransom Money* (1988*)*; *The Upper Crust* (1988). Last TV movie: *Express to Terror* (1979).	Died in Rancho Mirage, California, April 26, 1986, age 74.
Crawford, Joan	*Trog* (1970). Last TV movie: *Night Gallery* (1969). Last silent movie: *Our Modern Maidens* (1929)	Died in New York, New York, May 10, 1977, age 69.
Cregar, Laird	*Hangover Square* (1945).	Died in Los Angeles, California, December 9, 1944, age 28. Film released after his death.
Crews, Laura Hope	*The Man Who Came to Dinner* (1941).	Died in New York, New York, November 13, 1942, age 61.

Crisp, Donald	*Spencer's Mountain* (1963).	Died in Van Nuys, California, May 25, 1974, age 93.
Crosby, Bing	*Stagecoach* (1966). Last TV movie:*Dr.Cook's Garden* (1970). Last film appearance: *That's Entertainment!* (host-narrator, 1974). Last "Road" movie: *The Road to Hong Kong* (1962), the last of seven Road films.	Died in Madrid, Spain, October 14, 1977, age 76.
Currie, Finlay	*Bunny Lake is Missing* (1965).	Died in Buckinghamshire, England, May 9, 1968, age 90.
Cushing, Peter	*Biggles: Adventures in Time* (1986). Last film as Sherlock Holmes: *Masks of Death* (1986). Last film work: *Flesh and Blood* (documentary, narrator, 1994).	Died in Canterbury, Kent, England, August 11, 1994, age 81.
Dan George, (Chief)	*Nothing Personal* (1980).	Died in Vancouver, British Columbia, September 23, 1981, age 82.
Dandridge, Dorothy	*The Murder Men* (1961).	Died in West Hollywood, California, September 8, 1965, age 41.
Dangerfield, Rodney	*Angels with Angles* (2004).	Died in Los Angeles, California, October 5, 2004, Age 82.
Daniell, Henry	*My Fair Lady* (1964).	Died in Santa Monica, California, October 31, 1963, age 69, during filming of *My Fair Lady*.
Daniels, Bebe	*Life with the Lyons* (also a writer of the film, 1956). Last U.S. movie: *Music is Magic* (1935).	Died in London, England, March 16, 1971, age 70.
Dano, Royal	*The Dark Half* (1993). Last TV movie: *Once Upon a Texas Train* (1988).	Died in Los Angeles, California, May 15, 1994, age 71.
Darnell, Linda	*Black Spurs* (1965).	Died in Chicago, Illinois, April 10, 1965, age 43. Film was completed just before her death.
Darin, Bobby	*Happy Mother's Day...Love George* (1973).	Died in Los Angeles, California, December 20, 1973, age 37.
Darwell, Jane	*Mary Poppins* (1964).	Died in Woodland Hills, California, August 13, 1967, age 87.
Da Silva, Howard	*Garbo Talks* (1984). Last TV movie: *The Cafeteria* (1984).	Died in Ossining, New York, February 16, 1986, age 76.
Davenport, Harry	*Riding High* (1950).	Died in Los Angeles, California, August 9, 1949, age 83.
Davies, Marion	*Ever Since Eve* (1937). Last silent movie: *Marianne* (1929; both sound and silent versions released).	Last acting role: *Lux Radio Theater,* "The Brit" (1936). Died in Hollywood, California, September 22, 1961, age 64.
Davis, Bette	*Wicked Stepmother* (1989).	Died in Neuilly, France, October 6, 1989, age 81.

Davis, Brad	*The Player* (cameo, 1992). Last TV movie: *The Habitation of Dragons* (1992).	Died in Los Angeles, California, September 8, 1991, age 41.
Davis, Joan	*Harem Girl* (1952).	Died in Palm Springs, California, May 23, 1961, age 46.
Davis, Sammy (Jr.)	*Tap* (1989). Last TV movie: *The Kid Who Loved Christmas* (1990).	Died in Los Angeles, California, May 16, 1990, age 64.
Dean, James	*Giant* (1956).	Died in car crash in Paso Robles, California, September 30, 1955, age 24, shortly after making *Giant*.
DeCamp, Rosemary	*Saturday the 14th* (1981).	Died in Torrance, California, February 20, 2001, age 89.
Dehner, John	*Creator* (1985). Last TV work: *War and Remembrance* (mini-series, 1989).	Died in Santa Barbara, California, February 4, 1992, age 76.
Dekker, Albert	*The Wild Bunch* (1969).	Died in Hollywood, California, May 5, 1968, age 62.
del Rio, Dolores	*The Children of Sanchez* (1978).	Died in Newport Beach, California, April 11, 1983, age 77.
Demarest, William	*Won Ton Ton, The Dog Who Saved Hollywood* (1976). Last TV movie: *The Millionaire* (1978).	Died in Palm Springs, California, December 28, 1983, age 91.
Dennis, Sandy	*The Indian Runner* (1991).	Died in Westport, Connecticut, March 1, 1992, age 54.
Denny, Reginald	*Assault on a Queen* (1966). Last Bulldog Drummond film: *Bulldog Drummond's Bride* (1939).	Died in Surrey, England, June 16, 1967, age 75.
Devine, Andy	*The Mouse and His Child* (voice, 1977). Last movie as Jingles Jones: *The Counterfeit Ghost* (1958). Last movie as Cookie Bullfincher: *The Far Frontier* (1948).	Died in Orange, California, February 18, 1977, age 71.
Dewhurst, Colleen	*Dying Young* (1991); *Bed & Breakfast* (1992).	Appeared with son Campbell Scott in *Dying Young* (1991). Died in South Salem, New York, August 22, 1991, age 67.
DeWilde, Brandon	*Wild in the Sky* (1972).	Died in car accident, near Denver, Colorado, July 6, 1972, age 30, while appearing in stage production of *Butterflies are Free*
DeWolfe, Billy	*World's Greatest Athlete* (1973). Last TV movie: *Free To Be…You and Me* (voice, 1974).	Died in Los Angeles, California, March 5, 1974, age 67.
Diamond, Selma	*All of Me* (1984). Last TV movie: *The Ratings Game* (1984).	Died in Los Angeles, California, May 14, 1985, age 64.
Dietrich, Marlene	*Just a Gigolo* (cameo, 1979). Last silent movie: *Ship of Lost Men* (1929).	Died in Paris, France, May 6, 1992, age 90. Fell and broke her leg in Sydney, Australia in September 1975, in her last stage appearance.

Divine (Harris Glenn Milstead)	*Out of the Dark* (1989); *Hairspray* (1988).	Died in Los Angeles, California, March 7, 1988, age 42, *Hairspray* opened just before he died.
Dix, Richard	*The Thirteenth Hour* (seventh and last Whistler film, 1947).	Died in Los Angeles, California, September 20, 1949, age 56.
Donat, Robert	*The Inn of the Sixth Happiness* (1958).	Died in London, England, June 9, 1958, age 53.
Donlevy, Brian	*Pit Stop* (1969).	Died in Woodland Hills, California, April 5, 1972, age 71.
Douglas, Melvyn	*Ghost Story* (1981); *The Hot Touch* (1981).	Died in New York, New York, August 4, 1981, age 80.
Douglas, Paul	*The Mating Game* (1959).	Died in Hollywood, California, September 11, 1959, age 52.
Drake, Tom	*Savage Abduction* (1975). Last TV movie: *Mayday at 40,000 Feet* (1976).	Died in Torrance, California, August 11, 1982, age 63.
Dressler, Marie	*The Late Christopher Bean* (1933).	*Tugboat Annie* and *Dinner at Eight* also released in 1933. Died in Santa Barbara, California, July 28, 1934, age 64.
Dru, Joanne	*Super Fuzz* (1981).	Died in Beverly Hills, California, September 10, 1996, age 74.
Duggan, Andrew	*Doctor Detroit* (1983). Last TV movie: *J. Edgar Hoover* (1987).	Died in Westwood, California, May 15, 1988, age 64.
Dumont, Margaret	*What a Way to Go* (1964). Last of seven Marx Brothers films: *The Big Store* (1941).	Last appearance with Groucho Marx: TV, *The Hollywood Palace,* 1965, shortly before she died in Hollywood, California, March 6, 1965, age 75.
Dunn, James	*The Oscar* (1966). Last TV movie: *Shadow Over Elverton* (1968).	Died in Santa Monica, California, September 3, 1967, age 61.
Dunn, Michael	*The Abdication* (1974).	Died in London, England, August 29, 1973, age 39, while working on *The Abdication.*
Dunne, Irene	*It Grows on Trees* (1952).	Died in Los Angeles, California, September 4, 1990, age 91.
Dunnock, Mildred	*The Pick-Up Artist* (1987). Last TV movie: *The Children's Story* (1982).	Died in Oak Bluffs, Massachusetts, July 5, 1991, age 90.
Durante, Jimmy	*It's A Mad, Mad, Mad, Mad World* (1963). Last TV movie: *Frosty, the Snowman* (narrator, 1969).	Died in Santa Monica, California, January 29, 1980, age 86.
Duryea, Dan	*The Bamboo Saucer* (1968).	Died in Hollywood, California, June 7, 1968, age 61.
Dvorak, Ann	*Secret of Convict Lake* (1951).	Died in Honolulu, Hawaii, December 10, 1979, age 67.
Ebsen, Buddy	*The Beverly Hillbillies* (1993), playing Barnaby Jones.	Died in Torrance, California, July 6, 2003, age 95.

Eddy, Nelson	*Northwest Outpost* (a.k.a. *End of the Rainbow*; 1947). Last TV appearance: *The Desert Song* (1955). Last of eight films with Jeanette MacDonald: *I Married an Angel* (1941).	Died in Miami Beach, Florida, March 6, 1967, age 65.
Elliott, Denholm	*Noises Off* (1992).	Died in Ibiza, Spain, October 6, 1992, age 70, soon after completing the film.
Elliott, William ("Wild Bill")	*Footsteps in the Night* (1957). Last Red Ryder movie: *Conquest of Cheyenne* (1946).	Died in Las Vegas, Nevada, November 26, 1965, age 62.
Emhardt, Robert	*Forced Vengeance* (1982).	Died in Ojai, California, December 29, 1994, age 80.
Erickson, Leif	*My Life as a Dog* (1987). Last TV movie: *Savage in the Orient* (1983).	Died in Pensacola, Florida, January 29, 1986, age 74.
Errol, Leon	*Chinatown Chump* (1951). Last Mexican Spitfire film: *Mexican Spitfire's Blessed Event* (1943).	Died in Hollywood, California, October 12, 1951, age 70.
Evans, Dale	*Pals of the Golden West* (1951); *Roy Rogers, King of the Cowboys* (as herself, 1992).	Died in Apple Valley, California, February 7, 2001, age 88.
Evans, Dame Edith	*Nasty Habits* (1977); *The Slipper and the Rose* (1977). Last TV movie: *QB VII* (miniseries, 1974).	Died in Cranbrook, Kent, England, October, 14, 1976, age 88. *Nasty Habits* and *The Slipper and the Rose* were released after her death.
Evans, Maurice	*The Jerk* (1979). Last TV movie: *A Caribbean Mystery* (1983).	Died in Sussex, England, March 12, 1989, age 87.
Ewell, Tom	*Easy Money* (1983). Last TV movie: *Terror at Alcatraz* (1982).	Died in Woodland Hills, California, September 12, 1994, age 85.
Fairbanks, Douglas (Jr.)	*Ghost Story* (1981). Last TV movie: *Strong Medicine* (1986). Last silent movies: *A Woman of Affairs* (1929); *The Jazz Age* (1929); *The Fast Life* (1929); *Careless Age* (1929); *Our Modern Maidens* (1929). Most were also released with sound.	Died in New York, New York, May 7, 2000, age 90.
Fairbanks, Douglas (Sr.)	*The Private Life of Don Juan* (1934). Last silent movie: *The Iron Mask* (1929).	Died in Santa Monica, California, December 12, 1939, age 56.
Farley, Chris	*Almost Heroes* (1998).	Died in Chicago, Illinois, December 18, 1997, age 33.
Farmer, Frances	*The Party Crashers* (1958).	Died in Indianapolis, Indiana, August 1, 1970, age 56.
Farnsworth, Richard	*The Straight Story* (1999). Last TV movie: *Best Friends for Life* (1998).	Died in Lincoln, New Mexico, October 6, 2000, age 80.
Farrell, Glenda	*Tiger By the Tail* (1968).	Died in New York, New York, May 1, 1971, age 66.

Faye, Alice	*Every Girl Should Have One* (1978); *The Magic of Lassie* (1978).	Died in Rancho Mirage, California, May 9, 1998, age 83.
Feld, Fritz	*Homer and Eddie* (1989).	Died in Los Angeles, California, November 18, 1993, age 93.
Feldman, Marty	*Yellowbeard* (1983).	Died in Mexico City, Mexico, December 2, 1982, age 48, while filming *Yellowbeard. Slapstick of Another Kind* also released after his death.
Ferrer, José	*Arrest the Restless* (1992); *Life of Sin* (1992). Last TV movie: *The Perfect Tribute* (1991).	Died in Coral Gables, Florida, January 26, 1992, age 83.
Fetchit, Stepin	*Won Ton Ton, the Dog Who Saved Hollywood* (1976).	Died in Woodland Hills, California, November 19, 1985, age 83.
Field, Betty	*Coogan's Bluff* (1968).	Died in Hyannis, Massachusetts, September 13, 1973, age 60.
Fields, W.C.	*Sensations of 1945* (1945). Last silent movies: *Fools for Luck* (1928); *Tillie's Punctured Romance* (1928).	Died in Pasadena, California, December 25, 1946, age 66.
Finch, Peter	*Network* (1976). Last TV movie: *Raid on Entebbe* (1977).	Died in Beverly Hills, California, January 14, 1977, age 60, while on promotional tour for *Network*. Won posthumous Academy Award for Best Actor for his final film.
Fitzgerald, Barry	*Broth of a Boy* (1959).	Died in Dublin, Ireland, January 4, 1961, age 72.
Fleming, Eric	*The Glass Bottom Boat* (1966).	Drowned in a canoeing accident while filming location shots in Peru, September 28, 1966, age 41,
Flynn, Errol	*Cuban Rebel Girls* (1959). Last of eight films with Olivia de Havilland: *Thank Your Lucky Stars* (as themselves; 1943).	Died in Vancouver, British Columbia, October 14, 1959, age 50.
Flynn, Joe	*The Rescuers* (voice; 1977).	Died in Hollywood, California, July 19, 1975, age 50, soon after finishing his work on the film.
Fonda, Henry	*On Golden Pond* (1981). Last TV movie: *Summer Solstice* (1981).	Died in Los Angeles, California, August 12, 1982, age 77.
Fong, Benson	*Jinxed* (1982). Last TV movie: *Kung Fu: The Movie* (1986).	Died in Los Angeles, California, August 1, 1987, age 70.
Ford, Wallace	*A Patch of Blue* (1965).	Died in Woodland Hills, California, June 11, 1966, age 68.
Foster, Preston	*Chubasco* (1968).	Died in La Jolla, California, July 14, 1970, age 69.
Frawley, William	*Safe at Home* (1962).	Died in Hollywood, California, March 3, 1966, age 79.
Gable, Clark	*The Misfits* (1961). Last of six films with Jean Harlow: *Saratoga* (1937). Last of eight films	Died in Los Angeles, California, November 16, 1960, age 59, shortly after finishing *The Misfits*.

	with Joan Crawford: *Strange Cargo* (1940).	
Garbo, Greta	Last silent movie: *The Kiss* (1929). *Two-faced Woman* (1941). Retired from show business in 1941.	Died in New York, New York, April 15, 1990, age 84.
Gardenia, Vincent	*The Super* (1991). Last TV movie: *Tragedy of Flight 103: The Inside Story* (1991).	Died in Philadelphia, Pennsylvania, December 9, 1992, age 70.
Gardiner, Reginald	*Do Not Disturb* (1965).	Died in Westwood, California, July 7, 1980, age 77.
Gardner, Ava	*Regina* (1983). Last TV movie: *Harem* (1986).	Died in London, England, January 25, 1990, age 67.
Garfield, John	*He Ran All the Way* (1951).	Died in New York, New York, May 21, 1952, age 39.
Garland, Judy	*I Could Go On Singing* (1963). Last of ten films with Mickey Rooney: *Words and Music* (1948).	Died in London, England, June 22, 1969, age 47.
Garner, Peggy Ann	*A Wedding* (1978). Last TV movie: *This Year's Blond* (1980).	Died in Woodland Hills, California, October 16, 1984, age 52.
Garson, Greer	*The Singing Nun* (1966); *The Happiest Millionaire* (1967). Last TV movie: *Little Women* (1978). Last of nine films with Walter Pidgeon: *Scandal at Scourie* (1953).	Died in Dallas, Texas, April 6, 1996, age 92.
Gaynor, Janet	*Bernardine* (1957). Last silent movies: *Christina* (1929); *Lucky Star* (1929).	Died in Palm Springs, California, September 14, 1984, age 77.
Genn, Leo	*The Martyr* (1973).	Died in London, England, January 26, 1978, age 72.
George, Gladys	*It Happens Every Thursday* (1953). Last silent movie: *Chickens* (1921).	Died in Los Angeles, California, December 8, 1954, age 54.
Gibson, Hoot	*The Horse Soldiers* (1959).	Died in Woodland Hills, California, August 23, 1962, age 70.
Gielgud, Sir John	*Elizabeth* (1998). Last TV movie: *The Quest for Camelot* (voice; 1998). Appeared in short film *Catastrophe* (2000).	Died in Buckinghamshire, England, May 21, 2000, age 96.
Gilbert, Billy	*Five Weeks in a Balloon* (1962).	Died in Hollywood, California, September 23, 1971, age 77.
Gilbert, John	*The Captain Hates the Sea* (1934). Fourth and last film with Greta Garbo: *Queen Christina* (1933).	Died in Los Angeles, California, January 9, 1936, age 41.
Gilford, Jack	*Cocoon: The Return* (1988). Last TV movie: *Young Again* (1986).	Died in New York, New York, June 4, 1990, age 81.
Gingold, Hermione	*Garbo Talks* (1984). Last TV movie: *How to be a Perfect Person in Just Three Days* (1983).	Died in New York, New York, May 24, 1987, age 89.

Gish, Dorothy	*The Cardinal* (1963). Last silent movie: *Madame Pompadour* (1927).	Died in Rapallo, Italy, June 4, 1968, age 70.
Gish, Lillian	*The Whales of August* (1987). Last TV movie: *The Adventures of Huckleberry Finn* (1985). Last silent movie: *The Wind* (1928).	Died in New York, New York, February 27, 1993, age 99.
Gleason, Jackie	*Nothing in Common* (1986). Last TV movie: *Izzy and Moe* (1985).	Died in Fort Lauderdale, Florida, June 24, 1987, age 71.
Gleason, James	*The Last Hurrah* (1958).	Died in Los Angeles, California, April 12, 1959, age 72.
Goddard, Paulette	*Time of Indifference* (1964). Last TV appearance: *The Snoop Sisters* (1972).	Died in Switzerland, April 23, 1990, age 78.
Gorcey, Leo	*The Phynx* (cameo as himself; 1970). Last Bowery Boys/East Side Kids film: *Crashing Las Vegas* (1956).	Died in Oakland, California, June 2, 1969, age 51.
Gordon, Gale	*The 'Burbs* (1989).	Died in Escondido, California, June 30, 1995, age 89.
Gordon, Ruth	*The Trouble with Spies* (1987); *The Ten Year Lunch* (1987); *Voyage of the Rock Aliens* (1988).	Died in Edgartown, Massachusetts, August 28, 1985, age 88. All three films released after her death.
Grable, Betty	*How to be Very, Very Popular* (1955).	Died in Santa Monica, California, July 2, 1973, age 56.
Grahame, Gloria	*The Nesting* (1981).	Died in New York , New York, October 5, 1981, age 57.
Granger, Stewart	*Hell Hunters* (1987). Last TV movie: *Fine Gold* (1990).	Died in Santa Monica, California, August 16, 1993, age 80.
Grant, Cary	*Walk, Don't Run* (1966). Retired after making the film.	Died in Davenport, Iowa, while on a lecture tour, November 29, 1986, age 82.
Greene, Richard	*Special Effects* (1984).	Died in Norfolk, England, June 1, 1985, age 66.
Greenstreet, Sydney	*Flamingo Road* (1949); *Malaya* (1949).	Died in Hollywood, California, January 18, 1954, age 74.
Greenwood, Charlotte	*The Opposite Sex* (1956); *Oklahoma* (1955).	Died, in Los Angeles, California, January 18, 1978, age 87.
Greenwood, Joan	*Little Dorritt* (1987). Last TV movie*: Melba* (miniseries, 1987).	Died in London, England, February 27, 1987, age 65.
Guardino, Harry	*Fist of Honor* (1991).	Died in Palm Springs, California, July 17, 1995, age 69.
Guinness, Sir Alec	*Mute Witness* (1994).	Died in Sussex, England, August 5, 2000, age 86.
Gwenn, Edmund	*The Rocket from Calabuch* (1956).	Died in Woodland Hills, California, September 6, 1959, age 83.
Gwynne, Fred	*My Cousin Vinny* (1992). Last TV movie: *Lincoln: The Making of the President 1860-1862* (voice 1992).	Died in Taneytown, Maryland, July 2, 1993, age 66.

Hackett, Buddy	*Little Mermaid II*: *The Return to the Sea* (voice, 2000). Last feature film: *Hey Babe!* (1980).	Died in Los Angeles, California, June 30, 2003, age 78.
Hackett, Joan	*Harnessing the Sun* (docudrama, 1980). Last feature film: *The Escape Artist* (1982).	Died in Encino, California, October 8, 1983, age 49.
Haden, Sara	*Andy Hardy Comes Home* (1958).	Died in Woodland Hills, California, September 15, 1981, age 81.
Hale, Alan (Jr.)	*Terror Night* (1987); *Back to the Beach* (1987).	Died in Los Angeles, California, January 2, 1990, age 71.
Hale, Alan (Sr.)	*Rogues of Sherwood Forest* (1950).	Died in Hollywood, California, January 22, 1950, age 57.
Haley, Jack	*Norwood* (1970). Last TV movie: *Rolling Man* (1971).	Died in Los Angeles, California, June 6, 1979, age 80. *Norwood* was produced and directed by son Jack Haley Jr.
Hall, Huntz	*Auntie Lee's Meat Pies* (1993). Last Bowery Boys/East Side Kids film: *In the Money* (1958).	Died in North Hollywood, California, January 30, 1999, age 79.
Hallahan, Charles	*Mind Rage* (2000). Last TV movie: *Things That Go Bump* (1996).	Died in Los Angeles, California, November 25, 1997, age 54.
Hamilton, Margaret	*The Anderson Tapes* (1971); *Journey Back to Oz* (voice, 1974). Last TV movie: *Letters from Frank* (1979).	Died in Salisbury, Connecticut, May 16, 1985, age 82.
Hamilton, Murray	*Whoops Apocalypse* (1986). Last TV movie: *The Last Days of Patton* (1986).	Died in Washington, North Carolina, September 1, 1986, age 63.
Hamilton, Neil	*Which Way to the Front?* (1970). Last TV movie: *Vanished* (1971). Last silent movies: *The Studio Murder Mystery* (1929); *Why Be Good?* (1929).	Died in Escondido, California, September 24, 1984, age 85.
Harding, Ann	*The Man in the Gray Flannel Suit* (1956); *I've Lived Before* (1956); *Strange Intruder* (1956). Last TV movie: *Young Man From Kentucky* (1957). Retired after making *Young Man From Kentucky*.	Died in Sherman Oaks, California, September 1, 1981, age 80.
Hardwicke, Sir Cedric	*The Pumpkin Eater* (1964).	Died in New York, New York, August 6, 1964, age 71.
Hardy, Oliver	*Utopia* (1951; a.k.a. *Atoll K*). *Utopia* was also the last film Laurel and Hardy appeared together. Last silent movie: *Angora Love* (1929).	Last public appearance of Laurel and Hardy: December 1, 1954, on Ralph Edwards' *This Is Your Life* TV program. Died in North Hollywood, California, August 7, 1957, age 65.
Harlow, Jean	*Saratoga* (1937). Last silent movies: *Bacon Grabbers* (1929); *Thundering Toupees* (1929);	Died in Los Angeles, California, June 7, 1937, age 26, during filming of *Saratoga*.

	Why is a Plum-ber? (1929); *Why Be Good?* (1929).	
Harrison, Sir Rex	*A Time to Die* (made 1979, released 1983). Last TV movies: *Heartbreak House* (1986); *Anastasia: The Mystery of Anna* (1986).	Died in New York, New York, June 2, 1990, age 82. Appeared on stage in *The Circle* (W. Somerset Maugham play) until a month before he died.
Hart, William S.	*Tumbleweeds* (also last silent movie, 1925).	Died in Newhall, California, June 24, 1946, age 81.
Hartman, Phil	*Small Soldiers* (1998). Voice of Captain Blasto in video game: *Blasto* (1998).	Died in Encino, California, May 28, 1998, age 49.
Harvey, Laurence	*Welcome to Arrow Beach* (director and actor, 1974).	Died London, England, November 25, 1973, age 45. He died before the film was released.
Hayakawa, Sessue	*The Daydreamer* (voice, 1966). Last silent movies: *The Great Prince Shan* (1924); *I Have Killed* (1924); *Sen Yan's Devotion* (1924); *The Danger Line* (1924).	Died in Tokyo, Japan, November 23, 1973, age 84.
Hayes, George ("Gabby")	*The Caribou Trail* (1950). Last film as Windy Halliday: *Renegade Trail* (1939). Last film as Gabby Whittaker: *Heldorado* (1946).	Died in Burbank, California, February 9, 1969, age 83.
Hayward, Louis	*Terror in the Wax Museum* (1973).	Died in Palm Springs, California, February 21, 1985, age 75.
Hayward, Susan	*The Revengers* (1972). Last TV movie: *Say Goodbye, Maggie Cole* (1972).	Died in Hollywood, California, March 14, 1975, age 56.
Hayworth, Rita	*The Wrath of God* (1972).	Died in New York, New York, May 14, 1987, age 68.
Heflin, Van	*Airport* (1970). Last TV movie: *The Last Child* (1971).	Died in Hollywood, California, July 23, 1971, age 60.
Henie, Sonja	*The Countess of Monte Cristo* (1948, as actress). *Hello London* (1958, as herself).	Died en route to Oslo, Norway, October 12, 1969, age 57.
Henreid, Paul	*The Exorcist II: The Heretic* (1977).	Died in Santa Monica, California, March 29, 1992, age 84.
Hepburn, Audrey	*Always* (1989). Last TV appearance: host of *Gardens of the World with Audrey Hepburn* (miniseries, 1993).	Died in Tolochenaz, Switzerland, January 20, 1993, age 63.
Hepburn, Katharine	*Love Affair* (1994). Last TV movie: *One Christmas* (1994). Last of nine films with Spencer Tracy: *Guess Who's Coming To Dinner* (1967).	Died in Old Saybrook, Connecticut, June 29, 2003, age 96.
Herbert, Hugh	*Gink at the Sink* (1952).	Died in North Hollywood, California, March 12, 1952, age 64.
Hersholt, Jean	*Run for Cover* (1955). Last Dr. Christian film: *Melody for Three*	Died in Hollywood, California, June 2, 1956, age 69.

	(1941). Last silent movies: *Modern Love* (1929); *The Younger Generation* (1929); *Girl on the Barge* (1929); *Abie's Irish Rose* (1929).	
Hickey, William	*Mouse Hunt* (1999).	Died in New York, New York, June 29, 1997, age 68.
Hodiak, John	*On the Threshold of Space* (1956).	Died in Los Angeles, California, October 19, 1955, age 41.
Holden, Fay	Last Andy Hardy film: *Andy Hardy Comes Home* (1958).	Died in Los Angeles, California, June 23, 1973, age 79.
Holden, William	*S.O.B.* (1981).	Died in Santa Monica, California, November 16, 1981, age 63.
Holliday, Judy	*Bells Are Ringing* (1960).	Died in New York, New York, June 7, 1965, age 42.
Holloway, Sterling	Last feature film: *Thunder and Lightning* (1977). Last animated film: *Tukiki and His Search for a Merry Christmas* (voice, 1979). Last TV movie: *Christmas at Walt Disney World* (voice, 1987).	Died in Los Angeles, California, November 22, 1992, age 87.
Holt, Jack	*Across the Wide Missouri* (1951).	Died in Los Angeles, California, January 18, 1951, age 62.
Holt, Tim	Last feature film: *This Stuff'll Kill Ya!* (1971). Last cowboy film: *Desert Passage* (1952).	Died in Shawnee, Oklahoma, February 15, 1973, age 55.
Homolka, Oscar	*The Tamarind Seed* (1974).	Died in Sussex, England, January 27, 1978, age 79.
Hope, Bob	Last starring feature: *Cancel My Reservation* (1972). Last film appearance: *Spies Like Us* (cameo, 1985). Last "Road" movie: *The Road to Hong Kong* (1962), the last of seven Road films.	Died in Toluca Lake, California, July 27, 2003, age 100.
Hopkins, Miriam	*The Savage Intruder* (a.k.a. *The Comeback*, 1968).	Died in New York, New York, October 9, 1972, age 69.
Horton, Edward Everett	*Cold Turkey* (1971).	Died in Encino, California, September 29, 1970, age 84.
Houseman, John	*The Naked Gun: From the Files of Police Squad!* (cameo; 1988); *Scrooged* (cameo; 1988).	Died in Malibu, California, October 31, 1988, age 86. Completed both films shortly before he died.
Howard, Leslie	*Spitfire* (a.k.a. *First of the Few*; director/actor, 1943). Narrated documentaries *The Gentle Sex* (1942); *War in the Mediterranean* (1943).	Killed in plane crash, en route from Portugal to London, England, June 1, 1943, age 50.
Howard, Trevor	*The Dawning* (1988).	Died in Hertfordshire, England, January 7, 1988, age 71.
Hudson, Rock	*The Ambassador* (1984). Last TV movie: *The Vegas Strip Wars* (1984).	Died in Los Angeles, California, October 2, 1985, age 59.

Hull, Josephine	*The Lady From Texas* (1951).	Died in New York, New York, March 12, 1957, age 71.
Hunnicutt, Arthur	*Winterhawk* (1975). Last TV movie: *The Daughters of Joshua Cabe Return* (1975).	Died in Woodland Hills, California, September 26, 1979, age 68.
Hunter, Jeffrey	*Viva America!* (a.k.a. *Cry Chicago;* 1969).	Died in Los Angeles, California, May 27, 1969, age 42.
Huston, John	*Momo* (1986). Last TV movie: *Mister Corbett's Ghost* (1987).	Died in Middletown, Rhode Island, August 28, 1987, age 81. At the time of his death, he was planning to film *Mr. North.*
Huston, Walter	*The Furies* (1950).	Died in Beverly Hills, California, April 7, 1950, age 66.
Hutton, Jim	*Psychic Killer* (1975).	Died in Los Angeles, California, June 2, 1979, age 45.
Hyde-White, Wilfrid	*Fanny Hill* (1983).	Died in Woodland Hills, California, May 6, 1991, age 87.
Ingram, Rex	*Journey to Shiloh* (1968). Last TV appearance: *The Bill Cosby Show,* "A Christmas Ballad" (1969).	Died in Hollywood, California, September 19, 1969, age 73.
Ireland, John	*Waxworks II: Lost in Time* (1992).	Died in Santa Barbara, California, March 21, 1992, age 78.
Ives, Burl	*Two Moon Junction* (1988).	Died in Anacortes, Washington, April 14, 1995, age 85.
Jaeckel, Richard	*Martial Outlaw* (1993).	Died in Woodland Hills, California, June 14, 1997, age 70.
Jaffe, Sam	*Rio abajo* (a.k.a. *On the Line,* 1984).	Died in Beverly Hills, California, March 24, 1984, age 93.
Jagger, Dean	*Evil Town* (1987).	Died in Santa Monica, California, February 5, 1991, age 87.
Janssen, David	*Inchon* (1981). Last TV movie: *City in Fear* (1980).	Died in Malibu, California, February 13, 1980, age 49, shortly after completing *City in Fear.*
Jenkins, Allen	*The Front Page* (1974).	Died in Santa Monica, California, July 20, 1974, age 74.
Johnson, Ben	*The Evening Star* (1996). Last TV movie: *Ruby Jean and Joe* (1996).	Died in Mesa, Arizona, April 8, 1996, age 77, before *The Evening Star* was released.
Jones, Buck	*Dawn on the Great Divide* (1942). Last silent movies: *The Big Hop* (1928); *The Branded Sombrero* (1928).	Film was released shortly after he died of burns November 30, 1942, age 47, after the Coconut Grove (night club) fire, Boston, Massachusetts.
Jones, Henry	*Arachnophobia* (1990).	Died in Los Angeles, California, May 17, 1999, age 86.
Jory, Victor	*The Mountain Men* (1980). Last TV movie: *Power* (1980).	Died in Santa Monica, California, February 12, 1982, age 79.
Joslyn, Allyn	*The Brothers O'Toole* (1973).	Died in Los Angeles, California, January 21, 1981, age 79.

Julia, Raul	*Street Fighter* (1994).	Died in Manhasset, New York, October 24, 1994, age 54, a few days before *Street Fighter* was finished, and while *Down Came a Blackbird* was in production.
Kahn, Madeline	*Judy Berlin* (1999).	Died in New York, New York, December 3, 1999, age 57, before the film was released.
Karloff, Boris	*Targets* (1969). Four Mexican films (1968) also among his last movies: *The Crimson Cult, The Fear Chamber, Dance of Death* and *The Sinister Invasion.* All his scenes were filmed at one time in California and spliced into the movies. Among last silent movies: *King of the Kongo* (1929, released as silent film, later with sound); *The Phantom of the North* (1929).	Died in Midhurst, Sussex, England, February 2, 1969, age 81.
Kasznar, Kurt	*The Ambushers* (1967). Last TV movie: *Suddenly Love* (1978).	Died in Santa Monica, California, August 6, 1979, age 65.
Kaye, Danny	*The Madwoman of Chaillot* (1969). Last TV movie: *Skokie* (1981).	Died in Los Angeles, California, March 3, 1987, age 74.
Keaton, Buster	*A Funny Thing Happened on the Way to the Forum* (1966); *War Italian Style* (1967). Last silent movie: *Spite Marriage* (1929).	Died in Woodland Hills, California, February 1, 1966, age 70.
Kellaway, Cecil	*Getting Straight* (1970). Last TV appearance: *Wacky Zoo of Morgan City* (1972).	Died in Hollywood, California, February 28, 1973, age 79.
Kelly, Gene	Last feature film: *Xanadu* (1980). Last TV work: *North and South* (miniseries, 1985); *Sins* (1985). Last screen appearance: *That's Entertainment III* (host, 1994).	Died in Los Angeles, California, February 2, 1996, age 83.
Kelly, Grace (Princess Grace of Monaco)	*High Society* (1956); *The Swan* (1956). Narrated *The Children of Theatre Street* (1977; documentary).	Died after automobile accident in Monaco, September 14, 1982, age 52.
Kelly, Patsy	*The North Avenue Irregulars* (1979).	Died in Woodland Hills, California, September 24, 1981, age 71.
Kelton, Pert	*The Comic* (1969).	Died in Ridgewood, New Jersey, October 30, 1968, age 61.
Kennedy, Arthur	*Grandpa* (1990).	Died in Branford, Connecticut, January 5, 1990, age 75.
Kennedy, Edgar	*My Dream is Yours* (1949).	Died in Woodland Hills, California, November 9, 1948, age 58.

Kibbee, Guy	*Three Godfathers* (1948).	Retired after making film. Died in East Islip, Long Island, New York, May 24, 1956, age 74.
Kilbride, Percy	*Ma and Pa Kettle at Waikiki* (1955).	Died in Los Angeles, California, December 11, 1954, age 76.
Kiley, Richard	*Patch Adams* (1998); *Blue Moon* (1999).	Died in Warwick, New York, March 5, 1999, age 76.
Kinsky, Klaus	*Paganini* (1989).	Died in Lagunitas, California, November 23, 1991, age 65.
Kovacs, Ernie	*Five Golden Hours* (1961).	Died in Los Angeles, California, January 13, 1962, age 42.
Kruger, Otto	*Sex and the Single Girl* (1964).	Died in Los Angeles, California, September 6, 1974, age 89.
Ladd, Alan	*The Carpetbaggers* (1964).	Died in Palm Springs, California, January 29, 1964, age 50.
Lahr, Bert	*The Night They Raided Minsky's* (1968).	Died in New York, New York, December 4, 1967, age 72, before production completed.
Lake, Arthur	*16 Fathoms Deep* (1948). Last Blondie movie: *Beware of Blondie* (1950).	Died in Indian Wells, California, January 9, 1987, age 81.
Lake, Veronica	*Flesh Feast* (1970).	Died in Burlington, Vermont, July 7, 1973, age 54.
Lamarr, Hedy	*The Female Animal* (1957).	Died in Orlando, Florida, January 19, 2000, age 86.
Lamas, Fernando	*The Cheap Detective* (1978) Last TV movie: *The Dream Merchants* (1980)	Died in Los Angeles, California, October 8, 1982, age 67.
Lamour, Dorothy	*Creepshow 2* (1987).	Died in Los Angeles, California, September 22, 1996, age 81.
Lancaster, Burt	*Field of Dreams* (1989). Last TV movie: *Separate But Equal* (1991).	Died in Century City, California, October 20, 1994, age 80.
Lanchester, Elsa	*Die Laughing* (1980).	Died in Woodland Hills, California, December 26, 1986, age 84.
Landis, Carole	*Brass Monkey* (1948); *Noose* (1948).	Died in Brentwood, California, July 5, 1948, age 29.
Landis, Jessie Royce	*Airport* (1970). Last TV movie: *Ceremony of Innocence* (1972).	Died in Danbury, Connecticut, February 2, 1972, age 67.
Laughton, Charles	*Advise and Consent* (1962).	Died in Hollywood California, December 15, 1962, age 63. The last and only film he directed was *The Night of the Hunter* (1955).
Laurel, Stan	*Utopia* (1951; a.k.a. *Atoll K*); also the last film Laurel and Hardy appeared together. Last silent movie: *Angora Love* (1929).	Last public appearance of Laurel and Hardy: December 1, 1954, on Ralph Edwards' *This Is Your Life* TV program. Laurel died in Santa Monica, California, February 23, 1965, age 74.
Lawford, Peter	*Where is Parsifal?* (1983).	Died in Los Angeles, California, December 24, 1984, age 61.

Lee, Brandon	*The Crow* (1993).	Killed in accidental shooting on set during filming in Wilmington, North Carolina, March 31, 1993, age 27.
Lee, Bruce	*Enter the Dragon* (1973); *Return of the Dragon* (1973); *The Chinese Connection* (1973).	Died in Hong Kong, July 20, 1973, age 32.
Lee, Canada	*Cry the Beloved Country* (1951).	Died in New York, New York, May 9, 1952, age 45.
Leigh, Janet	*A Fate Totally Worse Than Death* (2000).	Died in Beverly Hills, California, October 3, 2004, age 77.
Leigh, Vivien	Last starring role: *The Roman Spring of Mrs. Stone* (1962). Small role in *Ship of Fools* (1965).	Died in London, England, July 8, 1967, age 53.
Lemmon, Jack	*The Legend of Bagger Vance* (narrator, 2000). Last TV movie: *Tuesdays with Morrie* (1999).	Died in Los Angeles, California, June 27, 2001, age 76.
Leonard, Sheldon	*The Brinks Job* (1978).	Died in Beverly Hills, California, January 10, 1997, age 89.
Levant, Oscar	*The Cobweb* (1955).	Died in Beverly Hills, California, August 14, 1972, age 65.
Lindsay, Margaret	*Tammy and the Doctor* (1963).	Died in Los Angeles, California, May 9, 1981, age 70.
Little, Cleavon	*Goin' to Chicago* (1991). Last TV movie: *In the Nick of Time* (1991).	Died in Sherman Oaks, California, October 22, 1992, age 53.
Lloyd, Harold	*The Sin of Harold Diddlebock* (a.k.a. *Mad Wednesday;* 1947). Last silent film: *Speedy* (1928).	Died in Los Angeles, California, March 8, 1971, age 77.
Lockhart, Gene	*Jeanne Eagles* (1957).	Died in Santa Monica, California, March 31, 1957, age 65.
Lombard, Carole	*To Be or Not to Be* (1942).	Died in plane crash near Las Vegas, Nevada, January 16, 1942, age 33, before film was released.
Loo, Richard	*The Man with the Golden Gun* (1974).	Died in Burbank, California, November 20, 1983, age 80.
Lorne, Marion	*The Graduate* (1967).	Died in New York, New York, May 9, 1968, age 79.
Lorre, Peter	*The Patsy* (1964).	Died in Los Angeles, California, March 23, 1964, age 59.
Lovejoy, Frank	*Cole Younger, Gunfighter* (1958).	Died in New York, New York, October 2, 1962, age 48.
Lowe, Edmund	*Heller in Pink Tights* (1960).	Died in Woodland Hills, California, April 21, 1971, age 79.
Loy, Myrna	*Just Tell Me What You Want* (1980). Last TV movie: *Summer Solstice* (1981). Last Thin Man movie: *Song of the Thin Man* (1947).	Died in New York, New York, December 14, 1993, age 88.
Lugosi, Bela	*Plan 9 from Outer Space* (1956, released 1959). Last silent movie:	Died in Los Angeles, California, August 16, 1956, age 73, during

	The Veiled Woman (1928, no known surviving copies).	filming of *Plan 9 from Outer Space*. A stand-in completed his scenes.
Luke, Keye	*Alice* (1990); *Gremlins 2: The New Batch* (1990).	Died in Whittier, California, January 12, 1991, age 87.
Lundigan, William	*Where Angels Go, Trouble Follows* (1968).	Died in Los Angeles, California, December 20, 1975, age 61.
Lupino, Ida	*My Boys Are Good Boys* (1978).	Died in Los Angeles, California, August 3, 1995, age 77.
Lynde, Paul	*The Villain* (1979).	Died in Beverly Hills, California, January 10, 1982, age 55.
Lynn, Diana	*You're Never Too Young* (1955). Last TV movie: *Company of Killers* (a.k.a. *The Hit Team* 1970).	Died in Los Angeles, California, December 18, 1971, age 45.
MacDonald, Jeanette	*The Sun Comes Up* (1949). Last of eight films with Nelson Eddy: *I Married an Angel* (1942).	Died in Houston, Texas, January 14, 1965, age 63.
MacLane, Barton	*Arizona Bushwhackers* (1968).	Died in Santa Monica, California, January 1, 1969, age 67.
MacMahon, Aline	*I Could Go On Singing* (1963).	Died in New York, New York, October 12, 1991, age 92.
MacMurray Fred	*The Swarm* (1978). Last TV movie: *Beyond the Bermuda Triangle* (1975).	Died in Santa Monica, California, November 5, 1991, age 83.
MacRae, Gordon	*The Pilot* (a.k.a. *Danger in the Skies,* 1979).	Died in Lincoln, Nebraska, January 24, 1986, age 64.
Macready, George	*The Return of Count Yorga* (1971).	Died in Santa Monica, California, July 2, 1973, age 63.
Magnani, Anna	*Fellini's Roma* (as herself, 1972).	Died in Rome, Italy, September 26, 1973, age 65.
Main, Marjorie	*The Kettles on Old MacDonald's Farm* (1957). Last non-Kettle film: *Friendly Persuasion* (1956).	Died in Los Angeles, California, April 10, 1975, age 85.
Mansfield, Jayne	*Single Room Furnished* (1968).	Killed in highway accident near New Orleans, Louisiana, June 29, 1967, age 34. Film released after her death.
March, Fredric	*The Iceman Cometh* (1973).	Died in Los Angeles, California, April 14, 1975, age 77.
Marchand, Nancy	*Dear God* (1996). Last TV work: *The Sopranos* (1999-2000).	Died in Stratford, Connecticut, June 18, 2000, age 71.
Marley, John	*On the Edge* (1985). Last TV movie: *The Glitter Dome* (1984).	Died in Los Angeles, California, May 22, 1984, age 77.
Marlowe, Hugh	*The Last Shot You Hear* (1969).	Died in New York, New York, May 2, 1982, age 71.
Marshall, E.G.	*Absolute Power* (1997). Last TV movie: *The Defenders: Choice of Evils* (1998).	Died in Mount Kisco, New York, August 24, 1998, age 84.
Marshall, Herbert	*The Third Day* (1965).	Died in Beverly Hills, California, January 22, 1966, age 75.

Martin, Dean	*Cannonball Run II* (1984). Last Matt Helm film: *The Wrecking Crew* (1968). Last of 16 movies with Jerry Lewis: *Hollywood or Bust* (1956).	Died in Beverly Hills, California, December 25, 1995, age 78.
Martin, Strother	*Hotwire* (1980).	Died in Thousand Oaks, California, August 1, 1980, age 61.
Marvin, Lee	*Delta Force* (1986); *The Dirty Dozen: The Next Mission* (1985).	Died in Tucson, Arizona, August 29, 1987, age 63.
Marx, Chico	Last films with Marx Brothers: *Love Happy* (1950); *The Story of Mankind* (1957). Three Marx Brothers appeared in *The Story of Mankind,* but not together.	Last appearance as Marx Brother, *GE Theater:* "The Incredible Jewel Robbery" (TV, March 8, 1959) with Harpo and Groucho. Died in Hollywood, California, October 11, 1961, age 75.
Marx, Groucho	*Skidoo* (1968). Last films with Marx Brothers: *Love Happy* (1950). *The Story of Mankind* (1957). Three Marx Brothers appeared in *The Story of Mankind,* but not together.	Last appearance as Marx Brother, *GE Theater:* "The Incredible Jewel Robbery" (TV, March 8, 1959) with Harpo and Chico. Last public appearance with a Marx Brother: January 16, 1977, Wiltshire Hyatt House Hotel, Hollywood, when he and Zeppo appeared at the Marx Brothers Motion Picture Hall of Fame induction ceremonies. Died in Los Angeles, California, August 19, 1977, age 86.
Marx, Harpo	Last films with Marx Brothers: *Love Happy* (1950). *The Story of Mankind* (1957). Three Marx Brothers appeared in *The Story of Mankind,* but not together.	Last appearance as Marx Brother, *GE Theater:* "The Incredible Jewel Robbery" (TV, March 8, 1959) with Groucho and Chico. Died in Los Angeles, California, September 28, 1964, age 75.
Marx, Zeppo	*Duck Soup* (1933).	Last surviving Marx brother. Last public appearance with Marx Brother: January 16, 1977, Wiltshire Hyatt House Hotel Hollywood, when he and Groucho appeared at the Marx Brothers Motion Picture Hall of Fame induction ceremonies. Died in Palm Springs, California, November 30, 1979, age 78.
Masina, Giulietta	*A Day to Remember* (1991).	Died in Rome, Italy, March 23, 1994, age 73.
Mason, James	*The Shooting Party* (1984); *The Assisi Underground* (1985).	Died in Lausanne, Switzerland, July 27, 1984, age 75, just before *The Shooting Party* was released.
Massey, Ilona	*Jet Over the Atlantic* (1959).	Died in Bethesda, Maryland, August 20, 1974, age 62.
Massey, Raymond	*MacKenna's Gold* (1969).	Died in Los Angeles, California, July 29, 1983, age 86.

Mastroianni, Marcello	*Voyage to the Beginning of the World* (1997).	Died in Paris, France, December 19, 1996, age 72, soon after finishing the film.
Matthau, Walter	*Hanging Up* (2000).	Died in Santa Monica, California, July 1, 2000, age 79.
Mature, Victor	*Firepower* (1979). Last TV movie: *Samson and Delilah* (1984).	Died in Rancho Santa Fe, California, August 4, 1999, age 86.
Maxwell, Marilyn	*From Nashville with Music* (1969). Last TV movie: *Wild Women* (1970).	Died in Los Angeles, California, March 20, 1972, age 49.
Maynard, Ken	*The Marshal of Windy Hollow* 1972). Last silent movie: *California Mail* (1929).	Died in Woodland Hills, California, March 23, 1973, age 77.
McClure, Doug	*Riders in the Storm* (1995).	Died in Sherman Oaks, California, February 5, 1995, age 59.
McCoy, Tim	*Requiem for a Gunfighter* (1965). Last of the Rough Rider films: *Law of the West* (1941).	Died in Nogales, Arizona, January 29, 1978, age 86.
McCrea, Joel	*Mustang Country* (1976).	Died in Woodland Hills, California, October 20, 1990, age 84.
McDaniel, Hattie	*The Big Wheel* (1949).	Last TV appearance: lead role in a few episodes of the sitcom *Beulah* (1952), then became ill. Died in San Fernando Valley, California, October 26, 1952, age 57.
McDonald, Marie	*Promises! Promises!* (1963).	Died in Calabasas, California, October 21, 1965, age 42.
McDowall, Roddy	*Something to Believe In* (1998); *Keepers of the Frame* (documentary, as himself; 1999).	Last professional performances: Ebenezer Scrooge in *A Christmas Carol* in New York, New York (1997); PlayStation game, *A Bug's Life* (voice, 1998). Died in Los Angles, California, October 3, 1998, age 70.
McFarland, George ("Spanky")	*The Aurora Encounter* (1985).	Died in Grapevine, Texas, June 30, 1993, age 64.
McGiver, John	*The Apple Dumpling Gang* (1975). Last TV movie: *Twas the Night Before Christmas* (voice; 1974).	Died in West Fulton, New York, September 11, 1975, age 62.
McGuire, Dorothy	*Summer Heat* (narrator; 1987). Last TV movie: *The Last Best Year* (1990).	Died in Santa Monica, California, September 13, 2001, age 83.
McHugh, Frank	*Easy Come, Easy Go* (1967).	Died in Greenwich, Connecticut, September 11, 1981, age 83.
McLaglen, Victor	*Sea Fury* (1958).	Died in Newport Beach, California, November 7, 1959, age 72.
McMillan, Kenneth	*Three Fugitives* (1989).	Died in Santa Monica, California, January 8, 1989, age 56.

McNear, Howard	*The Fortune Cookie* (1966).	Died in Hollywood, California, January 3, 1969, age 63.
McQueen, Butterfly	*The Mosquito Coast* (1988).	Died in Augusta, Georgia, December 22, 1995, age 84.
McQueen, Steve	*The Hunter* (1980).	Died in Juarez, Mexico, November 7, 1980, age 50.
Medford, Kay	*Windows* (1980).	Died in New York, New York, April 10, 1980, age 59.
Meek, Donald	*Magic Town* (1947).	Died in Los Angeles, California, November 18, 1946, age 68. Film released after his death.
Meeker, Ralph	*Without Warning* (1980).	Died in Woodland Hills, California, August 5, 1988, age 67.
Menjou, Adolphe	*Pollyanna* (1960).	Died in Beverly Hills, California, October 29, 1963, age 73.
Meredith, Burgess	*Grumpier Old Men* (1995). Voice in video game *Ripper* (1996).	Died in Malibu, California, September 9, 1997, age 88.
Merkel, Una	*Spinout* (1966).	Died in Los Angeles, California, January 2, 1986, age 82.
Middleton, Charles	*The Last Bandit* (1949).	Died in Los Angeles, California, April 22, 1949, age 69.
Mifune, Toshiro	*Deep River* (1995); *Picture Bride* (1995).	Died in Tokyo, Japan, December 24, 1997, age 77.
Milland, Ray	*The Sea Serpent* (1984); *Masks of Death* (1984).	Died in Torrance, California, March 10, 1986, age 81.
Miller, Ann	Last big MGM musical: *Hit the Deck* (1955). Last dramatic role: *Mulholland Drive* (2001).	Died in Los Angeles, California, January 22, 2004, age 81.
Mineo, Sal	*Sonic Boom* (1974); *Hunters* (1974). Last TV movie: *Columbo: A Case of Immunity* (1975).	Killed outside his Hollywood, California, apartment after returning from rehearsal of play *P.S. Your Cat is Dead*, February 12, 1976, age 37.
Miranda, Carmen	*Scared Stiff* (1953).	Heart attack while taping *Jimmy Durante Show*; died in Beverly Hills, California, the following day, August 5, 1955, age 46.
Mitchell, Cameron	*Jack-O* (1995).	Died in Pacific Palisades, California July 6, 1994, age 75.
Mitchell, Thomas	*Pocketful of Miracles* (1961).	Died in Beverly Hills, California, December 17, 1962, age 70.
Mitchum, Robert	*James Dean, Race with Destiny* (1997); *Dead Men* (1996).	Died in Santa Barbara, California, July 1, 1997, age 79. Granddaughter Carrie Mitchum co-starred in *James Dean, Race with Destiny*.
Mix, Tom	*Rustler's Roundup* (1933). Last serial: *The Miracle Rider* (1935). Last silent movies: *The Big Diamond* (1929); *The Drifter*, (1929); *Outlawed* (1929).	Died near Florence, Arizona, October 12, 1940, age 60.

Mohr, Gerald	*Funny Girl* (1968).	Died in Stockholm, Sweden, November 10, 1968, age 54, while producing a TV series.
Monroe, Marilyn	*The Misfits* (1961).	Last day at Fox and last public appearance: June 1, 1962. Last photo shoot: July 6, 1962, with *Life* magazine photographer, Allan Grant. Last magazine cover while alive: *Life* magazine August 3, 1962. Died in Los Angeles, California, August 5, 1962, age 36, while working on the film *Something's Got to Give*.
Montand, Yves	*IP5, L'ile aux pachydermes* (1992).	Died in Senlis, France, during filming, November 9, 1991, age 70.
Montez, Maria	*Camorra* (a.k.a. *Schatten über Neapal*, 1951).	Died in Paris, France, September 7, 1951, age 34.
Montgomery, Robert	*Your Witness* (a.k.a. *Eye Witness*, 1950).	Died in New York, New York, September 27, 1981, age 77.
Moore, Clayton	*Missile Monsters* (1958). Last Lone Ranger film: *The Lone Ranger and the Lost City of Gold* (1958). Last serial: *Son of Geronimo* (1952). Many of his earlier western serials were repackaged and shown on TV in the 1960s under different names.	Died in Los Angeles, California, December 28, 1999, age 85.
Moore, Dudley	*The Mighty Kong* (voice, 1998).	Died in Plainfield, New Jersey, March 27, 2002, age 66.
Moore, Victor	*The Seven Year Itch* (1955).	Died in East Islip, Long Island, New York, July 23, 1962, age 86.
Moorehead, Agnes	*Dear Dead Delilah* (1972); *Charlotte's Web* (voice, 1973). Last TV movie: *Frankenstein: The True Story* (1972).	Died in Rochester, Minnesota, April 30, 1974, age 67.
More, Kenneth	*The Unidentified Flying Oddball* (1979); *A Tale of Two Cities* (1980).	Died in London, England, July 12, 1982, age 67.
Moreland, Mantan	*The Young Nurses* (1973).	Died in Los Angeles, California, September 28, 1973, age 71.
Morgan, Dennis	*Won Ton Ton, the Dog Who Saved Hollywood* (1976).	Died in Fresno, California, September 7, 1994, age 83.
Morgan, Frank	*Key to the City* (1950).	Died in Beverly Hills, California, September 18, 1949, age 58, while working on film version of *Annie Get Your Gun*.
Morley, Robert	*Istanbul* (1989).	Died in Reading, England, June 3, 1992, age 84.
Morris, Chester	*The Great White Hope* (1970). Last Boston Blackie movie:	Died in New Hope, Pennsylvania, September 11, 1970, age 69, while

	Boston Blackie's Chinese Venture (1949).	appearing in stage production of *Caine Mutiny Court Martial.*
Morris, Wayne	*Buffalo Gun* (1961).	Died in Los Angeles, California, September 14, 1959, age 45.
Morrow, Vic	*Twilight Zone: the Movie* (1983).	Killed in a helicopter crash at Indian Dunes, California, during the filming, July 23, 1982, age 50.
Moss, Arnold	*Gambit* (1966).	Died in New York, New York, December 15, 1989, age 79.
Mostel, Zero	*Watership Down* (voice, 1978); *Best Boy* (documentary, 1979). Last feature film: *The Front* (1976).	Died in Philadelphia, Pennsylvania, September 8, 1977, age 62.
Mowbray, Alan	*A Majority of One* (1956).	Died in Hollywood, California, March 25, 1969, age 72.
Mulhare, Edward	*Out to Sea* (1997). Last TV movie: *Hart to Hart: Secrets of the Hart* (1995).	Died in Los Angeles, California, May 24, 1997, age 74.
Mulligan, Richard	*Guess Who's Coming for Christmas?* (1990).	Died in Los Angeles, California, September 26, 2000, age 67.
Muni, Paul	*The Last Angry Man* (1959).	Died in Montecito, California, August 25, 1967, age 71.
Munson, Ona	*The Red House* (1947).	Died in New York, New York, February 11, 1955, age 48.
Murphy, Audie	*A Time for Dying* (1971).	Died in plane crash near Roanoke, Virginia, shortly after completing film, May 28, 1971, age 46.
Murphy, George	*Talk About a Stranger* (1952); *It's a Big Country* (1952); *Walk East on Beacon* (1952).	Retired from acting in 1952, became producer, later U.S. Senator. Died in Palm Beach, Florida, May 3, 1992, age 89.
Mustin, Burt	*Train Ride to Hollywood* (a.k.a. *Night Train,* 1978).	Died in Glendale, California, January 28, 1977, age 94.
Nagel, Conrad	*The Man Who Understood Women* (1959); *A Stranger in My Arms* (1959).	Died in New York, New York, February 24, 1970, age 72.
Naish, J. Carroll	*Dracula vs. Frankenstein* (1971).	Died in La Jolla, California, January 24, 1973, age 73.
Natwick, Mildred	*Dangerous Liaisons* (1988).	Died in New York, New York, October 25, 1994, age 86.
Nesbitt, Cathleen	*Never, Never Land* (1980).	Died in London, England, August 2, 1982, age 93.
Newton, Robert	*Around the World in Eighty Days* (1956).	Died in Los Angeles, California, March 25, 1956, age 51.
Niven, David	*Curse of the Pink Panther* (1983).	Died in Switzerland, July 29, 1983, age 74.
Nolan, Jeanette	*The Horse Whisperer* (1998).	Died in Los Angeles, California, June 5, 1998, age 86.
Nolan, Lloyd	*Hannah and Her Sisters* (1986).	Died in Los Angeles, California, September 27, 1985, age 83.

Novello, Jay	*The Domino Principle* (1977).	Died in North Hollywood, California, September 7, 1982, age 78.
Oakie, Jack	*Lover Come Back* (1961).	Died in Los Angeles, California, January 23, 1978, age 74.
Oates, Warren	*Blue Thunder* (1983). Last TV movie: *The Blue and the Gray* (miniseries, 1982).	Died in Hollywood Hills, California, April 3, 1982, age 53.
Oberon, Merle	*Interval* (1973).	Died in Los Angeles, California, November 23, 1979, age 68.
O'Brien, Edmond	*Lucky Luciano* (1973).	Died in Inglewood, California, May 9, 1985, age 69.
O'Brien, George	*Cheyenne Autumn* (1964).	Died in Tulsa, Oklahoma, September 23, 1985, age 85.
O'Brien, Pat	*Ragtime* (1981).	Died in Santa Monica, California, October 15, 1983, age 83.
O'Connell, Arthur	*The Hiding Place* (1975). Last TV movie: *Shootout in a One-Dog Town* (1974).	Died in Hollywood, California, May 18, 1981, age 73.
O'Connor, Carroll	*Return to Me* (2000). Last TV movie: *36 Hours to Die* (1999).	Died in Culver City, California, June 21, 2001, age 75.
O'Connor, Donald	*Out to Sea* (1997). Last "Francis" movie: *Francis in the Navy* (fifth in series, 1955).	Died in Calabasas, California, September 27, 2003, age 78.
O'Keefe, Dennis	*The Naked Flame* (1968).	Died in Santa Monica, California, August 31, 1968, age 60.
Oland, Warner	*Charlie Chan at Monte Carlo* (1937).	Died in Stockholm, Sweden, August 5, 1938, age 57.
Oliver, Edna May	*Lydia* (1941).	Died in Los Angeles, California, November 9, 1942, age 59.
Olivier, (Lord) Laurence	*War Requiem* (TV, narrator, 1988).	Died in Steyning, Sussex, England, July 11, 1989, age 82.
O'Malley, J. Pat	*Cheaper to Keep Her* (1980).	Died in San Juan Capistrano, California, February 27, 1985, age 80.
O'Sullivan, Maureen	*Good Ole Boy: A Delta Boyhood* (1988). Last Tarzan movie: *Tarzan's New York Adventure* (1942).	Died in Scottsboro, Arizona, June 23, 1998, age 87.
Ouspenskaya, Maria	*A Kiss in the Dark* (1949).	Died in Los Angeles, California, December 3, 1949, age 73.
Owen, Reginald	*Bedknobs and Broomsticks* (1971).	Died in Boise, Idaho, November 5, 1972, age 85.
Page, Geraldine	*My Little Girl* (1987). Last TV movie: *Nazi Hunter: The Beate Klarsfeld Story* (1986).	Died in New York, New York, June 13, 1987, age 62.
Pallette, Eugene	*Silver River* (1948).	Died in Los Angeles, California, September 3, 1954, age 65.
Palmer, Lilli	*The Holcroft Covenant* (1985). Last TV movie: *Peter the Great* (miniseries, 1986).	Died in Los Angeles, California, January 27, 1986, age 71.

Pangborn, Franklin	*The Story of Mankind* (1957).	Died in Santa Monica, California, July 20, 1958, age 65.
Parks, Larry	*Freud* (1962).	Died in Studio City, California, April 13, 1975, age 60.
Patrick, Gail	*The Inside Story* (1948).	Died in Los Angeles, California, July 6, 1980, age 69.
Patrick, Lee	*The Black Bird* (1975).	Died in Laguna, California, November 21, 1982, age 70.
Payne, John	*They Ran For Their Lives* (1968).	Died in Malibu, California, December 6, 1989, age 77.
Pearce, Alice	*The Glass-Bottom Boat* (1966).	Died in Hollywood, California, March 3, 1966, age 48.
Peck, Gregory	*Cape Fear* (1991). Last TV movie: *Moby Dick* (1998).	Died in Los Angeles, California, June 12, 2003, age 87.
Peppard, George	*The Tigress* (1992). Last TV movie: *Night of the Fox* (1970).	Died in Los Angeles, California, May 8, 1994, age 65.
Perkins, Anthony	*A Demon in My View* (1992); *In the Deep Woods* (1992).	Died in Hollywood, California, September 12, 1992, age 60.
Phoenix, River	*The Thing Called Love* (1993); *Silent Tongue* (1994).	Was filming *Dark Blood* when he died in Hollywood, California, October 31, 1993, age 23. Was scheduled to make *Interview with the Vampire*.
Pickens, Slim	*Pink Motel* (1983).	Died in Modesto, California, December 8, 1983, age 64.
Pickford, Mary	*Secrets* (1933). Last silent movie: *My Best Girl* (1927).	Retired from film acting in 1933. Died in Santa Monica, California, May 29, 1979, age 86.
Pidgeon, Walter	*Sextette* (1978). Last of nine films with Greer Garson: *Scandal at Scourie* (1953).	Died in Santa Monica, California, September 25, 1984, age 87.
Pitts, ZaSu	*The Thrill of It All* (1963). Last silent movie: *Her Private Life* (1929).	Died in Hollywood, California, June 7, 1963, age 65, shortly after appearing on the TV drama *Burke's Law*.
Pleasence, Donald	*Fatal Frames* (1995). Last Halloween film: *Halloween 6: The Curse of Michael Myers* (1995).	Died in St. Paul de Vence, France, February 2, 1995, age 75.
Powell, Dick	*Susan Slept Here* (1954).	Died in Los Angeles, California, January 1, 1963, age 58, a day after appearing on *The Dick Powell Show* (dramatic anthology).
Powell, Eleanor	*Sensations of 1945* (final starring role; 1944); *The Duchess of Idaho* (guest star, 1950).	Died in Beverly Hills, California, February 11, 1982, age 69.
Powell, William	*Mister Roberts* (1955). Last silent movie: *The Four Feathers* (1929).	Died in Palm Springs, California, March 5, 1984, age 91.
Power, Tyrone	*Witness for the Prosecution* (1957); *The Sun Also Rises* (1957); *Abandon Ship* (1957).	Died in Spain, November 15, 1958, age 45, while filming *Solomon and Sheba*.

Presley, Elvis	*Change of Habit* (1969). Last TV: two documentaries: *Elvis: That's the Way It Is* (1970); *Elvis on Tour* (1972).	Died in Memphis, Tennessee, August 16, 1977, age 42. *See also* Music—Popular Performers.
Preston, Robert	*The Last Starfighter* (1984). Last TV movie: *Outrage!* (1986).	Died in Santa Barbara, California, March 21, 1987, age 68.
Price, Vincent	*Arabian Knight* (*The Thief and the Cobbler,* voice, 1995). Last feature movie: *Edward Scissorhands* (1990).	Died in Los Angeles, California, October 25, 1993, age 82.
Pyle, Denver	*Maverick* (1994).	Died in Burbank, California, December 25, 1997, age 77.
Quayle, Sir Anthony	*King of the Wind* (1989).	Died in London, England, October 20, 1989, age 76.
Quinn, Anthony	*Avenging Angelo* (2001). Last TV film: *The Road to Santiago* (1999).	Died in Boston, Massachusetts, June 3, 2001, age 86.
Raft, George	*The Man with Bogart's Face* (1980).	Died in Los Angeles, California, November 24, 1980, age 85.
Raines, Ella	*Man in the Road* (1957).	Died in Los Angeles, California, May 30, 1988, age 67.
Rains, Claude	*The Greatest Story Ever Told* (1965).	Died in Laconia, New Hampshire, May 30, 1967, age 77.
Ramsey, Anne	*Homer and Eddie* (1989).	Died in Los Angeles, California, August 11, 1988, age 58.
Randall, Tony	*Down with Love* (2003).	Died in New York, New York, May 17, 2004, age 84.
Randolph, Lillian	*The Onion Field* (1979). Last TV movie: *Roots* (miniseries; 1977).	Died in Arcadia, California, September 12, 1980, age 65.
Rathbone, Basil	*Autopsy of a Ghost* (1967); *Hillbillies in a Haunted House* (1967). Last Sherlock Holmes movie: *Dressed to Kill* (1946).	Died in New York, New York, July 21, 1967, age 75.
Ray, Aldo	*Shock 'Em Dead* (1991).	Died in Martinez, California, March 27, 1991, age 64.
Raye, Martha	*The Concorde–Airport 79* (1979). Last TV movie: *Alice in Wonderland* (1985).	Died in Los Angeles, California, October 19, 1994, age 78.
Reagan, Ronald	*The Killers* (1964). Last TV performance as actor: "Raid on the San Francisco Mint," special episode of *Death Valley Days* (1967).	Died in Los Angeles, California, June 5, 2004, age 93.
Redfield, William	*One Flew Over the Cuckoo's Nest* (1975).	Died in New York, New York, August 17, 1976, age 49.
Redgrave, Sir Michael	*Rime of the Ancient Mariner* (1976). Last TV movie: *Dr. Jekyll and Mr. Hyde* (1973).	Died in Buckinghamshire, England, March 21, 1985, age 77.
Reed, Donna	*Yellow-Headed Summer* (1974). Last TV movie: *Deadly Lessons* (1983).	Died in Beverly Hills, California, January 14, 1986, age 64.

Reed, Oliver	*Gladiator* (2000); *Orpheus and Eurydice* (narrator, 2000). Last TV movie: *Jeremiah* (1998).	Died in Valetta, Malta, during filming of *Gladiator*, May 2, 1999, age 61.
Reeve, Christopher	Last film before accident: Village of the Damned (1995). Last Superman film: *Superman IV: The Quest for Peace* (1987). Last completed film as director: *The Brooke Ellison Story* (TV; 2004).	Died in Mount Kisko, New York October 10, 2004, age 52. Reeve was injured in a horse riding accident in May 1995 that left him without the use of his arms and legs. He had to use a ventilator to breath.
Reeves, George	*Westward Ho, the Wagons!* (1956). Last Superman film: *Stamp Day for Superman* (1954).	Died in Los Angeles, California, June 16, 1959, age 45.
Reid, Kate	*Deceived* (1991).	Died in Stratford, Ontario, March 27, 1993, age 62.
Remick, Lee	*The Vision* (1987). Last TV movie: *Young Catherine* (1991).	Died in Los Angeles, California, July 2, 1991, age 55.
Renaldo, Duncan	Last Cisco Kid film: *The Girl from San Lorenzo* (1950).	Died in Santa Barbara, California, September 3, 1980, age 76.
Rennie, Michael	*The Young, the Evil and the Savage* (1968).	Died in Harrogate, England, June 10, 1971, age 62.
Revere, Anne	*Birch Interval* (1977).	Died in Locust Valley, New York, December 18, 1990, age 87.
Richardson, Sir Ralph	*Invitation to the Wedding* (1985); *Greystoke: The Legend of Tarzan: Lord of the Apes* (1984).	Died in London, England, October 10, 1983, age 80. *Greystoke,* re-leased after he died, led to his second Academy Award nomination.
Rin Tin Tin	*Rin Tin Tin, the Lightning Warrior* (1931).	Died in Los Angeles, California, August 10, 1932, age 14.
Ritter, Thelma	*What's So Bad About Feeling Good?* (1968).	Died in Queens, New York, February 5, 1969, age 63.
Robards, Jason (Jr.)	*Magnolia* (1999). Last TV movie: *Going Home* (2000).	Died in Bridgeport, Connecticut, December 26, 2000, age 78.
Robeson, Paul	*Song of the Rivers* (voice, 1954). Last acting role: *Tales of Manhattan* (1942).	Died in Philadelphia, Pennsylvania, January 23, 1976, age 77. (*See also* Music—Classical Performers.)
Robinson, Bill ("Bojangles")	*Stormy Weather* (1943). Last of four films with Shirley Temple: *Just Around the Corner* (1938).	Died in New York, New York, November 25, 1949, age 71.
Robinson, Edward G.	*Soylent Green* (1973). Last TV movie: *The Old Man Who Cried Wolf* (1970).	Died in Hollywood, California, January 26, 1973, age 79.
Robson, Dame Flora	*Clash of the Titans* (1981).	Died in Brighton, England, July 7, 1984, age 82.
Robson, May	*Joan of Paris* (1942).	Died in Beverly Hills, California, October 20, 1942, age 84.
Rogers, Charles ("Buddy")	*The Parson and the Outlaw* (1957).	Died in Rancho Mirage, California, April 21, 1999, age 94.

Rogers, Ginger	*Harlow* (1965). Last of ten films with Fred Astaire: *The Barkleys of Broadway* (1949).	Died in Rancho Mirago, California, April 25, 1995, age 83.
Rogers, Roy	*Mackintosh and T.J.* (1975); *Kenny Rogers as the Gambler: The Adventure Continues* (1983). Last Sons of the Pioneers movie: *Night Time in Nevada* (1948).	Died in Apple Valley, California, July 6, 1998, age 86.
Rogers, Will	*Steamboat 'Round the Bend* (1935); *In Old Kentucky* (1935).	Killed in a plane crash in Alaska, August 15, 1935, age 55. Both films released after he died.
Roland, Gilbert	*Barbarosa* (1982).	Died in Beverly Hills, California, May 15, 1994, age 88.
Rolle, Esther	*Train Ride* (2000). Last TV movie: *To Dance with the White Dog* (1993).	Died in Los Angeles, California, November 17, 1998, age 78.
Rollins, Howard E. (Jr.)	*Drunks* (1997). Last TV movie: *In the Heat of the Night: Who was Geli Bendi?* (1994).	Died in New York, New York, December 8, 1996, age 46.
Romero, Cesar	*Simple Justice* (1990); *Mortuary Academy* (1989).	Died in Santa Monica, California, January 1, 1994, age 86.
Ruggles, Charles	*Follow Me, Boys* (1966). Last TV movie: *Carousel* (1967).	Died in Los Angeles, California, December 23, 1970, age 84.
Rumann, Sig	*The Last of the Secret Agents* (1966).	Died in Julian, California, February 14, 1967, age 82.
Russell, Gail	*The Silent Call* (1961).	Died in Los Angeles, California, August 26, 1961, age 36.
Russell, Rosalind	*Mrs. Pollifax—Spy* (1971). Last TV movie: *The Crooked Hearts* (1972).	Died in Beverly Hills, California, November 28, 1976, age 69.
Rutherford, Dame Margaret	*Countess from Hong Kong* (1967). Last of four films starring Miss Marple: *Murder Ahoy* (1964). Last appearance as Miss Marple: *Alphabet Murders* (cameo, 1965).	Died in Buckinghamshire, England, May 22, 1972, age 80.
Ryan, Irene	*Don't Worry, We'll Think of a Title* (1966).	Died in Santa Monica, California, April 26, 1973, age 70, while appearing in stage production of *Pippin*.
Ryan, Robert	*Executive Action* (1973).	Died in New York, New York, July 11, 1973, age 63.
Sabu	*A Tiger Walks* (1964).	Died in Los Angeles, California, December 3, 1963, age 39.
Sakall, S.Z. ("Cuddles")	*The Student Prince* (1954).	Died in Los Angeles, California, February 12, 1955, age 71.
Salmi, Albert	*Breaking In* (1989). Last TV movie: *Till We Meet Again* (miniseries; 1989).	Died in Spokane, Washington, April 23, 1990, age 62.
Sampson, Will	*Poltergeist II* (1986); *Firewalker* (1986). Last TV movie: *Roanoak* (1986).	Died in Houston, Texas, June 3, 1987, age 51.

Sanders, George	*Psychomania* (1973). Last Saint (Simon Templar) movie: *The Saint in Palm Springs* (1941). Last Falcon movie: *The Falcon's Brother* (1942).	Died in Barcelona, Spain, April 25, 1972, age 65.
Sargent, Dick	*Frame Up* (1991). Last TV movie: *Acting on Impulse* (1993).	Died in Los Angeles California, July 8, 1994, age 64.
Schildkraut, Joseph	*The Greatest Story Ever Told* (1965).	Died in New York, New York, January 21, 1964, age 68.
Scott, George C.	*Angus* (1995). Last TV movie: *Inherit the Wind* (1999).	Died in Westlake Village, California, September 22, 1999, age 71.
Scott, Randolph	*Ride the High Country* (1962).	Died in Los Angeles, California, March 2, 1987, age 89.
Scott, Zachary	*It's Only Money* (1962).	Died in Austin, Texas, October 3, 1965, age 51.
Seberg, Jean	*The Wild Duck* (1976).	Died in Paris, France, September 8, 1979, age 40.
Sellers, Peter	*The Fiendish Plot of Dr. Fu Manchu* (1980).	Died in London, England, July 24, 1980, age 54. *Trail of the Pink Panther* (1982), sixth in the Pink Panther series, was released after his death.
Shaw, Robert	*Avalanche Express* (1979); *Force Ten from Navarone* (1978).	Died in County Mayo, Ireland, August 28, 1978, age 5 1, before *Avalanche Express* sound track was completed.
Shearer, Norma	*Her Cardboard Lover* (1942). Last silent film: *Lady of Chance* (1928).	Died in Woodland Hills, California, June 12, 1983, age 82.
Sheridan, Ann	*The Woman and the Hunter* (1957).	Died in San Fernando, California, January 21, 1967, age 51.
Shields, Arthur	*The Pigeon That Took Rome* (1962).	Died in Santa Barbara, California, April 27, 1970, age 74.
Shirley, Anne	*Murder, My Sweet* (1944).	Died in Los Angeles, California, July 4, 1993, age 75.
Sidney, Sylvia	*Mars Attacks* (1996); *Fantasy Island* (1998).	Died in New York, New York, July 1, 1999, age 88.
Silvera, Frank	*Valdez is Coming* (1971). Last TV movie: *Perilous Voyage* (1976).	Died in Pasadena, California, June 11, 1970, age 56.
Silverheels, Jay	*The Man Who Loved Cat Dancing* (1973).	Died in Woodland Hills, California, March 5, 1980, age 67.
Silvers, Phil	*The Happy Hooker Goes Hollywood* (1980).	Died in Century City, California, November 1, 1985, age 73.
Sim, Alastair	*The Littlest Horse Thieves* (a.k.a. *Escape From the Dark,* 1976).	Died in London, England, August 19, 1976, age 75.
Sinatra, Frank	Last movie role: *Cannonball Run II* (1984). Last TV film: *Young at Heart* (guest appearance, 1993).	Died in Los Angeles, California, May 14, 1998, age 82. (*See also* Music—Popular Performers; Radio.)
Skelton, Richard ("Red")	*Those Magnificent Men in Their Flying Machines* (cameo, 1965). Last feature film: *Public Pigeon No. One* (1957).	Died in Rancho Mirage, California, September 17, 1997, age 84.

Slezak, Walter	*Treasure Island* (1973).	Died in Long Island, New York, April 22, 1983, age 80.
Sloane, Everett	*The Disorderly Orderly* (1964). Last TV movie: *Hercules and the Princess of Troy* (1965).	Died in Los Angeles, California, August 6, 1965, age 55.
Smith, Alexis	*The Age of Innocence* (1993). Last TV movie: *Marcus Welby, M.D.: A Holiday Affair* (1988).	*The Age of Innocence* released after she died in Los Angeles, California, June 9, 1993, age 72.
Smith, Sir C. Aubrey	*Little Women* (1949).	Died in Beverly Hills, California, December 20, 1948, age 85.
Sondergaard, Gale	*Echoes* (1983).	Died in Woodland Hills, California, August 14, 1985, age 86.
Soo, Jack	*Return from Witch Mountain* (1978) Last TV movie: *She Lives!* (1973)	Died in Los Angeles, California, January 11, 1979, age 63.
Sothern, Ann	*The Whales of August* (1987). Last Maisie film: *Undercover Maisie* (1947). Last TV movie: *A Letter to Three Wives* (1985).	Died in Ketchum, Idaho, March 15, 2001, age 92. Daughter Tish Sterling appeared in *The Whales of August.*
Soule, Olan	*The Shaggy D.A.* (1976). Last TV movie: *Code Red* (1982).	Died in Los Angeles, California, February 1, 1994, age 85.
Sparks, Ned	*Magic Town* (1947).	Died in Victorville, California, April 3, 1957, age 73.
Stack, Robert	*Killer Bud* (2001); *Recess: School's Out* (voice, 2001). Last TV movies: *H.U.D.* (2000); *Butt-Ugly Martians* (voice, series; 2001).	Died in Beverly Hills, California, May 14, 2003, age 84.
Stander, Lionel	*The Last Good Time* (1994). Last TV movie: *Hart to Hart: Secrets of the Hart* (1995).	Died in Los Angeles, California, November 30, 1994, age 86.
Stanwyck, Barbara	*The Night Walker* (1964); *Roustabout* (1964). Last TV role: *Dynasty II: The Colbys* (1986).	Died in Santa Monica, California, January 20, 1990, age 82. Ex-husband Robert Taylor co-starred in *The Night Walker.*
Starrett, Charles	*Hollywood Bronc Busters* (as himself; 1956). Last Durango Kid film: *Kid From Broken Gun* (1952).	Died in Borrego Springs, California, March 22, 1986, age 82.
Steele, Bob	*Nightmare Honeymoon* (1973). Last Tucson Smith film: *Riders of the Rio Grande* (1943).	Died in Burbank, California, December 21, 1988, age 82.
Steiger, Rod	*Poolhall Junkies* (2002); Last TV movie: *Animated Epics: Moby Dick* (voice; 2000).	Died in Los Angeles, California, July 9, 2002, age 77.
Stephenson, Henry	*A Challenge to Lassie* (1949).	Died in San Francisco, California, April 24, 1956, age 85.
Stevens, Inger	*A Dream of Kings* (1969). Last TV movie: *Run, Simon, Run* (a.k.a. *Savage Run;* 1970).	Died in Hollywood, California, April 30, 1970, age 35.

Stewart, James	*An American Tail: Fievel Goes West* (voice, 1991). Last TV movie: *North and South II* (miniseries, 1986).	Died in Beverly Hills, California, July 2, 1997, age 89.
Stone, Fred	*The Westerner* (1940).	Died in Hollywood, California, March 6, 1959, age 85.
Stone, Lewis	*All the Brothers Were Valiant* (1953). Last of 14 films as Judge Hardy: *Love Laughs at Andy Hardy* (1946).	Died in Beverly Hills, California, September 12, 1953, age 73.
Strauss, Robert	*Dagmar's Hot Pants* (1972).	Died in New York, New York, February 20, 1975, age 61.
Strode, Woody	*The Quick and the Dead* (1995).	Died in Glendora, California, December 31, 1994, age 80.
Strudwick, Shepperd	*Cops and Robbers* (1973).	Died in New York, New York, January 16, 1983, age 75.
Sullavan, Margaret	*No Sad Songs for Me* (1950).	Died in New Haven, Connecticut, January 1, 1960, age 49, while appearing in the play *Sweet Love Remembered*.
Sullivan, Francis L.	*The Prodigal* (1955).	Died in New York, New York, November 19, 1956, age 53.
Summerville, George ("Slim")	*The Hoodlum Saint* (1946).	Died in Laguna Beach, California, January 6, 1946, age 53.
Swanson, Gloria	*Airport '75* (as herself, 1975). Last TV movie: *The Killer Bees* (1974). Last silent movie: *Queen Kelly* (1929).	Died in New York, New York, April 4, 1983, age 84.
Switzer, Carl ("Alfalfa")	*The Defiant Ones* (1958).	Died in Mission Hills, California, January 21, 1959, age 31.
Talbot, Lyle	*Sunrise at Campobello* (1960); *The Haunted World of Ed Wood Jr.* (as himself, 1995).	Died in San Francisco, California, March 3, 1996, age 94.
Tamiroff, Akim	*The Great Train Robbery* (1969).	Died in Palm Springs, California, September 17, 1972, age 72.
Tandy, Jessica	*Camilla* (1994); *Nobody's Fool* (1994). Last TV movie: *To Dance with the White Dog* (1994).	Died in Easton, Connecticut, September 11, 1994, age 85.
Taylor, Dub	*Maverick* (1994). Last TV movie: *Conagher* (1991).	Died in Los Angeles, California, October 3, 1994, age 87.
Taylor, Robert	*The Hot Line* (1969).	Died in Santa Monica, California, June 8, 1969, age 57.
Teal, Ray	*Run for the Roses* (1975).	Died in Santa Monica, California, April 2, 1976, age 74.
Terry-Thomas	*The Hound of the Baskervilles* (1978).	Died in Surrey, England, January 8, 1990, age 78.

Tierney, Gene	*The Pleasure Seekers* (1964). Last TV movie: *Scruples* (mini-series, 1980).	Died in Houston, Texas, November 6, 1991, age 70.
Tobias, George	*The Phynx* (1970). Last TV movie: *The Waltons* (1972).	Died in Los Angeles, California, February 27, 1980, age 78.
Toler, Sidney	*The Trap* (1947).	Died in Los Angeles, California, February 12, 1947, age 72.
Tone, Franchot	*Nobody Runs Forever* (1968).	Died in New York, New York, September 18, 1968, age 63.
Townes, Harry	*The Check is in the Mail* (1986).	Died in Huntsville, Alabama, May 23, 2001, age 86.
Tracy, Lee	*The Best Man* (1964).	Died in Santa Monica, California, October 18, 1968, age 70.
Tracy, Spencer	*Guess Who's Coming to Dinner?* (also the last of nine films with Katharine Hepburn;1967).	Died in Beverly Hills, California, June 10, 1967, age 67.
Travers, Henry	*The Girl From Jones Beach* (1949).	Died in Hollywood, California, October 18, 1965, age 91.
Treacher, Arthur	*Mary Poppins* (1964).	Last telecast as Announcer, *The Merv Griffin Show*, February 11, 1972. Died in Manhasset, New York, December 14, 1975, age 81.
Trevor, Claire	*Kiss Me Goodbye* (1982). Last TV film: *Breaking Family Ties* (1987).	Died in Newport Beach, California, April 8, 2000, age 91.
Truex, Ernest	*Fluffy* (1965).	Died in Fallbrook, California, June 27, 1973, age 82.
Tucker, Forrest	*Thunder Run* (1985). Last TV movie: *Timestalkers* (1987).	Died in Woodland Hills, California, October 25, 1986, age 67.
Tufts, Sonny	*Cottonpickin' Chickenpickers* (1967).	Died in Santa Monica, California, June 4, 1970, age 58.
Turner, Lana	*Thwarted* (1991).	Died in Century City, California, June 29, 1995, age 74.
Tuttle, Lurene	*Testament* (1983). Last TV movie: *It Came Upon a Midnight Clear* (1984).	Died in Encino, California, May 28, 1986, age 79.
Ustinov, Sir Peter	*Luther* (2003). Last TV movie: *Winter Solstice* (2003).	Died in Genolier, Switzerland, March 28, 2004, age 82.
Valentino, Rudolph	*Son of the Sheik* (silent movie, 1926).	Died in New York, New York, August 23, 1926, age 31, shortly before the film was released.
Van Cleef, Lee	*Thieves of Fortune* (1990).	Died in Oxnard, California, December 14, 1989, age 64.
Varney, Jim	*Toy Story 2* (1999; voice); *Atlantis: The Lost Empire* (voice, videogame, 2001). Last feature film: *Daddy and Them* (2001).	Died in White House, Tennessee, February 10, 2000, age 50.
Veidt, Conrad	*Above Suspicion* (1943). Last silent movie: *The Last Performance* (1929).	Died in Los Angeles, California, April 3, 1943, age 50.

Velez, Lupe	*Ladies' Day* (1944). Last Mexican Spitfire film: *Mexican Spitfire's Blessed Event* (1943).	Died in Hollywood, California, December 14, 1944, age 36.
Vera-Ellen	*Let's Be Happy* (1957).	Died in Los Angeles, California, August 30, 1981, age 55.
Walburn, Raymond	*The Spoilers* (1955).	Died in New York, New York, July 26, 1969, age 81.
Walker, Nancy	*Murder by Death* (1976); *Won Ton Ton, the Dog Who Saved Hollywood* (1976). Last TV sitcom: *True Colors* (1990).	Died in Studio City, California, March 25, 1992, age 69.
Walker, Robert	*My Son John* (1952).	Died in Santa Monica, California, August 28, 1951, age 32, while working on the film.
Walsh, J.T.	*The Negotiator* (1998).	Died in La Mesa, California, February 27, 1998, age 54.
Walston, Ray	*Early Bird Special* (2000). Last TV movie: *Swing Vote* (1999).	Died in Beverly Hills, California, January 1, 2001, age 86.
Waters, Ethel	*The Sound and the Fury* (1959).	Died in Chatsworth, California, September 1, 1977, age 80.
Wayne, David	*The Survivalist* (1987); *Poker Alice* (1987).	Died in Santa Monica, California, February 9, 1995, age 81.
Wayne, John	*The Shootist* (1976). Last known silent film: *Words and Music* (1929).	Died in Los Angeles, California, June 11, 1979, age 72.
Webb, Clifton	*Satan Never Sleeps* (1962).	Died in Beverly Hills, California, October 13, 1966, age 76.
Weidler, Virginia	*Best Foot Forward* (1943); *The Youngest Profession* (1943).	Died in Los Angeles, California, July 1, 1968, age 42.
Weissmuller, Johnny	*Won Ton Ton, the Dog Who Saved Hollywood* (1976). Last film as Jungle Jim: *Jungle Man-Eaters* (1954). Last Tarzan film: *Tarzan and the Mermaids* (1948).	Died in Acapulco, Mexico, January 20, 1984, age 79.
Welles, Orson	Last feature film as actor: *Someone to Love* (1987).	Died in Los Angeles, California, October 9, 1985, age 70.
Werner, Oskar	*Voyage of the Damned* (1976).	Died in Marburg, Germany, October 23, 1984, age 61.
West, Mae	*Sextette* (1978).	Died in Los Angeles, California, November 22, 1980, age 87.
Weston, Jack	*Short Circuit 2* (1988).	Died in New York, New York, May 3, 1996, age 70.
White, Jesse	*Matinee* (1993).	Died in Los Angeles, California, January 9, 1997, age 79.
Whitty, Dame May	*The Return of October* (1948).	Died in Beverly Hills, California, May 29, 1948, age 82.
Wickes, Mary	*Little Women* (1994); *The Hunchback of Notre Dame* (animated, voice, 1996).	Died in Los Angeles, California, October 22, 1995, age 85, while working on *The Hunchback of Notre Dame*.

Wilcoxon, Henry	*Sweet 16* (1981). Last TV movie: *Enola Gay: The Men, The Mission, The Atomic Bomb* (1980).	Died in Los Angeles, California, March 6, 1984, age 78.
Wilde, Cornel	*Flesh and Bullets* (1985).	Died in Los Angeles, California, October 16, 1989, age 74.
Wilding, Michael	*Lady Caroline Lamb* (1972). Last TV movie: *Frankenstein: The True Story* (1972).	Died in Chicester, England, July 8, 1979, age 66.
Williams, Emlyn	*The Walking Stick* (1970).	Died in London, England, September 25, 1987, age 81.
Williams, Rhys	*The Sons of Katie Elder* (1965).	Died in Santa Monica, California, May 28, 1969, age 71.
Wills, Chill	*Mr. Billion* (1977); *Stubby Pringle's Christmas* (1978).	Died in Encino, California, December 15, 1978, age 75.
Wilson, Marie	*Mr. Hobbs Takes a Vacation* (1962).	Died in Hollywood, California, November 23, 1972, age 55.
Windsor, Marie	*Commando Squad* (1987).	Died in Beverly Hills, California, December 10, 2000, age 80.
Winninger, Charles	*Raymie* (1960).	Died in Palm Springs, California, January 27, 1969, age 84.
Winters, Roland	*Loving* (1970). Last TV movie: *You Can't Go Home Again* (1979).	Died in Englewood, New Jersey, October 22, 1989, age 84.
Winwood, Estelle	*Murder By Death* (1976).	Died in Woodland Hills, California, June 20, 1984, age 101.
Wong, Anna May	*Portrait in Black* (1960); *The Savage Innocents* (1960). Last silent movie: *Piccadilly* (1929).	Died in Santa Monica, California, February 2, 1961, age 56.
Wood, Natalie	*Brainstorm* (1983).	Drowned in boating accident off Santa Catalina Island, California, November 29, 1981, age 43, before production was completed.
Wood, Peggy	*The Sound of Music* (1965).	Died in Stamford, Connecticut, March 18, 1978, age 86. Received Academy Award nomination for her final film.
Woolley, Monty	*Kismet* (1955).	Died in Albany, New York, March 6, 1963, age 74.
Worth, Irene	*Onegin* (1999).	Last theatrical appearance: *I Take Your Hand in Mine* (2001), London, England. Died in New York, New York, March 11, 2002, age 85
Wynn, Keenan	*Hyper Sapiens: People from Another Star* (1986).	Died in Brentwood, California, October 14, 1986, age 70.
York, Dick	*Inherit the Wind* (1960).	Died in Grand Rapids, Michigan, February 20, 1992, age 63.
Young, Gig	*Game of Death* (1978).	Died in New York, New York, October 19, 1978, age 64.
Young, Loretta	*It Happens Every Thursday* (1953). Last TV movie: *Lady in the Corner* (1989). Last silent	Died in Los Angeles, California, August 12, 2000, age 87.

	movies: *The Forward Pass* (1929); *The Care-less Age* (1929); *Fast Life* (1929); *Seven Footprints to Satan* (1929).	
Young, Robert	*Secret of the Incas* (1954). Last TV movie: *Marcus Welby, M.D.: A Holiday Affair* (1988).	Died in Westlake Village. California, July 21, 1998, age 91.
Young, Roland	*St. Benny the Dip* (1951); *That Man from Tangier* (1953).	Died in New York, New York, June 3, 1953, age 65.

Music

Notes on the music tables: A cross section of prominent deceased composers and performers is presented. Groups are included if the group's leader has died, or if the group has ceased to exist in its original form and it will not exist again in its original form. **Last film score** refers to the last time the composer was the primary or one of the primary composers of original music for a film. **Last film** indicates a film in which the person appeared as himself or herself or as an actor. **Last Broadway show** indicates the last original work of the composer or performer. Revivals and revues are excluded. **Last recording** indicates the final recording a musician actually participated in, as opposed to another person's recording of his or her work. **Last album** refers to the final work recorded (though not necessarily released) during a performer's lifetime. Later compilation works are excluded. **Last Top 40 hits** and **No. 1 hits** are the general pop charts, unless otherwise indicated.

Music—Composers

Albéniz, Isaac	Spanish pianist/composer Isaac Manuel Francisco Albéniz died in Cambo-les-Bains, France, on May 19, 1909, age 48. • **Last completed composition:** *Quatre Melodies*.
Anderson, Leroy	American composer Leroy Anderson died in Woodbury, Connecticut, on May 18, 1975, age 66. • **Last Broadway show:** *Goldilocks*. Last performance of original run: February 28, 1959, at the Lunt-Fontanne Theater in New York, New York. • **Last composition:** *March of the Two Left Feet* (1970). In 1973, he made an arrangement of the *Second Regiment Connecticut National Guard March*.
Arlen, Harold	American composer/pianist Harold Arlen (Hyman Arluck) died in New York, New York, on April 23, 1986, age 81. • **Last Broadway show:** *Saratoga*. Last performance of original run: February 13, 1960, at the Winter Garden Theater in New York, New York. • **Last score for full-length film:** *Gay Purr-ee* (1962). Retired after writing original music for the animated feature film. • **Last film score:** *Mago de Oz Cuento de Frank Baum* (Mexican TV, 1985).
Bach, Johann Sebastian	German composer Johann Sebastian Bach died in Leipzig, Germany, on July 28, 1750, age 65. • **Last major composition:** *Art of the Fugue* (BWV 1080), published in

	1752, two years after his death. • **Last composition (undocumented):** The chorale "Vor deinen Thron tret ich allheir" (BWV 668)—said to have been dictated to a pupil during Bach's final days—is most often credited as his last composition. However, a manuscript discovered in a neglected family archive in Kiev, Ukraine, in the year 2000 might actually be Bach's last work. "Lieber Herr Gott, Wecke Uns Auf" (Dear Lord God, Awaken Us) was originally composed in 1672 by Johann Christoph Bach, Johann Sebastian's uncle. A new arrangement for double choir, wind and strings was made by Johann Sebastian Bach in his final days for his own funeral. • **Last position:** Director of music at Leipzig and Kantor of the Thomasschule from 1723 to 1750. • **Last pupil:** Johann Gottfried Müthel, who died in 1788.
Balakirev, Mily	Russian composer/pianist Alexeyevich (Mily) Balakirev died in Saint Petersburg, Russia, on May 29, 1910, age 73. • **Last composition:** *Concerto No. 2 in E Flat Major,* begun in 1909 (unfinished, opus posthumous). It was completed by his pupil Sergei Liapunov. • **Last performance as pianist**: October 1894, when Balakirev played Chopin's *B Flat Minor Sonata* in Warsaw, Poland.
Barber, Samuel	American composer Samuel Barber died in New York, New York, on January 23, 1981, age 70. • **Last work for the stage:** *Antony and Cleopatra* (opera, 1966), commissioned for the opening of the Metropolitan Opera House in Lincoln Center for the Performing Arts, New York, New York. • **Last composition:** *Canzonetta,* Opus 48 (1978-81).
Bartók, Béla	Hungarian composer/pianist Béla Bartók died in New York, New York, on September 26, 1945, age 64. • **Last composition (completed):** *Piano Concerto No. 3* (1945), composed while Bartók was in exile in the United States during World War II. • **Last work (unfinished):** *Viola Concerto,* commissioned in 1944. Bartók died before it was finished. His wife and son arranged for Tibor Sérly to complete the work. • **Last performance as pianist:** first performance of the *Concerto for Two Pianos and Orchestra* with Bartók and his wife as soloists, January 21, 1943, in New York, New York.
Beethoven, Ludwig van	German composer Ludwig van Beethoven died in Vienna, Austria, on March 26, 1827, age 56 (?). • **Last completed composition:** *String Quartet No. 16 in F Major,* Opus 135, composed in 1826. • **Last piano concerto:** *Concerto No. 5 in E Flat* (nicknamed *Emperor Concerto*). • **Last piano sonata:** *Sonata No. 32 in C Minor,* Opus 111 (1821-22). • **Last symphony:** *Symphony No. 9* ("Ode to Joy"), first performed in Vienna in 1824. Beethoven made notes for a 10th symphony but never completed it. • **Last public performance as pianist:** January 25, 1815, playing a concert marking the birthday of the Empress of Russia. • **Last appearance on a concert stage (scheduled):** May 7, 1824, for the

	premiere performance of his last completed symphony, *Symphony No. 9.* • **Last appearance on a concert stage (unscheduled):** September 5, 1825. Beethoven was attending a performance of one of his string quartets. Something about the performance bothered him, so he took a performer's violin and played the passage himself. • **Last piano owned by Beethoven:** in the possession of the Beethoven Haus, Bonn, Germany. It was made by the Viennese court piano-maker Conrad Graf around 1823. • **Last surviving person who knew Beethoven:** Gerhard von Breuning, who died in 1892.
Bellini, Vincenzo	Italian opera composer Vincenzo Bellini died in Puteaux, France, near Paris, on September 24, 1835, age 34. • **Last opera:** *I Puritani* (1835).
Berg, Alban	Austrian composer Alban Berg died in Vienna, Austria, on December 24, 1935, age 50. • **Last completed composition:** *Violin Concerto* finished in August 1935, a few months before he died. He left unfinished his second opera *Lulu.* Act III was later orchestrated by Friedrich Cerha, and a completed version of the opera was performed for the first time in 1979 in Paris, France.
Berlin, Irving	Russian-born American songwriter Irving Berlin (Isadore Baline) died in New York, New York, on September 22, 1989, age 101. • **Last Broadway show:** *Mr. President* (1962). Last performance of original run: June 8, 1963, at the St. James Theater, in New York, New York. • **Last new Broadway song**: "An Old-Fashioned Wedding," written for the 1966 revival of *Annie Get Your Gun* at the Music Theater of Lincoln Center in New York, New York. • **Last film music:** title song for *Sayonara* (1957). • **Last film as performer:** *This is the Army* (1943, uncredited). • **Last Broadway show as performer:** *This is the Army* as Sergeant Irving Berlin. Last performance of original run: September 26, 1942, at the Broadway Theater in New York, New York. • **Last public performance:** At the White House in 1974, when Berlin sang "God Bless America" in honor of returning Vietnam War prisoners.
Berlioz, Hector	French composer/conductor Hector Berlioz died in Paris, France, on March 8, 1869, age 65. • **Last composition:** *Béatrice et Bénédict* (1860-62), an opera based on Shakespeare's *Much Ado About Nothing.* Berlioz's opera *Les Troyens,* completed in 1858, received a very poor reception when it was premiered at the new Paris Opera House in 1863. It was withdrawn after less than two dozen performances. Berlioz was so discouraged by its failure that he wrote no more after the *Les Troyens* debacle.
Bernstein, Elmer	American composer/conductor Elmer Bernstein died in Ojai, California, on August 18, 2004, age 82. • **Last film score:** *Far From Heaven* (2002), for which he received an Academy Award nomination. • **Last film as himself:** *Cecil B. De Mille: American Epic* (2004).
Bernstein, Leonard	American composer/conductor/pianist Leonard Bernstein died in New York, New York, on October 14, 1990, age 72.

	• **Last composition:** *Dance Suite* (1990), premiered by the Empire Brass Quintet at the Metropolitan Opera, New York, New York. • **Last Broadway show:** *1600 Pennsylvania Avenue* (1976). Last performance of original run: May 8, 1976, at the Mark Hellinger Theater, in New York, New York. • **Last film score:** *On the Waterfront* (1954). • **Last film:** *Bernstein Conducts Candide* (TV, commentator, 1989). • **Last concert with the Israel Philharmonic:** June 22, 1989. • **Last concert with the New York Philharmonic:** October 31, 1989. • **Last concert at Tanglewood, Massachusetts:** August 19, 1990. • **Last concert in New York City:** March 11, 1990 at Carnegie Hall. • **Last Unitel production:** December 25, 1989. Berlin Celebration Concert, commemorating the fall of the Berlin Wall. Beethoven's *Symphony No. 9* was performed. Bernstein reworked "Ode to Joy" as "Ode to Freedom."
Bizet, Georges	French composer Alexandre César Léopold (Georges) Bizet died in Bougival, near Paris, France, on June 3, 1875, age 36. • **Last composition:** The opera *Carmen*. When it premiered at the Opéra Comique in Paris in March 1875, critics panned it and the public reacted with indifference. The failure to gain acceptance in his hometown caused Bizet to fall into a depression. He was also suffering from a throat infection and was in failing health. In May, he moved to a suburb of Paris, hoping to improve his condition. He died there a short time later, after suffering two heart attacks.
Blake, Eubie	American composer/pianist/bandleader James Hubert ("Eubie") Blake died in New York, New York, on February 12, 1983, age 100. Blake is considered the last of the ragtime pioneers. • **Last Broadway show as composer:** *Eubie!* (1978). Last performance of original run: October 7, 1979, at the Ambassador Theater in New York, New York. • **Last Broadway show as performer:** *Shuffle Along* (1952). Last performance: May 10, 1952, at the Broadway Theater in New York, New York. • **Last film score:** *Eubie Blake Plays His Fantasy on Swanee River* (1923). A TV film version of Eubie! was made in 1980, which he worked on. • **Last film as performer:** *Scott Joplin* (1977). • **Last recording as bandleader:** "Eubie Blake Song Hits" (1976), when he was 93. • **Last public appearance:** Lincoln Center in New York, New York, June 19, 1982, at the age of 99.
Bloch, Ernest	Swiss-born American composer Ernest Bloch died in Portland, Oregon, on July 15, 1959, age 78. • **Last compositions:** Two *Last Poems for Flute Solo and Orchestra* (1958); *Suite No. 1 for Violin Solo* (1958*); Suite No. 2 for Violin Solo* (1958). He left unfinished a *Suite for Viola.*
Borodin, Alexander	Russian composer/scientist Alexander Porfiryevich Borodin died in Saint Petersburg, Russia, on February 27, 1887, age 53. • **Last completed composition:** *String Quartet No. 2 in D* (1881-87). • **Last major unfinished compositions:** the opera *Prince Igor* and *Symphony No. 3.* Borodin's friends Nikolai Rimsky-Korsakov and Alexander

	Glazunov completed *Prince Igor*. It was produced in 1890. Glazunov finished and orchestrated the symphony.
Brahms, Johannes	German composer/pianist Johannes Brahms died in Vienna, Austria, on April 3, 1897, age 63. • **Last compositions:** *Four Serious Songs,* Opus 121, written shortly before he died and inspired by the final illness of Clara Schumann. *Eleven Chorale Preludes for Organ,* Opus 122 (published posthumously). The final piece—No. 11, "O Welt ich muss dich lassen," ("Oh world I must leave thee")—is considered Brahms's last composition. • **Last orchestral composition:** *Double Concerto for Violin and Cello*, Opus 102 (1887). • **Last piano composition:** *Klavierstücke,* Opus 119 (four pieces in B minor, E minor, C and E Flat). • **Last public appearance:** March 7, 1897. He attended a performance of his *Symphony No. 4.* • **Last surviving pupil:** Carl Friedberg, who died in 1955.
Britten, Benjamin	English composer/conductor/pianist Edward Benjamin Britten (Lord Britten of Aldeburgh) died in Aldeburgh, England, on December 4, 1976, age 63. • **Last choral work:** *Sacred and Profane* (medieval lyrics for unaccompanied voices). • **Last composition:** *String Quartet No. 3*, completed just a few months before his death. • **Last Broadway show:** *Let's Make an Opera* (1950). Last performance of original run: December 16, 1950, at the John Golden Theater, in New York, New York. • **Last music for radio production:** *The Dark Tower* (BBC, 1946). • **Last film score:** *Love From a Stranger* (1937). • **Last opera:** *Death in Venice* (1973).
Bruch, Max	German composer/conductor Max Christian Friedrich Bruch died in Friedenau, Germany, on October 20, 1920, age 82. • **Last composition:** *String Octet* (1920), completed seven months before Bruch died.
Bruckner, Anton	Austrian composer/organist Anton Bruckner died in Vienna, Austria, on October 11, 1896, age 72. • **Last compositions:** *Mass No. 2 in E* (fourth revision, 1896) and *Symphony No. 9* (unfinished). Bruckner was working on the symphony when he died. The first three movements were completed by November 30, 1894. • **Last public appearance:** January 12, 1896, a performance of his *Te Deum.*
Caesar, Irving	American lyricist Irving Caesar died in New York, New York, on December 17, 1996, age 101. • **Last Broadway show:** *My Dear Public* (1943). Last performance of original run: October 16, 1943, at the 46th Street Theater, New York, New York. • **Last film score:** *If I Forget You* (1940). • **Last Top 40 *Billboard* hit (Pop Charts) as composer during his lifetime:** "Just A Gigolo," recorded by David Lee Roth. Caesar was 90 years old when it entered the charts on April 20, 1985.
Cahn, Sammy	American lyricist/composer/performer Sammy Cahn (Samuel Cohen) died in Los Angeles, California, on January 15, 1993, age 79.

	• **Last original music for film:** "It's a Woman's World," *All Hands on Deck* (1961). • **Last film as performer:** *Boardwalk* (1979). • **Last Broadway show:** *Words and Music* (1974). Last performance of original run: August 3, 1974, at the John Golden Theater in New York.
Carmichael, Hoagy	American songwriter/singer/actor Hoagland Howard ("Hoagy") Carmichael died in Rancho Mirage, California, on December 17, 1981, age 82. • **Last film as actor:** *The Wheeler Dealers* (uncredited, 1963). • **Last original music for film:** "Just for Tonight," *Hatari* (1962). Lyrics by Johnny Mercer.
Chabrier, Emmanuel	French composer/pianist Alexis Emmanuel Chabrier died in Paris, France, on September 13, 1894, age 53. • **Last completed compositions:** *Ode a la musique* and *Bourree fantastique.* Both were completed during his last three years, while he suffered from paralysis. • **Last unfinished composition:** *Briséis.*
Cherubini, Luigi	Italian composer Maria Luigi Carlo Zenobio Salvadore Cherubini died in Paris, France, on March 15, 1842, age 81. • **Last opera:** *Ali Baba* (premiered in Paris, 1833).
Chopin, Frédéric	Polish composer/pianist Fryderyk Franciszek (Frédéric François) Chopin died in Paris, France, on October 17, 1849, age 39. • **Last compositions:** *Mazurka in F Minor*, Opus 68, and *Mazurka in G Minor*, Opus 67. Both were composed in the summer of 1849. • **Last public performance as pianist:** November 16, 1848, at the Guildhall, London, where he played for the benefit of Polish refugees. • **Last piano owned by Chopin:** on display in the Frederick Chopin Museum at the Frederick Chopin Society of Warsaw. The piano is on loan from the National Museum in Warsaw.
Cohan, George M.	American composer/lyricist/producer/performer George Michael Cohan died on November 5, 1972, in New York, New York, age 64. • **Last Broadway musical:** *Billie* (1928) at the Erlanger Theater in New York, New York. • **Last Broadway show as playwright/producer/performer:** *The Return of the Vagabond* (melodrama). Last performance of original run: May 18, 1940, at the National Theater in New York, New York. • **Last film score:** *Yankee Doodle Dandy* (1942). • **Last film as actor:** *Gambling* (1934). • **Last film as writer:** *So This Is London* (1940).
Copland, Aaron	American composer Aaron Copland died in North Tarrytown, New York, on December 2, 1990, age 90. • **Last composition:** *Proclamation* (for piano, 1982). • **Last ballet:** *Dance Panels,* commissioned in 1959 by Jerome Robbins. The ballet, in seven sections, is the only one Copland wrote without a story line. • **Last film score:** *Something Wild* (1961). Later reworked as the suite *Music for a Great City,* commissioned by the London Symphony. • **Last public performance:** 1982, conducting the New Haven Symphony. • **Last public appearance:** July 24, 1985, Aaron Copland Day celebration at the Berkshire Music Center in Tanglewood, Massachusetts.

Creston, Paul	American composer Paul Creston (Giuseppe Guttoveggio) died in San Diego, California, on August 24, 1985, age 78. • **Last major compositions:** *Symphony No. 6,* premiered 1982; *Prelude and Dance* for two pianos (1983).
Debussy, Claude	French composer Achille Claude Debussy died in Paris, France, on March 25, 1918, age 55. • **Last major compositions:** three sonatas: cello (1915); flute, viola and harp (1915); and violin (1916-17). Debussy left four operas unfinished. Two were based on stories by Edgar Allan Poe. He had begun working on *Fall of the House of Usher* in 1908. • **Last public performance as a pianist:** May 1917, when he accompanied violinist Gaston Poulet at the premiere of his *Violin Sonata.* • **Last piano recordings:** November 1, 1913. Debussy recorded several pieces, including "The Engulfed Cathedral," as piano rolls using the Welte-Mignon reproducing piano system.
Delibes, Léo	French composer/organist Clément Philibert Léo Delibes died in Paris, France, on January 16, 1891, age 54. • **Last composition:** *Kassya,* unfinished. Orchestrated by Massenet and premiered posthumously in 1893.
Delius, Frederick	English composer Fritz Theodor Albert (Frederick) Delius died in Grez-sur-Loing, France, on June 10, 1934, age 72. • **Last compositions:** Delius had a debilitating illness during his later years, but he continued to compose with the help of Eric Fenby, who wrote down his work for him. Among Delius's works during this time were *A Song of Summer* (1930), *Fantastic Dance* (1931) and his third *Violin Sonata* (1930). • **Last opera:** *Fennimore and Gerda* (1908-10). • **Last public appearance:** 1929, at a festival of his music in London, England.
Donizetti, Gaetano	Italian opera composer Gaetano Donizetti died in Bergamo, Italy, on April 8, 1848, age 50. • **Last opera produced in his lifetime:** *Dom Sébastien, roi de Portugal* (1843).
Dukas, Paul	French composer Paul Dukas died in Paris, France, on May 17, 1935, age 69. • **Last known composition:** *Sonnet de Ronsard* (published 1924). Dukas continued composing but was highly critical of his music and destroyed much of it before he died.
Duke, Vernon	Russian-born American composer Vernon Duke (Vladimir Dukelsky) died in Santa Monica, California, on January 16, 1969, age 65. • **Last major completed work:** *Anima Eroica (Ode to St. Brigitte,* 1966). • **Last original score for a Broadway show:** *Two's Company* (1952). Last performance of original run: March 8, 1953, Alvin Theater, New York, New York. • **Last incidental music for a Broadway show:** *Time Remembered.* Last performance of original run: June 14, 1958, at the Morosco Theater in New York, New York. • **Last film score:** *She's Working Her Way Through College* (1952).
Dvořák, Antonín	Czech Bohemian-born composer Antonín Leopold Dvořák died in Prague, Czechoslovakia, on May 5, 1904, age 62.

	• **Last composition:** *Armida* (staged 1904). • **Last performance:** April 4, 1900, conducting the Czech Philharmonic Orchestra. • **Last surviving pupil:** Rudolf Karel.
Elgar, Sir Edward	English composer Sir Edward William Elgar died in Worcester, England, on February 23, 1934, age 76. • **Last completed composition:** *Mina* (1934), a short piece for small orchestra, named for his Cairn terrier. He left unfinished works that were completed in various interpretations after his death. These include *Symphony No. 3,* Opus 88; *The Spanish Lady,* Opus 89 (opera); and a piano concerto, Opus 90.
Ellington, Duke	American composer/conductor/pianist Edward Kennedy ("Duke") Ellington died in New York, New York, on May 24, 1974, age 75. • **Last Broadway show:** *Pousse-Café* (1966). Last performance of original run: March 26, 1966, at the 46th Street Theater in New York, New York. • **Last film score:** *Change of Mind* (1969). • **Last film as actor:** *Anatomy of a Murder* (uncredited, 1959). • **Last film as himself:** *On the Road with Duke Ellington* (1974). • **Last major composition:** *Third Sacred Concert*, premiered October 1973 at a United Nations-sponsored event in Westminster Abbey, London, England. Ellington composed the three *Sacred Concerts* between 1965 and 1973. • **Last recording:** *Eastborne Performance* (from a concert in England), released 1973.
Fain, Sammy	American composer Sammy Fain (Samuel Feinberg) died in Los Angeles, California, on December 6, 1989, age 87. • **Last Broadway show:** *Something More!* (1964). Last performance of original run: November 21, 1964, at the Eugene O'Neill Theater in New York, New York. • **Last film score:** *The Rescuers* (animated, 1977). • **Last film as actor:** *Special Valentine with the Family Circus* (voice, animated, 1978).
Faith, Percy	Canadian-born composer/conductor/arranger Percy Faith died in Encino, California, on February 9, 1976, age 67. • **Last film score:** *The Oscar* (1966). • **Last song for film:** "Welcome To St. Crispin," from the movie *P.J.* (1968)
Falla, de, Manuel	Spanish composer Manuel Maria de Falla y Matheu died in Alta Gracia de Cordoba, Argentina, on November 14, 1946, age 69. • **Last composition:** *Atlántida* (cantata, unfinished). De Falla spent 20 years working on it. His pupil Ernesto Halffter completed the work and it was premiered in Milan in 1962.
Fauré, Gabriel	French composer/organist Gabriel Urbain Fauré died in Paris, France, on November 4, 1924, age 79. • **Last composition for piano:** *Thirteenth Nocturne*, Opus 119 (1921). • **Last composition:** *String Quartet in E Minor,* Opus 121 (1923).
Field, John	Irish composer/pianist John Field died in Moscow, Russia, in January 1837, age 54. • **Last compositions:** *Nocturnes* (1837) and *Andante in E-Flat* (published posthumously).

Fields, Dorothy	American lyricist/writer/composer Dorothy Fields died in New York, New York, on March 28, 1974, age 68. • **Last Broadway show (provided lyrics):** *See Saw* (1973). Last performance of original run: December 8, 1973, at the Mark Hellinger Theater in New York, New York. • **Last Broadway show (provided book):** *Redhead* (1959). Last performance of original run: March 19, 1960, at the 46th Street Theater in New York, New York. • **Last film score:** *So This is Paris* (1954). • **Last film as herself:** *Stage Door Canteen* (uncredited, 1943).
Foster, Stephen	American composer Stephen Collins Foster died in New York, New York, on January 13, 1864, age 37. • **Last song:** unknown. "Beautiful Dreamer" is often cited as Foster's last song. He sold "Beautiful Dreamer" to Firth, Pond & Company, his main publisher, in 1862, two years before he died. The company had it engraved but did not publish it. In 1864, William A. Pond & Co. (formerly Firth, Pond) published "Beautiful Dreamer" as Foster's last song. What is certain is that Foster did not compose "Beautiful Dreamer" a few days before his death, as Pond advertised. What is not certain is Foster's last song. It may have been one of several that were published in *The Athenaeum Collection of Tunes for Church and Sunday School* in December 1863, just a month before he died.
Franck, César	Belgian-born French composer César Auguste Jean Guillaume Franck died in Paris, France, on November 12, 1890, age 67. • **Last opera:** *Ghisèle* (1888-89). Franck had finished the orchestration only to the end of the first act when he died. • **Last completed compositions:** *Quartet* (1889) and *Chorales for Organ* (1890). He wrote his first and only quartet the year before he died. Franck did his final composing in the summer of 1890. • **Last pupil:** Charles Tourenmire (1870-1939).
Friml, Rudolf	Bohemian-born composer Charles Rudolf Friml died in Hollywood, California, on November 12, 1972, age 92. • **Last Broadway show:** *Music Hath Charms* (1934). Last performance of original run: 1935, at the Majestic Theater in New York, New York. • **Last film score:** *Northwest Outpost* (a.k.a. *End of the Rainbow,* 1947).
Gershwin, George	American composer/pianist George Gershwin (Gershovitz) died in Beverly Hills, California, on July 11, 1937, age 38. He frequently collaborated with his brother lyricist Ira Gershwin. • **Last completed film score:** *A Damsel In Distress* (1937). • **Last unfinished film score:** *The Goldwyn Follies* (1938). • **Last completed George and Ira Gershwin song:** "Love Walked In" (1936). • **Last unfinished George and Ira Gershwin song:** "Our Love is Here to Stay." Ira completed the song after George's death. It appeared in *The Goldwyn Follies* posthumously in 1938. • **Last concert piece:** *Cuban Overture* (1932). • **Last Broadway show:** *The Show is On* (opened posthumously). Last performance of original run: 1937, at the Winter Garden Theater in New York, New York. • **Last production Gershwin saw of *Porgy and Bess*:** March 1936, at

	the National Theater in Washington, D.C. • **Last surviving lyricist who worked with George Gershwin:** Irving Caesar, who died on December 17, 1996, age 101.
Gershwin, Ira	American lyricist Ira Gershwin (Israel Gershovitz) died in Beverly Hills, California, on August 17, 1983, age 86. He frequently collaborated with his brother composer George Gershwin. • **Last Broadway show (original music):** *Park Avenue* (1946). Last performance of original run: January 4, 1947, at the Shubert Theater in New York, New York. • **Last Broadway show:** *My One and Only* (1983), which recycled music from *Funny Face,* produced in 1927. Last performance of original run: March 3, 1985, at the Saint James Theater in New York, New York. • **Last completed George and Ira Gershwin song:** "Love Walked In" (1936). • **Last unfinished George and Ira Gershwin song:** "Our Love is Here to Stay." Ira completed the song after George's death. It appeared in *The Goldwyn Follies* in 1938.
Gilbert, William S.	English librettist/playwright William Schwenck Gilbert died in Middlesex, England, on May 29, 1911, age 74. • **Last collaboration with Arthur S. Sullivan:** *The Grand Duke* (1896). They collaborated for 28 years on 14 light operas. Gilbert wrote the lyrics. Sullivan composed the music. • **Last opera:** *Fallen Fairies* with music by Edward German, opened in 1909.
Glazunov, Alexander	Russian composer Alexander Konstantinovich Glazunov died in Paris, France, on March 21, 1936, age 70. He is considered the last of the great composers of the Russian national school. • **Last composition:** *Saxophone Concerto* (1934).
Glinka, Mikhail	Russian composer Mikhail Ivanovich Glinka died in Berlin, Germany, on February 15, 1857, age 52. • **Last opera:** *Ruslan and Ludmilla.* When it premiered in 1842, the audience hissed and the critics panned it. The failure of the opera to gain acceptance embittered Glinka; he gave up on writing operas. • **Last major composition:** *Festival Polonaise* for the coronation ball of Tsar Alexander II (1855). • **Last public appearance:** February 14, 1857, when the trio from his opera *A Life for the Tsar* was sung. He died the following day.
Gluck, Christoph Willibald von	German composer Christoph Willibald von Gluck died in Vienna, Austria, on November 15, 1787, age 73. • **Last opera:** *Echo et Narcisse*, written in 1779. It was not a success when it premiered in Paris, France. Disappointed, Gluck returned to his home in Vienna. He had a stroke that prevented him from working on anything else.
Goldsmith, Jerry	American composer Jerrald K. ("Jerry") Goldsmith died in Beverly Hills, California, on July 21, 2004, age 75. • **Last film score:** *Timeline* (2003).
Gottschalk, Louis Moreau	American composer/virtuoso pianist Louis Moreau Gottschalk died in Tijuca, Brazil, on December 18, 1869, age 40. • **Last public performance:** A farewell extravaganza in Brazil on November 25, 1869, with 650 musicians and 16 pianos. Gottschalk finished

	performing his composition "La Morte" (Death) and began to play another of his popular compositions, "Tremelo," then collapsed on stage. He died a few weeks later of a ruptured appendix.
Gounod, Charles	French composer Charles François Gounod died in Saint Cloud, France, on October 18, 1893, age 75. • **Last opera:** *Le Tribut de Zamora* (1881). • **Last composition:** *Requiem* in memory of his grandson. He was working on it when he died. • **Last public appearance:** April 4, 1890, conducting a concert of his own works.
Grainger, Percy	Australian-born American composer/pianist Percy Aldridge Grainger (George Percy Grainger) died in White Plains, New York, on February 20, 1961, age 78. • **Last public concert performance:** April 29, 1960.
Grieg, Edvard	Norwegian composer Edward Hagerup Grieg died in Bergen, Norway, on September 4, 1907, age 64. • **Last composition:** *Four Psalms* (mixed choir, 1906). Grieg completed three of the psalms during the summer. The final psalm, "How Fair is Thy Face," was written that autumn. • **Last public appearance:** London, England, in 1906.
Grofé, Ferde	American composer Ferdinand Rudolf (Ferde) von Grofé died in Santa Monica, California, on April 3, 1972, age 80. • **Last symphonic work:** *World's Fair Suite* (1964). • **Last film scores:** *The Return of Jesse James* (1950) and *Rocketship X-M* (a.k.a. *Expedition Moon,* 1950).
Hammerstein II, Oscar	American librettist/producer Oscar Hammerstein II died in Doylestown, Pennsylvania, on August 23, 1960, age 65. • **Last Broadway collaboration with Richard Rodgers:** *The Sound of Music* (1959). Last performance of original run: June 15, 1963, at the Mark Hellinger Theater in New York, New York. He collaborated with Rodgers on many great musicals, beginning with *Oklahoma* in 1943. Their songs have often appeared in later musicals, including some completely new shows written around their music. • **Last Broadway show:** *The Sound of Music.* • **Last song of Hammerstein:** "Edelweiss," written during the Boston, Massachusetts, tryout of *The Sound of Music.* • **Last film score collaboration with Richard Rodgers:** *State Fair* (1945).
Handel, George Frideric	German composer George Frideric Handel died in London, England, on April 14, 1759, age 74. • **Last instrumental composition:** *Organ Concerto No. 3 in B Flat,* (1751) • **Last oratorio:** *Jephtha* (composed 1751, first performed 1752). • **Last compositions:** Handel lost his eyesight while working on the oratorio *Jephtha*. There were no new compositions after that. He made additions to an earlier work by dictating them to a pupil: he augmented his 1708 Italian oratorio *Il Trionfo del Tempo e die Disinganno* with an English version, *Triumph of Time and Truth,* which was produced at Covent Garden, London, England, in 1757. • **Last opera:** *Deidamia* (1741). • **Last performance of a Handel opera under his direction:** *Deidamia* on February 10, 1741.

	• **Last public performance as an organist:** May 1, 1753, at a performance of his oratorio *The Messiah* for a foundling hospital charity. Handel played an organ concerto and voluntary that day. • **Last performance of *The Messiah* under Handel's direction:** May 15, 1754. • **Last performance of a Handel opera during his lifetime:** April 6, 1754, a performance of *Admeto* at King's Theatre, Haymarket, London, England.
Handy, W. C.	Blues composer/author W(illiam) C(hristopher) Handy died in New York, New York, on March 28, 1958, age 84. He is known as the "Father of the Blues." • **Last blues composition:** "Wall Street Blues" (1929). In 1940, he did a new arrangement of "The Memphis Blues" (or "Mister Crump"), written originally in 1912. After 1929, Handy concentrated mainly on writing spirituals. The last was "Jesus Goin' a Make Up My Dying Bed" (1939). • **Last book on music:** *Unsung Americans Sung* (1944). • **Last film:** *Satchmo the Great* (as himself, 1957). • **Last film score:** *St. Louis Blues* (1929). Handy produced the film.
Hart, Lorenz	American lyricist Lorenz Hart died in New York, New York, on November 22, 1943, age 48. • **Last Hart Broadway collaboration with Richard Rodgers:** *By Jupiter* (1942). Last performance of original run: June 12, 1943, at the Shubert Theater in New York, New York. This was also Hart's last Broadway show. He collaborated with Richard Rodgers on about 400 songs and 29 shows, beginning in 1925. • **Last film score collaboration with Richard Rodgers:** *Higher and Higher* (1943). Rodgers and Hart contributed the song "Disgustingly Rich." Their last substantial film collaboration was *They Met in Argentina* (1941). • **Last song:** "To Keep My Love Alive," written for the 1943 revival of *A Connecticut Yankee.*
Haydn, Franz Joseph	Austrian composer Franz Joseph Haydn died in Vienna, Austria, on May 31, 1809, age 77. He wrote his last compositions in 1802 and 1803. • **Last completed compositions:** *Harmoniemesse* (*Mass No. 12 in B Flat*, 1802); *String Quartet No. 83* (1802-03); vocal quartet "My strength is gone: old and weak am I." • **Last symphony:** *Symphony No. 104 in D* (*The London*, 1795). • **Last public performance:** December 26, 1803. Haydn conducted *The Seven Last Words* at a concert for a Viennese hospital fund. • **Last public appearance:** March 27, 1808. Haydn attended a performance of his *The Creation* by the Society of Amateur Concerts at the University of Vienna celebrating his 76th birthday.
Herbert, Victor	Irish-born American composer/conductor/cellist Victor Herbert died in New York, New York, on May 26, 1924, age 65. • **Last symphonic work:** *Columbus Suite*, part of which was commissioned originally for the World's Columbian Exposition in Chicago, Illinois, in 1893. Herbert later added three movements and premiered it in 1903, while he was conductor of the Pittsburgh Symphony. • **Last opera:** *Madeleine* (1914). • **Last completed score for Broadway show:** *The Dream Girl* (1924), at

	the Ambassador Theater in New York, New York. • **Last music for a Broadway show:** a number for the *Ziegfeld Follies of 1924*, which opened on June 24, 1924, at the New Amsterdam Theater in New York, New York. Herbert was working on it when he died. • **Last film scores:** *Little Old New York* (special theater music, 1923); *When Knighthood was in Full Flower* (1922).
Herrmann, Bernard	American composer/conductor Bernard Herrmann died in Los Angeles, California, on December 24, 1975, age 64. • **Last film scores:** *Taxi Driver* (1976) and *Obsession* (1976), both released posthumously.
Hindemith, Paul	German composer/conductor/violist Paul Hindemith died in Frankfurt, Germany, on December 28, 1963, age 68. • **Last composition:** *Mass* for unaccompanied chorus (1963). • **Last operas:** *The Harmony of the World* (1951) in five acts; *The Long Christmas Dinner* (1960) in one act, set to a libretto by Thornton Wilder.
Holst, Gustav	English composer Gustav Theodore Holst died in London, England, on May 25, 1934, age 59. • **Last compositions:** *Lyric Movement* (1933) and *Brook Green Suite* (1933). In 1934, Holst scored a *Scherzo* that he had begun in 1933: he planned for it to be part of a symphony but died before he finished it. • **Last ballet:** *The Morning of the Year* (1927), a choral ballet. • **Last film score:** *The Bells* (1931). It was not released in the United Kingdom or United States, and no copies are known to exist. • **Last opera:** *The Wandering Scholar*, Opus 50 (finished in 1930, premiered in 1934).
Honegger, Arthur	French composer Arthur Honegger died in Paris, France, on November 27, 1955, age 63. • **Last composition:** *Une Cantate de Noël.* Honegger began collaborating on it with Swiss poet Caesar von Arx in 1940 but put it aside when Arx died. He was commissioned to finish the work in 1953, and it premiered that December. • **Last Broadway show:** *Maitresse De Roi,* a play with music by Honegger; opened on November 30, 1926, at the Cosmopolitan Theater in New York, New York. • **Last film score:** *Storm Over Tibet* (1952).
Humperdinck, Engelbert	German composer Engelbert Humperdinck died in Neustrelitz, Germany, on September 27, 1921, age 67. • **Last composition:** the opera *Gaudeamus* (1919). It was completed with the help of his son Wolfram. • **Last public appearance:** September 26, 1921, at a production of Weber's *Der Freischutz,* his son Wolfram's first production as director. Humperdinck had a heart attack during the performance and died the next day.
Ibert, Jacques	French composer Jacques François Antoine Ibert died in Paris, France, on February 5, 1962, age 71. • **Last major composition:** *Symphony No. 2,* ("Bostoniana," unfinished, 1955-61, premiered in Paris, 1963). • **Last film score:** *Invitation to the Dance* (1956).
Ireland, John	English composer/pianist John Nicholson Ireland died in Sussex, England, on June 12, 1962, age 82.

	• **Last composition:** *Meditation on John Keble's Rogationtide Hymn* (1958) • **Last film score:** *The Overlanders* (1946). The score was later arranged as a suite by Sir Charles Mackerras.
Ives, Charles	American composer Charles Edward Ives died in New York, New York, on May 19, 1954, age 79. Ives did very little composing after he had the first of a series of heart attacks in 1918. • **Last composition:** "A Farewell to Land" (1925), a song with words by the poet Byron.
Janácek, Leos	Czech composer/conductor/organist Leos Eugen Janácek died in Ostrava, Czechoslovakia, on August 12, 1928, age 74. • **Last opera:** *From the House of the Dead* (produced posthumously, 1930) • **Last composition:** *String Quartet No. 2, "Intimate Letters"* (1928), finished shortly before he died. • **Last pupil:** Rudolf Firkusny.
Johnson, James P.	American-born composer/stride pianist/bandleader James Price Johnson died in New York, New York, on November 17, 1955, age 61. • **Last Broadway show as a composer:** *Sugar Hill* (1931). Last peformance of original run: 1932, at the Forrest Theater in New York, New York. • **Last film score:** *Yamekraw* (1930). • **Last film as actor:** *St. Louis Blues* (uncredited, 1929).
Joplin, Scott	American ragtime composer/pianist Scott Joplin died in New York, New York, on April 1, 1917, age 48. • **Last rag:** *Magnetic Rag* (1914). Joplin spent his last six years in New York, working on his opera *Treemonisha*. During that time, he wrote only four rags. *Treemonisha* was not produced on Broadway until 1975. • **Last performance of initial Broadway run of *Treemonisha*:** December 15, 1975, at the Palace Theater in New York, New York..
Kabalevsky, Dmitri	Russian composer Dmitri Borisovich Kabalevsky died in Moscow, Russia, on February 16, 1987, age 83. • **Last piano concerto:** *Piano Concerto No. 4,* ("Prague Concerto") Opus 99 (1975). • **Last composition:** "Cry of the Song," Opus 101 (voice and piano, 1978-79). • **Last film score:** *Khmuroye utro* (a.k.a. *Gloomy Morning* and *Grey Dawn,* 1959).
Kahn, Gus	German-born stage and film lyricist Gus Kahn (Gustav Gerson) died in Beverly Hills, California, on October 8, 1941, age 54. • **Last film score:** *Ziegfeld Girl* (1941). • **Last Broadway show:** *Show Girl* (1929). Last performance of the original run: October 5, 1929, at the Ziegfeld Theater in New York, New York.
Kálmán, Emmerich	Hungarian composer Emmerich (Imre) Kálmán died in Paris, France, on October 30, 1953, age 71. • **Last composition:** *Arizona Lady* (operetta, premiered posthumously, 1954). • **Last Broadway show:** *Marinka* (1945). Last performance of the original run: December 8, 1945, at the Ethel Barrymore Theater in New York, New York. • **Last film score:** *The Csardas Princess* (1951).
Kern, Jerome	American composer Jerome David Kern died in New York, New York, on November 11, 1945, age 60.

	• **Last Broadway show:** *Very Warm for May* (1939). Last performance of original run: January 6, 1940, at the Alvin Theater in New York, New York. Kern had signed to write the score for *Annie Get Your Gun* but had a stroke and died. • **Last film scores:** *Centennial Summer* (1946) and *The Man I Love* (1946), both released posthumously. • **Last song:** "All Through The Day," posthumously featured in the film *Centennial Summer* (1946).
Khachaturian, Aram	Armenian composer/conductor Aram Ilyich Khachaturian died in Moscow, Russia, on May 1, 1978, age 74. • **Last composition:** *Vocalise in C Major* (for piano, 1978). • **Last film score:** *Nakanune* (a.k.a. *On the Eve,* 1959).
Kodály, Zoltán	Hungarian composer/educator Zoltán Kodály died in Budapest, Hungary, on March 6, 1967, age 84. • **Last completed composition:** *Laudes Organi* (1966). • **Last film score:** *Háry János* (1966).
Korngold, Erich Wolfgang	Austrian-born American composer Erich Wolfgang Korngold died in Hollywood, California, on November 29, 1957, age 60. • **Last film score:** *Magic Fire* (a.k.a. *Frauen um Richard Wagner,* 1956). Korngold arranged Wagner's music for a film about him. • **Last opera:** *Kathrin* (1937). • **Last symphonic work:** *Symphony in F Sharp,* Opus 40 (premiered 1954). • **Last composition:** *Theme and variations,* Opus 42 (1953).
Kreisler, Fritz	Austrian violinist/composer Friedrich (Fritz) Kreisler died in New York, New York, on January 29, 1962, age 86. • **Last Broadway show:** *Rhapsody* (1944). Last performance of original run December 2, 1944, at the New Century Theater in New York, New York • **Last film score:** *The King Steps Out* (1936). • **Last public performance as violinist:** November 1, 1947, concert at Carnegie Hall, New York, New York.
Lalo, Édouard	French composer Édouard Victor Antoine Lalo died in Paris, France, on April 22, 1892, age 69. • **Last compositions:** *Piano Concerto in F Minor* (1889), opera *La Jacquerie* (unfinished, 1892). Completed by Arthur Coquard and premiered in Monte Carlo, Monaco, in 1895.
Lehár, Franz	Hungarian composer Ferencz (Franz) Lehár died in Bad Ischl, Austria, on October 24, 1948, age 78. • **Last composition:** the operetta *Giuditta,* produced at the Vienna State Opera in 1934. • **Last Broadway show:** *Yours is My Heart* (1946). Last performance of original run: October 5, 1946, at the Shubert Theater in New York, New York. • **Last film score:** *Shadow of a Doubt* (uncredited, 1943), contributed original music.
Leoncavallo, Ruggiero	Italian composer Ruggiero Leoncavallo died in Montecatini, Italy, on August 9, 1919, age 61. • **Last Broadway production:** *I Pagliacci.* Leoncavallo contributed to a short version performed at Daly's Theater in New York, New York, in 1908. The full opera was produced posthumously at the Center Theater in New York, New York, in 1944.

	• **Last opera:** *Edipo Re*, premiered in Chicago, Illinois, the year after his death.
Lerner, Alan Jay	American lyricist/librettist/playwright Alan Jay Lerner died in New York on June 14, 1986, age 67. He frequently collaborated with composer Frederick Loewe. • **Last Lerner and Loewe Broadway collaboration:** *Gigi* (1973). Last performance of original run: February 19, 1974, at the Uris Theater in New York, New York. • **Last Lerner and Loewe film score collaboration:** *The Little Prince* (1974). It was also Lerner's last film score. • **Last Broadway show:** *Dance a Little Closer.* Music by Charles Strouse (1983). Last performance of original run: May 11, 1983, at the Minskoff Theater in New York, New York.
Liadov, Anatoli	Russian composer Anatoli Konstantinovich Liadov (or Lyadov) died in Novgorod, Russia, on August 28, 1914, age 59. • **Last orchestral composition:** *Skorbnayapesn* (*Nénie*) a symphonic poem
Liszt, Franz	Hungarian composer/pianist Franciscus (Franz or Ferencz) Liszt died in Bayreuth, Germany, on July 31, 1886, age 74. • **Last composition:** a few bars of Mackenzie's *Troubadour,* on which he had planned to write a fantasy. Liszt was active as a composer until the end of his life. Works he wrote during the year before he died include *Mephisto Waltz No. 4, Hungarian Rhapsodies Nos. 18* and *19* and *Salve Regina.* • **Last concert performance (for his own benefit):** 1847, at Elisabethgrad. Liszt then retired from concert performances. • **Last public performance:** July 19, 1886, in Sondershausen, Germany. Liszt was asked to perform at the end of a concert he was attending. He played a fantasia and *Soiree de Vienne.* • **Last piano owned by Liszt:** Found in a religious institution in Rome in 1991 by Carlo Dominici. The piano, which is also the last playable piano owned by Liszt, has been restored. It was made by the French piano maker Erard c. 1865. • **Last surviving pupil:** José Vianna Da Motta, who died in 1948. Two others who have been named as Liszt's last pupil are Emil von Sauer, who died in 1942 and Alexander Siloti, who died in 1945.
Loesser, Frank	American composer Frank Loesser died in New York, New York, on July 28, 1969, age 59. • **Last Broadway show:** *How to Succeed in Business Without Really Trying* (1961). Last performance of original run: March 6, 1965, at the 46th Street Theater in New York, New York. • **Last non-Broadway musical score:** *Pleasures and Palaces* (1965). The show closed during an out of-town tryout before making it to New York. • **Last film score:** *Hans Christian Anderson* (1952).
Loewe, Frederick	Austrian-born American composer Frederick Loewe died in Palm Springs, California, on February 14, 1988, age 83. He frequently collaborated with lyricist/librettist/playwright Alan Jay Lerner. • **Last Lerner and Loewe Broadway collaboration:** *Gigi* (1973). Last performance of original run: February 19, 1974, at the Uris Theater in New York, New York. • **Last Lerner and Loewe film score collaboration:** *The Little Prince*

	(1974). • **Last film score:** *Galateya* (TV, 1977). Loewe collaborated with Timur Kogan. • **Last Broadway show:** *Lerner and Loewe: A Very Special Evening* (1979). Last performance of original run: May 14, 1979, a benefit concert at the Winter Garden Theater in New York, New York.
Lully, Jean-Baptiste	Italian-born French composer Jean-Baptiste Lully died in Paris, France, on March 22, 1687, age 54. • **Last opera:** *Armide* (1686). • **Last public performance:** January 8, 1687, at a performance of his *Te Deum*. A few weeks later Lully died of gangrene caused by an injury sustained at the concert. He accidentally stabbed his foot with his baton (a long staff) while conducting.
Lutoslawski, Witold	Polish composer/conductor/pianist Witold Lutoslawski died in Warsaw, Poland, on February 7, 1994, age 81. • **Last composition:** *Symphony No. 4* (premiered 1993). • **Last recording:** *Symphony No. 3,* with Lutoslawski conducting the Polish National Radio Symphony Orchestra (1992).
MacDowell, Edward	American composer/pianist Edward MacDowell died in New York, New York, on January 23, 1908, age 47. • **Last compositions:** *10 New England Idyls* (for piano), *Six Fireside Tales*, and *Summer Wind* (for women's chorus), all written in 1902.
Mahler, Gustav	Bohemian-born composer Gustav Mahler died in Vienna, Austria, on May 18, 1911, age 50. • **Last compositions:** *Das Lied von der Erde* (*The Song of the Earth*) and *Symphony No. 9,* both completed the year before he died. *Symphony No. 10* remained uncompleted at the time of his death He finished only the Adagio. • **Last appearance of Mahler as conductor of his own work:** January 20, 1911, in New York, New York, at a performance of his *Symphony No. 4* • **Last public performance:** February 21, 1911, in New York, New York. Mahler collapsed immediately afterward and died three months later.
Mancini, Henry	American composer Enrico Nicola (Henry) Mancini died in Los Angeles, California, on June 14, 1994, age 70. • **Last Broadway show:** *Victor/Victoria* (opened posthumously, 1995). Last performance of original run: July 27, 1997, at the Marquis Theater in New York, New York. • **Last film scores:** *Son of the Pink Panther* (1993) and *A Memory for Tino* (1993). • **Last Top 40 *Billboard* hit (Pop Charts) as performer:** "[Theme from] Love Story," which entered the charts on February 6, 1971. Credited as Henry Mancini and His Orchestra.
Mascagni, Pietro	Italian composer/conductor Pietro Mascagni died in Rome, Italy, on August 2, 1945, age 82. • **Last composition:** "O Roma felix" (1942). • **Last Broadway show:** *The Eternal City* (1902). Last performance of original run: 1903, at the Victoria Theater in New York, New York. • **Last opera:** *Nerone* (produced 1935).
Massenet, Jules	French composer Èmile Frédéric (Jules) Massenet died in Paris, France, on August 23, 1912, age 70.

	• **Last opera:** *Cléopâtre* (1912; premiered posthumously 1914). • **Last Massenet opera performed in his lifetime:** *Roma,* at the Paris Opera in 1911.
Mendelssohn, Felix	German composer/conductor/pianist Jakob Ludwig Felix Mendelssohn-Bartholdy died in Leipzig, Germany, on November 4, 1847, age 38. • **Last orchestral composition:** *Violin Concerto in E Minor, Opus 64 (1844).* • **Last completed major work:** *String Quartet No. 6 in F Minor,* Opus 80 (1846). • **Last composition:** "Nachtlied" (Night Song), written for a friend's birthday in October 1847. Mendelssohn died a month later. He left several uncompleted works, including the opera *Lorelei* and an oratorio, *Christus.*
Mercer, Johnny	American songwriter/lyricist John Herndon (Johnny) Mercer died in Los Angeles, California, on June 25, 1976, age 66. • **Last major collaboration:** Musical with Andre Previn, based on the J.P. Priestley novel *The Good Companions.* Opened in London, England in July 1974. • **Last recording:** *That's What Life is All About* (1976), Bing Crosby with the Pete Moore Orchestra (Special Guest Johnny Mercer). Two duets with Crosby and Johnny Mercer: "The Pleasure of Your Company" and "Good Companions." • **Last Broadway shows as composer:** *Foxy* (1964). Last performance of original run: April 18, 1964, at the Ziegfeld Theater in New York, New York. *Seven Brides for Seven Brothers* was turned into a stage musical posthumously. Last performance of original run: July 11, 1982, at the Alvin Theater in New York. • **Last Broadway show as performer:** *Hello Worship* (1928). Last performance of original run: May 11, 1928, at the Frolic Theater in New York, New York. • **Last film scores:** *The Facts of Life* (1960), *Something's Got to Give* (unfinished, 1962). He also wrote lyrics for many later films. The last was *Walt Disney's Robin Hood* (animated, 1973). • **Last film as himself:** *Screen Snapshots Series 25, No. 6: Wendell Niles and Don Prindle Show* (short, 1946). • **Last film as actor:** *To Beat the Band* (1935). • **Last song:** "Twilight World," music by Marian McPartland (1973).
Meyerbeer, Giacomo	German composer Giacomo Meyerbeer (Jakob Liebmann Beer) died in Paris, France, on May 2, 1864, age 72. • **Last opera:** *L'Africaine.* Meyerbeer began working on it in 1838 and devoted many years to it. *L'Africaine* was in rehearsal when he died. It was premiered posthumously in 1865. • **Last opera written for the Italian stage:** *Il Crociato in Egitto* (premiered in 1824). It was also the last opera for which a solo role was written for a soprano castrato.
Milhaud, Darius	French composer/pianist Darius Milhaud died in Geneva, Switzerland, on June 22, 1974, age 81. • **Last composition:** *Quintet for Winds,* Opus 443 (1973). • **Last film score:** *Rentrée des classes* (short, 1956). • **Last film as actor:** *Entr'acte* (short, 1924).

Monteverdi, Claudio	Italian composer Claudio Monteverdi died in Venice, Italy, on November 29, 1643, age 76. • **Last opera:** *The Coronation of Poppea* (1642, premiered posthumously). Several Monteverdi's compositions were first published in 1642, shortly before he died. Others were first published in 1649 and 1650, after his death.
Morton, "Jelly Roll"	American pioneer jazz composer/pianist "Jelly Roll" Morton (Ferdinand Joseph Le Mothe Mouton) died in Los Angeles, California, on July 10, 1941, age 50 or so. His last name is also shown as La Menthe and LaMott. Some sources list his birth year as 1885; others, as 1890. • **Last studio recording:** *Last Sessions: The Complete General Recordings,* released December 1939. • **Last performance of original Broadway run of *Jelly's Last Jam*:** September 5, 1993, at the Virginia Theater in New York, New York. The show was a posthumously produced revue of his music.
Mozart, Wolfgang Amadeus	Austrian composer Wolfgang Amadeus Mozart died in Vienna, Austria, on December 5, 1791, age 35. • **Last compositions:** Mozart was living in Vienna in the summer of 1791, when he received a mysterious commission to compose a *Requiem*. He had a foreboding of death and believed the *Requiem* was intended for him. His health began to deteriorate in the fall of 1791. During his final days, he worked intensely to finish the *Clarinet Concerto* (K622, 1791) and *Eine kleine Freimaurer Kantata* (*Masonic Cantata*, K623, 1791). He completed a short motet, *Ave Verum Corpus,* (K618, 1791) and was working on the *Requiem* (K626, 1791) when he died. • **Last symphony:** *No. 41 in C Major* (*Jupiter*, K551, 1788). • **Last piano concerto:** *No. 27 in B Flat* (K595, 1791). • **Last opera:** *La Clemenza di Tito* (*The Clemency of Titus*, K621, 1791), an opera seria. • **Last public performance:** March 4, 1791, in Vienna. Mozart played the first performance of his *Piano Concerto No. 27.*
Mussorgsky, Modest	Russian composer Modest Mussorgsky died in Saint Petersburg, Russia, on March 28, 1881, age 42. • **Last compositions:** He left two unfinished operas: *Khovantchina* and *The Fair at Sorochinsk. Khovantchina* was completed by Rimsky-Korsakov and premiered in 1886. Cesar Cui produced a version of *The Fair at Sorochinsk* in 1917. Nicholai Tcherepnin also produced a version of it in 1923. • **Last public appearance of Mussorgsky:** February 15, 1881, when Rimsky-Korsakov conducted one of his works.
Newman, Alfred	American composer/director Alfred Newman died in Hollywood, California, on February 18, 1970, age 69. • **Last film score:** *Airport* (1970). He died shortly afterward. • **Last Broadway show:** *Funny Face* (1927-28). Last performance of original run: January 23, 1928, at the Alvin Theater in New York, New York. • **Last Academy Award:** *Camelot* (1967). Newman was nominated for more Oscars than any other composer of film music. He won nine.
Nielson, Carl	Danish composer Carl August Nielson died in Copenhagen, Denmark, on October 3, 1931, age 66.

	• **Last major work:** *Commotio,* Opus 58, for organ, composed a few months before he died.
Offenbach, Jacques	German-born composer Jacques Offenbach (Jacob Levy Eberst) died in Paris, France, on October 5, 1880, age 61. • **Last composition:** the opera *The Tales of Hoffman.* Offenbach worked on his opera during his last two years but died before it was finished. It was completed by Ernest Guirard and presented the following year.
Orff, Carl	German composer/conductor Carl Orff died in Munich, Germany, on March 29, 1982, age 87. • **Last composition for the stage:** *De temporum fine comoedia* (*Comedy About the End of Time,* 1969-71). It premiered in Salzburg, Austria, in 1973. • **Last film score:** *Die Bernauerin* (TV, 1958).
Ornstein, Leo	Russian-born American composer/pianist Leo Ornstein died in Green Bay, Wisconsin, on February 24, 2002, age 109. • **Last composition:** *Eighth Piano Sonata,* finished in September 1990, when he was in his 90s.
Paderewski, Ignace Jan	Polish composer/piano virtuoso Ignace Jan Paderewski died in New York, New York, on June 29, 1941, age 80. • **Last composition:** a hymn, "Hey, White Eagle" (1917). • **Last film:** *Moonlight Sonata* (1937). • **Last piano used by Paderewski:** a Steinway & Sons piano now on display in the Paderewski Room in the Polish Museum of America, Chicago, Illinois. • **Last surviving pupil:** Henryk Sztompka. • **Last resting place:** Paderewski was a fervent Polish nationalist who worked to see his homeland established as an independent state. When Poland was invaded by Germany at the beginning of World War II, Paderewski relocated to the United States, where he headed the Polish government-in-exile. When he died, he was buried in Arlington National Cemetery at the request of President Franklin D. Roosevelt. His heart was removed and kept elsewhere. Paderewski asked in his will that his body be returned to a free Poland, but he wanted a part of him to stay always in America. His heart was later enshrined in a bronze monument at the Our Lady of Czestochowa, Doylestown, Pennsylvania. Paderewski's body was returned to his homeland on June 27, 1992, and placed in Saint John's Cathedral in Krakow.
Paganini, Niccolò	Italian composer/virtuoso violinist Niccolò Paganini died in Nice, France, on May 27, 1840, age 57. • **Last composition:** waltz (May 1840). Most of his works were published posthumously. • **Last violin performance**: June 9, 1837, in Turin, Italy, with guitarist Luigi Legnani.
Piston, Walter	American composer/teacher Walter Hamor Piston died in Belmont, Massachusetts, on November 12, 1976, age 82. • **Last composition:** *Concerto for String Quartet, Winds and Percussion* (1976).
Poulenc, Francis	French composer Francis Poulenc died in Paris, France, on January 30, 1963, age 64. • **Last composition:** *Sonata for Oboe and Piano* (1962), the last of three woodwind sonatas written in his final year.

	• **Last opera:** *The Human Voice* (1959) a one-act tragedy.
Prokofiev, Sergei	Russian composer Sergei Sergeyevich Prokofiev died in Moscow, Russia, on March 5, 1953, age 61. He died on the same day as Stalin, and his death went unpublished and unknown to all but close friends for days. • **Last symphony:** *Symphony No. 7 in C Sharp Minor,* Opus 131, premiered in 1952. • **Last completed piano sonata:** *Piano Sonata No. 9 in C,* Opus 103, completed in 1947 and premiered by Russian pianist Svyatoslav Richter. • **Last completed composition:** a revision of *Piano Sonata No. 5 in C Major* (a revision of Opus 38, renumbered Opus 135), finished in 1953. • **Last ballet:** *A Tale of the Stone Flower,* Opus 118 (1948-53), unfinished. It was in rehearsal when Prokofiev died. Dmitri Kabalevsky finished part of it. • **Last film score:** *Ivan the Terrible* (1945). • **Last opera:** *The Story of a Real Man,* Opus 117 (1948). • **Last public performance:** January 13, 1945. Prokofiev conducted the Moscow Philharmonic Orchestra in a performance of his *Symphony No. 5.* He suffered a concussion soon afterward. The injury created health problems that prevented Prokofiev from further performances during his remaining eight years. • **Last public appearance:** October 11, 1952, at the premiere of his *Symphony No. 7 in C Sharp Minor,* Opus 131.
Puccini, Giacomo	Italian composer Giacomo Puccini died in Brussels, Belgium, on November 29, 1924, age 65. Puccini is considered the last great Italian Romantic opera composer. • **Last opera:** *Turandot.* Puccini was working on it when he died. The score was completed by Franco Alfano, and *Turandot* had its first performance in 1926.
Purcell, Henry	English composer/organist Henry Purcell died in London, England, on November 21, 1695, age 36. • **Last composition:** *Funeral Music for Queen Mary* (1694).
Rachman- inoff, Sergei	Russian composer/pianist/conductor Sergei Vasilyevich Rachmaninoff died in Beverly Hills, California, on March 28, 1943, age 69. Rachmaninoff is considered the last great Russian Romantic composer. • **Last compositions:** Among his last works were a revision of his 1909 *Piano Concerto No. 4 in G Minor,* Opus 40 (1941) and a piano arrangement of a Tchaikovsky lullaby (1941). • **Last orchestral composition:** *Symphonic Dances,* Opus 45 (1940). • **Last completed work for solo piano:** *Variations on a Theme of Corelli* (1931). • **Last major work for piano and orchestra:** *Rhapsody on a Theme of Paganini,* Opus 43 (1934). • **Last opera:** *Monna Vanna* (unfinished, 1907). • **Last performance as a conductor:** March 14, 1941, Chicago, Illinois. A performance of his *Symphony No. 3,* Opus 44. • **Last performance as a pianist:** In 1942-43, during World War II, Rachmaninoff made a concert tour for the benefit of war relief. He became ill after playing a concert at the University of Tennessee Alumni Gymnasium in Knoxville on February 17, 1943. He died a few weeks later.

Rameau, Jean Philippe	French composer Jean-Philippe Rameau died in Paris, France, on September 12, 1764, age 80. • **Last opera:** *Abaris ou les Boréades* (1763). Symphonic excerpts were performed in 1896. A concertante version was performed in 1964. But it was not until 1982, in Aix-en-Provence, that the opera was given its first performance under John Eliot Gardiner.
Ravel, Maurice	French composer Maurice Joseph Ravel died in Paris, France, on December 27, 1937, age 62. • **Last public performance:** 1933. Ravel was in a traffic accident in 1932. Within a few months, he lost his coordination, was in great pain and was partially paralyzed. He underwent brain surgery in 1937 in an attempt to help him, but he never regained consciousness. He died nine days later. • **Last work for solo piano:** *Le Tombeau de Couperin,* published in 1917. • **Last ballet:** *Bolèro*, premiered in 1928 as a concert piece. • **Last film score:** *Don Quichotte à Dulcinée* (songs for voice and piano, 1932-33), commissioned for a film but not used. • **Last surviving pupil:** Polish-born French pianist Vlado Perlemuter, who died September 23, 2002, age 98.
Resphigi, Ottorino	Italian composer Ottorino Resphigi died in Rome, Italy, on April 18, 1936, age 56. • **Last composition:** *Lucrezia,* a one-act opera. Resphigi died before he completed the orchestration. *Lucrezia* was finished by his widow with the help of composer Ennio Porrino and was produced posthumously at La Scala, Milan, Italy, on February 24, 1937.
Riddle, Nelson	American composer/arranger/conductor Nelson Smock Riddle died in Los Angeles, California, on October 6, 1985, age 64. • **Last Top 40 *Billboard* hit (Pop Charts) during his lifetime:** "Route 66 Theme," which entered the charts on August 4, 1962. His last No. 1 hit was "Lisbon Antiqua" (1955). Both were credited as Nelson Riddle and His Orchestra. • **Last film score:** *Chattanooga Choo Choo* (1984). In 1985, he wrote the score for the TV special *The International Championship of Magic*. • **Last film:** *Linda Ronstadt in Concert: What's New* (as himself, 1984).
Rimsky-Korsakov, Nikolai	Russian composer/conductor Nikolai Andreyevich Rimsky-Korsakov died in Lyubensk, Russia, on June 21, 1908, age 64. • **Last composition:** *The Golden Cockerel* (1906-07), an opera based on a work of Pushkin. It was banned during Rimsky-Korsakov's lifetime because it satirized the autocratic government of Russia. It was produced for the first time in Moscow in 1909. • **Last public appearance:** 1907, festival of Russian music in Paris, France.
Rodgers, Richard	American composer Richard Rodgers died in New York, New York, on December 30, 1979, age 77. Rodgers collaborated with lyricist Lorenz Hart on 29 shows and about 400 songs from 1925 until Hart's death in 1943. He then collaborated with Oscar Hammerstein II until Hammerstein's death in 1960. • **Last Broadway collaboration with Lorenz Hart:** *By Jupiter* (1942). Last performance of original run: June 12, 1943, at the Shubert Theater in New York, New York. • **Last film score with Lorenz Hart:** *Higher and Higher* (1943); Rod-

	gers and Hart contributed only the song "Disgustingly Rich." Their last major film collaboration was *They Met in Argentina* (1941). • **Last Broadway collaboration with Oscar Hammerstein II:** *The Sound of Music* (1959). Last performance of original run: June 15, 1963, at the Mark Hellinger Theater in New York, New York. • **Last film score collaboration with Oscar Hammerstein II:** *State Fair* (1945). • **Last Broadway show:** *Rex* (1976), a collaboration with Sheldon Harnick. Last performance of original run: June 5, 1976, at the Lunt-Fontanne Theater in New York, New York. • **Last film score:** *Androcles and the Lion* (TV, 1967).
Rodrigo, Joaquín	Spanish composer Joaquín Rodrigo died in Madrid, Spain, on July 6, 1999, age 97. • **Last composition:** *Ecos de Sefarad* for guitar (1987). • **Last work in concerto form:** *Concierto para un fiesta* (1982). • **Last orchestral composition:** *Palillos y panderetas* (1982). • **Last film score:** *The House of Exorcism* (1973).
Romberg, Sigmund	Hungarian-born composer Sigmund Romberg died in New York, New York, on November 9, 1951, age 64. • **Last Broadway show:** *The Girl in Pink Tights* (produced posthumously). Last performance of original run: June 12, 1954, at the Mark Hellinger Theater in New York, New York. Romberg died soon after he completed the score. • **Last film score:** *Up in Central Park* (1948).
Rossini, Gioacchino	Italian composer Gioacchino Antonio Rossini died in Passy near Paris, France, on November 13, 1868, age 77. • **Last opera:** *William Tell*, his 38th opera, completed in 1829. Although he lived 39 more years, Rossini never wrote another opera. Instead, he composed songs, piano pieces and sacred music. • **Last composition:** a cantata that includes the hymn *À Napoleon III et Son Vaillant Peuple*, composed for the Paris Universal Exposition of 1867.
Rota, Nino	Italian composer Nino Rota died in Rome, Italy, on April 10, 1979, age 67. He wrote all the film scores for Federico Fellini's films from 1952 until 1979. • **Last Fellini film score:** *The Orchestra Rehearsal* (TV, 1979).
Rózsa, Miklós	Hungarian-born American composer Miklós Rózsa died in Los Angeles, California, on July 27, 1995, age 88. • **Last orchestral composition:** *Viola Concerto*, premiered in 1984 by Pinchas Zukerman. • **Last film score:** *Gesucht: Monika Ertl* (1989). • **Last film as himself:** *Billy Wilder* (1970). • **Last film as actor:** *The Private Life of Sherlock Holmes* (uncredited, as the conductor, 1970).
Rubinstein, Anton	Russian composer/pianist Anton Grigorevich Rubinstein died in Peterhof, Russia, on November 20, 1894, age 64. • **Last composition:** *Suite in E Flat for Orchestra* in six movements, No. 119. • **Last public appearances in London, England:** Farewell recitals in May/June 1887, at Saint James Hall.

Saint-Saëns, Camille	French composer/pianist/organist Charles Camille Saint-Saëns died in Algiers, Algeria, on December 16, 1921, age 86. • **Last composition:** three sonatas—for oboe, bassoon and clarinet—written shortly before he died. • **Last film score:** *L' Assassinat du duc de Guise (short, 1908).* • **Last film as himself:** *Ceux de chez nous* (1915). • **Last public performance:** August 6, 1921 in Dieppe, France, a few months before he died. At the end of his concert, he announced that he had performed before an audience for the last time.
Satie, Erik	French composer/pianist Erik Alfred Leslie Satie died in Paris, France, on July 1, 1925, age 59. • **Last composition:** the ballet, *Relache* (1924). The ballet *Mercure* was completed earlier that year. • **Last film score:** *Entr'acte* (1924, short, uncredited). Satie wrote *Cinéma: Entr'acte Symphonique de Relâche* to accompany René Clair's film *Entr'acte.* The film was made to be shown during the intermission of Satie's ballet *Relâche*
Scarlatti, Alessandro	Italian composer Alessandro Scarlatti died in Naples, Italy, on October 25, 1725, age 65. • **Last opera:** *La Griselda* (1721).
Scarlatti, Domenico	Italian composer/harpsichordist Guiseppe Domenico Scarlatti died in Madrid, Spain, on July 23, 1757, age 71. • **Last composition:** *Salve Regina* (for single voice, 1754).
Schoenberg, Arnold	Austrian-born American composer/conductor Arnold Schoenberg died in Los Angeles, California, on July 13, 1951, age 76. • **Last composition:** During his last year, Schoenberg worked on *Moses und Aron,* an opera he began in 1930. He completed only the first two acts and a few bars for Act III before he died. • **Last instrumental composition:** *Phantasy for Violin with Piano Accompaniment,* Opus 47 (1949). • **Last film score:** *Under Cover of Night* (1937).
Schubert, Franz	Austrian composer Franz Schubert died in Vienna, Austria, on November 19, 1828, age 31. • **Last public concert:** March 26, 1828. It was also his only public concert. He used the money he earned from it to buy a piano. • **Last compositions:** Schubert composed three piano sonatas in September 1828: *Sonata in C Minor, Sonata in A Major* and *Sonata in B Flat Major.* He also completed *String Quintet in C Major* in September. He wrote several sacred works in October 1828: *Benedictus in A Minor, Tantum ergo in E Flat Major* and *Offertory Intende voci in B Flat Major.* He also wrote the songs "Der Hirt auf dem Felsen" and "Die Taubenpost." • **Last musical activity:** On November 14, fatally ill with typhoid fever, Schubert was able to sit up in his bed and correct the proof of *Winterreise,* his song cycle. He left an huge amount of unpublished work. • **Last opera:** *Der Graf von Gleichen* (1827), left unfinished.
Schumann, Robert	German composer Robert Schumann died in a private asylum at Endenich near Bonn, Germany, on July 29, 1856, age 46. • **Last major works:** *Mass,* Opus 147, and *Requiem,* Opus 148, both in 1852. *Violin Concerto in D Minor* (published posthumously, 1853). • **Last composition:** Mentally ill and delusional, Schumann spent the end

	of his life at the asylum in Endenich. During his final days, he imagined the ghosts of Schubert and Mendelssohn had given him a musical theme. The last music he composed was a set of variations for piano using this theme. The work remains unfinished. • **Last opera:** *Genoveva*, Opus 81 (1847-49, premiered in 1850). • **Last musical position:** Musical director in Düsseldorf, Germany, from 1850 to 1853, before he was fired.
Scriabin, Alexander	Russian composer/pianist Alexander Nikolayevich Scriabin died in Moscow, Russia, on April 27, 1915, age 47. • **Last symphonic work:** *The Poem of Fire: Prometheus* (1910). Scriabin left unfinished *Preparation for the Final Mystery*, begun in 1903. • **Last piano composition:** *Preludes,* Opus 74 (1914). • **Last performance:** April 15, 1915, at Petrograd (Saint Petersburg).
Shostakovich, Dmitri	Russian composer Dmitri Shostakovich died near Moscow, Russia, on August 9, 1975, age 68. • **Last completed composition:** *Sonata for Viola and Piano,* Opus 147, finished a month before he died. It was first performed posthumously on October 1, 1975. • **Last symphony:** *Symphony No. 15 in A Major*, Opus 141 (1971). He left *Symphony No. 16,* Opus 147C, unfinished at the time of his death. • **Last ballet:** *The Dreamers* (1975). • **Last film score:** *King Lear* (1969). • **Last opera:** *Katerina Izmailova*, Opus 114 (1963), a revision of his earlier opera, *Lady Macbeth of the Mtsensk District*, Opus 29.
Sibelius, Jean	Finnish composer Johan Julian Christian (Jean) Sibelius died in Järvenpää, Finland, on September 20, 1957, age 91. • **Last compositions:** tone poem, *Tapiola*, Opus 112 (1926). His last published pieces were for piano, violin and organ (1931). • **Last film score:** *Vastaus* (1952). • **Last film as himself:** *Jean Sibelius kotonaan* (1927, silent).
Smetana, Bedrich	Czech composer Bedrich Smetana died in Prague, Czechoslovakia, on May 12, 1884, age 60. • **Last composition:** the opera *The Devil's Wall*, first performed in 1882. Smetana left unfinished the opera *Viola* (1883-84), based on Shakespeare's *Twelfth Night*.
Sousa, John Philip	American composer/bandmaster John Philip Sousa died in Reading, Pennsylvania, on March 6, 1932, age 77. He assumed leadership of the U.S. Marine Band in 1880 and led it for 12 years. • **Last of the Sousa Band:** After he left the U.S. Marine Band in 1892, Sousa formed the Sousa Band and toured with it for many years. The band folded in 1931, a victim of the Great Depression. He continued to perform with other bands. • **Last surviving member of the original Sousa Band:** Rudolph Becker, who joined the band as a clarinetist during the band's formation in 1892 and continued with the band until 1918. Becker later played with the Philadelphia Orchestra. He died in Philadelphia, Pennsylvania, on April 17, 1961, age 95. • **Last appearance of Sousa as bandmaster:** March 6, 1932. Sousa died after conducting a rehearsal of the Ringgold Band in Reading, Pennsylvania. The last piece of music he conducted was one of his greatest

	marches, "The Stars and Stripes Forever."
	• **Last appearance with a military band:** February 22, 1932, when Sousa conducted the U.S. Navy Band at the United States Capitol in Washington D.C., commemorating the bicentennial of George Washington's birth.
	• **Last appearance at Willow Grove Amusement Park:** 1926. Sousa appeared at the Pennsylvania park every year from 1901 to 1926, except for the year 1911.
	• **Last film as himself:** *John Philip Sousa* (silent, 1900).
	• **Last composition:** "The Library of Congress March," the last march Sousa began. It remained unfinished when he died. The march was reconstructed by composer Stephen Bulla under the supervision of Sousa authority Loras John Schissel. The march premiered at the Library of Congress in Washington, D.C., on May 6, 2003.
	• **Last Broadway show:** *Everything* (1918). Last performance of original run: Hippodrome Theater in New York, New York.
Steiner, Max	Austrian-born American composer Maximilian Raoul (Max) Steiner died in Hollywood, California, on December 28, 1971, age 83.
	• **Last film scores:** *Those Calloways* (1965), *Two on a Guillotine* (1965).
Straus, Oscar	Austrian composer Oscar Straus died in Bad Ischl, Austria, on January 11, 1954, age 83.
	• **Last film score:** *Le Ronde* (*The Roundabout,* 1950). Straus contributed to the score of *The Earring of Madame de* (1953).
	• **Last Broadway show:** *The Last Waltz* (1921). Last performance of original Broadway run: 1921 at the Century Theater in New York, New York.
Strauss, Johann (Jr.)	Austrian composer Johann Strauss Jr. died in Vienna, Austria, on June 3, 1899, age 73.
	• **Last composition:** the operetta *Die Götten der Vernunft* (1897). Two Strauss works were published posthumously: *Aschenbrodel* (*Cinderella,* ballet) and *Traumbilder* (orchestral piece).
	• **Last public appearance:** May 22, 1899, at a festival in Vienna.
Strauss, Richard	German composer/conductor/pianist Richard Strauss died in Garmisch-Partenkirchen, West Germany, on September 8, 1949, age 85.
	• **Last composition:** *Four Last Songs from Hermann Hesse and Joseph von Eichendorff*, Opus 150, completed in 1948. A fifth song remained unfinished.
	• **Last opera:** *Capriccio,* Opus 85, staged in Munich, Germany, in 1942.
	• **Last public performance:** June 1949, conducting *Der Rosenkavalier,* the day before his 85th birthday.
Stravinsky, Igor	Russian composer/conductor/pianist Igor Fyedorovich Stravinsky died in New York, New York, on April 6, 1971, age 88.
	• **Last major composition:** *The Requiem Canticles,* (1965-66). Stravinsky also arranged two sacred choral songs from Hugo Wolf's *Spanisches Liederbuch* (1968-69) and composed *The Owl and the Pussycat,* a song for voice and piano, based on Edward Lear's poem (1966).
	• **Last ballet:** *Agon* (1957).
	• **Last opera:** *The Rake's Progress* (1951).
	• **Last public performance as conductor:** 1967, Massey Hall in Toronto, Canada. Stravinsky conducted *Pulcinella* for the only time in his career, and he remained seated throughout.

	• **Last recording:** *The Firebird Suite* (1967). • **Last film as himself:** *A Stravinsky Portrait* (1966).
Strayhorn, Billy	American composer/pianist/arranger Billy Strayhorn died in New York, New York, on May 31, 1967, age 51. He was a frequent collaborator with Duke Ellington. • **Last composition:** "Blood Count," finished while in the hospital, shortly before he died.
Sullivan, Arthur S.	English librettist Arthur Seymour Sullivan died in London, England, on November 22, 1900, age 58. • **Last collaboration with William S. Gilbert:** *The Grand Duke* (1896). They collaborated for 28 years on 14 light operas. Gilbert wrote the lyrics. Sullivan composed the music. • **Last opera:** *The Emerald Isle* (unfinished); completed by Edward German after Sullivan's death and premiered in 1901.
Tchaikovsky, Peter Ilich	Russian composer Peter Ilich Tchaikovsky died in Saint Petersburg, Russia, on November 6, 1893, age 53. • **Last completed composition:** *Symphony No. 6 in B minor,* Opus 74 (*Pathétique*), completed two months before he died. It had its first performance on October 28, 1893. • **Last unfinished compositions:** Tchaikovsky began work on *Symphony No. 7* in 1892, but was displeased with it and set it aside. He used the first movement for his *Piano Concerto No. 3*. His pupil Sergi Taneyev later added an andante and a finale to the concerto from Tchaikovsky's symphony notes. Soviet musicologist Semyon Bogatyriev reconstructed *Symphony No. 7* in 1956, and it premiered the following year. In the second half of 1893, Tchaikovsky worked on a piano arrangement of a Russian folk song, "Tis Not the Wind that Bends the Branch," and a concertante piece, *Andante and Finale*, Opus 79, which was left unfinished at the time of his death along with some other fragments. • **Last ballet:** *The Nutcracker*, Opus 71 (1892). • **Last opera:** *Iolanta,* Opus 69 (1891). • **Last public appearance:** October 16, 1893, when Tchaikovsky conducted his *Piano Concerto No. 1* in Saint Petersburg.
Tiomkin, Dmitri	Russian-born composer/pianist Dmitri Tiomkin died in London, England, on November 12, 1979, age 81. • **Last film score:** *Chaikovsky* (*Tchaikovsky*, 1969).
Tippett, Sir Michael	English composer Sir Michael Kemp Tippett died in London, England, on January 8, 1998, age 93. • **Last composition:** *Caliban's Song* (1995). • **Last orchestral work:** *The Rose Lake* (1993). • **Last film score:** *Let My People Go* (short, 1965).
Turina, Joaquin	Spanish composer/conductor/pianist Joaquín Turina died in Madrid, Spain, on January 14, 1949, age 66. • **Last composition:** *From My Terrace* (1947). • **Last film score:** *Una Noche en Blanco* (1949).
Vaughan Williams, Ralph	English composer/conductor/organist Ralph Vaughan Williams died in London, England, on August 26, 1958, age 85. • **Last composition:** *Symphony No. 9 in E Minor* (1958). • **Last film score:** *The Vision of William Blake* (1958).

Verdi, Giuseppe	Italian operatic composer Giuseppe Fortunino Francesco Verdi died in Milan, Italy, on January 27, 1901, age 87. • **Last composition:** A musical setting for a prayer written by Queen Margherita after the assassination of her husband, Humbert I (1900). • **Last opera:** *Falstaff* (1885-92), the last of 26 operas. Verdi was 72 when he began working on it. *Falstaff* premiered at La Scala, Milan, when he was 79.
Villa-Lobos, Heitor	Brazilian composer/conductor Heitor Villa-Lobos died in Rio de Janeiro, Brazil, on November 17, 1959, age 72. • **Last composition:** *Forest of the Amazon* (symphonic poem, late 1958/early 1959). It was created from music originally composed for the film *Green Mansions* but little of the score was used. • **Last Broadway show:** *Magdalena* (1948). Last performance of original Broadway run: December 4, 1948, at the Ziegfeld Theater in New York, New York. • **Last film score:** *Green Mansions* (1959). • **Last film as himself:** *South of the Border with Disney* (short, 1940).
Vivaldi, Antonio	Italian composer/violinist Antonio Lucio Vivaldi died in Vienna, Austria, on July 28, 1741, age 65 to 72 (birth date uncertain). • **Last compositions:** Cantatas composed just before he left Venice, Italy, for Vienna in 1741.
Wagner, Richard	German composer Richard Wagner died in Venice, Italy, on February 13, 1883, age 69. • **Last composition:** "Good Friday Spell" from *Parsifal.* • **Last opera:** *Parsifal,* premiered at the 1882 Bayreuth Festival. • **Last performance:** December 24, 1882. While in Venice, Wagner conducted—as a birthday gift for his wife Cosima—a private performance of a symphony he had composed as a young man.
Waller, Thomas ("Fats")	American composer/pianist/arranger/leader Thomas Wright ("Fats") Waller died aboard a train near Kansas City, Missouri, on December 15, 1943, age 39. • **Last recording:** September 1943, on a V-Disc. • **Last public performance:** Zanzibar Room, Hollywood, California, December 1943. Afterward, he boarded a train for New York. Waller was not feeling well, but he wanted to be home with his family for Christmas. He died of bronchial pneumonia en route. • **Last composition:** Broadway musical *Early to Bed* (1943). Last performance of original run: May 13, 1944, at the Broadhurst Theater in New York, New York. • **Last film as himself:** *Stormy Weather* (1943). • **Last film as actor:** *Ain't Misbehavin'* (1941).
Walton, Sir William	English composer Sir William Turner Walton died in Ischia, Italy, on March 8, 1983, age 80. Walton is considered one of Great Britain's last great Romantic composers. • **Last composition:** *Prologo e Fantasia* (1981-82) written for Mstislav Rostropovich. • **Last film score:** *Three Sisters* (1970). • **Last film as actor:** *Wagner* (1983).
Warren, Harry	American composer/songwriter Harry Warren (Salvatore Anthony Guaragna) died in Los Angeles, California, on September 22, 1981, age 87.

	• **Last Broadway show:** *42ⁿᵈ Street* (1980). Last performance of original run: January 8, 1989, at the Saint James Theater in New York, New York. • **Last film score:** *Busby Berkeley* (1974). • **Last film as himself:** *Go Into Your Dance* (uncredited, 1935). • **Last film as actor:** *A Very Honorable Guy* (uncredited, 1934).
Waxman, Franz	German-born American composer Franz Waxman died in Los Angeles, California, on February 24, 1967, age 60. • **Last composition:** *Dr. Jekyll and Mr. Hyde,* opera, unfinished. • **Last film score (documentary):** *The Longest Hundred Miles* (*Escape from Bataan*, TV, 1967). • **Last film score (feature film):** *Lost Command* (1966). • **Last film as actor:** *Love in the Afternoon* (uncredited, 1957).
Weber, Carl Maria von	German composer Carl Maria von Weber died in London, England, on June 5, 1826, age 39. • **Last completed composition:** the march "Zu den Fluren des heimischen Herdes," a reworking of an earlier work. • **Last uncompleted composition:** the song "From Chindara's warbling fount I come." It was reconstructed for performance after his death. • **Last major composition:** the opera *Oberon* (premiered April 12, 1826).
Webern, Anton	Austrian composer/conductor Anton Friedrich Wilhelm von Webern died after being shot accidentally by an American soldier on sentry duty in Mittersill, Austria, on September 15, 1945, age 61. • **Last completed composition:** *Cantata No. 2, for soprano, bass, choir and orchestra*, Opus 31 (1943). Webern began working on Opus 32, another cantata, but died before completing it. It was later finished by John Beckwith as *After Images, after Webern*. Its premiere on September 15, 1995, coincided with the fiftieth anniversary of Webern's death.
Weill, Kurt	German-born American composer Kurt Weill died in New York, New York, on April 3, 1950, age 50. • **Last opera:** *Lost in the Stars* (1949), a musical version of *Cry, the Beloved Country*. Libretto by Maxwell Anderson. Last performance of original Broadway run: July 1, 1950, at the Music Box Theater in New York, New York. Weill was collaborating with Anderson on an adaptation of *Huckleberry Finn* when he died. • **Last film score:** *Down in the Valley* (TV, 1950).
Wolf, Hugo	Austrian composer Hugo Wolf died in Vienna, Austria, on February 22, 1903, age 42. • **Last compositions:** the opera *Manuel Venegas* (unfinished, 1897); three Michelangelo sonnets set to music (composed March 1897).
Young, Victor	American composer/violinist Victor Young died in Palm Springs, California, on November 10, 1956, age 56. • **Last Broadway show:** *Seventh Heaven* (1955). Last performance of ori-ginal run: July 2, 1955, at the ANTA Playhouse in New York, New York. • **Last film score:** *China Gate* (unfinished). Young died while working on the score. It was completed by Max Steiner and released in 1957. • **Last Top 40 *Billboard* hit (Pop Charts) as performer:** "(Main Theme) Around the World in 80 Days," which entered the charts on July 8, 1957, posthumously. Credited as Victor Young and His Singing Strings.

Music—Classical—Composers—The Five/The Mighty Handful

In the 1860s, Russian music critic Vladimir Stasov dubbed a group of Russian nationalist composers "The Mighty Handful." Also known as "The Five," they included: Mily Balakirev, Alexander Borodin, César Cui, Modest Mussorgsky and Nikolai Rimsky-Korsakov.

• **Last surviving member of The Five:** César Cui, who died in Petrograd (Saint Petersburg), Russia, on March 24, 1918, age 83.

Music—Classical—Composers—Les Six

"Les Six" were a group of French composers who banded together after World War I to protest the impressionistic music of Debussy and others. They were given that name by music critic Henri Collet in 1920. Les Six were: Georges Auric, Louis Durey, Arthur Honegger, Darius Milhaud, Germaine Tailleferre and Francis Poulenc. The group lost their cohesiveness in the 1920s.

• **Last surviving member of Les Six:** Germaine Tailleferre, who died in Paris, France, on November 7, 1983, age 91.

Music—Classical Performers

Anderson, Marian	American contralto Marian Anderson died in Portland, Oregon, on April 8, 1993, age 96. • **Last concert performance:** recital on Easter Sunday, April 19, 1965, at Carnegie Hall in New York, New York. In 1976, she toured as an actress in Aaron Copland's *A Lincoln Portrait*. • **Last film:** *Marian Anderson* (1991).
Björling, Jussi	Swedish operatic tenor Jussi Björling died in Siaroe, Sweden, on September 9, 1960, age 49. • **Last opera performance:** *Il Trovatore,* Stockholm Royal Opera, March 6, 1960. • **Last New York concert performance:** recital at Hunter College, New York, New York, December 27, 1959. • **Last U.S. concert performance:** recital in Pasadena, California, April 5, 1960. • **Last recording:** *Requiem* (Verdi) in Vienna, Austria, June 12-18, 1960. • **Last concert performance:** recital, August 20, 1960, in Stockholm, Sweden.
Callas, Maria	American operatic soprano Maria Callas (Kalogeropoulos) died in Paris, France, on September 16, 1977, age 53. • **Last concert performance:** with tenor Giuseppe di Stefano, in Sapporo, Japan, November 11, 1974. • **Last opera performance:** *Tosca* (Puccini) at Covent Garden, London, England, July 5, 1965. • **Last film:** *Medea* (1969).
Caruso, Enrico	Italian operatic tenor Enrico Caruso died in Naples, Italy, on August 2, 1921, age 48. • **Last concert performance:** Brooklyn School of Music, New York, December 11, 1920. • **Last opera performance:** December 24, 1920, portraying Eleazar in Jacques Halevy's *La Juive* at the Metropolitan Opera House, New York, New York. He was taken ill on stage. • **Last recording:** Victor Records, Camden, New Jersey, September 16, 1920.

	• **Last film:** *Splendid Romance* (silent, 1919). • **Last surviving person who performed in a recital with Caruso:** Nina Morgana, a soprano who studied voice in Milan, Italy, and later worked as an assistant artist on Caruso's concert tours. Morgana sang for the Metropolitan Opera from 1920 to 1935. She died in Ithaca, New York, on July 8, 1986, age 94.
Casals, Pablo	Spanish cellist/conductor/composer Pablo Casals died in Rio Piedras, Puerto Rico on October 22, 1973, age 96. • **Last public performance:** at the Jerusalem Music Center workshop and performance three weeks before he died. He played cello and conducted a youth orchestra especially created for the occasion.
Chaliapin, Feodor	Russian operatic bass Feodor Ivanovich Chaliapin died in Paris, France, on April 12, 1938, age 65. • **Last New York concert performance:** March 3, 1935. • **Last concert performance:** London Palladium, March 21, 1937. • **Last film:** *Don Quixote* (1933). • **Last resting place:** Chaliapin left Russia in 1921, after the revolution and eventually settled in Paris, where he died and was buried in 1938. In 1984, his body was disinterred and was taken to the Novodevichy Monastery Cemetery in Moscow.
Farrar, Geraldine	American operatic soprano Geraldine Farrar died in Ridgefield, Connecticut, on March 11, 1967, age 85. • **Last Metropolitan Opera performance:** *Zaza* (Leoncavallo), 1922. • **Last concert performance:** Carnegie Hall, New York, New York, 1931. Farrar retired in 1931. • **Last film:** *The Woman and the Puppet* (1920).
Fiedler, Arthur	American conductor Arthur Fiedler died in Brookline, Massachusetts, on July 10, 1979, age 84. He began conducting the Boston Pops concerts in 1930. • **Last Boston Pops recording:** *Capriccio Italian* and *Capriccio Espagnole* (1977). • **Last film as himself:** *Arthur Fiedler: Just Call Me Maestro* (TV, 1979). • **Last film as actor:** *Mary's Incredible Dream* (TV, 1976).
Flagstad, Kirsten	Norwegian operatic soprano Kirsten Flagstad died in Oslo, Norway, on December 7, 1962, age 67. • **Last Metropolitan Opera performance:** *Alceste* (Gluck), April 1, 1952. • **Last opera performance:** *Dido* (Purcell), Mermaid Theater, London, 1952. • **Last U.S. concert performance:** Wagnerian music, benefit for Symphony of the Air, March 22, 1955. • **Last film:** *The Big Broadcast of 1938* (as herself, 1938).
Gigli, Beniamino	Italian operatic tenor Beniamino Gigli died in Rome, Italy, on November 30, 1957, age 67. He was an accomplished actor and made many films. • **Last opera performance:** Messina, Italy. He sang both Turiddu in *Cavalleria Rusticana* (Mascagni) and Canio in *Pagliacci* (Leoncavallo), August 22, 1954. • **Last concert performance:** recital in Washington, D.C., on May 25, 1955, the last of 41 farewell performances worldwide. • **Last film as singer:** *Puccini* (1952, voice, reissued in 1956 as *Two Loves Had I*). • **Last film as himself:** *Soho Conspiracy* (1950). • **Last film as actor:** *Taxi di notte* (a.k.a. *The Singing Taxi Driver,* 1950).

Gould, Glenn	Canadian concert pianist/conductor/composer Glenn Herbert Gould died in Toronto, Canada, on October 4, 1982, age 50. • **Last concert performance:** recital at the Wilshire Ebell Theater in Los Angeles, California, April 10, 1964. After that, Gould concentrated on making recordings. A few months before he died, he formed a chamber orchestra in Toronto. • **Last album:** *Glenn Gould Conducts Wagner's Siegfried Idyll* (1982). • **Last film as himself:** *The Music of Man* (TV miniseries, 1978). • **Last film as actor:** *Cities* (TV miniseries, 1979). • **Last film score:** *The Wars* (1983).
Hofmann, Josef	Polish-born American concert pianist/composer Josef Hofmann (Kasimierz) died in Los Angeles, California, on February 16, 1957, age 81. • **Last Carnegie Hall performance:** January 20, 1946, on his 70th birthday.
Horowitz, Vladimir	Ukrainian-born concert pianist Vladimir Horowitz died in New York, New York, on November 5, 1989, age 86. • **Last live performances:** 1987. • **Last film:** *Horowitz Plays Mozart* (1987). • **Last recording:** 1989. Horowitz recorded works by Haydn, Liszt, Liszt/Wagner and Chopin for Sony Classical. Released as *The Last Recording,* it went on to win the 1990 Grammy for the best solo classical album.
Jeritza, Maria	Czech operatic dramatic soprano Maria Jeritza (Mizzi Jedlitzka) died in Orange, New Jersey, on July 10, 1982, age 94. • **Last Metropolitan Opera performance:** *Tosca* (Puccini), for the 66th time, February 6, 1932. • **Last film:** *Großfüsterin Alexandra* (1933).
Kapell, William	American concert pianist William Kapell, age 31, was killed in a plane crash near San Francisco, California, on October 29, 1953, on the way home from a concert tour in Australia. • **Last concert performance:** Goolong, Australia, October 22, 1953, the last of 37 concerts in 14 weeks. The concert was broadcast live and recorded. The last piece Kapell performed was Chopin's *Sonata in B-Flat Minor*, known as the "Funeral March" sonata.
Lanza, Mario	American operatic tenor/actor Mario Lanza (Alfredo Arnold Cocozza) died in Rome, Italy, on October 9, 1959, age 38. • **Last Hollywood film:** *Serenade* (1955). • **Last European film:** *For the First Time* (1959). • **Last concert performance:** Kiel, West Germany, April 13, 1959. • **Last recording:** included "The Lord's Prayer," recorded September 10, 1959.
Lehmann, Lotte	German operatic soprano Lotte Lehmann died in Santa Barbara, California, on August 26, 1976, age 87. • **Last Metropolitan Opera performance:** the Marschallin in *Der Rosenkavalier* (Strauss), February 17, 1945. • **Last opera performance:** *Der Rosenkavalier* (Strauss), Los Angeles, California, November 1, 1946. • **Last New York concert performance:** recital, February 16, 1951: The recital was recorded. • **Last concert performance:** recital, Pasadena, California, November 11, 1951. • **Last film as actress:** *Big City* (1948).

Levant, Oscar	American concert pianist/actor/composer Oscar Levant died in Beverly Hills, California, on August 12, 1972, age 65. • **Last concert performance:** August 2, 1958. • **Last recording:** *Oscar Levant at the Piano* (1958). • **Last musical film as actor:** *The 'I Don't Care' Girl* (1953). • **Last dramatic film as actor:** *The Cobweb* (1955). • **Last film score:** *Romance on the High Seas* (1948).
Lind, Jenny	Swedish-born soprano Jenny Lind (the "Swedish Nightingale") died in Malvern, England, on November 2, 1887, age 67. • **Last U.S. performance:** Castle Garden, New York, New York, May 24, 1852. • **Last concert performance:** *Robert le Diable* (Meyerbeer), London, England, May 10, 1849. • **Last professional performance:** January 20, 1870. Lind sang the soprano role in her husband Otto Goldschmidt's oratorio *Ruth* in Düsseldorf, Germany. • **Last public performance:** Charity concert, Malvern, England, July 23, 1883.
Martinelli, Giovanni	Italian operatic tenor Giovanni Martinelli died in New York, New York, on February 2, 1969, ago 83. • **Last Metropolitan Opera performance:** *Norma* (Bellini), March 8, 1945. • **Last opera performances:** Martinelli formally retired after a performance in *Samson and Delilah* (Saint-Saëns) in Philadelphia, Pennsylvania, on January 25, 1950; however, he made appearances afterward. His last was as the Emperor Altoum in *Turandot* (Puccini) in 1965 when he was 80. • **Last film:** *Italian Songs* (Vitaphone short, 1931).
McCormack, John	Irish lyric tenor John McCormack died in Dublin, Ireland, on September 16, 1945, age 61. • **Last U.S. concert performance:** Buffalo, New York, March 17, 1937. • **Last concert performance:** Farewell Concert, Royal Albert Hall, London, England, November 27, 1938. • **Last film as himself:** *Wings of the Morning* (1937). • **Last film as actor:** *Song O' My Heart* (1930).
Melba, Dame Nellie	Australian soprano Dame Nellie Melba (Helen Porter Mitchell) died in Sydney, Australia, on February 23, 1931, age 69. • **Last performance in England:** Covent Garden, London, 1926. She performed at a charity concert at the Brighton Hippodrome on October 5, 1929. • **Last performance in Australia:** Geelong, November 1928.
Melchior, Lauritz	Danish-born American tenor Lauritz Melchior died in Santa Monica, California, on March 18, 1973, age 82. • **Last Metropolitan Opera performance:** *Lohengrin* (Wagner), February 2, 1950. • **Last film as actor:** *The Stars are Singing* (1952).
Moore, Grace	American operatic soprano Grace Moore was killed in a plane crash in Copenhagen, Denmark, on January 26, 1947, age 48. • **Last Broadway performance:** *The Dubarry*, 1932. • **Last film as herself:** *A Dream Comes True* (uncredited, 1935). • **Last film as actress:** *Louise* (1939). • **Last concert performance:** January 25, 1947, before an audience of

	more than 4,000 people in Copenhagen, Denmark. The following day, her plane crashed on take-off.
Ormandy, Eugene	Hungarian-born American conductor Eugene Ormandy (Jeno Blau) died in Philadelphia, Pennsylvania, on March 12, 1985, age 85. He led the Philadelphia Orchestra for 44 years. • **Last concert performance:** with the Philadelphia Orchestra at Carnegie Hall, New York, New York, January 10, 1984. • **Last film:** *Night Song* (1948). • **Last professional appearance:** as an honoree at *The Kennedy Center Honors: A Celebration of the Performing Arts* (TV, 1982).
Peerce, Jan	American operatic tenor Jan Peerce (Jacob Pincus Perelmuth) died in New Rochelle, New York, on December 15, 1984, age 80. • **Last Metropolitan Opera performances:** 1966-67 season. • **Last concert performance:** Carnegie Hall, 1982. • **Last film:** *Goodbye, Columbus* (cameo, 1969). The film was directed by his son Larry
Pinza, Ezio	Italian operatic bass Fortunato ("Ezio") Pinza died in Stamford, Connecticut, on May 9, 1957, age 64. • **Last Metropolitan Opera performance:** *Don Giovanni* (Mozart). December 6, 1948. • **Last film:** *Tonight We Sing* (1953). • **Last Broadway appearance in *South Pacific*:** January 16, 1954. He originated the role of Emile de Becque in 1949. After *South Pacific*, Pinza appeared in the theatrical show *Fanny*.
Pons, Lily	French operatic coloratura soprano Lily (Alice Josephine) Pons died in Dallas, Texas, on February 13, 1976, age 71. • **Last opera performance:** The Mad Scene from *Lucia di Lammermoor* (Donizetti) with Placido Domingo, at the Will Rogers Auditorium, Fort Worth, Texas, November 26 and 30, 1962. • **Last concert performance:** Promenade Concert of the New York Philharmonic, with Andre Kostelanetz conducting, May 1972. • **Last film:** *Carnegie Hall* (as herself, 1947).
Ponselle, Rosa	American operatic soprano Rosa Ponselle died in Baltimore, Maryland, on May 25, 1981, age 84. • **Last Metropolitan Opera performance:** *Carmen* (Bizet), Cleveland, Ohio, April 17, 1937. • **Last concert performance:** February 1939. • **Last film:** *Broadway Highlights No 2* (short, as herself, 1935).
Robeson, Paul	American singer/actor/activist Paul Robeson died in Philadelphia, Pennsylvania, on January 23, 1976, age 77. • **Last Broadway performance:** *Othello* (1943-44). Last performance of revival run: July 1, 1944, at the Shubert Theater in New York, New York. • **Last concert performances:** October-November 1960, in Australia and New Zealand, with accompanist Lawrence Brown. • **Last public appearance:** *Freedomways* magazine celebration of Robeson's 67th birthday at Hotel Americana, New York, New York, April 22, 1965. Because of failing health, Robeson made no further public appearances. (*See also* Movies—Performers.)
Rubinstein, Arthur	Polish-born American concert pianist Arthur Rubenstein died in Geneva, Switzerland, on December 20, 1982, age 95.

	• **Last concert performance:** Wigmore Hall, London, England, June 10, 1976. • **Last film:** *Arthur Rubinstein—The Love of Life* (1969).
Sayao, Bidu	Brazilian-born American operatic soprano Bidu Sayao died in Lincolnville, Maine, March 12, 1999, age 94. • **Last opera role:** *La Demoiselle Elue* (Debussy). • **Last Metropolitan Opera performance:** 1951. She retired from live performances in 1954. • **Last recording:** Brazilian composer Heitor Villa-Lobos's *The Forest of the Amazon* (1959). Sayao came out of retirement to record with him. • **Last film:** *Toscanini: The Maestro* (as herself, 1988).
Schumann-Heink, Ernestine	Czech-born American operatic contralto Ernestine Roessler Schumann-Heink died in Hollywood, California, on November 17, 1936, age 75. • **Last Broadway performance:** *Love's Lottery* (1904). Last performance of original run: 1904, at the Broadway Theater in New York, New York. • **Last Metropolitan Opera performance:** Erda in *Siegfried* (Wagner), March 11, 1932. • **Last Victor Company recording:** "My Heart Ever Faithful" (Bach) and "Taps" (Pasternack), January 1931. She recorded with Victor for 25 years. • **Last film:** *Here's to Romance* (1935).
Segovia, Andrés	Spanish classical guitarist/composer Andrés Segovia died in Madrid, Spain, on June 2, 1987, age 94. • **Last concert performance:** Miami Beach, Florida, in 1987, just weeks before his death. He spent part of his 90th year concertizing in Japan and the United States.
Solti, Sir Georg	Hungarian conductor Sir Georg Solti died in Antibes, France on September 5, 1997, age 84. • **Last orchestral performance:** Royal Opera House, Zurich, Switzerland, July 12 and 13, 1997. • **Last opera performance:** *Simon Boccanegra* (Verdi) at Covent Garden, London, England, 1997. • **Last recording:** *Don Giovanni* (Mozart) with the London Philharmonic, 1996. • **Last films:** *Anna Karénine* (*Anna Karenina,* conductor, 1997). He also appeared in a segment of *The Great Conductors* TV series in 1997.
Stokowski, Leopold	English-born conductor Leopold Stokowski died in Nether Wallop, Hampshire, England, on September 13, 1977, age 95. • **Last live performance:** 1975, Venice, Italy. • **Last recording:** 1977, a few weeks before he died. Stokowski led the National Philharmonic Orchestra, a specially formed group made up of top London-area musicians. Among the works recorded in that session: *Symphony No. 2* (Brahms) and *Symphony No. 4* (Mendelssohn). • **Last film:** *Moments in Music* (as himself, 1950).
Swarthout, Gladys	American operatic mezzo soprano Gladys Swarthout died in Florence, Italy, on July 7, 1969 age 68. • **Last Metropolitan Opera performance:** *Carmen* (Bizet) March 7, 1945. • **Last film as actress:** *Ambush* (1939).
Szell, George	Hungarian-born American conductor George Szell died in Cleveland, Ohio, on July 30, 1970, age 73. • **Last studio recording:** Dvorák's *Symphony No. 8* with the Cleveland Orchestra, Severance Hall, Cleveland, April 28-29, 1970.

	• **Last live recording:** *La Damnation de Faust* (Berlioz) with the Cleveland Orchestra, May 22, 1970, at Ueno Bunka-Kaikan Culture Center, Tokyo, Japan.
Tauber, Richard	Austrian-born British tenor/conductor/composer Richard Tauber died in London, England, on January 8, 1948, age 56. • **Last opera performance:** *Don Giovanni* (Mozart) at Covent Garden, London, September 27, 1947. • **Last film as actor:** *Lisbon Story* (1946).
Tibbett, Lawrence	American operatic baritone Lawrence Tibbett died in New York, New York, on July 15, 1960, age 63. • **Last Metropolitan Opera performance:** *Khovantchina* (Mussorgsky), 1950. • **Last Broadway performance:** *Fanny.* Last performance of original run: December 16, 1956, at the Belasco Theater in New York, New York. • **Last film:** *House of Strangers* (voice, uncredited, 1949).
Toscanini, Arturo	Italian conductor/cellist Arturo Toscanini died in New York, New York, on January 16, 1957, age 89. • **Last appearances in Italy and England:** 1952. La Scala, Milan, and Royal Festival Hall, London with the London Philharmonia Orchestra. • **Last live performance:** with the NBC Symphony, April 4, 1954. At the end of the concert, Toscanini let his baton fall to the floor and walked off the stage. He did not return to acknowledge the applause. • **Last studio performance:** recording session of the NBC Symphony on June 5, 1954. • **Last opera broadcast:** *Un Ballo in Maschera* (Verdi) in 1954. • **Last film:** *Hymn of Nations* (1944).
Traubel, Helen	American operatic soprano Helen Traubel died in Santa Monica, California, on July 28, 1972, age 73. • **Last Metropolitan Opera performance:** *Tristan und Isolde* (Wagner) in 1953. • **Last film as actress:** *Gunn* (1967).
Tucker, Richard	American operatic tenor Richard Tucker died in Kalamazoo, Michigan, while preparing for a concert on January 8, 1975, age 60. • **Last Metropolitan Opera performance:** *Pagliacci* (Leoncavallo), a few weeks before he died. • **Last film:** *Carmen* (TV, 1953).
Walter, Bruno	German-born American conductor/pianist Bruno Walter (Schlesinger) died on in Beverly Hills, California, on February 17, 1962, age 85. • **Last recording:** Mozart overtures with the Columbia Orchestra in Los Angeles, California, March 29, 31, 1961. • **Last Metropolitan Opera performance:** conducting Verdi's *Requiem,* March 27, 29, 1959. • **Last public appearance:** December 4, 1960, Los Angeles Philharmonic with pianist Van Cliburn. • **Last film:** *Bruno Walter, The Maestro, The Man* (TV, 1958).
Wunderlich, Fritz	German lyric tenor Friedrich Karl ("Fritz") Wunderlich died in an accidental fall down stone steps in a castle in Heidelberg, Germany, on September 17, 1966, age 35. • **Last performance:** Usher Hall, Edinburgh, Scotland, September 4, 1966, performing Robert Schumann's *Dichterliebe,* Opus 48, and Franz

Schubert's *Lieder,* accompanied by pianist Hubert Giesen. Wunderlich was to have made his New York Metropolitan Opera debut as Don Ottavio in *Don Giovanni* (Mozart) on October 8, 1966.
• **Last recording of live performance:** Wunderlich's Edinburgh performance was recorded and later released as *Fritz Wunderlich's Last Concert.*
• **Last studio recording:** *The Creation* (Haydn) with Herbert von Karajan and the Berlin Philharmonic Orchestra, 1966. Wunderlich died before the recording was completed. The remaining recitatives were taken over by Werner Krenn.

Music—Classical—Performers—Castrati Singers

Castrati singers were adult male sopranos whose youthful voices were retained by castration. Centuries ago, the Roman Catholic Church banned women from singing in church services. Since soprano voices were needed for liturgical music, one solution was to castrate young males before puberty to preserve their high voices. The castrati also found roles in operas. As the popularity of opera grew in the 1700s, the practice of castrating men for their voices began to draw critics. The practice fell into disrepute after Voltaire, Rousseau and others attacked it as a crime against nature. Castrati singers began to disappear from opera in the late 18th century.
• **Last castrati allowed by the Roman Catholic Church:** In the Roman Catholic church, Pope Benedict XIV (1740-58) spoke out against the practice of castrating singers. Pope Clement XIV (1769-74) threatened with excommunication those who continued the practice. Despite the ban, castrati could still be found into the early 20th century. As late as 1900, there were 16 castrati in Italian church choirs and the Sistine Chapel choir. They were banned from singing in the Vatican in 1903.
• **Last surviving castrato:** Allessandro Moreschi, who had the surgery in 1865. He joined the Sistine Chapel Choir in 1883, became its conductor in 1898 and retired in 1913. He died in Vatican City in 1922, age 64. He is the only castrato for whom recordings survive.
• **Last operatic castrato:** Giovanni Velluti. When he performed in an opera in London in

1825, Velluti caused considerable controversy.
• **Last opera written for a castrato:** *Il Crociato in Egitto* by Giacomo Meyerbeer. It premiered in 1824.

Music—Classical—Performers—Orchestras—Vienna Philharmonic

• **End of ban on women musicians:** February 27, 1997, when members of the Vienna Philharmonic voted to admit women to the orchestra. It ended the Philharmonic's 155-year policy of excluding women. The orchestra was preparing for an overseas tour and made the move to avert protests.

Music—Popular—Auditoriums—Grand Ole Opry

Ryman Auditorium in Nashville, Tennessee, became the home of the Grand Ole Opry in 1941.
• **Last performance of Grand Ole Opry at Ryman Auditorium:** March 9, 1974. The show moved to the new Opryland.

Music—Popular—Disc Jockeys—Freed, Alan

Alan Freed broke barriers by playing the music of black artists for primarily white audiences. He coordinated the first Rock concert and is credited with coining the term "Rock & Roll." He died in Palm Springs, California, on January 20, 1965, age 42.
• **Last Rock & Roll movie of Freed:** *Go Johnny Go* (producer, 1959). It featured performances by the Flamingos, the Cadillacs, Chuck Berry, Eddie Cochran, Harvey Fuqua, Ritchie Valens and Jackie Wilson.
• **Last day Freed was at station WINS in New York:** May 9, 1958. Freed quit one day after being indicted for inciting unlawful de-

struction of property in Boston, Massachusetts.

• **Last day Freed was at station WABC in New York:** November 20, 1959. He was fired for refusing to say that he never accepted payola.

• **Last day Freed was at station WNEW-TV in New York:** November 28, 1959. He was fired for refusing to say that he never accepted payola.

Music—Popular—Promoters—Graham, Bill

Rock promoter Bill Graham was involved in many musical milestones, including Woodstock and Live Aid. He was killed in a helicopter crash on October 25, 1991, age 60.

• **Last major project of Graham:** He was killed while he was working on his book: *Bill Graham Presents: My Life Inside Rock and Out.*

Music— Popular—Performers
(Includes Bluegrass, Country & Western, Folk, Gospel, Jazz, Pop, Rap, Rhythm & Blues, Rock & Roll, Soul. Performers are American unless stated otherwise. See also Movies—Performers)

Aaliyah	Rhythm & Blues/pop singer/actress Aaliyah Dana Haughton died in a plane crash in Marsh Harbour, Abaco Island, Bahamas, on August 25, 2001, age 22. • **Last album:** *Aaliyah*, released July 17, 2001, a month before she died. A compilation of tracks Aaliyah had been working on was released posthumously as *I Care 4 U* in December 2002. • **Last Top 40 *Billboard* hit (Pop Charts) during Aaliyah's lifetime:** "We Need a Resolution" (2001). Several additional hits were released posthumously. The last was "Miss You" (2003). • **Last music video:** "Rock the Boat." Aaliyah was killed while returning from the filming. • **Last film:** *Queen of the Damned* (released posthumously, 2002). Aaliyah's last film role was Queen Akasha. Just before she was killed, she had started to film two sequels to the *Matrix*: *The Matrix Reloaded* (2003) and *The Matrix Revolutions* (2003).
Acuff, Roy	Country music pioneer Roy Claxton Acuff died in Nashville, Tennessee, on November 23, 1992, age 89. • **Last Top 40 *Billboard* hit (Country Charts) during Acuff's lifetime:** "Old Time Sunshine Song" (1974). • **Last film as himself:** *Bill Monroe: Father of Bluegrass Music* (TV, 1993). Acuff also appeared as an honoree in *The Kennedy Center Honors: A Celebration of the Performing Arts* (TV, 1991). • **Last film as actor:** *Country Comes Home* (TV, 1982).
Adderley, Julian ("Cannonball")	Alto saxophonist bandleader Julian Edwin ("Cannonball") Adderley died in Gary, Indiana, on August 8, 1975, age 46. • **Last recording:** original music for *Big Man,* a folk musical based on the life of John Henry (1975). • **Last Top 40 *Billboard* hit (Pop Charts) during Adderley's lifetime:** "Mercy, Mercy, Mercy," which went on the charts on January 28, 1967. • **Last film:** *Save the Children* (as himself, 1973).
Allen, Peter	Australian composer/performer Peter Allen (Woolnough) died in San Diego, California, on June 18, 1992, age 48. • **Last album:** *Make Every Moment Count* (1990).

	• **Last Broadway show as composer and performer during Allen's lifetime:** *Legs Diamond* (1988). Last performance of original run: February 19, 1989, the Mark Hellinger Theater in New York, New York. • **Last Broadway musical as composer:** *The Boy from Oz* (opened posthumously, 2003). • **Last film score:** *The Trap* (TV, 1991). • **Last film as actor:** *The First Olympics: Athens 1896* (TV, 1984). • **Last performance:** concert in Sydney, Australia, January 1992.
Ames Brothers	The four singing Urick brothers, known professionally as The Ames Brothers, were Ed, Gene, Joe and Vic. Vic Ames died on January 23, 1978. Gene Ames died in 1997. • **Last Ames Brothers Top 40 *Billboard* hit (Pop Charts):** "China Doll," which made the charts on February 22, 1960. Ed Ames last charted as a solo performer with "Who Will Answer?," which debuted on the charts on December 30, 1967.
Andrews Sisters	The three singing Andrews Sisters were LaVerne, Maxene and Patty. • **Last surviving Andrews Sister:** Patty (Patricia Marie). LaVerne Sofia Andrews died on May 8, 1967, age 55. Maxene Angelyn Andrews died on October 21, 1995, age 79. • **Last performances together as the Three Andrews Sisters:** 1966. Ill health caused LaVerne to retire. She was replaced by Joyce DeYoung. The second group disbanded with the death of LaVerne. • **Last performance of Maxene and Patty Andrews together**: *The Andrews Sisters in Over Here* (a.k.a. *Over Here*), opened March 6, 1974. Last performance of original run: January 4, 1975, the Shubert Theater, New York, New York. • **Maxene Andrews's last performance**: the show *Swing Time Canteen* at the Blue Angel Theater, New York, New York, October 8, 1995. • **Last Andrews Sisters No. 1 hit:** "I Want To Be Loved" (1950). • **Last film:** *Melody Time* (voices only, 1948).
Armstrong, Louis ("Satchmo")	Jazz trumpeter/vocalist Louis ("Satchmo") Armstrong died in New York, New York, on July 6, 1971, age 69. • **Last recording:** A reading of the poem "A Visit From St. Nicholas" for the HBO special *'Twas the Night.* The recording was made at his home in Corona, New York, in 1971. • **Last albums:** *Disney Songs the Satchmo Way* (1968), *Louis Armstrong and His Friends* (1970) and *Country and Western* (1970). • **Last Top 40 *Billboard* hits (Pop Charts) during Armstrong's lifetime:** "Hello Dolly," which went on the charts on February 29, 1964. ("What a Wonderful World," recorded in 1968, reached the charts on March 19, 1988, after being featured in the film *Good Morning Viet Nam*). • **Last performance:** two-week engagement, Empire Room, Waldorf-Astoria Hotel, New York, New York, February 1971. • **Last Broadway show as performer:** *Swingin' the Dream* (1939). Last performance of original run: December 9, 1939, at the Center Theater in New York, New York. • **Last film:** *Hello Dolly* (1969).
Bailey, Pearl	Singer/actress/dancer Pearl Bailey died in Philadelphia, Pennsylvania, on August 17, 1990, age 72. • **Last telecast of *The Pearl Bailey Show*:** May 8, 1971.

	• **Last feature film:** Disney's *The Fox and the Hound* (voice, 1981). • **Last TV movie:** *Peter Gunn* (1989). • **Last Broadway show:** farewell tour with *Hello Dolly* in 1975. Last Broadway performance of that revival: December 28, 1975, at the Minskoff Theater in New York, New York. Bailey announced her retirement in 1976.
Baker, Chet	Jazz singer/trumpeter Chesney Henry ("Chet") Baker Jr. was killed in a fall from a hotel room window in Amsterdam, Holland, on May 13, 1988, age 58. • **Last albums:** *Diane* (with Paul Bley, 1985), *Chet Baker Trio* (1985). • **Last film score:** *Lapsus* (short, released posthumously, 1991). • **Last recording:** *My Favorite Songs, Vols. 1-2: The Last Great Concert* (recorded April 25, 1988, Funkhaus, Hanover, Germany. Released posthumously). • **Last concert:** at the Thelonious in Rotterdam, Holland, May 1988, a few days before his death. • **Last film:** *Let's Get Lost* (as himself, 1988), a documentary about Baker made during his last year.
Baker, Josephine	Singer/dancer/entertainer Josephine Baker (Freda Josephine Carson) died in Paris, France, on April 12, 1975, age 68. • **Last professional appearance:** April 8, 1975, Bobino Theater, Paris; a revue of routines from her 50-year career as an entertainer. • **Last Broadway show as performer:** *A Evening with Josephine Baker* (1973). Last performance of original run: January 6, 1974, at the Palace Theater in New York, New York. • **Last film:** *Carosello del varietà* (1955).
Basie, Count	Jazz pianist/organist/bandleader William ("Count") Basie died in Hollywood, California, on April 26, 1984, age 79. • **Last Top 40 *Billboard* hit (Pop Charts) during Basie's lifetime:** "April in Paris," which went on the charts on February 4, 1956. • **Last Grammy:** *88 Basin Street* (his ninth, 1984). • **Last musical activity:** Basie had a heart attack in 1976. Despite deteriorating health, he continued to perform. He gave some of his final concerts while in a wheelchair. He spent his last years working on his autobiography, which was published posthumously. • **Last Broadway show as performer:** *Frank Sinatra, Ella Fitzgerald, and Count Basie* (1975). Last performance of original run: September 20, 1975, at the Uris Theater in New York, New York. • **Last film score:** *Killer Diller* (1948). • **Last films:** *Last of the Blue Devils* (as himself, 1979). Basie later appeared in a televised Carnegie Hall concert and multiple televised Kennedy Centers Honors presentations.
Beatles, The	Known in 1958 as The Quarrymen, the British Rock group changed their name to Silver Beatles and then to The Beatles in 1960. • **Last time Stuart Sutcliffe was a Beatle:** April 1961. Sutcliffe, who played bass, died on April 10, 1962, age 21. • **Last appearance of Pete Best as a Beatle:** August 15, 1962. The following day, he was dismissed from the group and replaced on drums by Ringo Starr. The other three Beatles at that time were John Lennon, Paul McCartney and George Harrison. All three played guitar. • **Last Beatles gig at the Cavern Club:** August 3, 1963. The Beatles had

made many early appearances at the Cavern Club, in Liverpool, England, and it was there that they were first seen by future manager Brian Epstein.

• **Last Beatles concert in the United Kingdom:** May 1, 1966, *The New Music Express 'Poll Winners' Show* at Wembley Stadium in London, England, along with The Rolling Stones and The Who.

• **Last U.S. tour:** Began at International AmphiTheater, Chicago, Illinois, August 12, 1966. Ended later that month in San Francisco, California.

• **Last full-scale scheduled live concert of The Beatles:** August 29, 1966, at Candlestick Park (later renamed 3Com Park) in San Francisco, before a crowd of 25,000 people. The last song they sang that night: "Long Tall Sally." After the concert, The Beatles concentrated on studio recordings.

• **Last time The Beatles were managed by Brian Epstein:** August 1967. On August 31, 1967, the group formally announced they would handle their own affairs following the death of Epstein four days earlier.

• **Last performance of the four Beatles as a group:** January 30, 1969, on the roof of Apple Studios, 3 Saville Row, London. Billy Preston played organ. The show was stopped after 42 minutes when police arrived after receiving a noise complaint from the nearby Royal Bank of Scotland. The roof performance was filmed for the movie *Let It Be*, which would be The Beatles' last feature film.

• **Last episode of "The Beatles" cartoon show:** April 20, 1969. The ABC Saturday morning cartoon show premiered four years earlier. It featured Beatles songs but not the real Beatles' speaking voices.

• **Last time all four Beatles recorded together in a studio:** August 20, 1969. The last track recorded by the group as a unit was "I Want You (She's So Heavy)."

• **Last photo session of The Beatles together:** August 22, 1969, at the new home of John Lennon.

• **Last album released while The Beatles were still together:** *Let It Be.* Released in the United Kingdom on May 8, 1970. It was recorded 15 months earlier.

• **Last film:** *Let It Be* (1970), a documentary about how The Beatles made music and the conflict that led to their break-up.

• **Last album recorded by The Beatles:** *Abbey Road,* their 13th. It was released on September 26, 1969, and quickly reached the No. 1 spot, where it remained almost three months.

• **Last song The Beatles recorded together:** "I, Me Mine," on January 3, 1970, recorded by Harrison, McCartney and Starr. Lennon was away on a holiday. Harrison later used this song as the title of his autobiography.

• **Last Top 40 *Billboard* hit (Pop Charts) before the Beatles disbanded:** "The Long and Winding Road" and "For You Blue" went on the charts on May 23, 1970, while *Let it Be* held the No. 1 album spot. The group had filmed a video short for "The Long and Winding Road" on August 22, 1969.

• **Last Top 40 *Billboard* hit (Pop Charts) after The Beatles disbanded:** Several Beatles records have made the Pop Charts after the group disbanded. The last new Top 40 Billboard Chart hit (Pop Charts) was "Real Love," which went on the charts on March 23, 1996. "Real Love," was a demo recorded by John Lennon in 1979.

The other Beatles added new parts in the studio in 1995. It was The Beatles' 52nd Top 40 hit.

- **Last Grammy Award for The Beatles as a group:** 1970, "Best Original Score Written for a Motion Picture or TV Special" for *Let It Be*. Paul and Linda McCartney accepted the awards on behalf of the group.
- **Last of The Beatles as a group:**   disbanded after Paul McCartney announced on April 10, 1970, that he was leaving the group. McCartney filed a writ in the London High Court on December 30, 1970, seeking the legal dissolution of the partnership. Legal dissolution procedures took several years to complete.
- **Last of Wings:** officially disbanded April 1981. Paul McCartney formed the group Wings in 1971.
- **End of Lennon's immigration battle:** John Lennon fought a long immigration battle in the United States beginning in 1972. The battle finally ended on July 27, 1976, when he was awarded his green card.
- **Lennon's last Top 40 *Billboard* hit (Pop Charts) during his lifetime:** "(Just Like) Starting Over," which went on the charts on November 11, 1980, a month before he died and remained there 19 weeks. Several of Lennon's solo recordings entered the charts posthumously. The last, "Nobody Told Me," entered the charts on January 21, 1984. It was his 13th solo Top 40 Hit.
- **Lennon's last live performance:** the Elton John concert, Madison Square Garden, New York, New York, November 28, 1974. Lennon joined Elton John to sing "Whatever Gets You Through the Night," "Lucy In The Sky With Diamonds" and "I Saw Her Standing There."
- **Lennon's last single recording:** "(Just Like) Starting Over" released in the United Kingdom on October 24, 1980.
- **Lennon's last album:** *Double Fantasy* (released in the United States on November 15, 1980). On December 8, 1980, just three weeks after the album was released, Lennon, age 40, was shot to death outside his apartment at The Dakota in New York City by Mark David Chapman, a fan for whom he had signed an autograph earlier that day.
- **Lennon's last film as producer:** *Erection* (1971).
- **Lennon's last film as actor:** *Fire in the Water* (1977).
- **Lennon's last film as director:** *Imagine* (1973).
- **Lennon's last film as himself:** *The Day the Music Died* (1977).
- **Lennon's last piano:** Steinway & Sons upright piano delivered to his New York apartment on May 9, 1979.
- **Harrison's last recording:** Vocal track for "Horse to the Water," co-written by his son Dhani for the Jools Holland Big Band Rhythm and Blues album *Small World Big Band* at his home in Switzerland on October 1, 2001.
- **Harrison's last album:** *Brainwashed,* completed by Dhani Harrison and Jeff Lynne and released in November 2002. George Harrison had been working on it when he died of cancer in Los Angeles, California, on November 29, 2001, age 58.
- **Harrison's last Top 40 *Billboard* hit (Pop Charts) as performer during his lifetime:** "When We Was Fab" (1988). It was his 15th solo Top 40 Hit.
- **Harrison's last film as actor:** *Shanghai Surprise* (1986).
- **Harrison's last film as producer:** *Cold Dog Soup* (1990).
- **George Martin's last album:** Beatles record producer Sir George Martin released his last album of Beatles songs on October 20, 1998, called *George Martin In My Life* (MCA Music America).

Bechet, Sidney	American-born jazz clarinetist/soprano saxophone virtuoso Sidney Joseph Bechet lived for many years in France and died in Paris on his 62nd birthday, May 14, 1959. • **Last recording:** July 1958, at the World's Fair in Brussels, Belgium. • **Last Broadway show as performer:** *Hear that Trumpet* (1946). Last performance of original run: October 12, 1946, at the Playhouse Theater in New York, New York. • **Last film score:** *Ah, quelle équipe! (1957). It was also Bechet's last film as an actor.*
Beiderbecke, Bix	Jazz cornetist/composer Leon Bismarck ("Bix") Beiderbecke died in New York, New York, August 6, 1931, age 28. • **Last recording session:** September 8, 1930, with friend Hoagy Carmichael, for Victor. They recorded four songs together, including Carmichael's "Georgia on My Mind." • **Last performance:** During the summer of 1931, Beiderbecke played some East Coast college engagements. In early August, he became ill with pneumonia and was bed-ridden. Despite failing health, he did not want to disappoint those who were expecting him to play. His last performance was at Princeton University. He died a week later.
Benton, Brook	Rhythm & Blues singer Brook Benton (Benjamin Franklin Peay) died in New York, New York, on April 9, 1988, age 56. • **Last Top 40 *Billboard* hit (Pop Charts) during Benton's lifetime:** "Rainy Night in Georgia," which went on the charts on January 31, 1970. It was his 24th Top 40 hit. • **Last Top 100 *Billboard* hit (Pop Charts) during Benton's lifetime:** "Shoes" and "The Dixie Flyers," which peaked at No. 67. • **Last albums:** *16 Golden Classics* (1986) and *His Greatest Hits* (1986). • **Last film:** *Mister Rock and Roll* (as himself, 1957).
Blackwood Brothers Quartet	The legendary Gospel group Blackwood Brothers Quartet was founded in 1934. The original members were brothers Roy, Doyle and James Blackwood and Roy's oldest son R.W. Blackwood. Their home base was Choctaw County, Mississippi. • **Last surviving founding Blackwood Brothers member:** James Blackwood, who died on February 3, 2002, age 82. A tribute album to Blackwell, entitled *We Called Him Mr. Gospel Music: The James Blackwood Tribute Album*, won the 2003 Grammy for The Jordanaires, Larry Ford and The Light Crust Doughboys.
Blakey, Art	Bandleader/drummer Art Blakey (Abdullah ibn Buhaina) died in New York, New York, on October 16, 1990, age 71. • **Last recording of Art Blakey and the Jazz Messengers:** *One for All,* recorded April 1990, just months before he died. • **Last film:** *Jazz at the Smithsonian: Art Blakey & The Jazz Messengers (released posthumously, 1991).*
Brown, Ray	Jazz bassist Raymond Matthews ("Ray") Brown died in Indianapolis, Indiana, on July 2, 2002, age 75. He remained active as a performer until his death, shortly before he was to perform in Indianapolis. • **Last albums:** *Some of My Best Friends are Guitarists* (2002), *Ray Brown, Monty Alexander and Russell Malone* (2002).
Calloway, Cab	Bandleader/songwriter Cabell ("Cab") Calloway III died in Hockessin, Delaware, on November 18, 1994, age 86.

	• **Last film score:** *Hi-De-Ho* (1947). Some of Calloway's other works were later included in films and TV productions. • **Last film:** Janet Jackson's *Alright* (1989, music video). • **Last non-Broadway show performance:** *His Royal Highness of Hi-De-Ho: the Legendary Cab Calloway* (1987). • **Last Broadway show as performer:** *The Pajama Game* (1973). Last performance was February 3, 1974, at the Lunt-Fontanne Theater in New York, New York. • **Last concert appearance:** with grandson C. Calloway Brooks at a benefit for Associated Black Charities, Baltimore, Maryland, in 1992.
Carle, Frankie	Bandleader/pianist Frankie Carle (Francis Nunzio Carlone) died in Mesa, Arizona, on March 7, 2001, age 97. • **Last tour:** 1983, with Russ Morgan's Orchestra as part of the Big Band Cavalcade. Among his last public appearances was the annual reunion of the Big Band Academy in 1997, when he was in his 90s. • **Last film:** *Champ Butler Sings* (1954).
Carpenters, The	Brother and sister team Karen and Richard Carpenter made up the pop duo known as The Carpenters. Karen died in Downey, California, on February 4, 1983, age 32. • **Last album of new material:** *Made in America* (1981). • **Last Top 40 *Billboard* hit (Pop Charts) as performers during Karen's lifetime:** "Touch Me When I'm Dancing," which entered the charts on July 4, 1981. It was the pair's 20th Top 40 hit. • **Last TV special by The Carpenters:** *Music, Music, Music* (May 1980). • **Last recording session by The Carpenters:** April 1982. The song "Now" was the last one recorded. • **Last public singing appearance by Karen Carpenter:** singing Christmas carols at the Buckley School in Sherman Oaks, California, December 17, 1982. • **Last TV appearance by Karen Carpenter:** 25th Annual Grammy Awards (1983).
Carter, Benny	Virtuoso Jazz alto saxophonist/trumpeter/composer/bandleader Bennett Lester ("Benny") Carter died in Los Angeles, California, July 12, 2003, age 95. He was the last surviving major Jazz figure from the 1930s. • **Last public performance:** Catalina Bar & Grill, Hollywood, California, March 1998. • **Last TV show for which Carter composed music:** *O Canada* (1997). • **Last film as actor:** *The View from Pompey's Head* (1955). • **Last film as himself:** *Jazz Seen: The Life and Times of William Claxton* (2001). Carter also appeared as an honoree on *The Kennedy Center Honors: A Celebration of the Performing Arts* (1996).
Chapin, Harry	Folk-Rock singer/composer/storyteller Harry Chapin died on July 16, 1981, when his car was hit by a tractor-trailer near Jericho, New York, age 38. • **Last Top 40 *Billboard* hit (Pop Charts) as performer during Chapin's life:** "Sequel" (sequel to the hit song "Taxi"), which debuted on the charts on November 22, 1980. • **Last concert:** at Anna Bananas (coffee house) in Honolulu, Hawaii, in July 1981, two weeks before he died. • **Last Broadway show as composer and performer:** *The Night That Made America Famous* (1975). Last performance of original run: April 5,

	1975, at the Ethel Barrymore Theater in New York, New York. • **Last film score:** *Cutting Loose* (1980). • **Last film as actor:** *Mother and Daughter: The Loving War* (1980). • **Last completed song:** "The Last Stand." • **Last TV appearance:** June 25, 1981, with Tom Chapin.
Charles, Ray	Blues singer/pianist Ray Charles Robinson died in Los Angeles, California, on June 10, 2004, age 73. • **Last of 12 Grammy Awards while alive:** "A Song For You" (1993). • **Last public appearance:** April 30, 2004, at the dedication of his 40-year-old studio in Los Angeles as a historic landmark.
Cherry, Don	Cornetist/flutist/bandleader Donald Eugene ("Don") Cherry died in Malaga, Spain, on October 19, 1995, age 58. • **Last studio recording:** *Dona nostra* (1993). • **Last film score:** *Die Ratte* (1993).
Cline, Patsy	Country singer Patsy Cline (Virginia Patterson Hensley) died when her plane crashed near Camden, Tennessee, on March 5, 1963, age 30. • **Last Top 40 *Billboard* hit (Pop Charts) during Cline's lifetime:** "She's Got You," which entered the charts on February 24, 1962. • **Last recording session:** Bradley Studios, Nashville, Tennessee, February 7, 1963. The last song on Cline's last recording was "I'll Sail My Ship Alone" • **Last public appearance:** benefit concert for disc jockey Cactus Jack Call at the Memorial Building in Kansas City, Kansas, March 3, 1963. Call had died in a car accident in January.
Clooney, Rosemary	Jazz and ballad singer/actress Rosemary Clooney died in Beverly Hills, California, on June 29, 2002, age 74. • **Last recording:** with the Honolulu Symphony Pops Orchestra in Hawaii on November 16, 2001. The orchestra made a demo recording of the concert. It would turn out to be her last recording. This was her final performance before being diagnosed with cancer. • **Last Top 40 *Billboard* hit (Pop Charts) during Clooney's lifetime:** "Mangos," which entered the charts on April 13, 1957. • **Last performance:** Count Basie Theater, Red Bank, New Jersey, December 15, 2001. • **Last Broadway show as performer:** *Bing Crosby on Broadway* (1976). Last performance of original run: December 19, 1976, at the Uris Theater in New York, New York. • **Last films as herself:** *Edith Head: The Paramount Years* (short, 2002) and *Marlene Dietrich: Her Own Song* (2001), both documentaries. • **Last film as actress:** *Radioland Murders* (1994).
Cochran, Eddie	Vocalist/guitarist Edward Ray ("Eddie") Cochran died in a car crash in Chippenham, England, on April 17, 1960, age 21. • **Last Top 40 *Billboard* hit (Pop Charts) during Cochran's lifetime:** "C'mon Everybody," which hit the charts on January 5, 1959. • **Last recording session:** Goldstar Studio, Hollywood, California, January 8, 1960. • **Last performance:** concert at the Hippodrome, Bristol, Somerset, England, April 16, 1960. • **Last single:** "Three Steps to Heaven," released three months before Cochran was killed. • **Last film as himself:** *Go, Johnny, Go!* (1958).

	• **Last film as actor:** *Hot Rod Gang* (a.k.a. *Fury Unleashed*, uncredited, 1958).
Cole, Nat "King"	Singer/pianist/actor Nat "King" Cole (Nathaniel Adams Coles) died in Santa Monica, California, on February 15, 1965, age 47. • **Last used name Coles:** 1939. He dropped the "s" from his name when he formed the King Cole Trio. • **Last Top 40 *Billboard* hit (Pop Charts) during Cole's lifetime:** "I Don't Want to See Tomorrow," which entered the charts on October 24, 1964. A recording of "Unforgettable," recorded in 1961 with new vocals added by his daughter Natalie in 1991, entered the charts on July 27, 1991. It was credited as Natalie Cole with Nat "King" Cole and was his 29th Top 40 hit. • **Last film as actor:** *Cat Ballou* (1965). • **Last film as himself:** *Premier Khrushchev in the USA* (1959).
Coltrane, John	Jazz tenor saxophonist/leader/composer John William Coltrane died on Long Island, New York, on July 17, 1967, age 40. • **Last recording with Miles Davis:** *Someday My Prince Will Come* (March 1961). • **Last performance:** Left Bank Jazz Society, Baltimore Maryland, May 7, 1967, two months before he died. • **Last recording before an audience:** "Olatunji Concert" at Babatunde Olatunji's Center for African Culture in New York, New York, April 23, 1967. • **Last recordings in a studio:** "Kulu Se Mama" and "Meditations." Coltrane approved release of the album *Expression* just before he died. • **Last released works:** Several of Coltrane's compositions were released for the first time after he died. The last was "First Meditations (for Quartet)" in 1977.
Columbo, Russ	Singer/bandleader/composer/actor Ruggerio Eugenio de Rodolpho ("Russ") Columbo died in Los Angeles, California, on September 2, 1934, age 26. • **Last recording:** "I See Two Lovers" on August 31, 1934. A few days later, he died in a shooting accident. While a friend was showing him an antique gun, it fired and killed him. • **Last film as actor:** *Wake Up and Dream* (1934). • **Last film as himself:** *Moulin Rouge* (1934). • **Last film score:** *Hello Sister* (1930).
Como, Perry	Singer Pierino ("Perry") Como died in Jupiter, Florida, on May 12, 2001, age 88. • **Last Top 40 *Billboard* hit (Pop Charts) during Como's lifetime:** "And I Love You So," which entered the charts on May 19, 1973. It was his 31st Top 40 hit. • **Last film as himself:** *Frank Sinatra: The Best Is Yet To Come* (TV, 1990) • **Last film as actor:** *Words and Music* (1948).
Cooke, Sam	Soul singer Sam Cooke died in a shooting incident in Los Angeles, California, on December 11, 1964, age 33. • **Last Top 40 *Billboard* hit (Pop Charts) during Cooke's lifetime:** "Cousin of Mine," which entered the charts on October 24, 1964. Several of his songs charted shortly after his death. The last was "Sugar Dumpling," which entered the charts on August 28, 1965. It was his 29th Top 40 hit.

	• **Last recording released in his lifetime:** "At the Copa," released a month before he died. • **Last film:** *Buddy Bregman's Music Shop* (as himself, TV, 1963).
Croce, Jim	Singer/guitarist/composer Jim Croce died in a plane crash in Natchitoches, Louisiana, on September 20, 1973, age 30. • **Last concert:** Northwestern Louisiana University, September 20, 1973. After the concert, Croce and five others were killed when their plane crashed during take-off. • **Last recording session:** Hit Factory, September 13, 1973. • **Last Top 40 *Billboard* hit (Pop Charts) during Croce's lifetime:** "Bad, Bad Leroy Brown," which entered the charts on June 2, 1973. Several of his other songs charted just after his death. The last was "Workin' at the Car Wash Blues," which entered the charts on June 29, 1974.
Crosby, Bing	Singer/actor Harry Lillis ("Bing") Crosby died in Madrid, Spain, on October 14, 1977, age 74. • **Last Top 40 *Billboard* hit (Pop Charts) during Crosby's lifetime:** "White Christmas," which re-entered the charts for the sixth time in December 1962. It was first recorded in 1947. • **Last TV appearance:** *Barbara Walters Special*, May 31, 1977. • **Last TV performance:** Recorded in London, England, September 1977, co-starring David Bowe and Twiggy. It aired after Crosby's death. • **Last Broadway show as performer:** *Bing Crosby on Broadway* (1976). Last performance of original run: December 19, 1976, at the Uris Theater in New York, New York. • **Last album:** *Seasons,* with the Pete Moore Orchestra, September 1977. • **Last recording:** BBC studios in England, October 11, 1977. Crosby recorded eight songs with the Pete Moore Orchestra. The last was "Once in a While." The songs were released as *Bing: The Final Chapter.*
Cugat, Xavier	Spanish-born bandleader/musician/arranger Xavier Cugat (Francisco de Asís Javier Cugat Mingall de Brue y Deulofeo) died in Barcelona, Spain, on October 27, 1990, age 90. • **Last film score:** *The Lightship* (1962). • **Last film as himself:** *Una Rosa al Viento* (as himself, 1984). • **Last film as actor:** *Nunca en horas de clase* (1978).
Darin, Bobby	Singer/songwriter/actor Bobby Darin (Walden Robert Cassotto) died in Los Angeles, California, on December 20, 1973, age 37, while undergoing surgery to correct a congenital heart defect. • **Last Top 40 *Billboard* hit (Pop Charts) as performer during Darin's lifetime:** "Lovin You," which entered the charts on February 11, 1967. It was his 22nd Top 40 hit. • **Last film score:** *Gunfight in Abilene* (1967). • **Last film as actor:** *Happy Mother's Day...Love George* (1973). • **Last *The Bobby Darin Show* telecast:** April 27, 1973. • **Last live performance:** Las Vegas Hilton, August 16-25, 1973.
Davis, Miles	Jazz trumpeter/composer/organist/bandleader Miles Dewey Davis III died in Santa Monica, California, on September 28, 1991, age 65. • **Last appearance:** surprise appearance at the Montreux Jazz Festival with Quincy Jones in 1991, a few months before he died. • **Last album (live performance):** *Miles & Quincy Live at Montreux,* recorded from the 1991 concert performance.

	• **Last studio album:** *Doo-Bop* (released posthumously, 1992). • **Last film score:** *Dingo* (1991). • **Last film as actor:** *Dingo* (1991).
Davis, Sammy (Jr.)	Singer/dancer/actor Sammy Davis Jr. died in Los Angeles, California, on May 16, 1990, age 64. • **Last Top 40 *Billboard* hit (Pop Charts) as performer during Davis's lifetime:** "The Candy Man," which entered the charts on April 15, 1972. It was credited as Sammy Davis Jr. with the Mike Curb Congregation. • **Last telecast of *The Sammy Davis Jr. Show*:** April 22, 1966. • **Last episode of *Sammy and Company*:** produced 1977. The syndicated show was first released in 1975. • **Last Broadway show as performer:** *Stop the World–I Want to Get Off* (revival; 1978). Last performance was August 27, 1978, at the New York State Theater in New York, New York.
Denver, John	Singer/songwriter/entertainer John Denver (Henry John Deutschendorf) died in a plane crash near Monterey Bay, California, on October 12, 1997, age 53. • **Last song:** believed to be "Yellowstone, Coming Home," about the wolves returning to Yellowstone. He wrote the song for an episode of the PBS *Nature* series, filmed a few months before he died. It was released as "John Denver: Let This Be a Voice." • **Last Top 40 *Billboard* hit (Pop Charts) during Denver's lifetime:** "Shanghai Breezes," which went on the charts on April 24, 1982. It was his 15th Top 40 hit. • **Last film score:** *The Bears and I* (1974). • **Last film as actor:** *Walking Thunder* (1997).
Doors, The	The Rock group The Doors, led by James Douglas ("Jim") Morrison, was formed in Los Angeles, California, in 1965. Morrison died in Paris, France, on July 3, 1971, age 27. Ray Manzarek, Robbie Krieger and John Densmore—the three surviving members of The Doors—officially broke up in January 1973. • **Last Doors appearance with Jim Morrison:** New Orleans, Louisiana, November 12, 1970. Lead singer Morrison left the group in December. • **Last Top 40 *Billboard* hit (Pop Charts) during Morrison's lifetime:** "Riders on the Storm," which went on the charts on July 24, 1971. • **Last Doors album with Jim Morrison:** *L.A. Woman* (released April 1971, three months before his death). • **Last recording by Jim Morrison:** a recording made in Paris, France, by Jomo & The Smoothies: believed to be Jim Morrison and two street musicians, June 16, 1971. • **Morrison's last film as actor:** *Gli Intoccabli* (1968, a.k.a. *Machine Gun McCain,* 1970).
Dorsey Brothers, Jimmy and Tommy	Trombonist/bandleader Thomas Francis ("Tommy") Dorsey died in Greenwich, Connecticut, on November 26, 1956, age 51. Saxophonist/bandleader James Francis ("Jimmy") Dorsey died in New York, New York, on June 12, 1957, age 53. • **Last of the Dorsey brothers' reunion:** 1956. The Dorsey brothers went their separate ways after a dispute in 1935. Jimmy formed his own band. He reunited with Tommy in 1953 to cut overhead when big bands were fading in popularity. The brothers' reunion ended three years later with

	Tommy's death.
	• **Tommy Dorsey's last feature-length film:** *Disc Jockey* (as himself, 1951).
	• **Last film as Dorsey brothers:** *Universal Musical Featurette: The Dorsey Brothers Encore* (short, 1953).
	• **Last film for which Tommy Dorsey contributed original music:** *Broadway Rhythm* (1944).
	• **Last Top 40 *Billboard* hits (Pop Charts) as performers during Jimmy Dorsey's lifetime:** "So Rare," which entered the charts on April 13, 1957. "June Night" was cut five days after Jimmy's death and released as the Jimmy Dorsey Orchestra. "Tea for Two Cha Cha," with the Tommy Dorsey Orchestra starring Warren Covington, entered the charts on September 15, 1958.
Duchin, Eddy	Bandleader/pianist Eddy Duchin died in New York, New York, on February 9, 1951, age 40.
	• **Last film as actor:** *Hit Parade of 1937* (1937).
	• **Last film as himself:** *Coronado* (1935).
Eckstine, Billy	Pop singer/bandleader William Clarence ("Billy") Eckstine died in Pittsburgh, Pennsylvania, on March 8, 1993, age 78.
	• **Last recording:** *Billy Eckstine Sings with Benny Carter* (1986).
Eldridge, Roy	Jazz trumpeter David Roy Eldridge died in Valley Stream, New York, on February 26, 1989, age 78.
	• **Last album:** *Roy Eldridge and Vic Dickenson* (1978).
	• **Last film:** *After Hours* (as himself, 1961).
Fitzgerald, Ella	Jazz vocalist/composer Ella Jane Fitzgerald died in Beverly Hills, California, on June 15, 1996, age 79. She was the last of the four great female singers who are considered to have defined the Jazz vocal style (the others: Billie Holiday, Sarah Vaughan and Carmen McRae).
	• **Last album:** *All That Jazz* (1990), for which she received her 13th and last Grammy.
	• **Last Broadway show as performer:** *Frank Sinatra, Ella Fitzgerald, and Count Basie* (1975). Last performance of original run: September 20, 1975, at the Uris Theater in New York, New York.
	• **Last film as herself:** *Listen Up: The Lives of Quincy Jones* (1990).
	• **Last film as actress:** *Let No Man Write My Epitaph* (1960).
	• **Last TV special:** *The Apollo Theater Hall of Fame* (1993).
Foggy Mountain Boys (Flatt and Scruggs)	The Foggy Mountain Boys were the Bluegrass musicians Lester Raymond Flatt and Earl Scruggs. Flatt died in Nashville, Tennessee, on May 11, 1979, age 64.
	• **Last of the Foggy Mountain Boys:** disbanded in 1969.
	• **Last Broadway show as performers:** *Hayride* (1954). Last performance of original run: October 2, 1954, at the 48th Street Theater in New York, New York.
	• **Last appearance on *The Beverly Hillbillies*:** November 20, 1968, episode: "Bonnie, Flatt, and Scruggs" It was their seventh episode. They also performed the show's theme song.
	• **Last film together:** *Country Music on Broadway* (as themselves, 1963).
Ford, "Tennessee Ernie"	Country singer Ernest Jenning ("Tennessee Ernie") Ford died in Reston, Virginia, on October 17, 1991, age 72.
	• **Last Top 40 *Billboard* hit (Pop Charts) as performer during Ford's lifetime:** "In the Middle of an Island," which went on the charts on Sep-

	tember 23, 1957. • **Last telecast of** *The Ford Show*: June 29, 1961. Ford hosted the variety show for five seasons. • **Last films:** *The Mouse and the Mayflower* (TV, animated, narrator, 1968); *Opryland* (TV, 1973).
Garner, Erroll	Jazz pianist/composer Erroll Louis Garner died in Los Angeles, California, on January 2, 1977, age 55. • **Last album:** *Magician* (1974). • **Last concert:** Chicago, Illinois, 1975. Garner retired after this concert due to ill health. He died two years later. • **Last film score:** *A New Kind of Love* (1963). • **Last film as actor:** *My Bed Is Not for Sleeping* (1968).
Gaye, Marvin	Rock vocalist/composer Marvin Gaye (Marvin Pentz Gay Jr.) was shot to death in Los Angeles, California, on April 1, 1984, a day before his 45th birthday. • **Last film score:** *Mensonge* (a.k.a. *Lie*, 1983). • **Last Top 40** *Billboard* **hit (Pop Charts) during his lifetime:** "Sexual Healing," which entered the charts on November 20, 1982 as his 40th Top 40 hit. It appeared on his comeback album *Midnight Love* (recorded in 1982). • **Last album:** *Greatest Hits* (compilation album, 1983). • **Last performance:** 1984 NBA All-Star Game, where he sang the national anthem. • **Last films as himself:** *The Day the Music Died* (1977), *Motown 25: Yesterday, Today, Forever* (TV special, 1983). • **Last film as actor:** *Chrome and Hot Leather* (1971).
Getz, Stan	Jazz tenor saxophonist Stan Getz (Stanley Gayetzby) died in Malibu, California, on June 6, 1991, age 64. • **Last live performance:** Philharmonic Hall in Munich, Germany, July 1990. Other performers included Kenny Barron, Alex Blake and Eddie Del Barrio. The concert was recorded and released as The Final Concert. • **Last recording:** *People Time* (1991), recorded three months before he died. • **Last Top 40** *Billboard* **hit (Pop Charts) during Getz's lifetime:** "The Girl From Ipanema," which made the charts on June 20, 1964. It was credited as Getz/Astrud Gilberto (Brazilian vocalist). • **Last film score:** *In Defense of a Married Man* (TV, 1990). • **Last film as himself:** *The Exterminator* (1980).
Gillespie, Dizzy	Bebop Jazz trumpeter/leader John Birks ("Dizzy") Gillespie died in Englewood, New Jersey, on January 6, 1993, age 75. • **Last recording:** *To Bird With Love: Live at the Blue Note,* January 1992, when Gillespie was 74. • **Last appearance:** Seattle, Washington, February 1992. • **Last film music:** *Voyage to Next* (1974). • **Last film as actor:** *My Universe Inside Out* (short, animated, voice, 1996). • **Last film as himself:** *The Spitball Story* (1998).
Goodman, Benny	Clarinetist/bandleader Benjamin David ("Benny") Goodman died in New York, New York, on June 13, 1986, age 77. • **Last album:** *Let's Dance*, a TV sound track that earned him a Grammy

	nomination for Best Jazz Instrumental Performance, Big Band. • **Last Top 40** *Billboard* **hit (Pop Charts) during Goodman's lifetime:** "Memories of You," which entered the charts on March 17, 1956. It was credited as The Benny Goodman Trio with Rosemary Clooney. • **Last Broadway show as performer:** *Seven Lively Arts* (1944). Last performance of original run: May 12, 1945, at the Ziegfeld Theater in New York, New York. • **Last film:** *Åke Hasselgård Story* (1983).
Gordon, Dexter	Jazz tenor saxophonist/actor Dexter Gordon died in Philadelphia, Pennsylvania, on April 25, 1990, age 67. • **Last recording:** sound track album from the 1986 film *'Round Midnight* for which he received an Oscar nomination. • **Last film score:** *Pornography: A Musical* (1971). • **Last film as actor:** *Awakenings* (1990).
Grappelli, Stéphane, and the Hot Club de France	French jazz violinist Stéphane Grappelli died in Paris, France, on December 1, 1997, age 89. Grappelli was the last surviving member of the Hot Club de France, a major internationally known Jazz quintet organized in the 1930s. The other members were: Louis Vola (double bass); Roger Chaput (rhythm guitar); Django Reinhardt (gypsy guitar) and his brother Joseph Reinhardt (rhythm guitar). • **Last film score by Grappelli:** *Autumn* (short film, 1997). • **Last film by Grappelli as actor:** *King of the Gypsies* (1978).
Grateful Dead, The	The Grateful Dead, led by Jerry Garcia, formed in San Francisco, California, in 1966. Ron ("Pigpen") McKernan (organ and harmonica) died on March 8, 1973, age 27. Keith Godchaux (keyboardist) died in Marin County, California, on July 23, 1980, age 32. Grateful Dead leader Jerome John ("Jerry") Garcia died in Forest Knolls, California, on August 10, 1995, age 53. • **Last Grateful Dead concert with Pigpen:** Hollywood Bowl, Los Angeles, California, June 17, 1972. • **Last studio album with Garcia:** *Built to Last,* released October 31, 1989. • **Last live album with Garcia:** *Without a Net*, released September 1990. • **Last concert with Garcia:** July 9, 1995, at Soldier Field in Chicago, Illinois. The group ended the concert with an encore of "Box of Rain." It would be the last verse sung at a Grateful Dead concert. Garcia died a month later. On December 8, 1995, surviving members of the Grateful Dead disbanded the group. • **Last studio recording by Garcia:** "Standing On The Corner" ("Blue Yodel No. 9") for the album *Jimmie Rodgers–A Tribute* (recorded in 1995, released in 1997). • **Last Top 40** *Billboard* **hit (Pop Charts) of The Grateful Dead as performers during Garcia's lifetime:** "Touch of Grey," which went on the charts on August 15, 1987. • **Last films:** *The History of Rock N' Roll Vol. 6* (TV, 1995) and *Rock and Roll* (mini-series TV). • **Last film score by Garcia:** *Zabriske Point* (1970).
Guthrie, Woody	Folk singer/composer Woodrow Wilson ("Woody") Guthrie died in New York, New York, on October 4, 1967, age 55. He suffered from Huntington's chorea, a degenerative disease that eventually robbed him of his ability to perform. He was in and out of hospitals during his last 13 years.

	• **Last major song:** "Deportee—Goodbye Juan—Plane Wreck at Los Gatos Canyon" (1948), about a crash that killed Mexican migrant workers.
Hackett, Bobby	Jazz cornetist Robert Leo ("Bobby") Hackett died in Chatham, Massachusetts, on June 7, 1976, age 61. • **Last studio album:** *Strike Up the Band* (1974). It included his last recording of "Embraceable You." • **Last film:** *Orchestra Wives* (uncredited, 1942).
Haley, Bill and His Comets	Rock-and-Roll pioneer William John Clifton ("Bill") Haley Jr. died in Harlingen, Texas, on February 9, 1981, age 55. Danny Cedrone (lead guitarist) died on June 10, 1954. Rudy Pompili (saxophonist) died on February 5, 1974, age 47. Several of the original Comets are still performing. • **Last time the Comets were styled as a Country & Western group:** 1952. The group changed their name from the Saddlemen and got rid of their Stetson hats and cowboy boots before the Thanksgiving holiday that year. • **Last recorded performance of "(We're Gonna) Rock Around the Clock" with Bill Haley:** part of a Royal Variety Command Performance for Queen Elizabeth II, November 26, 1979. • **Last album with Bill Haley:** *Everyone Can Rock'n'Roll* recorded at Fame Studios, Muscle Shoals, Alabama, in the summer of 1979. • **Last Top 40 *Billboard* hit (Pop Charts) during Haley's lifetime:** "(We're Gonna) Rock Around The Clock," which re-entered the charts on May 25, 1974, after being featured as the theme song for the TV sitcom *Happy Days*. It was originally recorded in 1954. • **Last film score by Bill Haley:** *Adios cuñado! (1966).* • **Last film with Bill Haley:** *Blue Suede Shoes* (1980).
Hampton, Lionel	Vibraphonist/drummer/bandleader Lionel Leo Hampton died in New York, New York, on August 31, 2002, age 94. Hampton is considered the last of the Big-Time Jazz Bandleaders. • **Last appearance:** February 25, 2002, at a Jazz festival named in his honor at the University of Idaho, Moscow, Idaho. • **Last film:** *Jazz* (as himself; Ken Burn's TV miniseries, 2001). • **Last film score:** *No Maps on My Taps* (1979).
Hawkins, Coleman	Jazz tenor saxophonist Coleman Hawkins died in New York, New York, on May 19, 1969, age 64. • **Last appearance:** *Jazz at the Philharmonic* (1969). Hawkins stopped performing in 1965. After that, he made only this one appearance. • **Last film:** *After Hours* (short, as himself, 1961).
Henderson, Fletcher	Bandleader/arranger/pianist Fletcher Hamilton Henderson Jr. died in New York, New York, on December 29, 1952, age 55. • **Last recording:** *Fletcher Henderson's Sextet* (1950). Henderson's musical career ended a few days after he made the recording when he suffered a stroke that left him partially paralyzed.
Hendrix, Jimi	Blues guitarist/composer James Marshall ("Jimi") Hendrix died in London, England, on September 18, 1970, age 27. • **Last song:** "The Story of Life." Hendrix was working on it the night he died. • **Last concert with The Jimi Hendrix Experience:** June 29, 1969, final day of the Denver Pop Festival at Mile High Stadium. • **Last public performances:** Isle of Wight Pop Festival, August 26, 1970, and Isle of Fehmarn, Germany, September 6, 1970. Hendrix made a minor public appearance sitting in with Eric Burdon and War at Ronnie

	Scott's club in London on September 16, 1970. • **Last back-up group:** Band of Gypsys, formed by Hendrix in 1970. • **Last album recorded by Hendrix:** *Cry of Love,* recorded at Hendrix's studio, Electric Lady, in Greenwich Village, New York City. The album was unfinished when Hendrix died but was pieced together by Mitch Mitchell and Eddie Kramer and released posthumously in 1971. • **Last Top 40 *Billboard* hit (Pop Charts) as performer during Hendrix's lifetime:** "All Along The Watchtower," which entered the charts on September 28, 1968. It was credited as The Jimi Hendrix Experience. • **Last film score:** *O Abismo* (1970). • **Last film as performer:** *Jimi Plays Berkeley* (1971), a posthumously released 1970 concert film.
Herman, Woody	Bandleader/clarinetist/saxophonist Woodrow Charles ("Woody") Herman died in Los Angeles, California, on October 29, 1987, age 74. He was the last working leader of the Big Band Era. He celebrated his 50th anniversary as a performer in 1986 and was still on the road in 1987. • **Last recording:** "Woody's Gold Star," released 1987. • **Last film:** *Herman's Herd* (short, as himself, 1949).
Hines, Earl ("Fatha")	Jazz pianist/composer Earl Kenneth ("Fatha") Hines died in Oakland, California, on April 22, 1983, age 79. He remained active as performer until his death. • **Last album:** *Earl Hines in New Orleans*, recorded in 1977, when he was 73. • **Last film:** *The Strip* (uncredited, 1951).
Hirt, Al	Dixieland and Jazz trumpeter Alois Maxwell ("Al") Hirt died in New Orleans, Louisiana, on April 27, 1999, age 76. • **Last Top 40 *Billboard* hit (Pop Charts) during Hirt's lifetime:** "Sugar Lips," which entered the charts on August 1, 1964. • **Last telecast of *Fanfare*:** September 11, 1965. Hirt hosted and performed on the musical variety show. It first aired in June 1965. • **Last film:** *The Manhunter* (TV, as himself, 1972).
Holiday, Billie	Jazz singer Billie Holiday (Eleanora Fagan Gough) died in New York, New York, on July 17, 1959, age 44. • **Last public appearance:** CBS TV program "Sound of Jazz," at the Phoenix Theater, New York, New York, May 25, 1959. • **Last accompanist:** Malcolm Earl ("Mal") Waldron (1926-2002), who served as Holiday's accompanist from 1957 until her death. • **Last album:** A collection of Holiday's great songs was released in 1959 as *Last Recordings*. It was reissued in 1988. • **Last film as herself:** *"Sugar Chile" Robinson, Billie Holiday, Count Basie and His Sextet* (short, as herself, 1951). • **Last film as actress:** *New Orleans* (1947).
Holly, Buddy	Rock-and-Roll pioneer Buddy Holly (Charles Hardin Holley) was killed in a plane crash near Mason City, Iowa, on February 3, 1959, age 22. • **Last studio recording session:** New York, October 21, 1958. Three songs were recorded: "True Love Ways," "Raining In My Heart" and "It Doesn't Matter Anymore." The last two songs—released on Coral Records on January 5, 1959—were the last singles released while Holly was alive. • **Last performance on *American Bandstand*:** October 28, 1958. The Crickets lip-synched to "Heartbeat" and "It's So Easy."

	• **Last of The Crickets:** The group broke up in the fall of 1958. Holly had formed his backup group in 1957. • **Last Top 40 *Billboard* hit (Pop Charts) as The Crickets:** "Think It Over," which entered the charts on August 4, 1958. • **Last album featuring Holly released during his lifetime:** *Buddy Holly* (Castle), released February 20, 1958. It featured his Top 10 single "Peggy Sue" and included "Rave On," which would hit the Top 40 Chart later that year. • **Last Holly recordings:** made with an acoustic guitar and tape recorder at his home in the Brevoort Apartments, Greenwich Village, New York, on January 18, 1959, two weeks before he died. The songs included "Peggy Sue Got Married," "That's What They Say," "Crying, Waiting, Hoping," "What to Do," "Learning the Game" and "That Makes It Tough." They were overdubbed and released posthumously as *Buddy Holly Story 2*. • **Last Holly performance:** At the Surf Ballroom in Clear Lake, Iowa, February 2, 1959, while on tour. Following the concert, Holly, the Big Bopper (Jiles Perry Richardson, age 29) and Ritchie Valens died in a plane crash. • **Last Top 40 *Billboard* hit (Pop Charts) during Holly's lifetime:** "Early in the Morning" which entered the charts on August 11, 1958. The song "It Doesn't Matter Anymore" entered the charts on March 9, 1959, after Holly's death. • **Last album (solo):** *Early in the Morning.* • **Last album with The Crickets:** *The Chirping Crickets* (1957).
Howlin' Wolf	Southern Blues singer/guitarist/harmonica player Howlin' Wolf (Chester Arthur Burnett) died in Hines, Illinois, on January 10, 1976, age 65. He remained active as a performer until 1975, when he was forced to retire because of ill health. • **Last live recording:** July 25–27, 1975, at the 1815 Club, Chicago, Illinois. Released in 1989 on the Wolf label as *Live 1975*. • **Last studio album:** *The Back Door Wolf* (1973). • **Last performance:** Chicago Amphitheater, Chicago, Illinois, with B.B. King, November 1975. • **Last film:** *Festival* (as himself, 1967).
Ink Spots (Original)	The popular singing quartet The Ink Spots was formed in the 1930s with Jerry Daniels, Charlie Fuqua, Orville ("Hoppy") Jones and Ivory ("Deek") Watson. Daniels became ill and was replaced by Bill Kenny. Fuqua died on December 21, 1971, age 60. Jones died on October 10, 1944, age 39. Watson died on November 4, 1969, age 60. • **Last film with original Ink Spots:** *Pardon My Sarong* (1942). • **Last surviving original member:** Bill Kenny's death on March 23, 1978, age 55, brought an end to the "original" Ink Spots. The Ink Spots, with newer members, are still active.
Ives, Burl	Folk singer/actor Burl Icle Ivanhoe Ives died in Ancortes, Washington, on April 14, 1995, age 85. • **Last Top 40 *Billboard* hit (Pop Charts) as performer during Ives's lifetime:** "Mary Ann Regrets," which entered the charts on December 8, 1962. • **Last concert performance:** 92nd Street YMCA 50th Anniversary Folk Festival, New York, New York. • **Last Broadway show as performer:** *Dr. Cook's Garden* (1967). Last performance of original run: September 30, 1967, at the Belasco Theater

	in New York, New York. • **Last film as actor:** *Two Moon Junction* (1988). • **Last film as himself:** *Herbie Day at Disneyland* (TV, 1974). • **Last album:** *The Magic Balladeer* (1993).
Jackson, Mahalia	Gospel singer Mahalia Jackson died in Evergreen Park, Illinois, on January 27, 1972, age 60. • **Last concert tour:** Europe, 1971. • **Last film as herself:** *The Best Man* (1964). • **Last film as actress:** *Imitation of Life* (1959).
Jackson, Milt	Jazz vibraphonist Milton ("Milt") Jackson died in New York, New York, on October 9, 1999, age 76. • **Last album:** *Explosive!* (1997). • **Last film:** *Jivin' in Be-Bop* (as himself, 1946).
James, Harry	Trumpeter/bandleader Harry Haag James died in Las Vegas, Nevada, on July 5, 1983, age 67. • **Last time James played with the Benny Goodman Orchestra:** 1938. • **Last performance:** June 26, 1983. Century Plaza Hotel, Los Angeles, California. • **Last film as himself:** *The Lady's Man* (1961). • **Last film as actor:** *The Sting II* (1983).
Jennings, Waylon	Country singer/songwriter Waylon Arnold Jennings died in Chandler, Arizona, on February 13, 2002, age 64. • **Last film scores:** *Mackintosh and T.J.* (1975) and *Moonrunners* (1975). • **Last film as actor**: *Tom Sawyer* (animated, voice, 2000). • **Last song recorded:** "The Dream." • **Last Top 40 *Billboard* hit (Pop Charts) as performer during his lifetime:** "Theme From The Dukes of Hazzard (Good Ol' Boys)," which entered the charts on November 1, 1980. It was credited only as Waylon. Most of his hits were on the Country charts, where he had 16 No. 1 hits. • **Last performance with Buddy Holly:** Surf Ballroom in Clear Lake, Iowa, February 2, 1959, while on the GAC Winter Show tour. Jennings was Holly's bass player. He gave up his seat on the plane to the Big Bopper, who was killed in the crash that also killed Holly and Ritchie Valens. • **Last Broadway show as performer:** *Broadway Opry '79* (1979). Last performance of original run: August 2, 1979, at the Saint James Theater in New York, New York.
Johnson, J.J.	Jazz trombonist James Louis ("J.J.") Johnson died in Indianapolis, Indiana, on February 4, 2001, age 77. Johnson recorded a series of critically hailed albums for Verve in the 1990s. He retired from performing in 1997. • **Last recording with Kai Winding:** *Great Kai and J.J.* Recorded in November 1960. The trombone duo recorded together often from 1954 to 1956 then again in a 1960 reunion. • **Last live performance with Kai Winding:** All-Star Jam Live, the Aurez Jazz Festival in 1982. • **Last performance:** William Patterson College in New Jersey, November 1996. • **Last film score:** *Murder Me, Murder You* (TV, 1983).
Johnson, Robert	Legendary Delta Blues guitarist Robert Johnson died in Greenwood, Mississippi, on August 16, 1938, age 27, after being poisoned a few days earlier. • **Last recordings:** Johnson only spent five sessions in the recording stu-

	dio: three were in San Antonio, Texas (November 23, 26 and 27, 1936) and two were in Dallas, Texas (June 19 and 20, 1937). Eleven recordings (78 rpm) were released from these sessions during his life and one posthumously. The last of Johnson's 12 original recordings was released by Vocalion in February 1939, six months after his death. • **Last performance:** Three Forks, Greenwood Mississippi, August 13, 1938. Johnson is believed to have been poisoned that night.
Jones, Spike	Bandleader/entertainer Lindley Armstrong ("Spike") Jones died in Bel Air, California, on May 1, 1965, age 54. • **Last big hits:** "I Went to Your Wedding," "Pal-Yat-Chee." • **Last telecast of** *The Spike Jones Show*: September 25, 1961. The show aired in 1954, 1957, and 1961, and featured the City Slickers. • **Last album:** *Persuasive Concussion* (unfinished when Jones died in 1965). Some of the tracks were released in 1993 as *Spiked!* • **Last film as actor:** *Fireman Save My Child* (1954). • **Last film as himself:** *Screen Snapshots: Ha! Ha! From Hollywood* (1953).
Joplin, Janis	Blues singer Janice Lyn Joplin died in Hollywood, California, on October 4, 1970, age 27. • **Last performance with Big Brother & the Holding Company:** December 7, 1968, in Hawaii. In September 1968, Her manager announced Joplin would leave the group after fulfilling current obligations. However, she did appear with Big Brother at the Fillmore West and Winterland Ballroom in San Francisco, California, in April 1970. • **Last back-up group:** Full-Tilt Boogie Band. • **Last concert:** Harvard Stadium, Cambridge, Massachusetts, August 12, 1970. • **Last TV appearance:** *The Dick Cavett Show*, August 3, 1970. • **Last album:** *Pearl,* Joplin's second album, unfinished when she died. • **Last Top 40** *Billboard* **hit (Pop Charts) during Joplin's lifetime:** "Piece of My Heart," which entered the charts on September 28, 1968. It was credited as Big Brother & The Holding Company. Joplin's last Top 40 hit was "Me and Bobby McGee," which entered the charts on February 20, 1971, four months after her death. • **Last film:** *Woodstock* (as herself, 1970).
Jordan, Louis	Saxophonist/bandleader/singer Louis Thomas Jordan died in Los Angeles, California, on February 4, 1975, age 67. • **Last major appearance:** Newport Jazz Festival (1973). • **Last recording:** *Santa Claus, Santa Claus* (1968). • **Last film as himself:** *Look-Out Sister* (1947). • **Last film as actor:** *Reet, Petite, and Gone* (1947).
Kenton, Stan	Bandleader/composer/pianist Stanley Newcomb ("Stan") Kenton died in Los Angeles, California, August 25, 1979, age 67. • **Last Top 40** *Billboard* **hit (Pop Charts) during Kenton's lifetime:** "Mama Sang a Song," which entered the charts on November 17, 1962. • **Last major appearance:** California State University at Northridge, a reunion of many of his former band members, including Milt Bernhart, Laurindo Almeida, Lennie Neihaus and Richard Maltby. • **Last recording:** recorded live at the Coconut Grove in Los Angeles, March 18, 1978. Released as *Stan Kenton: The Lost Concert*.

	• **Last film score:** *The Wedding in Monaco* (wedding of Grace Kelly and Prince Rainier, 1956). • **Last film:** *Spotlight No. 5* (short, uncredited, 1954).
Krupa, Gene	Jazz drummer Eugene Bertram ("Gene") Krupa died in Yonkers, New York, on October 16, 1973, age 64. Krupa's band broke up in 1951. He went into semi-retirement in the 1960s due to failing health. • **Last appearance:** a reunion of the old Goodman Quartet in Saratoga, New York, on August 18, 1973, a few months before he died. • **Last recording:** *Jazz at the New School* with Eddie Condon and Wild Bill Davison, recorded in November 1972. • **Last films:** *The Benny Goodman Story* (as himself, 1955). *The Gene Krupa Story* (1959). He recorded the drums for the sound track.
Kyser, Kay	Bandleader James King Kern ("Kay") Kyser died in Chapel Hill, North Carolina, on July 23, 1985, age 79. • **Last radio/TV shows:** radio: 1948; TV, 1954. Kyser's *Kollege of Musical Knowledge* was a popular radio show from 1938 to 1948. He took the show to TV in 1949, where it ran for a year. It was brought back briefly during the summer of 1954. Kyser retired in 1950 and devoted his life to the Christian Science Church as a reader and later as head of the Broadcast and Television division. • **Last film as himself:** *Screen Snapshots: Hula From Hollywood* (short, 1954). • **Last film as actor:** *Carolina Blues* (1944).
Led Zeppelin	The British Heavy-Metal group Led Zeppelin was formed in 1968 with Robert Plant, Jimmy Page, John Bonham and John Paul Jones. Bonham died on September 25, 1980, age 32, on the eve of a U.S. tour. • **Last film with original Led Zeppelin members:** *The Song Remains the Same* (1976). • **Last album during Bonham's lifetime:** *In Through The Out Door* (1979). • **Last Top 40 *Billboard* hit (Pop Charts) during Bonham's lifetime:** "Fool In The Rain," which entered the charts on January 12, 1980. • **Last of Led Zeppelin:** On December 4, 1980, Page, Plant and Jones announced they would not re-establish Led Zeppelin after Bonham's death. • **Last concert in the United States:** Oakland Coliseum (California), July 24, 1977. • **Last concert in the United Kingdom:** Knebworth, England, August 4, 1979. • **Last concert with original Led Zeppelin members:** at the Eissporthalle in West Berlin, East Germany, July 7, 1980. The last song they played was "Whole Lotta Love."
Ledbetter, Huddie ("Leadbelly")	Blues guitarist/composer/folk singer Huddie ("Leadbelly") Ledbetter died in New York, New York, on December 6, 1949, age around 60. While in Paris, France, in 1949, he suffered persistent muscle pain that led to a diagnosis of amyotrophic sclerosis (a.k.a. ALS, Lou Gehrig's disease). • **Last recordings:** *Leadbelly's Last Sessions,* recorded over the course of three nights in 1948, about a year before he died. • **Last concert:** University of Texas, June 15, 1949, six months before he died.
Lee, Peggy	Singer/actress Peggy Lee (Norma Delores Egstrom) died in Bel Air, California, on January 21, 2002, age 81. • **Last Top 40 *Billboard* hit (Pop Charts) during her lifetime:** "Is That All There Is," which entered the charts on October 11, 1969.

	• **Last film as actress:** *Disney's Halloween Treat* (animated, 1984). • **Last film as herself:** *The Quintessential Peggy Lee* (1984). • **Last Broadway show as composer and performer:** *Peg* (1983). Last performance of original run: December 17, 1983, at the Lunt-Fontanne Theater in New York, New York.
Liberace	Classical Pop pianist Wladziu Valentino Liberace, who was known professionally as Liberace, died in Palm Springs, California, on February 4, 1987, age 67. • **Last public performance:** October 16-November 2, 1986, Radio City Music Hall, New York, New York. After that engagement, he began a tour to promote his fourth book, *The Wonderful Private World of Liberace*. • **Last appearance:** 1986 Christmas telecast of *The Oprah Winfrey Show*. • **Last film as actor:** *The Loved One* (1965). • **Last film as himself:** *When the Boys Meet the Girls* (1965). • **Last telecast of *The Liberace Show*:** September 16, 1969.
Lombardo, Guy	Canadian-born bandleader Gaetano Albert ("Guy") Lombardo died in Houston, Texas, on November 5, 1977, age 75. The playing of "Auld Lang Syne" by Lombardo and his Royal Canadians on New Year's Eve was a long-standing tradition. • **Last New Year's Eve broadcast:** December 31, 1976, from the Waldorf-Astoria Hotel in New York, New York. • **Last televised concert:** Stork Club, Port Stanley, Ontario, Canada, June 1977. • **Last film:** *The Phynx* (1970). • **Last major competition as speedboat racer:** 1955, Indiana Governor's Cup at Madison in his boat *Tempo VII*. • **Last surviving member of the musical Lombardo family:** saxophonist Victor Lombardo, who died in Boca Raton, Florida, in January 1994, age 82.
Lunceford, Jimmy	Alto saxophonist/bandleader James Melvin ("Jimmy") Lunceford collapsed in a Seaside, Oregon, record shop while signing autographs in July 1947. He died a few days later, on July 12, age 45. • **Last recording:** *Margie* (1946-47). • **Last film as actor:** *Blues in the Night* (1941). • **Last film as himself:** *Melody Master: Jimmy Lunceford and His Orchestra* (1937).
Lymon, Frankie, and The Teenagers	The Doo Wop group Frankie Lymon and The Teenagers came together in 1955 with Franklin ("Frankie") Lymon, Herman Santiago, Jimmy Merchant, Joe Negroni and Sherman Garnes. Lymon died in New York, New York, on February 27, 1968, age 25. Negroni died on September 5, 1978, age 37. Garnes died on February 26, 1977, age 36. • **Last Top 40 *Billboard* hit (Pop Charts) during Lymon's lifetime:** "Goody Goody," which entered the charts on August 26, 1957. • **Last film of Lymon as actor:** *Mister Rock and Roll* (1957). • **Last film of Lymon as himself:** *Rock, Rock, Rock* (1956).
Mamas & The Papas, The	The original "The Mamas & the Papas"—John Phillips, Holly Gilliam Phillips, Dennis Doherty and Cass Elliot—formed in 1963. "Mama" Cass Elliot (Ellen Naomi Cohen) died in London, England, on July 29, 1974, age 32. John Phillips died in Los Angeles, California, on March 18, 2001, age 65. • **Last Top 40 *Billboard* hit (Pop Charts) as "The Mamas & the Papas":** "Glad to be Unhappy," which entered the charts on November 4, 1967.

	• **Last Top 40 *Billboard* hit (Pop Charts) by Cass Elliot:** "Make Your Own Kind of Music," which entered the charts on November 15, 1969. • **Last Broadway show by John Phillips as composer:** *Man in the Moon* (1974). Last performance of original run: February 1, 1975, at the Little Theater in New York, New York. • **Last film score by John Phillips:** *The Myth of Fingerprints* (1997). • **Last film by Cass Elliot as actress:** *Pufnstuf* (1970).
Manone, Wingy	Dixieland trumpeter/vocalist Joseph Matthews ("Wingy") Manone died in Las Vegas, Nevada, on July 9, 1982, age 82. • **Last full album:** 1966 (for Storyville). Manone toured and performed until near the end of his life. • **Last film as actor:** *Rhythm Inn* (1951). • **Last film as himself:** *Trocadero* (1944).
Marley, Bob The Wailers	Reggae great Bob Marley died in Miami, Florida, on May 11, 1981, age 36. In 1964, he was one of the founders the trio that evolved into the Wailers. • **Last surviving founding member of The Wailers:** Bunny Wailer (Neville O'Riley Livingston). The other founding member of the trio was Peter Tosh, who died on September 17, 1987, age 43. • **Last film of Marley as himself:** *Bob Marley* (a.k.a. *Bob Marley in Concert*, 1981). • **Last film of Marley as actor:** *Third World* (a.k.a. *Prisoner in the Streets*, 1980). • **Last film with Peter Tosh:** *Bob Marley and the Wailers: The Bob Marley Story* (as himself, 1986). • **Last concert of Marley:** Stanley Theater, Pittsburgh, Pennsylvania, September 23, 1980. Marley died of a brain tumor several months later.
Martin, Dean	Singer/actor Dean Martin (Dino Paul Crocetti) died in Beverly Hills, California, on December 23, 1995 age 78. • **Last Top 40 *Billboard* hit (Pop Charts) during Martin's lifetime:** "Little Ole Drinker, Me," which entered the charts on September 9, 1967. It was his 17th solo Top 40 Hit. • **Last charted album:** *You're the Best Thing* (1973). • **Last performance with Jerry Lewis:** the Copacabana in New York, New York, July 24, 1956.
Mayfield, Curtis	Rhythm-and-Blues singer/songwriter Curtis Mayfield died in Dunwoody, Georgia, on December 26 1999, age 57, nine years after he was left a quadriplegic when scaffolding fell on him while performing in Brooklyn, New York. • **Last album:** *New World Order* (1996). Nominated for a Grammy. • **Last album with the Impressions:** *The Young Mods' Forgotten Story* (1969). • **Last Top 40 *Billboard* hit (Pop Charts) during his lifetime:** "Kung Fu," which entered the charts on August 3, 1974. • **Last film score:** *The Return of Superfly* (1990). • **Last film as actor:** *Short Eyes* (a.k.a. *Slammer*, 1977). He also appeared as a guest in *Sgt. Pepper's Lonely Hearts Club Band* (1978).
McRae, Carmen	Jazz singer/actress Carmen Mercedes McRae died November 10, 1994, in Beverly Hills, California, age 74. • **Last album:** *Sarah: Dedicated to You* (recorded 1990).

	• **Last performance:** Blue Note, New York, New York, 1991. • **Last film as actress:** *Jo Jo Dancer, Your Life is Calling* (1986). • **Last film as herself:** *Carmen McRae: Live* (TV, 1986).
Merman, Ethel	Singer/actress Ethel Merman (Ethel Agnes Zimmermann) died in New York, New York, on February 15, 1984, age 76. • **Last Broadway show (benefit):** *Together on Broadway (Mary Martin and Ethel Merman)*, May 15, 1977, single-show benefit performance at the Broadway Theater in New York, New York. • **Last Broadway show (commercial):** 1966 revival *of Annie Get Your Gun.* Last performance of revival: November 26, 1966, at the Broadway Theater in New York. • **Last film as actress:** *Airplane!* (1980). • **Last film as herself:** *Night of 100 Stars* (TV, 1982).
Miller, Glenn/Glenn Miller Army Band	Bandleader/trombonist Alton Glenn Miller entered the U.S. Army Air Force in 1942, during World War II. He put together a military band that was sent to England in 1943, where it made hundreds of appearances and broadcasts. In 1944, a few days before his band was scheduled to leave for France, Miller flew there to check on arrangements for a Christmas broadcast. • **Last civilian radio broadcast by Miller before entering the service:** September 24, 1942. *The Glenn Miller Show,* also known as *Music that Satisfies,* sponsored by Chesterfield cigarettes. • **Last civilian engagement of Miller and his orchestra:** Central Theater in Passaic, New Jersey, on September 26, 1942. • **Miller's last film:** *Orchestra Wives* (1942). • **Miller's last recording:** Six propaganda programs recorded at Abbey Road Studio in England by Miller and his Army Air Force Band in the summer of 1944. The recordings were released for broadcast in Europe in October and November 1944. • **Last concert of the band led by Miller:** Twinwood Airfield, Bedford, England, just hours before he disappeared. Miller ended the concert with "The Star-Spangled Banner." • **Last time Miller was seen:** December 15, 1944, when the plane in which he was flying disappeared and is presumed to have crashed over the English Channel. The last person to see Glenn Miller alive was the band's manager Lieutenant Don Haynes. • **Last performance of the Glenn Miller Army Air Force Band:** National Press Club dinner for President Harry S. Truman, Washington, D.C., November 13, 1945. After World War II, the band carried on the Miller name.
Miller, Roger	Country singer/songwriter Roger Miller died in Los Angeles, California on October 25, 1992, age 56. • **Last Top 40 *Billboard* hit (Pop Charts) during his lifetime:** "Little Green Apples," which entered the charts on March 16, 1968. It was his 12th Top 40 hit. • **Last Broadway show as composer and performer:** *Big River* (1983). Last performance of original run: September 20, 1987, at the Eugene O'Neill Theater in New York, New York. • **Last film score:** *Robin Hood* (animated, 1973). • **Last film:** *Lucky Luke* (narrator, 1991). Miller also wrote the theme song for the TV show in 1991.

Milli Vanilli	Rob Pilatus and Fabrice Morvan formed the pseudo-Pop duo Milli Vanilli in Germany. They sold 30 million singles and won a Grammy for Best New Artist before it was discovered that they never sang a note as performers. Pilatus died in Frankfurt, Germany, on April 5, 1998, age 32. • **Last time Milli Vanilli were listed as Grammy holders:** November 1990. They returned the Grammy award at a press conference. • **Last Top 40 *Billboard* hit (Pop Charts) during Pilatus' lifetime:** "All or Nothing," which entered the charts on January 13, 1990. • **Last album:** *Rob and Fav* (1993). A few years after their the Grammy debacle, the duo regrouped as Rob and Fav and cut an album doing their own singing. It sold only 2,000 copies.
Mills Brothers (original)	The original Mills Brothers—John Jr., Herbert, Harry and Donald—began singing professionally in the 1920s. When John Mills Jr. died in 1936, at age 25, he was replaced by his father, John Mills Sr. John Sr. left the group in 1956. He died December 8, 1967, age 85. Harry died on June 28, 1982, in Los Angeles, California, age 68, Herbert died April 12, 1989, in Las Vegas, Nevada, age 77. • **Last surviving member of the original Mills Brothers:** Donald Mills, who died in Los Angeles on November 13, 1999, age 84. Donald was honored with a Grammy in 1998 for his 70-year career. • **Last Top 40 *Billboard* hit (Pop Charts) as performers:** "Cab Driver," which entered the charts on March 2, 1968. Their last No. 1 hit (pre-*Billboard* charts) was "Glow Worm" in 1952. • **Last film with John Mills Jr.:** *Broadway Gondolier* (1935). • **Last film of the Mills Brothers:** *The Big Beat* (as themselves, 1959). They also made an appearance on the 20th Annual Grammy Awards presentation in 1978.
Mingus, Charles	Jazz bassist/composer/bandleader Charles Mingus Jr. died in Cuernavaca, Mexico, on January 5, 1979, age 56. He was diagnosed with amyotrophic lateral sclerosis (a.k.a. ALS, Lou Gehrig's disease) in 1977. By 1978, he was unable to play bass and was confined to a wheelchair. Mingus was honored at the White House in June 1978. • **Last album:** *Me, Myself an Eye* (1978). • **Last project:** collaboration on the album *Mingus* (1979) with folk rock singer Joni Mitchell, who put lyrics to his last melodies. • **Last film score:** *Stations of the Elevated* (documentary, 1979). • **Last film:** *Mingus: Charles Mingus 1968* (as himself, 1968).
Monk, Thelonious	Jazz composer/pianist Thelonious Sphere Monk died at the Weehawken, New Jersey, home of friend and music patron Baroness Pannonica de Koenigswarter on February 17, 1982, age 64. • **Last musical activity:** After Monk disbanded his group around 1970, he appeared with the Giants of Jazz (1971-72). He retired in 1973 and spent his final years in seclusion, making only a few appearances that included the Newport Jazz Festival in 1975 and 1976, and three appearances at Carnegie Hall. • **Last appearance of Monk:** unannounced and informal. Monk sat in at Bradley's on University Place in New York, New York, in 1976. • **Last recording:** made in London, England, in 1971 for Black Lion while on a world tour with the Giants of Jazz: solo piano and trio with Art Blakey and Al McKibbon. The recordings filled three CDs and were re-

	leased as *The London Collection, Vols. 1, 2, and 3.* • **Last film score:** *The Homecoming* (1973). • **Last film:** *Newport Jazz Festival* (TV, as himself, 1968).
Monroe, Bill	Bluegrass musician William Smith ("Bill") Monroe died in Nashville, Tennessee, on September 9, 1996, age 84. • **Last recording:** "My Last Days on Earth" (1981), while battling cancer. He conquered the cancer and lived 15 more years. • **Last film as actor:** *That's Country* (1977). • **Last film as himself:** *High Lonesome: The Story of Bluegrass Music* (1994). In 1996, he appeared as an honoree on the TV special, *An Evening of Country Greats: A Hall of Fame Celebration.*
Monroe, Vaughn	Bandleader/singer/trumpeter Vaughn Monroe died in Stuart, Florida, on May 21, 1973, age 61. • **Last Top 40 *Billboard* hit (Pop Charts) during his lifetime:** "In the Middle of the House," which entered the charts on September 8, 1956. • **Last radio and TV shows:** Monroe had *The Vaughn Monroe Show* radio program from 1946 to 1954. The show made the transition to TV, where it aired intermittently from 1950 to 1955. The last telecast was September 8, 1955. Monroe also hosted the musical variety show *Air Time '57* (1956-57). It was last televised on April 4, 1957. • **Last film as actor:** *The Toughest Man in Arizona* (1952). • **Last film as himself:** *Carnegie Hall* (1947).
Montgomery, Wes	Jazz guitarist John Leslie ("Wes") Montgomery died in Indianapolis, Indiana, on June 15, 1968, age 43. He had just completed a tour. • **Last albums:** Montgomery made three pure pop albums in 1967-68: *A Day in the Life; Down Here on the Ground;* and *Road Song.* He died a month after recording *Road Song.* • **Last film score:** *Maidstone* (released posthumously, 1969).
Morgan, Helen	Singer Helen Morgan (Helen Riggins) died in Chicago, Illinois, on October 9, 1941, age 41. • **Last Broadway performance:** a revival of *Show Boat.* Last performance of revival in 1932 at the Casino Theater in New York, New York. • **Last film as actress:** *Show Boat* (1936). • **Last film as herself:** *Sweet Music* (1935).
Mulligan, Gerry	Jazz saxophonist/arranger/composer/pianist Gerald Joseph ("Gerry") Mulligan died in Darien, Connecticut, on January 20, 1996, age 68. • **Last performances:** Mulligan was active in music until a few weeks before he died. During his final years, he worked with Wynton Marsalis and wrote music for the *Jazz at Lincoln Center* concerts. He also performed in Chicago, Illinois, and at the JVC Jazz Festival in New York, New York. • **Last studio recording:** *Dragonfly* (1995). • **Last film score:** *I'm Not Rappaport* (1996). • **Last film as himself:** *A Great Day in Harlem* (1994). • **Last film as actor:** *The Rat Race* (1960).
Nelson, Rick	Singer/actor/teen idol Eric Hilliard ("Rick") Nelson was killed in a plane crash in DeKalb, Texas, on December 31, 1985, age 45. • **Last performance:** Gunnersville, Georgia, December 30, 1985. • **Last Top 40 *Billboard* hit (Pop Charts) during Nelson's lifetime:** "Garden Party," which entered the charts on September 16, 1972. It was credited as Rick Nelson & The Stone Canyon Band. It was his 36th Top 40

	hit. His last No. 1 hit was "Travelin Man" (1961). • **Last time Nelson used the name Ricky professionally:** 1961. "Hello Mary Lou" (May 1961) was his last *Billboard* Top 40s hit as Ricky Nelson. He dropped the "y" and became "Rick." • **Last film as actor:** *A Tale of Two Wishes* (TV, 1981). • **Last film as himself:** *Easy to be Free* (1973). (*See also* Television.)
Newley, Anthony	English composer/director/actor George Anthony Newley died in Jensen Beach, Florida, on April 14, 1999, age 67. • **Last Broadway show as composer and performer:** *Anthony Newley/Henry Mancini* (1974). Last performance of original run: November 10, 1974, at the Uris Theater in New York, New York. He did not perform in the 1978 revival of his show, *Stop The World–I Want to Get Off*. • **Last film score:** *Can Hieronymus Merkin Ever Forget Mercy Humppe and Find True Happiness?* (1967). His revival of *Stop The World–I Want to Get Off* was made into the film *Sammy Stops the World* (1978). • **Last film as himself:** *Blondes: Diana Dors* (TV, 1999). • **Last film as actor:** *Boris and Natasha* (1992).
Nichols, Red	Bandleader/cornetist Ernest Loring ("Red") Nichols died in Las Vegas, Nevada, on June 28, 1965, age 60. • **Last recording:** *Blues and Old Time Rags* (1963). • **Last Broadway show as a performer:** *Strike Up the Band.* Last performance, June 28, 1930, at the Times Square Theater in New York, New York. • **Last film:** *The Gene Krupa Story* (as himself, 1959).
Nirvana	Nirvana, a Grunge-Rock trio from Seattle, Washington, was led by Kurt Donald Cobain. He died in Seattle on April 5, 1994, age 27. • **Last album released during Cobain's lifetime:** *In Utero* (1993). When Cobain died, he left more than one hundred unreleased recorded songs and fragments. • **Last Top 40 *Billboard* hit (Pop Charts) during Cobain's lifetime:** "Come As You Are," which entered the charts on April 18, 1992. Other songs entered the charts after Cobain's death. The last was "The Man Who Sold The World," which made the charts on March 11, 1995. • **Last performance:** Terminal I, Munich, Germany, March 1, 1994. • **Last performances in the United States:** Seattle Center Arena, January 8, 1994. • **Last film:** *Nirvana Live! Tonight! Sold Out!* (1994).
Norvo, Red	Jazz vibraphonist/xylophonist/bandleader Red Norvo (Kenneth Norville) died in Santa Monica, California on April 6, 1999, age 91. • **Last album:** *Just Friends* (1983), released when he was 75. • **Last film as actor:** *Ocean's Eleven* (uncredited, 1960). • **Last film as himself:** *Screaming Mimi* (1958).
Notorious B.I.G./ Biggie Smalls	Rapper Christopher Wallace, known professionally as Biggie Smalls (a.k.a. The Notorious B.I.G.), died after being shot in Los Angeles, California, on March 9, 1997, age 24. • **Last Top 40 *Billboard* hit (Pop Charts) during Biggie Smalls' lifetime:** "One More Chance/Stay With Me," which entered the charts on June 24, 1995. Other songs entered the charts after his death. The last was "Victory," on March 28, 1998. It was credited as Puff Daddy & The Family Featuring The Notorious B.I.G. & Busta Rhymes. It was his 13th Top 40 hit. His last No. 1 hit was "Mo Money Mo Problems" (1997). It was posthumous

	and credited as The Notorious B.I.G. Featuring Puff Daddy & Mase. • **Last film as himself:** *Rhyme & Reason* (1997).
Oliver, Joe ("King")	Cornetist/bandleader Joseph ("King") Oliver died in Savannah, Georgia, on April 8, 1938, age 52. • **Last of the Creole Jazz Band:** 1924. Oliver had formed the group in 1922. After it folded, he took over another band and renamed it the Dixie Syncopators. • **Last of the Dixie Syncopators:** 1929. • **Last Oliver recordings:** 1931. Dental problems forced Oliver to give up music. He spent his final years as a janitor in a pool room in Savannah, Georgia. He left nearly 40 recordings and a number of compositions.
Orbison, Roy	Singer-songwriter Roy Kelton Orbison died in Madison, Tennessee, on December 6, 1988, age 52. • **Last Top 40 *Billboard* hit (Pop Charts) during Orbison's lifetime:** "Twinkle Toes," which entered the charts on May 21, 1966. The song "You Got It" made the charts posthumously on February 18, 1989. It was his 23rd Top 40 hit. His last No. 1 hit was "Oh, Pretty Woman" (1964), which was credited as Roy Orbison & The Candy Men. • **Last solo album:** *Mystery Girl*, recorded just prior to his death in 1988 hit the charts posthumously in February 1989. • **Last group album:** *The Traveling Wilburys* (recorded in November 1988 with Bob Dylan, Tom Petty, George Harrison and Jeff Lynne). • **Last TV appearance:** November 19, 1988, Diamond Awards Festival in Antwerp, Belgium. • **Last public performance:** December 4, 1988, Front Row Theater, Highland Heights, Ohio. He died two days later. • **Last film score:** *The Fastest Guitar Alive* (1967). • **Last film as actor:** *The Fastest Guitar Alive* (1967). • **Last film as himself:** *Roy Orbison and Friends: Black & White Night* (1988).
Ory, Kid	Jazz innovator/trombonist/composer Edward ("Kid") Ory retired from performing in 1966 and moved to Hawaii. He died in Honolulu on January 23, 1973, age 86. • **Last recording:** *Storyville Nights,* recorded in December 1961, a few weeks before his 75th birthday.
Parker, Charlie "Bird"/ "Yardbird"	Topnotch Jazz innovator/alto saxophonist Charles Christopher ("Charlie") Parker Jr. (a.k.a. "Bird" and "Yardbird") died at the New York, New York, home of friend and music patron Baroness Pannonica von Koenigswarter on March 12, 1955, age 34. • **Last recording released during his lifetime:** *The Genius of Charlie Parker, Vol. 5; C.P. Plays Cole Porter,* December 1954. • **Last appearance:** March 4, 1955, at Birdland, a New York City nightclub named in his honor. He died a week later.
Pepper, Art	Alto/tenor saxophonist/clarinetist Arthur ("Art") Edward Pepper died in Panorama City, California, on June 15, 1982, age 56. • **Last album:** *Tete-a-Tete,* one of two made shortly before he died. • **Last film:** *Art Pepper: Notes from a Jazz Survivor* (as himself, 1982).
Perkins, Carl	Rockabilly singer/songwriter/guitarist Carl Perkins (Carl Lee Perkings) died in Jackson, Tennessee, on January 18, 1998, age 65. • **Last album:** *Go Cat Go* (1996).

	• **Last Top 40 *Billboard* hit (Pop Charts) as performer during his life-time:** "Blue Suede Shoes," which made the charts on March 10, 1956. • **Last film as himself:** *All Star Concert for Montserrat* (TV, 1997). • **Last film as actor:** *Into the Night* (1985).
Presley, Elvis	Rock singer Elvis Aaron Presley died at Graceland, his mansion in Memphis, Tennessee, on August 16, 1977, age 42. • **Last appearance on *The Ed Sullivan Show* (TV):** January 6, 1957; his eighth appearance. The program devoted 20 minutes to Presley, who performed "Hound Dog," "Don't Be Cruel," "Love Me Tender," "Heartbreak Hotel," "Peace in the Valley," "Too Much" and "When My Blue Moon Turns to Gold Again." • **End of Presley's military career:** discharged on March 5, 1960. Presley entered the U.S. Army on March 24, 1958. His last rank was sergeant. • **Last live show before Presley's 1968 "comeback":** benefit show at Block Arena in Pearl Harbor, Hawaii, on March 25, 1961, that raised money for the USS *Arizona* memorial fund. It was Presley's first post-Army musical appearance. After the show, he stopped performing live until 1968. • **Last film as himself:** *Elvis in Concert* (TV, 1977). • **End of Presley's marriage:** Elvis and his wife Priscilla filed for divorce on August 11, 1972. The divorce was final on October 9, 1973. • **Last Top 40 *Billboard* hit (Pop Charts) during Presley's lifetime:** "Way Down," which entered the charts on July 16, 1977. Some songs also entered the charts posthumously. The last was "Guitar Man" on February 28, 1981. It was his 114th Top 40 hit. His last No. 1 hit was "Suspicious Minds" (1969). • **Last album:** *From Elvis Presley Boulevard, Memphis, Tennessee* (released May 1976); made in his studio at Graceland. Among the songs recorded were "The Last Farewell" and "Never Again." • **Last single:** "Way Down," made in his Graceland studio, October 29, 1976 • **Last live performance recording by Presley:** April 25, 1977, at a concert at Saginaw, Michigan Civic Center. Three songs recorded at the show appeared on the posthumously released album *Moody Blue* (1977). • **Last live performance by Presley:** June 26, 1977, Market Square Arena, Indianapolis, Indiana. The arena was demolished on July 8, 2001. • **Last Las Vegas performance by Presley:** Las Vegas Hilton, December 1-12, 1976. • **Last resting place:** At his funeral on August 18, 1977, Presley was entombed in a white marble mausoleum near the grave of his mother at Forest Hill Cemetery in Memphis. On October 2, 1977, his body and that of his mother were moved to Graceland after an apparent attempt to steal his body.
Puente, Tito	Latin and Afro-Cuban bandleader/vibraphonist/percussionist/ composer Ernest Anthony ("Tito") Puente died in New York, New York, on May 31, 2000, age 77. • **Last concert:** with Puerto Rico's Orquesta Sinfónica, April 29, 2000. Puente began experiencing shortness of breath during the performance and entered the hospital immediately afterward. • **Last albums:** *Mambo Birdland* (released September 1999) and *Por Fin* (*Finally*) with Eddie Palmieri (released posthumously June 2000). • **Last film score:** *The Best of Latin Jazz* (TV, 1997).

	• **Last film as himself:** *Americanos: Latino Life in the United States* (2000). • **Last film as actor:** *Radio Days* (1987).
Queen	The British rock group Queen was formed in 1972. Zanzibar-born lead singer Freddie Mercury (Frederick Bulsara) died in London, England, on November 25, 1991, age 45. • **Last Queen concert appearance with Freddie Mercury:** Knebworth Park, England, August 9, 1986. • **Last Top 40 *Billboard* hit (Pop Charts) during Mercury's lifetime:** "Radio Ga-Ga," which entered the charts on March 3, 1984. "Bohemian Rhapsody" re-entered the charts in 1992, after Mercury's death, when it was featured in the film *Wayne's World*. It was the last chart entry with Mercury. The last song to make the charts was "Somebody To Love," which re-entered the charts on May 22, 1993. It was a live performance from the Wembley Stadium Freddie Mercury Tribute Concert. It was credited as George Michael and Queen. It was Queen's 14th Top 40 hit. Queen's last No. 1 hit was "Another One Bites The Dust" (1980). • **Last Queen video released in Mercury's lifetime:** *Queen's Greatest Flix II* (October 1991). • **Last Queen film score:** *Highlander* (1986). • **Last Queen film during Mercury's lifetime:** *Queen Live at Wembley '86* (released posthumously, 1990). • **Last Queen album:** *Innuendo* (released 1991). • **Last of Queen:** disbanded in 1995.
Rainey, Ma	Pioneer Blues singer Gertrude Pridgett, who was known professionally as Ma Rainey, died in Columbus, Georgia, on December 22, 1939, age 53. Known as "The Mother of the Blues," she retired from performing in 1933. • **Last recording:** December 28, 1928.
Redding, Otis	Soul singer/songwriter Otis Redding was killed when the plane he was traveling in crashed into a Wisconsin lake on December 10, 1967. He was 26. Also killed were four members of the tour band the Bar-Kays: Ronnie Caldwell, Carl Cunningham, Pholon Jones and James King. • **Last recording:** "(Sittin' On the) Dock of the Bay," recorded on December 7, 1967, three days before Redding died. • **Last Top 40 *Billboard* hit (Pop Charts) during Redding's lifetime:** "Knock On Wood," which entered the charts on September 23, 1967. It was credited as Otis & Carla. A number of Redding's songs entered the charts shortly after he died. The last was a live recording of "Papa's Got a Brand New Bag," which made the charts on December 14, 1968. It was his 11th Top 40 hit. His last No. 1 hit was "(Sittin' On the) Dock of the Bay" (1968). • **Last film:** *Monterey Pop* (released posthumously, 1968).
Reinhardt, Django	French Gypsy jazz guitarist/violinist Jean Baptiste ("Django") Reinhardt died in Fontainebleau, France, on May 16, 1953, age 43. • **Last album:** *Brussels and Paris* (1953), a series of recordings made in sessions in Belgium and France, beginning in March 1947. The last session was on April 8, 1953, a month before Reinhardt died. • **Last film score:** *Le village de la colère* (1946).
Rich, Buddy	Jazz drummer Bernard ("Buddy") Rich died in New York, New York, on April 2, 1987, age 69. • **Last albums**: Rich recorded two sets in April 1985 at One Pass Production's King Street Studio in San Francisco, California. One set was re-

	leased in 1985 as *Mr. Drums: Live on King Street, San Francisco.* The second set was not released, but instead the master tapes were stored in a vault. They were believed to have been lost in a fire that destroyed the studio in 1990. The master tapes were discovered in 2000, recovered and released as *Buddy Rich and His Band—The Lost West Side Story Tapes*. • **Last film as himself:** *Artie Shaw: Time is All You've Got* (1985). • **Last film as actor:** *How's About It* (1943).
Riperton, Minnie	Singer Minnie Julia Riperton died in Los Angeles, California, on July 12, 1979, age 31. • **Last recording:** *Minnie.* After her death, instrumental backing was added to unreleased vocal tracks Riperton recorded in 1978. They were issued in 1980 as the album *Love Lives Forever*. • **Last Top 40 *Billboard* hit (Pop Charts) during Riperton's lifetime:** "Lovin' You," which entered the charts on February 15, 1975. • **Last film:** *Sgt. Pepper's Lonely Hearts Club Band* (1978).
Rodgers, Jimmie	Country music singer and pioneer James Charles ("Jimmie") Rodgers died in New York, New York, on May 26, 1933, age 35. • **Last recording:** May 24, 1933, in New York City two days before his death. He recorded 12 songs during the session. The last was a solo, "Years Ago." • **Last film:** *The Singing Brakeman* (1930).
Run-DMC	The pioneer rap trio Run-DMC was formed in Queens, New York, in 1982. Jason Mizell, who was known professionally as Jam Master Jay, died after he was shot in his Queens studio on October 30, 2002, age 37. Remaining members of the group announced there would be no Run-DMC without Mizell. • **Last album of Jay with Run-DMC:** *Crown Royal* (2001). • **Last performance of Jay with Run-DMC:** with Aerosmith, at the Verizon Wireless Music Center in Noblesville, Indiana, September 22, 2002. • **Last Top 40 *Billboard* hit (Pop Charts) during Jay's lifetime:** "Down With The King," which entered the charts on April 3, 1993. • **Last film of Jay:** *Who's the Man* (uncredited, 1993).
Selena	Tejano-pop singer Selena Quintanilla-Pérez was murdered in Corpus Christi, Texas, on March 31, 1995, age 23. • **Last stage appearance:** Chicago AmphiTheater on March 19, 1995. Selena made several appearances shortly before that, including the "Stay in School" benefit at the Alamodome on March 18 and the Tejano Rodeo on March 16. • **Last live recording:** The Astrodome concert on February 25, 1995, was recorded and later released as *Live: The Last Concert*. • **Last studio recording:** "A Boy Like That," for the album *The Songs of West Side Story,* based on the music of Leonard Bernstein, made three weeks before she was killed. • **Last film:** *Don Juan DeMarco* (1995).
Sex Pistols, The	The Punk-Rock group The Sex Pistols was created in 1975. The group's bassist John Simon Ritchie, who was known professionally as Sid Vicious, died in New York, New York, on February 2, 1979, age 21. • **Last concert:** January 14, 1978, at Winterland, San Francisco, California. The performance was recorded as *The Last Winterland Concert*. • **Last of the original Sex Pistols:** On January 15, 1978, lead vocalist

	Johnny Rotten (John Lydon) announced the group was finished. The surviving Sex Pistols later reunited for an unsuccessful tour.
Shakur, Tupac (2 Pac)	Rapper/actor Tupac (2 Pac) Amaru Shakur died after he was shot in Las Vegas, Nevada, on September 13, 1996, age 25. • **Last album released during Shakur's lifetime:** *All Eyez on Me* (1996). *The Don Killuminati: The 7 Day Theory* (1996), under the pseudonym Makiaveli, was released two months after his death. • **Last Top 40 *Billboard* hit (Pop Charts) during Shakur's lifetime:** "California Love," which entered the charts on June 22, 1996. It was credited as 2 Pac (featuring Dr. Dre and Roger Troutman). A number of songs featuring Shakur entered the charts posthumously. The last was "Changes," which hit the charts on December 26, 1998. His last No. 1 hit was "How Do You Want It" (1996). It was credited as 2 Pac (featuring KC and JoJo). • **Last music video:** "I Ain't Mad at Cha." • **Last films:** *Gridlock'd* and *Gang Related*, released in 1997. He had leading roles in both films.
Shore, Dinah	Singer/actress Frances Rose ("Dinah") Shore died in Beverly Hills, California, on February 24, 1994, age 77. • **Last Top 40 *Billboard* hit (Pop Charts) during Shore's lifetime:** "I'll Never Say 'Never Again' Again," which entered the charts on December 2, 1957. • **Last film as actress:** *Death Car on the Freeway* (TV, 1979). • **Last film as herself:** *HealtH* (1982). She also later appeared in a number of television specials, including *Pee-Wee Herman's Christmas Special* (1988) and *Comedy in Bloom* (1992).
Sinatra, Frank	Singer/actor/entertainer Francis Albert ("Frank") Sinatra died in Los Angeles, California, on May 14, 1998, age 82. • **Last recording with the Harry James Band:** November 8, 1939; Sinatra recorded "Every Day of My Life" and "Ciribiribin." He left the James band in January 1940, while they were performing in Buffalo, New York. • **Last recording with the Tommy Dorsey Orchestra:** July 30, 1942; Sinatra recorded "There Are Such Things." He left Dorsey and the Victor label in September 1942 and moved to Columbia and a solo career. • **Last Broadway performance:** *Frank Sinatra, Ella Fitzgerald, and Count Basie* (1975). Last performance of original run: September 20, 1975, at the Uris Theater in New York, New York. • **Last Top 40 *Billboard* hit (Pop Charts) as performer during Sinatra's lifetime:** "Theme From New York, New York," which entered the charts on May 31, 1980. It was his 28th Top 40 Hit. His last No. 1 hit was "Somethin' Stupid" (1967), credited as Nancy Sinatra & Frank Sinatra. • **Last albums:** *Duets,* released in 1993. Sinatra followed it in 1994 with *Duets II,* which won him a Grammy for traditional pop performance. • **Last full concert:** with Natalie Cole in Japan, December 19-20, 1994. He retired from performing in 1995, during his 80th year. • **Last TV appearance:** the sitcom *Who's the Boss* (1989). The episode: "Party Double." (*See also* Movies—Performers; Radio.)
Smith, Bessie	Blues and jazz singer Elizabeth ("Bessie") Smith was killed in an automobile accident in Clarksdale, Mississippi, on September 26, 1937, age 43. • **Last recording session:** 1933, under the direction of John Hammond. The record featured Jack Teagarden and Benny Goodman.

	• **Last hit song during her lifetime:** "Nobody Knows You (When You're Down and Out)" (1929). • **Last Broadway show as performer:** *Pansy* (1929). Last performance of original run: May 1929, at the Belmont Theater in New York, New York. • **Last New York appearance:** 1936. Sunday afternoon jam session sponsored by United Hot Clubs of America at Famous Door on 52nd Street. • **Last film:** *St. Louis Blues* (as herself, 1929).
Smith, Kate	Singer Kathryn ("Kate") Elizabeth Smith died in Raleigh, North Carolina, on June 17, 1986, age 77. She introduced the Irving Berlin song "God Bless America" in 1938. • **Last Broadway show as performer:** *Flying High*. Last performance of original run: 1931, at the Apollo Theater in New York, New York. • **Last live performance at a Philadelphia Flyers hockey game:** May 13, 1975. The Flyers won every game when Smith sang "God Bless America" live. And they won or tied about 82 percent of their games when a Kate Smith recording of "God Bless America" was played before the game. • **Last performance:** sang "God Bless America" at a U.S. Bicentennial special, just before July 4, 1976. • **Last film:** *This is the Army* (as herself, 1943). • **Last telecast of** *The Kate Smith Show*: July 18, 1960. The weekly half-hour musical series first aired on January 25, 1960.
Smith, Willie ("The Lion")	Stride pianist William ("Willie") Henry Joseph Bonaparte Bertholoff ("The Lion") Smith died in New York, New York, on April 18, 1973, age 75. Smith was one of the creators of the stride piano style. • **Last recording:** made in Paris, France, in June 1972. Smith was active in music until he died. • **Last film:** *Jazz Dance* (short, as himself, 1954).
Springfield, Dusty	English soul singer Dusty Springfield (Mary Isobel Catherine Bernadette O'Brien) died in Henley-on-Thames, Oxfordshire, England, on March 2, 1999, age 59. • **Last Top 40** *Billboard* **hit (Pop Charts) during her lifetime:** "What Have I Done to Deserve This?," which entered the charts on December 26, 1987. It was credited as Pet Shop Boys and Dusty Springfield. It was her 11th Top 40 hit. • **Last album:** *A Very Fine Love* (released 1995). Springfield was diagnosed with cancer after she made the album.
Stitt, Sonny	Jazz saxophonist Edward ("Sonny") Stitt died in Washington, D.C., on July 22, 1982, age 58. • **Last recording:** *Last Stitt Sessions,* made June 8-9, 1982. He died a short time later. • **Last performance:** July 1982, in Japan, a few days before he died. • **Last film:** *Jazz on a Summer's Day* (as himself, 1959).
Tatum, Art	Jazz pianist Art Tatum (Arthur Taylor Jr.) died in Los Angeles, California, on November 5, 1956, age 47. • **Last studio recording:** *Art Tatum—Ben Webster Quartet,* released September 11, 1956, two months before he died. • **Last film:** *The Fabulous Dorseys* (as himself, 1947).
Teagarden, Jack	Jazz trombonist/singer Weldon Leo ("Jack") Teagarden died in New Orleans, Louisiana, on January 15, 1964, age 58. • **Last public performance:** The Dream Room, New Orleans. He died of

	bronchial pneumonia in his hotel room after a performance. • **Last film as himself:** *Jazz on a Summer's Day* (1959). • **Last film as actor:** *Sliphorn King of Polaroo* (1945).
Temptations, The	The Motown Rhythm-and-Blues group The Temptations had numerous line-ups; however, the classic five were Eddie Kendrick(s), David Ruffin, Paul Williams, Otis Williams and Melvin Franklin. Additionally, Dennis Edwards is recognized as a "classic-era" member, and those six have been inducted into the Rock n' Roll Hall of Fame. Paul Williams died in Detroit, Michigan, on August 17, 1973, age 34. Davis Eli ("David") Ruffin died in Philadelphia, Pennsylvania, on June 1, 1991, age 50. Eddie James Kendrick died in Birmingham, Alabama, on October 5, 1992, age 52. (Kendrick dropped the "s" from his last name.) David Melvin English, who was known professionally as Melvin Franklin, died in Los Angeles, California, on February 23, 1995, age 52. • **Last surviving original member of The Temptations:** Otis Williams. • **Last Top 40 *Billboard* hit (Pop Charts) as performers:** "The Motown Song," which was charted by Rod Stewart with The Temptations on July 27, 1991. It was the group's 38th Top 40 hit. Their last No. 1 hit was "Papa Was a Rollin' Stone" (1972). • **Last Top 40 *Billboard* hit (Pop Charts) with Ruffin and Kendrick:** "A Nite At The Apollo Live! The Way You Do The Things You Do/My Girl," which entered the charts on August 14, 1985. It was credited as Daryl Hall & John Oates with David Ruffin and Eddie Kendrick. Kendrick's last solo No. 1 was "Keep on Truckin' (Part 1)" (1973).
Tormé, Mel	Singer/songwriter/pianist/drummer/actor Melvin ("Mel") Howard Tormé, died in Los Angeles, California, on June 5, 1999, age 73. • **Last recording:** *Swingin' at the Blue Note Bar & Grille* (released 2000). He sang the duet "Straighten Up and Fly Right" with his son Steve Marsh Tormé. The recording was made before he had a stroke in 1996. • **Last Top 40 *Billboard* hit (Pop Charts) during his lifetime:** "Comin' Home Baby," which entered the charts on December 15, 1962. • **Last film score:** *Walk Like a Dragon* (1960). • **Last film as actor:** *The Magic of Christmas* (TV, 1995). • **Last film as himself:** *A Spinal Tap Reunion: The 25th Anniversary London Sell-Out* (TV, 1992).
Twitty, Conway	Country singer/songwriter Conway Twitty (Harold Lloyd Jenkins) died in Springfield, Missouri, on June 5, 1993, age 59. • **Last Top 40 *Billboard* hit (Pop Charts) during Twitty's lifetime:** "You've Never Been This Far Before," which entered the charts on August 15, 1973. His last No. 1 on the Pop Charts was "It's Only Make Believe," which entered the charts on September 29, 1958. He switched from Pop to Country in 1965. Most of his hits were on the Country charts where he had 41 No. 1 hits. His last No. 1 Country hit was *Desperado Love* (1986). • **Last album:** *Final Touches* (1993), released after his death. • **Last public appearance:** Branson, Missouri, June 4, 1993. He collapsed and died on his tour bus en route to his home in Nashville. • **Last films:** *College Confidential* (1960) and *Platinum High School* (1960).
Valens, Ritchie	Rock singer/guitarist Ritchie Valens (Richard Stephen Valenzuela) died in a plane crash near Mason City, Iowa, on February 3, 1959, age 17.

	• **Last Top 40 *Billboard* hit (Pop Charts) during Valens' lifetime:** "La Bamba," which entered the charts on January 19, 1959. • **Last performance:** Surf Ballroom in Clear Lake, Iowa, February 2, 1959, while on tour. Following the concert, Valens, Buddy Holly and the Big Bopper were killed in the crash. • **Last film:** *Go, Johnny, Go!* (as himself, 1958).
Vaughan, Sarah	Pop and Bebop singer Sarah Lois Vaughan died in Hidden Hills, California, on April 3, 1990, age 66. • **Last recording:** *Brazilian Romance* (1987). • **Last Top 40 *Billboard* hit (Pop Charts) during Vaughan's lifetime:** "Broken-Hearted Melody," which entered the charts on August 17, 1959. • **Last film:** *Listen Up: The Lives of Quincy Jones* (as herself, 1990).
Vaughan, Stevie Ray	Blues and Rock guitarist Stevie Ray Vaughn died in a helicopter crash in East Troy, Wisconsin, on August 27, 1990, age 35. • **Last album:** *Family Style* (released 1990; artists listed as the Vaughan Brothers). • **Last film:** *Back to the Beach* (as himself, 1987).
Walker, T-Bone	Blues guitarist/bandleader/singer Aaron Thibeaux ("T-Bone") Walker died in Los Angeles, California, on March 16, 1975, age 64. He stopped performing after he suffered a stroke in 1974. • **Last album:** *Very Rare* (released 1974).
Waring, Fred	Conductor/bandleader Frederick ("Fred") Malcolm Waring died in State College, Pennsylvania, on July 29, 1984, age 84, just after videotaping a concert with The Pennsylvanians and completing his summer workshops. • **Last film score:** *Varsity Show* (1937). • **Last public performance:** concert for Penn State University's public TV station, July 1984. • **Last Broadway show as performer:** *Hello Yourself*. Last performance of original run: 1929, at the Casino Theater in New York, New York. • **Last film:** Disney's *Melody Time* (voice, 1948). • **Last telecast of *The Fred Waring Show*:** May 30, 1954. The program, which featured Waring and His Pennsylvanians, first aired in April 1949.
Washington, Dinah	Jazz, Blues, Gospel singer/pianist Dinah Washington (Ruth Lee Jones) died in Detroit, Michigan, on December 4, 1963, age 39. • **Last *Billboard* Top 40s hit during Washington's lifetime:** "Where Are You," which entered the charts on June 23, 1962. • **Last film:** *Jazz on a Summer's Day* (as herself, 1959).
Washington, Grover (Jr.)	Jazz, Rhythm & Blues saxophonist Grover Washington Jr. suffered a heart attack and died in New York, New York, on December 17, 1999, while taping an appearance on the CBS-TV *Saturday Early Show*. He was 56. • **Last album:** *Aria,* released posthumously March 2000. • **Last Top 40 *Billboard* hit (Pop Charts) during Washington's lifetime:** "Just The Two Of Us," which entered the charts on March 7, 1981. It was credited as Grover Washington Jr. with Bill Withers. • **Last film:** *Blues Brothers 2000* (1998).
Waters, Ethel	Blues singer/actress Ethel Waters died in Chatsworth, California, on September 1, 1977, age 80. • **Last performances:** In her later years, Waters avoided Blues songs such as "Stormy Weather" (which she had introduced and made famous) and instead performed only religious songs. She was active with Billy Gra-

	ham's Crusades for many years and retired in 1972 due to ill health. • **Last Broadway show as performer:** *At Home with Ethel Waters* (1953). Last performance of original run: October 10, 1953, at the 48th Street Theater in New York, New York. • **Last film as actress:** *The Sound and the Fury* (1959). • **Last film as herself:** *The Voice That Thrilled the World* (1943).
Waters, Muddy	Blues guitarist/singer/leader/writer/arranger McKinley Morganfield ("Muddy") Waters died in Westmont, Illinois, on April 30, 1983, age 68. • **Last recording:** *King Bee* (1981). • **Last public appearance:** Eric Clapton Concert, Sportatorium, Miami, Florida, June 30, 1982. • **Last film:** *Eric Clapton and his Rock and Roll Hotel* (as himself, 1980).
Weavers, The	The Weavers folk group first appeared as the No-Name Quartet. They became The Weavers in 1949. Original members were Pete Seeger, Lee Hayes, Fred Hellerman and Ronnie Gilbert. Hayes died in Tarrytown, New York, on August 26, 1981, age 67. • **Last concert:** November 1980 at Carnegie Hall in New York, New York, organized by Pete Seeger. PBS produced and broadcast a documentary of the performance. • **Last album:** *Reunion at Carnegie Hall 1963, Part 2* (1965); other compilation albums were released later.
Whiteman, Paul	Bandleader/violinist Paul Whiteman died in Doylestown, Pennsylvania on December 29, 1967, age 77. • **Last Broadway show as performer:** *Ziegfeld Follies of 1923* (1923) at the New Amsterdam Theater in New York, New York. • **Last film:** *The Fabulous Dorseys* (as himself, 1947). • **Last telecast of *Paul Whiteman's Goodyear Revue*:** March 30, 1952. The musical variety show first aired in November 1949. • **Last telecast of *Paul Whiteman's TV Teen Club:*** March 28, 1954. The teen talent show first aired in April 1949. • **Last telecast of *On the Boardwalk with Paul Whiteman*:** August 1, 1954. The variety show first aired on May 30, 1954. • **Last telecast of *America's Greatest Bands*:** September 24, 1955. Whitman hosted the music show that first aired on June 25, 1955.
Who, The	The British Rock band The Who was formed in London, England, in 1964. Keith Moon (drummer) died in London on September 7, 1978, age 31. John Entwistle (bassist) died in Las Vegas, Nevada, on June 27, 2002, age 57. • **Last performance of Moon with The Who:** May 25, 1978. The concert was filmed for The Who documentary *The Kids Are Alright*. • **Last Top 40 *Billboard* hit (Pop Charts) during Moon's lifetime:** "Squeeze Box," which entered the charts on January 3, 1976. "Who Are You" hit the charts about a week after his death. • **Last film with all original members of The Who:** *The Kids Are Alright* (1979, released after Moon's death). • **Last Top 40 *Billboard* hit (Pop Charts) as performers during Entwistle's lifetime:** "Athena," which entered the charts on October 9, 1982. It was The Who's 16th Top 40 hit. • **Last performance of Entwistle with The Who:** February 8, 2002, Royal Albert Hall, London, England.

	• **Last Broadway performance of The Who's _Tommy_:** last performance of original run: June 17, 1995, at the Saint James Theater in New York, New York.
Williams, Hank	Country singer/guitarist Hiram King ("Hank") Williams died at Oak Hill, West Virginia, on January 1, 1953, age 29. He was on his way to a concert in Canton, Ohio. • **Last single released in his lifetime:** "I'll Never Get Out of This World Alive." It reached No. 1 just after he died. • **Last recording session:** September 23, 1952, Castle Studios, Nashville, Tennessee. • **Last public appearance:** Casino Lounge in the Elite Cafe in Montgomery, Alabama, for the American Federation of Musicians, December 28, 1952.
Williams, Mary Lou	Jazz pianist/composer/arranger Mary Lou Williams died in Durham, North Carolina, on May 28, 1981 age 71. • **Last album:** _Solo Recital: Montreux Jazz Festival_ (1978). • **Last Broadway show as performer:** _Blue Holiday_ (1945). Last performance of original run: May 26, 1945, at the Belasco Theater in New York, New York.
Wilson, Jackie	Rock & Roll singer Jackie Wilson died in Mount Holly, New Jersey, on January 21, 1984, age 49. • **Last performance:** September 25, 1975. Wilson was singing "Lonely Teardrops" at the Latin Casino in Cherry Hill, New Jersey, when he had a heart attack. He sustained brain damage from oxygen deprivation and was hospitalized for the rest of his life. • **Last _Billboard_ Top 40s hit during his lifetime:** "I Get the Sweetest Feeling," which entered the charts on August 31, 1968. Wilson had 24 _Billboard_ Top 40 hits during his career. • **Last film as actor:** _The Teenage Millionaire_ (1962). • **Last film as himself:** _Go, Johnny, Go!_ (1958).
Winding, Kai	Danish-born jazz trombonist Kai Chresten Winding died in New York, New York, on May 6, 1983, age 59. • **Last album:** _Trombone Summit_ (1981). • **Last Top 40 _Billboard_ hit (Pop Charts) during Winding's lifetime:** "More," which entered the charts on July 27, 1963. It was credited as Kai Winding & Orchestra. • **Last recording with J.J. Johnson:** _Great Kai and J.J._, recorded in November 1960. The trombone duo recorded together often from 1954 to 1956 then again in a 1960 reunion. • **Last live performance with J.J. Johnson:** All-Star Jam Live, the Aurez Jazz Festival in 1982. • **Last film:** _A Man Called Adam_ (as himself, 1966).
Wynette, Tammy	Country singer Tammy Wynette (Virginia Wynette Pugh) died in Nashville, Tennessee, on April 6, 1998, age 55. • **Last recording with George Jones:** _One_ (1995). • **Last recording:** "In My Room," a tribute to Brian Wilson of the Beach Boys (1996). • **Last Top 40 _Billboard_ hit (Pop Charts) during Wynette's lifetime:** "Justified and Ancient," which entered the charts on February 15, 1992. It was credited as The KLF featuring Tammy Wynette.

	• **Last film:** *The Beach Boys: The Nashville Sound* (as herself, 1996). In 1997 and 1998, she lent her voice to a character on a few episodes of the animated TV series *King of the Hill.* Her last episode was "The Unbearable Blindness of Laying," December 21, 1997.
Young, Lester	Jazz saxophonist Lester Willis Young died in New York, New York, on March 15, 1959, age 49. • **Last recording with the Count Basie Band:** Newport Jazz Festival, Newport, Rhode Island, July 7, 1957, live concert recording. • **Last recording with Billie Holiday:** TV program, *The Sound of Jazz,* December 8, 1957. They recorded "Fine and Mellow." • **Last recording of Young:** March·4, 1959, with the Lester Young Quintet in Paris, France. • **Last album:** *Laughin' to Keep from Cryin'* (1958). • **Last film as himself:** *Jammin' the Blues* (short, 1944). • **Last film as actor:** *Policy Man* (1938).
Zappa, Frank Mothers of Invention	Singer/guitarist/composer Frank Zappa formed The Mothers of Invention in 1965. He died in Laurel Canyon, California, on December 4, 1993, age 52. • **Last Mothers of Invention album with Zappa:** *Bongo Fury* (1975). • **Last Zappa Mothers of Invention album with Howard Kaylan and Mark Volman:** *Just Another Band from L.A.* (1971). The two left to record on their own as Flo and Eddie. • **Last albums of Zappa:** *The Yellow Shark,* orchestral music, released in 1993, just before he died. *Civilization III* was released posthumously in 1995. • **Last Top 40 *Billboard* hit (Pop Charts) during Zappa's lifetime:** "Valley Girl," which entered the charts on September 4, 1982. It featured his daughter Moon Unit Zappa. • **Last concert appearance:** *Yellow Shark* concert in Frankfurt, Germany, September 17, 1992, performed by the Ensemble Modern. Zappa made only one short appearance due to his illness. • **Last public performance as a guitarist:** Budapest, Hungary, as a guest guitarist, June 29, 1991. • **Last major tour:** 1988. Last concert of the tour, June 9, 1988, Genoa, Italy. Zappa limited his live appearances after 1988. • **Last film score:** *Peef eeyatko* (1991), a documentary about himself that he also starred in and produced. • **Last film as himself:** *The Revenge of the Dead Indian* (1993). • **Last film Zappa wrote and directed:** *The True Story of Frank Zappa's 200 Motels* (1988). In 1991, he lent his voice to a character in an episode of the animated series *The Ren and Stimpy Show.*

Nations

(*see also* United States)

Nations—Afghanistan, (Transitional) Islamic State of

Afghanistan is north of Pakistan and east of Iran in southern Asia.

• **End of the Anglo-Afghan Wars:** 1919. Afghanistan engaged in three wars with Great Britain. The first began in 1839 and ended in 1842 with Great Britain withdrawing from Afghanistan. The second war began in 1878 and ended in 1880 with a pro-British ruler. The third war was waged in 1919 over whether Afghanistan should be independent.

• **End of British control over Afghan foreign affairs:** August 8, 1919, when Afghanistan proclaimed its independence with an Anglo-Afghan treaty signed at Rawalpindi. Great Britain did not formally recognize Afghanistan's independence until November 22, 1921, with the signing of the Anglo-Afghan Treaty at Kabul.

• **Last emir of Afghanistan:** Amanullah Khan, from 1919 to 1926. He was the first padash (king) of Afghanistan, from 1926 to 1929, when he was forced to abdicate. He died in Zurich, Switzerland, on April 25, 1960, age 67.

• **Last padash (king) of Afghanistan:** Muhammed Zahir Shah, who ascended to the throne in 1933. Afghanistan's monarchy was overthrown by a bloodless coup on July 17, 1973, and a republic was installed.

• **End of the Afghanistan Republic:** April 30, 1978, when a bloody coup led to the creation of a Marxist state, the Democratic Republic of Afghanistan.

• **End of occupation of Afghanistan by the Soviet Union:** February 15, 1989. Soviet troops had invaded Afghanistan in December 1979.

• **End of the Democratic Republic of Afghanistan:** April 15, 1992, when the Soviet-backed Marxist government was replaced by the Islamic State of Afghanistan by the Mujahideen. The Taliban, a fundamentalist Islamic group, gained control of much of the country in the 1990s.

• **End of Taliban control:** Fall of 2001, when the Taliban was driven from power.

Nations—Albania, Republic of

Albania borders the Adriatic and Ionian seas between Greece and Montenegro in southeastern Europe.

• **End of control by the Ottoman Empire:** November 28, 1912, during the First Balkan War, when Albania proclaimed its independence. Albania became a republic in 1925. A monarchy was established in 1928.

• **Last king of Albania:** King Zog I, who ruled Albania until Italy annexed the country in 1939, during World War II, and forced him into exile. King Victor Emmanuel III of Italy assumed the title of "King of Albania" by concordat and ruled from April 16, 1939,

to September 3, 1943. After the war ended, King Zog was unable to reclaim the throne. He abdicated in January 1946, and the country became the People's Republic of Albania.

• **End of Italian annexation:** September 8, 1943, during World War II, when Italy surrendered unconditionally to the Allies. Germany then seized control of Albania.

• **End of World War II occupation by Germany:** November 29, 1944, when the last German troops left Albania and the Communists gained control.

• **Last of the People's Republic of Albania:** December 28, 1976, when the country was renamed the Socialist People's Republic of Albania.

• **Last of the Socialist People's Republic of Albania:** April 30, 1991, when the country was renamed the Republic of Albania.

Nations—Algeria (People's Democratic Algerian Republic)

Algeria borders the Mediterranean Sea between Morocco and Tunisia in northern Africa. Ottoman (Turkish) rule was established in 1518.

• **End of Ottoman (Turkish) rule:** July 5, 1830, when France ousted the last dey (governor) and established French rule.

• **Last dey (governor):** Husein III, who governed from March 1, 1818, to July 5, 1830. He died in 1848.

• **End of French rule:** July 5, 1962, when Algeria declared itself an independent nation. On September 25, 1962, by proclamation, the country was named the People's Democratic Algerian Republic.

• **Last high commissioner (executive French official):** Christian Fouchet, who governed from March 19, 1962, to July 3, 1962. He died in 1974.

Nations—Andorra, Principality of

Andorra is between France and Spain in southwestern Europe. In 1278, the Spanish bishop of Urgel claimed Andorra as part of his cathedral. The French argued that the tiny state belonged to them. An agreement was reached allowing the Spanish bishop

and the head of France to have joint sovereignty over Andorra. This arrangement worked for 715 years.
• **End of Andorra's joint sovereignty system:** March 14, 1993, when the people adopted a parliamentary system of government and Andorra became an independent nation.

Nations—Angola, Republic of
Angola borders the Atlantic Ocean between Namibia and the Democratic Republic of the Congo in southern Africa. The first Portuguese settlement began in 1575.
• **End of Portuguese control:** November 11, 1975, when Angola gained its independence as the People's Republic of Angola.
• **Last high commissioner/governor-general (highest executive Portuguese official):** Leonel Silva Cardoso, who governed from August 26, 1975, to November 10, 1975.
• **Last known as the People's Republic of Angola:** August 27, 1992, when a new government took office as the Republic of Angola.

Nations—Antigua and Barbuda
The Caribbean island nation of Antigua and Barbuda is at the southern end of the Leeward Islands, east-southeast of Puerto Rico. The Spanish claimed Antigua in 1493. The British colonized the island in the 1600s. The nearby island of Barbuda was colonized by the British in 1661.
• **End of British control:** November 1, 1981, when both islands became independent as the nation of Antigua and Barbuda.

Nations—Argentina (Argentine Republic)
Argentina is between Chile and Uruguay in southern South America, bordering the Atlantic Ocean. The first Spanish settlement was in 1535. Spain established the Viceroyalty of Rio de la Plata in 1776.
• **End of the Viceroyalty of Rio de la Plata:** May 25, 1810, when the viceroyalty was ousted by Argentine revolutionaries. The last two viceroys—those after 1810—were viceroys in name only. The junta president who took power on May 25,
1810, claimed to rule on behalf of the deposed Spanish king.
• **Last viceroy of Rio de la Plata:** Francisco Javier Elío, who held the post from February 12, 1811, to July 9, 1816. He died in 1822.
• **End of Spanish control:** July 9, 1816, when Argentina's independence was formally recognized. Argentina went through a long period of political turmoil as various factions vied for control. In 1946, Juan Perón was elected president. His popular wife Eva (Evita) died on July 26, 1952, age 33. Juan Perón was overthrown by a military faction on September 19, 1955. He regained the presidency in 1973. Perón died on July 1, 1974, and his third wife María Estela ("Isabel") Martínez Cartas de Perón, who was vice-president, succeeded him as president.
• **End of Perón rule:** March 24, 1976, when Isabel Perón was removed from office.
• **End of the War of the Triple Alliance,** *see* Wars and Battles—Triple Alliance, War of the.
• **End of Argentina's occupation of the Falkland Islands (Islas Malvinas):** June 14, 1982. The occupation began on April 2, 1982. (*See also* Wars and Battles—Falkland Islands.)

Nations—Armenia, Republic of
Armenia is east of Turkey and Iran in southwestern Asia. Over the centuries, Armenia was under the control of the Roman, Byzantine and Ottoman empires. In 1828, Armenia was incorporated into Russia. Armenia, Azerbaijan and Georgia were part of the Viceroyalty of the Caucasus from 1844 to 1881 and again from 1905 to 1917. In 1917, they were joined to form the Transcaucasian Federation.
• **Last of the Transcaucasian Federation:** May 26, 1918, when it dissolved into three separate republics. Armenia was made a Soviet republic in 1920. It joined with the Georgian and Azerbaijani Soviet Socialist Republics in 1922 to became the Transcaucasian Soviet Federated Socialist Republic, one of the founding components of the Soviet Union.

• **Last of the Transcaucasian Soviet Federated Socialist Republic:** December 5, 1936, when Armenia became the Armenian Soviet Socialist Republic.

• **Last of the Armenian Soviet Socialist Republic:** September 23, 1991, when Armenia declared its independence from the Soviet Union as the Republic of Armenia. Armenian independence became effective on December 25, 1991, when the USSR was dissolved.

Nations—Australia

Australia is a continent in Oceania, between the Indian and South Pacific oceans. Australia's colonial settlement began when a penal colony was established in New South Wales in 1788.

• **Last convicts transported to Australia:** January 9, 1868, when the final 269 convicts arrived on the *Hougoumont*.

• **End of the ban on citizenship for Australian Aborigines:** 1967.

• **End of the policy of banning immigration of non-whites:** 1973. A European language dictation requirement ended in 1958. The White Australia Policy had been in effect since 1901.

• **Last surviving male Tasmanian Aborigine:** William Lanney (or Lanne) who died on March 2, 1968. The Tasmanian Aborigines were rounded up in the mid-1800s and moved to Flinders Island. Later, they were moved to Oyster Cove in southern Tasmania, where the last Tasmanian Aboriginal settlement was established in 1847. The Aborigines gradually died out from European diseases. No full-blood Tasmanian Aborigines are alive today.

• **Last surviving female Tasmanian Aborigine**: Believed by some to be Trucanini (or Truganini), who died in 1876. One hundred years later, in 1976, her ashes were scattered on the D'Entrecasteaux Channel. Other evidence suggests that the last female Tasmanian Aborigine who was born and raised in a traditional tribal setting died on Kangaroo Island in 1916.

Nations—Austria, Republic of

Austria is south of Germany and west of Hungary in west-central Europe. In 1526, Austria formed a union with Hungary. Austria and Hungary became a dual monarchy as the Austro-Hungarian Empire in 1867.

• **Last of the Austro-Hungarian Empire:** 1918, with the end of Hapsburg rule. On October 21, 1918, delegates met to establish an Austrian state. They formally signed an armistice on November 3, 1918, ending Austro-Hungarian participation in the war. The Republic of Austria was declared on November 12, 1918.

• **Last emperor of Austria (and king of Hungary):** Charles I (Charles Francis Joseph), who reigned from 1916 to 1918. When the Austro-Hungarian Empire was defeated in World War I, he did not formally abdicate. He went into exile in Switzerland under British protection. Charles made two unsuccessful attempts to regain the throne in 1921. During his second attempt, he was arrested and exiled to Madeira. He died there on April 1, 1922, age 34.

• **Last Austro-Hungarian empress:** Zita, wife of Charles I. She was left a widow in 1922. Zita died in Switzerland on March 14, 1989, age 96.

• **Last known as the (First) Republic of Austria:** July 1, 1934, when the country became the Federated State of Austria.

• **Last known as the Federated State of Austria:** March 13, 1938, when Austria was annexed by the German Reich.

• **End of German annexation:** April 27, 1945, as World War II was ending in Europe, when a provisional government was established. (*See also* Wars and Battles—World War II—Austria.)

Nations—Azerbaijan (Azerbaijani Republic)

Azerbaijan is in southwestern Asia, between Iran and Russia, with a small European portion north of the Caucasus Mountains and bordering the Caspian Sea. Azerbaijan, Georgia and Armenia were part of the Viceroyalty of the Caucasus from 1844 to 1881, and again from 1905 to 1917. In 1917, they were joined to form the Transcaucasian Federation.

• **Last of the Transcaucasian Federation:** dissolved on May 26, 1918. On May 28, 1918, Azerbaijan became the Azerbaijan People's Republic. Azerbaijan was made a Soviet republic in 1920. It joined with the Georgian and Armenian Soviet Socialist Republics in 1922 to became the Transcaucasian Soviet Federated Socialist Republic, one of the founding components of the Soviet Union.

• **Last of the Transcaucasian Soviet Federated Socialist Republic:** December 5, 1936, when Azerbaijan became the Azerbaijan Soviet Socialist Republic.

• **Last of the Azerbaijan Soviet Socialist Republic:** November 19, 1990, when the country became the Azerbaijani Republic. On August 30, 1991, Azerbaijan declared its independence from the Soviet Union. The independence became effective on December 25, 1991, when the Soviet Union was dissolved.

Nations—Bahamas (Commonwealth of the Bahamas)

The Bahamas are a chain of Caribbean islands southeast of Florida and northeast of Cuba. England began a settlement in the Bahamas in 1647. Pirates began to rule the islands in 1706.

• **End of pirate rule:** July 26, 1718, when the islands became a British crown colony. The Bahamas were briefly under American occupation beginning on March 3, 1776.

• **End of American occupation:** March 17, 1776. The Bahamas were under Spanish occupation twice: 1684 and again beginning on May 8, 1782.

• **End of Spanish occupation:** April 19, 1783. The Bahamas were returned to Great Britain in exchange for eastern Florida. In 1969, the colony became the Commonwealth of the Bahama Islands.

• **End of British rule:** July 10, 1973, when The Bahamas gained its independence.

Nations—Bahrain, Kingdom of

Bahrain is an archipelago in the Persian Gulf, east of Saudi Arabia. The Portuguese began to occupy the country in 1521.

• **End of Portuguese occupation:** 1602. Persia controlled Bahrain after the Portuguese left.

• **End of Persian control:** 1783, when the Khalifah dynasty was established. Great Britain and Bahrain signed a treaty of friendship in 1820 to suppress piracy and slave trade. In 1861, Bahrain became a British protectorate.

• **End of British protectorate:** August 15, 1971, when Bahrain regained its independence. It adopted the name State of Bahrain on August 16, 1971.

• **Last known as the State of Bahrain:** February 14, 2002, when the nation became the Kingdom of Bahrain. The ruler's title was changed to king.

Nations—Bangladesh, People's Republic of

Bangladesh is between India and Myanmar (Burma) and borders the Bay of Bengal in southern Asia. When India gained its independence in 1947, it was partitioned into two countries: India and Pakistan. Pakistan became a republic within the British Commonwealth in 1956. Pakistan was a divided country, separated by more than a thousand miles of India. The eastern part was called East Pakistan.

• **Last of East Pakistan:** On March 21, 1971, Sheik Mujibur Rahman (Mujeebur Rehman) declared East Pakistan independent of Pakistan. On March 26, 1971, the nation proclaimed its independence, taking the name People's Republic of Bangladesh.

• **Last governor of Bangladesh:** Abdul Motaleb Malik, who governed from August 31, 1971, to December 14, 1971. He died in 1977.

Nations—Barbados

Barbados is a Caribbean island northeast of Venezuela. It became a British colony in 1627.

• **End of British control:** November 29, 1966, when independence was granted and Barbados became a parliamentary democracy.

• **Last governor of Barbados:** Sir John Montague Stow, who served from October

8, 1959, to November 29, 1966. At that time, his title was changed to governor-general. He continued to serve until May 18, 1967. He died in 1997.

• **Last chief minister of Barbados:** Errol Barrow, who served from December 8, 1962, to November 18, 1966. At that time, his title was changed to prime minister. He continued to serve until September 8, 1976. He died in 1987.

Nations—Belarus, Republic of

Belarus is east of Poland and north of the Ukraine in eastern Europe. In 1922, most of the country became part of the Soviet Union as the Byelorussian Soviet Socialist Republic. In June 1941, the Germans invaded during Operation Barbarossa and captured the capital at Minsk.

• **End of World War II occupation of Minsk by Germany:** July 3, 1944. The date was later celebrated as the Byelorussian Independence Day.

• **Last of the Byelorussian Soviet Socialist Republic:** 1991. Independence was declared on August 25, 1991. On September 19, 1991, the country became the Republic of Belarus.

Nations—Belgium, Kingdom of

Belgium borders the North Sea between France and the Netherlands in western Europe. Belgium was under Hapsburg control from the 1400s until 1555, when it was taken over by Spain.

• **End of Spanish control:** May 8, 1713, when the Spanish Netherlands (Belgium) were ceded to Austria after the War of the Spanish Succession.

• **End of status as an Austrian province:** August 18, 1797, when Belgium was officially annexed to France by Austria.

• **End of French annexation:** February 15, 1814, when Belgian territory separated from France, creating the Government General of Belgium. In 1815, the Belgian lands and Liège were incorporated into the Kingdom of the Netherlands.

• **End of Netherlands control:** October 4, 1830, when a provisional government de-

clared independence from the Netherlands. The name Kingdom of Belgium was officially adopted on June 4, 1831.

• **End of Belgian control in Africa:** July 1, 1962, when Burundi and Rwanda gained their independence. Until 1960, Belgium also controlled the Belgian Congo, later known as Zaire, and now named the Democratic Republic of the Congo.

Nations—Belize

Belize borders the Caribbean Sea between Guatemala and Mexico in Central America. It became a British crown colony as British Honduras in 1862.

• **Last known as British Honduras:** June 1, 1973, when the country was renamed Belize.

• **End of British control:** September 21, 1981, when Belize gained its independence.

• **Last governor of Belize:** Sir James Patrick Ivan Hennessy, who served from 1980 to September 21, 1981. At that time, the title was changed to governor-general.

Nations—Benin, Republic of

Benin borders the Atlantic Ocean between Nigeria and Togo in western Africa. The French began establishing protectorates there in the 19th century.

• **End of French control:** August 1, 1960, when the country became fully independent as the Republic of Dahomey.

• **Last known as the Republic of Dahomey:** November 30, 1975, when the country was renamed the People's Republic of Benin.

• **Last known as the People's Republic of Benin:** March 1, 1990, when the country was renamed the Republic of Benin.

Nations—Bhutan, Kingdom of

Bhutan is on the slopes of the Himalayas between China and India in southern Asia. Great Britain invaded the country in 1772 and 1865. A monarchy was established in 1907. Bhutan was granted full autonomy by Britain and became a British protectorate in 1910.

• **End of the British protectorate:** August 15, 1947. After 1949, Bhutan accepted guid-

ance from India in foreign affairs.
• **End of the Indian protectorate:** September 31, 1971.

Nations—Bolivia, Republic of
Bolivia is a landlocked nation in central South America southwest of Brazil. Its people were conquered by the Spanish in the 1530s.
• **Last organized Inca resistance to Spanish:** 1538, when Spanish conquistador Francisco Pizarro completed his conquest of the Incas.
• **Last major Indian uprising against Spanish rule:** ended with the death of Tupac Amaru in July 1783.
• **Last time Bolivia was part of the Viceroyalty of Peru:** 1776, after which it was part of the Viceroyalty of Rio de la Plata. (The Viceroyalty of Peru was created in 1542 and included most of Spanish-controlled South America.)
• **Last time Bolivia was part of the Viceroyalty of Rio de la Plata:** August 1825, when Bolivia, then known as Upper Peru, gained its independence.
• **Last known as Upper Peru:** 1825, when Bolivian independence was proclaimed, and the country's name was changed to Bolivar to honor Simón Bolivar, who helped to liberate the region. The name Bolivar was later changed to Bolivia at the suggestion of liberator Antonio Jose dé Sucre.
• **Last time Bolivia's capital was known as Chuquisaca:** 1840, when the name was changed to Sucre to honor the first president of Bolivia.
(*See also* Wars and Battles—Chaco War; Pacific, War of the.)

Nations—Bosnia and Herzegovina, Republic of,
The nation of Bosnia and Herzegovina is in southeastern Europe, bordering Croatia and the Adriatic Sea. It became part of the Ottoman Empire in the 15th century.
• **End of Ottoman control:** July 13, 1878, when Austro-Hungary, France, Italy, Germany, Russia and Great Britain signed an agreement with the Ottoman Empire at the Congress of Berlin. Austria-Hungary was given the administration of Bosnia-Herzegovina. In 1908, Austria-Hungary annexed Bosnia-Herzegovina, creating a hostility that was a precipitating factor of World War I.
• **End of Austro-Hungarian annexation of Bosnia and Herzegovina:** 1918. The Kingdom of Serbs, Croats and Slovenes was created on December 1, 1918, after World War I ended. Bosnia and Herzegovina were made part of the union.
• **End of the Kingdom of Serbs, Croats and Slovenes:** October 3, 1929, with creation of the Kingdom of Yugoslavia. After World War II, Yugoslavia was reestablished with six republics. Bosnia and Herzegovina were federated as a single state. On March 3, 1992, Bosnia-Herzegovina declared its independence. The declaration led to a military conflict among Bosnians, Croats and Serbs.
• **End of Bosnian military conflict:** October 12, 1995, when a cease-fire went into effect, although fighting continued over contested towns in northwest Bosnia. The peace agreement was initialed at Wright-Patterson Air Force Base in Dayton, Ohio, on November 21, 1995, and formally signed in Paris, France, on December 14, 1995.

Nations—Botswana, Republic of
Botswana is in southern Africa, north of the Republic of South Africa and east of Namibia. In 1885, when threatened by the Boers, the people of the region asked Great Britain to establish a protectorate for their country. The Protectorate of Bechuanaland was created.
• **End of the Protectorate of Bechuanaland:** September 30, 1966, when Bechuanaland gained its independence from Great Britain as the Republic of Botswana.
• **Last commissioner of Bechuanaland:** Sir Hugh Selby Norman-Walker, who served from 1965 to September 30, 1966. His office was replaced by a president. He died in 1985.

Nations—Brazil, Federative Republic of
Brazil is in eastern South America, bordering the Atlantic Ocean. In 1500, explorer

Pedro Alvares Cabal claimed Brazil for Portugal. The office of governor-general was established in 1549.

• **Last governor-general of Brazil:** Pedro de Vasconcellos e Sousa, who governed from October 14, 1711, to July 13, 1714. The office of governor-general was replaced by a viceroy.

• **End of the Viceroyalty of Brazil:** December 16, 1815, when the last viceroy, Prince João de Bragança, was replaced by the monarch of Portugal, creating the Kingdom of Brazil (part of the United Kingdom of Portugal, and of Brazil, and Algarves).

• **End of Portuguese control:** September 7, 1822, when the Kingdom of Brazil declared its independence from Portugal. Portugal did not recognize Brazilian independence until May 13, 1825.

• **End of the Kingdom of Brazil:** October 12, 1822, when the title of king was changed to constitutional emperor and perpetual defender of the Empire of Brazil. Henceforth, the nation was the Empire of Brazil.

• **End of the Empire of Brazil:** November 15, 1889, when Emperor Dom Pedro II was overthrown in a bloodless revolution. Brazil then became a republic as the United States of Brazil. Dom Pedro II was the last emperor in the Western Hemisphere.

• **End of the United States of Brazil:** March 15, 1967, when the nation became the Federative Republic of Brazil.

• **Last time the Brazilian capital was in Salvador (São Salvador da Baía de Todos os Santos):** 1763, when it was moved to Rio de Janeiro.

• **Last time the Brazilian capital was in Rio de Janeiro:** April 21, 1960, when it was moved to the new city of Brasilia.

(*See also* Wars and Battles—Triple Alliance, War of the.)

Nations—Brunei (State of Brunei Darussalam)

Brunei is on the island of Borneo in southeastern Asia, bordering the South China Sea and Malaysia. It became a British protectorate in 1888 and a British dependency in 1905. The Japanese invaded Brunei in December 1941, during World War II, and occupied it completely by January 6, 1942.

• **End of World War II occupation by Japan:** June 14, 1945.

• **End of the British protectorate:** January 1, 1984, when Brunei became a fully sovereign and independent sultanate. British responsibility for defense and foreign affairs terminated at the end of 1983.

• **Last chief minister of Brunei:** Pehin Orang Kaya Laila Wijaya Dato, who served from September 1981 to December 31, 1983. With independence, the title of chief minister was changed to prime minister.

Nations—Bulgaria, Republic of

Bulgaria borders the Black Sea between Romania and Turkey in southeastern Europe. In 1395, Bulgaria was overrun by the Ottoman Turks, who would dominate the country for the next 500 years. The Principality of Bulgaria was established in 1879.

• **End of Ottoman (Turkish) domination:** October 5, 1908, when Bulgaria declared its independence from the Ottoman Empire (later Turkey). Bulgaria became a tsardom and the prince was renamed tsar.

• **Last prince of Bulgaria:** Ferdinand I, who was prince from August 14, 1887, to October 5, 1908. He became the first tsar, reigning until October 3, 1918, when he abdicated in favor of his son Boris. Ferdinand died in 1948. In 1912, during Ferdinand's reign, the First Balkan War broke out between members of the Balkan League—Serbia, Bulgaria, Greece and Montenegro—and the Ottoman Empire.

• **End of the First Balkan War:** The fighting ended on March 26, 1913, when Bulgaria captured Adrianople. The war ended officially with the Treaty of London signed on May 30, 1913. The Second Balkan War began in June 1913, when Bulgaria defeated Greek and Serbian troops and fighting broke out between Bulgaria and its ex-allies Greece and Spain.

• **End of the Second Balkan War:** August 10, 1913, with the Treaty of Bucharest

• **Last of the Kingdom of Bulgaria:** September 15, 1946, after the monarchy was abolished in a referendum called by Communists installed by the Soviet Army. A Soviet-style People's Republic of Bulgaria was established.

• **Last king of Bulgaria:** nine-year-old Simeon II, who lost his throne on September 8, 1946. Simeon Saxe-Coburgotski (former King Simeon II) was named prime minister of Bulgaria on July 12, 2001.

• **Last of the People's Republic of Bulgaria:** November 15, 1990, when the country became the Republic of Bulgaria.

Nations—Burkina Faso, Democratic Republic of

Burkina Faso is north of Ghana and Côte d'Ivoire in western Africa. The country was dominated by the Mossi people until the late 19th century. The Mossi are believed to have migrated there from central or eastern Africa in the 11th century.

• **End of Mossi control:** February 20, 1895, when Upper Volta became a French protectorate. Mossi resistance ended after the French arrived and captured their capital at Ouagadougou. Upper Volta became French colony in 1919 and an autonomous republic in 1958.

• **End of French control:** August 5, 1960, when the country gained independence from France as the Republic of Upper Volta.

• **Last governor of Upper Volta:** Max Berthet, who served from July 15, 1958, to December 11, 1958, when his title was changed to high commissioner. He continued to serve until February 1959.

• **Last known as the Republic of Upper Volta:** August 4, 1984, when Upper Volta was renamed Burkina Faso, meaning "the country of honorable people."

Nations—Burma, *see* Myanmar, Union of.

Nations—Burundi, Republic of

Burundi is east of the Democratic Republic of the Congo and south of Rwanda, bordering Lake Tanganyika in central Africa. It was ruled by the Tutsi kingdom in the 16th century. Germany took over Burundi and neighboring Rwanda and made both part of German East Africa in 1890.

• **End of German control:** June 1916, when Belgian forces took over the area during World War I. Ruanda-Urundi became part of a League of Nations Belgian mandate in 1922 and a United Nations trusteeship territory in 1946.

• **End of Belgian control:** July 1, 1962, when the United Nations trusteeship under Belgian administration ended and Urundi separated from Ruanda-Urundi to create the Kingdom of Burundi.

• **Last of the Kingdom of Burundi:** November 28, 1966, when the monarchy was overthrown and the Republic of Burundi was created.

• **Last king (mwami) of Burundi:** Ntare V Ndizeye (Charles Ndizeye), who reigned from September 1, 1966, to November 28, 1966.

• **Last prime minister of Burundi:** Pascal-Firmin Ndimira, who served from July 31, 1996, to June 12, 1998, when the post was abolished.

Nations—Cambodia, Kingdom of

Cambodia is in southeastern Asia, surrounded by Thailand, Vietnam, Laos and the Gulf of Thailand. Cambodia became a French protectorate in 1863 and an associated state in the French Union in 1949.

• **End of French control:** November 9, 1953, when Cambodia gained full independence as a constitutional monarchy and withdrew from the French Union. France did not recognize Cambodia's independence until December 20, 1954.

• **End of Cambodia's first constitutional monarchy:** October 9, 1970, when Prince Norodom Sihanouk was deposed and the Khmer Republic was created.

• **Last of the Khmer Republic:** January 6, 1976, when the country's name was changed to the Republic of Democratic Kampuchea, after the Khmer Rouge, led by Pol Pot, seized control.

• **End of the Khmer Rouge regime:** January 7, 1979, when Vietnam and Cambodian rebels seized the capital at Phnom Penh and established the People's Republic of Kampuchea (PRK). The United Nations did not recognize the PRK.

• **End of the Killing Fields:** January 1979, with the end of Pol Pot's regime. The Killing Fields were the mass graves in the countryside where Cambodians killed by the Khmer Rouge were buried. Nearly one fourth of the Cambodian population died from starvation, disease, overwork and execution from 1974 to 1979.

• **Last of the People's Republic of Kampuchea:** 1989, when a new constitution created the State of Cambodia.

• **Last of the State of Cambodia:** September 24, 1993, when the monarchy was reestablished with the return of Norodom Sihanouk. The country's official name was changed to the Kingdom of Cambodia.

• **Last of the Khmer Rouge movement:** In 1997, Pol Pot was denounced by his former comrades and placed under house arrest. In December 1998, Khieu Samphan and the last of the Khmer Rouge surrendered to the Cambodian government. On December 29, 1998, the remaining leaders of the Khmer Rouge apologized for the genocide of more than 1 million Cambodians in the 1970s.

Nations—Cameroon, Republic of

Cameroon is in western Africa, between Equatorial Guinea and Nigeria, bordering the Bight of Biafra. In 1884, Kamerun was created as a German protectorate .

• **End of the German protectorate:** March 4, 1916, during World War I, when Allied forces gained control. In 1922, Kamerun was given to France and Britain as the League of Nations mandates of French Cameroun and British Cameroons. In 1946, the mandates were changed to United Nations trusteeships.

• **Last governor of German Kamerun:** Karl Ebermaier, who served from 1914 to March 4, 1916. He died in 1943.

• **Last of French Cameroun:** January 1, 1960, when French Cameroun became independent as the Republic of Cameroon.

• **Last high commissioner of French Cameroun:** Xavier Antoine Torré, who held the post from February 19, 1958, to January 1, 1960. He died in 2003.

• **Last of British Cameroons:** October 1, 1961, when the Federal Republic of Cameroon was created after unification of the Republic of Cameroon (former French Cameroun) with the southern part of British Cameroons. (The northern part of British Cameroons joined Nigeria in 1961.)

• **Last premier of British Cameroons:** John Ngu Foncha, who served from February 1, 1959, to October 1, 1961. He died in 1999.

• **Last of the Federal Republic of Cameroon:** June 2, 1972, when the country was renamed the United Republic of Cameroon.

• **Last of the United Republic of Cameroon:** February 4, 1984, when the country was renamed the Republic of Cameroon.

Nations—Canada

Canada extends from the Atlantic to the Pacific oceans and covers more than half of the North American continent. The French claimed the Saint Lawrence River region as New France in 1534.

• **End of French control of New France:** February 10, 1763. France lost Canada in the French and Indian War. Great Britain gained control and renamed the region British North America. The Constitutional Act in 1791 split the two regions of Quebec at the Ottawa River to form Upper and Lower Canada.

• **End of Upper Canada (Canada West or Ontario) and Lower Canada (Canada East or Quebec):** February 5, 1841, when the two Canadas were united under one government by the Act of Union.

• **Last joint premiers of Canada:** Sir John Alexander Macdonald, who served from July 30, 1865, to June 30, 1867, along with Sir Narcisse Fortunat Belleau. On July 1, 1867, the joint premiers were replaced with a single prime minister: Macdonald. Macdonald died in 1891. Belleau died in 1894.

• **Last governor of the Province of Canada:** Charles Stanley, Viscount Monck of Ballytrammon, who served from October 25, 1861, to June 30, 1867, when the position was changed to governor-general. Stanley held that post until 1868.

• **End of a non-confederated Canada:** July 1, 1867, when the British North American Act joined Nova Scotia and New Brunswick with the Province of Canada (Quebec and Ontario) to establish the Dominion of Canada. Other parts of Canada were added in later years. July 1st is celebrated as Canada Day.

• **Last addition to the Dominion of Canada:** Newfoundland in 1949. It became Canada's tenth province at midnight on March 31st.

• **Last official use of the term "Dominion":** 1967.

• **End of British constitutional powers:** April 17, 1982, when the Constitution Act went into effect. The constitution ended the British North America Act of 1867 that had been the nation's constitution up to that time.

• **Last time Sverdrup Islands (Arctic Archipelago) belonged to Norway:** 1931. That year, Norway relinquished its claims to the islands to Canada.

• **Last time part of Vancouver Island belonged to the United States:** 1846, when the entire island went to Canada by terms of the Oregon Treaty.

• **Last use of primogeniture in Canada:** December 31, 1850. Primogeniture—the system by which the eldest son receives the larger part of a deceased father's property—was abolished the following day.

• **Last time Canada operated on a non-decimal currency system:** December 31, 1857, when a decimal currency system was formally adopted. On July 1, 1871, Parliament made the decimal currency system uniform across Canada.

• **Last time paper $1 bills were issued in Canada:** June 30, 1989, when the Bank of Canada started replacing the paper bills with $1 coins (often called "loonies").

Nations—Canada—Old Place Names

New Name	Old Name	Last Used
Cambridge	Galt	1973
Kenora	Rat Portage	1905
Kitchener	Berlin	1916
Niagara Falls	Clinton	1881
Nova Scotia	Acadia	1622
Ottawa	Bytown	1854
Prescott	Johnstown	1869
Prince Edward Island	Saint John Island	1798
Regina	Pile O' Bones	1882
Thunder Bay	Fort William and Port Arthur	1970
Toronto	York	1834
Vancouver	Gastown	1885
Winnipeg	Red River Colony	1866

Nations—Cape Verde, Republic of

Cape Verde is a group of islands in the Atlantic Ocean, west of Senegal in west Africa. Portuguese explorers arrived on the islands in 1455.

• **Last time Portuguese Guinea (Guinea-Bissau) was part of the Cape Verde colony:** 1879, when it became a separate colony.

• **End of Portuguese control:** July 5, 1975, when the Republic of Cape Verde gained its independence.

• **Last governor of Cape Verde:** Vicente Almeida d'Eça, who served from December 31, 1974, to July 5, 1975, when the post of governor was replaced by that of president.

Nations—Central African Republic

Central African Republic is in central Africa, north of the Democratic Republic of the Congo. When the French arrived in 1887, the region was named Ubangi-Shari for its two main rivers. In 1906, Ubangi-Shari was united with Chad. In January 1910, the colony joined Gabon and Middle Congo to become one of the territories of French Equatorial Africa.

• **Last time Ubangi-Shari was part of Ubangi-Shari-Chad:** April 12, 1916.

• **Last known as Ubangi-Shari:** December 1, 1958, when the colony became an autonomous republic within the French Community and changed its name to the Central African Republic.

• **Last governor of the Central African Republic:** Paul Camille Bordier, who served

from January 29, 1958, to 1959. He also served as the last and only high commissioner, from 1959 to August 1960, when a president was installed.
• **End of French control:** August 13, 1960, when the Central African Republic declared its independence from France. The Central African Empire was created in 1976.
• **Last emperor of the Central African Empire:** Bokassa I (Jean-Bédel Bokassa; Islamic name: Eddina Ahmed Bokassa), who reigned from December 4, 1976, to September 20, 1979, when he was overthrown. Earlier, he served as president.
• **End of the Central African Empire:** September 21, 1979, when Bokassa's regime was overthrown and the Central African Republic was restored. He died in November 1996, age 75.

Nations—Chad, Republic of
Chad is south of Libya and west of Sudan in central Africa. From 1906 to 1916, Chad was part of the Ubangi-Shari-Chad colony. In 1910, the colony joined Gabon and Middle Congo to become part of French Equatorial Africa.
• **Last time Chad was part of the Ubangi-Shari-Chad colony:** April 12, 1916, when Chad became a separate colony. Chad became an autonomous republic within the French Community on November 28, 1958.
• **End of French control:** August 11, 1960, when the country declared its independence as the Republic of Chad.
• **Last governor of Chad:** René Troadec, who served from November 3, 1956, to January 22, 1959. He was followed by the last and only high commissioner, Daniel Marius Doustin, who served until August 11, 1960, when a president was installed. Troadec died in 1986.

Nations—Chile, Republic of
Chile is west of Argentina and south of Peru in southern South America, with a long border along the Pacific Ocean. Before the Spanish arrived in the 1530s, northern Chile was part of the Inca Empire. Chile declared its independence from Spain in 1810 but

was reconquered by the Spanish in 1814.
• **End of Spanish control:** February 12, 1818, when the State of Chile declared its independence from Spain. Spain finally recognized Chile's independence on April 25, 1844.
• **Last known as the State of Chile:** July 9, 1826, when the country became the Republic of Chile. It became the Socialist Republic of Chile in June 4, 1932.
• **Last known as the Socialist Republic of Chile:** September 13, 1932, when the nation once again became the Republic of Chile.
(*See also* Wars and Battles—Pacific, War of the.)

Nations—China, People's Republic of
China is in eastern Asia, bordering the East China, Yellow, and South China seas and the Korea Bay. China's last dynasty, the Ch'ing (or Manchu) began in 1644. China went through a long time of prosperity. But as the population grew, the Manchus were not up to the task of providing jobs and improved agriculture. Moreover, Europeans were beginning to carve China into spheres of influence, with each nation demanding exclusive rights to trade. (*See also* Empires and Kingdoms—China.)
• **Last of the Ch'ing (Manchu) dynasty:** February 12, 1912, when China's last emperor abdicated, thus ending China's last dynasty. A year earlier, China was swept by revolution and a republic was declared.
• **Last emperor of China:** Hsüan T'ung (imperial name), who also used the anglicized name Henry P'u-yi (or P'u-I). He became emperor in 1908 when he was three and held the office until February 12, 1912. Hsüan T'ung was permitted to live in the Forbidden City—the walled complex in Beijing that held the imperial palace—and retain his title until November 5, 1924. His power was restored briefly, from July 1, 1917, to July 12, 1917, but it never extended outside the Forbidden City. In March 1934, he was crowned Emperor Kang Teh of Manchukuo (Japan's name for Manchuria). P'u-yi died in Beijing on October 15, 1967, age 61. His life was the subject of the movie

The Last Emperor (1987). (*See also* Nations—Japan—End of the Manchukuo Empire.)

• **End of the pigtail (queque):** December 7, 1911, when it was abolished by revolutionary edict as a symbol of Manchu feudalism. Beginning in the 17th century, Chinese men were required to wear their hair in long pigtails as a sign of their submission to Manchu rule.

• **End of the Long March:** October 25, 1935, in northern Senshi. The Long March began more than a year earlier, in October 1934, when Mao Tse-tung and about 90,000 to 100,000 Chinese Communists set out from Kiangsi in southeastern China to Yenan in the northwest seeking refuge in the Communist stronghold in Shensi. Less than one third survived the journey.

• **End of the Great Leap Forward:** 1961. The Great Leap Forward was an economic plan introduced in 1958, whose goal was to convert China into an industrial nation in the shortest possible time. It did not work as the planners had hoped. Instead of increasing food production, it brought shortages, famine and starvation.

• **End of the Cultural Revolution:** August 1977. Eleven years earlier, in August 1966, Chinese leader Mao Tse-tung officially launched the repressive Great Proletarian Cultural Revolution in an attempt to rid China of all foreign influences and to abolish the prevailing education system. The first step toward ending the Cultural Revolution came in July 1968, when the Chinese army began to disband the Red Guard. The militant militia group had been created in 1966 to put forth the goals of the revolution. The Cultural Revolution effectively ended in 1976 with the death of Mao Tse-tung and the subsequent arrest of the Gang of Four. It ended officially at the Eleventh Party Congress in August 1977. In 1981, the Communist party denounced the Cultural Revolution as a grave error.

• **Last of the Gang of Four:** probably Yao Wenyuan who was the group's propagandist. He was convicted in 1981 and was given the most lenient sentence of the group.

He was released from prison on in 1991. Two of the others are known to be dead. The third was reported dead but unconfirmed. (The Gang of Four were individuals led by Mao's wife, Jiang Qing, who promoted revolution and class struggle under Chairman Mao during the Cultural Revolution.)

• **Last surviving founding member of the Chinese Communist party:** Chang Kuo-tao. In the 1930s, he served as an army commander. After political disagreements with Mao Tse-tung, he broke with the Communists and joined the Chinese Nationalists. He later spent many years in exile in Asia and Canada. Chang Kuo-tao died in Toronto on December 3, 1979, age 82.

• **Last surviving marshal of the ten who led China's Communist Revolution:** Nie Rongzhen (Nieh Jung-chen). He was a member of the Communist party for 69 years and oversaw the development of China's first atomic bomb. From 1956 to 1974, he served as deputy premier and was a member of the Politburo from 1977 to 1985. Nie Rongzhen died in Beijing on May 16, 1992, age 92.

• **End of restriction on travel to China by Americans:** November 1972, when the U.S. lifted a 22-year restriction on ship and plane travel to China. President Richard M. Nixon paved the way by visiting China in February 1972. In December 1978, President Jimmy Carter extended full diplomatic recognition to China.

• **Last U.S. prisoners released:** 1973. The last two known U.S. prisoners held by China at that time arrived at Clark Air Force Base, Philippines, on March 15, 1973. Air Force Major Philip E. Smith, 38, of Illinois had been held seven and a half years. Navy Lieutenant Commander Robert J. Flynn, 35, of Minnesota had been a prisoner five and a half years.

(*See also* Empires and Kingdoms—China)

Nations—China, People's Republic of—Hong Kong

Hong Kong, borders the South China Sea in eastern Asia. The British occupied Hong Kong in 1841. It was ceded to them the following year by the Treaty of Nanking. In 1898, a 355-square-mile piece of land called the New Territories was leased from China for 99 years.

• **End of British dependency over Hong Kong:** June 30, 1997.

• **Last governor of Hong Kong:** Christopher Francis Patten, who served from July 9, 1992, to June 30, 1997.

• **Last British troops in Hong Kong:** August 10, 1994. British troops had been stationed there since September 1841.

Nations—China, People's Republic of—Tibet

Tibet is an autonomous region of China. In the south, it shares a border with India, Nepal and Bhutan. Buddhism was introduced in the 7th century. Before it was invaded by China in 1949, Tibet had a long history as an independent state.

• **Last time Tibet was independent:** 1950. In 1949, Chinese Red Army invaded Tibet under the pretense of liberating the peasants. Chinese forces occupied Tibet in 1950. Since that time, the Tibetan people have been resisting Chinese subjugation. In March 1959, demonstrations staged in Lhasa, the capital, led to open fighting throughout Tibet, forcing the Dalai Lama—the Buddhist spiritual leader and temporal ruler of Tibet—to seek asylum elsewhere.

• **End of the Dalai Lama's journey to India:** March 31, 1959. His 300-mile trek on foot through mountainous terrain with 80 followers took 12 days. On April 3, 1959, the Indian government confirmed that he had reached India four days earlier and that asylum had been granted. He remains in exile.

Nations—Colombia, Republic of

Colombia borders the Caribbean Sea and the Pacific Ocean in northern South America. The Spanish began to colonize the area in the early 1500s, and Colombia became part of the Viceroyalty of Peru. In 1717, Colombia separated from Peru and became part of the Viceroyalty of New Granada, which also

ruled Ecuador and Venezuela. In 1724, Colombia briefly reincorporated with Peru.

• **Last time Colombia was part of the Viceroyalty of Peru:** 1739, with restoration of the Viceroyalty of New Granada. In 1811, local juntas began to revolt against the Spanish king and on November 27, 1811, Colombia became part of the Federated Provinces of New Granada (later called the United Provinces of New Granada). A reconquest by Spain began in 1815.

• **Last president of the United Provinces of New Granada:** Manuel Fernando Serrano y Uribe, who served in 1816.

• **Last viceroy of New Granada:** Juan de la Cruz Mourgeon y Achet, who held the position from 1819 to 1821. The viceroyalty ended with the end of Spanish rule.

• **End of Spanish control:** December 17, 1819, when Simon Bolivar proclaimed the Gran Colombia (Great Colombia) Confederation. It was made up of the present nations of Colombia, Venezuela, Ecuador and Panama. In 1830, Venezuela and Ecuador withdrew to become separate nations. The rest of Gran Colombia (Colombia and Panama) became the State of New Granada.

• **Last known as the State of New Granada:** April 20, 1843, when the state became the Republic of New Granada.

• **Last known as the Republic of New Granada:** May 22, 1858, when the republic became the Granadine Confederation.

• **Last known as the Granadine Confederation:** July 18, 1861, when the confederation became the United States of New Granada.

• **Last known as the United States of New Granada:** September 20, 1861, when the union became the United States of Colombia.

• **Last known as the United States of Colombia:** August 5, 1886, when the union became the Republic of Colombia.

• **Last time Panama was a part of Colombia:** November 4, 1903, when Panama broke away and proclaimed its independence.

Nations—Comoros, Union of

The Comoros is an island nation in the Mo-

zambique Channel between northern Madagascar and northern Mozambique in southern Africa. In 1886, the islands of Njazidja, Nzwani and Mwali became French protectorates. In 1887, the three islands were renamed the Protectorate of the Comoros.
• **End of World War II occupation by Great Britain:** October 13, 1946. The British began occupying the islands on September 25, 1942. In 1947, the islands were made a French overseas territory.
• **End of French control:** July 6, 1975, when the islands declared their independence as the State of Comoros. Later, the island of Mayotte (Maoré) voted to remain under French control.
• **Last known as the State of Comoros:** May 24, 1978, when the nation became the Federal and Islamic Republic of Comoros.
• **Last known as the Federal and Islamic Republic of Comoros:** December 23, 2001, when the nation became the Union of Comoros.

Nations—Congo, Democratic Republic of the (Congo-Kinshasa)
The Democratic Republic of the Congo is northeast of Angola in central Africa. The King of Belgium began to colonize the area in 1876 and set up the independent Congo Free State in 1885.
• **Last known as the Congo Free State:** November 15, 1908, when the Congo Free State was annexed by Belgium and became known as the Belgian Congo.
• **End of Belgian control:** July 1, 1960, when the Belgian Congo gained independence as Republic of The Congo. The country was renamed the Democratic Republic of the Congo in July 1, 1966. Then, in October 27, 1971, the name was changed to the Republic of Zaire.
• **Last known as the Republic of Zaire:** May 17, 1997, when the Republic of Zaire once again became the Democratic Republic of the Congo.
• **Last governor-general of the Belgian Congo:** Henri Arthur Adolf Marie Christopher Cornelis, who held the post from July 12, 1958, to June 30, 1960.

Nations—Congo, Republic of (Congo-Brazzaville)
Republic of Congo borders the Atlantic Ocean between Angola and Gabon in western Africa. It became a French colony in 1880, and was known as the French Middle Congo Territory in 1883. As Middle Congo, the colony was part of French Equatorial Africa.
• **End of French control:** August 15, 1960, when it gained independence as Republic of the Congo. On January 3, 1970, it was renamed People's Republic of Congo.
• **Last French high commissioner:** Guy Noël Georgy, who served from January 7, 1959, to August 15, 1960. He died in 2003. From 1888 to 1959, the position was called lieutenant governor.
• **Last known as the People's Republic of Congo:** March 15, 1992, when the name of the nation was changed back to Republic of Congo.
• **Last prime minister:** Bernard Kolelas, who served from September 8, 1997, to October 15, 1997, when the post was abolished.

Nations—Costa Rica, Republic of
Costa Rica borders the Caribbean Sea and the Pacific Ocean between Nicaragua and Panama in Central America. After the Spanish claimed the region in 1509, it was administered as part of the colonial kingdom of Costa Rica.
• **End of Spanish control:** November 12, 1821, when Costa Rica proclaimed its independence from Spain. In 1824, it became the Free State of Costa Rica. From 1825 to 1888, Costa Rica was a member of the Central American Federation. (*See also* Alliances, etc.—Central American Federation.)
• **Last governor of Costa Rica:** Juan Manuel de Cañas y Trujillo, who served as interim governor from 1819 to October 29, 1821. His title was then changed to political patriotic chief. He continued to serve until November 12, 1821, when his office was replaced by that of president.
• **Last known Free State of Costa Rica Republic:** March 7, 1847, when the country

became the State of Costa Rica.
• **Last known as the State of Costa Rica Republic:** August 31, 1848, when the country became the Republic of Costa Rica.

Nations—Côte d'Ivoire, République de (Republic of Ivory Coast)

Côte d'Ivoire borders the Atlantic Ocean between Ghana and Liberia in western Africa. France declared protectorates over the area in 1842.
• **End of French control:** August 7, 1960, when the country declared its independence from France.
• **Last time the name Ivory Coast was used officially:** October 1985, when the government declared other nations should call the country by its French name, Côte d'Ivoire.

Nations—Croatia, Republic of

Croatia borders the Adriatic Sea in southern Europe between Slovenia and Bosnia-Herzegovina. In December 1918, at the end of World War I, Croatia joined with other Balkans states as the Kingdom of the Serbs, Croats and Slovenes.
• **End of the Kingdom of the Serbs, Croats and Slovenes:** October 3, 1929, when the name was changed to the Kingdom of Yugoslavia by royal decree of King Alexander I.
• **End of the Kingdom of Yugoslavia:** November 29, 1945, when the government of Marshal Tito was recognized and the monarchy was abolished. Croatia became the People's Republic of Croatia within Yugoslavia.
• **Last of the People's Republic of Croatia:** July 7, 1963, when it became Socialist Federal Republic of Croatia within Yugoslavia.
• **Last known as the Socialist Federal Republic of Croatia:** August 1990, when it became the Republic of Croatia.
• **Last time Croatia was part of Yugoslavia:** June 25, 1991, when Croatia and Slovenia declared their independence. Afterward, ethnic Serbs and Croats battled for control of the region.

Nations—Cuba, Republic of

Cuba is a Caribbean island nation about 90 miles south of Key West, Florida. It was first visited by Christopher Columbus in 1492.
• **End of Spanish control:** October 10, 1898, when independence was declared as the Republic of Cuba after an insurrection against Spanish control. On January 1, 1899, Spain ceded colonial authority to the United States.
• **Last surviving member of the Cuban junta that campaigned for liberation from Spain in the 1890s:** Horatio Seymour Rubens, who died in Garrison, New York, on April 8, 1941, age 71.
• **End of U.S. control:** May 20, 1902, when the Republic of Cuba was granted independence from the United States and a protectorate was established.
• **End of U.S. protectorate:** May 29, 1934.
• **Last surviving framer of the 1901 Cuban Constitution:** Dr. Antonio Bravo Correoso, who died in Santiago, Cuba, on January 2, 1944.
• **Last governor:** Charles Edward Magoon, who served as a provisional governor from October 13, 1906, to January 28, 1909. He died in 1920.
• **Last constitutionally elected president:** Carlos Prío Socarrás, who was overthrown by Fulgencio Batista on March 10, 1952. Socarrás died in Miami, Florida, on April 4, 1977, age 74.
• **End of the rule of Fulgencio Batista (Rubén Fulgencio Batista y Zaldívar):** January 1, 1959, when he resigned. Fidel Castro became premier of Cuba on February 16, 1959. Batista died in Guadalmina, Spain, on August 6, 1973, age 72.
• **Last U.S. ambassador to Cuba:** Philip Wilson Bonsal, who served from 1959 to 1960. He was recalled after Fidel Castro allied with the Soviet Union. Bonsal later served as U.S. ambassador to Morocco. He died in 1995.
• **End of U.S. diplomatic relations:** January 1961. Cuban exiles made an unsuccessful attempt to overthrow Castro later that year by invading the Bay of Pigs.
• **Last Bay of Pigs prisoner to be released:**

Ramon Conte Hernandez, who was released from jail by the Cuban government on October 18, 1986. After his release, Hernandez was flown to Miami International Airport on a chartered plane.

• **End of the Cuban Missile Crisis:** November 20, 1962, when President John F. Kennedy announced the U.S. naval blockade of Cuba was being lifted. Americans became aware of the crisis on October 22nd when Kennedy announced that Soviet missiles had been installed in Cuba. The U.S. ordered a naval and air blockade on the shipment of all offensive military equipment to Cuba until the missiles were removed. The blockade was lifted when U.S. surveillance showed the missiles were being crated and the bases were being removed.

• **Last time the U.S. navy base in Cuba was known as Guantanamo Bay Naval Station:** April 1, 1941, when it was renamed Guantanamo United States Naval Operating Base. (Cuba leased the base to the U.S. in 1903.)

• **Last time the U.S. base in Cuba was known as Guantanamo Bay U.S. Naval Operating Base:** June 18, 1952, when it was renamed Guantanamo Bay U.S. Naval Base.

Nations—Cyprus, Republic of

Cyprus is an island in the Mediterranean Sea, south of Turkey. It came under the control of the Ottoman Empire in the 1500s.

• **End of Ottoman control:** July 12, 1878, when Cyprus was leased to Great Britain. Cyprus was annexed by the British on November 5, 1914, and became a crown colony on March 10, 1925.

• **End of British control:** August 16, 1960, when Cyprus proclaimed its independence.

• **Last British governor of Cyprus:** Sir Hugh Mackintosh Foot, who served from December 3, 1957, to August 16, 1960. He died in 1990.

Nations—Czech Republic

The Czech Republic is in central Europe, southeast of Germany. When the Austro-Hungarian Empire collapsed at the end of World War I, Czechoslovakia was created

from some of the lands of Bohemia and Moravia. The Czechoslovak State was declared on October 28, 1918.

• **Last of the Czechoslovak State:** November 14, 1918, when the nation became the Czechoslovak Republic. From March 1939 until 1945, during World War II, Czechoslovakia was occupied by the Nazis.

• **End of World War II occupation by Germany:** May 4, 1945, when the Czechs expelled the Germans.

• **End of World War II control of the Sudetenland by Germany:** May 8, 1945, when the Sudetenland was restored to the Czechs. (Germany had seized the Sudetenland from Czechoslovakia in October 1938.)

• **Last known as the Czechoslovak Republic:** July 11, 1960, when the nation became the Czechoslovak Socialist Republic. The Czechoslovak Socialist Republic began to fall apart in 1989 with the downfall of the Soviet Union.

• **End of the Velvet Revolution/end of Communist control:** December 29, 1989. The Velvet Revolution started in mid-November 1989, when students began gathering at Wenceslas Square in Prague to protest police brutality. The crowds grew to hundreds of thousands in Prague and elsewhere throughout the country. The revolution ended with the collapse of Communism in the Czechoslovak Socialist Republic without a shot being fired. An election held on December 29th, gave the country its first non-Communist president since 1948: Vaclav Havel.

• **Last known as the Czechoslovak Socialist Republic:** March 29, 1990, when the nation became the Czechoslovak Federal Republic.

• **Last known as the Czechoslovak Federal Republic:** April 20, 1990, when the nation became the Czech and Slovak Federal Republic.

• **Last of the Czech and Slovak Federal Republic:** December 31, 1992. The following day, the nation was officially separated into two nations: the Czech Republic and the Slovak Republic.

• **Last prime minister of the Czech and**

Slovak Federal Republic: Jan Strásky who served from July 1, 1992, to December 31, 1992.

Nations—Denmark, Kingdom of

Denmark is on a peninsula north of Germany (Jutland) in northern Europe, bordering the Baltic and North seas. Denmark, Sweden and Norway were united in 1397 in the Union of Kalmar. Sweden left the union in 1523. That year, Denmark began to share its monarch with Norway.

• **Last monarch who ruled both Denmark and Norway:** Frederick VI, who began his reign in 1808. He ruled Norway until 1814, when Denmark was forced to cede Norway to Sweden after the Napoleonic Wars.

• **Last time the Danish West Indies were owned by Denmark:** December 12, 1916, when the United States purchased the islands (Saint Croix, Saint Thomas, Saint John). Danish administration of the islands ended and United States sovereignty began officially on March 31, 1917.

• **End of Denmark's union with İceland:** June 17, 1944. (*See also* Nations—Iceland.)

Nations—Denmark, Kingdom of—Greenland

Greenland (Greenlandic name: Kalaallit Nunaat) is an island northeast of Canada between the Arctic and Atlantic oceans. It is a self-governing province of Denmark. Norse immigrants colonized the area beginning in the 10th century.

• **Last bishop of Greenland:** died in 1378. No replacement was sent.

• **Last record of the early Norse in Greenland:** 1408, a marriage record at the Hvalsey Church in the East Settlement.

• **Last Norwegian claim in Greenland:** April 5, 1933. Norway withdrew its claim after the Permanent Court of International Justice awarded sovereignty over the east coast to Denmark. (In 1932, Norway had proclaimed annexation of the east coast of Greenland—Eric the Red's land.)

• **End of Danish sovereignty:** May 1, 1979, when Denmark granted home rule to Greenland.

Nations—Djibouti, Republic of

Djibouti is between Eritrea, Ethiopia and Somalia in eastern Africa, bordering the Gulf of Aden and the Red Sea. France gained control of the region in the late 19th century. It was established as the Territory of Obock and Protectorate of Tadjoura in 1884.

• **Last known as Territory of Obock and Protectorate of Tadjoura:** 1888, when the name was changed to French Somaliland. On October 27, 1946, French Somaliland became an overseas territory within the French Union.

• **Last known as French Somaliland:** July 3, 1967, when the name was changed to the French Territory of the Afars and the Issas.

• **Last known as the French Territory of the Afars and Issas:** June 27, 1977, when the territory gained independence from France as the Republic of Djibouti.

• **Last French high commissioner:** Camille d'Orano, who served from February 9, 1976, to June 27, 1977. The position was known as governor from 1887 to 1967.

Nations—Dominica, Commonwealth of

Dominica is a Caribbean island nation between Puerto Rico and Trinidad and Tobago. Dominica was the last of the Caribbean islands to be colonized by Europeans, due chiefly to the fierce resistance of the native Caribs. Great Britain and France both claimed jurisdiction over the island. Britain gained sovereignty in 1784. Dominica became part of the Leeward Islands colony in 1833.

• **Last time Dominica was part of the Leeward Islands colony:** January 1, 1940, when it became part of the Windward Islands colony.

• **Last time Dominica was part of the Windward Islands colony:** January 1, 1960.

• **End of British control:** February 27, 1967, when Dominica was granted self-government as an associated state.

• **End of associated state status:** November 3, 1978, when it declared its independence as the Commonwealth of Dominica.

Nations—Dominican Republic

The Dominican Republic occupies two thirds of the Caribbean island of Hispaniola. The western third is occupied by Haiti. On December 1, 1821, the Dominican Republic gained independence as the Independent State of the Spanish Part of Haiti in Colombia. On February 9, 1822, it was incorporated into Haiti.

• **End of Haitian domination:** February 27, 1844, when it established its independence as the Dominican Republic. In 1861, it became part of the Spanish colony of Santo Domingo.

• **End of Spanish control:** September 14, 1863, when independence was declared. It was not recognized by Spain until July 11, 1865. The U.S. occupied the island several times, beginning in 1903. The last occupation began on April 28, 1965.

• **End of last U.S. occupation:** September 21, 1966.

• **Last time Santo Domingo was known as Cuidad Trujillo:** 1961. Santo Domingo is the original (1496) name of the capital of the Dominican Republic. The name was changed to Cuidad Trujillo in 1936 for General Rafael Leonidas Trujillo y Molina, and then changed back to Santo Domingo in 1961, after he was assassinated.

Nations—East Timor, Democratic Republic of

The island of Timor is in the Malay Archipelago, about 360 miles northwest of Australia. Portuguese traders arrived in the early 16th century. Dutch settlers also arrived and claimed the region. A treaty in 1859 divided the island. Portuguese Timor, or East Timor, occupied the eastern half.

• **End of Portuguese control:** 1975, when Indonesia invaded East Timor. It annexed the land the following year.

• **End of Indonesian control:** August 1999, when East Timor was placed under United Nations administration. On May 20, 2002, the former Portuguese colony gained its independence as the Democratic Republic of East Timor (Timor-Leste in Portuguese).

Nations—Ecuador, Republic of

Ecuador is between Colombia and Peru in western South America, bordering the Pacific Ocean at the Equator. The area was conquered by the Spanish in the 1530s and was later part of the Viceroyalty of Peru.

• **Last time Ecuador was part of the Viceroyalty of Peru:** 1717, when the Viceroyalty of New Granada (Colombia, Ecuador, Panama and Venezuela) became a separate colony.

• **End of Spanish control:** 1822, when Simon Bolivar defeated a Spanish army at the Battle of Pichincha, and Ecuador gained its independence as part of the Gran Colombia (Great Colombia) Confederation. Gran Colombia was created in 1819 by Bolivar. It also included Colombia, Venezuela and Panama. Ecuador withdrew in 1830 to become a separate nation as the State of the South of Colombia. On September 22, 1830, the name was changed to the State of Ecuador.

• **Last known as State of Ecuador:** August 8, 1835, when the name was changed to the Republic of Ecuador.

Nations—Egypt, Arab Republic of

Egypt is in north Africa, bordered by Libya, the Sudan, Israel and the Red and Mediterranean seas. In 1517, the Ottoman Turks gained control of the region.

• **End of Ottoman control:** World War I. (*See also* Empires and Kingdoms—Ayyubid Sultanate, Fatimid Caliphate, Ottoman Empire.)

• **End of the French occupation of Cairo:** June 28, 1801. The French occupation of Cairo under Napoleon had begun in 1798 with the conquest of Upper Egypt.

• **End of the French occupation of Alexandria:** September 2, 1801. The French occupation of Alexandria under Napoleon had begun in 1798 with the conquest of Upper Egypt.

• **Last khedive (viceroy) of Egypt:** Abbas Hilmi Pasha (Abbas II), who ruled from January 8, 1892, to December 19, 1914. He was deposed when Great Britain established

a protectorate over Egypt. He died in 1944.
• **End of British control:** February 28, 1922, when Egypt's status as a British protectorate ended. The Egyptian kingdom was declared independent on March 16, 1922. British troops were withdrawn from all but the Suez Canal in 1936.
• **Last sultan of Egypt:** Ahmad Fuad Pasha, who was sultan from October 9, 1917, to March 16, 1922. He then became King Fuad I and ruled until he died in Cairo on April 28, 1936.
• **Last king of Egypt:** Fuad II, the young son of King Farouk who succeeded his father when Farouk was forced to abdicate on July 26, 1952, after a military coup. Fuad II abdicated on June 18, 1953, and Egypt became a republic.
• **End of the Suez Canal Crisis:** March 1957, with the withdrawal of Israeli troops. The crisis began when Egyptian President Gamal Abdel Nasser nationalized the Suez Canal on July 26, 1956. The Israelis invaded Egypt on October 30, 1956, then British and French forces landed at Port Said and Port Faud. The last British and French troops withdrew on December 22, 1956.
• **End of the United Arab Republic (with Syria):** September 28, 1961. Egypt and Syria had formed the United Arab Republic (UAR) in 1958. After the union ended, Egypt retained the name United Arab Republic.
• **Last known as the United Arab Republic:** September 11, 1971, when the country was renamed the Arab Republic of Egypt.

Nations—El Salvador, Republic of
El Salvador is between Guatemala and Honduras in Central America, bordering the Pacific Ocean. The area was conquered by the Spanish in the 1520s.
• **End of Spanish control:** September 21, 1821, when El Salvador proclaimed its independence. It was annexed to Mexico in 1822.
• **End of Mexican annexation:** July 1, 1823, when El Salvador and the other Central American nations proclaimed their independence. From 1825 to 1838, El Salvador

was part of the Central American Federation. (*See also* Alliances, etc.—Central American Federation.)
• **Last supreme chief of state:** Juan Nepomuceno Fernández Con Lindo y Zelaya, who served as a provisional supreme chief of state from January 7, 1841, to February 22, 1841. He then became president and served until February 1, 1842. He died in 1857. The Republic of El Salvador was proclaimed in 1859.

Nations—Equatorial Guinea, Republic of
Equatorial Guinea borders the Atlantic Ocean between Cameroon and Gabon in western Africa. The islands of Fernando Pó and Annobón became Portuguese colonies in 1474.
• **End of Portuguese control:** March 11, 1778, when the land was ceded to Spain and ruled as Spanish Guinea.
• **End of Spanish control:** October 12, 1968, when Spanish Guinea gained its independence as the Republic of Equatorial Guinea.
• **Last governor of Spanish Guinea:** Francisco Núñez Rodríguez, who served from 1962 to December 15, 1963. The position was replaced by a prime minister.
• **Last high commissioner of Equatorial Guinea:** Víctor Suances Díaz del Río, who served from 1966 to October 12, 1968. The position was replaced by a president.
• **Last time the capital city was known as Santa Isabel:** 1973, when it was renamed Malabo.
• **Last time the island name Fernando Pó was used:** 1973, when it was renamed Macias Nguema Bitogo. It was later renamed Bioko Island.

Nations—Eritrea, State of
Eritrea is between Djibouti and the Sudan in eastern Africa, bordering the Red Sea. The area was taken over by Italy in the 1880s. Eritrea was organized with Ethiopia and Italian Somaliland as Italian East Africa after Italy invaded Ethiopia in 1935.
• **End of Italian control:** May 5, 1941, when Eritrea came under British control.

• **End of British control:** September 1952, when Eritrea formally was federated to Ethiopia.
• **End of Ethiopian control:** May 29, 1991, when a provisional government was instituted that established a de facto independence. On May 24, 1993, the people voted to become the independent State of Eritrea.

Nations—Estonia, Republic of
Estonia is north of Latvia in eastern Europe, bordering the Baltic Sea and Gulf of Finland. The area was ceded to Russia by Sweden in 1721. Estonia was subordinated to the administrators of the Baltic Provinces until November 1917, when it proclaimed its own governing body. On February 24, 1918, Estonia became an independent republic. In 1940, it was incorporated into the Union of Soviet Socialist Republics (USSR) as the Estonian Soviet Socialist Republic.
• **Last of the Estonian Soviet Socialist Republic:** August 20, 1991, when Estonia declared its independence. The USSR recognized the independence of the Republic of Estonia on September 6, 1991.
• **End of World War II occupation by Germany:** September 18, 1944. The occupation began in July 1941.

Nations—Ethiopia, Federal Democratic Republic of
Ethiopia is northwest of Somalia in eastern Africa. After Italy invaded on October 3, 1935, Ethiopia's emperor Haile Selassie was driven from power and Ethiopia was annexed to Italy. It was organized with Eritrea and Italian Somaliland as Italian East Africa.
• **End of Italian control:** November 27, 1941, during World War II, when the last Italian administrators surrendered to the Allies. Emperor Haile Selassie returned to power.
• **End of the Ethiopian monarchy:** March 21, 1975, when it was officially abolished. On September 12, 1974, Emperor Haile Selassie was deposed in a military coup and a semi-official socialist state was established. On September 10, 1987, the nation became the People's Democratic Republic of Ethiopia.

• **Last known as the People's Democratic Republic of Ethiopia:** 1991, when the country became known as Ethiopia. It became the Federal Democratic Republic of Ethiopia on August 22, 1995.
• **Last emperor of Ethiopia:** Asfa Wossen (Crown Prince Asfa Wossen Haile Selassie), who was designated emperor from September 12, 1974, to March 21, 1975, although he never took office. He died in 1997. Haile Selassie I (Ras Tafari), who began to rule in 1930, is regarded as the last true emperor. He died on August 27, 1975, age 83, while under house arrest in Addis Ababa, Ethiopia.

Nations—Fiji Islands, Republic of the
Fiji is an island group in the southwest Pacific Ocean. Great Britain annexed the islands in 1874 at the request of local tribal chiefs, and Fiji became a dependency of the British crown. In 1877, Fiji became part of the British Western Pacific Territories.
• **Last time Fiji was part of the British Western Pacific Territories:** 1952.
• **End of British control:** October 10, 1970, when independence was granted as the Dominion of Fiji.
• **Last known as the Dominion of Fiji:** October 7, 1987, when Fiji's military leader declared the nation the Republic of Fiji and removed it from the British Commonwealth. Britain accepted the declaration on October 15, 1987, and on July 25, 1990, the country became the Sovereign Democratic Republic of Fiji.
• **Last known as the Sovereign Democratic Republic of Fiji:** July 27, 1998, when the nation was renamed the Republic of the Fiji Islands.

Nations—Finland, Republic of
Finland borders the Baltic Sea and the Gulfs of Bothnia and Finland in northern Europe. Sweden began its conquest of Finland in the 12th century. In 1581, Finland was made a grand duchy of Sweden.
• **End of Swedish control:** September 17, 1809, when a peace treaty gave Russia control of Finland after a war with Sweden.
• **Last grand duke of Finland:** Nikolay II, who held the title from November 1, 1894,

to March 15, 1917. He died in 1918. The Russian provisional government exercised grand ducal authority until November 7, 1917.

• **Last king of Finland:** Väinö I (Friedrich Karl von Hessen), who was elected king on October 7, 1918, but declined the throne on December 4, 1918. He died on May 28, 1940.

• **End of Russian control:** December 6, 1917, when Finland formally declared its independence from Russia. On January 4, 1918, Russia recognized Finland's independence.

• **End of the Winter War (Russo-Finnish War):** March 12, 1940, with Finland's defeat and the loss of some of its land to the USSR. The annexed territories were reintegrated into Finland in 1941. (The war began in November 1939, when Russian troops invaded Finland.)

Nations—France (French Republic)
France is in western Europe bordering the Bay of Biscay, English Channel and Mediterranean Sea. The Kingdom of the Franks dates back to the 5th century. In 987 A.D., the region became the Kingdom of France.

• **Last Carolingian monarch:** Louis V, who was the last direct descendant of Charlemagne to rule. When he died in 987, he left no heirs. He was succeeded by Hugh Capet, whose monarchy lasted 13 generations.

• **Last Capet king:** Charles IV (1294-1328). The multi-generational succession was broken when Charles IV died and the line passed to the Valois branch of the family.

• **Last House of Valois monarch to rule France:** Henry III. When he was murdered in August 1589, he left no heirs. The French crown passed to the Bourbon family. Henry of Navarre, became the first Bourbon king of France as Henry IV.

• **Last Bourbon king to rule France as absolute monarch:** Louis XVI, who ascended to the throne in 1774. He was deposed in 1792 and guillotined on January 21, 1793, age 38. Queen Marie Antoinette was guillotined on October 16, 1793, age 37.

• **Last Bourbon king:** Charles-Philippe,

Count d'Artois, younger brother of Louis XVI. He ascended to the throne as Charles X in 1824 but was ousted during a revolt in July 1830. He abdicated on August 2, 1830, and spent his remaining years in exile. Charles died in Goritz, Austria, on November 6, 1836, age79.

• **Last Dauphin:** Louis Antoine de Bourbon, Duc d'Angoulême, who renounced the title in 1830 after his father Charles X abdicated. (The "Dauphin" was the eldest son of the French king or that son's eldest son.)

• **Last of the Lost Dauphin:** Louis Charles de France, the second son of Louis XVI and Marie Antoinette, became Dauphin in 1789, after the death of his older brother. Because his fate was unknown, he became known as the Lost Dauphin. He was imprisoned with his family in 1792. Some accounts say he died in prison in 1795, but other stories claim another child was substituted for him in prison, while he escaped to America. These stories gave rise to several people claiming to be the Lost Dauphin. DNA tests performed in 2000 revealed that the child who died in prison was the Dauphin.

• **Last surviving person who could identify the Lost Dauphin:** Etienne de Grellet du Mabillier (a.k.a. Stephen Grellet), a French nobleman-in-exile who fled to the United States and settled in Burlington, New Jersey. Grellet died there in 1855.

• **Last use of the fleur-de-lis as the French national symbol:** 1830, when it was removed from the French flag for the final time and replaced by the tricolor. The fleur-de-lis had been used as the emblem of France since the reign of Clovis in 496.

• **Last of king the House of Orleans:** Louis Philippe, the Citizen King. The House of Orleans, a branch of the Bourbons, began and ended with his reign, which started with a revolution in 1830 and ended with his abdication on February 24, 1848. The Second Republic was established after his abdication. Louis Philippe died in Surrey, England, on August 26, 1850, age 76.

• **Last surviving son of King Louis Philippe of France:** Prince François, Duke of Joinville, who died in Paris on June 16,

1900, age 81. He was one of eight children.

• **End of the Second Republic:** December 2, 1852. It was replaced by the Second Empire, when Napoleon's nephew Louis Napoleon overthrew the republic and became Napoleon III. (The Second Republic had been established in 1848, after the abdication of King Louis Philippe.)

• **End of the Second Empire:** September 4, 1870, when the republican deputies of Paris set up a provisional government after the siege of Paris during the Franco-Prussian War. With the fall of the Second Empire of Napoleon III, the Third Republic was formed.

• **End of the Third Republic:** 1940. It collapsed with the fall of France during World War II. (*See also* Wars and Battles—World War II—France.)

• **End of the Fourth Republic:** September 1958. The Fourth Republic had been established on October 13, 1946, when the new French constitution was adopted. It replaced the provisional government that was set up following collapse of the Vichy government in June 1944. It was a continuation of the Third Republic (1870-1940). The Fifth Republic began when a new French constitution was adopted on September 28, 1958.

• **Last president of the Fourth Republic:** René Coty, who served from 1954 to 1958. He died in Le Havre, France, on November 22, 1962, age 80.

• **End of the French Union:** 1958. The French Union—a federation of French overseas territories and departments—was established by the Constitution of the Fourth Republic in 1946. The French Community—an association of former French colonies—replaced the French Union in 1958.

• **End of the French Community:** 1995, when it was dissolved by the French constitution. The French Community began to disintegrate as French territories sought independence.

• **Last time Alsace-Lorraine was separated from France:** January 1945, when French and U.S. troops liberated the region from German control during World War II. Alsace-Lorraine is a region in eastern France that shares borders with Germany and Luxembourg. France was forced to cede most of it to Germany in 1871, after the Franco-Prussian War. It was returned to France in 1918, at the end of World War I. Then Germany annexed it in 1940. Alsace-Lorraine remained under German control until it was once again returned to France in 1945.

Nations—France—Napoleon I

Napoleon Bonaparte rose to the rank of brigadier general during the French Revolution. He gained a reputation as a military genius when he was given command of French troops in Italy in 1796. His influence grew during the next few years. In 1799, he seized power in France.

• **End of the Directory:** November 9, 1799, after Napoleon's coup d'etat. The Directory had controlled France since 1795. It ended when the Consulate was created.

• **End of the Consulate:** December 2, 1804, when Napoleon crowned himself Emperor Napoleon I. The Consulate had ruled France since 1799.

• **End of the First Republic:** December 2, 1804, when Napoleon crowned himself emperor and created the First Empire. The First Republic had been proclaimed on September 21, 1792, when the French Revolution toppled the monarchy.

• **End of the First Empire:** 1814, with the abdication of Napoleon I (Napoleon Bonaparte) and restoration of the Kingdom of France. The First Empire had begun when Napoleon declared himself emperor in 1804 and thrust France into the Napoleonic Wars. He was forced to abdicate on April 6, 1814, and was sent into exile on the Mediterranean island of Elba.

• **Last day Napoleon was on Elba:** February 26, 1815. He escaped to fight a final battle. After his defeat at Waterloo on June 15, 1815, he was sent into exile on the remote island of Saint Helena in the South Atlantic Ocean, where he died in 1821. (*See also* Wars and Battles—French Revolution; Napoleonic Wars.)

• **Last legitimate heir of Napoleon:** Napoleon II of France (Napoleon Francis Joseph Charles Bonaparte), the only legitimate son of Napoleon Bonaparte and his second empress, Marie-Louise. He died in Vienna, Austria, on July 22, 1832, age 21, and was buried in the Hapsburg family vault in Vienna. His body was moved to Paris in 1940, at Hitler's request. He was placed near the tomb of his father in the Hôtel des Invalides. Napoleon also had illegitimate children who had descendants.

• **Last resting place of Napoleon:** Hôtel des Invalides in Paris, France. When Napoleon died on May 5, 1821, he was buried on the island of Saint Helena. On October 15, 1840, his body was taken to France. The government built a tomb for him at the Church of the Dome in the Hôtel des Invalides. A million people witnessed the reburial.

• **Last American Bonaparte:** Jerome Napoleon Bonaparte, a descendant of Napoleon's brother Jerome. He died in New York, New York, in 1945, age 67.

• **Last of the Bonaparte family to carry the name:** Marie Bonaparte who died in Saint-Tropez, France, on September 21, 1962, age 80. She was the daughter of the emperor's great nephew. She married Prince George of Greece.

Nations—Gabon (Gabonese Republic)

Gabon is in western Africa, between the Republic of the Congo and Equatorial Guinea, bordering the Atlantic Ocean at the Equator. France colonized the area in the 19th century.

• **Last known as the Gabon Colony:** January 15, 1910, when it became part of the French Equatorial Africa (AEF) colony. It was later known as the Gabon Region within the AEF, and still later as an overseas territory of France in the AEF.

• **End of French control:** Autonomy was granted on November 28, 1958. The Gabonese Republic gained full independence from France on August 17, 1960.

• **Last high commissioner:** Jean Risterucci, who held the post from July 1959 to August 17, 1960. He was replaced by a president. Risterucci died in 1982.

Nations—Gambia, Republic of The

The Gambia in western Africa is surrounded by Senegal except where it borders the Atlantic Ocean. The area was occupied or controlled by the Dutch, English and French at different times beginning in the 17th century. It became part of the British West African Settlements in 1866.

• **Last French settlement in the area:** Albreda, ceded to the British in 1857.

• **Last time The Gambia was part of the British West African Settlements:** 1888, when The Gambia became a separate colony. In 1894, Britain proclaimed a protectorate over the interior of The Gambia.

• **End of British control:** October 3, 1963, when self-rule was achieved. The nation was granted full independence on February 18, 1965, as the Dominion of The Gambia.

• **Last known as the Dominion of the Gambia:** April 24, 1970, when it became the Republic of The Gambia. On February 1, 1982, The Gambia and Senegal formed the confederation of Senegambia while maintaining individual sovereignty.

• **End of the Senegambia confederation:** dissolved on September 30, 1989, after diplomatic problems led to the withdrawal of Senegalese troops.

• **Last governor-general of The Gambia:** Sir Farimang Mamadi Singateh, who served from February 9, 1966, to April 24, 1970.

• **Last prime minister:** Sir Dawda Kairaba Jawara, who served from June 12, 1962, to April 24, 1970. At that time, his title was changed to president, a position he held until July 22, 1994.

Nations—Georgia

Georgia is along the Black Sea in southwestern Asia, bordered by Armenia, Azerbaijan, Turkey and Russia. Beginning in the 16th century, Georgia was under Persian and later Ottoman control. In 1801, Georgia became part of the Russian Empire. Georgia, Armenia and Azerbaijan were part of the Viceroyalty of the Caucasus from 1844 to 1881, and again from 1905 to 1917.

• **End of the Viceroyalty of the Caucasus:** September 20, 1917, when Georgia, Armenia and Azerbaijan formed the Transcaucasian Federation.

• **End of the Transcaucasian Federation:** May 26, 1918, when the federation was dissolved into three separate republics. Georgia was made a Soviet republic in 1920. It joined with the Armenian and Azerbaijani Soviet Socialist Republics in 1922 to became the Transcaucasian Soviet Federated Socialist Republic, one of the founding components of the Soviet Union.

• **Last known as the Transcaucasian Soviet Federated Socialist Republic:** December 5, 1936, when Georgia became the Georgian Soviet Socialist Republic.

• **Last chairman of the Central Executive Committee of the Transcaucasian Soviet Federated Socialist Republic:** Filipp Yeseyevich Makharadze, who served from May 27, 1935, to December 5, 1936. He died in 1941.

• **Last of the Georgian Soviet Socialist Republic:** April 1991, when it declared its independence as the Republic of Georgia. When the USSR dissolved in December 1991 the Republic of Georgia gained its independence.

• **Last known as the Republic of Georgia:** November 26, 1995, when the nation became Georgia.

Nations—Germany, Federal Republic of
Germany is in western Europe, bordered by Denmark, the Netherlands, France, Austria, Switzerland, Poland, the Czech Republic, the Baltic and North seas. Germany began as a political entity in the 9th century as part of the Holy Roman Empire. This marked the beginning of the First Reich.

• **End of the First Reich (Holy Roman Empire):** August 6, 1806, with the dissolution of the Holy Roman Empire. On July 25, 1806, the Confederation of the Rhine—an association of German states—was founded under French rule.

• **End of the Confederation of the Rhine:** abolished on October 19, 1813, after Napoleon's defeat. The German Confederation was founded two years later, in 1815.

• **End of the German Confederation:** August 24, 1866. It was followed by the North German Confederation, founded in 1867. This marked the beginning of the Second Reich.

• **End of the North German Confederation:** January 1, 1871, when the German Empire was created.

• **Last emperor of Germany/end of the Second Reich:** November 9, 1918, when Kaiser Wilhelm II (Friedrich Wilhelm Viktor Albrecht von Hohenzollern) abdicated as German Emperor and King of Prussia. At the same time, other ruling sovereigns also abdicated or were forced to step down. Germany became the Weimar Republic, a republican regime created by the Treaty of Versailles. (It was named for Weimar, the city where the constitution was adopted in 1919.) Kaiser Wilhelm II died in Doorn, Netherlands, on June 5, 1941, age 82. (*See also* Wars and Battles—World War I—Germany.)

• **End of the Weimar Republic:** 1933, with the rise to power of the National Socialist Party (Nazis) under then-chancellor Adolf Hitler (appointed on January 30, 1933). Hitler turned Germany into a totalitarian state ruled by the Nazis. The treaty that created the Weimar Republic was not entirely invalidated until after World War II, but Hitler's legal measures taken in 1933 substantially destroyed the democratic political system. The Third Reich began in 1933 with Hitler's rise to power. (*See also* Wars and Battles—World War II—Germany.)

• **Last chancellor of the pre-Weimar German Empire:** Friedrich Ebert, who was appointed imperial chancellor after Prince Max of Baden resigned on November 9, 1918. Ebert held the title briefly before he became the first president of the Weimar Republic in 1919, a post he held until 1925.

• **End of East Germany (German Democratic Republic) and West Germany:** October 3, 1990, when the two nations merged as the Federal Republic of Germany. (For the partition of Germany, see Wars and Battles—World War II—Germany.)

• **Last general secretary of the Socialist Unity (Communist) Party of East Ger-**

many/last full president: Egon Krenz, who served from October 18, 1989, to December 3, 1989, and played a leading role in abolishing the party on December 1, 1989. He was also the last chairman of the Council of State of East Germany. Krenz served from October 24, 1989, to December 6, 1989, making him the last full president of East Germany.

• **Last president of the People's Chamber of East Germany:** Sabine Bergmann-Pohl, who served from April 5, 1990, to October 2, 1990. She was the last acting president of East Germany.

• **Last chancellor of West Germany:** Helmut Michael Kohl, who served from October 1, 1982, until Germany was reunified in October 1990. He continued to serve as chancellor of the united Federal Republic of Germany until October 27, 1998.

• **Last president of West Germany:** Richard von Weizsäcker, who served from July 1, 1984, until reunification in October 1990. He continued to serve as president of the united Federal Republic of Germany until June 30, 1994.

• **Last U.S. ambassador to West Germany:** Vernon Anthony Walters, who served from 1989 to 1991 as U.S. ambassador to West Germany and later to the united Federal Republic of Germany. He died in West Palm Beach, Florida, on February 10, 2002, age 85.

• **Last king of Bavaria:** Louis III (German name Ludwig), the last reigning monarch of the house of Wittelsbach. He ruled from 1913 until 1918. When Germany lost World War I, a revolution broke out in Bavaria but Louis refused to abdicate. He died in exile in Sárvár, Hungary, on October 18, 1921, age 76.

• **Last king (kaiser) of Prussia:** Kaiser Wilhelm II (German name: Friedrich Wilhelm Viktor Albrecht von Hohenzollern), who abdicated as German emperor and king of Prussia on November 9, 1918.

• **Last prime minister of Prussia:** Adolf Hitler. He became the de facto head of Prussia on April 24, 1945, after he stripped Hermann Goering of all of his offices and had him placed under arrest on April 25. Hitler killed himself five days later.

• **End of the state of Prussia:** abolished on February 25, 1947, by Allied Control Council Decree No. 46, which stated: "The state of Prussia, which has forever been the carrier of militarism and reaction in Germany...shall herewith be dissolved."

• **Last use of the goose-step by German military troops:** 1990, shortly before East and West Germany reunified. The goose-step was a military step used by the Prussian army. Both the Nazis and the Italian army used it during World War II. It was used after the war by Eastern European armies.

• **Last surviving witness of the death of King Ludwig II of Bavaria:** Jacob Liebl, a fisherman who recovered the bodies of Ludwig and his physician-caretaker Dr. Gudden, from Lake Starnberg on June 13, 1886, a day after Ludwig had been committed to Berg Castle. Liebl died in Starnberg, Germany, on October 18, 1933. (King Ludwig II (Louis II) of Bavaria, in southern Germany, was known for building magnificent palaces, including the ultimate fairytale castle Neuschwanstein. His spending was so excessive that he almost bankrupt the state of Bavaria. Ludwig was declared insane in 1886 and committed to Berg Castle. He escaped in June 1886 and drowned in Lake Starnberg at age 40. The circumstances of his death are shrouded in mystery.)

Nations—Ghana, Republic of
Ghana is between Côte d'Ivoire and Togo in western Africa, bordering the Gulf of Guinea. The 19th-century gold trade there gave the region the name Gold Coast. Ghana became a British crown colony as the British Gold Coast in 1821.

• **End of British control:** Self-rule was achieved on February 8, 1951. On March 6, 1957, the Gold Coast and the British Togoland Trust Territory gained independence as the Dominion of Ghana. It was the first black African colony to become independent.

• **Last known as the Dominion of Ghana:** July 1, 1960, when it became the Republic of Ghana.

• **Last governor of the Gold Coast:** Sir Charles Noble Arden-Clarke, who served from August 11, 1949, to March 6, 1957. He then became the first governor-general of Ghana and served until June 24, 1957. Arden-Clarke died in 1962.

Nations—Great Britain, *see* Nations—United Kingdom of Great Britain and Northern Ireland.

Nations—Greece (Hellenic Republic)
Greece is surrounded by Albania, Bulgaria, Macedonia and Turkey in southern Europe and borders the Aegean and Ionian seas. The Greek city-states fell under Roman control beginning in 197 B.C. Greece was part of the Roman Empire until the 300s A.D., then part of the Byzantine Empire until 1453. Greece then became part of the Ottoman Empire.

• **End of Ottoman control:** February 3, 1830. The Greeks began their war for independence against the Ottoman Turks in 1821. The Kingdom of Greece was established on February 6, 1833. In March 1924, the monarchy was abolished and Greece became a republic. The monarchy was restored in 1935. A military junta took control of Greece in 1967 and sent the last king into exile.

• **End of the Greek monarchy:** June 1, 1973. A republican form of government was instituted that year.

• **Last king of Greece:** Constantine II, who went into exile in December 1967. He held the title from March 6, 1964, to June 1, 1973. In December 1974, Greek voters chose not to restore the monarchy.

• **Last of the Communist party of Greece provisional Democratic government:** August 28, 1949, when the last remnants of the Communist provisional government were driven out of Greece. (In 1947, the Communist party of Greece had declared the provisional Democratic government in the areas of northern Greece under its control.)

• **Last time the Ionian Islands were independent of Greece:** June 1, 1864, when they were incorporated into Greece. They previously were a British protectorate.

• **Last time Crete was independent of Greece:** May 30, 1913, when it was incorporated into Greece. Crete had declared its independence in 1908.

• **Last time the Dodecanese Islands and Rhodes were independent of Greece:** March 7, 1948, when they were incorporated into Greece. They were previously under Italian sovereignty. On September 15, 1947, they came under Greek administration.

Nations—Grenada
Grenada is a Caribbean island north of Trinidad and Tobago. It is the most southerly of the Windward Islands. French settlers arrived in 1650. The island changed ownership between France and Great Britain twice: in 1762 and 1779.

• **End of French control:** 1783, when Grenada was ceded to the British.

• **End of British control:** February 27, 1974, when Grenada was granted independence from the United Kingdom. It had become an associated state within the British Commonwealth in 1967.

• **End of Operation Urgent Fury:** November 21, 1983. Operation Urgent Fury began on October 23, 1983, after a military coup and the assassination of Grenada's president on October 19, 1983, caused members of the Organization of Eastern Caribbean States to seek help from the United States. About 1,900 U.S. troops and a small contingent of troops from Barbados, Jamaica, Saint Lucia, Dominica and Saint Vincent landed in Grenada on October 25, 1983.

• **End of U.S. occupation:** June 1985, when the last U.S. troops left Grenada.

Nations—Guatemala, Republic of
Guatemala is in Central America, surrounded by El Salvador, Mexico, Honduras Belize, the Pacific Ocean and the Gulf of Honduras (Caribbean Sea). Guatemala became a Spanish colony in 1524 and was administered by Spain as part of the Captaincy General of Guatemala.

• **End of Spanish control:** September 15,

1821, when independence was proclaimed. In 1822, Guatemala became part of the Mexican Empire.

• **Last Spanish leader of Guatemala:** Carlos de Urrutia y Montoya, who served from March 28, 1818, to September 15, 1821.

• **End of Mexican control:** 1823, when Guatemala seceded from Mexico, and its independence was restored. From 1825 until 1838, Guatemala was part of the Central American Federation. (*See also* Alliances, etc.—Central American Federation.)

• **Last time Ciudad Vieja was the capital of Guatemala:** 1542, when it was ruined by floods and an earthquake. The survivors founded Antigua as the capital in 1543.

• **Last time Antigua was the capital of Guatemala:** 1773, when it was destroyed by two earthquakes. Guatemala City was founded as the capital in 1776, after Antigua was abandoned.

Nations—Guinea, Republic of

Guinea is between Guinea-Bissau and Sierra Leone in western Africa, bordering the Atlantic Ocean. It became a French protectorate in 1849.

• **End of French control:** October 2, 1958, when the independent Republic of Guinea was established. The People's Revolutionary Republic of Guinea was created on January 1, 1979.

• **Last known as the People's Revolutionary Republic of Guinea:** May 25, 1984, when the nation once again became the Republic of Guinea.

• **Last great African colonial warrior:** Samory Touré, known as the Black Napoleon of the Sudan. He was born near Sarranko, Upper Guinea (now Guinea), and is considered the last of the great warriors of that region of Africa. He fought French rule but was finally captured on September 28, 1898. Touré died in Gabon, French Congo, on June 2, 1900, age about 70. He was a direct ancestor of Sekou Touré, the first president of the Republic of Guinea.

Nations—Guinea-Bissau, Republic of

Guinea-Bissau is surrounded by the nations of Guinea and Senegal in western Africa, bordering the Atlantic Ocean. The Portuguese explored the region in the 1440s and colonized it beginning in 1687.

• **End of Portuguese control:** September 24, 1973, when independence was unilaterally declared by Guinea-Bissau. Portugal did not formally recognize the independence until September 10, 1974.

• **Last governor of Guinea-Bissau:** Carlos Fabião, who served in 1974.

• **Last secretary-general of the African Independence (Communist) Party of Guinea (-Bissau) and Cape Verde:** João Bernardo Vieira, who held the position from November 14, 1980, to 1991.

Nations—Guyana, Co-operative Republic of

Guyana is between Suriname and Venezuela in northern South America, bordering the Atlantic Ocean. The British and the Dutch began to establish settlements in the area in the 17th century.

• **End of Dutch control:** November 20, 1815, when the land was officially ceded to Britain by the Dutch. Self-rule was achieved on August 26, 1961.

• **End of British control:** May 26, 1966, when the colony of British Guiana became independent as the Dominion of Guyana.

• **Last known as the Dominion of Guyana:** February 23, 1970, when it proclaimed itself the Co-operative Republic of Guyana (effective March 17, 1970).

• **Last governor of British Guiana:** Sir Richard Edmonds Luyt, who served from March 7, 1964, to May 26, 1966. He then became the first governor-general of Guyana and held that position until December 16, 1970. He died in 1994.

• **Last governor-general of Guyana:** Sir Edward Victor Luckhoo, who was acting governor-general from November 10, 1969, to February 22, 1970. He then became acting president of Guyana and served until March 17, 1970. He died in 1998.

• **Last premier of Guyana:** Linden Forbes Sampson Burnham, who held the position from December 12, 1964, to May 26, 1966.

He then became the first prime minister of Guyana and served until October 6, 1980. He died in 1985.

Nations—Haiti, Republic of

Haiti is on the western third of the Caribbean island of Hispaniola, which it shares with the Dominican Republic. The Spanish arrived there in 1492 with Columbus. The French arrived in the 1600s and settled part of the island.

• **End of Spanish control:** 1697, when Spain recognized the French possession of Saint Domingue. The British began occupying the western part of the island in 1793.

• **End of British occupation:** October 1798.

• **Last governor of British-occupied Saint Domingue:** Thomas Maitland, who served from March 1797 to October 1798. He died in 1824.

• **Last governor-general of Saint Domingue:** Jean-Jacques Dessalines, who served from November 30, 1803, to December 31, 1803. He became the first governor-general of the independent Haiti on January 1, 1804. Dessalines died in 1806. When Haiti declared its independence from France, civil war broke out between competing "North" and "South" governments. The North existed from 1804 to 1820. The South overlapped from 1806 to 1820. On December 28, 1806, the Republic of Haiti was created in the North. Henry Christophe was provisional chief of the Haitian government from October 17, 1806, to February 17, 1807, when northern Haiti became the State of Haiti. He served as president until March 28, 1811, when the State of Haiti (northern Haiti) became the Kingdom of Haiti. He then ruled as King Henry I.

• **End of the Kingdom of Haiti/end of "North" and "South" governments:** October 8, 1820, with the death of King Henry I (Henry Christophe) of the Kingdom of Haiti (northern Haiti). After King Henry I died, General Jean Pierre Boyer stepped in and ended the Haitian civil war. The kingdom was re-incorporated into the Republic of Haiti (southern Haiti).

• **End of French control:** 1820, when General Boyer purchased the official independence of Haiti from France for 150 million French francs. On February 9, 1822, Haiti gained control of the former colony of Santo Domingo, which occupied the rest of the island of Hispaniola.

• **End of Haitian control of Santo Domingo:** February 27, 1844, when Santo Domingo declared itself a separate nation as the Dominican Republic. The Republic of Haiti became the Empire of Haiti on August 26, 1849.

• **End of the Empire of Haiti:** December 23, 1858, when Haiti once again became the Republic of Haiti.

• **Last emperor of Haiti:** Faustin I (Faustin Éli Soulouque), who ruled from August 26, 1849, to 1858, when the Republic of Haiti was re-established. He served as president of the earlier Republic of Haiti (March 1, 1847, to August 26, 1849). Faustin I died on August 6, 1867, age about 82.

• **End of occupation by the United States (World War I and U.S. protectorate years):** August 15, 1934, when the last U.S. troops pulled out of Haiti. A series of violent deaths of Haitian presidents had led U.S. President Woodrow Wilson to send troops there from January 29, 1914, to October 19, 1914. Another much longer occupation began on July 28, 1915, with the sixth assassination, that of Haitian President Jean Vilbrun Guillaume Sam.

• **End of the Duvalier regime:** February 7, 1986, when the regime collapsed and Baby Doc fled to France. The Duvaliers came to power with François ("Papa Doc") Duvalier in 1957. When he died in 1971, he was succeeded by his son, Jean Claude ("Baby Doc") Duvalier.

Nations—Honduras, Republic of

Honduras is between Guatemala, El Salvador and Nicaragua in Central America, bordering the Caribbean Sea on the eastern side and the Pacific Ocean on the west. The area was claimed by Spain in 1502.

• **End of Spanish control:** September 1821, when Honduras (Comayagua and Tegucigalpa) declared its independence from

Spain. In December 1821, Comayagua was incorporated into Mexico, followed by Tegucigalpa in 1822.

• **End of Mexican control:** 1823, when Comayagua and Tegucigalpa became independent again. On September 16, 1824, the State of Honduras was created. In 1825, Honduras became a member of the Central American Federation. (*See also* Alliances, etc.—Central American Federation.)

• **Last known as the State of Honduras:** September 28, 1865, when it became the Republic of Honduras.

• **End of Bay Islands control by Great Britain:** July 14, 1860, when the islands were ceded to Honduras. Honduras formally took possession on June 1, 1861.

• **End of Swan Islands control by the United States:** September 1, 1972, when the U.S. signed over to Honduras ownership of the islands. The U.S. had annexed the islands in 1863.

• **End of U.S. occupations in Honduras:**

March 31, 1903 (occupation began on March 23, 1903);

June 8, 1907 (occupation began on March 18, 1907);

September 12, 1919 (occupation began on September 8, 1919);

April 21, 1925 (occupation began on February 28, 1924).

• **End of status as a U.S. protectorate:** September 12, 1919. The U.S. had set up the protectorate status in Honduras on March 28, 1911.

Nations—Hong Kong *see* China, People's Republic of—Hong Kong.

Nations—Hungary, Republic of
Hungary is east of Austria, Croatia and Slovenia in central Europe. In 1526, Hungary formed a union with Austria. Austria and Hungary became a dual monarchy as the Austro-Hungarian Empire in 1867.

• **End of the Austro-Hungarian Empire:** November 13, 1918, when Hungarian independence was proclaimed. On November 16, 1918, it became the Hungarian People's Republic, and then from March 21, 1919, to

August 1919, the Hungarian Conciliar Republic (Hungarian Soviet Federated Socialist Republic), before again becoming the Hungarian People's Republic.

• **Last king of Hungary:** Károly IV of Hungary (Charles I, Emperor of Austria), who ruled from 1916 to 1918. In 1921, he made two unsuccessful attempts to regain the throne. During his second attempt, he was arrested and exiled to Madeira. He died there on April 1, 1922, age 34.

• **End of World War II occupation by Germany:** April 4, 1945. Occupation began on April 1, 1944. Hungary became the Hungarian State on December 21, 1944.

• **Last known as the Hungarian State:** February 2, 1946, when the nation became the Republic of Hungary. On August 20, 1949, it was renamed the Hungarian People's Republic.

• **End of the Hungarian Revolt:** November 5, 1956, by which time most of Hungary was under Soviet control. (The anti-Communist rebellion had begun on October 1, 1956, when police tried to break up a student demonstration. Soviet tanks and troops moved in to suppress the revolt.)

• **Last of Imre Nagy:** the Hungarian politician was taken away by Soviet troops, brought to trial in secret and executed in June 1958. In 1989, the ruling socialist Workers' party announced that Nagy's trial had been unlawful and in June 1989, Nagy was reburied with full honors.

• **Last known as the Hungarian People's Republic:** October 23, 1989, when the nation again became the Republic of Hungary, a name it used from 1946 to 1949.

• **End of Soviet occupation:** June 1991, when the last Soviet troops withdrew after nearly 47 years.

Nations—Iceland, Republic of
Iceland is near the Arctic Circle in northern Europe, between the Greenland Sea and the Atlantic Ocean. A settlement was established in 930 A.D., and the Althing, a general assembly, was founded. Iceland came under Norwegian authority in the 1260s.

• **End of Norwegian control:** 1380, when

both Iceland and Norway came under Danish rule. Iceland became autonomous on February 1, 1904. The Kingdom of Iceland was granted independence in a personal (or nonpolitical) union with Denmark on December 1, 1918.

• **End of Danish control/end of the Kingdom of Iceland:** June 17, 1944, when Iceland became a republic.

• **Last king of Iceland:** Christian X of Denmark, who reigned until the Icelandic republic was established. Sveinn Björnsson, served as regent from June 17, 1941, to June 16, 1944. He became the first president of the new republic on June 17, 1944, and held that position until he died on January 24, 1952. King Christian X died in Copenhagen, Denmark, on April 20, 1947, age 76.

• **End of the World War II occupation of Iceland by Allied forces:** December 1944. Allied occupation began on May 10, 1940.

• **End of the Cod Wars:** June 1, 1976, when Iceland and Great Britain signed an accord. The Althing approved the agreement on November 11, 1976. The two nations had been involved in a series of disagreements on offshore fishing limits known as the Cod Wars since the 1950s. The first Cod War extended the fishing limit to 12 miles in 1958. The second Cod War in 1972-73 extended the limit to 50 miles. The third and last Cod War began in November 1975. When it ended, the offshore fishing limit was 200 miles.

Nations—India, Republic of

India is in southern Asia, bordering the Arabian Sea and the Bay of Bengal. Dynastic rule existed in the area until the Mongol leader Babur founded the Mogul Empire (or Mughal Empire) in 1526.

• **Last ruling dynasty before the Mogul Empire:** Lodi. The Delhi sultanate, under Ibrahim Lodi, ended with the defeat of Ibrahim Lodi by Babur in a battle on April 21, 1526. Babur's victory resulted in the creation of the Mogul Empire. The Moguls controlled India into the 19th century but faced interference from Europeans who began arriving in the 1500s.

• **End of the Mogul Empire:** 1858. It officially ended with the exile of Seraj ad-Din Abu'l Mozaffar Muhammad (Bahadur Shah II); however, the empire effectively ended in 1748 with the death of Roshan Akhtar (Muhammad Shah).

• **Last Mogul emperor of India:** Seraj ad-Din Abu'l Mozaffar Muhammad (Bahadur Shah II) who ruled from 1838 until he was deposed by the British on March 29, 1858, during the Sepoy Mutiny. He was tried for rebellion and sentenced to life in prison, where he died in 1862. In August 1858, a British act of Parliament annexed the empire, creating British India, effective November 1, 1858.

• **End of the Sepoy Mutiny:** the last rebels were defeated on June 20, 1858, in Gwalior. The Sepoy were Indian soldiers who served in the Indian Army under British officers while India was under British rule. The mutiny began in 1857, when many Sepoys were imprisoned for refusing to use cartridges that were greased with animal fat. This practice offended both Hindus and Muslims. The British said vegetable fat had been used. Rebellious troops set the mutineers free the next day. The mutiny quickly spread throughout the Indian army.

• **End of British India:** August 15, 1947, with passage of the Indian Independence Act. India became a self-governing dominion within the British Commonwealth of Nations. India was split into two states along religious lines: Dominion of India (Hindus) and Dominion of Pakistan (mostly Muslims).

• **Last British secretary of state for India:** William Francis Hare, Earl of Listowel, who served from April 17, 1947, to August 15, 1947 (and to January 4, 1948, as Secretary for Burma).

• **Last British viceroy of India:** Louis Francis Mountbatten, Viscount Mountbatten of Burma, who served from February 21, 1947, to August 15, 1947. His title was then changed to Earl Mountbatten of Burma, and he became the first governor-general of India after the transfer of power. Mountbatten, age 79, was killed when the Irish Republican

Army bombed his boat off the coast of Ireland on August 17, 1979.

• **Last known as the Dominion of India:** January 26, 1950, when India became a republic.

• **Last governor-general of India:** Chakravarti Rajagopalachari, who served from June 21, 1949, to January 26, 1950, when his office was replaced by that of president. He died in 1972.

• **End of French control of French India:** November 1, 1954, when France transferred Pondicherry, Karikal, Mahe and Yanam to India.

• **Last time English was India's official language:** January 26, 1950, when the Constitution of India came into force and made Hindi the official language. A grace period of 15 years was provided for non-Hindi people to learn the language and to allow English to operate as the associate official language. The changeover to Hindi was completed in January 26, 1965. It was accompanied by rioting among Tamil-speaking Indians in Madras.

• **End of royal titles and privileges in India:** 1972, when a constitutional amendment enacted on July 31, 1971, became effective. It abolished all royal titles and privileges, including the privy purse and payment of special pensions.

• **Last fast of Mohandas Karamchand Gandhi:** began on January 13, 1948, to bring peace to warring factions within his country. It ended after five days when leaders of the groups pledged peace. A few weeks later, on January 30, 1948, Gandhi, age 72, was murdered in New Delhi by a Hindu radical. Gandhi, a Hindu nationalist and spiritual leader, had used fasts to call attention to injustices.

• **Last time suttee (sati) was allowed:** 1829, when the British government made it a crime. Suttee is the practice of widows killing themselves by leaping onto the fiery funeral pyres of their dead husbands. Sometimes they did so willingly. Sometimes they were forced to do so. A few instances of modern-day suttee have occurred; however, the practice is illegal.

Nations—Indonesia, Republic of

Indonesia is a southeastern Asian archipelago of more than 13,000 islands straddling the Indian and Pacific oceans. The Dutch arrived there in the late 16th century.

• **Last known as Netherlands East Indies:** September 20, 1948, when the land was renamed Indonesia.

• **End of Dutch sovereignty:** December 27, 1949, with the independence of the Republic of the United States of Indonesia, which comprised the Republic of Indonesia (parts of Java and Sumatra) and various states and autonomous territories.

• **End of the Republic of the United States of Indonesia:** dissolved on August 17, 1950.

• **Last time Papua was known as Irian Jaya:** January 1, 2000, when it was renamed. It had been known as Irian Jaya since March 1973. Before that, it was known as Netherlands New Guinea (or West Papua).

• **Last time Jakarta was known as Batavia:** December 1949. The spelling was changed from Djakarta to Jakarta in 1972 when Indonesia adopted a common writing method.

Nations—Iran, Islamic Republic of

Iran is west of Afghanistan, Turkmenistan and Pakistan in the Middle East, bordering the Gulf of Oman, Persian Gulf and Caspian Sea.

• **Last time Iran used the name Persia:** March 21, 1935, when the Iranian government specified that Iran was to be the country's official and diplomatic name. "Iran" is the name used by the Iranian people. The name Persia evolved from a Greek word for the region.

• **Last Kajar shah/end of the Kajar dynasty:** Ahmed Shah, who was deposed by the National Assembly in 1925. He was regent from 1909 to 1914, when he was crowned. Ahmed Shah was the last of seven Kajar shahs. The first was Agha Muhammed Khan, who founded the Kajar dynasty in 1794.

• **End of the Pahlavi dynasty:** Muhammad

Reza Pahlavi, who was overthrown and fled Iran on January 16, 1979. The Pahlavi dynasty had gained control in 1925, when Reza Khan Pahlavi was chosen shah by the National Assembly to replace the deposed Ahmed Shah. Reza Shah Pahlavi was succeeded by his son Muhammad Reza Pahlavi in 1941. In the late 1970s, conservative Muslims opposed the shah's leadership and spurred a revolution. For a few days after he left office—from January 16, 1979, to January 22, 1979—the shah was replaced with a regency council chairman, Sayyed Jalaleddin Tehrani. Shah Muhammad Reza Pahlavi died in Egypt on July 27, 1980, age 60.

• **End of the Ayatollah Ruhollah Khomeini's exile** : February 1, 1979, when he returned to Iran. He had been in exile for 15 years. The Islamic Republic of Iran was created on April 1, 1979. The Islamic constitution vested the Ayatollah with the authority to run the country. In November 1979, Iranians seized the U.S. Embassy in Teheran and held 52 Americans as hostages.

• **End of the Iranian hostage crisis:** January 20, 1981. Just minutes after Ronald Reagan's inauguration as U.S. president, the hostages were flown to freedom, ending 444 days in captivity. An agreement had been reached on January 19, 1981, but the release was postponed one day, to coincide with Reagan's inaugural.

Nations—Iraq, Republic of

Iraq is north of Saudi Arabia, and west of Iran in the Middle East. Iraq was once known as Mesopotamia (a Greek word meaning "land between the rivers"). Its location straddling the Tigris and Euphrates rivers also earned the region the name the Fertile Crescent. Iraq was the center of the ancient Babylonian and Assyrian empires. The Ottoman Empire began to exercise control in the 17th century. By 1831, the region was under direct Ottoman rule.

• **End of Ottoman control:** 1917-18, during World War I, when the British drove out the Ottoman Turks. British troops occupied Baghdad on March 11, 1917. In November 1920, after the war, the State of Iraq was created as a British League of Nations mandate. The Kingdom of Iraq was established on August 23, 1921.

• **End of British control:** October 3, 1932, when Iraq declared full independence.

• **End of the Kingdom of Iraq and the Hashemite monarchy:** July 14, 1958, when a revolution established a republic.

• **Last king of Iraq:** Faysal II, Hashemite King of Iraq from April 4, 1939, to July 14, 1958, when he was assassinated in Baghdad during a military coup.

• **End of the Iran-Iraq War:** cease-fire: August 8, 1988; truce: August 20, 1988. The war between Iraq and Iran began on September 22, 1980, when Iraqi planes attacked Iran's airfields. (*See also* Wars and Battles—Gulf War.)

• **End of old Iraqi national holidays:** July 13, 2003, when a 25-member governing council of Iraqis abolished a number of old holidays and established April 9, the fall of Baghdad and Saddam Hussein's regime, as a new national holiday. The abolished holidays included:

April 7 (Baath Party founding date);

April 17 (Battle for Faw/Iran-Iraq War);

April 28 (Saddam Hussein's birthday);

July 17 (Arab Socialist Baath Party coup in Iraq

August 8 (Iran-Iraq War Cease-Fire).

Nations—Ireland, Republic of

Ireland is an island in the North Atlantic Ocean, west of Great Britain. The United Kingdom of Great Britain and Ireland was created in 1801. Independence of the Irish Republic was declared on January 21, 1919. On December 6, 1922, the Irish Free State was established as a British dominion.

• **End of the Irish Free State:** December 29, 1937, when southern Ireland became the State of Éire (Gaelic for Ireland). Six northern counties (Northern Ireland) remained within the United Kingdom.

• **End of Ireland's membership in the British Commonwealth:** December 21, 1948, when Ireland declared itself and Northern Ireland a republic. On April 18, 1949, Great Britain recognized the independence of the Republic of Ireland but refused to return the six northern counties.

• **End of the Irish ban on divorce:** February 27, 1997, when the ban was lifted and divorce became legal in Ireland.

• **End of Bobby Sands' hunger strike:** May 5, 1981, when he died on the 66th day of his hunger strike in the prison hospital at Long Kesh, Ireland. Sands was protesting his classification as a criminal for his political activities. He was the first of several men to die in the protest.

• **Last surviving member of the Fianna Fail party government from the Easter Rising:** Sean MacEntee, who fought against the British in the 1916 Easter Rising and was sentenced to death but reprieved in 1917. In 1927, he was elected to the Irish Free State Parliament and held numerous positions in the Fianna Fail government before he retired in 1969. MacEntee died in Dublin, Ireland, on January 9, 1984, age 94.

Nations—Israel, State of

Israel is between Egypt, Jordan, Syria and Lebanon in the Middle East, bordering the Mediterranean Sea. When the area was controlled by the Roman Empire it was known as Judea Palestine. As Palestine, the area became a British League of Nations mandate in 1923.

• **Last lieutenant-governor of Jerusalem:** Midhad Bey, who served from 1916 to December 9, 1917, when he was replaced by a British military administrator.

• **Last high commissioner:** Sir Alan Gordon Cunningham, who served from November 21, 1945, to May 14, 1948, when the chairman of Israel's Provisional State Council took over. He died in 1983.

• **End of the British mandate:** May 14, 1948, when a decree partitioned Palestine between Jews and Arabs and the independent State of Israel was proclaimed.

• **Last surviving signatory of the May 1948 Declaration of the Establishment of the State of Israel:** Meir Vilner, a member of the Israeli Knesset from 1949 to 1990. He died in Tel Aviv, Israel, on June 5, 2003, age 84.

Nations—Italy (Italian Republic)

Italy is a peninsula in southern Europe bordering the Adriatic and Tyrrhenian seas. In 1802, Napoleon Bonaparte unified the many Italian city-states into the Italian Republic. It became the Kingdom of Italy in 1805. After the fall of Napoleon in 1815, the independent states were restored. The Kingdom of Italy was reestablished in 1861.

• **Last king of Italy:** Humbert II. As Prince Humbert, he was regent under Victor Emmanuel III, beginning on June 5, 1944. He reigned as King Humbert II from May 9, 1946, to June 18, 1946, when the Italian Republic was created and he was replaced by a provisional head of state. He died in Geneva, Switzerland, on March 18, 1983, age 78.

• **Last Medici grand duke of Tuscany (last of the male line):** Giovan Gastone de' Medici, who died childless in 1737. After his death, Tuscany was annexed by Austria. (The Medicis, a Florentine family, rose to power in northern Italy in the 15th century.)

• **Last of the Medici family:** Anna Maria Ludovica de' Medici, who bequeathed the accumulated personal property, including the art and treasures of the Medicis, to the province of Florence, under the stipulation that nothing was to be removed from Florence. She died in 1743.

• **Last doge of Venice:** Ludovico Manin, who held the title from 1789 until he was overthrown by Napoleon in May 1797. He was the 120th and last doge of Venice. Manin died in 1802. (The doge had been the leader of Venetian Republic since the 7th century. He was selected by the aristocracy and lived in the ornate Doge's Palace on the Grand Canal.)

• **Last doge of Genoa:** Girolamo Luigi Francesco Durazzo (Count Jerome-Louis-Francois-Joseph-Marie Durazzo), who held the title from July 3, 1802, to June 4, 1805. Durazzo died in 1809. Genoa was annexed by Napoleon and the position of doge was eliminated. (Genoa had been ruled by doges since 1339.)

• **Last king of the Kingdom of the Two Sicilies:** Giuseppe Garibaldi, who held that title from September 7 1860, to November 8, 1860. He deposed King Francis II, who went into exile until he died in 1894. Garibaldi died in 1882.

• **End of Italy's colonial empire:** On February 10, 1947, Italy signed a peace treaty that removed all of its colonies. The treaty went into effect on September 15, 1947. Italy's colonial empire included Libya, Libyan Sahara, Eritrea and Italian Somaliland. In 1949, the United Nations decided the fate of Italy's former colonies.

• **End of Italy's ban on divorce:** December 18, 1970, when Italy's new divorce law went into effect. The law removed the ban on divorce and made it legal for the first time since 1815. The decision was confirmed by popular referendum in 1974, but was vigorously opposed by the Vatican.

Nations—Ivory Coast, *see* Côte d'Ivoire.

Nations—Jamaica

Jamaica is a Caribbean island nation south of Cuba. Columbus arrived in 1494, and Spanish colonization began in 1509.

• **End of Spanish colonialism:** 1655, when the English captured Jamaica.

• **Last of Port Royal:** On June 7, 1692, most of the city sank to the bottom of the sea when an earthquake struck the Caribbean. At that time, Port Royal was known as the richest city in the world. On January 9, 1702, a major fire destroyed the remaining part of Port Royal. The destruction of the 1702 fire was so severe that the assembly ordered the residents to re-settle in Kingston.

• **End of British colonialism:** August 6, 1962, when Jamaica won full independence from Great Britain after more than 300 years.

Nations—Japan

Japan is an archipelago off the east coast of Asia between the Sea of Japan and the Pacific Ocean. By the 300s A.D., competing clans had begun to seek control of central and southern Japan. The feudal system of military government known as the shogu-

nate began in the 12th century with the warrior Yoritomo. He founded the Yamakura shogunate in 1192.

End of Historic Japanese Eras and Shogunates

Name	End of Rule
Jomon	300 B.C.
Yayoi	300 A.D.
Kofun (Yamato)	645
Asuka	710
Nara	794
Heian	1185
Kamakura	1333
Muromachi	1568
Azuchi-Momoyama Ma	1603
Edo (Tokugawa)	1868
Meiji	1912
Taisho	1926
Showa	1989

• **End of the shogunates:** 1868. The last shogunate to rule Japan was the Tokugawa, founded by Iyeyasu in 1603.

• **Last Tokugawa shogun:** Tokugawa Yoshinobu (Hitotsubashi), who died in 1913.

• **Last Tokugawa armies defeated:** at the Battle at Ueno on July 4, 1868. In 1868, the emperor regained power, replacing the local military and civic rulers who had controlled Japan for many centuries. On January 4, 1868, Emperor Meiji issued an edict abolishing the office of shogun.

• **Last tairo (chief advisor to the shogun):** Tadashige Sakai, who held the position from February to December 29, 1865. He died in 1895.

• **Last roju (senior shogun councilor):** Tadatoshi Sakai and acting roju Taneyuki Tachibana, who both held the position from January to February 27, 1868. (The chairmanship rotated monthly.) Sakai died in 1907. Tachibana died in 1905.

• **Last kampaku (imperial chief advisor):** Nariyuki Nijo, who held the position from Jan-uary 1864 to January 3, 1868. He died in 1878.

• **End of feudalism:** 1871, when fiefs were abolished by imperial decree. In 1869, many of the daimyos (feudal lords) voluntarily surrendered their feudal rights.

• **End of Japan's isolation:** July 8, 1853, when U.S. Commodore Matthew Perry's ships sailed into Yeddo harbor, ending Japan's detachment from the outside world. The Treaty of Kanagawa in 1854 officially ended Japanese isolation from the West and opened some Japanese ports to U.S. ships.

• **End of the Manchukuo Empire:** August 1945, when Soviet troops invaded Manchuria at the end of World War II. Japanese control ended and the Manchukuo Empire fell apart. Japan had occupied Manchuria in northeastern Asia in 1931. The Manchukuo Empire was set up by Japan as a puppet state in 1932. Henry P'u-yi, last of China's Manchu (Ch'ing) dynasty, was inaugurated as chief executive of the new government on March 9, 1932. He was proclaimed Emperor Kang Teh on March 1, 1934. (*See also* Nations—China, People's Republic of—Last Emperor.)

• **End of the Japanese emperor's divine rights:** 1946, when Emperor Hirohito disavowed his divinity and Shinto, the state religion, was disestablished

• **End of U.S. control of Okinawa:** May 15, 1972, when Okinawa was returned to Japan after 27 years of U.S. rule. The United States retained troops and bases there.

• **End of the occupation of Japan by Allied forces:** April 28, 1952. Allied forces had occupied Japan since September 2, 1945. (*See also* Wars and Battles—World War II—Japan.)

Nations—Jordan, Hashemite Kingdom of
Jordan is in the Middle East, northwest of Saudi Arabia and east of Israel. The area was conquered by the Arabs in the 600s and the Ottoman Turks in the 1500s.

• **End of Ottoman control:** 1916. The region became a British League of Nations mandate after World War I. In 1921, the British recognized Abdullah ibn-Husein as the ruler of Transjordan, and the Hashemite dynasty was established.

• **End of the British mandate:** May 22, 1946. On May 25, 1946, Transjordan gained independence from Great Britain and became a kingdom. In 1957, it ended its special defense treaty relationship with the United Kingdom.

• **Last time Transjordan was part of Palestine:** May 26, 1923, when it was separated by the British.

• **Last known as Transjordan:** 1950.

• **Last emir:** Abdullah I, who held the title from April 11, 1921, to May 25, 1946, when it was changed to king. Abdullah I remained king until his death on July 20, 1951.

Nations—Kazakhstan, Republic of
Kazakhstan is in central Asia, northwest of China. A small portion is west of the Ural River in eastern Europe. The land was controlled by the Mongols and later the Russians for many centuries. In 1920, it became an autonomous republic within the Russian Soviet Federated Socialist Republic.

• **Last known as the Kazakh Autonomous Soviet Socialist Republic:** December 5, 1936, when it became a republic of the USSR as the Kazakh Soviet Socialist Republic.

• **Last known as the Kazakh Soviet Socialist Republic:** December 10, 1991, when it became the Republic of Kazakhstan. Independence was proclaimed on December 14, 1991. When the Soviet Union dissolved on December 25, 1991, Kazakhstan gained full independence.

Nations—Kenya, Republic of
Kenya is in eastern Africa, between Somalia and Tanzania, bordering the Indian Ocean. In 1895, Great Britain established a protectorate over the region as British East Africa, which also included Tanganyika, Zanzibar and Uganda.

• **End of British control:** December 12, 1963, when Kenya gained its independence. The Republic of Kenya was established on December 12, 1964.

• **Last British governor:** Malcolm John MacDonald, who served from January 4, 1963, to December 12, 1963, at which time his title was changed to governor-general. He continued to serve until December 12,

1964, when his position was replaced by that of the Kenyan president. MacDonald died in 1981.

Nations—Kiribati, Republic of
The island nation of Kiribati straddles both the Equator and the International Date Line in the Pacific. It is composed of 33 coral atolls. Kiribati became a British protectorate as the Gilbert Islands in 1892. It was made a British crown colony in 1916 and was granted self-rule by the British in 1971.
• **Last time Kiribati included the Ellice Islands:** October 1, 1975, when they were separated as the nation of Tuvalu.
• **End of British control:** July 12, 1979, when the Gilbert Islands gained independence as the Republic of Kiribati.
• **Last British governor:** Reginald James Wallace, who served from 1978 to July 12, 1979. His position was then replaced by that of president.

Nations—Korea, Democratic People's Republic of (North Korea) and Korea, Republic of (South Korea)
Korea is on the Korean Peninsula in eastern Asia, bordering Korea Bay, the Yellow Sea and the Sea of Japan. Northern Korea shares most of its northern border with China. For centuries, Korea's isolation earned it the name the Hermit Kingdom.
• **End of Korean isolation:** 1882, when Emperor Kojong permitted trade with outsiders. That year, the United States signed a peace and trade treaty with Korea.
• **End of the Yi dynasty:** 1910, when Korea was annexed to Japan. The Yi dynasty held power since 1392.
• **Last emperor of the Yi dynasty:** Yi Ch'ok, who ruled from July 20, 1907, to August 29, 1910.
• **Last Yi dynasty crown prince:** Yi Un, who died in Seoul, on May 1, 1970, age 72.
• **Last surviving member of Korea's monarchy:** Princess Yi Pangja, widow of the late Prince Yi Un. She died at the Naksunje Palace in Seoul on April 30, 1989, age 87.
• **End of Japanese control:** 1945, when Japan was defeated at the end of World War

II. Japan seized Korea in 1910 and renamed it Chosen. In November 1943, at the Cairo Conference during World War II, the decision was made by Great Britain, the U.S., China and the USSR that once Korea/Chosen was free of Japanese rule it would be given its freedom.
• **Last time Korea was united:** 1948, when the Allied powers agreed to divide Korea into two sections at the 38th parallel: the Democratic People's Republic of Korea (formed September 3, 1948) in the north; the Republic of Korea (formed August 15, 1948) in the south. Soviet troops were placed in the north, while U.S. troops were stationed in the south. In 1950, when North Korea invaded South Korea, the United Nations requested military aid for South Korea.
• **End of the United Nations-United States occupation of North Korea:** December 5, 1951. The UN-U.S. occupation began on October 19, 1950.
(*See also* Wars and Battles—Korean War.)

Nations—Kuwait, State of
Kuwait is between Iraq and Saudi Arabia, at the northern end of the Persian Gulf. Kuwait became a British protectorate in 1899.
• **End of the British protectorate:** June 19, 1961, when Kuwait gained full independence from the United Kingdom.
• **End of the annexation of Kuwait by Iraq:** February 27, 1991. Iraq had occupied Kuwait in August 1990. A U.S.-led coalition routed Iraqi forces and liberated Kuwait.
(*See also* Wars and Battles—Gulf War.)

Nations—Kyrgyz Republic (Kyrgyzstan)
The Kyrgyz Republic is in central Asia, west of China, south of Kazakhstan and north of Tajikistan. The land was annexed to Russia in 1864. It was known as the Kara-Kirghiz Autonomous Oblast from 1924 to 1925. The Kirghiz Autonomous Soviet Socialist Republic was formed in 1926.
• **Last known as the Kirghiz Autonomous Soviet Socialist Republic:** December 5, 1936, when it became the Kirghiz Soviet Socialist Republic, a constituent republic of the USSR.

• **Last known as the Kirghiz Soviet Socialist Republic:** December 15, 1990, when it became the Republic of Kyrgyzstan. On August 31, 1991, it declared its final independence. It became effective when the Soviet Union dissolved on December 25, 1991. Kyrgyzstan was renamed the Kyrgyz Republic on May 5, 1993.

Nations—Laos (Lao People's Democratic Republic)

Laos is in southeastern Asia, northeast of Thailand and west of Vietnam. The French established a protectorate there in 1893.

• **End of the French protectorate:** Laos originally declared independence from France by royal proclamation on April 8, 1945, but the independence effort was thwarted. Laos declared independence again, on October 22, 1953, as the Kingdom of Laos. France recognized this independence on July 21, 1954.

• **End of the Laotian monarchy:** December 2, 1975, when the Communist Pathet Lao gained control of the government and the Lao Peo-ple's Democratic Republic was proclaimed.

• **Last king (rath) of Laos:** Sri Savang Vatthana, who served from October 30, 1959, to his abdication on December 2, 1975. In 1977, he was sent to a reeducation camp, where he reportedly died of starvation. His death date is not known.

Nations—Latvia, Republic of

Latvia is between Estonia and Lithuania in eastern Europe, bordering the Baltic Sea. Latvia became an independent republic in 1918. It was annexed by the USSR in 1940 as the Latvian Soviet Socialist Republic. Independence was attempted unsuccessfully in the 1940s.

• **Last known as the Latvian Soviet Socialist Republic:** August 1991, when it declared its independence from the USSR and became the Republic of Latvia. The Soviet Union recognized its independence on September 6, 1991.

• **Last Russian troops left Latvia:** August 31, 1994.

Nations—Lebanon, Republic of

Lebanon is between Israel and Syria in the Middle East, bordering the Mediterranean Sea. The state of Lebanon was created in 1920, following the fall of the Ottoman Empire and was administered under a French League of Nations mandate. In 1926, the country was reorganized as the Lebanese Republic.

• **End of the French mandate:** November 26, 1941, when the Lebanese Republic declared its independence from France. France recognized Lebanon's independence on November 22, 1943.

• **End of World War II occupation by Allied forces:** December 31, 1946, when the French withdrew. The British withdrew their troops on April 17, 1946. (The occupation had begun in 1941.)

• **Last U.S. Marines left Lebanon (1958 occupation):** October 25, 1958, after the inauguration of President Faud Chehab. U.S. President Dwight D. Eisenhower had ordered 5,000 U.S. Marines to Lebanon, at the request of Lebanon's previous president Camille Chamoun in July 1958.

• **End of the 1982-84 multinational peacekeeping mission:** April 1984, when the force left Lebanon. (Israel had invaded Lebanon in June 1982 to destroy Palestine Liberation Organization (PLO) strongholds. Killings in Palestinian refugee camps led to the stationing of a multinational peacekeeping force. The first troops arrived in August 1982.)

• **End of the Lebanese Civil War:** October 1990, when the government gained control of the south and disbanded all the private militias. Lebanon's civil war began in 1975.

• **Last Lebanese Civil War U.S. hostage freed:** Associated Press correspondent Terry Anderson, released on December 4, 1991.

• **Last Lebanese Civil War European hostages freed:** German relief workers Thomas Kemptner and Heinrich Struebig, released on June 17, 1992.

Nations—Lesotho, Kingdom of

Lesotho is in southern Africa, surrounded by the Republic of South Africa. The land once known as Basutoland became a British protectorate in 1868.

• **End of the British protectorate of Basutoland:** October 4, 1966, when Basutoland gained independence as the Kingdom of Lesotho.

• **End of the exile of King Moshoeshoe II:** reinstated on January 25, 1995. He had been exiled by the military government in 1990. He died in a car accident on January 15, 1996, age 57.

• **Last British government representative:** Alexander Falconer Giles, who served as British resident commissioner from 1961 to April 30, 1965 and then as British government representative until October 4, 1966. He died in 1989.

Nations—Liberia, Republic of

Liberia is between Côte d'Ivoire and Sierra Leone in western Africa, bordering the Atlantic Ocean. Liberia is Africa's oldest independent republic. It has its roots in the American Colonization Society that was established in the United States in 1816 to send freed slaves back to western Africa. The first ex-slaves arrived in 1821 at Providence Island (now Monrovia). In 1824, the settlers chose the name Liberia for their colony, and Monrovia (for President James Monroe) for their capital. (*See also* Slavery and Involuntary Servitude.)

• **End of colonial status:** July 27, 1847, when Liberian settlers separated from the American Colonization Society and declared Liberia an independent state. From 1847 to 1980, Liberia was a one-party state run by the Americo-Liberian controlled True Whig party.

• **End of the True Whig Party/Americo-Liberian-dominated government:** April 12, 1980, when Sergeant Samuel K. Doe, from the Krahn ethnic group, seized power in a coup d'etat.

Nations—Libya (Socialist People's Libyan Arab Jamahiriya)

Libya borders the Mediterranean Sea between Egypt and Tunisia in northern Africa. Italy seized control of Libya during the Turko-Italian War (1911-12).

• **End of Italian control:** May 13, 1943, during World War II, when Libya was conquered by Allied forces and placed under Anglo-French control, and later United Nations control. The country gained independence as the United Libyan Kingdom on December 24, 1951, with Idris I as Libya's first king.

• **End of the United Libyan Kingdom:** April 25, 1963, when the nation was transformed from a federal to a unitary state as the Libyan Kingdom.

• **End of the Libyan Kingdom:** September 1, 1969, when a coup overthrew the monarchy. Muammar al-Qaddafi deposed King Idris and the Libyan Arab Republic was proclaimed.

• **Last king of Libya:** Idris I (Sidi Muhammad Idris-al-Mahdi as-Sanusi), who was deposed on September 1, 1969. He died in Cairo, Egypt, on May 25, 1983, age 93.

• **Last known as the Libyan Arab Republic:** March 2, 1977, when the nation's name was changed to Socialist People's Libyan Arab Jamahiriya (state of the masses).

Nations—Liechtenstein, Principality of

Liechtenstein is between Austria and Switzerland in central Europe. The Principality of Liechtenstein was created within the Holy Roman Empire on January 23, 1719.

• **End of control by the Holy Roman Empire:** July 12, 1806, when Liechtenstein became a sovereign state.

Nations—Lithuania, Republic of

Lithuania borders the Baltic Sea between Latvia and Russia in eastern Europe. Russia acquired the region through a series of partitions of Poland in the 1700s. Germany occupied the area in World War I.

• **End of German and (pre-USSR) Russian control:** February 16, 1918, when the Lithuanian Regional Council declared full independence. Lithuania was annexed to the USSR on August 3, 1940, as the Lithuanian Soviet Socialist Republic.

• **Last king of Lithuania:** Mindaugas II, who never assumed the throne. The monarchy was abolished on November 2, 1918. He died in Italy in 1928.

• **Last known as the Lithuanian Soviet Socialist Republic:** March 11, 1990, when independence was declared from the Soviet Union, as the Republic of Lithuania. On September 6, 1991, Lithuania's independence was recognized by the Soviet Union.

• **Last Russian troops left Lithuania:** August 31, 1993.

Nations—Luxembourg, Grand Duchy of

Luxembourg is between France, Germany and Belgium in western Europe. It became a grand duchy in 1815 with the Congress of Vienna. The Grand Duchy of Luxembourg was divided by the 1839 Treaty of London. The western part was annexed by Belgium. The remaining part later joined the German Confederation.

• **End of the German Confederation:** 1866.

• **End of Belgian annexation:** September 9, 1867, when Luxembourg became an independent neutral state.

• **End of World War II occupation by Germany:** September 11, 1944. Germany invaded Luxembourg on May 10, 1940.

• **End of neutrality:** 1949, when Luxembourg became a charter member of the North Atlantic Treaty Organization.

Nations—Macedonia

Macedonia is north of Greece in southeastern Europe. More than 500 years of Ottoman rule ended in 1913, at the end of the Balkan Wars. With the collapse of the Austro-Hungarian Empire in 1918, Macedonia became part of the Kingdom of Serbs, Croats and Slovenes.

• **End of the Kingdom of Serbs, Croats and Slovenes:** October 3, 1929, when King Alexander renamed it the Kingdom of Yugoslavia and divided it into provinces. Macedonia became the Banovina (province) of Vardar.

• **End of World War II occupation by Bulgaria:** September 8, 1944. The Bulgarian occupation of Macedonia began in 1941.

• **End of the Kingdom of Yugoslavia:** November 29, 1945, when Yugoslavia was declared a federative people's republic and Macedonia became the People's Republic of Macedonia within it.

• **Last of the People's Republic of Macedonia:** July 7, 1963, when it became a socialist republic within the Socialist Federal Republic of Yugoslavia.

• **End of the Socialist Republic of Macedonia in Yugoslavia:** April 15, 1991, when it became the Republic of Macedonia. On September 18, 1991, Macedonia declared its independence.

Nations—Madagascar, Republic of

Madagascar is an island nation in the Indian Ocean, east of Mozambique in southern Africa. France set up a protectorate in 1885. In 1896, France annexed Madagascar and subsequently deposed its monarch.

• **Last king of Madagascar:** Radama II, who ruled from 1861 to March 12, 1863. After he died in 1863, his successors were all females.

• **Last queen of Madagascar:** Queen Ranva-lona III, who ruled from 1883 to February 27, 1897, and was then exiled. She died in 1917. On October 14, 1958, the island was established as the Malagasy Republic, an autonomous state within the French Community.

• **End of the French protectorate:** June 26, 1960, when Madagascar became an independent nation as the Malagasy Republic.

• **End of the Malagasy Republic:** December 30, 1975, when the country was renamed the Democratic Republic of Madagascar.

• **End of the Democratic Republic of Mada-gascar:** September 12, 1992, when the country became the Republic of Madagascar.

Nations—Malawi, Republic of

Malawi is east of Zambia in southern Africa. It became a British Central African Protectorate in 1891. In 1907, it was renamed Nyasaland. The Federation of Rhodesia and Nyasaland was formed in 1953, linking Nyasaland, Southern Rhodesia and Northern Rhodesia (now Zambia).

• **End of the Federation of Rhodesia and Nyasaland:** dissolved on December 31, 1963.
• **End of the British protectorate:** July 6, 1964, when Nyasaland became the independent state of Malawi. Two years later, on July 6, 1966, it was renamed the Republic of Malawi when it became a republic within the British Commonwealth.
• **Last British governor:** Sir Glyn Smallwood Jones, who served as governor from 1961 until July 6, 1964, at which time his title was changed to governor-general. He held that position until it was eliminated on July 6, 1966. He died in 1992.

Nations—Malaysia

Malaysia is on the Malay Peninsula and on the northern third of the island of Borneo in southeastern Asia, bordering Indonesia and the South China Sea. The Portuguese arrived in 1511 and occupied Malacca. Great Britain established the Strait Settlements (Penang, Malacca, Singapore) in 1867. North Borneo (Sabah), Sarawak and Brunei became British protectorates in 1888. The states came together as the Federated Malay States in 1895. The term "British Malaya" describes all the Malayan possessions held during British domination.
• **End of World War II occupation by Japan:** 1945, at the end of the war. Japanese occupation began in January 1942.
• **End of the Federated Malay States:** April 11, 1946, when the Union of Malaya was created among Penang, Malacca and nine Malay states.
• **End of the Union of Malaya:** February 1, 1948, when the union was replaced by the Federation of Malaya.
• **End of British Malaya/end of British control:** August 31, 1957, when Malaya gained independence and became a member of the British Commonwealth.
• **Last British high commissioner:** Sir Donald Charles MacGillivray, who held the position from May 31, 1954, to August 31, 1957. He died in 1966.
• **End of the Federation of Malaya:** September 1963, when the Federation of Malay-

sia was created. It consisted of Malaya, Singapore, Sabah and Sarawak.
• **End of Singapore's participation in the Federation of Malaysia:** August 9, 1965, when Singapore withdrew to become a separate nation.

Nations—Maldives, Republic of

The Maldives are a group of atolls in the Indian Ocean southwest of India. A sultanate was established there in 1153. The islands were occupied by the Portuguese in the 16th century. Later, they were taken over by the Dutch. Great Britain gained control in the 19th century, and the islands became a British protectorate in 1887.
• **End of the British protectorate:** July 26, 1965, when the country gained its independence.
• **End of the sultanate:** 1968, when the sultanate was replaced by a republic. (The sultanate had been abolished in 1953 but was restored in 1954.)
• **Last sultan of the Maldives:** Muhammad Farid Didi, who held the title from March 7, 1954, to November 11, 1968. He died in 1969.

Nations—Mali, Republic of

Mali is southwest of Algeria in western Africa. In 1880, it became the French Territory of Upper Senegal. It was named the French Sudan Territory in 1890. The name French Sudan was dropped when the land was divided in 1899; however, it was again named French Sudan in 1920, when the region was reorganized.
• **End of French Sudan:** November 24, 1958, when French Sudan became the Sudanese Republic within the French Community. On April 4, 1959, the Sudanese Republic united with Senegal to form the Mali Federation.
• **End of the Mali Federation:** August 20, 1960, when Senegal withdrew.
• **End of French control/end of the Sudanese Republic:** September 22, 1960, when the newly independent Sudanese Republic withdrew from the French Community and renamed itself the Republic of Mali.

• **Last French high commissioner:** Jean-Charles Sicurani, who held the position from November 1958 to June 20, 1960. He died in 1977.

Nations—Malta, Republic of
Malta is a group of islands in the Mediterranean Sea, south of Sicily. Sicilians seized Malta in 1090. After Holy Roman Emperor Charles V gave control of the islands to the Knights Hospitalers in 1530, the knights became known as the Knights of Malta.
• **End of control by the Knights of Malta:** June 12, 1798, when Malta was captured by Napoleon. The Knights were expelled as French occupation began.
• **End of French occupation:** September 1800, when the British and Maltese removed the French. Malta became a British possession with the Treaty of Paris in 1814. That year it became a British crown colony.
• **End of British crown colony status:** September 21, 1964, when Malta gained its independence as the Sovereign State of Malta.
• **Last known as the Sovereign State of Malta:** December 13, 1974, when the nation became the Republic of Malta.

Nations—Marshall Islands, Republic of the
The Marshall Islands are a group of atolls and reefs in the Pacific Ocean, midway between Hawaii and Australia. They include Bikini Atoll. The islands were first visited by Europeans in 1788. They were purchased by Germany and became a German protectorate in 1885.
• **End of the German protectorate:** October 3, 1914, during World War I, when the islands were occupied by Japan. Japan received a League of Nations mandate over the islands in 1920 and later claimed sovereignty over them. During World War II, the Marshall Islands were the scene of major fighting.
• **End of World War II occupation by Japan:** February 23, 1944, when the islands were captured by the United States. Beginning on July 18, 1947, the Marshall Islands were administered by the U.S. as part of the Trust Territory of the Pacific Islands.
• **End of the Trust Territory of the Pacific Islands:** dissolved on November 3, 1986. On December 22, 1990, the United Nations Security Council ratified the termination of the Trusteeship. With its ending, the islands gained their independence. On September 17, 1991, the islands were admitted to the UN as the Republic of the Marshall Islands.
• **Last high commissioner of the Trust Territory of the Pacific Islands:** Janet J. McCoy, who held the position from 1981 to November 3, 1986. She later served as Assistant Secretary of the Interior. McCoy died on August 4, 1995.

Nations—Mauritania, Islamic Republic of
Mauritania borders the Atlantic Ocean between Senegal and Western Sahara in northwest Africa. France established a protectorate there in 1903 as part of French West Africa. Mauritania became a French colony in 1920.
• **End of French control:** November 28, 1960, when the nation won its independence as the Islamic Republic of Mauritania.
• **Last French high commissioner:** Pierre Anthonioz, who held the position from February 1959 to November 28, 1960. He died in 1996.

Nations—Mauritius, Republic of
Mauritius is an island nation in the Indian Ocean east of Madagascar. The Dutch began to colonize the region in 1638 but abandoned it. The French East India Company claimed it in 1721 and called it Ile de France. It became a French crown colony in 1767.
• **End of French control:** December 3, 1810, when the Britain took control. British possession was confirmed by the Treaty of Paris on May 30, 1814.
• **End of British control:** March 12, 1968, when Mauritius declared its independence as an independent sovereign state within the British Commonwealth. On March 12, 1992, the Republic of Mauritius was created.
• **Last governor-general:** Sir Veerasamy

Ringadoo, who served from January 17, 1986, to March 12, 1992. He died in 2000.

Nations—Mexico (United Mexican States)
Mexico is south of the United States, bordering the Pacific Ocean, Caribbean Sea and Gulf of Mexico. After the Spanish began their conquest of Mexico in the early 1500s, Mexico City became the seat of government for the Viceroyalty of New Spain.
• **End of Spanish control:** September 28, 1821, when Mexico achieved its independence as the Mexican Empire, and Agustin de Iturbide set himself up as emperor. He was forced to abdicate in 1823 and the United Mexican States were established in 1824. France established another empire in Mexico in 1864 and sent Maximilian as emperor. (He was an Austrian cousin of Napoleon III.)
• **End of the (second) Mexican Empire:** May 15, 1867, after the French withdrew support and the United Mexican States were restored.
• **Last emperor and empress of Mexico:** Maximilian and his wife Carlota. Carlota went to Europe in 1866 to seek help to save the empire. Maximilian was executed in Mexico on June 19, 1867, age 34. Carlota died in Belgium on January 19, 1927, age 86. Benito Juarez, who was president of Mexico prior to Maximilian's arrival, again served as president of Mexico until 1872. Porfirio Díaz came to power in 1876 and had a long rule as president of Mexico: 1876-80 and 1884-1911. His dictatorial regime began to disintegrate in 1910, when the Mexican people revolted.
• **End of Díaz regime:** May 25, 1911, when Díaz was forced out of office. He went into exile in Paris, France, and died there on July 2, 1915, age 84. Diaz had been pursued by Mexi-can rebel leader Francisco ("Pancho") Villa.
• **Last military action of Pancho Villa:** 1920, when he ended his rebellion against the Mexican government and accepted land in northern Durango. Villa (born Doroteo Arango), was assassinated in Parral, Chihuahua, Mexico, on July 20, 1923, age 45.

Nations—Micronesia, Federated States of
Micronesia is an island nation in the western Pacific Ocean, between Hawaii and Indonesia. It was once known as the Caroline Islands. The islands came under Spanish control in 1886.
• **End of Spanish control:** 1899, after the Spanish-American War. The islands were sold to Germany and became part of German New Guinea.
• **End of German control:** October 3, 1914, when the islands were occupied by the Japanese. In 1920, Japan was granted a League of Nations mandate over them.
• **End of Japanese control:** 1944. The islands were administered by the U.S. Navy from 1944 to 1951, and then by the U.S. Department of the Interior until 1981. They became part of the United Nations Trust Territory of the Pacific Islands in 1947.
• **End of the Trust Territory of the Pacific Islands:** dissolved on November 3, 1986. On December 22, 1990, the UN Security Council ratified the termination of the Trusteeship and the islands gained their independence. On September 17, 1991, they were admitted to the UN as the Federated States of Micronesia.

Nations—Moldova, Republic of
Moldova is northeast of Romania in Eastern Europe. It came under Ottoman control in the 1500s. Russia acquired the land in 1812, when Turkey gave up Bessarabia. In 1918, it proclaimed its independence as the Moldavian Democratic Republic.
• **Last of the Moldavian Democratic Republic:** October 11, 1924, when the USSR established the Moldavian Autonomous Soviet Socialist Republic within the Ukrainian Autonomous Soviet Socialist Republic.
• **End of the Moldavian Autonomous Soviet Socialist Republic:** August 2, 1940, when the country became the Moldavian Soviet Socialist Republic.
• **End of the Moldavian Soviet Socialist Republic:** August 27, 1991, when independence was declared and the country adopted the Romanian spelling of Moldova. The Republic of Moldova gained its inde-

pendence when the USSR was dissolved on December 25, 1991.

Nations—Monaco, Principality of

Monaco borders the Mediterranean Sea along the southern coast of France near the Italian border. The House of Grimaldi gained control of Monaco in the 10th century when the land was conferred upon the family by Holy Roman Emperor Otto I.

• **End of the direct male Grimaldi line:** 1731. The direct male line of the Grimaldi family died out with Antoine I. His daughter Louise Hippolyte succeeded to the throne. She was followed by her husband, Jacques de Goyon-Matignon (Jacques I), who took the Grimaldi name. Monaco's monarchy were deposed in 1793, during the French Revolution, when France annexed the principality.

• **End of French annexation:** June 17, 1814, when Monaco's sovereignty was re-established. However, Monaco remained a protectorate of France until November 20, 1815, when it became a protectorate of the Kingdom of Sardinia.

• **End of Sardinian control:** July 17, 1860, when Monaco once again became a protectorate of France.

• **End of the monarch's absolute power:** 1911, when the constitution gave that power to a cabinet and a national council. A treaty signed with France in 1919 required that France approve all successions to the throne.

• **End of World War II occupation by Italy:** September 8, 1943. The Italian occupation began on November 11, 1942. The Germans took over occupation of Monaco when the Italians left.

• **End of World War II occupation by Germany:** September 3, 1944.

Nations—Mongolia, State of

Mongolia is in northern Asia, between China and Russia. The ancient nomadic Mongol tribes of Mongolia, Siberia and China were united in the 13th century under Genghis Khan. After his death in 1227, his empire was divided and eventually fell apart. Mongolia was subsequently ruled by

China for several centuries.

• **End of Chinese rule:** 1911, when the Chinese Manchu dynasty collapsed. The Chinese were finally driven out in early 1921. Mongolia was proclaimed an independent state later that year. It remained a monarchy until 1924.

• **End of the monarchy in Mongolia:** 1924, when Jebtsun Damba Khutukhtu, the Living Buddha of Urga, died. On November 28, 1924, the Mongolian People's Republic was proclaimed and Communist rule was introduced.

• **Last known as the Mongolian People's Republic:** February 12, 1992, when Mongolians adopted a new constitution and renamed their country the State of Mongolia.

• **Last time Mongolia's capital was known as Urga:** 1924, when it was renamed Ulan Bator (Red Hero).

• **Last chairman of the Council of Ministers (premier):** Sharavyn Gungaadorj, who served from March to September 11, 1990. The title was then changed to prime minister.

Nations—Morocco, Kingdom of

Morocco is west of Mauritania and Algeria in northern Africa and borders the Mediterranean Sea and the Atlantic Ocean. In ancient times, it was part of the Empire of Carthage. It was conquered by the Arabs in the 7th century A.D. Portugal invaded Morocco in 1415.

• **Last Portuguese stronghold in Morocco:** Magazan, abandoned in 1769. Part of Morocco fell under Spanish rule in the 19th century. In 1906, France gained control of the rest of the country. In 1912, it was divided into Spanish Morocco and French Morocco and made a protectorate of the two nations. The sultan was exiled in 1953 but allowed to return in 1955.

• **End of French Morocco and Spanish Morocco:** March 2, 1956, when the Kingdom of Morocco gained its independence.

• **Last sultan of Morocco:** Muhammad V, who ruled as sultan until August 14, 1957. He then exchanged the title sultan for king, and ruled until February 26, 1961.

• **Last French resident-general:** André Louis Dubois, who held the office from November 1955 to March 2, 1956. Dubois died in 1998.

• **End of Spanish control of Ifni:** January 4, 1969. Ifni is a small district along the Atlantic coast of Morocco. Spain occupied the region in 1934, basing its claim on an agreement signed in 1860 with the Sultan of Morocco. Although Morocco gained its independence in 1956, it was unable to regain control of Ifni for another 13 years.

• **End of Tangier's status as an international zone:** October 29, 1956, when it was returned to Morocco. The seaport of Tangier had been taken from Morocco in 1923 and established as an international zone.

Nations—Mozambique, Republic of

Mozambique is in southeastern Africa, bordering the Mozambique Channel between Tanzania and the Republic of South Africa. Portuguese explorers arrived in 1498 and were followed by traders in the early 1500s.

• **End of Portuguese control:** June 25, 1975, when Mozambique gained its independence as the People's Republic of Mozambique. It was the last colonial holding that made up what was once Portuguese East Africa.

• **Last known as the People's Republic of Mozambique:** December 1, 1990, when the nation became the Republic of Mozambique.

• **Last Portuguese high commissioner/ governor-general:** Victor Crespo, who held the position from September 1974 to June 25, 1975.

Nations—Myanmar, Union of (former Burma)

Myanmar borders the Bay of Bengal and the Andaman Sea in southeastern Asia. It was administered as part of British India beginning in 1824, after the first Burma War. Upper Burma was annexed in 1886, and the British ruled both parts as a province of British India.

• **End of British annexation:** April 1, 1937, when Burma was detached from British India and made a crown colony. Japan invaded in 1942, during World War II, and expelled the British from most of the country.

• **End of World War II occupation by Japan:** June 14, 1945, when Burma was liberated by the British.

• **End of British crown colony status:** January 4, 1948, when the nation gained its independence as the Union of Burma.

• **Last known as the Union of Burma:** June 18, 1989, when the nation was renamed the Union of Myanmar.

Nations—Namibia, Republic of

Namibia borders the Atlantic coast in southwestern Africa. The land became a protectorate of Germany as German Southwest Africa in 1884.

• **End of German control:** July 1915, during World War I, when the Germans surrendered and South African forces occupied Namibia. In December 1920, the Union of South Africa was given a mandate over Namibia as South-West Africa.

• **Last known as South-West Africa:** June 12, 1968, when South-West Africa was renamed Namibia by the United Nations. Namibia was not recognized by the Republic of South Africa and was the scene of guerrilla fighting for many years as Namibian factions worked to end South African control.

• **End of South African control:** March 21, 1990, when Namibia gained its independence as the Republic of Namibia.

• **End of South African control of Walvis Bay:** March 1, 1994, when South Africa gave to Namibia control of the deep-water port at Walvis Bay, which it had administered since 1922.

Nations—Nauru, Republic of

Nauru is an island nation in the Pacific Ocean just south of the Equator. An American whaling ship that visited the island in 1798 called it Pleasant Island.

• **Last use of the name Pleasant Island:** 1888, when Germany annexed the island as part of the Marshall Islands and gave it its native name: Nauru. In 1906, Nauru became part of German New Guinea.

• **End of German annexation:** 1914. During World War I, Australia and later Great

Britain took control of Nauru. In 1920, after the war, Nauru became a League of Nations mandate administered by Australia.

• **End of World War II occupation by Japan:** September 13, 1945, when Australia reoccupied the island. The Japanese World War II occupation of Nauru began in August 1942. Nauru was made a United Nations trust territory in 1947.

• **End of United Nations Trust Territory status:** January 1968, when the island (8.2. square miles) became the world's smallest independent nation as the Republic of Nauru.

Nations—Nepal, Kingdom of

Nepal is north of India in central Asia. Modern Nepal was established in 1768, when Prithur Narayan Shan, the ruler of Gorkha, added the valley of Nepal to his kingdom. His descendants established most of Nepal's present boundaries and introduced Hinduism as the state religion. In 1816, after the Anglo-Nepalese War, the British established a de facto protectorate over Nepal. A British residency was established at Katmandu.

• **End of the de facto British protectorate:** 1923, when Great Britain recognized the full independence of Nepal.

• **Last British resident (envoy):** William Frederick Travers O'Connor, who served from 1920 to 1923. He died in 1943.

Nations—Netherlands, Kingdom of the

The Netherlands border the North Sea in western Europe. They were part of Charlemagne's empire until the 9th century, when they were absorbed into the Low Countries with Belgium. In the 1400s, they were taken over by the House of Burgundy.

• **End of House of Burgundy rule:** 1482, when the House of Hapsburg gained control after Mary of Burgundy wed Maximilian, son of Holy Roman Emperor Frederick III. In 1556, a Spanish branch of the Hapsburgs gained the throne. In 1568, the Netherlands began the Eighty Year War with Spain to end persecution and gain its freedom. In 1579, the seven northern provinces signed the Union of Utrecht, declaring their independence as the United Provinces of the Netherlands.

• **End of the Eighty Years War against Spain:** January 30, 1648, with the Peace of Munster. The treaty recognized the independence of the United Provinces of the Netherlands.

• **End of the United Provinces of the Netherlands:** 1795, after the French invaded the Netherlands and set up the Republic of Batavia.

• **End of the Republic of Batavia:** 1806, when Louis Bonaparte incorporated Holland into his empire. In 1815, the Congress of Vienna established the United Kingdom of Netherlands, comprised of Belgium and the United Provinces. Belgium revolted in 1830, and gained its independence in 1839.

• **End of World War II occupation by Germany:** May 5, 1945, when the last German troops surrendered to the Allies. (The Netherlands had been invaded by the Germans in May 1940. The liberation of the country began when U.S. troops captured Maastricht on September 15, 1944.)

• **Last Dutch overseas dependencies:** The Netherlands Antilles and Aruba in the Caribbean. Both are self-governing regions of the Kingdom of the Netherlands. The Netherlands Antilles gained complete autonomy in 1954. Aruba separated from the Netherland Antilles in 1985 and sought its own autonomy.

Nations—New Zealand

New Zealand is an island nation southeast of Australia in the southern Pacific Ocean. Dutch explorer Abel Tasman was the first European to see New Zealand in 1642, but the Dutch made no attempt at colonization because the Maoris who lived there were hostile to outsiders. British explorer James Cook visited the islands in 1769 and claimed the land for Great Britain. Soon afterward, British whalers established settlements along the coast. In 1841, New Zealand officially became a separate British colony. Fighting began soon afterward as Maoris and colonists disputed ownership of the land. The first Maori War was fought from 1845 to

1847. The second and third wars were fought from 1860 to 1869. After that, fighting was sporadic.

• **End of the Maori Wars:** 1872, when progovernment forces attempted to capture Maori leader Te Kooti. He was formally pardoned by the government in 1883 and in 1891 was given some land. He died in 1893.

• **End of British control:** September 26, 1907, when the Dominion of New Zealand was established. New Zealand gained full sovereignty on November 25, 1947.

• **Last official use of the term "Dominion":** January 1, 1987.

Nations—Nicaragua, Republic of

Nicaragua is between Honduras and Costa Rica in Central America, bordering the Pacific Ocean and Caribbean Sea. Spanish colonialism began in Nicaragua with the arrival of the first Spaniards in 1522. The country was administered as part of the Captaincy-General of Guatemala.

• **End of Spanish control:** 1821, when Nicaragua proclaimed its independence from Spain. Nicaragua was annexed to Mexico, along with the rest of Central America in 1821.

• **End of Mexican annexation:** 1823, when Nicaragua and the other Central American countries formed the Central American Federation. Nicaragua became an independent republic on February 28, 1854. In November 1909, it became a U.S. protectorate. (*See also* Alliances, etc.—Central American Federation.)

• **End of U.S. protectorate:** January 3, 1933.

Nations—Niger, Republic of

Niger is south of Algeria in the Sahara region of west-central Africa. It came under French domination in the late 1800s and was part of French West Africa. Niger became an autonomous republic within the French Community on December 19, 1958.

• **End of French control:** August 3, 1960, when the country gained its independence as the Republic of Niger.

Nations—Nigeria, Federal Republic of

Nigeria is between Benin and Cameroon bordering the Gulf of Guinea on the western coast of Africa. It was the site of British and Portuguese slave trade from the 1600s to the 1800s. In the 19th century, Great Britain established administrative control over Nigeria as part of British West Africa.

• **End of British control:** October 1, 1960, when Nigeria became an independent federal state within the British Commonwealth. A year later, the northern part of British Cameroons voted to join Nigeria. In 1963, Nigeria became a federal republic within the British Commonwealth.

• **Last governor-general of Nigeria:** Ibo leader Dr. Nnamdi Azikiwe, who served from 1960 to 1963. He then became the first president of Nigeria from 1963 to 1966. His term was interrupted when he was overthrown in a military coup. Nigeria was plunged into a civil war on May 30, 1967, when the eastern region seceded and formed the Republic of Biafra.

• **End of the Biafran Civil War:** January 12, 1970, with the surrender of the last Biafran troops and the loss of about 2 million people. The Republic of Biafra was reintegrated into Nigeria.

Nations—Norway, Kingdom of

Norway is on the western part of the Scandinavian Peninsula, bordering the Norwegian Sea and Arctic Ocean. Norway was a united kingdom by the 11th century. It joined Denmark and Sweden as the Kalmar Union in 1397. Sweden left the union in 1523.

• **End of the union with Denmark:** 1814, when the Napoleonic Wars ended. Norway lost and was ceded to Sweden.

• **End of the union with Sweden:** June 7, 1905, when Norway became independent.

• **Last time Oslo was named Christiania:** 1924. The name of Norway's capital was changed from Oslo to Christiania (or Kristiania) after a major fire in the city in 1624. The name was officially changed back to Oslo in 1924.

• **End of World War II occupation by Germany:** May 1945 when World War II ended in Europe. The Kingdom of Norway was restored on May 9, 1945. (Germany had invaded Norway on April 9, 1940, and abolished the monarchy in September 1940. The Kingdom of Norway became simply Norway.)

Nations—Oman, Sultanate of

Oman is on the southeastern Arabian peninsula in the Middle East, bordering the Gulf of Oman and the Arabian Sea. The Portuguese seized Muscat, along the coast, in 1515.
• **End of Portuguese control:** 1650, when the Portuguese were driven out by the Ottoman Turks.
• **End of control by the Ottoman Turks:** 1749, when Ahmed Ibn Said ousted the Turks and founded the Sultanate of Muscat and Oman. He was the ancestor of the present ruling family. In 1891, the sultanate came under informal British protection.
• **End of informal British protection:** December 2, 1971. The protection had begun with a treaty in 1891.
• **Last British consul-general:** David Gordon Crawford, who served from 1969 to December 2, 1971. He died in 1981.
• **Last use of the name Muscat and Oman:** August 1970, when Sultan Said bin Taimur was overthrown by his son Qabus Bin Said, who began a program of modernization and changed the nation's name to the Sultanate of Oman.

Nations—Pakistan, Islamic Republic of

Pakistan is in the western corner of the Indian subcontinent, between India, Iran and Afghanistan, and bordering the Arabian Sea. In August 1947, shortly after World War II ended, India was partitioned by the British into the independent nations of India and Pakistan. The division was made along religious lines: Hindu and Muslim. From the beginning, Pakistan was a divided country. Its two parts, West Pakistan and East Pakistan, were separated by more than a thousand miles of Indian territory. Pakistan became an Islamic republic within the British Commonwealth on March 23, 1956.
• **Last known as West Pakistan:** March 26,

1971, when East Pakistan declared its independence as the People's Republic of Bangladesh. West Pakistan dropped the "west" but retained the name Pakistan.

Nations—Palau, Republic of

Palau (native name: Belau) is a group of islands in the western Pacific, southeast of the Philippines. The Spanish visited the islands in 1543 but did not claim them until 1875.
• **End of Spanish control:** 1899, when Spain sold the islands to Germany. They became part of German New Guinea.
• **End of German control:** 1914, during World War I, when Japan occupied Palau. In 1920, the Japanese were given a League of Nations mandate over them.
• **End of Japanese control:** after intensive fighting between September 6 and October 13, 1944, during World War II. The Allies took over occupation of the islands. In 1947, Palau became part of the Trust Territory of the Pacific Islands.
• **End of Trust Territory status:** 1994, when Palau voted to end its trustee status. It declared its independence on October 1, 1994. Palau was the last Trust Territory district.

Nations—Panama, Republic of

Panama is at the southern end of Central America, between Costa Rica and Colombia, bordered by the Caribbean Sea and Pacific Ocean. Columbus arrived in 1502 and claimed the region for Spain. Panama was ruled as part of the Viceroyalty of Peru from 1542 until 1717, when it became part of the Viceroyalty of New Granada that also included Colombia, Ecuador and Venezuela.
• **End of Spanish control:** December 17, 1819, when Simon Bolivar proclaimed the Gran Colombia Confederation. It included the present nations of Colombia, Ecuador, Panama and Venezuela. The confederation ended in 1830, when Ecuador and Venezuela separated, and Panama and Colombia became the State of New Granada. Panama seceded on November 18, 1840, to form the State of Panama.
• **End of the State of Panama:** March 20,

1841, when Panama became the State of the Isthmus.

• **End of the State of the Isthmus:** December 31, 1841, when Panama was reincorporated into the State of New Granada with Colombia.

• **Last known as the State of New Granada:** April 20, 1843, when the state became the Republic of New Granada.

• **Last known as the Republic of New Granada:** May 22, 1858, when the republic became the Granadine Confederation.

• **Last known as the Granadine Confederation:** July 18, 1861, when the confederation became the United States of New Granada.

• **Last known as the United States of New Granada:** September 20, 1861, when the union became the United States of Colombia.

• **Last known as the United States of Colombia:** August 5, 1886, when the union became the Republic of Colombia.

• **Last time Panama was a part of Colombia:** November 4, 1903, when Panama broke away and proclaimed its independence as the Republic of Panama.

Nations—Papua New Guinea, Independent State of
Papua New Guinea is on the eastern half of New Guinea and many outlying islands, north of Australia. It became a British protectorate as British New Guinea in 1884.

• **End of the British protectorate:** September 1906, when control passed to Australia and it was renamed the Territory of Papua.

• **End of the Territory of Papua:** July 1, 1949, when Papua (an Australian territory) combined administration with New Guinea (a UN trust territory) as the Territory of Papua and New Guinea.

• **Last of the Territory of Papua and New Guinea:** July 1, 1971, when the "and" was dropped and the name officially became the Territory of Papua New Guinea.

• **End of the Territory of Papua New Guinea:** September 16, 1975, when it gained its freedom as the Independent State of Papua New Guinea.

Nations—Paraguay, Republic of
Paraguay is in south-central South America, surrounded by Argentina, Brazil and Bolivia. It is one of the two landlocked nations of South America. The Spanish founded a settlement there in 1537. Beginning in 1542, it was ruled as part of the Viceroyalty of Peru. It became part of the Viceroyalty of the Rio de la Plata in 1776.

• **End of Spanish control:** May 14, 1811, when the country declared its independence. The Republic of Paraguay was established on October 12, 1813.

(*See also* Wars and Battles—Chaco War.)

Nations—Peru, Republic of
Peru is in western South America, bordered by Chile, Bolivia, Brazil, Ecuador, Colombia and the Pacific Ocean. When the Spanish explorer Francisco Pizarro arrived in 1532, Peru, was the center of the Inca Empire that extended from northern Ecuador to northern Chile. The Spaniards toppled the empire and ruled Peru as part of the Viceroyalty of Peru. Peru began its fight for independence in 1820, when General José de San Martin of Argentina arrived with an army to help end Spanish rule. Peru declared its independence from Spain on July 28, 1821, but fighting lasted for three more years.

• **End of Spanish control:** December 9, 1824, at the battle of Ayacucha, during Peru's struggle to remain independent. The Spaniards were defeated, guaranteeing that Peru would keep its independence. (*See also* Wars and Battles—Pacific, War of the.)

Nations—Philippines, Republic of the
The Philippines are an archipelago of more than 7,000 islands in the Pacific Ocean about 600 miles from southeastern Asia. Ferdinand Magellan, the first European to reach the islands, claimed them for Spain in 1521. When the Spanish assumed control, they named them for King Philip of Spain.

• **End of Spanish control:** August 13, 1898, when control of the Philippines was ceded to the United States after the Spanish-American War. On November 15, 1935, the Philippines were granted commonwealth status.

• **End of the Commonwealth of the Philippines:** July 4, 1946, when the Republic of the Philippines was proclaimed.
• **Last occupation of Clark Air Base by the United States:** November 26, 1991. The U. S. installation at Clark Air Base was so heavily damaged when Mount Pinatubo erupted in June 1991, that the U.S. decided to abandon the site.
• **Last U.S. occupation of Suvac Bay Naval Base:** October 1, 1992.
• **Last U.S. military forces in the Philippines:** November 24, 1997.

Nations—Poland, Republic of
Poland borders the Baltic Sea in north-central Europe. The Poles united in the 900s A.D. under the Piast dynasty, the first ruling dynasty in Poland.
• **Last Piast ruler:** Jadwiga, granddaughter of Casimir III the Great. The Piast dynasty ended in 1386, when she married Ladislav Jagiello, Grand Duke of Lithuania, starting the Jagellon (Jagiellonian) dynasty.
• **Last Jagellon ruler:** Sigismund II, who reigned from 1548 until he died on July 6, 1572. He was also Poland's last hereditary monarch. Polish influence waned in the 1700s. Prussia, Austria and Russia divided Poland among themselves in 1772. A second partition was made in 1793. Thaddeus Kosciusko tried to reunite Poland in 1794, but his revolt failed. When Poland was partitioned again in 1795, it ceased to exist as a nation.
• **Last elective king:** Stanislav II, who served from 1764 to 1795. Poland was then partitioned among Russia, Prussia and Austria. Napoleon created the Duchy of Warsaw in 1807 from lands he seized from Prussia and Austria.
• **End of the Duchy of Warsaw:**   1815. With Napoleon's defeat, Poland was partitioned again among Russia, Austria and Prussia. The Poles revolted unsuccessfully against Russian rule in 1831 and 1863-64.
• **End of Russian control:** November 11, 1918, when Poland was reconstituted as a sovereign state and gained its independence as a republic. Germany and the USSR allied

to invade Poland on September 1, 1939. The country was again partitioned. After Germany attacked the USSR in 1941, all of Poland fell under German domination.
• **End of German control:** January 17, 1945, when the last German troops were driven from Poland during World War II. By 1947, Poland was under Communist control. The country became the Polish People's Republic on August 1, 1952. Solidarity, a union headed by Lech Walesa, launched a drive away from Communism in the early 1980s.
• **Last of the Polish People's Republic:** December 30, 1989, when the nation became the Republic of Poland. Walesa was elected president of Poland in 1990 and held the position until 1995.

Nations—Portugal (Portuguese Republic)
Portugal borders the Atlantic Ocean on the western side of the Iberian Peninsula. It was known as Lusitania when it was conquered by Julius Caesar and Augustus. Roman rule ended in the 6th century A.D., when the Visigoths seized the region. Visigoth control ended in 711, when most of the region fell to the Moors. The House of Burgundy gained control in 1095.
• **Last Burgundy ruler:** Ferdinand I, who ruled from 1367 to 1383. The House of Burgundy was replaced by the House of Aviz (or Avis) in 1385.
• **Last Aviz ruler:** Henry, who ruled from 1578 to 1580. His throne was seized by the king of Spain and Portugal was made a Spanish dependency.
• **End of Spanish control:** December 1, 1640, when the House of Braganza (Bragança) gained control of the throne. In 1807, when Napoleon invaded Portugal, the Braganza royal family fled to Brazil.
• **Last House of Braganza ruler:** Maria II, who ruled from 1833 to 1853. With her marriage to Duke Ferdinand of Saxe-Coburg-Gotha in 1836, the line became the House of Braganza-Coburg.
• **Last House of Braganza-Coburg ruler:** Manuel II, who ruled from February 1, 1908, to October 5, 1910, when he was de-

posed by a revolution in Portugal. He spent the rest of his life in exile in England and died there in July 1932, age 43.

• **End of the Portuguese monarchy:** October 5, 1910, when Manuel II fled and Portugal became a republic.

• **End of Portugal's African empire:** November 11, 1975, when Angola gained its independence. The disbanding of the Portuguese empire marked the end of the last of the world's great colonial empires.

• **Last Portuguese colony in Asia:** Macao. It was also was the last remaining European-ruled colony in Asia. Macao, located at the mouth of the Pearl River in China, was set up as a Portuguese trading colony in 1557. In 1987, China and Portugal agreed that Macao would revert to China on December 20, 1999.

Nations—Qatar, State of

Qatar is on a small peninsula in the Persian Gulf in the Middle East. The Ottoman Turks arrived in 1872.

• **End of Ottoman occupation:** 1916, in the waning years of the Ottoman Empire. That year, Qatar signed a treaty with Great Britain, by which Britain agreed to grant protection. Oil was discovered in Qatar in the 1940s.

• **End of British protection:** September 3, 1971, when Qatar gained its independence. At that time, the treaty with Great Britain was terminated.

• **Last British political officer:** Edward Firth Henderson, who served from 1969 to 1971. When Qatar became an independent state, Henderson was the first ambassador from the United Kingdom. He died in April 1995.

Nations—Romania

Romania borders the Black Sea in southeastern Europe. The region was part of the Roman Empire until the 200s A.D. After the Romans withdrew, the land was overrun by Huns, Goths, Slavs, Mongols and other invaders. When the Mongols withdrew in the 1200s, the principalities of Walachia and Moldavia were created. In 1861, the princi-

palities merged as the United Rumanian Principalities. The Kingdom of Rumania was established in 1881.

• **Last Rumanian monarch:** King Michael I, who ruled from July 20, 1927, to June 8, 1930, upon the death of his grandfather Ferdinand I. He was replaced by his father Carol II but became king again in 1940, when Germany seized Romania during World War II. King Michael abdicated on December 30, 1947, and the Rumanian People's Republic was established.

• **Last of the Rumanian People's Republic:** August 21, 1965, when the Socialist Republic of Rumania was created.

• **Last use of "Rumania" spelling:** February 1966, when the official spelling was changed to "Romania."

• **Last of the Socialist Republic of Romania:** December 29, 1989, when the country began its transition to a free-market economy and changed its name to Romania.

Nations—Russia (Russian Federation)

Russia occupies much of eastern Europe and northwestern Asia. It borders the Baltic Sea, Pacific Ocean, Black Sea and Arctic Ocean. The earliest Russian state was established in the 9th century. The first tsar was proclaimed in the 16th century. In 1917, the monarchy collapsed with the Russian Revolution.

• **Last Russian tsar:** Grand Duke Mikhail Romanov, who held the title of tsar for just one day—March 16, 1917. He was informed that he was tsar when his brother Tsar Nicholas II abdicated on March 15, 1917.

• **End of the Russian monarchy:** ended with the resignation of Grand Duke Mikhail Romanov on March 16, 1917. A provisional government then took control of the country.

• **Last of the Romanov dynasty:** March 16, 1917, when the monarchy was overthrown. The Romanov dynasty had ruled Russia since Mikhail Romanov became Tsar Mikhail I in 1613.

• **Last of the tsar's family:** The family of Tsar Nicholas were taken prisoners in 1917. In April 1918, they were moved to Ekaterinburg, Russia. On July 16 (or 17), 1918, Nicholas, his wife Alexandra and their children Alexis, Olga, Tatiana, Marie and possibly Anastasia were assassinated and their bodies were burned by Bolsheviks. In 1991, the graves of the family were found. DNA tests conducted in 1993 confirmed that the bodies were those of the royal family.

• **Last of Anastasia, Grand Duchess of Russia:** The daughter of Nicholas and Alexandra was last seen July 16 (or 17), 1918, and is believed to have been executed with her family by Bolsheviks at Ekaterinburg, Russia. Anna Anderson (1902-84), of Pomerania, claimed to be Anastasia. Her suit was rejected by the West German Federal Supreme Court in 1970. In 1995, DNA tests proved conclusively that Anderson was not Anastasia.

• **Last pre-Soviet U.S. ambassador to Russia:** David Rowland Francis. He served from 1916 until after the 1917 Russian Revolution. He was a former mayor of St. Louis, Missouri (1885-89), governor of Missouri (1889-93) and Secretary of the Interior (1896-97). Francis died in St. Louis on January 15, 1927, age 77.

• **Last surviving Soviet official of those who joined the Communist (Bolshevik) party before the 1917 Russian Revolution:** Lazar M. Kaganovich, who served as a top adviser to Josef Stalin and was viewed as one of his possible successors. Kaganovich died in Moscow on July 25, 1991, age 97.

• **Last surviving Red Army commander from the Russian Revolution:** Marshal Semyon M. Budenny, Cossack/Bolshevik cavalry officer who played a significant role in defeating White Russian armies. He died in Moscow on October 27, 1973, age 90.

Nations—Russia—Russian Soviet Federated Socialist Republic

The Russian Soviet Federated Socialist Republic was the largest of the 15 unions that made up the USSR. It was created in January 1918 as the first Soviet republic. In December 20, 1922, it joined with Ukraine, Transcaucasia and Byelorussia to form the USSR.

• **Last of the Russian Soviet Federated Socialist Republic:** December 1991. On December 8, 1991, Belarus, Russia and Ukraine formed a confederacy of independent states. Independence became effective on December 25, 1991, with the dissolution of the USSR.

• **Last president of the Russian Soviet Federated Socialist Republic:** Boris Yeltsin in 1991. He served as Russia's first post-Soviet president, from 1991 to 1999.

• **Last time Saint Petersburg was known as Petrograd:** February 1924, when the name was changed to Leningrad. (The city of Saint Petersburg was founded in western Russia in 1703 by Tsar Peter the Great. The name was changed to Petrograd in August 1914.)

• **Last time Saint Petersburg was known as Leningrad:** July 1991, when the name reverted to Saint Petersburg.

• **Last time the Russian capital was in Saint Petersburg:** March 9, 1918, when the capital was moved to Moscow.

Nations—Rwanda, Republic of

Rwanda is in the interior of eastern Africa, north of Burundi and Tanzania. It became a German protectorate in 1884, and part of German East Africa in 1890.

• **End of German control:** May 1916, when Belgium occupied the country during World War I. In 1922, Rwanda was ceded to Belgium as part of the League of Nations mandate of Ruanda-Urundi. Rwanda became part of the United Nations trust territory of Ruanda-Urundi under Belgium in 1946.

• **End of the Belgian trusteeship:** July 1, 1962, when Rwanda gained full independence.

• **Last high representative:** Guillaume Logiest, who held the post from January 1962 to July 1, 1962. Prior to that, he was special military resident in Rwanda from November 1959 to January 1962.

Nations—Saint Kitts and Nevis, Federation of

The islands of Saint Kitts and Nevis are part of the Leeward Islands in the Caribbean. Saint Kitts, also known as Saint Christopher, was visited by Columbus in 1493. British settlers arrived in 1623. In the 1700s, Great Britain and France disputed ownership of the islands.

• **End of French-British ownership dispute:** 1783, when all of the islands came under British control by the Treaty of Versailles.

• **End of British control:** February 27, 1967, when the islands gained self-government as an associated state in the United Kingdom.

• **End of associated state status:** September 19, 1983, when the nation gained its independence as the Federation of Saint Kitts and Nevis.

• **Last governor:** Sir Clement Arrindell, who held the post from November 1981 to September 19, 1983. After independence, he held the post of governor-general until December 31, 1995.

Nations—Saint Lucia

Saint Lucia is one of the Windward Islands in the eastern Caribbean. Great Britain tried unsuccessfully to settle the island in 1605 and 1638 but met resistance from the fierce Caribs who lived there. France had better luck in 1650. After that, Britain and France fought over ownership.

• **End of French control:** 1814, when the island was ceded to Britain by the Treaty of Paris. Saint Lucia became a crown colony in 1838.

• **End of British control:** February 27, 1967, when Saint Lucia was granted self-government as an associated state in the United Kingdom.

• **End of associated state status:** February 22, 1979, when Saint Lucia gained its independence.

• **Last governor:** Sir Allen Montgomery Lewis, who held the post from 1974 to February 22, 1979. After independence, he served as governor-general from 1979 to 1980 and again from 1982 to April 30, 1987.

Nations—Saint Vincent and the Grenadines

Saint Vincent is a large island in the Windward Islands of the Caribbean. The Grenadines are a chain of about 600 small islands northeast of Grenada. Great Britain claimed Saint Vincent in 1627; however, there was no attempt to settle the island. France claimed and occupied the island in 1779.

• **End of French claim:** 1783, when it was returned to Britain by the Treaty of Versailles.

• **End of British control:** October 27, 1969, when Saint Vincent and the Grenadines became an associated state within the British Commonwealth.

• **End of associated state status:** October 27, 1979, when the nation of Saint Vincent and the Grenadines gained its independence.

• **Last governor:** Sir Sidney Gun-Munro, who held the post from 1976 to October 27, 1979. After independence, he served as governor-general until February 28, 1985.

Nations—Samoa, Independent State of

Samoa is an island group in the South Pacific, northeast of New Zealand. It was once Western Samoa. Nearby is a cluster of islands known today as American Samoa. The islands of Samoa were divided by treaty in 1899. Germany received the western islands (Western Samoa). The U.S. received the rest (American Samoa).

• **End of German control:** August 29, 1914, when New Zealand occupied Western Samoa at the outbreak of World War I. A League of Nations mandate in December 1920 gave New Zealand administration over Western Samoa. In January 1947, Western Samoa became a United Nations Trust Territory administered by New Zealand.

• **End of New Zealand administration:** January 1, 1962, when the Independent State of Western Samoa was established.

• **Last known as the Independent State of Western Samoa:** July 2, 1997, when "Western" was dropped and the nation became the Independent State of Samoa.

Nations—San Marino, Most Serene Republic of

San Marino is a small (23.4 sq. acres) landlocked republic in north-central Italy. It is believed to be the oldest republic in the

world and to have been founded in the 4th century A.D. by Marinus, a stonecutter who was later canonized. Italy recognized its independence in 1862. Despite its declared position of neutrality at the beginning of World War II, San Marino was invaded by the German army in August 1944 and was the scene of heavy fighting.
• **End of World War II occupation by Germany:** September 21, 1944, when Allied forces liberated San Marino.

Nations—São Tomé and Príncipe, Democratic Republic of

The nation of São Tomé and Príncipe is on two islands off the west-central coast of Africa. Portugal first visited the islands in 1470 and established a colony there. The two islands united as a Portuguese crown colony in 1753 and as an overseas province in 1951.
• **End of Portuguese control:** July 12, 1975, when the islands gained their independence as the Democratic Republic of São Tomé and Príncipe.
• **Last governor:** António Elisio Capelo Pires Veloso, who held the position in 1974. He held the position of high commissioner from December 18, 1974 to July 12, 1975.

Nations—Saudi Arabia, Kingdom of

Saudi Arabia borders the Red Sea, Arabian Gulf and the Gulf of Aqaba and occupies about nine-tenths of the Arabian Peninsula. It was the home of nomadic Semitic tribes for thousands of years. Muhammad, founder of Islam, was born there, at Mecca, c. 570 A.D. The nation of Saudi Arabia began to come together as a political entity with the Saud family, when Abd al-Aziz Ibn Saud gained power in 1902. By 1926, the country had reached its present boundaries. Oil became an important industry after it was discovered in 1938.
• **Last known as Arabia:** 1926, when the country was renamed Saudi Arabia. The country was unified on September 23, 1932, as the Kingdom of Saudi Arabia.

Nations—Senegal, Republic of

Senegal is in the westernmost point of Africa, surrounded by Mauritania, Guinea-Bissau, Mali, Guinea and the Atlantic Ocean. France began exerting influence on Senegal in the 1650s. In 1895, Senegal became part of French West Africa. In 1946, Senegal and the rest of French West Africa became part of the French Union.
• **End of French control:** November 25, 1958, when Senegal became an autonomous republic within the French Community. Senegal joined a federation with the Sudanese Republic (now Mali) in 1959. On June 20, 1960, the Mali Federation declared its independence from France.
• **End of Senegal's membership in the Mali Federation:** August 20, 1960. Senegal formed a confederation with The Gambia known as Senegambia on February 1, 1982.
• **End of Senegambia:** September 30, 1989.

Nations—Serbia and Montenegro

Serbia and Montenegro are in southwestern Europe, surrounded by Bosnia-Herzegovina, Croatia, Romania, Bulgaria, Hungary, Macedonia and Albania and bordering the Adriatic Sea. Until 1991, Serbia and Montenegro were two of the six republics of the Socialist Federal Republic of Yugoslavia. (Yugoslavia was created as the Kingdom of Serbs, Croats and Slovenes in 1918 after World War I ended. It also included Bosnia-Herzegovina, Croatia, Slovenia and Macedonia.)
• **End of the Kingdom of the Serbs, Croats and Slovenes:** October 3, 1929, when the name was changed to the Kingdom of Yugoslavia by royal decree of King Alexander I.
• **End of the Kingdom of Yugoslavia:** November 29, 1945, when the government of Marshal Tito was recognized and the monarchy was abolished. The Kingdom of Yugoslavia became the Socialist Federal Republic of Yugoslavia on January 31, 1946.
• **Last king of Yugoslavia:** Peter Karageorevich, who died on November 5, 1970, in Los Angeles, California, age 47. As Peter II, he acceded to the throne upon the death of his father King Alexander in 1934. His

reign ended in 1945 when the Tito government won the election on November 11th.

• End of the Socialist Federal Republic of Yugoslavia: June 25, 1991, after Croatia and Slovenia declared their independence. The Republic of Bosnia and Herzegovina declared its independence in February 1992. The republics of Serbia and Montenegro became the Federal Republic of Yugoslavia on April 27, 1992, under President Slobodan Milosevic. He attempted unsuccessfully to unite some of the surrounding republics into a Serbian state and was arrested in 2001. In 2002, Serbia and Montenegro began negotiations to form a looser confederation. In 2003, the United Nations restructured Yugoslavia into two republics called Serbia and Montenegro.

Nations—Seychelles, Republic of

The Seychelles are a group of islands in the Indian Ocean, 700 miles north of Madagascar. Portuguese seafarers were the first Europeans to see the islands in 1505. Portugal made no attempt to colonize the islands. France settled them in the 1770s.

• End of French control: 1794, when the Seychelles were occupied by Great Britain after the French Revolution. The Seychelles were made a dependency of the British colony of Mauritius in 1810. The Seychelles were ceded to Britain in 1814 by the Treaty of Paris. They became a British crown colony in 1903. The Seychelles were granted self-rule on October 1, 1975.

• End of British control: June 29, 1976, when the islands declared their independence as the Republic of Seychelles.

• Last governor: Colin Hamilton Allen, who held the post from 1973 to October 1, 1975, when the Seychelles became self-governing. He then held the post of high commissioner from October 1975 to June 29, 1976.

Nations—Sierra Leone, Republic of

Sierra Leone borders the Atlantic Ocean between Guinea and Liberia on the west coast of Africa. The British established a settlement for freed slaves at Freetown in 1787. The coastal region was renamed Sierra Leone in 1799. It became a British crown colony in 1808 and a British protectorate in 1895.

• End of British control: April 27, 1961, when Sierra Leone gained its independence as a state within the British Commonwealth.

• End of commonwealth status: April 19, 1971, when the Republic of Sierra Leone was declared.

• Last governor: Sir Maurice Henry Dorman, who served from September 1956 to April 27, 1961. He then held the position of governor-general until April 27, 1962. He died in 1993.

Nations—Singapore, Republic of

Singapore is on the tip of the Malay Peninsula in southeastern Asia. It was founded by Sir Thomas Stamford Raffles, a British colonial administrator, in 1819. From 1858 to 1867, it was part of British India, then became a separate crown colony.

• End of World War II occupation by Japan: September 12, 1945. The occupation began on February 15, 1942. Singapore was under British military rule from September 12, 1945, until April 1, 1946.

• End of British crown colony status: June 3, 1959, when Singapore became a self-governing state within the British Commonwealth. Singapore joined the Federation of Malaysia in September 1963.

• End of membership in the Federation of Malaysia: August 9, 1965, when Singapore withdrew to become a separate nation as the Republic of Singapore.

Nations—Slovak Republic (Slovakia)

The Slovak Republic is in central Europe north of Hungary. It fell under Hungarian control in 907 A.D. when the Magyars conquered the region.

• End of Hungarian control: October 28, 1918, when Slovakia united with Czechoslovakia as World War I was ending and the Austro-Hungarian Empire was disintegrating. It became the Slovak Socialist Republic within Czechoslovakia on January 1, 1969.

• End of the Slovak Socialist Republic

within **Czechoslovakia:** March 29, 1990, Slovakia became the Slovak Republic within Czechoslovakia.

• **Last time Slovakia was within Czech o-slovakia:** January 1, 1993, when it declared its independence as the Slovak Republic.

Nations—Slovenia, Republic of
Slovenia is between Austria and Croatia in southern Europe. It was once a province within the Kingdom of Hungary. Slovenia became part of the Austrian Hapsburg empire in 1526, when the Ottoman Turks defeated Hungary. When the Austro-Hungarian Empire was created in 1867, Slovenia and Croatia became part of it.

• **Last time Slovenia was part of the Austro-Hungarian Empire:** November 1918 when the empire was defeated in World War I. On December 1, 1918, Slovenia joined with other Balkans states as the Kingdom of Serbs, Croats, and Slovenes.

• **End of the Kingdom of the Serbs, Croats, and Slovenes:** October 3, 1929, when King Alexander renamed it the Kingdom of Yugoslavia and divided it into provinces. Slovenia became the Banovina (province) of Dravska.

• **End of the Kingdom of Yugoslavia:** November 29, 1945, when the People's Republic of Slovenia was created as one of the six constituent republics within the Federal People's Republic of Yugoslavia.

• **Last known as the People's Republic of Slovenia:** July 7, 1963, when it became the Socialist Republic of Slovenia.

• **Last known as the Socialist Republic of Slovenia:** March 8, 1990, when the Republic of Slovenia was declared.

• **Last time Slovenia was part of Yugoslavia:** June 25, 1991, when Slovenia officially declared its independence.

Nations—Solomon Islands
The Solomon Islands are in the southwestern Pacific Ocean, east of Papua New Guinea. A Spanish explorer came across them in 1567, but no attempt was made to colonize them for two centuries. Germany claimed some of the northern islands in 1885 but renounced claim to all but two of them in 1899. The British established a protectorate over the southern islands in 1893 as part of the British Western Pacific Territories. After World War I, the German-owned section of the islands became part of the Australian mandated territory of New Guinea. The Solomons saw heavy fighting during World War II. The Japanese occupied the islands in 1942.

• **End of World War II occupation by Japan:** February 8, 1943 on Guadalcanal, when U.S. troops captured the island. The Japanese held onto the island of Bougainville until 1945.

• **Last known as the British Solomon Islands Protectorate:** June 22, 1975, when Great Britain shortened their name to the Solomon Islands.

• **End of British control:** On January 2, 1976, the islands were granted self-government. They gained their independence from Great Britain on July 7, 1978.

• **Last British governor:** Sir Colin Hamilton Allan, who served from January 1976 to July 8, 1978. He died in 1993.

Nations—Somalia (Somali Democratic Republic)
Somalia is on the horn of East Africa, bordering the Gulf of Aden and the Indian Ocean. Great Britain created the British Somaliland protectorate in the north in 1887. Italy created Italian Somalia (Italian Somaliland) in the south in 1905.

• **End of British control:** June 26, 1960, when British Somaliland gained its independence as the State of Somaliland.

• **End of Italian control:** July 1, 1960, when Italian Somaliland and the State of Somaliland were united as the independent Somali Republic (Somalia). The country was renamed the Somali Democratic Republic in 1969. It became the Somali Republic again in 1991. The country lost its government in 1991, when it was thrown into anarchy. The northern part (former British Somaliland) broke away and declared itself the Republic of Somaliland. Several warlords set up their own mini-states. In 1992, the United Nations declared

Somalia a country without a government. U.S. and UN troops were sent to Somalia to protect the delivery of food to the famine-stricken population.

• **End of U.S. and United Nations military presence in Somalia:** U.S. forces withdrew on March 25, 1994. UN forces pulled out on March 3, 1995.

Nations—South Africa, Republic of

South Africa is at the southern tip of the African continent, bordering the Atlantic and Indian oceans. The earliest Dutch settlers arrived in 1652 and established Cape Colony. Later Dutch arrivals founded the republics of Transvaal and Orange Free State. In May 1910, the Union of South Africa was created by the British Parliament when Cape Colony, Orange Free State and Transvaal joined together. In 1931, South Africa became a sovereign state within the British Commonwealth.

• **End of Dutch rule in Cape Town:** 1814, when Great Britain gained control of Cape Colony after the Napoleonic Wars. Britain annexed Zululand in 1887. In 1897, it became a part of Natal, which in 1910 joined the Union of South Africa.

• **Last Zulu king recognized by the British:** King Cetshwayo (Cetewayo), who was captured by the British in 1879, following his defeat in the Zulu War. He regained his throne in 1883 but was deposed. He died in Eshowe, South Africa, in February 1884, age around 58.

• **End of British control and end of the Union of South Africa:** May 31, 1961, when the Union of South Africa withdrew from the British Commonwealth. and became a republic.

• **End of apartheid:** removed in stages, beginning in 1990. In October 1990, the Separate Amenities Act was abolished. On June 5, 1991, the South African Parliament repealed the apartheid laws on property ownership (Land Acts). On June 17, 1991, the law that classified all Africans by race at birth (Population Registration Act) was scrapped. Apartheid ended formally in 1994, when the first all-race elections were held

and the African National Congress was elected. (Apartheid, a policy of racial separation, had become official in 1948 with enactment of laws severely restricting the rights of black South Africans.)

• **End of Mandela's imprisonment:** February 11, 1990. Black nationalist leader Nelson Mandela was released from jail after 27 years in prison. He was elected president of South Africa in 1994 and served from May 10, 1994, to June 1999.

• **End of the United Nations embargo:** May 25, 1994, shortly after Nelson Mandela was elected South Africa's first black president. When the UN Security Council lifted a 10-year ban on weapons exports from South Africa, it was the last of the apartheid-era embargoes.

Nations—Spain, Kingdom of

Spain shares the Iberian Peninsula in southwestern Europe with Portugal. It also borders the Atlantic Ocean and Mediterranean Sea. Spain created a vast colonial empire through a series of explorations, beginning in the late 1400s. The Council of the Indies was created in 1524 by Emperor Charles V as the supreme governing body of the Spanish Empire in America and the Philippines.

• **End of the Council of the Indies:** abolished on March 24, 1834. By the 19th century, its powers had become so eroded it served only an advisory role.

• **End of French occupation:** December 1813, when the French were driven out of Spain. Napoleon I had invaded Spain in 1808 and placed his brother Joseph Bonaparte on the throne.

• **Last Spanish monarch of the House of Hapsburg:** Charles II, who served from 1665 to 1700. He left no heirs when he died on November 1, 1700, age 38. He was succeeded by Philip V, who founded the Bourbon dynasty in Spain. Philip's accession to the throne caused the War of the Spanish Succession.

• **End of the Spanish First Republic:** December 29, 1874, when the monarchy was restored. The First Republic had been established in February 1873, when King

Amadaus of the House of Savoy abdicated after a brief civil war. His predecessor, Isabella, had been a member of the House of Bourbon. His successor, Alfonso XII, was also a member of the House of Bourbon.

• **End of the Spanish Second Republic:** July 23, 1936, when a military uprising led to civil war. The Second Republic was established on April 14, 1931, when King Alfonso XIII was deposed. It lasted five years. Francisco Franco controlled Spain after the civil war. In July 1947, he announced that Spain would become a monarchy after his death or retirement. For the next 29 years, Spain was a nominal (name only) monarchy.

• **End of nominal monarchy in Spain:** November 22, 1975, when the Spanish monarchy was restored, after Franco died and his designated successor Prince Juan Carlos Bourbon, grandson of Alfonso XIII, ascended to the throne.

(*See also* Wars and Battles—Spanish Civil War; Spanish Succession, War of the.)

Nation—Sri Lanka, Democratic Socialist Republic of

Sri Lanka is an island nation in the Indian Ocean off the southeastern coast of India. It was known as Ceylon when the Portuguese arrived in 1505. They controlled the coastal areas until the Dutch arrived in 1658.

• **End of Dutch control:** 1796, when the British occupied the island. The British made Ceylon a crown colony in 1802.

• **Last native ruler:** the King of Kandy, who was defeated by the British in 1815. In 1931, Great Britain granted Ceylon limited self-rule.

• **End of British control:** February 4, 1948, when Ceylon became a self-governing dominion within the British Commonwealth.

• **Last known as Ceylon:** May 22, 1972, when the nation resumed its original name, Sri Lanka, which means "resplendent island" in Sinhalese.

Nations—Sudan, Republic of the

Sudan shares part of its northern border with Egypt. In ancient times, northern Sudan was part of the Kingdom of Nubia. Egypt conquered, occupied and annexed Sudan in the early 1820s. In 1881, Muhammad Ahmed ibn-Seyyid Abdullah—a Muslim zealot who called himself the Mahdi (leader of the faithful)—revolted against Egyptian rule. By 1885, he controlled of most of Sudan. He died shortly after his followers captured the city of Khartoum.

• **End of Mahdi control:** September 2, 1898, when an Anglo-Egyptian army defeated the Mahdi's followers. Sudan was placed under Anglo-Egyptian control with a governor appointed by Egypt and approved by Great Britain.

• **End of Anglo-Egyptian control:** January 1, 1956, when Sudan was proclaimed an independent nation as the Republic of The Sudan. On May 25, 1969, the country became the Democratic Republic of the Sudan.

• **Last known as the Democratic Republic of the Sudan:** December 15, 1985, when the nation once again became the Republic of the Sudan.

Nations—Suriname, Republic of

Suriname is on the northern coast of South America, bordering Guyana, French Guiana, Brazil and the Atlantic Ocean. The region was involved in a land swap between the British and Dutch in 1667. The British took New Netherland (New York). In exchange, the Dutch received Dutch Guiana (or Netherlands Guiana).

• **Last known as Dutch Guiana:** September 20, 1948, when the colony was renamed Suriname.

• **End of Dutch control:** November 25, 1975, when Suriname gained its independence as the Republic of Suriname.

• **Last governor-general:** Johan Henry Eliza Ferrier, who held the post from August 1968 to November 1975. He was Suriname's president from November 1975 until August 10, 1980.

Nations—Swaziland, Kingdom of

Swaziland is almost entirely surrounded by the Republic of South Africa. Independence was promised by the British in 1881 and 1884, but political instability kept Swaziland from gaining its freedom. In 1902, after the Boer Wars ended, Swaziland became a protectorate as one of the High Commission Territories.

• **End of British control:** April 25, 1967, when Swaziland won self-government. It became an independent nation on September 6, 1968. The Kingdom of Swaziland was Britain's last territory in Africa.

Nations—Sweden, Kingdom of

Sweden borders the Gulf of Bothnia and the Baltic Sea on the eastern side of the Scandinavian Peninsula. It shares much of its western border with Norway. Sweden joined Norway and Denmark in the Kalmar Union in 1397.

• **End of Sweden's membership in the Kalmar Union:** 1523. Sweden left the union and severed its ties with the Roman Catholic Church. It marked the beginning of control by the House of Vasa, a royal dynasty.

• **End of the House of Vasa in Sweden:** June 6, 1654, when Queen Christina abdicated. She moved to Rome, Italy, renounced her Lutheran faith and became a Roman Catholic. She died in Italy on April 19, 1689, age 62.

• **End of Sweden's union with Norway:** June 1905, when Norway became independent.

• **Last operation of the Falu Copper Mine:** closed December 8, 1992, when the mine ran out of workable ore. The Falu Copper Mine in central Sweden had been used for more than 1,000 years and is believed to have been the world's oldest continuously operated industrial worksite.

Nations—Switzerland (Swiss Confederation)

Switzerland is a mountainous nation in central Europe, west of France and south of Germany. It was once the Roman province of Helvetica. The Franks gained control in the 6th century. It was split between Swabia and Burgundy in the 9th century but reunited as part of the Holy Roman Empire in 1033. Switzerland's modern history begins in 1291, when three cantons formed a league

for their common defense against encroachment by the Hapsburgs. The popular legend of William Tell is connected to this union. During the next century, other cantons joined the league, and by 1388, a strong confederation had emerged. The Swiss gained their independence from the Holy Roman Empire in 1499. In 1798, Switzerland was invaded by France and the Helvetic Republic was formed. Switzerland was placed under French supervision.

• **End of the Helvetic Republic:** March 10, 1803. The Swiss Confederation was reestablished by Napoleon.

• **End of French control:** 1815, with the defeat of Napoleon. That year, the Congress of Vienna granted perpetual neutrality to Switzerland. In 1848, the cantons drafted a new constitution that made the country a powerful federalized, centralized state.

Nations—Syria (Syrian Arab Republic)

Syria's location on the Mediterranean Sea in the Middle East made it a prime target for ancient invaders. Hebrews, Assyrians, Chaldeans, Persians, Greeks and Romans all conquered the land. Rome vanquished Syria c. 64 B.C. After the Roman Empire was divided, Syria became part of the Byzantine Empire. Syria was conquered by the Arabs in the 630s A.D. Beginning in 661, it was the center of Islamic power with the Ommaid (or Omayyud) caliphate.

• **End of the Ommaid (Omayyad) dynasty:** 750 A.D., when the Ommaid dynasty was replaced by the Abbasids in Iraq, and Syrian dominance faded. Christian Crusaders gained power over the coastal regions of Syria in the 1100s.

• **End of Ottoman control:** October 1, 1918. The Ottoman Empire controlled Syria for 400 years, except for a brief occupation by Ibrahim Pasha of Egypt in the 1830s. Syria became a French League of Nations mandate in 1920.

• **End of the French mandate:** April 17, 1946, when the last French troops left Syria. On February 1, 1958, Syria formed the United Arab Republic (UAR) with Egypt.

• **End of the United Arab Republic:** September 28, 1961, when Syria withdrew following a military coup.

Nations—Taiwan (Republic of China)
Taiwan is an island nation off the southeast coast of mainland China. When the Portuguese arrived in 1590, they named the land Ihla Formosa (beautiful island). The Chinese, however, have called the island Taiwan (terraced bay) for centuries. The Dutch were the first Europeans to settle the island in 1624. The Portuguese established small colonies in the north.
• **End of Dutch control:** September 22, 1683, when the Manchus of China annexed the region as part of the Chinese Empire.
• **End of Manchu control:** May 8, 1895, when Taiwan was ceded to Japan under terms of the Treaty of Shimonoseki after the Sino-Japanese War.
• **End of Japanese control:** October 25, 1945, when Taiwan was restored to China at the end of World War II. Japan formally renounced its claim to the island with the 1951 San Francisco Peace Treaty.
• **Last Japanese governor general:** Admiral Kiyoshi Hasegawa who was appointed in 1940. He died on September 2, 1970, age 87.
• **Last time Taiwan was part of China:** 1949, when China was divided into two nations: the People's Republic of China and Taiwan (Republic of China). On December 7-8, 1949, the Nationalist Chinese (Republic of China), led by Chiang Kai-shek, moved from mainland China and established their government in Taiwan.
• **Last time Taiwan was in the United Nations:** November 15, 1971. Taiwan was removed from the United Nations, and the People's Republic of China gained its seat. On December 15, 1978, President Jimmy Carter announced that the United States would formally recognize the People's Republic of China.
• **End of U.S. diplomatic relations with Taiwan:** December 31, 1978.

Nations—Tajikistan, Republic of
Tajikistan is in southeast central Asia, west

of China and north of Afghanistan. The Soviet Union gained control of Tajikistan in 1918, after the Russian Revolution. The Tadzikh Autonomous Soviet Socialist Republic was created within the Uzbek Soviet Socialist Republic in 1925.
• **End of the Tadzikh Autonomous Soviet Socialist Republic:** December 5, 1929, when the Tadzikh Soviet Socialist Republic was proclaimed within the USSR.
• **End of the Tadzikh Soviet Socialist Republic:** September 9, 1991, when it gained its independence from the USSR as the Republic of Tajikistan. Independence became effective on December 25, 1991, when the USSR was dissolved.

Nations—Tanzania, United Republic of
Tanzania borders the Indian Ocean south of Kenya on the east coast of Africa and includes the islands of Zanzibar and Pemba. Tanganyika, on the mainland, was made a German protectorate in 1885 as part of German East Africa.
• **End of German East Africa and German control:** 1918, during World War I, after Great Britain occupied German East Africa. In 1922, the area was mandated to the British by the League of Nations. German settlers were ousted and the region's name was changed to Tanganyika. The British League of Nations mandate became a United Nations trust territory in December 1946.
• **End of British control:** December 9, 1961, when Tanganyika gained its independence from Great Britain. Zanzibar became independent on December 19, 1963.
• **Last governor of Tanganyika:** Sir Richard Gordon Turnbull, who served from 1958 to December 9, 1961. After independence, he served as governor-general until December 9, 1962. He died in December 1998.
• **Last time Tanganyika and Zanzibar were separate nations:** April 26, 1964, when Tanganyika and Zanzibar merged to form the United Republic of Tanganyika and Zanzibar.
• **Last known as the United Republic of Tanganyika and Zanzibar:** October 29,

1964, when the nation's name was changed to the United Republic of Tanzania.

Nations—Thailand, Kingdom of
Thailand occupies the Indochinese peninsula and part of the Malay Peninsula in southeastern Asia. The Thais, from southwestern China, migrated southward possibly as early as the 800s A.D. and gave the country its name. By 1238, they had established Thailand's first independent state with the capital at Sukhothai.
• **End of Sukhothai era:** 1350, when Thailand was annexed by the Kingdom of Ayutthaya and the capital was moved to the port city of Ayutthaya.
• **End of the Ayutthaya era:** 1767, when Burmese invaders destroyed the capital. The capital then was moved to Thon Buri (Dhonburi) and finally to Bangkok in 1782.
• **Last Ayutthaya king:** King Ekatat, who was removed from power in 1767 by Phraya Taksin. King Rama I was installed in 1782 as the first monarch of the Chakri dynasty.
• **End of the reign of Rama IV (King Mongkut):** 1868. He ruled from April 1851, and became known to many readers in the Western world through a book about the experiences of English teacher Anna Leonowens, who traveled to Siam in 1862 to tutor his children. The book was the basis for the musical show *The King and I* and several books and films. King Mongkut died on October 18, 1868, his 64th birthday. His son Chulalongkorn (Rama V) ruled from 1868 until 1910.
• **End of Thailand's absolute monarchy:** 1932, when Thailand replaced its monarchy with a constitutional government after a military coup d'etat that began in June. The new constitution promulgated in December 1932, included the appointment of a prime minister. A king in title remains.
• **Last time Thailand was officially named Siam:** May 11, 1949, by proclamation. The country was known as the Kingdom of Siam until June 23, 1939, then was renamed the Kingdom of Thailand (which means "land of the free" in Thai). In 1946, the country was once again known as the Kingdom of Siam.

That lasted just a few years. Siam reverted to the name Thailand in 1949.

Nations—Togo (Togolese Republic)
Togo is in western Africa, bordered by Ghana, Burkina Faso, Benin and the Bight of Benin. A German protectorate was established there as Togoland in 1884.
• **End of the German protectorate of Togoland:** August 26, 1914, when French and British troops captured the area during World War I. The land was divided between the two nations in 1916. In 1922, after the war, the land was mandated to Great Britain and France by the League of Nations as British Togoland and French Togoland.
• **End of British Togoland:** December 13 1956, when it became part of the Gold Coast (now Ghana).
• **End of French Togoland:** April 27, 1960, when it gained independence as the Republic of Togo.

Nations—Tonga, Kingdom of
Tonga is a group of islands in the southern Pacific Ocean. Polynesians are believed to have arrived there more than 2,500 years ago. In 1616, the Dutch were the first outsiders to see the islands. James Cook visited them in 1777 and named them the Friendly Islands. They became a British protectorate in 1900. Tongo has had a supreme ruler since its earliest days. In 1875, the Kingdom of Tonga was established.
• **End of the British protectorate:** June 4, 1970, when the kingdom became an independent nation in the British Commonwealth as the Kingdom of Tonga.

Nations—Trinidad and Tobago, Republic of
The islands of Trinidad and Tobago are in the southern Caribbean, off the coast of Venezuela. Both were visited by Columbus in 1498. Spain claimed Trinidad at that time.
• **End of Spanish control:** February 21, 1797, after a war with Great Britain. Trinidad was ceded to Britain in 1802 by the Treaty of Amiens.
• **Last time Trinidad and Tobago were**

separate colonies: January 1, 1899, when they united.

• **End of British control:** August 31, 1962, when Trinidad and Tobago gained its independence as a sovereign state within the British Commonwealth. On August 1, 1976, Trinidad and Tobago became an independent republic.

• **Last governor-general:** Sir Ellis Emmanuel Innocent Clarke, who held the position from February 1973 until August 1, 1976. After Trinidad and Tobago gained its independence, Clarke served as president from 1976 to March 13, 1987.

Nations—Tunisia, Republic of

Tunisia borders the Mediterranean Sea between Algeria and Libya in northern Africa. The Berbers were already living there when the Phoenicians visited the area as early as the 1100s B.C. The Hafsid dynasty gained control of the region in 1228 A.D. and ruled for more than three centuries.

• **End of Hafsid rule:** 1570-74, when the Hafsids were overpowered by the Ottoman Empire. During Ottoman Turkish rule, power was placed in the hands of a bey (provincial governor). The Hussein dynasty was established in 1705, and the position of bey became hereditary. Tunisia became a French protectorate in 1881.

• **End of the French protectorate:** March 20, 1956, when France recognized the independence of Tunisia.

• **End of the Hussein dynasty:** July 25, 1957, when the bey was deposed, Tunisia was declared a republic and a president was elected.

• **Last bey:** Muhammad al-Amin, who served as bey from May 1943 to March 20, 1956. He then served as king from March 1956 until July 25, 1957, when he was deposed.

Nations—Turkey, Republic of

Turkey is in southeastern Europe and southwestern Asia. It was part of the Ottoman Empire from 1453 until the empire collapsed at the end of World War I. Modern Turkey was created in 1923 from the Turkish remnants of the Ottoman Empire. Turkey became an independent republic on October 29, 1923.

• **End of the sultanate:** November 1, 1922, when the sultan was deposed.

• **Last sultan of Turkey:** Muhammad VI, who ruled from 1918 to November 1, 1922. The caliphate and sultanate were separated later that month.

• **End of the caliphate:** March 3, 1924, when Abdul-Mejid II, the last caliph, was deposed.

• **End of the Seriat in Turkey:** April 20, 1924. The Seriat (Islamic-inspired laws) and the traditional religious schools were abolished with the adoption of the Turkish constitution.

• **Last official use of old-style Arabic letters and numbers:** 1928. In June 1928, new numerals were adopted. In August 1928, the modern Turkish alphabet was adopted.

• **End of the use of the fez as standard male headwear:** November 25, 1925, by an Assembly bill sometimes known as the Hat Law, that made the wearing of standard hats compulsory.

• **Last time Constantinople was known as Byzantium:** 330 A.D., when the Roman emperor Constantine I moved his capital there from Rome. Byzantium was founded around 660 B.C. by the Greeks.

• **Last time Istanbul was known as Constantinople:** 1930, when the name was officially changed to Istanbul.

• **Last time Ankora was known as Angora:** 1930, when the city's name was officially changed to Ankora.

• **Last time the Koran (Quran) was read in Arabic in public:** 1933, when it became required that the Islamic call to worship and public readings of the Koran (Quran) had to be in Turkish.

Nations—Turkmenistan, Republic of

Turkmenistan is in central Asia, bordered by Iran, Kazakhstan, Uzbekistan, Afghanistan and the Caspian Sea. In ancient times, it was part of the Persian Empire. In 1881, it was made part of Russian Turkistan. It became part of the Soviet Union in 1924 as the

Turkmen Soviet Socialist Republic.
• **End of the Turkmen Soviet Socialist Republic:** October 27, 1991 when it declared its independence as the Republic of Turkmenistan. Independence became effective on December 25, 1991, when the USSR was dissolved.

Nations—Tuvalu
Tuvalu is made up of a chain of nine islands scattered over a half million square miles in the western Pacific. They were once known as the Ellice Islands. They became a British protectorate in 1892 as part of the British colony of the Gilbert and Ellice Islands. They were annexed by Great Britain in 1916 as part of the Gilbert and Ellice Islands crown colony. (*See also* Nations—Kiribati.)
• **Last known as Ellice Islands:** October 1, 1975, when they were separated from the Gilberts and renamed Tuvalu.
• **End of British control:** October 1, 1978, when the islands were granted full independence.
• **Last time the U.S. claimed the islands of Nurakita, Nukulaelae, Nuykefetau and Funafuti:** February 7, 1979, when a treaty was signed ending the U.S. claim.

Nations—Uganda, Republic of
Uganda is a landlocked nation in eastern Africa, north of Tanzania. It was the early home of the Kingdom of Buganda. In 1894, Great Britain established a protectorate over Buganda and in 1902, over the rest of Uganda. The region comprising the British colonies of Kenya, Tanganyika, Zanzibar and Uganda was known as British East Africa.
• **End of British control:** October 9, 1962, when Uganda gained its independence. The Kingdom of Buganda was made a federated state within Uganda.
• **End of Idi Amin rule:** April 11, 1979, when he was deposed by a force of Ugandan rebels, exiles and Tanzanians. He had assumed power in February 1971 when he ousted President Milton Obote. Amin died in Saudi Arabia on August 16, 2003, age 77 or 80.

Nations—Ukraine
Ukraine is in southeastern Europe, south of Russia and bordering the Sea of Azov and the Black Sea. As early as the 800s, the city of Kiev was known as Rus and was an important commercial hub in Eastern Europe. It lost its influence when the Mongols arrived in the 1200s. Poland conquered part of the region in 1387. In the 16th century, it began to be called Ukraine. The Ukrainians revolted against Poland in 1648 but were weakened by the Cossack Revolt. In 1654, Ukraine asked the tsar of Muscovy for protection. Ukraine remained a province of Russia until the overthrow of the tsar in March 1917. The Ukrainian People's Republic was created in 1918.
• **End of the Ukrainian People's Republic:** January 6, 1919, when the Ukrainian Soviet Socialist Republic was established. On December 20, 1922, the Ukrainian SSR became one of the founding constituents of the USSR.
• **End of the Ukrainian Soviet Socialist Republic:** 1991. Ukraine declared its independence on August 24, 1991. Independence became effective on December 25, 1991, when the USSR was dissolved.

Nations—Union of Soviet Socialist Republics (USSR)
The Union of Soviet Socialist Republics (USSR), a union of 15 soviet republics, was established in 1922. It occupied the eastern half of Europe and the northern part of Asia. The largest was the Russian Soviet Federated Socialist Republic, with more than half of the population of the USSR. The USSR was dissolved in 1991.
• **End of Cominterm:** dissolved by Josef Stalin on May 22, 1943. Cominterm, an organization of world Communist parties, was founded in 1919.
• **End of Cominform:** dissolved on April 16, 1956. Cominform had been set up in 1947 as the Communist Information Bureau.
• **Last of the USSR:** dissolved December 25, 1991. Final steps toward ending the USSR began in September 1991, when the Congress of People's Deputies voted to dis-

solve it. On September 6, the USSR officially recognized that Estonia, Latvia and Lithuania were no longer constituent republics of the Soviet Union. On December 8, Belarus, Russia and Ukraine formed a confederacy of independent states. By December 21, the confederacy comprised 11 of the 12 remaining former Soviet republics. Soviet President Mikhail Gorbachev resigned on December 25, 1991, and was not replaced, as the country he once ruled no longer existed. Also on December 25th, the United States recognized the rest of the Soviet Union as independent nations. (*See also* Armenia, Azerbaijan, Belarus, Estonia, Georgia, Kazakhstan, Kyrgyz Republic, Latvia, Lithuania, Moldova, Russia, Tadzhikstan, Turkmenistan, Ukraine, Uzbekistan.)

• **Last Central Intelligence Service director:** Yevgeny M. Primakov, in November-December 1991. He was the first director of Foreign Intelligence Service from 1991 to 1996. Primakov was Russian foreign minister from 1996 to 1998 and prime minister of Russia from 1998 to 1999.

• **Last KGB chairman:** Vadim V. Bakatin, from August to November 1991. He was Soviet interior minister from 1988 to 1990 and became the first chairman of the Interrepublican Security Service in 1991.

• **Last of the KGB:** ceased to exist on November 6, 1991. The KGB (Komitet Gosudarstvennoi Bezopasnosti (Committee for State Security) was the main national security and intelligence agency of the USSR.

• **Last NKVD/MVD chairman:** General Sergei N. Kruglov. He was the last chairman of the NKVD from 1945 to 1953 (MVD after 1946) and the first chairman of the KGB from 1953 to 1954. The NKVD was the People's Commissary for Internal Affairs. The MVD was the Ministry of Internal Affairs.

• **Last secretary-general of the Soviet Communist party:** Mikhail Gorbachev, who was also president of the USSR. When he resigned on August 24, 1991, he severed the link between the Communist party and the government that had existed during the entire history of the USSR.

• **Last Soviet foreign minister:** Boris D. Pankin, who held the post from August 28 to November 14, 1991. He was the former editor of Komsomolskaya Pravda, chairman of the Soviet Copyright Agency and Soviet ambassador to Sweden and later to Czechoslovakia. Pankin served as Russian ambassador to Great Britain from 1991 to 1994.

• **Last Soviet ambassador to the United Nations:** Yuli M. Vorontsov from 1990 to 1991. He was the first Russian ambassador to the United Nations from 1991 to 1994. Vorontsov served as Russian ambassador to the United States from 1994 to 1999.

• **Last United States ambassador to the USSR:** Robert S. Strauss, in 1991. He was the first post-Soviet Union U.S. Ambassador to Russia and served from 1991 to 1993.

Nations—United Arab Emirates

The United Arab Emirates are on the eastern Arabian Peninsula and extend along part of the Gulf of Oman and the Persian Gulf. The Trucial States emerged through a series of treaties in the late 19th century.

• **End of the Trucial States:** December 2, 1971, when six of the sheikdoms—Abu Dhabi, Ajman, Dubai, al-Fujairah, Sharjah and Umm al-Qaiwain—united as the United Arab Emirates. The seventh, Ras al-Khaimah, joined in 1972.

Nations—United Kingdom of Great Britain and Northern Ireland

The United Kingdom is comprised of England, Scotland, Wales and Northern Ireland. England became part of the Roman Empire in 43 A.D. The beginning of the end of Roman rule was around 407, when Constantine III was appointed emperor of Britain. He began to withdraw the last of the Romans stationed there.

• **End of Roman rule:** by 410, when the Romans were just about gone from England. After they left, England was invaded by others, including Angles, Saxons and Jutes.

• **Last Anglo-Saxon king:** Harold II, born c. 1020. He was killed on October 14, 1066, at the Battle of Hastings, following the Norman invasion led by William of Normandy (William the Conqueror). The Battle of Hastings ended Anglo-Saxon rule in England and established Norman rule.

• **Last successful invasion of Great Britain:** The Norman invasion led by William of Normandy (William the Conqueror) in 1066.

• **Last Norman king:** Stephen, who ruled from 1135 to 1154. He was replaced by Henry II, the first Plantagenet (or House of Anjou) king.

• **Last Plantagenet king:** Richard II. He was deposed by Parliament and imprisoned in 1399, and was probably murdered in prison the following year. The Plantagenets were replaced by Henry IV of the House of Lancaster.

• **Last monarch of the House of Lancaster:** Henry VI, who was deposed on March 4, 1461, when Edward, son of the Duke of York, claimed the throne as Edward IV.

• **Last monarch of the House of York:** Richard III, who was killed at the Battle of Bosworth Field in 1485. The House of Tudor followed, beginning with the reign of Henry VII. He ruled until 1509 then was succeeded by his son Henry VIII.

• **Last wife of Henry VIII:** Catherine Parr, who married Henry VIII on July 12, 1543. She was his sixth wife. Henry died on January 28, 1547, age 55. Catherine married Sir Thomas Seymour a few months later. She died during childbirth on September 7, 1548, age around 36.

• **Last Tudor ruler:** Queen Elizabeth I, only child of Henry VIII and Anne Boleyn. She died unmarried and with no heirs on March 24, 1603, age 69. The Tudors were followed by James I of the House of Stuart. His son Charles I was beheaded in 1649 and the monarchy was abolished. Oliver Cromwell declared England to be a Commonwealth, or republic. He became Lord Protector in December 1653 and died in September 1658.

• **End of the Commonwealth:** 1660. Richard Cromwell succeeded to his father Oliver's title of Lord Protector in September 1658. The Commonwealth fell apart and Richard resigned on May 24, 1659. The House of Stuart was restored when Charles II acceded to the throne on May 29, 1660.

• **Last male ruler in the direct Stuart line:** James II, who lost his throne on December 11, 1688, in the Glorious Revolution. He attempted to regain the throne but was halted by William of Orange at the Battle of the Boyne in July 1690. James II spent the rest of his life in France, where he died on September 6, 1701, age 67. His followers, the Jacobites, tried to regain the throne for him and his descendants for more than a century.

• **Last ground battle fought in Britain and last battle of the Jacobites:** the Battle of Culloden Moor, near Inverness, Scotland, fought on April 16, 1746. The Jacobites were defeated by the Duke of Cumberland. After James II died, the Jacobites supported his son James III (Prince James Francis Edward Stuart)—known as the Old Pretender—as the rightful claimant to the throne. When James III died in 1766, he was succeeded by his son Charles Edward (the Young Pretender). When Charles died in 1788, he left no legitimate heirs. The succession passed to his brother Henry, Duke of York, who was a Catholic cardinal in Italy.

• **Last of the Jacobite pretenders:** Henry Benedict Maria Clement Stuart (Henry, Duke of York), who died in Frascati, Italy, on July 13, 1807, age 82. He was the last of the direct male line of James II and the last to try to claim the throne.

• **Last Stuart ruler:** Queen Anne, the daughter of James II. She had many children, but only one—William, Duke of Gloucester—survived infancy. William died in 1700, when he was 10 years old. When Anne died on August 1, 1714, age 49, without leaving an heir, the House of Hanover took the throne.

• **Last monarch of the House of Hanover:** Queen Victoria, who died on the Isle of Wight on January 22, 1901, age 81. She reigned for 63 years, 7 months and 2 days, the longest of any British monarch to that time. She was succeeded as monarch by her son Edward VII.

• **Last surviving son of Queen Victoria:** Arthur, Duke of Connaught, who died on

January 12, 1942, age 91.

• **Last surviving child of Queen Victoria:** Beatrice Marie Victoria Fedora, Princess of Battenberg, who died on October 26, 1944, age 87.

• **Last surviving grandchild of Queen Victoria:** Princess Alice (Alice Mary Victoria Augusta Pauline, Countess of Athlone). She lived through six reigns, attended four coronations and rode in both the carriage procession for Queen Victoria's Diamond Jubilee in 1897 and the Silver Jubilee procession of Queen Elizabeth II in 1977. She died in London, England, on January 3, 1981, age 97.

• **Last British monarch to use the Saxe-Coburg name:** Edward VII, King of Great Britain and Ireland, who ruled from 1901 to May 6, 1910. He was also the first to use the Saxe-Coburg name. The name of the royal family was changed to Windsor by proclamation on July 17, 1917. Edward was succeeded by his son, who began his reign as George V on May 6, 1910.

• **End of the reign of King George V:** January 20, 1936. He was succeeded by his son Edward VIII.

• **End of the reign of King Edward VIII:** abdicated on December 11, 1936. He was crowned on January 20, 1936, but subsequently renounced the throne to marry Wallis Warfield Simpson, a commoner. He was succeeded by his brother, the Duke of York, who ruled as George VI. Edward, the Duke of Windsor, died on May 28, 1972, age 78.

• **End of the reign of King George VI:** February 6, 1952. He was succeeded by his daughter Elizabeth II.

• **Last use of the title Emperor or Empress of India:** June 22, 1947, when George VI issued a proclamation abandoning the title. The title Empress of India was first used by Victoria by a proclamation issued on May 1, 1876.

• **Last use of the name United Kingdom of Great Britain:** January 1, 1801, when Great Britain and Ireland were merged by Act of Union and renamed the United Kingdom of Great Britain and Ireland. (The name United

Kingdom of Great Britain had been given to England and Scotland in 1707 by the Act of Union. Wales had become part of England in 1536 by an earlier Act of Union.)

• **Last use of the name United Kingdom of Great Britain and Ireland:** April 1927, when a Parliamentary act provided that the name was to be changed to the United Kingdom of Great Britain and Northern Ireland. (*See also* Nations—Ireland.)

Nations—United States of America, *see* United States of America.

Nations—Uruguay, Eastern Republic of
Uruguay is between the nations of Argentina and Brazil in eastern South America, bordering the Rio de la Plata and Atlantic Ocean. The first outsiders were the Spanish who visited the area in 1516. Spain established a major colony in Montevideo, Uruguay, in 1726, and incorporated the territory of Uruguay into the Viceroyalty of the Rio de la Plata in 1777. Uruguay's war of independence from Spain began in 1811.

• **End of Spanish rule:** June 1814, when a Spanish fleet was defeated and Uruguayan liberator General José Artigas captured Montevideo. Portugal conquered the country in 1817. In 1821, Uruguay was annexed to Brazil by Portugal.

• **End of Brazilian rule:** August 25, 1825, Uruguay declared its independence from Brazil and became part of the United Provinces of the Rio de la Plata as the State of Montevideo.

• **End of membership in the United Provinces of the Rio de la Plata:** December 1, 1828, when it seceded as the State of Montevideo. On July 18, 1830, the Eastern Republic of Uruguay was established. (*See also* Wars and Battles—Triple Alliance, War of the.)

Nations—Uzbekistan, Republic of
Uzbekistan is in northwestern central Asia, north of Turkmenistan. It was once part of the Persian Empire. The land was later conquered by Alexander the Great and Genghis Khan. It became part of the USSR as the

Uzbek Soviet Socialist Republic in 1924.
• **End of the Uzbek Soviet Socialist Republic:** August 31, 1991, when the nation declared its independence as the Republic of Uzbekistan. Independence became effective in December 1991, when the USSR was dissolved.

Nations—Vanuatu, Republic of
Vanuatu is an archipelago between Fiji and New Caledonia in the southern Pacific. A Spanish expedition saw the islands in 1606, but did not settle there. British explorer James Cook arrived in 1774 and named them New Hebrides. After the Britain established a protectorate in 1824, the French also sent traders, missionaries and planters. In 1887, a joint Anglo-French protectorate was established. The New Hebrides Condominium was created in 1906.
• **Last of the New Hebrides Condominium:** July 30, 1980, when it gained its independence as the Republic of Vanuatu.

Nations—Vatican, State of the (Vatican City)
The State of the Vatican covers about 108 acres within the city of Rome, Italy. The early history of the Vatican is tied with the Papal States, lands in central Italy over which the popes traditionally have exercised temporal authority.
• **End of the Papal States:** September 20, 1870, when the Italian Army occupied Rome and annexed the Papal States. The Law of Papal Guarantees, enacted by the Italian parliament on May 13, 1871, granted the pope free use of the Vatican and the Lateran palaces. From 1871 until 1929, the sovereignty of Vatican City was in dispute.
• **End of the dispute on the sovereignty of the Vatican:** February 11, 1929, with the Lateran Treaty. The dispute ended when the independent State of the Vatican, headed by the pope, was recognized by the treaty.
• **End of the Lateran Treaty:** June 3, 1985, when a concordat, or church-state treaty, was signed replacing the 1929 document. The concordat reaffirmed the independence of the Vatican but ended the status of the Roman Catholic Church as the state religion of Italy.
• **Last time Rome had Sacred City status:** June 3, 1985, when it ended as part of the concordat that replaced the Lateran Treaty of 1929.
• **Last of the Papal Military Corps:** September 14, 1970, when Pope Paul VI disbanded all military units but the Swiss Guards. The internal security of the Vatican City is provided by the Gendarmerie of the State of Vatican City and the Pontifical Swiss Guard. (*See also* Religion—Roman Catholicism.)

Nations—Venezuela, Republic of
Venezuela occupies a large portion of the northern coast of South America along the Caribbean Sea. It was visited by Columbus on his third voyage in 1498. The first Spanish settlement was in 1499. The German House of Welser sent settlers to establish a colony in Venezuela in the 1520s.
• **End of German colonialism:** 1556, when, the contract of the German House of Welser was terminated. The settlers left and the colony reverted to Spanish control. The second Spanish settlement began in 1567.
• **End of Spanish control:** July 5, 1811, when a congress convoked by a junta declared Venezuelan independence from Spain. The December 1811 constitution was the official beginning of Venezuela's First Republic. In 1819, Simon Bolivar proclaimed the Gran Colombia Confederation. The union included Venezuela, Colombia, Ecuador and Panama.
• **Last time Venezuela was part of the Gran Colombia Confederation:** 1830, when Venezuela withdrew to become a separate nation.

Nations—Vietnam, Socialist Republic of
Vietnam is in southeastern Asia, surrounded by Laos, China, Cambodia and the South China Sea. It saw numerous invasions over the centuries, most notably by the Chinese and the Mongols. The French began seizing parts of Vietnam in the mid-1800s and occupied all of it by 1884. (French holdings Southeast Asia were known as French Indochina.)

• **End of French control:** March 9, 1945, when Japanese troops occupied the country during World War II. After the Japanese left and the war ended, Vietnam's empire ended and the country was divided into north and south. (*See* Wars and Battles—Indochina War.)

• **Last emperor of the Empire of Viet Nam:** Bao Dai (Nguyen Vinh Thuy), who abdicated on August 25, 1945. He died in Paris, France, on July 31, 1997, age 83. On August 1, 1954, when the Indochina War ended, the Geneva Accords formally partitioned the country into North Vietnam (Democratic Republic of Vietnam) and South Vietnam (Republic of Vietnam) at the 17th parallel. Political conflict between North and South escalated into a full-scale war in the 1960s. (*See* Wars and Battles—Vietnam War.)

• **End of North and South Vietnam:** July 2, 1976, when North Vietnam and South Vietnam were officially unified as the Socialist Republic of Vietnam.

• **Last time Ho Chi Minh City was known as Saigon:** 1976. It was officially renamed with the proclamation that unified the Socialist Republic of Vietnam. Unofficially, the city was renamed after the fall of South Vietnam in 1975.

• **End of U.S. travel ban to Vietnam:** December 1991.

• **End of U.S. trade embargo:** February 3, 1994. It was lifted by President William Jefferson Clinton.

Nations—Yemen, Republic of
The nation on the southwestern corner of the Arabian Peninsula that is the Republic of Yemen was two separate nations until 1990: Yemen Arab Republic (North Yemen) and People's Republic of Southern Yemen (South Yemen). North Yemen has been autonomous since the early 20th century. South Yemen is made up of the city of Aden, and several surrounding sheikdoms, sultanates and emirates that formed the Federation of South Arabia.

• **End of the Federation of South Arabia:** November 28, 1967, when it gained independence as the People's Republic of Southern Yemen.

• **End of the People's Republic of Southern Yemen:** November 30, 1970, when the country became the People's Democratic Republic of Yemen.

• **Last king or imam of the Yemen Arab Republic (North Yemen):** Crown Prince Muhammad al-Badr, who held the post from September 19, 1962, to September 27, 1962. The monarchy was replaced and a republic was declared.

• **Last president of the Yemen Arab Republic (North Yemen):** Colonel Ali Abdullah Saleh, who held the post from July 17, 1978, to May 22, 1990.

• **Last prime minister of the Yemen Arab Republic (North Yemen):** Abdul Aziz Abdel Ghani, who served his second term from November 13, 1983, to May 22, 1990.

• **Last prime minister of the People's Democratic Republic of Yemen (South Yemen):** Yasin Said Numan, who held the position from February 8, 1986, to May 22, 1990.

• **End of the People's Democratic Republic of Yemen (South Yemen) and Yemen Arab Republic (North Yemen):** May 22, 1990, the two nations merged to form the Republic of Yemen.

• **Last chairman of the Presidium of the Supreme People's Council of the People's Democratic Republic of Yemen (South Yemen):** Haidar Abu Bakr al-Attas, who served as chairman from January 1986 to May 22, 1990. After unification, he became the prime minister of the Republic of Yemen.

Nations—Yugoslavia, Federal Republic of, *see* Serbia and Montenegro.

Nations—Zambia
Zambia is east of Angola in south-central Africa . The Portuguese explored part of the country in 1514. After David Livingston of Scotland came across Victoria Falls in 1855, the British began to colonize the region. Cecil Rhodes was given a charter for the British South Africa Company in 1889. The Rhodesian Protectorate was established in

1895. In 1911, it was divided into Northern and Southern Rhodesia. The Federation of Rhodesia and Nyasaland was formed in 1953, linking Southern Rhodesia (now part of Zimbabwe), Northern Rhodesia and Nyasaland (now Malawi).
• **End of the Federation of Rhodesia and Nyasaland:** December 31, 1963. In January 1964, Northern Rhodesia gained self-rule.
• **End of Northern Rhodesia:** October 24, 1964, when it became independent as the Republic of Zambia. Southern Rhodesia remained a British colony. (*See also* Nations—Zimbabwe.)

Nations—Zimbabwe, Republic of

Zimbabwe is in south-central Africa, east of Botswana. As Southern Rhodesia, it became a British colony in 1923, when Great Britain took control of the region from the British South Africa Company. The Federation of Rhodesia and Nyasaland was formed in 1953, linking Southern Rhodesia, Northern Rhodesia (now Zambia) and Nyasaland (now Malawi).
• **End of the Federation of Rhodesia and Nyasaland:** December 31, 1963. Northern Rhodesia and Nyasaland gained independence as Zambia and Malawi.
• **Last known as Southern Rhodesia:** Renamed Rhodesia after Northern Rhodesia and Nyasaland gained their independence in December 1963. Rhodesia declared its independence, but the British did not recognize it. In June 1979, the interim state of Zimbabwe Rhodesia was created.
• **Last of Zimbabwe Rhodesia:** September 2, 1979, when "Rhodesia" was dropped from the country's name and a new flag was adopted. On April 17, 1980, the country gained its independence from Great Britain as Zimbabwe.

Native Americans

The following "lasts" are documented last North American native speakers of distinct languages, last full-blooded members of tribes that are considered "extinct" and other significant lasts relating to the tribe's history. (*See also* Wars and Battles—World Wars I and II—Code Talkers.)

Adai
The Adai once lived in what is now Natchitoches Parish, Louisiana. They had contact with Europeans as early as 1699. By 1778, the tribe was almost extinct; however a small settlement was reported in 1805. In 1825, the population had dwindled to about 27. • **Last of the Adai:** Lost their identity and their language became extinct when the last of them merged with the southern Caddoans around 1830.
Atakapa
The Atakapa (a.k.a. Attakapa, Attacapa) lived in the bayou and coastal areas of southwestern Louisiana and southeastern Texas until the early 1800s. They were devastated by European diseases. Their population, estimated at about 3,500 in 1698, dropped to 175 in 1805. By 1908, only nine known descendants survived. The Atakapa language is among the better-recorded Native American languages. The Smithsonian Institution published *A Dictionary of the Atakapa Language* in 1932. • **Last Atakapa speaker:** documented around 1935. The language is now extinct but a number of descendants today claim Atakapa heritage.
Beothuk
The Beothuk, a group of Algonquian-speaking hunter-gatherers, were the original inhabitants of Newfoundland. They probably numbered less than 1,000 at the time of European contact. Their population was greatly diminished by invading French and English and the Micmac Indians. The Beothuk numbered about 450 by 1768 and 72 by 1814. By 1823, only a few were left. • **Last of the Beothuk:** Shanawdithit, or Nancy April, and her mother and sister, who sur-

rendered to trappers in 1823. Her mother and sister died a short time later. Shanawdithit died from tuberculosis in Saint John's, Newfoundland, on June 6, 1829.

Biloxi

The Biloxi Indians (a.k.a. Baluxa, Beluxi, Bilocchi, Bolixe) were first recorded living near present Biloxi, in southern Mississippi. Around 1763, some of the Biloxis moved to western Louisiana and later to Texas. Some also lived with the Choctaws and Creeks in Indian Territory (now Oklahoma). Their language is now extinct.

• **Last Biloxi camp:** 1846, on Little River in Bell County, Texas.

Cahuilla

The Cahuilla live around the Sonoran and Mohave deserts in southern California. Some are on the Morongo Reservation at the foot of San Gorgonio Pass, near Banning. They were once designated as Pass, Mountain and Desert Cahuilla. Today, no one speaks Pass Cahuilla. Only five or so Mountain Cahuilla speakers are left, and most are in their 70s. Perhaps a dozen Desert Cahuilla remain, but only one, an octogenarian, is fully fluent in the Cahuilla language.

• **Last fluent speaker of Cahuilla on the Morongo Reservation:** Katherine Silva Saubel, a Native American activist and scholar who has been working for more than a half century to preserve her native language.

Calapooya (Kalapuya)

The Calapooya or Kalapuya (a.k.a. Santiam, Lukamiute, Wapatu) lived around the headwaters of the Willamette River in Oregon. In 1855, a treaty ceded all of their land to the United States, and the remaining Calapooya were removed to the Grand Ronde Reservation.

• **Last full-blooded Calapooya:** Eliza, who died in 1922 at age 115.

• **Last known native speaker of Kalapuya:** John Hudson, a Santiam Kalapuya who once lived on the Grand Ronde Reservation. He was a translator for linguist Melville Jacobs, who interviewed him in detail about Kalapuya ways in 1928.

Calusa

The Calusa lived from Tampa Bay to the Florida Keys in southwestern Florida. They were among the first Indians the Spanish encountered in North America. Diseases such as measles and smallpox, introduced by the Spanish and French, wiped out entire villages.

• **Last of the Calusa:** One source writing in 1775 mentioned that the last of the Calusa emigrated to Cuba in 1763, when Spain ceded Florida to England. Some researchers disagree that they were true Calusans. They believe the Calusa remained in Florida until the 1800s, after which nothing is known about them. They are now extinct.

Catawba

The Catawba, a southeastern Siouan tribe, probably numbered around 4,400 when they first had contact with European outsiders. Like other tribes, their numbers were reduced by smallpox. Today, several hundreds of people of Catawba descent live mostly in South Carolina but do not speak their native language.

• **Last full-blooded Catawba:** Robert Lee Harris, who died in 1954. He was chief of the Catawba Nation in 1895 and 1939-40.

• **Last fluent speaker of Catawba:** When Red Thunder Cloud (Cromwell Ashbie Hawkins West, a.k.a. Carlos Westez) died in January 1996, age 76, he was described as the last fluent speaker of Catawba. However, when Red Thunder Cloud died, Chief Gilbert Blue of the Catawba Reservation in Rock Hill, South Carolina, announced he was still speaking Catawba and several others also knew the language.

Cayuse

The Cayuse once lived in the Blue Mountain region of northeastern Oregon and in parts of Washington. They were probably the first North American Indians to domesticate the bronco, which is often called the Cayuse, or Indian pony. By 1830, younger Cayuse could no longer speak their language. Many of the tribe died during a smallpox epidemic in 1847. In 1888, ethnologist Henry Henshaw made a Cayuse word list, He believed only six people remained who spoke the language. The Cayuse adopted the Nez Percé language when theirs died out.

• **Last two Cayuse speakers:** believed to have died in the 1940s. Remnants of the Cayuse live on the Umatilla Reservation in Oregon and have intermarried with other tribes. In 1990, 126 people claimed Cayuse descent.

Chetco

The Chetco lived near the mouth of the Chetco River in Oregon. They were sent to the Siletz Reservation after the Indian uprisings of the mid-1850s. By 1910, their numbers had dwindled to nine.

• **Last of the Chetcos:** believed to be Lucy Dick, daughter of the chief of the tribe. She was born between 1841 and 1847 and died in 1940. Her Indian name was lost after she moved to the Siletz Reservation and was renamed by whites.

Chickasaw

The Chickasaw were living in the Mississippi Valley when the Spanish began exploring the region in 1540. They were known as one of the Five Civilized Tribes, along with the Choctaw, Cherokee, Creek and Seminole. In the mid-19th century, the Chickasaw were resettled in Indian Territory (now Oklahoma).

• **Last chief from when the Chickasaw lived in the Southeast:** Tishomingo, who died around 1838, when his group was moving from the Mississippi Valley to Indian Territory.

Chippewa (Ojibwa)

Early explorers and settlers had difficulty pronouncing the name Ojibwa, so they simplified it to Chippewa. The Ojibwa/Chippewa lived in the Midwest and spoke an Algonquian language.

• **Last full-blooded Chippewa:** Victoria Cadaract, who died on March 23, 1915. She was the last of the Chippewa tribe and may have been the last surviving full-blooded Native American in northwestern Ohio.

Chumash

The Chumash lived along the coast of California from San Luis Obispo to Ventura and on the offshore islands of Santa Barbara Channel. They may have numbered 15,000 before the Spanish missions were established in the 1770s. The Chumash were greatly reduced through intermarriage and disease. Only 50 descendants of mixed blood remained on the Santa Ynez Reservation in 1972. The Chumash language had numerous dialects including Obispeño, Ineseño, Purisimeño, Barbareño, Ventureño, Canaliño and Isleño (Island Chumash).

• **Last speaker of Obispeño Chumash:** Mrs. Rosario Cooper of Arroyo Grande, California.

• **Last native Chumash speaker of any dialect:** Mary Yee, who spoke the Barbareño dialect. She died in 1965.

• **Last Chumash island governor:** Maria Leqte, who was born c. 1783 and was living in 1852, when a census was taken.

• **Last traditional Chumash fiesta:** recorded in 1869.

• **Last original Chumash tomols (boats) used for fishing:** made about 1850. In 1913, Fernando Librado made a tomol replica for linguist/ethnographer John P. Harrington to show how they were constructed. This boat is now on exhibit in the Santa Barbara Museum of Natural History.

• **Last of the Chumash weavers:** died around 1915. The Chumash were known for their basketry. Petra Pamishkimait, a well-known basketmaker, was one of the last traditional Chumash weavers selling baskets to American tourists at the Ventura mission site.

• **Last intact Chumash village site:** Humaliwu in Malibu, California. It also contains burial sites. The land has been continuously used by the Chumash for several thousand years.
• **Last full-blooded Chumash medicine man:** Semu Huaute, who was born around 1908.
• **Last full-blooded Canaliño Chumash:** Tomas Ygnacio Aquino (1871-1952), who is buried in the mausoleum at Santa Barbara Cemetery, in Santa Barbara, California. His inscription identifies him as the "Last Canaliño Indian."

Comanche

The Comanches lived entirely on the Southwestern Plains of the United States. Their language is so similar to the Shoshone that some ethnologists believe the two groups were once part of the same tribe. The Comanches were the last of the Plains tribes to be placed on a reservation. Between 9,000 and 12,000 Comanches are living today. Many are farmers and ranchers in Oklahoma.
• **Last Comanche chief:** Chief Quanah Parker, who was the son of Chief Peta Nocona and Cynthia Ann Parker, a white captive. Parker was in his 60s when he died near Fort Sill, Oklahoma, on February 22, 1911.

Coos (Kusan)

The Coos (a.k.a. Kus, Kusan) lived along the Oregon coast between the Coos and Coquille rivers. The northern group (Hanis) lived around the Coos River. The southern group (Miluk) settled around the Coquille. The Coos numbered about 2,000 in 1780 but had dwindled to 93 when the 1910 federal census was taken. Today, about 300 people claim Coos ancestry, but the Coos language is extinct.
• **Last Coos speaker:** believed to have died in 1976.

Delaware (Lenni-Lenape)

The Delaware Indians (a.k.a. Lenape, Lenni-Lenape), originally lived in the Delaware and Hudson River valleys between Delaware and New York. Displaced by European settlers, they moved westward and eventually settled in Oklahoma, where several thousand descendants live today.
• **Last fluent speaker of the language of the Western Delaware tribe:** Bessie Snake, who was 104 when she died in 1999. Two nonagenarian members of the Eastern Delaware Tribe still speak the language.
• **Last Lenape in New Jersey:** Ann Roberts, known as Indian Ann. She lived at the Indian reservation in Indian Mills, New Jersey, where she died in 1894, age 90.

Dena'ina (Tanaina)

Dena'ina (Tanaina) is an Athabascan language with four dialects spoken around Cook Inlet on the Kenai Peninsula of Alaska.
• **Last fluent native speaker of Dena'ina:** Peter Kalifornsky, who lived in the village of Kalifornsky, Alaska. He was the last person born in the village and the last one buried there. He spent the last two decades of his life preserving his native tongue. With the help of a linguist, he worked out a written form of the language and then became its first author. Kalifornsky wrote several books about his tribe's traditions, legends and recollections. He also taught the Dena'ina language to the people of his region. Kalifornsky died in June 1993, age 81.
• **Last speaker of Dena'ina in the Eklutna/Matanuska area:** Shem Pete of Susitna Station Alaska, a colorful raconteur who was in his 90s when he died in 1989. His recollections have been published in the book *Shem Pete's Alaska.*

Esselen

The Esselen lived in southern and central California. Their numbers were greatly reduced after they were forced to live and work on a mission in the 1770s. Many died in measles and diphtheria epidemics in the early 19th century. The few who survived were indentured to Mexican landowners. The Esselen culture is now extinct, but some descendants remain in California.

• **Last native Esselen speaker:** Isabel Meadows, who died in 1939 at around age 93. She referred to her people and her language as "Carmeleño."

Eyak

The Eyak lived on the southern coast of Alaska between Prince William Sound and the mouth of the Copper River. Their numbers were greatly reduced beginning in the 1890s, when canneries built on the Copper River Delta took away their livelihood. Soon after that, a railroad was built atop of the last major Eyak village site in Cordova. The Eyak were so devastated by the 1918 Spanish influenza epidemic that their numbers dropped to about 50 by 1920. By the 1960s, only five speakers of the Eyak language were left in the villages of Yakutat and Cordova. A few descendants remain at Cordova.

• **Last full-blooded Eyak/last native speaker of the Eyak language:** Marie Smith Jones.

Hawaiian/'Ōlelo Hawai'I

In 1896, Hawaii's newly established, predominantly white provisional government banned the Hawaiian language, 'Ōlelo Hawai'I, from being taught in all private and public schools. Hawaiian could be taught only as a foreign language. By 1980, fewer than 2,000 native speakers remained, and of them, just a few dozen were under the age of 18.

• **Last year the Hawaiian language was banned in schools:** 1986, when the 90-year-old law was rescinded. In 1987, the first public-school Hawaiian-language immersion classes were established in the state.

Juaneño

The Juaneño were a Shoshonean tribe that lived between San Juan Creek and San Luis Rey River in the coastal region of southern California. They were missionized at San Juan Capistrano. When the missions were secularized in 1834, they merged with other groups as Mission Indians.

• **Last fluent speaker of the Juaneño language:** Anastacia de Majel, who recorded the language for linguist/ethnographer John P. Harrington in the mid-1930s. She died in 1938.

Kaw (Kansa)

The Kaw (a.k.a. Kansa, Kanza, Konza) lived in northeastern Kansas, northwestern Missouri and Iowa. They gave the state of Kansas its name. Their numbers were reduced by diseases such as smallpox. Although a Kaw Nation still exists, none of the 2,500 people on tribal rolls are full-blooded Kaw.

• **Last full-blooded Kaw:** William Mejojah ("Little Star"), who died in Omaha, Nebraska, on April 23, 2000, age 82.

• **Last remaining speaker of the Kaw language:** University of Kansas linguistics professor Robert Rankin, who has spent more than two decades compiling a dictionary and grammar of the Kaw language. He is computerizing the data with the hope that the tribe might be able to revive their language.

Kwaaymii

The Kwaaymii lived in the Laguna Mountains east of San Diego, California. Most died in the 1860 smallpox epidemic and the 1918 Spanish influenza epidemic.

• **Last full-blooded Kwaaymii:** Tom Lucas, who died in 1989, about age 86.

Maidu

The Maidu lived in north-central California. Like the other Native Americans in the state, they were dispossessed and reduced in numbers after the Gold Rush. Today, about 2,500 claim Maidu ancestry, but none speak the language fluently.

• **Last fluent speaker of Maidu:** Dr. William Shipley, who became interested in Maidu in his early days as a professor of linguistics at the University of California at Santa Cruz. He has compiled a Maidu dictionary and grammar and is endeavoring to rescue the nearly extinct language for future generations.

Makah

The Makah Nation is on the Olympic Peninsula in Washington State in the northwestern-most point of the contiguous United States

• **Last fully fluent speaker of the Makah language:** Tribal Elder and basketweaver Ruth E. Claphanhoo, who died at her home in Neah Bay, Washington, on August 21, 2002, age 100. She was also the oldest surviving member of her tribe.

Mandan

The ancestral homeland of the Mandan was along the Missouri River in what is now North Dakota. The Mandan were farmers who lived in small villages. Their population was approximately 15,000 before they were devastated by a smallpox epidemic in 1782. They had been reduced from nine to only two villages by the time Lewis and Clark encountered them in 1804. The Mandan were hit with smallpox again in 1837. About 400 people of Mandan descent live on the Fort Berthold Reservation in North Dakota.

• **Last full-blooded Mandan:** Mattie Grinnell, who died in Twin Buttes, North Dakota, on January 6, 1975, age 108.

• **Last fluent speaker of the Mandan language:** Edwin Benson (Ma-doke-wa-des-she, or Iron Bison), who teaches the Mandan language.

Miami

The Miami lived in central Indiana. During the 18th century, they were reduced to three small tribes: Wea, Piankashaw and Miami. Throughout the 19th century, they were reduced even more. Between 1832 and 1840, the Miami moved to reservations in Kansas, where the Wea and Piankashaw united as the Peoria. The Peoria and the Miami moved to Oklahoma in 1867.

• **Last Piankashaw village:** along the Wabash River a few miles west of Owensville, Indiana. It was destroyed by white settlers in 1807, and the Piankashaw fled to the other side of the river.

• **Last Miami chief before the Miami were removed from Indiana:** Francis La Fontaine, for whom the town of La Fontaine, Indiana, was named. The town is on the site of the Miami Indian Reservation.

• **Last full-blooded Piankashaw:** George Washington Finley, who died in 1932, age around 74. He was raised as a Peoria and was one of the last native speakers of the Peoria language.

• **Last fluent speaker of the Miami language:** Ross Bundy, who died in 1964. His knowledge of the Miami language was so important that the Smithsonian Institution asked him to travel to Washington, D.C., and record it. But unfortunately he was too ill to make the trip and a recording was never made. With his death, the language almost became extinct, but recently it is being revived.

Miwok

The Coast Miwok were a small group within the Miwok tribe who lived in central California. They disappeared or were absorbed into Spanish culture. Only a few survived into the 20th century.

• **Last fluent speaker of the Bodega dialect of the Coast Miwok:** Mrs. Sarah Ballard, who worked with linguists to document her language in the 1960s and early 1970s.

• **Last surviving legitimate Miwok:** Rhonda Pope, who in 1995 documented her claim, based upon a 1928 court order filed by her great-grandfather Louis Oliver. In the 1928 case, Oliver won tribal recognition for himself and his family in federal court.

Mohegan-Pequot

Mohegan-Pequot was an eastern Algonquian language spoken originally along the Thames River in southeastern Connecticut. The Mohegans began to lose their language after their first contact with white settlers. In the 1700s, missionaries wanted it banned. Other laws prohibited teaching it in schools. By the mid-1800s, Mohegans spoke mostly English. Mo-

hegan children who did not learn English were taken away from their families and raised by white settlers.
• **Last speaker of the Mohegan-Pequot language:** Fidelia Hoscott Fielding of Mohegan, Connecticut, who died in 1908, age around 81. She learned the language from her grandmother, Martha Uncas, a traditional elder who raised her and taught her the ways of the Mohegans.
• **Last full-blooded Mohegans:** Medicine Woman Gladys Tantaquidgeon, who was 101 in 2000, and her sister Ruth Tantaquidgeon, who was ten years younger. The sisters helped the Mohegan tribe gain federal recognition in 1994.

Montauk
The Montauk tribe lived on the eastern tip of Long Island, New York. In 1660, they sold the last of their lands to a group of settlers.
• **Last chief of the Montauk Indians:** John Hannibal (a.k.a. "King Pharoah"), who died on June 16, 1894, age 87. The Pharaoh Museum on Montauk Highway in Montauk, New York, has family artifacts from the last of the Montauk tribe.

Musqueam
The Musqueam lived in what is now the greater Vancouver area of British Columbia.
• **Last fluent speaker of Musqueam:** Adeline Point. She spent the last few years of her life working with University of British Columbia linguists to preserve her dialect. She died on the Musqueam Indian Reserve in South Vancouver on August 6, 2002, age 92.

Mutsun
The Mutsun lived near San Juan Bautista and in the San Juan Valley in central California. The Mutsun language was one of eight Ohlone dialects. (*See* Native Americans—Ohlone).
• **Last fluent Mutsun speaker and last full-blooded Mutsun:** Ascension Solorsano Cervantes, who died in 1930. She worked closely with linguist/ethnographer John P. Harrington to document her language. An herbalist, she explained the many ways her people had used native plants. Although the Mutsun language died out in the 1930s, it is being revived today by people of Mutsun descent.

Nanticoke
The Nanticoke Indians once lived on land that is now Maryland and Delaware. The last villages and reservations on the Delmarva peninsula were uprooted during the 1740s. The people from Delmarva were relocated in the North and West. Some families remained and were assimilated into the white community.
• **Last speaker of Nanticoke:** Mrs. Lydia Clark, who died between 1840 and 1850 (or in 1856).

Natchez
The Natchez once lived around Natchez, Mississippi and were the largest and most powerful of the Lower Mississippi Indian groups. They may have numbered 4,000. After they lost a war with the French in 1730, they were forced to disperse. Many were sent as slaves to Santo Domingo. Others fled and joined the Cherokee, Creek and Chickasaw. Those who lived with the Creeks settled not far from Eufaula, Oklahoma.
• **Last speaker of the old Natchez language:** Alkini, an elderly woman who lived with the Creeks. She died about 1890. The Cherokee Natchez preserved their language longer.
• **Last speaker of Natchez:** died in the 1970s. His grandchildren grew up among the Cherokee and spoke some Cherokee, but mostly they spoke English.

Nooksack
The Nooksack lived in northwestern Washington. In 1855, they were forced to move to the Lummi Reservation.
• **Last fluent speaker of Nooksack:** Sindick Jimmy, who died in 1977. By the 1980s, just a few people knew less than 40 words. But recently Nooksack has been revived in language classes with the hope that students will soon be fluent.

Ohlone

The name Ohlone is used to describe the California Indians of the San Francisco Bay area and inland around 60 miles. They numbered perhaps 7,000 in 1750 but were drastically affected by the changes introduced by the Spanish, as well as by diseases brought by the Europeans. By 1832, the Ohlone numbered about 2,000. Many of them merged with other Native Americans and Mexicans throughout the 19th century. However, about 150 greatly mixed descendants survive.
• **Last known Ohlone tribal dance:** held in Alisal, California, in 1897. Alisal stood on what was then property of William R. Hearst.
• **Last Ohlone sweat house:** torn down in 1900 and not rebuilt.
• **Last speaker who had a significant grasp of an Ohlone language:** died in the 1930s. Ohlone has been extinct since the 1950s.

Omaha

The Omaha, who live in northeastern Nebraska, are part of the Sioux family.
• **Last full-blooded Omaha chief:** Big Elk, who died in 1846 and is buried in Belleville, Nebraska. He traveled to Washington, D.C., during the administration of President James J.K. Polk. A portrait of Big Elk was painted by American artist George Catlin during that visit.

Otoe-Missouria

The Otoe and Missouria lived in northeast Kansas, Missouri, Iowa and Nebraska before the white settlers displaced them. The Missouria were absorbed by the Otoe in the 1850s.
• **Last fluent speaker of Otoe-Missouria:** Truman Washington Dailey, who died on December 16, 1996, age 98. About six semi-fluent speakers remain, and all were born 50 or more years ago.

Ozette

The Ozette were a subgroup of the Makah that lived around the mouth of the Ozette River in Washington. By 1872, about 200 were left. A reservation was set up for them at Cape Alava in 1893.
• **Last of the Ozette:** only one person remained by 1937.

Pawtuxet

The Pawtuxet lived in Massachusetts and Rhode Island and were part of a larger group called the Wampanoag.
• **Last of the Pawtuxet:** Squanto, who was kidnapped in 1615 and taken to Europe. He spent two years England, where he learned the English language. When he returned to his Pawtuxet village in 1619, he found no survivors. Every one of the Pawtuxets had died in a smallpox epidemic while he was away. Over the next few years, Squanto acted as a guide and interpreter for the Pilgrims and taught them how to plant and find food. He contracted smallpox and died in 1622.

Penobscot

The Penobscot were the principal tribe of the Wabanaki (Eastern) Confederacy of Maine, They have kept their name, territory and tribal identity. Most of the 3,000 Penobscots living today are still in Maine.
• **Last native Penobscot speaker:** renowned basketmaker Madeline Tomer Shay. After her death in 1993, medical pathologist and ethnolinguist Dr. Frank T. Siebert Jr. became the only living person who knew the language well. He developed a transcription system for Penobscot and compiled a dictionary of the language. He died in Bangor, Maine, in 1998 at age 85. Efforts are now underway in the Penobscot Nation to revive the language.

Pequaket

The Pequaket were a subgroup of the Algonquians of central Maine. They were friendly to the French and hostile to the English, and that caused them to be nearly eradicated by the late 17th century. Their survivors settled in French Canada.

• **Last of the Pequakets:** Molly Ockett (Mollocket), who died in 1816 in Andover, Maine. The inscription on her gravestone identified her as the "last of the Pequakets." The book *A Walk With Molly Ockett* was written about her life.

Pomo

At one time, the Pomo people spoke seven languages, including Southern, Central, Northern, Eastern, Northeastern, Southeastern and Southwestern Pomo (Kashaya). The Northern Pomo language was native to Sonoma and Mendocino counties in northern California.
• **Last Northern Pomo speaker:** a woman in her late 80s who died in January 1995, while she was teaching her language to a younger member of the tribe. The Northern Pomo language is now extinct.

Poosepatuck

The Poosepatuck are part of the Unkechaug, one of the tribes that were living on Long Island, New York, when the white settlers arrived. The early Poosepatuck lived near Mastic on the east side of the island, overlooking the bay, and were called the Beach Indians.
• **Last surviving full-blooded Poosepatuck:** Aunt Martha Mayne. When she died, she was described, and had been previously honored, as the "last full-blooded Poosepatuck Indian." She died in Mystic, Long Island, New York on July 7, 1933, age 98.

Powhatan

Powhatan was the language of Pocahontas. Today several thousand people living in Virginia claim Powhatan descent, but the language is extinct.
• **Last Powhatan speaker:** alive in 1907. The speaker gave some words in the Nansemond dialect to a linguist.

Quinault

Quinault was Salish Indian language spoken in western Washington. Several elders know some parts of the language and the culture.
• **Last speaker with an extensive knowledge of Quinault:** Oliver Mason, hereditary leader of the Quinault. He died on April 27, 1996.

Saponi and Tutelo

The Saponi lived in Virginia and North Carolina. As their numbers dwindled through wars with colonists and other tribes, they chose to migrate to survive. The Saponi and another tribe, the Tutelo, were reported to have gone north to join with their former enemy, the Iroquois. The American Revolution destroyed their settlement.
• **Last of the Saponi:** By 1763, only 30 Saponi were alive and scattered throughout northern Pennsylvania and New York. After 1780, the Saponi were extinct.
• **Last known surviving full-blooded Tutelo:** Nikonha, who was thought to be 106 years old when he died in 1871. A photograph was taken of him in Ontario in 1870.

Sinkyone

The Sinkyone lived mostly along the northwestern California coast about 140 miles north of San Francisco. They were dispossessed from their land and reduced in population by the California Gold Rush. They are no longer a distinct group.
• **Last full-blooded Sinkyone who lived on the Lost Coast:** believed to be Sally Bell, who saw her family massacred by U.S. troops. The Sally Bell Grove, one of the last surviving old-growth redwood groves on the Lost Coast of California, was named for her. (The Lost Coast is an extremely rocky and steep section of the shoreline in Humboldt County where the highway turns inland, leaving the coast untouched.)

Sioux (Lakota, Dakota, Nakota)

The Sioux Nation is made up of three tribes: Lakota, Dakota and Nakota. The Dakota division is also known as the Santee Sioux. The Nakota are also known as the Yankton Sioux.
• **Last Sioux chief to reside in Iowa Territory:** Chief War Eagle (tribal name Wambdi Okicize), a Santee Sioux who was elected chief of the Yankton Sioux. War Eagle was a

courier and interpreter for the U.S. Army and later was scout for fur trader John Jacob Astor's American Fur Company. He died in Iowa in 1851, around age 74.

Siuslaw Alsean (Yankonan)

The Siuslaw Alsean or Yankonan lived around the Siuslaw River on the Oregon coast and included the Yaquina, Alsea, Siuslaw and Kuitsh. They may have numbered as many as 5,000 in 1780, before they began to die from smallpox, measles and other infectious diseases brought from the outside world. The last remnants of these groups were moved to the Siletz Reservation in Oregon. In 1910, only 29 Alsea, 19 Yaquina, and 7 Siuslaw were identified. By 1930, only nine Kuitsh remained. They were later grouped into the "Confederated Siletz Indians of Oregon."
• **Last full-blooded member of the Kuitsh and Siuslaw:** Marge Severy of Florence, Oregon.
• **Last Siuslaw speakers:** the Barrett family and Billy Dick of Florence, Oregon.
• **Last Alsea speaker:** John Albert, who was interviewed by linguist/ethnographer John P. Harrington in 1942.

Takelma

The Takelma lived in southwest Oregon and are now extinct.
• **Last fluent speaker of Takelma:** Frances Johnson, who worked with linguist Edward Sapir in 1906 and was the source of the material he incorporated into his Takelma grammar and texts. She was interviewed and recorded by linguist/ethnographer John P. Harrington in 1933 and 1934.

Tataviam

Tataviam was spoken by Native Americans who lived along the upper Santa Clara River beyond Piru in California. When the Spanish first made contact with the Tataviam, they numbered less than 1,000. In the 19th century, contagious diseases and marriage outside their group further diminished their population.
• **Last surviving Tataviam speaker:** Juan José Fustero, who died on June 30, 1921, near Rancho Camulos. He claimed to be the last full-blooded Tataviam; however, there may have been others. A newspaper article in the *Los Angeles Herald Examiner* in 1965 stated that Fustero was married to a full-blooded Tataviam and they had children.

Tillamook

The Tillamook lived along the Oregon coast from Nehalin to the Salmon River. Lewis and Clark first encountered the tribe in 1805. By the mid-19th century, the Tillamook had declined to about 200 people. By 1930, only 12 were left.
• **Last fluent Tillamook speaker:** Minnie Adams Scovell, who died in 1972.

Tualatin

The Tualatin lived along the Willamette River in Oregon. Many were killed by an epidemic in the 1830s. By 1890, only 28 remained on the Grand Ronde Reservation. The full-blooded Tualatin disappeared through death and intermarriage.
• **Last known native speaker of Tualatin:** Louis Kenoyer, who died in 1936.

Wampanoag

The Wampanoag once lived in eastern Massachusetts, Cape Cod, Nantucket and Martha's Vineyard and numbered about 12,000. Many on the mainland were killed by epidemics in the 1600s. About two thirds of those who lived on Martha's Vineyard were killed by fever in 1763. An unknown epidemic wiped out the Wampanoags on Nantucket by the mid-1800s.
• **Last Wampanoag on Nantucket:** died in 1855.
• **Last surviving member of the Nantucket tribe:** Abraham Quary, whose portrait was painted by Massachusetts artist Jerome Thompson in 1834.
• **Last native speaker of Wampanoag:** Chief Wild Horse, a Medicine Man. He recorded

the Lord's Prayer in his native language in New Bedford, Massachusetts, in 1961. Although about 3,000 claim Wampanoag descent, their Algonquian language became extinct. However, members of the tribe are working to revive it.

Wanapum

The Wanapum lived above the confluence of the Snake and Columbia rivers, a prime salmon-fishing area in what is now east-central Oregon. Lewis and Clark spent two days with them in 1805. About 60 members of the Wanapum tribe are now living in Washington State.
• **Last full-blooded Wanapum:** Tribal Elder Robert Tomanawash.

Wappo

The Wappo once lived in the Napa and Russian River valleys in northern California. They lived near Spanish missions and settlements, and many intermarried before white settlers from the east moved into the region. By 1910, only 73 Wappos remained. About 50 descendants survived by 1970.
• **Last speaker of Wappo:** well-known basketweaver Laura Somersal, who died in 1990.

Wiyot

The Wiyot lived on the northwest California coast between the Mad and Eel River estuaries. They had little or no contact with outsiders before 1850. At the time of their first significant encounter with whites, they numbered about 1,500 to 2,000. Their numbers dwindled quickly through disease, slavery and exploitation. In 1910, only 58 people were described as full-blooded Wiyot. They are all gone now; however, a sizable group of mixed descendants survives.
• **Last Wiyot speaker:** Mrs. Della Henry Prince, who died in 1962. Through conversations with her, the language was documented in the book *The Wiyot Language* (University of California Press, 1964). Some Wiyot tribe members are working to revive the language.

Wyandot

The Wyandot (a.k.a. Wandat, Wendat, Wyandotte, Guyandot) of Ohio and Indiana began their mandatory removal of the region in the 1840s. They settled first in Kansas then in Oklahoma.
• **Last Wyandot land in Ohio:** 12-square-mile area in Upper Sandusky, ceded to the United States by a treaty with the Wyandots on March 17, 1842.
• **Last Wyandot church service in Ohio:** July 9, 1843, conducted before the entire Wyandot Nation (664 members) at the mission church by Wyandot spiritual leader Square Grey Eyes. He opposed the removal of his people until the very last.
• **Last Wyandot in central Ohio:** Bill Moose, who died in 1937, age 100. His family moved to the Columbus. Ohio, area when most of his tribe was relocated to Kansas in 1843. His death marked the end of the Native Americans of that area. He is commemorated by a memorial in Columbus.

Yahi

The Yahi, a subgroup of the Yana Indians, once lived in northern California. Two massacres at Mill Creek in the 1860s all but eradicated them, and the survivors were thought to have died out not long afterward. In 1911, a middle-aged Indian later known as Ishi walked into the town of Oroville starving and alone. News of his appearance reached University of California anthropologists Alfred Kroeber and Thomas Waterman, who came to Oroville to learn more about Ishi and the Yahi. Kroeber took Ishi to San Francisco, where he lived in the Museum of Anthropology until his death from tuberculosis on March 25, 1916. Artifacts crafted by Ishi are housed at the museum (now at the Hearst Museum of Anthropology in Berkeley).
• **Last surviving Yahi:** Generations of California schoolchildren have been taught that Ishi was the last full-blooded Yahi, but he may actually have been of mixed blood. Steven

Shackley, research archaeologist at the University of California at Berkeley, observed that the arrowheads Ishi made were not Yahi but very possibly Nomlaki or Wintu. The many projectile points Ishi made while living at the museum had long blades, concave bases and side notches, whereas Yahi arrowheads are short and squat, with contracting stems and base notches.

Newspapers
Last of Some Major American Newspapers

Title	Last Issue	Description
American Weekly Mercury	May 22, 1746	Founded in 1719, in Philadelphia, Pennsylvania. First newspaper published in Pennsylvania and only the fourth in America.
Arkansas Gazette	October 18, 1991	Founded in 1865 as *Arkansas State Gazette*. Published as *Little Rock Daily Gazette* (1865-66), *Daily Arkansas Gazette* (1866-89), *Arkansas Gazette* (1889-1991).
Baltimore Evening Sun	September 15, 1995	*Evening Sun* founded on April 4, 1910. Ceased publication after 85 years. The *Morning Sun* began on May 17, 1837, and is still published as *The Sun*.
Baltimore News American	May 27, 1986	Created when the *Baltimore American* and *Baltimore News Post* merged in 1964.
Boston Evening Transcript	April 30, 1941	Founded in 1830 as *Daily Evening Transcript*. Other early names: *Boston Transcript* (1854-66) and *Boston Daily Evening Transcript* (1866-72). Issued as *Boston Evening Transcript* since 1872.
Brooklyn Daily Eagle (New York)	January 28, 1955	Founded 1841. Never missed an issue for 114 years then ceased publication after it experienced a prolonged strike.
Chicago Daily News	March 4, 1978	Founded in 1875. Absorbed by *Post & Mail* in 1878, *Journal* in 1929 and *Evening Post* in 1932.
Chicago Today	September 13, 1974	Founded as *Chicago American* in 1900. Published as *Herald American* (1939-58), *Chicago's American* (1958-69) and *Chicago Today* (1969-74).
Dallas Times Herald	December 9, 1991	*Dallas Daily Times* was founded in 1879. *Dallas Daily Herald* was first published in 1873. The two papers merged in 1888 as the *Dallas Times Herald*.
Elizabeth Daily Journal (New Jersey)	January 3, 1992	Founded in 1779. New Jersey's oldest newspaper and the nation's second oldest.
Evening News (Newark, New Jersey)	August 31, 1972	Founded in 1873. Once New Jersey's largest and most important newspaper. It closed shortly after an 11-month strike.

Indianapolis Times	October 11, 1965	Began as the *Indianapolis Sun* in 1878. Published as *Indianapolis Times* since 1924.
Los Angeles Herald Examiner	November 2, 1989	Weekly and daily *Los Angeles Herald* founded in 1873. Weekly folded in 1918. Daily was bought by Hearst in 1922. Merged with *Evening Express* in 1931. Merged with *Examiner* in 1962 as *Los Angeles Evening and Sunday Herald Examiner*. Merged with *Los Angeles Examiner* as *Los Angeles Herald Examiner* in 1977.
Louisville Times (Kentucky)	February 14, 1987	Founded 1884. Sold to Gannett in 1986, along with the *Courier-Journal*.
Massachusetts Gazette and Boston Weekly News-Letter	February 29, 1776	First continuously published newspaper in America. Founded in 1704 as *Boston News-Letter*. Other early names: *Weekly News-Letter* (1727-30), *Boston Weekly News-Letter* (1730-57), *Boston News-Letter* (1757-62), *Boston News-Letter and New-England Chronicle* (1762-63), *Massachusetts Gazette and Boston News-Letter* (1763-68), *Boston Weekly News-Letter* (1768- 69). Last title: *Massachusetts Gazette and Boston Weekly News-Letter* (1769-76).
Minneapolis Times	May 15, 1948	Founded 1889 as an evening paper.
National Intelligencer (Washington, D.C.)	December 31, 1869	Founded in October 1800 as *National Intelligencer and Washington Advertiser*. Renamed *National Intelligencer* in 1810.
New-York Gazette	November 19, 1744	Founded in 1725. New York's first newspaper.
New York Herald-Tribune	April 14, 1966	*New York Herald* was founded in 1835. *New York Tribune* was founded in 1841. Merged to form *New York Herald-New York Tribune* in 1924. Published as *New York Herald-Tribune* (1926-66). Merged with *New York Journal-American* and *New York World-Telegram & the Sun* in 1966 to form *New York World-Journal-Tribune*.
New York Journal-American	April 14, 1966	Founded as *New York Morning Journal and Advertiser* in 1882. Purchased by William Randolph Hearst in 1895 and renamed *New York Journal-American*. Merged with *New York World-Telegram & the Sun* and *New York Herald-Tribune* in 1966 to form *New York World-Journal-Tribune*.
New York Mirror	October 16, 1963	Published as *Daily Mirror* (1937-57) and *New York Mirror* (1957-63).
New York Sun (original)	January 4, 1950	Founded 1830. Purchased by *New York World-Telegram* in 1950 and renamed *New York World-Telegram & the Sun*.
New York Telegram	February 26, 1931	Founded as *Evening Telegram* in 1867. Renamed *New York Telegram and Evening*

		Mail in 1924 and *New York Telegram* in 1925. Merged with *New York World* as *New York World-Telegram* in 1931.
New York World	February 26, 1931	Founded in 1860. Purchased by Joseph Pulitzer in 1883. Sold to Scripps-Howard in 1930. Morning edition ceased and afternoon edition merged with *New York Telegram* as *New York World-Telegram* in 1931.
New York World-Journal-Tribune	May 5, 1967	Earlier names: *New York Tribune* (1841-42), *New York Daily Tribune* (1842-66), *New York Tribune* (1866-1924). Merged with *New York Herald* to form *New York Herald-New York Tribune* (1924-26). Published as *New York Herald-Tribune* (1926-66). Merged with *New York Journal-American* and *New York World-Telegram & the Sun* in 1966 to form *New York World-Journal-Tribune*. When it folded, it left New York City with just one evening newspaper.
New York World-Telegram	January 4, 1950	*New York World-Telegram* created in 1931 by a merger of *New York World* and *New York Telegram*. Renamed *New York World-Telegram & the Sun* in 1950, when owner purchased *New York Sun*.
New York World-Telegram & the Sun	April 14, 1966	Merged with *New York Journal-American* and *New York Herald-Tribune* in 1966 to form *New York World-Journal-Tribune*.
Oregon Journal	September 4, 1982	Published as *Oregon Daily Journal* from 1902 to 1972 and as *Oregon Journal* from 1972 to 1982.
Palm Beach Evening Times	May 1, 1987	Founded in 1922 as *Palm Beach Times,* an afternoon paper. Renamed *Evening Times* in 1979. *Palm Beach Post* and *Evening Times* merged into single newspaper, *Palm Beach Post,* in 1987.
Pennsylvania Gazette	October 11, 1815	Founded in 1728 as *The Universal Instructor in all Arts and Sciences* in Philadelphia, Pennsylvania. Renamed *Pennsylvania Gazette* and published by Benjamin Franklin from 1729 to 1766. Renamed *Pennsylvania Gazette, and Weekly Advertiser* in 1779 and *Pennsylvania Gazette* in 1782.
Philadelphia Evening and Sunday Bulletin	January 29, 1982	Founded in 1847 as *Cummings Telegraphic Evening Bulletin*. Renamed *Daily Evening Bulletin* in 1856 and *Evening Bulletin* in 1870. Renamed *Evening and Sunday Bulletin* after it purchased the *Philadelphia Record* in 1947.
Philadelphia Public Ledger	January 5, 1942	Founded in 1836. Merged with *North American* as *Public Ledger & North Ameri-*

		can in 1926. Merged with *Philadelphia Inquirer* in 1934. *Evening Public Ledger* ceased publication January 1942.
Philadelphia Record	January 31, 1947	Founded in 1870. Ceased publication when it was purchased by *Evening Bulletin*.
Pittsburgh Press	January 1993	Founded in 1884 as *Penny Press*. Renamed *Pittsburgh Press* in 1888. Ceased publication soon after it was sold to its rival, *Pittsburgh Post-Gazette*.
Saint Louis Globe-Democrat	October 31, 1986	Founded in 1843 as *Missouri Democrat*. Renamed *Saint Louis Democrat* in 1873. Merged with *Saint Louis Globe* in 1875.
United States Gazette (Philadelphia, Pennsylvania)	June 30, 1847	Founded as *Gazette of the United States and Daily Evening Advertiser* in 1794. Other early names: *Gazette of the United States* (1795-96), *Gazette of the United States and Philadelphia Daily Advertiser* (1796-1800), *Gazette of the United States and Daily Advertiser* (1800-01), *Gazette of the United States* (1801-04) and *United States Gazette* (1804-18). Merged with *True American* to form *United States Gazette and True American* (1818-23) and *United States Gazette* (1823-47). Merged with *North American* as *North American and United States Gazette*.
Washington Star (Washington, D.C.)	August 7, 1981	Earlier names: *Daily Evening Star* (1852-54); *Evening Star* (1854-1972); *Evening Star and the Washington Daily News*, formed by merger of *Evening Star* and *Washington Daily News* (1972-73). Renamed *Washington Star-News* (1973-75), *Washington Star and Daily News* (1975) and *Washington Star* (1975-81).

Phonographs and Tapes

Phonographs and Tapes—Cylinders

When Thomas A. Edison demonstrated his first workable phonograph in 1877, it was an elongated cylinder. The cylinder was difficult to duplicate and fragile to store. Emil Berlinger's disc, introduced in the 1890s, solved both problems. By the early 1900s, cylinders were on their way out and discs were in.

• **Last of the phonograph cylinders:** 1929. Columbia stopped making cylinders in 1912. United States Phonograph Company ceased production of its Everlasting cylinders in 1913, leaving Edison Company as the last cylinder maker. Edison continued to make Blue Amberol cylinders until the company closed its entertainment phonograph division in 1929.

Phonographs and Tapes—Records

78 rpm records

By the 1920s, disc phonograph records were the standard. They spun at 78 revolutions per minute (rpms) and produced four minutes of sound. The 78 rpm records were made of shellac and were very fragile. In 1948, Columbia Records introduced $33\frac{1}{3}$

rpm long-play (LP) records. They were made of durable vinyl and played for more than 20 minutes. Within a decade, the industry abandoned 78 rpm records.
• **Last widespread use of 78 rpm records:** The industry began phasing out 78s in 1957. By 1959, only a few companies were making them. Some sources list Chuck Berry's "Too Pooped to Pop" (Chess Records, February 1960) as the last 78 rpm record. However, others were made later. Seventy-eight rpm records by The Beatles were released in India in the mid-1960s.

45 rpm records
RCA Victor introduced the 7-inch 45 rpm extended-play vinyl record and player in 1949. The small discs could be stacked on a player to provide the listener up to 50 minutes of uninterrupted music.
• **Last widespread use of 45 rpm records:** mid 1980s. They began to be displaced by compact discs (CDs) after 1982; however, many labels produced them until the 1990s.

$33^1/3$ rpm records
The $33^1/3$ rpm records were introduced in 1948. When compact discs (CDs) were introduced in 1982, the $33^1/3$ vinyl discs seemed bulky and more likely to scratch.
• **Last widespread use of $33^1/3$ rpm records:** mid 1980s. The $33^1/3$s can still be purchased and at least one company is still making them.

Phonographs and Tapes—Eight-track Tapes
Eight-track tapes were the preeminent portable and car audio format of the 1970s.
• **Last widespread use of eight-track tapes:** 1988. They began to be replaced with smaller and more durable cassettes at end of the 1970s. Most major labels removed their eight-track tapes from stores by 1983; however, members of the Columbia and RCA record clubs could still buy new releases on eight-track through 1988.
• **Last eight-track tape released on a major label:** Believed to be *Fleetwood Mac's Greatest Hits,* released November 1988.

Photography

Photography—Film—Cellulose Nitrate Film
Camphor plasticized cellulose nitrate film was first manufactured in 1889. It proved to be highly flammable.
• **Last cellulose nitrate film produced:** 1951, when it was replaced by cellulose acetate or other slow-burning film.

Photography—Photographs—Albumen Prints
Albumen prints began to be used in 1855. The process used paper that was sensitized by a coat of egg white mixed with chlorine, bromine or iodine salts then immersed in silver nitrate. The prints tended to fade and turn yellow if they were exposed to light.
• **Last widespread use of albumen prints:** c. 1895, when albumen paper was gradually replaced by gelatin paper.

Photography—Photographs—Ambrotypes
Ambrotypes were made by imaging a negative on glass backed by a dark surface. They had brass frames and were enclosed in decorative cases. They were first made in 1851 and hit their peak between 1857 and 1859.
• **Last widespread use of ambrotypes:** 1865. The process was used on a minor scale until the 1890s.

Photography—Photographs—Cabinet Photographs
Cabinet photographs were introduced around 1860. They were generally $6^1/2$" x $4^1/2$" cards. The photographer's name and address was almost always printed at the bottom. Cabinet photographs were popular from the post-Civil War era until the 1890s.
• **Last widespread use of cabinet photographs:** early 20th century.

Photography—Photographs—Cartes-de-visite
Cartes-de-visite were first made in 1858 and were among the earliest paper photographs. Their name derives from the fact that the palm-size pictures resembled visiting cards.

The photographer's name and address was almost always on the back of the card.
• **Last widespread use of cartes-de-visite:** Most were made between 1859 and 1866. They were not used after around 1900-05.

Photography—Photographs—Cyanotypes
Cyanotype photographs or blueprint-type photographs were first produced in 1841. The process uses light-sensitive iron salts. Photographers who were away from their studio could make a quick print of a picture to check the quality of the image.
• **Last widespread use of cyanotype photographs:** 1880-1900. They are still produced on a small scale.

Photography—Photographs—Daguerreotypes
Daguerreotypes were named for Louis J.M. Daguerre and were the earliest commercial photographs. The first were made in 1839. By the 1840s, daguerreotype portrait studios were in most large cities. The daguerreotype process, which used toxic mercury vapor, required a high level of expertise, so its use was limited to professional photographers.
• **Last widespread use of daguerrotypes:** Late 1860s. By around 1851, daguerreotypes began to face competition from the wet collodian process; however, daguerreotypes continued to be made until after the Civil War.

Photography—Photographs—Tintypes/Ferrotypes
Tintypes or ferrotypes were introduced in the United States by 1860. Production hit its peak by 1863 and waned after the Civil War.
• **Last widespread use of tintypes:** 1930s. They were in use from the late 1800s until just prior to World War II. Most tintypes were taken by itinerant photographers at county fairs and other places where crowds gathered.

Photography—Photographs—Wet Collodion Process
Collodion—a mix of gun cotton (nitrocellulose), ethyl alcohol and ethyl ether—was used to coat glass plates that were then sen-sitized by a bath of silver nitrate. The wet collodion process came into use around 1851.
• **Last widespread use of the wet collodion process:** 1880s, when gelatin dry plates came into use.

Political Machines and Organizations

Political Machines and Organizations—American Liberty League
The American Liberty League was established in 1934. It was a reactionary organization that combated radical movements and was against New Deal programs.
• **Last of the American Liberty League:** 1940, when it was dissolved.

Political Machines and Organizations—Long, Huey
Huey Long of Louisiana built a powerful political organization and was elected governor and U.S. senator. His hopes for the U.S. presidency ended when he was shot to death in the Louisiana capitol on September 8, 1935, age 41.
• **Last survivor of the Huey Long political machine:** Senator Allen J. Ellender (D-LA), who died in Bethesda, Maryland, on July 27, 1972, age 81.

Political Machines and Organizations—Tammany Hall
Tammany Hall was the powerful Democratic party organization that thrived in the late 19th and early 20th centuries in New York City and County. It was marred by corruption and scandals and began to decline in the early 1930s.
• **Last boss of Tammany Hall:** Carmine De Sapio, who revived the organization after World War II. De Sapio was later challenged by reformers who accused him of corruption and ties with organized crime. The charges led to the dissolution of Tammany Hall and a stay in a federal penitentiary for De Sapio beginning in 1971. He died in New York, New York, on July 27, 2004, age 95.

Political Machines and Organizations— Tweed Ring

William Marcy Tweed ("Boss Tweed") was a New York City chairmaker who used his connections with the volunteer fire department as a stepping stone to political power. He and his three cohorts gained control of city government and city finances and ruled New York City from 1860 to 1871. They amassed several million dollars and managed to run the city into a debt of more than $100 million.

• **End of the Tweed Ring:** Overthrown by reformers in 1871. In 1874, Tweed was convicted of fraud and sentenced to 12 years in prison. He managed to be released on a technicality in 1875. The state of New York then filed a civil suit against him and he was rearrested and imprisoned. Tweed escaped to Cuba and was headed for Spain when he was caught. He was extradited and imprisoned at Ludlow Street Jail in New York in 1876. He died there on April 12, 1878, age 55.

Political Parties (U.S)

Political Parties (U.S.)—American party, *see* Know-Nothing party.

Political Parties (U.S.)—Anti-Masonic party

The Anti-Masonic party was formed in New York State in 1828, in opposition to the secretive Masonic society, which claimed as its members President Andrew Jackson and many Democrats. The party came into existence not long after the 1826 mysterious disappearance of William Morgan, a Mason from western New York who had planned to publish an expose of the society's secrets. The Anti-Masonic party held its first national nominating convention in Baltimore, Maryland, in September 1831.

• **Last of the Anti-Masonic party:** began to decline after the 1836 elections. It eventually was absorbed into the Whig party along with the National Republican party.

Political Parties (U.S.)—Anti-Monopoly party

The Anti-Monopoly party was organized in Chicago, Illinois, in May 1884. It nominated Benjamin F. Butler as its presidential candidate that year. The Greenback Party also nominated Butler. The Anti-Monopoly party advocated federal regulation of monopolies in interstate commerce, repeal of all tariffs, a graduated income tax and the banning of land grants to corporations.

• **Last of the Anti-Monopoly party:** disbanded after the 1884 election in which Butler was soundly defeated.

Political Parties (U.S.)—Barnburners

The Barnburners were a radical group within the Democratic party that was influential between 1842 and 1848. They took their name from the old Dutch legend about the farmer who burned down his barn to solve his rat problem. The Barnburners stood in contrast to the Hunkers, the party regulars who pledged to support the party candidate.

• **Last of the Barnburners:** 1848. When they were refused recognition at the 1848 Democratic convention, they joined two other anti-slavery groups as the Free Soilers and nominated Martin Van Buren for president. After the election, some of the Barnburners remained with the Free Soilers. Others returned to the Democratic fold.

Political Parties (U.S.)—Bull Moose party, *see* Progressive party.

Political Parties (U.S.)—Constitutional Union party

The Constitutional Union party had only one convention in Baltimore, Maryland, in May 1860, where it nominated John Bell of Tennessee for president and Edward Everett of Massachusetts for vice president. The party was represented in only one election the following November.

• **Last of the Constitutional Union party:** disappeared in 1861, at the beginning of the Civil War.

Political Parties (U.S.)—Democratic-Republican party

The Democratic-Republican party was rooted in the late 18th-century Anti-

Federalist movement. It emerged as an opposition political party in the 1790s and won the election of 1800 for Thomas Jefferson.

• **Last of the Democratic-Republican party:** held power until 1824, when its candidate was defeated by John Quincy Adams. The party regained power in 1828 with the election of Andrew Jackson. After that election, the party gradually became known as the Democratic party.

Political Parties (U.S.)—Equal Rights party (Locofoco party)

The Equal Rights party was formed in October 1835, when a group split from the Democratic party over banking and labor issues. Party members were called "Locofocos" as a term of derision. The gas lights were turned off at an Equal Rights party meeting in an attempt to halt them. The party continued to nominate its slate by candlelight. The candles were lit by newly invented friction matches known as locofocos.

• **Last of the Equal Rights party:** After the party held a state convention in New York in 1836, Martin Van Buren adopted many of their policies, especially on finance and labor, leaving them without a platform. During the 1840s, the party lost its momentum. Gradually members returned to the Democratic party.

Political Parties (U.S.)—Federalist party

The Federalist party's roots go back to ratification of the U.S. Constitution in 1787. Federalists were those who supported a strong constitutional government. They coalesced as a party in the 1789 election.

• **Last of the Federalist party:** The last meeting to field a presidential candidate was held in 1812. The party had no presidential candidates in the 1816 election. It disbanded at the national level but held on at the local level until the mid-1820s. By 1828, the Federalist party had disappeared.

Political Parties (U.S.)—Free Soil party

The Free Soil party was founded in 1848 by dissatisfied Whigs and Democrats who wanted to prevent the spread of slavery into the new territories recently acquired from

Mexico. (*See* Barnburners, above.)

• **Last of the Free Soil party:** by 1854, Free Soilers found they were unable to have an impact on the slavery question, so they joined the newly created Republican party.

Political Parties (U.S.)—Greenback party

The Greenback party was created after the Panic of 1873 to encourage the distribution of more paper money. In May 1876, the party nominated a candidate for president who encouraged the issuance of U.S. notes. He did not win, but the party attracted many followers. In 1878, the party merged with the National Labor Reform party and succeeded in having 14 members elected to the House of Representatives.

• **Last of the Greenback party:** 1884. The party dissolved when its candidate Benjamin Butler did poorly at the polls. Some party members later joined the Union Labor party.

Political Parties (U.S.)—Know-Nothing party

The Know-Nothing party was organized in the 1850s as the American party. The party nominated Millard Fillmore for president in the 1856 election but had a poor showing. He carried only one state.

• **Last of the Know-Nothing party:** fell apart shortly after the 1856 election. Some members joined the Constitutional Union party in 1860.

Political Parties (U.S.)—Liberal Republican party

The Liberal Republican party was organized in 1872 by Republicans who were displeased with the first administration of Ulysses S. Grant. They nominated Horace Greeley for president. The Democrats adopted the same platform and chose the same candidate.

• **Last of the Liberal Republican party:** the 1872 election, when Greeley had a poor showing and Grant won. The party disappeared shortly afterward.

Political Parties (U.S.)—Liberty party

The Liberty party was organized in April 1840 by abolitionists from six northeastern

states. That year, they nominated James G. Birney for president. He garnered fewer than 7,000 votes. He did better in the 1844 election, with more than 62,000 votes, but it was not enough to gain any electoral votes. The party could not get the support it needed from the abolitionists.
• **Last of the Liberty party:** nominated Senator John P. Hale of New Hampshire as its last presidential candidate in the 1848 election, but before the election members of the party merged with anti-slavery Democrats and Whigs to form the Free Soil party.

Political Parties (U.S.)—National Democratic party (Gold Bugs/Gold Democrats)
After the 1896 Democratic convention, a conservative group that favored the gold standard, left the party to oppose the nomination of the pro-silver platform of Democratic presidential candidate William Jennings Bryant. The Gold Bugs, or Gold Democrats, formed the National Democratic party and nominated their own candidate, John M. Palmer, a senator from Illinois.
• **Last of the National Democratic party:** disappeared after one election. After the Spanish-American War (1898), currency was no longer an issue.

Political Parties (U.S.)—National Equal Rights party
The National Equal Rights party was organized in 1872 and nominated Victoria Woodhull for president that year. Its platform included women's suffrage, temperance, civil service reform, uniform marriage, divorce and property laws and an anti-war policy. The party nominated Belva Ann Lockwood in the 1884 campaign. She garnered less than 5,000 votes.
• **Last of the National Equal Rights party:** dissolved in 1888 after a poor voter turnout in the election.

Political Parties (U.S.)—National Republican party
The National Republican party was an opposition party to the Jacksonian Democratic Republican party. It was created when that party split and Henry Clay supported John

Quincy Adams in the 1824 presidential election. The party chose Henry Clay as Jackson's opponent for the 1832 election.
• **Last of the National Republican party:** Jackson defeated Clay in the 1832 election and National Republican party members became part of the Whig party in 1834.

Political Parties (U.S.)—National Union party
The Republican party used the name National Union party during the 1864 presidential campaign in an attempt to build a coalition of Republicans, war Democrats and independents. Lincoln was nominated for president by the National Union party.
• **Last of the National Union party:** disappeared after the 1864 election. The National Union name was used again in 1866 by a another group: supporters of President Andrew Johnson who tried to unite moderate Republicans.

Political Parties (U.S.)—People's party (Populists)
The People's party, also known as Populists, was formed in 1892. Primarily farmers, the Populists sought agrarian reforms that would control overproduction and depressed agricultural prices. They had a strong showing in the Midwest and West in the election of 1892 and were successful in electing six senators and seven representatives to Congress.
• **Last of the People's party:** 1908. Although they accepted the Democratic party platform and supported its candidate, William Jennings Bryant, in 1896, the Populists continued to nominate their own presidential candidates for 12 more years.

Political Parties (U.S.)—Progressive party (Bull Moose)
When President William Howard Taft was nominated for a second term on the first ballot at the June 1912 Republican convention, supporters of former President Theodore Roosevelt believed he had been cheated out of the nomination. The dispute led to a split in the party. Roosevelt supporters created the Progressive party. Early in the campaign, Roosevelt commented that he felt as

fit as a bull moose, hence the party's nickname.

• **Last of the Progressive party:** 1916 election, when Theodore Roosevelt turned down the Progressive nomination and supported the Republican candidate. Lacking his leadership, the Progressive party disappeared.

Political Parties (U.S.)—States' Rights Democratic party (Dixiecrats)

In the 1948 presidential campaign, a group of conservative southern Democrats bolted from the Democratic party and formed their own party. At the root of their dissent was the civil rights platform of Democratic presidential candidate Harry S. Truman that promoted desegregation. The Dixiecrats strongly opposed it and wanted to maintain their segregated way of life.

• **Last of the States' Rights Democratic party:** ceased to exist after Truman was elected president in 1948.

Political Parties (U.S.)—Union party

The Union party surfaced briefly in 1936 to oppose the programs and policies of President Franklin D. Roosevelt's New Deal. One of the prime movers was Rev. Charles Coughlin, the "Radio priest." (*See* Radio—Radio Priest.)

• **Last of the Union party:** fell apart in 1936, when the party's candidate failed to get on the ballot.

Political Parties (U.S.)—Whig party

The Whig party came together in 1834 to oppose Andrew Jackson and the Democrats. The party put up several candidates for the election of 1836 but failed to produce a winner. The Whigs did better in the 1840 election, when their candidate William Henry Harrison won the presidency. The Whig candidate Zachary Taylor won the presidency in 1848. Winfield Scott, the Whig candidate in 1852, received only 42 electoral votes; he was no match for Franklin Pierce, who garnered 254. Whig members split over the issue of slavery. Southern Whigs supported the 1854 Kansas-Nebraska Act, while northern Whigs did not. Many southern Whigs left the party.

• **Last of the Whig party:** 1856, with their support of the Know-Nothing presidential candidate Millard Fillmore. Fillmore lost. Remnants of the Whig party formed the Constitutional Union party in 1860 in an attempt to hold the Union together. Their candidate, John Bell, garnered only 39 electoral votes.

Population—Immigration, U.S.

Population—Immigration, U.S.— Castle Garden Immigration Center

Castle Garden was located in Battery Park, at the southern tip of Manhattan in New York, New York. It was first used as an immigration center in 1855.

• **Last immigrants received at Castle Garden:** December 31, 1891. On January 1, 1892, Ellis Island opened as an immigration center. Castle Garden was the site of the New York Aquarium from 1896 to 1941.

Population—Immigration, U.S.— Ellis Island

Ellis Island is in New York Bay, about one mile southwest of Manhattan Island, New York, and about 1,300 feet from the New Jersey shore. It replaced Castle Garden as the main U.S. immigration center in 1892.

• **Last immigrants received at Ellis Island:** 1943. It served as a detention center for deportees until it was closed in November 1954. Ellis Island became part of Statue of Liberty National Monument in 1965. It was opened to tourists in 1976.

Population—Immigration, U.S.— National Origins Quota System

For many years, a quota system based on national origins was used as the basis for selecting immigrants to be admitted to the United States. The first major restrictions on who could enter the U.S. were imposed in the 1920s. They were further codified in 1952, with the McCarran-Walter Act.

• **End of national origins quota system of immigration:** with the Immigration and Naturalization Amendments to the 1952 McCarran-Walter Act signed by President

Lyndon B. Johnson on October 3, 1965. It went into effect on December 1, 1965.

Population—United States

Last time U.S. population was below	Year	Federal census count
10 million	1820	9,638,453
50 million	1870	38,558,371
100 million	1910	91,972,266
150 million	1940	131,669,275
200 million	1960	179,325,671
250 million	1990	248,709,873

Source: Bureau of the Census, U. S. Dept. of Commerce.

Population—Worldwide

Last time world population was below	Year
1 billion	1804
2 billion	1927
3 billion	1960
4 billion	1974
5 billion	1987
6 billion	1999

Source: UN population estimates.

Postal Service (U.S.)

Postal Service (U.S.)—Mail Trains

Mail trains began to be used in the United States in the 1860s, during the Civil War. The mail was sorted in transit. The system came to be known as Railway Post Offices or RPOs. The Railway Post Office (RPO) system also included trolley lines in some cities.
• **Last RPO train in the United States:** last ran on July 1, 1977, between Washington, D.C., and New York, New York.
• **Last RPO trolley in the United States:** last ran on May 6, 1950, between Los Angeles and San Bernardino, California, as part of the Pacific Electric line.

Postal Service (U.S.)—Mule Mail Delivery

The U.S. Postal Service provides a variety of ways to get mail delivered, and it delivers the mail to some very remote regions.
• **Last mule delivery in the U.S.:** the Supai route in Arizona that delivers mail to the Havasupai Indian Reservation. The tribe's members live below the south rim of the Grand Canyon. Only those on foot, mule or horseback can use the eight-mile trail that provides the only way in and out of the reservation.

Postal Service (U.S.)—Pony Express

The Pony Express was created to carry the U.S. mail between the Midwest and California. Riders on the first Pony Express trip between Saint Joseph, Missouri, and Sacramento, California, started from each place at 5 p.m. on April 3, 1860. The journey took just short of 10 days and ended on April 13. The horses were changed every 10 miles along the 1,900-mile route.
• **Last of the Pony Express:** discontinued on October 24, 1861, when the first transcontinental telegraph lines were completed. The Pony Express service lasted slightly more than 18 months.
• **Last surviving Pony Express rider:** Julius Mortimer (also known as Bronco Charlie Miller and Bronco Carlos), a runaway who joined the Pony Express at age 11. He later performed with Buffalo Bill Cody's Wild West Show. At age 92, he rode a horse from New York City to San Francisco, California, with letters for Mayor Rossi, collected from Mayor Walker. Mortimer died in New York, New York, on January 15, 1955, age 105.
• **Last surviving Pony Express station at its original location:** Home Station No. 1, Marysville, Kansas. Other stations have survived, but they have been removed from their original location.

Postal Service (U.S.)—Postal Savings System

The U.S. Postal Savings System was a savings bank for small accounts operated by the U.S. Post Office Department. It began in 1911.
• **Last day of operation of the U.S. Postal Savings System:** June 30, 1967. The system ended officially the following day.

Postal Service (U.S.)—U.S. Post Office Department

The first Post Office Department was established in Philadelphia, Pennsylvania, in 1775. The U.S. Congress gave the department permanent status in the 1790s. It became an executive department in 1872.

• **Last of the U.S. Post Office Department:** abolished by Congress with the Postal Reorganization Act of 1970. The law created the U.S. Postal Service that began operation July 1, 1971.

Postal Service (U.S.)—ZIP Codes

In 1963, the U.S. Postal Service introduced the Zoning Improvement Plan, or ZIP Code, a postal addressing system aimed at speeding up the processing of mail. Mr. ZIP, an advertising character, was created to promote the new system. Mr. ZIP became one of the most successful trademark identification campaigns in history.

• **Last use of Mr. ZIP image by the United States Postal Service:** 1980, when the character was retired with the introduction of the ZIP +4 system.

• **Last time United States mail was processed without ZIP codes:** 1963. The five-digit ZIP code system for sorting mail faster and more efficiently began to be phased in that year. When the ZIP code was introduced, the United States Post Office also introduced two-letter abbreviations for all states.

Postal Service (U.S.)—Postal Rates (U.S.)
First-Class Postage

Old Rate	Last Date at Old Rate	New Rate	Date Effective
2 cents	July 5, 1932	3 cents	July 6, 1932
3 cents	July 31, 1958	4 cents	August 1, 1958
4 cents	January 6, 1963	5 cents	January 7, 1963
5 cents	January 6, 1968	6 cents	January 7, 1968
6 cents	May 15, 1971	8 cents	May 16, 1971
8 cents	March 1, 1974	10 cents	March 2, 1974
10 cents	December 30, 1975	13 cents	December 31, 1975
13 cents	May 28, 1978	15 cents	May 29, 1978
15 cents	March 21, 1981	18 cents	March 22, 1981
18 cents	October 31, 1981	20 cents	November 1, 1981
20 cents	February 16, 1985	22 cents	February 17, 1985
22 cents	April 2, 1988	25 cents	April 3, 1988
25 cents	February 2, 1991	29 cents	February 3, 1991
29 cents	December 31, 1994	32 cents	January 1, 1995
32 cents	January 9, 1999	33 cents	January 10, 1999
33 cents	January 6, 2001	34 cents	January 7, 2001
34 cents	June 29, 2002	37 cents	June 30, 2002

Postal Service (U.S.)—Postal Rates (U.S.)
Postcards

Old Rate	Last Date at Old Rate	New Rate	Date Effective
1 cent	December 31, 1951	2 cents	January 1, 1952
2 cents	July 31, 1958	3 cents	August 1, 1958
3 cents	January 6, 1963	4 cents	January 7, 1963
4 cents	January 6, 1968	5 cents	January 7, 1968
5 cents	May 15, 1971	6 cents	May 16, 1971
6 cents	March 1, 1974	8 cents	March 2, 1974

8 cents	September 13, 1975	7 cents	September 14, 1975
7 cents	December 30, 1975	9 cents	December 31, 1975
9 cents	May 28, 1978	10 cents	May 29, 1978
10 cents	March 21, 1978	12 cents	March 22, 1981
12 cents	October 31, 1981	13 cents	November 1, 1981
13 cents	February 16, 1985	14 cents	February 17, 1985
14 cents	April 2, 1988	15 cents	April 3, 1988
15 cents	February 2, 1991	19 cents	February 3, 1991
19 cents	December 31, 1994	20 cents	January 1, 1995
20 cents	June 30, 2001	21 cents	July 1, 2001
21 cents	June 29, 2002	25 cents	June 30, 2002

Radio

Radio—Networks

During the 1930s, two radio giants, National Broadcasting Company (NBC) and Columbia Broadcasting System (CBS), gained major market power by way of their networks. NBC had two networks—Red and Blue—that controlled their member stations.
• **Last time NBC controlled the Blue Network:** May 3, 1941, when the FCC ordered NBC to sell one of its networks and reduce the power of its remaining network. The Blue Network was sold off and eventually became the American Broadcasting Company (ABC).

Radio—Radio Priest (Father Coughlin)

Roman Catholic priest the Rev. Charles Edward Coughlin, known as "the Radio Priest" and as "Father Coughlin," was pastor of the Shrine of the Little Flower in Royal Oak, Michigan. He began his radio broadcasts in 1926 and by the early 1930s had become an outspoken critic of American political and economic issues. He was an archconservative who attacked Communists, Jews and big business. Coughlin was particularly critical of President Franklin D. Roosevelt's New Deal programs and called the president the "great betrayer and liar." At the peak of his fame, Coughlin's Sunday afternoon broadcasts had millions of listeners. Coughlin also published a magazine called *Social Justice.*
• **Last of Coughlin's radio programs:** 1940. When he strayed from messages of morality and Christian virtues to political issues that included the bitter attacks on President Roosevelt, his superiors removed him from the airwaves.
• **Last time *Social Justice* was sent through the mail:** 1942. When World War II began, Coughlin was viewed as a Nazi sympathizer. Citing a violation of the Espionage Act, *Social Justice* was banned from the mail by the U.S. government. Coughlin retired from his pastoral duties in 1966. He died in Bloomfield Hills, Michigan, on October 27, 1979, age 88.

Radio—Programs
Last Broadcast of Some Popular American Programs
(*See also* Movies—Performers; Music—Popular Performers; Television—Programs.)

Title	Type of Show	First Aired	Last Show	Description
A & P Gypsies	music	1926	1936	Began as local New York show in 1924. Featured the orchestra of Harry Horlick, who died in Cedarhurst, New York, July 1970, age 74.

Abbott and Cos-tello Show, The	comedy/ variety	1942	1949	Began as a summer replacement for Fred Allen's show in 1940.
Abie's Irish Rose	sitcom	1942	1944	Based on the long-running Broadway play by Ann Nichols. Last episode: September 1944.
Against the Storm	soap opera	1939	1952	Off the air 1942. Revived 1949. Last episode: June 27, 1952.
Al Jolson Shows	music/ variety	1932	1949	Jolson, a radio pioneer, was featured in many programs, including *Presenting Al Jolson Show* (1932), *Shell Chateau* (1935- 36), and *Lifebuoy Program* (1936-39). His last radio show was *Kraft Music Hall* (1933-34, 1947-49). Jolson, died in San Francisco, California, October 23, 1950, age 64, the night before he was to tape an appearance on the Bing Crosby Show.
Al Pearce and His Gang	comedy	1928	1946	Off the air 1942. Revived 1943-46. Pearce died in Newport Beach, California, June 3, 1961, age 60.
Aldrich Family, The	sitcom	1939	1953	Based on characters in Clifford Gold-smith's play, *What a Life!* Last episode: April 26, 1953.
Amanda of Honeymoon Hill	soap opera	1940	1946	Last episode: May 1, 1946.
American Album of Familiar Music	music	1931	1951	Sunday evening programs of classical and semiclassical music.
American Forum of the Air	discus-sion	1935	1956	Began as *Mutual Forum Hour* (1935-37).
American Radio Warblers	music	1938	1945	Also titled *The Hartz Mountain Canar-ies Show.* Featured singing canaries. Sponsored by Hartz Mountain, birdseed maker
America's Town Meeting of the Air	current events	1935	1956	Guests discussed questions posed by the audience.
Amos 'n' Andy Show, The	sitcom	1926	1960	Longest running radio series. Began as *Sam and Henry* in Chicago, Illinois, in 1926. Title changed to *Amos 'n' Andy* when the show changed networks (1929) Used new format and new title, *Amos and Andy Music Hall,* in 1955. Last epi-sode: November 25, 1960. Freeman F. Gosden (Amos) died in Los Angeles, California, December 10, 1982, age 83. Charles Correll (Andy), died in Chicago, Illinois, September 26, 1972, age 82.
Answer Man, The	informa-tion	1937	1956	Popular 15-minute evening show that answered questions sent in by listeners.
Archie Andrews, The Adventures of	teen sitcom	1943	1953	Based on Bob Montana comic strip. Be-gan as 15-minute daily show and

				changed to half-hour Saturday morning show in 1946.
Armstrong Theater of Today, The	drama anthology	1941	1954	Weekly half-hour dramas heard on Saturdays at noon.
Arnold Grimm's Daughter	soap opera	1937	1942	Popular Cinderella-type story of a hard-working shopkeeper.
Arthur Godfrey Shows	talk/ variety/ music	1934	1972	Godfrey hosted several radio shows, including *The Arthur Godfrey Digest, The Arthur Godfrey Show* and *Arthur Godfrey's Talent Scouts*. His last show, *Arthur Godfrey Time,* aired April 30, 1972. Godfrey died in New York, New York, March 16, 1983, age 79.
Aunt Jenny's Real-Life Stories	soap opera	1937	1956	A different story each week, told in five 15-minute episodes. Last episode: September 28, 1956.
Author Meets the Critics	literary discussion	1946	1951	Half-hour weekly show. The TV version ran from 1947 to 1954.
Baby Snooks Show, The	comedy	1944	1951	Based on Baby Snooks character introduced by Fanny Brice on *Ziegfeld Follies of the Air* in 1936. It became a separate program in 1944. Last show: May 29, 1951, a memorial to Brice who had died that day following a cerebral hemorrhage five days earlier. She was 59.
Backstage Wife	soap opera	1935	1959	Also titled *Mary Noble Backstage Wife*. Last episode: January 2, 1959. Three other soaps ended that day.
Barry Craig, Confidential Investigator	crime drama	1951	1955	Half-hour weekly series. Last episode: June 30, 1955.
Battle of the Sexes	quiz show	1938	1943	Men and women competed, answering gender-specific question in half-hour weekly quiz show.
Beat the Band	musical quiz	1940	1944	Listeners mailed in questions about songs. Band tried to guess the tunes.
Believe It or Not	odd and unusual	1930	1948	Based on Robert L. Ripley's newspaper feature. Ripley died in New York, New York, May 27, 1949, age 55.
Bell Telephone Hour	music	1940	1958	Hour-long weekly concerts of classical and semiclassical music; also titled *The Telephone Hour.*
Ben Bernie Show, The	music/ variety	1930	1943	Also titled *Ben Bernie and All His Lads*. Bernie died in Beverly Hills, California, October 20, 1943, age 52.
Best Seller	serial drama	1960	1960	Five-part dramatizations of popular novels. Radio's last serial drama.
Betty and Bob	soap opera	1932	1940	One of radio's earliest soap operas. Last episode: March 18, 1940.
Beulah	sitcom	1945	1954	Spin-off from *Fibber McGee and Molly* as *Marlin Hurt and Beulah Show*. After

				Hurt's death on March 21, 1946, the show was renamed. Beulah was played by Hattie McDaniel, Louise Beavers and Lillian Randolph.
Bickersons, The	sitcom	1946	1951	Began as sketch on *Edgar Bergen and Charlie McCarthy Show.* Last episode: August 28, 1951.
Big Jon and Sparkie	juvenile adventure	1950	1958	One of the last radio programs for children.
Big Show, The	comedy/ variety	1950	1952	The 90-minute weekly program was the last major network radio show.
Big Sister	soap opera	1936	1952	Last episode: December 26, 1952.
Big Story, The	newspaper drama	1947	1955	Half-hour weekly dramatization of stories from newspapers.
Big Town	newspaper drama	1937	1952	Half-hour weekly series set in a newspaper office, co-starring Edward G. Robinson and Claire Trevor. Last episode: June 25, 1952.
Billie Burke Show, The	comedy	1944	1946	Title changed to *The Gay Mrs. Featherstone* (1945).
Bing Crosby Show, The	music/ variety	1931	1956	Also titled *The Woodbury Program* and *Philco Radio Time.* Crosby also appeared on *Kraft Music Hall* (1936-46).
Blind Date	meeting people	1943	1946	Show arranged blind dates for people and paid for a chaperoned night on the town.
Blondie	sitcom	1939	1950	Weekly series based on Chic Young's comic strip characters.
Bob and Ray Shows	comedy	1946	1984	Bob Elliott and Ray Goulding began working together on radio in the late 1940s and appeared in several shows. Goulding died in Manhasset, New York, March 24, 1990, age 68.
Bob Burns Show, The	comedy/ variety	1941	1947	Also titled *The Arkansas Traveler.* Comedian Bob Burns, who coined the word "bazooka," died in Encino, California, February 2, 1956, age 59.
Bob Hawk Show, The	quiz show	1942	1953	Began as *Thanks to the Yanks* in World War II. Renamed in 1945. Hawk died in Laguna Hills, California, July 4, 1959, age 81.
Bob Hope Show, The	comedy/ variety	1935	1955	Began as *The Pepsodent Show.* Last show: April 21, 1955.
Bobby Benson's Adventures	adventure	1932	1955	Children's program. Off the air 1936-49. Returned in 1949 as *Bobby Benson and the B-Bar-B Riders.*
Boston Blackie	detective drama	1944	1950	Based on the movie series that began in 1942. Last episode: October 25, 1950.
Box 13	detective drama	1948	1949	Box 13 was the post office box of former newsman Dan Holiday. Last episode: "Round Robin," August 14, 1949.

Break the Bank	quiz	1945	1955	Both audience and call-in contestants could win.
Breakfast Club, The	morning show	1933	1968	Last show aired December 27, 1968, after a 34-year run.
Breakfast in Hollywood	morning show	1941	1949	Began as *Breakfast at Sardi's*. Also titled *Tom Breneman's Hollywood*. Breneman died in Encino, California, April 28, 1948, age 45.
Bride and Groom	audience participation	1945	1950	Audience listened to newlywed couples and picked their favorites.
Bright Horizon	soap opera	1941	1945	Spin-off of soap opera *Big Sister*.
Brighter Day, The	soap opera	1948	1956	One of the last network radio soaps to go on the air. Last episode: June 29, 1956. The TV version aired 1954-62.
Broadway Is My Beat	detective drama	1949	1954	One of the last network detective shows to go on the air. Last episode: August 1, 1954.
Buck Rogers in the 25ᵗʰ Century	sci-fi adventure	1932	1947	Based on the comic strip character created by Philip Nowlan. Last episode: March 28, 1947.
Bulldog Drummond, The Adventures of	detective drama	1941	1954	Off the air 1944-45 and 1947-53.
Burns and Allen Show, The	comedy/ variety	1934	1950	Husband-and-wife comedy team George Burns and Gracie Allen first appeared on radio in 1932 and had their own shows beginning in 1934, with several titles, including *New Swan Show* and *Maxwell House Coffee Time*. Last *Burns and Allen Show* broadcast: May 17, 1950. Burns and Allen made the transition to TV in 1950.
Calling All Cars	police drama	1933	1938	Stories were based on crimes from Los Angeles police files. Last episode: "Murder in the Morning," September 8, 1938.
Calling All Detectives	mystery solving	1945	1950	Listeners were given a chance to solve mysteries and win prizes.
Camel Caravan (Comedy Caravan)	comedy/ variety/ quiz	1933	1954	Blanket title for several shows, including *Benny Goodman's Swing School* (1937-39), *Vaughn Monroe Show* (1946-54) and *The Bob Hawk Show* (1946-53).
Can You Top This?	joke swapping	1940	1954	Comedians matched wits and humor with audience.
Candid Microphone	audience participation	1947	1950	Off the air in 1948 but brought back in 1950 as summer replacement. Forerunner to TV's *Candid Camera*.
Captain Midnight	juvenile adventure	1939	1949	Children's program. Aired locally in Chicago, Illinois, in 1939. Last episode: December 15, 1949.

Carnation Contented Hour	music	1932	1951	Half-hour weekly series.
Casey, Crime Photographer	mystery/ adven- ture	1943	1955	Based on the novels of George Harmon Coxe. Show ran as *Flashgun Casey*; *Casey, Press Photographer*; *Casey, Crime Photographer* and *Crime Photographer*. Last episode: April 22, 1955.
Cavalcade of America	drama anthology	1935	1953	Weekly historic dramas. Last episode: "A Time to Grow—Louisiana Purchase," March 31, 1953.
CBS Radio Mystery Theater, The	mystery	1974	1982	Hour-long dramatizations of mysteries. Last original episode in series: "The Boat-man and the Devil," December 7, 1982. Last broadcast series, December 31, 1982.
CBS Radio Workshop, The	drama anthology	1956	1957	Half-hour experimental dramas based on *The Columbia Workshop* of the 1930s and 1940s. Last episode: "Young Man Axelrod," September 22, 1957.
Ceiling Unlimited	wartime drama	1942	1944	Patriotic 15-minute dramas about aviation.
Chamber Music Society of Lower Basin Street, The	music/ comedy	1940	1952	Last regular season was 1944. Revived as summer series 1950, 1952.
Chandu, the Ma- gician	mystery adven- ture	1932	1950	First series ran 15 minutes. Changed to half-hour in 1949. Last episode: September 6, 1950
Chaplain Jim	wartime drama	1942	1946	World War II drama series.
Charlie Chan, The Adventures of	detective	1932	1948	Off the air 1933-37, 1938-44, 1945-47. Series ended June 21, 1948.
Chesterfield Supper Hour, The	music	1944	1949	Fifteen-minute show, five days a week.
Chicago Theater of the Air, The	drama/ music	1940	1955	Opera translated into English and presented as drama.
Chick Carter, Boy Detective	adven- ture	1943	1945	Children's program.
Cinnamon Bear, The	children's series	1937	1962	Syndicated holiday stories aired each year, beginning about a month before Christmas.
Cisco Kid, The	western adven- ture	1942	1956	Based on character created by O. Henry. Off the air 1944-47. Returned 1947 as syndicated series. Syndicated TV series produced 1950-56.
Cities Service Concerts	music	1937	1956	Classical and semiclassical music. Originally an hour, cut to half hour in 1940. Title changed to *Highways in Melody* in 1944 and to *Cities Service Band of America* in 1948.

Clara, Lu 'n' Em	soap opera	1931	1945	Off the air 1936. Returned 1942-43. Syndicated series ran 1943-45.
Claudia	weekly serial drama	1941	1948	Based on play *Claudia* by Rose Franken. Also titled *Claudia and David.* Off the air after first season. Syndicated 1947-48.
Clock, The	suspense drama	1946	1948	Time-oriented stories. Last episode: May 23, 1948.
Coast to Coast on a Bus	juvenile music/ drama	1924	1948	Began as *Horn and Hardart's Children's Hour*, then became *The Children's Hour.* Final series title was *Coast to Coast on a Bus.*
Colgate Sports Newsreel, The	sports/ celebrity inter- views	1937	1956	Also titled *Bill Stern's Sports Newsreel* and *Bill Stern's Sportsreel.* Stern died in Harrison, New York, November 19, 1971, age 64.
College Quiz Bowl	quiz	1953	1955	Later became popular TV show (1959-70, 1987).
Collier Hour, The	variety	1927	1932	Dramatization of stories from *Collier's* magazine.
Columbia Workshop, The	experi- mental drama	1936	1957	Works by known and unknown authors. Last dramatization: "The Natural History of Nonsense," January 25, 1947. Returned in 1956 as *CBS Radio Workshop.*
Count of Monte Cristo, The	adventure	1946	1952	Based on character created by Alexander Dumas.
Counterspy	adventure	1942	1957	Also titled *David Harding Counterspy.* Last episode: November 29, 1957.
Court of Missing Heirs, The	unclaimed fortunes	1937	1947	Off the air 1938-39 and 1942-46. Revived one season.
Crime Doctor	crime	1940	1947	Half-hour series aired on Sunday evening.
Crime Does Not Pay	crime	1949	1951	Last original show: "Violets, Sweet Violets," April 11, 1951. The show was syndicated in 1952.
Curtain Time	dramas	1938	1949	Weekly half-hour original dramas. Off the air 1939-45.
Daily Dilemma	quiz	1946	1948	Audience solved dilemma posed in drama.
Damon Runyon Theater, The	drama series	1949	1949	Based on Runyon characters. Syndicated series. Last show: "Dream Sweet Rose," December 25, 1949.
Dangerous Assignment	spy drama	1949	1953	Last episode: July 1, 1953.
Date With Judy, A	teen sitcom	1941	1950	Began as summer replacement. Became regularly scheduled program in 1943.
David Harum	soap opera	1936	1951	Based on 1934 Will Rogers film.
Day in the Life of Dennis Day, A	sitcom	1946	1951	Day, a vocalist on the *Jack Benny Show* for many years, died in Bel Air, California, June 22, 1988, age 71.

Death Valley Days	western anthology	1930	1945	Dropped in 1945, when Borax, the sponsor switched to new show *The Sheriff.*
Dick Tracy, The Adventures of	detective drama	1935	1948	Based on Chester Gould comic strip. Off the air 1939-43.
Dimension X	sci-fi	1950	1951	Last episode of original series: "Nightfall" September 29, 1951. Retitled *X Minus One* when it was revived in 1955-58.
Dinah Shore Shows	music/ variety	1939	1955	Shore's many radio shows included *Songs by Dinah Shore, Call for Music, In Person, Dinah Shore, Birdseye Open House* and *The Ford Show.* Her last radio show, *The Dinah Shore Show* (1953-55), used soundtracks from her TV show.
Dr. Christian	drama series	1937	1954	Jean Hersholt played the role of Dr. Paul Christian all 16 years on radio and in several films.
Dr. I.Q., the Mental Banker	quiz	1939	1950	Audience tried to outwit Dr. I.Q. with tough questions.
Dr. Kildare	medical drama	1950	1951	Based on Dr. Kildare films. Last episode: August 3, 1951. Later became TV series.
Don Winslow of the Navy	adventure	1937	1943	Children's program. Off the air 1940-42.
Double or Nothing	quiz	1940	1952	Became TV program in 1953.
Dragnet	crime drama	1949	1957	Last episode: "The Big Mustache," February 26, 1957. Dragnet spawned feature films and two TV series.
Dreft Star Playhouse, The	drama series	1943	1945	Movies were adapted to 15-minute weekday episodes that ran from a week to two months. Last episode: March 30, 1945.
Duffy's Tavern	sitcom	1941	1951	Created by comedian Ed Gardner who portrayed Archie the Manager. Last episode: December 28, 1951. Gardner died in Los Angeles, California, August 17, 1963, age 62.
Dunninger the Mentalist	mind-reading	1943	1944	Last show: December 27, 1944. Dunninger later had a TV show, *The Amazing Dunninger* (1955-56). He died in Cliffside Park, New Jersey, on March 9, 1975, age 82.
Easy Aces, The	sitcom	1931	1949	Off the air 1945-48. Revived 1948-49 as *Mr. Ace & Jane.* Show's creators and actors were Goodman and Jane Ace. Goodman Ace died in New York, New York, March 25, 1982, age 83. Jane Ace died in New York, November 11, 1974, age 69.
Ed Sullivan Show, The	variety	1932	1946	Aired 1932, 1941, 1943-44, 1946. Sullivan's TV show began in 1948. He died

				in New York, New York, October 13, 1974, age 72.
Ed Wynn Shows	comedy	1932	1945	Wynn appeared several radio shows, including *Texaco Fire Chief* (1932-35), *Gulliver the Traveler* (1935-36) and *Happy Island* (1944-45). *The Ed Wynn Show* ran on TV in 1949-50. Wynn died in Los Angeles, California, June 19, 1966, age 79.
Eddie Cantor Shows	comedy/ variety	1931	1954	Cantor appeared on many radio shows, including *The Eddie Cantor Show* (1935-39, 1946-49, 1951-54), *Time to Smile* (1940-46), *Pabst Blue Ribbon Show* (1946-48) and *Take It or Leave It* (1949- 50). He hosted *The Colgate Comedy Hour* on TV (1950-54). He died in Beverly Hills, California, October 10, 1964, age 72.
Edgar Bergen and Charlie McCarthy Show, The	comedy/ variety	1937	1956	In 1937, the *Chase and Sanborn Show* was retitled *The Edgar Bergen-Charlie McCarthy Show*. Bergen left the show in 1948 and returned to radio in 1949 with a show that ran until July 1, 1956. He died in Las Vegas, Nevada, September 30, 1978, age 75.
Ellery Queen, The Adventures of	detective drama	1939	1948	Based on a character created by Frederic Dannay and Manfred Lee.
Emily Post	etiquette advice	1930	1939	Based on Emily Post's popular etiquette book. Post died in New York, New York, on September 25, 1960, age 86.
Eno Crime Club, The	mystery thriller	1931	1936	Also titled *Eno Crime Clues*.
Escape	adven- ture	1947	1954	Last episode: "Heart of Kali," September 25, 1954.
Falcon, The	detective drama	1943	1954	Based on character created by Michael Arlen in a short story in 1940. Last episode: November 27, 1954.
Family Theater	drama	1947	1969	Hosted by Father Patrick Peyton of the Holy Cross Fathers. The series continued on TV.
Famous Jury Trials	crime drama	1936	1949	Dramatizations of important trials.
Fat Man, The	detective drama	1946	1951	Character created by Dashiell Hammett for radio. Last episode: September 26, 1951.
Father Knows Best	sitcom	1949	1954	Last episode: March 25, 1954. Robert Young remained with the show when it transitioned to TV in 1954.
FBI in Peace and War, The	crime drama	1944	1958	Last episode: September 28, 1958.

Fibber McGee and Molly	sitcom	1935	1959	Half-hour show until June 30, 1953; 15-minutes from 1953 to 1957. In the late 1950s, *Fibber McGee and Molly* appeared in five-minute sketches on *Monitor*. Last appearance: September 6, 1959. Show created two spin-offs: *Beulah* and *The Great Gildersleeve*. Fibber McGee was played by Jim Jordan who died in Los Angeles, California, April 1, 1988, age 91. His wife Marian Jordan (Molly) died in Encino, California, April 7, 1961, age 63.
Fireside Chats	presidential messages	1933	1944-45	A series of radio talks by U.S. President Franklin D. Roosevelt to the American people. After he gave the 21st talk, the White House did not always designate which radio speech was a *Fireside Chat,* so there is some debate as to how many he actually gave and which was the last. The number of chats range from 28 to 33. Roosevelt's last *Fireside Chat* was either made on June 12, 1944, on "Opening the Fifth War Loan Drive," or his radio speech made on January 6, 1945.
First Nighter, The	drama	1930	1953	Half-hour dramas. Show off the air 1944-45, 1946-47 and 1949-52 seasons. Show finally left the air in 1953.
Fitzgeralds, The	morning talk show	1940	1972	Husband and wife Pegeen and Ed Fitzgerald broadcast the show from their New York City apartment. Ed died in 1972, age 87. Pegeen continued broadcasting until April 1988. She died January 30, 1989, age 78.
Ford Theater, The	drama	1947	1949	Last episode: "Cluny Brown," July 1, 1949
Fort Laramie	western	1956	1956	Last episode: "Army Wife," October 28, 1956.
Frank Merriwell, The Adventures of	teen adventure	1934	1949	Aired three days a week in 1934. Off the air 1934-46. Revived in 1946 as half-hour Saturday show.
Frank Sinatra Shows	music/ variety/ drama	1942	1958	Sinatra's radio shows included: *Songs by Sinatra* (1943, 1945-47), *Your Hit Parade* (1943-44, 1947-49), *Frank Sinatra Show* (1944-47), *Light-Up Time* (1949-50) and *Rocky Fortune* (1953-54). Last program of *The Frank Sinatra Show (The Bobbi Show)* aired July 1, 1955. His last radio show was on ABC (1956-58).

Fred Allen Shows	comedy/ variety	1932	1949	Allen had several shows, including *Linit Bath Club Revue* (1932-33), *Town Hall Tonight* (1934-39), *Fred Allen Show* (1939, 1945-49) and *Texaco Star Theater* (1940-44). Last *Fred Allen Show* aired June 26, 1949. He made the transition to TV but semiretired in 1952. Allen died in New York, New York, March 17, 1956, age 61.
Front Page Farrell	newspaper drama	1941	1954	Night-time soap opera.
Frontier Gentleman	western	1958	1958	Last episode: "Random Notes," November 16, 1958.
Fu Manchu	mystery	1927	1940	Character created by British novelist Sax Rohmer. Aired on *The Collier Hour* (1929- 31); last episode: May 17, 1931. Became separate show as *Fu Manchu Mysteries* (1932-33); last episode: April 24, 1933. Syndicated series *The Shadow of Fu Manchu* was produced beginning in 1939; last broadcast: September 11, 1940.
Gang Busters	police drama	1935	1957	Began as a show titled *G-Men* in 1935. Title changed in 1936.
Garry Moore Show, The	talk/ music/ variety	1942	1961	Show moved to TV in 1950. Moore retired in 1968. He died on Hilton Head Island, South Carolina, November 28, 1993, age 78.
Gay Nineties Revue	music/ comedy	1940	1945	Featured music of the 1890s. Retitled *Gaslight Gaieties* in 1944.
Gene Autry's Melody Ranch	western/ music	1940	1956	Off the air 1942-45, while Autry was in the service during World War II. Last show aired May 13, 1956.
GI Journal	music/ variety/ comedy	1942	1946	Program for U.S. military personnel during World War II.
Gillette Cavalcade of Sports	sports	1947	1957	Friday night sporting events.
Ginny Simms Shows	music	1943	1947	Simms was featured vocalist on many radio shows, including *Kollege of Musical Knowledge* (1938-41), *Johnny Presents Ginny Simms* (1943-45) and *Borden Presents Ginny Simms* (1945-47). She died in Palm Springs, California, April 4, 1994, age 77.
Goldbergs, The	comedy/ drama	1929	1950	Created and written by Gertrude Berg, who starred as Molly Goldberg. Off the air 1945-49. Returned for one season. The TV version aired 1949-54. Berg

				died in New York, New York, September 14, 1966, age 66.
Grand Central Station	drama anthology	1937	1954	Off the air 1942-44. Last episode: April 2, 1954.
Grand Hotel	drama anthology	1933	1945	Off the air 1940-44. Revived one season.
Grand Marquee	drama series	1946	1947	Last episode: "The Remarkable Talents of E. Haw," September 11, 1947.
Great Gildersleeve, The	sitcom	1941	1957	Spin-off of *Fibber McGee and Molly*. Hal Peary created Throckmorton P. Gildersleeve and played the role until June 14, 1950. The role was taken over by Willard Waterman. Last episode: March 21, 1957. Peary died in Torrance, California, March 30, 1985, age 79. Waterman died in Burlingame, California, February 2, 1995, age 80.
Greatest Story Ever Told, The	Bible stories	1936	1956	Aired locally in Detroit, Michigan, in 1936. Aired on ABC beginning in 1947. Sunday evening program.
Green Hornet, The	juvenile adventure	1938	1952	Last episode: December 5, 1952.
Guiding Light, The	soap opera	1937	1956	Last episode: June 29, 1956. Show made the transition to TV in 1952.
Gunsmoke	western	1952	1961	One of the last popular dramatic programs on network radio. Last episode: "Letter of the Law," June 18, 1961.
Hallmark Playhouse, The	drama anthology	1948	1955	Titled *Hallmark Radio Hall of Fame* until February 1953. Last episode: "Christina Grenville," March 27, 1955.
Halls of Ivy, The	sitcom	1950	1952	Co-starred British actor Ronald Colman and his wife Benita Hume. TV version aired 1954-55.
Happiness Boys, The	music/ comedy	1921	1940	The Happiness Boys were Billy Jones and Ernie Hare. Hare died in Jamaica, New York, March 9, 1939, age 55. Jones continued the show with Hare's daughter. Jones died in New York, New York, November 23, 1940, age 53.
Harvest of Stars	music/ drama	1945	1950	Featured concert music.
Have Gun, Will Travel	western	1958	1960	Last new radio network show to go on air. The radio show began after the TV version. Last episode: "From Here to Boston," November 27, 1960.
Hedda Hopper Show, The	Hollywood gossip	1939	1951	Show aired 1939-42, 1944-46 and 1950-51 in formats ranging from 5 to 30 minutes. Hopper also had a newspaper gossip column. She died in Hollywood, California, February 1, 1966, age 75.

Helen Hayes Shows	drama	1935	1963	Hayes's radio appearances included *The New Penny* (1935-36), *Helen Hayes Theater* (1940-42), *This is Helen Hayes* (1945), *Textron Theater* (1945-46) and *The Electric Theater* (1949). Last radio series: *The General Electric Theater* (1963). Hayes died in Nyack, New York, March 17, 1993, age 92
Henry Morgan Shows	comedy/ variety	1940	1950	Morgan's first show was *Meet Mr. Morgan* (1940). *Here's Morgan* aired 1941-43. He was off the air (1943-45), while in the service during World War II. *The Henry Morgan Show* aired 1946-47, 1949-50. He later appeared on TV. Morgan died New York, New York, May 19, 1994, age 79.
Herb Shriner Time	comedy/ variety	1948	1949	Daily 15-minute show. Shriner's shows aired on TV in the 1950s. He died in Delray Beach, Florida, April 24, 1970, age 51.
Hermit's Cave, The	super-natural	1940	1943	Syndicated show.
Hilltop House	soap opera	1937	1957	Originally titled *Hilltop House*. Retitled *The Story of Bess Johnson* in 1941. Off the air 1942-48. Returned again as *Hilltop House*.
His Honor, The Barber	drama series	1945	1946	Half-hour weekly series starred Barry Fitzgerald.
Hitchhiker's Guide to the Galaxy	sci-fi adventure	1978	1980	Last episode: "Fit the Twelfth," January 25, 1980.
Hobby Lobby	interesting hobbies	1937	1949	Off the air 1946. Revived briefly in 1949.
Hollywood Hotel	drama-variety	1934	1938	Last episode: "Canary Murder Case," December 2, 1938. Revived as *Hollywood Premiere* and aired from March to November 28, 1941.
Hollywood Star Preview	drama	1947	1950	Title changed to *Hollywood Star Theater* in 1948.
Hollywood Star Time	celebrity interviews	1944	1944	Stars were interviewed while they ate lunch
Home Sweet Home	soap opera	1934	1936	Last episode: November 16, 1936.
Honest Harold	sitcom	1950	1951	Hal Peary's show after he left *The Great Gildersleeve*. Lasted just one season.
Hop Harrigan	juvenile adventure	1942	1948	Based on All-American Comics character.
Hopalong Cassidy	western	1950	1952	A hit TV show before it aired on radio.
Horace Heidt's Youth Opportunity Program	talent show	1947	1953	Show traveled from town to town seeking young amateur talent. Bandleader Heidt died in Los Angeles, California, December 1, 1986, age 85.

Hour of Charm, The	music	1935	1948	Hour-long show featured Phil Spitalny and his All-Girl Orchestra performing semiclassical and classical music. Spitalny died in Miami, Florida, October 11, 1970, age 79.
House of Mystery	mystery	1945	1949	Directed toward a young audience.
House Party	audience partici-pation	1945	1967	Also titled *General Electric House Party, Pillsbury House Party* and *Art Linkletter's House Party.* Last show: October 13, 1967.
I Love a Mystery	mystery-adven-ture	1939	1952	Off the air 1941-43 and 1944-49. Last episode: "Find Elsa Holberg, Dead or Alive," December 1952. The characters Doc Long, Jack Packard and Reggie Yorke also appeared in a summer series entitled *I Love Adventure* (April 25-July 18, 1948). Last episode of that series: "The Ambassador Ricardo Santos Affair."
I Love Lucy	sitcom	1951	1952	The TV version was already a big hit when the radio series aired.
I Was a Communist for the FBI	drama	1952	1954	Stories about Cold War espionage.
Information Please!	quiz show	1938	1952	Listeners mailed in questions to stump a panel of experts. The show aired on television as a summer replacement in 1952.
Inner Sanctum Mysteries	mystery	1941	1952	Last full season was 1950-51. Aired as a summer replacement in 1952. Last episode: "Death Pays the Freight," October 5, 1952.
Irene Rich Dramas	drama	1933	1944	Actress Irene Rich appeared in original radio plays. She died in Hope Ranch, California, April 22, 1988, age 96.
It Pays to be Ignorant	comedy	1942	1951	A spoof of quiz shows. The series ran on network TV in 1949-51 and was syndicated in 1973.
Jack Armstrong, the All-American Boy	juvenile adven-ture	1933	1950	Last daily 15-minute serial ended August 22, 1947. Program ran 30 minutes twice a week until 1950. A sequel, *Armstrong of the SBI,* with Jack Armstrong as an adult, ran just one season (1950-51). Last episode: June 28, 1951.
Jack Benny Show, The	comedy/variety	1932	1955	One of the longest running comedies in radio history. Last original show: May 22, 1955. Reruns aired until 1958. Benny's show was on radio and TV at same time during part of the 1950s.

Jack Carson Shows	comedy/ variety	1943	1956	Carson's show was first heard in 1943-47. During 1947-48, he was on the *New Sealtest Village Store*. *The Jack Carson Show* aired in 1948-49 and in 1955-56. Carson also had his own TV show (1954-55) and hosted others. He died in Encino California, on January 2, 1963, age 52.
Jack Pearl Show, The	comedy/ variety	1932	1951	Pearl's radio appearance on the *Ziegfeld Follies of the Air* as Baron Munchausen in 1932 led to other shows. *The Jack Pearl Show* ran 1936-37, 1948-49, and 1951. Pearl died in New York, New York December 25, 1982, age 88.
Jack Smith Show, The	music	1945	1953	Daily 15-minute evening program of music.
Jimmy Durante Show, The	comedy/ variety	1943	1950	Durante made the transition to TV in 1950. His performing career ended in 1972, when he had a stroke. He died in Santa Monica, California, January 29, 1980, age 86.
Jimmy Fidler Show, The	gossip	1932	1950	Fidler also had a long-running newspaper column. He remained active into the 1970s. He died in Los Angeles, California, August 9, 1988, age 87.
Joan Davis Shows	comedy/ sitcom	1943	1950	Davis's radio shows included *Sealtest Village Store* (1943-45), *Joanie's Tea Room* (1945-47) and *Leave It to Joan* (1949-50). She died in Palm Springs, California, May 23, 1961, age 53.
Joe Penner Show, The	comedy/ variety	1933	1940	Retitled *The Penners of Park Avenue* in 1939-40. Penner returned to the stage when his radio show ended. He was 36 when he died on January 10, 1941, while performing in the show *Yokel Boy* in Philadelphia, Pennsylvania.
Johnny Presents	variety	1939	1947	Johnny Roventini dressed as a bellhop and was a spokesperson for Philip Morris cigarettes. He died in Suffern, New York, November 30, 1998, age 88.
John's Other Wife	soap opera	1936	1942	The other wife was John's secretary, and she was a "wife" in name only .
Johnson Family, The	soap opera	1936	1950	Jimmy Scribner, a white man, wrote the scripts and played all the roles in the African-American Johnson family that lived in the mythical Southern town of Chicazola.
Joyce Jordan, Girl Intern	soap opera	1938	1956	After Jordan passed her medical exams in the 1942-43 season, the show was retitled *Joyce Jordan, M.D.* It was off

				the air 1948-51 and 1952-55, then returned for one season.
Judy Canova Show, The	comedy/ variety	1943	1953	Last show: May 28, 1953. Canova also appeared on the Paul Whiteman and Charlie McCarthy shows. She died in Los Angeles, California, August 5, 1983, age 66.
Jungle Jim	juvenile adventure	1935	1954	Based on the comic strip character by Alex Raymond. Last episode: August 1, 1954.
Just Plain Bill	soap opera	1932	1955	The story of a small-town barber had a strong following. Last episode: September 30, 1955.
Juvenile Jury	juvenile problem solvers	1946	1953	Panel of young people told how they would solve problems other children posed.
Kate Smith Shows	music/ variety/ talk	1931	1952	Smith's shows included *Kate Smith and Her Swanee Music* (1931-34), *Kate Smith Revue* (1934-47, 1951-52) and *Kate Smith Speaks* (daily daytime show, 1938-51). She made the transition to TV in 1950.
Kay Kyser's Kollege of Musical Knowledge	music/ variety/ quiz	1938	1949	Contestants could win prizes by answering Bandleader Kay Kyser's questions. His show appeared on TV in 1949-50 and 1954.
Kitty Keene, Incorporated	soap opera	1937	1941	Last episode: April 25, 1941.
Knickerbocker Playhouse	drama	1939	1942	Show became *Abie's Irish Rose* in 1942.
Kraft Music Hall, The	music/ variety	1933	1949	Aired as one-hour show until 1942, then as half hour show.
Ladies Be Seated	audience participation	1944	1950	Daily afternoon show with pranks, contests and quizzes that offered money as prizes.
Land of the Lost	juvenile fantasy	1943	1948	Adventures of a brother and sister who lived at the bottom of the sea.
Lassie	canine adventure	1947	1950	Inspired by the film *Lassie Come Home* (1943). Last episode: May 27, 1950. Lassie made the transition to TV in 1954.
Leave It to the Girls	panel discussion	1945	1949	Aired on Saturday evening until 1947, then on Friday evening. Show moved to TV in 1949.
Leonidas Witherall	detective drama	1944	1945	Aired for two years as a summer replacement. Witherall, an amateur detective, was a dead ringer for William Shakespeare.
Let George Do It	detective drama	1946	1955	Detective George Valentine ran ads in newspapers to find cases. Last episode: January 12, 1955.

Let's Pretend	juvenile drama	1933	1954	Popular children anthology series was last heard on October 23, 1954.
Life Begins at Eighty	panel discussion	1948	1953	Octogenarians and older people discussed major issues. Aired originally as summer replacement (1948-49). Returned 1952-53.
Life Can Be Beautiful	soap opera	1938	1954	Popular radio soap.
Life of Mary Sothern, The	soap opera	1934	1938	Last episode: April 22, 1938.
Life of Riley, The	sitcom	1944	1951	Lionel Stander originated the role in 1944; however, William Bendix played Riley most of the time it was on radio. Last episode: June 29, 1951. The show went to TV while still on radio.
Life with Luigi	sitcom	1948	1953	The show was still on radio when it went to TV (1952-53). Last episode: May 23, 1953. J. Carroll Naish played Luigi on both radio and TV.
Light of the World	Bible stories	1940	1950	Fifteen-minute daily serialized dramatizations of the Bible.
Lights Out	horror tales	1934	1947	Off the air 1939. Revived 1942-43. Two summer airings in 1945, 1946. Last series in 1947 aired one month, ending August 6. TV version aired 1949-52.
Lincoln Highway	drama	1940	1942	Half-hour shows centered on life along the highway.
Linda's First Love	drama serial	1937	1950	Listeners could win prizes if they answered questions about what characters should do.
Lindlahr Food and Nutrition Show, The	health/ nutrition	1936	1953	Victor Lindlahr died in Miami Beach, Florida, January 26, 1969, age 71.
Listening Post	drama	1944	1948	Plots drawn from *Saturday Evening Post* human-interest stories.
Little Orphan Annie	adventure	1931	1943	Based on the Harold Gray comic strip character.
Lone Journey	soap opera	1940	1952	Off the air 1943-46, 1947-51.
Lone Ranger, The	western	1933	1956	Last of the radio series aired September 3, 1954. The TV version began in 1949.
Lorenzo Jones	soap opera	1937	1955	Actor Karl Swenson played Lorenzo the entire run of the series. He died in Torington, Connecticut, October 8, 1978, age 70.
Louella Parsons	Hollywood gossip	1945	1951	Parsons also had a newspaper gossip column. She died in Santa Monica, California, December 9, 1972, age 91.
Lum and Abner	rustic humor	1931	1954	Last episode: May 7, 1954. Chester Lauck, who portrayed Lum, died in Hot Springs Arkansas, February 22, 1980,

				age 78. Abner was played by Norris Goff, who died in Palm Desert, California, June 7, 1978, age 72.
Lux Radio Theater, The	drama	1934	1955	One-hour movie adaptations. Hosted by Cecil B. DeMille until January 22, 1945. Last episode: "Edward, My Son," June 7, 1955.
Ma Perkins	soap opera	1933	1960	Last episode: November 25, 1960. Actress Virginia Payne played the role of Ma Perkins the entire run of the series. She died in Cincinnati, Ohio, February 10, 1977, age 66.
Magic Key, The	music/ variety	1935	1939	Classical and semiclassical music mixed with popular radio acts.
Magnificent Montague, The	sitcom	1950	1951	Monty Woolley played Montague. He also appeared on the *Monty Woolley Program* (1943-44) and *The Drene Show* (1944-45).
Maisie (The Adventures of Maisie)	sitcom	1945	1952	Off the air 1947-48. Syndicated series aired 1948-49. Returned to network one season (1951-52). Maisie was played by Ann Sothern, who also portrayed the character in 10 films.
Major Bowes' Original Amateur Hour	talent show	1934	1946	Major Edward Bowes died in Rumson, New Jersey, June 14, 1946, age 71. The show went off the air when he died. It was revived in 1948 with Ted Mack as emcee. The show went to TV at the same time as *Ted Mack's Original Amateur Hour* and lasted until 1970.
Major Hoople	sitcom	1942	1944	Based on the comic strip character in *Our Boarding House,* created by Gene Ahren.
Man Behind the Gun, The	war stories	1942	1944	Dramatization of true World War II stories.
Man Called X, The	espionage drama	1944	1952	Off the air 1945-47 and 1948-50. Last series ran 1950-52. Last episode: May 27, 1952.
Mandrake the Magician	adventure	1940	1942	Based on King Features comic strip character created by Lee Falk and Phil Davis. Last episode: February 6, 1942.
Manhattan Merry-Go-Round, The	music/ comedy	1932	1949	A Sunday evening fixture during its 17-year run.
March of Time, The	dramatization of news	1931	1945	Produced by *Time* magazine.
Mark Trail	adventure	1950	1952	Last episode: "The Wolf Trap," June 27, 1952.
Marriage for Two	soap opera	1949	1950	Last episode: March 31, 1950.

Martin Kane, Private Detective	crime drama	1949	1952	First aired as *Private Eye*. Last episode: December 21, 1952.
Mary Margaret McBride	talk show	1934	1954	Began in 1934 as *The Martha Dean Show*. Retitled *Mary Margaret McBride* in 1941. McBride died in West Shokun, New York, April 7, 1976, age 76.
Maxwell House Coffee Time	comedy/ variety	1940	1944	Aired as *Good News of 1938,* then *Good News of 1939*. Reformatted and retitled *Maxwell House Coffee Time* in 1940 and featured Frank Morgan and Fanny Brice. Show ended in 1944 when Brice left to star on the *Baby Snooks Show*.
Mayor of the Town	drama	1942	1949	Off the air 1943-44. Lionel Barrymore portrayed the mayor during the run of the show. He then hosted *Hallmark Playhouse* (1952-54).
Meet Corliss Archer	teen sitcom	1943	1955	Based on character created by F. Hugh Herbert in the stage play *Kiss and Tell*. Show was televised 1951-52.
Meet Me at Parky's	comedy	1945	1947	Harry Einstein's creation Nick Parkyakarkis was so popular on *The Eddie Cantor Show* that he was given his own show. Einstein died in Beverly Hills, California, November 24, 1958, age 50.
Meet the Press	news panel	1946	1956	Joint venture of network and *American Mercury* magazine. Made the transition to TV in 1947.
Mel Blanc Show, The	comedy	1946	1947	Half-hour show. Last episode: "The Missing Bread Slices," June 24, 1947. Blanc died in Los Angeles, California, July 10, 1989, age 81.
Mercury Theater on the Air (*Campbell Playhouse, Orson Welles Theater, Mercury Summer Theater*)	adaptations of classics	1937	1946	Last episode of *Mercury Theater on the Air* series: "Bridge of San Louis Rey," December 4, 1938. Renamed *Campbell Playhouse* (1938-40). Last episode of *Campbell Playhouse* series: "Jane Eyre," March 31, 1940. Returned as *Orson Welles Theater* (1941-42). Last episode of *Orson Welles Theater* series: "Between Americans," February 2, 1942. Returned final time June 1946 as *Mercury Summer Theater*. Last episode series: "King Lear," September 13, 1946.
MGM Theater of the Air	film adaptations	1949	1951	Last original episode: "We Who Are Young," April 20, 1951. Reruns aired until December 1952.
Michael Shayne, Private Detective	detective drama	1944	1953	Based on character created by Brett Halliday. Aired as *The New Adventures*

				of Michael Shayne (1948-50). Off the air 1950-52; returned for one season. Show was TV series in 1960-61.
Monitor	news magazine	1955	1975	Last show: January 26, 1975.
Mr. and Mrs. North, Adventures of	murder mystery	1942	1955	Off the air 1946-47. Last episode: April 18, 1955. The TV version ran 1952-54.
Mr. District Attorney	crime drama	1939	1952	Last episode: June 13, 1952. The show was on TV while on radio.
Mr. Keen, Tracer of Lost Persons	mystery	1937	1955	Last episode: April 19, 1955.
Mr. President	drama series	1947	1953	Dramatizations of the lives of U.S. presidents.
Mrs. Wiggs of the Cabbage Patch	soap opera	1935	1938	Last episode: December 23, 1938.
Murder and Mr. Malone	crime drama	1947	1951	Aired as *The Amazing Mr. Malone* in the fall of 1949.
Music Appreciation Hour, The	music	1928	1942	Classical and semiclassical music. Show's producer, director and commentator was Dr. Walter Damrosch.
My Favorite Husband	sitcom	1948	1951	Featured Lucille Ball. Last episode: March 31, 1951.
My Friend Irma	sitcom	1947	1954	Irma was portrayed by Marie Wilson, who also played the role on TV (1952-54) and in two films.
My Little Margie	sitcom	1952	1955	The TV version ran during the same years, with the same cast.
My True Story	serial dramas	1943	1961	Stories were adapted from *True Story* magazine and presented in 15-minute daily segments. TV version lasted only a few months in 1950.
Mysterious Traveler, The	supernatural stories	1943	1952	Last episode: "Treasure of Superstition Mountain," September 16, 1952.
Mystery in the Air	mystery	1947	1947	Summer replacement starring Peter Lorre that ran just one season. Last of the series: "Crime and Punishment," September 25, 1947. *Mystery in the Air* was also the name of a summer replacement that aired in 1945.
Mystery Theater, The	mystery	1943	1954	Began as *The Mollé Mystery Theater* (1943-47). Off the air 1947-51. Returned as *The Mystery Theater*.
National Barn Dance	music	1924	1960	Off the air 1946-48. Syndicated 1950-60. Last show aired April 30, 1960.
National Farm and Home Hour	information	1929	1958	Aired daily from 1929 to 1945. Aired once a week during its final years.
NBC Presents: Short Story	drama	1951	1952	Last show: March 14, 1952.

NBC University Theater of the Air, The	dramatic anthology	1948	1951	Dramatizations of great works of literature Began as *World's Great Novels* (1944-48). Retitled *NBC University Theater of the Air* (1948). Title changed to *NBC Theater* in 1949. Last episode: "The Withered Arm," February 14, 1951.
Nero Wolfe, The Adventures of	detective drama	1943	1951	Based on Rex Stout character. Off the air 1943-45. Revived as *The Amazing Adventures of Nero Wolfe.* Last series, *The New Adventures of Nero Wolfe,* ran 1950-51. Last episode: "The Case of Room 304," April 27, 1951.
Nick Carter, Master Detective	crime drama	1943	1955	Last episode: "The Case of the Counterfeit Passports," September 25, 1955.
Night Beat	newspaper drama	1950	1952	Last episode: "The Fire Bug Killers," September 25, 1952.
Nobody's Children	orphan adoptions	1939	1941	Orphans told their stories on the air with the hope of being adopted.
Official Detective	police drama	1946	1957	Began as a 15-minute program. Expanded to a half hour in 1947.
One Man's Family	serial drama	1932	1959	The saga of the Barbour family. Last episode: May 8, 1959, ending a 27-year run
O'Neills, The	soap opera	1934	1943	Last episode: June 18, 1943.
Orson Welles Shows	drama	1937	1952	Welles was featured in many radio programs, including *The Shadow* (1937-38), *Orson Welles Radio Almanac* (1944), *This is My Best* (1944-45) and *Black Museum* (1952). (*See also* Mercury Theater on the Air.)
Our Gal Sunday	soap opera	1936	1959	Last episode: January 2, 1959. One of four radio soaps that ended on that day.
Our Miss Brooks	sitcom	1948	1957	Last episode: July 7, 1957. *Our Miss Brooks* was heard on TV from 1952 to 1956, with most of the same cast. Eve Arden played Connie Brooks.
Ozzie and Harriet, The Adventures of	sitcom	1944	1954	Last radio show: June 18, 1954. Became a popular TV show in 1952. Ozzie Nelson died in San Fernando Valley, California, June 3, 1975, age 68. His wife Harriet Hilliard Nelson died in Laguna Beach, California, October 2, 1994, age 85.
Passing Parade, The	amazing stories	1938	1951	Created by John Nesbitt, who also hosted the show. A series of *The Passing Parade* short films was produced from 1938 to 1949. Nesbitt died in Carmel, California, August 10, 1960, age 49.
Pat Novak, For Hire	crime drama	1946	1949	Last episode: June 18, 1949.

Paul Whiteman Shows	music	1929	1954	Conductor Paul Whiteman was on radio as early as 1922. Among the many programs he was featured on were *Old Gold Hour* (1929-30), *Kraft Music Hall* (1933-35), *Philco Hall of Fame* (1943-46) and *Paul Whiteman Teen Club* (1947-48). He made the transition to TV in 1949 and hosted several series.
Pause That Refreshes on the Air, The	music	1934	1949	Program of classical and semiclassical music sponsored by Coca-Cola. Off the air 1935-40, 1944-47.
Penthouse Party	talk-variety	1934	1941	Off the air 1936-41. Revived briefly in 1941.
People Are Funny	audience participa-tion	1942	1959	Hosted during most of the show's run by Art Linkletter. Made transition to TV in 1954.
Pepper Young's Family	soap opera	1936	1959	Show began in 1932 as *Red Adams*. Retitled *Forever Young* in 1935. Retitled *Pepper Young's Family* in June 1936.
Perry Mason	crime mystery	1943	1955	Based on character created by Erle Stanley Gardner. TV version first aired in 1957.
Phil Baker Show, The	comedy/ variety	1933	1939	Baker emceed *Take It or Leave It* (1941-51). He died in Copenhagen, Denmark, December 1, 1963, age 67.
Phil Harris-Alice Faye Show	music/ variety	1948	1954	Part of the *Fitch Bandwagon* until 1948. Last show: June 18, 1954.
Philip Marlowe, The Adventures of	detective drama	1947	1951	Based on Raymond Chandler character. Began as summer replacement. Aired as regular program beginning 1949. Last episode: "The Sound and the Unsound," September 15, 1951.
Philip Morris Playhouse, The	drama	1939	1953	Off the air in 1943. Returned one season (1948-49), then off the air until 1951. On TV 1953-54.
Philo Vance, Detective	detective drama	1945	1950	Based on S.S. Van Dine character. Last episode: "The Muddy Murder Case," July 4, 1950.
Portia Faces Life	soap opera	1940	1951	Lucille Wall played Portia most of the time the program was on the air. The TV version lasted just one season (1954-55). Wall died in Reno, Nevada, July 11, 1986, age 88.
Pot o' Gold	game show	1939	1947	Off the air 1941-46. Revived 1946-47. Show phoned people. To win, they had be at home to answer the call.
Pretty Kitty Kelly	soap opera	1937	1940	Last episode: September 27, 1940.
Prudential Family Hour	music/ variety	1941	1949	Music format until 1948. Last season show was comedy/drama.

Pursuit	suspense	1949	1952	A TV version had a short run in 1958-59.
Queen for a Day	interview show	1945	1957	Popular daytime show. Made transition to TV (1956-64). Revived one season as syndicated series (1970).
Quick as a Flash	quiz	1944	1951	Panel members were given clues then were asked to identify a phrase or personality. TV version ran 1953-54.
Quiet, Please	mystery	1947	1949	Last episode: "Quiet Please," June 25, 1949.
Quiz Kids, The	quiz	1940	1953	Contestants were under 16. TV version aired 1949- 56.
Radio City Playhouse	drama	1948	1950	Last episode: "Reflections," January 1, 1950.
Radio Reader's Digest	drama	1942	1948	Last episode: "Why Housewives Have No Whiskers," June 3, 1948.
Railroad Hour, The	music-variety	1948	1954	Last program: June 21, 1954.
Red Ryder, The Adventures of	western	1942	1949	Based on short-story and comic strip character created by Fred Harman.
Red Skelton Show, The	comedy/variety	1941	1953	Made the transition to TV, where show lasted 20 years (1951-71).
Richard Diamond, Private Detective	crime drama	1949	1953	Last episode: September 20, 1953. A TV version ran in 1957-60.
Right to Happiness, The	soap opera	1939	1960	Last episode aired on November 25, 1960, a date known as "the last day of soap opera," when several soaps ended.
Rin Tin Tin	canine adventure	1930	1955	Off the air 1934-55. Returned for one season. The TV version aired from 1954 to 1959. Another series, *Rin Tin Tin, K-9 Cop* ran 1988-93. Rin Tin Tin, an Alsatian Shepherd, was introduced in silent films in the 1920s.
Road of Life, The	soap opera	1937	1959	Last episode: January 2, 1959. Three other soaps also ended that date. The TV version lasted from December 1954 to July 1955.
Rocky Fortune	adventure	1953	1954	Frank Sinatra played Rocky Fortune. Last episode: "Boarding House Double-cross," March 30, 1954.
Rogue's Gallery	crime drama	1945	1951	Last episode: November 21, 1951.
Romance of Helen Trent, The	soap opera	1933	1960	Last episode: June 24, 1960, ending a 27-year run.
Roses and Drums	drama	1932	1936	Dramatizations of historic events. Last episode: "Road's End," March 29, 1936.
Roxy and His Gang	variety	1922	1931	Roxy was played by the show's creator Samuel Lionel Rothafel, who died in

				New York, New York, January 13, 1936, age 54.
Roy Rogers Show, The	music/ variety	1944	1955	Aired on TV part of the time it was on radio (1951-57).
Rudy Vallee Shows	music	1929	1947	Singer/bandleader Rudy Vallee was featured in several radio shows, including *The Fleischmann Hour* (1929-39), *The Sealtest Show* (1940-43). *Villa Vallee* (1944-46) and *The Rudy Vallee Show* (1946-47). Vallee died in North Hollywood, California, July 3, 1986, age 84.
Saint, The	detective drama	1945	1951	Based on character created by Leslie Charteris. Last episode: October 21, 1951. The Saint returned to BBC radio in the 1990s.
Sam Spade, Detective, The Adventures of	detective drama	1946	1951	Based on Dashiell Hammett character. Last episode: "The Hail and Farewell Caper," April 27, 1951.
Sammy Kaye Shows	music	1930s	1956	Bandleader Sammy Kaye began broadcasting in the mid-1930s. He was featured on many shows, including *Sammy Kaye's Sunday Serenade* (1941-54), *So You Want to Lead a Band* (1946-48) and *The Sammy Kaye Show* (1950-56).
Scattergood Baines	sitcom/ soap opera	1937	1950	Off the air in 1942. Returned in syndication with new sitcom format (1949).
Sci–Fi Radio	sci-fi adventure	1989	1990	Last episode: "Yankee Doodle," March 18, 1990.
Screen Directors' Playhouse	film adaptations	1949	1951	Last episode: "Mother was a Freshman," August 30, 1951.
Screen Guild Theater	film adaptations	1939	1951	Last episode: "Apartment for Peggy," May 31, 1951.
Sea Hound, The	juvenile adventure	1942	1951	Off the air 1948-51, then revived one season.
Sealtest Village Store, The	sitcom	1943	1948	Spun off from *The Rudy Vallee Show* when Vallee left to enter the service during World War II.
Second Mrs. Burton, The	soap opera	1946	1960	One of the last radio soap operas to go on the air. One of several that ended November 25, 1960.
Sergeant Preston of the Canadian Mounted Police	juvenile adventure	1947	1955	Began as *The Challenge of the Yukon* (1947). Retitled in 1953. Last episode: June 9, 1955. Made transition to network TV in 1955. Syndicated 1958.
Seth Parker	music/ variety/ drama	1929	1939	Began as *Sunday Evening at Seth Parker's* (1929-33). Retitled *Cruise of the Seth Parker* (1933-34). Off the air 1934-35, 1936-38. *Seth Parker,* a four-

				masted schooner named for the radio character, attempted to make an around-the-world cruise but was destroyed in a storm February 1935.
Shadow, The	crime drama	1930	1954	Based on character created by Walter Gibson. Last episode: December 26, 1954.
Sheriff, The	western	1945	1951	Replaced *Death Valley Days.* Began as *Death Valley Sheriff.*
Sherlock Holmes, The Adventures of	detective drama	1930	1956	Off the air 1936-39, 1950-55. Last episode: September 4, 1956. Basil Rathbone portrayed Holmes from 1939 to 1946. His last appearance: "The Singular Affair of the Baconian Cipher," May 27, 1946.
Show Boat	music/ drama/ variety	1932	1941	Based on the Edna Ferber novel and Broadway musical. Cancelled in 1938 but brought back in 1940.
Silver Eagle	juvenile adventure	1951	1955	Last episode: March 10, 1955.
Singin' Sam, The Barbasol Man	music	1930	1947	Off the air 1937-41. Syndicated *Reminiscin' with Singin' Sam* was broadcast in 1945-47. Singing' Sam was Harry Frankel, who died in Richmond, Indiana, June 13, 1948, age 60.
Singing Story Lady, The	children's stories	1932	1941	The Singing Story Lady was Ireene Wicker. She died in West Palm Beach, Florida, November 17, 1987, age 86.
Six Shooter, The	western	1953	1954	James Stewart's only radio series lasted just one season. Last episode: "Myra Barker," June 24, 1954.
Skippy Hollywood Theater, The	drama	1940	1950	Skippy Peanut Butter was the sponsor of the syndicated series.
Sky King	aviation adventure	1946	1954	Last episode: June 3, 1954. *Sky King* made the transition to TV in 1953.
Smilin' Ed and His Buster Brown Gang	children's show/ music	1929	1953	Began as *The Smilin' Ed McConnell Show.* Off the air 1941-44. Returned as *Smilin' Ed and His Buster Brown Gang.* Ed McConnell died in Newport Beach, California, July 24, 1954, age 62.
Somebody Knows	crime	1950	1950	Aired one summer. Last episode: August 24, 1950, the unsolved 1947 murder of the Black Dahlia.
Space Patrol	adventure	1950	1955	Half-hour series first aired twice a week, then moved to Saturday in 1951.
Spotlight Bands	music	1941	1946	Began as *The Victory Parade of Spotlight Bands* during World War II. Off the air 1942-43. Returned as *Spotlight Bands.*

Stage Door Canteen	wartime entertain- ment	1942	1945	Celebrities entertained the troops during World War II.
Stella Dallas	soap opera	1937	1955	Last episode: December 2, 1955. Anne Elstner played Stella Dallas during the entire run of the series. She died in Doylestown, Pennsylvania, January 29, 1981, age 82.
Stepmother	soap opera	1938	1942	Last episode: July 10, 1942.
Stoopnagle and Budd	comedy	1931	1937	Began as *The Gloom Chasers*. Roles were played by Frederick Chase Taylor and Wilbur ("Budd") Hulick. Taylor died in Boston, Massachusetts, on May 29, 1950, age 52.
Stop Me If You've Heard This One	game show	1939	1948	Listeners sent in jokes and a panel pro- vided the punch lines. Cancelled 1940, revived 1947. TV version ran 1948-49.
Stop the Music	music quiz	1949	1955	Off the air 1952. Revived 1954-55.
Story of Mary Marlin, The	soap opera	1935	1952	Aired locally in Chicago, Illinois, in 1934 and on network the following year. Canceled in 1945 but revived for one season (1951-52).
Story of Myrt and Marge, The	soap opera	1931	1942	Syndicated version released in 1946.
Straight Arrow	juvenile adventure	1948	1951	Last episode: "Long Summer," June 21, 1951.
Strange Romance of Evelyn Winters, The	soap opera	1944	1948	One of the later soaps to air.
Strike it Rich	quiz	1947	1957	Off the air 1955 then revived for one sea- son (1957). The TV series ran 1951-58.
Studio One	drama	1947	1948	Last performance: "Constant Nymph," July 27, 1948. The TV version ran 1948- 58.
Superman, The Adventures of	fantasy adventure	1938	1951	Based on Action Comics character cre- ated by Jerry Siegel and Joe Shuster. Last episode: March 1, 1951. Moved to TV in 1951.
Suspense	mystery	1942	1962	Began as summer replacement, 1940. Last episode: "Devil Stone," September 30 1962. *Suspense* was the last of the old- time radio dramas to leave the air.
Take It or Leave It	quiz	1940	1950	Last person to host the show was Eddie Cantor (1949-50).
Tales of the Texas Rangers	western	1950	1952	Last episode: "Drive-In," September 14, 1952.
Tales of Tomorrow	sci-fi anthology	1953	1953	Last episode: "The Drop," April 9, 1953. *Tales of Tomorrow* was on TV 1951 to 1953.
Tarzan of the Apes	adventure	1932	1953	Based on Edgar Rice Burroughs charac- ter. Aired as *Tarzan of the Apes,* in

				1932-36 and as *Tarzan Lord of the Jungle* in 1951-53. Last episode of that series: June 27, 1953.
Terry and the Pirates	adventure	1937	1948	Based on comic strip character by Milton Caniff. First series aired 1937-39. Show revived in 1943. *Terry and the Pirates* had a short TV run in 1952
Tex and Jinx	talk	1949	1956	*Tex and Jinx* were husband Tex McCrary and wife Jinx Falkenburg. Falkenburg also hosted *Hi, Jinx!* in 1946-49. Their show made the transition to TV in 1957.
Texaco Star Theater, The	variety/ comedy	1938	1948	The show transitioned to TV in 1948 as the *Milton Berle Show*.
Theater Guild on the Air, The	drama	1945	1953	Last episode: "Julius Caesar," June 7, 1953.
Thin Man, The Adventures of the	mystery	1941	1950	Based on characters Nick and Nora Charles created by Dashiell Hammett. Last episode: September 1, 1950.
Third Man, The	mystery	1951	1952	Based on character created by Graham Greene. Also titled *The Lives of Harry Lime*. Last episode: "Greek Meets Greek," July 25, 1952. Syndicated TV series was produced 1959-62.
This Is My Best	drama	1944	1946	Last episode: "The Furious Bride," May 28, 1946. Orson Welles produced, directed, narrated and starred in shows that aired in 1944-45.
This Is Nora Drake	soap opera	1947	1959	Last episode: January 2, 1959. Three other radio soaps ended that date.
This Is Your FBI	crime-fighting dramas	1945	1953	Last episode: "The Red-headed Blackmailer," January 20, 1953.
This Is Your Life	celebrity biographies	1948	1950	Created by and hosted by Ralph Edwards. Made the transition to TV in 1952.
Those We Love	serial drama	1938	1945	Off the air 1941-43.
Today's Children	soap opera	1933	1950	Off the air 1938-1943; returned 1943 and ran until 1950. One of several soap operas created by Irna Phillips, who died in Chicago, Illinois, December 22, 1973, age 72.
Tom Corbett, Space Cadet	juvenile adventure	1952	1952	Show already on TV when radio series began.
Tom Mix Ralston Straightshooters	western	1933	1950	Off the air 1942-44. Last episode: June 23, 1950. After Tom Mix was killed in an auto accident in 1940, his role was played by several actors. The last "Tom Mix" was Joe ("Curley") Bradley, from 1944 to 1950. Bradley died June 3, 1985, in Long Beach, California, age 74.

Tommy Riggs and Betty Lou Shows	comedy	1938	1943	Comedian Tommy Riggs provided the voice for seven-year-old Betty Lou. The *Quaker Party with Tommy Riggs* aired in 1938-40. *Tommy Riggs and Betty Lou* aired in 1942-43. Riggs died in Pittsburgh, Pennsylvania, May 21, 1967, age 58.
Tony Wons' Scrapbook	poetry/ philoso- phy	1930	1942	Off the air several seasons. Final series aired 1940-42. Wons died in Iron Mountain, Michigan, July 1, 1965, age 73.
Town Crier, The	talk	1929	1937	Also titled *Radio's Town Crier*. Featured author/drama critic Alexander Woollcott. He had a heart attack while appearing on the radio program *People's Platform* in New York, New York, and died a few hours later, January 23, 1943, age 56.
True Detective Mysteries	detective drama	1929	1959	Based on stories from *True Detective* magazine. Several versions were broadcast: 1929-30, 1936-37, 1938-39 and 1944-59.
Truth or Consequences	game show	1940	1956	Created by Ralph Edwards, who hosted the show until 1954. The show made the transition to TV in 1950.
Twenty Questions	game show	1946	1954	Show made the transition to TV in 1949 and remained on the air until 1955.
Twenty Thousand Years in Sing Sing	crime drama	1933	1939	Narrated by Lewis E. Lawes, warden of New York State's Sing Sing Prison. Lawes died in Garrison, New York, April 23, 1947, age 63.
Two for the Money	quiz	1952	1956	TV version aired during same time but lasted longer (1952-57).
Uncle Don	children's show	1928	1949	Local New York show for most of its run. On network 1939-40. Uncle Don was Don Carney, who died in Miami, Florida, January 14, 1954, age 64.
Uncle Ezra's Radio Station	variety	1934	1941	Character originated on National Barn Dance.
Under Arrest	crime drama	1947	1954	Began as summer replacement. Regular series aired 1948-54.
Valiant Lady	soap opera	1938	1952	Off the air 1946. Revived unsuccessfully during 1951-52 season.
Vaughn de Leath Shows	music	1922	1939	Female singer and radio pioneer de Leath was featured on several early radio shows including *Voice of Firestone* (1928-30) and *The Vaughn de Leath Show* (1931-39). She died in Buffalo, New York, May 28, 1943, age 46.
Vic and Sade	sitcom	1932	1946	Last episode of daily daytime series: September 29, 1944. A weekly evening version aired a short time in 1946.

Victor Borge Show, The	comedy/ variety	1945	1947	Borge appeared earlier on the *Kraft Music Hall* (1941-43). The TV version of his show aired in 1951.
Voice of Firestone, The	music	1928	1957	A Monday evening fixture on radio for more than 27 years. On TV 1949-63. TV and radio shows simulcast until June 1957.
Vox Pop	interviews	1935	1948	*Vox pop* (Latin) is short for *vox populi,* voice of the people.
Voyage of Scarlet Queen, The	maritime adventure	1947	1948	Set aboard a five-masted sailing ship in the 19th century. Last episode: "Winchester Rifle and the Ambitious Groom," February 25, 1948.
Walter Winchell Show, The	news/ gossip	1932	1957	Titled *Jergens Journal* until 1948. Winchell died in Los Angeles, California, February 20, 1972, age 74.
We Love and Learn	soap opera	1942	1956	Began as *As the Twig is Bent*. Off the air 1951-55. Returned to the air in 1955 as *Story of Ruby Valentine* with an African-American cast and syndicated on the National Negro Network.
We, the People	human interest	1936	1951	The show aired on TV 1948-52.
Wendy Warren and the News	soap opera news	1947	1958	Show included news every day at noon.
What's My Name?	game show	1938	1949	Off the air 1943. Revived in 1949. A forerunner of the TV show *What's My Line?* Arlene Francis appeared on both shows.
What's the Name of That Song?	musical quiz	1944	1949	Contestants guessed the names of tunes played by show's musicians.
When a Girl Marries	soap opera	1939	1957	Last episode: August 30, 1957.
Whispering Streets	soap opera	1952	1960	Last episode: November 25, 1960.
Whistler, The	mystery	1942	1955	Aired nationally until 1948, then heard regionally. Last episode: "Design for Murder," September 8, 1955.
Wild Bill Hickok	juvenile western adventure	1951	1956	Last episode: February 12, 1956. When the show transitioned to TV in 1951, Guy Madison (Wild Bill) and Andy Devine (Jingles) played the same roles they played on radio.
Winner Take All	quiz	1946	1949	Show went to TV in 1948 while still on radio.
Witch's Tale, The	supernatural	1934	1938	Show first aired locally in New York (1931). Last episode: June 13, 1938.
Woman in My House, The	soap opera	1951	1959	The saga of a family created by Carlton E. Morse, who also created the popular series *One Man's Family*.
Woman in White, The	soap opera	1938	1948	Off the air 1942-44.

Woman of America	soap opera	1943	1946	Began as stories about historic women in soap opera format. Changed to modern soap.
Woman of Courage	soap opera	1940	1942	Set during the Great Depression.
X Minus One	sci-fi anthology	1955	1958	Last episode: "Gray Flannel Armor," January 9, 1958. A one-episode revival aired January 1973: "The Iron Chancellor." (See also *Dimension X.*)
You Are There	historical drama	1947	1950	Began as *CBS Is There.* Retitled *You Are There* in 1948. Last show: "Boston Tea Party," July 9, 1950. TV version aired 1953-57.
You Bet Your Life	quiz	1947	1956	Groucho Marx was host. The show transitioned to TV in 1950, also with Marx.
Young Dr. Malone	soap opera	1939	1960	Last episode: November 25, 1960. One of six soaps cancelled that day.
Young Widder Brown	soap opera	1938	1956	Last episode: June 29, 1956.
Your Hit Parade	music	1935	1959	Show made transition to TV in 1950. Last radio show: January 16, 1953. TV show simulcast over radio until 1959.
Yours Truly, Johnny Dollar	crime drama	1948	1962	The last major dramatic show on network radio. Last episode: "The Tip-Off Matter," September 30, 1962.
Zero Hour, The	thriller drama	1973	1974	Last episode: "Holdout, " July 26, 1974.
Ziegfeld Follies of the Air	music/ variety	1932	1936	Went off the air when Florenz Ziegfeld died in 1932. Returned in 1936 but did not last the year.

Railroads

(*See also* Engineering—Bridges, Tunnels.)

Railroads—Locomotives
• **Last surviving U.S. coal-fired passenger locomotive:** Norfolk & Western No. 611, Class J Steam Locomotive (1950), now at the Virginia Museum of Transportation in Roanoke.

Railroads—Rails Standardized
When construction began on the first transcontinental railroad in 1863, the gauge, or distance between rail tracks, was set at $56^1/2$ inches, the same gauge northern U.S. railroads and those in England were using. In the American South, however, tracks were 5 feet apart. And in the West, tracks known as narrow gauge were only 3 feet apart. After the Civil War, it became essential that all rails in the nation operate with a standardized gauge.

• **Last time rails were not standardized in the U.S.:** 1886. Between May 26 and June 1 1886, thousands of track workers moved more than 9,000 miles of Southern rails three inches closer to conform with the gauge north of the Mason-Dixon line. In the West, standardization moved more slowly. It was finally completed around 1900.

• **Last broad-gauge rail line in Canada:** Carillon and Grenville Railway. It was abandoned 1910. The following year, the line was purchased by the Canadian Northern Railway.

Railroads—Trains—Orient Express/Simplon-Orient Express

The Orient Express ran twice a week from Paris, France, to Constantinople, Turkey, beginning in 1883. When the train was inaugurated, passengers traveled by rail between Paris and Bucharest, Romania, and by ship from there to Constantinople. By 1889, the entire journey was by rail. Beginning in 1885, it provided weekly service to Vienna. The train took the name Simplon after it began running through the Simplon Tunnel in the Alps in 1906.

• **Last regular trip of the Orient Express:** May 22, 1977. It was discontinued because of declining passengers. In mid-1980s, the train began operating again, but this time as a tourist attraction.

Railroads
Last Year of Operation for Some Major American Railroads

Name of Railroad and Year Founded	Ended Operation	Description
Allegheny Portage Railroad and the Public Works (1834)	1857	First rail connection between Philadelphia and Pittsburgh, Pennsylvania. The railroad was dismantled in 1858 and the rails were shipped to Indiana.
Atchison, Topeka & Santa Fe Railway (1859)	1995	Chartered as Atchison & Topeka Railroad Company (1859). Renamed Atchison, Topeka & Santa Fe Railroad Company (1863). Renamed Atchison, Topeka & Santa Fe Railway (1895). Merged with Burlington Northern Railroad as Burlington Northern Santa Fe Railway (1995).
Atlantic Coast Line Railroad (1871)	1967	Merged with Seaboard Air Line Railroad to form Seaboard Coast Line Railroad (1967).
Baltimore & Ohio Railroad (1827; the B&O (railroad))	1986	First railroad chartered for commercial transportation of people and freight (1827). Integrated into Chessie System (1972). Merged with the Chesapeake & Ohio Railway, which then merged into CSX Transportation (1986).
Burlington Northern Railroad (1970)	1995	Created by merger of four railroads (1970). Became Burlington Northern Santa Fe Railway (1995) with merger of Atchison, Topeka and Santa Fe.
Central Railroad of New Jersey (1852)	1976	Filed for bankruptcy (1967). Taken over by Conrail (1976).
Chesapeake & Ohio Railway (1868; the C&O)	1986	Chartered as Chesapeake & Ohio Railroad when Virginia Central and Covington & Ohio merged (1868). Renamed Chesapeake & Ohio Railway (1878). Merged into CSX Transportation (1986).
Chessie System (1972)	1986	Created to operate Chesapeake & Ohio, Baltimore & Ohio and other rail lines. Merged with Seaboard System to became CSX Transportation (1986).
Chicago, Burlington & Quincy Railroad Company (1864)	1970	Existing Illinois railroad adopted the name Chicago, Burlington & Quincy Railroad Company (1864). It expanded after the Civil War and eventually extended to Denver, Colorado. Merged with three other railroads as Burlington Northern Railroad (1970).
Chicago, Milwaukee, St. Paul	1986	Chartered as Milwaukee & St. Paul Railway Company. Renamed Chicago, Milwaukee & St. Paul Railway Com-

& Pacific (1874)		pany (1874). Incorporated as Chicago, Milwaukee, St. Paul & Pacific (1927). Sold to Soo Line Railroad and renamed The Milwaukee Road, Inc. (1985). Absorbed into Soo Line Railroad (1986).
Chicago & North Western Railroad (1859)	1995	Merged with Union Pacific (1995).
Chicago, Rock Island & Pacific Railroad Company (1848)	1980	Earlier names: Rock Island & LaSalle Rail Road Company (1848-51), Chicago & Rock Island Rail Road Company (1851-66), Chicago, Rock Island & Pacific Railroad Company (1866-80), Chicago, Rock Island & Pacific Railway (1880-1947), Chicago, Rock Island & Pacific Railroad Company (1948-80). Bankruptcy led to liquidation of the railroad. Last train operated on March 31, 1980.
Delaware, Lacka-wanna & Western Railroad (1853)	1960	Created when two rail lines—Lackawanna & Western and the Delaware and Cobb—merged (1853). Merged with the Erie as Erie-Lackawanna (1960).
Denver & Rio Grande Western Railroad (1921)	1988	Merged with Southern Pacific Railroad (1988).
Erie Railroad Company (1832)	1960	Chartered as New York & Erie Railroad (1832). Name changed to Erie Railway (1861). Taken over by New York, Lake Erie and Western Railway (1878). Reorganized as Erie Railroad Company (1895). Merged with the Lackawanna as Erie-Lackawanna (1960). Declared bankrupt (1972). Reorganized as Erie Transportation (1973). Absorbed into Conrail (Consolidated Rail Corporation, 1976).
Great Northern Railway (1857)	1970	Chartered as Minnesota & Pacific Railroad Company (1857). Reorganized as St. Paul, Minneapolis & Manitoba Railway Company (1879). Renamed Great Northern Railway Company (1889). Merged with three other railroads as Burlington Northern Railroad (1970).
Kentucky & Indiana Terminal Railroad (1880)	1981	Chartered as Kentucky & Indiana Bridge Company (1880). Renamed Kentucky & Indiana Bridge & Railroad Company (1900). Renamed Kentucky & Indiana Terminal Railroad (1910). Sold to Southern Railway (1981).
Lehigh Valley Railroad Company (1846)	1976	Chartered as Delaware, Lehigh, Schuylkill and Susquehanna Railroad Company (1846). Renamed Lehigh Valley Railroad Company (1853). Ceased passenger service (1964). Filed for bankruptcy protection (1970). Absorbed into Conrail 1976.
Minneapolis, St. Paul & Sault Ste. Marie Railway (1888)	1961	Merged with Wisconsin Central to create Soo Line (1961).
Missouri-Kansas-Texas Railroad Company (1865; "Katy Line")	1989	Known as the "Katy Line." Chartered as Union Pacific Railway Company, Southern Branch (1865). Renamed Missouri, Kansas, and Texas Railway Company (1870). Reorganized as Missouri-Kansas-Texas Railroad Company of Texas (1923). Merged into Union Pacific (1989).

Nashville, Chattanooga & St. Louis Railway (1845)	1956	Chartered as Nashville & Chattanooga Railroad Company (1845). Reorganized and renamed Nashville, Chattanooga & St. Louis Railway (1873). Absorbed by Louisville & Nashville (1956).
New York Central Railroad Company (1853)	1968	Created when several short lines between Albany and Buffalo joined together (1853). Merged with Pennsylvania Railroad to create Penn Central, world's largest privately owned rail line (1968).
New York, Chicago & St. Louis Railroad (1881; "Nickel Plate Road")	1964	Known as the "Nickel Plate Road." Merged into Norfolk and Western Railway (1964).
New York, New Haven & Hartford Railroad (1872)	1969	Went into receivership (1961). Absorbed by Penn Central (1969).
Norfolk & Western Railway (1881)	1982	Created from Atlantic, Mississippi & Ohio Railroad (1881). Reorganized as Norfolk & Western Railway (1896). Consolidated with Southern Railway to form Norfolk Southern Corporation (1982).
Penn Central Railroad (1968)	1976	Created from merger of New York Central and Pennsylvania Railroad (1968). Declared bankruptcy (1970). Freight operations absorbed into Conrail (Consolidated Rail Corporation) with several other Northeastern rail lines (1976). Reorganized as Penn Central Corporation (1978).
Pennsylvania Railroad Company (1846)	1968	Merged with New York Central Railroad to form Penn Central Company (1968). • **Last steam locomotive entered service:** T1, 5546 (4-4-4-4) in 1946. • **Last of Broad Street Station, Philadelphia:** closed 1952, then demolished.
Pere Marquette Railroad (1900)	1947	A number of rail lines incorporated as Pere Marquette Railroad Company (1900). Reincorporated as Pere Marquette Railway (1917). Merged into Chesapeake & Ohio (1947).
Piedmont & Northern Railway (1911)	1969	Passenger service ended (1951). Merged into Seaboard Coast Line (1969).
Pittsburgh & Lake Erie Railroad (1875; "Little Giant")	1992	Known as the "Little Giant." Sold to CSX (1992).
Pittsburgh & West Virginia (1904)	1964	Chartered as Wabash Pittsburgh Terminal Railroad (1904). Went into receivership (1911). Renamed Pittsburgh & West Virginia. Merged into Norfolk & Western (1964).
Reading Company (1833)	1976	Chartered as Philadelphia & Reading Railroad (1833). Renamed Reading Company (1924). Went bankrupt (1971). Operations taken over by Conrail (1976).
St. Louis and San Francisco Railway (1849; "Frisco")	1980	Chartered as Pacific Railroad of Missouri (1849). Established as Saint Louis and San Francisco Railway (1876). Merged with Burlington Northern (1980).
Seaboard Air Line Railroad (1900)	1967	Created from consolidation of several lines as Seaboard Air Line Railway (1900). Reorganized as Seaboard Air Line Railroad (1946). Merged with Atlantic Coast Line as Sea-

		board Coast Line (1967).
Seaboard Coast Line Railroad (1967)	1982	Merged with Louisville & Nashville to form Seaboard System Railroad.
Seaboard System Railroad (1982)	1986	Created by merger of Seaboard Coast Line Railroad and Louisville & Nashville Railroad. Merged with Chessie system to become CSX Transportation (1986).
Soo Line (1961)	1990	Created when Minneapolis, St. Paul & Sault Ste Marie Railway merged with Wisconsin Central (1961). Sold to Canadian Pacific (1990).
Southern Railway (1894)	1982	Merged with Norfolk & Western as Norfolk Southern Railway (1982).
Southern Pacific Railroad Company (1865)	1996	Merged into Union Pacific.
Spokane, Portland & Seattle Railway Company (1905)	1970	Came under the control of the Northern Pacific and the Great Northern railroads soon after it was completed in 1909. Merged with three other railroads as Burlington Northern Railroad (1970).
Wabash Railroad Company (1877)	1964	Chartered as Northern Cross Railroad (1837). Reorganized as Wabash Railway Company (1877). Merged with St. Louis, Kansas City & Northern Railway and renamed Wabash, St. Louis & Pacific Railway (1979). Renamed Wabash Railroad Company (1889). Merged with New York, Chicago & St. Louis Railroad into Norfolk & Western Railway (1964).

Railroads—Last Spike Ceremonies

Often new structures or businesses commemorate the start of the venture with a "first," such as the laying of a cornerstone or a ribbon cutting. But many railroads celebrate their readiness to begin operating with a "last"—the driving of the "last spike" (often gold) to formally mark completion of the track construction. Golden Spike ceremonies began when the first transcontinental railroad was completed in 1869. The idea for the Golden Spike originated with San Francisco financier and contractor David Hewes, brother-in-law of California businessman and politician Leland Stanford.

Railroads—Last Spike Ceremonies— First Transcontinental Railroad

The first transcontinental railroad in North America was completed with the joining of the Union Pacific Railroad and the Central Pacific Railroad at Promontory Summit, Utah, on May 10, 1869. The ceremony took place between two locomotives facing each other with 3,000 government officials, railroad employees and track workers looking on. A special pre-bored polished California laurel railroad tie was used in the ceremony. Three special spikes were driven into the tie before the golden spike. The golden spike was driven by Leland Stanford with a silver hammer. After the ceremony, the laurel tie and the spikes were replaced with a normal tie and iron spikes.

• **Last of the ceremonial railroad tie and golden spike:** The laurel tie was destroyed during the 1906 San Francisco earthquake. The golden spike is now in the Leland Stanford Memorial Museum at Stanford University, Palo Alto, California.

• **Last of the track at Promontory Summit:** In 1942, during World War II, the orginal track was pulled and salvaged for the war effort. A ceremonial undriving of the last spike was enacted. In 1943, a commemorative marker was unveiled. In 1957, Promontory Summit became a National Historic Site.

Railroads
Last Spike Ceremonies for
Some Major United States and Canadian Railroads

Railroad and Location	Date and Place Last Spike Was Driven	Description
Alaska Railroad (connecting Seward and Anchorage, Alaska)	September 10, 1918, between Bird Creek and Girdwood, Alaska	• **Last spike:** presented to Colonel Mears in 1918. Now owned by the Southern California Arms Collectors Association.
(completion of railroad connecting Seward and Nenana, Alaska)	July 15, 1923 Nenana, Alaska	• **Last spike driven:** by President Warren G. Harding. Now on display at the Harding Home Museum, Marion, Ohio. Harding died while returning from this trip.
Baltimore & Ohio Railroad (connecting Baltimore, Maryland, and the Ohio River)	December 24, 1852, Roseby's Station, near Wheeling, West Virginia	• **Last spike location:** marked by a boulder with the inscription "Roseby's Rock, Track Closed. Christmas Eve, 1852." The rock is named for Roseby Carr, who was in charge of the construction teams.
Canadian Northern Railway (connecting Montreal, Quebec, and Vancouver, British Columbia)	January 23, 1915, Basque, British Columbia	Known as "Canada's second transcontinental railway." • **Last spike driven:** by railroad owner William Mackenzie.
Canadian Pacific Railway (connecting Lake Superior and Winnipeg, Manitoba)	June 19, 1882, Feist Lake, near Dryden, Ontario	• **Last spike driven:** by Jennie Fowler, sister of engineer Robert Fowler.
(connecting Winnipeg, Manitoba, and Montreal, Quebec)	May 16, 1885, Noslo, near Jackfish, Ontario	• **Last spike driven:** by Colonel Oswald of the Montreal Light Infantry.
(completion of railway connecting Atlantic and Pacific coasts)	November 7, 1885, Craigellachie, British Columbia	• **Last spike driven:** by Donald A. Smith, Lord Strathcona, a director of the Canadian Pacific Railway. The last spike was immediately removed, cut up and handed out as souvenirs. A small obelisk marks the spot. Event was the subject of Pierre Berton's book *The Last Spike.*
Chesapeake & Ohio Railway (connecting Richmond, Virginia, and Huntington, West Virginia)	January 29, 1873, Hawk's Nest, West Virginia	• **Last spike driven:** by General Williams C. Wickham. John Henry had his legendary contest against a machine while working on this rail line.
Chicago, Milwaukee & St. Paul Railroad	May 19, 1909, Garrison, Mon-	Through freight service between Chicago and Seattle was established July 4,

(connecting Chicago, Illinois, and Seattle, Washington)	tana	1909. Through passenger service was established on July 10, 1910.
Galveston, Harrisburg and San Antonio Railway (connecting Houston and San Antonio, Texas)	January 12, 1883, near Pecos River, Texas	• **Last spike driven:** by Thomas W. Peirce, president of the railway. A silver spike was used.
Grand Trunk Pacific Railway (connecting Halifax, Nova Scotia, and Prince Rupert, British Columbia)	April 7, 1914, Fort Fraser, British Columbia, Canada	• **Last spike driven:** by Peter Titiryn, construction foreman for the western crew, and E.J. Chamberlin, president of the Grand Trunk Pacific Railway.
Great Northern Railway (connecting Duluth, Minnesota, and Everett, Washington)	January 6, 1893, Scenic, Washington	• **Last spike driven:** by C. Shields general superintendent, and J.D. Farrell, division superintendent for the Great Northern Railway, without ceremony. An iron spike was used.
Illinois Central Railroad (connecting LaSalle and Cairo, Illinois)	September 27, 1856, Mason, Illinois	A marker on Illinois Highway 37 now identifies the spot. This was the first federal land grant railroad.
Lehigh Valley Railroad (connecting Lehigh Valley and Schuylkill Valley, Pennsylvania)	July 12, 1890, Renimont, West Penn Township, Pennsylvania	• **Last two gold spikes driven:** one by R.A. Wilder who conceived the project, and one by R.H. Sayre, a vice president of the Lehigh Valley Railroad.
New York, Texas and Mexican Railway (connecting Mexico City, Mexico, and New York, New York)	July 4, 1882 Garcitas Creek, Texas	• **Last spike ceremony:** attended by Italian backer Count Telfener and wife Ada. The railway is also known as the Macaroni Line because of the vast amounts of macaroni it carried to supply the 1,200 Italian laborers who migrated to Texas.
Northern Pacific Railroad (connecting Dakota Territory and Montana Territory)	November 11, 1880 Cantonment, Little Missouri, Dakota Territory	Two silver spikes were driven.
(connecting Great Lakes and Columbia River/Puget Sound, Washington)	September 8, 1883, Independence Creek, Montana Territory	• **Last spike driven:** by H.C. Davis, who had driven the first spike in 1876. The same iron spike was used.
Northwestern Pacific Railroad (connecting Sausalito and Eureka, California)	October 23, 1914, Cain Rock (near Garberville, California)	• **Last spike ceremony:** filmed as part of the 14-minute short called, *Redwood Empire Special and Lumber Mills.*
Rutland Railroad (connecting Burlington, Vermont, and Boston, Massachusetts)	December 18, 1849, Summit, Vermont	Trains from Burlington, Vermont and Boston, Massachusetts, converged for a celebration by company officials. Water from Boston Harbor was mixed with water from Lake Champlain.
Shenandoah Valley Railroad (connecting Hagerstown,	April 5, 1881, Luray, Virginia	• **Last spike driven:** by William Milnes, former president of the Shenandoah Valley Railroad. He dug the iron

Maryland, and Basic City/Waynesboro, Virginia)		on his property and forged the spike in his blacksmith shop.
Southern Pacific Railroad (connecting Los Angeles and San Francisco, California)	September 5, 1876, Lang Station, California	• **Last spike driven:** by Colonel Charles Crocker, president of the Southern Pacific Railroad. The spike was made of gold from San Gabriel, California. It is now at the California Historical Society in San Francisco.
Virginia and Truckee Railroad (connecting Virginia City, and Carson City, Nevada)	August 24, 1872 near Carson City, Nevada	• **Last spike driven:** by Henry M. Yerington, Superintendent of the Virginia and Truckee Railroad.
Western Pacific Railroad (connecting Salt Lake City, Utah, and Oakland, California)	November 1, 1909, Spanish Creek, near Keddie, California	• **Last spike driven:** by Leonardo di Tomasso, foreman.
(Inside Gateway section, connecting Western Pacific and Great Northern Railway)	November 10, 1931, Bieber, California	• **Last spike driven:** by Arthur Curtiss James. A gold spike was used.
White Pass & Yukon Route Railroad (connecting Skagway, Alaska, and White Horse, Yukon Territory)	July 29, 1900, Carcross, Yukon Territory	Samuel Graves attempted to drive the last spike, but was unsuccessful, so other dignitaries tried. The gold spike was bent and destroyed. The track foreman had to pound in a regular spike.

Railroads—Trains
Last Run of Some Famous American Trains

Train and Year of First Run	Last Run	Description
Black Diamond (1896)	May 11, 1959	Lehigh Valley's most famous train provided deluxe passenger service between Exchange Place in Jersey City, New Jersey, and Buffalo, New York.
Broadway Limited (1912)	September 9, 1995	Pennsylvania Railroad's luxury train on the New York-Philadelphia-Chicago route was first named "Pennsylvania Special," then renamed "Broadway Limited." Amtrak took over in 1971 and operated it until 1995.
California Zephyr (1949)	March 22, 1970	Operated between Chicago and Oakland, California. as a collaborative effort among three railroads: Western Pacific; Denver & Rio Grande; and Chicago, Burlington & Quincy.
Capitol Limited (1938)	May 1, 1971	Baltimore & Ohio's train ran between Chicago, Illinois, and Washington, D.C.
Dixie Flagler (1940)	November 1957	Chicago & Eastern Illinois's train ran between Chicago, Illinois, and Miami, Florida.
El Capitan (1937)	May 1, 1971	Domed-car train between Chicago and Los Angeles ended when the Atchison, Topeka & Santa Fe ended passenger service in 1971 with the Amtrak takeover.

Flying Yankee (1935)	May 7, 1957	Maine Central/Boston & Maine train that traveled between Portland, Maine, and Boston, Massachusetts.
Green Diamond (1936)	1967	Illinois Central Railroad's first diesel-powered streamliner.
Hiawatha (1935)	May 1, 1971	Chicago, Milwaukee, St. Paul & Pacific Railroad's luxury streamliner provided high-speed service between Chicago, Illinois, and Saint Paul, Minnesota.
Mark Twain Zephyr (1935)	May 1963	Chicago, Burlington & Quincy's train spent its last six years on the Saint Louis, Missouri, to Burlington, Illinois, route.
Panama Limited (1911)	May 1, 1971	Illinois Central's Chicago-New Orleans train. Went out of service in 1932, then returned in 1934 with the first air-conditioned cars in the U.S.
Pioneer Zephyr (1934)	March 20, 1960	First diesel-powered streamlined passenger train in the U.S. After completing more than 3 million miles of service, it made its final run, from Lincoln to Galesburg, Illinois. On May 26, 1960, the train was presented to Chicago's Museum of Science and Industry.
Rio Grande Zephyr (1971)	April 24, 1983	Denver & Rio Grande Western train that traveled between Chicago and San Francisco.
Royal Blue Line (1890)	April 1958	Baltimore & Ohio's deluxe passenger train between Washington and New York.
San Francisco Chief (1954)	May 1, 1971	Atchison, Topeka & Santa Fe's Chicago-San Francisco streamliner.
Silver Meteor (1939)	May 1, 1971	New York-Miami-Tampa train put into service by Seaboard Air Line. Ended with Amtrak takeover of passenger service.
Super Chief (1937)	May 1, 1971	Showcase train of Atchison, Topeka & Santa Fe Railway ran between Chicago and Los Angeles.
Twentieth Century Limited (1902)	December 2, 1967	New York Central's luxury train between New York, New York, and Chicago, Illinois, was the fastest long-distance train in the world when it was put into service in 1902. A streamliner was introduced in 1938. It fell victim to cheaper, faster airliners.
Twin Zephyrs (1935)	April 30, 1971	Chicago, Burlington & Quincy's Chicago-Minneapolis-Saint Paul train.
Wabash Cannon Ball (1880s)	April 30, 1970	The song "Wabash Cannon Ball" came before Norfolk & Western's Saint Louis-to-Detroit train.

Religion

Religion—Bible
The Apocalypse is found in the last book of the New Testament, Revelation 6:1-8. Part of it is believed to reveal secrets of future events.
• **Last of the Four Horsemen of the Apocalypse:** Death, rider of the pale horse. The other three are believed to be Christ on the white horse, War on the red horse, and famine on the black horse.

Religion—Boy Bishops
During the Middle Ages in England, a choir boy was elected bishop on Saint Nicholas Day, December 6th, and held the office until December 28th.
• **Last of the Boy Bishops:** abolished by Henry VIII in 1542, revived briefly by

Queen Mary in 1552, and finally abolished during the reign of Queen Elizabeth I, who ruled from 1558 to 1603.

Religion—Clergy (England)—Celibacy
• **Last time celibacy was required of English clergy:** 1547, during the reign of Edward VI. That year, members of the clergy were permitted to marry.

Religion—Clergy (England)— Monasteries, Religious Houses, Abbeys
The English Parliament renounced Papal authority in 1534, following a rift between King Henry VIII and the Roman Catholic Church in Rome.
• **Last of the small abbeys:** abolished by Henry VIII in 1536. The Franciscans had 50 abbeys and other houses at the time of the 1536 suppression.
• **Last of the religious houses:** abolished by Parliament with the Suppression Act of 1536, during the reign of King Henry VIII. The closure and confiscation of the monasteries took four years: 1536 to 1540. At the time of their closing, more than 10,000 monks, friars, and nuns lived in over 800 monasteries, abbeys, nunneries and friaries.
• **Last monastery to transfer allegiance to Church of England:** Waltham Abbey, an Augustinian abbey in Essex, on March 23, 1540.

Religion—Crusades
The Crusades were a series of Christian religious expeditions from western Europe to the Middle East. They had two goals: to ensure a safe trip for pilgrims wishing to visit the Holy Land (the holy sites in Palestine); and to remove the Holy Land from Muslim control and establish a Christian authority in its place. The first Crusade began in 1095.
• **Last Crusade:** began in 1270, when King Louis IX of France and King Edward I of England set out for the Holy Land with an army of men. Louis became ill and died in Carthage.
• **Last city in Holy Land held by Christians:** Acre (Akko, modern Israel). When it

fell in 1291, it marked the end of fighting in Palestine and Syria and the end of the era of the Crusades.

Religion—Harmony Society
The Harmony Society founded a religious community in Butler County, Pennsylvania, in 1804. Its residents were 600 emigrants from Germany who came to America with their leader George Rapp to escape religious persecution. In 1815, they founded a new community in Indiana known as Harmony. The settlement was torn by dissention as residents found it difficult to cope with frontier life, the climate, and the isolation. In 1824, the land and buildings were sold to Robert Owens, who named the Indiana settlement New Harmony and established his own communistic society. The Harmony Society returned to Pennsylvania and created a third village, near Pittsburgh. The society grew weaker after Rapp died in 1847. Membership dwindled to the point that only a few members were left by the end of the 1800s.
• **Last of the Harmony Society:** 1906, when it disbanded.
• **Last of New Harmony:** 1828, when dissention arose and the society was disbanded.

Religion—Methodism
English theologian and evangelist John Wesley, founder of Methodism, died in London, England, on March 2, 1791, age 87.
• **Last letter known to have been written to America by Wesley:** to Ezekiel Cooper on February 1, 1791, a month before Wesley died. Cooper was in his 80s when he died in 1847.
• **Last letter known to have been written by Wesley:** to William Wilberforce, February 24, 1791.
• **Wesley's last journal entry:** October 24, 1790. He began keeping his 55-year-long journal on October 14, 1735.
• **Wesley's last sermon:** February 22, 1791, at Leatherhead, England..

Religion—Mormonism
The Church of Jesus Christ of Latter-Day Saints (the Mormon Church) was founded

by Joseph Smith in 1830.

• **Last surviving witness of the *Book of Mormon:*** David Whitmer, who died in 1888.

• **Joseph Smith's last address to his followers:** June 18, 1844. A short time later, on June 27, 1844, Smith and his brother Hyrum were killed by a mob. They had been arrested and jailed in Carthage, Illinois.

• **Last president of Church of Jesus Christ of Latter-Day Saints to know Joseph Smith:** Lorenzo Snow, fifth president, from 1898 to 1901. He died in Salt Lake City, Utah, on October 10, 1901, age 87.

• **Last of the early Mormons in Nauvoo, Illinois:** 1846. After violent clashes with other settlers over polygamy, the Mormons began leaving their settlement in Nauvoo, Illinois, in February 1846 for the Salt Lake Valley in what is now Utah. The last group of the early Mormon settlers left Nauvoo in September 1846. The State of Deseret was founded in Utah in July 1847 by members of the Church of Jesus Christ of Latter-Day Saints.

• **Last of the State of Deseret:** April 5, 1851, when it was dissolved and the Utah Territory was established by the U.S. Congress.

• **Last of an all-white Mormon priesthood:** June 9, 1978, when the Mormons revoked their 148-year-old policy of excluding black men from the priesthood.

• **Last wife of Brigham Young:** Ann Eliza Webb, who was 23 when she married the 66-year-old Mormon leader on April 6, 1868. Brigham Young had 27 wives and 56 children.

• **Last surviving wife of Brigham Young:** Eliza Burgess Young, who died in Salt Lake City, Utah, on August 21, 1915, age 87.

• **Last surviving child of Brigham Young:** Mabel Young Sanborn, who was the 54th of Brigham Young's 56 children. She died in Salt Lake City, Utah, on September 20, 1950, age 87.

Religion—People's Temple

The People's Temple was founded in Indianapolis, Indiana, in 1956 by Jim Jones. He moved the Temple's headquarters to Ukiah, California, in 1965 and to Guyana in South America in 1977.

• **Last of the People's Temple commune:** November 18, 1978, when 913 followers of the People's Temple committed suicide by drinking a cyanide-spiked beverage in Jonestown, their settlement in a Guyana jungle. A tape recording made during the suicide indicated commune leader Jim Jones had told his followers they would be massacred by Guyanese soldiers for the earlier killing of U.S. congressman Leo Ryan. The People's Temple bodies were removed by the U.S. government and brought to the United States for burial.

• **Last Jonestown bodies buried:** May 24, 1979, in a common grave in Oakland, California. These last 48 bodies were not identified. Most are believed to be the children of commune members who died the previous November.

Religion—Roman Catholicism—Cardinals

Next to the office of pope, cardinals are the highest ecclesiastical officials in the Roman Catholic Church. They are appointed by the pope. Until 1917, laymen could be cardinals in the Roman Catholic Church.

• **Last cardinal who was not a priest:** Giacomo Antonelli (1806-76), who was secretary of state to Pope Pius IX. In 1962, Pope John XXIII decreed that all cardinals must first be consecrated bishops.

Religion—Roman Catholicism—Clergy—British Parliament

After the Reformation in England, the Church of England became the state church. Because of their allegiance to the pope, Roman Catholics were viewed as a threat to the monarchy. One of the laws passed to limit their rights banned priests from sitting in the House of Commons of Parliament.

• **Last time Roman Catholic priests were barred from sitting in House of Commons of Parliament:** March 5, 1829, when the law banning them was repealed by the Roman Catholic Relief Act.

Religion—Roman Catholicism—Clergy—Tonsure

Tonsure is a rite of shaving the head as a preliminary step to priesthood that dates back 1,500 years. Different religious orders had different tonsures. Some shaved only the crown of their head. Others retained a band of hair, others shaved their entire head.
• **Last of the tonsure:** September 14, 1972, when Pope Paul VI ordered the practice to be abolished.

Religion—Roman Catholicism—Council of Trent

The Council of Trent was called to condemn the teachings of theologian reformers John Calvin and Martin Luther. It convened in the Austrian city of Trent (now part of Italy) on December 13, 1545, and lasted almost 18 years.
• **End of the Council of Trent:** December 3, 1563.

Religion—Roman Catholicism—Fatima Visitations

Three young children—Lucia dos Santos, age 10, and her two cousins Francisco Marto, age 9, and his sister Jacinta Marto, age 7—reported seeing the Virgin Mary during six visitations in Fatima, Portugal, beginning on May 13, 1917.
• **Last visitation:** October 13, 1917.
• **Last survivor of the Fatima visitations:** Lucia dos Santos. The other two children, Francisco and Jacinta Marto, died of influenza while very young.

Religion—Roman Catholicism—Habits

Habits are the traditional religious attire worn by members of religious orders.
• **Last time nuns were required to wear religious habits:** the 1960s. After Vatican Council II (1962-65), the rules on religious habits were relaxed. Nuns were permitted to wear secular clothes if wearing religious habits would impede their daily activities.
• **Last time the Sisters of Charity wore large wing-like headpieces (bonnets):** 1963, when they exchanged their distinctive white bonnets for a simpler veil.

Religion—Roman Catholicism—Meatless Fridays

For centuries, Roman Catholics were obliged under pain of sin to abstain from eating meat on Fridays as a form of penance.
• **Last Friday Roman Catholics in U.S. were obliged to abstain from eating meat:** November 18, 1966. A decree from Pope Paul VI and a decision by American bishops allowed Catholics to substitute another penitential practice on Fridays, which still remains a special day of penance.

Religion—Roman Catholicism—Papacy

The pope is the highest ranking official in the Roman Catholic Church. He resides in Vatican City, within the city of Rome, Italy. His reign can be traced in a direct line back to Saint Peter in 64-67 A.D.
• **Last non-Italian pope prior to John Paul II of Poland:** Dutch pope Adrian VI, who held the office in 1522-23.
• **End of papal authority in England:** 1534, with the Act of Supremacy. The act abrogated pope's authority and declared that the king had always been the head of the Church of England. Adrian IV (Nicholas Breakspear), who reigned from 1154 to 1159, was the only Englishman to hold the office of pope.
• **Last married pope:** Adrian II, who ruled from 867 to 872. His wife and daughter were murdered by Roman nobles.
• **End of the Great Western Schism:** November 11, 1417. During the Great Western Schism, which started in 1378, two and sometimes three men claimed to be pope at the same time. One lived in Rome, Italy, the other in Avignon, France. Their dispute was political, not religious. The matter was resolved at the Council of Constance that convened in 1414. Two of the claimants were deposed and the papacy went to Cardinal Odo Colonna, who took the name Martin V. With his election, the Great Western Schism came to an end.

Religion—Roman Catholicism—Second Vatican Council

Second Vatican Council, often referred to as

Vatican II, was convened to examine the present and future roles of the Roman Catholic Church. It met in sessions during the autumn of four consecutive years, beginning in 1962. During the four sessions, the council issued declarations on issues such as religious liberty, non-Christian religions and education.

• **Last session of Vatican II:** began September 14, 1965, and ended December 8, 1965.

Religion—Roman Catholicism— Spanish Inquisition

The Roman Catholic Church has known two major inquisitions. One began in 1233, when Pope Gregory IX commissioned members of the Dominican clergy to investigate whether the secret religious practices of the Albigensians were heresy. The other, the Spanish Inquisition, was totally independent of the first one. It was harsher, better organized and more likely to put people to death. The Spanish Inquisition was established in 1478 by King Ferdinand V and Queen Isabella of Spain. It was totally controlled by the Spanish monarchs, with little or no input from the pope in Rome. It directed much of its rancor at the Jews and Moors living in Spain.

• **Last of the Spanish Inquisition:** abolished in 1808 by Joseph Bonaparte but restored by King Ferdinand VII of Spain. In 1834, the Spanish Inquisition was finally abolished by the Holy Office.

• **Last of Torquemada:** Tomás de Torquemada was named Grand Inquisitor of the Spanish Inquisition in 1483. Under his authority, thousands of people were brought into court and 2,000 were killed. Torquemada retired to a monastery in 1494. He died there on September 16, 1498, age 77 or 78.

Religion—Shakers

The Christian sect formally known as the United Society of Believers in Christ's Second Appearing originated in England in the 1770s as an offshoot of the Quaker movement. Its members emphasized celibacy, simple living and pacifism. The group earned the name "Shakers" from their practice of shaking, trembling and whirling during their religious services. The Shakers established about 20 communities in the eastern and midwestern United States by the mid-19th century with about 6,000 members. After the Civil War, the sect began to decline. By 1970, the Shakers were on the brink of extinction.

• **Last surviving eldress of the Shakers:** Bertha Lindsay, who died at the Shaker Village in Canterbury, New Hampshire, on October 3, 1990, age 93. Her death left only a handful of Shakers.

Religion—Shaker Communities in the United States

The Shaker communities are listed here in the order they were founded. Today, many are on the National Register of Historic Places. Those sites are marked with an asterisk [*]. Five villages are also National Historic Landmarks. These are noted in the "Comments" column.

Name of Shaker Community and Year Founded	Last Active	Description
Watervliet* near Albany, New York (1776)	1938	When the eldress died, the community was closed and the few remaining Shakers moved to Mount Lebanon and Hancock.
Harvard* Harvard, Massachusetts (1781)	1918	Buildings in the historic district are now private residences and not open to the public.
Mount Lebanon* Columbia County, New York (1787)	1947	National Historic Landmark.

Hancock* near Pittsfield, Massachusetts (1790)	1960	Once the center of Shaker authority in America. National Historic Landmark.
Tyringham* Tyringham, Massachusetts (1792)	1875	Buildings are privately owned and not open to the public.
Canterbury* Canterbury, New Hampshire (1792)	1992	National Historic Landmark. • **Last Canterbury Shaker:** Sister Ethel Hudson, who died on September 7, 1992, age 96.
Enfield* Enfield, Connecticut (1792)	1917	The eight remaining Shakers sold the land and moved to Hancock and New Lebanon. Some of the buildings are on the grounds of the Connecticut Department of Corrections and are not accessible to the public.
Shirley* Shirley, Massachusetts (1793)	1909	Fourteen of the original 26 buildings have survived. The village is now part of the Massachusetts Correctional Institution complex.
Enfield* Enfield, New Hampshire (1793)	1923	The Great Stone Dwelling, built 1837-41, is the largest Shaker building ever built any community. Today it is an inn.
Alfred* Alfred, Maine (1793)	1931	Today it is part of the Alfred Shaker Historic District.
Sabbathday Lake* New Gloucester, Maine (1794)	still active	With the closing of Canterbury, Sabbathday Lake became the last active Shaker community. National Historic Landmark.
Union Village Warren County, Ohio (1805)	1912	Now the site of Otterbein Homes.
Watervliet near Dayton, Ohio (1806)	1900	Property later became a state farm. In 1981, it became the site of a research park, retreat center and private housing.
Pleasant Hill* Harrodsburg, Kentucky (1806)	1910	• **Last Pleasant Hill Shaker:** Sister Mary Settles, who died in 1923. A National Historic Landmark.
South Union* South Union, Kentucky (1807)	1922	The western-most Shaker community. Now maintained as the Shaker Museum at South Union.
West Union Busro, Indiana (1810)	1827	Remaining members went to Shaker communities in Ohio and Kentucky.
North Union* near Cleveland, Ohio (1822)	1889	All the village buildings were demolished. The site is now Shaker Heights.
White Water* New Haven, Ohio (1822)	1916	More than 20 buildings have survived.
Groveland Groveland, New York (1836)	1892	Land is now occupied by a state prison.

Religion—State Religions
Former State Religions of Nations

A state religion (also called an "established church" or "state church") is a religion or religious body or creed officially endorsed by the government as the official religion. Many nations have state religions. Only those nations that have disestablished their state religion are listed.

Country	State Church and Denomination	Last Year
Albania	Atheism	1991
Armenia	Armenian Orthodox Church (Oriental Orthodox)	1921
Austria	Roman Catholic Church (Catholic)	1918
Bulgaria	Bulgarian Orthodox Church (Eastern Orthodox)	1946
Cambodia	Buddhism	1975
China	Confucianism	1912
Estonia	Church of Estonia (Lutheran)	1940
Ethiopia	Ethiopian Orthodox Church	1974
France	Roman Catholic Church (Catholic)	1905
Georgia	Georgian Orthodox Church (Eastern Orthodox)	1921
Guyana	Anglican	1966
Ireland	Church of Ireland (Anglican)	1874
Italy	Roman Catholic Church (Catholic)	1984
Japan	Shintoism	1945
Latvia	Roman Catholic Church (Catholic)	1940
Lithuania	Roman Catholic Church (Catholic)	1940
Nepal	Hinduism	1990
Peru	Roman Catholic Church (Catholic)	1979
Portugal	Roman Catholic Church (Catholic)	1910
Romania	Romanian Orthodox Church (Eastern Orthodox)	1947
Russia	Russian Orthodox Church (Eastern Orthodox)	1917
Sweden	Church of Sweden (Lutheran)	1999
Turkey	Islam	1922
Wales	Church in Wales (Anglican)	1920

Religion—State Religions—United States
Former State Religions in the United States

Nine of the original 13 American colonies had established state religions by the beginning of the American Revolution. The 1st Amendment to the United States Constitution explicitly prohibited the federal government from establishing a state church. However, this amendment was often interpreted as allowing for state governments to maintain existing state churches. With the passage of the 14th Amendment in 1868, the prohibition on established churches was interpreted as a general prohibition on state support or endorsement of religion.

State	State Church and Denomination	Last Year
Connecticut	Congregational Church	1818
Georgia	Anglican Church	1777
Maryland	Anglican Church	1775

Massachusetts	Congregational Church	1833
New Hampshire	Congregational Church	1819
New York	Dutch Reform Church (1693); Anglican Church	1777
North Carolina	Anglican Church	1777
South Carolina	Anglican Church (termed "Christian Protestant Religion")	1790
Virginia	Anglican Church	1786

Restaurants, Taverns and Other Eateries

Restaurants, etc.—Boar's Head Tavern

The Boar's Head Tavern once stood in the Eastcheap section of London, England. Its construction date is not known, but it was standing during Shakespeare's time. He mentioned the tavern in *Henry IV*. It was destroyed in the Great Fire of London in 1666 and was rebuilt two years later.

• **Last of the Boar's Head Tavern:** demolished in 1831 to make room for the new London Bridge.

Restaurants, etc.—Brown Derby

The Brown Derby, one of Los Angeles's most popular restaurants, opened in 1929. It was a familiar hangout for many Hollywood celebrities. Its owner Robert Cobb created the Cobb Salad.

• **Last of the Brown Derby:** demolished in 1994. The restaurant had been damaged by a fire and later by an earthquake.

Restaurants, etc.—Burger Chef

Burger Chef hit its peak in 1971 when it had about 1,200 stores. In 1982, when the chain was acquired by Hardee's, all but about 100 stores were closed. The rest disappeared over time.

• **Last surviving Burger Chef restaurant:** Cookville, Tennessee. It closed on May 1, 1996, when its owner retired after it lost a franchising legal battle with the Hardee's Corporation. Some restaurants called Burger Chef are operating, but they have no connection with the original chain.

Restaurants, etc.—Coconut Grove

The Coconut Grove, in the Hotel Ambassador, in Los Angeles, California, opened in 1921 and soon became a magnet for celebrities and their fans.

• **Last of the Coconut Grove:** closed in 1989, along with the Hotel Ambassador. Robert F. Kennedy was shot in the hotel on June 5, 1968, while campaigning for the U.S. presidency. He died on June 6, 1968, age 42.

Restaurants, etc.—Delmonico's

Delmonico's, one of New York City's most famous restaurants, opened in 1830 and relocated several times. It moved to Fifth Avenue and 44th Street in 1896.

• **Last located on Fifth Avenue and 44th Street:** 1923. It closed, a victim of Prohibition. The site was demolished. Delmonico's later reopened in lower Manhattan.

Restaurants, etc.—Horn and Hardart Automat

The Horn and Hardart Automat was a self-serve restaurant where food such as a sandwich, salad or piece of pie was placed on a plate in a compartment behind a small glass window. Patrons accessed what they wanted by placing nickels in a slot. The Horn and Hardart Company opened its first Automat at 818 Chestnut Street in Philadelphia, Pennsylvania, in 1902. Although the Automats are no longer operated, the Horn and Hardart name remains in use.

• **Last Horn and Hardart Automat:** closed April 9, 1991. It was at 200 East 42nd Street, New York, New York.

Restaurants, etc.—McDonald's

The early McDonald's had red-and-white tile stripes, canted windows and a sharply angled roof framed by soaring yellow arches.

• **Last remaining example of a vintage McDonald's:** Lakewood Boulevard and

Florence Avenue in Downey, California. The restaurant was earmarked for demolition after it sustained damage in the 1994 earthquake. Downey's Mayor Joyce Lawrence and the Los Angeles Conservancy persuaded McDonald's to preserve and restore the c. 1953 restaurant. It reopened in 1996 with an adjacent museum, gift shop and dining facility.

Restaurants, etc.—Tabard/Talbot
The Tabard in Southwark, London, England, dates back to the early 1300s. It was the starting place for the pilgrims in Chaucer's *Canterbury Tales*. After a fire in 1676, it was torn down and rebuilt as The Talbot.
• **Last of the Tabard/Talbot:** demolished in 1875 despite protests.

Restaurants, etc.—Windows on the World
The landmark restaurant complex Windows on the World opened on the 107th floor of the North Tower of the World Trade Center in New York, New York, in 1976. It offered patrons a spectacular view of the city.
• **Last of the original Windows on the World:** destroyed September 11, 2001, in the terrorist attack on the two towers. (*See also* Crime—Terrorism—September 11, 2001.)

Roads, Trails and Highways

Roads, Trails and Highway—Alaska Highway/Alcan Highway
The Alaska Highway, originally known as the Alcan Military Highway, extends nearly 1,600 miles from rail and highway terminals at Dawson Creek, British Columbia, Canada, to Fairbanks, Alaska. It was built between March and October of 1942, during World War II. The highway was opened only to military traffic when it was completed.
• **Last time the Alcan Highway was restricted to military traffic:** 1946, soon after World War II ended, when it was opened to civilians for the first time.

Roads, Trails and Highways— Appalachian Trail
The 2,160-mile-long continuously marked footpath known as the Appalachian Trail was built by volunteers between 1922 and 1937. One terminus is at Mount Katahdin, Maine. The other is at Springer Mountain in northern Georgia. The first section opened in October 1923.
• **Last part of the Appalachian Trail opened:** August 14, 1937.

Roads, Trails and Highways—Chisholm Trail
The Chisholm Trail was the main route between Texas and Kansas that ranchers used to get their cattle to market after the Civil War. The trail began in southern Texas and ran through San Antonio, Austin, and Fort Worth. It cut through the center of Indian Territory (Oklahoma) and extended into Kansas. There, it passed through Wichita and Newton, ending at Abilene, where it connected with the Union Pacific (Kansas Pacific) Railroad. As it passed through Indian Territory, it followed a wagon path made by trader Jesse Chisholm in 1866, hence the trail's name. The Chisholm Trail reached its peak of usage in 1871. After that, another trail farther west siphoned off some of the traffic. Also, railroads were built, spelling the end of the trail's usefulness for cattle drives.
• **Last use of the Chisholm Trail for cattle drives:** 1884, when it was closed by barbed wire. During its last year, it was open only as far as Caldwell in southern Kansas. By then, farmers had settled the lands along the trail and fenced off their properties.

Roads, Trails and Highways—Mormon Trail
The Mormon Trail, also known as the Salt Lake Trail, was an old trail reopened in 1846 by Brigham Young and a group of Mormons he was leading from Illinois to Utah. The trail started in Nauvoo, Illinois, crossed Iowa, and followed the Platte River to Fort Laramie, where it followed the old Oregon Trail to Fort Bridger, Wyoming.

From there, it went through Echo Canyon to Emigration Canyon, then onto the Great Salt Lake Plain.

• **Last major use of the Mormon Trail:** 1869. With completion of the transcontinental railroad that year, the route became less important. It received only limited use after that.

Roads, Trails and Highways—National Road

The National Road, also known as the Cumberland Road and National Pike, was the first federally funded road built in the United States. Construction began in Cumberland, Maryland, in 1811. The first stretch of the road opened as far as Wheeling, West Virginia, in 1818. As more government funds were appropriated, the road extended farther west.

• **End of federal funding:** 1852. By then, the Cumberland Road extended to Vandalia, Illinois. The state of Illinois extended the road to Saint Louis, Missouri. Today, much of the road follows U.S. Highway 40.

Roads, Trails and Highways—New Jersey Turnpike

Construction on the New Jersey Turnpike began in January 1950. The original turnpike extended 118 miles from Deepwater Township to the Raritan River in New Brunswick. Spurs and extensions were added later.

• **Last stretch of the original New Jersey Turnpike completed:** January 15, 1952.

Roads, Trails and Highways—Oregon Trail

The Oregon Trail was about 2,000 miles long. The first pioneers used the trail in 1836. The eastern terminus was in Independence, Missouri. It was originally the route fur trappers used when traveling from the Missouri River to the Columbia River. It followed part of the Santa Fe Trail to Fort Laramie, then ran to Fort Bridger, Wyoming, and through the Rocky Mountains at South Pass. On the Pacific side of the mountains, it went through the Grande

Ronde Valley then to the Umatilla River and onto Fort Vancouver.

• **Last use of the Oregon Trail as a major transportation route:** 1870s, when the railroad reached San Francisco, California. From there, travelers would journey by boat up the coast. Some wagons used the Oregon Trail as late as the 1880s.

• **Last wagon to travel the Oregon Trail:** 1906, driven by Ezra Meeker who made the journey to publicize the trail and remind people of its importance. Meeker retraced the journey he made originally in 1852.

Roads, Trails and Highways— Pennsylvania Turnpike

The Pennsylvania Turnpike was the first highway of its kind in the United States. Construction began in October 1938. It extended 160 miles from Irwin, east of Pittsburgh, to Middlesex, west of Harrisburg.

• **Last stretch of the original Pennsylvania Turnpike completed:** October 1, 1940.

• **Last surviving original (1940) Pennsylvania Turnpike toll booth:** A booth from Exit 15 at Blue Mountain that is now preserved at the Smithsonian Institution in Washington, D.C.

Roads, Trails and Highways—Route 40

Route 40 once extended 3,200 miles from Atlantic City, New Jersey, to San Francisco California.

• **Last time Route 40 was used as a transcontinental highway:** 1964, when portions of it were decommissioned with the opening of Interstate 80. Much of Route 40 was absorbed by I-80. Today, the western terminus of Route 40 is in Silver Creek Junction, Utah.

Roads, Trails and Highways—Route 66

Route 66 opened in 1924 and extended 2,400 miles from Chicago, Illinois, to Los Angeles, California. The popular route was immortalized in a song and was the title of a TV series.

• **Last portion of Route 66 to be paved:** 1938, when the section of the road between Adrian and Glenrio, Texas, was surfaced.

• **Last use of Route 66 as a major trans-**

portation route: October 13, 1984, when the final section at Williams, Arizona, was bypassed and Route 66 was officially decommissioned. As a major highway, Route 66 began to disappear in the mid 1950s as superhighways were built. Only isolated stretches of the old 66 remain.

Roads, Trails and Highways—Santa Fe Trail

The Santa Fe Trail was for many years the main gateway to the Southwest. It opened in 1821, soon after Mexico gained its independence from Spain. The trail's eastern terminus was in Franklin, Missouri. It passed through the valley of the Arkansas River, southwest through Raton Pass, Colorado, to Santa Fe, New Mexico. When the steamboats arrived, the trail's eastern starting place was moved to Independence, Missouri. A stagecoach began traveling along the trail from Independence to Santa Fe in 1850.

• **Last use of the Santa Fe Trail as a major transportation route:** 1880, when the Atchison, Topeka and Santa Fe Railroad reached Santa Fe.

• **Last surviving stagecoach stop on the Santa Fe Trail that is still open to the public:** Mahaffie Stagecoach Stop and Farm in Olathe, Kansas. The site is on the National Register of Historic Places.

Science
Last Works of Some Major Scientists

Ampère, André-Marie	French physicist André-Marie Ampère was one of the discoverers of electromagnetism. The term *ampere,* a unit of measurement of electric current, was named for him. • **Last work of Ampère:** a classification of the sciences (*Essai sur la philosophie des sciences, ou exposition analytique d'une classification naturelle de toutes les connaissances humaines*), published a month after he died. Ampère died in Marseilles, France, on June 10, 1936, age 61.
Bell, Alexander Graham	Scottish-born inventor Alexander Graham Bell gained his greatest fame with the invention of the telephone in 1875. He had many interests, including flight and solar energy. Bell was granted 18 patents in his own name and 12 with collaborators. In his later years, he became interested in watercraft. • **Last invention of Bell:** HD-4 hydrofoil, invented jointly with Casey Baldwin. With speeds up to 71 miles per hour, the hydrofoil was the fastest watercraft at that time. Bell was 75 when his last patent was granted. He died in Baddeck, Nova Scotia, on August 2, 1922, age 75.
Boyle, Robert	Irish-born English scientist/philosopher Robert Boyle formulated Boyle's Law of Gases, which states that the pressure of a gas is inversely proportional to the volume it occupies. • **Last works of Boyle:** *Discourse Against Customary Swearing* (1695), one of several works published posthumously. Boyle died in London, England, on December 31, 1691, age 64. He was a religious man who spent his last years dealing with theological matters and endeavoring to reconcile religion with science. One of his last works was *The Christian Virtuoso* (1691), in which he put forth the view that studying nature is a religious duty.
Darwin, Charles	British naturalist Charles Darwin left England on the HMS *Beagle* on December 27, 1831, on an expedition that lasted nearly five years. The purpose of the journey was to explore the flora and fauna of the western coast of South America and the Southern Pacific. • **End of the *Beagle* voyage:** October 2, 1836. Darwin's discoveries were

	published as *On the Origin of Species by Means of Natural Selection* in 1859. His revolutionary findings challenged the prevailing scientific view of evolution. • **Last of the *Beagle:*** HMS *Beagle* was 25 years old when she was transferred out of the Royal Navy in 1845. She was renamed *W.V.7* in 1863 and was used by the Preventive Service as a stationary vessel. She was moored at Paglesham at the mouth of the River Roach on the coast of Essex. *W.V.7* was sold in May 1870 and probably was broken up for scrap. • **Last major work of Darwin:** *Formation of Vegetable Mould through the Action of Worms with Observations on their Habits*, in 1881, showing the importance of worms to soil fertility. Darwin died in Kent, England, on April 19, 1882, age 73.
Descartes, Rene	French mathematician/scientist/philosopher Rene Descartes laid the groundwork for the scientific method with his guideline on how to seek knowledge in any scientific field. • **Last philosophical activity of Descartes:** In the fall of 1649. Descartes accepted an invitation to go to Sweden to instruct Queen Christina in philosophy. He died there on February 11, 1650, age 53. • **Last book:** *The Passions of the Soul*, written by Descartes in the winter of 1645-46 and published late in 1649.
Edison, Thomas Alva	American inventor/businessman Thomas Alva Edison gained fame for his many inventions, which included the first workable phonograph and the first practical light bulb. • **Last research by Edison:** a way to obtain rubber economically from domestic plants. Edison experimented on thousands of different plants while searching for a substitute for costly imported rubber. • **Last patent by Edison:** patent for a way to make rubber from goldenrod, granted when he was 83. Edison applied for the patent in January 1931 and received it that year. It was his 1,093rd. He died in West Orange, New Jersey, on October 18, 1931, age 84. • **Last surviving member of Edison's team that developed the incandescent light bulb:** Francis Jehl, who died on February 9, 1941, in St. Petersburg, Florida, age 80. His memoirs are recorded in the book *Menlo Park Reminiscences* published in 1937.
Einstein, Albert	German-born American theoretical physicist Albert Einstein won the Nobel Prize in Physics in 1921. He died in Princeton, New Jersey, on April 18, 1955, age 76. • **Last theoretical concerns of Einstein:** he spent his last years searching for a unified field theory that would connect gravitation with electromagnetic and subatomic forces. His last notebook contains his final calculations, made just before he died. • **Last letter of Einstein:** to Bertrand Russell, giving permission to use his name on a manifesto asking all nations to give up nuclear weapons. It was written in 1955, a week before Einstein died.
Faraday, Michael	English chemist/physicist Michael Faraday is known as the Father of Electrical Engineering for his work in areas such as electromagnetic induction, electromagnetic rotations and the magneto-optical effect. Faraday ended his scientific research around 1862, and spent his last years at Hampton Court, in England, where he died on August 25, 1867, age 76. • **Last chemistry publication of Faraday:** "Experimental relations of gold

	and other metals to light" (1857). • **Last physics publication of Faraday:** on the influence of magnetic field on spectral lines of sodium, and on lines of force and the concept of a field (1862). • **Last of Faraday's Christmas lectures**: "The Natural History of a Candle" (1860).
Goddard, Robert	American physicist/rocket pioneer Robert Hutchings Goddard is considered the Father of Modern Rocketry. He began his work on rockets in 1909 and fired his first liquid-fueled rocket in 1926. He died in Baltimore, Maryland, on August 10, 1945, age 63. • **Last major work of Goddard:** *Rocket Development: Liquid-Fuel Rocket Research, 1929-1941*, published posthumously in 1948.
Harvey, William	English physiologist William Harvey discovered how blood circulated in the body. He died in Essex, England, on June 3, 1657, age 79. • **Last publication of Harvey:** "Essay on the generation of animals" (*Exercitationes de Generatione Animalium*), based on his study of embryology and baby chicks. It appeared in 1651.
Herschel, William	German-born British astronomer William Herschel discovered the planet Uranus and more than 2,500 stars. • **Last astronomical observation of Herschel:** a comet on July 4, 1819. • **Last scientific lecture of Herschel:** presented when he was 80 years old. Herschel died near Windsor, England, on August 25, 1822, age 83.
Kepler, Johannes	German astronomer/astrologer/ mathematician Johannes Kepler discovered the laws of planetary motion that showed planets move in ellipses, not circles. • **Last work of Kepler:** *Rudolphine Tables,* a set of astronomical tables of planetary motion prepared for King Rudolf II. The tables were completed in 1624 but not published until 1627. Kepler died in Regensberg, Germany, on November 15, 1630, age 58.
Lavoisier, Antoine-Laurent	French chemist Antoine-Laurent Lavoisier developed a way to classify elements. He also wrote *Elements of Chemistry,* which is considered the first modern chemistry textbook. He was the inventor of plaster of Paris and discovered the role oxygen plays in combustion. His accomplishments have earned for him the title Father of Modern Chemistry. During the French Revolution, Lavoisier was found guilty of conspiracy against the people of France. • **Last days of Lavoisier:** In November 1793, during the French Revolution, he was arrested, tried and found guilty of conspiracy against the people of France. He spent his last five months in prison awaiting his execution. He was sent to the guillotine on May 8, 1794, age 51.
Linnaeus, Carolus	Swedish botanist Carolus Linnaeus (a.k.a. Carl von Linné) designed the first system for naming, ranking and classifying living organisms. For his accomplishment, he is often called the Father of Taxonomy. He put his findings in the book *Systema Naturae* in 1735. He revised the book many times with additions. • **Last edition of *Systema Naturae* written by Linnaeus:** the 12th, published in Stockholm in 1766-68. By then, Linnaeus recognized he would never be able to accomplish his goal of naming, ranking and classifying all the species. He died on January 10, 1778, age 70. A 13th edition was published ten years after his death.

Mendel, Gregor	Augustinian monk and biologist Gregor Johann Mendel was born in Hein-zendorf, Austrian Silesia (now the Czech Republic). His experiments on heredity in plants laid the groundwork for the field of genetic research. • **Last years of Mendel:** His plant hybridization research was published in 1866 but had little impact during his lifetime. From 1874 until his death ten years later, Mendel was isolated from his fellow monks in St. Thomas Monastery and from the public because of a solitary stance he took in opposition to a tax on the monasteries to cover the expenses of church institutions. Mendel died in Brünn (Brno, now in the Czech Republic) on January 6, 1884, age 61.
Newton, Isaac	English mathematician/scientist/natural philosopher Isaac Newton discovered the law of gravity and is credited with inventing differential and integral calculus. He was knighted in 1705 and died in London, England, on March 20, 1727, age 85. • **Last work on calculus by Newton:** "On the Quadrature of Curves," an essay written in 1691-93. It was published as an appendix in the 1704 edition of Newton's *Opticks*.
Pasteur, Louis	French chemist Louis Pasteur invented pasteurization, a process for heating milk and other liquids to kill bacteria and molds present in them. He is considered the Father of Microbiology and Immunology. • **Last major research of Pasteur:** on rabies. In 1885, he successfully treated a patient with a vaccine against rabies (also known as hydrophobia). Pasteur suffered from a stroke when he was 46 that paralyzed his left side and made lab work difficult for him. He died on September 28, 1895, age 72.
Planck, Max	German physicist Max Karl Ernst Ludwig Planck won a Nobel Prize in physics in 1918 for his work on quantum theory. • **Last years of Planck:** Planck lost all his papers, books and his home in an Allied bombing of Berlin, Germany, during World War II. And he was buried for hours in an air-raid shelter. His younger son was executed by the Nazis in 1945 for allegedly attempting to assassinate Hitler. Planck lived long enough to see the war end. He was elected president of the Max Planck Gesellschaft in 1946. He died in Gottingen, West Germany, on October 4, 1947, age 89.
Priestley, Joseph	English chemist/Unitarian theologian/minister Joseph Priestley is known for his discovery of oxygen. He left England for political reasons in 1794 and settled in Northumberland, Pennsylvania, where he died on February 6, 1804, age 70. • **Last scientific paper of Priestley:** on nitric acid in the atmosphere as it is carried down by snow. It was published November 1803, three months before he died.
Tesla, Nikola	Electrician/inventor Nikola Tesla was born in Croatia (then part of the Austro-Hungarian Empire). His work on alternating current made possible the long-distance transmission of electricity and revolutionized electrical technology. • **Last scientific work of Tesla:** Teleforce death-beam weapon, a particle beam so powerful it could destroy an army 200 miles away. Tesla mentioned he was working on the weapon in an article in the *New York Sun* in July 1934. • **Last years of Tesla:** After he was hit by a taxi in New York City in 1937, Tesla refused to seek medical treatment, believing he could heal the injury he sustained. He never fully recovered from the accident and became increasingly reclusive. During his final years, he seldom left his room in the

	Hotel New Yorker. In 1943, shortly before he died, he claimed he had perfected the death-beam weapon. He died in his New York City hotel room on January 7, 1943, age 86.
Volta, Alessandro	Italian physicist Alessandro Giuseppe Antonio Anastasio Volta was 55 when he invented the electric battery in 1800. Later, the term *volt* would be applied to a measurement of electricity in his honor.
	• **Last research of Volta:** Volta did very little research after he invented the electric battery. He stopped teaching in 1813 and retired in 1819 and died in Camnago, near Lake Como, Italy, on March 5, 1827, age 82.

Science—Geology—Mohole Project

The aim of the Mohole Project was to obtain rock samples from the upper mantle of the Earth through a hole drilled in the ocean floor. Phase I began in 1961 with drillings off the coast of Mexico.

• **Last of the Mohole Project:** abandoned in 1966. The project was too expensive, and technical difficulties were encountered that could not be overcome.

Science—Mathematics—Fermat's Last Theorem

In the 17th century, French mathematician Pierre de Fermat observed that it was not possible for a cube to be the sum of two cubes, a fourth power to be the sum of two fourth powers, or for any number that is a power greater than the second to be the sum of two like powers. In other words, for any number greater than two, no whole numbers can satisfy the equation: $a^n + b^n = c^n$. Many people tried to prove Fermat's theorem but with no success.

• **Last time Fermat's last theorem lacked proof:** 1995. In June 1993, Andrew Wiles, an English mathematician at Princeton University, claimed he had done so. When a gap was found in his solution, Wiles and Richard Taylor corrected it and provided a revised proof that was deemed complete. In 1995, Wiles and Taylor presented the long elusive proof for Fermat's last theorem at a conference at Boston University in Massachusetts.

Science—Mathematics—Slide Rules

The slide rule is a mechanical device that enables the user to make quick mathematical calculations. It dates back to the 17th century. Modern slide rules evolved in the mid-1800s. During the early 1970s, electronic calculators made the slide rule obsolete.

• **Last slide rules produced by major manufacturers:** the 1970s. In 1972, the Frederick Post Company made its last slide rule. Its successor, Teledyne Post, ceased selling slide rules a few years later. In 1975, Keuffel & Esser manufactured their last slide rules. The last slide rule they produced was donated to the Smithsonian Institution. Aristo ended slide rule production in 1978.

Ships

Ships—Barques/Barks

Barques, or barks, are sailing ships with three to five masts, all square-rigged except the after mast, which is rigged fore and aft.

• **Last five-masted barque built:** *Kobenhavn,* launched in 1921 in Denmark. When she was lost at sea in December 1928, she was also the last five-masted barque still sailing. (*See also* Disappearances–Marine)

• **Last French five-masted barque:** *France,* launched in 1911. Wrecked in New Caledonia in 1922, she was finally totally destroyed when used as target practice for U.S. bombers in 1944.

• **Last German five-masted barques:** *R.C. Rickmers,* launched in 1906, was the last German five-masted barque built. She was sunk on March 27, 1917, by the German submarine *U-66* off the coast of Ireland. *Potosi,* another German five-master, was built in Geestemünde in 1895. She was given to France after World War I and renamed *Flora.* She sank on October 19, 1925, after her cargo caught fire and the crew was forced to abandon ship. She was the last German five-masted barque still sailing.

• **Last cargo-carrying four-masted barque:** *Krusenstern* (formerly named *Padua*), launched in Germany in 1926.

• **Last British four-masted barque:** *Archibald Russell*, launched in 1905 in Scotland. She was broken up and scrapped in 1949.

• **Last Danish four-masted barque:** *Viking*, launched in 1907. She was sold to the city of Gothenburg, Sweden, in 1950 to be used as a stationary school ship. She is now preserved in Gothenburg.

• **Last Dutch four-masted barque:** *Geertruida Gerarda*, launched in 1904 and later renamed *Olympia*. She was broken up in Genoa, Italy, in 1926.

• **Last German four-masted barque:** *Hussar*, launched in 1931 in Kiel. Later renamed *Sea Cloud* (1935), *Angelita* (1955), *Patria, Antarna* (1964) and *Sea Cloud of Cayman* (1974). She is still in service as a passenger cruiser.

• **Last Italian four-masted barque:** *Regina Elena,* launched in Genoa, Italy, in 1903. She was renamed *Ponape* (1911), *Bellhouse* (1914) and *Ponape* (1925) and was broken up in Latvia in 1936.

• **Last Japanese four-masted barques:** *Nippon Maru* II (launched 1984) and *Kaiwo Maru* II (launched 1989). Both are replicas of ships of the same names built in 1930 that were later rigged as four-masted barques. They are used as school ships. The original ships now serve as museums.

Ships—Brigantines

Brigantines are two-masted sailing ships with the fore mast square-rigged and the main mast fore-and-aft rigged. A number of brigantines still can be found throughout the world.

• **Last brigantine registered in Great Britain:** *Zebu*, built in 1938. Originally a Baltic trader with fore-and-aft rig, she became square-rigged in 1983 to be more efficient for trade-wind operations. She served as flagship of Operation Raleigh Zebu,

which circumnavigated the world between 1984 and 1988, sailed 69,000 miles and visited 41 countries. She is now based at Preston, Lancashire, England.

Ships—Bugeyes (Chesapeake Bay)

Bugeyes were two-masted sailing vessels used for dredging oysters. Many of the bugeyes were converted to "buy boats." Buy boats followed other boats and purchased their oysters and took them to the shucking houses.

• **Last Chesapeake Bay bugeye to retain its sailing rig and working appearance:** *Edna E. Lockwood*, built in 1889. She is the only unaltered representative of the fleet that once harvested Chesapeake oysters. She was donated to the Chesapeake Bay Maritime Museum in 1973.

• **Last converted bugeye oyster buy boat on the Chesapeake:** *Wm. B. Tennison,* built in 1899 by Frank Laird at Crabb Island (near Oriole), Maryland. She was converted into a buy boat in 1908-09.

Ships—Clipper Ships

Clipper ships were tall-masted, sharp-bowed sailing vessels built in the mid-19th-century for great speed. They were at their peak in the 1850s. Many clipper ships met their end during the Civil War. The opening of the Suez Canal in 1869 also hastened their demise. The great square-riggers had to be towed through the canal. Clipper ships had different designations, according to their cargo. In addition to the tea clippers and wool clippers, a number were designated opium clippers.

• **Last American clipper ship:** No fully intact American clipper ships have survived; however, a portion of one remains. *Snow Squall,* built in Cape Elizabeth, Maine, in 1851. She went aground near the Falkland Islands in March 1864, was condemned and was left to rot. In the 1980s, the bow of the ship was recovered during Operation Snow Squall. It is now on display in Portland Harbor Museum in Maine.

• **Last great commercial clipper ship:** *Cutty Sark.* She is also the only surviving intact clipper ship. She was built in 1869 at Dumbarton, Scotland, for the tea trade with China. She carried her last tea cargo in 1877. Cutty Sark was later used to carry wool out of Australia (1885-95). She was sold to a buyer in Portugal and renamed *Ferreira.* Another buyer in 1920 renamed her *Maria di Amparo.* In 1922, Wilfred Dowman, a British buyer, took the ship back to England and restored her original name. His widow later donated *Cutty Sark* to the Thames Nautical Training College. After restoration by the Cutty Sark Preservation Society, *Cutty Sark* was opened as a museum in Greenwich, England, in 1957.

• **Last surviving tea clipper captain:** Andrew Shewan, who sailed on many British clippers. When he was in his seventies, he described his experiences in the book *The Great Days of Sail.* He died in 1917.

Ships—Clipper Ships
Last of Some of the Clipper Ships of Donald McKay
(Listed in the order they were built.)

The clipper ships of Canadian-born American master shipbuilder Donald McKay were among the fastest, finest and largest ever built. McKay was forced to close his East Boston, Massachusetts, shipyard during a financial panic in 1857. During the Civil War, he made steam-powered war ships for the U.S. government. His last clipper ship, *Glory of the Seas,* would be his financial downfall. It bankrupted him and forced him to close his yard again. McKay remained a shipbuilder until 1874. (*See also* Shipbuilders.)

Ship and Year Built	Details of Last Voyage and Fate
Stag Hound (1850)	Cargo of coal caught fire October 12, 1861, about 45 miles south of Pernambuco (Recife), Brazil. Ship was abandoned. The crew reached Pernambuco.
Flying Cloud (1851)	One of the fastest clipper ships ever built. *Flying Cloud* made the journey from New York, New York, to San Francisco, California, in a record 89 days. *Flying Cloud* went aground at Beacon Island, St. John's, New Brunswick, Canada, June 19, 1874, and was condemned and sold for scrap the following year.
Flying Fish (1851)	Left China November 23, 1858, bound for New York, New York. Wrecked en route, then condemned. The wreck was sold to a Manila merchant, rebuilt and renamed *El Bueno Suceso.* She later sailed between Manila in the Philippines and Spain. Her end came when she foundered in the China Sea.
Staffordshire (1851)	Left Liverpool, England, for Boston, Massachusetts, December 30, 1853. Struck a rock at Seal Islands, Cape Sable, Nova Scotia, Canada, and sank. The ship did not carry enough lifeboats, and 170 people died.
Bald Eagle (1852)	Left Hong Kong for San Francisco, California, October 15, 1861. Disappeared. Fate unknown.
Sovereign of the Seas (1852)	Grounded on Pyramid Shoal, Straits of Malacca, en route from Hamburg, Germany, to China, August 6, 1859. Crew rescued by the American ship *Eloisa.* Cargo was salvaged.
Westward Ho! (1852)	Burned in the harbor of Callao, Peru, on February 27, 1864.
Chariot of Fame (1853)	Abandoned January 1876, en route from Chincha Islands, Peru, to Cork, Ireland.

Great Republic (1853)	McKay's largest clipper ship. Renamed *Denmark* in 1869. Caught in a hurricane near Bermuda en route from Rio de Janeiro, Brazil, to St. John's, New Brunswick. The ship sprang a leak and was abandoned.
Romance of the Seas (1853)	Disappeared en route from Hong Kong to San Francisco, California, December 31, 1862.
Lightning (1854)	Caught fire in Geelong, Australia, October 31, 1869, while preparing to sail for London England. She was scuttled and broken up for scrap.
Champion of the Seas (1854)	Sprang a leak January 3, 1877, en route from Chile to Ireland. Abandoned off Cape Horn. Crew were rescued by the British ship *Windsor*.
Commodore Perry (1854)	Caught fire August 27, 1869, while transporting coal from England to India. Beached at Bombay, India.
James Blaine (1854)	Destroyed by a fire while docked at Liverpool, England, April 21, 1857. Sold to a shipbuilder who converted the hull into a coal barge.
Donald McKay (1855)	Burned and later broken up in 1888. The figurehead of McKay that adorned *Donald McKay* survived and is at Mystic Seaport, Connecticut.
Mastiff (1856)	Destroyed by fire September 15, 1859, en route to Hawaii. The crew was rescued by the British ship *Achilles* and taken to Honolulu.
Glory of the Seas (1869)	McKay's last clipper ship was sold in Victoria, British Columbia in 1911 for use as a floating salmon cannery. In 1923, she was burned for her metal in Seattle, Washington. Her figurehead was placed in India House in New York, New York. The builder's half-model is at the Mariners Museum, Newport News, Virginia. • **Last captain:** Joshua S. Freeman, who purchased her in 1885 and sailed her on her last voyage from Liverpool, England, to San Francisco, California. He used her for coal trade along the west coast until 1902.

Ships—East Indiamen

East Indiamen were large merchant ships built from the 16th to the 19th centuries for use on the trade route between Europe and India.
• **Last remaining Indian-built East Indiaman:** *Edwin Fox*, built in Bengal, India, in 1853. The ship is now moored in Picton, New Zealand. *Edwin Fox* holds several other "lasts" claims, including: last surviving Crimean War troop ship; last surviving convict ship to Australia; and last surviving wooden immigrant ship to New Zealand.

Ships—Galleons

Galleons were large sea-going vessels with three or more masts and usually two or more decks. The ships were used mainly by Spain for commerce or as warships during the 16th through 19th centuries. Between 1565 and 1815, Manila galleons carried goods from Asia to the West in exchange for silver from the Americas and the manufactured goods from Europe. The prosperous trade route came to an end when the ports in the Philippines opened to foreign trade.
• **Last Manila galleon:** *Magallanes,* which left Manila in 1811 and returned to the Philippines four years later.

Ships—Galleys

Galleys were large seagoing vessels propelled primarily by oars in battle and equipped with sails for cruising.
• **Last major battle fought with galley ships:** Battle of Lepanto in October 1571, in which two great galley armadas, Christian and Turkish, fought for control of the eastern Mediterranean near the Greek town of Lepanto. The Turkish armada was larger but not as well-equipped as the Christian armada (Spain and the Papal States). Although this was the last of the great galley battles, galleys would continue to be built. They finally were replaced by galleons in the 1700s.

Ships—Gundalows

Gundalows are heavy flat-bottomed boats.

They were common in the Piscataqua River region in New England, where they began as simple barges in the 1600s. They evolved into fully decked cargo carriers with cabins and flexible lateen sails in the 1800s.

• **Last original working gundalow:** *Fanny M.*, launched in 1889 and skippered by Captain Edward H. Adams (1860-1950). *Fanny M.* ended her days rotting in the mud, but Adams and his son began building a new gundalow named *Driftwood* in 1930. It was launched in 1950 and burned in 1970. The only gundalow in the region now is a reproduction built in the 1980s and named in Adams' honor. It is operated by the Piscataqua Gundalow Project, Strawbery Banke Museum, in Portsmouth, New Hampshire.

• **Last remaining gundalow built and manned by U.S. forces during the American Revolution:** the Continental gunboat *Philadelphia*, part of Benedict Arnold's fleet. Built in Skenesborough, New York, in 1776, she sank during a battle in Lake Champlain that year. The hull was raised in 1935, exhibited in New York until 1961 and later placed on display at the Smithsonian Institution.

Ships—Hijackings—*Achille Lauro*

The Italian-owned cruise liner *Achille Lauro* was en route from Alexandria, Egypt, to Port Said, Egypt, when she was seized by four Palestinian terrorists on October 7, 1985. They demanded the release of 50 Palestinian prisoners held by Israel. During the two days they held the ship, they murdered Leon Klinghoffer, an American wheelchair-bound passenger, and threw his body overboard.

• **End of the *Achille Lauro* hijacking:** October 9, 1985. The terrorists surrendered in exchange for safe passage. The plane provided for them was forced to land in Sicily, where they were taken into custody.

• **Last of the *Achille Lauro*:** caught fire on November 30, 1994, and sank three days later off the coast of Somalia. All but two of the passengers and crew were rescued.

Ships—Hijackings—*Santa Maria*

The Portuguese luxury liner *Santa Maria* was seized by 26 terrorists on January 22, 1961, and held for 10 days. The ship had just left Curaçao, Netherland Antilles carrying 607 passengers. The hijackers had taken the ship to protest the Salazar regime.

• **End of the *Santa Maria* hijacking:** February 2, 1961, when hijackers were granted asylum by Brazil and left the ship at Recife. The passengers reached Lisbon, Portugal, on the 16th.

• **Last of the *Santa Maria*:** retired in 1973 and scrapped in Taiwan.

Ships—Mutinies—*Bounty*

The mutiny on the British ship HMS *Bounty* has been the subject of many books and films. It began April 28, 1787, and was led by Master's Mate Fletcher Christian and involved 12 crew members. Captain William Bligh and 18 sailors were put in a launch and set adrift in the South Pacific.

• **Last of the *Bounty* mutineers:** Nine of the mutineers lived in Tahiti for a while, then sailed the *Bounty* to Pitcairn Island in 1790. Six were killed on the island. One died of asthma. One committed suicide. The last survivor was Alexander Adams, who used the name John Adams. When the HMS *Briton* visited Pitcairn Island in 1812, Adams was the only crew member they found. He died in 1829.

• **Last of the *Bounty*:** The mutineers burned the *Bounty* at Pitcairn Island after unloading food and tools. The ship's remains were found in 1957, off the southern end of the island.

• **Last of Captain Bligh and the *Bounty* crew that was set adrift:** after rowing more than 3,600 miles, Bligh and his 18 crewmen reached Timor, near Java, where they were picked up by a passing ship. Twelve men returned to England with him; one died on the way home. The other six men stayed in the South Pacific. One stayed in the East Indies. One died at Coupang, Timor. Three died at Batavia, Java. One was killed by natives at Tofoa. Bligh eventually rose to the rank of admiral. He died in London in 1817 at age 63.

Ships—Naval—Battleships—British
• **Last battleship built for the British Royal Navy:** HMS *Vanguard,* completed in 1946. She was fitted with the 15-inch turrets from the HMS *Courageous* and HMS *Glorious* that had been converted to aircraft carriers. HMS *Vanguard* was scrapped in 1960.

Ships—Naval—Battleships—United States

The following chart includes all United States battleships of the modern era (generally speaking, the 20th century) or after the sinking of the battleship *Maine*. The Treaty for the Limitation of Naval Armaments mentioned frequently below was the result of a conference held in Washington, D.C., a few years after World War I ended. The conference convened in 1921-22 and included the United States, Great Britain and its Dominions, Japan, France, Italy, the Netherlands, Portugal, Belgium and China. The naval treaty reduced the naval tonnage of the five leading naval powers. The treaty originally was set to expire after 10 years, but it was extended by five years. The Treaty for the Limitation of Naval Armaments expired on December 31, 1936.

Battleship, Hull Number and Year Commissioned	Last Service and Fate
Alabama, **USS** BB-8 (1900)	• **Last World War I service:** conducting recruit-training missions in Chesapeake Bay and Atlantic coastal waters. • **Last of the USS *Alabama* (BB-8):** decommissioned May 7, 1920. Struck from the Navy List and transferred to the War Department September 15, 1921, for use as a target. Sunk September 27, 1921. Sold for scrap March 19, 1924.
Alabama, **USS** BB-60 (1942)	• **Last World War II service:** off the southern coast of Honshu, Japan. • **Last of the USS *Alabama* (BB-60):** decommissioned January 9, 1947, at Seattle, Washington. Struck from the Navy List June 1, 1962. Transferred to the state of Alabama for use as a memorial June 16, 1964. Arrived at permanent berth, Mobile, Alabama, September 14, 1964.
Arizona, USS BB-39 (1916)	• **Last World War I service:** gunnery training ship; also patrolled East Coast from Virginia capes to New York. Served as part of escort for USS *George Washington* during President Woodrow Wilson's journey to Europe for the Paris Peace Conference in December 1918. • **Last full commission:** March 1, 1931. • **Last flag change of command:** January 23, 1941, when Rear Admiral Wilson was relieved as Commander, Battleship Division 1 by Rear Admiral Isaac C. Kidd. • **Last voyage to the West Coast:** departed Pearl Harbor for Long Beach, California, June 11, 1941, and returned July 8, 1941. • **Last training exercise:** conducting night firing exercise December 4, 1941, with *Nevada* (BB-36) and *Oklahoma* (BB-37). All three ships were moored at quays (keys) along Ford Island December 5, 1941. • **Last World War II service and last of the USS *Arizona* (BB-39):** sank during Japanese attack on Pearl Harbor December 7, 1941. Of the 1,400 on board the ship, 1,103 lost their lives. Struck from the Navy List December 1, 1942. Later designated a national shrine. The *Arizona* Memorial was dedicated May 30, 1962.

Arkansas, USS BB-33 (1912)	• **Last World War I service:** escorted German High Seas Fleet to Firth of Forth November 1918. Part of naval escort for USS *George Washington* carrying President Woodrow Wilson to France for the Paris Peace Conference in December 1918. • **Last World War II service:** fire support during invasion of Okinawa. After a month at Apra Harbor, *Arkansas* sailed to Leyte Gulf and remained there until the end of the war. Transported 800 troops home to the United States as part of Operation Magic Carpet. • **Last of the USS *Arkansas* (BB-33):** sunk as a target in atomic bomb tests at Bikini Atoll July 25, 1946. Decommissioned July 29, 1946. Struck from the Navy List August 15, 1946.
California, USS BB-44 (1921)	• **Last World War II service:** at Okinawa before joining TF 95 to cover East China Sea minesweeping and before assisting Sixth Army occupation force in Honshu, Japan. • **Last of the USS *California* (BB-44):** decommissioned February 14, 1947. Sold for scrap July 10, 1959.
Colorado, USS BB-45 (1923)	• **Last World War II service:** off Okinawa before assisting with the occupation of Japan, covering airborne landings at Atsugi Airfield in Tokyo. Transported more than 6,000 troops home to the United States as part of Operation Magic Carpet. • **Last of the USS *Colorado* (BB-45):** decommissioned January 7, 1947. Sold for scrap July 23, 1959.
Connecticut, USS BB-18 (1906)	• **Last full commission:** October 3, 1916, flagship of Fifth Division, Battleship Force Atlantic Fleet after repairs at Philadelphia Naval Yard. • **Last World War I service:** trained midshipmen and gun crews for merchant ships. • **Last of the USS *Connecticut* (BB-18):** decommissioned March 1, 1923 and scrapped November 1, 1923, in compliance with the Washington Treaty for the Limitation of Naval Armaments.
Delaware, USS BB-28 (1910)	• **Last World War I service:** escort for British destroyers before returning to U.S., arriving at Hampton Roads, Virginia, August 1918. Remained there until the war ended. • **Last of the USS *Delaware* (BB-28):** entered Norfolk Navy Yard August 30, 1923, decommissioned November 10, 1923, and scrapped February 5, 1924, in compliance with the Washington Treaty for the Limitation of Naval Armaments.
Florida, USS BB-30 (1911)	• **Last World War I service:** convoy duty with the Sixth Battle Squadron. Part of fleet that escorted German High Seas Fleet into the Firth of Forth in November 1918. Part of naval escort for USS *George Washington* carrying President Woodrow Wilson to France for the Paris Peace Conference December 1918. • **Last of the USS *Florida* (BB-30):** decommissioned February 16, 1931, and sold for scrap in compliance with the 1930 London Naval Treaty.
Georgia, USS BB-15 (1906)	• **Last World War I service:** escorted convoys. • **Last of the USS *Georgia* (BB-15):** decommissioned July 15, 1920. Scrapped November 1, 1923, in compliance with the Washington Treaty for the Limitation of Naval Armaments. Struck from the Navy List November 10, 1923.
Idaho, USS BB-24	• **Last decommissioned:** July 30, 1914; turned over to the Royal Hellenic Navy of Greece and renamed *Kilkis*.

(1908)	• **Last World War II service and last of the USS *Idaho* (BB-24):** sunk by German aircraft in Salamis harbor, April 1941.
***Idaho*, USS** BB-42 (1919)	• **Last World War II service:** support at Okinawa until June 20, 1945; returned to Leyte Gulf until end of the war. *Idaho* was present at the signing of the Japanese surrender in Tokyo, September 2, 1945. • **Last of the USS *Idaho* (BB-42):** decommissioned July 3, 1946. Placed in reserve until sold for scrap November 24, 1947.
***Illinois*, USS** BB-7 (1900)	• **Last recommissioned:** November 2, 1912. • **Last decommissioned:** May 15, 1920, after which *Illinois* was used by the state of New York. • **Last service:** quarters for Naval Reserve unit, New York, until December 31, 1955. • **Last of the USS *Illinois* (BB-7):** towed to Baltimore, Maryland, for scrapping May 18, 1956.
***Indiana*, USS** BB-1 (1895)	• **Last recommissioned:** May 24, 1917. • **Last World War I service:** training ship for gun crews off Tomkinsville, New York, and in the York River, Virginia. • **Last decommissioned:** January 31, 1919, at Philadelphia, Pennsylvania. Reclassified as *Coast Battleship No. 1* on March 29, 1919, so that the name *Indiana* could be assigned to a newly authorized battleship. • **Last of the USS *Indiana* (BB-1):** sank while being used as a target in tests designed to determine effectiveness of aerial bombs in November 1920. Sold for scrap March 19, 1924.
***Indiana*, USS** BB-50	Not built, in compliance with the Washington Treaty for the Limitation of Naval Armaments.
***Indiana*, USS** BB-58 (1942)	• **Last World War II service:** member of Task Group 38.1 from July 1 to August 15, 1945, supporting air strikes against Japan and bombing coastal targets. • **Last of the USS *Indiana* (BB-58):** decommissioned September 11, 1947, and placed in reserve. Struck from the Navy List June 1, 1962, and sold for scrap. Her mast is at Indiana University in Bloomington. Her anchor is at Fort Wayne. Various other relics of the *Indiana* are in museums and schools in the state.
***Iowa*, USS** BB-4 (1897)	• **Last recommissioned:** April 23, 1917. • **Last World War I service:** training ship and guarding entrance to Chesapeake Bay. Decommissioned for last time March 31, 1919. • **Last reclassified:** April 30, 1919, as *Coast Battleship No. 4.* • **Last use:** as first radio-controlled target ship in fleet exercise. • **Last of the USS *Iowa* (BB-4):** sunk March 23, 1923, in Panama Bay.
***Iowa*, USS** BB-53	Unfinished in compliance with the Washington Treaty for the Limitation of Naval Armaments. Sold for scrap November 8, 1923.
***Iowa*, USS** BB-61 (1943)	• **Last World War II service:** strikes on the Japanese city of Hitachi on July 17-18, 1945, and supporting carrier strikes during August 1945. • **Last Korean War service:** combat operations off the coast of Korea, bombarding enemy targets at Songjin, Hunguam and Kojo, North Korea. *Iowa* departed Yokosuka, Japan, October 19, 1952, for overhaul at Norfolk, Virginia. Decommissioned in 1958. Spent two and a half decades mothballed. • **Last recommissioned:** April 28, 1984, modernized. • **Last decommission:** October 26, 1990.

	• **Last voyage of the USS *Iowa* (BB-61):** under tow from Newport, Rhode Island, arriving April 21, 2001, in San Francisco, California, where the *Iowa* is now berthed.
***Kansas*, USS** BB-21 (1907)	• **Last World War I service:** engineering training ship in the Chesapeake Bay. Occasionally made escort and training cruises to New York. • **Last of the USS *Kansas* (BB-21):** decommissioned December 16, 1921. Struck from the Navy List on August 24, 1923. Sold for scrap in compliance with the Washington Treaty for the Limitation of Naval Armaments.
Kearsarge, **USS** BB-5 (1900)	*Kearsarge* was the last battleship not named for a State in the Union. By an act of Congress, the ship was named *Kearsarge* to commemorate the famed steam sloop-of-war. • **Last recommissioned as battleship:** June 23, 1915. • **Last World War I service:** rescued survivors of Norwegian ship *Nordhav* that had been sunk by German submarine U-117 on August 18, 1918. • **Last decommissioned as battleship:** May 10, 1920, Philadelphia Naval Yard. • **Last reclassification:** August 5, 1920, as crane ship *AB-1*. Name changed for the last time November 6, 1941, to *Crane Ship No. 1*. • **Last of the USS *Kearsarge* (BB-5):** decommissioned as a crane ship. Struck from the Navy List June 22, 1955. Sold for scrap August 9, 1955.
Kentucky, **USS** BB-6 (1900)	• **Last recommissioned:** June 23, 1915. • **Last World War I service:** training recruits. • **Last of the USS *Kentucky* (BB-6):** decommissioned in Philadelphia, Pennsylvania, May 29, 1920, in compliance with the Washington Treaty for the Limitation of Naval Armaments. Sold for scrap January 23, 1924.
Louisiana, **USS** BB-19 (1906)	• **Last World War I service:** gunnery and engineering training ship off mid-Atlantic coast. Made four voyages carrying troops home from Europe to the United States beginning December 1918. • **Last of the USS *Louisiana* (BB-19):** decommissioned at Philadelphia Naval Yard October 20, 1920. Scrapped November 1, 1923, in compliance with the Washington Treaty for the Limitation of Naval Armaments.
***Maine*, USS** BB-10 (1902)	• **Last recommissioned:** June 15, 1911. • **Last World War I service:** training ship for engineers, armed guard crews and midshipmen. • **Last of the USS *Maine* (BB-10):** decommissioned May 15, 1920. Sold in January 23, 1922, and scrapped in compliance with the Washington Treaty for the Limitation of Naval Armaments.
Maryland, **USS** BB-46 (1921)	• **Last World War II service:** ended April 14, 1945, after serving as an escort for retiring transports. Entered Navy Yard at Bremerton, Washington, May 1945 for extensive overhaul. Part of Operation Magic Carpet, from August to December 1945. *Maryland* transported more than 9,000 American troops to the West Coast. • **Last of the USS *Maryland* (BB-46):** decommissioned April 3, 1947. Sold for scrap July 8, 1959. Maryland Governor J. Millard Tawes dedicated a monument on the grounds of the State House at Annapolis to the memory of *Maryland* and the battleship's fighting men, June 2, 1961.
Massachusetts, **USS** BB-2	• **Last recommissioned:** June 9, 1917. • **Last World War I service:** heavy gun target practice ship in the Chesapeake Bay and coastal Atlantic waters.

(1896)	• **Last reclassification:** as *Coast Battleship No. 2* March 29, 1919. • **Last of the USS *Massachusetts* (BB-2):** decommissioned March 31, 1919. Struck from the Navy List November 22, 1920, and loaned to the War Department as a target ship. *Massachusetts* was scuttled off Pensacola Bar, Florida, January 6, 1921, then bombarded by batteries from Fort Pickens for four years. She was returned to the Navy February 20, 1925, and offered for sale as scrap. No acceptable bids were received. The *Massachusetts* was declared property of the state of Florida in November 1956.
Massachusetts, USS BB-54	Unfinished in compliance with the Washington Treaty for the Limitation of Naval Armaments. Sold for scrap November 8, 1923.
Massachusetts, USS BB-59 (1942)	• **Last World War II service:** returned to Kamaishi, Japan, where on August 9, 1945, *Massachusetts* fired what was probably the last 16-inch shell discharged in combat in the war. • **Last of the USS *Massachusetts* (BB-59):** decommissioned March 27, 1947. Remained part of Atlantic Reserve Fleet at Norfolk, until struck from Navy List June 1, 1962. Transferred to *Massachusetts* Memorial Committee June 8, 1965, and preserved as a memorial in August 1965.
Michigan, USS BB-27 (1910)	• **Last World War I service:** gunnery training. • **Last of the USS *Michigan* (BB-27):** sailed to Philadelphia, Pennsylvania, August 31, 1921. Decommissioned February 11, 1922. Struck from the Navy List November 10, 1923. Sold for scrap in 1924 in compliance with the Washington Treaty for the Limitation of Naval Armaments.
Minnesota, USS BB-22 (1907)	• **Last World War I service:** gunnery and engineering training ship. Service was interrupted when *Minnesota* struck a German mine near Fenwick Island Shoal Lighthouse and was seriously damaged. *Minnesota* was repaired in time to make three voyages to France, returning more than 3,000 troops to the United States after the war ended. • **Last of the USS *Minnesota* (BB-22):** decommissioned December 1, 1921. Struck from the Navy List the same day. Dismantled at Philadelphia Naval Shipyard in compliance with the Washington Treaty for the Limitation of Naval Armaments and sold for scrap January 23, 1924.
Mississippi, USS BB-23 (1908)	• **Last of the USS *Mississippi* (BB-23):** decommissioned July 21, 1914; turned over to the Royal Hellenic Navy of Greece. Renamed *Lemnos* and served as coastal defense ship until sunk by German aircraft in Salamis harbor April 1941. After World War II, she was salvaged as scrap.
Mississippi, USS BB-41 (1917)	• **Last World War II service:** supporting troops at Okinawa until June 16, 1945. *Mississippi* was present in Tokyo Bay for the signing of the Japanese surrender before returning home on September 6, 1945. Assisted in final evaluation of *Petrel*, a radar-homing missile in February 1956. • **Last of the USS *Mississippi* (BB-41):** decommissioned at Norfolk, Virginia, September 17, 1956. Sold for scrap November 28, 1956.
Missouri, USS BB-11 (1903)	• **Last recommissioned:** April 23, 1917. • **Last World War I service:** training ship in the Chesapeake Bay arm of the Atlantic Fleet. • **Last of the USS *Missouri* (BB-11):** decommissioned September 8, 1919, at Philadelphia Navy Yard. Sold for scrap January 26, 1922, in compliance with the Washington Treaty for the Limitation of Naval Armaments.

Missouri, USS BB-63 (1944)	• **Last World War II service:** Japanese surrender ceremonies held on the USS *Missouri* in Tokyo Harbor, September 2, 1945. For a while in 1950, *Missouri* was the only U.S. battleship in commission. • **Last Korean War service:** Kojo area, March 23, 1953. Decommissioned 1955. Entered Pacific Reserve Fleet. • **Last recommissioned:** May 1986, San Francisco, California. • **Last wartime service:** February 1991, during the Gulf War when *Missouri* fired on Faylaka Island and Kuwait City in support of the ground offensive. • **Last decommissioned:** March 31, 1992, at Long Beach, California. USS *Missouri* was the last battleship completed by the U.S. Navy and the last on active duty. • **Last location of the USS *Missouri* (BB-63):** Pearl Harbor, Hawaii, 1,000 yards from the *Arizona* Memorial. *Missouri* was opened as museum January 1999.
Montana, USS BB-51	Unfinished in compliance with the Washington Treaty for the Limitation of Naval Armaments. Sold for scrap October 25, 1923.
Nebraska, USS BB-14 (1907)	• **Last full commission:** April 3, 1917. • **Last World War I service:** principal escort for convoys across the Atlantic in autumn 1918. • **Last of the USS *Nebraska* (BB-14):** decommissioned July 2, 1920. Scrapped November 30, 1923, in compliance with the Washington Treaty for the Limitation of Naval Armaments.
Nevada, USS BB-36 (1916)	• **Last World War I service:** with British Grand Fleet. Arrived at Bantry Bay, Ireland, August 1918; made a sweep of the North Sea. Part of the naval escort for USS *George Washington* carrying President Woodrow Wilson to France for the Paris Peace Conference in December 1918. • **Last World War II service:** off Okinawa until June 30, 1945, and from July 10 to August 7 with the Third Fleet. Used as a target in atomic bomb tests at Bikini Atoll July 1, 1946, and July 25, 1946. Survived both blasts. • **Last of the USS *Nevada* (BB-36):** decommissioned August 29, 1946. Sunk as a target off Hawaii July 31, 1948.
New Hampshire, USS BB-25 (1908)	• **Last World War I service:** two convoy escort missions, guarding transports from New York to rendezvous point off the coast of France beginning September 15, 1918. From December 1918 to June 1919, *New Hampshire* made four trips transporting troops home from France. • **Last of the USS *New Hampshire* (BB-25):** decommissioned May 21, 1921. Scrapped November 1, 1923, in compliance with the Washington Treaty for the Limitation of Naval Armaments.
New Jersey, USS BB-16 (1906)	• **Last World War I service:** trained gunners and seamen recruits in the Chesapeake Bay. After the Armistice until June 1919, *New Jersey* made four trips and transported 5,000 troops home from Europe. • **Last of the USS *New Jersey* (BB-16):** decommissioned August 6, 1920, at Boston Naval Yard. Transferred to the U.S. Army. Sunk in bomb tests off Cape Hatteras, North Carolina, September 5, 1923.
New Jersey, USS BB-62 (1943)	• **Last World War II service:** conducted bombardment and preparing invasion beaches in late March 1945, for an assault a week later. Spent the last months of war being overhauled at Puget Sound Naval Shipyard, then sailed for San Pedro, Pearl Harbor, Eniwetok and Guam July 4, 1945.

	• **Last Korean War service:** destroyed large-caliber guns, bunkers, caves and trenches at Wonsan, two days before truce. Recommissioned in 1968 and refitted for service in Vietnam. Became the only active battleship in the world at that time. • **Last Vietnam War service:** ended April 1969, after six months of bombardment and fire support missions along Vietnamese coast. Decommissioned in 1969. Recommissioned for the last time December 28, 1982, Long Beach, California, for service in Middle East. • **Last decommissioned:** February 8, 1991, Long Beach; towed to Bremerton, Washington. • **Last service of the USS *New Jersey* (BB-62):** towed to Philadelphia, Pennsylvania, by the tug *Sea Victory*, arriving November 11, 1999. In January 2000, the *New Jersey* was donated to Home Port Alliance of Camden, New Jersey, to be used as a museum. The museum opened to the public in 2001.
New Mexico, **USS** BB-40 (1918)	• **Last World War I service:** part of naval escort for the USS *George Washington* that transported President Woodrow Wilson home from the Paris Peace Conference, February 1919. • **Last World War II service:** encountered Japanese suicide missions at Hagushi on May 12, 1945. Was in Tokyo Bay for the surrender of Japan, September 2, 1945. • **Last of the USS *New Mexico* (BB-40):** decommissioned July 19, 1946. Sold for scrap October 13, 1947.
New York, **USS** BB-34 (1914)	• **Last World War I service:** present for surrender of the German High Seas Fleet in the Firth of Forth November 21, 1918. Escorted USS *George Washington* carrying President Woodrow Wilson to France, December 1918 for the Paris Peace Conference. • **Last World War II service:** support at assault on Okinawa before returning to Pearl Harbor for a planned invasion of Japan. Used as a target in atomic bomb tests at Bikini Atoll (Operation Crossroads) July 1, 1946, and July 25, 1946. Survived both blasts. • **Last of the USS *New York* (BB-34):** decommissioned August 29, 1946, after being taken to Kwajalein Atoll and then to Pearl Harbor, Oahu, Hawaii. Sunk as target 40 miles off Pearl Harbor July 8, 1948.
North Carolina, **USS** BB-52	Unfinished in compliance with the Washington Treaty for the Limitation of Naval Armaments. Sold for scrap October 25, 1923.
North Carolina, **USS** BB-55 (1941)	• **Last World War II service:** a month of air strikes and naval bombardment on Japanese home islands, firing on major industrial plants near Tokyo. *North Carolina's* scout planes performed a daring rescue of a downed carrier pilot under heavy fire in Tokyo Bay. • **Last of the USS *North Carolina* (BB-55):** decommissioned June 27, 1947, in New York. Struck from the Navy List June 1, 1960. Transferred to the state of North Carolina September 6, 1961. Dedicated as a memorial in Wilmington, North Carolina, April 29, 1962.
North Dakota, **USS** BB-29 (1910)	• **Last World War I service:** trained gunners and engineers, York River, Virginia, and New York. • **Last of the USS *North Dakota* (BB-29):** decommissioned November 22, 1923. Struck from the Navy List January 7, 1931. Sold for scrap March 16, 1931.

***Ohio*, USS** BB-12 (1904)	• **Last World War I service:** trained crews taking part in battleship maneuvers out of Norfolk, Virginia. • **Last of the USS *Ohio* (BB-12):** decommissioned May 31, 1922. Sold for scrap March 24, 1923.
***Oklahoma*, USS** BB-37 (1916)	• **Last World War I service:** protected Allied convoys in European waters in August 1918. Part of naval escort for USS *George Washington* carrying President Woodrow Wilson to France for the Paris Peace Conference in December 1918. *Oklahoma* also escorted the president's ship back to the United States after his second visit to Europe in July 1919. • **Last World War II service:** sank at Pearl Harbor December 7, 1941. Later raised and entered dry dock December 28, 1943. • **Last of the USS *Oklahoma* (BB-37):** decommissioned September 1, 1944. Stripped of guns and superstructure and sold December 5, 1946. Sank about 540 miles from Pearl Harbor en route to San Francisco, May 17, 1947.
***Oregon*, USS** BB-3 (1896)	• **Last service:** recommissioned August 21, 1919, to serve as reviewing ship for President Woodrow Wilson during arrival of the Pacific Fleet at Seattle, Washington. • **Last decommissioned:** October 4, 1919. Rendered incapable of future combat service January 4, 1924. Retained on the Navy List as a naval relic with a classification of "unclassified." Loaned to the state of Oregon June 1925. Restored and moored at Portland as a floating museum. Reclassified for the last time February 17, 1941, as *IX- 22*. • **Last of the USS *Oregon* (BB-3):** struck from the Navy List November 2, 1942, and sold for scrap December 7, 1942. Scrapping began in Kalima, Washington, March 1943. Scrapping stopped at the main deck and *Oregon* was returned to Navy for use in Guam as a storage hulk for ammunition and breakwater. Hulk remained in Guam until a typhoon broke the mooring and drifted *Oregon* 500 miles out to sea. She was towed back. *Oregon* was sold March 15, 1956, and towed to Kawasaki, Japan, where she was scrapped.
***Pennsylvania*, USS** BB-38 (1916)	• **Last World War I service:** training maneuvers in Chesapeake Bay area. Part of the naval escort for USS *George Washington* carrying President Woodrow Wilson to the Paris Peace Conference December 1918. • **Last World War II service:** Okinawa, where *Pennsylvania* was heavily damaged by a Japanese torpedo. Used as a target in atomic bomb tests at Bikini Atoll July 1, 1946 and July 25, 1946. Survived both blasts. • **Last of the USS *Pennsylvania* (BB-38):** decommissioned August 29, 1946, but remained at Kwajalein Atoll. Struck from the Navy List and sunk off Kwajalein February 19, 1948.
***Rhode Island*, USS** BB-17 (1906)	• **Last full commission:** Hampton Roads, Virginia, March 27, 1917. • **Last World War I service:** participated in torpedo proving trials in June 1918. Transported more than 5,000 troops from France home to the United States between December 1918 and July 1919. • **Last of the USS *Rhode Island* (BB-17):** decommissioned June 30, 1920. Rendered incapable of further combat service October 4, 1923. Scrapped November 1, 1923 in compliance with the Washington Treaty for the Limitation of Naval Armaments.
South Carolina,	• **Last World War I service:** engaged in gunnery training until the Armistice. Transported more than 4,000 troops home from Europe to the

USS BB-26 (1910)	United States between February and June 1919. • **Last of the USS *South Carolina* (BB-26):** decommissioned in Philadelphia, Pennsylvania, December 15, 1921, after completing midshipmen's summer training course at Annapolis, Maryland. Struck from the Navy List November 10, 1923. Sold for scrap April 24, 1924, in compliance with the Washington Treaty for the Limitation of Naval Armaments.
South Dakota, USS BB-49	Unfinished in compliance with the Washington Treaty for the Limitation of Naval Armaments. Sold for scrap October 25, 1923.
South Dakota, USS BB-57 (1942)	• **Last World War II service:** supported carriers in strikes against northern Honshu, Japan, August 10, 1945, and in Tokyo area on August 13 and 15. The August 15 strike was the last strike of World War II. Japan surrendered later on that day. • **Last of the USS *South Dakota* (BB-57):** decommissioned January 31, 1947. Struck from the Navy List June 1, 1962. Sold for scrap October 25, 1962.
Tennessee, USS BB-43 (1920)	• **Last World War II service:** minesweeping in East China Sea. Patrolled the waters off Shanghai during the last two months of the war. • **Last of the USS *Tennessee* (BB-43):** decommissioned February 14, 1947. Struck from the Navy List; sold for scrap July 10, 1959.
Texas, USS (1895)	Considered the first true United States naval battleship, although it was the last battleship without a designated battleship hull number. • **Last decommissioned:** February 1, 1911. Renamed *San Marcos* on February 15, 1911, to allow the name *Texas* to be assigned to BB-35. • **Last of the USS *Texas*:** struck from the Navy List October 10, 1911; sunk as target in Tangier Sound in Chesapeake Bay.
Texas, USS BB-35 (1914)	*Texas* is the last Dreadnought-type battleship remaining in the world. • **Last World War I service:** with the Grand Fleet in the Sixth Battle Squadron. Part of naval escort for USS *George Washington* carrying President Woodrow Wilson to the Paris Peace Conference December 1918. • **Last World War II service:** provided support at Okinawa before heading to Leyte for the remainder of the war. • **Last of the USS *Texas* (BB-35):** decommissioned April 21, 1948. Struck from the Navy List April 30, 1948, and transferred to the state of Texas to serve as a permanent memorial at San Jacinto State Park.
Utah, USS BB-31 (1911)	• **Last World War I service:** operated from Bantry Bay, Ireland, covering Allied convoys approaching the British Isles. • **Last recommissioned:** April 1, 1932, at Norfolk, Virginia. • **Last voyage:** advanced anti-aircraft gunnery cruise in Hawaiian waters in early December 1941, where *Utah* was moored for the last time at Pearl Harbor in berth F-11 off Ford Island. Sank during the Japanese attack on Pearl Harbor December 7, 1941. • **Last person to leave the USS *Utah* (BB-31):** Fireman John B. Vaessen, who remained on his post in the dynamo room to provide lights as long as possible. • **Last of the USS *Utah* (BB-31):** placed under control of Pearl Harbor Base Force on December 29, 1941. Partially righted to clear an adjacent berth, *Utah* was declared out of commission, not in service, on September 5, 1944, and struck from the Navy List November 13, 1944. *Utah*'s par-

	tially submerged rusting hulk still rests at Pearl Harbor with the remains of 58 crew members trapped inside.
Vermont, USS BB-20 (1907)	• **Last World War I service:** engineering training ship in Chesapeake Bay region. • **Last of the USS *Vermont* (BB-20):** decommissioned June 30, 1920, at Mare Island Naval Shipyard, California. Struck from the Navy List November 10, 1923. Scrapped November 30, 1923, in compliance with the Washington Treaty for the Limitation of Naval Armaments.
Virginia, USS BB-13 (1906)	• **Last World War I service:** escorted convoys more than halfway across the Atlantic in autumn 1918. From December 1918 to July 1918, *Virginia* transported more than 6,000 troops from France home to the United States. • **Last of the USS *Virginia* (BB-13):** decommissioned August 13, 1920. Transferred to the Army and sunk by bombing off Diamond Shoals, North Carolina, September 5, 1923.
Washington, USS BB-47	Unfinished in compliance with the Washington Treaty for the Limitation of Naval Armaments. Used as a target and sunk November 25, 1924.
Washington, USS BB-56 (1941)	• **Last World War II service:** San Pedro Bay, Leyte, Philippines. Sailed to the west coast of the U.S. June 6, 1945, making stops at Guam and Pearl Harbor before reaching Puget Sound Navy Yard on June 23. *Washington* was assigned to Operation Magic Carpet and transported more than 1,500 troops from England to New York in November 1945. • **Last of the USS *Washington* (BB-56):** decommissioned June 27, 1947. Struck from the Navy List on June 1, 1960. Sold for scrap May 24, 1961.
West Virginia, USS BB-48 (1923)	Sank December 7, 1941, during the Japanese attack on Pearl Harbor, Oahu, Hawaii. Refloated May 17, 1942, and modernized. • **Last World War II service:** running drills in preparation for landing in Japan. *West Virginia* was present for the final surrender of Japan and played a part in the occupation that followed. *West Virginia* made the last of three runs transporting troops home to the United States as part of Operation Magic Carpet in December 1945. • **Last of the USS *West Virginia* (BB-48):** decommissioned January 9, 1947. Sold for scrap August 24, 1959.
Wisconsin, USS BB-9 (1901)	• **Last recommissioned:** April 23, 1917, after spending time moored at Philadelphia Naval Yard. • **Last World War I service:** engineering school ship on training cruises in the Chesapeake Bay and York River. • **Last of the USS *Wisconsin* (BB-9):** decommissioned May 15, 1920. Sold for scrap January 26, 1922, in compliance with the Washington Treaty for the Limitation of Naval Armaments.
Wisconsin, USS BB-64 (1944)	• **Last World War II service:** part of TF 38 raids on Japanese industrial facilities, airfields and merchant and naval shipping. • **Last Korean War service:** off Songjin, Korea, March 15, 1952, where *Wisconsin* received a direct hit but subsequently destroyed enemy battery before continuing her mission. After lending support to First Marine Division, *Wisconsin* returned to Japan March 19, 1952. Conducted training for remainder of the war. When decommissioned in 1958, *Wisconsin* was the last active battleship in service, leaving the U.S. Navy without an active battleship for first time since 1898. • **Last recommissioned:** 1988, at Philadelphia Naval Shipyard.

Wyoming, USS BB-32 (1912)	• **Last Gulf War service:** fired on Faylaka Island and Kuwait City in support of a ground offensive in late February 1991. • **Last of the USS *Wisconsin* (BB-64):** decommissioned for the last time September 30, 1991. Moored at National Maritime Center, Norfolk, Virginia, since December 7, 2000. Opened to the public April 16, 2001.
Wyoming, USS BB-32 (1912)	• **Last World War I service:** guarded Allied minelayers as they planted a North Sea mine barrage. • **Last World War II service:** Casco Bay, July 1945, as part of a force established to study methods and dealing with Japanese kamikazes. • **Last of the USS *Wyoming* (BB-32):** decommissioned August 1, 1947. Struck from the Navy List September 16, 1947. Sold for scrap October 30, 1947.

Ships—Naval—Battleships, United States
• **Last U.S. battleship on active duty:** USS *Missouri* (BB-63), decommissioned on March 31, 1992. No battleships are left in the U.S. Navy. The Navy made the decision to do away with them because of the high cost of operation and less need for them with the more modern powerful cruisers and destroyers of today's Navy.

Ships—Naval—Carriers—United States
Modern American Carriers
(Chart includes all retired United States carriers.)

Carrier, Hull Number and Year Commissioned	Last Service and Fate
America, USS CV-66 (1965)	• **Last Vietnam War service:** strike operations against North Vietnam September and October 1972. • **Last service:** *America*'s 20th and final deployment was to the Mediterranean Sea and Indian Ocean, beginning August 28, 1995, and ending on February 24, 1996. • **Last of the USS *America* (CV-66):** decommissioned August 9, 1996. Struck from the Navy List. Presently in Naval Inactive Ship Maintenance Facility, Philadelphia, Pennsylvania. Will be scrapped.
Antietam, USS CV-36 (1945)	• **Last World War II service:** Newly commissioned in 1945, *Antietam* was three days out of Oahu, Hawaii, en route to Eniwetok Atoll when Japan surrendered. Upon arrival at Eniwetok August 19, 1945, her mission was changed from combat to occupation support duty. • **Last recommissioned:** January 17, 1951. • **Last Korean War service:** March 21, 1952, following completion of nearly 6,000 sorties. *Antietam* returned to Yokosuka and then to the United States. • **Last of the USS *Antietam* (CV-36):** decommissioned for the last time May 8, 1963; berthed in reserve fleet at Philadelphia, Pennsylvania. Struck from the Navy List May 1, 1973. Sold for scrap February 28, 1974.
Bataan, USS CV-29 (1943)	• **Last World War II service:** participated in the final raid on the Japanese home islands, July 10 to August 15, 1945. • **Last Korean War service:** operated off Korea from October 1952 until

	May 10, 1953. *Bataan* then departed for San Diego. She sailed via Pearl Harbor to Kobe and Yokosuka, Japan, July 31, 1953, before returning to the United States. • **Last of the USS *Bataan* (CV-29):** decommissioned in San Francisco, California, April 9, 1954. Struck from the Navy List September 1, 1959. Sold for scrap May 1961.
***Belleau Wood*, USS CV-24 (1943)**	• **Last World War II service:** participated in the final raid on Japanese home islands, July 10 to August 15, 1945. • **Last service:** decommissioned January 13, 1947. Transferred to France September 5, 1953. Served in the French Navy under the name *Bois Belleau*. Returned to the United States in 1960. • **Last of the USS *Belleau Wood* (CV-24):** struck from the Navy List October 1, 1960. Sold for scrap.
***Bennington*, USS CV-20 (1944)**	• **Last World War II service:** participated in the final raids on Japanese home islands, July 10 to August 15, 1945. • **Last recommissioned:** November 13, 1952. • **Last major service:** recovered Apollo 4 spacecraft in the Pacific Ocean, November 9, 1967. • **Last of the USS *Bennington* (CV-20):** decommissioned January 15, 1970. Struck from the Navy List in 1989. Sold for scrap December 1, 1994.
***Bon Homme Richard*, USS CV-31 (1944)**	• **Last World War II service:** air strikes on Japan between July 2 and August 15, 1945. • **Last Korean War service:** operations against North Korean targets, concluding December 18, 1952. • **Last recommissioned:** September 1955. • **Last Vietnam War service:** *Bon Homme Richard's* fifth Southeast Asia combat tour in six years. Deactivated after her 1970 deployment. • **Last of the USS *Bon Homme Richard* (CV-31):** decommissioned July 2, 1971. Became part of reserve fleet at Bremerton, Washington. Struck from the Navy List in 1989. Sold for scrap February 4, 1992.
***Boxer*, USS CV-21 (1945)**	USS *Boxer* was completed too late to take part in World War II. • **Last Korean War service:** commenced March 30, 1953, when *Boxer* departed for Far East and took part in the last actions of the Korean War, remaining in until November. • **Last major service:** assisting in recovering the first unmanned Apollo spacecraft in Atlantic Ocean, February 26, 1966. • **Last of the USS *Boxer* (CV-21):** decommissioned December 1, 1969. Struck from the Navy List the same day. Sold for scrap March 13, 1971.
***Bunker Hill*, USS CV-17 (1943)**	• **Last World War II service:** May 11, 1945, supporting Okinawa invasion. Hit and severely damaged by two suicide planes. Returned to Bremerton, Washington, via Pearl Harbor and participated in Magic Carpet fleet after the war. Decommissioned January 9, 1947. Reclassified three times, although not recommissioned. • **Last reclassification:** August 1953 as AVT-9. • **Last of the USS *Bunker Hill* (CV-17):** struck from the Navy List November 1, 1966, Retained as moored electronic test ship in San Diego, California, until November 1972. Sold for scrap May 1973.
***Cabot*, USS CV-28**	• **Last World War II service:** made strikes on Wake Island, August 1, 1945, en route to Eniwetok. Remained on training duty until the end of

(1943)	the war. Decommissioned January 21, 1955. Reclassified as AVT-3 May 15, 1959. Loaned to Spain August 30, 1967, where she served as *Dedalo*. Sold to Spain in 1972. • **Last of the USS *Cabot* (CV-28):** struck from the Spanish Navy List August 1989. Donated to a private U.S. organization for use as a museum. Organization had credit difficulties and was unable to accept. Auctioned by U.S. Marshals Service September 10, 1999. *Cabot* was the last surviving "light carrier" when scrapped in December 2000.
Coral Sea, USS CV-43 (1947)	• **Last recommissioned:** January 25, 1960. • **Last Vietnam War service:** July 17, 1972 deployment. *Coral Sea* was in the Western Pacific-Vietnam area almost continuously from December 1964 to July 1975. • **Last major service:** assisting USS *Iowa* (BB-61) after a gun turret explosion killed 47 crew April 19, 1989. • **Last of the USS *Coral Sea* (CV-43):** decommissioned April 26, 1990. Sold for scrap May 7, 1993.
Cowpens, USS CV-25 (1943)	• **Last World War II service:** participated in final raid on Japanese home islands, July 10 to August 15, 1945. *Cowpens* made two voyages transporting troops home from Pearl Harbor, Guam and Okinawa as part of Operation Magic Carpet. • **Last of the USS *Cowpens* (CV-25):** decommissioned January 13, 1947. Reclassified as AVT-1 May 1959. Struck from the Navy List November 1, 1959. Sold for scrap.
Enterprise, USS CV-6 (1938)	• **Last World War II service:** May 14, 1945, when a suicide plane destroyed the forward elevator of *Enterprise*, killing 14 and wounding 34. Sailed to Puget Sound Navy Yard for repairs and was later part of Operation Magic Carpet that transported more than 10,000 troops home from Europe after the war. Entered New York Naval Shipyard January 18, 1946, for inactivation. • **Last of the USS *Enterprise* (CV-6):** decommissioned February 17, 1947. Sold July 1, 1958, and dismantled.
Essex, USS CV-9 (1942)	• **Last World War II service:** final raids against Japanese home islands from July 10 to August 15, 1945. • **Last recommissioned:** January 16, 1951. • **Last Korean War service:** sailing China Sea with Peace Patrol beginning December 1, 1953. • **Last of the USS *Essex* (CV-9):** decommissioned for the last time June 30, 1969. Struck from the Navy List June 1, 1973. Sold for scrap June 1, 1975.
Forrestal, USS CV-59 (1955)	• **Last Vietnam War service:** bombed July 29, 1967, after just five days in combat. A fire on board killed 134 crewmen and caused major damage. • **Last operational deployment:** *Forrestal*'s 21st and final deployment, May 30, 1991; provided air power presence and airborne intelligence support during Operation Provide Comfort. • **Last activity:** arrived in Philadelphia, Pennsylvania, in September 1992 for a 14-month, $157 million overhaul. The overhaul was canceled in early 1993. • **Last of the USS *Forrestal* (CV-59):** decommissioned September 11, 1993. Struck from the Navy List the same day. Since 1998, *Forrestal* has

	been at the Naval Education and Training Center, Newport, Rhode Island, on hold as a museum/memorial donation.
Franklin, USS CV-13 (1944)	• **Last World War II service:** March 19, 1945, when *Franklin* was severely damaged by enemy fire within 50 miles of the Japanese mainland. Although 724 were killed, the *Franklin* survived and was taken to Brooklyn, New York, and later Bayonne, New Jersey. • **Last of the USS *Franklin* (CV-13):** decommissioned February 17, 1947. Reclassified as AVT-8, May 15, 1958. Struck from the Navy List October 10, 1964.
Franklin D. Roosevelt, USS CV-42 (1945)	• **Last recommissioned:** February 1957. • **Last major service:** supported first overseas operational commitment on carrier for AV-8A *Harrier* October 4, 1976. • **Last of the USS *Franklin D. Roosevelt* (CV-42):** decommissioned September 30, 1977. Struck from the Navy List the next day. Sold for scrap by Defense Reutilization and Marketing Service April 1, 1978.
Hancock, USS CV-19 (1944)	• **Last World War II service:** August 15, 1945, the day Japanese surrendered. *Hancock* recalled planes from missions before they reached their targets. Later that day, planes of *Hancock*'s air patrol shot down a Japanese torpedo plane as it attacked a British task force. *Hancock* transported more than 7,500 troops home to California as part of Operation Magic Carpet. • **Last recommissioned:** November 15, 1956. • **Last Vietnam War service:** awaited possible evacuation of refugees from South Vietnam in 1975 and stood alert, although not utilized, during recovery of the *SS Mayaguez* in May 1975. • **Last of the USS *Hancock* (CV-19):** decommissioned January 30, 1976. Struck from the Navy List January 31, 1976. Sold for scrap September 1, 1976.
Hornet, USS CV-8 (1941)	• **Last World War II service and last of the USS *Hornet* (CV-8):** sank after enemy action at the Battle of Santa Cruz Islands October 27, 1942. Struck from the Navy List January 13, 1943.
Hornet, USS CV-12 (1943)	• **Last World War II service:** support to ground troops on Okinawa and raids to destroy the industrial capacity of Japan in April and May 1945. • **Last recommissioned:** September 11, 1953. *Hornet* spent most of the Korean War being converted into an attack aircraft carrier. • **Last Vietnam War service:** operated in Vietnamese waters most of summer 1967. • **Last major service:** recovery carrier for Apollo 11 and Apollo 12 missions in July and November 1969. • **Last of the USS *Hornet* (CV-12):** decommissioned June 26, 1970. Struck from the Navy List July 25, 1989. Originally sold for scrap April 1993 but then donated to Aircraft Carrier Hornet Foundation for use as a museum in Alameda, California, in 1998.
Independence, USS CV-22 (1943)	• **Last World War II service:** participated in the last carrier strikes against Japan in July and August 1945. Used as a test target at Bikini Atoll (Operation Crossroads) July 25, 1946. Did not sink. • **Last of the USS *Independence* (CV-22):** taken to Kwajalein Atoll. Decommissioned August 28, 1946. Sunk as target in weapons tests off the California coast June 29, 1951.

Independence, **USS** CV-62 (1959)	• **Last Vietnam War service:** seven-month stint beginning May 10, 1965, when *Independence* became first Atlantic Fleet carrier stationed in the South China Sea off the coast of Vietnam. • **Last Gulf War service:** August to December 1990, when *Independence* embarked with Carrier Air Wing 14 and became the first carrier to enter the Arabian Gulf since 1974. • **Last major service:** deployed in Arabian Gulf January 1998 to support negotiations between the United Nations and Iraq and to participate in Operation Southern Watch. • **Last of the USS *Independence* (CV-62):** decommissioned September 30, 1998, at Puget Sound Naval Shipyard, Bremerton, Washington, as the Navy's oldest active ship. Presently on inactive reserve in Naval Inactive Ship Maintenance Facility, Bremerton. The *Independence*'s "Don't Tread on Me" jack was transferred to the Navy's next oldest ship, the *Kitty Hawk* (CV-63).
Intrepid, **USS** CV-11 (1943)	• **Last World War II service:** hit by a diving Japanese plane April 16, 1945, doing extensive damage and requiring repairs that would continue until the end of the war. • **Last Vietnam War service:** seven months with the 7th Fleet off Vietnam, ending in June 1967. • **Last service:** flagship for Commander Carrier Group 16 at Quonset Point, Rhode Island. • **Last of the USS *Intrepid* (CV-11):** decommissioned March 15, 1974. Saved from being scrapped by the *Intrepid* Museum Foundation campaign. Established as a floating museum in New York City August 1982. Designated a National Historic Landmark in 1986.
Kearsarge, **USS** CV-33 (1946)	• **Last recommissioned:** February 15, 1952. • **Last Korean War service:** February 1953. *Kearsarge's* planes flew nearly 6,000 sorties against North Korea. *Kearsarge* returned to Asia July 1, 1953, and operated with the 7th Fleet during the Korean truce. • **Last of the USS *Kearsarge* (CV-33):** decommissioned February 13, 1970. Struck from the Navy List May 1, 1973. Sold for scrap 1974.
Lake Champlain, **USS** CV-39 (1945)	• **Last World War II service:** part of Operation Magic Carpet, transporting troops home from Europe to New York after the war. • **Last recommissioned:** September 19, 1952. • **Last Korean War service:** off western Korea from June 14, 1953 until the truce on July 27, 1953. • **Last major service:** primary recovery ship for Gemini 5 spacecraft, August 5, 1965. • **Last of the USS *Lake Champlain* (CV-39):** decommissioned in Philadelphia, Pennsylvania, May 2, 1966. Struck from the Navy List December 1, 1969. Sold for scrap April 28, 1972.
Langley, **USS** CV-1 (1912)	Commissioned as *Jupiter*. Name changed to *Langley,* April 11, 1920. • **Last recommissioned:** March 20, 1922. • **Last World War II service and last of the USS *Langley* (CV-1):** February 27, 1942, when *Langley* was sunk as a result of enemy action about 75 miles south of Tjilatjap, Java.
Langley, **USS** CV-27 (1943)	• **Last World War II service:** Okinawa invasion and strikes on Kyushu, Japan, to destroy kamikaze bases in southern Japan until May 11, 1945. • **Last of the USS *Langley* (CV-27):** decommissioned February 11,

	1947. Transferred to France January 8, 1951. Served the French Navy as *Lafayette*. Returned to the United States March 20, 1963. Sold for scrap February 19, 1964.
Lexington, USS CV-2 (1927)	• **Last World War II service and last of the USS *Lexington* (CV-2):** sank May 8, 1942, as a result of enemy action at the Battle of the Coral Sea.
Lexington, USS CV-16 (1943)	• **Last World War II service:** air strikes on Japanese home islands through August 15, 1945. Transported troops from Japan to San Francisco, California, December 1945. • **Last recommissioned:** August 15, 1955. • **Last service:** on January 1, 1969, *Lexington* was redesignated as CVT-16 and spent its last 22 years as a training carrier in Pensacola, Florida, Corpus Christi, Texas, and New Orleans, Louisiana. • **Last of the USS *Lexington* (CV-16):** decommissioned November 8, 1991. Struck from the Navy List November 30, 1991. Now a museum in Corpus Christi.
Leyte, USS CV-32 (1946)	• **Last Korean War service:** February 25, 1951, when *Leyte* returned to Norfolk, Virginia, for overhaul, after pilots had accumulated 11,000 hours in the air during combat. For the remainder of the war, *Leyte* was in the Caribbean and Mediterranean seas. Departed Quonset Point, Rhode Island, in January 1959 for New York Navy Yard. Overhauled then decommissioned May 15, 1959. Reclassified as AVT-10 same day. Assigned to Philadelphia group of the Atlantic Reserve Fleet with a berth in New York. • **Last of the USS *Leyte* (CV-32):** struck from the Navy List June 1, 1969. Sold for scrap September 1970.
Midway, USS CV-41 (1945)	• **Last recommissioned:** January 31, 1970. • **Last Gulf War service:** March 11, 1991, when *Midway* left the Persian Gulf for Yokosuka, Japan. Sailed to Pearl Harbor August 1991. Replaced by *Independence* (CV-62) as forward deploying carrier. • **Last of the USS *Midway* (CV-41):** decommissioned in San Diego, California, April 11, 1992. Struck from the Navy List March 17, 1997. Taken to the Navy Inactive Ship Maintenance Facility, Bremerton, Washington, where she is on donation hold for use as a museum and memorial.
Monterey, USS CV-26 (1943)	• **Last World War II service:** air strikes against Japanese home islands July 1 to August 15, 1945. • **Last recommissioned:** September 15, 1950. • **Last major service:** flood rescue mission in Honduras October 1-11, 1954. • **Last of the USS *Monterey* (CV-26):** departed Pensacola, Florida, June 9, 1955, to rejoin the Atlantic Reserve Fleet, Philadelphia Group. Decommissioned January 16, 1956. Reclassified as AVT-2 May 1959. Struck from the Navy List June 1970. Sold for scrap May 1971.
Oriskany, USS CV-34 (1950)	• **Last Korean War service:** air strikes April 1953, after which *Oriskany* left Korea on April 22. Sailed again for Asia September 14, 1953. Operated with the 7th Fleet during the Korean truce. • **Last recommissioned:** March 7, 1959, San Francisco Naval Yard, California.

	• **Last Vietnam War service:** final deployment to Asia April 1969. • **Last of the USS *Oriskany* (CV-34):** decommissioned September 30, 1975. Struck from the Navy List July 1989. Sold for scrap on September 9, 1995, but the contractor defaulted. Repossessed by the Navy. Currently at Beaumont Reserve Fleet in Beaumont, Texas.
Philippine Sea, USS CV-47 (1946)	• **Last Koran War service:** participated in air strikes beginning in late December 1951. Returned to San Diego, California, August 8, 1952. Sailed west on last 7th Fleet deployment January 1958. • **Last of the USS *Philippine Sea* (CV-47):** decommissioned December 28, 1958. Reclassified as AVT-11 May 15, 1959. Struck from the Navy List December 1 1969. Sold for scrap March 1971.
Princeton, USS CV-23 (1943)	• **Last World War II service and last of the USS *Princeton* (CV-23):** sank as a result of enemy action in the Sibuyan Sea, near the Philippines, October 24, 1944.
Princeton, USS CV-37 (1945)	• **Last Korean War service:** launched planes for close air support from February 1953 until the end of the conflict. Remained in Korea until September 7, 1953. • **Last Vietnam War service:** May to December 1968 as flagship for Amphibious Ready Group Alpha, providing amphibious assault carrier services for operations Fortress Attack III and IV, Proud Hunter, Swift Pursuit and Eager Hunter. • **Last major service:** main recovery ship for Apollo 10 spacecraft April 1969. • **Last of the USS *Princeton* (CV-37):** decommissioned January 30, 1970. Struck from the Navy List on January 30, 1970. Sold for scrap May 1971.
Randolph, USS CV-15 (1944)	• **Last World War II service:** participated in strikes on Kisarazu Airfield and surrounding installations that concluded on August 15, 1945, the day Japanese surrendered. Made two trips to the Mediterranean to transport troops home as part of Operation Magic Carpet. • **Last recommissioned:** July 1, 1953. • **Last of the USS *Randolph* (CV-15):** berthed in Philadelphia, Pennsylvania. Decommissioned February 13, 1969. Struck from the Navy List June 1, 1973. Sold for scrap April 1, 1975.
Ranger, USS CV-4 (1934)	• **Last World War II service:** trained pilots for combat duty operating out of San Diego, California. • **Last of the USS *Ranger* (CV-4):** decommissioned October 18, 1946, at Norfolk Naval Shipyard, Virginia. Struck from the Navy List October 29, 1946. Sold for scrap January 28, 1947.
Ranger, USS CV-61 (1957)	• **Last Vietnam War service:** part of Operation Linebacker II, ending December 29, 1972. Some later scheduled sorties in January 1973 were cancelled January 27, 1973 in accord with Vietnam cease-fire. Relieved on station December 19, 1992, by the USS *Kitty Hawk* (CV-63). • **Last Gulf War service:** 228 U.S. Navy sorties were launched from the USS *Ranger* in the Persian Gulf. *Ranger* left the gulf in December 1992 for Somalia to participate in Operation Restore Hope, a relief effort.

	• Last of the USS *Ranger* (CV-61): decommissioned in San Diego, California, July 10, 1993. On inactive reserve in the Naval Inactive Ship Maintenance Facility, Bremerton, Washington.
***Reprisal,* USS** CV-35	Unfinished. (Hull, 53 percent complete). Sold for scrap November 1949.
***Saipan,* USS** CV-48 (1946)	Name changed to *Arlington* (AGMR-2) April 8, 1965. Served as a communications relay ship. **• Last Vietnam War service and last major service:** June 27, 1969, when she returned to the Vietnamese coast but was ordered east after just seven days to participate in her last major duty—supporting the recovery of the Apollo 11 spacecraft. **• Last of the USS *Saipan/Arlington* (CV-48):** decommissioned January 14, 1970. Struck from the Navy List August 15, 1975. Sold for scrap June 1, 1976.
***San Jacinto,* USS** CV-30 (1943)	**• Last World War II service:** attacks on Hokkaido and Honshu, Japan, July 9, 1945. Continued to operate off the coast of Japan until the end of the war. Later participated in mercy air missions over Allied prisoner-of-war camps. Returned to Alameda, California, September 14, 1945. **• Last of the USS *San Jacinto* (CV-30):** decommissioned March 1, 1947. Berthed at San Diego, California. Reclassified as AVT-5 May 15, 1959. Struck from the Navy List June 1, 1970. Sold for scrap December 15, 1971.
***Saratoga,* USS** CV-3 (1927)	**• Last World War II service:** training pilots at Pearl Harbor beginning June 3, 1945, and concluding September 6, 1945, after the Japanese surrender. *Saratoga* participated in Operation Magic Carpet and carried home to the United States more than 29,000 Pacific war veterans, more than any other ship. **• Last of the USS *Saratoga* (CV-3):** used as test target and sunk at Bikini Atoll as part of Operation Crossroads, July 25, 1946. Struck from the Navy List August 15, 1946.
***Saratoga,* USS** CV-60 (1956)	**• Last Vietnam War service:** autumn 1972. *Saratoga's* aircraft battered North Vietnam for more than a week. She left Vietnam for Subic Bay, Philippines, January 7, 1973. **• Last Gulf War service:** on March 11, 1991, *Saratoga* left the Persian Gulf after nearly eight months. While there, *Saratoga* compiled a record of 11,700 arrested landings, 12,700 sorties flown, 36,382 miles traveled and six Suez Canal crossings. **• Last of the USS *Saratoga* (CV-60):** last deployment ended June 24, 1994, at Mayport, Florida. Decommissioned at Mayport August 20, 1994. Struck from the Navy List the same day. Since August 7, 1998, *Saratoga* has been berthed at the Naval Education and Training Center, Newport, Rhode Island, on donation hold.
***Shangri-La,* USS** CV-38 (1944)	**• Last World War II:** air strikes against Japan, beginning July 10, 1945, and ending with Japan's surrender on August 15, 1945. **• Last recommissioned:** January 10, 1955. **• Last Vietnam War service:** seven months at Yankee Station from which *Shangri-La* departed for Subic Bay, Philippines, November 9, 1970. **• Last of the USS *Shangri-La* (CV-38):** decommissioned July 30, 1971.

	Placed in Atlantic Reserve Fleet and berthed at Philadelphia, Pennsylvania. Struck from the Navy List July 15, 1982. Disposed of by the Marine Administration August 9, 1988.
Tarawa, USS CV-40 (1945)	• **Last recommissioned:** February 3, 1951, at Newport, Rhode Island. Reactivated in response to the Korean War but never saw service in that conflict. *Tarawa*'s last years were spent serving the Atlantic Fleet, operating out of Quonset Point, Rhode Island, Norfolk, Virginia, and the Caribbean, including barrier patrols for Soviet fleets and training pilots. • **Last of the USS *Tarawa* (CV-40):** decommissioned May 13, 1960, and placed on reserve at Philadelphia, Pennsylvania. Reclassified May 1961 as AVT-12. Struck from the Navy List June 1, 1967. Sold for scrap October 3, 1968.
Ticonderoga, USS CV-14 (1944)	• **Last World War II service:** attack on Tokyo that was in progress when the Japanese surrendered in August 1945. *Ticonderoga* remained near Tokyo until the formal surrender, then transported more than 1,000 troops home as part of Operation Magic Carpet. • **Last recommissioned:** September 11, 1954. • **Last Vietnam War service:** in the Sea of Japan. Concluded deployment in Subic Bay, Philippines, September 4, 1969. • **Last major service:** recovery carrier for Apollo 17 spacecraft in December 1972, after which *Ticonderoga* sailed to San Diego, California, for her last active service. • **Last of the USS *Ticonderoga* (CV-14):** decommissioned September 1, 1973. Struck from the Navy List November 16, 1973. Sold by the Defense Reutilization and Marketing Service for scrap September 1, 1975.
Valley Forge, USS CV-45 (1946)	• **Last Korean War service:** June 25, 1953, when *Valley Forge* left Korea for San Diego, California, after dropping 3,700 tons of bombs on the enemy. • **Last Vietnam War service:** September 3, 1969, when *Valley Forge* left Danang for Yokosuka, Japan. She left Yokosuka September 11, 1969, and arrived in Long Beach, California, October 31, 1969. • **Last of the USS *Valley Forge* (CV-45):** decommissioned January 16, 1970. Struck from the Navy List the same day. Sold for scrap October 29, 1971.
Wasp, USS CV-7 (1940)	Construction on the *Wasp* began in 1936, while the 1921-22 Washington Treaty for the Limitation of Naval Armaments was still in effect. *Wasp* was the last U.S. carrier whose size was limited by the treaty. • **Last World War II service and last of the USS *Wasp* (CV-7):** sank September 15, 1942, as result of enemy action about 150 miles southeast of San Cristobal. Hit by two Japanese torpedoes, killing 193 of the crew.
Wasp, USS CV-18 (1943)	• **Last World War II service:** August 15, 1945, when Japan surrendered. Two Japanese planes tried to attack *Wasp*'s task group. *Wasp* pilots shot down both planes. • **Last recommissioned:** September 10, 1951. • **Last of the USS *Wasp* (CV-18):** decommissioned July 1, 1972. Sold for scrap.
Wright, USS CV-49 (1947)	• **Last recommissioned:** May 11, 1963, at Puget Sound, Washington. • **Last major service:** stand alert at Norfolk during *Pueblo* (AGER-2) crisis in February 1969.

	• **Last of the USS *Wright* (CV-49):** decommissioned May 27, 1970. Placed on reserve at Philadelphia Naval Shipyard. Struck from the Navy List on December 1, 1977. Sold for scrap August 1, 1980.
Yorktown, USS CV-5 (1937)	• **Last World War II service and last of the USS *Yorktown*:** sank June 7, 1942, as a result of enemy action at the Battle of Midway. On May 19, 1998, underwater explorer Dr. Robert Ballard and his National Geographic Battle of Midway expedition team found *Yorktown* under three miles of water. The carrier was reported to be well preserved.
Yorktown, USS CV-10 (1943)	• **Last World War II service:** August 13, 1945, when *Yorktown* aircraft attacked Tokyo for the last time, two days before the Japanese surrendered. • **Last recommissioned:** October 14, 1955. • **Last Vietnam War service:** in Vietnamese waters June 16, 1967, before heading for Yokosuka, Japan. *Yorktown* last served as the flagship for Commander Carrier Group 16 at Quonset Point, Rhode Island. She was relieved by *Intrepid* (CV-11). • **Last of the USS *Yorktown* (CV-10):** decommissioned June 27, 1970, at Philadelphia, Pennsylvania. Struck from the Navy List June 1, 1973. Towed from Bayonne, New Jersey, to Charleston, South Carolina, June 1975. Established as floating memorial in Charleston, October 13, 1975, on the 200th Anniversary of the U.S. Navy.

Ships—Naval—Cruisers—Great Britain
• **Last of the big gun cruisers that protected Great Britain before and during World War II:** HMS *Belfast*, commissioned in 1938 and built by Harland & Wolff in Belfast, Ireland. She held a crew of more than 950 men. During World War II, she sank the German battle cruiser *Scharnhorst* at the Battle of North Cape on December 26, 1943. *Belfast* was one of the ships that fired the first shots on June 6, 1944, D-Day, attacking a battery at Ver sur Mer, France. Today the *Belfast* is a floating museum in London, England.

Ships—Naval—Destroyers—Tribal Class
The Tribal Class destroyers were built between 1937 and 1945 for the Royal Canadian Navy, the Royal Navy and the Royal Australian Navy. The Tribals used some of most advanced naval architecture, marine propulsion systems and weaponry of their time.
• **Last Tribal Class destroyer:** HMCS *Haida.* Once almost sold for scrap, today the *Haida* is a designated historic site in Toronto, Canada.

Ships—Naval—Warships
• **Last sailing ship used in a major naval battle:** *Seeadler*, built in 1888 as the *Pass of Balmaha*, a fully rigged sailing ship. She was captured by a German submarine in 1915, during World War I, and refitted as a raider. Under the command of Count Felix von Luckner, *Seeadler* was responsible for sinking several merchant ships in the South Atlantic and Pacific. In August 1917, *Seeadler* sank off the coast of Mopelia, one of the French Society Islands. Luckner was captured and placed in a prisoner-of-war camp in New Zealand. He died in Malmo, Sweden, on April 14, 1966, age 84.
• **Last engagement involving wooden men-of-war sailing ships:** Battle of Navarino, October 20, 1827, off the coast of Greece. A Turkish and Egyptian fleet was destroyed by French, Russian and British ships.
• **Last active British former screw-driven wooden battleship:** the British ship HMS *Conway*. She was commissioned in 1839 as HMS *Nile*. She was converted to a screw-driven ship in 1853 when an engine and propellers were added. She became a training ship in 1876. *Conway* was accidentally wrecked in the Menai Straits of North Wales in 1953.
• **Last remaining example of a wooden hybrid steam and sail fighting ship:** the

Danish screw frigate *Jylland*, launched in Copenhagen, Denmark, in 1860. She was also the last ship in the Danish Navy made of wood. *Jylland* took part in the Battle of Helgoland in 1864, during a war between Denmark and Germany over ownership of Schleswig and Holstein. The battle was the last engagement of wooden-built, hybrid steam/sail warships in a sea battle. *Jylland* has been restored and is on permanent display in Ebeltoft, Denmark.

Ships—Naval—Warships—16th Century
• **Last surviving preserved 16th-century warship:** *Mary Rose,* built in England between 1509 and 1511. She sank in July 1545 off the coast of Portsmouth, England, during an engagement with the French fleet. The hull was located in 1971. The ancient ship was raised from the seabed in 1982 and was found to be extremely well preserved. She is now at the Mary Rose Museum in Portsmouth and is the only 16th-century warship on display anywhere in the world.

Ships—Naval—Warships—17th Century
• **Last surviving preserved 17th-century warship:** *Vasa*, a royal warship built in Sweden between 1625 and 1628. *Vasa* sank in 1628, just minutes after being launched in Stockholm's harbor. Excavation of the *Vasa* was completed in 1962. The ship is now on display at the Vasa Museum in Stockholm, Sweden.

Ships—Naval—Warships—18th Century
• **Last surviving seagoing 18th-century British naval ship:** HMS *Victory*, launched in 1765 but not commissioned until 1778. In 1921, when *Victory* was in disrepair, a decision was made to preserve her because of her long history. Restoration began soon afterward. Today, HMS *Victory* is the flagship of the Second Sea Lord and Commander in Chief Naval Home Guard. She is in drydock at Portsmouth Naval Base, Portsmouth, England.
• **Last surviving seagoing 18th-century U.S. naval ship:** the frigate USS *Constitution* ("Old Ironsides"), launched in 1797.

(*See table below:* Ships—Naval—Frigates — United States.)

Ships—Naval—Warships—Frigates
Frigates built during the 18th and 19th centuries were three-masted, full-rigged, high-speed, medium-sized sailing warships with 28 to 60 guns on the main deck, raised quarter deck and forecastle. Their use declined when steam was introduced. Today's frigates are warships larger than destroyers but smaller than cruisers.
• **Last frigate used by the U.S. service:** *Joseph Conrad*, a fully rigged three-masted frigate launched at the shipyard of Burmeister & Wain, Copenhagen, Denmark, in 1882 as the *Georg Stage*. From 1939 to 1945, as *Joseph Conrad,* she served as a U.S. Merchant Marine school ship. Since 1947, she has been at Mystic Seaport in Connecticut. *Joseph Conrad* is listed on the National Register of Historic Places.
• **Last frigate used by the Portuguese Navy:** the *D. Fernando II e Glória*. Launched in 1838, she was the last warship on the "India Run," a military route between Portugal and India. In 1878, she made her last mission at sea: a training voyage for ensigns to the Azores. *D. Fernando II e Glória* then served as the Naval Artillery School until 1938. A fire partially destroyed the ship in 1963. In 1992, the hull was refloated, taken to Lisbon and restored to its 1850s appearance. It is now a museum.
• **Last frigate used by the Royal Danish Navy:** HDMS *Peder Skram,* commissioned May 25, 1966. She was removed from duty in 1988 and decommissioned on July 5, 1990. She was subsequently preserved as a museum ship and is now berthed at Holmen Navy Base, Copenhagen, Denmark.

Ships—Naval—Warships—Ships-of-the-Line
A ship-of-the-line is a sailing vessel with two or more complete decks of guns, generally mounting 64 or more guns.
• **Last surviving ship-of-the-line:** HMS *Victory*, which served as Admiral Lord Nel-

son's flagship during the Battle of Trafalgar in 1805. *Victory* is still commissioned. In 1922, she was drydocked and opened as a museum. *Victory* sustained her last battle scar from a German bomb that landed in the drydock during World War II.

• **Last U.S. Navy ship-of-the-line:** the 74-gun warship USS *Vermont*, which was finished at the Boston Navy Yard around 1825 but not commissioned until 1862. She saw action in the Civil War then remained in New York for 37 years as a store and receiving ship. *Vermont* was condemned and struck from the Navy List in December 1901. The following April, she was sold in New York.

Ships—Naval—Warships—Wind-powered

• **Last ship built for the U.S. Navy that was powered solely by wind:** the second USS *Constellation*, built in 1854. The ship was idle for a while during the early 20th century then was recommissioned in 1940 to serve as a flag ship for the U.S. Navy's Atlantic Fleet. *Constellation* was decommissioned in 1955 and designated a National Historic Landmark. In 1999, the Constellation Foundation completed a restoration, returning the ship to her appearance as she was at the beginning of the Civil War. USS *Constellation* is now in the Inner Harbor in Baltimore, Maryland.

Ships—Naval—Warships—Frigates—United States
Last of America's First Warships

In March 1794, the United States Congress authorized the construction of America's first six warships, the frigates *Chesapeake, Congress, Constellation, Constitution, President* and *United States*.

Ship Name	Description and Fate
USS *Chesapeake* (36 guns)	Built at Gosport Navy Yard, Portsmouth, Virginia, and launched on August 15, 1799. *Chesapeake* saw action with France (1800-01) and patrolled the southern United States and West Indies. She was sent to the Mediterranean during the Barbary War. During the War of 1812, *Chesapeake* was captured by the British off the coast of Massachusetts. She was towed to Halifax and repaired then sailed to England, where she saw action in the Royal Navy. • **Last of the USS *Chesapeake*:** sold in Portsmouth, England, and broken up for scrap in 1820. Some of the ship's timbers were used in the construction of a flour mill in Wickham, near Portsmouth. The timbers are still there in the Chesapeake Mill.
USS *Congress* (36 guns)	Built in Portsmouth, New Hampshire, by J. Hackett and launched on August 16, 1799. *Congress* saw military action in 1800, when she escorted U.S. merchant ships to the East Indies. In 1804, during the Barbary War, she was sent to the Mediterranean. *Congress* patrolled the North Atlantic during the War of 1812. • **Last of the USS *Congress*:** In 1834, the Navy determined *Congress* was not fit for repair. The Navy Commissioner ordered the ship to be broken up at the Norfolk Navy Yard in Virginia. She was scrapped in 1836.
USS *Constellation* (36 guns)	Launched in Baltimore, Maryland, on September 7, 1797. *Constellation* was the first ship commissioned in the U.S. Navy. She was also the first to put to sea and the first to engage an enemy vessel. She saw action with France (1798-1800), in the Barbary War (1802-05) and in the War of 1812 (1812-15). *Constellation* was part

	of Stephen Decatur's squadron in the Mediterranean in 1815. From 1819 to 1845, she sailed the Pacific, Caribbean, Atlantic and Mediterranean. In 1840-45, she traveled around the world. • **Last of the USS *Constellation*:** taken out of service and dismantled in Virginia in 1854. By then, she needed extensive repair. When the sloop of war *Constellation* was built in 1854, some of the timbers from the old *Constellation* were included in her construction.
USS *Constitution* (44 guns)	The USS *Constitution* is the last surviving seagoing 18th-century U.S. frigate, and she is the oldest commissioned ship in the U.S. Navy. *Constitution* was built at Edmund Hartt's Shipyard in Boston, Massachusetts, and launched on October 21, 1797. She saw action in the Barbary War (1802-05) and the War of 1812 and was the victor in a contest with the British ships *Guerrière, Java, Cyane* and *Levant. Constitution* saw more action and won more battles than any other early U.S. warship. She earned the nickname "Old Ironsides" because her hull held up so well in her many encounters. By 1830, the ship was about to be condemned as unseaworthy, but the public—inspired by Oliver Wendell Holmes's poem "Old Ironsides"—refused to let her be scrapped. *Constitution* was spared and rebuilt. She served as a training ship during and after the Civil War. In 1878-79, she transported U.S. exhibits to the Paris Exposition. *Constitution* was taken to Boston in 1897 to celebrate her 100th birthday. She escaped being scrapped in 1905. In 1925, she was restored through the efforts of patriotic groups and school children. The USS *Constitution* Museum opened in Boston in 1976.
USS *President* (44 guns)	USS *President* was the last of the six frigates to be built. She was launched in New York on April 1, 1800. *President* saw action in the Barbary War and later patrolled the east coast of the United States. *President* captured HMS *Highflyer* during the War of 1812. In 1815, *President* was captured by a squadron of British ships. • **Last of the USS *President*:** taken into the British Royal Navy and used until 1817, when she was broken up at Portsmouth, England.
USS *United States* (44 guns)	Built in at Joshua Humphreys' Shipyard in Philadelphia, Pennsylvania, and launched May 10, 1797. *United States* saw action with France from 1798 to 1801. While under the command of Captain Stephen Decatur during the War of 1812, she defeated HMS *Macedonian*. She was modernized in 1832 and saw service in the Mediterranean, the Pacific and Africa. In 1849, *United States* was sent to the Norfolk Navy Yard, where she remained until the Civil War. In April 1861, the Norfolk Navy Yard was captured by Confederate troops. The Confederate Navy repaired the ship and renamed her CSS *United States.* • **Last of the USS *United States*:** sunk in the Elizabeth River by the Confederate Navy to prevent her from being captured and used by the Union Navy. After the Confederates abandoned Norfolk in 1862, the U.S. government raised the ship and towed it back to Norfolk Navy Yard. In December 1865, after the war ended, *United States* was ordered broken up. Her timbers were sold.

Ships—Naval—Warships—Oared
• **Last oared warship built for the Royal Navy:** the British galley *Royal Anne,* launched in 1709. In 1721, while carrying the governor of Barbados to the West Indies she was wrecked off Stag Rocks, Lizard Point in Cornwall, England, as she attempted to return to Falmouth during a storm. The wreck site was located in 1991.

Ships—Naval—Warships—Paddle Steamers
• **Last remaining paddle steamer warship:** The former *Lieutenant Commander Vasile Paun,* renamed *Republica,* now on the Danube River at Tulcea, Romania.

Ships—Naval—Warships—Steam-Sail Hybrids, *see* Ships—Naval—Warships

Ships—Ocean Liners
Last Voyages and Fate of Some Major Ocean Liners

The table details the last voyage and fate of the vessel. Marine disappearances and marine disasters are listed elsewhere. *See* Disappearances, Disasters

Albert Ballin
Built in 1923 at Blohm & Voss Shipyards, Hamburg, Germany, for the Hamburg-America Line. She was a sister ship of the *Deutschland* and named for Hamburg-America's managing director. As the *Albert Ballin,* she had her first voyage in July 1923. Because Ballin was a Jew, the Nazis changed the ship's name in October 1935 to the *Hansa.* She remained in Germany for much of World War II.   • **Last of the *Albert Ballin/Hansa*:** struck a mine in shallow water off Warnemunde on March 6, 1945. Around 1949, the Soviet Union salvaged the *Hansa* and refitted her as the *Sovetsky Sojus.* The *Albert Ballin/Hansa/Sovetsky Sojus* was scrapped in 1981.
America
Built by Newport News Shipbuilding and Drydock, in Virginia. *America* entered service in 1940. When the United States entered World War II, the ship was painted gray and became the troop ship USS *West Point.* In 1946, she was decommissioned, refitted and renamed *America.* She was sold to a Greek company in November 1964 and renamed *Australis* by her new owner. She was next sold to an American firm and again renamed *America.* After a financially disastrous cruise, she was pulled from service and auctioned off. She was repurchased by the Greek company that had owned her earlier and was renamed *Italis.* She was sold once again in 1980 and named *Noga.* Four years later, a new name: *Alferdoss.* In 1993, another sale brought the name *American Star.*   • **Last of the *America*:** scheduled to go to Thailand but grounded and wrecked off the coast of the Canary Islands during a storm in January 1994. The ship with many names—*America/West Point/Australis/America/Italis/Noga/Alferdoss/American Star*—was declared a total loss in July 1994 and subsequently scrapped.
Aquitania
Last of the four-funnel ships. She was built by John Brown & Co. Yards, Clydebank, Scotland, for Cunard Line as a sister ship to the *Mauretania* and *Lusitania.* She was launched April 21, 1913. From 1915 to 1918, during World War I, she served as both a troop ship and a hospital ship. In 1919, she returned to commercial service. The *Aquitania* was a troop ship again during World War II.   • **Last voyage of the *Aquitania*:** completed on December 1, 1949. It was *Aquitania's* 443rd voyage during 35 years of service.   • **Last of the *Aquitania*:** taken to Faslane, Scotland, in February 1950 to be scrapped.

Bismarck

Built by Blohm & Voss Shipyard in Hamburg, Germany, as one of the sister ships of *Vaterland* and *Imperator*. After World War I, the *Bismarck* was renamed *Majestic* when she was given to Great Britain under the war reparation terms of the Treaty of Versailles to compensate for Britain's loss of the *Britannic*. White Star Line acquired her in February 1921. When White Star and Cunard merged in 1934, *Majestic* was marked for disposal. The British Admiralty purchased the ship and renamed her *Caledonia*.

• **Last of the *Bismarck/Majestic/Caledonia*:** sank after a fire in 1939. She was sold and scrapped in 1940. The remains were towed to Inverkeithing, Scotland, in 1943, where the demolition was completed.

Bremen

Built by AG Weser Yards in Bremen, Germany, for North German Lloyd. She made her maiden voyage on July 16, 1929. She was moved to Hamburg at the beginning of World War II.

• **Last of the *Bremen*:** destroyed by a fire on March 16, 1941. An angry crew member may have started the blaze in a storeroom. Scrappers took the steel from the ship to German munitions factories to be used for war materials. What remained of the *Bremen* was taken to the Weser River and blown up with explosives.

Canberra

Built in Belfast, Ireland, for P&O Lines. She was the largest ship built since White Star Line's *Britannic*. She entered service in 1961. *Canberra* was used as a troop ship during the Falkland Islands Conflict in 1982.

• **Last of the *Canberra*:** taken out of service on September 30, 1997, and sold to ship breakers in Pakistan. The scrapping took almost a year.

Cleveland

Built at Blohm & Voss Shipyard in Hamburg, Germany, for Hamburg-America Line. Her maiden voyage was March 1909. After World War I, she went to the United States as part of war reparations. The U.S. converted her into a troop ship and renamed her USS *Mobile*. In 1920, she was sold to Britain and renamed *King Alexander*. She was sold again in 1923 to a U.S. company and renamed *Cleveland*. In 1926, she was purchased by her original owner, Hamburg-America Line, to be used for transatlantic service.

• **Last of the *Cleveland/Mobile/King Alexander/Cleveland*:** retired in 1931 and scrapped in Hamburg in 1933.

Columbus

Built for North German Lloyd at Schichau Shipyards in Danzig, Germany, between 1914 and 1924. Construction was halted at the beginning of World War I then resumed in 1920. The ship was originally called *Hindenburg* but was renamed *Columbus* in the final stages of construction. Her maiden voyage was in April 1924.

• **Last of the *Columbus*:** scuttled in 1939 by the Germans 400 miles off Delaware Bay on the U.S. East Coast to avoid capture by a British warship. The 579 crew members who were aboard were rescued by a U.S. ship.

Cristoforo Colombo

Built as a sister ship to the *Andrea Doria* by Ansaldo Shipyards, Genoa, Italy. Her maiden voyage was to New York in 1954. *Cristoforo Colombo* transported Michelangelo's *Pieta* to the New York World's Fair in 1964. She was taken out of transatlantic service in the 1970s and placed in Adriatic service. By 1977, the ship was uneconomical to operate and was used as a hotel in Venezuela.

• **Last of the *Cristoforo Colombo*:** ordered to be towed to Kaohsiung, Taiwan, and scrapped in 1981. When the ship had a potential buyer, she was towed to Hong Kong. The deal fell through, so *Cristoforo Colombo* was towed back to Taiwan in the fall of 1982 and scrapped.

Deutschland

Built by Vulcan Shipbuilding Company of Stettin for Hamburg-America Line in 1900. She was taken out of service in 1910 because of a serious vibration problem. She was rebuilt and renamed *Victoria Luise*. After World War I, she was renamed *Hansa* and used for transatlantic service for four years.

• **Last of the *Deutschland/Victoria Luise/Hansa*:** sold and scrapped in 1925.

Empress of England

Made her maiden voyage for Canadian Pacific Line from Liverpool, England, to Quebec, Canada, in 1957. As transatlantic travel declined, the ship was used more for cruises than passenger crossings. In 1970, she was withdrawn from service by Canadian Pacific and sold. The new owner renamed her *Ocean Monarch* and refitted her as a full cruise ship The ship began losing money in 1971, so she made only one Mediterranean cruise. She was sent to New Zealand. After two years there, she operated out of Sydney, Australia. Mechanical problems caused her to be taken out of service in 1975.

• **Last of the *Empress of England/Ocean Monarch*:** left Southampton in June 1975 for Kaohsiung, Taiwan, where she was broken up for scrap.

Europa

Built for North German Lloyd by Blohm & Voss Shipyard, Hamburg, as a sister ship of the *Bremen*. Her maiden voyage was on March 19, 1930. *Europa* was converted to a warship in 1939. In 1940, she was slated to be part of Germany's Operation Sea Lion, but the United States took possession and used her as a troop ship. After the war, she was given to France by a reparations commission and was renamed *Liberté*.

• **Last of the *Europa/Liberté*:** retired in 1958 and scrapped at La Spezia, Italy, in 1962.

Flandre

The first new French liner launched after World War II. She was built for transatlantic service but by the late 1950s was beginning to lose money. She was sold by French Line in the late 1960s and renamed *Carla C* but marketed by Princess Cruise Lines as *Princess Carla*. In 1986, she was renamed *Carla Costa*. When she was sold in 1992, she was renamed *Pallas Athena* by her new owners.

• **Last of the *Flandre/Carla C/Carla Costa/Pallas Athena*:** a fire in March 1994 caused the ship to be a total loss. She was scrapped in Turkey in December 1994.

Great Eastern

Considered by some naval historians to be the most extraordinary ship ever to sail the seas. She was designed by Isambard K. Brunel and built at John Scott Russell's shipyard on the River Thames in London, England, between 1854 and 1857. Originally named *Leviathan,* she was renamed *Great Eastern* prior to launching in 1858. At 693 feet, she was five times longer than any ship afloat and could carry 4,000 passengers. She was made of iron and had both a paddle wheel and screw propellers. She also had six masts, rigged for both square and fore-and-aft sails. She could travel round-trip from England to Ceylon without refueling. *Great Eastern* soon proved to be an economic disaster as a passenger ship. She was sold and renovated. The new owner used her to lay the first Atlantic cable in 1865-66. *Great Eastern* was the only ship that could hold the entire length of cable. Later, she laid cable between Bombay, India, and Suez, Egypt.

• **Last of the *Leviathan/Great Eastern*:** docked in Liverpool in 1872. In 1885, a new owner used her as a floating billboard on the River Mersey. Finally, in 1888, the great ship was sold for scrap. The demolition took three years.

Great Britain

The second of three ships designed by Isambard K. Brunel made her first voyage in December 1844. The six-masted *Great Britain* was the first iron-hulled, screw-propeller driven, steam-powered passenger liner.

• **Last commercial voyage:** February 1886. *Great Britain* ran into problems and was condemned in 1888 while in the Falkland Islands. After serving as a coal and storage hulk for many years, she was abandoned in 1937. In 1970, she was taken to Bristol, England, and restored. She is now at the National Maritime Museum, Greenwich, England.

Great Western
The paddle-wheeler *Great Western* was the first steamship built for transatlantic travel. She was designed by Isambard K. Brunel and made her maiden voyage from Bristol, England, to New York in April 1838. *Great Western* was sold in 1846 to a company that used her for West Indies passenger service. She was used as a troop ship during the Crimean War.
• **Last of the *Great Western*:** scrapped in August 1856 at Castle's yard on the Thames at Vauxhall, England.

Gripsholm I
Built for Swedish-American Line in 1925. She was the first diesel-engine transatlantic liner. During World War II, Sweden was neutral. *Gripsholm I* was operated by the International Red Cross and carried prisoners of war and civilian internees. She returned to commercial service in 1946. *Gripsholm I* was sold to a German company in 1954 and began service between Bremen, Germany, and New York. She was renamed *Berlin* in 1955 and taken over by North German Lloyd.
• **Last of the *Gripsholm I/Berlin*:** made her last voyage from New York to Bremerhaven, Germany, in 1966. She was broken up for scrap later that year in La Spezia, Italy.

Ile de France
Built in St. Nazaire, France. Began her maiden voyage on June 22, 1927. She was refitted as a troop ship during World War II. *Ile De France* was rebuilt after the war and a smokestack was removed. In July 1956, she rescued 753 survivors of the *Andrea Doria* collision.
• **Last passenger voyage of the *Ile de France*:** November 1958, from New York.
• **Last of the *Ile de France*:** sold to a Japanese scrap firm that renamed her *Furansu Maru* when they took possession of the ship for scrapping. Before she completed her final journey, she was chartered by a Hollywood film company and renamed *Claridon* for the movie *The Last Voyage*. After filming, the *Ile de France/Furansu Maru/Claridon* was taken to Osaka, Japan, where she was scrapped in 1959.

Imperator
Built at Vulcan Shipyards in Hamburg, Germany, for Germany's Hamburg-America Line. Her maiden voyage began on June 10, 1913. The United States took possession of the ship during World War I as USS *Imperator*. She was used as a troop ship until August 1920. She was later sold to Cunard/White Star. After Cunard gained sole control of the ship, her name was changed to RMS *Berengaria*.
• **Last of the *Imperator/Berengaria*:** By late 1930s, she needed a major overhaul and was put up for sale. She was sold to a scrapper at Jarrow, England, in 1939 and cut down to the water line. Demolition was interrupted by World War II but was completed at Rosyth, Scotland, in 1946.

Kaiser Wilhelm der Grosse
The first of four four-stack steamships named for the German imperial family that were built by Vulcan Shipbuilding Company of Stettin for North-German Lloyd. Her maiden voyage was in 1897, from Bremerhaven to New York.
• **Last trip of the *Kaiser Wilhelm der Grosse* from New York:** July 1914. During World War I, she was taken over by the German navy and refitted as an auxiliary cruiser.
• **Last of the *Kaiser Wilhelm der Grosse*:** sank while loading coal in West Africa in 1914. The British claimed their ship *Highflyer* sank *Kaiser Wilhelm der Grosse*. The Germans claimed *Kaiser Wilhelm der Grosse* was scuttled to avoid capture.

Kaiser Wilhelm II

One of the four four-stack steamships named for the German imperial family that were built by Vulcan Shipbuilding Company of Stettin, Germany, for North-German Lloyd. She made her maiden voyage on April 14, 1903. *Kaiser Wilhelm II* was in a New York port at the beginning of World War I and was seized by the United States. She was refitted as a troop ship and renamed *Agamemnon*. In October 1917, she was struck by the USS *Von Steuben* (the former *Kronprinz Wilhelm,* another German ship that was seized during the war). In 1919, after the war ended, *Kaiser Wilhelm II/Agamemnon* was released from service but was never used again. She remained mothballed from 1919 to 1940. She was renamed *Monticello* in 1929 and plans were made to refurbished her as a cruise ship, however, the Great Depression intervened and the project was canceled.
• **Last of the *Kaiser Wilhelm II/Agamemnon/Monticello*:** made her last voyage to Baltimore, Maryland, in 1940, where she was scrapped.

Kronprinz Wilhelm

One of the four four-stack steamships named for the German imperial family that were built by Vulcan Shipbuilding Company of Stettin, Germany, for North-German Lloyd. When the United States entered World War I, she was tied up in a U.S. port. She was seized by the U.S. government and renamed USS *Von Steuben*. After the war, she was decommissioned by the U.S. Navy and turned over to the United States Shipping Board, which operated her for several years, first as *Baron Von Steuben,* then as *Von Steuben.*
• **Last of the *Kronprinz Wilhelm/Baron Von Steuben/Von Steuben*:** broken up in 1923 and sold for scrap in Baltimore, Maryland.

Kronprinzessin Cecilie

One of the four four-stack steamships named for the German imperial family that were built by Vulcan Shipbuilding Company of Stettin, Germany, for North-German Lloyd. She made her maiden voyage on August 6, 1907. She was in a New York port at the beginning of World War I and was seized by the U.S. government. She was held in Boston for three years. When the United States entered the war, *Kronprinzessin Cecilie* was refitted as a troop ship and renamed USS *Mount Vernon.*
• **Last voyage of the *Kronprinzessin Cecilie/Mount Vernon*:** to Vladivostock, Russia, in 1919 to evacuate refugees and troops stranded there by a civil war. She returned to the United States and was laid up for many years. Several attempts to use her commercially fell through. She was offered to the British at the beginning of World War II but was found to unfit for service.
• **Last of the *Kronprinzessin Cecilie/Mount Vernon*:** scrapped in Baltimore, Maryland, in 1940.

Leonardo da Vinci

Built at Ansaldo Shipyards, Genoa, Italy, and operated by Italian Line. *Leonardo da Vinci* made her maiden voyage in July 1960. She ended transatlantic service in 1976 and became a cruise ship. She was put up for sale in 1978.
• **Last of the *Leonardo da Vinci*:** hit by a serious fire in July 1980 that burned for four days, causing the ship to capsize. She was later was towed to La Spezia, Italy, and scrapped.

Mauretania I

Built for Cunard Line by Swan, Hunter & Wigham Richardson Ltd. as a sister ship of the *Lusitania* and *Aquitania*. Her maiden voyage was in November 1907. *Mauretania I* was converted into a war ship in 1915 during World War I. She also served as a hospital ship. In 1919, she returned to commercial service.
• **Last voyage of the *Mauretania I*:** New York to Southampton, England, September 1934.
• **Last of the *Mauretania I*:** sold to scrappers at Rosyth, Scotland, in 1935. Her fittings and furniture were auctioned off.

Mauretania II

Launched at Cammell Laird, Birkenhead, England. Made her maiden voyage from Liverpool to New York in June 1939. She was taken over as a troop ship during World War II. *Mauretania II* was returned to commercial service in 1949. By 1962, she was unprofitable for transatlantic trips, so she was converted to a cruise ship, traveling from New York to the Mediterranean.

• **Last cruise of the *Mauretania II***: September 1965.

• **Last of the *Mauretania II***: sold and taken to Inverkeithing, Scotland, to be scrapped.

Michelangelo

Built at Ansaldo Shipyard in Genoa, Italy, in 1955. Made her maiden voyage in 1965. By the early 1970s, the ship was losing money.

• **Last transatlantic crossing of the *Michelangelo***: June 1975. *Michelangelo* was sold to the Shah of Iran in 1977, along with *Raffaello*. She was rebuilt as a military ship.

• **Last of the *Michelangelo***: sold to Pakistan in 1991 to be scrapped.

Normandie

Built at Chantiers de L'Atlantique, St. Nazaire, France, by the French government. She was the first of the big ocean liners to exceed 1,000 feet. *Normandie* entered service in May 1935. In 1939, at the beginning of World War II, she was laid up at a pier in New York City. In December 1941, she was seized by the U.S. government, transferred to the U.S. Navy and renamed USS *Lafayette*.

• **Last of the *Normandie/Lafayette***: hit by a fire on February 9, 1942, while being refitted. The fire spread quickly. Firefighters dumped so much water onto the ship that her mooring lines snapped and she capsized. She was righted in late summer 1943 and towed to a drydock in Brooklyn. She remained there until the end of the war. The cost to make her seaworthy was too high so in October 1945 *Normandie/Lafayette* was stricken from the Navy List of ships. She was sold in October 1946 and towed to Port Newark, New Jersey, where she was scrapped in 1946-47.

Olympic

One of three ships built for White Star Line as competition for Cunard Line's *Mauretania I, Aquitania* and *Lusitania*. The other two were *Titanic* and *Gigantic* (later renamed *Britannic*). *Olympic* made her first voyage on June 14, 1911. She was a troop ship during World War I.

• **Last transatlantic crossing of the *Olympic***: May 1934.

• **Last of the *Olympic***: decommissioned in 1935 and taken to Jarrow, England, where she was partially scrapped. The demolition was completed at Inverkeithing, Scotland, in 1937. All the fittings were sold. Many went to the White Swan Hotel in Alnwick, England.

Paris

French liner built at Chantiers & Ateliers de St. Nazaire. She made her maiden voyage in June 1921.

• **Last of the *Paris***: ruined by fire on April 18, 1939, as she was about to leave Le Havre for New York with statuary and paintings for the New York World's Fair. So much water was used to fight the fire that the ship eventually capsized. She remained on her side during World War II. *Paris* was broken up for scrap in 1947.

Queen Mary

Last of the three-stackers (three-funnel ships). She is also the last surviving major pre-World War II transatlantic liner. RMS *Queen Mary* was built for Cunard Line by John Brown & Company. Her maiden voyage began on May 27, 1936, from Southampton, England, to New York. In 1941, during World War II, she became a troop transport. *Queen Mary* resumed commercial service in 1946. By 1967, she was operating at a loss.

• **Last commercial voyage of the *Queen Mary* for Cunard:** ended on September 27, 1967, when she arrived in England from New York. She was put up for sale and purchased by the City of Long Beach, California, to be used as a tourist attraction. • **Last voyage of the *Queen Mary*:** left Southampton, England, on October 31, 1967. She arrived in Long Beach Harbor via Cape Horn on December 31, 1967. After an extensive renovation, she was opened to the public on May 10, 1971.
Raffaello Italian liner. Made her maiden voyage from Genoa to New York in 1965. Italian Line discontinued North Atlantic service in 1974. Afterward, *Raffaello* was used mainly for cruising, but she continued to lose money. • **Last crossing to New York:** April 1975. *Raffaello* and *Michelangelo* were sold to the Shah of Iran and moved to Bushire, Iran. • **Last of the *Raffaello*:** hit during an air attack in 1983, during the Iran-Iraq War.
Rex Built by Ansaldo Shipyards in Genoa, Italy, in 1932. Her maiden voyage began on September 27, 1932, from Genoa. During World War II, *Rex* was towed to Trieste, Italy, where she remained. • **Last of the *Rex*:** bombed by the British Royal Air Force on September 8, 1944. She burned and sank. Demolition for scrap began in 1947 and was completed by 1958.
Vaterland Built in 1914 by Blohm & Voss Shipyard, Hamburg, Germany, for Hamburg-America Line. She was in an American port at the beginning of World War I. When the U.S. entered the war in 1917, she was seized and renamed *Leviathan*. She served as a major troop transport. She returned to passenger service in 1923 but lost money. She was withdrawn from service in 1934, a victim of the Great Depression. • **Last of the *Vaterland/Leviathan*:** ordered to be scrapped by her owner, United States Lines, in 1937. She was demolished at Rosyth, Scotland, in 1938.

Ships—Packet Ships

Packet ships were vessels that made regular voyages between the same ports with mail and passengers.

• **Last packet ship to sail out of South Street Sea Port in New York City:** the *Charles Cooper*. The American-built square-rigger began her service sailing in the Layton & Hurlbut Line of Antwerp Packets in 1856. Leaking and need of repair en route from Liverpool, England, to Melbourne, Australia, she pulled into Port Stanley, Falkland Islands, on September 25, 1866. Her repairs were too costly, so her captain sold her. She has decayed there ever since and only parts of her partially submerged hull remain.

Ships—Schooners

Schooners are fore-and-aft rigged sailing vessels with two or more masts. Many still exist, although certain types and designs have fallen out of use, leaving the following notable last examples:

Ships—Schooners—Coastal

The coastal schooner was a vessel that traded between ports on the same stretch of coast. Only five two-masted coastal schooners remain in the United States.

• **Last surviving Maine-built 19th-century coaster schooner:** the Lewis R. French. She has worked continuously since she was launched into Christmas Cove, Maine, in 1871. Her home port is Camden, Maine. She is listed on the National Historic Register.

• **Last surviving U.S.-built traditional coasting schooner and last surviving sailing cable ship in the world:** *Western Union,* launched in 1939. She is also the last schooner constructed in Key West, Florida. The ship served the Western Union Telegraph Company for 35 years. She later survived a run-in with Cuban gunboats, a hurricane and efforts to scrap her. She also helped to transport Cubans to freedom during the Mariel Boatlift. Today, *Western*

Union is the flagship of Key West.

Ships—Schooners—Fishing

• **Last fishing schooner working under sail in commercial use:** *Kathryn M. Lee,* built in 1923, in Dorchester, New Jersey, by Henry Stowman and Sons, and launched as a sail-powered schooner for oystering. She still dredges for oysters under sail on the Chesapeake Bay. After the restoration she is undergoing has been completed, she will be used for educational cruises and excursion day sails when she is not oystering. *Kathryn M. Lee* is listed on the National Historic Register.

• **Last surviving 19th-century Gloucester-built fishing schooner:** *Ernestina*, built in Essex, Massachusetts, in 1894 as the *Effie M. Morrissey.* During World War II, she was an Arctic supply and survey ship for the U.S. Navy. She was renamed *Ernestina* after the war and sailed regularly between the Cape Verde Islands and the U.S. She is the last Atlantic sailing packet: she made her last voyage in 1965. She became the property of the newly independent African Cape Verde Republic in 1976. The government restored and returned the ship to the U.S. in 1982. *Ernestina* is the oldest surviving Grand Banks fishing schooner, one of two remaining examples of the Fredonia-style schooner and one of two Arctic exploration schooners still afloat (the *Bowdoin* is the other). *Ernestina* is on the National Historic Register. Her home port is New Bedford, Massachusetts.

• **Last surviving knockabout-style schooner afloat in the U.S.:** *Adventure,* built in 1926 at Essex, Massachusetts. She is one of the last Gloucester (Massachusetts) fishing schooners. Before retiring from fishing in 1953, *Adventure* was the last dory trawler. She was subsequently refitted as a windjammer. She carried passengers along the coast of Maine until 1987. Since 1988, *Adventure* has served as Gloucester's historic tall ship. She is listed in the National Historic Register and has been designated a National Historic Landmark.

• **Last commercial fishing schooner on the Great Lakes:** *Helen MacLeod II,* built as a Great Lakes schooner between 1923 and 1926 in Bayfield, Ontario, Canada, and launched in 1926. She operated as a fishing vessel until 1945, long after other commercial sail fishing had disappeared from the Great Lakes. *Helen MacLeod II* has been owned by the Bayfield Historical Society since 1996 and is presently being restored.

Ships—Schooners—Lumber-Trade

During the 19th and early 20th centuries, 225 steam schooners specifically designed for the lumber trade were in use along the Pacific coast of the United States.

• **Last remaining wooden-hulled, steam-propelled single-ended lumber-trade schooner:** *Wapama* (also known as *Tongass*), built by St. Helen's Ship Building Company of Oregon in 1915. She was in operation until 1949. She was rehabbed in 1959, and between 1987 and 1994 her condition was stabilized to prevent further disintegration. Today, *Wapama* is at the San Francisco Maritime National Historical Park in California.

Ships— Schooners—Seven-Masted

Only one seven-masted fore-and-aft schooner was ever built: the *Thomas W. Lawson,* constructed in 1902 by the Fore River Ship & Engine Building Company in Quincy, Massachusetts. She was also the largest schooner ever built.

• **Last of the *Thomas W. Lawson*:** Originally used in the coal trade, she was rebuilt for carrying oil in 1906 by the Newport News Shipbuilding & Drydock Co. She was bound for London, England, loaded with oil, when she sank on Hellweather Reef, Scilly Islands, south of England, on December 13, 1907, during a storm. Fifteen of the 17 crew members were lost.

Ships—Schooners—Six-Masted

Six-masted schooners were built to maximize profits as cargo vessels in the Atlantic coastal coal trade. With their smaller crews, they were economical to operate. However, their lifetime was sometimes short and was often disastrous. Ten six-masters were constructed between 1900 and 1909. Most sank within 20 years after they were launched.

• **Last six-masted schooner built:** the

Wyoming, built at the Percy & Small shipyard in Bath, Maine, and launched in 1909. She was also the largest six-master. *Wyoming* was lost with her entire crew off the coast of New England in 1924.

• **Last surviving six-masted schooner:** the *William L. Douglas,* launched at the Fore River shipbuilding yard in Quincy, Massachusetts in 1903. She was the only one with steel construction. She ended her long period of service de-masted, as an oil barge.

Ships—Schooners—Five-Masted

In all, 58 five-masted schooners were built along the East Coast of the United States between 1888 and 1920.

• **Last of the U.S. five-masted schooners:** *Edna Hoyt,* built in 1920 by Dunn & Ellicott in Maine. She sustained storm damage off the coast of Portugal in November 1937 and was towed to Lisbon where she was condemned.

Ships—Schooners—Pungy

The pungy was a Chesapeake Bay schooner built in Maryland and Virginia mainly between 1840 and 1880. Its name may have derived from Pungateague, a creek on the Eastern Shore of Maryland. No original pungies survive today. However, a replica, the *Lady Maryland,* was built in 1985 by the Living Classroom Foundation.

• **Last original pungy schooner to sail the Chesapeake Bay:** taken to the Great Lakes and abandoned there in 1959.

• **Last remains of a pungy schooner:** recovered from Watts Creek and placed on exhibit at Martinak State Park, Maryland, in 1964 and 1969.

Ships—Schooners—Ram

The first ram schooner was built in 1889 in Bethel, Delaware. The origin of the name "ram" is not known. It may have been a description of the way one of the schooners moved through a canal. By 1911, 26 had been built, mainly in Bethel. Many of the ram schooners disappeared after World War I. By 1933, only 13 remained on the Chesapeake Bay. Fire, stranding and other disasters reduced that number to two by 1945.

• **Last surviving Chesapeake Bay-built**

ram schooner: *Victory Chimes*, launched in 1900 as *Edwin and Maud.* She carried mostly lumber until her owner sold her to a passenger cruise firm. In 1987, Domino's Pizza began a restoration of the ship, then known as *Domino Effect.* In 1990, she was sold to her current owners. Today, as *Victory Chimes,* the ship is an operating windjammer and is on the National Historic Register.

• **Last Bethel (Delaware)-built ram schooner:** *Granville R. Bacon,* built in 1911. She was stranded at Weekapaug, Rhode Island, in 1934 and later burned.

Ships—Schooners—Scow

Scow schooners were used in the United States in the late 19th century. The last one was built in 1906. By the 1920s, most scows had been rigged down to one mast. Some, further changed, continued to work as barges or oyster-shell dredges.

• **Last intact, floating U.S. scow schooner:** *Alma,* a flat-bottomed vessel built in 1891 at Hunters Point, San Francisco, California. When she retired from work in the San Francisco Bay in 1957, *Alma* was the last American scow schooner in use. She was transferred to the National Park Service in 1978, and is on the National Historic Register. She is now part of the fleet of historic vessels at Hyde Street Pier in San Francisco Maritime National Historical Park.

Ships—Skipjacks

The skipjack is the last ocean-going American vessel to fish under sail in significant numbers. The skipjacks originated in the late 1800s along the Eastern Shore of Maryland. The shallow-draft vessels have a centerboard, single mast, two sails and are 25 to 50 feet long. These historic Chesapeake Bay wooden oyster dredge boats have almost disappeared from Maryland waters.

• **Last surviving commercial fleet of skipjacks in North America:** Dogwood Harbor, Tilghman Island, Maryland.

• **Last 19th-century skipjack still dredging for oysters in Chesapeake Bay:** the *Rebecca T. Ruark,* built on Maryland's Eastern Shore in 1886. She is on the National Historic Register and is docked in Dogwood Harbor, Tilghman, Maryland.

Ships—Slave Ships, *see* Slavery and Servitude.

Ships—Sloops

A sloop is a single-masted vessel with the mast fore-and-aft rigged with a mainsail and jib and usually a gaff topsail and forestay sail.

• **Last sloop to carry a gaff rig:** the Chesapeake Bay sloop *J.T. Leonard*, built in 1882 and launched at James Island, Maryland. She was broken up in 1976.

Ships—Smacks

The smack was a fishing vessel that was designed to keep the catch alive in an internal wet well until reaching port. The smacks were used along the East and Gulf coasts of the United States.

• **Last surviving American smack:** the smack *Emma C. Berry*, built at the R. & J. Palmer shipyard at Noank, Connecticut, and launched in 1866. *Emma C. Berry* is also one of the oldest surviving commercial vessels in America. She was acquired and restored by Mystic Seaport Museum in Connecticut in 1969.

Ships—Square-riggers

The square-rigger is a sailing ship that has her sails extended on yards suspended horizontally at the center. To be full-rigged, a ship must have its three or more masts square-rigged.

• **Last remaining four-masted full-rigged ship:** *Falls of Clyde,* built in Great Britain in 1878. While under the British flag, she made several voyages to American ports, notably San Francisco, California, and Portland, Oregon. Later, under the U.S. flag, she was involved in the Hawaiian transpacific sugar trade. After 1907, *Falls of Clyde* transported fuel as a sailing oil tanker and is now the last surviving sailing oil tanker left afloat in the world. Re-masted in 1970 and subsequently re-rigged, *Falls of Clyde* was operated by the Bernice P. Bishop Memorial Museum and was turned over to the Hawaii Maritime Center where she is the centerpiece of a maritime museum.

• **Last full-rigged vessel on the U.S. West Coast:** *Balclutha* a three-masted, full-rigged ship, built in 1886 in Glasgow, Scotland. She was the last ship to fly the flag of the Kingdom of Hawaii. After she went aground in 1904, the Alaska Packers Association purchased her and renamed her *Star of Alaska*. She was sold again in 1933 and renamed *Pacific Queen*. In 1935, she appeared in the film *Mutiny on the Bounty*. In 1954, the San Francisco Maritime Museum purchased and restored her and returned her original name. *Balclutha* has been designated a National Historic Landmark and is on view in San Francisco Maritime National Historic Park.

Ships—Steamboats

The first successful steamboats began operating in the early 1800s. Many still exist, although certain types and designs have fallen out of use, leaving the following notable last examples:

Ships—Steamboats—Coastal

• **Last surviving tall-stacked U.S. coastal steamship:** SS *Nobska,* built by the Bath Iron Works in Bath, Maine, in 1925 for the New England Steamship Company and named for the point of land on the southeastern tip of Woods Hole. She was known as *Nantucket* from 1928 to 1956. She remained active calling on New England ports and islands until 1973. *Nobska* is presently being restored by the New England Steamship Foundation in New Bedford, Massachusetts.

• **Last of the U.S. East Coast sidewheelers:** the Hudson River side-wheelers *Alexander Hamilton* and *Peter Stuyvesant*. *Alexander Hamilton* made her final round-trip voyage from Manhattan to Poughkeepsie, New York, on September 6, 1971. An attempt to convert her into a casino in New Jersey failed. She sank at Leonardo, New Jersey, in the late 1970s or early 1980s. *Peter Stuyvesant* was moved to Boston, Massachusetts, where she was moored near Anthony's Pier 4 Restaurant. She was destroyed in a blizzard on February 7, 1978.

Ships—Steamboats—Great Lakes
• **Last surviving classic Great Lakes steamboat:** *Keewatin,* once owned by the Canadian Pacific Line. She was built in Scotland in 1907 and operated for 57 years between Georgian Bay and upper Lake Superior. She retired from service in 1965 and was sold to a museum. She is now at the Keewatin Maritime Museum in Saugatuck, Michigan. Her sister ship, the SS *Assiniboia,* was sold for off-lake use. She was destroyed by fire while docked at Soupy Island, near Philadelphia, Pennsylvania, on November 17, 1969.

• **Last Great Lakes vessel built as a steam-powered ship:** The *Edward L. Ryerson* built by Manitowoc Shipbuilding Company in Wisconsin, in 1960. The lack of a self-unloading rig made her less competitive in the ore trade. She made her last voyage in December 1998 and has since been on lay-up at Sturgeon Bay, Wisconsin.

Ships—Steamboats—Ocean-going Paddle-Wheel
• **Last ocean-going paddle-wheel steamboat:** *Waverley,* built for the London & North Eastern Railway Company and launched at A. & J. Inglis's yard on the Clyde at Glasgow, Scotland, in 1947. She replaced a vessel of the same name that was lost in 1940 while returning from Dunkirk with troops. In 1974, she was sold to the Paddle Steamer Preservation Society that set up the Waverley Steam Navigation Company to run her.

• **Last paddle-wheel steamboat built to cross the Atlantic:** *Scotia,* launched in 1862 for Cunard Line. In 1876, her paddles and a funnel were removed and she was fitted with twin screws. *Scotia* worked for many years as a telegraph cable-laying ship. She was wrecked on May 11, 1904, in Guam.

Ships—Steamboats—River Paddle-Wheel
• **Last remaining original overnight paddle-wheel river steamboat in operation:** *Delta Queen* built in 1927 at the C.N.& L. Shipyard in Stockton, California. The hull was built in Scotland. She operated first on the Sacramento River in California then was requisitioned by the U.S. Navy during World War II. After the war, she was sold and moved to the Mississippi River system. She is operated by Delta Queen Steamboat Company, the last overnight steamboat company, and is now on the National Historic Register.

• **Last of the *Robert E. Lee*:** dismantled in 1876 at Portland, Kentucky. The ship's hull became a wharf boat at Memphis, Tennessee. The side-wheel steamer *Robert E. Lee* was one of the most famous Mississippi steamboats and was immortalized in a popular song. She was built in New Albany, Indiana, in 1866, and could carry more than 5,000 bales of cotton in a single load. *Robert E. Lee* beat the *Natchez,* in a celebrated 1,200-mile race from New Orleans, Louisiana, to Natchez, Mississippi, in 1870.

• **Last paddle-wheel steamboat built in Great Britain:** *Maid of the Loch,* launched by A. & J. Inglis in Glasgow, Scotland, in 1953 for service on Loch Lomond, Scotland's largest lake. She was withdrawn from service in 1981 and began to deteriorate. She was rescued from further decay in 1993. *Maid of the Loch* is owned by Loch Lomond Steamship Company in Balloch and is currently undergoing restoration.

• **Last New Zealand paddle-wheel steamboat:** *Waimarie* ("Good fortune" in Maori), built in 1900 as *Aotea* and renamed in 1902. *Waimarie* sank at her moorings at Hattrick's Wharf on the Whanganui River in 1952. In 1990, the Whanganui Riverboat Restoration and Navigation Trust was organized. *Waimarie's* hull was salvaged in 1993 and she was restored. The steamer went back into service in 2000.

Ships—Steamboats—Showboat
Showboat steamboats were a major part of the Mississippi paddle-wheel boat trade in the 19th and early 20th centuries.

• **Last old-time Mississippi River showboat:** the *Goldenrod,* built in 1908-09 by Pope Dock Company as *Markle's New Showboat.* She is the largest showboat steamer ever built and is said to have been the inspiration for Edna Ferber's novel *Show*

Boat. The city of Saint Charles, Missouri, purchased her in 1988. *Goldenrod* was moved to the Missouri River, restored and renovated in 1991. She was used as a dinner theater but closed in 2001. She is moored at a storage dock until her future is determined. *Goldenrod* is on the National Historic Register.

• **Last of the old Mississippi River paddle-wheel showboat captains:** Captain Bill Menke, who died in Saint Louis, Missouri, on July 15, 1968, age 88. He once operated the *Goldenrod.*

• **Last surviving classic excursion steamboats in the U.S.:** *Columbia* and *Ste. Claire.* They are also the last essentially unaltered passenger ships designed by Frank E. Kirby. *Columbia* and *Ste. Claire* shared the run from Detroit to Bob-Lo Island for 81 years. Both ships are on the National Historic Register and are National Historic Landmarks. *Columbia* is in Wayne County, Michigan. *Ste. Claire* is in Toledo, Ohio.

Ships—Tugboats

Tugboats are still a common mainstay of waterfronts and harbors throughout the world; however, certain types are no longer used, leaving the following notable last examples:

• **Last functioning 19th-century wooden-hulled tugboat in the U.S.:** *Arthur Foss,* built in 1889 by the Oregon Railway and Navigation Company, Portland, Oregon, as the *Wallowa.* She was sold in 1929 and renamed *Arthur Foss* by the new owners. In 1933, she was appeared as the *Narcissus* in the film *Tugboat Annie.* During World War II, she was chartered to the U.S. Navy and was the last vessel to escape Wake Island in January 1942, before Japanese forces captured the island. In 1963, she was renamed *Theodore Foss.* After she was decommissioned by the Foss Company in 1970, she was again named *Arthur Foss.* Today, she is at the Maritime Heritage Center in Seattle, Washington. *Arthur Foss* is on the National Historic Register.

• **Last functioning steam-powered, coal-fired, twin-screw tugboat in the United**

Kingdom: the *Portwey,* built 1927 and owned by the Maritime Trust. At one time, hundreds of these vessels were working in Great Britain. *Portwey* is docked at North Quay, West India Dock Road in London, England.

Ships—Whalers

Whales were once hunted commercially for the oil that was extracted from their bodies. Whale oil was widely used for fuel for lamps and as a lubricant. Whaling declined in the late 19th century when petroleum was found to be a cheap substitute.

• **Last surviving wooden sailing whaler:** *Charles W. Morgan,* built by Hillman Brothers of New Bedford, Massachusetts, in 1841, and named for Charles Waln Morgan, a part owner. She ended her last whaling voyage on May 28, 1921. The *Charles W. Morgan* has appeared in several films, including *Miss Petticoats* (1916), *Down to the Sea in Ships* (1922) and *Java Head* (1935). She was acquired by Mystic Seaport in Connecticut in 1941 and is now on the National Historic Register.

Ships—Wherries

The wherry was a light boat used in England as a fast, efficient way to transport cargo. The demise of the wherries began with the advent of the railroad. Today, only seven wherries of any type have survived.

• **Last trading wherry:** *Ella,* built in 1912. She was the last commercial craft to use the North Walsam and Dilham Canal in 1934.

• **Last black-sail trading wherry available for charter:** *Albion,* built in Lowestoft in 1898. She was acquired by a trust in 1949 and now carries passengers from spring to early autumn.

• **Last wherry yacht:** *White Moth,* launched in 1915. She was rescued in 1986 and restored. She is now available for hire.

• **Last pleasure wherry:** *Ardea,* launched in 1927. She was taken to France, in 1959. Customs and excise authorities impounded her in the mid-1960s. Wherry enthusiasts found *Ardea* in 1991 in the Seine, where her mast and sailing gear had been removed and she was being used as a houseboat.

Last Ships of Some Noted Shipbuilders

Builder	Description
Brunel, Isambard K.	Isambard Kingdom Brunel, chief engineer of England's Great Western Railway, was largely responsible for creating a regular transatlantic service. As founder of the Great Western Steamship Company of Bristol, his name is linked to three famous transatlantic liners*: Great Western, Great Britain* and *Great Eastern. (See* Ships—Ocean Liners.) • **Last ship built by Brunel:** *Great Eastern*, an iron steamship built in 1858. Designed to carry 4,000 passengers, she failed financially as a passenger ship and had success only when laying transatlantic cable.
McKay, Donald	Canadian-born Donald McKay immigrated to America and built a shipyard in East Boston, Massachusetts. He would become one of the most important and well-known 19th-century shipbuilders working in the United States. He died in Hamilton, Massachusetts, on September 20, 1880, age 70. • **Last ship built by McKay:** U.S. sloop-of-war *Adams*. After completing the *Adams*, McKay retired from shipbuilding and became a farmer. • **Last remaining McKay ship:** wreckage of the USS *Essex*, an armed naval sloop built between 1874 and 1876. The *Essex* served the U.S. Navy from 1876 to 1903. From 1904 to 1927, she was used by the Toledo Naval Militia. In 1927, she was transferred to the Naval Reserve of the State of Minnesota. The *Essex* was removed from the Navy List on October 27, 1930, and sold for scrap. She was partially dismantled and pieces were sent as souvenirs to former officers and enlisted men. The *Essex* was towed to Minnesota Point on October 13, 1931, where she was burned. What remained of the ship was towed to shore. The wreckage is still visible on the shoreline of Lake Superior at Park Point, Minnesota. The remains of the *Essex* were listed on the National Historic Register in 1994. (*See also* Ships—Clipper Ships.)
Roach, John	John Roach is sometimes called the Father of Iron Shipbuilding in America. He founded his shipyard in 1859 in Chester, Pennsylvania. Roach constructed about 114 iron vessels for private companies and foreign governments. He also built the sectional dock at Pensacola, Florida, and the iron bridge over the Harlem River at Third Avenue in New York, New York. Roach died in New York, New York, on January 10, 1887. • **Last vessels built by Roach:** three armored cruisers, USS *Atlanta, Boston* and *Chicago,* and the gunboat USS *Dolphin* (gunboat) for the U.S. Navy. At first, the government refused to accept the *Dolphin*. That rejection, plus a financial crisis, forced Roach to shut down his shipyard on July 18, 1885. The shipyard later became Delaware River Iron Shipbuilding Works.
Sewall, Arthur	American shipbuilder Arthur Sewall, of Bath, Maine, built 80 wooden ships, including the *Roanoke, Rappahannock, Susquehanna* and *Shenandoah*. In 1894, he launched *Dirigo,* the first steel sailing ship built in the U.S. The Germans sank *Dirigo* on May 31, 1917, during World War I. Sewall died in Maine on September 5, 1900, age 64. • **Last wooden ship built by Sewall:** the massive four-masted wooden bark *Roanoke,* built in 1892 in Bath, Maine. She was the largest square-rigged wooden ship ever built in the U.S. A fire destroyed *Roanoke* in August 1905, while at anchor in New Caledonia.

Ships—Ship Owners—White Star Line

White Star Line was established in 1845. In 1936, it merged with Cunard Steamship Company as Cunard-White Star Steamship Company. In 1957, Cunard dropped the White Star name and returned to its original name: Cunard Steamship Company, Inc.

• **Last of the original White Star Line ships in service**: the third ship known as *Britannic*. She was scrapped in 1961.

• **Last remaining White Star Line vessel :** *Nomadic,* built in 1911 as a tender to transport or shuttle passengers and baggage from the dock to the ship. *Nomadic* served the *Olympic* and *Titanic.* She is privately owned and is being restored

Ships—Shipyards
Last Year of Operation of Some Major United States Shipyards

Shipyard	Location and Date Opened	Year Closed	Description
American International Shipbuilding Corp.	Hog Island, Philadelphia, Pennsylvania (1917)	1921	Produced more than 100 ships during World War I. Later used as a storage facility for surplus war ships. The city of Philadelphia took over the land in 1930. It is now occupied by Philadelphia International Airport.
Charlestown Navy Yard	Boston, Massachusetts (1800)	1973	Formally disestablished July 1, 1974. Boston National Historic Park opened on part of the site later in 1974. USS *Constitution* and USS *Cassin Young* are on display there.
Long Beach Naval Shipyard	Long Beach, California (1940)	1997	Constructed as Moreell Dry Dock. Known as Terminal Island Naval Shipyard (1945-48).
Mare Island Naval Shipyard	San Francisco Bay (1854)	1996	Mare Island was the U.S. Navy's oldest West Coast base. • **Last vessel launched:** nuclear-powered submarine USS *Drum,* launched in 1970.
New York Naval Shipyard	Brooklyn, New York (1801)	1966	Also known as Brooklyn Navy Yard; New York Navy Yard; and United States Navy Yard. • **Last Fleet Rehabilitation and Modernization (FRAM) job:** the USS *Intrepid.* The shipyard closed while the overhaul was in progress. Remaining work was finished at Naval Supply Depot, Bayonne, New Jersey.
New York Shipbuilding	Camden, New Jersey (1900)	1967	Originally was to have been on Staten Island, New York. After naming his yard, the owner opted instead to build it in New Jersey. • **Last ship launched:** USS *Kitty Hawk,* in 1961 • **Last submarine:** USS *Pogy* (SSN-657), unfinished. The *Pogy* was completed at Ingalls Shipbuilding in Mississippi.
Philadelphia Naval Shipyard	Southwark, Philadelphia County, Pennsylvania (1801-76);	1996	Joshua Humphreys opened his shipbuilding company in Southwark, Philadelphia County, Pennsylvania, in 1797. Four years later, the U.S. Navy built the first naval shipyard on the site of Humphreys' shipyard. In 1876, Philadelphia Naval Shipyard moved to

	League Island, Philadelphia (1876-1996)		League Island in south Philadelphia. • **Last ship built from the keel up:** USS *Blue Ridge* in 1970. • **Last overhaul project:** USS *John F. Kennedy,* completed September 13, 1995.
San Francisco Naval Shipyard	Hunters Point, San Francisco Bay, south of San Francisco (1868)	1974	Also known as Hunters Point Naval Shipyard. After the shipyard closed on June 30, 1974, it was leased to a commercial ship repair company that operated until 1986.
Sun Shipbuilding & Drydock Company	Chester, Pennsylvania (1917)	1977	Made 543 ships, including 40 percent of the tankers produced in the U.S. during World War II. Built the *Glomar Explorer* (1973).
William Cramp & Sons Ship & Engine Building Company	Port Richmond, Philadelphia, Pennsylvania (1830)	1946	Major producer of iron ships. Launched the first modern U.S. battleship: USS *Indiana* (1893). Closed 1927-40. Reactivated 1940 for World War II.

Ships—Shipyards—Canadian— Amherstburg Navy Yard

• **Last ship built at the Navy Yard in Amherstburg, Ontario:** the HMS *Detroit,* launched in August 1813. It was also the largest. The *Detroit* had been commissioned by King George III in honor of the capture of Fort Detroit (Michigan). She was to serve as the flagship of the British Fleet; however, she was captured by the U.S. Navy's Commodore Oliver Hazard Perry during the Battle of Lake Erie on September 10, 1813. *Detroit* was taken to Presque Isle and sunk. She was raised in 1837 and refitted as a merchant vessel. She was later sold to a group of merchants in Niagara Falls, New York. She sailed down the Niagara River and eventually broke up when she went over the falls. The flags from the *HMS Detroit* are at the U.S. Naval Academy in Annapolis. A full-size replica of the ship is in the planning stages.

Ships—Submarines—United States
Last of Some Modern American Submarine Classes

Commission date is based upon first commissioning of each vessel. Decommissioning is based on date of last decommissioning from the U.S. Navy. Excluded are commissions later held under service in another country's navy. A number of these classes have surviving examples that, although now are decommissioned, serve as training and museum vessels.

Submarine Class	Last of Class Commissioned and Year Commissioned	Last of Class to be Decommissioned	Date Decommissioned
A	A-7 USS *Shark* (SS-8), 1903	A-3 USS *Grampus* (SS-4); A-5 USS *Pike* (SS-6)	July 25, 1921
B	B-3 USS *Tarantula* (SS-12), 1907	B- 1 USS *Viper* (SS-10)	December 1, 1921

C	C-5 USS *Snapper* (SS-16), 1910	C-2 USS *Stingray* (SS-13); C-3 USS *Tarpon* (SS-14); C-5 USS *Snapper* (SS-16)	December 23, 1919
D	D-3 USS *Salmon* (SS-18), 1910	D-3 USS *Salmon* (SS-18)	March 20, 1922
E	E-1 USS *Skipjack* (SS-24) E-2 USS *Sturgeon* (SS-25), 1912	E-1 USS *Skipjack* (SS-24); E-2 USS *Sturgeon* (SS-25)	October 20, 1921
F	F-4 USS *Skate* (SS-23), 1913	F-2 USS *Barracuda* (SS-21); F-3 USS *Pickerel* (SS-22)	March 15, 1922
G	G-3 USS *Turbot* (SS-31), 1915	G-3 USS *Turbot* (SS-31)	May 5, 1921
H	H-9 (SS-152), 1918	H-8 (SS-151)	November 17, 1922
K	K-7 (SS-38); K-8 (SS-39), 1914	K-6 (SS-37)	May 21, 1923
L	L-5 (SS-44), 1918	L-11 (SS-51)	November 28, 1923
M	M-1 (SS-47), 1916	M-1 (SS-47)	March 15, 1922
N	N-6 (SS-58), 1918	N-1 (SS-53); N-2 (SS-54); N-3 (SS-55)	April 30, 1926
O	O-13 (SS-74), 1918	O-8 (SS-69)	October 11, 1945
R	R-23 (SS-100), R-25 (SS-102), R-26 (SS-103), 1919	R-6 (SS-83); R-20 (SS-97)	September 27, 1945
S	S-47 (SS-158), 1925	S-15 (SS-120)	June 11, 1946
T	T-2 (AA2/SS-60), 1922	T-2 (AA2/SS-60)	July 16, 1923
Barracuda	USS *Bonita* (V-3/SS-165), 1926	USS *Bonita* (V-3/SS-165)	March 3, 1945
Argonaut	USS *Argonaut* (V-4/SS-166), 1928	USS *Argonaut* V-4/SS-166)	Lost: January 10, 1943
Narwhal	USS *Nautilus* (V-6/SS-168), 1930	USS *Nautilus* (V-6/SS-168)	June 30, 1945
Dolphin	USS *Dolphin* (V-7/SS-169), 1932	USS *Dolphin* (V-7/SS-169)	October 2, 1945
Cachalot	USS *Cuttlefish* (V-9/SS-171), 1934	USS *Cuttlefish* (V-9/SS-171)	October 24, 1945
Porpoise	USS *Pike* (SS-173), 1935	USS *Porpoise* (SS-172); USS *Pike* (SS-173)	November 15, 1945
Shark	USS *Tarpon* (SS-175), 1936	USS *Tarpon* (SS-175)	November 15, 1945
Perch	USS *Pompano* (SS-181), 1937	USS *Permit* (SS-178); USS *Plunger* (SS-179)	November 15, 1945
Salmon	USS *Skipjack* (SS-184), 1938	USS *Skipjack* (SS-184)	August 28, 1946
Sargo	USS *Spearfish* (SS-190), 1939	USS *Sargo* (SS-188); USS *Saury* (SS-189); USS *Spearfish* (SS-190)	June 22, 1946
Seadragon	USS *Sea Lion* (SS-195), 1939	USS *Seadragon* (SS-194)	October 29, 1946

Searaven	USS *Seawolf* (SS-197), 1939	USS *Searaven* (SS-196)	December 11, 1946
Tambor	USS *Thresher* (SS-200), 1940	USS *Tuna* (SS-203)	December 11, 1946
Mackerel	USS *Marlin* (SS-205), 1941	USS *Mackerel* (SS-204); USS *Marlin* (SS-205)	November 9, 1945
Gar	USS *Grayback* (SS-208), 1941	USS *Gar* (SS-206)	December 11, 1945
Gato	USS *Croaker* (SS-246), 1944	USS *Rasher* (SS-269)	December 20, 1971
Balao	USS *Tiru* (SS-416), 1948	USS *Clamagore* (SS-343)	June 12, 1975
Tench	USS *Grampus* (SS-523), 1949	USS *Tigrone* (SS-419)	June 27, 1975
SSK	USS *Bass* (K2/SS-551), 1952	USS *Bonita* (K3/SS-552)	November 7, 1958
Tang	USS *Gudgeon* (SS-567), 1952	USS *Gudgeon* (SS-567)	September 30, 1983
Albacore	USS *Albacore* (AGSS-569), 1953	USS *Albacore* (AGSS-569)	December 2, 1972
SST	USS *Marlin* (T2/SST-2), 1953	USS *Mackerel* (T1/SST-1); USS *Marlin* (T2/SST-2)	January 31, 1973
Sailfish	USS *Salmon* (SS-573), 1956	USS *Sailfish* (SS-572)	September 30, 1978
Grayback	USS *Growler* (SSG-577), 1958	USS *Grayback* (SSG-574)	June 16, 1984
Darter	USS *Darter* (SS-576), 1956	USS *Darter* (SS-576)	December 1, 1989
Barbel	USS *Blueback* (SS-581), 1959	USS *Blueback* (SS-581)	April 1, 1990
Nautilus	USS *Nautilus* (SSN-571), 1954	USS *Nautilus* (SSN-571)	March 30, 1980
Seawolf	USS *Seawolf* (SSN-575), 1957	USS *Seawolf* (SSN-575)	March 30, 1987
Skate	USS *Seadragon* (SSN-584), 1959	USS *Swordfish* (SSN-579)	June 2, 1989
Triton	USS *Triton* (SSN-586), 1959	USS *Triton* (SSN-586)	May 3, 1969
Halibut	USS *Halibut* (SSN-587), 1960	USS *Halibut* (SSN-587)	June 30, 1976
Permit	USS *Gato* (SSN-615), 1968	USS *Gato* (SSN-615)	October 1, 1995
Tullibee	USS *Tullibee* (SSN-597), 1960	USS *Tullibee* (SSN-597)	June 18, 1988
Glenard P. Lipscomb	USS *Glenard P. Lipscomb* (SSN-685), 1974	USS *Glenard P. Lipscomb* (SSN-685)	July 11, 1990
George Washington	USS *Abraham Lincoln* (SSBN-602), 1961	USS *George Washington* (SSBN-598)	January 24, 1985

Ethan Allen	USS *Thomas Jefferson* (SSBN-618), 1963	USS *John Marshall* (SSBN-611)	July 22, 1992
Lafayette	USS *Nathanael Greene* (SSBN-636), 1964	USS *Stonewall Jackson* (SSBN-634)	February 9, 1995
Benjamin Franklin	USS *Will Rogers* (SSBN-659), 1967	USS *Mariano G. Vallejo* (SSBN-658)	March 9, 1996

Ships—Submarines

Ships—Submarines—German
German submarines are known familiarly as U-boats. "U" is an abbreviation for the German word *Unterseeboot,* or undersea boat. Type IX U-boats were designed in 1935-36 in Germany as large ocean-going submarines. Type IX-C was a refinement built to hold extra fuel.
• **Last surviving Type IX-C submarine:** the U-505, brought to the surface with a depth charge attack from the USS *Chatelain* on June 4, 1944. U-505 was the first enemy ship boarded and captured by U.S. forces on the high seas since the War of 1812. Since 1954, the U-505 has been opened to the public in her dry berth exhibit at the Chicago Museum of Science & Industry. The submarine is on the National Historic Register. (*See also* Wars and Battles— World War II—Submarines.)

Ships—Submarines—United States— Conning Tower
The conning tower of a submarine is a raised bridge frequently used as an entrance, exit or observation post.
• **Last U.S. submarine with a conning tower:** USS *Triton* (SSN-586), commissioned in 1959. *Triton* was also the last submarine to have any significant deck superstructure, or casing, twin screws and a stern torpedo room. She was decommissioned on May 3, 1969, and towed to Norfolk, Virginia, where she remained into the 1980s. She was then transferred to the Puget Sound Naval Shipyard, Bremerton, Washington.

Ships—Submarines—United States— Diesel Electric Propelled
The last diesel electric propelled submarines built by the U.S. Navy were three submarines of the Barbel class in 1959: *Barbel* (SS-580), *Blueback* (SS-581) and *Bonefish* (SS-582).
• **Last Barbel-class submarine to be decommissioned:** *Blueback* (SS-581) on April 1, 1990.

Ships—Submarines—United States— Polaris System
On December 3, 1956, the U.S. Navy terminated participation in the U.S. Army's *Jupiter* missile program and began working of the Polaris missile submarine, which was operational by 1960.
• **End of the Polaris system:** March 1, 1982, when the USS *Robert E. Lee* (SSBN-601), the U.S. Navy's last *Polaris* ballistic missile submarine was redesignated as SSN-601.

Ships—Submarines—United States— Regulus Missile Program
The U.S. Navy Regulus Missile Program, begun in 1947, was operational by 1953.
• **End of the Regulus Missile Program:** 1957, to allow funding for the Polaris project. All SSGN submarines on order were recast as SSN-593 class attack submarines, and all existing Regulus submarines continued operations. In 1960, USS *Halibut* (SSGN-587), the first and only nuclear powered, Regulus-guided missile submarine, was commissioned.
• **Last Regulus patrol of the *Halibut*:** 1964. With the Polaris submarines on line, the Regulus submarines were phased out.

Slavery and Involuntary Servitude

Abolition of Slavery Worldwide

Country	Year Slavery Was Abolished
Afghanistan	1923
Angola	1858
Argentina*	1813/1825/1853
Austria* (Austrian domains; later Austro-Hungary)	1781 (serfdom; edict) 1848-9 (serfdom; Constitution of Austria)
Bechuanaland	1936
Belgian Congo	1910
Bohemia*	1780 (serfdom)
Bolivia	1831
Brazil**	1871 (newborns of slaves: Rio Banco Law) 1885 (slaves over 60) 1888 (Golden Law)
British Colonies* (including Belize, British West Africa, British West Indies, Antigua, Barbuda, Guyana and Jamaica)	1833 (Abolition Act) 1834 (children under 6 years) 1838 (everyone else)
Burma	1926
Cambodia*	1877/1884
Cameroon	1923
Canada*	1791/1818 Upper Canada 1833/1838 (rest of Canada: Abolition Act of 1833)
Central America, United Provinces of	1824
Chile	1823
China*	1910 (chattel) 1950s (ximlim)
Colombia	1851-52
Cuba*	1870 (slaves over 60; newborns back to 1868: Moret Law) 1878 (veterans: Treaty of Zanjon) 1886 (royal decree; end of 8-year patronato)
Danish Colonies (including Danish West Indies)	1847 (newborns) 1848 (everyone else)
Denmark	1788 (serfdom)
Dutch Colonies (Dutch West Indies)	1860
Ecuador	1851-52
Ethiopia	1942
France ***	1848
French Colonies (including French Guiana, Guadeloupe, Martinique and Réunion)	1848
Gold Coast (Africa)	1874
Great Britain	1833 (Abolition Act) 1834 (children under 6 years) 1838 (everyone else; end of 5-year apprenticeship)
Haiti (Saint Domingue)	1803 (Sonthonax abolished slavery) 1804 (decree of 16 pluviôse II, abolishing "Negro slavery in the colonies")
Holland	1863
Hungary	1780 (serfdom)
India*	1843 (abolishment as a legal institution) 1860 (prohibition of slave ownership) 1976 (bonded labor)
Iran	1928
Iraq	1923

Jordan	1928
Korea	1801 (public slavery)
	1894 (private slavery)
Malaya	1915
Mauritania	1980-81
Mexico	1829
Nepal	1929
	2000 (bonded labor)
Nigeria, Northern*	1901/1936
Peru	1854-55
Oman	1970
Portugal	1761
Portuguese Colonies* (including Cape Verde)	1869 (abolished with condition of liberto) 1876 (liberto ended)
Prussia*	1811/1823 (serfdom)
Puerto Rico	1870 (newborns and people over 60) 1873 (everyone else)
Qatar	1952
Russia	1858/1861 (serfdom)
Saudi Arabia*	1936/1962
Sierra Leone	1926-27
Somaliland (Italian colony)	1903-04
Spain	1870 (newborns)
Suriname	1863
Sweden	1846
Swedish Colonies (including St. Barthelemy)	1847
Uruguay	1842
Venezuela*	1821/1854
Yemen	1962
Zanzibar and Pemba	1897

* The emancipation of slaves was gradual. Years shown are when emancipation began and when slavery was finally abolished.

** Brazil was the last nation in the Western Hemisphere to abolish slavery.

*** France outlawed slavery in 1791. It was reinstated by Napoleon in 1801 and finally outlawed in 1848.

End of the Slave Trade Worldwide

Country	Year Slave Trade Was Abolished
Angola	1836
Bolivia	1843
Brazil	1850 (law passed) 1851 (implemented)
British Colonies (including Belize, British West Africa, British West Indies, Antigua, Barbuda, Guyana, Jamaica and Canada)	1807 (law passed) 1808 (implemented) 1813 (import of slaves to Java)
Chile	1843
Cuba	1888
Danish Colonies (including Danish West Indies	1792 (edict issued) 1803 (implemented)
Denmark	1792 (edict issued) 1803 (implemented)
Dutch Colonies (including Dutch East and West Indies and Suriname)	1814 1818 (import of slaves to Dutch Indonesia)
Ecuador	1848
France	1817
French Colonies (including French Guiana, Guadeloupe, Martinique and Réunion)	1848
Great Britain	1807 (act passed) 1808 (implemented)
Holland	1818
India	1798 (export from Bengal) 1790s (export from Bombay and Madras) 1811 (import to Bengal) 1813 (import to Bombay and Madras) 1843 (universal prohibition)

Notable Last Facts

	1922 (indentured labor to most countries)
Mauritius	1835
Mexico	1843
Ottoman Empire	1857
Portugal	1815 (to Brazil and north of the equator) 1830 (everywhere else) 1836 (export banned)
Saudi Arabia	1936 (import of slaves by sea banned)
Sierra Leone	1896
Spain	1817 (to Caribbean) 1820 (south of the Equator) 1821 (everywhere else)
Sweden	1813
Swedish Colonies (including St. Barthelemy)	1813
Zanzibar	1845 (slave trade abolished) 1873 (public slave market closed) 1876 (access to coast port denied)

Abolition of Slavery in the United States

State, Colony or Territory	Year abolished
Alabama*	1863
Arkansas*	1863
California	1850
Connecticut***	1784/1848
Delaware	1865
District of Columbia	1862
Florida*	1863
Georgia*	1863
Illinois**	1787
Indiana**	1787
Iowa	1846
Kansas	1861
Kentucky	1865
Louisiana*	1863

Maine	1820
Maryland	1864
Massachusetts	1781
Michigan**	1787
Mississippi*	1863
Missouri	1865
Nevada	1864
New Hampshire	1784
New Jersey***	1804/1846
New York***	1799/1827
North Carolina*	1863
Pennsylvania***	1780/1808
Ohio**	1787
Oregon	1848
Rhode Island***	1784/1840s
South Carolina*	1863
Tennessee	1864
Texas*	1863
Vermont	1777
Virginia*	1863
West Virginia	1863
Wisconsin**	1787

* The Emancipation Proclamation of 1863 technically ended slavery in Virginia, North and South Carolina, Georgia, Florida, Alabama, Mississippi, Louisiana, Texas and Arkansas. In practice, slavery was not abolished completely until December 6, 1865, with the ratification of the 13th Amendment to the U.S. Constitution. Section 2 gave Congress the power to enforce the amendment by appropriate legislation.
** Slavery was abolished by the Northwest Ordinance of 1787.
*** Emancipation of slaves was gradual. Years shown are when emancipation began and when slavery was finally abolished.

Slavery and Involuntary Servitude—American Anti-Slavery Society
The American Anti-Slavery Society was the first national abolitionist organization. It was founded in Philadelphia, Pennsylvania, on December 4, 1833.
• **Last surviving American Anti-Slavery Society founder:** Robert Purvis, who was one of its 60 founders. He signed its declaration of sentiments and was the society's vice-president. Purvis died in Philadelphia on April 15, 1898, age 87.
• **Last of the American Anti-Slavery Society:** formally dissolved in 1870, after the group had achieved its goals.

Slavery and Involuntary Servitude— American Colonization Society

The American Colonization Society was founded on December 21, 1816, to help freed black slaves emigrate from the United States to Africa. The society purchased a tract of land in western Africa and named it Liberia. About 11,000 blacks were resettled there beginning in 1821. In 1860, the society built a permanent headquarters on Pennsylvania Avenue in Washington, D.C.

• **Last American Colonization Society group relocated to Liberia:** 1891. It numbered 154 people.

• **Last of the American Colonization Society Washington, D.C., headquarters:** the building was torn down in 1930. The site is roughly where the Canadian Embassy was later built.

• **Last of the American Colonization Society:** disbanded in 1964. The society turned over its records to the Library of Congress. (*See also* Nations—Liberia.)

Slavery and Involuntary Servitude— *Amistad* and Cinque

In July 1839, a group of African slaves led by Cinque, seized control of the *Amistad,* a Cuban schooner, and ordered the owners to take them back to Africa. The ship was intercepted off the coast of Long Island, New York, and the Africans were imprisoned in New Haven, Connecticut, charged with the murder of two crew members. The resulting lawsuit eventually reached the U.S. Supreme Court, with John Quincy Adams arguing on behalf of the Africans. The court ruled in their favor.

• **Last of the *Amistad* slaves:** Cinque and the other mutineers raised money for their return trip to Africa by touring and appearing before sympathetic audiences in the North. They were able to charter the brig *Gentlemen* and sail for Sierra Leone in December 1841. Thirty-five of the original 53 mutineers reached their homeland. The rest died while in America or at sea. Back in his homeland, Cinque became an interpreter for a Christian missionary for a few years. He died in 1879 in his 60s.

• **Last of the original *Amistad:*** After she was intercepted, the *Amistad* was retained at a wharf in New London, Connecticut, for 18 months. In October 1840, she was auctioned off by the U.S. Marshall to a sea captain from Rhode Island. He changed her name to *Ion* and used her for a few years to transport goods to and from the West Indies. He sold *Ion* in Guadeloupe in 1844. Nothing more is known of her fate. A replica of the *Amistad* was built in the 1990s.

Slavery and Involuntary Servitude— Anti-slavery Gag Rule—U.S. Congress

The anti-slavery gag rule was adopted by the U.S. House of Representatives on motion of John C. Calhoun in 1836. It required that all anti-slavery petitions be laid on the table without action to prevent a flood of such petitions after creation of the American Anti-Slavery Society in 1833.

• **Last of the anti-slavery gag rule:** December 3, 1844, when John Quincy Adams's motion to strike it was carried by a vote of 108 to 80.

Slavery and Involuntary Servitude— Importation of Slaves into the United States

The U.S. Slave Trade Act, passed by Congress in March 1794, prohibited anyone from carrying slave trade from the United States to any foreign place or country.

• **Last time slave ships were permitted to outfit in American ports:** 1794.

• **Last time U.S. allowed the legal importation of slaves:** December 31, 1807. On January 1, 1808, by act of Congress, the importation of slaves into any port within the jurisdiction of the United States was prohibited. The law did not prevent the smuggling of slaves into the U.S. As many as 250,000 slaves are believed to have been brought into the U.S. illegally during the next half century.

Slavery and Involuntary Servitude— *The Liberator*

The Liberator was a weekly newspaper published by abolitionist William Lloyd

Garrison in Boston, Massachusetts, beginning on January 1, 1831.

• **Last issue of *The Liberator*:** published on December 29, 1865, eight months after the end of the Civil War. Garrison died in New York, New York, on May 23, 1879, age 73.

Slavery and Involuntary Servitude— Slave Ships

• **Last slave ship known to deliver slaves to the United States:** *Clotilde*. She docked at Mobile Bay, Alabama, with 116 slaves from Dahomey (now Benin), West Africa, on July 9, 1860, more than 50 years after the importation of slaves had been outlawed. *Clotilde* was financed by Mobile steamship-maker Timothy Meaher and captained by William Foster. Some of the slaves reportedly became property of the Meaher family. *Clotilde* is believed to have been scuttled in the Mobile or Spanish river. The National African-American Archives Museum in Mobile houses artifacts from the *Clotilde*.

• **Last surviving slave from the *Clotilde*:** Cudjoe Kazoola Lewis, who died in Mobile in 1935. He was born in Dahomey around 1847. Many of his descendants still live in the Mobile area.

• **Last slave ship in Georgia:** *Wanderer*, a yacht that was specially outfitted to transport slaves in 1858. She docked off the coast of West Africa in September 1858 and took on a cargo of around 490 slaves. As many as 70 are believed to have died during the six-week voyage. *Wanderer* reached Cumberland Island, Georgia, in November 1858 and disembarked her cargo onto nearby Jekyll Island. The ship's owner, Charleston, South Carolina, planter William C. Corrie, then converted her back to a pleasure craft.

• **Last of the *Wanderer*:** wrecked off the coast of Cuba on January 21, 1871, while carrying a cargo of bananas.

Space

Space—Animals—Astro-Chimps
In the early days of the U.S. space program, chimpanzees were sent into space ahead of

the astronauts to determine whether the flights were safe for humans. The first astro-chimp was 3-year-old Ham, who flew in January 1961. Later that year, 5-year-old Enos rocketed into orbit.

• **Last surviving astro-chimp from the early U.S. space program:** Minnie, who died on March 14, 1998, age 41. She was the only female chimp trained for the Mercury program but never flew in space. She was a backup for Ham and Enos. Minnie was buried next to fellow chimp Ham at the Space Center in Alamogordo, New Mexico.

Space—Astronomy—Planets—Jupiter
In July 1994 Comet Shoemaker-Levy 9 encountered the planet Jupiter. Data from the Hubble Space Telescope and other observatories enabled astronomers to see the encounter firsthand. At least 21 discernable fragments with diameters up to 2 kilometers hit the planet. The first impacted with Jupiter on July 16, 1994.

• **Last of the large Comet Shoemaker-Levy 9 fragments:** Fragment W, which struck Jupiter on July 22, 1994.

Space—Astronomy— Planets—Pluto
• **Last planet discovered in the solar system:** Pluto, the ninth planet, discovered in 1930 by American astronomer Clyde W. Tombaugh at Lowell Observatory in Flagstaff, Arizona. Pluto is also the smallest planet in the solar system (smaller than Earth's Moon) and is usually the farthest from the sun. Pluto is one of only two planets in the solar system that cannot be seen without a telescope (the other is Neptune).

Space—Cape Canaveral/Cape Kennedy
In Florida, the name Canaveral goes back more than 400 years. Cabo de Canaveral along the Atlantic Ocean, was so named by the Spanish for the many canes and reeds found on its beaches. In 1949, the U.S. government established the Joint Long Range Proving Ground at Cape Canaveral. It later became Cape Canaveral Auxiliary Air Force Base. Construction on the NASA Launch Operations Center began in 1961.

• **Last known as NASA Launch Operations Center/Cape Canaveral Auxiliary Air Force Base:** December 20, 1963, when the two facilities were renamed John F. Kennedy Space Center a month after the death of the president. Later, the two facilities were renamed John F. Kennedy Space Center NASA and Cape Kennedy Air Force Station. In May 1973, Florida changed Cape Kennedy Air Force Station to Cape Canaveral Air Force Station; however, John F. Kennedy Space Center's name remained the same. In 1992, Cape Canaveral Air Force Station was renamed Cape Canaveral Air Station.

• **Last known as Cape Canaveral Air Station:** 2000, when the name was changed back to Cape Canaveral Air Force Station.

Space—Jet Propulsion Laboratory (JPL)—Original Group

Several graduate students at California I n-stitute of Technology (Caltech) conducted liquid-propellant rocket tests between 1936 and 1938 near Pasadena. Their studies helped generate the interest in and viability of rocketry that led to the formation of the Jet Propulsion Laboratory in 1944.

• **Last surviving member of the early rocket testing group that lead to the formation of JPL:** Apollo M.O. Smith, who died on May 1, 1997, age 85.

Space—Manned Space Missions—Apollo

The United States Apollo space program was announced in 1960. It included the Mercury and Gemini missions. The goal of Apollo was to land human beings on the Moon and return them safely to Earth. Six of the Apollo spacecraft did land on the Moon: Apollos 11, 12, 14, 15, 16 and 17.

• **Last lunar landing mission in the Apollo program:** Apollo 17, launched December 7, 1972. The astronauts were Eugene A. Cernan (commander), Ronald E. Evans (command module pilot), and Harrison H. ("Jack") Schmitt (lunar module pilot). The last manned lunar landing was on December 11, 1972, at 2:54 p.m. (EST). The last manned lunar liftoff was 75 hours later, on December 14, 1972, at 5:54 p.m. (EST).

• **Last astronaut on the Moon in the 20th century:** Eugene A. Cernan. As he left the Moon on December 14, 1972, his last words were: "As we leave the Moon at Taurus-Littrow, we leave as we came, and, God willing, we shall return, with peace and hope for all mankind. God speed the crew of Apollo 17." Apollo 17 returned to Earth December 19, 1972.

Space—Manned Space Missions—Gemini

The Gemini space mission was part of the Apollo program. It followed the Mercury mission and preceded the Apollo lunar landings. The first two Gemini flights, Gemini 1 and 2, were unmanned. They were followed by 10 two-manned Gemini flights, beginning with Gemini 3 on March 23, 1965.

• **Last Gemini flight:** Gemini 12, from November 11 to November 15, 1966, with U.S. astronauts James A. Lovell and Edwin E. ("Buzz") Aldrin. Recovery was in the Atlantic Ocean by the USS *Wasp.*

Space—Manned Space Missions—Mercury

Project Mercury, part of the Apollo program, was NASA's first manned space mission. It was initiated in 1958 and involved six manned flights between 1961 and 1963. The flights were: Freedom 7, Liberty Bell 7, Friendship 7, Aurora 7, Sigma 7 and Faith 7.

• **Last of the original seven U.S. astronauts to be chosen in 1959 for Project Mercury:** Donald K. ("Deke") Slayton. The others were: Alan B. Shepard, Virgil I. ("Gus") Grissom, John H. Glenn Jr., M. Scott Carpenter, Walter ("Wally") M. Schirra and L. Gordon Cooper Jr.

• **Last Mercury flight:** May 15-16, 1963, when U.S. astronaut L. Gordon Cooper Jr. completed 22 orbits in Mercury Faith 7 to evaluate the effects of one day in space. Mercury was replaced by the Gemini program. Faith 7 splashed down in the Pacific Ocean on May 16, 1963, about 80 miles southwest of Midway Island near the recovery ship USS *Kearsarge.* Cooper remained in the capsule until it was hoisted onto the deck of the *Kearsarge*. The 22-orbit flight of Faith 7 lasted 1 day, 10 hours, 19 minutes and 49 seconds.

• **Last Mercury astronaut to travel in space as part of Apollo program:** Donald ("Deke") Slayton in the Apollo-Soyuz Test Project in July 1975.

• **Last of the original Mercury astronauts to travel in space:** John J. Glenn Jr., from October 29 to November 7, 1998, as part of the STS-95 mission of the Space Shuttle Discovery. At age 77, Glenn, then U.S. senator from Ohio, became the oldest astronaut to travel in space. He retired from the U.S. Senate in January 1999.

Space—Manned Space Missions— Mir Space Station

The Russian space station Mir proved long-duration space flight was possible. Mir ended nearly 15 years in space on March 23, 2001, when Russian Mission Control guided fragments of the space station safely into the South Pacific Ocean about 1,800 miles east of New Zealand.

• **Last crew on Mir:** Russian cosmonauts Viktor Afanasyev (commander) and Sergei Avdeyev and French astronaut Jean-Pierre Haignere left Mir Space Station on August 27, 1999, after the Russian government decided to abandon the aging station.

• **Last American astronaut on Mir:** Dr. Andrew ("Andy") Thomas, who was the seventh U.S. astronaut to join the Russian crew on Mir. Thomas left Mir on the shuttle Discovery on June 12, 1998, after 141 days in space.

Space—Manned Space Missions—Salyut

Salyut 1, the first Earth-orbiting space laboratory, was launched by the Soviet Union on April 19, 1971. The station remained in orbit until October 16, 1971.

• **Last Salyut space station:** Salyut 7, launched April 19, 1982. It remained in orbit until February 7, 1991, then fell apart over Argentina and Chile upon reentry, lighting up the ski with hundreds of fiery metal fragments.

Space—Manned Space Missions—Skylab

Skylab, the first Earth-orbiting U.S. space station, was launched unmanned on May 14, 1973. Three three-man crews visited the station between 1973 and 1974. Skylab burned as it reentered the Earth's atmosphere on July 11, 1979. Parts of it landed in the Australian Outback and the Indian Ocean.

• **Last crew to occupy Skylab:** Gerald P. Carr, Edward G. Gibson and William Pogue. They were at the space station from November 16, 1973, to February 8, 1974.

Space—Manned Space Missions—Soyuz

The Soyuz spacecraft were part of the Soviet space program. The first Soyuz spacecraft was launched on April 23, 1967.

• **Last first-generation Soyuz spacecraft:** Soyuz 11.

• **Last crew to travel on Soyuz 11:** cosmonauts Georgi Dobrovolsky (commander), Vladislav Volkov (flight engineer) and Viktor Patsayev (research) , who were killed when Soyuz 11 depressurized while re-entering the Earth's atmosphere on June 29, 1971. After the disaster, the Soyuz spacecraft were redesigned.

• **Last second-generation Soyuz spacecraft:** Soyuz 40.

• **Last to travel on Soyuz 40:** Leonid Ivanovich Popov (commander) and Dumitru Dorin Prunariu, the first cosmonaut from Romania. They returned to Earth from the Soviet Salyut space station on May 22, 1981.

Space—Manned Space Missions— Voskhod

Voskhod, the second series of manned Soviet space flights, followed the Vostok flights.

• **Last Voskhod mission:** Voskhod 2, launched March 18, 1965. The crew were Lieutenant Colonel Aleksei A. Leonov, who made the first space walk, and Colonel Pavel Belyayev.

Space—Manned Space Missions—Vostok

Vostok was a series of six manned Soviet

space flights made in 1961-63. Vostok 1, launched in April 12, 1961, carried the first human into space—cosmonaut Yuri Gagarin.

• **Last Vostok mission:** Vostok 6, launched June 16, 1963. It carried Valentina Tereshkova, the first woman in space. She was also the first woman commander.

Space—Unmanned Space Missions—Biosatellite

Biosatellite (a.k.a. Biosat) was a U.S. Earth-orbiting biological laboratory whose purpose was to study the biological effects of the space environment on living organisms. Biosatellite 1 was launched December 14, 1966. Biosatellite 2 was launched on September 7, 1967.

• **Last Biosatellite:** Biosatellite 3, launched on June 28, 1969. It spent only nine of the planned 30 days in orbit. The flight was cut short when the monkey on board became ill. Further Biosat launches were cancelled.

Space—Unmanned Space Missions—Luna

The USSR's Luna probes of the surface of the Moon began with the launching of the lunar flyby Luna 1 in January 1959. Luna 1 was the first spacecraft to go into solar orbit.

• **Last Luna probe:** Luna 24, launched August 9, 1976. It was the third of the Luna spacecraft to retrieve lunar samples. The mission ended when Luna 24 returned to Earth on August 22, 1976.

Space—Unmanned Space Missions—Lunar Orbiters

Five unmanned U.S. lunar orbiter spacecraft were sent to the Moon to photograph and map the lunar surface prior to the manned Apollo landings. The first lunar orbiter was launched August 10, 1966.

• **Last lunar orbiter:** Lunar Orbiter 5, launched August 1, 1967. The orbiter took photographs from August 6th to the 18th, then provided readout until the 27th. Lunar Orbiter 5 impacted the lunar surface on command on January 31, 1968.

Space—Unmanned Space Missions—Mariner

The Mariner spacecraft were launched by the U.S. and were designed to fly near or orbit Mercury, Venus and Mars and provide new information about them. Seven Mariner vehicles were successful. Three were lost.

• **Last Mariner spacecraft:** Mariner 10, launched November 3, 1973. It flew past Venus on February 5, 1974, and reached Mercury on March 29th. It had a second encounter with Mercury on September 21, 1974. The third and last Mercury encounter was on March 16, 1975. Mariner 10 is still orbiting the Sun. What would have been Mariner 11 and 12 evolved into Voyager 1 and 2.

Space—Unmanned Space Missions—Mars Pathfinder

The Mars Pathfinder was launched by the U.S. on December 4, 1996. It delivered the rover Sojourner to the surface of Mars on July 4, 1997.

• **Last Mars Pathfinder transmission:** 3:23 a.m. (Pacific Daylight Time) on September 27, 1997. Engineers were able to detect a signal as late as October 7th but could not restore communications.

Space—Unmanned Space Missions—Orbiting Geophysical Observatory (OGO)

Six orbiting geophysical observatories (OGOs, a.k.a. Pogos) were launched by the United States, starting in September 1964. They performed systematic explorations of space between Earth and the Moon.

• **Last OGO:** OGO-6, launched June 5, 1969. It ceased operating on October 12, 1979.

Space—Unmanned Space Missions—Orbiting Solar Observatory (OSO)

Eight Orbiting Solar Observatories (OSOs) were launched by the United States, beginning in March 1962. They studied the Sun and cosmic radiation.

• **Last OSO:** OSO-8, launched June 21, 1975. It ceased operating on October 1, 1978.

Space—Unmanned Space Missions—Pioneer

The U.S. Pioneer space program was started in 1958 to study how the environment of the solar system would impact on space travel. The earliest Pioneer spacecraft were sent to the Moon and into orbit around the Sun. Some of them are still operating, although their signals have been lost.

• **Last transmission from Pioneer 10:** January 23, 2003. By then it had traveled an estimated 7.6 billion miles. Pioneer 10 was launched on March 2, 1972. It passed within 81,000 miles of Jupiter in December 1973 then became the first spacecraft to move out of the solar system.

• **Last transmission from Pioneer 11:** September 30, 1995. Pioneer 11 was launched on April 5, 1973. It followed Pioneer 10 to Jupiter, then made the first direct observations of Saturn in 1979.

• **Last of Pioneer 12 (Pioneer Venus 1):** ran out of propellant and burned up in the atmosphere of Venus. Pioneer 12 was launched toward Venus on May 20, 1978. Although designed to last just a year and a half, Pioneer 12 operated for 14 years.

• **Last of Pioneer 13 (Pioneer Venus 2):** entered the Venusian atmosphere on December 9, 1978, and sent out four scientific probes before burning up in the upper atmosphere. Pioneer 13 was launched toward Venus on August 8, 1978.

Space—Unmanned Space Missions—Ranger

The U.S.-launched Ranger spacecraft provided photographic information about the lunar surface. Each Ranger was equipped with six TV cameras that transmitted images of the Moon back to Earth.

• **Last in the Ranger Series:** Ranger 9, launched March 21, 1965. It reached the Moon on March 24, 1965, and sent back more than 5,800 images of the lunar surface.

Space—Unmanned Space Missions—Sputnik

Sputnik 1, the world's first spacecraft, was launched by the Soviet Union on October 4, 1957. Sputnik 2 was launched a month later, on November 3, carrying the first animal into space, a dog named Laika. Other Sputniks were launched later.

• **Last of Sputnik 1:** disintegrated January 4, 1958.

• **Last of Sputnik 2:** disintegrated April 14, 1958.

Space—Unmanned Space Missions—Surveyor

The Surveyor program, launched by the U.S., was a series of lunar probes that determined the surface of the Moon was safe for landing the astronauts.

• **Last in the Surveyor series:** Surveyor 7, launched January 7, 1968. It touched down on the Moon near the crater Tycho on January 10, 1968, and televised the area.

Space—Unmanned Space Missions—Vanguard

Vanguard was the first U.S. satellite program. The Vanguard satellites provided information on the Earth's space environment, including data on the Earth's magnetic field and the Van Allen radiation belts. The first Vanguard satellite went into orbit on March 17, 1958.

• **Last Vanguard satellite:** Vanguard III, launched September 18, 1959.

Space—Unmanned Space Missions—Venera

The Soviet Venera program explored the planet Venus. The first planetary probe was launched on February 12, 1961, with Venera 1.

• **Last Venera satellite:** Venera 16, launched on June 7, 1983. It reached Venus on October 14, 1983. Venera 16 worked in conjunction with Venera 15, which was launched five days earlier. They entered into Venus orbit four days apart and together mapped the planet's northern hemisphere.

Space—Unmanned Space Missions—Viking

The Viking spacecraft were Mars orbiters and landers. Viking 1 was launched by the United States on August 20, 1975, and reached Mars on July 20, 1976.

• **Last transmission from Viking I:** the

orbiter shut down on August 7, 1980, after it ran out of propellant. The lander lasted until November 13, 1982, when a command was sent by mistake to shut down. Further attempts to regain communication failed.

• **Last transmission from Viking 2:** April 12, 1980. Viking 2 was launched toward Mars on September 9, 1975. The lander reached the Martian surface on September 3, 1976. The orbiter shut down in July 1978. The lander shut down on April 12, 1980.

Space—Unmanned Space Missions—Voyager

The Voyager outer planet flybys involved two spacecraft. Voyager 2 was launched on August 20, 1977, before Voyager 1. It reached Neptune in August 1989.

• **Last of the Voyager flights:** Voyager 1, launched September 5, 1977. It flew by Saturn on November 13, 1980. Both Voyager 1 and 2 are now in deep space.

Sports

Sports—Automobile Racing

Sports—Automobile Racing—AAA

The American Automobile Association (AAA) organized the first national championship racing series in 1909. The races were held mostly on roads, not tracks.

• **Last AAA-sanctioned auto races on roads:** 1916. Automobile manufacturers preferred tracks that were more profitable and safer.

• **Last AAA-backed auto racing on race tracks:** 1955. The AAA stopped backing the races so that it could concentrate more on its membership program.

Sports—Automobile Racing—Formula One—Front Engine Cars

Formula cars are single-seater racing cars.

• **Last year a front-engine car won a Formula One victory:** 1960. The car was a Dino Ferrari 246 driven by Phil Hill on the Monza banked track at the Grand Prix of Italy.

Sports—Automobile Racing—Indy 500—Front-Engine Cars

The Indianapolis 500 is held on Memorial Day in Indianapolis, Indiana.

• **Last year a front-engine car won the Indianapolis 500:** 1964. A.J. Foyt drove the No. 1 car, racing for the Sheraton-Thompson team. Front-engine cars had won every Indy 500 from 1911 to 1964.

Sports—Automobile Racing—Indy 500—Pole Position

• **Last year pole position at the Indianapolis 500 was not determined by qualifying speed:** 1914. Until then, pole position was determined by the order that the entries were received and for one year by drawing. Qualifying speeds began determining pole position in 1915.

Sports—Automobile Racing—Indy 500—Racers

Mario Andretti

Mario Andretti is the only auto racer to win the Daytona 500 (1967), Indy 500 (1961) and Formula One world title (1978).

• **Last racing season:** 1994, dubbed the "Arrivederci Tour."

• **Last Indy car race:** September 1994. It was Andretti's 407th race.

• **Last Indy car victory:** Phoenix 200 in April 1993. It was Andretti's 52nd victory.

• **Last CART championship**: 1984. (CART is an acronym for Championship Auto Racing Teams, Inc.)

A.J. Foyt

A(nthony) (J)oseph Foyt is the only auto racer to drive in the Indy 500 for 35 consecutive years. He won seven Indy championships

• **Last Indy car national championship:** 1979, the same year Foyt won the USAC's stock car championship, becoming the only driver to win both titles in the same year.

• **Last Indy car victory:** Pocono 500 in 1981.

• **Last racing season:** 1992. Foyt practiced at Indy in 1993 but retired on the first qualifying day.

• **Last race at the Indianapolis Motor Speedway:** 1992. Foyt finished ninth, five laps off the pace.

Sports—Automobile Racing—NASCAR

The National Association for Stock Car Racing (NASCAR) was founded in Daytona Beach, Florida, in 1947.
• **Last surviving founding NASCAR member:** Sammy Packard, who died in Daytona Beach, Florida, on March 23, 2003, age 83.

Sports—Automobile Racing—NASCAR— Racers

Dale Earnhardt

Dale Earnhardt won the NASCAR Winston Cup seven times. He was career victories leader at Daytona and won the 1998 Daytona 500.
• **Last race:** Daytona 500, February 18, 2001. Earnhardt died at age 49 from injuries sustained during a crash in the last turn of the last lap. He was running interference so that fellow team members Michael Waltrip and son Dale Earnhardt Jr. could take the first and second-place finishes.

Richard Petty

Richard Petty won more NASCAR races than any other racer. He had 200 wins when he retired in 1992 after a career that spanned three decades.
• **Last Winston Cup:** 1979.
• **Last Daytona 500 victory:** 1981.
• **Last track where Petty competed in official competition:** Atlanta Motor Speedway.
• **Last racing victory:** July 4, 1984, at the Firecracker 400 (Daytona International Speedway). It was his 200th victory.
• **Last racing season:** 1992. Petty retired after a 29-race Fan Appreciation Tour.

Sports—Automobile Racing—Road Racers—Cannonball Baker

Erwin G. ("Cannonball") Baker was a test driver who won many speed and endurance tests.
• **Last record:** set in 1948, when Baker drove up Mount Washington, New Hampshire, in 15 minutes, 12.75 seconds in a Nash. He died on May 10, 1960, age 78.

Sports—Automobile Racing— Steam-powered Automobiles

• **Last steam-powered automobile to set a land speed record:** the Wogglebug, driven by Fred Marriot at Ormond Beach, Florida, on January 26, 1906, traveling at 127.659 miles per hour.

Sports—Baseball

Sports—Baseball—All-Star Games

All-Star Games have been played since 1933. For a while, two games were played in one year to raise money for the players' pension fund.
• **Last year two All-Star games were played in one season:** 1962. All-Star Game No. 1 was played in Washington, D.C. The National League won 3-1. Game No. 2 was played at Wrigley Field in Chicago, Illinois, on July 30, 1962. The American League won 9-4.

Sports—Baseball—Ballparks
Last of Some Major American Ballparks

Anaheim, California
The stadium in Anaheim, California, is home to the Anaheim Angels.
• **Last known as Anaheim Stadium:** 1997. That year, the name was changed to Edison International Field.

Arlington, Texas
Arlington Stadium was home to the Texas Rangers.
• **Last known as Turnpike Stadium:** 1971. The park was renamed Arlington Stadium when the Washington Senators moved to Texas and became the Rangers.

- **Last Texas Rangers game at Arlington Stadium:** October 3, 1993. Since then, the Rangers have played at The Ballpark in Arlington.
- **Last of Arlington Stadium:** demolished in 1994.

Atlanta, Georgia
The Braves began to use Atlanta-Fulton County Stadium when they arrived in 1966.
- **Last Atlanta Braves game in Atlanta-Fulton County Stadium:** October 24, 1996. It is the only ballpark to close with a World Series game. The following year, the Braves moved to Turner Field, which had been constructed for the 1996 Olympics.
- **Last of Atlanta-Fulton County Stadium:** demolished August 2, 1997. It is now a parking area for Turner Field.

Baltimore, Maryland
- **Last Baltimore Orioles game at Memorial Stadium:** October 6, 1991. Since 1992, the Orioles have played at Oriole Park at Camden Yards.
- **Last of Memorial Stadium:** demolition began in November 2000 and was completed on April 21, 2001. The Memorial Wall was demolished in February 2002. Some of the stadium concrete was used to build an oyster reef in the Chesapeake Bay.

Bloomington, Minnesota
- **Last Minnesota Twins game at Metropolitan Stadium:** September 30, 1981. Since 1982, the Twins have played at the Hubert H. Humphrey Metrodome in Minneapolis.
- **Last of Metropolitan Stadium:** demolished in 1984-85 to make room for the Mall of America.

Boston, Massachusetts
- **Last Boston Red Sox game at Huntington Avenue Grounds:** October 7, 1911. The Red Sox began playing there in 1901.
- **Last of Huntington Avenue Grounds:** demolished and replaced by a YMCA. Northeastern University acquired the land in the 1950s. A memorial for the park is on the campus. The Red Sox have played most of their home games at Fenway Park since 1912.
- **Last Boston Braves game at South End Grounds:** August 11, 1914. The Boston Red Stockings began playing there in 1872; the Braves arrived in 1876. The park burned down during a game in 1894. It was rebuilt and reopened later that year. The Braves moved to Braves Field in 1914.
- **Last of South End Grounds:** demolished. It is now the site of the Ruggles Station, Orange Line of the Massachusetts Bay Transportation Authority.
- **Last surviving Boston Braves player to play at South End Grounds:** James Francis ("Frank") O'Rourke, who played for the Braves in 1912. He died in Chatham, New Jersey, on May 14, 1986, age 91.
- **Last Boston Braves game at Braves Field:** September 21, 1952.
- **Last of Braves Field:** Purchased by Boston University and renamed Nickerson Field.
- **Last of the Braves Field scoreboard:** Installed at Kansas City's Municipal Stadium in 1955.
- **Last Boston Red Sox game at Braves Field:** June 1932.
- **Last ads removed from Fenway Park's "Green Monster":** 1947, when the left field wall was painted green.

Brooklyn, New York
- **Last Brooklyn Dodgers game at Washington Park:** 1912. The Brooklyn Dodgers began playing at Washington Park in 1890. They moved to Ebbets Field in 1913.
- **Last Brooklyn Dodgers game at Ebbets Field:** September 26, 1957. The Dodgers beat the Pirates 2-0 in front of a crowd of 6,702. The winning pitcher was Danny McDevitt; the losing pitcher was Bennie Daniels.
- **Last World Series game at Ebbets Field:** Game Seven of the 1956 World Series, when

the Yankees took the series. That game was also Jackie Robinson's last in the majors.
• **Last home run hit at Ebbets Field:** September 24, 1957, by Duke Snider off Robin Roberts of the Philadelphia Phillies.
• **Last of Ebbets Field:** demolition began on February 23, 1960. Eight light towers were moved to Downing Stadium on Randall's Island. The scoreboard clock was moved to McCormick Field in Asheville, North Carolina. The stadium grounds became home to the Ebbets Field Apartments and Intermediate School 320. The apartments were renamed Jackie Robinson Apartments in 1972.
• **Last Brooklyn Dodgers game at Roosevelt Stadium:** September 3, 1957, a 3-2 loss to the Philadelphia Phillies in 12 innings. Fifteen Dodgers games were played at Roosevelt Stadium in Jersey City, New Jersey, during 1956 and 1957. In 1958, the Dodgers moved to Los Angeles, California.
• **Last of Roosevelt Stadium:** demolished in 1985. The land is now the site of a housing development known as Society Hill.

Chicago, Illinois
• **Last Chicago White Sox game at South Side Park:** June 27, 1910, after which the White Sox moved to the old Comiskey Park. The Chicago White Sox began playing at South Side Park in 1901.
• **Last of South Side Park:** burned down on December 25, 1940. A housing project now occupies the stadium grounds.
• **Last Chicago White Sox game at old Comiskey Park:** September 30, 1990.
• **Last of old Comiskey Park:** demolished in 1991. Also known as Charles A. Comiskey's Baseball Palace and White Sox Park. The infield dirt (550 tons) was moved to New Comiskey Park. In 1991, the White Sox began playing at New Comiskey Park.
• **Last known as New Comiskey Park:** 2003, when it was renamed US Cellular Park.
• **Last Chicago Cubs game at State Street Grounds:** 1877. The Cubs first played there in 1876.
• **Last Chicago Cubs game at Lakefront Park:** 1884. The Cubs first played there in 1878.
• **Last Chicago Cubs game at Westside Park:** 1891. The Cubs first played there in 1885.
• **Last Chicago Cubs game at Brotherhood Park:** 1893. The Cubs first played there in 1891.
• **Last Chicago Cubs game at West Side Grounds:** 1915. The Cubs first played there in 1893. In 1916, they moved to Weeghman Park.
• **Last known as Weeghman Park:** 1919, when it was renamed Cubs Park.
• **Last known as Cubs Park:** 1926, when it was renamed Wrigley Field in honor of American industrialist William Wrigley Jr.

Cincinnati, Ohio
• **Last Cincinnati Reds game at Lincoln Park Grounds:** 1876.
• **Last Cincinnati Reds game at Avenue Grounds:** 1879. The Reds first played there in 1876.
• **Last Cincinnati Reds game at Bank Street Grounds:** 1883. The Reds first played there in 1880.
• **Last Cincinnati Reds game at League Park:** 1901. The Reds first played there in 1884.
• **Last Cincinnati Reds game at Palace of the Fans:** October 6, 1911. The Reds first played there in 1902.
• **Last of Palace of the Fans:** burned down in the fall of 1911.
• **Last Cincinnati Reds game at Redland Field/Crosley Field:** June 24, 1970. The Reds first played at Redland Field in 1912. During the 1970 season, the team began playing at

Riverfront Stadium.
- **Last known as Redland Field:** 1933, when it was renamed Crosley Field.
- **Last of Crosley Field:** torn down in 1970. An industrial park now occupies the former playing ground. The old home plate was moved to Riverfront Stadium. A replica of Crosley Field was constructed on a farm near Union, Kentucky. A replica also has been constructed at Blue Ash, Ohio.
- **Last known as Riverfront Stadium:** 1996, when it was renamed Cinergy Field.
- **Last Cincinnati Reds game at Cinergy Field:** September 22, 2002.
- **Last of Cinergy Field:** demolished by implosion on December 29, 2002. The site became part of the Great American Ballpark.

Cleveland, Ohio
- **Last Cleveland Indians game at League Park:** 1946. In 1947, the Indians began playing all their games at Cleveland Stadium. Until then, they played only Sunday and holiday games at Cleveland Stadium. The rest were played at League Park.
- **Last Cleveland Indians game at Cleveland Stadium:** October 3, 1993. The stadium was also known as Lakefront Stadium and Cleveland Public Municipal Stadium. Since 1994, the Indians have played at Jacobs Field.
- **Last of Cleveland Stadium:** demolished beginning in November 1996, after the last occupants, the Cleveland Brown football team, vacated and moved to Baltimore.

Denver, Colorado
- **Last Colorado Rockies game at Mile High Stadium:** August 11, 1994. The Colorado Rockies played at Mile High Stadium from 1993 to 1994. Since then, they have played at Coors Field.

Detroit , Michigan
- **Last Detroit Tigers game at Bennett Park:** September 10, 1911. The Tigers began playing there in 1901.
- **Last of Bennett Park:** demolished in 1912. Navin Field was built on the site.
- **Last known as Navin Field:** 1938, when it was renamed Briggs Stadium.
- **Last known as Briggs Stadium:** 1961, when it was renamed Tiger Stadium.
- **Last Detroit Tigers game at Tiger Stadium:** September 27, 1999. Detroit beat Kansas City 8-to-2. Brian Moehler was the winning pitcher and Jeff Suppan, the loser. In the eighth inning, Robert Fick hit a grand slam that was also the last hit, last run, last RBI and last home run in the stadium. The Tigers moved to Comerica Park in 2000.

Houston, Texas
- **Last Houston Colt 45s game at Colt Stadium:** September 27, 1964.
- **Team last known as Colt 45s:** 1965, when they moved to The Astrodome, a space-age megastadium, and changed their name to the Astros.
- **Last of Colt Stadium:** purchased by a Mexican League team in the early 1970s and moved to Gomez Palacio, Mexico. It was moved a second time to Tampico, Mexico.
- **Last Houston Astros game in The Astrodome:** October 9, 1999. In 2000, the Astros moved to Enron Field.
- **Last known as Enron Field**: 2002, when it was renamed Minute Maid Park.

Kansas City, Missouri
Muehlebach Field opened in 1923.
- **Last known as Muehlebach Field:** 1938, when it was renamed Ruppert Stadium
- **Last known as Ruppert Stadium:** 1943, when it was renamed Blues Stadium.
- **Last known as Blues Stadium:** 1955, when it was renamed Municipal Stadium.
- **Last Kansas City Athletics game at Municipal Stadium:** September 27, 1967. The Kansas City Athletics had played there since 1955. In 1968, the team moved to Oakland, California.

- **Last Kansas City Royals game at Municipal Stadium:** October 4, 1972. Beginning in 1973, the Royals played at Royals Stadium.
- **Last known as Royals Stadium:** 1993, when it was renamed Kauffman Stadium.
- **Last of Municipal Stadium:** demolished in 1976. A municipal garden is now on the site.

Los Angeles, California
- **Last Los Angeles Angels game at Los Angeles's Wrigley Field:** October 1, 1961. The Los Angeles Angels began playing at Chavez Ravine/Dodger Stadium in 1962.
- **Last of Los Angeles's Wrigley Field:** demolished 1966. The site is now occupied by a park, recreation center, mental health center and senior citizens center.
- **Last Los Angeles Angels game at Chavez Ravine/Dodger Stadium:** September 22, 1965. In 1966, the Angels moved to Anaheim, California.
- **Last Los Angeles Dodgers game at Los Angeles Memorial Coliseum:** September 20, 1961. The Los Angeles Dodgers began playing there in 1958. Beginning in 1962, the Los Angeles Dodgers played at Dodger Stadium (previously known as Chavez Ravine).

Milwaukee, Wisconsin
- **Last Milwaukee Brewers game at Milwaukee County Stadium:** September 28, 2000. The Brewers moved to Miller Park in 2001.
- **Last of Milwaukee County Stadium:** demolished February 21, 2001.

Montreal, Canada
- **Last Montreal Expos game at Jarry Park:** September 26, 1976. The Expos then moved to Olympic Stadium (Stade Olympique). Jarry Park (Parc Jarry) was used as a tennis stadium for many years after the Expos left.
- **Last of Jarry Park**: torn down in 1995.

New York, New York
Four New York City ball parks were known as the Polo Grounds:
Polo Grounds (I) was outside northern Central Park from 5th to 6th Avenues and 110th to 112th Streets.
- **Last New York Giants game at the Polo Grounds (I):** October 13, 1888.
- **Last of the Polo Grounds (I):** the City of New York took over the site for street construction in 1889.
Polo Grounds (II) was between 155th and 157th streets at the southern half of South Coogan's Hollow.
- **Last New York Giants game at the Polo Grounds (II):** September 13, 1890.
- **Last of the Polo Grounds (II):** moved to the other end of Coogan's Hollow to gain a larger field.
Polo Grounds (III) was at the northern half of Coogan's Hollow, between 157th and 159th streets.
- **Last New York Giants game at the Polo Grounds (III):** April 13, 1911.
- **Last of the Polo Grounds (III):** destroyed by a fire that burned for two days, April 14-15, 1911.
Polo Grounds (IV) was built on the same area as Polo Grounds (III). It opened in June 1911 as Brush Stadium.
- **Last known as Brush Stadium:** 1920, when it was renamed Polo Grounds (IV).
- **Last New York Giants game at the Polo Grounds (IV):** September 29, 1957. The Giants lost the game 9-1 to the Pittsburgh Pirates. In 1958, the Giants moved to San Francisco, California.
- **Last New York Yankee game at the Polo Grounds (IV):** October 8, 1922. The Yankees used the Polo Grounds between 1913 and 1922, as well as for one game in 1912.
- **Last Major League baseball game at Polo Grounds (IV):** September 18, 1963. The Philadelphia Phillies beat the Mets, 5-1.

- **Last home run hit at the Polo Grounds (IV):** September 18, 1963, by Jim Hickman of the New York Mets, off Chris Short of the Philadelphia Phillies.
- **Last of the Polo Grounds (IV):** demolition began on April 10, 1964. Today, the grounds are the site of Willie Mays Field (playground) and Polo Grounds Towers (four 30-story apartment buildings).
- **Last New York Giants games at Saint George Cricket Grounds:** 1890. The Giants began playing there in 1889, while the Polo Grounds was being constructed.
- **Last New York Highlanders game at Hilltop Park (New York American League Park):** October 5, 1912. The Highlanders began playing there in 1903. They moved to the Polo Grounds in 1913 and were renamed the New York Yankees.
- **Last of Hilltop Park:** demolished in 1914. The park was between Broadway and Fort Washington Avenue, 165th and 168th streets. The land is now part of the Columbia University campus.
- **Last surviving New York Highlander player who played at Hilltop Park:** Chester ("Chet") Cornelius Hoff, who joined the Highlanders in 1911. Hoff died in Daytona, Florida, on September 17, 1998, age 107.

Philadelphia, Pennsylvania
- **Last Philadelphia A's game at Columbia Park:** 1908. The Philadelphia Athletics began playing there in 1901. In April 1909, the Athletics moved to Shibe Park and took the sod and home plate with them.
- **Last known as Shibe Park:** 1953, when it was renamed Connie Mack Stadium.
- **Last Philadelphia Athletics game at Connie Mack Stadium:** September 19, 1954. In 1955, the Athletics moved to Kansas City, Missouri.
- **Last Phillies game at Connie Mack Stadium:** October 1, 1970. Home plate was moved to Veterans Stadium, the Phillies' new park, in 1971. Many of the Connie Mack Stadium seats were moved to Duncan Park in Spartanburg, South Carolina, and to War Memorial Stadium in Greensboro, North Carolina.
- **Last of Connie Mack Stadium:** damaged by fire on August 20, 1971. The stadium was demolished in June 1976. The land is now the site of the Deliverance Evangelistic Church.
- **Last Phillies game at Veterans Stadium:** September 28, 2003. The Phillies moved to the new Citizens Bank Park in 2004.
- **Last of Veterans Stadium:** demolished by implosion on March 21, 2004.
- **Last Philadelphia Phillies game at Baker Bowl:** June 20, 1938. When it opened in 1887, the park was officially called National League Park. Informally, it was known as Huntingdon Street Baseball Grounds and as Philadelphia Base Ball Park. The park was destroyed by fire in 1894. It was rebuilt and dedicated on May 2, 1895. In 1913, the park was renamed Baker Bowl for its new owner, William F. Baker. The Phillies moved to Shibe Park in 1938.
- **Last of Baker Bowl:** demolished in 1950. The old Baker Bowl grounds now hold a parking lot, car wash, gas station and bus garage.

Pittsburgh, Pennsylvania
- **Last Pittsburgh Pirates game at Exposition Park:** June 29, 1909. The team moved to Forbes Field and played their first game there on June 30th, 1909.
- **Last Pittsburgh Pirates game at Forbes Field:** June 28, 1970. Pittsburgh beat the Chicago Cubs 3-2 and 4-1. The Pirates then moved to Three Rivers Stadium.
- **Last of Forbes Field:** damaged by fires on December 24, 1970, and July 17, 1971. Demolition of the park began on July 28, 1971. University of Pittsburgh buildings now occupy the grounds. Home plate was kept at the site and encased in glass in the Galleria of the Forbes Quadrangle.
- **Last Pirates game at Three Rivers Stadium:** October 1, 2000. The Pirates moved to

PNC Park, which opened in the spring of 2001.
• **Last of Three Rivers Stadium:** demolished by implosion February 11, 2001.

Saint Louis, Missouri
• **Last Saint Louis Cardinals game at Robison Field:** June 6, 1920. The park was abandoned that year and the Cardinals moved to Sportsman's Park.
• **Last Saint Louis Browns game at Sportsman's Park:** September 27, 1953. The Browns moved to Baltimore in 1954 and became the Orioles. Sportsman's Park was also known as Busch Stadium from 1953 to 1966.
• **Last Saint Louis Cardinals game at Sportsman's Park/Busch Stadium:** May 8, 1966. After the game, a helicopter carried the home plate from the old stadium to Busch Memorial Stadium.
• **Last of Sportsman's Park/Busch Stadium:** demolished in 1966. The grounds now house the Herbert Hoover Boys' Club. A baseball diamond is now where the Major League diamond was once located.

San Diego, California
San Diego Stadium opened in August 1967. The San Diego Padres began playing there in 1969.
• **Last known as San Diego Stadium:** 1980, when it was renamed Jack Murphy Stadium.
• **Last known as Jack Murphy Stadium:** 1997, when it was renamed Qualcomm Stadium.
• **Last Padres game at Qualcomm Stadium:** September 28, 2003. The Padres moved to Petco Park in 2004.

San Francisco, California
• **Last San Francisco Giants game at Seals Stadium:** September 20, 1959. The San Francisco Giants moved to Candlestick Park in 1960.
• **Last known as Candlestick Park:** 1996 when it was renamed 3Com Park.
• **Last known as 3Com Park:** 2004, when the name was changed to Monster Park.
• **Last Giants game at 3Com Park:** September 30, 1999. The Giants played their first game at Pacific Bell Park in 2000.

Seattle, Washington
• **Last Seattle Pilots game at Sick's Stadium:** October 2, 1969. In 1970, the Pilots moved to Milwaukee and became the Brewers.
• **Last of Sick's Stadium:** demolished in 1979. A home improvement center is now on the site. The Sick's Stadium home plate was placed in the Royal Brougham trophy case at the Seattle Kingdome. Box seats and grandstand benches were moved to the Growden Memorial Park in Fairbanks Alaska, where the Fairbanks Goldpanners play their home games.
• **Last Seattle Mariners game at the Kingdome:** June 27, 1999. The Mariners moved to Safeco Field in July 1999.
• **Last of the Kingdome:** Demolished by implosion on March 26, 2000.

Toronto, Canada
• **Last Toronto Blue Jays game at Exhibition Stadium:** May 28, 1989. Since 1989, the Blue Jays have played at the SkyDome.
• **Last of Exhibition Stadium:** demolished by implosion on February 1, 1999.

Washington, D.C.
• **Last Washington Senators game at original American League Park:** September 27, 1902. The stadium was built in 1901 and was the first home of the Washington Senators. The Senators moved in 1902 to what would later be known as Griffith Stadium.
• **Last (original) Washington Senators game at Griffith Stadium:** October 2, 1960. Griffith Stadium has also been known as American League Park, Beyer's Seventh Street Park, League Park, National Park (until 1920) and Clark Griffith Park (1922). In 1961, the original Senators moved to Minnesota and became the Twins. A new Washington Senators

baseball franchise was created.
- **Last game played by (new) Washington Senators at Griffith Stadium:** September 21, 1961. The Senators moved to D.C. Stadium in 1962.
- **Last of Griffith Stadium:** demolished between January and August 1965. Some of the seats were moved to Tinker Field in Orlando, Florida. A statue of Walter Johnson from the stadium was moved to Walter Johnson High School in Bethesda, Maryland, and a statue and memorial to Clark Griffith were moved to D.C. Stadium. The old Griffith Stadium grounds are now the site of the Howard University Medical Center and the Howard University College of Dentistry.
- **Last known as D.C. Stadium:** 1969, when the name was changed to Robert F. Kennedy Stadium to honor Senator Robert F. Kennedy who was assassinated in 1968.
- **Last Washington Senators game at Robert F. Kennedy Stadium:** September 30, 1971. In 1972, the team moved to Arlington, Texas, and renamed the Texas Rangers.

Sports—Baseball—Ballparks—Lights

Major League baseball introduced games under lights in 1935, when Cincinnati and Philadelphia played the first night game at Crosley Field.
- **Last Major League ballpark to add lights for night games:** Wrigley Field, Chicago, Illinois. Lights were in the park ready to be installed in December 1941, but Philip K. Wrigley donated them to the war effort soon after the United States entered World War II that month. All games were played during the day until August 1988, when light were finally introduced.

Sports—Baseball—Ballparks—Wooden Structures

The early baseball stadiums were made of wood that burned to the ground. The move toward more substantial fireproof structures began with the opening of Shibe Park, the first concrete and steel stadium, in Philadelphia, in 1909.
- **Last all-wooden structure used in the Major Leagues:** Robison Field in Saint Louis, Missouri. The field was last used for professional baseball in 1920.

Sports—Baseball—Equipment—Gloves

Baseball gloves came into use in the 1870s. By 1895, rules began to specify their size and use.
- **Last barehanded Major League player:** Jeremiah Dennis Eldredge, who played ball as Jerry Denny. His Major League career

ended with the Louisville Colonels of the National League in 1894, but he continued playing in the Minors until 1902, retiring at age 43. He avoided wearing a glove because it would have affected his two-handed throws. Denny died in Houston, Texas, on August 16, 1927, age 68.

Sports—Baseball—Equipment—Uniform Numbers

The Cleveland Indians experimented by placing uniform numbers on the sleeves of their baseball players' uniforms in 1916. Seven years later, the Saint Louis Cardinals also made a trial run with a similar numbering system. This was the last of the sleeve-only numbering system. The New York Yankees introduced numbers sewn on the backs of players' jerseys in 1929.
- **Last time road uniforms were numberless:** By 1931, all the American League road uniforms were numbered. In 1932, all National League teams were required to number their players' road uniforms.
- **Last team to add numbers to their home uniforms:** Philadelphia Athletics in 1937.

Sports—Baseball—Hall of Fame

The Baseball Hall of Fame is in Cooperstown, New York. The original five players were inducted in 1936.
- **Last surviving member of the original Baseball Hall of Fame inductees:** Ty Cobb. (*See* Sports—Baseball—Players.)

Sports—Baseball—Leagues
(*See also* Sports—Baseball—Little League; Negro Leagues; Women's Leagues.)

Sports—Baseball—Leagues—American Association
The American Association became a Major League rival to the National League in 1882. American Association teams varied over the years. In its final season, it fielded teams in Baltimore, Boston, Cincinnati, Columbus, Louisville, Milwaukee, Philadelphia, Saint Louis and Washington.
• **Last of the American Association:** went out of existence in 1891. On December 18, 1891, the remaining five teams were bought out and absorbed into the National League.

Sports—Baseball—Leagues—American League
The American League of Professional Baseball Clubs was formed in 1901 with clubs in Baltimore, Boston, Chicago, Cleveland, Detroit, Milwaukee, Philadelphia and Washington.
• **Last surviving player from American League's first season:** Patrick Joseph ("Paddy") Livingston, who played for Cleveland that year. Livingston died in Cleveland, Ohio, on September 19, 1977, age 97.

Sports—Baseball—Leagues—Federal League
The Federal League operated as an independent league in 1913 and as a third league in competition with the National and American Leagues in 1914-15. It had teams in Baltimore, Brooklyn, Buffalo, Chicago, Indianapolis, Kansas City, Pittsburgh and Saint Louis.
• **Last of the Federal League:** ceased operation for financial reasons at the end of the 1915 season.
• **Last surviving player from the Federal League:** Edd J. Roush, who died in Bradenton, Florida, on March 21, 1988, age 94.
• **Last surviving ballpark where the Federal League played:** Wrigley Field. The park was built for the Chicago Federals as Weeghman Park and opened in April 1914. After the Federal League folded, it was sold to William Wrigley Jr. The park was renamed in his honor in 1926.

Sports—Baseball—Leagues—National Association
The National Association of Professional Base Ball Players was formed in March 1871 and was open to all professional or semi-professional teams. The league had from eight to thirteen teams at the beginning of each season.
• **Last of the National Association:** lasted just five seasons. On February 2, 1876, the National League was created, replacing the National Association.
• **Last surviving player from the National Association:** John Wellington McKelvey, who played with a New Hampshire team. McKelvey died in Rochester, New York, on May 31, 1944, age 96.

Sports—Baseball—Leagues—National League
The National League, created in 1876, is the last surviving professional baseball league from the 19th century.
• **Last surviving player from the National League's first season:** Tommy Bond, who played for Boston that year. He died in Boston, Massachusetts, on January 24, 1941, age 84.

Sports—Baseball—Leagues—Players League
The Players League was created in 1890 with teams in eight cities: Boston, Brooklyn, Buffalo, Chicago, Cleveland, New York, Philadelphia and Pittsburgh. It lasted just one season.
• **Last of the Players League:** the National League and American Association bought out the Players League in December 1890.

Sports—Baseball—Leagues—Union Association
The Union Association was created in 1884. It had teams in Altoona (Pennsylvania),

Baltimore, Boston, Chicago, Cincinnati, Philadelphia, Saint Louis and Washington, D.C. The league lasted just one season.
• **Last of the Union Association:** formally disbanded on January 15, 1885.

Sports—Baseball—Little League
Little League baseball for boys nine to twelve years old was organized in Williamsport, Pennsylvania, in 1939.
• **Last time females could not play in Little League:** June 1974, when National Little League Baseball, Inc. announced girls would be allowed to play in its games.

Sports—Baseball—Negro Leagues
The Negro Leagues were made up of several groups that played at different times. The first teams date back to the 1860s. The main groups during the heyday of the Negro Leagues were the Negro National League (NNL), Negro American League (NAL) and Eastern Colored League (ECL).
• **Last of the Negro National League (NNL):** folded in 1948 and absorbed into the Negro American League in 1949. When the NNL was founded in 1933, it had teams in Baltimore, Brooklyn, Chicago, Columbus, Cleveland, Detroit, Indianapolis, Nashville and Pittsburgh.
• **Last of the Negro American League (NAL):** formally ended in 1960. When it was founded in 1937, the NAL had teams in Birmingham, Chicago, Cincinnati, Detroit, Indianapolis, Kansas City, Memphis and Saint Louis.
• **Last of the Eastern Colored League (ECL):** folded after the 1928 season. The ECL was formed in 1923 and included East Coast teams in Atlantic City, Baltimore, Brooklyn, Darby (near Philadelphia), Harrisburg, New York, Washington, D.C., and a traveling Cuban team.
• **Last black player in the Major Leagues before the color barrier:** Moses Fleetwood ("Fleet") Walker, a catcher who signed with the Toledo Blue Stockings of the Northwestern League in 1883. A year later, the Blue Stockings joined the American Association, which was considered a Major

League. Until 1947, Moses and his brother Welday Wilberforce Walker were the only black players who played in the Major Leagues. Fleet Walker died in Cleveland, Ohio, on May 11, 1924, age 67. Welday Walker died in Steubenville, Ohio, on November 23, 1937, age 78.
• **Last black Minor League player before full integration:** outfielder Bill Galloway, who played 20 games for Woodstock of the Canadian League in 1899. Jackie Robinson played Minor League baseball for Montreal in 1946 on his way to the Majors.
• **Last Major League baseball team to be integrated after the color barrier ended:** Boston Red Sox. The Red Sox did not have their first African-American player until 1959, when they brought infielder Elijah ("Pumpsie") Green up from the Minors.
• **Last Negro League player to enter the Majors:** Isaac ("Ike") Brown. He ended his Negro League career with the Kansas City Monarchs as an All-Star shortstop in 1960. He was signed by the Detroit Tigers in 1961 but did not play his first game in the Major Leagues until June 17, 1969. Brown played his last game with the Tigers in 1974. He died in Memphis, Tennessee, on May 17, 2001, age 59.
• **Last former Negro League player in the Majors:** Saturnino Orestes Arrieta Armas ("Minnie") Minoso. Although his career waned in the early 1960s, the White Sox brought Minoso back in 1976 and again in 1980. In 1993, the White Sox activated Minnie for the last game of the season to allow him to play a sixth decade, but the Major League Players Association raised an objection, so he did not have a chance to play. On June 30, 1993, Minoso became the last Negro League player to play in a Minor League game when he pinch-hit for the Saint Paul Saints of the Northern Baseball League, against the Thunder Bay Whiskey Jacks. The 70-year-old Minoso faced 19-year-old pitcher Yoshi Seo.
• **Last regularly playing former Negro League player in the Major Leagues:** Henry Louis ("Hank") Aaron. He played for the Indianapolis Clowns of the Negro

Leagues in 1952, at the beginning of his career, and he finished his career with the Milwaukee Brewers in 1976.

• **Last Negro League All-Star Game:** 1963, in Kansas City. Satchel Paige was the Winning Pitcher and MVP for the winning West team. The Negro League All-Star Games matched the Eastern All-Stars versus the Western All-Stars.

• **Last surviving female Negro League player:** Mamie ("Peanut") Johnson, who joined the Indianapolis Clowns in 1953 and pitched for three years. She was one of three women who played professional baseball with the men of the Negro Leagues.

• **Last black team to play in a white league:** the Acme Colored Giants of Celoron, New York. They disbanded and left the Iron and Oil League in 1898.

• **Last surviving owner of a Negro Leagues baseball team:** William ("Sou") Bridgeforth, who purchased the Baltimore Elite Giants in the mid-1940s. He later owned the Birmingham Black Barons. Bridgeforth died in Nashville, Tennessee, on July 22, 2004, age 97.

• **Last surviving female Negro League owner:** Effa Manley, who became co-owner of the Brooklyn Eagles in 1935, after she married Abe Manley, with whom she co-founded the team. In 1936, they purchased the Newark Dodgers franchise and moved the Eagles to Newark. They owned the team until 1948. Effa Manley died on April 16, 1981, age 81.

• **Last Negro League team:** the Indianapolis Clowns. After the Negro Leagues folded, the Clowns and a few other teams continued as novelty barnstorming attractions. The Clowns were active into the 1970s.

Sports—Baseball—Players
Last Events for Some Major Players

Aaron, Hank Henry ("Hank") Aaron spent almost all of his career as a member of the Braves, first in Milwaukee. Wisconsin, and then in Atlanta, Georgia. In 1975, he returned to Milwaukee and played his last games as a Brewer. During his playing career, he appeared in a record 24 All-Star Games. • **Last home run:** his 755th, on July 20, 1976, against pitcher Dick Drago of the California Angels. • **Last Major League game:** October 3, 1976, against the Detroit Tigers as a Designated Hitter. Aaron singled off Dave Roberts in the sixth inning and was removed by Manager Alex Grammas for pinch-runner Jim Gantner.
Cobb, Ty Tyrus Raymond ("Ty") Cobb played his last games with the Philadelphia A's. He died in Atlanta, Georgia, on July 17, 1961, age 74. • **Last steal:** June 15, 1928, when Cobb stole home for the 50th time. • **Last hit:** September 3, 1928, while pinch-hitting for Joe Boley against Washington Senators pitcher Bump Hadley. • **Last Major League game:** September 11, 1928. While facing Yankees pitcher Henry Johnson, Cobb, pinch-hitting for Jimmy Dykes, popped out to shortstop Mark Koenig. • **Last surviving player who pitched to Cobb:** Melvin Leroy ("Mel") Harder of the Cleveland Indians, who pitched to Cobb in 1928, when Cobb was playing his last season with the Philadelphia A's. Harder died in Chardon, Ohio, on October 20, 2002, age 94.
Gehrig, Lou Henry Louis ("Lou") Gehrig played 2,130 games for the New York Yankees without missing an appearance. He set a record for career grand slams that still stands. Gehrig's tearful "luckiest man on the face of the earth" speech was given on the July 4, 1939, at Yankee Stadium. He died of amyotrophic lateral sclerosis (ALS) in New York, New York,

on June 2, 1942, shortly before his 38th birthday.

- **Last grand slam:** his 23rd; off Lee Ross of the Philadelphia A's on August 20, 1938.
- **Last home run:** September 23, 1938, his 493rd, off Dutch Leonard of the Washington Senators.
- **Last game:** April 30, 1939. Although Gehrig said farewell to his fans at the July 4, 1939 game, he had stopped playing on April 30th. A ticket stub from Gehrig's final game was sold at auction on eBay in 2000 for $2,969.
- **Last glove Gehrig used in a Major League game:** sold at the 1999 Sotheby's Halper baseball auction for $387,500.

Mantle, Mickey

Mickey Charles Mantle, one of the greatest switch hitters of all times, was voted Most Valuable Player three times: 1956, 1957 and 1962. He played with the New York Yankees 18 years and retired after the 1968 season. Mantle died in Dallas, Texas, on August 13, 1995, age 63.

- **Last home run:** his 536th, September 20, 1968.
- **Last Major League game:** September 28, 1968, his 2,401st game.
- **Last ball:** a ball used in that last game sold at auction in 1997 for $8,050.
- **Last bat:** The bat used in Mantle's last game sold at Sotheby's Halper auction in 1999 for $40,250.

Mays, Willie

New York (and San Francisco) Giants great Willie Howard Mays Jr. led the National League in home runs four times and had a career batting average of .302. He was traded to the New York Mets in 1972 and retired after the 1973 season, ending a 22-year playing career.

- **Last home run:** Mays's 660th; off Don Gullett of Cincinnati on August 17, 1973.
- **Last Major League hit:** October 14, 1973, in the 12-inning Game 2 of the World Series, a Mets 10-7 victory over the Oakland A's.

Paige, Satchel

The legendary Leroy Robert ("Satchel") Paige began his professional career in the 1920s playing in the Negro Leagues. After the color barrier was broken, Paige was signed by the Cleveland Indians. In 1952, while playing with the Saint Louis Browns, he was named an American League All-Star.

- **Last Major League game:** September 25, 1965. Paige was 59 when he played his last Major League game for the Kansas City A's against the Boston Red Sox. He started and allowed just one hit, a double to Carl Yaztrzemski in the first inning. Paige struck out one player and did not walk any in three scoreless innings.
- **Last hitter to face Paige:** Jim Gosger, who grounded out on September 25, 1965. Paige was replaced by Diego Segui and the Red Sox came back to win 5-2.
- **Last season:** 1968. When it was learned that Paige was just shy of the required time to obtain a $3,000 Major League pension, he was placed again on the Kansas City roster; however, the 62-year-old Paige did not play that year. He became a coach and remained with Atlanta for a year. Paige died in Kansas City, Missouri, on June 8, 1982, age around 75.

Ruth, Babe

George Herman ("Babe") Ruth began his playing career in 1914 with the Boston Red Sox. He played for the New York Yankees from 1919 to 1934. Ruth ended his career with the Boston Braves. He had a remarkable lifetime total of 714 home runs and 2,213 RBIs.

- **Last man to pinch-hit for Ruth**: Ben Paschal. New York Yankees Manager Miller Huggins had put Paschal up for Ruth on the opening day of the 1927 season, after Ruth had gone 0 for 3, striking out twice. Paschal delivered a single in the pinch-hit appearance.

- **Last time as pitcher:** October 1, 1933. Ruth pitched all nine innings of the Yankees' 1-0 victory over the Boston Red Sox. The losing pitcher was Bob Kline.
- **Last home game as a New York Yankee:** September 24, 1934, at Yankee Stadium. The Red Sox beat the Yankees 5-0.
- **Last road game as a New York Yankee:** September 30, 1934, in a 5-3 loss to the Washington Nationals. Ruth left the Yankees the following February when he realized he was not going to be named club manager.
- **Last home runs:** May 25, 1935, while playing for the Boston Braves. He hit three home runs that day, one off Red Lucas and the final two off Guy Bush. Ruth's last home run, his 714th, set a record that lasted 39 years; it was topped by Hank Aaron in 1974.
- **Last game as player:** May 30, 1935, Boston Braves against the Philadelphia Phillies at Baker Bowl in Philadelphia. Ruth injured his knee and played only the first inning of the opener of a doubleheader, The Phillies won 11-6. On June 2, 1935, Ruth announced his retirement. He closed his career with a .181 average for the season and never played again.
- **Last man to pitch to Ruth:** Jim Bivin in the first game of a doubleheader between the Braves and the Phillies on May 30, 1935. In the first inning, Ruth grounded out to Phillies first baseman Dolph Camilli and was replaced in the game by Hal Lee.
- **Last uniform worn by Ruth:** The uniform Ruth is said to have worn in his last game as a player on May 30, 1935, was sold at a Robert Edwards auction in 1997 for $56,025.
- **Last activity in professional baseball:** 1938, as a coach with the Brooklyn Dodgers. The white glove that Ruth used during that season as a coach was sold at a private auction in 1999 for $94,817.
- **Last appearance of Ruth at Yankee Stadium:** June 13, 1948, at a celebration of the 25th anniversary of Yankee Stadium, "the house that Ruth built." The appearance was captured in the Pulitzer Prize-winning photograph by *New York Herald* photographer Nathaniel Fein. The bat that Ruth used during his June 1948 farewell appearance at Yankee Stadium sold for $107,000 at Sotheby's auction of the Halper collection in 1999. A ticket stub from that game was sold on eBay for $1,539 in 2000.
- **Last public appearance by Ruth:** premiere of the movie *The Baby Ruth Story,* in New York, July 26, 1948. Ruth died in New York City less than a month later on August 16, 1948, age 53.
- **Last surviving player who witnessed Babe Ruth's last home runs:** Richard ("Gus") Suhr of the Pittsburgh Pirates, who played against Ruth on May 25, 1935, when Ruth hit his last home runs (Nos. 712, 713 and 714). Suhr died in Scottsdale, Arizona, on January 15, 2004, age 98.
- **Last surviving photographs from Ruth's last game:** were those taken by Philadelphia *Evening Bulletin* photographer Bruce Murray Sr. Ruth's last game was unplanned, and as such, it received little press coverage. Murray's photos are the only known pictures of Ruth's last game.
- **Last surviving Yankee teammate of Babe Ruth:** William Murray ("Billy") Werber, who played with Ruth in New York during the 1930 and 1933 seasons.
- **Last surviving Yankee teammate from Ruth's 1932 championnship season:** Charles Devens, who pitched for the Yankees from 1932 to 1934. He witnessed Ruth's famous called shot against the Cubs in the World Series. Devens died in Milton, Massachusetts, on Agust 13, 2003, age 93.
- **Last surviving Red Sox teammate of Babe Ruth:** James Edward ("Jimmy") Cooney, who played with Ruth in Boston during the 1917 season. Cooney died in Warwick, Rhode Island, on August 7, 1991, age 96.
- **Last surviving Braves teammate of Babe Ruth:** Ray Coleman Mueller, who played with Ruth in 1935. Mueller made his Braves debut two weeks before Ruth's last game. He

died in Lower Paxton Township, Pennsylvania, on June 29, 1994, age 82. Another player on the 1935 Braves team lived longer but did not make his debut until three months after Ruth's last game: Prosper Albert Bilangio—who played professionally under the name Al Blanche—played during part of the 1935 season. He died in Melrose, Massachusetts, on April 2, 1997, age 87.
• **Last copy of the movie** *Headin' Home*: sold at auction in 1999 for $39,704. Ruth had a number of acting and cameo appearances in films during his career. *Headin' Home* was a biography of Ruth made in 1920.

Williams, Ted

Theodore Samuel ("Ted") Williams gained a reputation as one of baseball's greatest hitters. He joined the Boston Red Sox in 1939 and was with them when he retired in 1960. In 1941, his third season, he batted .406.
• **Last Major League game as player:** September 26, 1960, against the Baltimore Orioles in Boston. In his last plate appearance, Williams hit a home run off Orioles pitcher Jack Fisher at Boston's Fenway park. The home-run sparked a late-inning rally that would lead to a Red Sox victory. Williams died in Crystal River, Florida, on July 5, 2002, age 83.

Sports—Baseball—Players—Delahanty Brothers

Five Delahanty Brothers played professional baseball: Ed, Frank, Jim, Joe and Tom.
• **Last surviving Delahanty brother:** Frank George ("Pudgie"), who played outfield for four different teams between 1905 and 1915. Frank Delahanty died in Cleveland, Ohio, on July 22, 1966, age 83.

Sports—Baseball—Players—19th Century

• **Last surviving 19th-century professional baseball player:** Ralph Miller, who appeared in 29 games during 1898 and 1899. He died in Cincinnati, Ohio, on May 8, 1973, age 100. Miller was the first player to reach the age of 100.

Sports—Baseball—Players—"Tinker to Evers to Chance"

The famed Chicago Cubs double-play combination Joe Tinker, Johnny Evers and Frank Chance were the subject of the poem "Baseball's Sad Lexicon," written in 1908 by New York sportswriter Franklin P. Adams.
• **Last survivor of the Tinker-to-Evers-to-Chance trio:** Joseph Bert ("Joe") Tinker, who died in Orlando, Florida, on July 27, 1948, age 68.
• **Last game Tinker, Evers and Chance played together:** April 12, 1912. Chance was replaced by Vic Saier.

Sports—Baseball—Rules—Bounce Home Run

• **Last player to be awarded a home run on a ball that bounced over the fence:** Al Lopez of the Brooklyn Dodgers on September 12, 1930. The ground rule double rule was introduced in 1931.

Sports—Baseball—Rules—Games

In the early days of baseball, the rule was that the winner was the first team that scored 21 runs.
• **Last year baseball games were not established at nine innings:** 1856.
• **Last year baseball was played without much regard for the rules:** 1856. Beginning in April 1857, the rules of the National Association of Base Ball Players governed the game.

Sports—Baseball—Rules—Pitching

• **Last year the distance from home plate to the pitcher's mound was less than 60 feet, 6 inches:** 1892, when it was 50 feet.

Sports—Baseball—Rules—Spitballs

The spitball—a ball to which a pitcher has applied a foreign substance to better control its motion—is now illegal in baseball.
• **Last time the spitball was legal:** 1920. When it was outlawed that year, those al-

ready throwing it were permitted to continue using it.

• **Last players allowed to use spitball:** At the time of the ruling in 1920 that outlawed the spitball, 17 men were deemed to be legalized spitballers: Doc Ayers, Ray Caldwell, Stan Coveleski, Bill Doak, Phil Douglas, Red Faber, Dana Fillingim, Ray Fisher, Marv Goodwin, Burleigh Grimes, Dutch Leonard, Jack Quinn, Clarence

Mitchell, Dick Rudolph, Allan Russell, Urban Shocker and Allen Sothoron.

• **Baseball's last legal spitball:** thrown on September 20, 1934, by Hall of Famer Burleigh Grimes of the New York Yankees. He pitched one inning, striking out Joe Stripp, the last batter he ever faced. Grimes ended his career as the last of the legalized spitballers. The spitball has been used since then, but not legally.

Sports—Baseball—Records—Streaks
Last Games of Some Winning and Losing Streaks

Consecutive Complete Games—Pitcher

The Major League record for most consecutive complete games pitched was set by John W. ("Jack") Taylor of the Saint Louis Cardinals. He pitched 187 complete games in a row, not counting 15 additional relief appearances.

• **Last full game of Taylor's streak:** August 9, 1906. The streak had begun on June 13, 1901, and ended with an incomplete game on August 13, 1906.

Consecutive Games Played

The Major League record for most consecutive games played was set by Cal Ripken Jr.

• **Last game of Ripken's consecutive game streak:** September 19, 1998, his 2,632nd game. Ripken's streak eclipsed what was thought to be an unbeatable record set of 2,130 games by Lou Gehrig.

Consecutive Games with a Hit

Joe DiMaggio set the Major League record for most consecutive games won.

• **Last game of DiMaggio's 56-game hitting streak:** July 16, 1941. He went 3 for 4 that day against the Cleveland Indians. DiMaggio went hitless on July 17, 1941 against Al Smith and Jim Bagby of the Cleveland Indians.

Consecutive Games Won by a Team

The Major League record for the most consecutive victories by a team is 26 (+ 1 tie) held by the New York Giants in 1916.

• **Last game of the Giants winning streak:** September 30, 1916. The Giants won the first game of a doubleheader against the Braves, 4-0. Boston broke the streak in the second game with an 8-3 win.

Consecutive Games Lost by a Team

The Major League record for the most consecutive losses by a team is 23 by the Philadelphia Phillies in 1961.

• **Last game of the Phillies losing streak:** August 20, 1961. They lost the first game of a double header to the Milwaukee Braves 5-2, but broke the streak by winning the second game, 7-4.

Consecutive Games Won by a Pitcher

The Major League record for most consecutive games won by a pitcher is by Carl Hubbell.

• **Last game of Hubbell's winning streak:** May 27, 1937. On May 31, 1937, Hubbell lost to the Brooklyn Dodgers, ending his winning streak of 24 consecutive victories that began in July 1936 and stretched over two seasons.

Consecutive Games Lost by a Pitcher

The Major League record for most consecutive games lost by a pitcher was set by Anthony

---

Young of the New York Mets.
• **Last game of Young's losing streak:** June 24, 1993. Young's losing streak of 27 consecutive losses by a pitcher began on May 6, 1992.

Consecutive Scoreless Innings
Orel Hershiser set a Major League record for most consecutive scoreless innings.
• **Last game of Hershiser's consecutive scoreless innings streak:** September 28, 1988, when he pitched 10 scoreless innings, boosting his total to 59 consecutive innings for the Los Angeles Dodgers in a game the San Diego Padres eventually won 2-1 in 16 innings. Hershiser continued for eight more innings in the League Championship series, but that was post-season play.

Sports—Baseball—Defunct or Relocated Teams
Last Games, Use of Names and Players
and Other Events of Former Teams

Baltimore Orioles (I)
In 1903, the original Baltimore Orioles moved to New York and became the New York Highlanders (later known as the Yankees).
• **Last game as the Baltimore Orioles (I):** September 29, 1902, losing to the Boston Americans in Baltimore, 9-5.
• **Last Baltimore Orioles (I) manager:** Wilbert Robinson.
• **Last former Baltimore Orioles (I) player to retire from the Majors:** Roger Bresnahan.
• **Last surviving Baltimore Orioles (I) player:** Andrew ("Andy") Paul Oyler, who joined the team in 1902. Oyler died in East Pennsboro Township, Pennsylvania, on October 24, 1970, age 90.

Boston Braves
Known as the Braves twice in the franchise's history: 1912-35 and 1941-52. When the franchise began in 1876, the team was known as the Boston Red Caps.
• **Last known as the Boston Red Caps:** 1882.
• **Last known as the Boston Beaneaters:** 1906.
• **Last known as the Boston Doves:** 1910.
• **Last known as the Boston Rustlers:** 1911.
• **Last known as the Boston Bees:** 1940.
• **Last game as the Boston Braves:** September 28, 1952, against the Brooklyn Dodgers in Brooklyn. The 12-inning game was called due to darkness with the score tied 5-5. In 1953, the Braves moved to Milwaukee.
• **Last Boston Braves manager:** Charlie Grimm.
• **Last Boston Braves player to hit a home run:** Eddie Matthews on September 27, 1952.
• **Last former Boston Braves player to retire from the Majors:** Eddie Matthews.

Brooklyn Dodgers
Known as the Dodgers twice in the franchise's history: 1911-13 and 1932-57.
• **Last known as the Brooklyn Atlantics:** 1884.
• **Last known as the Brooklyn Grays:** 1887.
• **Last known as the Brooklyn Bridegrooms:** 1898. Known as the Brooklyn Grooms from

1891 to 1895.
- **Last known as the Brooklyn Infants:** 1910.
- **Last known as the Brooklyn Superbas:** 1926, known as Superbas twice in franchise history: 1899-1910 and 1913.
- **Last known as the Brooklyn Robins:** 1931.
- **Last game as the Brooklyn Dodgers:** September 29, 1957, losing to the Philadelphia Phillies in Philadelphia. In 1958, the Dodgers moved to Los Angeles.
- **Last game winning/losing pitchers:** winning pitcher: Seth Morehead; losing pitcher: Roger Craig.
- **Last Brooklyn Dodgers manager:** Walter Alston, who managed the Dodgers beginning in 1955 and continued after the team moved to Los Angeles, until he retired in 1976.
- **Last Brooklyn Dodgers player to hit a home run:** Randy ("Handsome Ransom") Jackson on September 28, 1957.
- **Last former Brooklyn Dodgers player to retire from the Majors:** Bob Aspromonte.

Kansas City Athletics (A's)
- **Last game as the Kansas City A's:** October 1, 1967, losing to the New York Yankees in New York, 4-3. In 1968, the A's moved to Oakland, California.
- **Last game winning/losing pitchers:** winning pitcher: Mel Stottlemyre; losing pitcher: Jim ("Catfish") Hunter.
- **Last Kansas City A's manager:** Luke Appling, who finished the 1967 season after Alvin Dark was fired.
- **Last Kansas City A's player to hit a home run:** Dave Duncan on October 1, 1967.
- **Last former Kansas City A's player to retire from the Majors:** Reggie Jackson.

Milwaukee Braves
- **Last game as the Milwaukee Braves:** October 3, 1965, losing to the Los Angeles Dodgers in Los Angeles, 3-0. In 1966, the Milwaukee Braves moved to Atlanta.
- **Last game winning/losing pitchers:** winning pitcher: Bob Miller; losing pitcher: Bob Sadowski.
- **Last Milwaukee Braves manager:** Bobby Bragan.
- **Last Milwaukee Braves player to hit a home run:** Gene Oliver on October 2, 1965.
- **Last former Milwaukee Braves player to retire from the Majors:** Phil Niekro.

New York Giants
- **Last known as the New York Gothams:** 1884.
- **Last game as the New York Giants:** September 29, 1957, losing to the Pittsburgh Pirates at the Polo Grounds in New York, 9-1. In 1958, the New York Giants moved to San Francisco.
- **Last game winning/losing pitchers:** winning pitcher: Bob Friend; losing pitcher: Johnny Antonelli.
- **Last New York Giants manager:** Bill Rigney.
- **Last New York Giants player to hit a home run:** Gail Harris, who hit a pair of home runs in the second game of a double-header on September 21, 1957.
- **Last former New York Giants player to retire from the Majors:** Willie Mays.

Philadelphia Athletics (A's)
- **Last game as the Philadelphia A's:** September 26, 1954, beating the New York Yankees in New York, 8-6. In 1955, the Philadelphia A's moved to Kansas City.
- **Last game winning/losing pitchers:** winning pitcher: Art Ditmar (his first major league victory); losing pitcher: Tommy Byrne.
- **Last Philadelphia A's manager:** Eddie Joost during the 1954 season. Cornelius Alexander McGillicuddy ("Connie Mack") retired in 1953 after managing the team for 50 years.

He died in Philadelphia, Pennsylvania, on February 8, 1956, age 93.
- **Last Philadelphia A's player to hit a home run:** Lou Limmer on September 25, 1954. It was his last home run in the Majors.
- **Last former Philadelphia A's player to retire from the Majors:** Vic Power.

Saint Louis Browns
- **Last game as the Saint Louis Browns:** September 27, 1953, losing to the White Sox in Saint Louis in 11 innings, 2-1. The Browns owner Bill Veeck sold the team to a group of Baltimore investors on October 29, 1953, and in 1954 the Browns moved to Baltimore and were renamed the Orioles.
- **Last game winning/losing pitchers:** winning pitcher: Billy Pierce; losing pitcher: Duane Pillette.
- **Last Saint Louis Browns manager:** Marty Marion.
- **Last Saint Louis Browns player to hit a home run:** Billy Hunter, September 26, 1953.
- **Last Saint Louis Browns player to play in an All-Star game:** Satchel Paige, who pitched the eighth inning of the 1953 All-Star game in Cincinnati.
- **Last former Browns player to retire from the Majors:** Don Larsen.

Seattle Pilots
- **Last game as the Seattle Pilots:** October 2, 1969, losing to the Oakland A's in Seattle, 3-1. In 1970, the Seattle Pilots moved to Milwaukee and became the Brewers.
- **Last game winning/losing pitchers:** winning pitcher: Jim Roland; losing pitcher: Steve Barber.
- **Last Seattle Pilots manager:** Dave Bristol.
- **Last Seattle Pilots player to hit a home run:** Steve Whitaker on September 27, 1969.
- **Last former Pilots player to retire from the Majors:** Fred Stanley.

Washington Senators (I)
- **Last game as the Washington Senators (I):** October 2, 1960, losing to the Baltimore Orioles, 2-1. In 1961, the Senators moved to Minnesota and became the Twins.
- **Last game winning/losing pitchers:** winning pitcher: Milt Pappas; losing pitcher: Pedro Ramos.
- **Last original Washington Senators manager:** Cookie Lavagetto.
- **Last original Washington Senators player to hit a home run:** Bobby Allison on September 28, 1960.
- **Last former original Washington Senators player to retire from the Majors:** Jim Kaat.

Washington Senators (II)
- **Last game as the Washington Senators (II):** September 30, 1971, losing to the New York Yankees by forfeiture, 9-0, after fans rushed the field during the game. In 1972, the Senators moved to Texas and were renamed the Rangers.
- **Last game winning/losing pitchers:** None. The last game was forfeited because of fans rushing the field. A victory was assigned to New York, but no winning or losing pitchers were designated.
- **Last Washington Senators (II) manager:** Ted Williams.
- **Last Washington Senators (II) player to hit a home run:** Frank Howard on September 30, 1971. The home run did not count in the game results due to the forfeiture; however, rules provide for it to count for player statistics.
- **Last former Washington Senators (II) player to retire from the Majors:** Toby Harrah.

Sports—Baseball—Current Teams
Last Games, Use of Names and Players and Other Events of Current Teams

Anaheim Angels • **Last known as the Los Angeles Angels:** 1964. • **Last known as the California Angels:** 1996.
Atlanta Braves (*See above*: Boston Braves and Milwaukee Braves.)
Baltimore Orioles (*See above*: Saint Louis Browns.)
Boston Red Sox • **Last known as the Boston Americans:** 1907.
Chicago Cubs • **Last known as the Chicago White Stockings:** 1889. • **Last known as the Chicago Colts:** 1897. • **Last known as the Chicago Orphans:** 1902.
Chicago White Sox **1919 Chicago White Sox ("The Black Sox")** In 1920, eight Chicago White Sox players were accused of fixing the 1919 World Series, allowing the Cincinnati Reds to win. • **Last day the banned 1919 White Sox were eligible to play professional baseball:** September 28, 1920. The eight were indicted that day and immediately suspended by Chicago White Sox owner Charles Comiskey. Although they were eventually acquitted, they were banned from baseball for life. After the indictment, the 1919 team became known as the Black Sox. • **Last surviving member of the 1919 "Black Sox" group:** Charles August ("Swede") Risberg. He played shortstop in the 1919 World Series. Following his ban from baseball, Risberg continued to play in outlaw leagues and semiprofessional teams. He later worked on a Minnesota dairy farm. He died in Red Bluff, California, on October 13, 1975, age 81.
Cincinnati Reds The team has been known as the Cincinnati Reds four times in their history: 1876-80; 1890-1943; 1945-53 and 1960-present. • **Last known as the Cincinnati Red Stockings:** 1889. • **Last known as the Cincinnati Redlegs:** 1959.
Cleveland Indians • **Last known as the Cleveland Blues or Bluebirds:** 1901. • **Last known as the Cleveland Bronchos:** 1902. • **Last known as the Cleveland Naps:** 1914. • **Last surviving member of the Cleveland Naps:** William Adolph ("Bill") Wambsganss, who joined the Naps in 1914, the last season before they became known as the Indians. He died in Lakewood, Ohio, on December 8, 1985, age 91.
Houston Astros • **Last known as Houston Colt 45s:** 1964.
Milwaukee Brewers (*See above*: Seattle Pilots I.)
Minnesota Twins (*See above*: Washington Senators I.)
New York Yankees • **Last known as the New York Highlanders:** 1912. • **Last surviving member of the New York Highlanders:** Chester ("Chet") Cornelius Hoff, who joined the Highlanders in 1911. Hoff died in Daytona, Florida, September 17, 1998, age 107. • **Last surviving team member of the 1927 New York Yankees (a.k.a. "Murderers' Row"):** Mark Anthony Koenig, who played second base for the team that also included Babe Ruth and Lou Gehrig. Koenig died in Willows, California, on April 22, 1993, age 88.

Many baseball scholars consider the '27 New York Yankees the best team in baseball history. (*See above*: Baltimore Orioles I.)
Oakland Athletics (A's) (*See above*: Philadelphia Athletics (A's) and Kansas City Athletics (A's.)
Philadelphia Phillies   The team has been known as the Phillies twice in the franchise's history:1890-1943; 1946-present.   • **Last known as the Philadelphia Quakers:** 1889.   • **Last known as the Philadelphia Blue Jays:** 1945.
Pittsburgh Pirates   • **Last known as the Pittsburgh Alleghenies:** 1889.   • **Last known as the Pittsburgh Innocents:** 1890.
Saint Louis Cardinals   • **Last known as the Brown Stockings:** 1877.   • **Last known as the Saint Louis Browns (I):** 1882 (a later team also used this name).   • **Last known as the Saint Louis Brown Stockings:** 1898.   • **Last known as the Saint Louis Perfectos:** 1899.   • **Last surviving team member of the 1934 Saint Louis Cardinals (a.k.a. "The Gashouse Gang"):** Clifford Rankin ("Pat") Crawford. The team also included Dizzy Dean and Ducky Medford. Crawford died in Morehead City, North Carolina, on January 25, 1994, age 91.
San Francisco Giants (*See above*: New York Giants.)
Texas Rangers (*See above*: Washington Senators II.)

Sports—Baseball—Teams—All-White
• **Last all-white team to win the World Series:** 1950 New York Yankees.
• **Last all-white National League team to win the Pennant:** the 1950 Philadelphia Phillies, a.k.a. "the Whiz Kids."

Sports—Baseball—Teams—1934 Touring All-Stars
• **Last surviving member of the 1934 All-Star Team that toured Japan:** Joseph Thomas Cascarella, who played for the Philadelphia A's in the 1934 season. That year, he traveled to Japan with the noted touring American All-Star team that included Babe Ruth, Lou Gehrig and Jimmy Foxx among others. Cascarella died in Baltimore, Maryland, on May 22, 2002, age 94.

Sports—Baseball—Women—All-American Girls Professional Baseball League (AAGPBL)
The All-American Girls Professional Baseball League (AAGPBL) was an all-women's professional baseball league that began in 1943. It was an alternative to men's Major League baseball, which had been affected by

the large number of players who had gone into the service during World War II. The league was the subject of the 1992 movie *A League of Their Own*.
• **Last AAGPBL batting champion:** Joanne Weaver of the Fort Wayne Daisies. She posted a batting average of .429 in 1954, the final season for the league.
• **Last AAGPBL "Player of the Year":** Joanne Weaver of the Fort Wayne Daisies.
• **Last AAGPBL pitching leader:** Jan Rumsey of the South Bend Blue Sox.

Sports—Baseball—World Series
The first World Series in 1903 and the series from 1919 to 1921 were best of nine.
• **Last Best-of-Nine World Series:** 1921.
• **Last surviving participant of the first baseball World Series (1903):** Frederick ("Freddy") Alfred Parent, who was shortstop for the winning team (Boston). Parent died in Biddeford, Maine, on November 2, 1972, age 96.
• **Last surviving participant of the 1919 ("Black Sox") World Series:** Edd J. Roush, who played for the Cincinnati Reds against

Notable Last Facts

the Chicago White Sox. Roush was later inducted into the Baseball Hall of Fame. He died in Bradenton, Florida, on March 21, 1988, age 94.

Sports—Basketball—Arenas and Stadiums
Last of Some Major American Basketball Arenas and Stadiums

Atlanta, Georgia

The Atlantic Hawks began playing at Alexander Memorial Coliseum (Georgia Institute of Technology campus) in 1968 and continued until 1972. That year, they moved to the Omni. From 1997 to 1999, the Hawks split their games between the Alexander Memorial Coliseum and the Georgia Dome.
- **Last Atlanta Hawks game at Alexander Memorial Coliseum (Georgia Institute of Technology campus):** 1999.
- **Last Atlanta Hawks game at the Omni:** April 19, 1997; a post-season semi-final playoff game against the Chicago Bulls.
- **Last of the Omni:** demolished by implosion on July 26, 1997.
- **Last Atlanta Hawks game at the Georgia Dome:** 1999. Since 1999, the Atlanta Hawks have played at Philips Arena.

Baltimore, Maryland

The Bullets began playing at the Civic Center in 1963.
- **Last Baltimore Bullets game at the Civic Center:** 1973. That year, they moved to Landover, Maryland, and were renamed the Washington Bullets.
- **Last known as the Civic Center:** 1986, when it was renamed Baltimore Arena.
- **Last known as the Baltimore Arena:** 2003, when it was renamed 1st Mariner Arena.

Boston, Massachusetts

The Boston Celtics began playing at the Boston Garden in 1946. The Celtics logo was placed on center court in 1973.
- **Last Boston Celtics game at the Boston Garden:** May 5, 1995, a post-season playoff game against the Orlando Magic. The Celtics were eliminated from the playoffs with a 95-92 loss.
- **Last of the Boston Garden:** demolished in November 1997. The parquet floor was installed in the Boston Arena in 1946 then moved to the Boston Garden in 1952, and moved again to the Fleet Center in Boston in 1995. It was replaced in 2000. The last game played on the floor was on December 22, 1999. The 20-foot-by-20-foot section of the floor that featured the Celtics logo was auctioned off by Sotheby's in 2000 for $331,100.

Chicago, Illinois

The Chicago Bulls began playing at the Chicago Stadium in 1928.
- **Last Chicago Bulls game at the Chicago Stadium:** 1994.
- **Last of the Chicago Stadium:** demolished in 1994 and replaced by the United Center.

Cincinnati, Ohio

The Cincinnati Royals began playing at the Cincinnati Gardens in 1958.
- **Last Cincinnati Royals game at the Cincinnati Gardens:** 1972. That year, they moved to Kansas City and were renamed the Kings.

Cleveland, Ohio

The Cleveland Cavaliers began playing at the Cleveland Arena in 1970.
- **Last Cleveland Cavaliers game at the Cleveland Arena:** 1974. They moved to the Richfield Coliseum for the 1974-75 season.
- **Last of the Cleveland Arena:** demolished in April 1977. Today, the Red Cross area headquarters occupies the site.

• **Last Cleveland Cavaliers game at the Richfield Coliseum:** 1994. The Cleveland Cavaliers moved to the newly built Gund Arena.
Detroit, Michigan The Detroit Pistons began playing at the Olympia Stadium in 1957. • **Last Detroit Pistons game at the Olympia Stadium:** 1961. That year, the team moved to the Cobo Arena. • **Last of the Olympia Stadium:** closed in December 1979; demolished in September 1986. • **Last Detroit Pistons game at the Cobo Arena:** 1978. The Pistons moved to the Silverdome in Pontiac, Michigan. • **Last Detroit Pistons game at the Silverdome:** 1988. That year, they moved to the Palace in Auburn Hill, Michigan.
East Rutherford, New Jersey The New Jersey Nets moved from the Rutgers Athletic Center in Piscataway, New Jersey, to the Brendan Byrne Arena in East Rutherford, New Jersey, in 1981. • **Last known as Brendan Byrne Arena:** January 1996, when it was renamed Continental Airlines Arena.
Indianapolis, Indiana The Indiana Pacers began playing at Market Square Arena in 1974. • **Last Indiana Pacers game at Market Square Arena:** 1999. Since that year, they have played at the Conseco Field House. • **Last of the Market Square Arena:** demolished by implosion on July 8, 2001.
Landover, Maryland The Washington Bullets began playing at USAir Arena (a.k.a. US Airways Arena) in 1973. • **Last Washington Bullets game at USAir Arena:** 1997, when they moved to MCI Center in Washington, D.C. and were renamed the Washington Wizards.
Miami, Florida The Miami Heat began playing at the Miami Arena in 1988. • **Last Miami Heat game at Miami Arena:** 1999. Since January 1, 2000, the team has played at the American Airlines Arena.
Milwaukee, Wisconsin The Milwaukee Bucks began playing at The Mecca in 1968. • **Last Milwaukee Bucks game at The Mecca:** 1988. Since that year, they have played at the Bradley Center. • **Last known as The Mecca:** 1998, when it was renamed Wisconsin Center.
Milwaukee, Wisconsin The Milwaukee Hawks began playing the Milwaukee Arena in 1951. • **Last Milwaukee Hawks game at the Milwaukee Arena:** March 14, 1955. That year, they moved to Saint Louis, Missouri.
New York, New York The New York Nets began playing at the Nassau Veterans Memorial Coliseum in 1971. • **Last New York Nets game at the Nassau Veterans Memorial Coliseum:** 1977. They moved to New Jersey, playing first in Piscataway, after they went from the ABA to the NBA.
Philadelphia, Pennsylvania The Philadelphia 76ers began playing at Convention Hall in 1963. • **Last Philadelphia 76ers game at Convention Hall:** 1967. The 76ers then moved to the newly built Spectrum. • **Last Philadelphia 76ers game at the Spectrum:** 1996. The 76ers moved to the nearby newly constructed First Union Center. • **Last known as First Union Center:** 2003, when it was renamed Wachovia Center.

Piscataway, New Jersey
The New Jersey Nets began playing at the Rutgers Athletic Center (Rutgers University campus) in 1977.
• **Last New Jersey Nets game at the Rutgers Athletic Center:** 1981. That year, the team moved to the Brendan Byrne Arena in East Rutherford, New Jersey.
• **Last known as the Rutgers Athletic Center:** 1985, when it was renamed the Louis Brown Athletic Center.
Saint Louis, Missouri
The Saint Louis Hawks began playing at the Kiel Auditorium in 1955.
• **Last Saint Louis Hawks game at the Kiel Auditorium:** 1968. that year, the team moved to Atlanta, Georgia.
Syracuse, New York
The Syracuse Nationals began playing at the New York State Fair Coliseum in 1949.
• **Last Syracuse Nationals game at the New York State Fair Coliseum:** 1951. That year, the team moved to the Onondaga War Memorial Coliseum.
• **Last Syracuse Nationals game at the Onondaga War Memorial Coliseum:** 1963. That year, the Nationals moved to Philadelphia and were renamed the Philadelphia 76ers.
Toronto, Canada
The Raptors began playing at the SkyDome in 1995.
• **Last Toronto Raptors game at the SkyDome:** February 19, 1999. Since that year, the team has played at the Air Canada Centre.

Sports—Basketball—Exhibition—Harlem Globetrotters

The Harlem Globetrotters have compiled some phenomenal streaks over the years.

• **End of the Harlem Globetrotters' 2,495-game winning streak:** January 5, 1971, in Martin, Tennessee, when Red Klotz of the New Jersey Reds hit a shot with seconds to play to beat the Harlem Globetrotters 100-99.

• **End of the Harlem Globetrotters' 24-year, 8,829-game winning streak:** September 12, 1995, in Vienna, Austria, when they lost 91-85 to the Legendary All-Stars, a team led by former NBA great Kareem Abdul-Jabbar. The Globetrotters had beaten the All-Stars in two previous appearances.

• **Last surviving original member of the Harlem Globetrotters:** Albert ("Runt") Pullins, who traveled with the Globetrotters from the time of their founding in 1929 to 1934, when he founded the Harlem Clowns. He died in Chicago, Illinois, on October 21, 1985, age 74.

Sports—Basketball—First Team

The first basketball team was formed by James Naismith, who invented the game in his gym class at the International YMCA Training School in Springfield, Massachusetts, in 1891. Naismith died in Lawrence, Kansas, on November 28, 1939, age 79.

• **Last surviving member of Naismith's original team of basketball players:** Raymond Pimlott Kaighn, who died in July 1962, age 92.

Sports—Basketball—Intercollegiate—Rules

• **Last time teams had a designated foul shooter:** 1922-23 season. Beginning the next season, a fouled player was required to take his own foul shots.

• **Last time a jump ball followed every score in NCAA play:** 1936.

• **Last time it was illegal to shoot off the dribble:** the 1914-15 season. The rule was changed for the 1915-16 season.

Sports—Basketball—Intercollegiate—Streaks

The UCLA Bruins set a record for the longest winning streak in college basketball history.

• **End of the UCLA 88-game Bruins win-**

ning streak: January 19, 1974, when the Bruins lost 71-70 to the Fighting Irish of Notre Dame. The Bruins were up by 11 with less than four minutes left to play, but the Irish took the lead with 29 seconds on the clock on Dwight Clay's jump shot from the corner.

Sports—Basketball—Professional—Leagues—American Basketball Association (ABA)

The American Basketball Association was created in 1967. It lasted nine seasons.

• **Last ABA game:** May 13, 1976, the final game of the ABA championship, when the New York Nets beat the Denver Nuggets 112-106, winning the series 4-2. The next month, four former ABA teams—San Antonio, Denver, New York and Indiana—were admitted into the National Basketball Association.

Sports—Basketball—Professional—Streaks

The Los Angeles Lakers set a record for the longest winning streak in major professional sports history with 33 games.

• **Last game of the Los Angeles Lakers winning streak:** January 7, 1972, when the Lakers beat the Atlanta Hawks 134-90. The streak ended on January 10, 1972, when the Lakers lost to the Milwaukee Bucks, 120-104. It was the Lakers' first loss since October 31, 1971. Milwaukee player Kareem Abdul-Jabbar, who would later become a Laker great, sealed the Milwaukee victory by scoring 39 of the points.

Sports—Basketball, Professional—Teams, All White

• **Last all-white team to win the NBA championship:** 1957-58 Saint Louis Hawks. They later became the Atlanta Hawks.

Sports—Basketball—Professional—Players
Last Events for Some Major Players

Abdul-Jabbar, Kareem   Kareem Abdul-Jabbar began his career as Ferdinand Lewis ("Lew") Alcindor Jr.   • **Last used name Lew Alcindor Jr.:** 1971. He legally changed his name to Kareem Abdul-Jabbar that year.   • **Last game as a Laker:** April 23, 1989. The Lakers beat Seattle 121-117.
Chamberlain, Wilt   Wilton Norman ("Wilt the Stilt") Chamberlain retired from the NBA on March 28, 1972.   • **Last team as a player:** Los Angeles Lakers. He joined the San Diego Conquistadors as coach for the 1973-74 season. Chamberlain died in Los Angeles, California, on October 12, 1999, age 63.
Cousy, Bob   Bob Cousy retired in 1963 after 13 seasons in the NBA.   • **Last game as a Boston Celtic:** April 24, 1963, age 34. In that final game, Cousy scored 18 points, leading the Boston Celtics over the Los Angeles Lakers for their sixth World Championship. Technically, it was not Cousy's last game. He made a brief comeback as a player-coach, during the 1969-70 season, but played only seven games.
Erving, Julius   Julius Winfield Erving ("Dr. J.") played with the Philadelphia 76ers from 1976 to 1987.   • **Last game as a Philadelphia 76er:** May 3, 1987, in the deciding playoff game against the Milwaukee Bucks in Milwaukee, Wisconsin. The Bucks beat the Philadelphia 76ers in Game 5 of a best-of-five series to advance to the Eastern Conference semifinals.
Johnson, Earvin, Jr.   Earvin Johnson Jr. ("Magic") retired from basketball on November 7, 1991, after announcing that he had tested positive for HIV. He did go on to play in the 1992 All-Star game and in the 1992 Olympics as part of the United States team. He coached the Lakers

for part of the 1993-94 season.
- **Last playing season:** 1995-96. Johnson made a brief comeback, playing part of the 1995-96 season before announcing his retirement for the last time, on May 14, 1996.

Sports—Basketball—Professional—Defunct Teams
Last Season of Some Defunct Teams

Basketball Association of America (BAA), National Basketball League (NBL), American Basketball Association (ABA) and National Basketball Association (NBA)

The basketball leagues are so intertwined that a separate list would be cumbersome. The Basketball Association of America (BAA) was formed in 1946-47. The National Basketball Association (NBA) came out of a merger between the BAA and the National Basketball League (NBL) in 1949. The American Basketball Association (ABA) was established in 1967. The following list represents NBA teams that have moved or no longer exist. Also listed are BAA teams and NBL teams that never made the final transition to the NBA but existed at the time of the merger of the leagues. These teams are listed only with their last name and location; all of their earlier incarnations have been excluded. The same hold true for ABA teams that did not merge into the ABA during the merger of those leagues in 1976. "Last Season" represents each team's final season in that city and the team's name in the BAA, NBL, ABA or NBA, wherever it ended up last. If the team left the NBA for another league such as the National Professional Basketball League (NPBL), that information is not given.

Team	Last Season	Details of Last Season
Anaheim Amigos	1967-68	ABA team moved to Los Angeles, California, in 1968 and was renamed the Stars.
Anderson Packers	1949-50	Team was with the NBL before playing one season in the NBA. Played in the NPBL in 1950-1951.
Baltimore Bullets (I)	1954-55	Team formerly with the BAA. It played six seasons in the NBA before folding.
Baltimore Bullets (II)	1972-73	NBA team moved to Landover, Maryland, in 1973 and became the Capitol Bullets. In 1974, the team was renamed the Washington Bullets.
Baltimore Claws	1975	ABA team moved from Memphis, Tennessee, in 1975 and was renamed the Claws.
Buffalo Braves	1977-78	Team moved to San Diego, California, in 1978 and became the Clippers.
Carolina Cougars	1973-74	ABA team moved to Saint Louis. Missouri, in 1974 and was renamed the Saint Louis Spirits.
Chicago Packers/ Zephyrs	1962-63	Team was originally the Packers but was renamed the Zephyrs in 1962. In 1963, the Chicago Zephyrs moved to Baltimore, Maryland, and became the second incarnation of the Baltimore Bullets.
Chicago Stags/Bruins	1949-50	Team formerly with BAA. It played one season in the NBA. It changed its name from the Stags to the Bruins during 1950.
Cincinnati Royals	1971-72	Team moved from Rochester. Later moved farther west, dividing home games between Kansas City, Missouri, and Omaha, Nebraska, and was renamed the Kings in 1972.

Cleveland Rebels	1946-47	Team played one season in the precursor BAA.
Dallas/Texas Chaparrals	1972-73	ABA team moved from Houston, Texas. In 1973, the team moved to San Antonio and became the Spurs, which joined the NBA in 1976. The team was known as the Texas Chaparrals during the 1970-71 season.
Denver Nuggets (I)	1949-50	Team played one season in the NBA. A later Denver Nuggets team in the ABA merged into the NBA in 1976.
Denver Rockets	1973-74	ABA team renamed the Denver Nuggets in 1974. The team moved to the NBA in 1976.
Detroit Falcons	1946-47	Team started out in Indianapolis, Indiana, in 1946 and played only one season in the precursor BAA.
Fort Wayne Pistons	1956-57	Team was formerly with the BAA. It played eight seasons in the NBA before moving to Detroit in 1957.
Houston Mavericks	1968-69	ABA team moved to North Carolina in 1969 and renamed the Carolina Cougars.
Indianapolis Jets	1948-49	Team came from the NBL and played one season in the NBA before folding.
Indianapolis Olympians	1952-53	Team played four seasons in the NBA before folding.
Kansas City-Omaha Kings	1984-85	Team was the Cincinnati Royals before moving to the Midwest and dividing home games between Kansas City, Missouri, and Omaha, Nebraska. It was renamed the Omaha Kings in 1972. In 1975, the team settled in Kansas City. It moved to Sacramento, California, in 1985.
Kentucky Colonels	1975-76	ABA team folded with the league in 1976.
Los Angeles Stars	1969-70	ABA team moved to Salt Lake City, Utah, in 1970.
Memphis Pros/ Tams/Sounds	1974-75	ABA team moved from New Orleans, Louisiana, and was renamed the Tams in 1972 and the Sounds in 1974. Team moved to Baltimore, Maryland, in 1975 and was renamed the Baltimore Claws.
Miami Floridians	1971-72	ABA team moved from Minnesota. The team was known simply as the Floridians from 1970 to 1972.
Milwaukee Hawks	1954-55	Team was the Tri-Cities Blackhawks before moving to Milwaukee, Wisconsin, and becoming the Milwaukee Hawks. It moved to Saint Louis, Missouri, in 1955.
Minneapolis Lakers	1959-60	Team came from the BAA and played 11 seasons in the NBA before moving to Los Angeles, California, in 1960.
Minnesota Muskies	1967-68	ABA team moved to Miami in 1968 and was renamed the Floridians.
Minnesota Pipers	1968-69	ABA team moved from Pittsburgh, Pennsylvania, to Minnesota in 1968. In 1969, team moved back to Pittsburgh.
New Jersey Americans	1967-68	ABA team moved to New York in 1968 and changed name to the Nets. The Nets joined the NBA in 1976.
New Orleans Buccaneers	1969-70	ABA team moved to Memphis in 1970 and was renamed the Pros.

New Orleans Jazz	1978-79	Team moved to Salt Lake City, Utah, in 1979 and became the Utah Jazz.
New York Nets	1976-77	Team had been an ABA team that merged into the NBA in 1976. The team moved from Uniondale, New York, to Piscataway, New Jersey, in 1977 and became the New Jersey Nets. Later moved to East Rutherford, New Jersey.
Oakland Oaks	1968-69	ABA team moved to Washington in 1969 and was renamed the Caps.
Philadelphia Warriors	1961-62	Team came from the BAA and played 13 seasons in the NBA before moving to San Francisco, California, in 1962 to become the San Francisco Warriors.
Pittsburgh Ironmen	1946-47	Team played only one season in the earlier BAA.
Pittsburgh Pipers/ Condors	1971-72	ABA team moved to Minnesota in 1968. In 1969, team moved back to Pittsburgh, Pennsylvania. In 1970, it was renamed the Pittsburgh Condors.
Providence Steam Rollers	1948-49	Team played three seasons in the earlier BAA.
Rochester Royals	1956-57	Team came from the BAA and played eight seasons in the NBA before moving to Cincinnati, Ohio, in 1957.
Saint Louis Bombers	1949-50	Team came from the BAA and played only one season in the NBA.
Saint Louis Hawks	1967-68	NBA team moved from Milwaukee, Wisconsin. Moved to Atlanta, Georgia, in 1968.
Saint Louis Spirits	1975-76	ABA team moved from North Carolina. It folded with the league in 1976.
San Diego Clippers	1983-84	NBA team moved from Buffalo, New York, where it was the Buffalo Braves. Moved to Los Angeles, California, in 1984.
San Diego Conquistadors/Sails	1974-75	ABA team renamed the San Diego Sails in 1975. It folded the same year.
San Diego Rockets	1970-71	NBA team moved to Houston, Texas, in 1971.
San Francisco Warriors	1970-71	NBA team moved from Philadelphia, Pennsylvania, to San Francisco, California, in 1962. Moved to Oakland, California, in 1971 and became the Golden State Warriors.
Sheboygan Redskins	1949-50	Wisconsin team came from the NBL and played only one season in the NBA. Played in the NPBL in 1950-51.
Syracuse Nationals	1962-63	New York team came from the NBL and played 14 seasons in the NBA before moving to Philadelphia, Pennsylvania, in 1963 to become the Philadelphia 76ers.
Toronto Huskies	1946-47	Canadian team played only one season in the earlier BAA.
Tri-City /Tri-Cities Blackhawks	1950-51	Team came from the NBL before playing two seasons in the NBA. The team originally was the Tri-City Blackhawks. It changed its name to the Tri-Cities Blackhawks during its second season. The team di-

		vided home games between Moline and Rock Island Illinois, and Davenport, Iowa. It moved to Milwaukee, Wisconsin, in 1951 and become the Milwaukee Hawks.
Utah Stars	1974-75	ABA team moved from Los Angeles, California, and folded in 1975.
Virginia Squires	1975-76	ABA team moved from Washington and folded with the ABA in 1976.
Washington Bullets	1996-97	NBA team previously was the Baltimore Bullets and the Capitol Bullets. The team's name was changed to Washington Wizards in 1997.
Washington Capitols	1950-51	NBA team disbanded before the end of the 1950-51 season.
Washington Caps	1969-70	ABA team moved from Oakland, California. It moved to Virginia in 1970 and changed its name to Squires.
Waterloo Hawks	1949-50	Iowa team came from the NBL and played only one season in the NBA. Played in the NPBL in 1950-51.

Sports—Basketball—Professional—Rules
• **Last time a jump ball followed every score in NBA play:** 1938-39 season.
• **Last time the NBA played without the 24-second shot clock:** the 1953-54 season. On April 22, 1954, at their annual meeting, NBA owners agreed to adopt the 24-second shot clock for the 1954-55 season.

Sports—Bowling

Sports—Bowling—Anthony, Earl
Earl Anthony held the record as the all-time leader in Professional Bowling Association (PBA) National tour titles with 41 wins. Additionally, he had 43 second-place finishes. He retired from competition more than once, including 1984, after winning player of the year honors in 1983. Anthony died in New Berlin, Wisconsin, on August 14, 2001, age 63.
• **Last PBA Tour:** 1991. Anthony returned for a short unsuccessful appearance on the PBA Tour in 1987 then joined the new PBA Senior Tour in 1988 and won four tournaments. He retired again in 1991.

Sports—Boxing

Sports—Boxing—Bare-Knuckle
In bare-knuckle boxing the contenders did not wear gloves.

• **Last American bare-knuckle champion:** John L. ("Boston Strong Boy") Sullivan. He held the title until 1889, during the era of the transition of boxing to a gloved sport.
• **Last American bare-knuckle championship fight:** July 8, 1889, when John L. Sullivan beat Jake Kilrain in 75 rounds in Richburg, Mississippi, in a fight that lasted two hours and 16 minutes. It was the last bare-knuckle championship bout under the old London Prize Ring rules, as well as the last bare-knuckle championship fight of any jurisdiction. Sullivan died in Abingdon, Massachusetts, on February 2, 1918, age 59.
• **Last British bare-knuckle champion:** Jem ("the Gypsy") Mace, who vacated his English championship in 1871. Mace had held the title since Tom ("the Fighting Sailor") King retired in 1863, and is referred to by many as the "Father of Modern Boxing." Mace's last recorded exhibition was a three-round bout with Jack Valentine in Capetown, South Africa, on January 18, 1904. Mace died in England on November 30, 1910, age 79.
• **Last bare-knuckle world champion:** John L. ("Boston Strong Boy") Sullivan. He held the title during the transition to a gloved sport.
• **Last world bare-knuckle championship fight:** probably Sullivan's match with Charles Watson ("Charlie") Mitchell on March 10, 1888, in Chantilly, France. In

some references, this fight was reported as a Heavyweight Championship of the World that used London Rules and bare knuckles. The fight went 39 rounds before it was called after three hours and ten minutes. Sullivan scored the first knockdown of the fight, but Mitchell was the first to draw blood in Round 8.

Sports—Boxing
Last Events of Some Major Boxers

Ali, Muhammad

Muhammad Ali was born Cassius Marcellus Clay Jr. in 1942.

• **Last time Ali used the name Cassius Clay:** February 25, 1964, when he fought Sonny Liston in Miami Beach, Florida. After the fight, he announced he was a member of the Nation of Islam and used the name Cassius X briefly. In March, he changed his name to Muhammad Ali.

• **Last day Ali's draft evasion conviction held:** June 28, 1971, overturned by the U.S. Supreme Court by a vote of 8-0. (Ali had been convicted of draft evasion in 1967.)

• **Last time Ali won back the heavyweight championship:** September 15, 1975, in a 15-round victory over Leon Spinks in New Orleans, Louisiana. Ali held the heavyweight championship title three separate times.

• **Last title fight:** an 11th-round knockout loss to Larry Holmes on October 2, 1980, in Las Vegas, Nevada.

• **Last professional fight:** a 10-round decision loss against Trevor Berbick on December 11, 1981, in Nassau, Bahamas, hyped as "Drama in the Bahamas."

Corbett, James J.

James J. ("Gentleman Jim") Corbett died in Bayside, New York, on February 18, 1933.

• **Last held the heavyweight title:** March 17, 1897, when he was knocked out in the 14th round by Bob Fitzsimmons in Carson City, Nevada.

• **Last fight:** August 14, 1903, San Francisco, California, a 10th-round knockout to Jim Jeffries.

Dempsey, Jack

William Harrison ("Jack") Dempsey (a.k.a. "The Manassa Mauler") died May 31, 1983, just before his 88th birthday.

• **Last held the heavyweight title:** September 23, 1926, when he lost by decision to Gene Tunney in Philadelphia, Pennsylvania. Dempsey lost again to Tunney at Chicago's Soldier Field on September 22, 1927. Dempsey announced his retirement in March 1928. Between 1931 and 1940, he fought in a number of exhibition matches.

• **Last exhibition matches:** during the summer of 1940: July 29, 1940, in Charlotte, North Carolina, a second-round knockout to Ellis Bashara; August 15, 1940, at the New York World's Fair, Flushing Meadows, New York, two rounds against Mickey McAvoy. Afterward, Dempsey retired from participation in exhibition bouts.

Frazier, Joe

Joseph ("Joe") William Frazier (a.k.a. "Smokin' Joe") first won his heavyweight title in 1970.

• **Last held the heavyweight title:** January 22, 1973, when he lost in a second-round knockout to George Forman in Kingston, Jamaica.

• **Last fight:** a failed one-bout comeback on December 3, 1981, when Frazier drew with journeyman fighter Jumbo Cummings.

LaMotta, Jake

Jacob ("Jake") LaMotta (a.k.a. the "Bronx Bull") captured the middleweight title in 1949.

• **Last held the middleweight title:** February 14, 1951, when he lost to Sugar Ray Robin-

son in a fight that was stopped in the 13th round.
- **Last fight:** April 15, 1954, a loss to Billy Kilgore in Miami Beach, Florida.

Leonard, Sugar Ray

Charles ("Sugar Ray") Leonard suffered a detached retina and had surgery in 1982. He remained out of the ring until 1984. After one fight, he left the ring again until 1987. He retired again but returned to the ring in 1991. He made his last comeback in 1997.
- **Last fight:** March 1, 1997, a fifth-round TKO loss to Hector Camacho in Atlantic City, New Jersey.

Liston, Sonny

Charles ("Sonny") Liston died around December 30, 1970, of undetermined circumstances at his home in Las Vegas, Nevada. His body was found on January 5, 1971. There is some uncertainty about when and how he died.
- **Last fight:** June 29, 1970, a 10th-round knockout victory over Chuck Wepner in Jersey City, New Jersey.

Louis, Joe

Joseph Louis Barrow fought professionally as Joe Louis (a.k.a. the "Brown Bomber"). He retired undefeated on March 1, 1949, but returned to the ring the following year because he owed money to the government for taxes. On September 27, 1950, he returned to lose to Ezzard Charles. Louis fought nine more fights. He died in Las Vegas, Nevada, on April 12, 1981, age 66.
- **Last held the heavyweight title:** March 1, 1949.
- **Last fight:** October 26, 1951, an 8th-round knockout loss to Rocky Marciano at Madison Square Garden, New York.

Marciano, Rocky

Rocco Marchegiano, who fought professionally as Rocky Marciano, won all 49 of his fights, including 43 by knockouts. He formally retired on April 27, 1956, and was the first undefeated heavyweight of modern times. He was killed in a plane crash near Newton, Iowa, while en route to a party in his honor on August 31, 1969, a day before his 46th birthday.
- **Last fight:** September 21, 1955, in New York, a ninth-round knockout of Archie Moore.

Patterson, Floyd

Floyd Patterson was the first man to recapture the heavyweight title in modern times. He lost it to Ingemar Johansson in 1959 and regained it the following year.
- **Last held the heavyweight title:** September 25, 1962, when Patterson lost to Sonny Liston in Chicago.
- **Last fight:** September 20, 1972 in New York, a TKO loss to Muhammad Ali in a National American Boxing Federation (NABF) heavyweight title fight.

Robinson, Sugar Ray

Walker Smith Jr., who fought professionally as Sugar Ray Robinson, died on April 12, 1989, age 67. During his career, he won the middleweight title six times and fought 18 world champions. He retired in 1952. Robinson mounted a comeback in 1955 and suffered 16 of his 19 career defeats in the next ten years.
- **Last held the middleweight title:** March 4, 1961, when Robinson lost the NBA middleweight title to Gene Fulmer in Las Vegas.
- **Last fight:** November 10, 1965 in Pittsburgh, Pennsylvania, a 10th-round loss to Joey Archer. Robinson retired for the last time in December 1965.

Schmeling, Max

German boxer Maximilian ("Max") Adolph Otto Siegfried Schmeling held the world heavyweight championship from 1930 to 1932.
- **Last U.S. fight**: June 22, 1938, when Schmeling lost a world heavyweight championship

bout to Joe Louis in a first-round knockout in New York, New York.
• **Last fight:** October 31, 1948, in Berlin, Germany, a loss to Reidel Vogt.

Tunney, Gene
James Joseph ("Gene") Tunney was also known as "The Fighting Marine."
• **Last fight:** July 26, 1928, an 11th-round knockout against Tom Heeney. Tunney formally announced his retirement July 31, 1928.

Walcott, Jersey Joe
Arnold Raymond Cream, who fought professionally as Jersey Joe Walcott, died in Camden, New Jersey, on February 25, 1994, age 80.
• **Last held the heavyweight title:** September 23, 1952, when he lost to Rocky Marciano in a 13th-round knockout in Philadelphia, Pennsylvania.
• **Last fight:** May 15, 1953, in Chicago, Illinois, a first-round knockout loss to Rocky Marciano.

Sports—Football

Sports— Football—Intercollegiate—All-White
• **Last all-white collegiate football team to win a championship:** University of Texas Longhorns in 1969.

Sports—Football—Intercollegiate—Coaches—Rockne, Knute
Knute Rockne coached the Fighting Irish of Notre Dame for 13 years. He was killed in a plane crash in Bazaar, Kansas, on March 31, 1931, age 43.
• **Last game as coach at Notre Dame:** December 6, 1930. Notre Dame beat the University of Southern California Trojans 27-0 in Los Angeles, California, giving the Fighting Irish a perfect season record of 10-0 and Rockne a career record of 105 wins, 12 losses and 5 ties.

Sports—Football—Intercollegiate—Players—All Americans—Walter Camp's
In 1889, Walter Chauncey Camp and col-laborator Caspar Whitney began selecting annual All-American football teams composed of the best intercollegiate players in the U.S. Camp's lists were later published each year in *Collier's* magazine. They became the standard for outstanding gridiron performance. Camp died in New York while attending a Football Rules Committee meeting on March 14, 1925. He had regularly attended these meetings since 1878.
• **Last All-American list by Camp:** appeared in 1924, and consisted of:
[End] Charlie Berry (Lafayette)
[End] Henry Bjorkman (Dartmouth)
[Tackle] Ed Weir (Nebraska)
[Tackle] Ed McGinley (Pennsylvania)
[Guard] Ed Slaughter (Michigan)
[Guard] Babe Hornell (California)
[Center] Ed Garbisch (Army)
[Quarterback] Harry Stuhldreyer (Notre Dame)
[Half Back] Red Grange (Illinois)
[Half Back] Walt Koppisch (Columbia)
[Full Back] Homer Hazel (Rutgers).

Sports—Football—Intercollegiate—Defunct Bowl Games

Bowl Name and Location	Last Year	Last Game Results
All-American Bowl (Birmingham, Alabama)	1990	North Carolina State 31, Southern Mississippi 27
Aloha Bowl (Honolulu, Hawaii)	2000	Boston College 31, Arizona State 17
Aviation Bowl (Dayton, Ohio)	1961	New Mexico 28, Western Michigan 12
Bacardi Bowl (Havana, Cuba)	1937	Auburn 7, Villanova 7

Bluebonnet Bowl (Houston, Texas)	1987	Texas 32, Pittsburgh 27
Bluegrass Bowl (Louisville, Kentucky)	1958	Oklahoma State 15, Florida State 6
California Bowl (Fresno, California)	1991	Bowling Green 28, Fresno State 21
Camellia Bowl (Lafayette, Louisiana)	1948	Hardin-Simmons 49, Wichita State 12
Cherry Bowl (Pontiac, Michigan)	1985	Maryland 35, Syracuse 18
Delta Bowl (Memphis, Tennessee)	1949	William & Mary 20, Oklahoma State 0
Dixie Bowl (Birmingham, Alabama)	1949	Baylor 20, Wake Forest 7
Dixie Classic (Dallas, Texas)	1934	Arkansas 7, Centenary 7
Fort Worth Classic (Fort Worth, Texas)	1921	Centre 63, Texas Christian 7
Garden State Bowl (East Rutherford, New Jersey)	1981	Tennessee 28, Wisconsin 21
Gotham Bowl (New York, New York)	1962	Nebraska 36, Miami (Florida) 34
Great Lakes Bowl (Cleveland, Ohio)	1947	Kentucky 24, Villanova 14
Harbor Bowl (San Diego, California)	1949	Villanova 27, Nevada 7
Heritage Bowl (Atlanta, Georgia)	1999	Hampton 24, Southern 3
Los Angeles Christmas Festival (Los Angeles, California)	1924	Southern California 20, Missouri 7
Mercy Bowl (Los Angeles, California)	1961	Fresno State 36, Bowling Green 6
Micron PC Bowl (a.k.a. **Blockbuster Bowl, Carquest Bowl**) (Miami, Florida)	2000	North Carolina State 38, Minnesota 30
Oahu Bowl (Honolulu, Hawaii)	2000	Boston College 31, Arizona State 14
Oil Bowl (Houston, Texas)	1947	Georgia Tech 41, Saint Mary's (California) 19
Pasadena Bowl (Pasadena, California)	1971	Memphis State 28, San Jose State 9
Presidential Cup (College Park, Maryland)	1950	Texas A&M 40, Georgia 20
Raisin Bowl (Fresno, California)	1949	San Jose State 20, Texas Tech 13
Salad Bowl (Phoenix, Arizona)	1952	Houston 26, Dayton 21
San Diego East-West Christmas Classic (San Diego, California)	1922	West Virginia 21, Gonzaga 13
Shrine Bowl (Little Rock, Arkansas)	1948	Hardin-Simmons 40, Ouachita Baptist 12

Sports—Football—Intercollegiate—Players—First

The first intercollegiate football game was played between Rutgers and Princeton at College Field on the Rutgers campus in New Brunswick, New Jersey, on November 6, 1869. Rutgers won 6-4 but would not beat Princeton again for 69 years.

• **Last surviving player from the first Rutgers team:** George H. Large, who later served as a state senator in Hunterdon County, New Jersey. He died in 1939.

• **Last surviving player from the first Princeton team:** Robert Preston Lane, who died in Hagerstown, Maryland, on November 5, 1938. On that same day, in Piscataway, New Jersey, Rutgers beat Princeton for the first time since the original 1869 contest. George H. Large, Rutgers' last surviving player, was in attendance and was honored at halftime.

Sports—Football—Intercollegiate—Players—"The Four Horsemen of Notre Dame"

The "Four Horsemen of Notre Dame" was a nickname coined by sportswriter Grantland Rice to describe the legendary Notre Dame backfield of the early 1920s. The Four Horsemen were Jim Crowley, Elmer Layden, Don Miller and Harry Stuhldreyer.

• **Last game the Four Horsemen played together:** the Rose Bowl on January 1, 1925, when Notre Dame beat Stanford, 27-10. It was the culmination of a national championship and a 10-0 season under coach Knute Rockne.

• **Last surviving member of the Four Horsemen:** right halfback, James H. ("Sleepy Jim") Crowley. After Notre Dame, Crowley played professional football briefly, then went into coaching at Michigan State and Fordham University, where he coached Vince Lombardi. Crowley died in Scranton, Pennsylvania, on January 15, 1986, age 83.

Sports—Football—Intercollegiate—Players—Grange, Red

Harold Edward ("Red") Grange, who played for the University of Illinois, earned the nickname "The Galloping Ghost." He died on January 28, 1991, age 87.

• **Last game Grange played at the University of Illinois:** November 21, 1925, against Ohio, at Ohio Stadium. A few days later, on Thanksgiving, Grange played his first professional game with the Chicago Bears.

Sports—Football—Intercollegiate—Players—Thorpe, Jim

James Francis ("Jim") Thorpe, a Native American, is considered by many to be one of the greatest athletes of all time. He participated in the Olympics in track and played professional baseball and football. Thorpe died in Lomita, California, on March 28, 1953, age 64.

• **Last game Thorpe played with the Carlisle Indian School:** against Army in 1912. He completed six straight passes; the last for a touchdown. Carlisle won 27-6.

• **Last surviving teammate of Jim Thorpe at Carlisle:** Gus Welch, who died in Bedford, Virginia, on January 29, 1970, age 78.

• **Last game of Thorpe as a professional football player:** November 30, 1928, when the Chicago Cardinals played against the Chicago Bears.

Sports—Football—Intercollegiate—Rules

• **Last time the forward pass was illegal in college football:** 1906. On January 12, 1906, the American Intercollegiate Football Rules Committee legalized the forward pass. The change in the rules was made in an effort to open up the game and reduce the number of injuries.

• **Last time teams numbered more than 11 players:** 1880. Until then, a football team could number 11, 15, 20 or 25 players. The number was set at 11 at a football convention held that year at Yale University.

Sports—Football—Intercollegiate—Streaks—Shut-outs—University of Tennessee

The University of Tennessee shut-out streak began on November 5, 1938, in a game against Chattanooga.

• **Last shut-out game:** October 12, 1940, against Chattanooga with a 53-0 victory. The streak of consecutive shut-outs against opponents ended on October 19, 1940, after 17 games, when Tennessee beat Alabama, 27-12.

Sports—Football—Professional—Coaches—Lombardi, Vince

• **Last game as coach of the Green Bay Packers:** Super Bowl II, January 16, 1968, in a victory over the Oakland Raiders, 33-14 at Super Bowl Stadium in Florida. Lombardi formally resigned from the Packers on February 1, 1968, after nine seasons. He took over as coach of the Washington Redskins in 1969. Lombardi died in Washington, D.C., on September 3, 1970, age 57.

• **Last game as Washington Redskins coach:** December 21, 1969, when the Redskins lost to the Dallas Cowboys, 20-10.

Sports—Football—Professional—Hall of Fame

The Pro Football Hall of Fame was established in Canton, Ohio, in 1963. The original inductees included 11 players and six executives. They were inducted on January 29, 1963.

• **Last surviving member of the original Pro Football Hall of Fame inductees:** Sammy Baugh.

Sports—Football—Professional—Leagues—All-American Football Conference (AAFC)

The All-American Football Conference (AAFC) was organized for the 1946 season.

• **Last of the AAFC:** disbanded in 1949. On December 9, 1949, the NFL commissioner announced that three AAFC teams—the Baltimore Colts, Cleveland Browns and San Francisco 49ers—would be admitted into the NFL. The rest of the AAFC players were pooled and drafted by the 13 clubs.

• **Last AAFC game:** December 11, 1949. The Cleveland Browns defeated the San Francisco 49ers, 21-7 to win their fourth consecutive and last championship game in the four-year history of the AAFC.

Sports—Football—Professional—Leagues—American Football League (AFL)

The American Football League (AFL) was formed in 1959 with franchises in eight major cities. In 1966, the AFL champion began to play the NFL champion in the Super Bowl. The AFL was fully merged with the NFL by 1970.

• **Last AFL championship game:** January 4, 1970. The Kansas City Chiefs, with the help of four interceptions, beat the Oakland Raiders 17-7. The Chiefs went on to Super Bowl IV where they beat the Minnesota Vikings, 23-7.

Sports—Football—Professional—Leagues—American Professional Football Association (APFL)

The American Professional Football Association (APFL) was founded in 1920, with Jim Thorpe as president.

• **Last of the APFL:** On June 24, 1922, at the suggestion of George Halas, team owners agreed to change the name of the league to the National Football League (NFL).

• **Last APFL season:** 1921-22.

Sports—Football—Professional—Leagues—United States Football League (USFL)

The United States Football League (USFL) was a professional league that operated from 1983 to 1985 as a springtime football league.

• **Last USFL season:** 1985, when the league disbanded.

• **Last USFL game:** the July 14, 1985, USFL championship game in which the Baltimore Stars beat the Oakland Invaders 28-24.

Sports—Football—Professional—Leagues—World Football League (WFL)

The World Football League (WFL) was a professional league established in 1974 in competition with the NFL.

• **Last WFL champion:** Birmingham Americans, who won the 1974 World Bowl 22-21 against the Florida Blazers.

• **Last of the WFL:** disbanded in 1975.

Sports—Football—Professional—Leagues—Xtreme Football League (XFL)

The Xtreme Football League (XFL) was a professional league. It was operated by the World Wrestling Federation and NBC for just one season in 2001.

• **Last XFL game:** the XFL Championship game on April 21, 2001, in which the Los Angeles Xtremes defeated the San Francisco Demons, 38-6. Three weeks later, the league announced it was ceasing operations.

Sports—Football—Professional—Rules—Forward Pass

• **Last season without a forward pass rule:** 1932-33. On February 25, 1933, team owners voted to establish the rule that allowed a forward pass to be thrown from anywhere behind the line of scrimmage.

Sports—Football—Professional—Rules—Goal Posts

Prior to 1933, goal posts sat on the end line. On February 25, 1933, team owners voted to move the goals posts inward to the goal line, in the hope that it would increase scores with more field goals.

• **Last season goal posts were on the goal line:** 1973-74. On April 25, 1974, team owners voted to move the goal posts from the goal line back to the end line, with the hope that it would increase the number of touchdowns at the expense of field goals.

Sports—Football—Professional—Rules—Hash Marks

• **Last season there were no hash marks on the field (10 yards in from the sidelines):** 1932-33. On February 25, 1933, team owners voted to establish the marks.

Sports—Football—Professional—Rules—Helmets

• **Last season players were not required to wear helmets:** 1942-43. Helmets became mandatory in 1943.

• **Last season plastic helmets were permitted:** 1947-48. They were banned in 1948.

Sports—Football—Professional—Rules—Substitutions (Unlimited)

• **Last season without unlimited substitutions:** 1948-49. During the 1949 season, unlimited substitutions were used on a trial basis. On January 23, 1950, team owners voted to approve an unlimited substitution rule. This set the stage for modern two-platoon football and specialists.

Sports—Football—Professional—Rules—Sudden Death

• **Last season without a sudden death rule for play-off ties:** 1946-47. On January 24, 1947, team owners voted to adopt a sudden-death overtime in the event of a tie in a playoff game. However, it was not needed until the Baltimore Colts–New York Giants championship game in 1958.

• **Last season without a regular-season sudden death rule:** 1973-74. On April 25, 1974, team owners voted to adopt the 15-minute sudden-death quarter that would be played in the event that a regular-season game ended in a tie after the regulation four quarters.

Sports—Football—Professional—Streaks—Extra Points—Blanda, George

George Blanda of the Chicago Bears set a record with 156 consecutive extra points without a miss.

• **End of Blanda's streak:** October 21, 1956, in his first extra-point attempt of a game against the Baltimore Colts. The failed kick sailed off to the left, but the Bears won the game, 58-27.

Sports—Football—Professional—Streaks—Losing—Cardinals

The Chicago Cardinals had the longest losing streak in NFL history, with 29 losses.

• **End of the Chicago Cardinals losing streak:** October 14, 1945, when they beat the Chicago Bears 16-7.

Sports—Football—Professional—Streaks—Winning—Miami Dolphins

During the 1972 season, the Miami Dolphins won every game in the regular season and post season making them the only team in NFL history to have a perfect season.

• **Last victory in Miami Dolphins' perfect season:** Super Bowl VII, January 14, 1973, at the Los Angeles Memorial Coliseum. They beat the Washington Redskins 14-7.

Sports—Football—Professional—Defunct Teams (NFL and Predecessors)
Last Game, Season Record Head Coach, Win and Other Events of Some Former Teams

Akron Indians (Akron, Ohio)
• **Last known as Akron Pros:** 1925.
• **Last season record:** 1-4-3 (1926).
• **Last head coach:** Rube Ursella (Al Nesser also coached part of the last season).

- **Last win:** October 3, 1926, in Akron vs. Hammond Pros (Akron 17, Hammond 0).
- **Last game:** November 25, 1926, in Canton, Ohio, vs. Canton Bulldogs (Akron 0, Canton 0).

Akron Pros (Akron, Ohio)
- **Last season record:** 4-2-2 (1925). Became the Akron Indians in 1926.
- **Last head coach:** George Berry.
- **Last win:** November 1, 1925, in Akron vs. Dayton Triangles (Akron 17, Dayton 3).
- **Last game:** November 8, 1925, in Pottsville, Pennsylvania (Akron 0, Pottsville 21).

Baltimore Colts I (Baltimore, Maryland)
- **Last season record:** 1-11-0 (1950).
- **Last head coach:** Clem Crowe.
- **Last win:** November 5, 1950, in Green Bay, Wisconsin, vs. Green Bay Packers (Baltimore 41, Green Bay 21).
- **Last game:** December 10, 1950, in New York, New York, vs. New York Yankees (Baltimore 14, New York 51).

Baltimore Colts II (Baltimore, Maryland)
- **Last headquartered in Baltimore:** March 1984. The Baltimore Colts moved to Indianapolis, Indiana. Baltimore got another NFL franchise in 1996, when the Cleveland Browns moved to Baltimore and changed their name to the Ravens, an homage to Baltimore's Edgar Allen Poe.

Boston Bulldogs (Boston, Massachusetts)
- **Last known as the Pottsville Maroons:** 1928.
- **Last season record:** 4-4-0 (1929).
- **Last head coach:** Dick Rauch.
- **Last win:** November 17, 1929, in Boston vs. Buffalo Bisons (Boston 12, Buffalo 7).
- **Last game:** November 24, 1929, in Providence, Rhode Island, vs. Providence Steam Roller (Boston 6, Providence 20).

Boston Yanks (Boston, Massachusetts)
- **Last season record:** 3-9-0 (1948). Became the New York Bulldogs in 1949.
- **Last head coach:** Clipper Smith.
- **Last win:** December 5, 1948, in Boston vs. Philadelphia Eagles (Boston 37, Philadelphia 14)
- **Last game:** same.

Brooklyn Dodgers (Brooklyn, New York)
- **Last known as the Dayton Triangles:** 1929.
- **Last season record:** 2-8-0 (1943). Became the Brooklyn Tigers in 1944.
- **Last head coach:** Pete Cawthorn.
- **Last win:** November 14, 1943, in Brooklyn vs. Philadelphia-Pittsburgh Steagles (Brooklyn 13, Phil-Pitt 7). The Philadelphia-Pittsburgh Steagles were a combined team of Philadelphia Eagles and Pittsburgh Stealers. The two teams pooled players because of a player shortage during World War II.
- **Last game:** November 28, 1943, in New York, New York, vs. New York Giants (Brooklyn 7, Giants 24).

Brooklyn Lions (Brooklyn, New York)
- **Last season record:** 3-8-0 (1926). Became the New York Yankees in 1927.
- **Last head coach:** Punk Berryman.
- **Last win:** November 14, 1926, in Brooklyn vs. Canton Bulldogs (Brooklyn 19, Canton 0).
- **Last game:** November 28, 1926, in New York vs. New York Giants (Brooklyn 0, New York 27).

Brooklyn Tigers (Brooklyn, New York)
- **Last known as Brooklyn Dodgers:** 1943.
- **Last season record:** 0-10-0 (1944).

- **Last head coaches:** Pete Cawthorn, Ed Kuhale, Frank Bridges.
- **Last win:** none.
- **Last game:** December 3, 1944, in Philadelphia, Pennsylvania, vs. Philadelphia Eagles (Brooklyn 0, Philadelphia 34).

Buffalo All-Americans (Buffalo, New York)
- **Last season record:** 5-4-3 (1923). Became the Buffalo Bisons in 1924.
- **Last head coach:** Tommy Hughitt.
- **Last win:** December 1, 1923, in Rochester, New York, vs. Rochester Jeffersons (Buffalo 13, Rochester 0).
- **Last game:** December 2, 1923, in Canton, Ohio, vs. Canton Bulldogs (Buffalo 0, Canton 14).

Buffalo Bisons (Buffalo, New York)
- **Last known as the Buffalo All-Americans:** 1923.
- **Last known as the Buffalo Rangers:** 1926. Renamed the Buffalo Bisons for their final seasons (1927-29).
- **Last season record:** 1-7-1 (1929).
- **Last head coach:** Al Jolley.
- **Last win:** November 24, 1929, in Chicago, Illinois, vs. Chicago Bears (Buffalo 19, Chicago 7).
- **Last game:** same.

Canton Bulldogs (Canton, Ohio)
- **Last surviving member of the 1922 Canton Bulldogs (NFL's first championship team):** Arda Bowser, who was a punter, place kicker, linebacker and fullback. He was also the first NFL player to use a kicking tee. Bowser died in Winter Park, Florida, in September 1996, age 97.
- **Last season record:** 1-9-3 (1926).
- **Last head coach:** Pete Henry.
- **Last win:** October 3, 1926, in Canton, vs. Louisville Colonels (Canton 13, Louisville 0).
- **Last game:** November 28, 1926, in Chicago, Illinois, vs. Chicago Bears (Canton 0, Chicago 35).

Chicago Tigers (Chicago, Illinois)
- **Last season record:** 1-5-1 (1920).
- **Last head coach:** Guil Falcon.
- **Last win:** October 17, 1920, in Chicago vs. Detroit Heralds (Chicago 12, Detroit 0).
- **Last game:** November 25, 1920, in Chicago, vs. Decatur Staleys (Chicago 0, Decatur 6).

Cincinnati Celts (Cincinnati, Ohio)
- **Last season record:** 1-3-0 (1921).
- **Last head coach:** Bill Doherty.
- **Last win:** October 16, 1921 in Muncie, Indiana, vs. Muncie Flyers (Cincinnati 14, Muncie 0).
- **Last game:** November 27, 1921, in Evansville, Indiana, vs. Evansville Crimson Giants (Cincinnati 0, Evansville 48).

Cincinnati Reds (Cincinnati, Ohio)
- **Last season record:** 0-8-0 (1934).
- **Last head coach:** Algy Clark.
- **Last win:** December 2, 1934, in Saint Louis, Missouri, vs. Saint Louis Gunners (Cincinnati 21, St. Louis 14).
- **Last game:** same.

Cleveland Bulldogs I (Cleveland, Ohio)
- **Last known as the Cleveland Indians:** 1923.
- **Last season record:** 5-8-1 (1925).

- **Last head coach:** Cap Edwards.
- **Last win:** December 12, 1925, in Philadelphia, Pennsylvania, vs. Frankford Yellow Jackets (Cleveland 3, Frankford 0).
- **Last game:** December 20, 1925, in Cleveland vs. Frankford Yellow Jackets (Cleveland 7, Frankford 12).

Cleveland Bulldogs II (Cleveland, Ohio)
- **Last season record:** 8-4-1 (1927). Became the Detroit Wolverines in 1928.
- **Last head coach:** Roy Andrews.
- **Last win:** December 3, 1927, in Cleveland vs. Duluth Eskimos (Cleveland 20, Duluth 0).
- **Last game:** same.

Cleveland Indians I (Cleveland, Ohio)
- **Last known as the Cleveland Tigers:** 1920.
- **Last season record:** 3-5-0 (1921).
- **Last head coach:** Jim Thorpe.
- **Last win:** December 3, 1921, in New York, New York, vs. New York Brickley's Giants (Cleveland 17, New York 0).
- **Last game:** December 11, 1921, in Washington, D.C., vs. Washington Senators (Cleveland 0, Washington 7).

Cleveland Indians II (Cleveland, Ohio)
- **Last season record:** 3-1-3 (1923). Became the Cleveland Bulldogs I in 1924.
- **Last head coach:** Cap Edwards.
- **Last win:** November 18, 1923, in Cleveland, vs. Columbus Tigers (Cleveland 9, Columbus 3).
- **Last game:** November 25, 1923, in Cleveland, vs. Canton Bulldogs (Cleveland 10, Canton 46).

Cleveland Indians III (Cleveland, Ohio)
- **Last season record:** 2-8-0 (1931).
- **Last head coaches:** Al Cornsweet, Hoge Workman.
- **Last win:** October 18, 1931, in Providence, Rhode Island vs. Providence Steam Roller (Cleveland 13, Providence 6).
- **Last game:** November 28, 1931, in Chicago, Illinois, vs. Chicago Cardinals (Cleveland 0, Chicago 21).

Cleveland Tigers (Cleveland, Ohio)
- **Last season record:** 1-4-2 (1920). Became the Cleveland Indians in 1921.
- **Last head coaches:** Stan Cofall, Al Pierotti.
- **Last win:** October 31, 1920, in Cleveland vs. Columbus Panhandles (Cleveland 7, Columbus 0).
- **Last game:** November 28, 1920, in Buffalo, New York, vs. Buffalo All-Americans (Cleveland 0, Buffalo 7).

Columbus Panhandles (Columbus, Ohio)
- **Last season record:** 0-8-0 (1922). Became the Columbus Tigers in 1923.
- **Last head coach:** Herb Dell.
- **Last win:** December 4, 1921, in Columbus vs. Louisville Brecks (Columbus 6, Louisville 0).
- **Last game:** November 30, 1922, in Columbus vs. Oorang Indians (Columbus 8, Oorang 18).

Columbus Tigers (Columbus, Ohio)
- **Last known as the Columbus Panhandles:** 1922.
- **Last season record:** 1-6-0 (1926).
- **Last head coach:** Jack Heldt.

- **Last win:** September 26, 1926, in Canton, Ohio, vs. Canton Bulldogs (Columbus 14, Canton 2).
- **Last game**: November 7, 1926, in Buffalo, New York, vs. Buffalo Rangers (Columbus 0, Buffalo 26).

Dallas Texans (Dallas, Texas)
- **Last known as New York Yanks:** 1951.
- **Last season record:** 1-11-0 (1952).
- **Last head coach:** Jim Phelan.
- **Last win:** November 27, 1952, in Akron, Ohio, vs. Chicago Bears (Dallas 27, Chicago 23).
- **Last game:** December 13, 1952, in Detroit, Michigan, vs. Detroit Lions (Dallas 6, Detroit 41).

Dayton Triangles (Dayton, Ohio)
- **Last season record:** 0-6-0 (1929). Became the Brooklyn Dodgers in 1930.
- **Last head coach:** Fay Abbott.
- **Last win:** September 24, 1927, in Frankford, Pennsylvania, vs. Frankford Yellow Jackets (Dayton 6, Frankford 3).
- **Last game:** November 24, 1929, in Chicago, Illinois, vs. Chicago Cardinals (Dayton 0, Chicago 19).

Detroit Heralds (Detroit, Michigan)
- **Last season record:** 1-5-1 (1921).
- **Last head coach:** Bill Marshall.
- **Last win:** October 9, 1921, in Detroit vs. Dayton Triangles (Detroit 10, Dayton 7).
- **Last game:** November 13, 1921, in Dayton, Ohio, vs. Dayton Triangles (Detroit 0, Dayton 27).

Detroit Panthers (Detroit, Michigan)
- **Last season record:** 6-4-2 (1926).
- **Last head coach:** Jimmy Conzelman.
- **Last win:** October 31, 1926, in Detroit vs. Canton Bulldogs (Detroit 6, Canton 0).
- **Last game:** November 28, 1926, in Detroit vs. Green Bay Packers (Detroit 0, Green Bay 7).

Detroit Wolverines (Detroit, Michigan)
- **Last known as the Cleveland Bulldogs:** 1927.
- **Last season record:** 7-2-1 (1928).
- **Last head coach:** Roy Andrews.
- **Last win:** December 9, 1928, in New York, New York, vs. New York Yankees (Detroit 34, New York 6).
- **Last game:** same.

Duluth Eskimos (Duluth, Minnesota)
- **Last known as the Duluth Kelleys:** 1925. Became the Orange Tornadoes in 1929.
- **Last season record:** 1-8-0 (1927).
- **Last head coach:** Ernie Nevers.
- **Last win:** October 23, 1927, in Pottsville, Pennsylvania, vs. Pottsville Maroons (Duluth 27, Pottsville 0).
- **Last game:** December 11, 1927, in Chicago, Illinois, vs. Chicago Bears (Duluth 14, Chicago 27).

Evansville Crimson Giants (Evansville, Indiana)
- **Last season record:** 0-3-0 (1922).
- **Last head coach:** Frank Fausch.
- **Last win:** November 27, 1921, in Evansville vs. Cincinnati Celts (Evansville 48, Cincin-

nati 0).
• **Last game:** November 12, 1922, in Louisville, Kentucky, vs. Louisville Brecks (Evansville 6, Louisville 13).

Frankford Yellow Jackets (Philadelphia, Pennsylvania)
• **Last season record:** 1-6-1 (1931).
• **Last head coach:** Bull Behman.
• **Last win:** October 25, 1931, in Chicago, Illinois, vs. Chicago Bears (Frankford 13, Chicago 12).
• **Last game:** November 8, 1931, in New York, New York, vs. New York Giants (Frankford 0, New York 13).

Hammond Pros (Hammond, Indiana)
• **Last season record:** 0-4-0 (1926).
• **Last head coach:** Doc Young.
• **Last win:** September 27, 1925, in Chicago, Illinois, vs. Chicago Cardinals (Hammond 10, Chicago 6).
• **Last game:** November 21, 1926, in Pottsville, Pennsylvania, vs. Pottsville Maroons (Hammond 0, Pottsville 7).

Hartford Blues (Hartford, Connecticut)
• **Last season record:** 3-7-0 (1926).
• **Last head coach:** Jack Keogh.
• **Last win:** November 21, 1926, in Hartford vs. Dayton Triangles (Hartford 16, Dayton 0).
• **Last game:** November 27, 1926, in Hartford vs. Duluth Eskimos (Hartford 0, Duluth 16).

Kansas City Blues (Kansas City, Missouri)
• **Last season record:** 2-7-0 (1924). Became the Kansas City Cowboys in 1925.
• **Last head coach:** Roy Andrews.
• **Last win:** November 11, 1924, in Kansas City vs. Milwaukee Badgers (Kansas City 7, Milwaukee 3).
• **Last game:** November 16, 1924, in Rock Island, Illinois, v. Rock Island Independents (Kansas City 0, Rock Island 17).

Kansas City Cowboys (Kansas City, Missouri)
• **Last known as Kansas City Blues:** 1924.
• **Last season record:** 8-3-0 (1926).
• **Last head coach:** Roy Andrews.
• **Last win:** December 12, 1926, in Kansas City vs. Duluth Eskimos (Kansas City 12, Duluth 7).
• **Last game:** same.

Kenosha Maroons (Kenosha, Wisconsin)
• **Last known as the Toledo Maroons:** 1923.
• **Last season record:** 0-4-1(1924).
• **Last head coaches:** Earl Potteiger, Bo Handley.
• **Last win:** none.
• **Last game:** November 9, 1924, in Buffalo, New York, vs. Buffalo Bison (Kenosha 0, Buffalo 27).

Los Angeles Buccaneers (Los Angeles, California)
• **Last season record:** 6-3-1 (1926).
• **Last head coaches:** Tut Imlay, Brick Muller.
• **Last win:** November 25, 1926, in Detroit, Michigan, vs. Detroit Panthers (Los Angeles 9, Detroit 6).
• **Last game:** December 5, 1926, in Kansas City, Missouri, vs. Kansas City Cowboys (Los Angeles 3, Kansas City 7).

Louisville Brecks (Louisville, Kentucky)
• **Last season record:** 0-4-0 (1923).
• **Last head coach:** Jim Kendrick.
• **Last win:** November 12, 1922, in Louisville vs. Evansville Crimson Giants (Louisville 13, Evansville 6).
• **Last game:** December 9, 1923, in Louisville vs. Oorang Indians (Louisville 0, Oorang 19).

Louisville Colonels (Louisville, Kentucky)
• **Last season record:** 0-4-0 (1926).
• **Last head coach:** Lenny Sachs.
• **Last win:** none.
• **Last game:** November 14, 1926, in Green Bay, Wisconsin, vs. Green Bay Packers (Louisville 0, Green Bay 14).

Milwaukee Badgers (Milwaukee, Wisconsin)
• **Last season record:** 2-7-0 (1926).
• **Last head coach:** Johnny Bryan.
• **Last win:** October 10, 1926, in Racine, Wisconsin, vs. Racine Tornadoes (Milwaukee 13, Racine 2).
• **Last game:** November 14, 1926, in Chicago, Illinois, vs. Chicago Bears (Milwaukee 7, Chicago 10).

Minneapolis Marines (Minneapolis, Minnesota)
• **Last season record:** 0-6-0 (1924).
• **Last head coach:** Joe Brandy.
• **Last win:** November 25, 1923, in Rock Island, Illinois, vs. Rock Island Independents (Minneapolis 6, Rock Island 5).
• **Last game:** November 15, 1924, in Philadelphia, Pennsylvania, vs. Frankford Yellow Jackets (Minneapolis 7, Frankford 39).

Minneapolis Red Jackets (Minneapolis, Minnesota)
• **Last season record:** 1-7-1 (1930).
• **Last head coach:** George Gibson.
• **Last win:** October 12, 1930, in Minneapolis vs. Portsmouth Spartans (Minneapolis 13, Portsmouth 0).
• **Last game:** December 7, 1930, in Portsmouth, Ohio, vs. Portsmouth Spartans (Minneapolis 0, Portsmouth 42).

Muncie Flyers (Muncie, Indiana)
• **Last season record:** 0-2-0 (1921).
• **Last head coach:** Cooney Checkaye.
• **Last win:** none.
• **Last game:** October 16, 1921, in Muncie vs. Cincinnati Celts (Muncie 0, Cincinnati 14).

Newark Tornadoes (Newark, New Jersey)
• **Last known as Orange Tornadoes:** 1929.
• **Last season record:** 1-10-1 (1930).
• **Last head coach:** Andy Salata (Al McCall and Jack Fish also coached part of the last season).
• **Last win:** October 4, 1930, in Philadelphia, Pennsylvania, vs. Frankford Yellow Jackets (Tornadoes 19, Frankford 0).
• **Last game:** October 29, 1930, in New York, New York, vs. New York Giants (Tornadoes 7, Giants 34).

New York Brickley's Giants (New York, New York)
• **Last season record:** 0-2-0 (1921).

- **Last head coach:** Charlie Brickley.
- **Last win:** none.
- **Last game:** December 3, 1921, in New York vs. Cleveland Tigers (New York 0, Cleveland 17).

New York Bulldogs (New York, New York)
- **Last known as the Boston Yanks:** 1948. Became the New York Yanks in 1950.
- **Last season record:** 1-10-1 (1949).
- **Last head coach:** Charley Ewert.
- **Last win:** November 6, 1949, in New York vs. New York Giants (Bulldogs 31, Giants 24).
- **Last game:** December 11, 1949, in New York vs. Pittsburgh Steelers (New York 0, Pittsburgh 27).

New York Yankees (New York, New York)
- **Last known as the Brooklyn Lions:** 1926. Became the Staten Island Stapletons in 1929.
- **Last season record:** 4-8-1 (1928).
- **Last head coach:** Dick Rauch.
- **Last win:** December 16, 1928, in New York vs. New York Giants (New York Yankees 8, New York Giants 6).
- **Last game:** same.

New York Yanks (New York, New York)
- **Last known as the New York Bulldogs:** 1949. Became the Dallas Texans in 1952.
- **Last season record:** 1-9-2 (1951).
- **Last head coach:** Norman ("Red") Strader.
- **Last win:** December 2, 1951, in Green Bay, Wisconsin, vs. Green Bay Packers (New York 31, Packers 18).
- **Last game:** December 16, 1951, in New York vs. New York Giants (New York Yankees 17, New York Giants 27).

Oorang Indians (Marion, Ohio)
Oorang was not a location but rather a breed of Airedale terrier. The team was set up to promote the dog and was composed entirely of Native Americans. They played their home games in Marion, Ohio, hometown of then-President Warren G. Harding.
- **Last season record:** 1-10-0 (1923).
- **Last head coach:** Jim Thorpe.
- **Last win:** December 9, 1923, in Louisville, Kentucky, vs. Louisville Brecks (Oorang 19, Louisville 0).
- **Last game:** same.

Orange Tornadoes (Orange, New Jersey)
- **Last season record:** 3-5-4 (1929). Became the Newark Tornadoes in 1930.
- **Last head coach:** Jack Depler.
- **Last win:** October 20, 1929, in Boston, Massachusetts, vs. Boston Bulldogs (Orange 19, Boston 13).
- **Last game:** December 14, 1929, in Philadelphia, Pennsylvania, vs. Frankford Yellow Jackets (Orange 0, Frankford 10).

Pottsville Maroons (Pottsville, Pennsylvania)
- **Last season record:** 2-8-0 (1928). Became the Boston Bulldogs in 1929.
- **Last head coach:** Pete Henry.
- **Last win:** November 25, 1928, in Pottsville, vs. Green Bay Packers (Pottsville 26 , Green Bay 0).
- **Last game:** November 29, 1928, in Pottsville, vs. Providence Steam Roller (Pottsville 0, Providence 7).

Providence Steam Roller (Providence, Rhode Island)
- **Last season record:** 4-4-3 (1931).
- **Last head coach:** Ed Robinson.
- **Last win:** November 21, 1931, in Providence, vs. Cleveland Indians (Providence 13, Cleveland 7).
- **Last game:** November 29, 1931, in New York, New York, vs. New York Giants (Providence 0, New York 0).

Racine Tornadoes (Racine, Wisconsin)
- **Last known as Racine Legion:** 1924.
- **Last season record:** 1-4-0.
- **Last head coach:** Wally McIlwain (Shorty Barr also coached part of the last season).
- **Last win:** September 26, 1926, in Racine, vs. Hammond Pros (Racine 6, Hammond 3).
- **Last game:** October 24, 1926, in Green Bay, Wisconsin, vs. Green Bay Packers (Racine 0, Green Bay 35).

Rochester Jeffersons (Rochester, New York)
- **Last season record:** 0-5-1 (1925).
- **Last head coach:** Tex Grigg.
- **Last win:** November 20, 1921, in Rochester vs. Columbus Panhandles (Rochester 27, Columbus 13).
- **Last game:** November 15, 1925, in Pottsville, Pennsylvania, vs. Pottsville Maroons (Rochester 6, Pottsville 14).

Rock Island Independents (Rock Island, Illinois)
- **Last season record:** 5-3-3 (1925).
- **Last head coach:** Rube Ursella.
- **Last win:** November 26, 1925, in Detroit, Michigan, vs. Detroit Panthers (Rock Island 6, Detroit 3).
- **Last game:** November 29, 1925, in Chicago, Illinois, vs. Chicago Cardinals (Rock Island 0, Chicago 7).

Saint Louis All-Stars (Saint Louis, Missouri)
- **Last season record:** 1-4-2 (1923).
- **Last head coach:** Ollie Kraehe.
- **Last win:** November 11, 1923, in Saint Louis vs. Oorang Indians (Saint Louis 14, Oorang 0).
- **Last game:** November 24, 1923, in Saint Louis vs. Milwaukee Badgers (Saint Louis 0, Milwaukee 17).

Saint Louis Gunners (Saint Louis, Missouri)
- **Last season record:** 1-2-0 (1934).
- **Last head coach:** Chile Walsh.
- **Last win:** November 11, 1934, in Pittsburgh, Pennsylvania, vs. Pittsburgh Pirates (Saint Louis 6, Pittsburgh 0).
- **Last game:** December 2, 1934, in Saint Louis vs. Green Bay Packers (Saint Louis 14, Green Bay 21).

Staten Island Stapletons (Staten Island, New York)
- **Last known as the New York Yankees:** 1928.
- **Last season record:** 2-7-3 (1932).
- **Last head coach:** Hal Hanson.
- **Last win:** November 20, 1932, in Staten Island vs. Chicago Cardinals (Staten Island 21, Chicago 7).
- **Last game:** November 27, 1932, in Staten Island vs. Green Bay Packers (Staten Island 3, Green Bay 21).

> **Toledo Maroons** (Toledo, Ohio)
> - **Last season record:** 3-3-2 (1923). Became the Kenosha Maroons in 1924.
> - **Last head coach:** Guil Falcon.
> - **Last win:** November 24, 1923, in Rochester, New York vs. Rochester Jeffersons (Toledo 12, Rochester 6).
> - **Last game:** November 29, 1923, in Canton, Ohio, vs. Canton Bulldogs (Toledo 0, Canton 28).
>
> **Tonawanda Kardex** (Tonawanda, New York). Also known as the Lumbermen.
> - **Last season record:** 0-1-0 (1921).
> - **Last head coach:** Walter ("Tam") Rose.
> - **Last win:** none.
> - **Last game:** November 6, 1921, in Rochester, New York, vs. Rochester Jeffersons (Tonawanda 0, Rochester 45).
>
> **Washington Senators** (Washington, D.C.)
> - **Last season record:** 1-2-0 (1921).
> - **Last head coach:** Jack Hegerty.
> - **Last win:** December 11, 1921, in Washington, D.C., vs. Cleveland Indians (Washington 7, Cleveland 0).
> - **Last game:** December 18, 1921, in Washington, D.C., vs. Canton Bulldogs (Washington 14, Canton 28).

Sports—Football—Professional— Teams—All-White

- **Last NFL team to integrate:** the Washington Redskins in 1962.

Sports—Golden Age of Sports

Sports—Golden Age of Sports

The "Golden Age of Sports" was the decade of the 1920s when great American sports icons such as Babe Ruth, Jack Dempsey, Gertrude Ederle, Jim Thorpe, Man O' War, the Four Horsemen of Notre Dame, Red Grange and Big Bill Tilden rose to the forefront of the American media.

- **Last surviving sports icon of the Golden Age of Sports:** Gertrude Ederle, who gained fame as an Olympic swimmer and as the first woman to swim across the English Channel. She died in Wyckoff, New Jersey, on November 30, 2003, age 98.

Sports—Golf

Sports—Golf—Equipment

- **Last golfer to win a major with hickory-shafted clubs:** Johnny Fisher, who won the U.S. Amateur in 1936.

Sports—Golf—Golfers—Turnesa Brothers

The seven American Turnesa brothers were Phil, Frank, Joe, Mike, Jimmy, Doug and Willie. They dominated the game of golf for many years in the mid-20th century.

- **Last surviving Turnesa brother:** Willie ("the Wedge"), the youngest. He was the only brother who did not turn pro. Willie Turnesa won the United States Amateur Championship in 1938 and 1948, the British Amateur Championship in 1947, and was runner-up in the British in 1949. He was also a member of three winning Walker Cup teams and served as captain of the 1951 squad. He died in Sleepy Hollow, New York, on June 16, 2001, age 87.

Sports—Golf—Golfers—Zaharias, Babe

Mildred Ella ("Babe") Didrikson Zaharias won 31 Ladies Professional Golf Association (LPGA) tournaments in her six-year professional career. She was named Associated Press Woman Athlete of the Year six times. Zaharias died in Galveston, Texas, on September 27, 1956, age 42.

• **Last major championship win:** the U.S. Women's Open in 1954, her tenth.
• **Last Western Open win:** 1950, her fourth.
• **Last Titleholders championship win:** 1952. her third.
• **Last year she was named Associated Press Woman Athlete of the Year:** 1954. Zaharias also received the award in 1932, 1945, 1946, 1947 and 1950.
• **Last major professional victories:** Tampa Open and Peach Blossom Classic in 1955.

Sports—Golf—Streaks—Majors—Nicklaus, Jack

Jack Nicklaus joined the Professional Golf Association (PGA) tour in 1962 and did not miss a major between that year and 1998. During that time, he played in 146 consecutive majors championships.
• **Last of Nicklaus's consecutive majors championship streak:** July 7, 1998, when he announced he would not be competing in the 1998 British Open or PGA Championship.

Sports—Horse Racing
Last Events of Some Major Race Horses

Affirmed
Affirmed was the last Triple Crown winner of 20th century when he captured the 1978 Triple Crown. He won 22 of his 29 career races and was the first horse to win more than $2 million. He died on January 12, 2001, age 26.
• **Last race:** 1979 Jockey Club Gold Cup. Affirmed's saddle slipped and he wound up last, making it the only time in his career that he did not finish in the money. Affirmed retired to stud.

Citation
Citation, winner of the 1948 Triple Crown, won a record 16 straight races. He died on August 8, 1970, age 25.
• **Last race:** Hollywood Gold Cup in Inglewood, California, on July 14, 1951. Citation won by four lengths and pushed his winnings past $1 million.
• **Last public appearance at a race track:** July 28, 1951, at Arlington Park, when he was paraded before a crowd of 28,000, before being retired to stud.

Man O' War
Man O' War was one of the great stars of the "Golden Age of Sports." He won 20 of 21 starts. His only loss was due to a mix-up at the starting gate. He died on November 1, 1947, age 30.
• **Last race:** October 12, 1920, at Kenilworth Park, Windsor, Ontario. It was a match race with Sir Barton, the 1919 Triple Crown Winner. Man O' War won the $75,000 purse and $5,000 Gold Cup by seven lengths. He went on to stud for more than 20 years and produced 386 registered foals, including 1937 Triple Crown winner War Admiral and Clyde Van Dusen, the 1929 Kentucky Derby winner.

Seabiscuit
Seabiscuit, a grandson of Man O' War, retired at age 7 as an all-time money winner. Considered the underdog, he defeated Triple Crown winner War Admiral, a son of Man O' War, in a special two-horse race at Pimlico in 1938. He died in 1947 at age 14.
• **Last race:** March 2, 1940, the Santa Anita Handicap at Santa Anita Park in California.

Secretariat
Secretariat, winner of the 1973 Triple Crown, won the Belmont by an astonishing 31 lengths and set a record. Secretariat died in 1989.
• **Last race:** October 28, 1973, at the Canadian International Championship at Woodbine Race Course.

> • **Last public appearance at a race track:** November 6, 1973, when he was paraded before a crowd of 32,900, at Aqueduct in New York before going to stud. At the time of his death, an autopsy revealed that his heart was two and a half times larger than the average horse.

Sports—Horse Racing—Jockeys—Arcaro, Eddie

George Edward ("Eddie") Arcaro was the only jockey to ride two Triple Crown champions. He had 17 Triple Crown racing victories, including five Kentucky Derbies. In 24,092 races, Arcaro's earnings totaled more than $30 million, including 554 stakes victories. He retired because of bursitis in his right arm. After retiring, Arcaro served as a TV commentator and a public relations rep for the Golden Nugget Casinos. He died on November 14, 1997, age 81.

• **Last race:** November 18, 1961, at age 45, finishing third on Endymion in the Pimlico Futurity.

• **Last Kentucky Derby win:** 1952, riding Hill Gail.

• **Last victory in a Triple Crown race:** in the 1956 Preakness with Fabius, a son of Citation.

Sports—Horse Racing—Jockeys—Shoemaker, Willie

William Lee ("Willie") Shoemaker held the record as the winningest jockey in horse-racing. He retired with 8,833 wins. He then pursued a career as a trainer. In 1991, he was seriously injured an automobile accident. After months of rehabilitation, he returned to training and won a race two days later. He died in San Marino, California, on October 12, 2003, age 72.

• **Last victory as a jockey:** January 20, 1990, riding Beau Genius in the Hallandale Handicap at Gulfstream Park in Florida.

• **Last race as a jockey:** February 3, 1990, at Santa Anita Park, finishing fourth riding Patchy Groundfog in a race billed as "The Legend's Last Ride." It was Shoemaker's 40,350[th] race.

• **Last race as a trainer:** November 3, 1997. Shoemaker retired after the Oak Tree Meet at Santa Anita Park.

Sports—Horse Racing—Women Jockeys

• **Last year women were prohibited from being jockeys at major U.S. race tracks:** 1968. The following year, Diane Crump became the first woman to ride in a U.S. thoroughbred race.

Sports—Ice Hockey

Sports—Ice Hockey—Early (pre-NHL)

• **Last time professional and amateur hockey players played together:** 1910. That year, the National Hockey Association was formed and the mixed teams ended.

• **Last year of the National Hockey Association:** 1917, when it was replaced by the National Hockey League (NHL).

• **Last pre-NHL Stanley Cup winner:** Seattle Metropolitans in 1917. The Stanley Cup was first awarded in 1893.

Sports—Ice Hockey—NHL—Early Years and "Original Six Era"

The years 1942 to 1967 are known in ice hockey as the "Original Six Era." The Boston Bruins, Chicago Black Hawks, Detroit Red Wings, Montreal Canadiens, New York Rangers and Toronto Maple Leafs were the only teams in the league.

• **Last surviving NHL inaugural (1917-18) teams:** Montreal Canadiens and Toronto Maple Leafs. Other teams would come and go in the early years of the NHL. The four teams that joined the league during the 1920s were Boston, Chicago, Detroit and New York.

• **Last of the "Original Six Era":** ended at the beginning of the 1967-68 season, when several expansion teams were added to the league.

• **Last regular season goal in the "Original Six Era":** scored by Wayne Rivers of the Boston Bruins on April 1, 1967, at 19:18 of the third period in a 5-2 loss to the Toronto

Maple Leafs. Wayne Connelly got the last assist. This was the latest goal scored in the three NHL games played on the last day of the 1966-67 season.

• **Last regular season games of the "Original Six Era":** April 1, 1967, when the Toronto Maple Leafs beat the Boston Bruins 5-2; the Chicago Black Hawks beat the New York Rangers 8-0; and the Montreal Canadiens beat the Detroit Red Wings 4-2.

• **Last "Original Six Era" Stanley Cup winner:** the Toronto Maple Leafs, who beat the Montreal Canadiens 4-2 in 1967.

Sports—Ice Hockey—"Original Six Era" Teams
Last Team Events at the Original Six Arenas

Boston Bruins

The Boston Bruins began playing at the Boston Garden in 1928.

• **Last Bruins regular-season game at the Boston Garden:** May 1, 1995. The Boston Bruins beat the Ottawa Senators 5-4. The last goal of the game was scored by Pavol Demitra of the Senators.

• **Last Bruins playoff game at the Boston Garden:** May 14, 1995. The New Jersey Devils beat the Boston Bruins 3-2. The last goal of the game was scored by Adam Oates of the Bruins.

• **Last Bruins game at the Boston Garden:** September 26, 1995. The Bruins beat the Montreal Canadiens 3-0 in an NHL exhibition match.

Chicago Black Hawks

The Chicago Black Hawks began playing at Chicago Stadium in 1929.

• **Last regular-season Black Hawks game at Chicago Stadium:** April 14, 1994. The Maple Leafs beat the Black Hawks 6-4. The last goal of the game was scored by John Cullen of the Maple Leafs.

• **Last playoff game at Chicago Stadium:** April 28, 1994. The Toronto Maple Leafs beat the Black Hawks 1-0. The last goal of the game was scored by Mike Gartner of the Maple Leafs.

Detroit Red Wings

The Detroit Red Wings began playing at Olympia Stadium in 1927.

• **Last Red Wings game at Olympia Stadium:** December 15, 1979. The Detroit Red Wings tied the Quebec Nordiques 4-4. The last goal of the game was scored by Greg Joly of the Red Wings.

Montreal Canadiens

The Montreal Canadiens began playing at the Montreal Forum in 1924.

• **Last regular-season Canadiens game at the Montreal Forum:** March 11, 1996. The Montreal Canadiens beat the Dallas Stars 4-1. The last goal of the game was scored by Andrei Kovalenko of the Canadiens.

• **Last Canadiens playoff game at the Montreal Forum:** April 27, 1994. The Boston Bruins beat the Canadiens 3-2. The last goal of the game was scored by Al Iafrate of the Bruins.

New York Rangers

The New York Rangers began playing at the old Madison Square Garden in 1925.

• **Last Rangers game at old Madison Square Garden:** February 11, 1968. The New York Rangers tied the Detroit Red Wings 3-3. The last goal of the game was scored by Jean Ratelle of the Rangers.

> **Toronto Maple Leafs**
> The Toronto Maple Leafs began playing at Maple Leaf Gardens in 1931. It would become the last surviving hockey arena from the "Original Six Era."
> • **Last Maple Leafs game at Maple Leaf Gardens:** February 13, 1999. The Chicago Black Hawks beat the Toronto Maple Leafs 6-2. The last goal of the game was scored by Bob Probert of the Chicago Black Hawks.

Sports—Ice Hockey—NHL—Players—Gretzky, Wayne

When Wayne Douglas Gretzky retired in 1999, he held or shared 61 National Hockey League (NHL) records, including most goals, most assists and most points, both in one season and career. He was named Most Valuable Player on nine occasions, won 11 titles for most goals and played in 18 All-Star games. One day after he retired, he was nominated to the Ice Hockey Hall of Fame.

• **Last NHL season:** 1998-99, the year he collected his 2,800th point.

• **Last NHL game:** April 18, 1999, with the New York Rangers against Pittsburgh.

• **Last NHL point:** April 18, 1999, assist on goal by Brian Leetch at 19:30 of the second period.

• **Last NHL goal:** March 29, 1999 vs. New York Islanders.

• **Last NHL multi-goal game:** March 22, 1998, vs. Pittsburgh, two goals.

• **Last NHL hat trick:** October 11, 1997, vs. Vancouver.

• **Last NHL penalty shot:** January 5, 1991, vs. Toronto's Peter Ing. Gretzky did not score.

Sports—Ice Hockey—NHL—Players—Howe, Gordie

Gordon ("Gordie") Howe is one of the great forwards and is often known as "Mr. Hockey." He played his first pro hockey game in 1946 and appeared in a game for the last time in 1997 in a career that spanned six decades.

• **Last NHL season:** 1979-80, the year Howe collected his 800th goal.

• **Last regular-season NHL game:** April 6, 1980, with the Hartford Whalers against Detroit.

• **Last NHL playoff game:** April 11, 1980, in the playoffs with the Hartford Whalers against the Montreal Canadiens. The Canadiens swept the best-of-five series in three straight games.

• **Last NHL goal:** April 9, 1980, in the second game of the playoffs against the Montreal Canadiens at 13:59 of the third period. The Whalers lost that game to the Canadiens 8-4. Howe was playing alongside his son who drew the only assist.

• **Last All-Star appearance:** February 5, 1980, at the Joe Louis Arena in Detroit. The event drew the largest crowd ever to watch an NHL game up to that time. During his career, Howe played in 23 All-Star games.

• **Last pro game:** October 4, 1997, when he played 47 seconds in the opening game for the Detroit Vipers of the International Hockey League, at age 69. Howe did not touch the puck in the game but became the only player to compete during six decades of hockey.

Sports—Ice Hockey—NHL—Players—Goalie—Captains

In the history of the NHL, only six goalies have served as team captains: the team leader who is designated by wearing a "C." Today, goalies are the only players who cannot serve as team captains.

• **Last NHL goalie/team captain:** Bill Durnan of the Montreal Canadiens during the 1947-48 season. Durnan's tendency to leave the crease to question calls with referees upset opponents who saw the practice as a way to slow down or delay games by gaining unscheduled timeouts. NHL officials agreed and passed a rule the following season that prohibits goalies from serving as captains.

Sports—Ice Hockey—NHL—Rules—Face Masks

• **Last NHL goalie to play without a face mask:** Andy Brown of the Pittsburgh Penguins. He played his last game without a face mask on April 7, 1974, with the Penguins. They lost to the Atlanta Flames, 6-3. Brown went on to play three seasons in the World Hockey Association (WHA) and did not wear a face mask there either. He retired during the 1976-77 WHA season.

Sports—Ice Hockey—NHL—Rules— Helmets

The NHL began requiring players to use helmets with the 1979-80 season. However, players who were already active were permitted to continue to play without helmets, provided they sign a waiver absolving the league from responsibility in case of a head injury.

• **Last NHL player to play without a helmet:** Craig MacTavish, who retired from the Saint Louis Blues of the NHL on April 29, 1997. He was the last player to retire who signed the waiver. During 16 seasons, he scored 213 goals.

Sports—Ice Hockey—NHL—Rules— Long Pants

Although long pants enabled a team to skate faster, the long pants also caused players to slide into the boards with more force and injure themselves.

• **Last NHL teams to play with long pants:** Philadelphia Flyers and Hartford Whalers during the 1982-83 season. Long pants were banned after the season for safety reasons.

Sports—Ice Hockey—NHL—Rules— Overtime

In 1942, during World War II, regular-season overtime was discontinued because of wartime restrictions on travel.

• **Last of the "Original Six Era" overtime rules:** The last regular-season overtime game of the "Original Six Era" took place on November 10, 1942, in New York. The New York Rangers beat the Chicago Black Hawks 5-3 in a game with an overtime period that was played in its entirety, as opposed to sudden death. In overtime, both Bryan Hextall and Lynn Patrick scored for New York; Patrick scored the last goal. Regular season overtime was not re-

established until the 1983-84 season.

• **Last use of 1983-84 overtime rules:** during the 1998-99 season. Beginning with the 1999-2000 season, a new set of regular season overtime rules went into effect that required one skater to be removed from the ice.

Sports—Ice Hockey—NHL—Streaks— Games Played

Doug Jarvis earned the record for the most consecutive games played in the NHL with 964. During the 1986-87 season, he broke the record of 914 games that had been set by center Garry Unger.

• **Last game of Jarvis's consecutive-games-played streak:** October 10, 1987, with the Hartford Whalers against the New York Rangers. In his next game, Jarvis sat out and was replaced by Brent Peterson.

Sports—Ice Hockey—NHL—Streaks— Scoring

Wayne Gretzky scored a goal in 51 consecutive games during 1983-84.

• **Last game of Gretzky's scoring streak:** January 27, 1984, with the Edmonton Oilers against the New Jersey Devils. The streak was broken the following night in a game against the Los Angeles Kings.

Sports—Ice Hockey—NHL—Streaks— Winning

During the 1979-80 season, the Philadelphia Flyers set a record by playing 35 consecutive games without a loss. Their record during the streak was 25-0-10.

• **Last game of the Flyers 1979-80 winning streak:** January 6, 1980, when the Philadelphia Flyers beat the Buffalo Sabres 4-2. The Flyers lost the next game against the Minnesota North Stars on the following night. The previous record was held by the Montreal Canadiens with 28 games during the 1977-78 season.

Sports—Ice Hockey—NHL—Teams— All-Stars

• **Last season coaches were named to the end-of-the-season All-Star team:** 1945-46. That year, Dick Irvin of the Montreal Cana-

diens was selected as First Team coach, and Johnny Gottselig of the Chicago Black Hawks was selected as Second Team Coach.
• **Last season each All-Star team featured two goalies instead of three:** 1990-91. During the 1991-92 season, the All-Star teams were increased in size because additional expansion teams joined the league.

Sports—Ice Hockey—NHL Teams—Defunct or Relocated
Last Season, Game, Goal and Stanley Cup

Atlanta Flames

The Atlanta Flames played eight seasons in the NHL.
• **Last season:** 1979-80.
• **Last goal:** April 5, 1980, scored by Ken Houston, assisted by Don Lever and Kent Nilsson at 17:34 of the third period of a game against the Washington Capitals. The Flames and the Capitals tied 4-4. Wayne Stephenson was the opposing goalie. The next season the Flames moved to Calgary.
• **Last Stanley Cup:** none.
• **Last Stanley Cup appearance:** none.

Cleveland Barons

The Cleveland Barons played two seasons in the NHL. They merged with the Minnesota North Stars in 1978.
• **Last season:** 1977-78.
• **Last goal:** April 9, 1978, scored by Dennis Maruk assisted by Kris Manery and Mike Fidler at 15:28 of the third period of a game against the Pittsburgh Penguins. The Barons lost to the Penguins 3-2. Denis Haron was the opposing goalie.
• **Last Stanley Cup:** none.
• **Last Stanley Cup appearance:** none.

Colorado Rockies

The Colorado Rockies played six seasons in the NHL. In 1982, they moved to New Jersey and were renamed the New Jersey Devils.
• **Last season:** 1981-82.
• **Last goal:** April 3, 1982, scored by John Wensink assisted by Kevin Maxwell and Stan Weir at 16:22 of the third period of a game against the Calgary Flames. The Rockies beat the Flames 3-1. Pat Riggin was the opposing goalie.
• **Last Stanley Cup:** none.
• **Last Stanley Cup appearance:** none.

Detroit Cougars

The Detroit Cougars played four seasons before they were renamed the Detroit Falcons.
• **Last season:** 1929-30.
• **Last Stanley Cup:** none.
• **Last Stanley Cup appearance:** none.

Detroit Falcons

The Detroit Falcons played two seasons before they were renamed the Detroit Red Wings.
• **Last season:** 1931-32.
• **Last goal:** March 20, 1932, scored by Ebbie Goodfellow with an assist by Wally Kilrea at 1:35 in the third period in a game against the Toronto Maple Leafs. The Falcons lost to the Maple Leafs, 3-2. Lorne Chabot was the opposing goalie.
• **Last Stanley Cup:** none.
• **Last Stanley Cup appearance:** none.

Hamilton Tigers

The Hamilton Tigers played five seasons in the NHL and then went on strike after the

1924-25 season. The team was sold and moved to New York the next season, where it was renamed the New York Americans.
- **Last season:** 1924-25.
- **Last goal:** March 9, 1925, scored by Red Green in a game against the Montreal Canadiens. The Tigers lost to the Canadiens 4-1.
- **Last Stanley Cup:** none.
- **Last Stanley Cup appearance:** none.

Hartford Whalers
The Hartford Whalers played 18 seasons in the NHL.
- **Last season:** 1996-97.
- **Last goal:** April 13, 1997, scored by Kevin Dineen, assisted by Geoff Sanderson and Andrew Cassels at 0:24 of the third period in a game against the Tampa Bay Lightning. The Whalers beat the Lightning 2-1. Knowing it was the last game for the team in Hartford, the Whalers coaches allowed back-up goalie Jason Muzzatti to play the final second of the game so that his name could be recorded on the final fact sheet as well as the starting goalie. Muzzatti is recorded as playing 0:01 and teammate Sean Burke as playing 59:59 in the final game.
- **Last Stanley Cup:** none.
- **Last Stanley Cup appearance:** none.

Kansas City Scouts
The Kansas City Scouts played two season in the NHL.
- **Last season:** 1975-76.
- **Last goal:** April 4, 1976, scored by Craig Patrick with an assist by Dave Hudson at 5:42 of the third period in a game against the Vancouver Canucks. The Scouts lost to the Canucks, 6-2.
- **Last Stanley Cup:** none.
- **Last Stanley Cup appearance:** none.

Minnesota North Stars
The Minnesota North Stars played 26 seasons in the NHL and made the playoffs 17 times. The North Stars moved to Dallas in 1993 and was renamed the Dallas Stars.
- **Last season:** 1992-93.
- **Last goal:** April 15, 1993, scored by Ulf Dahlen assisted by Russ Courtnall and Dave Gagner at 19:11 of the third period of a game against the Detroit Red Wings. The North Stars lost to the Red Wings, 5-3. Tim Chevaldae was the opposing goalie.
- **Last Stanley Cup:** none.
- **Last Stanley Cup appearance:** 1991, losing to the Pittsburgh Penguins 4-2.

Montreal Maroons
The Montreal Maroons played 14 seasons in the NHL. They won the Stanley Cup twice.
- **Last season:** 1937-38.
- **Last goal:** March 17, 1938, scored by Jimmy Ward in a 6-3 loss to their rivals, the Montreal Canadiens. The goal came at 19:46 of the third period assisted by Paul Runge and Baldy Northcott. Wilf Cude was the opposing goalie.
- **Last Stanley Cup:** 1935, beating Toronto 3-0.
- **Last Stanley Cup appearance:** same.

Montreal Wanderers
The Montreal Wanderers team played only four NHL games and only won one game. The franchise ended after their rink burned down
- **Last season:** 1917-18.
- **Last of their rink, the Westmount Arena:** burned down on January 2, 1918. After the fire, the team folded.

- **Last pre-NHL Stanley Cup:** 1908.
- **Last Stanley Cup appearance:** none.

New York/ Brooklyn Americans

The New York/Brooklyn Americans played 17 seasons in the NHL, and only the last one was as Brooklyn. In their last season, they came in last place, but still produced Hart trophy winner Tommy Anderson.

- **Last season:** 1941-42.
- **Last goal:** March 17, 1942, scored by future Hall-of-Famer Harry Watson, who was then an 18-year-old rookie. Watson scored the goal at 10:09 of the third period of a game assisted by Norm Larson and Tommy Anderson. The Americans lost to the Boston Bruins 8-3. Frank Brimsek was the opposing goalie.
- **Last Stanley Cup:** none.
- **Last Stanley Cup appearance:** none.

Oakland Seals/California Golden Seals/California Seals

The Oakland/California Golden Seals played three seasons as the Oakland Seals. In August 1970, when the team was bought by Charlie O. Finley, the name was changed to the California Golden Seals. In February 1974, the NHL took over the franchise and renamed the team the California Seals

- **Last season:** 1975-76.
- **Last goal:** April 4, 1976, scored by Jim Moxey at 19:58 of the third period with an assist by Rick Hampton. The Seals beat the Los Angeles Kings 5-2. The next season, the Seals moved to Cleveland and became the Barons.
- **Last Stanley Cup:** none.
- **Last Stanley Cup appearance:** none.

Ottawa Senators

The Ottawa Senators won nine Stanley Cups during their 16 seasons in the NHL.

- **Last season:** 1933-34.
- **Last goal:** March 17, 1934, scored by Des Roche at 16:35 in the third period of a game against the Montreal Maroons. Des's brother Earl Roche and Syd Howe assisted. The Senators tied the Maroons 2-2. Dave Kerr was the opposing goalie. The next season, the team moved to Saint Louis, Missouri, and became the Saint Louis Eagles.
- **Last Stanley Cup:** 1927 beating Boston 2-0.
- **Last Stanley Cup appearance:** same.

Philadelphia Quakers

The Philadelphia Quakers played only one season and won only four games. In 1931, the team received permission from the NHL to cease operations for a season while they resolved some logistical and financial problems, but they fell victims to the Great Depression. In 1936, after having been shut down for five years, they folded.

- **Last season:** 1930-31.
- **Last goal:** March 22, 1931, scored by Gerry Lowrey at 15:30 of the third period with an assist by Wally Kilrea. The Quakers tied the Montreal Canadiens 4-4.
- **Last Stanley Cup:** none.
- **Last Stanley Cup appearance:** none.

Pittsburgh Pirates

The Pittsburgh Pirates played five seasons in the NHL.

- **Last season:** 1929-30.
- **Last goal:** March 18, 1930, scored by Herb Drury at 17:45 of the second period. The Pirates lost to the Detroit Falcons 4-2. The next season, the team moved to Philadelphia and became the Quakers.

- **Last Stanley Cup:** none.
- **Last Stanley Cup appearance:** none.

Quebec Bulldogs

The Quebec Bulldogs played only one season in the NHL and won only four games. They had won two Stanley Cups prior to joining the NHL.
- **Last season:** 1919-20.

Quebec Nordiques

The Quebec Nordiques played 16 seasons in the NHL. They moved to Denver in 1995 and were renamed the Colorado Avalanche.
- **Last season:** 1994-95.
- **Last game:** May 16, 1995.
- **Last goal:** May 3, 1995, scored by Sylvain Lefebvre, assisted by Owen Nolan and Craig Wolanin, at 9:25 of the third period of a game against the Hartford Whalers. The Nordiques beat the Whalers 4-1.
- **Last Stanley Cup:** none.
- **Last Stanley Cup appearance:** none.

Saint Louis Eagles

The Saint Louis Eagles played only one season.
- **Last season:** 1934-35.
- **Last goal:** March 19, 1935, scored by Carl Voss in the third period of a game against the Toronto Maple Leafs. The Eagles lost to the Maple Leafs 5-3. The opposing goalie was George Hainsworth.
- **Last Stanley Cup:** none.
- **Last Stanley Cup appearance:** none.

Toronto Arenas

The Toronto Arenas played only two seasons in the NHL but won the Stanley Cup in 1918.
- **Last season:** 1918-19.
- **Last game:** February 20, 1919, losing to the Ottawa Senators in Ottawa, 9-3.
- **Last Stanley Cup:** 1918, beating the Vancouver Millionaires 3-2.
- **Last Stanley Cup appearance:** same.

Toronto Saint Patricks

The Toronto Saint Patricks played beginning in 1919-20 and won the Stanley Cup in 1922.
- **Last season:** 1926-27.
- **Last game:** February 16, 1927, losing to Detroit 5-1 in Detroit, Michigan. The Saint Patricks became the Maple Leafs on February 17, 1927, when the team was taken over by Conn Smythe.
- **Last goal:** February 16, 1927, against the Detroit Red Wings.
- **Last Stanley Cup:** 1922, beating the Vancouver Millionaires 3-2.
- **Last Stanley Cup appearance:** same.

Winnipeg Jets

The Winnipeg Jets played 17 seasons in the NHL. The team moved to Arizona in 1996 and became the Phoenix Coyotes.
- **Last season:** 1995-96.
- **Last regular season goal:** April 14, 1996, scored by Darrin Shannon assisted by Mike Eastwood and Oleg Tverdovsky at 19:48 of the third period of a game against the Anaheim Mighty Ducks. The Jets lost 5-2. Guy Herbert was the opposing goalie.
- **Last playoff game:** April 28, 1996. The Jets lost to Detroit in the sixth game of their playoff series at Winnipeg Arena.
- **Last Stanley Cup:** none.
- **Last Stanley Cup appearance:** none.

Sports—Olympics—Events—Discontinued
Last year some major Olympic events were played before being discontinued

Olympic Event	Last Year
Cricket	1900
Croquet	1900
Cycling–440 Yard	1904
Cycling–1/3 Mile	1904
Cycling–880 Yard	1904
Cycling–1 Mile	1904
Cycling–660 Yard	1906
Cycling–5 Kilometer	1908
Cycling–10 Kilometer	1906
Cycling–20 Kilometer	1908
Cycling–50 Kilometer	1924
Cycling–100 Kilometer	1908
Cycling–12-Hour Race	1896
Diving–Plain High Diving	1924
Diving–Plunge	1904
Fencing–Sword and Sabre	1906
Field Handball	1936
Golf (Men's)	1904
Golf (Women's)	1900
Gymnastics–Calisthenics	1952
Gymnastics–Horizontal Parallel Bars (Team)	1896
Gymnastics–Indian Club	1932
Gymnastics–Rope Climb	1932
Gymnastics–Side Vault	1924
Gymnastics–Swedish/Free Systems (Team)	1920
Gymnastics–Tumbling	1932
Jeu de Paume (Court Tennis)	1908
Lacrosse	1908
Motorboating	1908
Polo	1936
Racquet (Men's)	1908
Roque	1904
Rowing–Inrigger Fours	1912
Rowing–Man-of-War	1906
Rugby	1924
Shooting–Army Gun	1936
Shooting–Disappearing Target	1912
Shooting–Dueling Pistol (30 Meter)	1912
Shooting–Free Pistol (Team)	1920
Shooting–Free Rifle	1924
Shooting–Live Pigeon Shooting	1900
Shooting–Military Revolver	1896
Shooting–Military Rifle	1920

Notable Last Facts

Shooting–Running Deer	1924
Shooting–Small-Bore Rifle	1920
Shooting–Trap Team	1924
Swimming–Relay Races	1906
Swimming–50 Yard Freestyle	1904
Swimming–200 Meter Freestyle	1900
Swimming–200 Yard Freestyle	1904
Swimming–400 Meter Breaststroke	1920
Swimming–880 Yard Freestyle	1904
Swimming–4,000 Meter Freestyle	1900
Track and Field (Men's)–60 Meter Dash	1904
Track and Field (Men's)–5 Mile Run	1908
Track and Field (Men's)–200 Meter Hurdles	1904
Track and Field (Men's)–Steeplechase 2,500 Meter	1900
Track and Field (Men's)–Steeplechase 2,590 Meter	1904
Track and Field (Men's)–Steeplechase 3,200 Meter	1908
Track and Field (Men's)–Steeplechase 4,000 Meter	1900
Track and Field (Men's)–3,000 Meter Team Run	1924
Track and Field (Men's)–Cross-Country (Individual) 8,000 Meter	1912
Track and Field (Men's)–Cross-Country (Individual) 10,000 Meter	1920
Track and Field (Men's)–Cross-Country (Individual) 10,650 Meter	1924
Track and Field (Men's)–Cross-Country (Team) 5,000 Meter	1900
Track and Field (Men's)–Cross-Country (Team) 6,437 Meter	1904
Track and Field (Men's)–Cross-Country (Individual) 8,000 Meter	1912
Track and Field (Men's)–Cross-Country (Individual) 10,000 Meter	1920
Track and Field (Men's)–Cross-Country (Individual) 10,650 Meter	1924
Track and Field (Men's)–Walking–1,500 Meter	1906
Track and Field (Men's)–Walking–3,000 Meter	1920
Track and Field (Men's)–Walking–3,500 Meter	1908
Track and Field (Men's)–Walking–10,000 Meter	1952
Track and Field (Men's)–Walking–10 Mile	1908
Track and Field (Men's)–Standing High Jump	1912
Track and Field (Men's)–Standing Broad Jump	1912
Track and Field (Men's)–Standing Hop, Step, Jump	1904
Track and Field (Men's)–16-Pound Shot Put Two Hands	1912
Track and Field (Men's)–56-Pound Weight Throw	1920
Track and Field (Men's)–Discus Greek Style	1908
Track and Field (Men's)–Discus Two Hands	1912
Track and Field (Men's)–Javelin Freestyle	1908
Track and Field (Men's)–Javelin Two Hands	1912
Track and Field (Men's)–Pentathlon	1924
Track and Field (Men's)–Tug-of-War	1920
Weightlifting–One Hand	1906
Weightlifting–Two Hand	1906
Yachting–6 Meter Class	1952
Yachting–6.5 Meter Class	1920
Yachting–7 Meter Class	1920
Yachting–8 Meter Class	1936

Yachting–10 Meter Class	1920
Yachting–12 Meter Class	1956
Yachting–18 Foot Centerboard	1920
Yachting–30 Meter Class	1920
Yachting–40 Meter Class	1920
Yachting–Firefly Class	1948
Yachting–Monotype Class	1936

Sports—Soccer

Sports—Soccer—Early Leagues— American Soccer Leagues (Pre-NASL)

After the World Cup was broadcast throughout North America in 1966, American sports promoters began to plan an American professional soccer league. Two were created in 1967: United Soccer Association (USA) and National Professional Soccer League (NPSL). The United Soccer Association imported entire teams from overseas.

• **Last of the United Soccer Association (USA):** 1968, when it merged with the National Professional Soccer League (NPSL) to form the North American Soccer League (NASL).

• **Last of National Professional Soccer League (NPSL):** 1968, when it merged with the United Soccer Association (USA) to form the North American Soccer League (NASL). The NPSL, which captured the American television contract and recruited players, lasted one year.

Sports—Soccer—Early Leagues—U.S.— North American Soccer League (NASL)

Numerous soccer leagues have come and gone in the United States. The league with the greatest impact and renown was the North American Soccer League (NASL), which operated from 1968 to 1984.

• **Last NASL championship team:** Chicago Sting.

• **Last NASL Most Valuable Player:** Steve Zungul, Golden Bay Earthquakes in 1984.

• **Last NASL Rookie of the Year:** Roy Wegerle of the Tampa Bay Rowdies in 1984.

• **Last NASL leading scorer:** Steve Zungul of the Golden Bay Earthquakes in 1984 with 20 goals and 10 assists.

• **Last NASL leading goal tender:** Paul Hammond of the Toronto Blizzards in 1984 with 60 saves, 7 shutouts, and a Goals Allowed Average (GAA) of 1.16.

• **Last NASL Coach of the Year:** Don Popovic of the Golden Bay Earthquakes in 1983. No coaching award was given in 1984.

• **Last of the NASL:** folded in March 1985, taking with it the teams from Toronto, Tampa Bay, Vancouver and Golden Bay.

Sports—Soccer—Early Leagues—U.S.— Other Soccer Leagues

After the North American Soccer League (NASL) folded in 1985, several of the old NASL teams joined the Major Indoor Soccer League (MISL). The MISL had been formed in 1978 as the first attempt to create an indoor professional soccer league in the United States.

• **Last season as MISL:** 1990, when the MISL changed its name to Major Soccer League (MSL). The MISL had been weakened by competition from the NASL for good players.

• **Last MSL season:** folded after the 1991-92 season.

• **Last MSL championship team:** the San Diego Sockers.

• **Last MSL teams:**
Baltimore Blast
Cleveland Crunch
Dallas Sidekicks
Kansas City Comets
San Diego Sockers
St. Louis Storm
Tacoma Stars
Wichita Wings

Cleveland and Wichita joined the National Professional Soccer League (NPSL), which had been founded in 1984 as the American Indoor Soccer League (AISL).
• **Last AISL season:** 1990, when it changed its name to NPSL (the second league to use this name). The San Diego and Dallas teams joined the Continental Indoor Soccer League (CISL), which was founded in 1993, in the wake of the MISL's collapse.
• **Last CISL season:** folded a few months after the end of the 1997 season.
• **Last CISL championship team:** Seattle Sea Dogs.
• **Last NPSL (II) season:** folded in late August 2000, along with some of the league's teams. A new league was created, Major Indoor Soccer League II (MISL II), consisting of the remaining eight NPSL (II) teams.
• **Last NPSL (II) championship team:** Milwaukee Wave.

Sports—Soccer—Leagues—Defunct or Relocated
North American Soccer League (NASL)—Teams

Team	Last Year
Atlanta Apollos (replaced the Atlanta Chiefs (I))	1973
Atlanta Chiefs (I) (replaced by the Atlanta Apollos)	1972
Atlanta Chiefs (II)	1981
Baltimore Bays	1969
Baltimore Comets (moved to San Diego; became the Jaws)	1975
Boston Beacons (replaced the Boston Rovers)	1968
Boston Minutemen	1976
Boston Rovers (replaced by the Boston Beacons)	1967
Calgary Boomers	1981
California Surf	1981
Chicago Mustangs	1968
Chicago Spurs (moved to Kansas City)	1967
Chicago Sting	1984
Cleveland Stokers	1968
Colorado Caribous (moved to Atlanta; became the Chiefs (II))	1978
Connecticut Bicentennials (moved to Oakland; became the Stompers)	1977
Dallas Tornado	1981
Denver Dynamos (moved to Minnesota; became the Kicks)	1975
Detroit Cougars	1968
Detroit Express	1980
Edmonton Drillers	1982
Fort Lauderdale Strikers (moved to Minnesota)	1983
Golden Bay Earthquakes (replaced the San Jose Earthquakes)	1984
Hartford Bicentennials (became the Connecticut Bicentennials)	1976
Hawaii/Team Hawaii (moved to Tulsa; became the Roughnecks)	1977
Houston Hurricane	1980
Houston Stars	1968
Jacksonville Tea Men	1982
Kansas City Spurs	1970
Las Vegas Quicksilver (moved to San Diego; became the Sockers	1977
Los Angeles Aztecs	1981
Los Angeles Toros (moved to San Diego)	1967

Los Angeles Wolves	1968
Memphis Rogues (moved to Calgary; became the Boomers)	1980
Miami Gators (replaced by the Miami Toros)	1972
Miami Toros (moved to Fort Lauderdale; became the Strikers)	1976
Minnesota Kicks	1981
Minnesota Strikers	1984
Montreal Manic	1983
Montreal Olympique	1973
New England Tea Men (moved to Jacksonville)	1980
New York Cosmos	1985
New York Generals	1968
New York Skyliners	1967
Oakland Clippers	1968
Oakland Stompers (moved to Edmonton; became the Drillers)	1978
Philadelphia Atoms	1976
Philadelphia Fury (moved to Montreal; became the Manic)	1980
Philadelphia Spartans	1967
Pittsburgh Phantoms	1967
Portland Timbers	1982
Rochester Lancers	1980
Saint Louis Stars (moved to California; became the Surf)	1977
San Antonio Thunder (moved to Hawaii; became Team Hawaii)	1976
San Diego Jaws (moved to Las Vegas; became the Quicksilver)	1976
San Diego Sockers	1984
San Diego Toros	1968
San Francisco Gales	1967
San Jose Earthquakes (became the Golden Bay Earthquakes)	1982
Seattle Sounders	1983
Tampa Bay Rowdies	1984
Toronto Blizzards (replaced the Toronto Metro-Croatia)	1984
Toronto City	1967
Toronto Falcons	1968
Toronto Metros (replaced by the Toronto Metros-Croatia)	1974
Toronto Metros-Croatia (replaced by the Toronto Blizzards)	1978
Tulsa Roughnecks	1984
Vancouver Canadians (replaced by the Vancouver Royals)	1967
Vancouver Royals (replaced the Vancouver Canadians)	1968
Vancouver Whitecaps	1984
Washington Darts (moved to Miami; became the Gators)	1971
Washington Diplomats	1981
Washington Whips	1968
Washington/Team America	1983

Sports—Soccer—Leagues—NASL—New York Cosmos

The New York Cosmos were once the premiere team of the NASL. At their peak, they played before crowds numbering as many as 80,000; however, the Cosmos diminished in later years.

• **Last New York Cosmos game:** June 16,

1985, before a crowd of about 3,000. The Cosmos lost to Lazio of Rome, Italy.

Sports—Soccer—Players—Pelé

Pelé (Edson Arantes Do Nascimento) retired after the Cosmos won the NASL Soccer Bowl in 1977.

• **Last pro soccer game played by Pelé:** October 1, 1977, an exhibition game between the Cosmos and Santos at Giants Stadium in New Jersey before a crowd of 75,000 that sold out six weeks beforehand. It was covered by 650 journalists and broadcast in 38 nations. Pelé played the first half of the game with the New York Cosmos and the second half with Santos of Brazil, his original team. He later became Brazil's Minister for Sports and worked for children's causes and UNICEF.

Sports—Track and Field

Sports—Track and Field—Nurmi, Paavo

Paavo Nurmi (a.k.a. "The Flying Finn") was perhaps the greatest distance runner ever. He won ten gold medals in three Olympics: 1920, 1924 and 1928.

• **Last race of Nurmi:** September 16, 1934, at Viipuri, Finland, a 10,000 meter victory. He became a contractor and opened a haberdashery in Helsinki. Nurmi died in Helsinki, Finland, on October 2, 1973, age 76.

Sports—Track and Field—Streaks—Moses, Edwin

Edwin Moses strung together the longest winning streak in track and field history, winning 122 consecutive races. His streak began on September 2, 1977.

• **End of Moses's winning streak:** June 4, 1987, when Moses lost by .13 seconds to Danny Harris in the 400-meter hurdles at a meet in Madrid, Spain.

Telecommunications

Telecommunications—Telegraph—Morse Code

• **Last commercial maritime Morse Code message from North America:** July 13, 1999, sent by Rory Davis, chief engineer at Globe Wireless, a California marine communications firm. It was the same message the telegraph's inventor Samuel F.B. Morse transmitted 155 years earlier: "What hath God wrought?" Ship-to-shore telegraph has been replaced by satellite communications, high frequency radios and e-mail.

• **Last time Morse Code was the official Maritime Distress Mode:** January 31, 1999. The following day, the International Maritime Organization stopped using the code as part of the international maritime distress and safety network after more than a century. The United States, the United Kingdom and some continental European nations had previously closed their stations.

• **Last North American Morse Code railroad circuit:** Milwaukee Railroad, between Milwaukee and LaCrosse, Wisconsin. It closed down in 1985.

• **Last surviving telegrapher who transmitted news stories via Morse Code:** Associate Press telegrapher Aubrey Keel. His job was replaced when the electromechanical teletypewriters began to be used in the 1920s. He died in Kansas City, Missouri, on June 25, 1999, age 97.

• **Last use of Morse Code by ships:** July 31, 1999. Until then, ships at sea were required to carry equipment so that they could send the Morse Code S-O-S signal when in distress. The Morse system was replaced by satellite technology.

Telecommunications—Telephones

• **Last hand-cranked phones in the U.S.:** Bryant Pond, Maine; they went out of service on October 11, 1983, when the town's 440 phones switched over to direct dial. The last call was made from the living room of the home of the Hathaway family, who owned the local phone company.

• **Last hand-cranked phones in Great Britain:** on the Isle of Jura; went out of service on October 16, 1974.

• **Last hand-cranked phones in Australia:** in Wanarring, in the Outback NSW; went out of service on December 12, 1991.

• **Last pay AT&T phones:** AT&T stopped manufacturing pay telephones in 1995. On February 2, 2001, BellSouth announced it was getting out of the pay phone business.

• **Last time AT&T manufactured rotary phones:** the mid-1980s. However, many dial phones continue to be used in the 21st century.

• **Last time AT&T made enclosed telephone booths:** 1974. The company had problems with both vandalism and wear and tear. The solution was a phone mounted to a steel post imbedded in concrete.

Television
Last Original Episode or Telecast of Some Popular Television Programs That Ran a Year or Longer

Title	Type	First Telecast	Last First-Run Episode or Last Telecast of Original Run
Adam-12	police drama	September 21, 1968	May 20, 1975, "Something Worth Dying For" (Part 2)
Addams Family, The	sitcom	September 18, 1964	April 8, 1966, "Ophelia's Career"
Adventures of Ozzie and Harriet, The	sitcom	October 3, 1952	March 26, 1966
Adventures of Robin Hood, The	adventure	September 26, 1955	September 22, 1958
Alan Young Show, The	comedy/ variety	April 6, 1950	June 21, 1953
Alcoa Hour, The	drama	October 16, 1955	September 22, 1957, "Night"
Aldrich Family, The	sitcom	October 2, 1949	May 29, 1953
Alf	sitcom	September 22, 1986	March 24, 1990, "Consider Me Gone"
Alfred Hitchcock Presents (1955-63); *Alfred Hitchcock Hour* (1963-65)	suspense	October 2, 1955	*Alfred Hitchcock Presents,* May 24, 1963, "Death of a Cop"; *Alfred Hitchcock Hour,* May 10, 1965, "Off-Season"
Alias Smith and Jones	western	January 5, 1971	January 13, 1973, "Only Three to a Bed"
Alice	sitcom	August 31, 1976	March 19, 1985, "Th-th-th-that's All, Folks"
All in the Family (1971-79); *Archie Bunker's Place* (1979-83)	sitcom	January 12, 1971	*All in the Family*: April 8, 1979, "Too Good Edith." *Archie Bunker's Place*: April 4, 1983, "I'm Torn Here"
Ally McBeal	sitcom	September 8, 1997	May 20, 2002, "Bygones"
Amen	sitcom	September 27, 1986	May 11, 1991, "Deliverance" (Part 2)
America's Funniest People	comedy/ human interest	September 8, 1990	August 28, 1994

Notable Last Facts

Amos 'n' Andy Show, The	sitcom	June 28, 1951	June 11, 1953, "The Chinchilla Business"
Andy Griffith Show, The (1960-68. *See also* *Mayberry, R.F.D.*)	sitcom	October 3, 1960	April 1, 1968, "Mayberry R.F.D."
Andy Williams Show, The	music/ variety	July 3, 1958	July 17, 1971
Angie	sitcom	February 8, 1979	October 2, 1980, "Angie and Joyce Go to Jail"
Ann Sothern Show, The	sitcom	October 6, 1958	September 25, 1961, "The Invitation"
Anything But Love	sitcom	March 7, 1989	June 3, 1992, "Marty Walks"
Archie Bunker's Place, see All in the Family.			
Armstrong Circle Theater	drama	June 6, 1950	August 28, 1963, "Escape to Nowhere"
Arsenio Hall Show, The	talk/variety	January 3, 1989	May 1994 (syndicated)
Arthur Godfrey and His Friends	music/ variety	January 12, 1949	April 28, 1959
Arthur Godfrey's Talent Scouts	talent	December 6, 1948	July 21, 1958
A-Team, The	adventure	January 23, 1983	March 8, 1987, "Without Reservations"
Avengers, The	spy drama	January 7, 1961	September 14, 1969, "Bizarre"
Baa, Baa, Black Sheep (1976-77) *Black Sheep Squadron* (1977-78)	war drama	September 21, 1976	April 6, 1978, "A Little Bit of England"
Bachelor Father	sitcom	September 15, 1957	September 25, 1962
Banacek	detective drama	September 13, 1972	March 12, 1974, "Now You See Me, Now You Don't"
Baretta	police drama	January 17, 1975	May 18, 1978, "The Bundle"
Barnaby Jones	detective drama	January 28, 1973	April 3, 1980, "The Killin' Cousin"
Barney Miller	sitcom	January 23, 1975	May 20, 1982, "Landmark" (Part 3)
Bat Masterson	western	October 8, 1958	June 1, 1961, "Jeopardy at Jackson Hole"
Batman	fantasy	January 12, 1966	March 14, 1968, "Minerva, Mayhem and Millionaires"
Baywatch	adventure	April 23, 1989	May 19, 2001, "Rescue Me"
Benson	sitcom	September 13, 1979	April 19, 1986, "And the Winner is…"
Beverly Hillbillies, The	sitcom	September 26, 1962	March 23, 1971, "Jethro Returns"
Beverly Hills 90210	serial drama	October 4, 1990	May 17, 2000, Two episodes aired as two-hour finale:

			"The Penultimate"; "Ode to Joy"
Bewitched	sitcom	September 17, 1964	March 25, 1972, "The Truth, Nothing But the Truth, So Help Me Sam"
Big Story, The	drama	September 16, 1949	June 28, 1957
Big Town	news drama	October 5, 1950	October 2, 1956
Big Valley	western	September 15, 1965	May 19, 1969, "Point and Counterpoint"
Bionic Woman, The	adventure	January 14, 1976	May 13, 1978, "On the Run"
Black Sheep Squadron, see Baa, Baa Black Sheep			
Blossom	sitcom	January 3, 1991	May 22, 1995, "Goodbye"
Bob Hope Presents The Chrysler Theater	drama	September 27, 1963	May 17, 1967, "Deadlock"
Bob Newhart Show, The	sitcom	September 16, 1972	April 1, 1978, "Happy Trails to You"
Bonanza	western	September 12, 1959	January 16, 1973, "The Hunter"
Bosom Buddies	sitcom	November 27, 1980	May 27, 1982, "Call Me Irresponsible"
Boy Meets World	sitcom	September 24, 1993	May 5, 2001, "Brave New World" (Part 2)
Bracken's World	drama	September 19, 1969	December 25, 1970, "Miss Isabel Blue"
Brady Bunch, The	sitcom	September 26, 1969	March 8, 1974, "The Hair-Brained Scheme"
Brooklyn Bridge, The	sitcom	September 20, 1991	August 6, 1993, "No Time Like the Future"
Buffy the Vampire Slayer	supernatu-ral	March 10, 1997	May 20, 2003, "The Cho-sen"
Cagney & Lacey	police drama	March 25, 1982	May 16, 1988, "A Fair Shake"
Cannon	detective drama	September 14, 1971	March 3, 1976, "Mad Man"
Captain Kangaroo	children	October 3, 1955	December 8, 1984
Car 54, Where Are You?	sitcom	September 17, 1961	April 14, 1963, "The Curse of the Snitkins"
Carol Burnett Show, The	comedy/ variety	September 11, 1967	March 29, 1978, "A Special Evening With Carol Burnett"
Caroline in the City	sitcom	September 21, 1995	April 26, 1999, "Caroline and the Big Move" (Part 2)
Cavalcade of Stars	comedy/ variety	June 4, 1949	September 26, 1952
Charlie's Angels	detective drama	September 22, 1976	June 24, 1981, "Let Our Angel Live"
Checkmate	crime drama	September 17, 1960	June 20, 1962, "Side by Side"

Cheers	sitcom	September 30, 1982	May 20, 1993, "One for the Road" (Part 3)
Cheyenne	western	September 20, 1955	December 17, 1962, "Showdown at Oxbend"
Chicago Hope	medical drama	September 18, 1994	May 4, 2000, "Have I Got a Deal for You"
Chico and the Man	sitcom	September 13, 1974	July 14, 1978, "The Peeping Tom"
China Beach	war drama	April 26, 1988	July 22, 1991, "Hello Goodbye" (Part 2)
CHiPs	police drama	September 15, 1977	May 1, 1983, "Return of the Brat Patrol"
Climax	drama	October 7, 1954	June 26, 1958, "Cabin B-13"
Clueless	sitcom	September 20, 1996	May 25, 1999, "All-Night Senior Party"
Coach	sitcom	February 28, 1989	May 14, 1997, "Leaving Orlando" (Part 3)
Colgate Comedy Hour/ Colgate Variety Hour	comedy/ variety	September 10, 1950	December 25, 1955. Retitled *Colgate Variety Hour* 1955.
Columbo	police drama	September 15, 1971	May 13, 1978, "The Conspirators"
Combat	war drama	October 2, 1962	March 14, 1967, "The Partisan"
Cosby	sitcom	September 16, 1996	April 28, 2000, "The Song Remains the Same"
Cosby Show, The	sitcom	September 20, 1984	April 30, 1992, "And So We Commence" (Part 2)
Courtship of Eddie's Father, The	sitcom	September 17, 1969	March 1, 1972, "We Love Annie"
C.P.O. Sharkey	sitcom	December 1, 1976	April 28, 1978, "The Used-Car Caper"
Crazy Like a Fox	detective drama	December 30, 1984	May 3, 1986, "A Fox at the Races"
Cybill	sitcom	January 2, 1995	July 13, 1998, "Ka-Boom!"
Daktari	adventure	January 11, 1966	January 15, 1969
Dallas	serial drama	April 2, 1978	May 3, 1991, "Conundrum" (Part 2)
Daniel Boone	adventure	September 24, 1964	May 7, 1970, "Israel and Love"
Danny Kaye Show, The	variety	September 25, 1963	June 7, 1967
Danny Thomas Show, The/Make Room for Daddy	sitcom	September 29, 1953	April 27, 1964, "The Persistent Cop." Titled *Make Room for Daddy* first three seasons.
Dark Shadows	supernatural	June 27, 1966	April 2, 1971. Returned January-March 1991.
Dave's World	sitcom	September 20, 1993	June 20, 1997, "The Creeping Peril"

Davis Rules	sitcom	January 27, 1991	May 13, 1992, "The Girl with Someone Extra"
Dawson's Creek	serial drama	January 20, 1998	May 14, 2003, "All Good Things" (Part 1); "… Must Come to an End" (Part 2)
Day by Day	sitcom	February 29, 1988	June 4, 1989, "Father Knows Best"
Days and Nights of Molly Dodd, The	drama	May 21, 1987	April 13, 1991, "Here's a little touch of harry in the night"
Dean Martin Show/ Dean Martin Comedy Hour	variety	September 16, 1965	February 21, 1974. Retitled *The Dean Martin Comedy Hour* final season.
Dear John	sitcom	October 6, 1988	July 22, 1992, "Poor John" (Part 2)
December Bride	sitcom	October 4, 1954	May 7, 1959, "Bald Baby"
Defenders, The	legal drama	September 16, 1961	May 13, 1965, "Only a Child"
Dennis the Menace	sitcom	October 4, 1959	July 7, 1963, "Aunt Emma Visits the Wilsons"
Designing Women	sitcom	September 29, 1986	May 24, 1993, "Gone with a Whim" (Part 2)
Dharma & Greg	sitcom	September 24, 1997	April 30, 2002, "The Mamas and the Papas" (a.k.a. "Finale," Parts 1 & 2)
Dick Van Dyke Show, The	sitcom	October 3, 1961	May 25, 1966, "The Gunslinger"
Different World, A	sitcom	September 24, 1987	July 9, 1993, "Great X-Pectations"
Diff'rent Strokes	sitcom	November 3, 1978	March 7, 1986, "The Front Page"
Dinah Shore Chevy Show, The	music/ variety	October 5, 1956	May 12, 1963
Dinah Shore Show, The	music	November 27, 1951	July 18, 1957
Doctor, Doctor	sitcom	June 12, 1989	July 6, 1991, "Two Angry Men"
Dr. Kildare	medical drama	September 28, 1961	April 5, 1966, "Reckoning"
Dr. Quinn, Medicine Woman	medical drama	January 1, 1993	May 16, 1998, "A New Beginning"
Donna Reed Show, The	sitcom	September 24, 1958	March 19, 1966, "By-Line—Jeffrey Stone"
Donny and Marie/ Osmond Family Show, The	music/ variety	January 23, 1976	May 6, 1979. Retitled *The Osmond Family Show* 1979.
Doogie Howser. M.D.	sitcom	September 19, 1989	March 24, 1993, "What Makes Doogie Run"
Doris Day Show, The	sitcom	September 24, 1968	September 10, 1973
Dragnet	police drama	December 16, 1951	August 23, 1959, "The Big Red." Returned 1967-70.

			Last show April 16, 1970, "D.H.Q.-The Victims"
Dukes of Hazzard, The	adventure	January 26, 1979	February 8, 1985, "Opening Night at the Boar's Nest"
Dynasty	serial drama	January 12, 1981	May 11, 1989, "Catch 22"
Eight Is Enough	sitcom	March 15, 1977	May 23, 1981, "Father Knows Best"
Ellen/These Friends of Mine	sitcom	March 29, 1994	July 22, 1998, "Vows." Original title: *These Friends of Mine*. Retitled after first season.
Emergency	medical drama	January 22, 1972	July 3, 1979, "The Convention"
Empty Nest	sitcom	October 8, 1988	April 29, 1995, "Life Goes On" (Part 2)
Evening Shade	sitcom	September 21, 1990	May 23, 1994, "I Left My Ring in Evening Shade"
F.B.I., The	crime drama	September 19, 1965	April 28, 1974, "Survival"
F-Troop	sitcom	September 14, 1965	April 6, 1967, "Is This Fort Really Necessary?"
Facts of Life, The	sitcom	August 24, 1979	May 7, 1988, "The Beginning of the Beginning"
Falcon Crest	serial drama	December 4, 1981	May 17, 1990, "Home Again"
Fall Guy, The	adventure	November 4, 1981	May 2, 1986, "The Bigger They Are"
Family Affair	sitcom	September 12, 1966	March 4, 1971, "You Can Fight City Hall"
Family Matters	sitcom	September 22, 1989	July 17, 1998, "Lost in Space" (Part 2)
Family Ties	sitcom	September 22, 1982	May 14, 1989, "Alex Doesn't Live Here Anymore" (Parts 1 & 2)
Fantasy Island	fantasy/ adventure	January 28, 1978	May 19, 1984, "Surrogate Mother/The Ideal Woman." Revived 1998-99. Last show: January 23, 1999, "Heroes."
Father Knows Best	sitcom	October 3, 1954	May 23, 1960, "Betty's Graduation"
1st and Ten	sitcom	December 2, 1984	January 23, 1991, "Championship Game"
Flintstones, The	cartoon	September 30 1960	April 1, 1966, "The Story of Rocky's Raiders"
Flip Wilson Show, The	comedy/ variety	September 17, 1970	June 27, 1974
Flipper	adventure	September 19, 1964	April 15, 1967, "Flipper's New Friends" (Part 2)

Flo	sitcom	March 21, 1980	April 22, 1981, "The Daynce"
Flying Nun, The	sitcom	September 7, 1967	April 3, 1970, "No Tears for Mrs. Thomas"
Ford Show, The, see *Tennessee Ernie Ford Show*			
Frasier	sitcom	September 16, 1993	May 13, 2004, "Goodnight, Seattle"
Fresh Prince of Bel Air	sitcom	September 10, 1990	May 20, 1996, "I, Done" (Parts 1 & 2)
Friends	sitcom	September 22, 1994	May 6, 2004
Fugitive, The	adventure	September 17, 1963	August 29, 1967, "The Judgment" (Part 2)
Full House	sitcom	September 22, 1987	May 23, 1995, "Michelle Rides Again" (Parts 1 & 2)
Gale Storm Show, The/ Oh! Susannah	sitcom	September 29, 1956	March 4, 1960. Original title: *Oh! Susannah*. Retitled 1958.
Garry Moore Show, The	variety	June 26, 1950	January 8, 1967
General Electric Theater	drama	February 1, 1953	September 16, 1962
Gentle Ben	adventure	September 10, 1967	August 31, 1969
George Burns and Gracie Allen Show, The	sitcom	October 12, 1950	September 15, 1958, "The Exchange Student"
George Gobel Show, The	comedy/ variety	October 2, 1954	June 5, 1960
Get a Life	sitcom	September 23, 1990	March 8, 1992, "Clip Show"
Get Smart	sitcom	September 18, 1965	May 15, 1970, "I Am Curiously Yellow." Returned January 8 to February 19, 1995. Last episode: "Liver Let Die."
Getting By	sitcom	March 5, 1993	June 18, 1994, "My Brilliant Career"
Ghost and Mrs. Muir, The	sitcom	September 21, 1968	March 13, 1970, "Wedding Day"
Gilligan's Island	sitcom	September 26, 1964	April 17, 1967, "Gilligan, the Goddess" (Part 2)
Gimme a Break!	sitcom	October 29, 1981	May 12, 1987, "Mama's Date"
Glen Campbell Goodtime Hour, The	music/ variety	January 29, 1969	June 13, 1972
Golden Girls, The	sitcom	September 14, 1985	May 9, 1992, "One Flew Out of the Cuckoo's Nest" (Part 2)
Gomer Pyle, U.S.M.C.	sitcom	September 25, 1964	May 2, 1969, "Goodbye Camp Handeson, Hello Sergeant Carter"

Good Times	sitcom	February 8, 1974	August 1, 1979, "The End of the Rainbow"
Goodyear TV Playhouse	drama	October 14, 1951	September 29, 1957, "The Best Wine"
Grace Under Fire	sitcom	September 29, 1993	February 17, 1998, "Down in the Boondocks"
Greatest American Hero, The	fantasy/ adventure	March 18, 1981	February 3, 1983, "Thirty Seconds Over Little Tokyo"
Green Acres	sitcom	September 15, 1965	April 27, 1971, "The Ex-Secretary"
Growing Pains	sitcom	September 24, 1985	April 25, 1992, "The Last Picture Show" (Parts 1 & 2)
Gunsmoke	western	September 10, 1955	March 31, 1975, "The Sharecroppers"
Hangin' with Mr. Cooper	sitcom	September 22, 1992	August 30, 1997, "Getting Personal"
Happy Days	sitcom	January 15, 1974	September 24, 1984, "Fonzie's Spots"
Hardcastle & McCormick	detective drama	September 18, 1983	May 5, 1986, "A Chip Off the Ol' Milt"
Hart to Hart	detective adventure	August 25, 1979	May 22, 1984, "Meanwhile, Back at the Ranch"
Have Gun, Will Travel	western	September 14, 1957	April 20, 1963, "Face of a Shadow"
Hawaii Five-O	police drama	September 20, 1968	April 5, 1980, "Woe to Wo Fat"
Hawaiian Eye	drama	October 7, 1959	April 2, 1963, "Passport"
Hazel	sitcom	September 28, 1961	April 11, 1966, "A Question of Ethics"
Head of the Class	sitcom	September 17, 1986	June 25, 1991, "It Couldn't Last Forever" (Part 2)
Hearts Afire	sitcom	September 14, 1992	February 1, 1995, "John and George's Not-So-Excellent Adventure"
Hee Haw	music/ variety	June 15, 1969	Last first-run show: July 13, 1971. First-run syndicated 1971- May 1993.
Here's Lucy	sitcom	September 23, 1968	March 18, 1974, "Lucy Fights the System"
Highway to Heaven	fantasy drama	September 19, 1984	August 4, 1989, "Merry Christmas from Grandpa"
Hill Street Blues	police drama	January 15, 1981	May 12, 1987, "It Ain't Over Till It's Over"
Hogan's Heroes	sitcom	September 17, 1965	April 4, 1971, "Rockets or Romance"
Home Improvement	sitcom	September 17, 1991	May 25, 1999, "Backstage Pass"
Homicide: Life on the Street	police drama	January 31, 1993	May 21, 1999, "Forgive Us Our Trespasses"

Honeymooners, The	sitcom	November 1, 1952	September 12, 1970, *Jackie Gleason Show*
Hopalong Cassidy	western	June 24, 1949	December 23, 1951. Syndicated September 1952-April 2, 1954. Last episode "Tricky Fingers"
Hotel	drama	September 21, 1983	May 5, 1988, "Aftershocks" (Part 2)
House Calls	sitcom	December 13, 1979	May 27, 1982, "In Norman We Trust"
Howdy Doody	children	December 27, 1947	September 24, 1960, "Clarabell Speaks." Clarabell's last (and only) words: "Goodbye, kids."
Hunter	police drama	September 18, 1984	April 26, 1991, "Little Man With a Big Reputation"
I Dream of Jeannie	sitcom	September 18, 1965	May 26, 1970, "My Master, the Chili King"
I Love Lucy	sitcom	November 5, 1951	May 6, 1957, "The Ricardos Dedicate a Statue"
I Married Joan	sitcom	October 15, 1952	April 6, 1955, "Mountain Lodge"
I Spy	espionage adventure	September 15, 1965	April 15, 1968, "Pinwheel"
In Living Color	comedy/ variety	April 15, 1990	August 25, 1994
In the Heat of the Night	police drama	March 6, 1988	May 11, 1994, "Give Me Your Life" (Parts 1 & 2)
Incredible Hulk, The	adventure	March 10, 1978	May 12, 1982, "A Minor Problem"
Ironside	crime drama	September 14, 1967	January 16, 1975, "The Faded Image"
It Takes a Thief	adventure	January 9, 1968	March 23, 1970, "Project X"
I've Got a Secret	quiz	June 19, 1952	July 5, 1976
Jack Benny Show, The	comedy	October 28, 1950	April 16, 1965. Guests: The Smothers Brothers.
Jack Paar Tonight Show, The	talk/ variety	July 29, 1957	March 29, 1962
Jackie Gleason Show, The	comedy/ variety	September 20, 1952	September 12, 1970
Jake and the Fatman	legal drama	September 26, 1987	May 6, 1992, "Beautiful Dreamer (a.k.a. Mickey Daytona)"
Jeffersons, The	sitcom	January 18, 1975	June 25, 1985, "Off-Off-Off-Off Broadway"
Jim Nabors Show, The	comedy/ variety	September 25, 1969	May 20, 1971
Joanie Loves Chachi	sitcom	March 23, 1982	September 13, 1983

John Larroquette Show, The	sitcom	September 2, 1993	October 30, 1996, "Isosceles Love Triangle"
Julia	sitcom	September 17, 1968	May 25, 1971
Just Shoot Me	sitcom	March 4, 1997	August 16, 2003. "Future Issues"
Kate and Allie	sitcom	March 19, 1984	May 22, 1989, "What a Wonderful Episode"
Knight Rider	adventure	September 26, 1982	April 4, 1986 "Voo Doo Knight"
Knots Landing	serial drama	December 27, 1979	May 13, 1993, "Just Like Old Times" (Parts 1 & 2).
Kojak	police drama	October 24, 1973	March 18, 1978, "In Full Command" (Parts 1 & 2). Several Kojak films aired in 1987-90. Last movie: *None So Blind,* March 16, 1990.
Kraft Television Theater/ Kraft Theater/ Kraft Mystery Theater	drama	May 7, 1947	October 1, 1958, "Presumption of Innocence." Retitled *Kraft Theater* April 1958. Retitled *Kraft Mystery Theater,* June 1958.
Kukla, Fran and Ollie	children	January 12, 1949	June 13, 1954
Kung Fu	western/ martial arts	October 14, 1972	April 26, 1975, "The Last Raid"
L.A. Law	legal drama	September 15, 1986	May 19, 1994, "Finish Line"
Lassie	adventure	September 12, 1954	March 24, 1973, "The Dawning." See also *The New Lassie.*
Late, Late Show with Tom Snyder, The	talk/ variety	January 9, 1995	March 26, 1999
Late Night with David Letterman	talk/variety	February 2, 1982	June 25, 1993. Guests: Tom Hanks, Bruce Springsteen, David Sanborn. *Late Show with David Letterman* began on CBS in August 1993.
Laugh-In, see Rowan & Martin's Laugh-In			
Laverne and Shirley	sitcom	January 27, 1976	May 10, 1983, "Here Today, Hair Tomorrow"
Lawrence Welk Show, The	music	July 2, 1955	September 4, 1971. Syndicated September 1971-February 1982.
Leave It to Beaver	sitcom	October 4, 1957	June 20, 1963, "Family Scrapbook"
Life and Legend of Wyatt Earp, The	western	September 6, 1955	September 26, 1961
Life Goes On	drama	September 12, 1989	May 23, 1993, "Life Goes On (and On and On)"

Life of Riley, The	sitcom	January 2, 1953	August 22, 1958 (William Bendix)
Life of Riley, The	sitcom	October 4, 1949	March 1950 (Jackie Gleason)
Lineup, The	crime	October 1, 1954	January 20, 1960, "Seven Sinners"
Little House on the Prairie	drama	September 11, 1974	March 21, 1983, "Hello and Goodbye"
Lone Ranger, The	western/ crime	September 15, 1949	June 6, 1957, "Outlaws in Greasepaint"
Loretta Young Show, The/ Letter to Loretta, A	drama	September 20, 1953	September 10, 1961. Original title: *A Letter to Loretta;* changed 1954.
Lost in Space	scifi/ space	September 15, 1965	March 6, 1968, "Junkyard of Space"
Lou Grant	news drama	September 20, 1977	September 13, 1982, "Charlie"
Love, American Style	comedy/ romance	September 29, 1969	January 11, 1974, "Love and the Competitors"
Love Boat	drama/ romance	September 24, 1977	May 24, 1986, "Happily Ever After/Have I Got a Job for You/Mrs. Smith Goes to Minikulu." Four specials aired 1986-87. Last special: February 27, 1987, "Who Killed Maxwell Thorn?"
Lucy Show, The	sitcom	October 1, 1962	March 11, 1968, "Lucy and the 'Boss of the Year' Award" Retitled 1968. See *Here's Lucy.*
Lux Video Theater	drama	October 2, 1950	September 12, 1957
*M*A*S*H*	sitcom	September 17, 1972	February 28, 1983, "Goodbye, Farewell and Amen"
M Squad	police drama	September 20, 1957	June 21, 1960, "The Bad Apple"
MacGyver	adventure	September 29, 1985	May 21, 1992, "Mountain of Youth"
Mad About You	sitcom	September 23, 1992	May 24, 1999, "The Final Frontier" (Parts 1 & 2)
Magnum, P.I.	detective drama	December 11, 1980	May 1, 1988, "Resolutions" (Part 1 & 2)
Major Dad	sitcom	September 17, 1989	April 16, 1993, "Oops, a Daisy"
Mama	sitcom	July 1, 1949	July 27, 1956. Aired live 1949 -56. Aired on film December 16, 1956-March 16, 1957.
Mama's Family	sitcom	January 22, 1983	March 12, 1990, "Bye-Bye—Baby!"
Man Against Crime	detective drama	October 7, 1949	August 19, 1956

Man from U.N.C.L.E., The	spy spoof	September 22, 1964	January 15, 1968, "The Seven Wonders of the World Affair " (Part 2)
Mannix	drama	September 16, 1967	April 13, 1975, "Hardball"
Many Loves of Dobie Gillis, The	sitcom	October 1, 1959	September 18, 1963, "The Devil and Dobie Gillis"
Marcus Welby, M.D.	medical drama	September 23, 1969	May 4, 1976. "Vanity Case" (Part 2)
Married...With Children	sitcom	April 5, 1987	May 5, 1997, "How to Marry a Moron"
Martin	sitcom	August 27, 1992	May 1, 1997, "California, Here We Come" (Parts 1 & 2)
Martin Kane, Private Eye	detective drama	September 1, 1949	June 17, 1954
Mary Tyler Moore Show, The	sitcom	September 19, 1970	March 19, 1977, "The Last Show"
Matlock	legal drama	September 23, 1986	May 7, 1995, "The Scam" (Parts 1 & 2)
Maude	sitcom	September 12, 1972	April 22, 1978, "Maude's Big Move" (Part 3)
Maverick	western	September 22, 1957	May 4, 1962, "The Hidalgo Thing"
Mayberry, R.F.D. See also The Andy Griffith Show.	sitcom	September 23, 1968	March 29, 1971, "Emmett's Invention"
McCloud	crime drama	September 16, 1970	April 17, 1977, "McCloud Meets Dracula"
McHale's Navy	sitcom	October 11, 1962	April 12, 1966, "Wally for Congress"
McMillan and Wife	detective drama	September 29, 1971	April 24, 1977, "Have You Heard About Vanessa?"
Medical Center	medical drama	September 24, 1969	March 15, 1976, "If Wishes Were Horses"
Melrose Place	serial drama	July 8, 1992	May 24, 1999, "Asses to Ashes"
Miami Vice	police drama	September 16, 1984	June 28, 1989, "Leap of Faith"
Millionaire, The	drama	January 19, 1955	September 28, 1960
Milton Berle Show, The	comedy/ variety	June 8, 1948	January 6, 1967
Mission: Impossible	foreign intrigue	September 17, 1966	March 30, 1973, "Imitation." Returned 1988-90. Last show: June 9, 1990, "The Sands of Seth."
Mister Ed	sitcom	January 5, 1961	February 6, 1966, "Ed Goes to College"
Mod Squad, The	crime drama	September 24, 1968	March 1, 1973, "And Once for My Baby"

Moesha	sitcom	January 23, 1996	May 14, 2001, "Paying the Piper"
Monkees, The	sitcom	September 12, 1966	March 25, 1968, "Mijacogeo (The Frodis Caper)." *The New Monkees* aired September-December 1987.
Moonlighting	comedy/ drama	March 3, 1985	May 14, 1989, "Lunar Eclipse"
Mork & Mindy	sitcom	September 14, 1978	May 27, 1982, "The Mork Report"
Munsters, The	sitcom	September 24, 1964	May 12, 1966, "A Visit from the Teacher"
Murder, She Wrote	detective drama	October 7, 1984	May 19, 1996, "Death by Demographics"
Murphy Brown	sitcom	November 14, 1988	May 18, 1998, "Never Can Say Goodbye" (Parts 1 & 2)
My Favorite Martian	sitcom	September 29, 1963	May 1, 1966, "Pay the Man the $24"
My Little Margie	sitcom	June 9, 1952	May 25, 1955, "Margie's Elopement"
My Sister Sam	sitcom	October 6, 1986	April 12, 1988, "Life, Death and Admiral Andy"
My Three Sons	sitcom	September 29, 1960	April 13, 1972, "Whatever Happened to Ernie?"
My Two Dads	sitcom	September 20, 1987	April 30, 1990, "See You in September?"
Naked City	police drama	September 30, 1958	May 29, 1963, "Barefoot on a Bed of Coals"
Naked Truth, The	sitcom	September 13, 1995	May 25, 1998, "The Day of the Locos"
Name of the Game, The	adventure	September 20, 1968	March 19, 1971, "The Showdown"
Name That Tune	music/ quiz	June 29, 1953	October 19, 1959. Syndicated versions, 1970-71, 1974-76; daytime version, 1974-75, 1977.
Nanny, The	sitcom	November 3, 1993	May 12, 1999, "The Finale" (Parts 1 & 2)
Nat "King" Cole Show, The	music/ variety	November 5, 1956	December 17, 1957
New Dick Van Dyke Show, The	sitcom	September 18, 1971	September 2, 1974
New Lassie, The	adventure	September 9, 1989	March 14, 1992, "A Friendship Forever"
New WKRP in Cincinnati	sitcom	September 14, 1991	May 22, 1993, "Father of the Groom." See also *WKRP in Cincinnati.*
Newhart	sitcom	October 25, 1982	May 21, 1990, "The Last Newhart"

NewsRadio	sitcom	March 21, 1995	May 4, 1999, "New Hampshire" (Part 2)
Night Court	sitcom	January 4, 1984	May 31, 1992, "The 1992 Boat Show"
9 to 5	sitcom	March 25, 1982	October 27, 1983, "Goodbye, Pops." Syndicated 1986-September 1988.
Northern Exposure	drama	July 12, 1990	July 26, 1995, "Tranquility Base"
Odd Couple, The	sitcom	September 24, 1970	March 7, 1975, "Felix Remarries"
One Day at a Time	sitcom	December 16, 1975	May 28, 1984, "Another Man's Shoes"
Our Miss Brooks	sitcom	October 3, 1952	May 11, 1956, "Travel Crazy"
Partridge Family, The	sitcom/ music	September 25, 1970	March 23, 1974, "..._ _ _ ...S.O.S." Animated version, *Partridge Family 2200 A.D.,* aired September 1974-September 1975.
Patty Duke Show, The	sitcom	September 18, 1963	May 4, 1966, "Patty, the Psychic"
Pee-Wee's Playhouse	comedy	September 13, 1986	July 27, 1991
People Are Funny	quiz	September 19, 1954	April 2, 1961. Returned March 1984. Last new show: July 21, 1984.
Perfect Strangers	sitcom	March 25, 1986	August 6, 1993, "Up, Up and Away" (Parts 1 & 2)
Perry Como Show, The	music/ variety	December 24, 1948	June 12, 1963
Perry Mason	legal drama	September 21, 1957	September 4, 1966, "The Case of the Final Fadeout." Returned September 1973-January 1974.
Peter Gunn	detective drama	September 22, 1958	September 18, 1961, "Murder on the Line"
Petticoat Junction	sitcom	September 24, 1963	April 4, 1970, "Betty Joe's Business"
Peyton Place	serial drama	September 15, 1964	June 2, 1969
Phil Silvers Show, The	sitcom	September 20, 1955	June 17, 1959, "Weekend Colonel
Philco Television Playhouse	drama	October 3, 1948	October 2, 1955, "A Man is Ten Feet Tall"
Phyllis	sitcom	September 11, 1975	March 13, 1977, "A Baby Makes Six"
Picket Fences	drama	September 18, 1992	June 26, 1996, "Liver Let Die"
Police Woman	police drama	September 13, 1974	March 30, 1978, "Good Old Uncle Ben"

Practice, The	legal drama	March 4, 1997	May 16, 2004, "Cheers, a.k.a. Adjourned: Series Finale"
Private Benjamin	sitcom	April 6, 1981	September 5, 1983
Private Secretary	sitcom	February 1, 1953	March 17, 1957, "Thy Name is Sands"
Providence	serial drama	January 8, 1999	December 20, 2002, "The Eleventh Hour" (Parts 1 &2)
Quantum Leap	scifi/ adventure	March 26, 1989	May 5, 1993, "Mirror Image—August 8, 1953"
Quincy, M.E.	medical drama	October 3, 1976	May 11, 1983, "The Cutting Edge"
Racket Squad	crime drama	June 7, 1951	September 28, 1953
Rat Patrol	war drama	September 12, 1966	March 18, 1968, "The Kill at Koorlea Raid"
Rawhide	western	January 9, 1959	December 7, 1965, "Crossing at White Feather"
Real McCoys, The	sitcom	October 3, 1957	June 23, 1963, "Pepino's Mama"
Real People	human interest	April 18, 1979	July 4, 1984
Red Buttons Show, The	comedy/ variety	October 14, 1952	May 13, 1955
Red Skelton Show, The	comedy/ variety	September 30, 1951	August 29, 1971
Remington Steele	detective drama	October 1, 1982	April 17, 1987, "Steeled with a Kiss" (Parts 1 & 2)
Restless Gun, The	western	September 23, 1957	September 14, 1959
Rhoda	sitcom	September 9, 1974	December 9, 1978, "The Total Brenda"
Rifleman, The	western	September 30, 1958	April 8, 1963, "Old Tony"
Riptide	detective drama	January 3, 1984	April 22, 1986, "Echoes"
Robert Montgomery Presents	drama	January 30, 1950	June 24, 1957
Rockford Files, The	detective drama	September 13, 1974	January 10, 1980, "Deadlock in Parma"
Rookies, The	police drama	September 11, 1972	March 30, 1976, "Journey to Oblivion"
Room 222	drama	September 17, 1969	January 11, 1974, "Cry Uncle"
Ropers, The	sitcom	March 13, 1979	May 15, 1980, "Mother's Wake"
Roseanne	sitcom	October 18, 1988	May 20, 1997, "Into That Good Night" (Parts 1 & 2)
Route 66	adventure	October 7, 1960	March 13, 1964, "Where There's a Will, There's a Way" (Parts 1 & 2). Returned June 8, 1993. Last new show: July 6, 1993, "The Stolen Bride."

Rowan & Martin's Laugh-In	comedy	January 22, 1968	March 12, 1973. Guest stars: Ernest Borgnine, Sammy Davis Jr., Robert Goulet, Rip Taylor, Jo Anne Worley.
Roy Rogers Show, The	western	December 30, 1951	June 9, 1957, "Johnny Rover"
Run For Your Life	adventure	September 13, 1965	March 27, 1968, "The Exchange"
Ryan's Hope	serial drama	July 7, 1975	January 13, 1989
Saint, The	mystery/ adventure	October 4, 1962	February 9, 1969, "The World Beater"
St. Elsewhere	medical drama	October 26, 1982	May 25, 1988, "The Last One"
Sanford and Son	sitcom	January 14, 1972	March 25, 1977, "School Daze"
Saved by the Bell	sitcom	August 20, 1989	May 22, 1993, "Graduation"
Scarecrow and Mrs. King	adventure/ espionage	October 3, 1983	May 28, 1987, "The Khrushchev List"
Seinfeld	sitcom	May 31, 1990	May 14, 1998, "The Finale" (Parts 1 & 2)
77 Sunset Strip	drama	October 10, 1958	February 7, 1964, "Queen of the Cats"
Silver Spoons	sitcom	September 25, 1982	March 4, 1986, "Let It Snow, Let It Snow"
Simon & Simon	detective drama	November 24, 1981	December 31, 1988, "First, Let's Kill All the Lawyers"
Sing Along with Mitch	music	January 27, 1961	September 21, 1964
Single Guy, The	sitcom	September 21, 1995	April 16, 1997, "Vegas Finale"
Sisters	drama	May 11, 1991	May 4, 1996, "War & Peace" (Parts 1 & 2)
Six Million Dollar Man	scifi/ adventure	January 18, 1974	March 6, 1978, "The Moving Mountain"
$64,000 Question, The	quiz	June 7, 1955	November 2, 1958
Smothers Brothers Comedy Hour, The	comedy/ variety	February 5, 1967	June 8, 1969. Returned 1988-89. Last new show: August 23, 1989.
Smothers Brothers Show, The		January 13, 1975	May 26, 1975
Smothers Brothers Summer Show, The		July 15, 1970	September 16, 1970
Soap	sitcom	September 13, 1977	April 20, 1981
Sonny and Cher Comedy Hour, The/ The Sonny and Cher Show	music/ variety	August 1, 1971

February 1, 1976 | May 29, 1974

August 29, 1977 |
| *Soul Man* | sitcom | April 15, 1997 | May 26, 1998, "Little Black Dress" |

Spike Jones Show, The	comedy/ variety	January 2, 1954	September 25, 1961
Star Trek	scifi/space	September 8, 1966	June 3, 1969, "Turnabout Intruder"
Star Trek: Deep Space Nine	scifi/space	January 3, 1993	June 2, 1999, "What You Leave Behind" (Parts 1 & 2)
Star Trek: The Next Generation	scifi/space	September 28, 1987	May 23, 1994, "All Good Things…" (Parts 1 & 2)
Starsky & Hutch	police drama	September 10, 1975	May 15, 1979, "Sweet Revenge"
Stop the Music	quiz/music	May 5, 1949	June 14, 1956
Streets of San Francisco, The	police drama	September 16, 1972	June 9, 1977, "The Canine Collar"
Strike It Rich	quiz	May 7, 1951	January 3, 1958
Suddenly Susan	sitcom	September 19, 1996	December 26, 2000, "The Finale" (Parts 1 & 2)
Sugarfoot	western	September 17, 1957	April 17, 1961, "Trouble at Sand Springs"
Suspense	mystery/ suspense	March 1, 1949	August 17, 1954, "Barn Burning"
T.J. Hooker	police drama	March 13, 1982	May 28, 1986, "Deadly Force"
Tales of Wells Fargo	western	March 18, 1957	September 8, 1962, "Vignette of a Sinner"
Tarzan	adventure	September 8, 1966	April 4, 1968, "Trina"
Taxi	sitcom	September 12, 1978	June 15, 1983, "Simka's Monthlies"
Tennessee Ernie Ford Show, The *Ford Show, The*	music/ variety	January 3, 1955 October 1956	March 26, 1965. Aired daytime 1955-57, 1962-65. June 29, 1961
Texan, The	western	September 9, 1958	September 12, 1960
Texas	serial drama	August 4, 1980	December 31, 1982
That Girl	sitcom	September 8, 1966	March 19, 1971, "The Elevated Woman"
That's Incredible	human interest	March 3, 1980	April 30, 1984
3rd Rock from the Sun	sitcom	January 9, 1996	May 22, 2001, "The Thing That Wouldn't Die" (Parts 1 & 2)
thirtysomething	comedy/ drama	September 29, 1987	May 28, 1991, "California"
This is Your Life	biography	October 1, 1952	September 10, 1961
Three's Company	sitcom	March 15, 1977	September 18, 1984, "Friends and Lovers" (Parts 1 &2)
Thunder Alley	sitcom	March 9, 1994	July 4, 1995, "No Swing Set"
Toast of the Town/ Ed Sullivan Show, The	music/ variety	June 20, 1948	March 28, 1971. Guests: Melanie, David Frye, Sandler & Young. Retitled *The Ed Sullivan Show* 1955.

Tonight! with Steve Allen	talk/ variety	September 27, 1954	January 25, 1957
Tonight Show Starring Johnny Carson, The	talk/ variety	October 1, 1962	May 22, 1992. Last guest: Bette Midler.
Too Close for Comfort	sitcom	November 11, 1980	September 15, 1983, "Monroe's Critical Condition"
Topper	sitcom	October 9, 1953	July 15, 1955, "Topper's Vacation"
Touched by an Angel	fantasy/ drama	September 21, 1994	April 27, 2003, "I Will Walk With You" (Part 2)
Trapper John, M.D.	medical drama	September 23, 1979	September 4, 1986, "The Elusive Butterfly"
Treasury Men in Action	crime drama	September 11, 1950	September 30, 1955
Twenty Questions	quiz	November 26, 1949	May 3, 1955
21 Jump Street	police drama	April 12, 1987	June 18, 1990, "Blackout." Syndicated October 13, 1990-April 27, 1991. Last episode: "Second Chances."
Twilight Zone, The	scifi/super-natural	October 2, 1959	June 19, 1964, "The Bewitchin' Pool"
Twin Peaks	serial drama	April 9, 1990	June 10, 1991, Episode 29, a.k.a. "Beyond Life and Death"
Two Guys and a Girl	sitcom	March 11, 1998	May 16, 2001, "The Internet Show"
227	sitcom	September 14, 1985	May 6, 1990, "No Place Like Home"
Untouchables, The	police drama	October 15, 1959	May 21, 1963, "A Taste of Pineapple"
Virginian, The	western	September 19, 1962	March 24, 1971, "Jump-Up." Retitled *The Men from Shiloh* 1970.
Wagon Train	western	September 18, 1957	May 2, 1965, "The Jarbo Pierce Story"
Waltons, The	drama	September 14, 1972	June 4, 1981, "The Revel"
Wanted—Dead or Alive	western	September 6, 1958	March 29, 1961, "Barney's Bounty"
Webster	sitcom	September 16, 1983	March 10, 1989, "Webtrek"
Welcome Back, Kotter	sitcom	September 9, 1975	June 8, 1979, "The Bread-winners"
What's Happening	sitcom	August 5, 1976	April 28, 1979, "The Benefit Show." Revived as syndi-cated show *What's Happening Now!!* 1979.
What's My Line?	quiz	February 2, 1950	September 3, 1967
Who's the Boss?	sitcom	September 20, 1984	April 25, 1992, "Savor the Veal" (Parts 2 & 3).

Wild, Wild West	western	September 17, 1965	April 4, 1969, "The Night of the Plague"
Wings	sitcom	April 19, 1990	May 21, 1997, "Final Approach" (Parts 1 & 2)
WKRP in Cincinnati	sitcom	September 18, 1978	April 21, 1982, "Up and Down the Dial." See also *New WKRP in Cincinnati.*
Wonder Woman	adventure/ fantasy	April 21, 1976	September 11, 1979, "Phantom of the Roller Coaster" (Part 2)
Wonder Years, The	sitcom	January 31, 1988	May 12, 1993, "Summer" (Part 1); "Independence Day" (Part 2)
X Files	fantasy drama	September 10, 1993	May 19, 2002, two-hour episode, "The Truth"
You Bet Your Life	quiz/ comedy	October 5, 1950	June 29, 1961
Your Hit Parade	music	October 7, 1950	April 24, 1959. Returned August 1974. Last new show: August 30, 1974.
Your Show of Shows	comedy/ variety	February 25, 1950	June 5, 1954
Zorro	western/ adventure	October 10, 1957	July 2, 1959, "Finders Keepers." Four *Walt Disney Presents* episodes: 1960-61. Last episode: April 2, 1961, "Auld Acquaintance." Revived 1990-92. Last new episode: December 2, 1992, "My Word Is My Bond." Animated series: 1997-98. Last episode: December 12, 1998, "Adios, Mi Capitan."

Television—Executives

• **Last survivor of the "Big Three" founders of network television:** Leonard H. Goldenson, who founded ABC television. The other two were William Paley of CBS and David Sarnoff of NBC. Goldenson died in Sarasota, Florida, in December 1999, at age 94.

Time

Time—Calendars—Julian and Gregorian

The Julian calendar was introduced in Rome by Julius Caesar in 45 B.C. It set the year as 365.25 days, giving an error of one day every 128 years. The Gregorian calendar was adopted by Pope Gregory XIII in 1582. It established the year as 365.2425 days, giving an error of one day in approximately 3,300 years. Many countries made the calendar adjustment in 1582.

Last Date Some Countries Used the Julian Calendar

Country	Date
Austria (Salzburg)	October 5, 1583
Belgium and Flanders	December 21, 1582

Bulgaria	October 31, 1915
Czech Republic	January 6, 1584
Denmark	February 18, 1700
Estonia	January 31, 1918
Finland	February 17, 1753
France	December 9, 1582
Germany (Protestant States)	February 18, 1700
Great Britain and colonies (including 13 American colonies)*	September 2, 1752
Greece	March 9, 1924
Hungary	October 21, 1587
Italy	October 4, 1582
Luxembourg	December 14, 1582
Norway	February 18, 1700
Poland	October 4, 1582
Portugal	October 4, 1582
Romania	March 31, 1919
Russia	January 31, 1918
Spain	October 4, 1582
Sweden	February 17, 1753

* The switch to the Gregorian calendar meant dropping 11 days. September 3 became September 14. Also, New Year's Day was moved from March 25 to January 1. In the old days, March 24, 1700, was followed by March 25, 1701. All days before the calendar change were marked O.S. for Old Style.

Time—Calendars—February 30th

Sweden switched back and forth between the Julian and Gregorian calendars, creating between 1700 and 1712 a calendar that was one day ahead of the Julian calendar and ten days behind the Gregorian calendar.
• **Last and only time the calendar had February 30th:** 1712 in Sweden (which then included Finland). The day was added so that Sweden could convert to the Julian calendar the following day, March 1, 1712.

Time—Calendars—Revolutionary

The Revolutionary calendar was adopted by France in November 1793, during the French Revolution and was made retroactive to September 22, 1792, the autumnal equinox and the date the French Republic was officially established. The Year 1 began on that date. The 12 months of the year each had 30 days. Each month was divided into three ten-day segments, the last day of which was a rest day. The excess five days (six in leap year) were national holidays.
• **Last of the Revolutionary calendar:** replaced by the Gregorian calendar on January 1, 1806.

Time—20th Century

Many people celebrated the beginning of a new century and a new millennium on January 1, 2000. But they were a year early.
• **Last day of the 20th century and end of the Second Millennium:** December 31, 2000. The 21st century and the Third Millennium technically did not began until January 1, 2001.

Time—War Time

On February 2, 1942, during World War II, all clocks in the United States advanced one hour in an effort to save energy.
• **End of U.S. War Time:** September 30, 1945.

Transportation
(*See also* Automobiles, Aviation, Railroads, Roads.)

Transportation—Cable Cars

Cable cars move by gripping and ungripping cables that run under the street. Their heyday was between 1880 and 1890. They declined after the electric trolley cars were perfected in 1888. Generally speaking, many of the cable car lines' last year corresponds to the beginning of trolley service in those cities.
• **Last city in the world to operate cable cars:** San Francisco, California. The city was also the first. The cars started rolling in August 1873. They survive due in part to the steep hills, but mostly because of nostalgia.

Transportation—Cable Cars

Last Year of Operation for Some Major American Cable Car Lines

City, First Year of Operation	Cable Car Line	Last Year
Baltimore, Maryland 1891	Baltimore Traction Company	1896
Baltimore, Maryland 1893	Baltimore City Passenger Railway	1899
Binghamton, New York 1885	Washington Street & State Asylum Railroad	1888
Brooklyn, New York 1887	Brooklyn Cable Company	1887
Brooklyn, New York 1891	Brooklyn Heights Railroad (Baltimore, Maryland)	1909
Butte, Montana 1889	Butte City Street Railroad	1897
Chicago, Illinois 1882	Chicago City Railway	1906
Chicago, Illinois 1886	Chicago West Division Railway	1886
Chicago, Illinois 1888	North Chicago Street Railroad	1906
Chicago, Illinois 1890	West Chicago Street Railroad	1906
Cincinnati, Ohio 1885	Mount Adams and Eden Park Railway	1898
Cincinnati, Ohio 1888	Mount Auburn Cable Railway	1902
Cincinnati, Ohio 1888	Vine Street Cable Railway	1898
Cleveland, Ohio 1890	Cleveland City Cable Railway/ Cleveland City Railway Co.	1901
Denver, Colorado 1888	Denver Tramway Company	1893
Denver, Colorado 1889	Denver City Cable Company	1900
Grand Rapids, Michigan 1888	Valley City Street and Cable Railway	1891
Hoboken, New Jersey 1886	North Hudson County Railway	1892
Kansas City, Missouri 1887	Grand Avenue Railway	1903
Kansas City, Missouri 1888	Interstate Consolidated Rapid Transit Company	1892
Kansas City, Missouri 1885	Kansas City Cable Railway	1906
Kansas City, Missouri 1887	Metropolitan Street Railway	1913
Kansas City, Missouri 1888	Peoples Cable Railway	1899
Kansas City, Missouri 1889	Union Cable Railway	1889
Los Angeles, California 1889	Los Angeles Cable Railway	1896
Los Angeles, California 1885	Second Street Cable Railway	1889
Los Angeles, California 1886	Temple Street Cable Railway	1902
New York, New York 1893	Metropolitan Street Railway	1901
New York, New York 1883	New York and Brooklyn Bridge Railway	1908

New York, New York 1885	Third Avenue Railroad	1899	**Saint Louis, Missouri** 1890	Saint Louis Railroad	1900
New York, New York 1868	West Side and Yonkers Patent Railway	1870	**Saint Paul, Minnesota** 1888	Saint Paul City Railway	1898
Newark, New Jersey 1888	Essex Passenger Railway/ Newark and Irvington Street Railway	1889	**San Diego, California** 1890	San Diego Cable Railway	1893
Oakland, California 1886	Oakland Cable Railway	1899	**San Francisco, California** 1873	Clay Street Hill Railroad	1891
Oakland, California 1890	Consolidated Cable Company	1896	**San Francisco, California** 1877	Sutter Street Railway	1906
Omaha, Nebraska 1887	Cable Tramway Company of Omaha	1895	**San Francisco, California** 1880	Geary Street Park and Ocean Railway	1912
Philadelphia, Pennsylvania 1885	Philadelphia Traction Company	1895	**San Francisco, California** 1880	Presidio and Ferries Railway	1906
Pittsburgh, Pennsylvania 1885	Pittsburgh Traction Company	1895	**San Francisco, California** 1883	Market Street Cable Railway	1906
Pittsburgh, Pennsylvania 1889	Citizens Traction Company	1897	**San Francisco, California** 1888	Omnibus Railroad and Cable Company	1899
Pittsburgh, Pennsylvania 1890	Central Traction Company	1896	**Seattle, Washington** 1888	Seattle City Railway	1940
Portland, Oregon 1890	Portland Cable Railway	1904	**Seattle, Washington** 1889	Front Street Cable Railway	1900
Providence, Rhode Island 1889	Providence Cable Tramway	1895	**Seattle, Washington** 1891	Union Trunk Line	1940
Saint Louis, Missouri 1887	Citizens Railway	1894	**Seattle, Washington** 1890	West Seattle Cable Railway	1897
Saint Louis, Missouri 1886	Saint Louis Cable and Western Railway	1891	**Seattle, Washington** 1891	Madison Street Cable Railway	1940
Saint Louis, Missouri 1888	Missouri Railroad	1901	**Sioux City, Iowa** 1889	Sioux City Cable Railway	1894
Saint Louis, Missouri 1890	Peoples Railway	1901	**Spokane, Washington** 1889	Spokane Cable Railway	1894
			Tacoma, Washington 1891	Tacoma Railway & Motor Company	1938

Washington, D.C. 1890	Washington and Georgetown Railroad	1898
Washington, D.C. 1895	Columbia Railway	1899

Transportation—Elevated Lines
• **Last day of operation for New York's Third Avenue "El":** May 12, 1955. It was the last elevated line in Manhattan.

Transportation—Horsecars
The first horsecar line began operating in New York, New York, in the 1830s. By the mid-1880s, most of the 400 or more street railway companies operating in North America used horses. Some horsecars were replaced with short-lived cable car lines and then electric trolley lines. But many went directly from horsecar to electrified routes. By the first decade of the 1900s, most cities had converted their transit systems to electricity.

Transportation—Horsecars
Last Year Horsecars Operated
in Some American Cities

City	Year
Albany, New York	1890
Boston, Massachusetts	1900
Buffalo, New York	1894
Chicago, Illinois	1906
Detroit, Michigan	1896
Los Angeles, California	1898
New York, New York	1917
Pasadena, California	1898
Philadelphia, Pennsylvania	1897
San Diego, California	1896
San Francisco, California	1913
Syracuse, New York	1900
Washington, D.C.	1900

• **Last horsecar lines in the U.S.:** the Metropolitan Railway's Bleecker Street line in New York City, which ran until 1917. The horsecar line in Middletown, Ohio, was in operation until 1918.
• **Last horsecar line in Canada:** Sarnia, Ontario, which ran until 1901 or 1902.

Transportation—Stagecoaches—Missouri-California Overland Stage
John Butterfield's Overland Stage Company began operating in 1858, giving the U.S. its first regular transcontinental mail service. The 2,800-mile trip between Saint Louis, Missouri, and San Francisco, California, by way of Texas, New Mexico and Arizona, took 25 days.
• **End of the southwestern route:** 1861. When the Civil War began, the U.S. Congress ordered the service to be moved farther north. Wells Fargo bought the company in 1866.
• **End of the Missouri-California Overland Stage:** 1869. It ceased operation when the Union Pacific Railroad was completed. Other stages continued to operate in less populated areas, but by the end of the 19th century, trains had taken over most of those routes.
• **Last use of Wells Fargo stagecoaches in California and Oregon:** 1895. As the railroads were completed, the company switched from stagecoaches to railroads.

Transportation—Subways—Beach's Pneumatic Underground Railroad
Beach's Pneumatic Underground Railroad was designed by Alfred E. Beach, owner of *Scientific American* magazine. The railroad, which used fans and suction to propel passengers in cars, ran a very short distance below Broadway in New York, New York. It began operation in 1870.
• **Last time Beach's Railroad was used:** 1873.
• **Last surviving part of Beach's Railroad:** a tunnel. In 1912, when workers were digging New York's new subway, they hit Beach's forgotten old tunnel. A part of it has been incorporated into the City Hall station, where it is marked with a plaque acknowledging Beach as the father of the New York subway system.

Transportation—Subways—Chicago Freight Subway
The Chicago Freight Subway, (a.k.a. Chi-

cago Tunnel Company) was fully operational by 1906. The company went bankrupt in 1956.

• **Last time the Chicago Freight Subway was used:** May 13, 1959, when the entire system was closed.

Transportation—Taxicabs—Checker Cab

Checker was the most prolific of the manufacturers of taxicabs in the United States. Checker taxicabs were most widely used in New York, New York.

• **Last time Checker Cab Company operated in New York:** July 8, 1982, when the company ceased operations.

• **Last New York Checker Cab:** taken out of service July 1999, with 994,050 miles. It was sold for $134,500 by Sotheby's Auction House in December 1999.

Transportation—Trolleys

Trolleys, sometimes called trolley cars, are streetcars that are connected with overhead power transmission lines called trolleys. They became popular in the mid-1880s. Many cities began removing their trolley systems in the 1940s, after World War II. Today, only seven American cities continue to run trolley service.

• **Last surviving trolley line in New Orleans:** The Saint Charles Avenue Route (home of the Streetcar Named Desire).

Transportation—Trolleys—Canada
Last Year Trolleys Operated in Some Canadian Cities

City	Year
Calgary, Alberta	1975
Montreal, Quebec	1966
Halifax, Nova Scotia	1969
Toronto, Ontario	1993

Transportation—Trolleys—U.S.
Last Year Trolleys Operated in Some American Cities

City	Year
Akron, Ohio	1959
Albuquerque, New Mexico	1928

Baltimore, Maryland	1962
Buffalo, New York	1950
Butte, Montana	1937
Charleston, West Virginia	1939
Charlotte, South Carolina	1938
Chattanooga, Tennessee	1947
Chicago, Illinois	1973
Cincinnati, Ohio	1951
Cleveland, Ohio	1954
Columbus, Ohio	1965
Corpus Christi, Texas	1931
Denver, Colorado	1950
Des Moines, Iowa	1964
El Paso, Texas	1974
Honolulu, Hawaii	1933
Houston, Texas	1940
Indianapolis, Indiana	1941
Kansas, City, Missouri	1959
Los Angeles, California	1963
Miami, Florida	1947
Milwaukee, Wisconsin	1965
New Haven, Connecticut	1948
New York, New York	1957
Pensacola, Florida	1931
Phoenix, Arizona	1948
Pittsburgh, Pennsylvania	1999
Providence, Rhode Island	1948
Rochester, New York	1956
Saint Louis, Missouri	1932
Seattle, Washington	1941
Sioux Falls, South Dakota	1929
Tacoma, Washington	1938
Troy, New York	1933
Washington, D.C.	1961

Transportation—Trolleys—Manufacturers

• **Last trolley built by Pullman Car Company:** 1951, #3321 delivered to Boston, Massachusetts.

• **Last trolley built by Yellow Coach:** 1938, Model 1208 delivered to Milwaukee Electric Railway & Light Company.

• **Last trolley built by Sunbeam:** 1962, Model MF2B, #301, delivered to Bournemouth, Dorset, England. This was also the last trolley delivered to any English company.

• **Last trolley built by Brill:** 1954.

United States of America
(*See also* Wars and Battles—
World War II—United States.)

United States—Agencies

United States—Agencies—Agricultural Adjustment Administration
The Agricultural Adjustment Administration was established within the U. S. Department of Agriculture in 1933 to help financially strapped farmers recover from the economic depression.
• **Last of the Agricultural Adjustment Administration:** 1946, when its functions were taken over by the USDA's Production and Marketing Administration.

United States—Agencies—Civilian Conservation Corps (CCC)
The Civilian Conservation Corps (CCC) was established by Congress in 1933. It provided jobs on public works projects such as reforestation, flood and fire control for young men from families on public welfare.
• **Last of the CCC:** June 30, 1942, when Congress voted to terminate it. Over the next six months, its assets were liquidated and all enrollees were discharged. By December 15, most of the equipment had been transferred to other agencies and the CCC came to an end.

United States—Agencies—Civil Works Administration (CWA)
The Civil Works Administration (CWA) was a temporary Roosevelt administration program created in 1933 to pump up the economy by providing jobs. Among the CWA projects were repairing rural schools and courthouses, updating school records and conducting health research.
• **Last of the CWA:** abolished April 1, 1934. Many of its projects were continued by the Federal Emergency Relief Administration.

United States—Agencies—Federal Emergency Relief Administration (FERA)
The Federal Emergency Relief Administration (FERA) was set up in 1933, during the early days of the Franklin D. Roosevelt administration to provide relief for needy people.
• **Last of the FERA:** abolished in 1935. As the hard times of the Great Depression diminished and people began to find jobs, the FERA was disbanded.

United States—Agencies—Federal Radio Commission (FRC)
The Federal Radio Commission (FRC) was created in 1927 to license radio stations and approve of locations and equipment.
• **Last of the FRC:** abolished in 1934. Its functions were transferred to the Federal Communications Commission, created that year.

United States—Agencies—Food and Drug Administration (FDA)
The Food and Drug Administration (FDA) was founded in 1928 as the Food, Drug and Insecticide Administration.
• **Last known as the Food, Drug and Insecticide Administration:** 1931, when the name was changed to Food and Drug Administration (FDA). It became part of the Federal Security Agency in 1940. It was moved to the Department of Health, Education and Welfare in 1953. FDA became part of the Department of Health and Human Services in 1980.

United States—Agencies—Interstate Commerce Commission ICC)
The Interstate Commerce Commission (ICC) was established in 1887 to regulate carriers engaged in interstate commerce.
• **Last of the ICC:** abolished on December 31, 1995, by the ICC Termination Act.

United States—Agencies—National Industrial Recovery Act (NIRA)
The National Industrial Recovery Act (NIRA), enacted in 1933, led to the creation of the National Recovery Administration (NRA), a U.S. federal agency. In *Schechter Poultry Corp.* v. *United States*, the U.S. Supreme Court ruled in May 1935 that the

NIRA was unconstitutional.
• **Last of the NIRA:** abolished on January 1, 1936.

United States—Agencies—National Youth Administration (NYA)

The National Youth Administration (NYA) was established by Executive Order of President Franklin D. Roosevelt in 1935 to help find work for high school and college students between the ages of 16 and 25. Originally within the WPA, the NYA was transferred to the Federal Security Agency in 1939. It came under the War Manpower Commission on September 17, 1942.
• **Last of the NYA:** terminated as of January 1, 1944.

United States—Agencies—Reconstruction Finance Corporation (RFC)

The Reconstruction Finance Corporation (RFC) was a federal corporation chartered by Congress in 1932, during the Great Depression, to ease financial problems by lending to banks, mortgage companies, insurance companies, municipalities, and other public agencies. The RFC was hit by scandal in 1952 and reorganized.
• **Last of the RFC:** abolished as of June 30, 1954.

United States—Agencies—Resettlement Administration

The Resettlement Administration was established in 1935, during the Great Depression, to help displaced farmers. It had the authority to help tenants become home owners.
• **Last of the Resettlement Administration:** reorganized in 1937 into the Farm Security Administration within the Department of Agriculture.

United States—Agencies—Social Security Administration

The act that set up Social Security was passed in August 1935. It provided that benefits were to be paid to retired workers over the age of 65 who were covered under the system. The first Social Security benefits were paid to nearly 28,000 beneficiaries in January 1940.

• **Last surviving original beneficiary:** William Howard Weamer. He was 66 when he received his first check for $17.44. He had paid $30 into the system. By 1980, Weamer, then living in a Doylestown, Pennsylvania, nursing home at the age of 106 was collecting a monthly check for $227.20. Weamer served as a two-time member of the Pennsylvania House of Representatives.

United States—Agencies—Works Projects Administration (WPA)

The WPA was created in 1935 by Executive Order of President Franklin D. Roosevelt as the Works Progress Administration. The agency's goal was to fund projects such as relief work, grants, loans on highways, reforestation, nonfederal projects and rural electrification.
• **Last known as the Works Progress Administration:** 1939, when the WPA was renamed the Works Projects Administration and placed under the Federal Works Agency.
• **Last of the WPA:** terminated on June 30, 1943, by an Executive Order issued the previous December. With increasing employment during World War II, the agency was no longer needed.

United States—Agencies—WPA Federal Theater

The WPA Federal Theater Project began January 1935 under the Civil Works Administration.
• **Last of the WPA Federal Theater:** terminated on July 31, 1939.

United States—Agencies—WPA Federal Writers' Project

The Federal Writers Project was created in 1935 as part of the Works Progress Administration It turned out 51 major books, including guides for all the states and several cities and about a thousand smaller books and pamphlets. After that, it dwindled in size and was renamed the Writers' Program.
• **Last of the WPA Federal Writers' Project:** 1943, during World War II. It was absorbed into the Office of War Information.

United States—
Boundaries and Frontiers

United States—Boundaries and Frontiers — Arizona-New Mexico Boundary

The Treaty of Guadalupe Hidalgo signed by the United States and Mexico in 1848 ended the Mexican War but led to a dispute over ownership of a portion of land along the Arizona-New Mexico boundary. The dispute stemmed from a misinterpretation of the boundary surveys.

• **End of the U.S.-Mexican Treaty of Guadalupe Hidalgo boundary dispute:** 1854, with ratification of the Gadsden Purchase. Mexico sold 29,600 acres to the U.S. for $10 million. The land along the Arizona-New Mexico boundary with Mexico extended as far north as the Gila River. The purchase averted the chance of another war and fixed the southern boundary of the United States at its present line.

United States—Boundaries and Frontiers —Maine-Canada Border

When the borders of the United States were established after the American Revolution, a boundary dispute arose between Maine and Canada. At stake were 12,000 square miles of valuable timber along the border.

• **End of the Maine-Canada boundary dispute:** August 9, 1842, with the Webster-Ashburton Treaty. The state of Maine and the U.S. gained 7,000 of the 12,000 disputed square miles that included the Aroostock Valley and the head of the Connecticut River.

United States—Boundaries and Frontiers —Mason-Dixon Line

The Mason-Dixon Line determined the Pennsylvania-Maryland boundary. English surveyors Charles Mason and Jeremiah Dixon laid out the line beginning in 1763 to settle a boundary dispute between the Calvert and Penn families, proprietors of Maryland and Pennsylvania. The original boundary extended from the eastern boundary of Maryland with Delaware west to Maryland's northwest corner. Some Native Americans prevented Mason and Dixon from going farther.

• **Last surveying of the Mason-Dixon Line:** 1784, when the line was extended to mark the boundary between Pennsylvania and Virginia. In the years before the Civil War, the Mason-Dixon Line came to mean the boundary between Northern and Southern states. During the Civil War, it marked the dividing line between free and slave states.

United States—Boundaries and Frontiers —Oregon Land Dispute

For more than a half century, beginning in 1790, the United States and Great Britain were engaged in a diplomatic dispute over who owned Oregon. Britain claimed all the territory west of the Rocky Mountains from Mexico to Alaska.

• **End of the U.S-British northwest border dispute:** June 18, 1846, with the Oregon Treaty. It set the 49th parallel as the border between the United States and British North America (Canada).

United States—Boundaries and Frontiers —San Juan Island Land Dispute

San Juan Island is in the Vancouver Channel. When a treaty in 1846 between the United States and Great Britain established the boundary between the U.S. and British Columbia, it awarded the island to Canada and gave rise to a land dispute.

• **End of the San Juan Island dispute:** 1872, when the island was awarded to the United States after almost 26 years of dispute. Kaiser Wilhelm I of Germany mediated the dispute.

United States—Cabinet

United States—Cabinet—Agriculture, Department of

The Department of Agriculture began as a division created within the U.S. Patent Office in 1832.

• **Last time the Department of Agriculture was a branch of the U.S. Patent Office:** May 15, 1862, when a new Department of Agriculture was created, administered by the Commissioner of Agriculture. The position had no cabinet rank until February 8, 1889.

United States—Cabinet—Commerce and Labor, Department of

The Department of Labor was created in 1887, but it did not have Cabinet status until 1903, when the Department of Commerce and Labor was established by Congress. In 1913, the department was split into two: Department of Commerce and Department of Labor.

• **Last Secretary of Commerce and Labor:** Charles Nagel, who served from 1909 to 1913.

• **Last time the Maritime Administration was part of the Department of Commerce:** 1981, when it became part of the Department of Transportation.

United States—Cabinet—Defense, Department of

The Department of Defense was originally designated the National Military Establishment (NME). It was created by the National Security Act of 1947.

• **Last time the Department of Defense was known as the National Military Establishment (NME):** August 10, 1949.

United States—Cabinet—Health, Education and Welfare

The Department of Health, Education and Welfare (HEW) was created in 1953.

• **Last of the Department of Health, Education and Welfare:** May 1980, when HEW was divided into two departments: Health and Human Services; Education.

• **Last Secretary of Health, Education and Welfare:** Patricia Roberts Harris. She was the first Secretary of Health and Human Services from 1979 to 1981. Previously, she was the first black woman to hold the position of U.S. Ambassador to Luxembourg (1965-67) and the first black woman to serve in the U.S. Cabinet. She was the Sec-

retary of the Department of Housing and Urban Development from 1977 to 1979.

United States—Cabinet—Interior, Department of

The Department of the Interior was established in 1849 as the Home Department. It included the Office of the Census, Office of Indian Affairs, General Land Office and Pension Office.

• **Last year the Census Bureau was part of the Department of the Interior:** 1903, when it became part of the Department of Commerce and Labor.

• **Last year the Patent Office was part of the State Department:** 1839, when it became part of the Department of the Interior.

• **Last year the Patent Office was part of the Department of the Interior:** 1925, when it became part of the Department of Commerce, where it has remained.

• **Last time the U.S. Patent Office required a miniature working model of an invention:** 1870. Submission of a model was at the discretion of the Commissioner of Patents. In 1880, the requirements were dropped altogether, except for flying machines; that requirement was dropped in 1903. The models took up so much space that the Patent Office had to get rid of them. Some were taken by the Smithsonian Institution. Others went back to the inventors, many thousands were sold at auction.

• **Last time the Pension Office was part of the Department of the Interior:** 1930, when it was transferred to the Veterans Administration.

United States—Cabinet—Navy, Department of

The Department of the Navy was created by Congress in April 1798.

• **Last time the Department of the Navy was a separate Cabinet office:** 1947. That year, under the National Security Act, it was incorporated into the Department of Defense. The Secretary of Defense replaced the Secretary of the Navy in the President's Cabinet.

• **Last member of the President's Cabinet to hold the title Secretary of the Navy:**

James Vincent Forrestal, from 1944 to 1947. When the Navy Department became a branch of the Department of Defense in 1947, Forrestal became Secretary of Defense.

United States—Cabinet—Post Office Department
The U.S. Post Office Department was established in 1782.
• **Last of the U.S. Post Office Department:** ended July 1, 1971, with creation of the U.S. Postal Service as a separate agency.
• **Last Postmaster General to hold a Cabinet-level position:** Winton M. Blount, who held the position from 1969 to 1971. He died on October 24, 2002, age 81.

United States—Cabinet—State Department
The State Department was established as the Department of Foreign Affairs in 1781 when the United States was ruled by the Articles of Confederation. The department was retained by the U.S. Congress in July 1789.
• **Last time the U.S. State Department was known as the Department of Foreign Affairs:** September 15, 1789.
• **Last Secretary of Foreign Affairs:** John Jay, jurist, co-author of the *Federalist Papers* and former president of the Continental Congress (1778-79), who held the position from 1784 to 1789.
• **Last Under Secretary of State:** John Nichol Irwin II, who held the title until July 13, 1972, when the position of Under Secretary of State was abolished. He was redesignated Deputy Secretary of State and held the position until February 1, 1973. He subsequently served as U.S. Ambassador to France (1973-74). Irwin died in New Haven, Connecticut, on February 28, 2000, age 86.

United States—Cabinet—War Department
The War Department was one of the executive departments established by the U.S. Congress in 1789.
• **Last of the War Department:** abolished in 1947, when it was made part of the Department of the Army and became a branch of the Department of Defense.
• **Last member of the president's Cabinet to hold the title of Secretary of War:** Kenneth C. Royall, appointed in 1947. He next served as the first Secretary of the Army when the War Department became part of the Department of the Army within the Department of Defense. The Secretary of the Army is not a Cabinet position. The secretary answers to the President through the Secretary of Defense.

United States—Capital

United States—Capitals of the Nation
From September 1774 to December 1776, the nation's capital was in Philadelphia, Pennsylvania. Over the next 24 years, it moved several times. The Continental Congress made its first move, to Baltimore, Maryland, in December 1776, when the Americans feared a British attack on the city of Philadelphia.
• **Last time the national capital was in Baltimore, Maryland:** March 4, 1777, when Congress returned to Philadelphia, where it met from March 5, 1777 to September 18, 1777. The Congress next went to Lancaster, Pennsylvania, and met in session in that city for just one day: September 27, 1777.
• **Last time the national capital was in Lancaster, Pennsylvania:** September 27, 1777. Congress moved from Lancaster to York, Pennsylvania, and reconvened on September 30, 1777. It remained in York for nine months.
• **Last time the national capital was in York, Pennsylvania:** June 27, 1778. The Continental Congress then returned to Philadelphia. By then, the British had evacuated the city. The capital remained in Philadelphia for the next five years. In June 1783, after the American Revolution ended, Congress left Philadelphia to escape an angry band of Pennsylvania veterans who had marched into the city demanding to be paid for their war services. The Congress recon-

vened in Princeton, New Jersey, on June 30, 1783, and remained there for four months.

• **Last time the national capital was in Princeton, New Jersey:** November 4, 1783, when Congress adjourned, with plans to meet a few weeks later in Annapolis, Maryland. Congress reconvened in Annapolis on November 26, 1783.

• **Last time the capital was in Annapolis, Maryland:** June 3, 1784. Congress next met in Trenton, New Jersey, in November and December 1784.

• **Last time the national capital was in Trenton, New Jersey:** December 24, 1784. Congress chose New York as a temporary capital. New York was the nation's capital from January 1785 to August 1790.

• **Last time the national capital was in New York, New York:** August 12, 1790. While meeting in New York, the Continental Congress ended on March 2, 1789, and the United States Congress convened two days later. After New York, the U.S. Congress assembled in Philadelphia in December 1790, where it remained until 1800.

• **Last time the national capital was in Philadelphia, Pennsylvania:** May 14, 1800, when the first session of the Sixth Congress ended. Congress reconvened in Washington, D.C., on November 17, 1800, for the second session.

United States—Colonial America
(*See also* United Sates—
Continental Congress)

United States—Colonial America—
Burgesses, House of
The House of Burgesses was the first representative legislative body in America. It sat in Jamestown, Virginia, for the first time in July 1619, with two burgesses, or citizens, from each of Virginia's seven boroughs.

• **Last time the House of Burgesses sat and transacted business:** June 1, 1775. Some members met on March 7, 1776, and again on May 6, 1776, but there was no quorum, and nothing was transacted at either session.

• **Last speaker of the House of Burgesses:** Peyton Randolph, from 1766 to 1775. Randolph served as the first president of the Continental Congress in 1774-75. He died in Philadelphia, Pennsylvania, on October 22, 1775, age 54.

United States—Colonial America—
London Company
The London Company, also known as the Virginia Company of London, was a trading company chartered 1606 to settle land between what is now Washington, D.C., and New York.

• **Last of the London Company:** dissolved in 1624, when England's King James revoked the charter. Virginia was made a royal colony.

United States—Colonial America—
Massachusetts Bay Company
The Massachusetts Bay Company was a group of merchants and others who were granted a charter in 1629 to trade and colonize New England between the Charles and the Merrimac rivers.

• **Last of the Massachusetts Bay Company:** 1684, when the charter was withdrawn and the colony was absorbed into the Dominion of New England.

United States—Colonial America—
Mayflower and Plymouth Colony
The *Mayflower* left Plymouth, England, in September 1620, carrying about 100 Pilgrims. It dropped anchor on Cape Cod in early November. Passengers chose a land site that would become Plymouth, Massachusetts. The Mayflower Compact was signed by 41 adult male passengers aboard the *Mayflower* on November 11, 1620. They promised to enact just and equal laws for the good of the Plymouth Colony.

• **Last time the Mayflower Compact was in force:** 1691, when the Plymouth Colony was absorbed by the Massachusetts Bay Colony.

• **Last surviving Mayflower Compact signer:** John Alden. He was also the youngest signer. He was around 21 when he signed. Alden died on September 22, 1687.

• **Last time passengers left the *Mayflower*:** March 21, 1621, after spending the winter on the ship. The *Mayflower* returned to England on April 5, 1621. It remained there until 1624. After that, the ship's history is unknown.

• **Last surviving female *Mayflower* passenger:** Mary Allerton Cushman, who died in 1699, age 90. She sailed to America with parents, her sister, Remember, and her brother, Bartholomew.

• **Last surviving male *Mayflower* passenger:** John Cooke, who died in Dartmouth, Massachusetts, on November 23, 1695, age 88.

• **Last remaining house once occupied by a Mayflower Pilgrim:** Alden House in Duxbury, Massachusetts. John and Priscilla Alden lived and died in the house.

• **Last of the Plymouth Colony:** October 1691, when it became part of the Massachusetts Bay Colony.

• **Last governor of the Plymouth Colony:** Thomas Hinckley. He began his term in 1681.

United States—Colonial America—New Netherland

New Netherland was the name the Dutch used for their colony in North America. It was founded in 1624 in the Hudson River Valley and originally extended from what is now New York City to Albany. When the Dutch conquered the lower Delaware River, that region also became part of New Netherland. New Amsterdam was founded in 1625 and became the capital of the colony.

• **Last of New Netherland:** 1664, when the English captured the region. New Amsterdam and New Netherland were renamed New York.

• **Last governor of New Netherland:** Peter Stuyvesant, who was in office when the colony surrendered to the English in 1664.

United States—Colonial America—New Sweden

New Sweden was a Swedish colony founded in 1638 along the Delaware River in what are now the states of Delaware, New Jersey and Pennsylvania.

• **Last of New Sweden:** 1655, when the Dutch conquered the region.

United States—Colonial America—Roanoke Island's Lost Colony

Roanoke Island is off the northeast coast of North Carolina. The earliest settlers landed in August 1585 but returned to England in June 1586. The following year, another group of men, women and children arrived, led by John White. White returned to England for supplies.

• **Last of the Roanoke Island colonists:** Unknown. When White returned to Roanoke Island in August 1590, all the colonists had vanished. The only clue they left was the word CROATAN carved on a tree. It would be another 17 years before the first permanent English colony would be established in the region—at Jamestown in southeastern Virginia in 1607.

United States—Confederation Era
(*See also* United Sates— Continental Congress)

The Confederation Era began on March 1, 1781, with ratification of the Articles of Confederation and Perpetual Union. The Articles were the first constitution of the United States and were the law of the land for eight years.

• **Last state to ratify the Articles of Confederation:** Maryland on March 1, 1781.

• **End of the Articles of Confederation:** March 2, 1789. The Articles were replaced with the new U.S. Constitution that went into effect with ratification by the needed number of states.

United States—Confederation Era— "Critical Period"

In 1888, American historian/philosopher John Fiske published a book about the Confederation Era entitled *The Critical Period of American History, 1783–1789*. Fiske's term "Critical Period" has subsequently been used to describe those troublesome years when the United States was controlled by a body of law that proved to be ineffec-

tive in governing the new nation.
• **End of the "Critical Period":** 1789, after the U.S. Constitution was signed and had become the law of the land.

United States—Congress

United States—Congress—Congressional Pages

The first Congressional pages served in Congress in the 1827 Congress. They began to be called pages in the late 1830s. They have many duties including answering phone calls and delivering envelopes, small packages, boxed flags, and such between the offices in the Capitol.
• **Last time Congressional pages were white only:** 1965, when the first black male pages were sworn in.
• **Last time Congressional pages were male only:** 1970, when the first female was sworn in.
• **Last time Congressional pages could be 14 years old:** 1983, when the minimum age was raised to 16.

United States—Congress—*Congressional Record*

The Congressional Record reports the pr o-ceedings and debates in both houses of Congress. It is issued daily when Congress is in session.
• **Last time the *Congressional Record* was known as the *Congressional Globe*:** 1873.

United States—Congress—Continental Congress

The Continental Congress met in 15 sessions in eight different cities between 1774 and 1789. (*See* United States—Capitals of the Nation.) The first session is known as the First Continental Congress. It convened in Philadelphia, Pennsylvania, on September 5, 1774, as an advisory council of representatives from the 13 colonies who gathered to decide on a course of action. The Continental Congress remained the governing body of the United States until the end of the Confederation Era.

• **Last session of the First Continental Congress:** October 26, 1774. When it adjourned, delegates made plans to meet again in May 1775.
• **Last session of the Second Continental Congress:** May 10, 1775, to December 12, 1776, in Philadelphia.
• **Last session of the Continental Congress:** November 3, 1788, to March 2, 1789, in New York, New York.
• **Last president of the Continental Congress:** Cyrus Griffin, who was elected on January 22, 1788, and served until April 30, 1789. Griffin died in Yorktown, Virginia, in 1810, age 62.
• **Last surviving Continental Congress president:** John Jay, who was elected on December 10, 1778, and served until September 28, 1779. He died in Bedford, New York, on May 17, 1829, age 83.
• **Last surviving member of the Continental Congress:** Paine Wingate, a delegate from New Hampshire in 1787 and 1788. He later served in the U.S. Senate and was a superior court judge. He died in Stratham, New Hampshire, on March 7, 1838, age 98.

United States—Congress—Army-McCarthy Hearings

In 1950, Senator Joseph R. McCarthy (R-Wis.) charged that the State Department had many Communists in its employ. He also attacked members of Congress and the Secretary of Defense. As his reputation grew, so did his attacks, which came to be known as "McCarthyism." In 1953, he accused the Army of being lax toward Communists. That prompted the Eisenhower administration to fight back. The Army-McCarthy hearings began in the spring of 1954 and lasted for five weeks.
• **Last of the Army-McCarthy hearings:** June 17, 1954. Although the outcome of the hearings was inconclusive, the hearings did cause people to question McCarthy's motives and methods.
• **Last of McCarthyism:** ended in December 1954, when the Senate voted 67-22 to censure McCarthy. He died in Bethesda, Maryland, on March 2, 1957, age 48.

United States—Congress—House Un-American Activities Committee

The House Committee on Un-American Activities was created in 1938 to investigate disloyalty, subversive activities and Communist links among organizations and private citizens. The agency was also called the Dies Committee for its chairman, Martin Dies Jr. of Texas. The name was later changed to House Un-American Activities Committee to create the acronym HUAC.

• **Last time the HUAC known by that name:** 1969, when the name was changed to the House Committee on Internal Security (HCIS).

• **Last of the HCIS:** abolished in 1975.

• **Last chair of the HCIS:** Representative Richard H. Ichord, of Missouri, who died in Texas, on December 18, 1992, age 66.

United States—Congress—Lame Duck Session

The lame duck session of Congress was a short session that began in December of even-numbered years and continued until March 4 of the following odd-numbered years. It enabled congressmen who failed to be reelected to continue to make laws to the end of the session in March.

• **Last of the lame duck session of Congress:** October 15, 1933, when it was abolished by the 20th Amendment. The amendment also moved the beginning of the sessions of Congress forward to January 3rd.

United States—Congress—Members— Calhoun, John C.

John C. Calhoun had a distinguished political career that included Secretary of War (1812-25) and Vice President (1825-32). He also served as representative and senator from South Carolina. Calhoun died in Washington, D.C., on March 31, 1850, age 68.

• **Last speech of Calhoun in the Senate**: Calhoun was too ill to deliver his last speech in the Senate on March 4, 1850. Someone read it for him. It was a denunciation of the Compromise of 1850.

• **Last appearance of Calhoun in the Sen-**ate: March 7, 1850, when Calhoun heard and approved an appeal by Daniel Webster for sectional unity.

United States—Congress—Members— Sumner, Charles

Senator Charles Sumner from Massachusetts was assaulted by Representative Preston Brooks of South Carolina while seated in Congress on May 22, 1856, and was seriously injured.

• **End of Sumner's absence due to injuries:** December 5, 1859.

• **Last public oration by Sumner:** at the New England Dinner in New York, New York, on December 22, 1873.

• **Last appeal by Sumner in the Senate:** January 27, 1874, when he appealed for civil rights for citizens of color.

• **Last appearance by Sumner in the Sen-**ate: March 10, 1874. Sumner died the following day, age 63.

United States—Congress—Members— Thurmond, Strom

When James Strom Thurmond of South Carolina died at age 100 on June 26, 2003, he was the longest serving member of the U.S. Senate.

• **End of Thurmond's final Senate term:** January 2003, after 48 years. He gave his farewell speech to the Senate in the fall of 2002.

United States—Constitution

United States—Constitution—Bill of Rights

The Bill of Rights are the first ten amendments to the U.S. Constitution. They were submitted to the states by the first U.S. Congress on September 25, 1789. Ten states ratified the ten amendments by December 15, 1791, making them enforceable on that date. Three states did not ratify by that time: Massachusetts, Georgia and Connecticut. It would be many years before they did. In 1939, Massachusetts ratified on March 2, and Georgia ratified on March 18th.

• **Last state to ratify the Bill of Rights:**

Connecticut, on April 19, 1939, almost 150 years after the document had been submitted by Congress.

United States—Constitution—Founding Fathers

"Founding Fathers" is the term given to the members of the Constitutional Convention who drafted the Constitution of the United States.

• **Last surviving "Founding Father":** James Madison, who died in Orange County, Virginia, on June 28, 1836, age 85.

United States—Constitution—Income Tax

Income tax became a permanent part of the U.S. tax system with ratification of the 16th Amendment. The amendment gave Congress the power to tax the income of both corporations and individuals. It states: "The Congress shall have power to lay and collect taxes on incomes, from whatever source derived, without apportionment among the several states, and without regard to any census or enumeration."

• **Last time the U.S. was without a permanent income tax:** 1914. The 16th Amendment was ratified in 1913. The federal income tax law was signed by President Woodrow Wilson in October 1913, and went into effect on March 1, 1914.

United States—Constitution—Ratification

The Constitution of the United States was drafted at a federal convention in Philadelphia, Pennsylvania, in the summer of 1787. In September 1787, delegates approved the document and sent it to the states for ratification.

• **Last of the 13 original states to ratify the Constitution:** Rhode Island on May 29, 1790, by a vote of 34 to 32.

• **Last amendment that did not require ratification within seven years of submission to the states:** The 17th Amendment. Beginning with the proposed 18th Amendment, Congress has included a provision requiring ratification within seven years from the time of the submission to the States.

United States— Declaration of Independence

United States—Declaration of Independence

In 1776, the Continental Congress appointed a committee to draft a declaration that stated the reasons the colonies were planning to revolt. The document was drafted in Philadelphia, Pennsylvania, and accepted by Congress on July 4, 1776.

• **Last man to sign the Declaration of Independence:** Thomas McKean of Delaware. He did not sign until 1781 by special permission because he was serving in the American Revolution.

• **Last state to ratify the Declaration of Independence:** New York, on July 9, 1776.

• **Last surviving signer of the Declaration of Independence:** Charles Carroll of Maryland, who died in Baltimore on November 14, 1832, age 95.

• **Last surviving widow of a signer of the Declaration of Independence:** Ann Thompson Gerry, widow of Elbridge Gerry of Massachusetts. She died in 1849. Elbridge Gerry died in Washington, D.C., on November 23, 1814, age 70.

United States—Flag

United States—Flag—Pledge of Allegiance

The Pledge of Allegiance was written in 1892 by Francis Bellamy, a Baptist minister. Soon after the pledge was published, public school students began saying it as part of a flag salute.

• **Last time the Pledge of Allegiance was changed:** 1954, when by act of Congress the words "under God" were added after "one nation." The pledge was emended once before, in 1925, when the words "my flag" were changed to "the flag of the United States.

United States—Flag—Stars and Stripes

By May 1, 1795, the United States flag had 15 stars and 15 stripes. As new states were added, it became obvious that limits had to be placed on changes to the design. Congress ordered the number of stripes to be limited to 13 after July 4, 1818; however, new stars would be added as states entered the Union. The act also provided that the changes would be made to the flag on the Independence Day after each new state was admitted to the Union.

Last Time Flag Had	Date	Reason for Change
13 stars	1795	That year, two were added for Vermont, Kentucky.
15 stars	1818	Five added for Indiana, Louisiana, Mississippi, Ohio, Tennessee.
20 stars	July 3, 1819	One added for Illinois, July 4, 1819.
21 stars	July 3, 1820	Two added for Alabama, Maine, July 4, 1820.
23 stars	July 3, 1822	One added for Missouri, July 4, 1822.
24 stars	July 3, 1836	One added for Arkansas, July 4, 1836.
25 stars	July 3, 1837	One added for Michigan, July 4, 1837.
26 stars	July 3, 1845	One added for Florida, July 4, 1845.
27 stars	July 3, 1846	One added for Texas, July 4, 1846.
28 stars	July 3, 1847	One added for Iowa, July 4, 1847.
29 stars	July 3, 1848	One added for Wisconsin, July 4, 1848.
30 stars	July 3, 1851	One added for California, July 4, 1851.
31 stars	July 3, 1858	One added for Minnesota, July 4, 1858.
32 stars	July 3, 1859	One added for Oregon, July 4, 1859.
33 stars	July 3, 1861	One added for Kansas, July 4, 1861.
34 stars	July 3, 1863	One added for West Virginia, July 4, 1863.
35 stars	July 3, 1865	One added for Nevada, July 4, 1865.
36 stars	July 3, 1867	One added for Nebraska, July 4, 1867.
37 stars	July 3, 1877	One added for Colorado, July 4, 1877.
38 stars	July 3, 1890	Five added for Idaho, Montana, North Dakota, South Dakota, Washington, July 4, 1890.
43 stars	July 3, 1891	One added for Wyoming, July 4, 1891.
44 stars	July 3, 1896	One added for Utah, July 4, 1896.
45 stars	July 3, 1908	One added for Oklahoma, July 4, 1908.
46 stars	July 3, 1912	Two added for Arizona, New Mexico, July 4, 1912.
48 stars	July 3, 1959	One added for Alaska, July 4, 1959.
49 stars	July 3, 1960	One added for Hawaii, July 4, 1960.

United States—Military

United States—Military—Billeting of Soldiers

In 1774, the Quartering Act—the last of several Intolerable Acts enacted by the British Parliament—required Americans to house and feed soldiers. The colonists viewed the action as a threat to their liberty. They called a congress to address the issue. It was one of the actions that led to the American Revolution.

• **End of peace-time billeting of soldiers in homes without consent of the homeowner:** December 15, 1791, with ratification of the 3rd Amendment to the U.S. Constitution. During wartime, the manner of quartering was to be prescribed by law.

United States—Military—Discipline
• **Last time branches of the armed forces had separate disciplinary laws:** 1951. The Uniform Code of Military Justice was passed by the U.S. Congress on May 5, 1950, and became effective May 31, 1951.

United States—Military—Pentagon
The Pentagon, in Alexandria, Virginia, is the headquarters of the U.S. Department of Defense and of the Air Force, Army and Navy. Begun in 1941, it was completed in January 1943 and covers 29 acres. The Pentagon is the world's largest office building.
• **Last surviving original employee of the Pentagon**: Marian Bailey, who began working at the Pentagon as a switchboard operator, when the building opened. She eventually became chief operator of the largest switchboard in the world. In later years, she gave tours and served as a goodwill ambassador. When she died at age 79 on January 22, 2001, she was the only remaining original employee still working at the Pentagon.

United States—Military—U.S. Air Force
The U.S. Air Force traces its origins to the Aeronautical Division of the U.S. Army Signal Corps on August 1, 1907. It was known as the Aviation Service when the U.S. entered World War I in April 1917. It was under the Signal Corps until 1918.
• **Last known as the Aviation Service:** 1918, when it was organized as the U.S. Air Service.
• **Last known as the U.S. Air Service:** 1926, when the U.S. Air Corps established.
• **Last known as the U.S. Air Corps:** 1941, when the name was changed to the U.S. Army Air Forces.
• **Last known as the U.S. Army Air Forces:** 1947, when the U.S. Air Force became a separate branch of the service.
• **Last surviving founder of the U.S. Air Force**: Eugene M. Zuckert. He was one of a small group of civilians and officers who created the Air Force and was the last survivor of the initial presidential appointees in the Department of Defense. Zuckert was named Assistant Secretary of the Air Force (management) in 1947. He served as Secretary of the Air Force from 1961 to 1965. Zuckert died on June 5, 2000, age 88.

United States—Military—U.S. Air Force —WASP
In August 1943, during World War II, two groups of civilian women pilots—the Women's Auxiliary Ferrying Squadron (WAFS) and the Women's Flying Training Detachment—were combined as the Women's Airforce Service Pilots (WASP). They ferried aircraft for the U.S. Army Air Force Ferrying Command, thus freeing male pilots for combat duty.
• **Last of the WASP:** officially disbanded by Congress on December 20, 1944.

United States—Military—U. S. Armed Forces—Draft (Conscription)
President Franklin D. Roosevelt signed the Military Selective Service Act in 1940, creating the Selective Service System. The agency was given the power to draft, or conscript, men to fill vacancies in the armed forces that could not be accomplished through voluntary enlistments.
• **End of the draft:** July 1, 1973, when the Selective Service System no longer had the authority to induct men into the military. The armed forces became all-volunteer organizations; however, men are still required to register for the draft. Mandatory registration was instituted in 1980, during the Carter administration.
• **Last men drafted into the U.S. Armed Forces prior to the expiration of the Selective Service Act:** June 30, 1973.

United States—Military—U.S. Armed Forces—Racial Segregation
On July 26, 1948, President Harry S. Truman issued an executive order to the U.S. armed forces to end racial segregation on all military posts by September 1, 1955. He also called for the end of discrimination in federal employment.
• **End of segregation in the U.S. armed forces:** September 30, 1954, when the

armed services were entirely desegregated.

• **Last U.S. conflict involving segregated units of the armed forces:** Korean War (1950-53).

• **Last all-black infantry:** U.S. Army 24th Infantry Regiment, 25th Division. It was the largest black unit to serve in Korea.

• **Last all-black combat unit in the U.S. Army to engage an enemy:** the 77th Engineer Combat Company, 25th Infantry, in Korea, on July 12, 1950. The unit was deactivated in June 1953.

United States—Military—U.S. Army—Cavalry

• **Last surviving cavalry horse on government rolls:** Chief, who was foaled in 1932, purchased by the U.S. Army in 1940 at Fort Robinson, Nebraska, placed in semi-retirement in 1949, and fully retired in 1958 at Fort Riley, Kansas.

• **Last horse issued to the Army by the Quartermaster:** Black Jack, who was also the last to carry the "U.S." brand that all army horses were given. He participated in the funerals of Presidents Hoover, Kennedy and Lyndon B. Johnson, General Douglas MacArthur and many others buried in Arlington National Cemetery. Black Jack died on February 6, 1976, age 29. His monument at Fort Meyer, Virginia holds his ashes.

• **Last large-scale U.S. Army mounted cavalry charge:** a two-hour encounter near the town of Ojo Azules, Mexico, on May 5, 1916. The charge was led by the Second Squadron, 11th U.S. Cavalry, commanded by Major Robert L. Howze against a band of Francisco ("Pancho") Villa's men. The U.S. troops were part of General John J. Pershing's expedition against Villa.

• **Last surviving member of Pershing's militia against Villa:** Willie Liddell, who died in Ardmore, Oklahoma, on November 24, 2003, age 106. Liddell was a member of the Oklahoma Militia.

• **Last known U.S. Army cavalry charge:** January 16, 1942, on the Bataan Peninsula after the fall of the Philippines during World War II. The charge was led against Japanese infantry and artillery by Edwin Price Ram-

sey, who had refused to surrender.

• **Last mounted cavalry camp built by the U.S. Army:** Camp Lockett, in Campo, California, in 1941.

• **Last U.S. Army Horse Cavalry Regiment:** 28th Cavalry, which was activated at Camp Lockett in February 1943, during World War II. It had its final review at a retreat parade in Algeria on March 24, 1944, and was inactivated the following week. The 28th Cavalry was disbanded on December 12, 1951.

United States—Military—U.S. Army—General Orders

General Orders are the rules of procedure a soldier is required to know before standing guard.

• **Last time soldiers were required to memorize 11 General Orders before going on sentry duty:** August 1967. That month, the number was dropped to three. Back in 1882, a soldier was required to memorize 22 General Orders.

United States—Military—U. S. Army—Mules

The U.S. Army used mules for more than a hundred years. The strong, hearty animals were used to haul weapons, ammunition and supplies. Not surprisingly, the mule became the Army mascot, and it is still the mascot of the U.S. Military Academy at West Point, New York.

• **Last U.S. Army mules:** mustered out of the service in December 1956 in Colorado.

• **Last U.S. Army mule to be deactivated:** Hambone, in 1956.

• **Last surviving U.S. Army mule:** probably Windriver, who was retired from the U.S. Army in 1956. She was purchased by a Shriners group and appeared at many functions. She retired again in 1978. Windriver died at age 46.

United States—Military—U.S. Army—Native American Scouts

• **Last surviving Pawnee Indian who served as a scout in the U.S. Army:** Rush

Roberts, who died in Pawnee, Oklahoma, in 1958, age 98.

• **Last surviving Kiowa Indian who served as a scout in the U.S. Army:** I-See-O (Plenty Fires), who is credited with averting a Kiowa and Comanche uprising in 1891, for which the U.S. Congress made him a sergeant for life. He was on active duty in the U.S. Army until his death at Fort Sill, Oklahoma, on March 10, 1927, age 75 to 80.

United States—Military—U. S. Army—WAAC/WAC

The Women's Army Auxiliary Corps (WAAC) was founded in May 1942 during World War II.

• **Last of the Women's Army Auxiliary Corps:** August 31, 1943, when the corps was disbanded. The following day, the newly created Women's Army Corps (WAC) enlisted those WAACs who wished to remain in the service. They were offered full military rank and benefits.

• **Last of the Women's Army Corps:** dissolved in 1978, when women became part of the regular army.

• **Last director of the Women's Army Corps:** General Mary Elizabeth Clarke, who had served as director since August 1975.

United States—Military—U.S. Coast Guard

From its founding in 1790, the U.S. Coast Guard was operated in peacetime by the U.S. Treasury Department.

• **Last time the U.S. Coast Guard was part of the Treasury Department:** April 1, 1967, when it became part of the newly created Department of Transportation.

• **Last time the U.S. Coast Guard was part of the Department of Transportation:** March 1, 2003, when it was transferred to the newly created Department of Homeland Security.

• **Last time the U.S. Coast Guard was two organizations:** 1915, when the U.S. Coast Guard was part of the Revenue Cutter Service (established 1790) and the Lifesaving Service (established 1878). In January 1915, the two agencies were united as the U.S.

Coast Guard. Two other organizations were added later: Bureau of Lighthouses (Federal Lighthouse Service) in 1939 and Bureau of Marine Inspection and Navigation in 1942.

• **Last use of Morse Code by a U.S. Coast Guard radio navigation station:** March 31, 1995. The event was commemorated with a ceremony at U.S. Coast Guard station NMN in Chesapeake, Virginia.

• **Last Lighthouse Service-era light keeper:** Frank P. Schubert, who served more than 60 years. He spent the last 43 years as a keeper and caretaker at the Coney Island Light Station in New York and was still at his post when he died on December 11, 2003, age 88.

• **Last U.S. lighthouse tender:** *Fir* (WLM 212), also the last working member of the U.S. Lighthouse Service fleet. Originally built with oil-burning steam engines, *Fir* was the last U.S. steam-powered lighthouse tender to be converted to diesel in 1951. Between 1950 and 1980, large buoys and lighthouses were automated and Pacific Northwest lightships were replaced. *Fir* became the last tender to serve numerous West Coast light stations.

• **Last of the "radioman" rating:** officially retired on July 1, 2003, at U.S. Coast Guard radio Station NMC in Point Reyes, California. The radioman rating, popularly known as "Sparks," was changed to "Telecommunications Specialist" in 1994.

United States—Military—U.S. Coast Guard—SPARS

SPARS, the Women's Reserve of the U.S. Coast Guard, was established on November 23, 1942, during World War II. The acronym SPAR is taken from the Coast Guard motto: Semper Paratus—Always Prepared.

• **Last of the SPARS:** disbanded within six months of the August 1945 surrender of Japan. The 1948 Women's Armed Service Integration Act did not include the Coast Guard; however, the Coast Guard established its own reserve training program for women in the late 1940s. And in 1973, women were allowed to serve in the regular Coast Guard.

United States—Military—U.S. Marine Corps—Campaign Hats

Beginning in 1898, all Marines wore campaign hats that resembled cowboy hats with slits down the center that made the tops slouch.

• **Last use of the campaign hat:** 1912, when it was replaced by the field hat (a.k.a. "Smokey"). It was the first American-style hat used by the Marines. (Previous hats were adopted from other countries.) The field hat was discontinued in 1942, during World War II. After the war, gunners were allowed to wear it. Since 1956, all drill instructors have worn the "Smokey."

United States—Military—U.S. Marine Corps—Women's Reserve

The U.S. Marine Corps approved the admission of women to the Marine Corps Reserve in November 1942, during World War II. Early training was conducted at Navy facilities used by the WAVEs. In July 1943, training was transferred to Camp LeJeune, a Marine base in North Carolina. The Marine Corps did not use an acronym such as WAC, WAVE or SPAR, as did other branches of the service. The women were known simply as Marines.

• **Last of the World War II women Marines:** Discharged by September 1946. In 1948, with passage of the Women's Armed Service Integration Act, women were permitted to enlist in the regular Marine Corps.

United States—Military—U.S. Navy—Ships, *see* Ships—Naval—Battleships, Carriers , Cruisers, Frigates—United States.

United States—Military—U.S. Navy—*Pueblo* Incident

The U.S. intelligence ship USS *Pueblo* was seized by North Korea in international waters off the North Korean coast on January 23, 1968; 83 officers and crewmen were imprisoned.

• **End of imprisonment of the *Pueblo* crew:** December 22, 1968, when 82 men and the body of one were returned to U.S. control. The North Koreans kept the *Pueblo* and they still hold it.

United States—Military—U.S Navy—WAVES

WAVES (Women Accepted for Voluntary Emergency Service) was established as a branch of the U.S. Navy in July 1942, during World War II.

• **Last of the WAVES:** Recruiting ended in 1945 with the end of the war. In 1948, with passage of the Women's Armed Service Integration Act, women were permitted to enlist in the regular navy, and the WAVES program was terminated.

• **Last surviving original officer of the WAVES program:** Laura Rapaport Borsten, who retired as a lieutenant commander in 1946. She died in Los Angeles, California, on August 11, 2003, age 91.

United States—National Anthem

United States—National Anthem

In 1814, during the British attack on Fort McHenry in Baltimore, Maryland, American lawyer/poet Francis Scott Key wrote the poem that would become "The Star-Spangled Banner," the national anthem of the United States. It was later set to music, using the English song "To Anacreon in Heaven."

• **Last day the U.S. was without a national anthem:** March 2, 1931. The following day, the U.S. Congress enacted legislation that made "The Star-Spangled Banner" the U.S. national anthem.

United States—Presidents

• **Last president inaugurated in the 18th century:** John Adams, who was inaugurated on March 4, 1797.

• **Last president inaugurated before the capital was in Washington, D.C.:** John Adams, who was inaugurated in Congress Hall in Philadelphia, Pennsylvania, on March 4, 1797.

• **Last surviving president who signed the U.S. Constitution:** James Madison.

• **Last surviving president who was a**

statesman of the Revolutionary era: John Quincy Adams, who was only 11 years old when he began a 70-year career of public service in 1778. He acted as his father's secretary during a diplomatic mission to France. Adams was president from 1825 to 1829. The following year, he was elected to the House of Representatives. He had a stroke in the Speaker's Room on February 21, 1848, and died two days later, age 80.

• **Last president born a British subject:** William Henry Harrison, who was born in 1773, three years before the Declaration of Independence was signed.

• **Last Whig president:** Zachary Taylor. He was the second of two Whig presidents. William Henry Harrison was the first.

• **Last U.S. president without any formal education:** Andrew Johnson. All the other presidents had some formal schooling. Johnson did not learn to write until he was 17.

• **Last president who was an indentured servant:** Andrew Johnson, who worked as a tailor for James J. Selby of Raleigh, North Carolina. In 1822, Johnson ran away and Selby posted a $10 reward for his return. Johnson went to South Carolina and opened his own shop. Millard Fillmore was the only other president to have been an indentured servant. He was a clothmaker.

• **Last president who was a slave owner:** Ulysses Simpson Grant. Ten of the first 18 U.S. Presidents were slave owners: George Washington, Thomas Jefferson, James Madison, James Monroe, Andrew Jackson, John Tyler, James K. Polk, Zachary Taylor, Andrew Johnson and Ulysses S. Grant.

• **Last president born in a log cabin:** James A. Garfield. Other presidents who were born in log cabins include Andrew Jackson, Millard Fillmore, James Buchanan and Abraham Lincoln.

• **Last president to be inaugurated in 19th century:** William McKinley, who was inaugurated on March 4, 1897.

• **Last U.S. president who never flew in airplane:** Calvin Coolidge, who was president from 1923 until 1929.

• **Last president whose term of office ended on March 3rd:** Herbert Hoover. The date was changed by the 20th Amendment ratified in 1933. It shortened the time between a president's election and inauguration with the president's term beginning at noon on January 20th.

• **Last president to be inaugurated in March:** Franklin D. Roosevelt, who was inaugurated for his first term on March 4, 1933. For his second term, he was the first president to be inaugurated on January 20 (in 1937). From 1783 until 1933, the president had been inaugurated on March 4th. With passage of the 20th Amendment, Inauguration Day was moved to January 20th.

• **Last time the president's terms could exceed two:** 1951. The 22nd Amendment, which became effective February 27, 1951, limited the number of terms a U.S. president could serve to two. The amendment states: "No person shall be elected to the office of the President more than twice, and no person who has held the office of President, or acted as President, for more than two years of a term to which some other person was elected President shall be elected to the office of the President more than once."

• **Last U.S. president to serve more than two terms:** Franklin Delano Roosevelt, who was elected in 1932, 1936, 1940 and 1944. He died in 1945, during his fourth term.

• **Last U.S. president to earn less than $100,000 per year:** Franklin Delano Roosevelt, who was paid $75,000 (taxable). The salary was increased to $100,000 when Truman was president. Lyndon B. Johnson was the last president to make under $200,000. The salary was raised to $200,000 during the Nixon administration. During the George W. Bush administration, it was increased to $400,000.

• **Last president born in the 19th century:** Dwight D. Eisenhower, who was born on October 14, 1890.

• **Last time Camp David was known as Shangri-La:** 1953, during the Eisenhower administration, when the presidential retreat in Maryland was renamed Camp David. The name David was chosen to honor

Eisenhower's father and grandson.

• **Last president to be inaugurated in the 20th century:** William Jefferson ("Bill") Clinton, who was inaugurated for a second term in 1997.

• **Last president to have Secret Service protection for life:** William Jefferson ("Bill") Clinton. In 1994, Congress enacted legislation providing that presidents elected after January 1, 1997, are limited to no more than 10 years of Secret Service protection after leaving office.

United States—Presidents—Kennedy, John F.

• **Last surviving passenger in the Kennedy assassination car:** Nellie Connally. Four people were riding in President Kennedy's car in Dallas, Texas, on November 22, 1963, when he was assassinated: The president and Mrs. Kennedy were in the back seat; Texas Governor John B. Connally and his wife Nellie were in front.

• **Last surviving member of the police detail that was escorting Lee Harvey Oswald the day he was shot by Jack Ruby:** retired Dallas police officer James R. Leavelle. In the films and photographs of the incident, Leavelle is in a white suit and hat to Oswald's immediate right.

• **Last surviving member of the Warren Commission:** President Gerald R. Ford. The Warren Commission, headed by Chief Justice Earl Warren, was created in 1963 to investigate the assassination of President John F. Kennedy. The commission's report issued September 24, 1964, concluded that Oswald acted alone. It recommended changing the way the president is protected.

United States—Presidents—Lincoln, Abraham

• **Last time Abraham Lincoln was beardless:** 1860. Lincoln grew a beard, presumably at the request of an 11-year-old girl who wrote to him in October 1860 during the presidential campaign saying she would ask her brothers to vote for him as president if he did. When Lincoln went to Washington in February 1861, he had a full beard.

• **Last Lincoln-Douglas debate:** October 15, 1858, in Alton, Illinois. Lincoln and Stephen A. Douglas had seven debates during the 1858 election campaign for U.S. senator from Illinois. They debated in Ottawa, Freeport, Jonesboro, Charleston, Galesburg, Quincy and finally in Alton. Lincoln lost the election. The two candidates met again in the 1860 presidential race. Douglas was the candidate of the northern wing of the Democratic party. He lost to Lincoln. Douglas was stricken with typhoid fever and died in Chicago a short time later, on June 3, 1861, age 48.

• **Last survivor of those who attended a Lincoln-Douglas debate:** believed to be Margaret Thomas McClenahan, who heard the debate at Galesburg in October 1858. In 1938, she was a guest of honor at the 80th anniversary of the debate. She died in Toulon, Illinois, on April 15, 1943, age 97.

• **Last surviving delegate to the 1860 convention that nominated Lincoln:** Addison G. Proctor, who was a delegate from Kansas. When he died in 1925, his physician claimed his death was due to exhaustion caused by giving numerous speeches throughout Illinois in celebration of Lincoln's birthday. Proctor died in Chicago, Illinois, of February 16, 1925, age 87.

• **Last surviving inaugural guard of Lincoln:** Louis Weintz, who as part of Company A, Engineers from West Point, was assigned to guard duty at the 1861 inauguration. Weintz died in Middletown, New York, on February 16, 1927, age 82.

• **Last presidential actions of Lincoln:** on the day he was assassinated, Lincoln met with Governor Swann and U.S. Senator Creswell about Maryland appointments. Lincoln pardoned Benjamin F. Twilly, a prisoner at Point Lookout, Maryland. He also held a cabinet meeting at which General Grant was present. He prepared a speech he intended to give the following day. He also deferred an appointment so he could attend the theater that evening.

• **Last surviving cast member at Ford's Theater:** William J. Ferguson, a cast member of *Our American Cousin,* the play that was being performed at Ford's Theater the night Lincoln was shot.

• **Last surviving person in Ford's Theater when Lincoln was assassinated:** Samuel J. Seymour of Arlington, Virginia. At the age of 5, his godmother, Mrs. George S. Goldsborough, had taken him to see *Our American Cousin*. The two sat in the balcony on the side opposite Lincoln's box. Seymour died in 1956 at age 96.

• **Last of the original Ford Theater (Ford's Old Opera House):** three floors collapsed on June 9, 1893, killing 22 and injuring 68. Nearly 500 government clerks were at work in the building at the time. It was being used by the Pension Bureau. The theater was later restored to how it looked the night Lincoln was shot. Officially known as Ford's Theater Lincoln Museum, it was dedicated in 1968. It is administered by the National Park Service.

• **Last surviving pallbearers who were at Lincoln's funeral**: General Henry Gaither Worthington, who served in the 38th Congress from October 1864 to March 1865. He died in Washington, D.C., on July 29, 1909, age 81. (His name is shown in some sources as Henry Clay Worthington). Also shown as Lincoln's last surviving pallbearer: Alexander Hamilton Coffroth, who was a member of the U.S. Congress in 1863-65, 1866 and 1879-81. He died in Markleton, Pennsylvania, on September 2, 1906, age 74.

• **Last surviving bodyguard of Lincoln:** Rufus Lewis, who was one of 25 lieutenants who were assigned to guard Lincoln's body when he died in 1865. Lewis was also one of the six who placed Lincoln's body into the tomb. He died in Naugatuck, Connecticut, on March 21, 1909, age 73.

• **Last burial of Lincoln:** September 26, 1901. In 1876, someone tried to steal Lincoln's body for ransom. The attempt failed but afterward precautions were taken to protect his tomb in Springfield, Illinois. In 1901, that tomb was torn down and a new one was built. Lincoln's son Robert feared another attempt would be made to steal his father's body, so he ordered Lincoln's coffin to be buried deep inside the tomb and cov-

ered with 20 inches of concrete. Twenty-three people (one source says 16) gathered for the re-interment.

• **Last survivor of the last people to see Lincoln's body:** Fleetwood Lindley, who was among the people present when Lincoln's coffin was opened inside the tomb in September 1901. Rumors persisted that Lincoln was not in the coffin, so public officials decided to open it before it was embedded in concrete. Lindley was 13 and the youngest person there. He died on February 1, 1963, age 75.

• **Last surviving Lincoln conspirator:** John Surratt, one of the six men who met with John Wilkes Booth on March 17, 1865, to thrash out plans for Lincoln's assassination. Surratt escaped arrest and fled to Canada and then to Europe. He was finally tracked down in Egypt and returned to the U.S. His trial in 1867 was in a civil court, not a military one. The jury was deadlocked, and Surratt was freed in 1868. He moved to Baltimore, Maryland, and worked as a school teacher. In 1872, he married and had several children. Surratt died on April 21, 1916, age 72.

United States—Presidents—White House
• **Last president who did not live in Washington, D.C., while holding office:** George Washington, who held the office from 1789 to 1797. The Executive Mansion (the White House) would not be occupied until 1800, after he left office.

• **Last president to be without running water in the White House:** Andrew Jackson. Running water was piped in for the first time in 1833 during the fourth year of Jackson's presidency.

• **Last president to live by candlelight in White House:** James K. Polk. The White House was not fitted with gas lights until 1849, the year Polk left office.

• **Last president to live in the White House without a bathroom and improved heating:** Millard Fillmore. Both improvements came during the administration of Franklin Pierce.

• **Last president to live in the White House without a telephone:** Ulysses S. Grant. The first telephone was installed in 1879 during the Rutherford B. Hayes administration.

• **Last president to live in the White House without electricity:** Grover Cleveland. Electricity was installed in 1891, during the Benjamin Harrison administration.

• **Last time the president's residence was known popularly as the Executive Mansion:** 1901. That year President Theodore Roosevelt changed the name to the White House. By then "White House" was the popular name for the president's house.

• **Last president to keep a cow at the White House:** William Howard Taft. He kept a cow on the White House lawn to supply him with fresh milk.

• **Last president without a radio in the White House:** Woodrow Wilson. The first radio was installed during the Warren G. Harding administration.

• **Last president without a television set in the White House:** Franklin D. Roosevelt. Two sets were installed during the Truman administration (1945-53).

United States— Programs and Policies

United States—Programs and Policies— New Deal

The New Deal, a program of the Franklin D. Roosevelt administration, promised to provide relief for the needy, economic recovery for the nation and the long-range reform of some economic institutions. New Deal relief and recovery programs included the Civilian Conservation Corps, Public Works Administration, National Recovery Administration (NRA), Agricultural Adjustment Administration (AAA) and the Works Projects Administration (WPA). (*See* United States—Agencies.) Its reform legislation included the Social Security Act of 1935 and the Fair Labor Standards Act of 1938. The New Deal began with Roosevelt's inauguration in 1933. It hit a snag when the U.S. Supreme Court began handing down rulings that were against New Deal programs: The NRA was invalidated in 1935; the AAA, in 1936. By 1937, reform programs began to decrease. As Europe moved closer to war in the late 1930s, New Deal programs met with increasing criticism. Democratic conservatives teamed up with Republicans in Congress after 1938 and prevented passage of any further major New Deal legislation.

• **Last of the New Deal:** December 23, 1943, when Roosevelt suggested dropping the New Deal label for his administration in favor of a "Win the War slogan.

• **Last New Deal politician:** Claude Pepper, who became a member of the U.S. Senate, representing Florida in 1936. In 1938, he played a key role in the passage of the first minimum wage act. He was active in politics until his death in Washington, D.C., on May 30, 1989, age 88.

United States—Programs and Policies— Open Door

By the end of the 19th century, major world powers, including Great Britain, France, Japan, Russia and Germany, had staked out their own spheres of interest in China, which they used to their advantage. The U.S. was hampered when it tried to establish trade with China. The Open Door policy began in 1899 during the McKinley administration when U.S. Secretary of State John Hay proposed these nations trade with China equally.

• **End of the Open Door policy:** 1943, when the United States renounced its extraterritorial rights in China.

United States—Scandals

United States—Scandals—Watergate Scandal

The Watergate scandal began on June 17, 1972, when the Democratic Party headquarters in the Watergate building in Washington, D.C., was burglarized. The involvement of the Nixon administration was uncovered in 1973. President Richard M.

Nixon's impeachment inquiry was held in 1974.

• **End of the Watergate Scandal:** August 9, 1974, with the resignation of Nixon.

• **Last Watergate prisoner:** Former Attorney General John Mitchell, who was released on parole on January 20, 1979. He served 19 months of a 2½-to-8-year sentence at the federal prison at Maxwell Air Force Base, near Montgomery, Alabama. He had been sentenced for conspiracy and obstruction of justice in the case. Altogether, 25 men served terms ranging from 25 days to 52 months.

United States—States

United States—Alabama

Alabama was once part of the Mississippi Territory that was created by Congress in 1798.

• **Last time Alabama was part of the Mississippi Territory:** 1817. The Alabama Territory was created that year.

• **End of Alabama's territorial status:** December 14, 1819, when Alabama entered the Union as the 22nd state

• **Last territorial governor:** William Wyatt Bibb, who served from 1817 to 1819. He was the first state governor, serving from 1819 to 1820.

• **Last time the Alabama capital was in Cahaba:** 1826. That year it was moved to Tuscaloosa.

• **Last time the Alabama capital was in Tuscaloosa:** 1846. That year, it was moved to Montgomery.

• **End of Alabama's secession:** June 25, 1868, when Alabama was readmitted to the Union. Alabama had seceded from the Union on January 11, 1861, as part of the Confederate States of America.

• **Last time Bibb County was known as Cahawba County:** December 4, 1820.

• **Last time Calhoun County was known as Benton County:** January 29, 1858.

• **Last time Chilton County was known as Baker County:** December 17, 1874.

• **Last time Covington County was known**

as **Jones County:** October 10, 1868.

• **Last time Etowah County was known as Baine County:** December 1, 1868.

• **Last time Lamar County was known as Sanford County:** February 8, 1877.

• **Last time Morgan County was known as Cotaco County:** June 14, 1821.

• **Last time Winston County was known as Hancock County:** January 22, 1858.

United States—Alaska

Alaska was first visited by Europeans in 1741, when Danish explorer Vitus Bering claimed the land for Russia.

• **Last time Russia owned Alaska:** March 30, 1867, when the United States purchased Alaska from the Russian government for $7.2 million (2¢ per acre). The deal was through the efforts of Secretary of State William H. Seward and Senator Charles Sumner. Both took heavy criticism for the sale that became known as Seward's Folly.

• **Last time Alaska was an unorganized territory:** 1884, when the laws of Oregon were extended to Alaska and a governor was appointed. The Alaska Territory was created in 1912.

• **End of Alaska's territorial status:** January 3, 1959, when Alaska entered the Union as the 49th state.

• **Last territorial governor of Alaska:** B. Frank Heintzleman, who served from 1953 to 1958.

• **Last territorial governor (acting) of Alaska:** Governor Waina Hendrickson, who served from 1958 to 1959.

United States—Arizona

Arizona was first explored by the Spanish in 1539. It was ruled by Spain as part of New Spain from 1598 to 1821. It then became part of Mexico.

• **Last time Arizona north of the Gila River was owned by Mexico:** 1848. The land was ceded to the United States at the end of the Mexican War under terms of the Treaty of Guadalupe Hidalgo and became part of New Mexico Territory. The Gadsden Purchase of 1854 gave the remainder of Arizona to the New Mexico Territory.

- **Last time Arizona was part of the New Mexico Territory:** 1863. That year the Arizona Territory was created.
- **End of Arizona's territorial status:** February 14, 1912, when Arizona entered the Union as the 48th state.
- **Last territorial governor of Arizona:** Richard E. Sloan, who served from 1909 to 1912.
- **Last surviving member of the Arizona Constitutional Convention of 1910:** Jacob Weinberger, who died in San Diego, California, on May 21, 1974, age 92.

United States—Arkansas
The exploration of Arkansas by DeSoto in 1540 gave France claim to the region. Part of the land was ceded to Spain in 1762.
- **Last time western Arkansas was owned by Spain:** 1800. That year, the Treaty of San Ildefonso ceded back to France land that Spain had held since 1762.
- **Last time Arkansas was owned by France:** 1803. That year, the United States bought the territory with the Louisiana Purchase. It was part of the Louisiana and Missouri territories until the Arkansas Territory was created in 1819.
- **End of Arkansas's territorial status:** June 15, 1836, when Arkansas entered the Union as the 25th state
- **Last territorial governor of Arkansas:** William S. Fulton, who served from 1835 to 1836.
- **End of Arkansas's secession:** June 22, 1868, when Arkansas was readmitted to the Union. (Arkansas had seceded from the Union on May 6, 1861, as part of the Confederate States of America.)
- **Last time Clay County was known as Clayton County:** December 6, 1875.
- **Last time Cleveland County was known as Dorsey County:** March 5, 1885.
- **Last time Logan County was known as Sarber County:** December 14, 1875.
- **Last time Marion County was known as Searcy County:** September 29, 1836.

United States—California
California was claimed by Spain in the 1540s It remained under Spanish control until 1821, when it became part of Mexico.
- **End of the Bear Flag Revolt:** July 9, 1846. The Bear Flag Revolt involved American settlers in the Sacramento Valley who were under Mexican rule. On June 14, 1846, they captured Sonoma and proclaimed the Republic of California. Their flag was that of a grizzly bear facing a star. While the revolt was going on, the U.S. became engaged in the Mexican War and U.S. troops occupied California. When the Bear Flag Revolt ended, the Bear flag was replaced with the U.S. flag.
- **Last time California was under Mexican jurisdiction:** February 2, 1848, with the Treaty of Guadalupe Hidalgo, in which Mexico ceded California to the United States. Although U.S. Naval forces occupied California in the early days of the Mexican War, Mexican jurisdiction did not end until the war ended. California entered the Union on September 9, 1850, as the 31st state.
- **Last governor of California under Mexican rule:** Don Pio de Jesus Nicol, who died in Los Angeles on September 11, 1894, age 93. He held office in 1832 and again in 1845-46.
- **Last mission built in California:** Mission San Francisco Solano, completed on July 4, 1823. Between 1769 and 1823, 21 missions were established a day's journey apart between San Diego and Sonoma.
- **Last time Santa Cruz County was known as Branciforte County:** April 5, 1850.

United States—Colorado
Colorado was once part of the territories of Utah, Kansas, Nebraska and New Mexico. French ownership of eastern Colorado began in 1684, when Robert La Salle claimed the region for France.
- **Last time eastern Colorado was owned by France:** 1803. The United States gained the land with the Louisiana Purchase.
- **Last time western Colorado was owned by Mexico:** 1848. The land was ceded to the U.S. by the Treaty of Guadalupe Hidalgo after the Mexican War.
- **Last of the Territory of Jefferson:** 1861.

The Territory of Jefferson was created by mining camp residents in 1859. Before the United States could approve, the residents drafted an organic act and elected a governor. The U.S. Congress dissolved the Territory of Jefferson when it created the Colorado Territory in February 1861 with boundaries that approximated those of the future state.
- **End of Colorado's territorial status:** August 1, 1876, when Colorado entered the Union as the 38th state.
- **Last territorial governor of Colorado:** John Long Routt, who served from 1875 to 1876.
- **Last time the Colorado capital was in Colorado City:** 1861. It was moved to Denver then in 1862 to Golden.
- **Last time the Colorado capital was in Golden:** 1867. That year it was permanently moved to Denver.
- **Last time Chaffee County was known as Lake County:** February 10, 1879.
- **Last time Conejos County was known as Guadalupe County:** November 7, 1861.
- **Last time Lake County was known as Carbonate County:** February 10, 1879.
- **Last time Ouray County was known as Uncompahgre County:** March 2, 1883.
- **Last time San Miguel County was known as Ouray County:** March 2, 1883.

United States—Connecticut
Connecticut was first settled in 1633. The colony obtained an English royal charter in 1662.
- **Last governor of the Connecticut colony:** Jonathan Trumbull Sr., who served from 1769 to 1776. He also was the first state governor, from 1776 to 1784. He died in Lebanon, Connecticut, on August 17, 1785, age 74. In 1781, Connecticut was one of the 13 former colonies that set up a central U.S. government under the Articles of Confederation.
- **End of Connecticut's confederation status:** January 9, 1788, when Connecticut became the fifth of the 13 original states to ratify the U.S. Constitution.

United States—Delaware
Delaware was once part of New Sweden and New Netherlands. It came under English control in 1664. In 1781, Delaware was one of the 13 former British colonies that set up a central U.S. government under the Articles of Confederation.
- **End of Delaware's confederation status:** December 7, 1787, when Delaware became the first of the original 13 states to ratify the U.S. Constitution.
- **Last time Wilmington was known as Willington:** 1739.
- **Last president of Delaware:** Joshua Clayton, who served from 1789 to 1793. Delaware abandoned the presidency and established a governor as its head in 1793.
- **Last time Kent County was known as Saint Jones County:** December 21, 1683.
- **Last time Sussex County was known as Deale County:** 1683.

United States—Florida
The colonies of East and West Florida were ceded to Great Britain by Spain in 1763, at the end of the Seven Years' War. They were returned to Spain in 1783, under the Treaty of Paris. A controversy over West Florida began with the Louisiana Purchase in 1803, when no clear boundary was established.
- **End of the West Florida controversy:** 1821, when the United States purchased Florida from Spain.
- **Last time any of Florida was owned by Spain:** 1821. With ratification of the Florida Purchase Treaty on February 21, 1821, Florida was ceded to the United States. It was organized as a territory the following year.
- **End of Florida's territorial status:** March 3, 1845, when Florida entered the Union as the 27th state
- **Last territorial governor of Florida:** John Branch, who served from 1844 to 1845.
- **End of Florida's secession:** June 25, 1868, when Florida was readmitted to the Union. (Florida had seceded from the Union January 10, 1861, as part of the Confederate States of America.)

- **Last time Bradford County was known as New River County:** December 6, 1861.
- **Last time Brevard County was known as Saint Lucie County:** January 6, 1855.
- **Last time Hernando County was known as Benton County:** December 24, 1850.
- **Last time Orange County was known as Mosquito County:** January 30, 1845.

United States—Georgia

The English claimed the land that is now Georgia in 1662 and began a settlement in 1733.

- **Last colonial governor of Georgia:** Sir James Wright, who served from 1760 to 1782. In 1781, Georgia was one of the 13 former British colonies that set up a central U.S. government under the Articles of Confederation.
- **End of Georgia's confederation status:** January 2, 1788, when Georgia became the fourth of the 13 original states to ratify the U.S. Constitution.
- **End of Georgia's secession:** July 15, 1870, when Georgia became the last Confederate state to reenter the Union. (Georgia had seceded from the Union on January 19, 1861, as part of the Confederate States of America.)
- **Last time the Georgia capital was in Savannah:** 1785. The last General Assembly was held there on February 22, then moved the capital to Augusta.
- **Last time the Georgia capital was in Augusta:** 1796, then the capital moved to Louisville.
- **Last time the Georgia capital was in Louisville:** 1804. The legislature moved the capital closer to the center of the state, at Milledgeville.
- **Last time the Georgia capital was in Milledgeville:** 1868. That year the capital moved to its fifth location, Atlanta.
- **Last time Bartow County was known as Cass County:** December 8, 1861.
- **Last time Jasper County was known as Randolph County:** December 10, 1812.
- **Last time Webster County was known as Kinchafoonee County:** February 21, 1856.

United States—Hawaii

In 1810, the warrior chief Kamehameha established the Kingdom of Hawaii.

- **Last of the Kamehameha line:** Kamehameha V, who was king of Hawaii from 1863 to 1872. The Kamehameha family ruled Hawaii for five generations.
- **Last monarch of Hawaii:** Queen Lilioukalani. She reigned from 1891 to 1893 but was deposed when the Republic of Hawaii was established by those who favored annexation by the United States. She was later arrested, sentenced to five years' imprisonment, then pardoned. Lilioukalani died on November 11, 1917, age 79. At her funeral, her farewell song, "Aloha Oe," which she had written, was played.
- **Last of the Republic of Hawaii:** August 12, 1898, when Hawaii was annexed to the United States. (The Republic of Hawaii was established by resident Americans in 1893 when they deposed Queen Lilioukalani.)
- **Last of the Republic of Hawaii:** August 12, 1898, when Hawaii was annexed to the United States. Hawaii became a U.S. territory on April 30, 1900.
- **End of Hawaii's territorial status:** August 21, 1959, when Hawaii entered the Union as the 50th state.
- **Last territorial governor of Hawaii:** William F. Quinn, who served from 1957 to 1959. Quinn was the first state governor, from 1959 to 1962.
- **Last royal palace in the United States:** Iolani Palace, built in Honolulu in 1879.
- **Last surviving performer of the authentic sacred hula ceremony:** Iolani Luahine. During her lifetime, she was dubbed a living National Treasure. Luahine died on the island of Hawaii on December 1, 1978, age 63.

United States—Idaho

When the Idaho Territory was created on March 3, 1863, it included land that is now Montana and Wyoming. In 1864, the eastern part of the territory was withdrawn to form Montana. In 1868, another portion of the territory was taken to form Wyoming, thus reducing the territory to what is now the

present state of Idaho.
- **End of Idaho's territorial status:** July 3, 1890, when Idaho entered the Union as the 43rd state.
- **Last territorial governor of Idaho:** George L. Shoup, who served from 1889 to 1890. He was the first state governor in 1890.

United States—Illinois
In 1673, French explorers Marquette and Jolliet explored the land that is now Illinois and claimed it for France
- **Last time Illinois was under French jurisdiction:** 1763. Great Britain acquired title to French territory east of the Mississippi with the Treaty of Paris (1763) that ended the French and Indian War.
- **Last time Illinois was under British jurisdiction:** 1783. Great Britain ceded Illinois to the United States at the end of the American Revolution.
- **Last Native American lands in Illinois:** acquired in 1833 through the Treaty of Chicago. The Indians were members of the Potawatoni, Chippewa and Ottawa nations.
- **End of Illinois's territorial status:** December 3, 1818, when Illinois entered the Union as the 21st state. The Illinois Territory was created in 1809 from land that also comprised Wisconsin. In 1818, Wisconsin was transferred to the Michigan Territory.
- **Last territorial governor of Illinois:** Ninian Edwards, who served from 1809 to 1818. Edwards later served as governor of the state, from 1826 to 1830.
- **Last time the Illinois capital was in Kaskaskia:** 1820. That year the capital moved to Vandalia.
- **Last time the Illinois capital was in Vandalia:** 1837. That year the capital moved to Springfield.
- **Last time Christian County was known as Dane County:** February 1, 1840.

United States—Indiana
Indiana was part of the French territory to which Great Britain acquired title east of the Mississippi with the 1763 Treaty of Paris that ended the French and Indian War.

- **Last time Indiana was under British jurisdiction:** 1783. Britain ceded Indiana to the United States at the end of the American Revolution under the terms of the Treaty of Paris (1783). The land became part of the Northwest Territory in 1787. The Indiana Territory was created in 1800.
- **End of Indiana's territorial status:** December 11, 1816, when Indiana entered the Union as the 19th state.
- **Last territorial governor of Indiana:** Thomas Posey, who served from 1813 to 1816.
- **Last time the Indiana capital was in Vincennes:** 1813. That year it moved to Corydon.
- **Last time the Indiana capital was in Corydon:** 1825. That year it was moved to Indianapolis.
- **Last time Howard County was known as Richardville County:** December 28, 1846.

United States—Iowa
By 1682, France claimed the entire Mississippi Valley and called it Louisiana. France ceded the part of Louisiana west of the Mississippi to Spain in 1762. It contained land that is now Iowa.
- **Last time Iowa was under Spanish jurisdiction:** 1800, when Spain ceded it back to France.
- **Last time Iowa was under French jurisdiction:** 1803. That year, France sold Iowa to the United States as part of the Louisiana Purchase. Iowa became part of the Louisiana Territory in 1805. In 1812, Iowa's land was part of the Missouri Territory. When Missouri entered the Union in 1821, Iowa was an unorganized territory for a while. In 1834, Congress attached Iowa to Michigan. When Michigan entered the union in 1836, the Wisconsin Territory was formed and Iowa became part of it. The Iowa Territory was created by Congress in 1838.
- **End of Iowa's territorial status:** December 28, 1846, when Iowa entered the Union on as the 29th state.
- **Last territorial governor of Iowa:** James Clarke, who served from 1845 to 1846.
- **Last time Calhoun County was known**

as Fox County: January 12, 1853.
• **Last time Lyon County was known as Buncombe County:** September 11, 1862.
• **Last time Monroe County was known as Kishkekosh County:** January 19, 1846.
• **Last time Washington County was known as Slaughter County:** January 25, 1839.
• **Last time Webster County was known as Risley County:** January 12, 1853.
• **Last time Woodbury County was known as Wahkaw County:** January 12, 1853.

United States—Kansas

Although Kansas was visited by Spanish explorers in 1540, France later claimed the region. Kansas was part of the land France called Louisiana.
• **Last time Kansas was under French jurisdiction:** 1803. That year, France sold Kansas to the United States as part of the Louisiana Purchase. The Kansas Territory was established by Congress with passage of the Kansas-Nebraska Act in May 1854. The act used the principle of popular sovereignty in allowing the state to chose whether all its citizens would be free or it would allow slavery. Kansas then became a battlefield for those for and against slavery.
• **End of Kansas's territorial status:** January 29, 1861, when Kansas opted to be a free state and was admitted as such to the Union as the 34th state
• **Last territorial governor (regularly appointed):** Samuel Medary, who resigned the governorship in December 1860.
• **Last territorial governor (acting):** George M. Beebe, who served from 1860 to 1861.
• **Last time Cherokee County was known as McGee County:** February 18, 1860.
• **Last time Cloud County was known as Shirley County:** February 26, 1867.
• **Last time Finney County was known as Sequoyah County:** February 21, 1883.
• **Last time Geary County was known as Davis County:** February 28, 1889.
• **Last time Jackson County was known as Calhoun County:** February 11, 1859.
• **Last time Logan County was known as**

Saint John County: February 24, 1887.
• **Last time Lyon County was known as Breckinridge County:** February 5, 1862.
• **Last time Miami County was known as Lykins County:** June 3, 1861.
• **Last time Morris County was known as Wise County:** February 11, 1859.
• **Last time Neosho County was known as Dorn County:** June 3, 1861.
• **Last time Norton County was known as Billings County:** February 19, 1874.
• **Last time Osage County was known as Weller County:** February 11, 1859.
• **Last time Wabaunsee County was known as Richardson County:** February 11, 1859.

United States—Kentucky

Most of the land that is now known as Kentucky was part of Virginia in the 1700s.
• **Last time Kentucky was part of Virginia:** 1792. Kentucky entered the Union as the 15th state on June 1, 1792, after Virginia dropped its claim to the area and the Virginia General Assembly passed an act allowing Kentucky to apply for statehood.

United States—Louisiana

Louisiana was explored by the Spanish before 1520, but Spain had made no claim to the land. It was claimed for France in the 1680s. In 1762, part of Louisiana was transferred from France to Spain by secret treaty. It was entirely under Spanish rule by 1768.
• **Last time Louisiana was under Spanish jurisdiction:** 1800, when the San Ildefonso Treaty, a secret negotiation by Napoleon, returned New Orleans to France.
• **Last time Louisiana was under French jurisdiction:** 1803. That year, France sold Louisiana to the United States as part of the Louisiana Purchase. In 1804, part of the Louisiana Purchase was organized as the District of Louisiana and the Territory of Orleans. The Orleans Territory made up what is now the state of Louisiana. The District of Louisiana later became the Louisiana Territory and still later the Missouri Territory.
• **End of Louisiana's territorial status:**

April 30, 1812, when the Territory of Orleans entered the Union as Louisiana, the 18th state.

• **End of Louisiana's secession:** June 25, 1868. Louisiana had seceded from the Union January 26, 1861, as part of the Confederate States of America.

• **Last post-Civil War federal troops withdrawn:** in 1877, ending Reconstruction in Louisiana. Home rule was restored.

• **Last of Storyville (New Orleans):** closed in 1917 by the U.S. Navy. The legendary Storyville opened in 1897. It was a section of New Orleans where prostitution was limited to a 38-block area near Canal, Basin, Iberville, Robertson and Saint Louis Streets.

United States—Maine

The land that is now Maine was claimed by Massachusetts in the 1620s and annexed to Massachusetts in 1652.

• **Last time Maine was part of Massachusetts:** 1820. Maine became a separate state that year and entered the Union on March 15, 1820, as the 23rd state.

United States—Maryland

The land that is Maryland was granted to Lord Baltimore by the English monarch in 1632. It was first settled in 1634. The proprietorship was overthrown in 1689 and Maryland became a royal colony. In 1715. the proprietorship was restored

• **Last proprietary governor of Maryland:** Robert Eden, who served from 1769 to 1776. The Convention and Council of Safety governed Maryland from 1776 to 1777. In 1781, Maryland was the last of the 13 original colonies to sign the Articles of Confederation that set up a central U.S. government.

• **End of Maryland's confederation status:** April 28, 1788, when Maryland became the seventh of the 13 original states to ratify the U.S. Constitution.

• **Last Native American land claims in Maryland:** relinquished by Native American chiefs of Six Nations on June 30, 1744, and purchased by the Maryland Assembly.

United States—Massachusetts

During its early history, Massachusetts was part of the Plymouth Colony and the Massachusetts Bay Colony. In 1691, the two colonies were united as the Province of Massachusetts.

• **Last colonial governor of Massachusetts:** Thomas Hutchinson, who served from 1771 to 1774. He was replaced by a military governor. Hutchinson was a historian and wrote *History of the Colony of Massachusetts Bay*. The third and last volume was not published until nearly 50 years after his death. He died in England on June 3, 1780, age 68.

• **Last royal military governor:** General Thomas Gage, who served from 1774 to 1775. In 1781, Massachusetts was one of the 13 former colonies that set up a central U.S. government under the Articles of Confederation.

• **End of Massachusetts' confederation status:** February 6, 1788, when Massachusetts became the sixth of the 13 original states to ratify the Constitution.

• **End of Shays's Rebellion:** February 4, 1787, at Petersham, Massachusetts, when Daniel Shays and 13 of his men were caught. Shays was tried and later pardoned. The rebellion began when Shays and a small army of farmers and laborers marched on Springfield, Massachusetts, during the summer of 1786, protesting heavy debt, high taxes and low farm prices. The following January, Shays and his supporters tried to seize the federal arsenal at Springfield.

United States—Michigan

French explorers, traders and missionaries visited Michigan in the 1600s, but France did not encourage settlement.

• **Last time Michigan was under French jurisdiction:** 1763. France ceded Michigan to Great Britain at the end of the French and Indian War under terms of the 1763 Treaty of Paris.

• **Last survivor of the French settlers in Michigan:** Joseph Campeau, a settler of Detroit, who died in 1863, age around 94.

• **Last time Michigan was under British**

jurisdiction: 1783. Britain ceded Michigan to the United States at the end of the American Revolution under the terms of the 1783 Treaty of Paris.

• **End of the British occupation of Detroit:** 1796. Although the American Revolution ended officially in 1783, the British did not evacuate Detroit until 13 years later. The Michigan Territory was created on July 1, 1805. A portion of the territory was detached to form the Wisconsin Territory in April 1836.

• **End of Michigan's territorial status:** January 26, 1837, when Michigan entered the Union as the 26th state.

• **Last territorial governor of Michigan:** Stevens T. Mason (ex officio, as secretary), who served from 1834 to 1835. He was the first governor of the state of Michigan from 1835 to 1840.

• **Last time the Michigan capital was in Detroit:** 1847. That year it was transferred to Lansing.

• **Last time Alcona County was known as Neewago County:** March 8, 1843.

• **Last time Alpena County was known as Anamickee County:** March 8, 1843.

• **Last time Antrim County was known as Meegisee County:** March 8, 1843.

• **Last time Charlevoix County was known as Reshkauko County:** March 8, 1843.

• **Last time Clare County was known as Kaykakee County:** March 8, 1843.

• **Last time Crawford County was known as Shawano County:** March 8, 1843.

• **Last time Emmet County was known as Tonedagana County:** March 8, 1843.

• **Last time Iosco County was known as Kanotin County:** March 8, 1843.

• **Last time Kalkaska County was known as Wabasee County:** March 8, 1843.

• **Last time Lake County was known as Aishcum County:** March 8, 1843.

• **Last time Mackinac County was known as Michilimackinac County:** March 8, 1843.

• **Last time Mason County was known as Notipekago County:** March 8, 1843.

• **Last time Menominee County was**

known as **Bleeker County:** March 19, 1863.

• **Last time Montmorency County was known as Cheonoquet County:** March 8, 1843.

• **Last time Osceola County was known as Unwattin County:** March 8, 1843.

• **Last time Otsego County was known as Okkuddo County:** March 8, 1843.

• **Last time Roscommon County was known as Mikenauk County:** March 8, 1843.

• **Last time Wexford County was known as Kautawaubet County:** March 8, 1843.

United States—Minnesota

French explorers visited Minnesota in the 1600s and claimed part of the land for France. In 1763, France ceded the land to Great Britain at the end of the French and Indian War under terms of the 1763 Treaty of Paris.

• **Last time Minnesota land east of the Mississippi River was under British jurisdiction:** 1783. All of Minnesota east of the Mississippi River became part of United States at the end of the American Revolution. It became part of the Northwest Territory in 1787.

• **Last time Minnesota land west of the Mississippi River was under French jurisdiction:** 1803, when the land became part of the United States with Louisiana Purchase.

• **End of Minnesota's territorial status:** May 11, 1858, when Minnesota entered the Union as the 32nd state. During its early history, Minnesota had been part of the territories of Michigan, Iowa, and Wisconsin. In 1849, the Minnesota Territory was created. Two years later, the Sioux ceded most of southern Minnesota to the United States.

• **Last territorial governor of Minnesota:** Samuel Medary, who served from 1857 to 1858.

• **Last time Clay County was known as Breckinridge County:** March 6, 1862.

• **Last time Kittson County was known as Pembina County:** March 9, 1878.

• **Last time Saint Louis County was**

known as **Superior County:** March 3, 1855.

United States—Mississippi

French explorer LaSalle claimed the entire Mississippi Valley for France in 1682.

• **Last time Mississippi was under French jurisdiction:** 1763. France ceded control of Mississippi to Great Britain at the end of the French and Indian War under terms of the 1763 Treaty of Paris.

• **Last time Mississippi was under British jurisdiction:** 1783. Britain ceded Mississippi to the United States at the end of the American Revolution. Congress established the Mississippi Territory in 1798. It included land that was also Alabama. In 1802, the territory was expanded northward to Tennessee and south to encompass West Florida.

• **End of Mississippi's territorial status:** The western part of the territory was admitted to the Union as Mississippi, the 20th state, on December 10, 1817, thus ending the Mississippi Territory. The remainder became the Alabama Territory.

• **Last territorial governor of Mississippi:** David Holmes, who served from 1809 to 1817. He was the first governor of the state of Mississippi from 1817 to 1820.

• **End of Mississippi's secession:** February 23, 1870, when Mississippi rejoined the Union. Mississippi had seceded from the Union January 9, 1861, as part of the Confederate States of America.

• **Last time Clay County was known as Colfax County:** April 10, 1876.

• **Last time Jefferson County was known as Pickering County:** January 11, 1802.

• **Last time Webster County was known as Sumner County:** January 30, 1882.

United States—Missouri

Missouri was claimed by France after French explorers visited the region in the 1670s and 1680s. France ceded the land to Spain in 1762.

• **Last time Missouri was under Spanish jurisdiction:** 1800. Spain retroceded the region to France.

• **Last time Missouri was under French jurisdiction:** 1803. The land was sold to the United States as part of the Louisiana Purchase. Congress organized the Missouri Territory in 1812.

• **End of Missouri's territorial status:** August 10, 1821, when Missouri entered the Union as the 24th state.

• **End of the Missouri Compromise:** repealed by the Kansas-Nebraska Act of 1854, and declared unconstitutional by the U.S. Supreme Court in the 1857 Dred Scott Case. The compromise had its beginning in February 1819, when the U.S. House of Representatives began to consider a bill to allow Missouri to form a state government. Representatives from free states wanted Missouri to enter the Union as a free state. Congress adjourned in March 1819, without resolving the issue. When Congress met the following year, the Missouri Compromise was submitted: Maine would enter the Union as a free state and Missouri would enter the Union as a slave state. A proviso of the Missouri Compromise banned slavery in territories north of 36°30'.

• **Last territorial governor of Missouri:** William Clark, who served from 1813 to 1820. He was Missouri's only territorial governor.

• **Last time Atchison County was known as Allen County:** February 14, 1845.

• **Last time Camden County was known as Kinderhook County:** February 23, 1843.

• **Last time Cass County was known as Van Buren County:** February 19, 1849.

• **Last time Dallas County was known as Niangua County:** December 16, 1844.

• **Last time Henry County was known as Rives County:** February 15, 1841.

• **Last time Holt County was known as Nodaway County:** February 15, 1841.

• **Last time Lafayette County was known as Lillard County:** February 16, 1825.

• **Last time Ozark County was known as Decatur County:** March 24, 1845.

• **Last time Texas County was known as Ashley County:** February 14, 1845.

United States—Montana

Montana was once part of the Idaho Territory that was created in 1863. On May 26, 1864, the Montana Territory was created from eastern Idaho.

• **End of Montana's territorial status:** November 8, 1889, when Montana entered the Union as the 41st state.

• **Last territorial governor of Montana:** Benjamin F. White, who served in 1889.

• **Last time the Montana capital was in Virginia City:** 1875. That year it was moved to Helena.

• **Last time Custer County was known as Big Horn County:** February 16, 1877.

• **Last time Lewis and Clark County was known as Edgerton County:** March 1, 1868.

United States—Nebraska

Nebraska was part of a vast French territory in North America west of the Mississippi River known as Louisiana. France ceded the region to Spain in 1762.

• **Last time Nebraska was under Spanish jurisdiction:** 1800, when Spain ceded Louisiana back to France.

• **Last time Nebraska was under French jurisdiction:** 1803. Nebraska was sold to the United States by France as part of the Louisiana Purchase. The Nebraska Territory was created in May 30, 1854, with the Kansas-Nebraska Act. It included all the land north of Texas to the Rocky Mountains. In 1861, with creation of the Dakota and Colorado territories, the Nebraska Territory was reduced to the size it is now.

• **End of Nebraska's territorial status:** March 1, 1867, when Nebraska entered the Union as the 37th state.

• **Last territorial governor of Nebraska:** Alvin Saunders, who served from 1861 to 1867.

• **Last time the Nebraska capital was in Omaha:** 1867. That year it was moved to Lancaster, which was renamed Lincoln to honor the late president.

• **Last of Nebraska's open range land opened to settlement:** 1904, with the Kinkaid Homestead Act.

• **Last time Nebraska had a bicameral legislature:** 1937. In 1934, Nebraskans voted to amend their Constitution to provide for a one-house legislature, making Nebraska the only state in the Union to adopt a unicameral legislature. In 1937, the first session of Nebraska's unicameral legislature met.

• **Last time Holt County was known as West County:** January 9, 1862.

• **Last time Knox County was known as Emmet County:** February 21, 1873.

• **Last time Lincoln County was known as Shorter County:** December 11, 1861.

• **Last time Nemaha County was known as Forney County:** March 1855.

• **Last time Saunders County was known as Calhoun County:** January 8, 1862.

• **Last time Seward County was known as Greene County:** January 3, 1862.

• **Last time Stanton County was known as Izard County:** 1862.

• **Last time Thayer County was known as Jefferson County:** March 1, 1871.

United States—Nevada

Nevada was the last state of the contiguous United States to be explored. Spanish missionaries visited the southern part of Nevada in the 1770s. But there was no major exploration until the 1820s, while Nevada was controlled by Mexico.

• **Last time Nevada was under Mexican jurisdiction:** 1848. The land of Nevada was ceded to the United States under the terms of the Treaty of Guadalupe Hidalgo that ended the Mexican War. The New Mexico and Utah territories were established in 1850. Nevada was part of the Utah Territory until 1861, when the Nevada Territory was created.

• **End of Nevada's territorial status:** October 31, 1864, when Nevada entered the Union as the 36th state.

• **Last territorial governor of Nevada:** James W. Nye, who served from 1861 to 1864.

United States—New Hampshire

New Hampshire's first settlement was in

1633. In 1649, the settlers placed themselves under the control of Massachusetts.

• **Last time New Hampshire was under Massachusetts's jurisdiction:** 1679. That year, New Hampshire was made a separate royal province.

• **Last royal governor of New Hampshire:** John Wentworth, who served from 1767 to 1775. He was forced to flee during the American Revolution. He was lieutenant governor of Nova Scotia from 1792 to 1808. In 1781, New Hampshire was one of the 13 former colonies that set up a central U.S. government under the Articles of Confederation.

• **End of New Hampshire's confederation status:** June 21, 1788, when New Hampshire became the ninth of the original 13 states to ratify the U.S. Constitution.

United States—New Jersey

New Jersey's first permanent settlement was made by the Dutch in 1660. The English seized control of the region in 1664, when they captured New Amsterdam and New Netherland (New York). In 1676, the New Jersey colony was split into two: East Jersey and West Jersey

• **Last time New Jersey was two separate colonies:** 1702. That year, East Jersey and West Jersey were united as the single colony of New Jersey. It was placed under the jurisdiction of the governor of New York.

• **End of New York jurisdiction over New Jersey:** 1738.

• **Last colonial governor of New Jersey:** William Franklin, who served from 1763 to 1776. His term as governor ended when he was arrested during the American Revolution. Franklin was the son of American patriot Benjamin Franklin. In 1781, New Jersey was one of the 13 former colonies that set up a central U.S. government under the Articles of Confederation.

• **End of New Jersey's confederation status:** December 18, 1787, when New Jersey became the third of the 13 original states to ratify the U.S. Constitution.

United States—New Mexico

New Mexico was visited by the Spanish explorer Coronado in 1540. A Spanish settlement began in 1598. When Mexico gained its independence from Spain in 1821, New Mexico came under Mexican control.

• **Last time New Mexico was under Mexican jurisdiction:** 1848. The land that is New Mexico became part of the United States with the Treaty of Guadalupe Hidalgo (1848) at the end of the Mexican War. The New Mexico Territory was created in 1850. It also included Arizona, southern Colorado, Nevada and Utah. In 1863, New Mexico was partitioned in half and the Arizona Territory was created.

• **End of New Mexico's territorial status:** January 6, 1912, when New Mexico entered the Union as the 47th state.

• **Last territorial governor of New Mexico:** William J. Mills, who served from 1910 to 1912.

United States—New York

New York's first permanent colony was the Dutch settlement at New Netherland in 1624. The English captured New Netherland in 1664.

• **Last colonial governor of New York:** William Tryon, who served from 1775 to 1780. (Tryon was also the British colonial governor of North Carolina, from 1765 to 1771.) In 1781, New York was one of the 13 former colonies that set up a central U.S. government under the Articles of Confederation.

• **End of New York's confederation status:** July 26, 1788, when New York became the 11th of the 13 original states to ratify the U.S. Constitution.

• **Last time Albany was known as Fort Orange:** 1652.

• **Last time Binghamton was known as Chenango Point:** 1834.

• **Last time Montgomery County was known as Tryon County:** April 2, 1784.

• **Last time Washington County was known as Charlotte County:** April 2, 1784.

United States—North Carolina

In 1663, North Carolina was part of Carolina, a grant bestowed by King Charles II of England on eight members of his court. It became a royal colony in 1729 when the proprietors sold their claim to the crown.

• **Last royal governor of North Carolina:** Josiah Martin, who served from 1771 to 1775. In 1781, North Carolina was one of the 13 former colonies that set up a central U.S. government under the Articles of Confederation.

• **End of North Carolina's confederation status:** November 21, 1789, when North Carolina became the 12th of the 13 original states to ratify the U.S. Constitution.

• **End of North Carolina's secession:** July 4, 1868, when North Carolina was readmitted to the Union. North Carolina had seceded on May 20, 1861, as part of the Confederate States of America.

• **Last time Beaufort County was known as Pamptecough County:** c. 1712.

• **Last time Craven County was known as Archdale County:** c. 1712.

• **Last time Hyde County was known as Wickham County:** c. 1712.

United States—North Dakota

In 1682, French explorer LaSalle claimed for France land that is now the southern part of North Dakota. Britain claimed northern North Dakota after an English geologist visited the area.

• **Last time southern North Dakota was under French jurisdiction:** 1803. The land was acquired by the United States with the Louisiana Purchase.

• **Last time northern North Dakota was under British control:** 1818. The United States acquired the land under terms of the London Convention with Great Britain. It established the 49th parallel as the border between the United States and British North America (Canada). The Dakota Territory was created in 1861 with its capital at Yankton. In February 1889, the territory was divided into North and South Dakota.

• **Last time Yankton was the territorial capital:** 1883. Bismarck replaced it that year.

• **End of North Dakota's territorial status:** November 2, 1889, when North Dakota entered the Union as the 39th state.

• **Last territorial governor of North Dakota:** Arthur C. Mellette in 1889.

• **Last time Wells County was known as Gingras County:** February 26, 1881.

United States—Ohio

Ohio was part of the Northwest Territory that was established as "The Territory Northwest of the River Ohio" by the Continental Congress in 1787. The Northwest Territory comprised all the land west of Pennsylvania and Virginia, between the Ohio and the Mississippi rivers.

• **Last of the Northwest Territory:** ended when it was divided in 1800 to create the Indiana Territory in the western part of the territory.

• **End of Ohio's territorial status:** March 1, 1803, when Ohio entered the Union as the 17th state.

United States—Oklahoma

Most of Oklahoma was part of the land purchased by the United States from France in the 1803 Louisiana Purchase. Oklahoma became part of the Missouri Territory when it was organized in 1812. It was later part of the Arkansas Territory. In 1834, a portion of the land was set aside as the Indian Territory. On May 2, 1890, the Oklahoma Territory was created from part of the Indian Territory.

• **End of Oklahoma's territorial status:** November 16, 1907, when Oklahoma entered the Union as the 46th state.

• **Last of the Indian Territory:** merged with the Oklahoma Territory in 1907, when Oklahoma became a state.

• **Last territorial governor of Oklahoma:** Frank Frantz, who served from 1906 to 1907.

• **Last time the Oklahoma capital was in Guthrie:** 1910. That year it was moved to Oklahoma City.

• **Last surviving homesteader of the 1893 Cherokee Strip:** Laura E. Crews, who died in Enid, Oklahoma, on March 25, 1976, age 105.

Notable Last Facts

United States—Oregon

Great Britain claimed the land that is now Oregon after it was abandoned by Spain in 1795. In 1818, the United States and Britain signed a treaty providing for joint occupation.

• **Last time Oregon as under British jurisdiction:** 1846, with the Oregon Treaty, when the two nations divided the land. Congress established the Oregon Territory in 1848.

• **End of Oregon's territorial status:** February 14, 1859, when Oregon entered the Union as the 33rd state.

• **Last territorial governor of Oregon:** George L. Curry, who served from 1854 to 1859.

• **Last time Marion County was known as Champeog County:** September 3, 1849.

• **Last time Washington County was known as Tuality County:** September 3, 1849.

United States—Pennsylvania

Swedish and Dutch colonists settled in Pennsylvania before the English arrived in 1664. In 1681, England's King Charles II granted to William Penn, as proprietor, land that is now the state of Pennsylvania

• **Last provincial governor of Pennsylvania:** John Penn, who served from 1773 to 1776. From 1777 to 1790, Pennsylvania was ruled by a Supreme Executive Council.

• **Last Supreme Executive Council president:** Thomas Mifflin, who served from 1788 to 1790. He was also the first state governor, from 1790 to 1799. In 1781, Pennsylvania was one of the 13 former colonies that set up a central U.S. government under the Articles of Confederation.

• **End of Pennsylvania's confederation status:** December 12, 1787, when Pennsylvania became the second of the original 13 states to ratify the U.S. Constitution.

• **Last time the Pennsylvania capital was in Lancaster:** 1812. That year the capital was moved to Harrisburg.

• **Last time Bradford County was known as Ontario County:** March 24, 1812.

United States—Rhode Island

The first settlement in Rhode Island was established in 1636 by Roger Williams. In 1663, scattered settlements united after King Charles II of England granted the region a charter. In 1781, Rhode Island was one of the 13 former colonies that set up a central U.S. government under the Articles of Confederation.

• **End of Rhode Island's confederation status:** May 29, 1790. when it became the last of the 13 original states to ratify the U.S. Constitution.

• **Last time Rhode Island had dual capitals:** 1900, in Providence and Newport. That year Providence became the only capital.

• **Last time Newport County was known as Rhode Island County:** June 16, 1729.

• **Last time Providence County was known as Providence Plantations County:** June 16, 1729.

• **Last time Washington County was known as King's County:** October 29, 1781.

United States—South Carolina

In 1663, South Carolina was part of Carolina, a grant bestowed by King Charles II of England on eight members of his court. It became a royal colony in 1729 when the proprietors sold their claim to the crown.

• **Last royal governor of South Carolina:** Lord William Campbell, who took office in 1775. In 1781, South Carolina was one of the 13 former colonies that set up a central U.S. government under the Articles of Confederation.

• **End of South Carolina's confederation status:** May 23, 1788, when South Carolina became the eighth of the 13 original states to ratify the U.S. Constitution.

• **End of South Carolina's secession:** June 25, 1868, when South Carolina was readmitted to the Union. South Carolina was the first state to secede from the Union on December 20, 1860, as part of the Confederate States of America.

• **Last time South Carolina counties were known as districts:** 1868.

United States—South Dakota
France claimed the land that is South Dakota after French explorers visited the region in the 1740s. Land west of the Mississippi was known as Louisiana. France ceded the land to Spain in 1762. It was retroceded to France in 1800.

• **Last time South Dakota was under French jurisdiction:** 1803. The land that is now South Dakota was acquired from France by the United States with the Louisiana Purchase. The Dakota Territory was created in 1861 with its capital at Yankton. In February 1889, the territory was divided into North and South Dakota.

• **End of South Dakota's territorial status:** November 2, 1889, when South Dakota was admitted to the Union as the 40th state.

• **Last territorial governor of South Dakota:** Arthur C. Mellette, who served in 1889. He also served as the first governor of the new state of South Dakota.

• **Last time Dewey County was known as Rusk County:** March 9, 1883.

• **Last time Union County was known as Cole County:** January 7, 1864.

United States—Tennessee
The State of Franklin (a.k.a. Frankland) embraced land that is now part of eastern Tennessee. North Carolina ceded the land to the United States in 1784. The U.S. Congress had two years to signify its intention of accepting. Meanwhile, a group of local people called a convention and set up the State of Franklin on the land. Its constitution banned lawyers, doctors and preachers from the legislature.

• **Last governor of the State of Franklin:** John Sevier, the only governor.

• **Last of the State of Franklin:** ceased to exist March 1788 when Sevier's term expired and no one was elected to succeed him. Sevier became the first governor of Tennessee in 1796 and later served in the U.S. House of Representatives. In 1789, Congress organized Tennessee as "The Territory of the United States South of the River Ohio" (a.k.a. Southwest Territory).

• **End of Tennessee's territorial status:** June 1, 1796, when Tennessee entered the Union as the 16th state.

• **Last territorial governor of Tennessee:** William Blount, who served from 1790 to 1796.

• **End of Tennessee's secession:** July 24, 1866, when Tennessee was readmitted to the Union. Tennessee had voted to secede from the Union to become part of the Confederate States of America on June 8, 1861. Tennessee was the last state to secede and the first to be readmitted to the Union.

• **Last time Loudon County was known as Christiana County:** July 7, 1870.

• **Last time Union County was known as Cooke County:** January 28, 1846.

United States—Texas
Spain claimed the land that is Texas in 1519. Texaco came under Mexican control in 1821.

• **Last time Texas was under Mexican jurisdiction:** 1836. Texans proclaimed their independence and declared their land the Republic of Texas. The following year, the United States recognized the republic.

• **Last major battle in the war for Texas independence:** Battle of San Jacinto on April 21, 1836. Texas forces, led by Sam Houston, routed the Mexican army. The battle lasted only 20 minutes, but it ended Mexican authority in Texas. The battle was a major victory in securing the freedom of Texas from Mexico. It led to the annexation of Texas and ultimately the Mexican War. It was at San Jacinto that the rally cry "Remember the Alamo," was first heard.

• **Last surviving veteran of the Battle of San Jacinto:** John G. Pickering, who died in Texas on February 4, 1917, age 99. Others have claimed or have been cited as the last surviving veteran of this battle. One is William Physick Zuber who died on September 22, 1913, age 93. His gravestone in Texas State Cemetery in Austin, Texas, states he was the last survivor. Another is Alphonso Steele, who died in July 1911, age 94. Steele referred to himself in a memoir, written late in his life, as "the last survivor of the Battle of San Jacinto." Surviving veterans of the battle gathered for their last reunion in Goliad, Texas, on April 21, 1906; both Zuber and Steele were at the last reunion.

• **Last survivor of the signers of the 1836 Texas Declaration of Independence:** William Crawford, originally from North Carolina. He died on September 3, 1895, age 90.

• **Last of the Republic of Texas:** December 29, 1845, when Texas was annexed as the 28th state of the Union.

• **End of Texas's secession:** March 30, 1870, when Texas was readmitted to the Union. Texas had voted on February 1, 1861, to secede from the Union and join the Confederate States of America.

• **Last time Brazos County was known as Navasoto County:** January 28, 1842.

• **Last time Cass County was known as Davis County:** May 16, 1871.

• **Last time Harris County was known as Harrisburg County:** December 28, 1839.

• **Last time Buchanan County was known as Stephens County:** December 17, 1861.

United States—Utah
The State of Deseret was founded in 1847 by members of the Church of Jesus Christ of Latter-Day Saints on land that is now part of Utah. The United States gained the land in 1848 after the Mexican War and refused to recognize the State of Deseret. (*See* Religion—Mormonism.)

• **Last of the State of Deseret:** ended when the U.S. created the Utah Territory in 1850.

• **End of Utah's territorial status:** January 4, 1896, when Utah entered the Union as the 45th state.

• **Last territorial governor of Utah:** Caleb W. West, who served from 1893 to 1896.

• **Last time Iron County was known as Little Salt Lake County:** December 3, 1850.

• **Last time Rich County was known as Richland County:** January 29, 1868.

• **Last time Salt Lake County was known as Great Salt Lake County:** January 29, 1868.

United States—Vermont
Vermont was the last of the New England states to be settled. The Republic of Vermont was created in 1777.

• **End of the Republic of Vermont:** March 4, 1791, when Vermont entered the Union as the 14th state.

• **Last time Washington County was known as Jefferson County:** November 8, 1814.

United States—Virginia
The English established Virginia's first settlement at Jamestown in 1607. Virginia became a royal colony in 1624.

• **Last royal governor of Virginia:** Earl of Dunsmore, who served from 1771 to 1776. In 1781, Virginia was one of the 13 former colonies that set up a central United States government under the Articles of Confederation.

• **End of Virginia's confederation status:** June 25, 1788, when Virginia was admitted to the Union as the 10th state to ratify the U.S. Constitution.

• **End of Virginia's secession:** January 26, 1870, when Virginia was readmitted to the Union. Virginia had seceded from the Union on April 17, 1861 as part of the Confederate States of America.

• **Last survivor of the 1861 Virginia secession convention:** James Clark McGrew, who voted against disunion. After the Civil War, he was Republican Representative to the U.S. Congress. He in died in Kingwood, West Virginia, on September 18, 1910, age 97.

• **Last time the Virginia capital was in Jamestown:** 1698. It moved to Williamsburg after the Jamestown statehouse burned down in October 1698.

• **Last time the Virginia capital was in Williamsburg:** 1779. That year, Richmond was designated the new capital.

• **Last time Arlington County was known as Alexandria County:** March 16, 1920.

• **Last time Shenandoah County was known as Dunmore County:** February 1, 1778.

• **Last time Northampton County was known as Accawmack County:** 1642.

• **Last time Isle of Wight County was**

known as Warrosquyoake County: 1637.
• Last time York County was known as Charles River County: 1643.

United States—Washington
Washington was originally part of the land that was organized as the Oregon Territory on August 14, 1848. On March 2, 1853, the part north of the Columbia River and the 46th parallel was organized as the Washington Territory.
• **End of Washington's territorial status:** November 11, 1889, when Washington entered the Union as the 42nd state.
• **Last territorial governor of Washington:** Miles Conway Moore, who served in 1889.
• **Last time Clark County was known as Vancouver County:** September 3, 1849.
• **Last time Grays Harbor County was known as Chehalis County:** March 15, 1915.
• **Last time Kitsap County was known as Slaughter County:** July 13, 1857.
• **Last time Mason County was known as Sawamish County:** January 8, 1864.

United States—West Virginia
West Virginia was part of Virginia when the Civil War began. People in the western part of the state objected when Virginia seceded from the Union in 1861 to join the Confederacy.
• **Last time West Virginia was part of Virginia:** June 20, 1863, when West Virginians formed their own government and entered the Union as the 35th state.
• **Last year the West Virginia capital was in Wheeling:** 1885. That year Charleston, which had been the capital from 1870 to 1875, became the permanent capital.

United States—Wisconsin
Wisconsin was part of the Northwest Territory until 1800. It was part of the Indiana Territory from 1800 to 1808, part of the Illinois Territory from 1809 to 1818 and part of the Michigan Territory from 1818 to 1836.
• **Last time Wisconsin was under French jurisdiction:** 1763. Great Britain took control at the end of the French and Indian War.

• **Last time Wisconsin was under British jurisdiction:** 1783, with the Treaty of Paris that ended the American Revolution. The Territory of Wisconsin was formed on July 3, 1836.
• **End of Wisconsin's territorial status:** May 29, 1848, when Wisconsin entered the Union as the 30th state.
• **Last territorial governor of Wisconsin:** Henry Dodge. who served from 1845 to 1848.
• **Last time Barron County was known as Dallas County:** March 4, 1869.
• **Last time Bayfield County was known as La Pointe County:** April 12, 1866.
• **Last time Langlade County was known as New County:** February 19, 1880.
• **Last time Rusk County was known as Gates County:** June 19, 1905.
• **Last time Vernon County was known as Bad Axe County:** March 22, 1862.

United States—Wyoming
The Wyoming Territory was created from part of the Dakota Territory on July 25, 1868.
• **End of Wyoming's territorial status:** July 10, 1890, when Wyoming entered the Union as the 44th state.
• **Last territorial governor of Wyoming:** Francis E. Warren, who served from 1889 to 1890. He was the first governor of the state of Wyoming in 1890.
• **Last time Johnson County was known as Pease County**: December 13, 1879.
• **Last time Sweetwater County was known as Carter County:** December 13, 1869.

United States—Territories

United States—Territories—Guam
The Pacific island of Guam was claimed by Spain in 1565.
• **Last time Guam was controlled by Spain:** 1899. That year, Guam was ceded to the United States, after the Spanish-American War. The U.S. Navy administered it except when it was occupied by the Japa-

nese during World War II. Japan captured Guam, December 10, 1941.

• **End of the Japanese occupation of Guam:** August 1944, when Guam was recaptured by the U.S. American forces landed on Guam on July 21, 1944, and reclaimed Guam three weeks later.

• **Last time Guam was administered by the U.S. Navy:** 1950.

• **Last time Guamians were not U.S. citizens:** 1950. The Organic Act passed that year by the U.S. Congress granted American citizenship to Guamians. Administration of the island was transferred to the U.S. Department of the Interior and a one-house legislature was established.

United States—Territories—Northern Mariana Islands

The Northern Mariana Islands were claimed by Spain after Magellan visited them in 1521.

• **Last time the Northern Marianas were controlled by Spain:** 1899. That year, the islands were sold to Germany.

• **Last time the Northern Marianas were controlled by Germany:** 1920. After World War I, the League of Nations assigned their jurisdiction to Japan.

• **Last time the Northern Marianas were controlled by Japan:** 1947, after World War II, when a UN mandate made them part of the UN Trust Territories of the Pacific Islands. In 1975, residents voted to establish a commonwealth with the United States. A new government went into effect in 1978. The islands were the last land to become a territory of the United States.

• **End of UN trusteeship over the Northern Marianas:** 1986, when the Commonwealth of the Northern Mariana Islands was created as part of the U.S.

United States—Territories—Puerto Rico

• **Last time Puerto Rico was administered by Spain:** 1898, when it was ceded to the United States.

• **Last time Puerto Ricans were not U.S. citizens:** 1917. Puerto Ricans were made U.S. citizens by the Jones Act that year.

• **Last known as Porto Rico:** 1932. That year, Congress made the Puerto Rico spelling official.

United States—Territories—Virgin Islands

• **Last time the Virgin Islands belonged to Denmark:** 1917. That year, the U.S. purchased Saint Thomas, Saint Croix, Saint John and about 50 islets for $25 million.

• **Last time the Virgin Islands were administered by the U.S. Navy:** 1931. That year, administration was transferred to the Department of the Interior.

• **Last time Virgin Islanders were not U.S. citizens:** 1927.

Wars and Battles

Wars and Battles—Alamo Siege

When the siege of the Alamo ended on March 6, 1836, in San Antonio, Texas, 189 American defenders were dead. Mexican casualties exceeded 1,500. Only about 15 people survived the Alamo siege, including a dozen Mexican women and three Americans—a woman, her child and her servant.

• **Last survivor of the Alamo:** Alejo Pérez Jr. He was the son of Juana Alsbury and her first husband, Alejo Pérez Sr. His mother brought him into the Alamo just before his first birthday. He died in San Antonio on October 19, 1918, age 83.

Wars and Battles—American Indian Wars

More than 100,000 American soldiers fought in a series of American Indian Wars between 1865 and 1898, with about a thousand battle deaths.

• **Last surviving U.S. Army veteran of the American Indian Wars:** Fredrak Fraske, who served in Cheyenne, Wyoming until 1897. He died in Chicago, Illinois, on June 18, 1973, age 101.

Wars and Battles—American Indian—Black Hawk's War

Black Hawk's War began in April 1832, when a band of Sauk and Fox Indians, led by Black Hawk, a Sauk chief, attempted to regain their lands in Illinois.

• **End of Black Hawk's War:** August 2, 1832, with the surrender of Black Hawk. The U.S. Army drove the Indians west across the Mississippi. Black Hawk was imprisoned but later released. He spent the last years of his life on a small tract of land in Keokuk, Iowa.

• **Last remains of Black Hawk:** When Black Hawk died on October 3, 1838, age 71, he was buried in a mound near his lodge. The following year, his body was stolen by an Illinois physician who planned to make money by putting it on exhibit. When Black Hawk's bones were recovered, they were placed in the Historical Society in Burlington, Iowa. The last remains of Black Hawk were lost in 1855, when the building was destroyed by fire.

Wars and Battles—American Indian— French and Indian War

The French and Indian War began in 1754, when the British, led by George Washington, tried to force the French out of Fort Duquesne in western Pennsylvania. The turning point of the war was the French loss of Quebec, the capital of New France, in 1759.

• **End of the French and Indian War:** 1763, when the Treaty of Paris ended the colony of New France and French control in North America. Great Britain gained Canada and all French lands east of the Mississippi. French lands west of the Mississippi went to Spain.

• **Last French and Indian War pensioner:** David Thompson, who died in Easton, Massachusetts, in October 1836, age 98 or older. Thompson enlisted when he was 16. He was at the massacre of Fort William Henry in 1757, where he lost an arm and for which he was granted a pension.

Wars and Battles—American Indian— King Philip's War

King Philip's War was named for Metacom, chief of the Wampanoag tribe, who was given the name Philip by the Pilgrims. Philip, troubled by their increasing encroachment on his people's hunting and fishing areas, led the Wampanoags and Narragansetts in an attack against the colonists in June 1675. The Narragansetts were nearly annihilated in the winter of 1675-76. Philip was killed on August 12, 1676, at Kingston, Rhode Island, by a Wampanoag working for the English.

• **End of King Philip's War:** August 28, 1676, when the Indians surrendered. Philip's head was placed on a pole and sent to Plymouth (Massachusetts), where it remained on display for many years. Philip's wife and child were sold into slavery in the West Indies. The end of King Philip's War marked the end of Native American power in New England.

Wars and Battles—American Indian— Little Bighorn (Custer's Last Stand)

The Battle of Little Bighorn on June 25, 1876, resulted in the defeat and death of U.S. 7th Cavalry officer George A. Custer and all the men under his command by Crazy Horse and a large number of Native Americans. Before the battle, Custer assigned three of his companies to Captain Frederick Benteen and three to Major Marcus Reno. Although none of the troops with Custer survived, there were survivors among the men with Benteen and Reno.

• **Last survivor of the Battle of Little Bighorn:** Charles A. Windolph, who was in Company H assigned to Benteen before the battle. His story is recounted in a book by Charles Windolph and Robert Hunt, *I Fought with Custer: The Story of Sergeant Windolph, Last Survivor of the Battle of Little Bighorn*. Windolph died in Lead, South Dakota, on March 11, 1950, age 98.

• **Last Native American survivors of Little Bighorn:** When Sitting Bull's son John died in May 1955, Sioux Dewey Beard (Wasu Maza) is believed to have become the last Native American survivor of the battle. He died the following November. Another claim among Native American participants came from Charles Sitting Man, who died in 1962.

• **Last surviving horse from the Battle of Little Bighorn:** Captain Myles Keogh's horse, Comanche, who was hit during the fighting but survived. After the battle, Comanche was taken to Fort Lincoln in the Dakota Territory and nursed back to health. Later, he was paraded at important ceremonies. Comanche died in Fort Riley, Kansas, on November 7, 1891. He was stuffed and placed in the University of Kansas's Dyche Museum of Natural History in Lawrence.

• **Last person to see Custer alive:** Curley, a Crow scout, who had been released from duty by Custer on the day of the battle. He saw an attack coming so he went to a nearby ridge where he watched much of it from a distance. When he saw that Custer was in trouble, he rode to get help from Generals Terry and Gibbon. In his later years, Curley lived at the Crow reservation in Montana, where he died on May 21, 1923. He was buried at the National Cemetery in Little Bighorn.

• **Last surviving child of any soldier who fought in the Battle of Little Bighorn:** Minnie Grace Mechling Carey, the daughter of Medal of Honor recipient Henry W.B. Mechling, who was with Company H, assigned to Captain Benteen during the battle.

Wars and Battles—American Indian—Modoc War

The Modoc War took place in southern Oregon and northern California in 1873. In the late 1860s, the Modocs were moved to a reservation in Oregon after their land in California was opened to settlement. A large group of them, led by Kintpuash (Captain Jack), fled the reservation in 1870 and lived in California for a few years. Early in 1873, the U.S. Army used force to get them to return to the reservation. The Modocs sought refuge at the lava beds near Tula Lake. In April, a parley was held. Two of the U.S. peace envoys were massacred.

• **End of the Modoc War:** May 1873, when many of the Modocs were taken back to the Oregon reservation. Captain Jack and five of his followers were caught, tried and condemned to death. They were hanged at Fort Klamath on October 3, 1873.

Wars and Battles—American Indian—Nez Percè War

As white settlers moved into the American Northwest in the 1860s and early 1870s, the Nez Percè were coerced into signing treaties that took from them large areas of their land in the Snake River Valley of Oregon and Idaho. Finally, their leader Chief Joseph refused to give up any more territory. The Nez Percè War began in July 1877, when the Nez Percè were forced to move to reservations in Oregon and Idaho.

• **End of the Nez Percè War:** October 5, 1877, at the Bear Paw Battle, when Chief Joseph negotiated an end to the extended siege by handing over his rifle to a United States Army colonel. The Nez Percè were taken first to Oklahoma then to reservations in Idaho and Washington. Chief Joseph died on the Colville Reservation in Washington on September 21, 1904, age about 64.

Wars and Battles—American Indian—Seminole Wars

The Seminole Wars were the most expensive wars the United States waged against the American Indians. They cost more than $30 million and took the lives of some 1,500 U.S. soldiers. The number of Seminoles who died is unknown. The first war began in 1817 and was fought in Florida and southern Georgia.

• **End of the First Seminole War:** April 1818, with a defeat of the Seminoles by forces commanded by General Andrew Jackson. The second Seminole war began in 1835, when U.S. Army forces arrived in Florida to enforce the Treaty of Payne's Landing (enacted in 1832). The Seminoles refused to give up their Florida land and move west.

• **End of the Second Seminole War:** 1842, although no peace treaty was signed. Some of the Seminoles were sent to Oklahoma. Others escaped to the Florida Everglades. A third Seminole War broke out in 1855 in a dispute over land occupied by Seminoles in Florida.

• **End of the Third Seminole War:** 1858, when all but a few Seminoles left Florida and migrated West.

Wars and Battles—American Indian—Tuscarora Wars

The Tuscarora Wars began when the Tuscarora Indians attacked English settlers in North Carolina in September 1711 in a dispute over continued English encroachment on their land.

• **End of the Tuscarora War:** 1713, when the Tuscaroras were defeated by a coalition of colonists and hostile Indians. The Tuscaroras signed a treaty and left the area, opening North Carolina for colonial expansion. They moved to New York and joined the Iroquois Confederation.

Wars and Battles—American Indian—Wounded Knee Siege

On February 27, 1973, 200 to 300 members of the American Indian Movement (AIM) seized the trading post and church on the Oglala Reservation in Wounded Knee, South Dakota, and held a demonstration to call attention to their grievances.

• **End of the Wounded Knee siege:** May 8, 1973, a few days after an agreement was reached by both sides. On September 16, 1974, charges against the leaders of AIM were dismissed in federal court.

Wars and Battles—American Indian—Yamasee War

The Yamasee War began in 1715 on the Carolina frontier. It was a struggle between the Yamasee Indians of the area and the English who wanted to colonize the land.

• **End of the Yamasee War:** 1718. The Yamasee were driven out of South Carolina and pushed southward through Georgia to northern Florida.

Wars and Battles—American Revolution—Battles

The American Revolution, or War of Independence, was a revolt of the 13 British colonies in North America. The first bloodshed was at Lexington. Massachusetts, in 1775. The fighting ended at Yorktown, Virginia, in 1781. The war officially ended with the Treaty of Paris in 1783,

• **Last survivor of Bunker Hill (Breed's Hill):** Ralph Farnham, a soldier from Lebanon, Maine. In 1780, he settled in Acton, Maine, and was said to be the first white inhabitant of that township. He died in Acton on December 26, 1861, age about 105.

• **Last in retreat at Bunker Hill (Breed's Hill):** Benjamin Gould, a commissioned captain in the Continental Army. After the Battle of Bunker Hill, he was the last man to cross Charlestown Neck in retreat. Gould died in Newburyport, Massachusetts, on May 30, 1841.

• **Last survivor of Lexington and Concord:** Jonathan Harrington, a fifer for the men who assembled at Lexington Green on April 19, 1775. He died in Lexington, Massachusetts, in 1854.

• **Last surviving Concord Minute Man:** Amos Baker of Lincoln, Massachusetts, who marched to Concord on April 19, 1775. In April 1850, his "Affidavit of the Last Survivor" was published.

• **Last surviving participant of the Boston Tea Party:** David Kenniston (or Kenison). He was born in Kingston, New Hampshire, and died in Chicago, Illinois, in February 1852.

• **Last survivor of the Wyoming (Pennsylvania) Massacre:** Asa A. Gore, who died in Preston, Connecticut, on December 1, 1859. Gore was a small child and was carried away from the scene in his mother's arms.

Wars and Battles—American Revolution—British Occupation

• **Last British occupation of Boston, Massachusetts:** March 17, 1776, when the British army under General Howe evacuated and General George Washington took possession of the city.

• **Last British occupation of New York, New York:** November 25, 1783, when the last British troops withdrew from the Battery in New York City. New York was the last major British outpost.

• **Last British occupation of Philadelphia, Pennsylvania:** June 18, 1778. Within an hour after the British left, American troops entered the city.

Wars and Battles—American Revolution —End of the War

• **End of hostilities:** February 4, 1783, when England declared an end to all hostilities with the United States. The U.S. Congress declared an end to the American Revolution on April 11, 1783. The main part of the U.S. Continental Army was disbanded on June 13, 1783.

• **Official end of the American Revolution:** January 14, 1784, when the United States ratified the Treaty of Paris that had been signed on September 3, 1783. The American representatives during the peace signing were Benjamin Franklin, John Jay and John Adams. The treaty established the Mississippi River as the western boundary of the United States.

Wars and Battles—American Revolution —Final Fighting

• **Last major battle of the American Revolution:** Yorktown, Virginia. The fighting ended on October 19, 1781, with the surrender of Lord Cornwallis and more than 7,000 British soldiers. When the British surrendered, an English band played "The World Turned Upside Down" as the color bearers relinquished their flags.

• **Last fighting of the American Revolution:** November 10, 1782, in Chillicothe, Ohio, when George Rodgers Clark attacked Shawnee Indians and Loyalists.

• **Last person killed in combat in the American Revolution:** Captain William Wilmott of the Second Maryland Regiment. He was killed by a British foraging party in a skirmish on James Island, South Carolina, on November 14, 1782.

Wars and Battles—American Revolution —*Gaspee*

The destruction of the British armed schoo-ner HMS *Gaspee* by Rhode Island patriots on June 9, 1772, was the first armed conflict leading to the American Revolution.

• **Last surviving participant in the attack on the *Gaspee*:** Ephraim Bowen, who died in Providence, Rhode Island, on September 2, 1841, age 89.

• **Last surviving witness to the attack on the *Gaspee*:** John Howland, who died in Providence, Rhode Island, on November 5, 1854, age 97.

Wars and Battles—American Revolution — Generals

• **Last surviving general:** General Thomas Sumter, known as the "Gamecock of the Revolution." After the war, he was elected to the South Carolina Senate, the Continental Congress, and the U.S. Congress. He served under the first four U.S. presidents. Sumter died at South Mount, near Strasburg, South Carolina, on June 1, 1832, age 97. The city and county of Sumter, South Carolina, both carry his name. So do counties in Alabama, Florida and Georgia.

• **Last headquarters of Washington:** the Rockingham mansion in Franklin Township, New Jersey, north of Princeton. Washington stayed at Rockingham from August to November 1783. While there, he wrote his Farewell to his troops. General George Washington officially resigned his commission to retire to private life on December 23, 1783.

• **Last of Washington's Life Guards:** Uzal Knapp, who was 18 when he entered the Continental Army. He fought at White Plains, wintered at Valley Forge, joined Lafayette's light infantry, and was with the French general at Monmouth, New Jersey. In 1780, Knapp was a sergeant in Washington's Life Guard and received a badge of merit for six years of faithful service. Knapp died on January 10, 1856, and was buried at Washington's headquarters in Newburgh, New York. His monument, erected in 1860, proclaims him "the Last of the Life Guards." Nathaniel Berry, who died on August 20, 1850, age 94, and Jesse Smith, who died in Salem, Massachusetts, in 1844, have also been identified as Washington's last Life Guards. Berry became a member of Washington's Life Guards in March 1778. He served at Valley Forge in the Commander-in-Chief's Guard under the command of Captain Caleb Gibbs and remained with the corps until he was discharged at Morristown, New Jersey, in 1780. Smith enlisted in 1775 and was transferred to the guard of the Commander-in-Chief under Captain Caleb Gibbs in 1776. He was at White Plains, Brandywine, Germantown, Monmouth and Valley Forge. Upon Smith's monument is inscribed: "He was the last survivor of the bodyguard of Washington."

• **Last of the Washington Elm:** fell down in 1923. Pieces of its wood were sent to museums and officials all over the United States. A small city park in Cambridge, Massachusetts, marks where the tree once stood. Tradition has it that on July 3, 1775, during the American Revolution, George Washington took command of his colonial troops under the tree.

• **Washington's Farewell to his Officers:** delivered on December 4, 1783, at Faunces Tavern, New York City, where Washington had set up headquarters for a few days.

Wars and Battles—American Revolution —Intolerable Acts

The Intolerable Acts, also known as the Coersive Acts, were passed in the spring of 1774 by the British Parliament to tighten control over the American colonists.

• **Last Intolerable Act:** an expansion of the Quartering Act, approved on June 2, 1774, affecting occupied buildings. The people of Massachusetts were required to house and feed soldiers. The colonists saw the acts as a threat to their liberty and responded by calling for a congress to seek redress of their grievances.

• **End of the Intolerable Acts:** September 17, 1774, when members of the First Continental Congress approved the Suffolk Resolves—resolutions made by the residents of Suffolk, Massachusetts—that declared the Intolerable Acts illegal and urged the colonists not to obey them.

Wars and Battles—American Revolution —Marines

• **Last Marine of the American Revolution mustered out:** Lieutenant Thomas Elwood (or Elmwood). He turned in his equipment on June 3, 1783. Elwood was on the frigate USS *Alliance*. After the Marines were mustered out in April 1783, he and a small guard remained aboard ship until Congress decided to sell the *Alliance*. Elwood died in Fairfield, Connecticut, in 1820 at about age 65. His name is shown in some sources as Elmwood and on DAR records as Elwood.

Wars and Battles—American Revolution —Navy

• **Last naval battle of the American Revolution:** March 10, 1783, after peace between the United States and Great Britain had been agreed upon. The USS *Alliance,* commanded by Captain John Barry, and the French vessel *Duc de Lauzon* left Cuba on March 7. Three days later, they encountered three British frigates, HMS *Alarm, Sybil* and *Tobago* and engaged two of them. None of the combatants were aware the war had ended.

• **Last surviving gunboat built and manned by American forces during the American Revolution:** the Continental gunboat *Philadelphia*, built in 1776. She was one of several vessels used by Benedict Arnold to fight British craft on Lake Champlain that October. *Philadelphia* sank on October 11, 1776, during the Battle of Valcour Island, but remained well preserved by the cold water. She was salvaged in 1935 and was taken to the Smithsonian Institution in 1961. *Philadelphia* is the oldest American fighting vessel in existence and is a National Historic Landmark.

Wars and Battles—American Revolution —Veterans

• **Last soldier of the American Revolution on a U.S. pension list:** Daniel Frederick Bakeman (or Beakman) of New Jersey. In 1778, he enrolled in the militia then served in the war. In 1867, Congress enacted special legislation that gave him a pension for the rest of his life. He died in Sandusky, New York, on April 5, 1869, age 109. His wife lived to be 105. The couple were married 85 years. In the Annual Report of the Commissioner of Pensions for the year 1874 the following paragraph appears: "With the death of Daniel F. Bakeman, of Freedom, Cattaraugas County, New York, April 5, 1869, the last of the pensioned soldiers of the Revolution passed away." A claim to being the last surviving soldier of the American Revolution was also made by John Gray, who was born January 6, 1764, in Fairfax County, Virginia, near Mount Vernon. He was 16 when he took up the musket of his father who had fallen at White Plains. Gray carried it until the war ended. He was at Yorktown for the final surrender. He later received a pension from the U.S. Congress. Gray died near Hiramsburg, Ohio, on March 29, 1868, age 104. His gravestone identifies him as "The Last of Washington's Companions."

• **Other last survivors:** In 1864, the Rev. Elias Brewster Hilliard endeavored to interview the last seven survivors of the American Revolution. By then, all were centenarians. Adam Link, 102, died in August 1864, before Hilliard could interview him. Another survivor could not be located. Of the remaining five, Lemuel Cook, at 105, was the oldest. Samuel Downing was 102. Alexander Milliner was 104. Daniel Waldo was 101. William Hutchins was 101. All died a short time after being interviewed. Hilliard's interviews were published as *The Last Men of the Revolution* (Hartford, CT: N.A. and R.A. Moore, 1864). The book was reprinted by Barre (MA) Publishers in 1968.

• **Last president who saw combat in the American Revolution:** James Monroe, who served in the American Revolution from 1776 until 1780. He saw military combat in New York, and was at the Battle of Monmouth. He spent time at Valley Forge during the winter of 1777-1778. Monroe died in 1831.

• **Last U.S. president who was a veteran of the American Revolution:** Andrew Jackson, who was born in 1767, joined the militia at the age of 13 during the American Revolution, and was captured. He did not see combat. Jackson died in 1845.

Wars and Battles—American Revolution —Veterans' Spouses and Descendants

• **Last surviving widow of an American Revolution veteran recognized by the U.S. Department of Veterans' Affairs:** Catharine S. Damon, who died on November 11, 1906, age 92.

• **Last surviving dependent of an American Revolution veteran recognized by the U.S. Department of Veterans' Affairs:** Phoebe M. Palmeter, who died April 25, 1911, age 90.

• **Last claimant for an American Revolution pension:** *The SAR Magazine* (publication of the Sons of the American Revolution) named Oliver N. Abbott of South Carolina, son of John Abbott who served in the South Carolina Militia. Oliver Abbott died on January 4, 1944, while his pension claim was being considered in the U.S. House of Representatives. *The SAR Magazine* (Winter 1991) also included a list of men who survived into the 20th century, whose fathers fought in the American Revolution.

• **Last surviving daughter of an American Revolution veteran:** Annie Knight Gregory, who died in Williamsport, Pennsylvania, on December 17, 1943, age 100. She was the daughter of Richard Knight, a drummer who was at Valley Forge with Washington. She was a member of the Conrad Weiser Chapter, Daughters of the American Revolution, Pennsylvania.

• **Last surviving granddaughter of an American Revolution veteran:** Zula Willemena Penny Morgan, the granddaughter of James Penny, who came to America with his father in 1775 and settled in Pennsylvania. Penny was only 14 when he enlisted in Captain James Morrison's Company of the 3rd Battalion in the militia of Lancaster County, Pennsylvania, commanded by Colonel Thomas Porter. His name appears on a company muster roll of that organization covering the period from December 17 to 26, 1776. Zula Morgan died in Ruston, Louisiana, on May 15, 1964, age 97.

Wars and Battles—Austrian Succession, War of the

The War of the Austrian Succession was a series of conflicts fought in Europe over claims to Austrian-held land after the death of Emperor Charles VI in 1740. The conflicts lasted until 1748.

• **Last battle in which a reigning British monarch led his troops:** Battle of Dettingen on June 27, 1743, during the War of the Austrian Succession. Great Britain's King George II, who was also the Elector of Hanover, led an army of British, Hessian and Hanoverian troops and defeated the French army near the Bavarian village of Dettingen in southern Germany.

• **End of the War of the Austrian Succession:** October 18, 1748, with the Treaty of Aix-la-Chapelle.

Wars and Battles—Barbary Wars

The Barbary Wars were conflicts fought by the United States against the Barbary States in the western Mediterranean Sea in 1801-05 and 1815. (The Barbary States were the north African kingdoms of Morocco, Algeria, Tunis and Tripolitania.) The first conflict, known as the Tripolitan War, began in May 1801 when the pasha of Tripolitania ordered the American flag removed from the U.S. consulate.

• **Last of the ship USS *Philadelphia*:** burned by Navy Captain Stephen Decatur in Tripoli harbor on February 16, 1804, to prevent the Barbary States from using it. The *Philadelphia* had hit a reef in October 1803 and the captain and crew were stranded there.

• **End of the Tripolitan War:** June 4, 1805, with a treaty signed aboard the USS *Constitution*. The United States paid a ransom for the release of the crew of the USS *Philadelphia*. Tripolitania agreed to abolish all future annual tribute payments to the pasha, but tributes were still to be paid to the other Barbary States. The second war, sometimes known as the Algerine War, began when the

dey of Algeria declared war on the U.S., claiming America had not paid enough tribute. Stephen Decatur launched an offensive on June 29, 1815, capturing two Barbary States ships.

• **End of the Algerine War and Barbary Wars:** June 30, 1815, with the signing of a treaty with Algeria that guaranteed the future safety of U.S. ships without tribute payments.

Wars and Battles—Boer Wars

The Boer Wars were two wars fought in South Africa between the descendants of Dutch settlers (Boers) and the British. (The Boers were also known as Afrikaners or Voortrekkers.) The first war began in 1880 when the Boers declared the Transvaal a republic.

• **End of the first Boer War:** February 1881, with a defeat for the British at Majuba Hill. The second Boer War (also known as the South African War) began in October 1899, when the Boers launched an attack in Cape Colony.

• **End of the second Boer War:** May 31, 1902, with the signing of the Treaty of Vereeniging. The Transvaal and Orange Free State—two independent republics founded by the Boers—became British colonies and were included in the Union of South Africa in 1910.

• **Last surviving British veteran of the Boer Wars:** George Ives, who died on April 15, 1993, age 111.

Wars and Battles—Chaco War

The Chaco War was waged between Bolivia and Paraguay over the Chaco Boreal, a vast wilderness region at the foot of the Bolivian Andes. Paraguay gained clear title to most of the disputed region; however, Bolivia was given a path to the Paraguay River and Puerto Casado.

• **End of Chaco War:** June 12, 1935 (truce); July 21, 1938 (peace treaty).

Wars and Battles—Civil War (U.S.)

The Civil War is also known as the War

Between the States, the War of the Rebellion and the War of Secession. It involved the northern States (the Union) and the southern states that seceded between December 1860 and June 1861 and formed the Confederate States of America (the Confederacy). After the South fired on Fort Sumter in April 1861, President Abraham Lincoln announced a state of insurrection existed. The war ended with the surrender of Confederate forces in April 1865.

Wars and Battles—Civil War—Andersonville Prison

Andersonville Prison, built by the Confederacy in Sumter County, Georgia, was known officially as Camp Sumter. The first Union prisoners arrived in February 1864. The initial pen was enlarged in June, 1864. By the time Andersonville shut down, more than 45,000 Union soldiers had been held there as prisoners of war, and almost 13,000 died from disease, malnutrition, injuries and deplorable camp conditions.

• **Last prisoners held at Andersonville Prison:** released in May 1865, when the prison was shut down soon after the war ended.

• **Last of Andersonville's camp commandant:** Captain Henry Wirz was executed on November 9, 1865, for mistreating Union soldiers during the war. Wirz was the only Civil War officer executed for war crimes.

• **Last time Andersonville was privately owned:** 1891. After the war, the land near Andersonville prison became a national cemetery. The rest of the land reverted to private ownership. The Grand Army of the Republic acquired that land in 1891 and installed monuments to show where the prison, stockade and gates once stood. Andersonville today is a National Historic Site. In 1970, it was designated a memorial to all Americans who were ever prisoners of war. In 1998, the National Prisoner of War Museum opened there.

Wars and Battles—Civil War—Battles and Generals

Union General William Tecumseh

Sherman's march from Atlanta to Savannah, Georgia, began on November 15, 1864. Approximately 68,000 Union soldiers marched 300 miles and left a 60-mile-wide swath of destruction.

• **End of Sherman's March to the Sea:** December 21, 1864, when General Sherman entered the city of Savannah, Georgia. After his March to the Sea, Sherman headed north.

• **Last Civil War military action of Sherman:** April 26, 1865, near Durham, North Carolina. against General Joseph E. Johnston's army. Sherman accepted the surrender of Johnston.

• **Last meeting of Robert E. Lee and Jefferson Davis:** November 26, 1867, two and a half years after the war ended. They met at the courthouse in Richmond, Virginia, where Davis was involved in a lawsuit: *United States v. Jefferson Davis.*

• **Last office of Robert E. Lee:** President of Washington College (now Washington and Lee University) from 1865 until his death. Lee died in Lexington, Virginia, on October 12, 1870, age 63. He is buried in Lee Chapel at Washington and Lee University. Lee's office at the college remains much as he left it for the last time on September 28, 1870.

• **Last surviving Union general:** Brigadier General Adelbert Ames, who died in Lowell, Massachusetts, on April 12, 1933, age 97. Ames fought at Gettysburg.

• **Last surviving Confederate general:** Brigadier General John McCausland, who died in Henderson, West Virginia, on January 22, 1927, age 91.

Wars and Battles—Civil War—Confederate States of America

Confederate States of America (CSA) delegates met for the first time on February 4, 1861, in Montgomery, Alabama, to form a new republic. After May 29, 1861, the permanent Confederate capital was Richmond, Virginia.

• **Last Confederate state to secede from the Union:** Tennessee on June 8, 1861.

• **Last session of the Congress of the Confederate States of America:** March 18, 1865.

• **Last day the Confederacy occupied Richmond, Virginia:** April 2, 1865, when the Confederate capital fell and the Confederate government abandoned the city. Confederates set fire to several buildings as they fled the city. Confederate president Jefferson Davis and his cabinet fled southward.

• **Last meeting of the Confederate cabinet under Jefferson Davis:** May 5, 1865. The meeting was held at the Georgia Branch Bank Building in Washington, Georgia. Davis was captured on May 10, 1865, near Irwinville, Georgia.

• **End of the Confederacy:** The Confederate States of America were not officially terminated. In *History of the Confederacy, 1832-1865,* Clifford Dowdey pointed out that the Confederate States of America never had an official end. The Confederate generals just surrendered. But there was no formal surrender of the Confederacy as a nation.

• **Last Confederate flag lowered:** aboard the CSS *Shenandoah* when the ship arrived in Liverpool, England, on November 6, 1865. At that time, she was turned over to United States authorities. *Shenandoah,* under the command of Lieutenant James I. Waddell, had completed a 58,000-mile raiding voyage in the Pacific during which time Waddell captured 11 American whalers near the Bering Strait. He did not receive word that the Civil War had ended until he encountered a British ship on August 2, 1865. Waddell decided to finish his nonstop voyage to Liverpool via Cape Horn.

• **Last Confederate Secretary of State:** Judah Philip Benjamin, known as "the Brains of the Confederacy." He served from March 1862 to the end of the war. Benjamin was a lawyer and former U.S. senator from Louisiana. He moved to England after the Civil War and established a successful law practice. His last great case was a suit against the London & Northwestern Railway. He retired in 1883 and died in Paris, France, in 1884, age 72.

• **Last Confederate Secretary of War:** Major General John C. Breckinridge of Kentucky, the fifth person to hold the office. He served from January to April 1865.

Breckinridge was Vice President of the United States from 1857 to 1861. He died in Lexington, Kentucky, on May 17, 1875, age 54.

• **Last Confederate Secretary of the Treasury:** George Alfred Trenholm of South Carolina, a cotton merchant who served from July 1864 to the end of the war.

• **Last Confederate Attorney General:** George Davis of North Carolina, the fourth person to hold the office. He served from January 1864 to the end of the war.

• **Last Confederate Secretary of the Navy:** Stephen R. Mallory, who was the only Secretary of the Navy in the Confederacy. He held the post from March 1861 to the end of the war.

• **Last Confederate Postmaster General:** John Henninger Reagan, who was the only Postmaster General of the Confederacy. He held the post from March 6, 1861 to the end of the war. Reagan was the last remaining member of the Confederate cabinet with Jefferson Davis when he was captured in May 1865.

• **Last surviving Confederate cabinet member:** John Henninger Reagan, Postmaster General of the Confederacy for the entire war. He died in Palestine, Texas on March 6, 1905, age 81.

• **Last Confederate state to be readmitted to the Union:** Georgia on July 15, 1870. Georgia reapplied in 1868, but representatives were unseated in 1869. The last state to be readmitted by order of reapplication was Texas, March 30, 1870.

• **End of the secession of Dade County, Georgia:** July 4, 1945, when the Free State of Dade, a county in northwestern Georgia, raised the United States flag for the first time in 85 years.

Wars and Battles—Civil War—Draft Riots

The first Civil War draft lottery in New York, New York, was held on July 11, 1863. The Draft Riots began a few days later, on July 13, 1863, when the draft lists were published in the newspaper. The public learned that the Republicans in charge of the draft had stuffed the lists with the names of Democrats. The public also learned that well-to-do New Yorkers were hiring substitutes to fight for them. Property damage during the rioting reached more than $1 million. The precise number of people killed is not known, but estimates range from 20 to more than 100. Several hundred were injured.

• **End of the Draft Riots:** July 16, 1863. The 7th New York Infantry joined local law enforcement in New York city and ended the rioting.

Wars and Battles—Civil War—End of the War

• **Last day of the Civil War:** April 9, 1865, when General Philip H. Sheridan and his cavalry surrounded General Robert E. Lee near the village of Appomattox Court House in Virginia. Lee sent a white flag through the lines carrying a letter of surrender to General Ulysses S. Grant, who was at the McLean farmhouse.

• **Last time the original McLean farmhouse was standing:** c. 1891-92, when the building was sold to a speculator. The McLean farmhouse was dismantled and packed in crates for shipment to Chicago to exhibit at the 1893 Columbian Exposition, but the plans did not work out. The house remained in pieces for almost a half century. In 1940, Appomattox Court House National Monument was created and work began on reconstructing the structure. Then World War II intervened (1941-45). In 1949, the reconstruction was completed and the house was opened to the public for the first time.

• **Last volley fired at Appomattox:** April 9, 1865, by the North Carolina Brigade of General William Ruffin Cox during the final surrender.

• **Last message of Lee to his army:** his Farewell to his Army on April 10, 1865.

• **Last major Civil War engagement/last men killed/last volley fired:** Palmetto Ranch (or Palmitto, Palmito), near Brownsville, Texas on May 13, 1865. Private John J. Williams of the 34th Indiana Infantry is generally identified as the last

man killed in battle in the Civil War. However, Bill Redman of the 62nd U.S. Colored Infantry died a few weeks after Williams of injuries sustained at the Battle of Palmetto Ranch (a.k.a. Battle of Palmetto Hill). The last volley was fired by the 62nd Infantry.

• **Last Confederate generals to surrender:** General Edmund Kirby-Smith and Brigadier General Stand Watie. On May 26, 1865, Kirby-Smith agreed to the terms of surrender for 43,000 scattered Confederate troops of the Department of the Trans-Mississippi to General E.R.S. Canby at Shreveport, Louisiana. The actual surrender was on June 2, 1865. Watie has the distinction of being the last Confederate general in the field to capitulate. He surrendered on June 23, 1865, at Doaksville, near Towson, in Indian Territory. Watie, who commanded the First Indian Brigade, was a chief of the Cherokee Nation and was the only Native American to attain the rank of general in the war.

• **Last casualties of the Civil War:** May 22, 1865, more than a month after the war ended. Three Confederate soldiers refused to accept Lee's surrender. They attacked Union troops at the courthouse in Floyd, Virginia. Two Union soldiers were wounded. After a chase, the Confederates were caught and shot. One was a Virginian named Bordunix.

• **End of the Civil War (official):** April 2, 1866, in all the United States except Texas. The Civil War officially ended in Texas on August 20, 1866. President Andrew Johnson issued proclamations stating the War of the Rebellion ended on those dates. The U.S. Supreme Court upheld the dates in *The Protector, 12 Wall, 700* (1872).

• **Last enrollments in the Union Army:** ended on April 12, 1865, when the Secretary of War announced the end of the draft and began mustering out troops.

Wars and Battles—Civil War—Postwar —Freedmen's Bureau

The Freedmen's Bureau (officially named the Bureau of Refugees, Freedmen, and Abandoned Lands) was established by Congress as part of the War Department on March 3, 1865. Its main function was to see to the welfare of former slaves and to administer abandoned lands in the South. The bureau was created originally for one year but was extended by Congress annually for several years. During its existence, the Freedmen's Bureau built hundreds of schools for black children and provided teachers. It faced bitter opposition from Southerners and was harassed by the Ku Klux Klan.

• **Last of the Freedmen's Bureau:** 1874, when educational activities ceased. The rest of the bureau's work was discontinued in 1869.

Wars and Battles—Civil War—Postwar —Reconstruction

Reconstruction began at the end of the Civil War with the Reconstruction Acts of 1867. It was a plan for restoring the state governments of the former Confederacy.

• **End of Reconstruction:** 1877, when Rutherford B. Hayes was elected president. On April, 24, 1877, a month after he entered office, the last federal troops were removed from the South. By then, former Confederates gained control of many of the state governments.

Wars and Battles—Civil War—Postwar —War Debt

In July 1864, Confederate General Jubal A. Early ransomed the city of Frederick, Maryland, for $200,000, money he needed to continue fighting in the war. The local banks provided the money. In exchange, Early spared the town.

• **Last Civil War debt payment:** July 1951, when the city of Frederick finally repaid to the banks the last of the money Early received.

Wars and Battles—Civil War—Ships

• **Last monitor (heavily clad armored ship):** USS *Canonicus,* built in Boston, Massachusetts, in 1864. She saw service until 1877, then was laid up. In 1907, *Canonicus* was towed to Hampton Roads, Virginia, and exhibited at the Jamestown Exposition. The following year she was scrapped.

• **Last Confederate naval encounter:** CSS *Shenandoah* against a whaling ship in the Bering Sea on June 28, 1865. On November 6, 1865, *Shenandoah* surrendered to British authorities in Liverpool. The ship was then seized by the U.S. government, sold to the Sultan of Zanzibar and renamed *El Majidi.* It foundered at sea while traveling from Zanzibar to Bombay. (*See above*: Last Confederate flag lowered.)

• **Last Civil War vessel afloat:** USS *Constellation.* See Ships—Warships—U.S. —Early.

Wars and Battles—Civil War—Ships— *Monitor* and *Virginia/Merrimac*

On March 9, 1862, the USS *Monitor* and the CSS *Virginia* fought to a draw in a four-hour battle at Hampton Roads, Virginia. The battle was the first between ironclad warships and showed their superiority over wooden ships. A day earlier, *Virginia* destroyed two wooden naval ships: USS *Cumberland* and USS *Congress.* The *Virginia* originally was the USS *Merrimac*, a Union ship that was captured in 1861 by the Confederacy when the Union troops evacuated Norfolk.

• **End of the CSS *Virginia/Merrimac*:** scuttled by her crew on May 11, 1862, after she ran aground in Virginia. She was abandoned and set afire. When the flames reached gunpowder aboard the ship, CSS *Virginia* was destroyed by an explosion. Parts of the *Virginia* are in several Virginia museums. Her ship's wheel is at the Mariners' Museum in Newport News. Her anchor is at the Museum of the Confederacy in Richmond. Her ship's bell is at the Chrysler Museum in Norfolk. And armor plates are at the Hampton Roads Naval Museum.

• **End of the USS *Monitor*:** December 31, 1862, when it was caught in a violent storm while being towed to North Carolina. *Monitor* sank, killing 16 of her 62 crew members. She went down in 230 feet of water. Duke University scientists confirmed in 1974 that they had found the *Monitor* the previous summer, resting on the ocean floor 15 miles south of Cape Hatteras Lighthouse. The ship's corroded condition made recovery too expensive. However, the Navy and the National Oceanic and Atmospheric Administration funded a project to raise parts of the ship. In 2001, *Monitor*'s steam engine was brought to the surface. The following year, the gun turret and cannons were salvaged.

• **Last surviving crew member of the *Virginia/Merrimac*:** John P. Kevill, who served as a powder boy at the age of 18 and fought in the battle at Hampton Roads on March 8, 1862. He died in Portsmouth, Virginia, on January 3, 1941, age 96.

• **Last to leave the *Monitor*:** Captain John Pyne Bankhead, commander of the *Monitor,* along with Lieutenant Green and several officers, as the ship foundered off Cape Hatteras on December 31, 1862. Bankhead died on April 27, 1867, on board the *Wyoming*, of which he had been captain since 1866.

• **Last surviving crew member of the *Monitor*:** Isaac H. Scott, who died in Buffalo, New York, on May 18, 1927, age 89.

Wars and Battles—Civil War— U.S. Army

• **Last man on active duty in the U.S. Army who fought in the Civil War:** John Lincoln Clem, also known as Johnny Shiloh. When he retired in 1916 with the rank of major general, Clem was the last man in the army who had fought in the Civil War. Clem joined the U.S. Army as a drummer when he was nine and was the youngest soldier ever to serve in the army. He became known as the "Drummer Boy of Chickamauga." Clem died in San Antonio, Texas, on May 13, 1937, age 85.

Wars and Battles—Civil War—Veterans

For many years, John B. Salling and Walter Washington Williams were accepted as the last surviving Confederate veterans. Salling, of Virginia, died on March 16, 1958. Williams of Houston, Texas, died on March 19, 1959. However, their claims were disputed by historian William Marvel in "The Great Impostors," in *Blue and Gray* magazine, February 1991. By checking census records,

Marvel determined Salling and Williams both would have been too young to serve.

• **Last surviving Confederate veteran:** Pleasant R. ("Riggs") Crump of Company A, 10th Alabama Infantry, who died in Alabama on December 31, 1951, age 104. He was the last of 1 million men who fought on the side of the Confederacy. At the time of his death, Crump was honored as the last Confederate soldier in Alabama and the last surviving soldier to have witnessed Lee's surrender at Appomattox.

• **Last surviving Union veteran:** Albert Henry Woolson, who enlisted in the 1st Minnesota Heavy Artillery in October 1864. He served as a private and as drum major, and witnessed Sherman's March to the Sea. Woolson died in Duluth, Minnesota, on August 2, 1956, age 109. He was the last of more than 2.6 million men who fought for the Union during the war.

Wars and Battles—Civil War—Veterans —Confederate States of America

• **Last major Confederate veterans reunion:** June 21-24 1932, in Richmond, Virginia. Although there would be smaller gatherings in later years, the 42nd assembly in 1932 marked the last great reunion of veterans of the Confederacy.

Wars and Battles—Civil War—Veterans —Grand Army of the Republic (GAR)

The Grand Army of the Republic (GAR) was an organization of veterans of the Civil War. It was created in Indianapolis, Indiana, shortly after the end of the war.

• **Last surviving GAR member:** Albert Henry Woolson. (*See above,* Last surviving Union veteran.)

• **Last GAR reunion:** Opened August 28, 1949, in Indianapolis, Indiana, where the first meeting had been held 82 years earlier. Six of the last 16 GAR survivors were there.

• **The last GAR commander:** Theodore A. Penland, who died in Vancouver, Washington, on September 13, 1950, age 101.

Wars and Battles—Civil War—Veterans —Dependents

• **Last surviving Confederate widow:** Alberta Martin, the third wife of William Jasper Martin. When she married Martin on December 10, 1927, she was 19, and he was 81. Martin served in Company, 4th Alabama Infantry. He died in 1932.

• **Last surviving widow of a white Union veteran:** Gertrude Grubb Janeway of Blaine, Tennessee. Her husband John served in the 14th Illinois Cavalry but used the name January, not Janeway, when he enlisted. Gertrude Grubb was 18 when she married the 81-year old veteran. She died on January 19, 2003, age 93.

• **Last surviving widow of a black Union veteran:** Daisy Anderson, who was 21 when she married 79-year-old Civil War veteran Robert Ball Anderson. Anderson served in the 125th Colored Infantry in the Union Army. He died in an automobile accident in 1930. Daisy Anderson died in Colorado in September 1998, age 97.

• **Last surviving Civil War widow:** Alberta Martin. With the death of Gertrude Grubb Janeway in 2003, Mrs. Alberta Martin became the last surviving Civil War widow. She died in Alabama on May 31, 2004, age 97.

• **Last U.S. president who was a Civil War veteran:** William McKinley. He was the last of six presidents who served in the Civil War: The others were Ulysses S. Grant, Rutherford B. Hayes, James A. Garfield, Chester A. Arthur and Benjamin Harrison.

Wars and Battles—Cold War

The Cold War was a political, economic and ideological war with limited military action between the Communist nations, led by the Union of Soviet Socialist Republics (USSR), and the capitalist nations, led by the United States. It began at the end of World War II and ended with the collapse of communism, beginning in 1989.

• **End of the Cold War:** February 1, 1992, at Camp David, Maryland, when U.S. President George Herbert Walker Bush and Russian President Boris Yeltsin jointly announced that the two nations do not regard each other as potential enemies. They both pledged to remove any remnants of Cold War hostility.

Wars and Battles—Cold War—Berlin Airlift

On June 24, 1948, the USSR placed a blockade on all land and water traffic between West Berlin and West Germany to protest U.S. policy on the economic recovery of Germany. Every road, waterway and rail line was shut down. The only access to West Berlin was by air. On June 26, a massive airlift got underway to keep the West Berliners supplied with food, medicine and other necessities.

• **End of the Berlin Airlift:** The USSR lifted the blockade on May 12, 1949. Phasing out continued until September 30, 1949. During its 15 months of operation, the airlift made more than 276,000 flights between West Berlin and West Germany, and transported more than 2 million tons of supplies.

• **Last Berlin Airlift plane:** a US C-54 Skymaster that flew from Rhein-Main Air Force Base (West Germany) to Tempelhof Air Field (West Berlin) on September 30, 1949, on the 276,926th flight. The last flight was made by Captain Perry Immel.

Wars and Battles—Cold War—Berlin Wall

The East Germans began construction of the wall along the border between East and West Berlin in August 1961 to put a halt to the many thousands of refugees fleeing East Berlin. The wall had several crossing checkpoints that could be used only with special permission. One of those was Checkpoint Charlie.

• **End of the Berlin Wall:** 1990. On November 9, 1989, the Berlin Wall was opened for the first time in 28 years, and East and West Berliners could pass freely from one part of the city to the other. The following day, East German troops began dismantling the wall. During 1990, the entire Berlin Wall was removed. For many people, removal of the wall represents a concrete end to the Cold War.

• **Last time Checkpoint Charlie was at the**

Berlin Wall: June 22, 1990, when it was carted away intact and placed in the Allied Museum in Berlin. Checkpoint Charlie was a small structure that served as one of the checkpoint/guardhouses at the Berlin Wall.

Wars and Battles—Cold War—Cuban Missile Crisis

The Cuban Missile Crisis began on October 14, 1962, when the United States was able to confirm from U-2 surveillance flights that medium- and intermediate-range missiles were being installed in Cuba. On October 22, U.S. President John F. Kennedy informed the world of the presence of the missiles.

• **End of the Cuban Missile Crisis:** October 28, 1962, when Soviet Premier Nikita Khrushchev ordered destruction of the missile sites in Cuba in return for a pledge that the U.S. would not interfere in Cuban affairs.

Wars and Battles—Cold War—East Germany

• **Last person killed by border guards while fleeing East Germany:** Chris Gueffroy on February 5, 1989. The four border guards responsible for the killing were decorated, given bonuses, extra vacation days and a celebratory meal. Two years later, in 1991, the guards were charged with manslaughter in the first trial of its kind. During the trial, the guards cited the Nuremberg defense: the claim that they were just following orders.

Wars and Battles—Cold War—Iron Curtain

The term "Iron Curtain" was made popular by British statesman Winston Churchill in a speech at Westminster College in Fulton, Missouri, on March 5, 1946. It was an imaginary line that ran from northern Poland to Trieste in southern Europe. The nations east of the line were Communist and cut themselves off economically, politically and ideologically from the capitalist nations of western Europe after World War II.

• **Last of the Iron Curtain:** 1989-90, with the demolition of the Berlin Wall. Removal of the wall that divided Berlin, Germany, spelled the end of the Iron Curtain as the ideological divider of East and West.

Wars and Battles—Crimean War

The Crimean War began as a dispute over the guardianship of holy shrines held by Turkey. The tsar of Russia extended protection to the Greeks. The Ottoman Turks declared war on October 4, 1853. Britain and France feared Russian expansion, so they entered the war on the side of the Turks in May 1854. They received help from Sardinia, Prussia and Sweden. Much of the fighting took place in the Crimea, hence the name. Russia lost the war.

• **End of the Crimean War:** March 30, 1856, with the Treaty of Paris. The war ended Russia's dominance in southeastern Europe.

• **Last survivor of the Charge of the Light Brigade:** Edwin Hughes, known as Balaclava Ned. The Charge of the Light Brigade was an attack on Russian troops at Balaclava, led by Lord Cardigan on October 25, 1854. Cardigan led more than 600 men into battle. About 40 percent of them were either killed or wounded. The event was memorialized in a poem, "Charge of the Light Brigade," by Alfred, Lord Tennyson (1854). Hughes died in Blackpool, England, in 1927.

• **Last surviving Crimean War troop ship:** *Edwin Fox*, built by William Henry Foster at Sukeali on the River Hooghly near Calcutta, India, in 1853. The *Edwin Fox* is now moored in Picton, New Zealand. (*See also* Ships—East Indiamen)

Wars and Battles—Falkland Islands Conflict

The Falkland Islands conflict was between the United Kingdom and Argentina over possession of the Falkland Islands, a British Dependent Territory in the South Atlantic Ocean. It began when Argentine forces occupied the Falkland Islands, South Georgia and the South Sandwich Islands on April 2-3, 1982. The UK imposed a sea and air blockade within 200 miles. British commandos seized South Georgia on April 25, and disabled an Argentine sub. A large force of British troops arrived on the islands on May 14th.

• **End of the Falklands Island Conflict:** June 14, 1982, with the surrender of Argentine forces and the restoration of British sovereignty.

Wars and Battles—Franco-Prussian War
The Franco-Prussian War began on August 4, 1870, when German troops marched into Alsace in northern France

• **End of the Franco-Prussian War:** January 28, 1871, with a defeat for France, when an armistice was signed. France lost most of the territories of Alsace and Lorraine and had to pay an indemnity of 5 billion francs ($1 billion). The war marked the end of the French Second Empire and the beginning of the French Third Republic. It also marked the beginning of the German Empire.

• **Last shots of the Franco-Prussian War:** fired February 1, 1871, near La Cluse in the Jura Mountains, along the border of France and Switzerland. The French army of more than 80,000 men marched into neutral Switzerland and were disarmed and interned.

• **Last casualty of the Franco-Prussian War:** a man known simply as Monty. Ironically, he had been the first person injured at the beginning of the war, according to Figuier's *Histoire de Mervelleux.* Later, a statue was erected to Monty in southern France by the French government.

Wars and Battles—French Revolution
The French Revolution had no clear-cut beginning and end. Some historians place the start at June 1789, when the Third Estate declared itself the National Assembly and agreed not to adjourn until France had a constitution. A month later, the Bastille was stormed. Others put the opening date earlier, in 1787, when a political crisis led to the emergence of two distinct factions: those loyal to the monarchy and those who favored democracy.

• **End of the French Revolution:** A major

phase of the revolution ended on July 27, 1794, when the Committee of Public Safety was abolished. Another phase ended in 1795 when a new constitution established the Directory. It lasted just four years. In 1799, Napoleon Bonaparte rose to power. His regime ended in 1815. For some historians, his downfall marked the end of France's revolutionary struggle. Others place the end of the revolution at 1799.

• **End of the Ancient Regime (Old Order):** October 5-6, 1789, when the French king and the National Assembly were sent to Versailles. The Ancient Regime was the socioeconomic and political system that existed in France under the old absolute monarchy before the Revolution.

• **Last of the Bastille:** destruction began when the Bastille was stormed by a mob on July 14, 1789. Within a few months, the demolition was complete. The Bastille had been built by Charles V as a chateau around 1370 in the eastern part of Paris. It became a state prison during the 17th century. The fall of the Bastille came to symbolize a triumph of the people over the power of the monarchy. In 1880, July 14th became a French national holiday as Bastille Day. Part of the site of the Bastille today is covered by the Place de la Bastille. Stones from the Bastille's foundation are visible in the subway station beneath the square.

• **Last of the Committee of Public Safety:** abolished July 27, 1794. It had been created in April 1793 to direct the army and was the chief executive body of the National Convention. The Committee of Public Safety played a key role in the Reign of Terror.

• **End of the Reign of Terror:** with the overthrow of Maximilien Robespierre and his associates on July 27, 1794, and his execution the following day. The Reign of Terror began with the fall of the Girondists when the Jacobins came to power on June 2, 1793. It was a time when the government used terror against its enemies. Thousands of people were brought before the Revolutionary tribunal, hastily tried and put to death by guillotine. (*See also* Nations—France.)

Wars and Battles—French Revolutionary Wars

The French Revolutionary Wars began in April 1792 when France declared war on Francis II, the king of Austria, who was also the Holy Roman Emperor. He had recently extended protection to Prussian states where French exiles were forming an anti-revolutionary army. In 1793, Great Britain, Spain, Holland and Prussia joined the fighting against France. When Napoleon defeated the Austrians in June 1800, Austria withdrew from the war. The British remained in the war and forced the French to surrender Egypt, which Napoleon had taken from the Ottoman Empire in 1798.

• **End of the French Revolutionary Wars:** October 1802, when France signed a treaty restoring Egypt to the Ottoman Empire.

Wars and Battles—Gulf War

The Gulf War, also known as the Persian Gulf War, was a conflict between Iraq and United Nations powers. Iraq, led by President Saddam Hussein, invaded Kuwait on August 2, 1990, and refused UN demands to withdraw. Military action was taken against Hussein after he ignored a UN resolution demanding his forces leave Kuwait by January 15, 1991. Operation Desert Shield was the code name for sending Allied troops to the Persian Gulf. Operation Desert Storm was the code name for the attack on Iraq by U.S. and coalition forces that began on January 16, 1991, with an air assault against military targets in Iraq and Kuwait. The ground war began on February 24, 1991. Two days later, the Allies entered and liberated Kuwait.

• **End of Operation Desert Storm:** March 3, 1991, when Iraqi representatives accepted terms for a provisional truce, ending offensive operations. On April 6, 1991, the official cease-fire was signed, and on April 11, 1991, the United Nations Security Council issued a formal cease-fire with Iraq to end the Gulf War.

• **Last U.S. ground troops returned to the U.S.:** June 13, 1991.

• **Last Kuwait oil fire extinguished:** November 6, 1991. The oil fires had been ignited by Iraq in Kuwait during the Gulf War.

Wars and Battles—Hundred Years' War

The Hundred Years' War was a series of conflicts fought during the Middle Ages between England and France. The fighting began in 1337 after a dispute arose between King Philip VI of the French House of Valois and England's King Edward III of the House of Plantagenet over the right to the throne of France.

• **End of the Hundred Years' War:** 1453, when England lost Gascony and had only one remaining holding in France, at Calais. The English held onto Calais until 1558, when the French seized control.

Wars and Battles—Indochina War

The Indochina War was waged in Southeast Asia by the Viet Minh (Vietnamese nationalists and Communist guerrillas) against French colonial rule beginning in 1945.

• **End of the Indochina War:** May 7, 1954, when the village of Dien Bien Phu in northern Vietnam was finally taken by the Vietnamese. Casualties exceeded 15,000 dead, injured, missing or captured. The defeat at Dien Bien Phu was the catalyst for France to end the Indochina War. An international conference in Geneva, Switzerland, in 1954 divided Vietnam into North Vietnam and South Vietnam along the 17th parallel. (*See also* Nations—Vietnam; Wars and Battles—Vietnam War.)

Wars and Battles—Iran-Iraq War

The Iran-Iraq War began on September 22, 1980, when Iraqi planes attacked Iranian airfields, including the airport at Teheran. One of the sources of conflict was control of the disputed Shatt al Arab waterway along the border Iran shared with Iraq.

• **End of Iran-Iraq War:** summer 1988, when Iran announced it accepted the United Nations Security Council's peace plan. The cease-fire went into effect on August 20, 1988. Iraq accepted peace terms in 1990.

Wars and Battles—King George's War

King George's War was named for Great Britain's King George II. It was the American colonies' equivalent of the War of the Austrian Succession in Europe. The fighting was mostly in New England and along the Canadian border. It was caused by British and French rivalry over factors such as fishing rights, trade and control of the Saint Lawrence and Mississippi rivers. It began when the French unsuccessfully attacked Port Royal in 1744. In 1745, the British seized Louisbourg on Cape Breton Island in northern Nova Scotia.

• **End of King George's War:** October 10, 1748, with the Treaty of Aix-la-Chapelle. Louisbourg was returned to France in exchange for giving Madras in India to the British.

Wars and Battles—King William's War

King William's War was the American counterpart of the War of the League of Augsburg in Europe (1688-97). It was a struggle between France and England for control of fisheries and the fur trade of North America. The war began in 1689 with a series of Native American massacres instigated by the French.

• **End of King William's War:** the Treaty of Ryswick in 1697. The war's outcome was indecisive. Within a few years both France and England would be warring again. (*See* Wars and Battles—Queen Anne's War.)

Wars and Battles—Korean War

The Korean War began when North Korean troops invaded South Korea on June 25, 1950. U.S. President Harry S Truman ordered General Douglas MacArthur to come to the aid of South Korea.

• **End of MacArthur's commands:** April 11, 1951, shortly after General Douglas MacArthur wrote to a member of the U.S. Congress criticizing White House policy in Korea. MacArthur favored stronger war measures, including attacking Communist military bases in China. President Truman relieved him of all three commands: Commander of Allied Occupation Forces in Japan; U.S. Commander-in-Chief, Far East Command; and Commander-in-Chief of UN Forces in Korea. MacArthur was replaced

by General Matthew B. Ridgway. MacArthur died in Washington D.C., on April 5, 1964, age 84.

• **Last U.S. ground combat of the Korean War:** July 24-26, 1953, in the Berlin Complex area controlled by the 1st and 7th U.S. Marine Regiments. The last Marine ground actions were on Hills 111 and 119.

• **End of the Korean War:** July 27, 1953 (July 26, EST), when an armistice was signed at Panmunjom, Korea.

• **End of the Korean War fighting:** 12 hours after the armistice was signed on July 27, 1953. Chinese troops withdrew from North Korea on October 26, 1958.

• **Last U.S. air strikes of the Korean War:** On July 22, 1953, Lieutenant Sam Young, flying an F-86, made the last MIG kill of the war. On July 27, 1953, the day the cease-fire was signed, Captain Ralph S. Parr Jr., flying an F-86, shot down an enemy transport. Lieutenant Denver S. Cook piloted the last Far East Air Forces (FEAF) Bomber Command sortie. The last bombs were dropped by a Douglas B-26 Invader 24 minutes before the cease-fire went into effect.

• **Last Korean Service Medal ship to be decommissioned:** U.S. Coast Guard Cutter *Ironwood*. Commissioned in October 1943, the ship is a 180-foot "B" Class (Mesquite class) buoy tender. She served in World War II, Korea and Vietnam and was the last ship awarded the Korean Service Medal that was still on active duty. *Ironwood* was decommissioned on October 6, 2000, at Kodiak, Alaska. Following a trip to San Pedro, California, she was sold to the Nigerian Navy.

• **Last day of eligibility for Korean veterans' benefits (GI Bill of Rights):** January 31, 1955. Public Law 550, the Veterans Readjustment Assistance Act of 1952 (a.k.a. Korean GI Bill of Rights), was granted to Korean War veterans who entered the service after June 27, 1950, and prior to February 1, 1955, who had at least 90 days of service and received other than a dishonorable discharge.

• **End of the Korean GI Bill of Rights program:** January 31, 1965. The program provided benefits for 1.3 million veterans.

Wars and Battles—Mexican War

In April 1846, Mexican troops entered Texas and attacked an American scouting party. Declaring the action an invasion, U.S. President James K. Polk requested a declaration of war from Congress. The U.S. declared war on Mexico on May 12, 1846.

• **Last major battle of Mexican War:** Chapultepec castle in Mexico City, Mexico, on September 13, 1847. The battle was a victory for the United States. Mexican resistance ended with the fall of the fortress. The following day Mexico surrendered.

• **End of the Mexican War:** February 2, 1848, when the Treaty of Guadalupe Hidalgo was signed. It was ratified by the U.S. Senate on March 10, 1848, and by Mexico in May 1848. Mexico was reduced in size by about two fifths. In exchange for $15 million, Mexico ceded land that is now portions of the states of Arizona, New Mexico, Colorado and Wyoming and the entire states of California, Nevada and Utah.

• **Last American troops left Mexico:** August 2, 1848.

• **Last surviving Mexican War veteran:** Owen Thomas Edgar, who died September 3, 1929, age 98.

• **Last surviving Mexican War widow:** Lena James Theobald, who died on June 20, 1963, age 89.

• **Last surviving Mexican War dependent:** Jesse G. Bivens, who died on November 1, 1962, age 94.

• **Last surviving officer of the Mexican War:** Brigadier General Horatio Gates Gibson, an 1847 graduate of the U.S. Military Academy at West Point. He died in Washington, D.C., on April 17, 1924, age 96.

• **Last U.S. president who was a veteran of the Mexican War:** Ulysses S. Grant, an 1843 West Point graduate who served in the war under Generals Zachary Taylor and Winfield Scott. Presidents Taylor and Pierce also served in the Mexican War.

Wars and Battles—Napoleonic Wars

The Napoleonic Wars were waged by Napoleon I between 1803 and 1815.

• **End of the Napoleonic Wars:** June 18, 1815, with Napoleon's defeat at Waterloo. After he surrendered and abdicated as emperor, he was exiled to the island of Saint Helena, where he died on May 5, 1821.

• **End of Napoleon's sea power:** the Battle of Trafalgar on October 21, 1805. The battle was a victory for Great Britain's Lord Nelson against a combined French and Spanish fleet. The British lost no ships and captured 20 enemy ships. The victory ended Spain's hope of recovering naval supremacy. It also ended any plans Napoleon might have had to invade England. (*See also* Nations—France—Napoleon.)

Wars and Battles—Pacific, War of the

The War of the Pacific began as a dispute between Chile and Bolivia over control of Bolivian territory along the Pacific seacoast that was rich in nitrate and guano. Bolivia sought the support of Peru. Chile declared war on Bolivia and Peru in April 1879.

• **End of the War of the Pacific:** October 20, 1883, when the Treaty of Ancon was signed between Chile and Peru, ceding Tarapaca province to Chile. A truce between Chile and Bolivia in 1884 gave Chile control of Bolivia's coastline, causing Bolivia to be landlocked. Another treaty signed in 1904, made the arrangement permanent. In return, Chile agreed to build a railroad between La Paz, the capital of Bolivia, and the port of Arica.

Wars and Battles—Peasants' War

The Peasants' War was the last in a long series of revolts by German peasants and poor urban dwellers against serfdom and the feudal system. It began in June 1524 near Stuhlingen, and spread throughout southern and western Germany.

• **End of the Peasants' War:** 1525. By the time the war ended, as many as 100,000 peasants had been killed. Some rebels in Austria continued the struggle until 1526. Among the factors that led to their defeat: they lacked leadership and unity and they did not have the support of Martin Luther. However, the peasant rebellion had some positive results: Serfdom was abolished in some regions, and feudalism was weakened in others.

Wars and Battles—Persian Gulf War, *see* Gulf War.

Wars and Battles—Punic Wars
The Punic Wars were three wars waged between Carthage (in northern Africa) and Rome. The first war began in 264 B.C. and ended in 241 B.C. The Second Punic War was from 218 to 202 B.C. The Third Punic War began in 149 B.C.
• **End of the Punic Wars:** 146 B.C. The wars gave Rome control of the northern African region of the Mediterranean.

Wars and Battles—Queen Anne's War
Queen Anne's War was a struggle between Great Britain and France in North America. It began in 1702, at the beginning of the reign of Queen Anne of England. The European phase of the war was the War of the Spanish Succession.
• **End of Queen Anne's War:** The fighting ended in 1712, after the British made two unsuccessful raids against the French. The war ended with the signing of the Treaty of Utrecht on April 11, 1713. Great Britain retained control of Nova Scotia and gained Newfoundland and the Hudson Bay area. Great Britain also gained exclusive trading rights in South America. France remained in control of Cape Breton Island and Prince Edward Island and agreed to have Great Britain act as a protectorate over the Iroquois Indians.

Wars and Battles—Roses, War of the
The War of the Roses is the name often used to describe the intermittent struggles that began in 1455 for control of the English throne between the houses of York (symbolized by the white rose) and Lancaster (associated with the red rose).
• **End of the War of the Roses:** Battle of Bosworth Field near Leicester, England, on August 22, 1485. Richard III was killed and Henry Tudor gained the English crown as Henry VII. When Henry married Elizabeth of York, daughter of Edward IV, who was a niece of Richard, he united the two battling houses and ended the War of the Roses.

Wars and Battles—Russo-Japanese War
The Russo-Japanese War, which began in February 1904, was caused by Russia and Japan both coveting the same land in Asia. When Russia acquired Port Arthur in China, Japan attacked Russian forces there. The Battle of Tsushima Strait, where the Russian fleet was destroyed, began on May 27, 1905, and ended on the 28th.
• **End of the Russo-Japanese War:** with the Portsmouth Treaty of September 1905, by which Russia surrendered Port Arthur. Japan emerged as a world power.

Wars and Battles—Russo-Turkish Wars
The Russo-Turkish Wars were a series of wars fought between Russia and the Ottoman Empire that began in the late 1690s. They were triggered by Russia's attempt to gain access to the land along the Black Sea that was controlled by the Ottoman Turks. The wars continued into the 20th century and ended with a treaty signed by Turkey and the USSR in 1921.
• **End of the Russo-Turkish War of 1768-74:** with the Treaty of Kuchuk Kainarji, signed on July 21, 1774. Russia gained the Crimea.
• **End of the Russo-Turkish War of 1828-29:** with the Treaty of Adrianople (a.k.a. Treaty of Edirne) signed on September 14, 1829. Russia gained most of the Caucasian coast on the Black Sea.
• **End of the Russo-Turkish War of 1877-78:** with the Treaty of San Stefano signed on March 3, 1878. Turkish control over Romania, Serbia and Montenegro was terminated. The Treaty of Berlin, signed July 13, 1878, abolished the Russian protectorate over Bulgaria.
• **End of the Russo-Turkish War of 1914-18:** with the Treaty of Brest-Litovsk, signed on March 3, 1918. It ended the state of war between Russia on one side and Germany, Austria-Hungary, Bulgaria and Turkey on the other. Russia lost to Turkey the Arme-

nian cities it had previously annexed. The Treaty of Brest-Litovsk also formally ended Russian participation in World War I. On November 13, 1918, the Russians officially abrogated the treaty. The Treaty of Moscow signed by Turkey and the Soviet Union on March 16, 1921, officially ended the Russo-Turkish Wars.

Wars and Battles—Seven Years' War

The Seven Years' War was primarily a conflict between the British and French for possession of North America. Its American counterpart was the French and Indian War (1754-63). The war aligned Prussia with Great Britain and Spain and Austria with France.
• **Last naval battle of the Seven Years' War:** Battle of Restigouche in New Brunswick, Canada, in June 1760.
• **End of the Seven Years' War:** February 10, 1763, with the signing of the Treaty of Paris by France, Great Britain and Spain.

Wars and Battles—Sino-Japanese Wars

The Sino-Japanese Wars were two conflicts between China and Japan. The First Sino-Japanese War began on August 1, 1894, when the Japanese sent troops to Korea after a revolt threatened the government.
• **End of the first Sino-Japanese War:** with the Treaty of Shimonoseki, signed on April 17, 1895. The treaty ended Chinese influence in Korea and gave Taiwan, the Pescadores and the Liaotung Peninsula to Japan. The second Sino-Japanese War began in 1931 when the Japanese occupied Manchuria and created the puppet state of Manchukuo. In 1937, the Japanese overran northeastern China and captured Shanghai and Nanjing.
• **End of the second Sino-Japanese War:** in September 1945, with the Japanese surrender at Nanjing after the end of World War II.

Wars and Battles—Six-Day War

The Six-Day War was waged between Israel and the neighboring Arab states of Egypt, Jordan and Syria. It began on June 5, 1967.

The Israelis captured the Sinai Peninsula, the Gaza Strip, East Jerusalem, the West Bank of the Jordan River and the Golan Heights of Syria.
• **End of the Six-Day War:** June 10, 1967, when Syria accepted a cease-fire.

Wars and Battles—Spanish-American War

The Spanish-American War was a brief conflict between Spain and the United States over Cuba. It began with the sinking of the U.S. battleship USS *Maine* in Havana Harbor on February 15, 1898.
• **End of the Spanish-American War:** December 10, 1898, with signing of the Treaty of Paris. Spain lost control of Philippines, Puerto Rico, Guam and other land.
• **Last battle of the Spanish-American War in Cuba:** Aguas Claras, on August 15, 1898.
• **End of the U.S. occupation of Cuba:** May 20, 1902.
• **Last surviving veterans of the Spanish-American War:** Nathan E. Cook, who died on September 10, 1992, age 106. He was the last surviving U.S. veteran of the Spanish-American War, according to data from the U.S. Department of Veteran Affairs. However, Jones Morgan outlived Cook by almost a year. Morgan, the son of freed slaves, was one of the Buffalo Soldiers who served in the black 9th and 10th Cavalry regiments. He died in Richmond, Virginia, on August 29, 1993, age 110.
• **Last surviving Rough Rider:** Jesse D. Langdon, of Lafayetteville, New York, who died on June 28, 1975, age 94. The Rough Riders were Lieutenant Colonel Theodore Roosevelt's First U.S. Volunteer Cavalry.
• **Last surviving U.S. soldier who was at San Juan Hill:** Ralph Waldo Taylor, who was 16 at the time. He was with the 71st New York Regiment. Taylor died in Florida on May 15, 1987, age 105.
• **Last of the USS *Maine*:** exploded and sank in the harbor of Havana, Cuba, on February 15, 1898; 260 American navy personnel were killed or lost. On March 12, 1914, the USS *Maine* was raised and sunk at sea

with full military honors. Many artifacts from the *Maine* were given to municipalities and organizations throughout the United States. The mainmast and an anchor are at Arlington National Cemetery; the foremast is at the U.S. Naval Academy; a gun is part of a monument in Portland, Maine; and the Union Jack is at Hampton Roads Museum in Virginia. Souvenir items such as key tags and memorial plaques were made of the ship's metal.

• **Last surviving Spanish-American War warship:** The cruiser USS *Olympia,* Admiral George Dewey's flagship at the Battle of Manila Bay. She is moored in the Delaware River in Philadelphia, Pennsylvania, and is part of the Independence Seaport Museum. *Olympia* is the third oldest U.S. naval vessel in existence and one of only two protected cruisers worldwide. The other is Russia's *Aurora. Olympia* is also the Navy's oldest steel ship.

Wars and Battles—Spanish Armada

The Spanish Armada was a fleet launched by Spain's King Philip II against England. It left Lisbon, Portugal, in May 1588 with approximately 130 ships and 30,000 soldiers and crew.

• **Last of the Spanish Armada:** halted on July 29, 1588. More than half of the ships were destroyed off the coast of France by English forces led by Sir Francis Drake and by heavy storms.

Wars and Battles—Spain—Spanish Civil War

The Spanish Civil War was a struggle between the Spanish government, led by General Francisco Franco, and leftist rebels. The war began with a rebellion led by Franco on July 17, 1936, protesting the election of the leftist Popular Front government. The capture of Barcelona and Catalonia in January 1939 marked the beginning of the end of the conflict.

• **End of the Spanish Civil War:** March 29, 1939, when Valencia, the last provincial capital in Spain, surrendered and the nationalists announced the war had ended.

Franco's regime had gained control and was recognized by Great Britain and France. Perhaps as many as 1 million people were killed in the fighting that began in July 1936.

• **Last of Guernica:** destroyed on April 26, 1937, by German bombers sent by Hitler to aid Franco. The devastation of Guernica, a town in northern Spain, shocked the world. Picasso painted his masterpiece *Guernica* two months later to memorialize the loss of the historic town.

Wars and Battles—Spanish Succession, War of the

In 1700, Spain's King Charles II, a Hapsburg, died without descendants, so he named Philip, Duke of Anjou and grandson of France's Louis XIV, as his heir. The duke took the Spanish throne as Philip IV. A coalition of Austria, Denmark, Great Britain, Holland and some of the German states challenged Philip's succession and went to war against France, Spain and Austria in 1701.

• **End of the War of Spanish Succession:** the Peace of Utrecht, which included the Treaty of Rastatt (1714) and the Treaty of Baden (1714), ended the fighting between France and the Holy Roman Empire. The war ended France's hopes of dominating Europe.

Wars and Battles—T'ai-p'ing Rebellion

The T'ai-p'ing Rebellion was a civil war in China. The T'ai-p'ings, led by Hung Hsiu-Ch'uan, tried to overthrow the Manchu dynasty and establish their own dynasty based on a militant form of Christianity. The rebellion began in January 1851 with a formal declaration proclaiming the new dynasty: T'ai-p'ing Tien-kuo (the Kingdom of Heavenly Peace).

• **End of the T'ai-p'ing Rebellion:** June 1864, with the suicide of its leader Hung Hsiu-Ch'uan.

Wars and Battles—Thirty Years' War

The Thirty Years' War was fought mainly in Germany, but it involved several nations and issues. It began in 1618 as a dispute between Protestants in Bohemia and their Catholic rulers. France, the German states, Denmark, and other nations were drawn into the conflict.

• **End of the Thirty Years' War:** October 24, 1648, with the Treaty of Westphalia. Switzerland's independence from the Holy Roman Empire was recognized; Sweden and the German states gained religious and political rights, and France received Hapsburg lands in the Alsace region. The war weakened the power of the Holy Roman Empire and the House of Hapsburg.

Wars and Battles—Triple Alliance, War of the

The War of the Triple Alliance—also known as the Paraguayan War—pitted the combined forces of Brazil, Argentina and Uruguay against Paraguay. Fighting began in late 1864. War was officially declared on May 1, 1865. It was the bloodiest war ever fought in Latin America. Paraguay lost more than 300,000 people (over half of its population) and 55,000 square miles of its territory.

• **End of the War of the Triple Alliance:** March 1, 1870, with the death of Paraguay's leader Francisco Solano López.

Wars and Battles—Tripolitan Wars, see Barbary Wars.

Wars and Battles—Vietnam War

The Vietnam War had its roots in the partitioning of Vietnam in 1954, after the Indochina War. U.S. involvement began in 1961, when American military advisors and support personnel were sent to South Vietnam during the Kennedy administration to help in a guerrilla war against the Viet Cong. On August 2, 1964, the U.S. announced that two American ships were attacked in the Gulf of Tonkin. On August 7th, the Gulf of Tonkin Resolution was passed by Congress. The resolution was the means by which President Lyndon B. Johnson was able to escalate military involvement in the Vietnam War.

• **End of the Battle of Hue:** February 25, 1968. The battle began after the Viet Cong captured the city of Hue on January 31, 1968. On the last day of the battle, the city was recaptured by U.S. and South Vietnamese forces. Known enemy casualties were more than 5,000.

• **End of the Gulf of Tonkin Resolution:** repealed by the U.S. Senate on June 24, 1970. Repeal of the resolution brought about the end of U.S. responsibility to protect South Vietnam.

• **End of the Vietnam War:** January 27, 1973, when a cease-fire was formally signed in Paris, France, by the United States, the Viet Cong and North and South Vietnam.

• **Last U.S. soldier killed before the cease-fire:** Army Lieutenant Colonel William B. Nolde, who died on January 27, 1973.

• **Last troops to leave Vietnam:** March 29, 1973, ending direct military role by the U.S. The troops were the last of 2.5 million Americans who served in Vietnam of whom more than 47,000 were killed in action.

• **Last POWs released in Operation Homecoming:** arrived at Travis Air Force Base, California: April 1, 1973. The last POW to be released was U.S. Army Captain Robert T. White, of Newport News, Virginia. White was captured by guerrilla forces in Vinh Binh Province in November 1969. Altogether, 591 POWs were released between February 12 and April 1, 1973, in Operation Homecoming.

• **End of U.S. aerial bombing of Cambodia:** August 15, 1973, ending its 13-year military involvement in Indochina. The halt came after Congress cut off funds as of that date for any U.S. combat activities in North and South Vietnam, Laos and Cambodia.

• **Last Americans to leave South Vietnam:** April 29-30, 1975, in Operation Frequent Wind, after President Gerald Ford ordered the total U.S. evacuation of South Vietnam. Eighty-one helicopters carried the last 395 Americans and about 4,000 Vietnamese in Saigon to U.S. ships offshore. South Vietnam fell to the Communists a short time later on April 30.

• **Last American service members to leave South Vietnam:** Eleven U.S. Marines who were on the roof of the U.S Embassy in Saigon on April 30, 1975, and boarded the last helicopter during Operation Frequent Wind.

• **Last members of U.S. military to die in the Vietnam War:** Corporal Charles McMahan and Lance Corporal Darwin Judge, two U.S. Marines who were killed in a rocket attack while guarding the Defense Attaché Office at Tan Son Nhut Airfield in Saigon on April 30, 1975.

• **Last Marine helicopter and crew lost in the Vietnam War:** a YT-14 (BuNo 154042) that crashed in the South China Sea near the USS *Hancock* on April 29, 1975, during Operation Frequent Wind, killing Captain William Craig Nystul and First Lieutenant Michael John Shea. Two crew members were rescued.

Wars and Battles—War of 1812

The War of 1812 was the second war between the United States and Great Britain. It was declared June 18, 1812, after a long dispute over the impressment of American soldiers by the British.

• **End of the Battle of Baltimore:** September 14, 1814. The attack on Baltimore began a day earlier. The British bombarded Fort McHenry for 25 hours. Francis Scott Key watched the entire battle. As the attack ended, he jotted down on a letter he had in his pocket the poem that would become the *Star-Spangled Banner.*

• **Last shot of the Battle of Lake Erie:** fired by Stephen Champlin, a naval officer who captured the *Little Belt* on September 13, 1813. He died in Buffalo, New York, on February 20, 1870, age 80.

• **Last battle of the War of 1812:** in New Orleans, Louisiana. It ended on January 8, 1815, when Major General Andrew Jackson defeated British forces led by Major General Sir Edward Pakenham. News had not reached either army that the war had ended two weeks earlier with the signing of the Treaty of Ghent. Pakenham was killed in the attack.

• **Last shots of War of 1812:** fired on June 30, 1815, in the Straits of Sunda, when Captain Lewis Warrington, commanding the

U.S. sloop of war *Peacock,* captured the British brig *Nautilus*.

• **End of the War of 1812:** December 24, 1814, with the Treaty of Ghent, signed in Belgium by Great Britain and the United States. Congress ratified the treaty in February 1815.

• **Last surviving crew member of the USS *Constitution* during the fight with HMS *Guerriere*:** William Dayton Salter. The battle took place on August 19, 1812. Salter commanded the Brooklyn Navy Yard in New York from 1856 to 1859 and was promoted to commodore in 1867. He died at Elizabeth, New Jersey, on January 3, 1869, age 74.

• **Last surviving witness to the *Constitution/Guerriere* battle:** John Adams, a sailor from Boston, Massachusetts. He was captured and confined in Dartmoor Prison in England until the end of the war. Adams died in Allston, Massachusetts, on March 17, 1886, age 89.

• **Last man-of-war engagement in the War of 1812:** the capture of the sloop HMS *Penguin* by the USS *Hornet* on March 23, 1815, in the South Atlantic off Tristan da Cunha. The *Hornet* was commanded by James Biddle. Neither ship was aware the war had ended.

• **Last survivor of those who served in the U.S. Navy in the War of 1812:** Duncan Nathaniel Ingraham. In 1863, during the Civil War, he broke the federal blockade of Charleston, South Carolina. Ingraham died in Charleston on October 16, 1891, age 88.

• **Last surviving War of 1812 veteran:** Hiram Cronk (He shortened his name from Crankheit/Cronkhite.) Cronk served as a drummer at Sackets Harbor, New York. He died on May 13, 1905, age 105, and was buried in Brooklyn, New York. His funeral was documented on film, and he was recognized at that time as the last surviving veteran of the war.

• **Last surviving War of 1812 officer:** Walter Bicker, who died in Far Rockaway, Long Island, New York, on June 3, 1886, age 90,

• **Last surviving War of 1812 widow:**

Carolina King, who died June 28, 1936.
• **Last surviving War of 1812 dependent:** Esther A.H. Morgan, who died on March 12, 1946, age 89.
• **Last U.S. president who was a veteran of the War of 1812:** James Buchanan, who was a volunteer in a Pennsylvania militia cavalry company. He saw service in the Baltimore Campaign during the war. Three other U.S. presidents fought in the War of 1812: Andrew Jackson, William Henry Harrison and John Tyler.

Wars and Battles—War of the Pacific, *see* Wars and Battles—Pacific, War of the.

Wars and Battles—War of the Roses, *see* Wars and Battles—Roses, War of the.

Wars and Battles—War of the Spanish Succession, *see* Wars and Battles—Spanish Succession, War of

Wars and Battles—War of the Triple Alliance, *see* Wars and Battles—Triple Alliance, War of the

Wars and Battles—Whiskey Rebellion
The owners of small stills in western Pennsylvania were angry when the U.S. Congress voted to put an excess tax on whiskey in 1791. They staged a rebellion that began in July 1794. When they burned down the house of the revenue inspector on August 1, President George Washington called out the militia from four states. The army of more than 12,000 quickly put down the rebellion.
• **End of the Whiskey Rebellion:** November 1794. Confronted by a force of more than 12,000 militia, the rebels put down their weapons and agreed to pay the whiskey tax. The leaders were tried and convicted of treason but later pardoned. The federal whiskey tax was repealed in 1801.

Wars and Battles—World War I
World War I was triggered by the June 28, 1914, assassination of Austro-Hungarian Archduke Franz Ferdinand in Sarajevo, capital of Bosnia. Most of the European nations aligned as either Central or Allied powers. Germany supported Austria-Hungary when it declared war on Serbia. France and Russia aligned with Serbia. Later Canada, Australia, New Zealand and the United States joined the conflict. Much of the fighting was in Western Europe, especially France. The war lasted four years.

Wars and Battles—World War I—Aviation—Australia, Canada
• **Last surviving Australian World War I fighter pilot (Australian Flying Corps):** Harold Edwards, who died in Brisbane in 1998, age 102. He was one of the Honor Guard at the burial of Baron Manfred von Richthofen (The Red Baron) in April 1918.
• **Last surviving Canadian World War I fighter pilot from the British Royal Naval Air Service:** Henry Botterell, who was commissioned by the British Royal Naval Air Service in 1917. He served in France and participated in seven dogfights with his Sopwith Camel. Botterell died in Toronto, Canada, on January 3, 2003, age 106.

Wars and Battles—World War I—Aviation—France
The Lafayette Escadrille was a volunteer group of 38 American pilots who flew with the French Air Service prior to U.S. involvement in World War I. The Escadrille came under American control in February 1918, after the U.S. entered the war.
• **Last surviving member of the Lafayette Escadrille:** Charles H. Dolan, who died in Honolulu, Hawaii, on December 31, 1981, age 86.
• **Last surviving ace of the Lafayette Escadrille:** Edwin C. ("Ted") Parsons, who joined the French Air Service in 1916. After World War I, he worked for the FBI and was an aviation advisor for Hollywood films. He also wrote magazine articles about the exploits of the Lafayette Escadrille. During World War II, he was an instructor at Pensacola Naval Air Station and fought in the Solomon Islands campaign. Parsons retired as a rear admiral in the U.S. Navy. He

died in Sarasota, Florida, on May 2, 1968, age 75.

• **Last surviving French World War I fighter ace (French Air Service):** Paul-Louise Weiller, who died in Geneva, Switzerland, on December 20, 1993, age 100.

Wars and Battles—World War I— Aviation—Germany

• **Last surviving German World War I fighter pilot (Imperial German Air Service):** Otto Roosen, who died in Heintsville, Ontario, Canada, on May 27, 1998, age 102.

• **Last German airship raid on Great Britain:** October 19, 1917, when 11 Zeppelins attacked. Five of the German airships were lost. *See also* Aviation—Airships.

• **Last aerial victory of German World War I ace Richthofen:** April 20, 1918, in a Fokker Dr.I Triplane. German aviator Baron Manfred von Richthofen, "The Red Baron," was credited with shooting down 80 aircraft during World War I. The baron's final two adversaries were both flying the Sopwith F-1 Camel.

• **Last airplane hit by Richthofen:** the Sopwith Camel flown by 19-year-old RAF pilot 2nd Lieutenant. D.G. Lewis, who survived the crash. The next day, April 21, Richthofen was killed in action. His plane was not badly damaged when it crashed, but the Australians found him dead in the cockpit. Souvenir hunters hacked apart the aircraft before the British Army Headquarters staff could reach the crash.

• **Last surviving witness to Richthofen's crash:** Eric Abraham, an Australian signaler who was on the ground. Abraham witnessed the shooting down of the Red Baron and asserted that Arthur Roy Brown brought down the plane. Abraham died in Brisbane, Australia, on March 20, 2003, age 104

Wars and Battles—World War I— Aviation—Great Britain

• **Last surviving pilot from the Royal Flying Corps** (RFC): Aviation ace Hubert Williams, a Welsh pilot who joined the RFC in 1915. He flew the legendary Sopworth Camel in combat. Williams died in Cardiff,

Wales, in September 2002, age 106.

Wars and Battles—World War I— Aviation—United States

• **Last surviving U.S. World War I Navy fighter pilot:** Herbert S. Kirk, who died in Bozeman, Montana, on October 3, 2001, age 106.

• **Last surviving U.S. World War I fighter ace:** James William Pearson, who joined the Royal Flying Corps in 1917. He may have shot down 33 enemy aircraft, but received credit for only 12. He was a recipient of the Distinguished Flying Cross. Pearson died in Montclair, New Jersey, on January 26, 1993, age 97. Some sources identify Arthur Raymond ("Ray") Brooks as the last surviving American fighter pilot ace from World War I. He was assigned to the 139th Aero Squadron and the 22nd Aero Squadron in France. Brooks was awarded the Distinguished Service Cross for downing six planes. He died in Summit, New Jersey, on July 17, 1991, age 95.

• **Last surviving U.S. World War I pilot (Army Air Corps):** Lieutenant Colonel John ("Jack") Potts. He was one of the five original Army aviators. Potts served as a flight instructor at Park Field in Tennessee in 1918. He later served in World War II and Korea and officially retired in 1957. Potts died in Florida on August 17, 2002, age 106.

• **Last World War I aerial victory of American ace Eddie Rickenbacker:** October 30, 1918. He brought down a Fokker at St. Juvin and a balloon at Remonville. Rickenbacker was America's top ace with 26 victories (24 planes and 2 balloons). Rickenbacker saw additional military service in World War II. His B-17 left Oahu, Hawaii, on October 21, 1942, then crashed in the Pacific Ocean north of Samoa. Rickenbacker and seven crew members were adrift for 24 days. They were found on November 14th. Rickenbacker died in Zurich, Switzerland, on July 23, 1973, age 82.

Wars and Battles—World War I— Battles

• **End of the Battle of Belleau Wood:** June

26, 1918. Belleau Wood, a forest near Châ-teau-Thierry, France, was the scene of heavy fighting between the German army and the U.S. 4th Marine Division, aided by French troops. The fighting, which began on June 1, 1918, resulted in more than 1,000 U.S. casualties and over 3,600 injured. The Allied victory at Belleau Wood prevented the Germans from advancing to Paris.

• **Last surviving Australian veteran of the Gallipoli campaign:** Alec Campbell of Hobart, Tasmania, who died in Hobart on May 16, 2002, age 103. In 2001, Campbell, Walter Parker and Roy Longmore were pictured as young soldiers on postage stamps issued in the Australian series. The Last Anzacs. Parker was 105 when he died a day after the stamps were issued. Longmore was 107 when he died on June 21, 2001.

• **Last surviving British veteran of the Gallipoli campaign:** Percy Goring, who moved to Bunbury, Western Australia, in 1948. Goring died in Bunbury on July 27, 2001, age 106.

• **Last surviving World War I Royal Welsh Fusilier:** Sergeant William Parkes, who died in San Francisco, California, on October 7, 2002, age 106. The Royal Welsh Fusiliers were formed in 1689 and have continuously served the British Crown and country.

• **End of the Battle of Meuse-Argonne:** November 11, 1918, with the end of the war. The Battle of Meuse-Argonne, an American offensive that began September 26, 1918, was the last major push of the Allied powers to destroy Germany and end the war.

• **Last Canadian soldier killed in World War I:** Private George Price, age 25, who was shot by a sniper in Mons, Belgium, at 10:58 a.m., two minutes before the Armistice was announced on November 11, 1918.

• **Last known surviving Canadian World War I combat veteran:** Clifford Holliday, who served with the Canadian Expeditionary Force in France. He died in Gardena, California, on May 4, 2004, age 105.

• **Last French casualties of World War I:** three French soldiers: Corporals Rene Beaufils and Jean Durocq and machine gun-ner Pierre Seyler, who fell at Dom-le-Mesnil on the Meuse, shortly before the bugles sounded the cease-fire at 11 a.m. on November 11, 1918.

• **Last Irish casualty of World War I:** Private G.E. Ellison, 55th Royal Irish Lancers, who was shot just a few seconds before 11 a.m. on November 11, 1918.

• **Last U.S. casualty of World War I:** U.S. Army Private Henry Gunther of Baltimore, Maryland, who was shot just one minute after the Armistice went into effect on November 11, 1918. Gunther was in Company A, 313th Infantry, 79th Division. As his platoon advanced on Metz near the German border, it ran into an ambush. Gunther charged the German position with fixed bayonet. He was shot at 11:01 a.m., just as a messenger arrived with word that the war was ending at 11 a.m. General John J. Pershing's order of the day named him the last American killed in the war. He received the Distinguished Service Cross posthumously.

• **Last known surviving combat-wounded U.S. veteran of World War I:** Alfred Pugh, who fought with the 77th Infantry Division. He was wounded during the Meusse-Argonne offensive in 1918. He died in Bay Pines, Virginia, on January 7, 2004, age 108.

• **Last surviving witness to the Christmas Truce in the Trenches:** Bertie Felstead, a British soldier. The event occurred on December 25, 1914, when British and German soldiers spontaneously emerged from the trenches near the village of Laventie in northern France on Christmas Day and called their own truce. They exchanged greetings and food and played football. Several hours later, the soldiers were ordered back to their trenches by their officers to continue fighting. Felstead died in England on July 22, 2001, age 106.

• **Last of the World War I Native American Code Talkers:** Solomon Lewis, Choctaw Code Talker who died in 1982 or 1983. The use of Native American Code Talkers began in late October 1918, during the closing days of World War I. Eight Choctaw members of the American Expeditionary

Force were asked by their commander to transmit messages in their native language after it was discovered that the Germans had broken the American radio codes. The Choctaw were successful in baffling the Germans during the last critical campaign of the war: the Battle of Meuse-Argonne.

• **Last successful wartime cavalry charge:** Battle of Beersheba, October 31, 1917, as part of the Palestine campaign, during World War I. The Australian 4th Light Horse Brigade charged at Turkish trenches and captured the wells at Beersheba.

Wars and Battles—World War I—End of the War

• **Last nation to declare war on Germany:** Honduras, on July 19, 1918, less than four months before the Armistice.

• **Last days of World War I:** Kaiser Wilhelm abdicated on November 9, 1918, and fled to the Netherlands. The Armistice was signed in Marshal Ferdinand Foch's railway coach in northern France, near the town of Compiègne at 5 a.m. on November 11th. At 11 a.m., the cease-fire went into effect. The German fleet surrendered to the British on November 21.

• **Official end of World War I:** June 28, 1919, when the Treaty of Versailles was signed. The U.S. Senate failed to muster the needed two-thirds majority needed for ratification, so the United States did not sign the treaty. Opposition centered on creation of a League of Nations. As a consequence of not signing, the U.S. never joined the League of Nations. (*See also* Nations—Germany.)

• **Official end of U.S. World War I hostilities:** occurred at different times with different nations.

Allied Peace treaty with Bulgaria (Treaty of Neuilly): signed November 27, 1919.

U.S. Peace Treaty with Austria: signed August 24, 1921.

U.S. Peace Treaty with Germany: signed August 25, 1921.

U.S. Peace Treaty with Hungary: signed August 29, 1921.

• **Official end of Russian World War I hostilities:** March 3, 1918, with the signing of the Treaty of Brest-Litovsk, ending the state of war with Germany, Austria-Hungary, Bulgaria and Turkey. On November 13, 1918, two days after the Armistice, the Russians officially abrogated the treaty. (*See also* Wars and Battles—Russo-Turkish War.)

• **End of Allied World War I occupation of Germany:** U.S. troops were in Germany until January 1923. British troops were there until December 1929. French and Belgians occupied Germany until June 1930. The Allied occupation of Germany had begun on December 1, 1918.

Wars and Battles—World War I—Ships and Submarines

• **Last World War I U.S. battleship:** the USS *Texas. See* Ships, Naval—Battleships.

• **Last World War I battle cruiser:** USS *Olympia.* (*See* Wars and Battles—Spanish American War—Ships.)

• **Last operational World War I ferry:** *Commander* built in 1917 for service between Rockaway and Brooklyn, New York. In 1918, *Commander* was leased by the U.S. Navy and used at the Brooklyn Navy Yard. From 1919 to 1981, *Commander* was operated by the Rockaway Boat Line. After that, the ferry was purchased by Hudson Highlands Cruises and Tours, Inc. and since then has been used as an excursion boat in the Hudson Highlands. *Commander* is listed on the National Register of Historic Places and the International Register of Historic Ships.

• **Last German U-boats sunk by enemy action in World War I:** U-116, sunk by a mine in the North Sea on October 28, 1918. Also, the U-34, shelled and destroyed by HMS *Privet* on November 9, 1918.

• **Last German U-boat to sink a ship in World War I:** The U-139, under the command of Lothar von Arnauld de la Periere, on October 1, 1918. The U-139 sank a ship in a British convoy crossing the Bay of Biscay.

• **Last of the German World War I fleet:** On November 21, 1918, the German High Seas Fleet surrendered its warships to the Allies. On June 21, 1919, the German crews scuttled most of the fleet at Scapa Flow, a bay in the southern part of the Orkney Irelands, near Scotland. The ships included 5 battle cruisers, 11 battleships, 8 cruisers, and 50 destroyers. The last ship scuttled at Scapa Flow was the SMS *Hindenburg* at 5 p.m. on June 21, 1919.

Wars and Battles—World War I— United States—Agencies—War Finance Corporation

The War Finance Corporation was established by Congress on April 5, 1918, to provide a source of credit for industries that were converting to war production. It was expanded after the war to aid agriculture.

• **Last of the War Finance Corporation:** abolished December 31, 1939.

Wars and Battles—World War I— United States—Agencies—War Industries Board

The War Industries Board was established by Congress in 1917 to coordinate U.S. industries in making goods for the war effort.

• **Last of the War Industries Board:** abolished on January 1, 1919, after World War I ended.

Wars and Battles—World War I— United States—Veterans

• **Last surviving World War I Congressional Medal of Honor recipient:** Thomas A. Pope. He earned the Medal of Honor while serving with Company E, 131st Infantry, 33rd Division, American Expeditionary Forces (AEF) at Hamel, France, on July 4, 1918, when he charged an enemy machine-gun nest. He was also the Army's first Medal of Honor winner in France. Pope died June 14, 1989, age 94.

• **Last U.S. president who was a veteran of World War I:** Dwight David Eisenhower. Harry S. Truman also served in World War I.

Wars and Battles—World War II

World War II began when Nazi Germany invaded Poland in September 1939, and Great Britain and France declared war on the Nazis. Germany next conquered Norway, Denmark, Holland, Belgium and Luxembourg. Italy and Japan joined the Germans, forming the Axis powers. After Germany invaded Russia in June 1941, the Soviet Union joined the fight. Britain, France, the USSR and the other nations that opposed Germany were known as the Allied powers. In December 1941, when the Japanese bombed Pearl Harbor in Hawaii, the United States became involved in the war as one of the Allied powers. World War II was fought mainly on two fronts: Europe and the Pacific. The European war ended in May 1945. The Pacific war ended in August 1945.

Wars and Battles—World War II— Austria—Anschluss

Anschluss—which means a *junction* or *connection* in German—is the term used to describe Germany's takeover of Austria in March 1938. On March 12, the Austrian government proclaimed a political and geographic union with Germany. It was later ratified by popular vote of the Austrian people.

• **End of the Anschluss:** May 1945, with Germany's defeat at the end of World War II.

• **End of the World War II occupation of Austria:** May 15, 1955, when Austria regained its sovereignty with ratification of the State Treaty of 1955. At that time, Austria's occupation by the four major Allied powers (France, U.S., Great Britain and the USSR) ended. National Day, October 26, commemorates when the last World War II troops left Austria.

Wars and Battles—World War II— Aviation—Europe

• **Last wartime acts of aerial resistance in Nazi-occupied Poland:** flown during the Battle of Kock on October 4, 1939. Two RWD8 parasol communication and liaison aircraft dropped hand grenades on the Nazis.

• **Last aircraft taken down by a biplane in Europe in World War II:** shot down near the village of Radvan in Slovakia on September 2, 1944. A Hungarian-flown Ju 52/3m was shot down by an Avia B.534 biplane piloted by Warrant Officer Frantisek Cyprich of the Slovak National Uprising.

• **Last World War II combat sortie in Europe:** flown by 124 Douglas A-26 Invaders on May 3, 1945. During the war in Europe, A-26s flew a total of 11,567 sorties.

• **Last World War II victory of the top German ace:** The Luftwaffe's Major Erich Hartmann, the top-scoring ace of all-time, flew 1,425 missions. He scored his 352nd and last victory on May 8, 1945, the last day of the war, when he shot down a Soviet fighter over Czechoslovakia. Hartmann surrendered to the British and was turned over to the Russians, who sentenced him to 10 years in a hard labor camp. He was released in 1955. Hartmann saw his last military service when he rejoined the new West German Air Force in 1959. He died in Stuttgart on September 19, 1993, age 71.

• **Last major Luftwaffe World War II action:** January 1, 1945, when the Luftwaffe flew 800 sorties against Allied airfields in France, Belgium and Holland and destroyed more than 300 Allied aircraft. The Luftwaffe lost 200 planes. The Luftwaffe, Germany's air force, had been built secretly after World War I in violation of the Treaty of Versailles.

• **Last of the Nazi Luftwaffe:** From April 5 to April 19, 1945, Allied air forces destroyed German planes on the ground and in the air and just about wiped out the Luftwaffe.

Wars and Battles—World War II— Aviation—Japan

• **Last surviving U.S. airplane involved in the Japanese attack on Pearl Harbor:** a Curtiss P-40B Tomahawk. The plane was at Wheeler Field during the attack. It was lost in January 1942 while on a training mission. In 1985, the plane was recovered and is the focus of Project Tomahawk, a restoration project in Torrance, California.

• **Last World War II B-29 sortie in Japan:** August 15, 1945, on Nippon Oil Company at Tsuchizakiminato. It was the last of 29,155 B-29 sorties. The plane returned to the Marianas Islands shortly after the formal announcement that the Japanese accepted the peace terms.

• **Last Japanese airplane shot down during World War II:** at 5:40 a.m. on August 15, 1945. U.S. Navy Lieutenant Commander T.H. Reidy, flying a Vought F4U, shot down a Nakajima C6N Saiun "Myrt" reconnaissance aircraft five minutes before the war was officially over. The last surviving Nakajima C6N1-S Saiun "Myrt" is in the Smithsonian Institution's National Air and Space Museum.

Wars and Battles—World War II— Aviation—United States

• **Last surviving AT-6 flown by the Tuskegee Airmen:** the "Double Vee," owned by Captain Steven Cowell. He restored the aircraft after he purchased it in 1997. The plane was built in 1943 and was at the Tuskegee Army Airfield in June 1946, when the base closed.

• **Last World War II victory of the top U.S. ace:** The top-scoring United States ace in Europe during World War II was Lieutenant Colonel Francis S. ("Gabby") Gabreski, who served with the 56th Fighter Group of the U.S. Army Air Force in England. He scored his 28th and last victory on July 5, 1944. A short time later, he was taken prisoner and was held in a stalag for 10 months. Gabreski later served in Korea, where he shot down 6.5 MIGs in aerial combat. His last military service ended in November 1967, when he retired as a colonel. He died in Dix Hills, New York, on January 21, 2002, age 83.

Wars and Battles—World War II— Battles—Alamein, El

Two major battles were fought near El Alamein in Egypt. They were waged by a German-Italian army led by German Field Marshal Erwin Rommel and the British 8th Army commanded by General Bernard Montgomery. The first battle began on July 1, 1942.

• **End of the first battle of El Alamein:**

July 27, 1942, after 27 days. The British Army was able to prevent the Germans and Italians from advancing. The second battle of El Alamein began October 23, 1942. Rommel began his retreat from El Alamein on November 4, 1942.

• **End of the second battle of El Alamein:** finished by November 6, 1942, when the Germans were in full retreat and more than 30,000 troops surrendered. The Allied victory saved the Suez Canal from being captured, and it prepared the way for an Allied invasion of North Africa.

• **Last of the Afrika Korps:** halted at El Alamein in Egypt and finally surrendered in May 1943. (The Afrika Korps, a specially trained German tank force, was formed in February 1941 and was commanded by Rommel during much of the African campaign.)

Wars and Battles—World War II—Battles—Bataan Death March

The Bataan Death March was the greatest mass surrender of American military forces in U.S. history. It began with the fall of Bataan on the Philippine Islands on April 9, 1942, when as many as 70,000 U.S. and Filipino soldiers surrendered to the Japanese. The death march began on April 10, 1942. Tens of thousands of the captives died when they were forced to march more than 60 miles to Camp O'Donnell, a concentration camp at San Fernando in Pampanga Province.

• **Last day of the Bataan Death March:** The march took six days. POWs arrived at Camp O'Donnell every day until April 24, 1942. By the end of the war, more than a third of the U.S. POWs who survived the march had either died of disease or starvation or had been killed by the Japanese.

• **End of detention of the Bataan Death March captives:** April 1945, during the liberation of the Philippines by U.S. forces led by General Douglas MacArthur. Japanese Lieutenant General Masaharu Homma, who ordered the Bataan Death March was tried for war crimes in Manila and executed on April 3, 1946.

Wars and Battles—World War II—Battles—Britain

The Battle of Britain was a series of air attacks waged by Germany against Great Britain in 1940. The Germans began bombing Royal Air Force (RAF) installations, aircraft factories and other strategic sites as a prologue to invading Great Britain. Unable to destroy the RAF, the Germans switched to bombing London. The RAF repelled the Germans, and Germany gave up its plan to invade England.

• **End of the Battle of Britain:** October, 31, 1940. The last attacks were over London and Kent. (The German air raids on Britain began on July 10, 1940, with attacks on Falmouth and Swansea and on a convoy in the English Channel.)

Wars and Battles—World War II—Battles—Bulge

The Battle of the Bulge was the last German counteroffensive of World War II. It was also the most heavily pitched battle of the war between the U.S. and Germany. It took place in the Ardennes region of Belgium and Luxembourg. The battle began in early December 1944, with a counterattack by 15 German divisions under General Karl von Rundstedt.

• **End of the Battle of the Bulge:** the last days of January 1945. (Dates for the end of the battle range from January 21 to 28.) Hitler had delayed the Allied invasion of Germany with the Battle of the Bulge, but he paid for it by using his last military reserves. Six weeks later, the Allies crossed into Germany.

Wars and Battles—World War II—Battles—Coral Sea

The Battle of the Coral Sea, which began on May 4, 1942, was the first Allied naval success in the Pacific. It prevented the Japanese from capturing Port Moresby, New Guinea, and ended Japan's hopes of invading Australia. The battle was the first naval engagement where all the fighting was done in the air by planes, not in the water by ships.

• **End of the Battle of the Coral Sea:** May 7, 1942.

Wars and Battles—World War II—Battles—Dunkirk

Dunkirk is a seaport on the Strait of Dover in France, near the Belgian border. About 400,000 British and French troops were trapped there when the city was surrounded by German forces on May 27, 1940. During the evacuation of Dunkirk, known as Operation Dynamo, about 350,000 of the troops were transported across the strait to England by a flotilla of small and large pleasure boats, yachts and fishing boats.

• **End of the Dunkirk evacuation:** June 4, 1940. About 85 percent of Dunkirk was later destroyed during the war.

• **Last person to leave Dunkirk:** Harold Rupert Leofric George Alexander, 1st Earl Alexander of Tunis, who directed the retreat effort. During World War II, he was a British field marshal and a commander in France, Burma (now Myanmar), North Africa and the Mediterranean. After the war, he was governor general of Canada (1946-52) and UK minister of defense (1952-54). He died on July 16, 1969, age 77.

Wars and Battles—World War II—Battles—Guadalcanal

Guadalcanal is one of the Solomon Islands in the Pacific Ocean. The battle began in August 1942 when the United States seized Henderson Field from the Japanese. A major sea battle took place off Guadalcanal from November 12 to 15, 1942. The final offensive on Guadalcanal began on January 15, 1943.

• **End of the Battle of Guadalcanal:** The Japanese began evacuating the island on February 3rd and were gone by February 7th. More than 1,600 Americans and 25,000 Japanese were killed in the battle. The capture of Guadalcanal is considered a turning point in the Pacific war in that it allowed the Allies to gain supremacy.

Wars and Battles—World War II—Battles—Iwo Jima

Iwo Jima, a volcanic island in the Pacific 600 miles southeast of Japan, was the location of one of the most famous war photographs of all time. On February 23, 1945, two flags were raised at Mount Suribachi. The second flag, put up hours after the first flag raising, was larger and became more famous because of the Pulitzer prize-winning photograph by Joe Rosenthal. Twelve Marines were involved in raising the two flags.

• **Last survivor of the men involved in the first flag raising:** Corporal Charles W. Lindberg.

• **Last survivor of the six Marines involved in the second raising:** Navy Corpsman John ("Doc") Bradley, who died in Wisconsin on January 11, 1994, age 70.

Wars and Battles—World War II—Battles—Leyte Gulf

Leyte is an island in the central Philippines. The Japanese occupied the region in 1942. The Battle of Leyte Gulf was the greatest naval battle of World War II and is considered the last great battleship engagement of all time. It began on October 23, 1944.

• **End of the Battle of Leyte Gulf:** October 26, 1944. The battle marked the end of the effectiveness of the Japanese navy and enabled U.S. forces to recapture the Philippines.

Wars and Battles—World War II—Battles—Midway

After U.S. military intelligence broke the Japanese secret code, the U.S. learned that the Japanese Navy was planning to occupy the island of Midway and destroy U.S. naval strength in the region. The battle to secure Midway began on June 4, 1942

• **End of the Battle of Midway:** June 7, 1942. Despite the loss of the USS *Yorktown,* the battle was a victory for the U.S. against the Japanese. It marked the end of the Japanese offensive in the Pacific.

• **Last survivors of Midway to be recovered:** Machinist A. Walter Winchell and his gunner Douglas M. Cossitt who were flying a USS *Enterprise* TBD (torpedo bomber). They were forced to ditch their plane when it ran out of fuel. After spending 17 days on a raft, Winchell and Cossitt were picked up

360 miles north of Midway on June 21, 1942.

Wars and Battles—World War II—Battles—Philippines

The Japanese invaded the Philippines in December 1941. In March 1942, U.S. troops commanded by General Douglas MacArthur were forced to leave the islands. MacArthur's departure took on special significance to the Philippine people when he pledged "I shall return."

• **End of the Japanese occupation of the Philippines:** General Douglas MacArthur invaded the Philippines in January 1945. Japanese troops in Manila were defeated in February. MacArthur announced on July 4, 1945, that the Philippines had been liberated from the Japanese.

Wars and Battles—World War II—Battles—Sandakan Death March

The Sandakan (or Borneo) Death March was Australia's worst military tragedy and the worst atrocity ever suffered by Australian soldiers. Of the 2,400 British and Australian prisoners held in Sandakan, Malaya, by the Japanese between 1942 and 1945, only six Australians made it out alive. There were no British survivors.

• **Last survivor of the Sandakan Death March:** Owen Campbell who had been taken prisoner when Singapore fell to the Japanese in February 1942. He was rescued on July 24, 1945. Campbell died in Adelaide, Australia, on July 3, 2003, age 87.

Wars and Battles—World War II—Battles—Wake Island

Wake Island is a small atoll in the Pacific Ocean between Hawaii and Guam. On December 23, 1941, the Japanese seized the island after a fierce 16-day battle with the U.S. Marines.

• **Last American off Wake Island in 1941:** Colonel Walter Bayler, who later was the first American to return to Wake Island in September 1945. His story is told in his book *Last Man Off Wake Island.*

Wars and Battles—World War II—Conferences
Last Date of Some of the Major Wartime Conferences

Name of Conference, Code Name and Location and Beginning Date	Purpose	Last Day of the Conference
Cairo (Sextant) Egypt November 22, 1943	Allied leaders U.S. President Franklin D. Roosevelt, British Prime Minister Winston Churchill and Nationalist Chinese General Chiang Kai-shek discussed war policy in Asia. They agreed on the purpose of the war: to strip Japan of the land claimed in the Pacific since World War II and the land taken from China.	November 26, 1943. Afterward, Roosevelt and Churchill went to Teheran to participate in a wartime conference with Stalin.
Casablanca Morocco January 14, 1943	British Prime Minister Churchill and U.S. President Franklin D. Roosevelt agreed on the invasion of Sicily and on an unconditional-surrender goal.	January 24, 1943
Potsdam (Terminal) Germany July 17, 1945	The last of the World War II conferences. U.S. President Harry S Truman, British Prime Minister Clement Atlee, Soviet Premier Josef Stalin, and former British Prime Minister Winston Churchill formulated the	August 2, 1945

	Potsdam Declaration outlining the terms under which Japan would be allowed to surrender. They agreed on postwar settlement in Germany and the division of Berlin into four occupation zones.	
Quebec (I) (Quadrant) Canada August 11, 1943	U.S. President Franklin D. Roosevelt, British Prime Minister Winston Churchill, Canadian Prime Minister W. L. Mackenzie King and Chinese Foreign Minister T.V. Soong discussed war planning and the creation of a far eastern theater of operations.	August 24, 1943
Quebec (II) (Octagon) Canada September 11, 1944	U.S. President Franklin D. Roosevelt, British Prime Minister Winston Churchill and their military advisors discussed the strategy for completing the war in Europe and for conducting the war in the Pacific.	September 16, 1944
Teheran Iran November 28, 1943	U.S. President Franklin D. Roosevelt, British Prime Minister Winston Churchill and Soviet Premier Josef Stalin discussed plans for the conquest of Germany. A few days before the conference, Roosevelt and Churchill met in Cairo.	December 2, 1943
Washington, D.C. (Arcadia) December 22, 1941	U.S. President Franklin D. Roosevelt and British Prime Minister Winston Churchill agreed to follow Churchill's "Europe first" strategy for fighting the war.	January 14, 1942
Washington, D.C. (Trident) May 11, 1943	U.S. President Franklin D. Roosevelt and British Prime Minister Winston Churchill discussed the invasion of Europe.	May 25, 1943
Yalta (Argonaut) Crimea, Ukrainian SSR, USSR February 4, 1945	U.S. President Franklin D. Roosevelt, British Prime Minister Winston Churchill and Soviet Premier Josef Stalin discussed the occupation and control of Germany.	February 11, 1945

Wars and Battles—World War II—Czechoslovakia—Lidice

The original village of Lidice was about 11 miles northwest of Prague, Czechoslovakia. It was destroyed during World War II.

• **Last of the original Czech village of Lidice:** eradicated by the Germans on June 10, 1942, in retaliation for the assassination of Reinhard Heydrich by the Czech underground. The SS shot 173 men and transported 196 women to Ravensbrück concentration camp. The village was then burned, dynamited and destroyed until every trace of it had been annihilated. In July 1942, the town of Stern Park Gardens near Joliet, Illinois, was renamed Lidice in memory of the Czech town. And in August, the Mexican village of San Geronimo-Aculdo was renamed for Lidice. The name Lidice also appeared in other nations and places, including parks, streets and even as the name of children. In Czechoslovakia, the land where the original village once stood is now a valley with trees and fields. Nearby is the postwar village of Lidice.

• **Last of Karl Hermann Frank:** Frank, who ordered the massacre and destruction of Lidice, was convicted of war crimes. He was publicly hanged in Prague on May 12, 1946.

Wars and Battles—World War II—End of the War in Europe

• **End of hostilities in Europe:** Berlin fell to the Russians on May 2, 1945. On the same day, an estimated 1 million German and Italian soldiers surrendered to U.S. General Mark Clark in northern Italy. On May 4, 1945, another 1 million men who made up the German army in Denmark, Holland and northeastern Germany also surrendered. On May 5, 1945, German troops in Austria were ordered to surrender. Admiral Karl Doenitz sent two emissaries—German Chief of Staff General Alfred Jodl and Admiral Hans-Georg von Friedeburg—to General Dwight D. Eisenhower's headquarters in Rheims, France.

• **Last shot fired in the European Theater of Operations in World War II:** fired at a German sniper before midnight on May 7, 1945, by Private First Class Domenic Mozzetto of Company B, 387th Infantry Regiment, 97th Division, U.S. Army, near Klenovice, Czechoslovakia.

• **End of the European phase of World War II (official):** Germany surrendered unconditionally to the Western Allies and the USSR on May 7, 1945, at 2:41 a.m. French time. (In the U.S., it was 8:41 p.m., May 6, Eastern War Time.) The signing took place in Rheims, France, at a schoolhouse being used as U.S. General Dwight D. Eisenhower's headquarters. The capitulation document was signed for the German High Command by Alfred Jodl and Hans-Georg von Friedeburg, and for the Supreme Allied Command by Lieutenant General Walter Bedell Smith, Eisenhower's Chief of Staff. It was signed for the USSR by General Ivan Susloparov and for France by General Francois Sevez. The following day, May 8, German Field Marshal Wilhelm Keitel, General Hans Stumpff and Admiral von Friedeburg met in Berlin in the presence of Soviet Marshal Georgi Zhukov to sign a similar document. Although the cease-fire order was given on May 8, they did not actually sign the document until a minute after midnight on May 9. Americans and the British were informed by radio simultaneously on May 8 that the war had ended. V-E (Victory in Europe) Day is celebrated on May 8. Officially, however, the war in Europe ended at 12:01 a.m., May 9, 1945.

• **Official end of the U.S. state of war with Germany:** October 19, 1951, by a Joint Resolution of the U.S. Congress.

• **End of the Allied military occupation of Western Germany:** May 5, 1955. After earlier conferences in London and Paris, the Paris Agreements were signed on October, 23, 1954. The agreements allowed the Allies to make provisions to terminate the military occupation of the Federal Republic of Germany (Western Germany) and restore its sovereignty as of May 1955.

• **End of World War II Soviet military occupation in East Germany:** September 21, 1955.

Wars and Battles—World War II—France

• **End of the Third Republic:** 1940. It collapsed with the fall of France during World War II.

• **Last president of the Third Republic:** Albert Lebrun, who served from 1932 to 1940. He died in Paris, France, on March 6, 1950, age 79.

• **Last act of the Third Republic:** met in Vichy on July 9, 1940, and voted itself out of existence. France then came under control of the Vichy government. This step was the result of the Germans having invaded France in May 1940 in the early days of World War II. An armistice was signed between the two nations on June 22nd.

• **Last Vichy regime president:** Henri Philippe Pétain, who was 84 when he became chief of state of the Vichy government in 1940. He was the first, last and only person to hold that position. The Vichy regime ended in 1944 when France was liberated. Pétain died on Ile d'Yeu off the coast of Brittany on July 23, 1951, age 95.

• **End of Vichy government relations with the U.S.:** November 8, 1942. It was the first time since 1778 that relations between the two countries had been interrupted.

• **Last surviving minister of the Vichy government:** Francois Lehideux, a French automobile businessman and politician who served as Minister of Industrial Production. He died in Paris, France, in June 1998, age 95.

• **Last surviving French World War II marshal:** Marshal Alphonse-Pierre Juin, who joined the Allies in 1942 after they landed in North Africa. Juin held the positions of Chief of the General Staff, Resident General in Morocco, Inspector General of the Armed Forces, and Commander-in-Chief of NATO's Central European Command. He died in Paris, France, on January 27, 1967, age 78.

• **Last American journalist to broadcast from Paris in 1940 before the German occupation:** Larry Lesueur, on June 10, 1940. He was later the first American to broadcast from a liberated Paris on August 25, 1944.

• **End of the World War II German occupation of Paris:** August 25, 1944, when the city was liberated by Allied forces. (The German occupation of Paris began on June 14, 1940.)

Wars and Battles—World War II—
Battles—Germany

• **Last surviving member of the 1933 Reichstag who voted against the transfer of power to Hitler:** Josef Felder. He was one of 94 legislators who voted in March 1933 not to cede the Reichstag's powers to Adolf Hitler's cabinet. Felder ended up spending a year in the Dachau concentration camp. He died in Munich, Germany, on October 28, 2000, age 100.

• **End of the Siegfried Line's impenetrability:** September 15, 1944, when American troops broke through the line near Aachen, Germany. On October 21, Aachen became the first German city to fall to the Allies. (The Siegfried Line was Germany's heavily fortified line of defense along the Belgium-Dutch-German border that the Germans believed could never be penetrated.)

• **Last bridge standing across the Rhine River:** Ludendorff Bridge over the Rhine at Remagen. In the final months of World War II, the Germans set out to destroy every bridge across the Rhine to prevent the invasion of Allied troops into their homeland. On March 7, 1945, U.S. Army advanced patrols found the Ludendorff Bridge still standing. The Germans were planning to detonate the bridge within 10 minutes. The Allies captured the bridge and used it for the next several days to allow Allied forces to pour into Germany. On March 17, the bridge collapsed from continued bombardment by German shells and artillery blasts, but by then, it had served its purpose. The last standing bridge at Remagen allowed the Allies to cross the Rhine, thus shattering German morale and shortening the war.

• **Last public appearance of Hitler:** March 20, 1945, to present awards to children who had shown bravery under Russian fire. The event was filmed in the last newsreel produced by Goebbels.

• **Last will of Hitler:** dictated on April 29, 1945, to his secretary Traudl Junge. He specified who was to be his executor, who was to receive his possessions and what was to be done with his body. Junge was later captured by Allied forces but was not tried for war crimes. She died in Munich, Germany, on February 10, 2002, age 81. Her story has been told in the book *Until the Final Hour: Hitler's Last Secretary* (2003).

• **Last surviving courier of Hitler:** Armin Dieter Lehrmann, who was in the Berlin bunker with Hitler during the führer's final days. Lehmann described his experience in the book *Hitler's Last Courier* (2001).

• **Last person to see Adolf Hitler and Eva Braun alive:** probably Artur Axmann, a German Nazi administrator and leader of the Hitler Youth. Axmann was captured by the Allies later in 1945 and imprisoned. In 1949, he was sentenced to 39 months in prison but released on time served. Hitler's death was confirmed in October 1955 by his valet Heinz Linge, who helped burn the body. A Soviet autopsy in 1968 disclosed 23 years after the event that Hitler took cyanide poison instead of shooting himself as hitherto believed. The report also revealed the badly charred bodies of Adolf Hitler and Eva Braun were found in a shell crater near his Berlin bunker.

• **Last radio broadcast of Axis Sally:** May 6, 1945. Axis Sally (Mildred Elizabeth Sisk Gillars) was an American who broadcasted pro-German propaganda radio programs to Allied troops from Berlin, beginning in December 1941. After the war, she was brought back to the U.S. and tried for treason: one of her broadcasts had threatened to jeopardize the invasion of Europe. She served time in prison and was released in 1961. Gillars died in Ohio on June 25, 1988, age 87.

• **Last radio broadcast of Lord Haw Haw:** April 30, 1945. Lord Haw Haw was American-born William Joyce who broadcasted pro-Nazi radio programs in Germany from 1939 to 1945. After the war, he was tried and found guilty of treason. He was hanged in London, England, on January 3, 1946, age 39. Lord Haw Haw was parodied by Mel Blanc in a 1943 American Loony Tunes cartoon as Lord Hee Haw, a donkey.

• **End of Nazi-controlled Germany and the Third Reich:** May 1945, when World War II ended with the defeat of Germany. With his armies in ruins and Russian forces descending on central Berlin, Adolf Hitler killed himself in Berlin, on April 30, 1945, age 56. Newly appointed Chancellor of Germany, Dr. Paul Joseph Goebbels killed himself on May 1, 1945, age 47.

• **Last führer:** Admiral Karl Doenitz (Dönitz) chief of the German navy. On April 29, 1945, the day before Hitler killed himself, he appointed Doenitz to be the new führer, or leader, of the Third Reich and Supreme Commander of the Armed Forces. Doenitz announced Hitler's death on May 1, 1945, and declared Hitler had designated him his successor. Doenitz held the post of führer until May 7, 1945, the day the Germans surrendered unconditionally. He died in Hamburg, West Germany, on December 24, 1980, age 89.

• **Last official seat of government and capital of World War II Germany:** Flensburg in northern Schleswig-Holstein, near the Danish border. After Hitler's suicide on April 30, 1945, Doenitz used the schoolhouse at Flensburg-Muerwik while he arranged the capitulation of German forces.

• **Last German forces in East Prussia and Pomerania surrendered to the Soviet Army:** May 9, 1945.

• **End of the Third Reich:** officially dissolved by the Allies on May 23, 1945, when Karl Doenitz and about 300 officers and civilian officials were taken into custody at Flensburg, in northern Germany. Doenitz was arrested and tried at Nuremberg.

• **Last of the Gestapo:** dissolved after the unconditional surrender of Germany in May 1945. At the Nuremberg Trials in 1946, the Gestapo was declared a criminal organization and charged with war crimes. (Gestapo is an acronym for Geheime Staatspolizei, the secret state police organization founded by Hermann Goering.)

Wars and Battles—World War II— Great Britain

• **End of the German occupation of the Channel Islands:** May 9, 1945, the day after the war ended in Europe. The Channel Islands were the only British territory to be occupied by the Germans during World War II. The Germans arrived on June 30, 1940, and occupied the islands nearly five years. During that time, 2,000 British subjects were shipped to Germany.

• **Last of the Cockleshell Heroes:** Corporal Bill Sparks, who died near Lewes, England, on November 30, 2003, age 80. The Cockleshell Heroes were 10 British Royal Marines who paddled 85 miles in kayaks to attack Hitler's merchant navy on the Gironde River at Bordeaux, France, in December 1942, as part of Operation Frankton. Only two of the men survived the attack: Sparks and Major Blondie Hasler.

• **End of British wartime rationing:** Clothing rationing ended on March 15, 1949. Sugar rationing ended on September 26, 1953. Meat and all food rationing ended on July 3, 1954. (Wartime rationing began

in Great Britain on January 8, 1940.)
• **Last V-2 to hit England:** 4:54 p.m., March 27, 1945. The last V-2 landed at Orpington, Kent. In all, 1,050 V-2s were targeted at England. More than 2,700 people were killed and 6,500 were seriously injured. (The V-2s—jet-propelled rockets—were used for the first time in September 1944. They were much more dangerous than their predecessors the V-1 buzz bombs in that they could not be heard and intercepted before they reached their target.)

Wars and Battles—World War II—Holocaust
The Holocaust is the term used to describe the systematic persecution, enslavement and extermination of Jews instigated by Adolf Hitler before and during World War II. As soon as Hitler was made chancellor of Germany in 1933, he began to implement his plan of ridding the nation of all the Jews by disenfranchising them and prohibiting Germans from having any business or social contact with them. Kristallnacht marked the first tangible attempt at annihilation, when Jewish-owned stores, homes and synagogues were looted and burned. Beginning in 1939, Jews were rounded up and shipped to labor camps. The massive exterminations known as the Final Solution started in 1942, when the Germans began gassing the Jews then burning their bodies in ovens in some of the concentration camps. The Holocaust caused the death of an estimated 6 million Jews.
• **End of Jewish citizenship under Nazi rule:** September 15, 1935. The ghettos were revived and the swastika became the German national flag.
• **End of Kristallnacht:** November 10, 1938. It began a day earlier. On November 9, 1938, German mobs began smashing the shop windows and houses of Jews all over Germany. They looted property and burned synagogues. For Germany's Jews, Kristallnacht symbolized the beginning of the end for them in Nazi Germany.
• **Last time Jewish students were permitted in Nazi German schools:** November 13, 1938. They were expelled the following day.

Wars and Battles—World War II—Holocaust
Last of Some of the German Concentration Camps

The German-run concentration camps were places of confinement for people whom the Nazis viewed as undesirable. They including Jews, Gypsies, Jehovah's Witnesses, homosexuals, political dissidents, the mentally ill, people with physical disabilities, prostitutes and habitual criminals. Hitler's storm troopers, the Sturm Abteilung (SA), established the camps soon after the Nazis rose to power. At first, the camps were prisons and labor camps. As the war progressed, some of them became places of execution. Millions were gassed at extermination camps in Bergen-Belsen, Sobibor, Auschwitz, Treblinka, Chelmno and elsewhere.

Auschwitz-Birkenau (near Krakow, Poland)
Opened 1941. Largest of the extermination camps. Estimates of the number of people murdered there range from 1 million to 2.5 million.
• **Last use of gas chambers at Auschwitz:** October 30, 1944.
• **Last of the crematoria:** Himmler ordered the demolition of the crematoria in November 1944. The last crematorium was destroyed the day before the camp was liberated in January 1945.
• **End of Nazi German control:** liberated January 27, 1945, by the Soviet Army. The camp was designated a memorial in 1946 and the Auschwitz-Birkenau State Museum opened in 1947.
• **Last surviving Auschwitz doctor:** Hans Muench, who was the only one of 40 defen-

---

dants cleared of charges during a war crimes trial in Krakow, Poland, in 1947. In 1998, prosecutors in Munich began investigating statements he made in an interview that appeared in *Der Spiegel*, a German news magazine. Prosecutors in Frankfurt also reopened multiple investigations into the wartime actions of Muench, who is alleged to have infected prisoners with malaria. The investigations against him were dropped when a medical examiner determined he was unfit to stand trial for murder. He was 88 and suffering from Alzheimer's disease.
• **Last surviving commander of the Soviet divisions that liberated Auschwitz:** General Vasily Petrenko, who died in Moscow, Russia, on March 2, 2003, age 91. Petrenko, a military historian, wrote about the liberation of the death camp in his memoirs.

Belzec (47 miles north of Lvov, Poland)
Opened April 1940 as a labor camp. Extermination camp began operating in March 1942. An estimated 600,000 people were killed there. Most were Jews. Some were Gypsies.
• **Last of Belzec:** liquidated by the Nazis in December 1942. The prisoners were transferred to Sobibor. The Germans tried to destroy evidence of the deaths by exhuming bodies from mass graves and cremating them.

Bergen-Belsen (between the villages of Bergen and Belsen in western Germany)
Opened in 1940 as a prisoner-of-war camp. Converted to a concentration camp in April 1943. Anne Frank died of typhus at Bergen-Belsen in March 1945.
• **End of Nazi German control of Bergen-Belsen:** liberated April 15, 1945, by the British army. British troops found 10,000 unburied corpses. They also found 40,000 inmates dying of tuberculosis, typhus and starvation. After the prisoners were freed, 28,000 died of malnutrition, disease and the consequences of torture. Among those responsible was camp commandant Josef Kramer, known as the Beast of Belsen. He was arrested the day the camp was liberated.
• **Last of camp commandant Josef Kramer:** On September 17, 1945, Kramer and 44 members of the SS (Schutzstaffel) went on trial in a British military court at Lüneberg, Germany, charged with conspiracy to commit mass murder in the camps at Bergen-Belsen and Auschwitz. Kramer and 10 others were convicted and hanged in Hameln, Germany, on December 14, 1945.

Buchenwald (Weimar, east-central Germany)
Opened July 1937. One of the largest German concentration camps. During its seven years and nine months of operation, Buchenwald operated many subcamps (estimates range from 87 and 174).
• **End of Nazi German control of Buchenwald:** evacuated by the Germans on April 6, 1945; liberated April 11, 1945, by U.S. forces who freed 21,000 inmates. On April 16, U.S. troops took about 2,000 German civilians from nearby Weimar to the camp so they could see how the inmates had been forced to live and die under Nazi rule. Dora-Mittelbau, near Nordhausen Germany, was a subcamp of Buchenwald. It opened in August 1943 and served as a concentration camp beginning in October 1944.
• **End of Nazi German control of Dora-Mittelbau:** evacuated by the Germans on April 1, 1945; liberated April 9, 1945.

Chelmno (Poland)
Opened December 7, 1941. Extermination camp where an estimated 320,000 people were killed. It was the first camp to use gas to kill prisoners. The Nazis closed it in March 1943 then reopened it in June 1944.
• **Last of Chelmno:** liquidated by the Nazis in July 1944.

Dachau (near Munich, western Germany)
Opened March 1933. Oldest of the concentration camps. More than 200,000 people were imprisoned at Dachau and an estimated 32,000 people died there.

- **End of Nazi German control of Dachau:** April 28, 1945. Liberated on April 29, 1945, by U.S. forces who found more than 65,000 prisoners there. After the war, Dachau served as a prisoner-of-war camp. The U.S. conducted the Dachau war crimes trials at the camp beginning in November 1945.
- **Last of the Dachau Nazi camp officials:** Forty-two former camp officials were tried for war crimes. All were found guilty. Twenty-three were hanged on May 28-29, 1946. The rest served various terms of imprisonment.

Flossenburg (southern Germany near the Czech border)
Opened in 1938. About 30,000 prisoners died there.
- **End of Nazi German control of Flossenburg:** liberated April 23, 1945, by U.S. forces.

Janowska (near Lvov, Ukraine)
Opened October 1941 to provide housing for forced laborers at a nearby factory. Liquidation of the Lvov ghetto began on June 1, 1943. About 3,000 Jews were killed during its destruction and another 7,000 were taken to Janowska, where they were murdered.
- **End of Nazi German control of Janowska:** liquidated by the Germans on November 13/14, 1943.

Majdanek (near Lublin, Poland)
Opened in 1942. Concentration and extermination camp. Executions began in October 1942. Estimates of the number of Jews murdered there are as many as 1.5 million.
- **End of Nazi German control of Majdanek:** liberated July 23, 1944, by Soviet troops. Majdanek was the first concentration camp to be liberated. Today, it is one of the best preserved. Large portions are still intact.

Maly Trostenets (near Minsk, Belarus)
Opened summer 1941 as a prisoner-of-war camp. Became an extermination camp in May 1942. Estimates of deaths range from a half million to more than 2 million.
- **End of Nazi German control of Maly Trostenets:** June 1944. As the Soviet Army approached the region, the Germans bombed the camp in an attempt to get rid of it. Maly Trostenets was liberated on June 28, 1944.

Ravensbrück (near Berlin, Germany)
Opened May 1939. The only major concentration camp for women. More than 132,000 women and children were imprisoned and perhaps as many as 92,000 died there.
- **End of Nazi German control of Ravensbrück:** evacuated April 27/28, 1945, when anyone who could walk was forced to leave. The Soviet Army liberated Ravensbrück on April 30, 1945.

Sobibor (near Lublin, Poland)
Extermination camp. Opened March 1942. An estimated 250,000 people were killed there. Sobibor shut down after a major revolt on October 14, 1943.
- **End of Nazi German control of Sobibor:** liquidated by the Nazis October 1943, after the prisoners revolted.

Theresienstadt (near Prague, then Czechoslovakia)
Opened November 1941. Prisoners were taken there before they were deported to death camps elsewhere. Although Theresienstadt was not an extermination camp, about 34,000 people died there from disease, starvation, overcrowding, lack of clothing and terrible sanitary conditions. The Jews of Denmark who did not manage to escape to Sweden were sent to Theresienstadt.
- **End of Nazi German control of Theresienstadt:** May 3, 1945. The Soviet Army liberated the camp on May 8, 1945.

Treblinka (near Treblinka, northeast of Warsaw, Poland)
Opened June 1942. Extermination camp. Estimates are that from 700,000 to 1.4 million Jews were murdered at Treblinka. Scene of a major revolt on August 2, 1943. Most of

Treblinka was burned down during the uprising. Afterward, the Germans ordered the dismantling of the camp. The prisoners who survived the revolt were forced to destroy all traces of Treblinka, then were killed.
• **End of Nazi German control of Treblinka:** shut down November 1943. Afterward, the Nazis disguised the land as a farm.

Wars and Battles—World War II—Holocaust—Concentration Camps

• **Last known surviving camp commander:** Dinko Sakic, who was convicted in Zagreb, Croatia, in 1999. He was given 20 years in prison—the maximum sentence under Croatian law for war crimes committed while running Croatia's Jasenovac camp. The Sakic trial was the first World War II war crimes trial in Eastern Europe.

• **Last concentration camp to be liberated by the Allies:** Stutthof, in Poland, near Gdansk. It was liberated by the Soviet Army on May 10, 1945.

Wars and Battles—World War II—Holocaust—Frank, Anne

During World War II, Anne Frank, a young Dutch Jewish girl, and her family spent two years hiding in a secret annex in a house in Amsterdam, Holland, to escape deportation to a Nazi concentration camp. She began keeping her diary on June 12, 1942, when she was 13 years old.

• **Last entry in the diary of Anne Frank:** August 1, 1944. Three days later, the police raided the house where the Frank family was hiding. Anne Frank died of typhus in Bergen-Belsen concentration camp in March 1945. Her diary was first published in Amsterdam in 1947.

• **Last surviving witness to the Frank family ordeal:** Miep Gies, Otto Frank's secretary, who brought the Frank family food as they hid for 25 months in a secret annex above Frank's office. On August 4, 1944, the Franks and others who were hiding with them were arrested by the Nazis and taken to concentration camps. Anne Frank left behind her diary. Gies found the book and saved it. After the war, when she learned Anne was dead, she gave the diary to Otto Frank.

Wars and Battles—World War II—Holocaust—Warsaw Ghetto

The ghetto in the city of Warsaw, Poland, was the largest of the Jewish ghettos. By 1942, it held a half million people. In July 1942, 300,000 Jews were deported to the Treblinka death camp. By early 1943, the ghetto's population had dwindled to 60,000. Beginning on April 18, the Jews in the ghetto engaged in a bloody 28-day struggle.

• **Last Jews killed in the Warsaw Ghetto:** May 16, 1943. The few survivors were sent to Treblinka. Warsaw was liberated by the Russian Army on January 17, 1945.

• **Last surviving leader/hero of the 1943 Warsaw Ghetto uprising:** Marek Edelman, who lives in Lotz, Poland. His story was told in the documentary: *The Lonely Struggle.*

Wars and Battles—World War II—Italy

Benito Mussolini, known as Il Duce (the Leader), was the prime minister of Italy for more than ten years. He was removed from power in 1943.

• **Last of Mussolini:** captured along with his mistress Clara Petacci as they tried to seek asylum in Switzerland. They were captured by Italian partisans near Lake Como and executed outside the village of Dongo on April 28, 1945. Their bodies were taken to Milan, Italy, where they were displayed in a piazza then buried in a cemetery in Milan. In April 1946, Mussolini's body was stolen. After it was recovered, it was interred at the Capuchin Monastery Cemetery at Cerro Maggiore, Italy. It remained there until 1957, when it was removed to San Cassiano Cemetery in Mussolini's birthplace, Predappio, Italy.

• **End of Italy as an Axis Power:** September 8, 1943, when U.S. General Dwight D. Eisenhower announced the unconditional surrender of Italy. (On September 3, 1943,

Marshall Pietro Badoglio had signed a secret armistice with the Allies as the British Eighth Army landed at Calabria, Italy.)

• **Last of the German Army in Italy:** May 2, 1945, when the German Army in Italy abided by the Caserta Agreement and surrendered to the Allies. (The Caserta Agreement was an unconditional surrender document signed by German forces on April 29, 1945.)

• **End of the German occupation of Rome:** June 4, 1944, the day Rome fell to the Allies. The Germans had occupied the city since September 10, 1943.

• **End of World War II hostilities in Italy:** May 2, 1945, three days after the Germans signed the terms of surrender at Caserta, near Naples. All German and Italian Fascist troops in northern Italy and western Austria surrendered.

Wars and Battles—World War II—Japan

• **Last air raid of Japan:** August 14, 1945, against Kumagaya and several other targets northwest of Tokyo.

• **Last shots of World War II:** fired by the submarine USS *Tigrone* (SS-419) on August 14, 1945. *Tigrone* was submerged when the cease-fire order was given. While in Tokyo Bay, she shelled a lighthouse. The USS *Heermann* (DD-532) also fired after the cease-fire became effective. *Heermann* was approximately 200 miles southeast of Tokyo and opened fire after being attacked by a Japanese plane.

• **Last U.S. vessel struck by a Kamikaze plane:** the destroyer USS *Cassin Young* (DD-793). The hit was the second Kamikaze hit the ship sustained during the Okinawa campaign. *Cassin Young* survived both hits and is now at Charlestown Navy Yard in Boston, Massachusetts.

• **Last Japanese-held North American outpost evacuated:** Kiska, in the Aleutian Islands, evacuated by August 15, 1943. Japan had occupied Kiska, Attu and Agattu since June 1942. The Allies began to recapture the Aleutians in May 1943 but bypassed Kiska. When Allied amphibious troops invaded Kiska on August 15, they found the Japanese had already withdrawn.

• **End of Japanese hostilities:** Emperor Hirohito accepted the U.S. terms of surrender on August 14, 1945. On September 2, 1945, Japanese envoys signed formal surrender documents aboard the USS *Missouri* anchored in Tokyo Bay. Foreign Minister Mamoru Shigemitsu signed for the Japanese government; U.S. General Douglas MacArthur signed for the Allies.

• **End of the state of war with Japan:** September 8, 1951, with the signing of the Treaty of San Francisco by 49 nations in San Francisco, California. The treaty went into effect on April 28, 1952, when the majority of nations ratified. Russia, Poland and Czechoslovakia did not sign.

• **End of the occupation of Japan:** April 28, 1952, when the Treaty of San Francisco went into effect.

• **Last Japanese troop hold-outs:**

Sergeant Shoichi Yokoi, a Japanese soldier, was found hiding on Guam on January 24, 1972, 28 years after the U.S. captured the island in World War II. He had not surrendered because he was obeying imperial Army orders never to do so. Yokoi died in Nagoya, Japan, on September 22, 1997, age 82.

Lieutenant Hiroo Onoda, a Japanese officer, held out for nearly 30 years in a jungle on Lubang Island in the Philippines. He was one of four men in his company who did not know the war had ended. The first of the four left the group in September 1949. The remaining three refused to believe the war was over, despite attempts by their families and friends to contact them. In May 1954, the second of the four was killed by a search party sent to find them. The third survivor was killed in a gun battle with government officials on October 19, 1972. Onoda, the last survivor, emerged from the jungle and surrendered on March 10, 1974. Onoda received a hero's welcome when he returned to Japan.

Private Teruo Nakamura, a Japanese soldier, held out until December 19, 1974, on the Indonesian island of Morotai. He feared that he would be killed if he were captured. Finally, he surrendered to Indonesian soldiers who had surrounded him. Nakamura died three years later in Taiwan.

Wars and Battles—World War II—Phony War

Germany's invasion of Poland in September 1939 was followed by a period of military inactivity that lasted several months. This time has come to be known as the Phony War.

• **End of the Phony War:** April 9, 1940, when Germany began a full-scale military attack known as the Blitzkrieg (lightning war) by invading Norway and Denmark. Then, on May 10, Germany invaded Belgium, the Netherlands, Luxembourg and France.

Wars and Battles—World War II—Postwar—Marshall Plan

The Marshall Plan, also known as the European Recovery Program, was a U.S. program of economic and technical assistance to 16 war-torn nations of Europe, implemented to enable them to regain their productivity. The plan was named for U.S. Secretary of State George C. Marshall, who urged help for them. The Marshall Plan began when President Harry S. Truman signed the first appropriation bill for $5.3 billion on April 3, 1948.

• **End of the Marshall Plan:** December 31, 1951. It was succeeded by the Mutual Security Administration.

Wars and Battles—World War II—Ships—Destroyers

• **Last surviving British World War II destroyer:** HMS *Cavalier*, launched in 1944. She was once the fastest ship in the Royal Navy. After years in drydock, the ship is now being prepared to become a major attraction at the Historic Dockyard in Chatham, England.

• **Last surviving U.S. ship of the group that entered Tokyo Bay on August 28, 1945:** the destroyer USS *Southerland* (DD-743), which was the first ship to anchor the American flag in Tokyo Bay at the end of World War II. *Southerland* was sunk as a target ship in the fall 1998.

Wars and Battles—World War II—Ships—Liberty Ships/Victory Ships

Liberty ships, or Victory ships, were built during World War II to transport troops and materials to Europe. In the United States they were called Liberty ships; in Canada they were Victory ships.

• **Last surviving Canadian Victory ship:** HMS *Flamborough Head*, launched in 1945. She served in the post-war Royal Navy as a fleet maintenance and repair ship. The ship was transferred to the Royal Canadian Navy in 1952 and renamed HMCS *Cape Breton*. She was declared surplus in the 1980s. In October 2001, she was demolished off Snake Island, Nanaimo, British Columbia, to create the world's second largest artificial reef.

• **Last surviving U.S. Liberty ship:** USS *Jeremiah O'Brien,* launched in Maine in 1943. She is also the last survivor of the 5,500-vessel Allied armada that stormed the Normandy beaches on D-Day in 1944 and the last of the 236 Maine-built Liberty ships to return home to the port where she was built. *Jeremiah O'Brien* was declared a National Historic Landmark in 1980 and is now berthed at Fort Mason in San Francisco, California.

Wars and Battles—World War II—Ships—Pearl Harbor

• **Last surviving warship from Pearl Harbor still afloat:** the U.S. Coast Guard Cutter *Taney,* built in 1936. *Taney* is now at the Baltimore Maritime Museum in Maryland.

• **Last surviving operable U.S. naval vessel that took part in the attack on Pearl Harbor:** the Navy tug *HOGA* (YT-146). The *HOGA* helped save the USS *Oglala* by pushing the ship away from the *Arizona* and helping the battleship *Nevada* to ground herself to avoid sinking in the harbor entrance channel. The *HOGA* is presently at a pier in San Francisco Bay awaiting disposition by the Navy. A preservation group is working to return the historic tug to Hawaii. (*See also* Ships—Battleships; Ships—Naval Carriers.)

Wars and Battles—World War II—Submarines—Germany

• **Last German submarine to be captured in World War II:** U-234 on May 15, 1945, eight days after the unconditional surrender of all German forces to the Allies. The mission of U-234 was to transport technology and scientists to Japan. On board were several top Nazi scientists, engineers and party members. The cargo included German weapons, technology, a disassembled Messerschmidt jet engine and 560 kilograms of uranium oxide. U-234 was captured by an American destroyer and her contents were taken to the naval yard at Portsmouth, New Hampshire. U-234 was sunk during trials off the eastern coast of the U.S. on November 20, 1947. The U-977 also has been identified as the last U-boat to be captured in World War II. It was seized at Mar Del Plata, Argentina, in August 1945, three months after the war in Europe was over. After a 66-day underwater escape to Argentina, the U-boat's captain was arrested and turned over to the Allies. He was accused of smuggling war criminals to South America. The U-977 was torpedoed and sunk in a test off the coast of Massachusetts on November 13, 1945.

• **Last surviving Type IX-C submarine:** U-505, which was brought to the surface with a depth charge attack from the USS *Chatelain* on June 4, 1944. A party from the USS *Pillsbury* boarded the submarine and retrieved valuable documents, including code books and the Enigma machine. Since 1954, U-505 has been open to the public in at the Chicago Museum of Science and Industry and is a National Historic Landmark.

• **Last surviving Type VII submarine:** U-995. The U-boat was surrendered to Great Britain, then transferred to Norway in October 1948, together with two other VII-C U-boats. She was converted into the Norwegian submarine KNM *Kaura* in December 1952 (NATO designation S-309). She was

decommissioned on December 15, 1962. In 1971, she was taken to Germany where she serves as a museum sub.

• **Last surviving Type XXI submarine:** the U-2540, built in 1945, at the end of the war. She was scuttled on May 4, 1945, near the Flensburg lightship. Her wreck was raised in 1957 and restored at Kiel Howaldtswerken. She was named *Wilhelm Bauer* and served as a research vessel in the Bundesmarine in 1960. She was decommissioned on December 15, 1962. Since 1984, she has been housed at the German Maritime Museum at Bremerhaven.

• **Last British/Canadian U-boat victim in World War II:** the frigate *Goodall* (K-479) torpedoed at the entrance to Kola Inlet (near Murmansk) on April 29, 1945. The attacking U-boat was the U-968.

• **Last U.S. World War II U-boat victim:** the collier SS *Black Point,* sunk near Point Judith, Rhode Island, en route to Massachusetts with a cargo of coal, on May 5, 1945, at 5:40 p.m., several hours after all U-boats were ordered to end attacks on Allied shipping. The attacking U-boat was the U-853. Eleven people were killed when the *Black Point* went down.

• **Last U-boats sunk by U.S. ships in World War II:** U-881 and U-853, both sunk on May 6, 1945. U-881 was sunk south of Newfoundland by the U.S. destroyer escort USS *Farquhar*. U-853 was sunk off the coast of New York by the U.S. destroyer escort USS *Atherton* and the patrol frigate *Moberly*.

• **Last ships of any type to be victims of German U-boats in World War II:** the merchant ships *Avondale Park* and *Sneland,* sunk off the Firth of Forth on May 7, 1945. The attacking U-boat was U-2336. The U-2336 surrendered on May 14, 1945, and was sunk near Ireland on January 2, 1946.

• **Last U.S. destroyer sunk by a German U-boat in World War II:** USS *Leary* (DD 158), sunk by the U-275 on December 24, 1943, during an escort mission in the North Atlantic. Ninety-seven of her crew were lost.

• **Last U-boat sunk by the British Royal Navy in World War II:** U-711, sunk off

Norway on May 4, 1945, by a Royal Navy task force of escort carriers (HMS *Queen,* HMS *Searcher* and HMS *Trumpeter)* with cruisers and destroyers . During the morning hours of May 4th German Admiral Doenitz gave the order that all U-boats were to cease fire at once and stop all hostile action against Allied shipping.

• **Last U-boat sunk in World War II:** the U-320, sunk west of Bergen, Norway, by a Royal Air Force Catalina plane of the No. 210 Squadron on patrol on May 8, 1945.

• **Last U-boat to leave Germany in World War II:** believed to be the U-534. It was rumored to have a fortune in loot on board when it sank near Denmark on May 5, 1945. Years later, a Danish investor bankrolled the recovery of the sub. There was no fortune on board, but the U-boat is now on display as a tourist attraction in Wirral, near Birkenhead (near Liverpool) in England.

• **Last U-boat sunk in Operation Deadlight:** U-3514, sunk by HMS *Loch Arkaig* on February 12, 1946. After the war, Great Britain had 110 German U-boats in its possession, based in Scotland and Northern Ireland. The British government made the decision to sink the subs in deep water by various means as part of Operation Deadlight. The operation began on November 14, 1945.

Wars and Battles—World War II— Submarines—Great Britain

• **Last submarine lost by the Royal Navy in World War II:** HMS *Porpoise.* She left Trincomale (Ceylon, now Sri Lanka) on January 2, 1945, to lay mines in the vicinity of Penang in Malaya. Japanese records show that a submarine spotted by aircraft in the vicinity of Penang was bombed. Although not destroyed in the bombing attack, *Porpoise* left a trail of leaking oil that allowed Japanese anti-submarine forces to find and destroy her, probably around January 16, 1945.

• **Last British submarine casualty in World War II:** HMS *Terrapin* on May 19, 1945. Although not sunk, *Terrapin* was damaged beyond repair as the result of

Japanese depth charges in the Java Sea. She was declared a loss and scrapped in 1946.

Wars and Battles—World War II— Submarines—United States

• **Last U.S. submarine to fire shots and sink a ship in World War II combat:** USS *Torsk* (SS-423). When she fired the last torpedoes of World War II on August 14, 1945 a day before the Japanese surrender, *Torsk* sank the last Japanese combat ships to be lost in the war. *Torsk* is now at the Baltimore Maritime Museum in Maryland.

• **Last U.S. submarine commissioned during World War II:** USS *Cochino* (SS-345). Commissioned on August 25, 1945, *Cochino* was lost in the Norwegian Sea during a storm on August 25, 1949.

• **Last surviving completely authentic World War II Gato Class submarine:** USS *Cod* (SS-224). She is a National Historic Landmark and is docked in Cleveland, Ohio. Gato Class submarines were produced at the beginning of the war. They were succeeded by the Balao class.

• **Last U.S. submarine lost in World War II:** USS *Bonefish* (SS-223), sunk after a heavy barrage of Japanese depth charges off Toyama Bay (Honshu, Japan) on June 18, 1945. Eighty-five men were lost.

Wars and Battles—World War II— Union of Soviet Socialist Republics

• **End of the siege of Leningrad:** January 27, 1944. German troops attempted to capture Leningrad (now St. Petersburg, Russia) in September 1941. After a siege that lasted almost 900 days, the Germans still had not taken the city. When the siege ended, perhaps as many as 800,000 Russians had died of disease, exposure, starvation or war-related injuries.

• **Last Nazi stronghold in the Ukraine:** Novograd-Volynski, captured by Soviet forces on January 3, 1944.

• **Last German troops in Stalingrad:** surrendered on February 2, 1943, despite Hitler's order that surrender was out of the question.

Wars and Battles—World War II—United States—Code Talkers

During World War II, the U.S. military used Native Americans to transmit by radio and telephone strategic messages coded in their native languages. The Japanese were not able to break their codes. Many of the Code Talkers were Navajos, but other tribes were also used.

• **End of secrecy for the Native American Code Talkers:** 1968, when the U.S. government declassified the project. For the first time, the Code Talkers were permitted to speak publicly of their role in World War II.

• **Last surviving Comanche Code Talker:** Charles Chibitty of Tulsa, Oklahoma, the last of the 16 original Comanches who made up part of the 4th Infantry Division, 4th Signal Corps, known as the "Code Talkers." In 1999, he was honored by the U.S. Departments of Defense and Interior.

• **Last surviving Lakota Code Talker:** believed to be Clarence Wolf Guts of Wanblee, South Dakota, He was one of 11 Lakota, Dakota and Nakota of South Dakota who served as Code Talkers in World War II.

• **Last surviving Meskwaki Code Talker:** Frank Sanache, who died in Tama, Iowa, on August 21, 2004, age 86. He was one of eight Meskwaki who were trained as Code Talkers in World War II. (*See also* World War I—Code Talkers.)

Wars and Battles—World War II—United States—Commanders

• **Last surviving top-level World War II U.S. Army commander:** General Mark Wayne Clark, who was General Dwight D. Eisenhower's deputy in the European Theater of Operations. In 1942, he helped plan the Allied invasion of North Africa. In 1944, he led the Fifth Army through the Italian campaign and the capture of Rome, and in 1945 he served as the Allied high commissioner in occupied Austria. In 1952, Clark succeeded General Matthew B. Ridgway as supreme commander of United Nations forces in Korea and signed the Korean armistice in 1953. He served as president of the Citadel in Charleston, South Carolina, until 1965. General Clark died in Charleston, South Carolina, on April 17, 1984, age 87.

• **Last surviving World War II U.S. Navy commander:** Admiral Arleigh ("31-Knot") Burke. During the war, he served as a captain in the Solomon Islands campaign and then as chief of staff assigned to the First Carrier Task Force, Pacific. He retired in 1961. Burke died in Bethesda, Maryland, on January 2, 1996, age 94.

• **Last surviving member of General MacArthur's World War II staff:** General Elliott Raymond Thorpe, who was also the last survivor of those who witnessed the signing of the peace treaties that ended both World Wars. In 1919, he was at Versailles, France, when the treaty ending World War I was signed. And in 1945, he was aboard the USS *Missouri* in Tokyo Bay, when the Japanese surrendered. Thorpe died in Sarasota, Florida on June 27, 1989, age 91.

• **Last command of U.S. General George S. Patton:** appointed military governor of Bavaria at the end of World War II. Patton created a controversy with his criticism of the denazification policies in Germany and was relieved as head of the Third Army in October 1945. He was then assigned to the 15th Army. On December 9, 1945, he was seriously injured in an automobile accident near Mannheim, Germany. Patton died at the 7th Army Hospital in Heidelberg on December 21, 1945, age 60.

Wars and Battles—World War II—United States—Japanese American Detention

The detention of 110,000 Japanese Americans began shortly after President Franklin D. Roosevelt signed Executive Order 9066 on February 19, 1942. Although many of the Japanese-American detainees were U.S. citizens, the federal government classified them as enemy aliens based solely on their ancestry. They were forcibly removed from their homes along the West Coast and placed in 10 detention camps in California, Arizona, Arkansas, Wyoming, Utah and Colorado.

• **End of Japanese-American detention:** The last internee left Tule Lake, California, on March 20, 1946. Tule was the last of the 10 detention centers to close. On August 10, 1988, the U.S. government officially apologized to the Americans of Japanese ancestry who were detained during World War II. Each camp survivor was given $20,000 to compensate for the time he or she lost while detained.

Wars and Battles—World War II— United States—Manhattan Project

Manhattan Project was the code name for the top-secret project that produced the first atomic bomb for the United States. Work began when the U.S. Army Corps of Engineers' Manhattan Engineer District was established in August 1942.

• **End of the Manhattan Project:** July 16, 1945, in Alamogordo, New Mexico, with the successful testing of an atomic bomb. A short time later, two atomic bombs were dropped on Japan, hastening the end of the war. The first atomic bomb, named Little Boy, was dropped from the B-29 Superfortress *Enola Gay* over Hiroshima, Japan, on August 6, 1945, killing more than 140,000 people. The plane was piloted by Colonel Paul W. Tibbets Jr. The second bomb was dropped three days later. The war ended a few days after that.

• **Last atomic bomb dropped on Japan:** on Nagasaki on August 9, 1945, from the B-29 Superfortress *Bock's Car*, piloted by Major Charles W. Sweeney. The plane flew to Japan from the Pacific island of Tinian. It met up with two other B-29s off the coast of Kyushu. One plane photographed the bombing. The other carried sensor instruments. The bomb, named Fat Boy, killed another 70,000 people. *Bock's Car* is now at the U.S. Air Force Museum in Ohio.

Wars and Battles—World War II— United States—Rationing

Automobiles (civilian passenger cars): production halted after January 31, 1942.

• **Last U.S. automobile maker to close down production to retool for the war effort:** Hudson. The '42 model Hudson produced in February 1942 was the last of the pre-war cars. Less than 6,000 were manufactured that year. As production wound down, models were produced with painted blackout trim in place of chrome and stainless steel.

• **End of the manufacturing ban on civilian passenger cars:** August 23, 1945, when the War Production Board revoked all controls on production.

Coffee: rationing began on November 29, 1942 (one pound every five weeks for consumers 15 years and older.

• **End of coffee rationing:** July 28, 1943.

Gasoline: rationing began in 17 eastern states in May 1942. The speed limit was lowered to 40 miles per hour to conserve gas and tires. In July, people received A, B or C stickers for their cars: An A sticker gave drivers 4 gallons a week. C was the most critical, given to those whose occupations were war-related. On October 1, 1942, the speed limit was lowered to 35 mph for passenger cars. On October 15, it was lowered for buses and other common carriers. By December 1, gas rationing had extended nationwide. Fuel oil rationing began in most of the United States on October 22, 1942.

• **End of gas and fuel oil rationing:** August 19, 1945, a few days after the war with Japan ended.

Meat: in short supply by the end of 1942 so an announcement was made in December that meat would be rationed as of March 1943. The rationing of some cuts of meat ended in May 1944 but was reinstated in December 1944.

• **End of meat rationing:** November 23, 1945. Butter rationing ended at the same time.

Rubber tires: rationing began on December 27, 1941.

• **End of tire rationing:** December 31, 1945.

Shoes: rationing began on February 7, 1943. Civilians were limited to three pairs of leather shoes a year. In September 1943, rations were cut to one pair every six

months.
- **End of shoe rationing:** October 30, 1945.

Sugar: rationing began in 1942. Ration books were ready by May 6 and distributed by an army of volunteers and students. The first ration coupon was for one pound of sugar (for two weeks).
- **End of sugar rationing:** June 11, 1947. Sugar was the last of the war-time ration controls to be lifted.

The dates some other wartime rationing controls were implemented:

Bicycles: May 15, 1942. Bicycles went only to those who could show a need.

Coal and oil stoves: December 18, 1942. They were sold only to those consumers who could show a need.

Farm machinery: September 15, 1942. Production had already been sharply curtailed.

Radios and phonographs: April 22, 1942. Production for civilians was banned for the duration of the war.

Refrigerators: April 30, 1942. Production was banned when the industry switched to war work.
- **End of all wartime production restrictions:** August 21, 1945, when the War Production Board ended controls on more than 200 items. By March 31, 1946, all of the wartime controls had been lifted except on sugar.

**Wars and Battles—World War II—
United States—Veterans—Presidents**
- **Last U.S. president who served in World War II:** George Herbert Walker Bush. A Navy pilot, Bush earned the Distinguished Flying Cross and three air medals for his service in the Pacific. Six other president were veterans of World War II: Eisenhower, Kennedy, Lyndon B. Johnson, Nixon, Ford and Reagan.
- **Last survivor of PT 109:** Gerard Zinser of Belleville, Illinois. The story of the sinking of President John F. Kennedy's PT 109 in World War II was told in Robert Donovan's book *PT 109* (McGraw-Hill, 1961) and in the 1963 movie with the same title. Zinser was an extra in the film. He died in Orange Park, Florida, on August 21, 2001, age 82.

**Wars and Battles—World War II—
United States—Veterans Benefits**
The starting date for training under the GI Bill for most World War II veterans was within four years of July 25, 1947, or the veteran's date of discharge.
- **Last day for World War II veterans to complete training under the GI Bill Benefits program:** July 25, 1956. Exceptions were made for GIs who enlisted between October 6, 1945, and October 5, 1946. Their GI benefit entitlement dates were tied to the end of their enlistment.

World War II—United States—Wartime Agencies

Name of Agency and Beginning Date	Purpose	Last of the Agency
Lend-Lease Administration March 1941	Empowered President Franklin D. Roosevelt to send goods and services to nations whose defense he deemed vital to defense of the U.S. Goods began to move immediately after the bill was passed by Congress and signed by the president.	• **End of Lend Lease:** August 21, 1945, when President Harry S. Truman ordered a halt to lend-lease operations to all Allied governments. While it was in operation, the program spent $41 billion.
National War Labor Board (NWLB) January 1942	Created within the Office for Emergency Management. The board handled labor disputes in industries that were involved with war work.	• **End of the NWLB:** September 1945, at war's end. The board was transferred to the Department of Labor and abolished the following year.

Office of Civilian Defense (OCD) May 1941	Established by Executive Order. It coordinated with the military civilian defense activities such as air raids, first aid and fire protection during World War II.	• **End of the OCD:** abolished as of June 30, 1945, by Executive Order of President Harry S. Truman. The OCD was among the first of the wartime agencies to be discontinued.
Office of Economic Stabilization (OES) October 1942	Established by Executive Order to formulate wartime policy for economic variables such as salaries, wages, prices, profits, and rents.	• **End of the OES:** assimilated into the Office of War Mobilization and Reconversion at war's end in 1945.
Office of Price Administration (OPA) August 1941	Established a few months before the U.S. entered World War II to provide a fair distribution of products in short supply and to prevent unfair price rises during wartime.	• **End of the OPA:** June 1, 1947.
Office of Scientific Research and Development (OSRD) June 1941	A temporary agency established to coordinate scientific research and mobilize needed personnel. Among its programs was the Manhattan Project.	• **End of the OSRD:** abolished in 1946 when it was absorbed into the U.S. Atomic Energy Commission.
Office of Strategic Services (OSS) June 1942	The first U.S. intelligence agency. Established by Executive Order to gather and evaluate strategic information for the Joint Chiefs of Staff.	• **End of the OSS:** abolished on October 1, 1945, soon after the war ended.
Office of War Information (OWI) June 1942	Created to serve as a clearing house and a coordinating agency for newspapers, magazines, radio and movies. It supervised the way the U.S. was presented to the world in the media during the war.	• **End of the OWI:** terminated August 31, 1945. Part of its program was transferred to the United States Information Agency.
War Manpower Commission (WMC) April 1942	Established by Executive Order. The agency coordinated recruitment of workers to fill critical labor shortages.	• **End of the WMC:** August 14, 1945, when all controls over employers and workers were abolished. The WMC was then absorbed into the Department of Labor.
War Production Board (WPB) January 1942	Established by Executive Order. Controlled the production and distribution of raw materials and manufactured items and how they were allocated between the military and civilians. The WPB halted production of some 300 items deemed non-essential to the public so that resources could be redirected to the war effort. The products included such items as household appliances, automobiles, radios, bicycles, beer cans and coat hangers. Sugar, coffee, and gasoline were rationed. Restric-	• **End of most WPB controls:** August 21, 1945, when the WPB ended 210 controls that had limited the production of certain categories of consumer goods in wartime. • **End of WPB:** November 3, 1945, when the board was absorbed into the Civilian Production Administration. Most war controls ended by March 31, 1946. (*See*: Wars and Battles—World War II— United States—Rationing)

	tions were placed on natural fiber cloth and shoe leather. Tuesdays and Fridays were designated as "meatless days."	
War Relief Control Board (WRCB) July 25, 1942	Established by Executive Order. Controlled the distribution of resources for war relief in the U.S. and abroad. Also controlled the solicitation and collection of funds. The agency licensed people and organizations that did the collecting and distributing.	• **End of the WRCB:** abolished June 30, 1945.

Wars and Battles—World War II—War Crimes Trials

• **Last of the Dachau war crimes trials:** August 1948. The Dachau war crimes trials began on November 15, 1945 in Western Germany. They were concerned with the atrocities at the Dachau concentration camp as well as cases of atrocities elsewhere such as the Malmedy Massacre.

• **Last of former Gestapo officer Adolf Eichmann:** captured in Argentina by Israeli agents in May 1960. Eichmann had played a major role in the extermination of Jews. After a four-month trial in Jerusalem for crimes against humanity, he was sentenced to death by an Israeli court on December 15, 1961. Eichmann was hanged in Ramle, Israel, on May 31, 1962. His body was cremated and his ashes were scattered in the Mediterranean Sea.

• **Last of Heinrich Himmler:** committed suicide by poison at Luneberg, Germany, on May 23, 1945, to escape being tried as a war criminal. Himmler headed the SS (Schutzstaffel), the Nazi secret police. He was arrested by British troops in May 1945, as the war was ending.

• **End of the first Nuremberg War Crimes Trial:** October 1, 1946. The first international war crimes trial involved the major war criminals. It began before the International Military Tribunal at Nuremberg, Germany, on November 14, 1945. The first trial ended when the tribunal found 22 top Nazis guilty of war crimes. Twelve, including Hermann Goering, were sentenced to death by hanging. Three were given life sentences; four received lesser prison sentences; three were acquitted. On October 15, 1946, Goering killed himself with poison a few hours before the others were executed. Twelve other Nuremberg trials were conducted by authority of the Allied Control Council for Germany beginning in December 1946, and 185 other war criminals were indicted. Of those, 177 who were tried, 24 were sentenced to death by U.S. tribunals; 20 were sentenced to life in prison; 98 received lesser prison sentences; and 35 were acquitted.

• **End of the last Nuremberg trial:** April 14, 1949.

• **Last surviving Nuremberg trial judge:** believed to be William Wilkins, the last of the 32 judges appointed to the Nuremberg trials by President Harry S. Truman. He died in Bellevue, Washington, on September 9, 1995 age 98.

• **End of the Tokyo War Crimes Trial:** November 12, 1948. The Tokyo (Japan) War Crimes Trial began on May 3, 1946, and tried 28 Japanese leaders. Two of the defendants died during the trial, and one was declared insane. The remaining 25 were found guilty of atrocities and other war crimes. Seven were sentenced to death; 16 received life imprisonment; two were given other terms. Hideki Tojo and six other Japanese war leaders were hanged in Tokyo on December 23, 1948.

Weapons

Weapons—Artillery—16-inch Coastal Defense Gun

The gun barrels of the 16-inch Coastal Defense Gun were originally built for a class of battle cruiser cancelled by the 1922 Washington Naval Treaty. The U.S. Navy had no immediate need for these massive guns, so it transferred them to the U.S. Army for coastal defense service. Between the 1920s and 1946, 16-inch guns were placed at major U.S. harbors in two-gun batteries to engage enemy battleships, aircraft carriers and heavy cruisers.

• **Last of these guns scrapped:** by 1950.

• **Last remaining example of a 16-inch Coastal Defense Gun:** at the U.S. Army Ordnance Museum at the Aberdeen Proving Grounds in Maryland.

Weapons—Biological Warfare

• **End of the legal development, production and stockpiling of bacteriological (biological) and toxin weapons:** 1975. The Convention on the Prohibition of the Development, Production and Stockpiling of Bacteriological (Biological) and Toxin Weapons and on their Destruction (a.k.a. Biological and Toxin Weapons Convention)—a treaty approved by the United Nations General Assembly in December 1971—opened to signing on April 10, 1972, and entered into force on March 26, 1975.

Weapons—Cadillac Tank

Cadillac produced the first M-24 tanks in 1942, shortly after World War I began.

• **Last Cadillac-built M-24 tank:** produced in August 1945, just a few days after World War II ended.

Weapons—Gatling Gun

The Gatling gun was adopted by the U.S. Army in 1866, after the Civil War. Changes in technology over the next four decades made the gun outmoded.

• **Last use of the Gatling gun by the U.S. Army:** 1911, when the U. S. Army declared the gun obsolete.

Weapons—Long Bows

Before the advent of firearms, the long bow was the weapon of choice on the battlefield. Even after firearms were introduced, the long bow still proved to be superior until guns were perfected. The change from bows to firearms took a long time.

• **Last of the long bows:** by end of 16th century; however, no records specifically indicate when the last long bows were regularly used. In 1589, the English Privy Council decided archers were no longer required in the standard militia company organization. However, archers could be formed into their own companies. In 1595, the Buckinghamshire (England) Commissioners of Musters reported that they were beginning to convert their archers into musketeers. The Privy Council instructed them to do so with all known archers.

Weapons—Nuclear Tests

• **Nuclear tests in space, air, water banned:** August 4, 1963, with the Nuclear Test Ban Treaty signed by the United States, the Soviet Union and Great Britain. The treaty prohibited testing of nuclear weapons in space, above ground or under water. Only underground tests were permitted.

Weapons—Pershing 1-A Missiles

The U.S. Army had begun destroying 169 Pershing 1A missiles in September 1988 under the terms of the 1987 Intermediate-Range Nuclear Forces Treaty.

• **Last of the Pershing 1A missiles:** destroyed by the U.S. Army at an ammunition plant in Karnack, Texas, on July 6, 1989, under the terms of the 1978 Intermediate Range Nuclear Forces Treaty.

Weather

Weather—Hurricanes and Tropical Storms—Names

When hurricane warning services developed to the point that tropical storms and hurricanes could be predicted, mariners and meteorologists began using numbers or letters to identify upcoming storms. Then, a storm tracker began to call the storms female names and the idea caught on.

• **Last year hurricanes had no names:** 1949. From 1950 to 1952, forecasters gave hurricanes names from the phonetic alphabet (A=Able; B=Baker; C=Charlie). In 1953, the U.S. National Weather Bureau began using female names for hurricanes in the Atlantic Ocean, Caribbean Sea and Gulf of Mexico. The following year, names such as Carol, Edna and Hazel made headlines as hurricanes hit American waters.

• **Last year only female names were used for hurricanes and tropical storms:** 1978. Male names were used the first time in 1979.

• **Last year only English names were used for hurricanes and tropical storms:** 1978. French and Hispanic names were used for the first time in 1979.

Weather—National Weather Service
The National Weather Service was established in 1870 as the Division of Telegrams and Reports for the Benefit of Commerce. It was originally under the jurisdiction of the U.S. Army Signal Service.

• **Last known as the Division of Telegrams and Reports for the Benefit of Commerce:** 1891. That year, the agency was transferred to the Department of Agriculture and renamed the U.S. Weather Bureau.

• **Last time the U.S. Weather Bureau was part of the Department of Agriculture:** 1940. That year, the agency was transferred to the U.S. Department of Commerce.

• **Last known as the U.S. Weather Bureau:** 1970. That year, the name was changed to the National Weather Service.

Index

A & P Gypsies (radio), 446
A. J. Beatty Glass Company, 168
A.W.H.C. Robertson (company), 165
Aaliyah, 319
Aalto, Alvar, 16
Aaron, Hank, 562, 563, 564
Aasáx language (Tanzania), 182
Abbas Hilmi Pasha (Abbas II), 373
Abbasid dynasty (Iraq), 413
Abbey's Theater (New York, New York), 149
abbeys and religious houses (England), 484
Abbie & Slats (comic strip), 70
Abbott and Costello Show, The (radio), 447
Abbott, Bud, 242
Abbott, Fay, 591
Abbott, John, 677
Abbott, Oliver N., 677
Abd al-Aziz Ibn Saud, 408
Abdul-Jabbar, Kareem, 575, 576
Abdullah I, King (Transjordan), 390
Abdul-Mejid II, Caliph (Turkey), 416
Abe, Kobo, 193
Abel, Walter, 242
Abie's Irish Rose (radio), 447, 461
Abie's Irish Rose (show), 148
Abington School District v. Schempp, 110
Aborigines, Australian, 358
Abraham Lincoln, USS (submarine), 541
Abraham, Eric, 696
Abu Dhabi (emirate), 418
Abu Simbel (Egypt), 132
AC/EA (airline), 46
Academy of Motion Picture Arts and Sciences (AMPAS), 236
Academy of Music (New York, New York), 149
Academy Theater (New York, New York), 150
Accawmack County, Virginia, 669
Ace (motorcycle maker), 232
Ace, Goodman, 453
Achaean League, 7
Achaemenid dynasty (Persia), 122
Achille Lauro (liner), 501
Achilles (sailing ship), 500
Acme Colored Giants (baseball), 563
Acme Theater (New York, New York), 150, 153
Acquired Immune Deficiency Syndrome (AIDS), 171
Acre (Akko, Israel), 484
Act of Supremacy, (England), 486
Act of Union (1707, England), 420
Act of Union (1841, Canada), 364
Actium, Battle of, 122
Acuff, Roy, 319
Adai (Native Americans), 423

Adam, Robert, 16
Adam-12 (TV), 612
Adams (sloop), 537
Adams, Alexander, 501
Adams, Edward H., 501
Adams, Franklin P., 566
Adams, John (mutineer), 501
Adams, John (president), 650, 675
Adams, John (sailor), 694
Adams, John Quincy, 441, 442, 546, 651
Adams, Major Michael, 44
Adams, Maude, 139
Adams, Nick, 242
Addams Family, The (TV), 612
Adderley, Julian "Cannonball", 319
Adena (Chillicothe, Ohio), 17
Adirondack Lodge (Clear Lake, New York), 175
Adrian II, Pope, 486
Adrian IV, Pope, 486
Adrian VI, Pope, 486
Adrianople, Treaty of, 690
Adrin (pesticide), 153
ADT, 63
Adventure (schooner), 532
Adventure Comics (comic book), 73
advertising legal services, 186
advertising, smoking, 173
Aeolia, 7
Aeronautical Division, U.S. Army Signal Corps, 647
Afanasyev, Viktor, 549
Affirmed (horse), 597
Afghanistan, 113, 543
Afghanistan, (Transitional) Islamic State of, 355
Afghanistan, Democratic Republic of, 356
AFLAC, Inc, 63
AFL-CIO, 181
Africa, 7, 121
Afrika Korps, 701
Afrikaners, 678
Against the Storm (radio), 447
Agamemnon (liner), 529
Agee, James, 193
Agricultural Adjustment Administration (AAA), 636, 654
Agricultural and Mechanical College of Kentucky, 106
Agricultural and Mechanical College of Kentucky University, 106
Agricultural College of Pennsylvania, 106
Agricultural College of Utah, 108
Agriculture, U.S. Department of, 636, 637, 638, 722
Aguas Claras, Battle of, 691
Ahern, Gene, 72
Ahern, Michael, 94
Ahmad Fuad Pasha (Fuad I), 374
Ahmed Ibn Said, Sultan (Muscat and

Oman), 402
Ahmed Shah (shah of Persia), 386
Ahren, Gene, 463
AIDS, 171
Ain't It a Grand and Glorious Feelin'? (comic strip), 70
Ain't Misbehavin' (show), 148
Ainu language (Japan), 182
Air Cal (airline), 46
Air California (airline), 46
Air Canada Centre (Toronto, Canada), 575
Air Cooled Motor Corp., 29
Air Corps, U.S., 647
Air Force Academy, U.S., 102
Air Force Museum, U.S, (Wright-Patterson Air Force Base, Dayton, Ohio), 37
Air Force Museum, U.S. (Wright-Patterson Air Force Base, Dayton, Ohio), 42, 43, 44
Air Force, U.S., 38, 40, 42, 647
Air France, 35
Air National Guard, U.S., 43, 45
Air Oregon (airline), 46
Air Service, U.S., 647
Air West (airline), 46
aircraft, civil, 34
aircraft, military, 37
aircraft, propeller-driven, 41
Airship, Age of the, 52
Aishcum County, Michigan, 662
Aix-la-Chapelle, Treaty of, 678, 688
Ajman (emirate), 418
AJS (Albert John Stevens) (motorcycle maker), 233
Akashi Kaikyo Bridge (Japan), 126
Akins, Claude, 242
Akkadian (language), 11
Akron (ZRS-4) (airship), 52, 92, 93
Akron Indians (football), 587
Akron Pros (football), 587
Akron, Ohio (trolleys), 635
Al Pearce and His Gang (radio), 447
Alabama, 545, 655
Alabama Agricultural and Mechanical College, 102
Alabama Colored People's University, 102
Alabama State College, 102
Alabama State College for Negroes, 102
Alabama State University, 102
Alabama Territory, 655, 663
Alabama, USS (battleship), 502
al-Adid (Fatimid caliph), 120
Alamein, El, 700
Alamo Siege, 671
Alan Young Show, The (TV), 612
Alarm, HMS (frigate), 676
Alaska, 112, 655
Alaska Air Transport, 46
Alaska Airlines, 46

American Colonization Society, 393, 546
American Diabetes Association, 174
American Dictionary of the English Language, An, 59
American District Telegraph Company, 63
American Expeditionary Force (World War I), 698
American Family Corporation, 63
American Federation of Labor (AFL), 181
American Flint Glass Manufactory, 164
American Football League (AFL), 586
American Forum of the Air (radio), 447
American Indian Movement (AIM), 674
American Indian Wars, 671
American Indians of All Tribes, 79
American Indoor Soccer League (AISL), 609
American International Shipbuilding Corp. (Pennsylvania), 538
American League of Professional Baseball Clubs, 561
American League Park (Washington, D.C.), 559
American Liberty League, 439
American Magazine, 220
American Mercury (magazine), 464
American Monthly (magazine), 221
American Motors Corp., 28, 30, 31
American National (CART) Championship (automobile race), 552
American party, 440, 441
American Porcelain Manufacturing Company, 164
American Pottery Company, 169
American Psychological Association, 174
American Radio Warblers (radio), 447
American Railway Union (ARU), 180
American Revolution, 640, 674, 675
American Samoa, 407
American Show Shop (theater, New York, New York), 150
American Society for Clinical Pathology, 174
American Star (liner), 525
American Stock Exchange, 58
American Telephone and Telegraph Company (AT&T), 61
American Terra Cotta and Tile Company, 164
American Terra Cotta Company, 164
American Weekly Mercury (newspaper), 434

American Woman Suffrage Association, 223
Ames (store), 62
Ames Brothers, 320
Ames, Adelbert, 679
Ames, Leon, 236, 242
AMF (American Metals Foundries), 236
Amherstburg Navy Yard (Amherstburg, Ontario), 539
Amiens, Treaty of, 415
Amin, Idi, 417
Amis, Sir Kingsley, 194
Amistad (slave ship), 546
Ammann, Othmar, 125
Amoco Building (Chicago, Illinois), 20
Amos 'n' Andy Show, The (radio), 447
Amos 'n' Andy Show, The (TV), 613
Amos and Andy Music Hall (radio), 447
Ampère, Andrè-Marie, 493
AmphiTheater (Queens, New York), 160
Amsterdam, Holland, 58
Amtrak, 482
Amundsen, Roald, 154
amusement parks, 143, 145
amusement parks, signs, 146
Anaheim Amigos (basketball), 577
Anaheim Angels (baseball), 553, 557, 571
Anaheim Mighty Ducks (ice hockey), 605
Anaheim Stadium (California), 553
Anamickee County, Michigan, 662
Anastasia, Grand Duchess (Russia), 406
Anchorage International Airport (Alaska), 51
Ancient Regime (Old Order), 686
ANCO Cinema (New York, New York), 151
Ancon, Treaty of, 689
And Her Name Was Maud(comic strip), 70
Andersen, Hans Christian, 194
Anderson Packers (basketball), 577
Anderson, Anna, 406
Anderson, Daisy, 684
Anderson, Dame Judith, 242
Anderson, Leroy, 282
Anderson, Maceo, 138
Anderson, Marian, 311
Anderson, Maxwell, 76, 194
Anderson, Robert Ball, 684
Anderson, Sherwood, 194
Anderson, Tommy, 604
Andersonville Prison, 679
Andorra, 113
Andorra, Principality of, 356
Andrea Doria (liner), 95, 526

Andrée, Salomon August, 154
Andrews Sisters, 320
Andrews, Edmund, 192
Andrews, Edward, 243
Andrews, Roy, 590, 591, 592
Andros, Edmund, 8
Andy Griffith Show, The (TV), 613
Andy Panda (cartoon character), 65
Andy Williams Show, The (TV), 613
Angel, Heather, 243
Angeli, Anna Maria Pier, 243
Angelita (sailing ship), 498
Angie (TV), 613
Anglican Code (England), 186
Anglo-Afghan Treaty (1921), 356
Anglo-Afghan Wars, 355
Anglo-Nepalese War, 400
Anglo-Saxon kings, 418
Angola, 113, 405, 543, 544
Angola, People's Republic of, 357
Angola, Republic of, 357
Angora Love (movie), 237
animals, endangered, 12
animals, extinct, 13
animation (movies), 236
Anjou, House of, 419
Ankora, Turkey, 416
Ann Sothern Show, The (TV), 613
Annapolis, Maryland (U.S. capital), 641
Anne, Queen (England), 419
Annie (show), 148
Anschluss, 699
Answer Man, The, 447
Antarctic expeditions, 159
Antarctic Peninsula, 15
Antarctica, 2, 15
Antarna (sailing ship), 498
Anthonioz, Pierre, 396
Anthony, Earl, 580
Anthony, Susan B., 69
Antietam, USS (carrier), 512
anti-evolution ("Monkey") law, 110
Antigua, 543, 544
Antigua and Barbuda, 11, 113, 223, 357
Antigua, Guatemala, 382
Antilles Clipper (aircraft), 37
Anti-Masonic party, 440
Anti-Monopoly party, 440
anti-slavery gag rule, 546
Antonelli, Giacomo, 485
Antony, Mark, 122
Antrim County, Michigan, 662
Anything But Love (TV), 613
Anzac Clipper (aircraft), 35
Aon Center (Chicago, Illinois), 20
Aotea (paddle steamer), 535
apartheid, 411
Apocalypse, last horseman of, 483
Apollo (theater, New York, New York), 150
Apollo 17, 548

Apollo space program, 548
Apollo-Soyuz Test Project, 549
Apostate, The (play), 140
Appalachian Trail, 491
Appleseed, Johnny. *See* Chapman, John
Appling, Luke, 569
Appomattox Court House, Virginia, 681
April, Nancy, 423
Aqua Alexandrine (aqueduct), 123
Aquarius, Age of, 1
aqueducts, 123
Aquino, Tomas Ygnacio, 425
Aquitania (liner), 525
Arab Republic of Egypt, 11
Arab Union, 7
Aransas National Wildlife Refuge, 13
Aransas/Wood Buffalo flock, 13
Arbuckle, Roscoe ("Fatty"), 243
Arcadia University, 102
Arcaro, Eddie, 598
Arch Street Theater (Philadelphia, Pennsylvania), 20
Archaean Era, 2
Archdale County, North Carolina, 666
Archer, Joey, 582
Archibald Russell (sailing ship), 498
Archie Andrews, The Adventures of (radio*)*, 447
Archie Bunker's Place (TV), 612
Arctic exploration, 157
Ardea (sailing ship), 536
Arden, Eve, 243, 466
Arden-Clarke, Sir Charles Noble, 381
Arequipa Pottery, 164
Argentina, 113, 223, 543, 693
Argentina/Argentine Republic, 357
Argonaut, USS (submarine), 540
Argosy All-Story (magazine), 222
Argyll, Earl of, 81
Ariel (motorcycle maker), 233
Aristo (manufacturer), 497
Aristocats, The (movie), 236
Arizona, 112, 655
Arizona Airways, 46
Arizona Territory, 656, 665
Arizona, USS (battleship), 502, 713
Arizona-New Mexico boundary dispute, 638
Arkansas, 112, 545, 656
Arkansas Gazette (newspaper), 434
Arkansas State Gazette (newspaper), 434
Arkansas Territory, 656
Arkansas Traveler, The (radio), 449
Arkansas, USS (battleship), 503
Arlen, Harold, 282
Arlen, Michael, 454
Arlen, Richard, 243
Arlington County, Virginia, 669

Arlington Stadium (Texas), 553
Arliss, George, 243
Armenia, 113, 489
Armenia, Republic of, 357
Armenian Soviet Socialist Republic, 358
Armistice (World War I), 697
Armistice Day, 175
Armstrong Circle Theater (TV), 613
Armstrong Cork Company, 63
Armstrong of the SBI (radio), 459
Armstrong Theater of Today, The (radio), 448
Armstrong Whitworth Argosy (aircraft), 34
Armstrong World Industries Inc., 63
Armstrong, Louis ("Satchmo"), 50, 320
Armstrong-Siddeley (automobile maker), 28
Army Air Corps, U.S., 37, 44
Army Air Force, U.S., 43
Army Air Forces, U.S., 647
Army, Department of the, 640
Army, Secretary of the, 640
Army, U.S., 56, 79, 648, 722
Army-McCarthy Hearings, 643
Arnauld de la Periere, Lothar von, 698
Arnaz, Desi, 243
Arnold Grimm's Daughter (radio), 448
Arnold, Benedict, 501, 676
Arnold, Dorothy, 89
Arnold, Edward, 243
Arrindell, Sir Clement, 407
Arriola, Gus, 71
Arrivederci Tour, 552
Arrivederci Roma (song), 95
Arsenio Hall Show, The (TV*)*, 613
Art Linkletter's House Party (radio), 459
Artef Theater (New York, New York), 150
Artemisia (wife of Mausolus), 134
Arthur Foss (tugboat), 536
Arthur Godfrey and His Friends (TV), 613
Arthur Godfrey Digest, The (radio), 448
Arthur Godfrey Time (radio), 448
Arthur Godfrey's Talent Scouts (radio), 448
Arthur Godfrey's Talent Scouts (TV), 613
Arthur, Chester A., 684
Arthur, Duke of Connaught, 419
Arthur, Jean, 243
Articles of Confederation, 640, 667, 669
Articles of Confederation and Perpetual Union, 642
Artigas, General José, 420

artist groups, 20
Artley, A. Sterl, 202
Aruba, 400
As the Twig is Bent (radio), 474
asbestos, 172
Asfa Wossen, Crown Prince (Ethiopia), 375
Ashanti, 7
Ashley County, Missouri, 663
Ashmolean Museum (Oxford, England), 14
Ashmun Institute, 106
Ashtabula Bridge (Ashtabula, Ohio), 127
Ashton, Sir Frederick, 135
Asimov, Isaac, 194
Asseo, Bertha, 138
Assiniboia, SS (steamboat), 535
Associated Tide Water Oil Company, 63
Assurbanipal, King (Assyrian Empire), 118
Assyrian Empire, 118
Astaire, Fred, 243
Astor Hotel (New York, New York), 176
Astor House (New York, New York), 176
Astor Place Opera House (New York, New York), 149
Astor Place Riot, 142, 149
Astor Theater (New York, New York), 150
Astor, Mary, 243
Astor, William Waldorf, 176
Astro-Chimp, 547
Astrodome, The (Houston, Texas), 348, 556
Asuka period (Japan), 389
Aswan High Dam, 132
AT&T, 612
AT-6 (aircraft), 700
Atahualpa (Inca emperor), 120
Atakapa (Native Americans), 423
Atchison County, Missouri, 663
Atchison, Topeka & Santa Fe Railway, 476, 482
A-Team, The (TV), 613
Athens, Greece, 186
Atherton, USS (destroyer escort), 714
Atitlan grebe, 13
Atkins, Charles ("Cholly"), 136
Atkinson's Casket (magazine), 220
Atkinson's Casket, Gems of Literature, Wit and Sentiment (magazine), 220
Atlanta Apollos (soccer), 609
Atlanta Baptist College, 106
Atlanta Baptist Seminary, 106
Atlanta Braves (baseball), 554, 571
Atlanta Chiefs I and II (soccer), 609
Atlanta Flames (ice hockey), 601, 602

Atlanta Hawks (basketball), 573, 576
Atlanta Motor Speedway (Georgia), 553
Atlanta, Georgia, 658
Atlanta, USS (cruiser), 537
Atlanta-Fulton County Stadium (Georgia), 554
Atlantic (ship), 96
Atlantic Beach Amusement Park (Atlantic Highlands, New Jersey), 143
Atlantic City Convention Center, 147
Atlantic City, New Jersey, 147
Atlantic Coast Line Railroad, 476, 478
Atlantic, Mississippi & Ohio Railroad, 478
Atlee, Clement, 703
Atomic Age, 3
Atomic Energy Commission, U.S., 719
Atwill, Lionel, 243
Auburn Automobile Company, 28
Auburn Polytechnic Institute, 102
Auburn University, 102
Audi NSU Auto Union AG, 31
Auer, Mischa, 243
Augusta Academy, 109
Augusta Institute, 106
Augusta, Georgia, 658
Augustan Age, 1
Augustus Caesar, 1
Aunt Jenny's Real-Life Stories (radio), 448
Auric, Georges, 311
auroch, 13
Aurora (cruiser), 692
Auschwitz-Birkenau (concentration camp), 708
Austen, Jane, 194
Austen, John, 81
Austin Maestro, 28
Austin Metro, 28
Austin Montego, 28
Austin, Herbert, 28
Austin-Rover Group, 28
Australia, 10, 15, 77, 183, 184, 223, 358, 695
Australian Flying Corps, 695
Australis (liner), 525
Austria, 79, 113, 489, 543
Austria (Salzburg), 630
Austria, Federated State of, 358
Austria, Republic of, 358
Austrian Succession, War of the, 678
Austro-Hungarian Empire, 358, 371, 384, 394, 409, 410, 543, 695
Author Meets the Critics (radio), 448
Autogiro (aircraft), 56
automobile registration, 34
Autry, Gene, 456
Autumn (hymn), 100
Avdeyev, Sergei, 549

Avengers, The (TV), 613
Avenue Grounds (Cincinnati, Ohio), 555
Avery Rock (lighthouse), 187
Avia B.534 (biplane), 700
Aviation Bowl (football), 583
Aviation Service, U.S. Army Signal Corps, 647
aviation, designers and manufacturers, 55
Aviz (or Avis), House of, 404
Avon (theater, New York, New York), 151
Avon Faience Pottery Company, 164
Avon Products, 63
Avondale Park (ship), 714
Avro 504 (aircraft), 38
Avro Anson (aircraft), 37
Avro Avian, 34
Axis Sally (Mildred Elizabeth Sisk Gillars), 707
Axmann, Artur, 706
Axton, Hoyt, 243
Ay, Evelyn, 147
Ayacucha, Battle of, 403
Ayers, Doc, 567
Ayutthaya era (Thailand), 415
Ayyubid sultanate, 120
Azerbaijan (Azerbaijani Republic), 113, 358
Azerbaijan People's Republic, 359
Azerbaijan Soviet Socialist Republic, 359
Azikiwe, Dr. Nnamdi, 401
Aztec Empire, 118
Azuchi-Momoya Ma period (Japan), 389
B. Smith Style (magazine), 220
B-29 (bomber aircraft), 700
Baa, Baa, Black Sheep (TV), 613
Babur (Mongol leader), 385
Baby Huey (cartoon character), 65
Baby Ruth Story, The (movie), 564
Baby Snooks Show, The (radio), 448, 464
Babylon, 118
Babylonian Captivity, 118
Babylonian Empire, 118
Bacardi Bowl (football), 583
Bacchanalia, The, 122
Bacchus, 122
Bach, Johann Sebastian, 1, 282
Bachelor Father (TV), 613
Back River (lighthouse), 187
Backstage Wife (radio), 448
Bacon, Henry, 16
Bacon, Lloyd, 238
Bad Axe County, Wisconsin, 670
Baddeley, Hermione, 243
Baden, Treaty of, 692
Badogli, Pietro, 712
Baer, Stanley, 72
Bagby, Jim, 567

Baghdad Pact, 8
Bahadur Shah II, 385
Bahamas, 113, 223, 359
Bahrain, 113, 223
Bahrain, Kingdom of, 359
Bahrain, State of, 359
bail, excessive, 80
Bailey, Bernard, 73
Bailey, Marian, 647
Bailey, Pearl, 320
Bailey, Ray, 70
Baine County, Alabama, 655
Bainter, Fay, 244
Bakatin, Vadim V., 418
Bakeman (or Beakman), Daniel Frederick, 676
Baker Bowl (Philadelphia, Pennsylvania), 558
Baker County, Alabama, 655
Baker, Amos, 674
Baker, Chet, 321
Baker, Erwin G. ("Cannonball"), 553
Baker, J.S., 70
Baker, Josephine, 321
Baker, Phil, 467
Baker, Ray Stannard, 222
Baker, Thomas, 178
Bakr al-Attas, Haidar Abu, 422
Balakirev, Mily, 283, 311
Balanchine, George, 136
Balbo, Italo, 160
Balbo's Column, 160
Balclutha (sailing ship), 534
Bald Eagle (clipper ship), 499
Baldwin, James, 194
Balkan League, 362
Balkan War, First, 356, 362
Balkan War, Second, 362
Ball, Lucille, 244, 465
Ball, Mrs. Martin Luther, 100
Ballard, Dr. Robert, 96, 100
Ballard, Mrs. Sarah (Miwok speaker), 428
Ballast Point (lighthouse), 187
Ballets Russes, 138
Ballpark, The (Arlington, Texas), 553
Balsam, Martin, 244
Baltic Provinces, 375
Baltimore & Ohio Railroad, 476, 480, 482
Baltimore American (newspaper), 434
Baltimore Arena (Baltimore, Maryland), 573
Baltimore Bays (soccer), 609
Baltimore Blast (soccer), 608
Baltimore Bullets (I) (basketball), 577
Baltimore Bullets (II) (basketball), 577
Baltimore City Passenger Railway (Baltimore, Maryland), 632

Baltimore Claws (basketball), 577
Baltimore Colts (football), 586, 587, 588
Baltimore Comets (soccer), 609
Baltimore Elite Giants, 563
Baltimore Evening Sun (newspaper), 434
Baltimore International College, 103
Baltimore News American (newspaper), 434
Baltimore News Post (newspaper), 434
Baltimore Orioles (baseball), 554, 559, 568, 570, 571
Baltimore Orioles (I) (baseball), 568
Baltimore Stars (football), 586
Baltimore Traction Company (Baltimore, Maryland), 632
Baltimore, Battle of, 694
Baltimore, Maryland (trolleys), 635
Baltimore, Maryland (U.S. capital), 640
Balzac, Honoré de, 194
Banacek (TV), 613
Banana Bottom (novel), 209
Bangladesh, People's Republic of, 113, 359, 402
Bank of Amsterdam (Netherlands), 58
Bank of Hamburg (Germany), 58
Bank of North America (Philadelphia, Pennsylvania), 58
Bank of the United States, First, 58
Bank of the United States, Second, 58
Bank Shot (movie), 136
Bank Street Grounds (Cincinnati, Ohio), 555
Bankhead, Pyne, 683
Bankhead, Tallulah, 244
banking and finance, 58
Banneker, Benjamin, 59
Banty Raids (cartoon), 66
Banyard's Museum (New York, New York), 150
Bao Dai, Emperor (Vietnam), 422
Bara, Theda, 244
Barbados, 11, 113, 223, 359
Barbary States, 678
Barbary Wars, 678
Barbel, USS (submarine), 542
Barber dime, U.S., 225
Barber half dollar, U.S., 226
Barber quarter, U.S., 226
Barber, Charles Edward, 226
Barber, Samuel, 283
Barber, Steve, 570
Barbier, Charlotte, 89
Barbuda, 543, 544
Bard College, 103
Bardeen, John, 118
Bare language (Brazil and Venezuela), 182

Barefoot in the Park (show), 148
Baretta (TV), 613
Bari, Lynn, 244
Barker gang, 84
Barker turbine engine, 133
Barker, Arizona Donnie Clark (Ma Barker), 84
Barker, Arthur, 84
Barker, Fred, 84
Barker, Herman, 84
Barker, Lloyd, 84
Barnaby (comic strip), 70
Barnaby Jones (TV), 613
Barnburners, 440
Barney Miller (TV), 613
Baron Von Steuben (liner), 529
Baroque Era, 1
barque/bark (sailing ship), 497
Barr, Shorty, 595
Barracuda, USS (submarine), 540
Barrett family (Siuslawan speakers), 432
Barrett, Michael, 81
Barrie, Sir James M., 194
Barrie, Wendy, 244
Barron County, Wisconsin, 670
Barrow, Clyde, 84
Barrow, Errol, 360
Barry Craig, Confidential Investigator (radio), 448
Barry, John, 676
Barry, Philip, 194
Barrymore, Ethel, 139, 244
Barrymore, Georgiana Drew, 140
Barrymore, John, 139, 244
Barrymore, Lionel, 139, 244
Barrymore, Maurice, 139
Barthelmess, Richard, 244
Bartholdi, Frederic Auguste, 232
Bartholomew, Freddie, 244
Bartók, Béla, 283
Bartow County, Georgia, 658
Barty, Billy, 244
Baryshnikov at the White House (TV), 136
Baseball Hall of Fame, 560
baseball, ballparks, 553
baseball, current teams, 571
baseball, defunct or relocated teams, 568, 571
baseball, early leagues, 561
baseball, equipment, 560
baseball, major players, 563
baseball, Negro leagues, 562
baseball, records and streaks, 567
baseball, rules, 566
baseball, women's leagues, 572
Basehart, Richard, 244
Bashara, Ellis, 581
Basie, Count, 321
Basketball Association of America (BAA), 577
basketball, defunct pro teams, 577

basketball, intercollegiate rules, 575
basketball, original team, 575
Basoalto, Neftalí Ricardo Reyes, 210
Bass, USS (submarine), 541
Bastille (Paris, France), 686
Basutoland, 393
Bat Masterson (TV), 613
Bataan Death March, 701
Bataan, USS (carrier), 512
Batavia, Republic of, 400
Bateman, Rev. Robert James, 100
Bates College, 103
Batista, Fulgencio, 370
Batman (TV), 613
Battle of the Sexes (radio), 448
Baucke, Friedrich Wilhelm, 183
Baugh, Sammy, 586
Bauhaus, 15
Baum, L. Frank, 195
Baxter, Anne, 244
Baxter, Warner, 244
Bay Islands, Honduras, 384
Bay Shore Park (Baltimore County, Maryland), 143
Bay View Park (Atlantic Highlands, New Jersey), 143
Bayadère, The (ballet), 138
Bayes, Nora, 139
Bayfield County, Wisconsin, 670
Bayler, Walter, 703
Bayou Bonfouca (lighthouse), 187
Baywatch (TV), 613
Beach Chalet at Golden Gate Park (San Francisco, California), 19
Beach Indians, 431
Beach's Pneumatic Underground Railroad, 634
Bear Flag Revolt, 656
Bear Paw Battle, 673
Bear Valley Dam, 132
Beard, Dewey (Wasu Maza), 672
Beard, Joe, 82
Beard, Maston, 117
Beat the Band (radio), 448
Beatles, The, 321
Beatrice Marie Victoria Fedora, Princess of Battenberg, 420
Beaufils, Rene (World War I casualty), 697
Beaufort County, North Carolina, 666
beauty pageants, 146, 147
Beauvoir, Simone de, 195
Beaver College, 102
Beaver College and Musical Institute, 102
Beaver Female Seminary, 102
Beavers, Louise, 244, 448
Bechet, Sidney, 324
Bechuanaland, 543
Beck, Ed, 86
Beckett, Samuel, 195
Beckett, Scotty, 244

Binns, Edward, 245
Biological and Toxin Weapons
  Convention, 721
biological warfare, 721
Bionic Woman, The (TV), 614
Biosatellite 3 (space laboratory), 550
Biosatellite/Biosat (space laboratory),
  550
biplanes, 37
Birdseye Open House (radio), 453
Birmingham Americans (football),
  586
Birmingham Black Barons, 563
Birmingham demonstrations (civil
  rights), 68
Birney, James G., 442
Biro, Charles, 71
Bishops and Clerks (lighthouse), 188
Bismarck (battleship), 96
Bismarck (liner), 526
Bismarck, North Dakota, 666
bison, 12
Bissell, Whit, 245
Bi-State Parks Airport (St. Louis,
  Missouri), 50
Bivens, Jesse G., 689
Bivin, Jim, 564
Bizet, Georges, 285
Bjorkman, Henry, 583
Björling, Jussi, 311
Björnsson, Sveinn, 385
Black and Blue (musical), 136
Black Bart, 84
Black Death, 171
Black Diamond (train), 482
Black Hawk, chief (Sauk tribe), 672
Black Hawk's War, 672
Black Hole of Calcutta, 78
Black Jack (cavalry horse), 648
Black Letter Script, 12
Black Museum (radio), 466
Black Point, SS (coal freighter), 714
Black September, 86
Black Sheep Squadron (TV), 613
Blackfriars Theatre (London,
  England), 149
Blackistone Island (lighthouse), 188
Blackwood Brothers Quartet, 324
Blair, Eric Arthur, 211
Blake of Scotland Yard (movie), 237
Blake, Eubie, 285
Blakely, Colin, 245
Blakely, David, 81
Blakey, Art, 324
Blakistone Island (lighthouse), 188
Blanc, Mel, 67, 707
Blanchard, Jean-Pierre, 54
Blanche, Al, 564
Blanda, George, 587
Blazing the Overland Trail (movie),
  237
Bleeker County, Michigan, 662
Bligh, William, 501

Blind Date (radio*)*, 449
Blitzkrieg (lightning war), 713
Blixen, Baroness Karen Christence,
  199
Bloch, Ernest, 285
Block, Herbert L. (Herblock), 67
Blockbuster Bowl (football), 584
Blondell, Joan, 245
Blondie (radio), 449
Bloom County(comic strip), 70
Bloomsburg Literary Institute, 103
Bloomsburg Literary Institute and
  State Normal School, 103
Bloomsburg State College, 103
Bloomsburg State Normal School,
  103
Bloomsburg State Teachers College,
  103
Bloomsburg University of
  Pennsylvania, 103
Bloomsbury Group, 192
Blore, Eric, 245
Blosser, Merrill, 71
Blossom (TV), 614
Blount College, 108
Blount, William, 668
Blount, Winton M., 640
bludgeoning (punishment), 81
Blue Amberol cylinders, 437
Blue and Gray (magazine), 683
Blue Angels, 41
Blue Network, 446
Blue Ridge, USS, 538
Blue, Gilbert (Catawba chief), 424
Blueback, USS (submarine), 541, 542
Bluebonnet Bowl (football), 584
Bluegrass Bowl (football), 584
Blues Stadium (Kansas City,
  Missouri), 556
Blythe, Herbert, 139
Boabdil, 122
Boar's Head Tavern (London,
  England), 490
Boardwalk (Atlantic City, New
  Jersey), 177
Bob and Ray Shows (radio), 449
Bob Burns Show, The (radio), 449
Bob Hawk Show, The (radio), 449,
  450
*Bob Hope Presents the Chrysler
  Theater* (TV), 614
Bob Hope Show, The (radio), 449
Bob Newhart Show, The (TV), 614
*Bobby Benson and the B-Bar-B
  Riders* (radio), 449
Bobby Benson's Adventures (radio),
  449
Bock's Car (B-29 aircraft), 717
Boeing 247 (aircraft), 35
Boeing 307 Stratoliner (aircraft), 35
Boeing 314 Clipper (aircraft), 35
Boeing 707 (aircraft), 35
Boeing 727 (aircraft), 35

Boeing Air Transport (airline), 46
Boeing B-17 Flying Fortress
  (aircraft), 38
Boeing B-29 Superfortress (aircraft),
  38
Boeing B-47 Stratojet (aircraft), 38
Boeing B-52 Stratofortress (aircraft),
  39
Boeing Museum (Seattle,
  Washington), 35
Boeing P-26A (monoplane fighter),
  37
Boer Wars, 678
Boers (Dutch settlers), 678
Bogarde, Sir Dirk, 245
Bogart, Humphrey, 245
Bogatyriev, Semyon, 308
Boggs, Hale, 89
Bohemia, 543
Bokassa I, Emperor (Central African
  Empire), 366
Bold King Cole (cartoon), 66
Boles, Charles E., 84
Bolger, Ray, 246
Bolivar, Simon, 9, 361, 368, 373,
  402, 421
Bolivia, 113, 543, 544, 689
Bolivia, Republic of, 361
Bolle, Frank, 71, 73
Bollman Truss Bridge (Savage,
  Maryland), 126
Bollman, Wendell, 126
Bolsheviks, 406
Bolton, Charles, 84
Bombay Hook (lighthouse), 188
Bon Homme Richard, USS (carrier),
  513
Bonanza (TV), 614
Bonanza Air Lines, 46
Bonanza Air Services, 46
Bonanza Creek (Yukon Territory,
  Canada), 170
Bonaparte, Jerome Napoleon, 378
Bonaparte, Joseph, 487
Bonaparte, Marie, 378
Bonaparte, Napoleon, 686. *See also*
  Napoleon I, Emperor
Bond, Tommy, 561
Bond, Ward, 246
bonded servants, 179
Bondi, Beulah, 246
Bonefish, USS (submarine), 542, 715
Boner's Ark (comic strip), 70
Bonham, John, 338
Bonita, USS (submarine), 540, 541
Bonnard, Pierre, 21
Bonney, William H., 75, 84
Bonnie and Clyde, 84
Bonnin and Morris (company), 163
Bonnin, Gousse, 163
Bonsal, Philip Wilson, 370
Boob McNutt (comic strip), 70
Book of Mormon, 485

Boone, Richard, 246
boot (punishment), 83
Booth, John Wilkes, 653
Booth, Junius Brutus (Sr.), 140
Boots and Her Buddies (comic strip), 70
Borden Presents Ginny Simms (radio), 456
Bordier, Paul Camille, 365
Borge, Victor, 474
Borges, Jorge Luis, 195
Borglum, Gutzon, 231, 232
Borglum, Lincoln, 232
Born Yesterday (show), 148
Borodin, Alexander, 285, 311
Borsten, Laura Rapaport, 650
Borzage, Frank, 238
Bosko (cartoon character), 65
Bosnia and Herzegovina, 113, 361
Bosnian military conflict, 361
Bosom Buddies (TV), 614
Bossey, Peter, 83
Bostitch, 63
Boston Airport (Massachusetts), 49
Boston Americans (baseball), 571
Boston and Sandwich Glass Company, 164
Boston Arena (Boston, Massachusetts), 573
Boston Ballet Company (play), 138
Boston Beacons (soccer), 609
Boston Beaneaters (baseball), 568
Boston Bees (baseball), 568
Boston Blackie (radio), 449
Boston Braves (baseball), 568
Boston Bruins (ice hockey), 598, 599, 604
Boston Bulldogs (football), 588
Boston Celtics (basketball), 576
Boston Conservatory of Elocution, Oratory, and Dramatic Art, 104
Boston Daily Evening Transcript (newspaper), 434
Boston Doves (baseball), 568
Boston Evening Transcript (newspaper), 434
Boston Garden (Boston, Massachusetts), 573, 599
Boston Minutemen (soccer), 609
Boston News-Letter (newspaper), 435
Boston Red Caps (baseball), 568
Boston Red Sox (baseball), 554, 571
Boston Red Stockings, 554
Boston Rovers (soccer), 609
Boston Rustlers (baseball), 568
Boston Strangler, 76
Boston Tea Party, 674
Boston Transcript (newspaper), 434
Boston Weekly News-Letter (newspaper), 435
Boston Wire Stitcher Company, 63
Boston Yanks (football), 588
Boston, British occupation of, 674

Boston, Massachusetts (horsecars), 634
Boston, USS (cruiser), 537
Boswell, James, 195
Bosworth Field, Battle of, 419, 690
Botswana, 114, 223
Botswana, Republic of, 361
Botterell, Henry, 695
Boulder Canyon Dam, 132
Boulder Canyon Project, 132
Boulder Dam, 132
Bounty, HMS (sailing ship), 501
Bourbon monarchs (France), 376
Bourbon, House of, 412
Bouzey Dam, 93
Bow, Clara, 246
Bowdoin (schooner), 532
Bowen, Catherine Drinker, 195
Bowen, Ephraim, 675
Bowes, Edward, 463
Bowie Normal and Industrial School for the Training of Colored Youth, 103
Bowie State College, 103
Bowie State University, 103
Bowling (magazine), 220
Bowser, Arda, 589
Box 13 (radio), 449
Boxer, USS (carrier), 513
boxers, major, 581
Boxhall, Joseph Groves, 101
boxing, bare-knuckle, 580
boy bishops, 483
Boy Meets World (TV), 614
Boyd, William (Hopalong Cassidy), 246
Boyer, Charles, 246
Boyer, General Jean Pierre, 383
Boyle, Robert, 493
Boyne, Battle of the, 419
Bracken, Eddie, 246
Bracken's World (TV), 614
Bradford County, Florida, 658
Bradford County, Pennsylvania, 667
Bradlees (store), 62
Bradley Center (Milwaukee, Wisconsin), 574
Bradley Polytechnic Institute, 103
Bradley University, 103
Bradley, Joe ("Curley"), 472
Brady Bunch, The (TV), 614
Brady, Scott, 246
Bragan, Bobby, 569
Braganza (Bragança), House of, 404
Braganza-Coburg, House of, 404
Brahms, Johannes, 286
Brainard, Brigadier General David L., 156
Branch, John, 657
Branciforte County, California, 656
Brand, Neville, 246
Brandenburg (ballet), 138
Brando, Marlin, 246

Brandy, Joe, 593
Brandywine Springs Amusement Park (Faulkland, Delaware), 143
Braniff Airlines, 46
Braniff Airways, 46
Braniff International Airways, 46
Branner, Martin, 73
Brannon, W.T., 76
Brasilia, Brazil, 362
Braun, Eva, 706
Braves Field (Boston, Massachusetts, 554
Brazil, 114, 182, 543, 544, 693
Brazil, Empire of, 362
Brazil, Federated Republic of, 361, 362
Brazil, Kingdom of, 362
Brazil, United States of, 362
Brazil, Viceroyalty of, 362
Brazilian Clipper (aircraft), 37
Brazos County, Texas, 669
Brazos Santiago (lighthouse), 188
Brazzaville Group, 7
break on wheel (punishment), 81
Break the Bank (radio), 450
Breakfast at Sardi's (radio), 450
Breakfast Club, The (radio), 450
Breakfast in Hollywood (radio), 450
Breakspear, Nicholas, 486
Brearley, Charles, 166
Breathed, Berke, 70
Breckinridge County, Kansas, 660
Breckinridge County, Minnesota, 662
Breckinridge, John C., 680
Breen, Joseph, 237
Breen, Margaret Isabella, 101
Breisacher, George, 72
Bremen (liner), 526
Bremen, Germany, 9
Brendan Byrne Arena (East Rutherford, New Jersey), 574, 575
Breneman, Tom, 450
Brennan, Walter, 246
Brenner, Victor D., 225
Brent, George, 246
Bresnahan, Roger, 568
Bressart, Felix, 246
Brest-Litovsk, Treaty of, 690, 698
Brethren's Normal School and Collegiate Institute, 105
Brevard County, Florida, 658
Brewster Buffalo (aircraft), 39
Brice, Fanny, 448, 464
Brick Bradford (comic strip), 70
Brickley, Charlie, 593
Bride and Groom (radio), 450
Bride, Harold Sydney, 100
bridge builders, 123
Bridgeforth, William ("Sou"), 563
bridges, Bollman truss, 126
bridges, covered, 124
bridges, Fink truss, 126
Bridges, Frank, 588

bridges, Haupt truss, 127
Bridges, Lloyd, 246
bridges, metal railroad, 126
bridges, suspension, 126
bridges, truss railroad, 126
Brigadoon (musical), 137
brigantines, 498
Briggs Stadium (Detroit, Michigan), 556
Briggs v. Elliot, 69
Briggs, Claire, 70
Bright Horizon (radio), 450
Brighter Day, The (radio), 450
Brill trolley, 635
Brimsek, Frank, 604
Bringing Up Father (comic strip), 70
Bristol Aero Engines Ltd. (automobile maker), 28
Bristol Aviation Heritage Museum (England), 35
Bristol, Dave, 570
Bristol-Siddeley Engines Ltd. (automobile maker), 28
Britain, Battle of, 701
Britannic (liner), 96, 526, 538
Britax (manufacturer), 233
British Airways, 35
British Cameroons, 7, 364
British Colonies, 543, 544
British Commonwealth, 11
British East Africa, 7, 390, 417
British East India Company, 62
British Gold Coast, 380
British Honduras, 360
British India, 399
British Leyland (automobile maker), 32
British Malaya, 395
British New Guinea, 403
British North America, 364
British North American Act (1867), 365
British Royal Naval Air Service, 695
British Sex Discrimination Act (1975), 102
British Solomon Islands Protectorate, 410
British South Africa Company, 422, 423
British Talbot (automobile maker), 32
British Togoland, 7, 380, 415
British West Africa, 7, 401, 543, 544
British West African Settlements, 378
British West Indies, 543, 544
British Western Pacific Territories, 375, 410
Briton HMS (sailing ship), 501
Britten, Benjamin, 286
Broadway After Dark (movie), 136
Broadway Central Hotel (New York, New York), 176

Broadway Is My Beat (radio), 450
Broadway Limited (train), 482
Broadway Theater (New York, New York), 150
Brocius, Curly Bill, 74
Brod, Max, 206
Bronson, Charles, 246
Brontë, Anne, 195
Brontë, Charlotte, 195
Brontë, Emily, 195
Bronze Age, 6
Brook, Clive, 247
Brooklyn Atlantics (baseball), 568
Brooklyn Bridegrooms (baseball), 568
Brooklyn Bridge (Brooklyn, New York), 124, 125
Brooklyn Bridge, The (TV), 614
Brooklyn Cable Company (Brooklyn, New York), 632
Brooklyn Daily (newspaper), 434
Brooklyn Dodgers (baseball), 554, 568
Brooklyn Dodgers (football), 588
Brooklyn Eagles (baseball), 563
Brooklyn Grays (baseball), 568
Brooklyn Grooms (baseball), 568
Brooklyn Infants (baseball), 568
Brooklyn Lions (football), 588
Brooklyn Navy Yard (New York), 538
Brooklyn Robins (baseball), 568
Brooklyn Superbas (baseball), 568
Brooklyn Tigers (football), 588
Brooks, Arthur Raymond, 696
Brooks, Henry, 157
Brooks, Louise, 247
Brooks, Richard, 238
Brotherhood Park (Chicago, Illinois), 555
Brough Superior (motorcycle), 233
Brougham, John, 140
Brougham's Theater (New York, New York), 150
Brown Derby restaurant (Los Angeles, California), 490
Brown University, 101, 103
Brown v. Board of Education of Topeka, Kansas, 69
Brown, Andy, 600
Brown, Arthur Roy, 696
Brown, F.E., 132
Brown, Isaac ("Ike"), 562
Brown, Joe E., 247
Brown, Johnny Mack, 247
Brown, Nicholas, 103
Brown, Ray, 324
Brown, Russ, 89
Brown's Schoolhouse (North Carolina), 104
Browne, Tom, 73
Browning, Elizabeth Barrett, 195
Browning, Robert, 196

Bruce Gentry (comic strip), 70
Bruce, Nigel, 247
Bruch, Max, 286
Bruckner, Anton, 286
Brunei, 223, 362, 395
Brunel, Isambard K., 123, 537
Brunelleschi, Filippo, 16
Brush Pottery Company, 164
Brush Stadium (New York, New York), 557
Brush, George S., 164
Brush-McCoy Pottery, 164
Bryan, Johnny, 593
Bryant Pond, Maine, 611
Bryant Theater (New York, New York), 150
Bryant, William Cullen, 196
Bryant, William Jennings, 442
Brynner, Yul, 247
Bryson, William, 134
BSA (Birmingham Small Arms), 233, 235
BSA Bantam (motorcycle), 233
bubonic plague, 171
Buchanan County, Texas, 669
Buchanan, Edgar, 247
Buchanan, James, 651, 695
Bucharest, Treaty of (1913), 362
Buchenwald (concentration camp), 709
Buck Rogers in the 25th Century (comic strip), 70
Buck Rogers in the 25th Century (radio), 450
Buck Ryan (comic strip), 70
Buck, Leffert Lefferts, 124
Buck, Pearl S., 196
Buckingham House, 18
Buckley, Will, 82
Bucknell University, 103
Bucknell, William, 103
Buckroe Beach Amusement Park (Hampton, Virginia), 143
Budenny, Marshal Semyon M., 406
Buffalo All-Americans (football), 589
Buffalo Bill Cody's Wild West Show, 444
Buffalo Bisons (football), 589
Buffalo Braves (basketball), 577, 579
Buffalo Creek Dam, 93
Buffalo nickel, U.S., 225
Buffalo Sabres (ice hockey), 601
Buffalo Soldiers, 691
Buffalo, New York (horsecars), 634
Buffalo, New York (trolleys), 635
Buffy the Vampire Slayer (TV), 614
Bug Light (lighthouse), 190
Buganda, Kingdom of, 417
Bugatti (automobile maker), 28
Bugatti Grand Prix, 28
Bugatti, Ettore, 28
Bugeyes (Chesapeake Bay ships),

498

Bugs Bunny (cartoon character), 65
Bugs in Love (cartoon), 67
Builders Square (store), 62
buildings, tallest, 61
Bulfinch, Charles, 16
Bulgaria, 11, 114, 489, 631, 690
Bulgaria, People's Republic of, 363
Bulgaria, Republic of, 362
Bulge, Battle of the, 701
Bull Moose party, 440
Bulldog Drummond, The Adventures of (radio), 450
bullion, gold, 170
Bullion, Laura, 85
Bullock School, 109
Bullock's (store), 62
Bullock's Point (lighthouse), 188
Buncombe County, Iowa, 660
Bundy, Ross (Miami speaker), 428
Bundy, Ted, 82
Bungle Family, The (comic strip), 70
Bunker Hill (Breed's Hill), Battle of, 674
Bunker Hill Covered Bridge (Claremont, North Carolina), 127
Bunker Hill, USS (carrier), 513
Buñuel, Luis, 238
Buono, Victor, 247
Burger Chef restaurant, 490
Burgess, Anthony, 196
Burgesses, House of, 641
Burgundy, House of, 400, 404
Burke, Arleigh ("31-Knot"), 716
Burke, Billie, 247
Burke, Edmund, 196
Burke, Sean, 603
Burkina Faso, 114, 223, 363
Burlington Northern Railroad, 476, 477, 478, 479
Burlington Northern Sante Fe Railway, 476
Burma, 399, 543
Burma-Shave Company, 61
Burn, Harry, 112
Burnett, Henry John, 81
Burnham and Company, 176
Burnham and Root, 16, 19
Burnham, Daniel H., 16
Burnham, Linden Forbes Sampson, 382
Burns and Allen Show, The (radio), 450
Burns, Bob, 449
Burns, George, 247, 450
Burns, Robert, 196
Burr, Aaron, 111
Burr, Raymond, 247
Burroughs Adding Machine Company, 63
Burroughs Corporation, 63
Burroughs, Edgar Rice, 196, 471
Burt, Harry, 162

Burton, Richard, 247
Burton's Gentleman's Magazine, 220
Burton's New Theater (New York, New York), 152
Burundi, 9, 114
Burundi, Kingdom of, 363
Burundi, Republic of, 363
Busch Gardens (Van Nuys, California), 143
Busch Memorial Stadium (Saint Louis, Missouri), 559
Busch Stadium (Saint Louis, Missouri), 559
Bush, George Herbert Walker, 232, 684, 718
Bush, George W., 651
Bush, Guy, 564
business and industry, 61
Buster Brown (comic strip), 70
Butler, Benjamin F., 440, 441
Butler, Jack, 183
Butler, Willis Pollard, 174
Butte City Street Railroad (Butte, Montana), 632
Butte, Montana (trolleys), 635
Butterfield, John, 634
Butterworth, Charles, 247
Buz Sawyer (comic strip), 70
Bye Bye Blackboard (cartoon), 66, 67
Byelorussian Soviet Socialist Republic, 360
Byington, Spring, 247
Byrd, Admiral Richard E., 154
Byrne, Tommy, 569
Byrne, William, 159
Byron, Lord (George Gordon), 196
Byte (magazine), 220
Byzantine Empire, 118, 413
Byzantium, 118, 416
C&O, the railroad), 476
C.P.O. Sharkey (TV), 615
cabinet photographs, 438
cable cars, 631
Cable Tramway Company of Omaha (Omaha, Nebraska), 633
Cabot, Bruce, 247
Cabot, Susan, 247
Cabot, USS (carrier), 513
Cadaract, Victoria, 425
Cadillac Eldorado, 33
Cadillac Motor Company, 30
Cadillac tank, 721
Caesar, Irving, 286
Caesar, Julius, 630
Cagney & Lacey (TV), 614
Cagney, James, 247
Cahaba, Alabama, 655
Cahawba County, Alabama, 655
Cahn, Sammy, 286
Cahuilla (Native Americans), 424
Cairo War Conference (Egypt), 703
Cairo, Egypt, 373
Calapooya (Native Americans), 424

Calcutta, India, 78
Caldor (store), 62
Caldwell, Ray, 567
Caledonia (liner), 526
Calgary Boomers (soccer), 609
Calgary Flames (ice hockey), 602
Calgary, Alberta (trolleys), 635
Calhern, Louis, 248
Calhoun County, Iowa, 659
Calhoun County, Kansas, 660
Calhoun County, Nebraska, 664
Calhoun, John C., 546, 644
Calhoun, Patrick, 101
Calhoun, Rory, 248
California, 12, 13, 112, 545, 656
California Academy of Science, 13
California Angels (baseball), 571
California Bowl (football), 584
California condor, 12
California Golden Seals (ice hockey), 604
California grizzly, 13
California Institute of Technology, 103
California Perfume Company, 63
California Surf (soccer), 609
California Zephyr (train), 482
California, Republic of, 656
California, USS (battleship), 503
Californian and Overland Monthly, The (magazine), 222
Californian, The (magazine), 222
Caligula, Emperor (Rome), 134
Calkin, Richard, 70
Call for Music (radio), 453
Callaghan, Ellen Natalia, 100
Callas, Maria, 311
Callimachus of Cyrene, 133
Calling All Cars (radio), 450
Calling All Detectives (radio), 450
Calloway, Cab, 324
Calusa (Native Americans), 424
Calvin and Hobbes (comic strip), 70
Calvin, John, 4, 486
Camacho, Hector, 582
Camark Pottery (company), 164
Cambodia, 8, 114, 223, 489, 543, 693
Cambodia, Kingdom of, 363
Cambodia, State of, 364
Cambrian Period, 2
Cambridge Glass Company, 164
Cambridge, Canada, 365
Cambridge, Godfrey, 248
Camden Art Tile and Pottery Company, 164
Camden County, Missouri, 663
Camel Caravan (*Comedy Caravan*, radio), 450
Camellia Bowl (football), 584
Cameron, Rod, 248
Cameroon, 10, 114, 543
Cameroon, Federal Republic of, 364
Cameroon, Republic of, 364

Camilli, Dolph, 564
Camp David (presidential retreat), 651
Camp O'Donnell (Philippines), 701
Camp Tuscazoar Foundation, 126
Camp, Walter Chauncey, 583
campaign hats (U.S. Marine Corps), 650
Campbell Bridge (Gowensville, South Carolina), 124
Campbell Playhouse (radio), 464
Campbell, Mary Katherine, 146
Campbell, Alec (Anzac veteran), 697
Campbell, Owen, 703
Campbell, William, 667
Camus, Albert, 196
Can You Top This? (radio), 450
Canada, 10, 114, 147, 364, 543, 544, 695
Canada, Dominion of, 365
Canada, place names, 365
Canada, Province of, 364
Canadian Arctic Expedition of 1913, 157
Canadian Group of Painters, 21
Canadian League (baseball), 562
Canadian Northern Railway, 480
Canadian Pacific Railway, 479, 480
Canaliño Chumash (Native Americans), 425
canals and waterways, 131
Canberra (liner), 526
Canby, E.R.S., 681
Candid Camera (TV), 450
Candid Microphone (radio), 450
Candlestick Park (San Francisco, California), 559
Candy, John, 248
Caniff, Milton, 71, 472
caning (punishment), 79
cannibalism, 178
Cannon (TV), 614
Canon Camera Company, 64
Canonicus, USS (armor clad ship), 682
Canonsburg Academy and Library Company, The, 109
Canonsburg Pottery (company), 168
Canova, Judy, 461
Canterbury Shaker community, 488
Canterbury Tales (Chaucer), 491
Canton Bulldogs (football), 589
Cantor, Eddie, 454, 471
Cape Breton Island, Canada, 690
Cape Breton, HMCS (Victory ship), 713
Cape Canaveral Air Station, 548
Cape Canaveral Auxiliary Air Force Base, 547
Cape Canaveral/Cape Kennedy, 547
Cape Cod Glass Works, 164, 165
Cape Colony, South Africa, 411
Cape Henlopen (lighthouse), 188

Cape Kennedy Air Force Station, 548
Cape Verde, Republic of, 114, 365, 544
Capek, Karel, 196
Capetown Clipper (aircraft), 35
Capital Airlines, 46
Capital Hotel (Johnstown, Pennsylvania), 176
capital punishment, 80
capital, United States, 640
Capitol Bullets (basketball), 577, 580
Capitol Limited (train), 482
Caplin, Elliot, 71
Capone, Alphonse ("Al"), 76
Capote, Truman, 196
Capp, Al, 71
Capra, Frank, 238
Captain and the Kids (comic strip), 70
Captain Brassbound's Conversion (play), 142
Captain Kangaroo (TV), 614
Captain Midnight (radio), 450
Captaincy-General of Guatemala, 401
Car 54, Where Are You? (TV), 614
Carbonate County, Colorado, 657
Carboniferous Period, 2
card catalogs, 187
Cardoso, Leonel Silva, 357
Carey, Harry (Sr.), 248
Carey, MacDonald, 248
Carey, Minnie Grace Mechling, 673
Carla C (liner), 527
Carla Costa (liner), 527
Carle, Frankie, 325
Carlisle Indian School, 585
Carlota, Empress (Mexico), 397
Carlson, Richard, 248
Carlson, W.A., 72
Carlyle, Thomas, 197
Carmeleño (Native Americans), 426
Carmichael, Franklin, 21
Carmichael, Hoagy, 287
Carnation Contented Hour (radio), 451
Carnegie Institute of Technology, 103
Carnegie Mellon University, 103
Carnegie Steel Company, 180
Carnegie Technical Schools, 103
Carney, Art, 248
Carney, Don, 473
Carol Burnett Show, The (TV), 614
Carol II, King (Romania), 405
Carolina Cougars (basketball), 577
Carolina parakeet, 13
Caroline in the City (TV), 614
Caroline Islands, 397
Carpathia (ship), 100
Carpenter, M. Scott, 548
Carpenters, The, 325
Carquest Bowl (football), 584

Carr, Gerald P., 549
Carr, Roseby, 480
Carradine, John, 248
Carrillo, Leo, 248
Carrington, Dora, 192
Carroll A. Deering (ship), 91
Carroll, Charles, 645
Carroll, Leo G., 248
Carroll, Les, 70, 72
Carroll, Lewis, 197
Carson, Jack, 248
Carter County, Wyoming, 670
Carter, Ad, 71
Carter, Benny, 325
Carter, Jimmy, 367, 414, 647
cartes-de-visite (photographs), 438
Carthage, 690
cartoonists, editorial/political, 67
cartoons, animated, 66
Caruso Cinema (New York, New York), 150
Caruso, Enrico, 311
Casa Coe da Sol (St. Petersburg, Florida), 18
Casa Manana (New York, New York), 150
Casa Mila (Barcelona, Spain), 17
Casablanca Charter, 10
Casablanca Group, 7
Casablanca War Conference (Morocco), 703
Casals, Pablo, 312
Cascarella, Joseph Thomas, 572
Case Institute of Technology, 103
Case School of Applied Science, 103
Case Western Reserve University, 103
Caserta Agreement, 712
Casey Court (comic strip), 70
Casey, Crime Photographer (radio), 451
Casey, Press Photographer (radio), 451
Casino Park (Kalamazoo, Michigan), 144
Casino Theater (New York, New York), 150 .
Casper the Friendly Ghost (cartoon character), 65
Casper's Birthday Party (cartoon), 65
Cass County, Georgia, 658
Cass County, Missouri, 663
Cass County, Texas, 669
Cass, Lewis, 222
Cass, Peggy, 248
Cassatt, Mary, 22
Cassavetes, John, 238
Casselman River Bridge (Grantsville, Maryland), 125
Cassels, Andrew, 603
Cassidy, Butch, 84
Cassidy, Jack, 248

Cassin Young, USS (destroyer), 538, 712

Cassius X, 581

Casson, A.J. (Alfred Joseph), 21

Castle Garden (New York, New York), 443

Castle, Irene, 136

Castle, Vernon, 136

castrati singers, 178, 318

Castro, Fidel, 370

Catawba (Native Americans), 424

Cather, Willa, 197

Cato Street conspirators, 80

Cats (show), 148

Cats & Bruises (cartoon), 66

Caucasus, Viceroyalty of the, 357, 378

caucus, congressional nominating, 110

Cavalcade of America (radio), 451

Cavalcade of Stars (TV), 614

Cavalier, HMS (destroyer), 713

cavalry charge (World War I), 698

cavalry charge, U.S. Army, 648

cavalry, U.S. Army, 648

Cawthorn, Pete, 588

Cayuse (Native Americans), 424

CBS Is There (radio), 475

CBS Radio Mystery Theater, The, 451

CBS Radio Playhouse No. 2 (New York, New York), 151

CBS Radio Workshop, 451, 452

Cedarburg Bridge (Wisconsin), 124

Cedrone, Danny, 333

Ceiling Unlimited (radio), 451

celibacy, clergy, 484

cellulose nitrate film, 438

Celoron Amusement Park (Jamestown, New York), 143

Cenozoic Era, 3

censorship, movies, 236

Census, Office of the, 639

Centenary Bible Institute, 106

Centennial Exposition (Philadelphia, Pennsylvania), 159

Centennial Park Bombing, 87

Central African Empire, 366

Central African Republic, 8, 10, 114, 365

Central Airways (airline), 46

Central America, 7

Central America, United Provinces of, 543

Central American Federation, 7, 369, 374, 382, 384, 401

Central Pacific Railroad, 479

Central Powers (World War I), 695

Central Railroad of New Jersey, 476

Central Theater (New York, New York), 150

Central Traction Company (Pittsburgh, Pennsylvania), 633

Central Treaty Organization (CENTO), 8

Central Vermont Airways, 46

Centre Le Corbusier (Heidi Weber Museum, Zurich, Switzerland), 18

Century (magazine), 223

Century Illustrated (magazine), 223

Century Magazine/ Scribner's Monthly (magazine), 223

Century Monthly (magazine), 223

Century of Progress International Exposition (Chicago, Illinois), 160

Ceramic Art Company, 165

Ceramics, Age of, 3

Cervantes, Ascension Solorsano (Mutsun speaker), 429

Cervantes, Miguel de, 197

Cetshwayo (Cetewayo), King (Zululand), 411

Ceylon, 412

Ch'in (Ts'in) dynasty (China), 119

Ch'in Shih Huang Ti, Emperor (China), 132

Ch'ing (Manchu) dynasty (China), 366

Chabot, Lorne, 602

Chabrier, Emmanuel, 287

Chaco Boreal, 678

Chaco War, 678

Chad, 8, 10, 114, 366

Chad, Republic of, 366

Chaffee County, Colorado, 657

Chagall, Marc, 22

Chakri dynasty (Thailand), 415

Chaley, Joseph, 127

Chaliapin, Feodor, 312

Challenge of the Yukon, The (radio), 469

Challenger Air Lines, 47

Challenger Oceanographic Expedition, 154

Challenger, HMS (ship), 154

Chamber Music Society of Lower Basin Street, The (radio), 451

Chamber of Commerce of the United States, 222

Chamberlain, Wilt, 576

Chamberlin, E.J., 481

Chamoun, Camille, 392

Champeog County, Oregon, 667

Champion Air (airline), 47

Champion of the Seas (clipper ship), 500

Champion, Gower, 136

Champlin, Stephen, 694

Chance, Frank, 566

Chandernagor, India, 8

Chandler, Jeff, 248

Chandler, Raymond, 197, 467

Chandu, the Magician, 451

Chaney, Lon (Jr.), 249

Chaney, Lon (Sr.), 248

Chang Kuo-tao, 367

Channel Islands, 707

Chanute, Octave, 126

Chao K'uang-yin (Kao Tsu), 119

Chapin, Harry, 325

Chaplain Jim (radio), 451

Chaplin, Sir Charles, 237, 238, 249

Chapman, John, 6

Charge of the Light Brigade, 685

Chariot of Fame (clipper ship), 499

Charity, Sisters of, 486

Charlemagne, 120

Charles Cartlidge and Company, 164

Charles Cooper (packet ship), 531

Charles Edward (Young Pretender), 419

Charles Hopkins Theater (New York, New York), 152

Charles I, Emperor (Austria), 384

Charles I, King (England), 419

Charles II, King (England), 5, 81, 419

Charles II, King (Spain), 411, 692

Charles IV, King (France), 376

Charles River County, Virginia, 670

Charles V, Holy Roman Emperor, 396

Charles V, King (France), 686

Charles VI, Emperor (Austria), 678

Charles W. Morgan (whaling ship), 536

Charles X, King (France), 376

Charles, Ezzard, 582

Charles, Mary Carmel, 183

Charles, Ray, 326

Charleston Hotel (Charleston, South Carolina), 176

Charleston, West Virginia (trolleys), 635

Charlestown Navy Yard (Massachusetts), 538

Charlevoix County, Michigan, 662

Charlie Chan stories, 195

Charlie Chan, The Adventures of (radio), 451

Charlie's Angels (TV), 614

Charlotte County, New York, 665

Charlotte Square, New Town (Edinburgh, Scotland), 16

Charlotte, South Carolina (trolleys), 635

Charlton Comics, 73

Charteris, Leslie, 469

Chase and Sanborn Show (radio), 454

Chase, Charles, 249

Chase, John Paul, 85

Chatelain, USS (ship), 542

Chattanooga, Tennessee (trolleys), 635

Chatterton, Ruth, 249

Chaucer, Geoffrey, 197

Chavez Ravine (Los Angeles, California), 557

Chavez, Cesar, 180
Checkaye, Cooney, 593
Checker Cab Compaany, 635
Checkmate (TV), 614
Checkpoint Charlie, 684
Cheers (TV), 615
Cheever, John, 197
Chehab, Faud, 392
Chehalis County, Washington, 670
Chekhov, Anton, 197
Chelmno (concentration camp), 709
Chelsea Keramic Art Works, 165
Chelsea Pottery (company), 165
Chemical Ko-Ko (cartoon), 66
Chemical Revolution, 3
Chenango Point, New York, 665
Cheonoquet County, Michigan, 662
Chernobyl Nuclear Power Plant, 95
Cherokee County, Kansas, 660
Cherokee Nation (Native
    Americans), 681
Cherry Blossom Grove (New York,
    New York), 152
Cherry Bowl (football), 584
Cherry, Don, 326
Cherrystone Bar (lighthouse), 188
Cherubini, Luigi, 287
Chesapeake & Ohio Railway, 476,
    478, 480
Chesapeake and Delaware Canal, 129
Chesapeake and Ohio Canal, 130
Chesapeake, USS (frigate), 523
chess, 163
Chessie System (railroad), 476
Chesterfield Supper Hour, The
    (radio), 451
Chesterton, G. K., 197
Chetco (Native Americans), 425
Chevaldae. Tim, 603
Chevalier, Maurice, 249
Chevrolet Camaro, 33
Chevrolet Corvair, 33
Cheyenne (TV), 615
Cheyney State College, 103
Cheyney State Teachers College, 103
Cheyney Training School for
    Teachers, 103
Cheyney University of Pennsylvania,
    103
Chiang Kai-shek, 414, 703
Chibitty, Charles, 716
Chicago & Eastern Illinois (railroad),
    482
Chicago & North Western Railroad,
    477
Chicago & Rock Island Rail Road
    Company, 477
Chicago & Southern Airlines, 47
Chicago American (newspaper), 434
Chicago Bears (football), 585, 587
Chicago Black Hawks (ice hockey),
    598, 599, 601, 602
Chicago Cardinals (football), 585,

587
Chicago City Railway (Chicago,
    Illinois), 632
Chicago Colts (baseball), 571
Chicago Cubs (baseball), 558, 571
Chicago Daily News (newspaper),
    434
Chicago Federals (baseball), 561
Chicago Freight Subway, 634
Chicago Hope (TV), 615
Chicago Hotel (Chicago, Illinois),
    176
Chicago Municipal Airport (Illinois),
    49
Chicago Mustangs (soccer), 609
Chicago O'Hare International Airport
    (Illinois), 49
Chicago Orchard Airport (Illinois),
    49
Chicago Orphans (baseball), 571
Chicago Packers/Zephyrs
    (basketball), 577
Chicago Republican (newspaper), 94
Chicago Spurs (soccer), 609
Chicago Stadium (Chicago, Illinois),
    573, 599
Chicago Stags/Bruins (basketball),
    577
Chicago Sting (soccer), 608, 609
Chicago Theater of the Air, The
    (radio), 451
Chicago Tigers (football), 589
Chicago Today (newspaper), 434
Chicago Tunnel Company, 635
Chicago West Division Railway
    (Chicago, Illinois), 632
Chicago White Sox (baseball), 555,
    571
Chicago White Stockings (baseball),
    571
Chicago, Burlington & Quincy
    Railroad Company, 476, 483
Chicago, Illinois (horsecars), 634
Chicago, Illinois (trolleys), 635
Chicago, Milwaukee & St. Paul
    (railroad), 476, 480
Chicago, Milwaukee, St. Paul &
    Pacific (railroad), 476, 483
Chicago, Rock Island & Pacific
    (railroad), 477
Chicago, Treaty of, 659
Chicago, USS (cruiser), 537
Chicago's American (newspaper),
    434
Chick Carter, Boy Detective (radio),
    451
Chickaloon River Bridge
    (Matanuska-Susitna, Alaska), 124
Chickasaw (Native Americans), 425
Chico and the Man (TV), 615
Chief, (cavalry horse), 648
child labor, United States, 178
Children's Hour, The (radio), 452

Chile, 114, 543, 544, 689
Chile, Republic of, 366
Chile, Socialist Republic of, 366
Chile, State of, 366
Chilton County, Alabama, 655
China, 114, 119, 121, 158, 489, 543,
    691, 692
China Beach (TV), 615
China, People's Republic of, 366,
    414
Chinese Nationalists, 367
Chiniquy, Gerry, 67
Chip n' Dale (cartoon character), 65
Chippewa (Native Americans), 425,
    659
ChiPS (TV), 615
Chips Ahoy (cartoon), 65
Chisholm Trail, 491
Chisholm, Jesse, 491
Chopin, Frédéric, 287
Choptank River Light, 188
Chorus Line, A (show), 148
Chosen (Korea), 391
Chou dynasty (China), 119
Christian County, Illinois, 659
Christian II, King (Sweden), 10
Christian X, King (Denmark), 385
Christian, Fletcher, 501
Christiana County, Tennessee, 668
Christiania (Kristiania), Sweden, 401
Christie, Dame Agatha, 197
Christie, James, 62
Christie's Auction House, 62
Christina, Queen (Sweden), 413
Christmas Truce (World War I), 697
Christy Minstrels (New York, New
    York), 150
Chrysler (automobile maker), 29
Chrysler Building (New York, New
    York), 61, 230
Chrysler turbine car, 27
Chrysler, Walter P., 31
Chu Yüan-chang (Hung Wu), 120
Chumash (Native Americans), 425
Church of Jesus Christ of Latter-Day
    Saints, 484, 669
Churchill, Winston, 88, 685, 703
Ciannelli, Eduardo, 249
Cierva C.8W Autogiro (aircraft), 56
Cierva, Juan de la, 56
cigarette commercial, 173
Cimmerians, 122
Cincinnati Celts (football), 589
Cincinnati Gardens (Cincinnati,
    Ohio), 573
Cincinnati Red Stockings (baseball),
    571
Cincinnati Redlegs (baseball), 571
Cincinnati Reds (baseball), 571
Cincinnati Reds (football), 589
Cincinnati Royals (basketball), 577,
    578
Cincinnati Zoo (Ohio), 13, 14

Colbert, Claudette, 249
Colby, Bainbridge, 112
Cold War, 684
Cole County, South Dakota, 668
Cole, Edward R., 13
Cole, Nat ("King"), 327
Colechurch, Peter of, 125
Coleridge, Samuel Taylor, 197
Coles, Charles ("Honi"), 136
Colette, 198
Colfax County, Mississippi, 663
Colgate Comedy Hour (TV), 454, 615
Colgate Sports Newsreel, The (radio), 452
Colgate University, 104
College and Academy of Philadelphia, 106
College of Agriculture and Mechanic Arts (Hawaii), 105
College of New Jersey, The, 104, 107
College of Physicians of Philadelphia (Pennsylvania), 175
College of South Jersey, 107
College Quiz Bowl (radio), 452
colleges, colonial, 101
Collegiate College, 109
Collier Hour, The (radio), 452, 456
Collier's (magazine), 25, 220, 452, 583
Collier's Once a Week (magzine), 220
Collier's the National Weekly (magazine), 220
Collins, Ray, 249
Collins, Wilkie, 198
Colman, Ronald, 249, 457
Colombia, 9, 114, 402, 543
Colombia, Republic of, 368, 403
Colombia, United States of, 368, 403
colonial empires, last of the world's great, 405
Colorado, 112, 656
Colorado Avalanche (ice hockey), 605
Colorado Caribous (soccer), 609
Colorado City, Colorado, 657
Colorado Fuel and Iron Works (Ludlow, Colorado), 180
Colorado Rockies (baseball), 556
Colorado Rockies (ice hockey), 602
Colorado Territory, 657
Colorado, USS (battleship), 503
Colored Normal Industrial, Agricultural and Mechanical College of South Carolina, 108
Colossus Bridge (Philadelphia, Pennsylvania), 127
Colossus of Rhodes, 133
Colt Stadium (Houston, Texas), 556
Coltrane, John, 327
Columbia (space shuttle), 50
Columbia (steamship), 536

Columbia Broadcasting System (CBS), 446
Columbia College, 104
Columbia Park (Philadelphia, Pennsylvania), 558
Columbia Pictures, 237
Columbia Pictures (movie studio), 237
Columbia Railway (Washington, D.C.), 634
Columbia Records, 437
Columbia Theater (New York, New York), 150
Columbia University, 101
Columbia Workshop, The (radio), 451, 452
Columbian Clipper (aircraft), 37
Columbian College, 105
Columbian University, 105
Columbo (TV), 615
Columbo, Russ, 327
Columbus (liner), 526
Columbus Circle (theater, New York, New York), 152
Columbus Panhandles (football), 590
Columbus Tigers (football), 590
Columbus, Christopher, 154
Columbus, Ohio (trolleys), 635
Comanche (cavalry horse), 673
Comanches (Native Americans), 426
Comayagua, Honduras, 384
Combat (TV), 615
Come Summer (musical), 137
comedy teams, 135
Comedy Theater (New York, New York), 150
Comerica Park (Detroit, Michigan), 556
Comet Shoemaker-Levy 9, 547
comics (cartoons), 70, 73
Cominform, 417
Cominterm, 417
Comiskey, Charles A., 555, 571
Commander (ferry), 698
Commemorative Air Force (Texas), 40, 43
Commerce and Labor, Department of (U.S.), 639
Commerce, Department of (U.S.), 639, 722
Committee of Public Safety, 686
Commodore Perry (clipper ship), 500
Commons, House of (Great Britain), 485
Commonwealth, English, 419
Communist party (USSR), 418
Community College of Baltimore, 103
Como, Perry, 327
Comoros, 114
Comoros, Federal and Islamic Republic of, 369
Comoros, Protectorate of the, 369

Comoros, State of, 369
Comoros, Union of, 368, 369
compact discs (CDs), 438
Company H, U.S. Cavalry, 673
Compromise of 1850, 644
Compute! (magazine), 220
Computer, Age of the, 3
computers, first generation, 117
Computer-Tabulating-Recording Company, 63
Comstock lode, 170
concentration camps, 711
Concorde (aircraft), 35
Condor (motorcycle maker), 233
Condor A250 (motorcycle), 233
Condors (basketball), 579
ConEd Building (New York, New York), 149
Conejos County, Colorado, 657
Conestoga, USS (ship), 91
Confederate States of America, 655, 656, 658, 661, 663, 666, 667, 679
Confederation Era, 642
Confederation of the Rhine, 379
Confucius, 119
Congo Brazzaville, 224
Congo Free State, 369
Congo, Democratic Republic of the (Congo-Kinshasa), 114, 369
Congo, Middle, 365
Congo, People's Republic of, 10, 369
Congo, Republic of (Congo-Brazzaville), 369
Congo, Republic of the, 8, 114, 369
Congregation for the Doctrine of the Faith, 60
Congress of Cúcuta (Colombia), 9
Congress of Industrial Organizations (CIO), 180, 181
Congress of Racial Equality, 68
Congress of the Confederation, 231
Congress of the United States, 227, 231, 641, 675
Congress, USS (frigate), 523, 682
Congressional Globe, 643
Congressional Medal of Honor, 699
Congressional pages, 643
Congressional Record, The, 643
Congreve, William, 198
Connally, John B., 652
Connally, Nellie, 652
Connecticut, 185, 489, 545, 657
Connecticut Agricultural College, 104
Connecticut Bicentennials (soccer), 609
Connecticut Colony, 10
Connecticut State College, 104
Connecticut, University of, 104
Connecticut, USS (battleship), 503
Connell, Mary Jean, 175
Connelly, Wayne, 599
Connie Mack Stadium (Philadelphia,

371
Czech Republic, 114, 371, 631
Czechoslovak Federal Republic, 371
Czechoslovak Republic, 371
Czechoslovak Socialist Republic, 371
Czechoslovak State, 371
Czechoslovakia, 11
D. Fernando II e Glória (frigate), 522
D. W. Griffith Theater (New York, New York), 150
D.C. Stadium (Washington, D.C.), 559
d'Orano, Camille, 372
Da Silva, Howard, 251
Dachau (concentration camp), 709
Dachau war crimes trials, 720
Dade, Free State of, 680
Daffy Duck (cartoon character), 65, 67
daguerrotypes, 439
Dahlen, Ulf, 603
Dahomey, 9, 10
Dahomey, Republic of, 360
Dailey, Truman Washington (Otoe-Missouria speaker), 430
Daily Arkansas Gazette (newspaper), 434
Daily Dilemma (radio), 452
Daily Mirror (New York newspaper), 435
Daily Normal and High School for Females (New York), 105
Daimler (automobile maker), 28
Daimler, Gottlieb, 28
Daimler-Benz (automobile maker), 31
daimyos (feudal lords), 179
Dakota (aircraft), 36
Dakota (Native Americans), 431
Dakota Agricultural College, 108
Dakota Territory, 666, 668
Daktari (TV), 615
Dalai Lama, 368
Dale Dyke Dam, 93
Dali, Salvador, 22
Dallas (TV), 615
Dallas County, Missouri, 663
Dallas County, Wisconsin, 670
Dallas Daily Herald (newspaper), 434
Dallas Daily Times (newspaper), 434
Dallas Pottery (company), 165
Dallas Sidekicks (soccer), 608
Dallas Stars (ice hockey), 603
Dallas Texans (football), 591
Dallas Times Herald (newspaper), 434
Dallas Tornado (soccer), 609
Dallas, Frederick, 165
Dallas/Texas Chaparrals (basketball), 578

Dalliger, John, 81
Dalmatian language (Croatia), 182
Dalton Gang, 85
Dalton, Cal, 67
Dalton, Emmett, 85
Daly's Fifth Avenue Theater (New York, New York), 150
Daly's Theater (New York, New York), 150
Damon Runyon Theater, The (radio), 452
Damon, Catharine S., 677
Damrosch, Walter, 465
Dan Air, 36
Dan George, (Chief), 251
Dana, Bill, 44
Dancin' (show), 148
Dandridge, Dorothy, 251
Dane County, Illinois, 659
Dangerfield, Rodney, 251
Dangerous Assignment (radio), 452
Daniel Boone (TV), 615
Daniel Deronda (novel), 200
Daniell, Henry, 251
Daniels, Bebe, 251
Daniels, Bennie, 554
Daniels, Jerry, 335
Daniels, Sidney E., 101
Danilova, Alexandra, 136
Danish West Indies, 372, 543
Dannay, Frederic, 454
Danny Kaye Show, The (TV), 615
Danny Thomas Show, The/Make Room for Daddy (TV), 615
Dano, Royal, 251
Dante Alighieri, 199
Danube Canal Bridge (Vienna, Austria), 127
Darin, Bobby, 251, 328
Darius III, Emperor (Persian Empire), 122
Darius the Great, 121
Dark Shadows (TV), 615
Dark, Alvin, 569
Darnell, Linda, 251
Darter, USS (submarine), 541
Dartmouth College, 101
Darwell, Jane, 251
Darwin, Charles, 493
Date With Judy, A (radio), 452
Dato, Pehin Orang Kaya Laila Wijaya, 362
Datsun (automobile), 29
Daughters of the American Revolution, 677
Dauphin (France), 376
Dave's World (TV), 615
Davenport, Fanny, 140
Davenport, Harry, 251
Davey, John, 182
David Harding Counterspy (radio), 452

David Harum (radio), 452
Davidson, Arthur, 236
Davies, Marion, 251
Davis County, Kansas, 660
Davis County, Texas, 669
Davis Rules (TV), 616
Davis, Arthur, 67
Davis, Bette, 251
Davis, Brad, 252
Davis, George, 680
Davis, Jack, 71
Davis, Jefferson, 232, 679, 680
Davis, Joan, 252, 460
Davis, Miles, 328
Davis, Phil, 463
Davis, Rory, 611
Davis, Sammy (Jr.), 252, 329
Davis-Monthan Air Force Base (Arizona), 38
Dawn Gawn (cartoon), 66
Dawson's Creek (TV), 616
Day by Day (TV), 616
Day in the Life of Dennis Day, A (radio), 452
Days and Nights of Molly Dodd, The (TV), 616
Dayton Triangles (football), 588, 591
DC Comics, 73
DDT (insecticide), 153
De Dion, Albert (Count), 29
De Dion-Bouton (automobile), 29
De Havilland Comet (aircraft), 36
de La Falaise, Henri, 237
de Leath, Vaughan, 473
de Lesseps, Ferdinand, 129
De Mille, Agnes, 137
De Sapio, Carmine, 439
De Sica, Vittorio, 238
de Silva, Candeláno, 182
De Soto, Hernando, 155
Deale County, Delaware, 657
Dean Martin Show, Dean Martin Comedy Hour (TV), 616
Dean, Allen, 71
Dean, Dizzy, 572
Dean, James, 252
Dear John (TV), 616
Dearborn Street Subway (Chicago, Illinois), 134
Death of Ocean View Park (movie), 144
death penalty, 80
Death Valley Days (radio), 453, 470
Death Valley Sheriff (radio), 470
Deathtrap (play), 148
Debaraz, Louis, 88
Debs, Eugene V., 180
debt, imprisonment for, 83
Debussy, Claude, 288
DeCamp, Rosemary, 252
Decatur County, Missouri, 663
Decatur House (Washington, D.C.), 17

Decatur, Stephen, 678
December Bride (TV), 616
Declaration of Independence, United States, 231, 645
Declaration of Paris (1856), 77
Dedham Pottery (company), 165
Deep Water Shoals (lighthouse), 189
Defenders, The (TV), 616
Defense Savings Bonds, U.S., 229
Defense, Department of (U.S.), 639
Defense, Secretary of, 639
Defoe, Daniel, 199
Dehner, John, 252
Dekker, Albert, 252
Del Monte Fishing Company, 12
del Rio, Dolores, 252
Delacorte, George, 71
Delage (automobile maker), 29
Delage, Louis, 29
Delahanty, Ed, 566
Delahanty, Frank, 566
Delahanty, Jim, 566
Delahanty, Joe, 566
Delahanty, Tom, 566
Delahaye (automobile maker), 29, 30
Delaware, 80, 545, 657
Delaware (Native Americans), 426
Delaware and Cobb (railroad), 477
Delaware and Hudson Canal, 130
Delaware and Raritan Canal, 130
Delaware Canal, 130
Delaware College, 104
Delaware Military Academy, 109
Delaware River Bridge (Philadelphia, Pennsylvania), 125
Delaware, Lackawanna & Western Railroad, 477
Delaware, Lehigh, Schuylkill and Susquehanna Railroad Company, 477
Delaware, University of, 104
Delaware, USS (battleship), 503
Delhi sultanate (India), 385
Delibes, Léo, 288
Delius, Frederick, 288
Dell Comics, 73
Dell, Herb, 590
Delmonico's restaurant (New York, New York), 490
DeLong, George Washington, 155
Delorean (automobile), 29
Delorean, John, 29
Delta Air Corporation (airline), 47
Delta Air Lines, Inc. (airline), 47
Delta Air Services (airline), 47
Delta Bowl (football), 584
Delta C&S Air Lines, 47
Delta Queen (paddle steamer), 535
Demand Notes, U.S., 228
Demarest, William, 252
DeMille, Cecil B., 238, 463
Democratic party, 652
Democratic-Republican party, 440

Demotic Script, 11
Dempsey, Jack, 581
Denishawn Dancers, 137
Denison University, 104
Denison, William S., 104
Denmark, 9, 10, 79, 114, 543, 631, 671
Denmark (clipper ship), 500
Denmark, Kingdom of, 372, 401
Dennis the Menace (TV), 616
Dennis, Sandy, 252
Dennison, Jo-Carroll, 147
Denny, Jerry, 560
Denny, Reginald, 252
Denver & Rio Grande Western Railroad, 477, 483
Denver City Cable Company (Denver, Colorado), 632
Denver Dynamos (soccer), 609
Denver Nuggets (basketball), 576, 578
Denver Rockets (basketball), 578
Denver Tramway Company (Denver, Colorado), 632
Denver, Colorado (trolleys), 635
Denver, John, 329
DePaul University, 104
Depler, Jack, 594
Der Spiegel (magazine), 708
DeRita, Joe, 135
Des Moines, Iowa (trolleys), 635
DeSalvo, Albert, 76
Descartes, Rene, 494
Deseret, State of, 485, 669
designated foul shooter (basketball), 575
Designer Accents (company), 167
Designing Women (TV), 616
DeSoto (automobile), 29
Dessalines, Jean-Jacques, 383
detention, Japanese American, 716
Detroit Cougars (ice hockey), 602
Detroit Cougars (soccer), 609
Detroit Express (soccer), 609
Detroit Falcons (basketball), 578
Detroit Falcons (ice hockey), 602, 604
Detroit Heralds (football), 591
Detroit Panthers (football), 591
Detroit Red Wings (ice hockey), 598, 599, 603, 605
Detroit Tigers (baseball), 556
Detroit Vipers (ice hockey), 600
Detroit Wolverines (football), 591
Detroit, HMS (sailing ship), 539
Detroit, Michigan (horsecars), 634
Dettingen, Battle of, 678
Deutschland (liner), 527
Devens, Charles, 564
Devereux, Robert, Earl of Essex, 78
Devil's Island (prison), 77
Devine, Andy, 252, 474
Devonian Period, 2

Dewey County, South Dakota, 668
Dewhurst, Colleen, 252
DeWilde, Brandon, 252
DeWolfe, Billy, 252
Dharma & Greg (TV), 616
di Tomasso, Leonardo, 482
Diaghilev, Sergei, 137
Diamond, Selma, 252
Díaz, Porfirio, 397
Dick Tracy, The Adventures of (radio), 453
Dick Van Dyke Show (TV), 616
Dick, Billy (Siuslawan speaker), 432
Dick, Lucy, 425
Dickens, Charles, 78, 79, 199
Dickenson, Fred, 72
Dickey, James, 199
Dickie Dare (comic strip), 71
Dickinson, Emily, 199
dictionaries, 59
Diderot, Denis, 60
Dieldrin (pesticide), 153
Dies Committee, 644
Dies, Martin (Jr.), 644
Diesel, Rudolf, 89
Dietrich, Marlene, 252
Diff'rent Strokes (TV), 616
Different World, A (TV), 616
Dillinger, John, 85
DiMaggio, Joe, 567
Dimension X (radio), 453
dimes, U.S., 228
Dinah Shore Chevy Show, The (TV), 616
Dinah Shore Show, The (radio), 453
Dinah Shore Show, The (TV), 616
Dineen, Kevin, 603
Dinesen, Isak, 199
Dingbat Family, The (comic strip), 71
Dino Ferrari 246 (race car), 552
dinosaurs, extinction of, 3
DiPetra, Tony, 71
Directors Guild of America, 236
directors, movie, 238
Directory, The (France), 377, 686
dirigibles, 92
Dirigo (sailing ship), 537
Dirks, John, 70
Dirks, Rudolph, 70
disappearances, 89
disasters, airships, 92
disasters, dams, 93
disasters, fire, 94
disasters, nuclear, 95
disasters, weather, 101
Discovery (Hudson's ship), 90
Discovery, HMS (Scott's ship), 159
Disney, Walt, 236
District of Columbia, 545
Ditmar, Art, 569
Divine (Harris Glenn Milstead), 253
diving (Olympic event), 606

divorce, 389
Dix, Richard, 253
Dixie Bowl (football), 584
Dixie Classic (football), 584
Dixie Flagler (train), 482
Dixie Syncopators, 345
Dixiecrats, 443
Dixmude (airship), 52, 92
Dixon, Jeremiah, 638
Dixon, L. Murray, 177
Djandoubi, Hamida, 80
Djibouti, Republic of, 114, 224, 372
DKW (das klein Wunder)
   (motorcycle maker), 233
Doak, Bill, 567
Dobrovolsky, Georgi, 549
Dochet's Island (lighthouse), 191
Doctor, Doctor, 616
Dodd, John (family), 6
Dodecanese Islands (Greece), 381
Dodge City Peace Commission, 74
Dodge, Henry, 670
Dodger Stadium (Los Angeles,
   California), 557
Dodgson, Charles Lutwidge, 197
dodo, 14
Doe, Sergeant Samuel K., 393
Doenitz, Karl, 707
Dog Island (lighthouse), 189
doge of Genoa, 388
doge of Venice, 388
Dogpatch USA (Arkansas), 143
Dogwood Harbor, Tilghman Island,
   Maryland, 533
Doherty, Bill, 589
Doherty, Dennis, 339
Dolan, Charles H., 695
Dolphin, USS (submarine), 540
Dom Pedro II, Emperor (Brazil), 362
Dom Pedro, Emperor (Brazil), 160
Dominica, 11, 114, 223
Dominica, Commonwealth of, 372
Dominican Republic, 114, 373, 383
Dominican University (Illinois), 104
Domino Effect (schooner), 533
Don Dixon and the Hidden Empire
   (comic strip), 71
Don Winslow of the Navy (comic
   strip), 71
Don Winslow of the Navy (radio),
   453
Donald Duck (cartoon character), 65
Donald McKay (clipper ship), 500
Donaldson, Stuart, 101
Donat, Robert, 253
Dondi (comic strip), 71
Donizetti, Gaetano, 288
Donlevy, Brian, 253
Donna Reed Show, The (TV), 616
Donne, John, 199
Donner party, 101
Donner, George, 101
Donny and Marie/Osmond Family

Show (TV), 616
Donovan, Robert, 718
Doodle Dandy of the U.S.A
   (musical), 137
Doogie Howser. M.D. (TV), 616
Doolin Gang, 85
Doolin, Bill, 75, 85
Doolittle, Hilda, 199
Doolittle, James, 43
Doors, The, 329
Dora-Mittelbau (concentration
   camp), 709
Dorians, 121
Doris Day Show, The (TV), 616
Dorman, Sir Maurice Henry, 409
Dorn County, Kansas, 660
Dorsetshire (ship), 96
Dorsey County, Arkansas, 656
Dorsey, Jimmy and Tommy, 329
Dos Passos, John, 200
Dosso Dossi, 21
Dostoyevsky, Feodor Mikhailovich,
   200
Double or Nothing (radio), 453
Douglas (motorcycle maker), 233
Douglas A-24 (aircraft), 40
Douglas A-26 Invader (aircraft), 700
Douglas A-26/B-26 Invader
   (aircraft), 40
Douglas A-4 Skyhawk (aircraft), 40
Douglas AD/A-1 Skyraider (aircraft),
   40
Douglas C-47 (aircraft), 36
Douglas DC-10 (aircraft), 36
Douglas DC-3 (aircraft), 36
Douglas Dragonfly (motorscooter),
   233
Douglas SBD Dauntless (aircraft), 40
Douglas, Melvyn, 253
Douglas, Paul, 253
Douglas, Phil, 567
Douglas, Stephen A., 652
Douglass College, 107
Doustin, Daniel Marius, 366
Dow Jones and Company, 222
Dowdey, Clifford, 680
Downing Stadium (Randall's Island,
   New York), 554
Downing, Samuel, 677
Doyle, Sir Arthur Conan, 200, 223
Dr. Christian (radio), 453
Dr. I.Q., the Mental Banker (radio),
   453
Dr. Kildare (radio), 453
Dr. Kildare (TV), 616
Dr. Quinn, Medicine Woman (TV),
   616
Dr. Seuss, 199
drachma (Greece), 224
Draco's laws, 186
Draft Riots (Civil War), 680
Dragnet (radio), 453
Dragnet (TV), 616

Drago (comic strip), 71
Drago, Dick, 563
Drake, Sir Francis, 156, 692
Drake, Stan, 71
Drake, Tom, 253
Dravska, Banovina of, 410
Dream Girls (show), 148
Dreamland Park (Coney Island, New
   York), 144
Dreamland Tower, The (amusement
   attraction), 144
Dred Scott Case, 663
Dreft Star Playhouse, The (radio),
   453
Dreiser, Theodore, 200
Drene Show, The (radio), 463
Dressler, Marie, 253
Drew, Georgiana, 139, 140
Drew, John, 140
Drexel Institute of Art, Science and
   Industry, 104
Drexel Institute of Technology, 104
Drexel University, 104
Dreyfus, Alfred, 77
Driftwood (sailing ship), 501
drinking age, minimum, 185
Droopy Dog (cartoon character), 66
Droopy Leprechaun (cartoon), 66
Drum, USS (submarine), 538
Drury Lane Theater (London,
   England), 149
Drury, Herb, 604
Dryden, John, 200
Du Maurier, Daphne, 200
Du Thèâtre au champ d'honneur
   (play), 139
Dubai (emirate), 418
Dubois, André Louis, 399
Duc de Lauzon (French ship), 676
Duchamp, Marcel, 22
Duchin, Eddy, 330
ducking stool, 83
dueling and duels, 101
Duesenberg Model J (automobile),
   29
Duesenberg, August, 29
Duesenberg, Frederick, 29
Duffy's Tavern (radio), 453
Duggan, Andrew, 253
Dukakis, Michael (Governor), 76
Dukas, Paul, 288
Duke University, 104
Duke, Vernon, 288
Dukes of Hazzard, The (TV), 617
Duluth Eskimos (football), 591
Duluth Kelleys (football), 591
Dumas, Alexandre (father), 200
Dumas, Alexandre (son), 200
Dumont, Margaret, 253
Dunbar, Paul Laurence, 200
Duncan Park (Spartansburg, South
   Carolina), 558

Duncan, Dave, 569
Duncan, Helen, 88
Duncan, Isadora, 137
Dunes Hotel and Casino (Las Vegas, Nevada), 176
Dunkirk, evacuation of, 702
Dunmore County, Virginia, 669
Dunn, Bob, 71
Dunn, James, 253
Dunn, John, 67
Dunn, Michael, 253
Dunne, Irene, 253
Dunninger the Mentalist (radio), 453
Dunnock, Mildred, 253
Dunsdon, Nicole, 147
Dunsmore, Earl of, 669
Duquesne University of the Holy Ghost, 104
Durand Glass (company), 165
Durand, Victor (Jr.), 165
Durant (automobile maker), 29
Durant, William C., 29
Durante, Jimmy, 253, 460
Durazzo, Girolamo Luigi Francesco, 388
Durey, Louis, 311
Durnan, Bill, 600
Durocq, Jean (World War I casualty), 697
Duryea wagon, 33
Duryea, Dan, 253
Duse, Eleanora, 141
Dust Bowl, 6
Dutch Colonies, 543
Dutch Creole language (Caribbean), 183
Dutch East India Company, 62
Dutch Guiana, 412
Dutch West Indies, 543
Duvalier, François ("Papa Doc"), 383
Duvalier, Jean Claude ("Baby Doc"), 383
Dvorak, Ann, 253
Dvořák, Antonín, 288
Dying Swan, The (ballet), 138
Dykes, Jimmy, 563
Dynasty (TV), 617
E & W. Bennett (company), 164
E. Bennett Chinaware Factory, 164
Eads Bridge (Saint Louis, Missouri), 124
Eads, James Buchanan, 124
Eakins, Thomas, 23
Earhart, Amelia, 57
Earl Carroll Theater (New York, New York), 150
Early Birds of Aviation, 57
Early Stone Age, 5
Early, Jubal A., 682
Earnhardt, Dale, 553
Earp, Morgan, 74
Earp, Virgil, 74
Earp, Wyatt, 74

East Alabama Male College, 102
East Berlin, 684
East Florida, 657
East Germany (German Democratic Republic), 11, 379, 685
East Indiaman (sailing ship), 77, 500
East Jersey, 665
East Pakistan, 402
East River Suspension Bridge (a.k.a. Williamsburg Suspension Bridge, New York), 124
East Tennessee College, 108
East Tennessee University, 108
Easter Rising (Ireland), 388
Eastern Airlines, 47
Eastern Airlines Shuttle, 47
Eastern Colored League (ECL) (baseball), 562
Eastern Europe, 121
Eastern State Penitentiary (Philadelphia, Pennsylvania), 79
Eastland, SS (ship), 96
Eastwood, Mike, 605
Easy Aces, The (radio), 453
Ebbets Field (Brooklyn, New York), 554
Ebermaier, Karl, 364
Ebert, Friedrich, 379
Ebsen, Buddy, 253
EC Comics, 73
Eckstine, Billy, 330
Economic Stabilization, Office of (OES), 719
Ecuador, 9, 114, 543, 544
Ecuador, Republic of, 373
Ecuador, State of, 373
Ed Sullivan Show, The (radio), 453
Ed Sullivan Show, The (TV), 628
Ed Wynn Show, The (TV), 454
Ed, Carl, 71
Eddie Cantor Show, The (radio), 454, 464
Eddy, Nelson, 254
Edelman, Marek, 711
Eden, Robert, 661
Ederle, Gertrude, 596
Edgar Bergen and Charlie McCarthy Show (radio), 449, 454
Edgar, Owen Thomas, 689
Edgerton County, Montana, 664
Edirne, Treaty of, 690
Edison International Field (Anaheim, California), 553
Edison, Thomas Alva, 437, 494
Edmonton Drillers (soccer), 609
Edna E. Lockwood (sailing ship), 498
Edna Hoyt (schooner), 533
Edo period (Japan), 389
Edsel (automobile), 29
Edson, Gus, 71
education, compulsory, 110
Education, Department of (U.S.), 639
education, racially segregated, 69

education, religious, 110
Edward I, King (England), 484
Edward III, King (England), 687
Edward IV, King (England), 419
Edward L. Ryerson (steamship), 535
Edward VI, King (England), 484
Edward VII, King (England), 2, 6, 419, 420
Edward VIII, King (England), 420
Edwardian Age, 2, 6
Edwards, Cap, 590
Edwards, Dennis, 351
Edwards, Harold, 695
Edwards, Ninian, 659
Edwards, Ralph, 472, 473
Edwards, Robert, 564
Edwards, Susannah, 88
Edwin Fox (ship), 500, 685
Edyth Totten Theater(New York, New York), 150
Effie M. Morrissey (schooner), 532
Egg Island Point (lighthouse), 189
Egg Rock (lighthouse), 189
Egypt, 7, 10, 114, 120, 691
Egypt, Arab Republic of, 373, 374
Eichmann, Adolf, 720
Eiffel Tower, 230
Eiffel, Alexandre Gustave, 230
Eight Is Enough (TV), 617
Eight, The (artist group), 20
eight-track tapes, 438
Einstein, Albert, 494
Einstein, Harry, 464
Éire, State of, 387
Eisenhower dollar coin, U.S., 227, 228
Eisenhower, Dwight D., 82, 232, 651, 699, 705, 711, 718
Eisenstein, Sergei M., 238
Eisman, Hy, 71
Eisner, Will, 72
Ekatat, King (Thailand), 415
El Bueno Suceso (clipper ship), 499
El Capitan (train), 482
El Majidi (sailing ship*)*, 682
El Paso, Texas (trolleys), 635
El Rancho Vegas Hotel-Casino (Las Vegas, Nevada), 176
El Salvador, 7, 114
El Salvador, Republic of, 374
Elamite (language), 11
Eldredge, Jeremiah Dennis, 560
Eldridge, Charles M., 99
Eldridge, Roy, 330
elections and voting, 110
Electoral College, 110, 111
Electric Theater, The (radio), 458
Electricity Building, 1933 Century of Progress Exhibition (Chicago, Illinois), 17
electrocution (punishment), 82
Elegy, The (movie), 237
Elgar, Sir Edward, 289

Elío, Francisco Javier, 357
Eliot Seminary, 109
Eliot, George, 200
Eliot, T.S., 200
Elizabeth Daily Journal (newspaper), 434
Elizabeth I, Queen (England), 419, 484
Elizabeth II, Queen (England), 420
Ella (sailing ship), 536
Ellen/These Friends of Mine (TV), 617
Ellender, Allen J., 439
Ellery Queen, The Adventures of (radio), 454
Ellice Islands, 391, 417
Ellington, Duke, 289
Elliot, "Mama" Cass, 339
Elliott, Bob, 449
Elliott, Denholm, 254
Elliott, William ("Wild Bill"), 254
Ellis Airlines, 47
Ellis Island (New York, New York), 230, 443
Ellis, Ruth, 81
Ellison, G.E. (World War I casualty), 697
Ellison, Ralph, 201
Elmer Fudd (cartoon character), 66
Eloisa (sailing ship), 499
Elstner, Anne, 471
Elwood (or Elmwood), Thomas, 676
Ely, Ron, 147
Emancipation Proclamation (1863), 545
embargo, oil (1973-74), 123
Embassy 49th Street Theater (New York, New York), 152
Embassy Five (theater, New York, New York), 151
Embezzled Heaven (play), 139
Emergency (TV), 617
Emergency Management, Office for (U.S.), 718
Emerson College, 104
Emerson College of Oratory, 104
Emerson, Ralph Waldo, 201
Emerson's Magazine and Putnam's Monthly, 222
Emhardt, Robert, 254
Emily Post (radio), 454
Emma C. Berry (ship), 534
Emmet County, Michigan, 662
Emmet County, Nebraska, 664
Empire Airlines, 47
Empire Pottery (company), 167
Empire State Building (New York, New York), 61, 178
Empire Theater (New York, New York), 150
Empress of England (liner), 527
Empress of India, 420
Empress of Ireland, RMS (ship), 97

Empty Nest (TV), 617
Encyclopédie (Diderot), 60
Endurance (ship), 159
energy, 123
Enfield, Connecticut, Shaker community, 488
Enfield, New Hampshire, Shaker community, 488
Engel v. *Vitale*, 110
England, 418
England, Church of, 485
England, wolves in, 13
English Field (Amarillo, Texas), 50
English, John, 94
English-language alphabet, 12
Enigma machine, 714
Enlightenment, Age of, 2
Eno Crime Club, The (radio), 454
Eno Crime Clues (radio), 454
Enola Gay (B-29 aircraft), 717
Enos (Astro-Chimp), 547
Enron, 63
Enron Field (Houston, Texas), 556
entail (property law), 186
Enterprise, USS (carrier), 514, 702
Entwistle, John, 353
environment, 153
Environmental Protection Agency, 153
Eocene Epoch, 3
epidemics, 171, 172
Epstein, Brian, 321
Equal Rights party (Locofoco party), 441
Equatorial Guinea, Republic of, 114, 374
Equifax Inc., 64
equipment, videorecording, 118
Eric the Red, 372
Erickson, Leif, 254
Erie Railroad Company, 477
Erie Railway, 477
Erie Transportation (railroad), 477
Erie-Lackawanna (railroad), 477
Eritrea, 114, 389
Eritrea, State of, 374
Ernestina (schooner), 532
Errol, Leon, 254
Erving, Julius ("Dr. J."), 576
Erwin Piscator's Dramatic Workshop (New York, New York), 150
Escape (radio), 454
Escenc, Tefvik, 184
escudo (Portugal), 224
Esherick, Joseph, 16
Esse (motorcycle maker), 234
Esselen (Native Americans), 426
Essex Passenger Railway (Newark, New Jersey), 633
Essex, USS (carrier), 514
Essex, USS (sloop), 537
Estonia, 114, 489, 631
Estonia (ship), 97

Estonia, Republic of, 375
Estonian Soviet Socialist Republic, 375
Ethiopia, 10, 224, 374, 489, 543
Ethiopia, People's Democratic Republic of, 375
Ethiopia, Federal Democratic Republic of, 375
Etowah County, Alabama, 655
Etruria Pottery (company), 167
Etruria, Kingdom of, 120
Etude Magazine, 221
Euclid Beach Park (Cleveland, Ohio), 144
eunuchs, 178
euro, 224
Europa (liner), 527
European Atomic Energy Commission (EAEC), 8
European Coal and Steel Community (ECSC), 8
European Community (EC), 8
European Economic Community (EEC), 8
European Recovery Program, 713
European Theater of Operations, 705, 716
European Union, 8
Evans, Dale, 254
Evans, Dame Edith, 254
Evans, George, 72, 163
Evans, Gwynne Owen, 81
Evans, Maurice, 254
Evans, Ronald E., 548
Evansville Crimson Giants (football), 591
Evening and Sunday Bulletin Building (Philadelphia, Pennsylvania), 17
Evening Shade (TV), 617
Evening Star (Washington newspaper), 437
Evening Telegram (New York newspaper), 435
Evening Times (Palm Beach newspaper), 436
Everett, Edward, 440
Evergreen Aviation Museum (McMinnville, Oregon), 55
Everlasting cylinders, 437
Evers, Johnny, 566
Everybody's Magazine, 221
Evita (show), 148
Ewell, Tom, 254
Ewert, Charley, 594
Ewing, Dr. Fayette Clay, 174
Excelsior (motorcycle maker), 233
Excelsior Supply Co., 234
Exchange Hotel (New Orleans, Louisiana), 177
executions, 78
Executive Mansion, 654
Exhibition of the Industry of All

Nations (new York, new York), 160

Exhibition Stadium (Toronto, Canada), 559

Exploration, Age of, 2

Exposed (movie), 138

Exposition Park (Pittsburgh, Pennsylvania), 558

expositions, 159

Eyak (Native Americans), 427

Eye of the Goddess, The (ballet), 137

Eyeball House (Woodland Hills, California), 17

F.B.I., The (TV), 617

Faber, Red, 567

face mask, ice hockey, 600

Facts of Life, The (TV), 617

Fain, Sammy, 289

Fair Labor Standards Act, 179, 181, 654

Fairbanks Goldpanners (baseball), 559

Fairbanks, Douglas (Jr.), 254

Fairbanks, Douglas (Sr.), 254

Fairmount Park (Philadelphia, Pennsylvania), 15, 159

Faith 7, 548

Faith, Percy, 289

Falcon Crest (TV), 617

Falcon, Guil, 589, 596

Falcon, The (radio), 454

Falk, Lee, 463

Falkenburg, Jinx, 472

Falkland Island wolf (warrah), 14

Falkland Islands, 357

Falkland Islands conflict, 685

Fall Guy, The (TV), 617

Falla, de, Manuel, 289

Falls of Clyde (sailing ship), 534

Falls View Bridge "Honeymoon Bridge" (Upper Steel Arch) (Niagara Falls, New York), 127

Falls View Suspension Bridge (No. 1) (Niagara Falls, New York), 127

Falls View Suspension Bridge (No. 2) (Niagara Falls, New York), 127

False Hare (cartoon), 65

Falu Copper Mine (Sweden), 413

Family Affair (TV), 617

Family Matters (TV), 617

Family Theater (radio), 454

Family Ties (TV), 617

Famous Jury Trials (radio), 454

Famous Studios (movie studio), 66

Fanny M. (sailing ship), 501

Fantastiks, The (show), 148

Fantasy Island (TV), 617

Faraday, Michael, 494

Farley, Chris, 254

Farm Security Administration, 637

Farmer, Frances, 254

Farmer, James, 68

Farnham, Ralph, 674

Farnsworth, Richard, 254

Farouk, King (Egypt), 374

Farquhar USS (destroyer escort), 714

Farrar, Geraldine, 312

Farrar, W. H., 167

Farrell, Glenda, 254

Farrell, J.D., 481

Fassbinder, Rainer Werner, 238

Fat Boy (bomb), 717

Fat Man, The (radio), 454

Father Knows Best (radio), 454

Father Knows Best (TV), 617

Fatima, 120

Fatima Visitations, 486

Fatimid caliphate, 120

Faulkner, Roy, 232

Faulkner, William, 201

Fauré, Gabriel, 289

Fausch, Frank, 591

Faustin I, Emperor (Haiti), 383

Fawcett-Munroe duel, 101

Faye, Alice, 255

FBI in Peace and War, The (radio), 454

Feast of Fools, 175

February 30th, 631

Federal Communications Commission, 636

Federal Deposit Insurance Corporation (FDIC), 58

Federal Emergency Relief Administration (FERA), 636

Federal Express, 64

Federal Express (airline), 47

Federal League (baseball), 561

Federal Lighthouse Service, 649

Federal Radio Commission (FRC), 636

Federal Reserve Bank Notes, 228

Federal Reserve Notes, 228

Federal Savings and Loan Insurance Corporation (FSLIC), 58

Federal Security Agency, 636

Federal Theater Project (WPA), 637

Federal Works Agency, 637

Federal Writers Project (WPA), 637

Federalist party, 441

Federated Malay States, 395

Federation of Malaysia, 395, 409

FedEx, 47, 64

Fedora (play), 140

Fein, Nathaniel, 564

Feininger, Lyonnel, 73

Feld, Fritz, 255

Felder, Josef, 706

Feldman, Marty, 255

Feldstein, Al, 71, 72

Felix the Cat (cartoon character), 66

Fellini, Federico, 238

Felstead, Bertie, 697

Felt, Edward, 87

Female Normal and High School

(New York), 105

fencing (Olympic event), 606

Fen-Phen, 172

Fenton, Christopher W., 169

Fenton's Works, 169

Fenway Park (Boston, Massachusetts), 554

Ferber, Edna, 201, 470

Ferdinand I, King (Romania), 405

Ferdinand I, Prince (Bulgaria), 362

Ferdinand II, King (Spain), 122

Ferdinand V, King (Spain), 487

Ferdinand VII, King (Spain), 487

Ferdinand, Emperor (Austria), 179

Ferguson, William J., 652

Fermat's Last Theorem, 497

Fernando Pó, Equatorial Guinea, 374

Ferreira (sailing ship), 499

Ferrer, José, 255

Ferrier, Johan Henry Eliza, 412

Ferris Wheel, 161

Ferris, George W., 161

ferrotypes, 439

Fertile Crescent, 387

Fetchit, Stepin, 255

feudalism, 119, 179, 389, 690

feuds, 75

Fianna Fail party (Ireland), 388

Fibber McGee and Molly (radio), 448, 455, 457

Fichtel & Sachs (manufacturer), 233

Fiddler on the Roof (show), 148

Fidler, Jimmy, 460

Fidler, Mike, 602

Fiedler, Arthur, 312

field handball (Olympic event), 606

field hat (U.S. Marine Corps), 650

Field, Betty, 255

Field, John, 289

Field, Lew, 151

Fielding, Fidelia Hoscott (Mohegan-Pequot speaker), 428

Fielding, Henry, 201

Fields, Dorothy, 290

Fields, W.C., 255

Fifth Avenue Hotel (New York, New York), 176

Fifth Avenue Opera House (New York, New York), 150

Fifth Cavalry, United States Army, 143

Fifth Republic (France), 377

fifty-cent coin, U.S. ("half dollar"), 226

Fiji Islands, Republic of, 114, 375

Fiji, Dominion of, 375

Fiji, Sovereign Democratic Republic of, 375

Fillingim, Dana, 567

Fillmore, Millard, 441, 443, 651, 653

Final Solution, 708

finance, 58

Finch, Peter, 255

Fine, Larry, 135
Finian's Rainbow (movie), 138
Fink, Albert, 126
Finland, 79, 114, 631
Finland, Republic of, 375
Finlandia Hall (Helsinki, Finland), 16
Finley, Charlie O., 604
Finley, George Washington, 428
Finley, James, 128
Finney County, Kansas, 660
Fir (WLM 212) (ship), 649
fire, Chicago (Illinois), 94
fire, Iroquois Theater, 95
fire, London, 78, 490
Firecracker 400 (automobile race), 553
Fireside Chats (radio), 455
First and Ten (TV), 617
First Carrier Task Force, Pacific, 716
First Continental Congress, 643
First Empire (France), 377
First Liberty Loan Parade, 231
First Mariner Arena (Baltimore, Maryland), 573
First National City Corporation, 64
First Nighter, The (radio), 455
First Reich (Holy Roman Empire), 379
First Republic (France), 377
First Republic (Spain), 411
First Union Center (Philadelphia, Pennsylvania), 574
Fish, Jack, 593
Fisher, H. C. ("Bud"), 72
Fisher, Ham, 71
Fisher, Jack, 566
Fisher, Johnny, 596
Fisher, Ray, 567
fishing schooner, 532
Fisk, Jim, 176
Fiske, John, 642
Fissore (automobile maker), 30
Fitch Bandwagon (radio), 467
Fitzgerald, Lionel LeMoine, 21
Fitzgerald, Barry, 255
Fitzgerald, Ed, 455
Fitzgerald, Edward, 135
Fitzgerald, Ella, 330
Fitzgerald, F. Scott, 4, 201, 221
Fitzgerald, Pegeen, 455
Fitzgeralds, The (radio), 455
Fitzroy, James, 81
Fitzsimmons, Bob, 581
five-cent coin, U.S. ("half dime"), 225
five-cent coin, U.S. ("nickel"), 225
five-dollar coin, U.S. ("half eagle"), 227
flag, United States, stars and stripes, 646
Flagstad, Kirsten, 312
Flair (magazine), 221
Flamborough Head, HMS (Victory

ship), 713
Flanders, 630
Flanders, Charles, 71
Flandre (liner), 527
Flashgun Casey (radio), 451
Flatt, Lester Raymond, 330
Flaubert, Gustave, 201
Fleet Center (Boston, Massachusetts), 573
Fleet Prison (London, England), 77
Fleet Rehabilitation and Modernization (FRAM), 538
Fleischmann Hour, The (radio), 469
Fleming, Eric, 255
Fleming, Ian, 201
Fleming, Victor, 239
Flensburg, Schleswig-Holstein, Germany, 707
fleur-de-lis (French symbol), 376
Flintstones, The (TV), 66, 617
Flip Wilson Show, The (TV), 617
Flipper (TV), 617
Flo (TV), 618
flogging (punishment), 79
Flor (sailing ship), 497
Florence, Italy, 5
Florida, 158, 545, 657
Florida Blazers (football), 586
Florida Everglades, 673
Florida Purchase Treaty (1827, 657
Florida, USS (battleship), 503
Floridians (basketball), 578
Flossenburg (concentration camp), 710
Fluff Brown (motorcycle maker), 233
fluoroscopes, shoe-fitting, 173
Flying Cloud (clipper ship), 499
Flying Eagle one-cent coin, U.S., 224
Flying Fish (clipper ship), 499
Flying Nun, The (TV), 618
Flying Tiger Line, 47
Flying Yankee (train), 483
Flynn, Errol, 255
Flynn, Joe, 255
Flynn, Robert J., 367
Foch, Ferdinand, 698
Focke-Wulf Fw-190 (aircraft), 41
Foggy Mountain Boys (Flatt and Scruggs), 330
Foghorn Leghorn (cartoon character), 66
Fokker 50 (aircraft), 55
Fokker D.VII Biplane, 41
Fokker D.VII Monoplane, 55
Fokker Dr. 1 Triplane, 41
Fokker, Anthony Herman, 55
Folies Bergere (New York, New York), 151
Foncha, John Ngu, 364
Fonda, Henry, 255
Fong, Benson, 255
Fontanne, Lynn, 141
Fonteyn & Nureyev on Broadway

(musical), 137
Fonteyn, Dame Margot, 137
Food and Drug Administration (FDA), 173, 636
Food, Drug and Cosmetic Act (1938), 162
Food, Drug and Insecticide Administration, 636
foot bnding, 178
Foot, Hugh Mackintosh, 371
football, defunct bowl games, 583
football, intercollegiate (first team), 584
football, intercollegiate, all-white, 583
football, professional, all-white, 596
football, team (number of players), 585
Forbes Field (Pittsburgh, Pennsylvania), 558
Ford Center for the Performing Arts (New York, New York), 150
Ford Model A (automobile), 33
Ford Model T (automobile), 33
Ford Motor Company, 27, 29, 33, 62
Ford Show, The (radio), 453
Ford Show, The (TV), 618, 628
Ford Theater (Ford's Old Opera House), 653
Ford Theater, The (radio), 455
Ford Thunderbird, 34
Ford Trimotor 5-AT, 36
Ford Willys do Brasil (automobile maker), 33
Ford, "Tennessee Ernie", 330
Ford, Charlie, 86
Ford, Edsel, 33
Ford, Ford Madox, 198
Ford, Gerald R., 102, 652, 693
Ford, Greg, 67
Ford, Henry, 33
Ford, John, 239
Ford, Wallace, 255
Ford's Theater Lincoln Museum, 653
Fordham University, 105
Foreign Affairs, Department of (U.S.), 640
foreign coins legal in U.S., 227
Forever Young (radio), 467
Forman, George, 581
Formhals, Henry, 71
Forney County, Nebraska, 664
Forrest, Edwin, 141, 142
Forrestal, James Vincent, 640
Forrestal, USS (carrier), 514
Forster, E.M., 192, 201
Fort Duquesne, 672
Fort Laramie (radio), 455
Fort Lauderdale Strikers (soccer), 609
Fort McHenry (Baltimore, Maryland), 694
Fort Orange, New York, 665

Fort Riley, Kansas, 172
Fort Sumter, 679
Fort Wayne Daisies (baseball), 572
Fort Wayne Pistons (basketball), 578
Fort William Henry, 672
Fort Worth Classic (football), 584
Fort Worth Meacham Airport (Texas), 49
Fort Worth Meacham International Airport (Texas), 49
Fort Worth Municipal Airport (Texas), 49
Forty-Eighth Street Theater (New York, New York), 150, 151
forty-five rpm records, 438
Forty-Fourth Street Theater (New York, New York), 153
Forty-Ninth Street Theater(New York, New York), 151
Forty-Second Street (musical), 136, 148
Forum (magazine), 223
Forum 47th Street Theater (New York, New York), 150
Forum Theater (New York, New York), 150
forward pass (football), 585, 586
Fosse, Bob, 137
Fossett, Bill, 85
Foster, Stephen, 290
Foster, Harold ("Hal"), 74
Foster, Preston, 255
Foster, Warren, 67
Foster, William, 547
Foster, William Henry, 685
Fostoria Glass Company, 165
Fouchet, Christian, 356
Founding Fathers, 645
Fountain, Albert J., 75
Four Horsemen of Notre Dame, 585
Fourth Republic (France), 377
Fowler, Jennie, 480
Fowler, Robert, 480
Fox (Native Americans), 672
Fox County, Iowa, 660
Fox, Fontaine, 72
Foxx, Jimmy, 572
Foxy Grandpa (comic strip), 71
Foy, Eddie, 135
Foy, Irving, 135
Foyt, A.J., 552
fractional currency, 228
fractions (stock exchange), 59
Fragment W (Comet Shoemaker-Levy 9), 547
Fraktur, 12
Frame Breaking Act (1812, Great Britain), 179
franc (Belgium), 224
franc (France), 224
franc (Luxembourg, Grand Duchy of), 224
France, 9, 10, 77, 114, 224, 376, 489,

543, 544, 631, 690, 691, 692, 695, 697
France (sailing ship), 497
France, Anatole, 201
Francesco II, King (Italy), 389
Francis I, Emperor (Austria), 120
Francis I, King (France), 24
Francis II, Emperor (Holy Roman Empire), 120
Francis II, King, (Austria), 687
Francis, Arlene, 474
Francis, David Rowland, 406
Francis, Willie, 82
Franck, César, 290
Franco, Francisco, 412, 692
François, Duke of Joinville, (Prince, France), 376
Franco-Prussian War, 377, 686
Frank Leslie Publishing House, 221
Frank Leslie's Popular Monthly Magazine, 220
Frank Merriwell, The Adventures of (radio), 455
Frank Sinatra Show (radio), 455
Frank, Anne, 709, 711
Frank, Karl Hermann, 704
Frank, Otto, 711
Franke, Radford, 187
Frankel, Harry, 470
Franken, Rose, 452
Frankford Yellow Jackets (football), 592
Frankland, 668
Franklin (automobile maker), 29
Franklin and Marshall College, 105
Franklin D. Roosevelt, USS (carrier), 515
Franklin Engine Company, 29
Franklin Expedition, 156
Franklin half dollar, U.S., 226
Franklin, Benjamin, 201, 665, 675
Franklin, Frederic, 136
Franklin, John (explorer), 156
Franklin, Melvin, 351
Franklin, State of, 668
Franklin, USS (carrier), 515
Franklin, William, 665
Frankton, Operation, 707
Franz Ferdinand, Archduke (Austria), 695
Fraser, Simon (Lord Lovat), 80
Frasier (TV), 618
Fraske, Fredrak, 671
fraud, 75
Fraudulent Mediums Act (Great Britain), 88
Frawley, William, 255
Frazee (theater, New York, New York), 151
Frazier, Joe, 581
Freckles and His Friends (comic strip), 71
Fred Allen Show (radio), 456

Frederick III, Holy Roman Emperor, 400
Frederick Post Company (manufacturer), 497
Frederick VI, King (Denmark), 372
Free Soil party, 440, 441, 442
Freed, Alan, 318
Freedman, Rose, 95
Freedmen's Bureau, 681
Freedomland (Bronx, New York), 144
Freeman, Don, 70
Freeman, Joshus S., 500
French Air Service, 696
French and Indian War, 364, 659, 661, 662, 663, 670, 672, 691
French Cameroun, 364
French Casino (New York, New York), 150
French Colonies, 543, 544
French Community, 8, 9, 365, 366, 377, 394, 395, 401, 408
French East India Company, 62, 396
French Empire, 120
French Equatorial Africa, 8, 365, 366, 369, 378
French Guiana, 77, 543, 544
French Guinea, 9
French India, 8
French Indochina, 8, 421
French Middle Congo Territory, 369
French Morocco, 398
French Panama Canal Company, 131
French Republic, 631
French Revolution, 2, 230, 377, 631, 686
French Revolutionary Wars, 687
French Second Empire, 686
French Somaliland, 372
French Spy, The (play), 142
French Sudan, 9, 395
French Territory of the Afars and the Issas, 372
French Togoland, 415
French Union, 9, 377
French West Africa, 9
Fresh Prince of Bel Air (TV), 618
Freudy Cat (cartoon), 66
Friday Foster (comic strip), 71
Friday, meatless, 486
Friedeburg, Hans-Georg von, 705
Friend, Bob, 569
Friendly Islands, 415
Friends (TV), 618
Friesland (Netherlands province), 11
Friml, Rudolf, 290
Frisco, the (railroad), 478
Fritz the Cat (cartoon character), 66
Fritz the Cat (comic strip), 71
Front Page Farrell (radio), 456
Front Street Cable Railway (Seattle, Washington), 633
front-engine race car, 552

Frontier Airlines, 47
Frontier Gentleman (radio), 456
Frontier Times Magazine, 123
Frost, Robert, 202
Frum, Elsie, 94
Fry, Roger, 192
F-Troop (TV), 617
Fu Manchu (radio), 456
Fuad I, King (Egypt), 374
Fuad II, King (Egypt), 374
Fugitive, The (TV), 618
Full House (TV), 618
Fuller, R. Buckminster, 16
Fuller, Ralph Briggs, 72
Fuller's City Hotel (Washington, D.C.), 178
Fulmer, Gene, 582
Fulper Pottery Company, 165, 168
Fulton Theater (New York, New York), 151
Fulton, William S., 656
Fults, Ralph Smith, 84
Fun Face (amusement park sign), 146
Fun with Dick and Jane series, 202
Funafuti (island), 417
Fung, Paul, 72
Funnies (II), The (comic book), 73
Funnies, The (comic strip), 71
Fuqua, Charlie, 335
Furansu Maru (liner), 528
Furgoneta Hispano SA (automobile maker), 30
Furness, Frank, 16
Fustero, Juan José (Tataviam speaker), 432
G. & C. Merriam Company, 60, 64
G. Binswanger and Company, 64
G.C. Murphy's (store), 63
Gable, Clark, 255
Gabon, 8, 10, 114, 365
Gabonese Republic (Gabon), 378
Gabreski, Francis S. ("Gabby"), 700
Gacy, John Wayne, 82
Gadsden Purchase, 638, 655
Gaelic (language), 193
Gaelic League, 193
Gagadju (Kakadu) language (Australia), 183
Gagarin, Yuri, 550
Gage, General Thomas, 661
Gagner, Dave, 603
Gaiety Theater (New York, New York), 151
Gaines, Bill, 71, 72
Gaite Parisienne (musical), 136
Gale Storm Show, The/ Oh! Susannah (TV), 618
Gallatin, Albert, 58
Gallaudet College, 105
Gallaudet, Thomas Hopkins, 105
galleon (sailing ship), 500
galley (sailing ship), 500
Gallipoli campaign (World War I), 697

Galloping Ghost, The, 585
Galloway, Bill, 562
Galsworthy, John, 202
Galveston Jetty (lighthouse), 189
Galveston, Harrisburg and San Antonio Railway, 481
Gama, Vasco da, 156
Gambia, Dominion of The, 378
Gambia, The, 7, 114, 223, 378, 408
games, 163
Gandhi, Mohandas Karamchand, 386
Gang Busters (radio), 456
Gang of Four, 367
Gantner, Jim, 563
Gar, USS (submarine), 541
Garbisch, Ed, 583
Garbo, Greta, 237, 256
García Lorca, Federico, 202
Garcia, Jerry, 332
Garden of Allah (Los Angeles, California), 176
Garden State Bowl (football), 584
Gardenia, Vincent, 256
Gardiner, Reginald, 256
Gardner, Ava, 256
Gardner, Ed, 453
Gardner, Erle Stanley, 202, 221, 467
Garfield, James A., 125, 651, 684
Garfield, John, 256
Garibaldi, Giuseppe, 388
Garland, Judy, 256
Garner, Erroll, 331
Garner, Peggy Ann, 256
Garrett, Pat, 75, 84
Garrison, William Lloyd, 547
Garry Moore Show, The (radio), 456
Garry Moore Show, The (TV), 618
Garson, Greer, 256
Gary, Jim, 71
Gashey, Jamal Al, 87
Gashouse Gang, The, 572
gaslight, 230
Gaslight Gaieties (radio), 456
gasoline, leaded, 153
Gaspe HMS (schooner), 675
Gass, Sergeant Patrick, 157
Gates County, Wisconsin, 670
Gateway Arch (St. Louis, Missouri), 19
Gatling gun, 721
Gato, USS (submarine), 541
Gaudi, Antonio, 17
Gauguin, Paul, 23
Gaul, 122
Gay Mrs. Featherston, The (radio), 449
Gay Nineties Revue (radio), 456
Gaye, Marvin, 331
Gaynor, Janet, 256
Gaza Strip, 691
Gazette of the United States (newspaper), 437

Gazette of the United States and Daily Evening Advertiser (newspaper), 437
Geary County, Kansas, 660
Geary Street Park and Ocean Railway (San Francisco, California), 633
Geertruida Gerarda (sailing ship), 498
Geheime Staatspolizei, 707
Gehrig, Lou, 563, 567, 572
Geisel, Theodor (Dr. Seuss), 199
Gelder, Aert de, 25
Gelderland (Netherlands province), 11
GEM and GEX (stores), 63
Gemini (show), 148
Gemini 12, 548
Gemini space program, 548
Gemini, Age of, 1
Gene Autry's Melody Ranch (radio), 456
General Assembly, UN, 721
General Electric Apparatus Company, 64
General Electric House Party (radio), 459
General Electric Theater (TV), 618
General Electric Theater, The (radio), 458
General Housewares Corporation, 166
General Land Office, 639
General Mitchell International Airport (Milwaukee, Wisconsin), 49
General Motors/United Auto Workers Sit-Down Strike, 180
General Orders, U.S. Army, 648
General Slocum (ship), 97
Genetic Engineering, Age of, 3
Geneva Agreement, 9
Genghis Khan, 119, 121, 398
Genn, Leo, 256
Gentle Ben (TV), 618
Gentlemen (sailing ship), 546
Gentlemen Prefer Blondes (musial), 136
Geological Time, 2
Geophysical Service, Incorporated, 64, 117
Georg Stag (frigate), 522
George (magazine), 221
George Burns and Gracie Allen Show, The (TV), 618
George Gobel Show, The (TV), 618
George II, King (England), 678, 687
George III, King (England), 4, 539
George IV, King (England), 4
George M. Cohan's Theater (New York, New York), 151
George V, King (England), 420
George VI, King (England), 420

George Washington Bridge (New York, New York), 126
George Washington University, 105
George Washington, USS (submarine), 541
George, Gladys, 256
Georgia, 489, 658
Georgia (nation), 114, 378
Georgia (state), 489, 545, 658
Georgia Dome (Atlanta, Georgia), 573
Georgia Female College, 109
Georgia Institute of Technology, 105
Georgia School of Technology, 105
Georgia, Republic of, 379
Georgia, USS (battleship), 503
Georgian Soviet Socialist Republic, 379
Georgy, Guy Noël, 369
German Confederation, 379, 394
German Democratic Republic, 379
German East Africa, 9, 406, 414
German Empire, 686
German High Seas Fleet, 698
German New Guinea, 397, 399, 402
German Southwest Africa, 399
Germanic black letter script, 12
Germany, 79, 114, 671, 689
Germany (Protestant States), 631
Germany, Federal Republic of, 379, 705
Gerry, Ann Thompson, 645
Gerry, Elbridge, 645
Gershwin, George, 290
Gershwin, Ira, 291
Gestapo, 707
Get a Life (TV*)*, 618
Get Smart (TV), 618
Getting By (TV), 618
Getty Oil Company, 63
Gettysburg College, 105
Getz, Stan, 331
Ghana, 7, 114
Ghana, Dominion of, 380
Ghana, Republic of, 380
Ghani, Abdul Aziz Abdel, 422
Ghent, Treaty of, 694
ghetto, Warsaw, 711
Ghost and Mrs. Muir, The (TV), 618
GI Bill Benefits program (Korean War), 688
GI Bill Benefits program (World War II), 718
GI Journal (radio), 456
Giacometti, Alberto, 23
Giant Dipper (amusement ride), 146
Gibbon, Edward, 202
Gibbons, Dave, 73
Gibbs, Caleb, 676
Gibbs, Dr. Charles Brook Flint, 174
Gibbs, May, 70
Gibran, Kahlil, 202
Gibson, Annie, 69

Gibson, Edward G., 549
Gibson, George, 593
Gibson, Hoot, 256
Gibson, Horatio Gates, 689
Gibson, Walter, 470
Gide, André, 202
Gielgud, Sir John, 141, 256
Gies, Miep, 711
Gigli, Beniamino, 312
Gilbert and Ellice Islands, 417
Gilbert Islands, 391
Gilbert, Billy, 256
Gilbert, Cass, 17
Gilbert, John, 256
Gilbert, William S., 291
Gilded Age, 3
Gilera (motorcycle maker), 234
Gilera, Giuseppe, 234
Giles, Alexander Falconer, 393
Gilford, Jack, 256
Gillespie, Dizzy, 331
Gillette Cavalcade of Sports (radio), 456
Gilligan's Island (TV), 618
Gilmore, Gary, 82, 83
Gimbel's (store), 63
Gimme a Break! (TV), 618
Gingold, Hermione, 256
Gingras County, North Dakota, 666
Ginny Simms Shows (radio), 456
Girard Trust Corn Exchange Bank (Philadelphia, Pennsylvania), 16
Girl Most Likely, The (movie), 136
Girondists, 686
Gish, Dorothy, 257
Gish, Lillian, 257
Glackens, William, 21
Glasgow Pottery (company), 166
Glass Menagerie, The (play), 142
Glassboro Normal School, 107
Glassboro State College, 107
Glazunov, Alexander, 291
Gleason, Jackie, 257
Gleason, James, 257
Gleason, Lev, 70
Glen Campbell Goodtime Hour, The (TV), 618
Glenard P. Lipscomb, USS (submarine), 541
Glendale Park (Nashville, Tennessee), 144
Glenn, John H. (Jr.), 548
Glessner House (Chicago, Illinois), 19
Glinka, Mikhail, 291
Globe (store), 63
Globe Stoneware Company, 169
Globe Theatre (London, England), 149
Globe Wireless, 611
Glomar Explorer (ship), 539
Gloom Chasers, The (radio), 471
Glorious Revolution, 5, 8, 184, 419

Glorious, HMS (ship), 502
Glory of the Seas (clipper ship), 499, 500
Gluck, Christoph Willibald von, 291
G-Men (radio), 456
goal posts (football), 587
Godchaux, Keith, 332
Goddard, Paulette, 257
Goddard, Robert, 495
Godey, Louis, 221
Godey's Lady's Book (magazine), 221
Godfrey, Arthur, 448
Godshall, Harry L., 146
Godwin, Frank, 72
Goebbels, Paul Joseph, 707
Goering, Hermann, 380, 707
Goethe, Johann Wolfgang von, 203
Goff, Bruce, 17
Goff, Norris, 462
Gogol, Nikolai, 203
Golan Heights, Syria, 691
gold, 170
Gold Bugs, 442
gold certificates, U.S., 228
Gold Coast, 7, 380, 415, 543
gold coins and notes, U.S., 227
Gold Democrats, 442
Gold Key Comics, 73
gold one-dollar coin, U.S., 227
Gold Rush, California, 170
Gold Rush, Klondike, 170
Goldberg, Rube, 70
Goldbergs, The (radio), 456
Golden Age (cartoons), 65, 73
Golden Age (sports), 596
Golden Bay Earthquakes (soccer), 608, 609
Golden Gate Bridge (San Francisco, California), 125, 126
Golden Girls, The (TV), 618
Golden Spike ceremonies (railroads), 479
Golden State Warriors (basketball), 579
Golden, Colorado, 657
Goldenrod (showboat), 535
Goldenson, Leonard H., 630
Goldsborough, Mrs. George S., 653
Goldsborough, Robert, 215
Goldsmith Oliver, 203
Goldsmith, Jerry, 291
golf (Olympic event), 606
golf, equipment, 596
Gomer Pyle, U.S.M.C. (TV), 618
Good Feelings, Era of, 2
Good Humor truck, 162
Good News of 1938 (radio), 464
Good News of 1939 (radio), 464
Good Times (TV), 619
Goodall (frigate), 714
Goodfellow, Ebbie, 602
Goodman, Benny, 331

Goodwin, Marv, 567
Goodyear TV Playhouse (TV), 619
Goofy (cartoon character), 66
Goofy's Freeway Trouble (cartoon), 66
goose step (military), 380
Gorbachev, Mikhail, 418
Gorcey, Leo, 257
Gordo (comic strip), 71
Gordon, Dexter, 332
Gordon, Gale, 257
Gordon, Ruth, 257
Gore, Asa A., 674
Goring, Percy, 697
Gorky, Maxim, 203
Gosden, Freeman F., 447
Gosger, Jim, 564
Gotham Bowl (football), 584
Gotham Theater (New York, New York), 150
Gothic (script), 12
Gothic Revival architecture, 15
Goths, 133
Gottschalk, Louis Moreau, 291
Gottselig, Johnny, 602
Goucher College, 105
Goucher, Dr. and Mrs. John Franklin, 105
Gould, Benjamin, 674
Gould, Glenn, 313
Gould's Island (lighthouse), 189
Goulding, Ray, 449
Gounod, Charles, 292
Goya, Francisco, 23
Grable, Betty, 257
Grace Cathedral (San Francisco, California), 23
Grace of Monaco, Princess, 262
Grace Under Fire (TV), 619
Graf Zeppelin I (airship), 52
Graf Zeppelin II (airship), 52
Graham, Bill, 319
Graham, Martha, 137
Graham's American Monthly Magazine of Literature and Art, 221
Graham's Lady's and Gentleman's Magazine, 220
Graham's Magazine of Literature and Art, 221
Grahame, Gloria, 257
Grammas, Alex, 563
Grampus, USS (submarine), 539, 541
Gran Colombia Confederation, 9, 368, 373, 402, 421
Granada, Kingdom of, 122
Granadine Confederation, 368, 403
Grand Army of the Republic (GAR), 679, 683
Grand Avenue Railway (Kansas City, Missouri), 632
Grand Canal (China), 119
Grand Central Station (radio), 457

Grand Hotel (radio), 457
Grand Marquee (radio), 457
Grand Ole Opry, 318
Grand Pont Suspendu (Fribourg, Switzerland), 127
Grand Trunk Pacific Railway, 481
Grand Union Hotel (Saratoga, New York), 176
grandfather clauses (voting), 111
Grange, Red, 583, 585
Granger, Stewart, 257
Grant, Cary, 257
Grant, Duncan, 192
Grant, Ulysses S., 160, 441, 651, 654, 681, 684, 689
Granville College, 104
Granville Literary and Theological Institution, 104
Granville R. Bacon (schooner), 533
Grape War, 180
Grappelli, Stéphane, 332
Grateful Dead, The, 332
Graves, Samuel, 482
Gray, Clarence, 70
Gray, Harold, 462
Gray, John, 677
Gray, Spalding, 203
Gray, Thomas, 203
Grayback, USS (submarine), 541
Grays Harbor County, 670
Grease (show), 148
Great American Ballpark (Cincinnati, Ohio), 555
Great American Smokeout, 163
Great Anthracite Coal Strike, 1902 (Pennsylvania), 180
great auk, 14
Great Belt Link (Denmark, 126
Great Britain, 6, 7, 8, 10, 78, 80, 543, 544, 631, 690, 691, 694
Great Britain (ship), 537
Great Colombia, Republic of, 9
Great Council of Basel, 175
Great Depression, 4
Great Eastern (ship), 527, 537
Great Gildersleeve, The (radio), 455, 457, 458
Great Lakes Bowl (football), 584
Great Law of the Quakers (Quaker Code of 1682), 186
Great Leap Forward, 367
Great Northern Hotel (Chicago, Illinois), 176
Great Northern Railway, 477, 479, 481
Great Proletarian Cultural Revolution, 367
Great Pyramid of Giza, 133
Great Republic (clipper ship), 500
Great Salt Lake County, Utah, 669
Great Stone Dwelling (Shaker building), 488
Great Wall of China, 119, 132

Great West Bay Light, 192
Great Western (ship), 528, 537
Great Western Schism, 486
Greatest American Hero, The (TV), 619
Greatest Story Ever Told, The (radio), 457
Greece, 7, 114, 381, 631
Greece, Kingdom of, 381
Greeley, Horace, 441
Greely Expedition, 156
Greely, Adolphus Washington, 156
Green Acres (TV), 619
Green Diamond (train), 483
Green Hornet, The (radio), 457
Green Monster (Fenway Park, Boston, Massachusetts), 554
Green Sergeant's Bridge (Flemington, New Jersey), 124
Green, Cecil Howard, 117
Green, Elijah ("Pumpsie"), 562
Green, Red, 602
Greenback party, 440, 441
greenbacks, 229
Greenbury Point Shoal (lighthouse), 189
Greene County, Nebraska, 664
Greene, Graham, 203, 472
Greene, Richard, 257
Greene, Ward, 72
Greenland, 372
Greenpeace, 154
Greenstreet, Lionel, 159
Greenstreet, Sydney, 257
Greenwood Pottery (company), 166
Greenwood, Charlotte, 257
Greenwood, Joan, 257
Gregorian calendar, 630
Gregory IX, Pope, 487
Gregory XIII, Pope, 630
Gregory XVI, Pope, 230
Gregory, Annie Knight, 677
Grellet, Stephen, 376
Grenada, 11, 114, 381
Grenadines, The, 407
Gretzky, Wayne, 600
Grieg, Edvard, 292
Griffin, Cyrus, 643
Griffith Stadium (Washington, D.C.), 559
Griffith, Clark, 559
Griffith, D. W., 239
Grigg, Tex, 595
Grimaldi, House of (Monaco), 398
Grimes, Burleigh, 567
Grimm, Charlie, 568
Grinnell, Mattie, 428
Gripsholm I (liner), 528
Grissom, Virgil I. ("Gus"), 548
Grofé, Ferde, 292
Groningen (Netherlands province), 11
Gropius, Walter, 17

Gross, Milt, 72
ground rule double (baseball), 566
Ground Zero (World Trade Center), 87
Group of Seven (artist group), 21
Groveland Shaker community, 488
Growden Memorial Park (Fairbanks Alaska), 559
Growing Pains (TV), 619
Growler, USS (submarine), 541
Grueby Faience Company, 166
Grueby, William H., 166
Grumman F-14 Tomcat (aircraft), 41
Grumman F3F-3 (aircraft), 37
Grumman F9F Panther (aircraft), 41
Grundy, George Debaun (Jr.), 57
Guadalcanal, Battle of, 702
Guadalupe County, Colorado, 657
Guadalupe Hidalgo, Treaty of, 638, 655, 656, 664, 665, 689
Guadeloupe, 543, 544
Guam, 670
Guantanamo Bay Naval Station, 371
Guantanamo Bay U.S. Naval Base, 371
Guantanamo United States Naval Operating Base, 371
Guardino, Harry, 257
Guatemala, 7, 114
Guatemala, Captaincy-General of, 401
Guatemala, Republic of, 381
Gudgeon, USS (submarine), 541
Gueffroy, Chris, 685
Guernica, Spain, 692
Guerriere (HMS), 694
Guiding Light, The (radio), 457
guilder (Netherlands), 224
Guinea, 7, 114
Guinea, People's Revolutionary Republic of, 382
Guinea, Republic of, 382
Guinea-Bissau, Republic of, 114, 382
Guinness, Sir Alec, 257
Gulf of Tonkin Resolution, 693
Gull Rocks (lighthouse), 189
Gullett, Don, 564
Gulliver the Traveler (radio), 454
Gumps, The (comic strip), 71
Gund Arena (Cleveland, Ohio), 573
Gundalow (sailing ship), 500
Gungaadorj, Sharavyn, 398
Gun-Munro, Sir Sidney, 407
Gunsmoke (radio), 457
Gunsmoke (TV), 619
Gunther, Henry, 697
Gustafson, Bob, 72
Gustavus I, King (Sweden), 10
Guthrie, Woody, 332
Guyan, Thomas, 81
Guyana, 115, 224, 489, 543, 544
Guyana, Co-operative Republic of, 382

Guyana, Dominion of, 382
Gwenn, Edmund, 257
Gwynne, Fred, 257
gymnastics (Olympic event), 606
Hackett, Bobby, 333
Hackett, Buddy, 258
Hackett, Joan, 258
Hadean Time, 2
Haden, Sara, 258
Hadley, Bump, 563
Hafsid dynasty (Tunisia), 416
Haida, HMCS (destroyer), 521
Haignere, Jean-Pierre, 549
haiku (Japanese poetry), 193
Haile Selassie I, Emperor (Ethiopia), 375
Hainsworth, George, 605
hair, 162, 367, 486
Hair (show), 148
Hairbreadth Harry (comic strip), 71
Haiti, 115, 224, 373, 543
Haiti, Empire of, 383
Haiti, Kingdom of, 383
Haiti, Republic of, 383
Haiti, State of, 383
Halas, George, 586
Hale, Alan (Jr.), 258
Hale, Alan (Sr.), 258
Hale, John P., 442
Haley, Bill, and His Comets, 333
Haley, Jack, 258
half dollar, U.S., 228
Half Hitch (comic strip), 71
half-cent coin, U.S., 224
Halibut, USS (submarine), 541, 542
Halifax, Nova Scotia (trolleys), 635
Hall of Fame (football), 586
Hall of Science (New York, New York), 161
Hall, Ada E., 100
Hall, Huntz, 258
Hallahan, Charles, 258
Halle Centrale, Main Railway Station (Brussels, Belgium), 17
Halliday, Brett, 464
Hallmark Playhouse (radio), 457, 464
Hallmark Radio Hall of Fame (radio, 457
Halls of Ivy, The (radio), 457
hallucinogenic drugs, 74
Halpern, Lee, 67
Ham (Astro-Chimp), 547
Hambone (U.S. Army mule), 648
Hambro, Carl, 10
Hamburg, Germany, 9, 58
Hamel, Veronica, 173
Hamilton Literary and Theological Institution, 104
Hamilton Tigers (ice hockey), 602
Hamilton, Margaret, 258
Hamilton, Murray, 258
Hamilton, Neil, 258

Hamlet (play), 140
Hammerstein, Oscar (I), 151
Hammerstein, Oscar (II), 292
Hammerstein's Lyric Theater (New York, New York), 151
Hammerstein's Victoria Theater (New York, New York), 151
Hammett, Dashiell, 72, 203, 454, 469, 472
Hammond Pros (football), 592
Hammond, Paul, 608
Hampshire Pottery (company), 166
Hampton, Lionel, 333
Hampton, Rick, 604
Hampton's (magazine), 221
Han dynasty (China), 119
Han River (Heavenly River), 119
Hancock County, Alabama, 655
Hancock Shaker community, 488
Hancock, USS (carrier), 515, 694
Hancock, Walter Kirtland, 232
Handel, George Frideric, 292
Handley, Bo, 592
Handy, W. C., 293
Hanford's Tri-State Airlines, 47
Hangin' with Mr.Cooper (TV), 619
hanging (execution), 82
Hanging Gardens of Babylon, 134
Hang-It-All, 16
Hanlon (manufacturer), 234
Hanna-Barbera Studio, 66
Hannibal, John (Montauk chief), 429
Hanover, Elector of, 678
Hanover, House of, 419
Hansa (liner), 525, 527
Hanseatic League, 9
Hanson, Hal, 595
Happiness Boys, The (radio), 457
Happy Days (TV), 619
Happy Hooligan (comic strip), 71
Happy Island (radio), 454
Hapsburg, House of, 120, 358, 360, 400, 411, 693
Harbor Bowl (football), 584
Hardcastle & McCormick (TV), 619
Hardee's Corporation, 490
Harder, Melvin Leroy ("Mel"), 563
Harding, Ann, 258
Harding, Warren G., 480, 653
Hardwicke, Sir Cedric, 258
Hardy, Oliver, 258
Hardy, Thomas, 203
Hare, William Francis, Earl of Listowel, 385
Hare, Ernie, 457
Haring, Keith, 23
Harlem Clowns (basketball), 575
Harlem Globetrotters (basketball), 575
Harlem Renaissance, 192
Harlem Suitcase Theater, 193
Harley, William S., 236
Harley-Davidson (motorcycle

maker), 234, 236
Harlow, Jean, 258
Harman, Fred, 72, 468
Harmony Society, 484
Harold II, Anglo-Saxon king, 418
Harold Teen (comic strip), 71
Harper & Brothers, 221
Harper's Weekly (magazine), 67, 221
Harrah, Toby, 570
Harrington, John P., 425, 427, 429, 432
Harrington, Jonathan, 674
Harris County, Texas, 669
Harris, Gail, 569
Harris, Joel Chandler, 203
Harris, Lawren S., 21
Harris, Patricia Roberts, 639
Harris, Robert Lee, 424
Harris, The (theater, New York, New York), 151
Harrisburg County, Texas, 669
Harrisburg, Pennsylvania, 667
Harrison Narcotics Act (1914), 74
Harrison, Benjamin, 654, 684
Harrison, George, 321
Harrison, Sir Rex, 259
Harrison, William Henry, 443, 651, 695
Hart to Hart (TV), 619
Hart, Eva, 100
Hart, Lorenz, 293
Hart, William S., 259
Hartford Bicentennials (soccer), 609
Hartford Blues (football), 592
Hartford Whalers (ice hockey), 600, 601, 603
Hartman, Phil, 259
Hartmann, Erich, 700
Hartz Mountain Canaries Show, The (radio), 447
Harvard Annex, 107
Harvard Shaker community, 487
Harvard University, 101
Harvest of Stars (radio), 457
Harvey (play), 141, 148
Harvey farm (Nova, Ohio), 6
Harvey Houses, 176
Harvey, Laurence, 259
Harvey, William, 495
Hasegawa, Admiral Kiyoshi, 414
Hasen, Irwin, 71
hash marks (football field), 587
Hashemite monarchy (Iraq), 387
Hasler, Blondie, 707
Hastings, Battle of, 418
Hat Law (Turkey), 416
Hatfields and McCoys, 75
Hathaway family, 611
Hathaway, Henry, 239
Hatlo, Jimmy, 71
Haunt of Fear, The (comic strip), 71
Haupt, Herman, 127
Havasupai Indian Reservation, 444

Have Gun, Will Travel (radio), 457
Have Gun, Will Travel (TV), 619
Haverford College, 105
Haverford School, 105
Hawaii, 2, 427, 658
Hawaii Five-O (TV), 619
Hawaii, Bicentennial quarter, 226
Hawaii, College of, 105
Hawaii, Republic of, 658
Hawaii, University of, 105
Hawaii/Team Hawaii (soccer), 609
Hawaiian Aye Aye (cartoon), 66
Hawaiian Eye (TV), 619
Hawk, Bob, 449
Hawker Hurricane (aircraft), 41
Hawker Siddeley Aviation, 34
Hawkins, Coleman, 333
Hawks, Howard, 239
Hawthorne, Nathaniel, 204
Hay, John, 654
Hayakawa, Sessue, 259
Haydn, Joseph, 293
Hayes, George ("Gabby"), 259
Hayes, Helen, 141, 458
Hayes, Rutherford B., 111, 654, 682, 684
Hayes-Tilden election dispute, 111
Haymarket riot, 181
Haynie, Jim, 94
Hays Code (movies), 236
Hays, Will H., 236
Hayward, Louis, 259
Hayward, Susan, 259
Hayworth, Rita, 259
hazardous materials, 153
Hazel (TV), 619
Hazel, Homer, 583
Head of the Class (TV), 619
head tax, 111
Headin' Home (movie), 564
Health and Human Services, Department of (U.S.), 636, 639
health hazards, 172, 173, 174
Health, Education and Welfare, Department of (U.S.), 636, 639
Hearst, William Randolph, 73
Hearst's Magazine, 221
Heart of Juliet Jones (comic strip), 71
Hearts Afire (TV), 619
heath hen, 14
Hechinger (store), 63
Heckle & Jeckle (cartoon characters), 66
Hedda Hopper Show, The (radio), 457
Hee Haw (TV), 619
Heeney, Tom, 583
Heermann, USS (destroyer), 712
Heflin, Van, 259
Hegedus, Andras, 11
Hegerty, Jack, 596
Heian period (Japan), 389

Heinlein, Robert A., 204
Heintzleman, B. Frank, 655
Heisey, A. H., Company, 166
Heisey, Augustus H., 166
Heldt, Jack, 590
Helen Hayes Theater (New York, New York), 151
Helen Hayes Theater (radio), 458
Helen MacLeod II (schooner), 532
Helena, Montana, 664
helicopters, 56
Hellenic Republic, 381
Heller, Joseph, 204
Hellman, Lillian, 204
Hello, Dolly! (show), 148
helmets (football), 587
helmets (ice hockey), 601
Help Me Dream (movie), 138
Helvetic Republic, 413
Helvetica, 413
Hemingway, Ernest, 204
Henderson (motorcycle maker), 234
Henderson Field, Guadalcanal, 702
Henderson, Bill, 234
Henderson, Edward Firth, 405
Henderson, Fletcher, 333
Henderson, Marge, 72
Henderson, Tom, 234
Hendon, Ernest, 175
Hendrickson, Waina, 655
Hendrix, Jimi, 333
Henie, Sonja, 259
Hennepin Canal, 130
Hennessy, Sir James Patrick Ivan, 360
Henreid, Paul, 259
Henri and Armand Sufaux & Cie (motorcycle maker), 235
Henri, Robert, 21
Henry County, Missouri, 663
Henry I (Henry Christophe), King (Haiti), 383
Henry II, King (England), 419
Henry III, King (France), 376
Henry IV (play), 490
Henry IV, King (England), 419
Henry Morgan Show, The (radio), 458
Henry Pete, 589
Henry V, King (Germany), 120
Henry VI, King (England), 419
Henry VII, King (England), 419, 484, 690
Henry VIII, King (England), 184, 419, 483
Henry, Duke of York, 419
Henry, King (Portugal), 404
Henry, O., 204, 222, 451
Henry, Pete, 594
Henshaw, Henry, 424
Henson, Matthew Alexander, 158
Hepburn, Audrey, 259
Hepburn, Katharine, 259

Horn and Hardart's Children's Hour (radio), 452
Hornell, Babe, 583
Hornet, USS (carrier), 515
Hornet, USS (man-of-war), 694
Horowitz, Vladimir, 313
horse racing, 597
horsecars, 634
horsepower, 6
horsepower tax, 34
horses, 6
Horta, Victor, 17
Horton, Edward Everett, 260
Horwitz, Curly, 135
Hot Club de France, 332
Hotchkiss (automobile), 29, 30
Hotchkiss-Brandt (automobile maker), 30
Hotel (TV), 620
Hotel Del Monte (Monterey, California), 176
hotels, 175
Hougoumont (ship), 358
Hour of Charm, The (radio), 459
Housatonic (ship), 97
House Calls (TV), 620
House of Mystery (radio), 459
House Party (radio), 459
House Un-American Activities Committee (HUAC), 644
Houseman, John, 260
Housing and Urban Development, U.S. Depament of, 639
Housman, A.E., 205
Houston Astros (baseball), 556
Houston Colt 45s (baseball), 556, 571
Houston Hurricane (soccer), 609
Houston Junior College, 105
Houston Mavericks (basketball), 578
Houston Stars (soccer), 609
Houston, Ken, 602
Houston, Sam, 668
Houston, Texas (trolleys), 635
Houston, University of, 105
Howard County, Indiana, 659
Howard, Frank, 570
Howard, John, 166
Howard, Leslie, 90, 260
Howard, Moe, 135
Howard, Robert, 166
Howard, Shemp, 135
Howard, Trevor, 260
Howdy Corporation, The, 64
Howdy Doody (TV), 620
Howe, George, 17
Howe, Gordie, 600
Howe, Syd, 604
Howells, William Dean, 205
Howland, John, 675
Howlin' Wolf, 335
Howze, Robert L., 648
HQ (store), 63

Hsüan T'ung, emperor (China), 366
Hu Hai, 119
Hu, King, 239
Huaute, Semu, 425
Hubbard, Michael, 71
Hubbell, Carl, 567
Hubble Space Telescope, 547
Hubert H. Humphrey Metrodome (Minneapolis, Minnesota), 554
Hudson (automobile maker), 28, 30, 31
Hudson Bay, Canada, 690
Hudson Essex (automobile), 30
Hudson Terraplane (automobile), 30
Hudson V8 Hornet (automobile), 30
Hudson, Dave, 603
Hudson, Ethel, 488
Hudson, Henry, 90
Hudson, John (Kalapuya speaker), 424
Hudson, Robert, 95
Hudson, Rock, 260
Hudson-Tailton (automobile), 30
Hue, Battle of, 693
Huffman Prairie Flying Field (Dayton, Ohio), 56
Huggins, Miller, 564
Hugh Capet, King (France), 376
Hughes Air West (airline), 46, 47
Hughes HK-1 "Hercules" NX37602 (aircraft), 55
Hughes, Edwin, 685
Hughes, Howard, 35, 46, 55
Hughes, Langston, 205
Hughitt, Tommy, 589
Hugo, Victor, 205
Hulick, Wilbur ("Budd"), 471
Hull, A.E., Pottery (company), 166
Hull, Josephine, 261
Hulme, John, 169
Hulme, T.E., 193
Humaliwu (Malibu, California), 425
human body, 178
Humber (automobile), 30
Humber River Bridge (England), 125, 126
Humber Sceptre (automobile), 30
Humbert II, King (Italy), 388
Humboldt Harbor (lighthouse), 189
Hume, Benita, 457
Humperdinck, Engelbert, 294
Humphreys, Joshua, 538
Humphries Weaving Company, de Vere Mill (Castle Hedingham, England), 223
Hundred Years' War, 687
Hung Hsiu-Ch'uan, 692
Hungarian People's Republic, 384
Hungarian State, 384
Hungary, 11, 115, 543, 631
Hungary, Republic of, 384
Hunkers, 440
Hunnicutt, Arthur, 261

Hunt, Richard Morris, 17
Hunt, Robert, 672
Hunter (TV), 620
Hunter College of the City of New York, 105
Hunter, Billy, 570
Hunter, Jeffrey, 261
Hunter, Jim ("Catfish"), 569
Hunter, Thomas, 105
Hunters Point Naval Shipyard (California), 539
Huntingdon Normal School, 105
Huntingdon Street Baseball Grounds (Philadelphia, Pennsylvania), 558
Huntington Avenue Grounds (Boston, Massachusetts), 554
Hupmobile (automobile maker), 30
Hupmobile Skylark (automobile), 30
Hurricane Georges (1998), 191
hurricanes, names for, 722
Husband, Rick, 50
Husein III, dey of Algeria, 356
Hussar (sailing ship), 498
Hussein dynasty (Tunisia), 416
Hussein, King (Jordan), 7
Hussein, Saddam, 687
Huston, John, 239, 261
Huston, Walter, 261
Hutchins, William, 677
Hutchinson, Thomas, 661
Hutton, Jim, 261
Huxley, Aldous, 205
Hyatt's Select School for Boys, 109
Hyde County, North Carolina, 666
Hyde, Bessie, 90
Hyde, Glen, 90
Hyde-White, Wilfrid, 261
hydrogen, 93
Hygrade Sylvania Corporation, 64
I Dream of Jeannie (TV), 620
I Love a Mystery (radio), 459
I Love Adventure (radio), 459
I Love Lucy (radio), 459
I Love Lucy (TV), 620
I Married Joan (TV), 620
I Spy (TV), 620
I Was a Communist for the FBI (radio), 459
I.F. Stone's Weekly (magazine), 221
I've Been to the Mountaintop (speech), 68
I've Got a Secret (TV), 620
I-5 Arroyo Pasajero Twin Bridges (Coalinga, California), 127
Ibert, Jacques, 294
Ibsen, Henrik, 205
Ice Age, 3
ice hockey, goalies, 600
ice hockey, original six teams, 599
ice hockey, overtime rules, 601
ice hockey, players, 600
ice hockey, teams, All-Star, 601
ice hockey, teams, defunct or

relocated, 602
Iceland, 10, 14, 115, 223, 372
Iceland, Kingdom of, 385
Iceland, Republic of, 384
Ichord, Richard H., 644
Idaho, 112, 658
Idaho State University, 105
Idaho Technical Institute, 105
Idaho Territory, 658, 664
Idaho, Academy of, 105
Idaho, USS (battleship), 503
Idlewild Airport (Queens, New York), 49
Idora Park (Youngstown, Ohio), 144
Idris I, King (Libya), 393
Ifni, Morocco, 399
Il Duce (the Leader), 711
Ile de France (liner), 95, 528
Ile de France (Mauritius), 396
Iliad (poem), 121
Illinois, 112, 545, 659
Illinois and Michigan Canal, 130
Illinois and Mississippi Canal, 130
Illinois Central Railroad, 481, 483
Illinois Industrial University, 105
Illinois Territory, 659, 670
Illinois, University of, 105, 585
Illinois, USS (battleship), 504
Imagism, 193
Imlay,Tut, 592
Immel, Perry, 684
Immigration and Naturalization Amendments (U.S.), 443
immigration, U.S., 443
impalement (punishment), 81
Imperator, USS (ship), 528
Imperial German Air Service, 696
Imperial Glass (company), 164, 166
Imperial Glass Corporation, 166
In Living Color (TV), 620
In Person (radio), 453
In the Heat of the Night (TV), 620
Inca Empire, 120, 361, 403
Incas (Carolina parakeet), 13
income tax, 645
Incredible Hulk, The (TV), 620
indentured servants, 179
Independence Day, 646
Independence Hall (Philadelphia, Pennsylvania), 231
Independence, USS (carrier), 515
Index of Forbidden Books, 60
India, 8, 115, 223, 543, 544
India Wharf (Boston, Massachusetts), 16
India, Dominion of, 385
India, Empress of, 6
India, Republic of, 385
Indian (motorcycle maker), 232, 234
Indian Ace (motorcycle), 232
Indian Affairs, Office of, 639
Indian Ann, 426
Indian Chief (motorcycle), 234

Indian Citizenship Act, 111
Indian Head dollar coin, U.S., 227
Indian Head eagle coin, U.S., 227
Indian Head half eagle coin, U.S., 227
Indian Head one-cent coin, U.S., 224
Indian Head quarter eagle coin, U.S., 227
Indian Princess dollar coin, U.S., 227
Indian Scout (motorcycle), 234
Indian Territory, 666
Indiana, 112, 545, 659
Indiana College, 105
Indiana State College, 105
Indiana State Normal School, 105
Indiana State Seminary, 105
Indiana State Teachers College, 105
Indiana State University, 105
Indiana Territory, 659, 670
Indiana University, 105
Indiana, USS (battleship), 504, 539
Indianapolis 500 (automobile race), 552
Indianapolis Clowns (baseball), 562
Indianapolis Jets (basketball), 578
Indianapolis Olympians (basketball), 578
Indianapolis Sun (newspaper), 435
Indianapolis Times (newspaper), 435
Indianapolis, Indiana (trolleys), 635
Indochina, 693
Indochina War, 687, 693
Indonesia, Republic of, 115, 386
Indonesia, United States of, 386
Industrial Age, 3
Industrial Revolution, 3
Industrial School for Colored Youth (Bowie State University), 103
infantile paralysis, 171
Information Age, 3
Information Agency, U.S., 719
Information Please! (radio), 459
Ing, Peter, 600
Inge, William, 205
Ingels, Graham, 71
Ingraham, Duncan Nathaniel, 694
Ingram, Rex, 261
Ink Spots (original), 335
Inklings, 193
Inman, Henry, 24
Inner Sanctum Mysteries (radio), 459
Institute for Colored Youth, The (Pennsylvania), 103
Interior Department Building (Washington, D.C.), 20
Interior, Department of the (U.S.), 639, 671
Inter-Island Airways Ltd., 47
Intermediate-Range Nuclear Forces Treaty, 721
Internal Security, House Committee on (HCIS), 644
International Business Machines

Corporation (IBM), 63
International Exhibition of Paris (1889), 230
International Federation of Trade Unions (IFTU), 181
International Hockey League, 600
International Maritime Organization, 611
International Military Tribunal (Nuremberg, Germany), 720
International Theater (New York, New York), 152
Interstate Commerce Commission ICC), 636
Interstate Consolidated Rapid Transit Company (Kansas City, Missouri), 632
Intolerable Acts, The, 676
Intra-Coastal Waterway, Delaware River to Chesapeake Bay, Delaware and Maryland, 129
Intrepid, USS (carrier), 516, 538
invention, miniature working model, 639
Iolani Palace (Honolulu, Hawaii), 658
Ion (sailing ship*)*, 546
Ionesco, Eugene, 205
Ionian Islands (Greece), 381
Iosco County, Michigan, 662
Iowa, 545, 659
Iowa State Agricultural College and Model Farm, 105
Iowa State University of Science and Technology, 105
Iowa Territory, 659
Iowa, State University of, 105
Iowa, University of, 105
Iowa, USS (battleship), 504
Iran, 8, 115, 543
Iran, Islamic Republic of, 386
Iran-Iraq War, 387, 687
Iraq, 7, 8, 115, 543
Iraq, Kingdom of, 387
Iraq, State of, 387
Ireland, 13, 115, 420, 489
Ireland, John, 261, 294
Irene Rich Dramas (radio), 459
Irian Jaya, Indonesia, 386
Irish Free State, 193, 387
Irish Literary Renaissance, 193
Iron Age, 6
Iron and Oil League (baseball), 563
Iron County, Utah, 669
Iron Curtain, 685
iron lung, 174
Ironside, 620
Ironwood, (U.S. Coast Guard cutter), 688
Iroquois Confederation (Native Americans), 674
Irvin, Dick, 601
Irving, Washington, 205

Irwin, John Nichol, II, 640
Isabella, Queen (Spain), 487
I-See-O (Plenty Fires), 649
Ishi, 433
Islam, 122
Islas Malvinas, 357
Isle of Wight County, Virginia, 669
Isotta-Fraschini (automobile maker), 30
Israel, 79, 115, 392, 691
Israel, State of, 388
Istanbul, Turkey, 416
Isthmus, State of the, 403
It Pays to be Ignorant (radio), 459
It Takes a Thief (TV), 620
Italia (airship), 154
Italian East Africa, 374, 375
Italian Somaliland, 389, 410
Italis (liner), 525
Italy, 10, 79, 115, 388, 489, 631, 711
Italy, Kingdom of, 388
Iturbide, Agustin de, 397
Ives, Burl, 261, 335
Ives, Charles, 295
Ives, George, 678
Ives, James Merritt, 22
Ivory Coast, 9, 10, 370
Iwo Jima, Battle of, 702
Iyeyasu (shogun founder), 389
Izard County, Nebraska, 664
J.J. Newberry's (store), 63
J.M. Fields (store), 63
J.T. Leonard *(sloop)*, 534
J.W. McCoy Pottery Company, 164
Jack Armstrong, the All-American Boy (radio), 459
Jack Benny Show, The (radio), 459
Jack Benny Show, The (TV), 620
Jack Carson Show, The (radio), 460
Jack Murphy Stadium (San Diego, California), 559
Jack Paar Tonight Show, The (TV), 620
Jack Pearl Show, The (radio), 460
Jack Smith Show, The (radio), 460
Jack the Ripper, 76
Jackie Gleason Show, The (TV), 620
Jackson County, Kansas, 660
Jackson, A.Y., 21
Jackson, Andrew, 58, 90, 440, 441, 443, 651, 653, 673, 677, 694, 695
Jackson, Mahalia, 336
Jackson, Milt, 336
Jackson, Reggie, 569
Jackson, Shirley, 205
Jackson, Thomas J. ("Stonewall"), 232
Jacksonian Democratic Republican party, 442
Jacksonville Tea Men (soccer), 609
Jacobins, 686
Jacobites, 419
Jacobs Creek Bridge (Uniontown,

Pennsylvania), 128
Jacobs Field (Cleveland, Ohio), 556
Jacobs, Melville, 424
Jacques I, Prince (Monaco), 398
Jadwiga (Piast ruler), 404
Jaeckel, Richard, 261
Jaffe, Sam, 261
Jagellon (Jagiellonian) dynasty (Poland), 404
Jagger, Dean, 261
Jakarta, Indonesia, 386
Jake and the Fatman (TV), 620
Jam Master Jay, 348
Jamaica, 11, 115, 223, 389, 543, 544
Jamaica Clipper (aircraft), 37
James (motorcycle maker), 234
James Blaine (clipper ship), 500
James I, King (England), 78, 88, 419
James II, King (England), 5, 81, 184, 419
James, Arthur Curtiss, 482
James, Frank, 86
James, Harry, 336
James, Henry, 206
James, Jesse, 86
James, Prince of Wales (Old Pretender), 419
Jamestown Exposition (1907), 682
Jamestown, Virginia, 669
Jamesway (store), 63
James-Younger Gang, 86
James-Younger Wild West Show, 86
Janácek, Leos, 295
Jane (comic strip), 71
Janeway, Gertrude Grubb, 684
Janissary, the, 121
Janowska (concentration camp), 710
Janssen, David, 261
January, John, 684
Japan, 115, 182, 224, 389, 489, 690, 691, 712
Japan Air Lines, 35
Jardin de Paris (theater, New York, New York), 152
Jarry Park (Montreal, Canada), 557
Jarvis, Deming, 164, 165
Jarvis, Doug, 601
Jasper County, Georgia, 658
Jawara, Sir Dawda Kairaba, 378
Jay, John, 640, 643, 675
Jazz Age, 4
Jeanneret-Gris, Charles Edouard. *See* Le Corbusier
Jeannette (ship), 155
Jebtsun Damba Khutukhtu, 398
Jeffers, Robinson, 206
Jefferson College, 109
Jefferson County, Mississippi, 663
Jefferson County, Nebraska, 664
Jefferson County, Vermont, 669
Jefferson Memorial (Washington, D.C.), 19
Jefferson nickel, U.S., 225

Jefferson Ward (store), 63
Jefferson, Joseph, III, 141
Jefferson, Thomas, 111, 186, 187, 441, 651
Jeffersons, The (TV), 620
Jeffries, Jim, 581
Jekyll & Hyde (show), 148
Jenkins, Allen, 261
Jennings, Waylon, 336
Jenny Lind Hall (New York, New York), 152
Jeremiah O'Brien, USS (Liberty ship), 713
Jergens Journal (radio), 474
Jeritza, Maria, 313
Jerome Robbins' Broadway (musical), 138
Jervis, John B., 132
Jest, The (play), 139
Jet Age, 3
Jet America (airline), 47
Jewell, Richard, 87
Jiang Qing, 367
Jim Nabors Show, The (TV), 620
Jimmy Durante Show, The (radio), 460
Jimmy Fidler Show, The (radio), 460
Jimmy, Sindick (Nooksack speaker), 429
Jinbilnggay, 184
Jiwarli language (Australia), 183
Joan Davis Shows (radio), 460
Joanie Loves Chachi (TV), 620
Jockey Club Gold Cup (1979), 597
jockeys, women, 598
Jodl, Alfred, 705
Joe and Asbestos (comic strip), 71
Joe Palooka (comic strip), 71
Joe Penner Show, The (radio), 460
John Deere and Company (Moline, Illinois), 19
John F. Kennedy International Airport (New York), 49
John F. Kennedy Space Center, 548
John F. Kennedy, USS, 538
John Larroquette Show, The (TV), 621
John Marshall, USS (submarine), 542
John Paul II, Pope, 486
John Wanamaker (store), 63, 160
John XXIII, Pope, 485
John's Other Wife (radio), 460
Johnny Hazard (comic strip), 71
Johnny Presents (radio), 460
Johnny Presents Ginny Simms (radio), 456
Johns-Manville Corporation, 64
Johnson County, Wyoming, 670
Johnson Family, The (radio), 460
Johnson, Andrew, 442, 651, 681
Johnson, Ben, 261
Johnson, Cornelius B., 13

Johnson, Crockett, 70
Johnson, Ferd, 72
Johnson, Frances (Takelma speaker), 432
Johnson, Frank B., 70
Johnson, Henry, 563
Johnson, J.J., 336
Johnson, James P., 295
Johnson, James Weldon, 206
Johnson, Lyndon B., 68, 444, 648, 651, 718
Johnson, Magic, 576
Johnson, Mamie ("Peanut"), 563
Johnson, Robert, 336
Johnson, Samuel (author), 206
Johnston, Frank, 21
Johnston, Joseph E., 679
Johnstown Flood, 94
Joint Long Range Proving Ground (Cape Canaveral), 547
joint-stock company, 65
Jolley, Al, 589
Jolson, Al, 447
Jomon period (Japan), 389
Jones Act, 671
Jones County, Alabama, 655
Jones, Billy, 457
Jones, Buck, 261
Jones, Henry, 261
Jones, James, 206
Jones, Jim, 485
Jones, John Paul, 338
Jones, Marie Smith (Eyak speaker), 427
Jones, Orville ("Hoppy"), 335
Jones, Sir Glyn Smallwood, 395
Jones, Spike, 337
Jonestown, Guyana, 485
Jonson, Ben, 206
Jonz, Don, 89
Joost, Eddie, 569
Joplin, Janis, 337
Joplin, Scott, 295
Jordaens, Jacob, 25
Jordan, 7, 115, 224, 544, 691
Jordan Marsh (store), 63
Jordan, Hashemite Kingdom of, 390
Jordan, Jim, 455
Jordan, Louis, 337
Jordan, Marian (Molly), 455
Jory, Victor, 261
Joseph Conrad (frigate), 522
Joseph Hemphill Porcelain Company, 169
Joseph, Chief (Nez Percè), 673
Joslyn, Allyn, 261
Joyce Jordan, Girl Intern (radio), 460
Joyce Jordan, M.D. (radio), 460
Joyce, James, 97, 206
Joyce, William, 707
Joyland Park (Atlantic Highlands, New Jersey), 143

Ju 52/3m (aircraft), 700
Juan Carlos Bourbon, Prince (Spain), 412
Juaneño (Native Americans), 427
Juarez, Benito, 397
Judea Palestine, 388
Judge, Darwin, 694
Judiciary Act (1789), 184
Judiciary Act (1801), 184
Judiciary Act (1802), 184
Judiciary Act (1869), 185
Judy Canova Show, The (radio), 461
Juin, Alphonse-Pierre, 706
Julia (TV), 621
Julia, Raul, 262
Julian calendar, 630
Julius Caesar (play), 140
Jumbo (elephant), 147
Jumbo (show), 151
jump ball (basketball), 575
Junge, Traudl, 706
Jungle Book, The (movie), 236
Jungle Jim (comic strip), 71
Jungle Jim (radio), 461
Juniata College, 105
Jupiter missile program, 542
Jupiter, planet, 547
Jura, Isle of, 611
Jurassic Period, 3
Just Kids (comic strip), 71
Just Plain Bill (radio), 461
Just Shoot Me (TV), 621
Justes, Alvin, 86
Juvenile Jury (radio), 461
Jylland (sailing ship), 522
Kaat, Jim, 570
Kabalevsky, Dmitri, 295
Kaczynski, Theodore ("Ted"), 88
Kafka, Franz, 206
Kaganovich, Lazar M., 406
Kahles, C.W., 71
Kahlo, Frida, 24
Kahn, Gus, 295
Kahn, Louis I., 17
Kahn, Madeline, 262
Kaighn, Raymond Pimlott, 575
Kaiser (automobile), 30
Kaiser Wilhelm der Grosse (liner), 528
Kaiser Wilhelm II (liner), 529
Kaiser, Henry J., 30
Kaiser-Jeep Corp., 33
Kaiwo Maru II (sailing ship), 498
Kajar dynasty (Iran), 386
Kalamazoo (lighthouse), 189
Kalapuya (Native Americans), 424
Kalifornsky, Peter, 426
Kalita Humphreys Theater (Dallas, Texas), 20
Kalkadoon language (Australia), 183
Kalkaska County, Michigan, 662
Kálmán, Emmerich, 295
Kalmar, Union of, 9, 372, 401, 413

Kamakura period (Japan), 389
Kamehameha V, King (Hawaii), 658
Kamen, Jack, 71
Kamerun (German protectorate), 364
Kamikaze, 712
Kampuchea, People's Republic of, 363
Kampuchea, Republic of Democratic, 363
Kanagawa Treaty of, 390
Kandy, King of, 412
Kane Expedition, 157
Kane, Elisha Kent, 157
Kane, Joseph Nathan, 206
Kang Teh, Emperor (Manchukuo), 366, 390
Kanotin County, Michigan, 662
Kansa (Native Americans), 427
Kansas, 112, 545, 660
Kansas City Athletics (baseball), 556, 558, 569
Kansas City Blues (football), 592
Kansas City Cable Railway (Kansas City, Missouri), 632
Kansas City Chiefs (football), 586
Kansas City Comets (soccer), 608
Kansas City Cowboys (football), 592
Kansas City Kings (basketball), 577
Kansas City Monarchs (baseball), 562
Kansas City Royals (baseball), 556
Kansas City Scouts (ice hockey), 603
Kansas City Spurs (soccer), 609
Kansas City-Omaha Kings (basketball), 578
Kansas State Agricultural College, 106
Kansas State College of Agriculture and Applied Science, 106
Kansas State University of Agriculture and Applied Science, 106
Kansas Territory, 660
Kansas, City, Missouri (trolleys), 635
Kansas, USS (battleship), 505
Kansas-Nebraska Act (1854), 443, 660, 663, 664
Kantor, MacKinlay, 207
Kapell, William, 313
Kara-Kirghiz Autonomous Oblast, 391
Karikal, India, 8, 386
Karloff, Boris, 262
Karluk Expedition, 157
Karluk, HMCS (ship), 157
Károly IV, King (Hungary), 384
Karpis, Alvin ("Old Creepy"), 84
Kaskaskia, Illinois, 659
Kasznar, Kurt, 262
Kate and Allie (TV), 621
Kate Smith and Her Swanee Music (radio), 461
Kate Smith Revue (radio), 461

Kate Smith Speaks (radio), 461
Kathryn M. Lee (schooner), 532
Katy, the (railroad), 477
Kauffman Stadium (Kansas City, Missouri), 556
Kaura, KNM (submarine), 714
Kautawaubet County, Michigan, 662
Kaw (Native Americans), 427
Kawabata, Yasunari, 207
Kay Kyser's Kollege of Musical Knowledge (radio), 461
Kaye, Danny, 262
Kaye, Sammy, 469
Kaykakee County, Michigan, 662
Kazakh Soviet Socialist Republic, 390
Kazakhstan, Republic of, 115, 390
Kealakekua Bay, Hawaii, 155
Kean, Edmund, 141
Kearsarge, USS (battleship), 505
Kearsarge, USS (carrier), 516, 548
Keaton, Buster, 239, 262
Keats, John, 207
Keel, Aubrey, 611
Keewatin (steamboat), 535
Kehoe, John ("Black Jack"), 179
Keitel, Wilhelm, 705
Kellaway, Cecil, 262
Kellum, John, 177
Kelly Barnes Dam, 93
Kelly Service, Inc., 64
Kelly, Gene, 262
Kelly, Grace (Princess Grace of Monaco), 262
Kelly, Patsy, 262
Kelly, Walt, 72
Kelly-Springfield Tire Company, 63
Kelton, Pert, 262
Kendrick(s), Eddie, 351
Kendrick, Jim, 593
Kennedy half dollar, U.S., 226
Kennedy, Arthur, 262
Kennedy, Edgar, 262
Kennedy, John F., 111, 371, 648, 652, 685, 718
Kennedy, Robert F., 490
Kenniston (or Kenison), David, 674
Kenora, Canada, 365
Kenosha Maroons (football), 592
Kenoyer, Louis (Tualatin speaker), 432
Kent County, Delaware, 657
Kent, William ("Pop"), 80
Kenton, Stan, 337
Kentucky, 545, 660
Kentucky & Indiana Bridge & Railroad Company, 477
Kentucky & Indiana Terminal Railroad, 477
Kentucky Colonels (basketball), 578
Kentucky Fried Chicken, 64
Kentucky, University of, 106
Kentucky, USS (battleship), 505

Kenya, 7, 115, 223
Kenya, Republic of, 390
Keogh, Jack, 592
Keogh, Myles, 673
Kepler, Johannes, 495
Keppler, Joseph, 222
Kern, Jerome, 295
Kerouac, Jack, 207
Kerr, Dave, 604
Ketcham, Hank, 71
Keuffel & Esser (manufacturer), 497
Kevill, John P., 683
Key, Francis Scott, 650, 694
Keynes, John Maynard, 192
KFC, 64
KGB (Committee for State Security), 418
Khachaturian, Aram, 296
Khmer Republic, 363
Khmer Rouge, 363
Khomeini, Ayatollah Ruhollah, 387
Khrushchev, Nikita, 685
Khufu (pharoah), 133
Kiangya (ship), 97
Kibbee, Guy, 263
Kid Antrim, 84
Kidder, Francis Turner, 81
Kiel Auditorium (Saint Louis, Missouri), 575
Kieslowski, Krzysztof, 239
Kilbride, Percy, 263
Kiley, Richard, 263
Kilgore, Billy, 581
Kill Devil Hill (North Carolina), 55
Killing Fields (Cambodia), 364
Kilpatrick, Ben, 85
Kilrain, Jake, 580
Kilrea, Wally, 602, 604
Kinchafoonee County, Georgia, 658
Kinderhook County, Missouri, 663
King Alexander (liner), 526
King and I, The (musical), 142, 415
King Features Syndicate, 73
King George's War, 687
King of the Carnival (movie), 237
King of the Royal Mounted (comic strip), 71
King Philip's War, 672
King Street Bridge (Melbourne, Australia), 128
King William's War, 688
King, Carolina, 695
King, Dennis, 142
King, Dr. Martin Luther (Jr.), 68
King, Henry, 236
King, Tom, 580
King, W.L. Mackenzie, 704
King's (store), 63
King's College, 104
King's County, Rhode Island, 667
Kingsford-Smith, Sir Charles Edward, 57
Kinkaid Homestead Act, 664

Kinsky, Klaus, 263
Kintpuash (Captain Jack) chief (Modoc tribe), 673
Kinzua Viaduct (Kushequa, Pennsylvania), 126
Kionga, 9
Kipling, Rudyard, 207, 222
Kirby, Jack, 73
Kirby-Smith, Edmund, 681
Kirghiz Autonomous Soviet Socialist Republic, 391
Kirghiz Soviet Socialist Republic, 391
Kiribati, Republic of, 115, 391
Kirk, Herbert S., 696
Kishkekosh County, Iowa, 660
Kiss and Tell (play), 464
Kiss for Cinderella, A (play), 139
Kiss, The (movie), 237
Kissel Industries (automobile maker), 30
Kissel Kar (automobile), 30
Kitsap County, Washington, 670
Kittson County, Minnesota, 662
Kitty Hawk, USS (carrier), 538
Kitty Keene, Incorporated (radio), 461
Klaw Theater (New York, New York), 151
Klee, Paul, 24
Kline, Bob, 564
Kling, Ken, 71
Klinghoffer, Leon, 501
Klotz, Red, 575
Kmart Corp., 64
Knapp, Uzal, 675
knee breeches, 161
Knickerbocker Playhouse (radio), 461
Knickerbocker Theater (New York, New York), 149
Knickerbocker, The (magazine), 221
Knight Errant (ballet), 139
Knight Rider (TV), 621
Knight, Richard, 677
Knights Hospitalers, 396
Knights of Labor, 181
Knights of Malta, 396
Knights of Saint Crispin, 181
Knights of Saint John, 134
Knights of the Golden Circle, 181
Knots Landing (TV), 621
Knowles, Isaac, 166
Knowles, Taylor and Knowles (company), 166
Know-Nothing party, 441
Knox College, 106
Knox County, Nebraska, 664
Knox Manual Labor College, 106
Kobenhavn (sailing ship), 91, 497
Kock, Battle of, 699
Kodama, Maria, 195
Koenig, Mark, 563, 571

Kofun (Yamato) period (Japan), 389
Kojak (TV), 621
Kojong, Emperor (Korea), 391
Koko the Clown, 66
Koldewey, Robert, 134
Kolelas, Bernard, 369
Kollege of Musical Knowledge (radio), 456
Kon-Tiki (raft), 156
Kon-Tiki Museum (Oslo, Norway), 156
Koppisch, Walt, 583
Koran (Quran), 416
Korea, 121, 544, 690, 691
Korea, Democratic People's Republic of (North Korea), 115, 391
Korea, Republic of (South Korea), 115, 391
Korean War, 391, 648, 688
Korngold, Erich Wolfgang, 296
Korvettes (store), 63
Korzeniowski, Jozef Teodor Konrad, 198
Kosciusko, Thaddeus, 404
Kovacs, Ernie, 263
Kraehe, Ollie, 595
Kraft Music Hall (radio), 447, 449, 461, 467, 474
Kraft Mystery Theater (TV), 621
Kraft Television Theater (TV), 621
Kraft Theater (TV), 621
Kramer, Josef, 709
Kramer, Stanley, 239
Krause Music Store (Chicago, Illinois), 20
Krazy Kat (comic strip), 71
Kreisler, Fritz, 296
Krenz, Egon (President of East Germany), 380
Kress Stores (store), 63
Krigstein, Bernie, 71
Kristallnacht, 708
Kroeber, Alfred, 433
Kronprinz Wilhelm (liner), 529
Kronprinzessin Cecilie (liner), 529
Kruger, Otto, 263
Kruglov, Sergei N., 418
Krupa, Gene, 338
Krusenstern (sailing ship), 498
Ku Klux Klan, 682
Kubert, Joe, 70
Kublai Khan, 119, 158
Kubrick, Stanley, 239
Kuchuk Kainarji, Treaty of, 690
Kuhale, Ed, 588
Kuhl, Ben, 86
Kuitsh (Native Americans), 432
Kukla, Fran and Ollie (TV), 621
Kung Fu (TV), 621
Kurosawa, Akira, 239
Kurtz, Frank, 38
Kusan (Native Americans), 426

Kuwait, 113, 391
Kwaaymii (Native Americans), 427
Kyrgyz Republic, 391
Kyrgyzstan, Republic of, 115, 392
Kyser, Kay, 338, 461
L.A. Law (TV), 621
L'Atlantique (ship), 97
La Cage aux Folles (show), 148
La Fontaine, Francis (Miami chief), 428
La Fontaine, Jean de, 207
La Gloire (play), 139
La Paz, Bolivia, 689
La Pérouse Expedition, 157
La Pointe County, Wisconsin, 670
La Salle, Robert, 656
La Voyante (movie), 139
labor, 181
Labor, Department of (U.S.), 719
Lac des Deux Montagnes (Montreal, Canada), 230
LaCava, Gregory, 239
Lackawanna & Western (railroad), 477
Lackawanna (railroad), 477
lacrosse (Olympic event), 606
Ladd, Alan, 263
Ladies Be Seated (radio), 461
Ladies Professional Golf Association (LPGA), 596
Ladies' Home Companion (magazine), 223
Lady from the Sea (play), 141
Lady Jane (Carolina parakeet), 13
Lady Maryland (ship), 533
Lady of the Lake (ship), 98
Lafayette County, Missouri, 663
Lafayette Escadrille, 695
Lafayette USS (ship), 530
Lafitte, Jean, 90
Lago de Celano, 133
Lago Fucino, 133
Lagonda (automobile), 30
LaGuardia Airport (New York), 49
LaGuardia, Fiorello, 49
Lahr, Bert, 263
Laird, Frank, 498
Lake Central Airlines, 47
Lake Champlain, USS (carrier), 516
Lake County, Colorado, 657
Lake County, Michigan, 662
Lake Erie, Battle of, 694
Lake Fucinus Emissarium, 133
Lake Geneva Inn (Lake Geneva, Wisconsin), 20, 176
Lake Maxinkuckee (lighthouse), 190
Lake Shore & Michigan Southern Railway, 127
Lake View Park (Kalamazoo, Michigan), 144
Lake, Arthur, 263
Lake, J.K., 135
Lake, Veronica, 263

Lakefront Park (Chicago, Illinois), 555
Lakefront Stadium (Cleveland, Ohio), 556
Lakota (Native Americans), 431
Lalo, Édouard, 296
Lamar County, Alabama, 655
Lamarr, Hedy, 263
Lamas, Fernando, 263
Lamb, Bertram, 72
Lamb, Charles, 207
Lambert, Gustaf E., 172
Lamberts Point (lighthouse), 190
lame duck session, 644
LaMotta, Jake, 581
Lamour, Dorothy, 263
Lancaster Colony Corporation, 165, 167
Lancaster, Burt, 263
Lancaster, House of, 419, 690
Lancaster, Pennsylvania, 640, 667
Lance Company, 162
Lanchester, Elsa, 263
Land of the Lost (radio), 461
land ownership, 186
land reclamation, 133
Landale, David, 101
Landis, Carole, 263
Landis, Jessie Royce, 263
Lane, Louisa, 140
Lane, Robert Preston, 584
Lang, Fritz, 239
Langdon, Jesse D., 691
Langfelder, Witmos, 90
Langlade County, Wisconsin, 670
Langley, USS (carrier), 516
languages, extinct world, 182
languages, Native American, 423, 424, 427
Lansing, Michigan, 662
Lantz, Walter, 66
Lanza, Mario, 313
Laos, 8, 115, 693
Laos (Lao People's Democratic Republic), 392
Laos, Kingdom of, 392
Lardner, Ring, 207
large denomination U.S. currency, 229
Large, George H., 584
large-size paper money, U.S., 229
Larkin Building (Buffalo, New York), 20
Larsen, Don, 570
Larson, Norm, 604
Las Vegas Quicksilver (soccer), 609
LaSalle (automobile), 30
LaSalle Hotel (Chicago, Illinois), 176
LaSalle Street Tunnel (Chicago, Illinois), 134
Lascaux caves (Montignac, France), 230
Lassie (radio), 461

Liberty Head twenty-five-cent coin, U.S., 226
Liberty Island (New York, New York), 232
Liberty party, 441
Liberty ships, 713
Librado, Fernando, 425
libraries, 186
Library of Congress, 187
Libya, 115, 389
Libya (Great Socialist People's Libyan Arab Jamahiriya), 393
Libyan Arab Republic, 393
Libyan Kingdom, 393
Libyan Sahara, 389
Liddell, Willie, 648
Liddil, Dick, 86
Lidice, Czechoslovakia, 704
Liebensraum (movie), 237
Liebl, Jacob, 380
Liechtenstein, Principality of, 115, 120, 224, 393
Life (magazine), 221
Life and Legend of Wyatt Earp, The (TV), 621
Life Begins at Eighty (radio), 462
Life Can Be Beautiful (radio), 462
Life Goes On (TV), 621
Life of Mary Sothern, The (radio), 462
Life of Riley, The (radio), 462
Life of Riley, The (TV), 622
Life with Father (show), 148
Life with Luigi (radio), 462
Lifebuoy Program (radio), 447
Lifesaving Service (U.S. Coast Guard), 649
Liggins, Brandy, 86
Light of Asia, The (musical), 137
Light of the World (radio), 462
Lighthouse at Alexandria, 134
Lighthouse Service, U.S., 649
lighthouses, 187
Lighthouses, Bureau of, 649
Lightnin' (play), 142
Lightning (clipper ship), 500
Lightoller, Charles Herbert, 100
Lights Out (radio), 462
lights, ballpark, 560
Light-Up Time (radio), 455
Lillard County, Missouri, 663
Limmer, Lou, 569
Lincoln Center (New York, New York), 19, 152
Lincoln County, Nebraska, 664
Lincoln Highway (radio), 462
Lincoln Memorial (Washington, D.C.), 16
Lincoln Memorial one-cent coin (Lincoln Memorial on back), 225
Lincoln Park Grounds (Cincinnati, Ohio), 555
Lincoln University, 106

Lincoln, Abraham, 231, 651, 652, 679
Lincoln, Mrs. Maurice, 85
Lincoln, Nebraska, 664
Lincoln, Robert, 653
Lincoln-Continental, 27
Lincoln-Douglas debate, 652
Lind, Jenny, 314
Linda's First Love (radio), 462
Lindbergh, Charles, 57
Lindlahr Food and Nutrition Show, The (radio), 462
Lindlahr, Victor, 462
Lindley, Fleetwood, 653
Lindsay, Bertha, 487
Lindsay, Margaret, 264
Lineup, The (TV), 622
Linge, Heinz, 706
Linit Bath Club Revue (radio), 456
Link, Adam, 677
Linkletter, Art, 467
Linnaeus, Carolus, 495
Lippincott's Magazine, 221
Liquid Paper Corporation, 64
lira (Italy), 224
Lismer, Arthur, 21
Listening Post (radio), 462
Liston, Sonny, 581, 582
Liszt, Franz, 297
Lit Brothers (store), 63
literacy tests, 111
literary movements and groups, 192
literature, 5, 192
Lithuania, 489
Lithuania, Republic of, 115, 393
Lithuanian Soviet Socialist Republic, 393
Little Audrey (cartoon character), 66
Little Bighorn, Battle of (Custer's Last Stand), 672
Little Boy (bomb), 717
Little Giant (railroad), 478
Little House on the Prairie (TV), 622
Little Iodine (comic strip), 71
Little Jimmy (comic strip), 71
Little King, The (comic strip), 71
Little Lulu (comic strip), 72
Little Meadow Creek (Concord, North Carolina), 170
Little Mermaid, The (movie), 236
Little Nemo in Slumberland (comic strip), 72
Little Ol' Bosko in Baghdad (cartoon), 65
Little Orphan Annie (radio), 462
Little Rock Daily Gazette (newspaper), 434
Little Salt Lake County, Utah, 669
Little Theater (New York, New York), 151
Little, Cleavon, 264
Lives of Harry Lime, The (radio), 472
Livingston, David, 422

Livingston, Patrick Joseph ("Paddy"), 561
Lloyd, Harold, 264
Lloyd, Temperance, 88
Loch Arkaig, HMS (ship), 715
Lockhart, Gene, 264
Lockheed Constellation (aircraft), 37
Lockheed Delta L-1011 TriStar (aircraft), 36
Lockheed F-104 Starfighter (aircaft), 42
Lockheed F-117 Nighthawk (aircraft), 42
Lockheed P-38 Lightning (aircraft), 42
Lockheed P-80 Shooting Star (aircraft), 42
Lockwood, Belva Ann, 442
Locofoco party, 441
Locomobile (automobile), 30
locomotive, coal-fired, 475
locomotive, steam, 478
Lodi, Ibrahim, 385
Loesser, Frank, 297
Loewe, Frederick, 297
Logan County, Arkansas, 656
Logan County, Kansas, 660
Logan International Airport (Boston, Massachusetts), 49
Logan, Joshua, 240
Logan, Lieutenant General Edward Lawrence, 49
Logiest, Guillaume, 406
Lombard, Carole, 264
Lombardi, Vince, 585
Lombardo, Guy, 339
Lonagron, Jorge, 71
London & Northwestern Railway, 680
London Company, 641
London, England, 76, 78, 147, 149
London, Jack, 208, 222
London, Treaty of, 362, 394
Lone Chipmunks, The (cartoon), 65
Lone Journey (radio), 462
Lone Ranger, The (radio), 462
Lone Ranger, The (TV), 622
long pants (ice hockey uniform), 601
Long Beach Naval Shipyard (California), 538
long bow, 721
Long Day's Journey Into Night (play), 141
Long March, The, 367
Long, Huey, 439
Longbaugh, Harry Alonzo, 84
Longfellow, Henry Wadsworth, 208, 222
Longmore, Roy (Anzac veteran), 697
Loo, Richard, 264
Look (magazine), 222
Lopez, Al, 566
Lord Haw Haw, 707

Notable Last Facts

Lorenzo Jones (radio), 462
Loretta Young Show, The (TV), 622
Lorne, Marion, 264
Lorrain, Claude, 24
Lorre, Peter, 264, 465
Los Angeles (airship), 51, 93
Los Angeles Angels (baseball), 557, 571
Los Angeles Aztecs (soccer), 609
Los Angeles Buccaneers (football), 592
Los Angeles Cable Railway (Los Angeles, California), 632
Los Angeles Christmas Festival (football), 584
Los Angeles Examiner (newspaper), 435
Los Angeles Herald Examiner (newspaper), 435
Los Angeles Kings (ice hockey), 604
Los Angeles Lakers (basketball), 576
Los Angeles Stars (basketball), 577, 578
Los Angeles Toros (soccer), 609
Los Angeles Wolves (soccer), 610
Los Angeles Xtremes (football), 586
Los Angeles, California (horsecars), 634
Los Angeles, California (trolleys), 635
Lost City of the Jungle (movie), 237
Lost Coast, 431
Lost in Space (TV), 622
Lothair, Duke (Saxony), 120
Lou Grant, 622
Loudon County, Tennessee, 668
Louella Parsons (radio), 462
Louis II (Ludwig), King of Bavaria, 380
Louis Antoine de Bourbon, Duc d'Angoulême, 376
Louis Armstrong New Orleans International Airport (Louisiana), 50
Louis Brown Athletic Center (Piscataway, New Jersey), 575
Louis C. Tiffany Furnaces (company), 168
Louis Cardinals (baseball), 559
Louis Charles de France, 376
Louis I, King (Etruria), 120
Louis III, King (Bavaria), 380
Louis IX, King (France), 484
Louis Penfield House (Ohio), 20
Louis Philippe, King (France), 376
Louis V, King (France), 376
Louis XIV, King (France), 2, 89
Louis XVI, King (France), 376
Louis, Duke of Parma, 120
Louis, Joe, 582
Louisiana, 545, 660
Louisiana Purchase, 157, 656, 657, 659, 660, 663, 664, 666, 668

Louisiana Purchase Exposition (St. Louis, Missouri), 160, 161
Louisiana State Bank (New Orleans, Louisiana), 17
Louisiana Territory, 659, 660
Louisiana, District of, 660
Louisiana, University of, 108
Louisiana, USS (battleship), 505
Louisville & Nashville (railroad), 478, 479
Louisville Brecks (football), 593
Louisville Colonels (baseball), 560
Louisville Colonels (football), 593
Louisville Times (newspaper), 435
Louisville, Georgia, 658
Love Boat (TV), 622
Love, American Style (TV), 622
Lovejoy, Frank, 264
Lovell, James A., 548
Low Countries, 400
Lowe, Edmund, 264
Lowell, Amy, 208
Lowell, James Russell, 208
Lowell, Robert, 208
Lower Canada, 364
Lowrey, Gerry, 604
Loy, Myrna, 264
Loyalists, 675
Loyola University (Chicago), 106
Lt. Commander Vasile Paun (paddle steamer), 525
Luahine, Iolani, 658
Lübeck, Germany, 9
Lubitsch, Ernst, 240
Lucas, Arthur, 80
Lucas, Red, 564
Lucas, Tom, 427
Luckhoo, Sir Edward Victor, 382
Lucky Stores (store), 63
Lucy Show, The (TV), 622
Lud, Ned, 179
Luddites, 179
Ludendorff Bridge (Germany), 706
Ludlow Coal Strike and Massacre, 180
Lufthansa, 37
Luftwaffe, 700
Lugosi, Bela, 264
Luke, Keye, 265
Luks, George, 21
Lully, Jean-Baptiste, 298
Lum and Abner (radio), 462
Lump, John, 140
Luna 24 (spacecraft), 550
Luna Park (Coney Island, New York), 144
Lunar Orbiter 5 (spacecraft), 550
Lunceford, Jimmy, 339
Lundigan, William, 265
Lunt, Alfred, 141
Lupino, Ida, 265
Lusitania (Portugal), 404
Lusitania (ship), 98

Luther, Martin, 4, 486
Lutoslawski, Witold, 298
Lux Radio Theater, The (radio), 463
Lux Video Theater (TV), 622
Luxembourg, Grand Duchy of, 10, 115, 224, 394, 631
Luyt, Richard Edmonds, 382
Lyceum Theater (New York, New York), 151
Lykins County, Kansas, 660
Lymon, Frankie, and The Teenagers, 339
Lynde, Paul, 265
Lynn, Diana, 265
Lynn, Wiley, 75
Lyon County, Iowa, 660
Lyon County, Kansas, 660
Lyric Theater (New York, New York), 151
Lyric Theatre (London, England), 142
LZ 2 (airship), 52
LZ 4 (airship), 52
LZ 5 (airship), 52
LZ 14 (airship), 52
LZ 18 (L2) (airship), 52
LZ 22 (Z-VII) (airship), 52
LZ 23 (Z-VIII) (airship), 52
LZ 24 (L3) (airship), 52
LZ 25 (Z-IX) (airship), 52
LZ 27 (L4) (airship), 52
LZ 29 (Z-X) (airship), 52
LZ 31 (L6) (airship), 52
LZ 32 (L7) (airship), 52
LZ 33 (L8) (airship), 52
LZ 36 (L9) (airship), 52
LZ 37 (airship), 52
LZ 38 (airship), 52
LZ 39 (airship), 53
LZ 40 (airship), 53
LZ 46 (L14) (airship), 53
LZ 47 (airship), 53
LZ 48 (L15) (airship), 53
LZ 50 (L16) (airship), 53
LZ 52 (L18) (airship), 53
LZ 53 (L17) (airship), 53
LZ 54 (L19) (airship), 53
LZ 61 (L21) (airship), 53
LZ 64 (L22) (airship), 53
LZ 66 (L23) (airship), 53
LZ 69 (L24) (airship), 53
LZ 72 (L31) (airship), 53
LZ 74 (L32) (airship), 53
LZ 76 (L33) (airship), 53
LZ 78 (L34) (airship), 53
LZ 79 (L41) (airship), 53
LZ 82 (L36) (airship), 53
LZ 84 (L38) (airship), 53
LZ 85 (L45) (airship), 53
LZ 86 (L39) (airship), 53
LZ 87 (L47) (airship), 53
LZ 89 (L50) (airship), 53
LZ 92 (L43) (airship), 53

LZ 93 (L44) (airship), 53
LZ 94 (L46) (airship), 53
LZ 95 (L48) (airship), 53
LZ 96 (L49) (airship), 53
LZ 97 (L54) (airship), 53
LZ 99 (L54) (airship), 53
LZ 100 (L53) (airship), 53
LZ 101 (L55) (airship), 54
LZ 102 (L57) (airship), 54
LZ 103 (L56) (airship), 54
LZ 104 (L59) (airship), 54
LZ 105 (L58) (airship), 54
LZ 108 (L60) (airship), 54
LZ 110 (L63) (airship), 54
LZ 111 (L65) (airship), 54
LZ 112 (L70) (airship), 54
LZ 113 (L71) (airship), 54
LZ 126 (airship), 54
LZ 126 (airship), 51
LZ 127 (airship), 54
LZ 129 (airship), 54
LZ 130 (airship), 54
M Squad (TV), 622
M*A*S*H (TV), 622
Ma Perkins (radio), 463
Maalin, Ali Maow, 171
Maastricht Treaty, 8
Mabillier, Etienne de Grellet du, 376
Macao, 405
Macaroni Line (railroad), 481
MacArthur, Douglas, 648, 688, 701, 703, 712
Macaulay, Thomas Babington, 208
Macbeth (play), 140, 141, 142
MacCashin, Eliza, 190
MacDonald, J.E.H, 21
MacDonald, Jeanette, 265
MacDonald, Malcolm John, 390
Macdonald, Sir John Alexander, 364
MacDowell, Edward, 298
Mace, Jem ("the Gypsy"), 580
Macedon, 7
Macedonia, 394
Macedonia, People's Republic of, 394
MacEntee, Sean, 388
MacGillivray, Sir Donald Charles, 395
MacGyver (TV), 622
Mack, Connie, 569
Mack, Ted, 463
Mackenzie, William, 480
Mackerel, USS (submarine), 541
Mackinac County, Michigan, 662
MacLane, Barton, 265
MacMahon, Aline, 265
MacMillan, Donald Baxter, 158
MacMurray Fred, 265
Macon (airship), 51, 93
MacRae, Gordon, 265
Macready, George, 142, 265
MacTavish, Craig, 601
Mad About You (TV), 622

Mad as a Mars Hare (cartoon), 66
Madagascar, 115
Madagascar, Democratic Republic of, 394
Madagascar, Republic of, 394
MADD (Mothers Against Drunk Driving), 185
Mademoiselle (magazine), 222
Madison Square Garden (New York, New York), 18, 151, 599
Madison Square Roof Garden (New York, New York), 152
Madison Street Cable Railway (Seattle, Washington), 633
Madison University, 104
Madison, Guy, 474
Madison, James, 645, 650, 651
Madrell, Edward ("Ned"), 183
Magallanes (sailing ship), 500
Magellan, Ferdinand, 158
Magic Key, The (radio), 463
Magic Show, The (show), 148
Magnani, Anna, 265
Magnat Debon (motorcycle maker), 235
Magnificent Montague, The (radio), 463
Magnificent Yankee, The (TV), 141
Magnum, P.I. (TV), 622
Magoon, Charles Edward, 370
Mahdi (Muhammad Ahmed ibn-Seyyid Abdullah), 412
Mahe, India, 8, 386
Mahler, Gustav, 298
Mahmud II, Sultan (Ottoman Empire), 121
Maid of the Loch (paddle steamer), 535
Maiden, the (torture instrument), 81
Maidu (Native Americans), 427
mail trains, 444
Main, Marjorie, 265
Maine, 545, 661
Maine State Seminary, 103
Maine, USS (battleship), 505, 691
Maine-Canada boundary dispute, 638
Maisie (The Adventures of Maisie) (radio), 463
Maitland, Thomas, 383
Majdanek (concentration camp), 710
Majel, Anastacia de, 427
Majestic (liner), 526
Majestic Theater (New York, New York), 152
Major Bowes' Original Amateur Hour (radio), 463
Major Dad (TV), 622
Major Hoople (radio), 463
Major Indoor Soccer League (MISL), 608
Major League Players Association, 562
Major Soccer League (MSL), 608

Makah (Native Americans), 428
Makharadze, Filipp Yeseyevich, 379
Malabo, Equatorial Guinea, 374
Malagasy Republic, 10, 394
Malamud, Bernard, 208
Malawi, 8, 115
Malawi, Republic of, 394
Malaya, 544
Malaya, Union of, 395
Malaysia, 115, 224, 395
Maldives, Republic of, 115, 395
Mali, 7, 115
Mali Federation, 395, 408
Mali, Empire of, 121
Mali, Republic of, 395
Malik, Abdul Motaleb, 359
Mall of America, 554
Malle, Louis, 240
Mallon, Mary, 172
Mallory, Stephen R., 680
Malpasset Dam, 94
Malta, 115, 223
Malta, Republic of, 396
Malta, Sovereign State of, 396
Maly Trostenets (concentration camp), 710
Mama (TV), 622
Mama's Family (TV), 622
Mamas, The & The Papas, 339
Mame (show), 148
Mamluks (Mamelukes), 120
mammoth, 14
Mamoulian, Rouben, 236, 240
Man Against Crime (TV), 622
Man Behind the Gun, The (radio), 463
Man Called X, The (radio), 463
Man from U.N.C.L.E., The (TV), 623
Man o' War, 597
Man of La Mancha (show), 148
Man or Devil (play), 139
Manchu dynasty (China), 120, 178, 390, 398, 414, 692
Manchukuo Empire, 367, 390, 691
Manchuria, 691
Mancini, Henry, 298
Mandan (Native Americans), 428
mandatory registration (draft), 647
Mandela, Nelson, 411
Mandrake the Magician (radio), 463
Manery, Kris, 602
Manet, Edouard, 24
Manhattan Merry-Go-Round, The (radio), 463
Manhattan Project, 717
Manin, Ludovico, 388
Mankiewicz, Joseph L., 240
Manley, Abe, 563
Mann, Anthony, 240
Mann, Thomas, 208
Manning, Michael, 81
Mannix (TV), 623
Manone, Wingy, 340

Mansa Musa, 121
Mansfield, Jayne, 265
Mantle, Mickey, 564
Manuel II, King (Portugal), 404
Manville Corporation, 64
Manx language (Isle of Man), 183
Many Loves of Dobie Gillis, The (TV), 623
Mao Tse-tung, 367
Maori (ship), 96
Maori Wars, 400
Maple Leaf Gardens (Toronto, Canada), 600
Marble Arch (London, England), 18
March of Time, The (radio), 463
March to the Sea, 679
March, Fredric, 265
Marchand, Nancy, 265
Marciano, Rocky, 582, 583
Marcus Aurelius, Emperor (Roman Empire), 122
Marcus Welby, M.D. (TV), 623
Marcus, Edwin, 67
Mare Island (lighthouse), 190
Mare Island Naval Shipyard (California), 538
Marguerite and Armand (ballet), 135, 137
Maria di Amparo (sailing ship), 499
Maria II, Queen (Portugal), 404
Mariano G. Vallejo, USS (submarine), 542
Marib Dam, 94
Marie Antoinette, Queen (France), 376
Marie-Louise, Empress (France), 378
Marijuana Tax Act, 74
Marine Corps Women's Reserve, U.S., 650
Marine Corps, U.S., 42, 650
Marine Inspection and Navigation, Bureau of, 649
Marine Mammal Protection Act, 12
Marine Protection, Research and Sanctuaries Act, 154
Marine Sulphur Queen (ship), 91
Marineland (Palos Verdes, California), 144
Mariner 10 (spacecraft), 550
Marion County, Arkansas, 656
Marion County, Oregon, 667
Maritime Administration (U.S.), 639
Maritime Distress Mode, 611
mark (Germany), 224
Mark Trail (radio), 463
Mark Twain Zephyr (train), 483
Market Square Arena (Indianapolis, Indiana), 574
Market Street Cable Railway (San Francisco, California), 633
Markle's New Showboat, 535
Marley, Bob, 340
Marley, John, 265

Marlin Hurt and Beulah Show (radio), 448
Marlin, USS (submarine), 541
Marlowe, Hugh, 265
Marquand, John P., 208
Marriage Act (1753, Great Britain), 78
Marriage for Two (radio), 463
marriage, interracial, ban on, 69
Married...With Children (TV), 623
Marriot, Fred, 553
Marriott Marquis Hotel (New York, New York), 150
Mars Pathfinder (spacecraft), 550
Marseilles-Rhone Canal (Arles, France), 135
Marshall Academy, 106
Marshall College, 106
Marshall Islands, 115, 399
Marshall Islands, Republic of the, 396
Marshall Plan, 713
Marshall University (West Virginia), 106
Marshall, Bill, 591
Marshall, E.G., 265
Marshall, George, 240
Marshall, George C., 713
Marshall, Herbert, 265
Marshall, James, 170
Marshall, Thurgood, 185
marsupials, 15
Martha (passenger pigeon), 14
Martha Dean Show, The (radio), 464
Martha's Vineyard, Massachusetts, 14
Martin (TV), 623
Martin 130 China Clipper (aircaft), 37
Martin B-10 (aircraft), 42
Martin B-26 Marauder (aircraft), 42
Martin Kane, Private Detective (radio), 464
Martin Kane, Private Eye (TV), 623
Martin V, Pope, 486
Martin, Alberta, 684
Martin, Dean, 266, 340
Martin, Edgar, 70
Martin, Strother, 266
Martin, William Jasper, 684
Martinek, Frank V., 71
Martinelli, Giovanni, 314
Martini (automobile maker), 31
Martini NF (automobile), 31
Martinique, 543, 544
Marto, Francisco, 486
Marto, Jacinta, 486
Martuthunira language (Australia), 183
Martyn, Grace Hanagan, 97
Maruk, Denns, 602
Marvel, William, 683
Marvin the Martian (cartoon

character), 66
Marvin, Lee, 266
Marx Brothers, 135, 253
Marx, Chico, 135, 266
Marx, Groucho, 135, 266
Marx, Gummo, 135
Marx, Harpo, 135, 266
Marx, Zeppo, 135, 266
Mary Celeste (sailing ship), 91
Mary Margaret McBride (radio), 464
Mary Noble Backstage Wife (radio), 448
Mary Perkins on Stage (comic strip), 72
Mary Rose (sailing ship), 522
Mary Tyler Moore Show, The (TV), 623
Mary, Mary (show), 148
Maryland, 489, 545, 661
Maryland State Normal School, 108
Maryland State Teachers College at Towson, 108
Maryland, USS (battleship), 505
Mascagni, Pietro, 298
Mascarene Islands, 14
Masina, Giulietta, 266
Mason County, Michigan, 662
Mason County, Washington, 670
Mason, Charles, 638
Mason, James, 266
Mason, Oliver (Quinault leader), 431
Mason, Stevens T., 662
Mason-Dixon Line, 638
Masonic University of Tennessee, 107
Masovia (Poland), 13
Massachusetts, 76, 490, 545, 661
Massachusetts Agricultural College, 106
Massachusetts Bay Colony, 10, 641
Massachusetts Bay Company, 641
Massachusetts Gazette and Boston Weekly News-Letter (newspaper), 435
Massachusetts State College, 106
Massachusetts, University of, 106
Massachusetts, USS (battleship), 505
Massenet, Jules, 298
Massey, Ilona, 266
Massey, Raymond, 266
Massine, Léonide, 138
Mastiff (clipper ship), 500
mastodon, 14
Mastroianni, Marcello, 267
Matchless (motorcycle maker), 233, 234
Matisse, Henri, 24
Matlock (TV), 623
Matthau, Walter, 267
Matthew Perry, Commodore, 390
Matthews, Eddie, 568
Mature, Victor, 267
Matz, Bob, 67

Meredith, George, 209
Merkel, Una, 268
Merman, Ethel, 341
Merriam-Webster Incorporated, 64
Merrill Lynch & Company, 62
Merrimac, USS (ship), 682
Merritt, Major General Wesley, 143
Mesolithic Age, 5
Mesopotamia, 118, 387
Mesozoic Era, 3
Messed-Up Movie Makers (cartoon), 66
Messerschmitt Bf-109 (aircraft), 43
Met Life Building (New York, New York), 151
Metacom, chief (Wampanoag tribe), 672
Methodism, 484
Metropolitan Hall (New York, New York), 152
Metropolitan Opera House (New York, New York), 152
Metropolitan Stadium (Bloomington, Minnesota), 554
Metropolitan Street Railway (New York, New York), 632
Metropolitan Theater (New York, New York), 150
Meuse-Argonne, Battle of, 697
Mexican Empire, 8, 382, 397
Mexican War, 655, 656, 668, 669, 689
Mexico, 115, 544, 545, 668
Mexico/United Mexican States, 397
Meyerbeer, Giacomo, 299, 318
MGM (movie studio), 65, 66, 237
MGM Grand Air (airline), 47
MGM Theater of the Air (radio), 464
Miami (Native Americans), 428
Miami and Erie Canal, 130
Miami Arena (Miami, Florida), 574
Miami County, Kansas, 660
Miami Dolphins, 587
Miami Floridians (basketball), 578
Miami Gators (soccer), 610
Miami Toros (soccer), 610
Miami Vice (TV), 623
Miami, Florida (trolleys), 635
Mianus River Bridge (Connecticut), 128
Michael I, King (Romania), 405
Michael Shayne, Private Detective (radio), 464
Michelangelo, 5, 24
Michelangelo (liner), 530
Michener, James, 209
Michigan, 112, 545, 661, 663
Michigan Central Railway Cantilever Bridge (Niagara Falls, New York), 128
Michigan Motors Corporation, 232
Michigan Territory, 659, 662, 670
Michigan, USS (battleship), 506

Michilimackinac County, Michigan, 662
Mickey Finn (comic strip), 72
Mickey Mouse, 67
Mickey's Christmas Carol (cartoon), 67
Mickey's Kangaroo (cartoon), 67
Micron PC Bowl (football), 584
Micronesia, Federated States of, 115, 397
Mid-Continent Airlines, 47
Middle Ages, 1, 4, 12
Middle Congo, 8, 369
Middle Stone Age, 5
Middlesex Canal, 131
Middleton, Charles, 268
Midget Theater (New York, New York), 150
Midway Airlines, 47
Midway Airport (Illinois), 49
Midway Gardens (Chicago, Illinois), 20
Midway, Battle of, 49, 702
Midway, USS (carrier), 517
Mies van der Rohe, Ludwig, 15, 18
Mifflin, Thomas, 667
Mifune, Toshiro, 268
MIG (aircraft), 700
Mikenauk County, Michigan, 662
Mikhail I, Tsar (Russia), 405
Mile High Stadium (Denver, Colorado), 556
Milestone, Lewis, 240
Milestones of Flight Gallery (National Air and Space Museum, Smithsonian Institution, Washington, D.C.), 57
Milhaud, Darius, 299, 311
Military Academy, U.S., 102, 648
Military College of South Carolina, The, 103
military discipline, 647
military draft, U. S. Armed Forces, 647
military schools, 102
Military Selective Service Act (1940), 647
Milland, Ray, 268
Millay, Edna St. Vincent, 209
Millbank Penitentiary (London, England), 78
Milledgeville, Georgia, 658
Miller and Arlington's Wild West Show, 143
Miller Park (Milwaukee, Wisconsin), 557
Miller, Ann, 268
Miller, Bob, 569
Miller, Bronco Charlie, 444
Miller, Don, 585
Miller, Glenn, 90, 341
Miller, John A., 145
Miller, Ralph, 566

Miller, Roger, 341
Millie Vanilli, 342
Milliner, Alexander, 677
Million Dollar Bridge (Portland, Maine), 128
Millionaire, The (TV), 623
Mills Brothers (Original), 342
Mills Field Municipal Airport (San Francisco, California), 51
Mills, John (Black Hole survivor), 78
Mills, Robert, 18, 232
Mills, William J., 665
Milne, A.A., 209
Milnes, William, 481
Milosevic, Slobodan, 409
Milton Berle Show (radio), 472
Milton Berle Show, The (TV), 623
Milton, John, 209
Milwaukee & St. Paul Railway Company, 476
Milwaukee Arena (Milwaukee, Wisconsin), 574
Milwaukee Badgers (football), 593
Milwaukee Braves (baseball), 569
Milwaukee Brewers (baseball), 557, 559, 570
Milwaukee Bucks (basketball), 576
Milwaukee County Airport (Wisconsin), 49
Milwaukee County Stadium (Milwaukee, Wisconsin), 557
Milwaukee Hawks (basketball), 578, 579
Milwaukee Road, Inc., The, 476
Milwaukee Wave (soccer), 609
Milwaukee, Wisconsin (trolleys), 635
Mineo, Sal, 268
mines, gold, 170
Ming dynasty (China), 120, 132
Mingus, Charles, 342
Minneapolis Lakers (basketball), 578
Minneapolis Marines (football), 593
Minneapolis Red Jackets (football), 593
Minneapolis Times (newspaper), 435
Minneapolis, St. Paul & Sault Ste. Marie Railway, 477
Minnelli, Vincente, 240
Minnesota, 662
Minnesota & Pacific Railroad Company, 477
Minnesota Kicks (soccer), 610
Minnesota Mining & Manufacturing Company, 64
Minnesota Muskies (basketball), 578
Minnesota North Stars (ice hockey), 601, 602, 603
Minnesota Pipers (basketball), 578
Minnesota Strikers (soccer), 610
Minnesota Territory, 662
Minnesota Twins (baseball), 554, 559, 570
Minnesota Vikings (football), 586

Minnesota, USS (battleship), 506
Minnie (Astro-Chimp), 547
Minoso, Minnie, 562
Minsky's Park Music Hall (New York, New York), 152
Minute Maid Park (Houston, Texas), 556
Minute Man, 674
Miocene Epoch, 3
Mir Space Station, 549
Mirabella (magazine), 222
Miranda, Carmen, 268
Mishima, Yukio, 209
Mispillion (lighthouse), 190
Miss America, 146
Miss Arkansas (1933), 146
Miss Canada Pageant, 147
Miss Congeniality (Miss America), 147
Miss Saigon (show), 148
Mission Indians, 427
Mission: Impossible (TV), 623
Mississippi, 185, 545
Mississippi Bubble, 64
Mississippi Normal College, 108
Mississippi Southern College, 108
Mississippi State Teachers College, 108
Mississippi Territory, 655, 663
Mississippi, USS (battleship), 506
Mississippian Period, 2
Missouri, 545, 663
Missouri Compromise, 663
Missouri Democrat (newspaper), 437
Missouri Railroad (Saint Louis, Missouri), 633
Missouri Territory, 659, 660, 663
Missouri, USS (battleship), 506, 712, 716
Missouria (Native Americans), 430
Missouri-California Overland Stage, 634
Missouri-Kansas-Texas Railroad Company, 477
Mistake Out Company, 64
Mister Ed (TV), 623
Mitchell, Cameron, 268
Mitchell, Charles Watson ("Charlie"), 580
Mitchell, Clarence, 567
Mitchell, General William ("Billy"), 49
Mitchell, John, 655
Mitchell, Margaret, 210
Mitchell, Thomas, 268
Mitchum, Robert, 268
Mitis, Ignaz von, 127
Mitsubishi (aircraft maker), 43
Mitsubishi Reisen A6M Zero-Sen (aircraft), 43
Miwok (Native Americans), 428
Mix, Tom, 75, 268, 472
Mizner, Addison, 18

Mizoguchi, Kenji, 240
Moberly (frigate), 714
Mobile USS (ship), 526
Mod Squad, The (TV), 623
Modern Times (movie), 237
Modjeska, Helena, 142
Modoc War, 673
Modocs (Native Americans), 673
Moesha (TV), 624
Moffett, Rear Admiral William A., 92
Mogul Empire, 385
Mohammad, Askia, 122
Mohammed XI (Kingdom of Granada), 122
Mohammed, Abu Abdullah, 122
Mohawk Airlines, 47
Mohegan (Native Americans), 428
Mohegan-Pequot (language), 428
Mohole Project, 497
Mohr, Gerald, 269
Moisant Field (New Orleans, Louisiana), 50
Moisant, John B., 50
Moksela language (Indonesia), 183
Moldavia (principality), 405
Moldavian Autonomous Soviet Socialist Republic, 397
Moldavian Democratic Republic, 397
Moldavian Soviet Socialist Republic, 397
Moldova, Republic of, 115, 116, 397
Molière, 210
Mollé Mystery Theater, The (radio), 465
Molly Maguires, The, 179
Monaco, Principality of, 115, 398
Monadnock Building (Chicago, Illinois), 19, 61
Monarch (California grizzly), 13
Monarch (motorcycle), 233
Monarch Air Lines, 47
Monark (motorcycle maker), 234
Mondrian, Piet, 24
Monet, Claude, 25
money, Canadian, 365
money, Europe, 224
money, non-decimal, 365
money, U.S., 224, 228
money, Union of Soviet Socialist Republics, 224
Mongkut, King (Thailand), 415
Mongol Empire, 119, 121
Mongolia, 115, 121
Mongolia, State of, 398
Mongolian People's Republic, 398
Monitor (radio), 455, 465
Monitor, USS (armor clad ship), 682
Monk, Jack, 70
Monk, Thelonious, 342
Monkees, The (TV), 624
Monmouth, Battle of, 677
Monmouth, James, Duke of, 81

Monona Terrace Convention Center (Madison, Wisconsin), 20
Monroe Conservatory of Oratory, 104
Monroe County, Iowa, 660
Monroe, Bill, 343
Monroe, James, 2, 161, 651, 677
Monroe, Marilyn, 269
Monroe, Vaughn, 343
Monrovia Group, 10
Monrovia, Liberia, 393
Monsanto, 64
Montana, 112, 664
Montana Territory, 664
Montana, Bob, 447
Montana, USS (battleship), 507
Montand, Yves, 269
Montauk (Native Americans), 429
Monterey, USS (carrier), 517
Monteverdi, Claudio, 300
Montevideo, State of, 420
Montez, Maria, 269
Montezuma (Aztec emperor), 118
Montgolfier, Jacques Etienne, 54
Montgolfier, Joseph, 54
Montgomery bus boycott, 68
Montgomery County, New York, 665
Montgomery Masonic College, 107
Montgomery Ward (store), 63
Montgomery, Alabama, 655
Montgomery, Bernard, 700
Montgomery, Robert, 269
Montgomery, Wes, 343
Monticello (liner), 529
Montmorency County, Michigan, 662
Montoya, Carlos de Urrutia y, 382
Montreal Canadiens (ice hockey), 598, 599, 600, 601, 602, 604
Montreal Expos (baseball), 557
Montreal Forum, 599
Montreal Manic (soccer), 610
Montreal Maroons (ice hockey), 603
Montreal Olympique (soccer), 610
Montreal Wanderers (ice hockey), 603
Montreal, Quebec (trolleys), 635
Montserrat, 11
Monty Woolley Program (radio), 463
monuments, 230
Moon Mullins (comic strip), 72
Moon, Keith, 353
Moonlight, Lardie, 183
Moonlighting (TV), 624
Moore, Alan, 73
Moore, Archie, 582
Moore, Bob, 71
Moore, Clayton, 269
Moore, Dudley, 269
Moore, Gary, 456
Moore, Grace, 314
Moore, Miles Conway, 670
Moore, Victor, 269

Moorehead, Agnes, 269
Moors, 121, 404
Moose, Bill, 433
moratorium (execution), 82
Morázan, Francisco, 8
More Fun Comics, 73
More, Kenneth, 269
Moreell Dry Dock (California), 538
Morehouse College, 106
Morehouse, Rev. Henry L., 106
Moreland, Mantan, 269
Moreschi, Allessandro, 318
Morgan College, 106
Morgan County, Alabama, 655
Morgan dollar coin, U.S., 226
Morgan State College, 106
Morgan State University, 106
Morgan, Dennis, 269
Morgan, Dr. Lyttleton F., 106
Morgan, Esther A.H., 695
Morgan, Frank, 269, 464
Morgan, George, 101
Morgan, George T., 226
Morgan, Helen, 343
Morgan, Henry, 458
Morgan, John Pierpont, 59
Morgan, Jones, 691
Morgan, William, 90, 440
Morgan, Zula Willemena Penny, 677
Moriori language (New Zealand), 183
Moriscos, 121
Mork & Mindy (TV), 624
Morley, Robert, 269
Mormon Trail, 491
Mormonism, 484
Morocco, Kingdom of, 115, 398
Morosco Theater (New York, New York), 152
morphine, 74
Morphy, Paul Charles, 163
Morris Canal, 131
Morris County, Kansas, 660
Morris Ital (automobile), 31
Morris, Willie, 206
Morris, Anthony, 163
Morris, Chester, 269
Morris, Wayne, 270
Morris, William, 31
Morrison, James, 677
Morrison, Jim, 329
Morro Castle (ship), 98
Morrow, Gray, 71
Morrow, Vic, 270
Morse Code, 611, 649
Morse, Carlton E., 474
Mortimer, Julius, 444
Mortimer, Sir Edward, 140
Morton, "Jelly Roll", 300
Morvan, Fabrice, 342
Mosaic Communications Corporation, 64
Moscow, Treaty of, 691

Moselle (ship), 98
Moses, Edwin, 611
Moses, Grandma, 25
Moses, James, 166
Moses, John, 166
Mosley, Zack, 72
Mosquito County, Florida, 658
Moss, Arnold, 270
Mossi (African people), 363
Mostar Bridge (Bosnia-Herzegovina), 128
Mostel, Zero, 270
Mothers of Invention, The, 355
Motion Picture Association of America (MPAA), 236
Motor Cycle (magazine), 233
motorboating (Olympic event), 606
Motosacoche (motorcycle), 235
Mott, Lucretia, 70
Mouly, Mercel, 25
Mount Adams and Eden Park Railway (Cincinnati, Ohio), 632
Mount Angel Abbey Library (St. Benedict, Oregon), 16
Mount Auburn Cable Railway (Cincinnati, Ohio), 632
Mount Clemens Pottery Company, 167
Mount Lebanon Shaker community, 487
Mount Pinatubo (volcano), 404
Mount Rushmore National Memorial, 231
Mount Saint Joseph College, 103
Mount Suribachi, 702
Mount Vernon Hotel (Cape May, New Jersey), 177
Mount Vernon, USS, 529
Mountain Park Hotel (Hot Springs, North Carolina), 177
Mountbatten of Burma, 1st Earl (Louis Mountbatten), 385
Mourgeon y Achet, Juan de la Cruz, 368
Movieland (New York, New York), 150
Mowbray, Alan, 270
Moxey, Jim, 604
Moyamensing Prison (Philadelphia, Pennsylvania), 79
Mozambique, 9, 115
Mozambique, People's Republic of, 399
Mozambique, Republic of, 399
Mozart, Wolfgang Amadeus, 300
Mozzetto, Domenic, 705
Mr. Ace & Jane (radio, 453
Mr. and Mrs. North, Adventures of (radio), 465
Mr. Blue Beard Jr. (play), 95
Mr. District Attorney (radio), 465
Mr. Keen, Tracer of Lost Persons (radio), 465

Mr. Magoo (cartoon character), 66
Mr. Peanut, 162
Mr. Potato Head, 163
Mr. President (radio), 465
Mrs. Wiggs of the Cabbage Patch (radio), 465
Muckrakers, 4, 222
Muehlebach Field (Kansas City, Missouri), 556
Mueller, Ray Coleman, 564
Muench, Hans, 708
Mugpi, (Inuit), 157
Muhammad, 120
Muhammad al-Amin, King (Tunisia), 416
Muhammad al-Badr, Crown Prince (Yemen), 422
Muhammad Ali, 120
Muhammad Farid Didi, Sultan (Maldives), 395
Muhammad Reza Pahlavi, Shah (Iran), 387
Muhammad Shah (Mogul emperor of India), 385
Muhammad V, Sultan/King (Morocco), 398
Muhammad VI, Sultan (Turkey), 416
Muhammed Zahir Shah, 356
Muhlenberg College, 106
Mujahideen, 356
mule mail delivery, 444
mules, U.S. Army, 648
Mulhare, Edward, 270
Muller, Brick, 592
Mulligan, Gerry, 343
Mulligan, Richard, 270
Muncie Flyers (football), 593
Muni, Paul, 270
Municipal Stadium (Kansas City, Missouri), 556
Munro, Hector Hugh, 213
Munsey's (magazine), 222
Munsey's Weekly (magazine), 222
Munson, Ona, 270
Munsters, The (TV), 624
Murder and Mr. Malone (radio), 465
Murder, She Wrote (TV), 624
Murderers' Row (baseball), 571
Murdoch, Dame Iris, 210
Murnau, F.W., 237, 240
Muromachi period (Japan), 389
Murphy Brown (TV), 624
Murphy, Audie, 270
Murphy, Christian/Bowman, 81
Murphy, George, 270
Murphy, Jim, 72
Murray, Bruce (Sr.), 564
Murray, Gilbert, 88
Muscat and Oman, Sultanate of, 402
Muscle Shoal (lighthouse), 190
Museum of Decorative Arts (Chicago, Illinois), 20
Museum of Flight (Seattle,

Washington), 55

Music Appreciation Hour, The (radio), 465

Musqueam (Native Americans), 429

Mussel Island (lighthouse), 190

Mussolini, Benito, 711

Mussorgsky, Modest, 300, 311

Mustin, Burt, 270

mutiny, 82

Mutiny on the Bounty (movie), 534

Mutsun (Native Americans), 429

Mutt and Jeff (comic strip), 72

Mutual Forum Hour (radio), 447

Mutual Security Administration, 713

Muzzatti, Jason, 603

MVD (Ministry of Internal Affairs), 418

Mwali (island), 369

My Dear Children (play), 139

My Fair Freddy (Episode 165) (cartoon), 66

My Fair Lady (show), 148

My Favorite Husband (radio), 465

My Favorite Martian (TV), 624

My Friend Irma (radio), 465

My Little Margie (radio), 465

My Little Margie (TV), 624

My One and Only (musical), 136

My Sister Sam (TV), 624

My Three Sons (TV), 624

My True Story (radio), 465

My Two Dads (TV), 624

Myanmar, Union of, 57, 115, 399

Mycenaean civilization, 121

Myerson, Bess, 147

Mysterious Mr. M, The (movie), 237

Mysterious Traveler, The (radio), 465

Mystery in Space (comic strip), 72

Mystery in the Air (radio), 465

Mystery Theater, The (radio), 465

N|u language (South Africa), 183

Nabokov, Vladimir, 210

Nabonidus, King (Babylon), 118

Nagel, Charles, 639

Nagel, Conrad, 270

Nagy, Imre, 384

Naish, J. Carroll, 270, 462

Naismith, James, 575

Nakajima (aircraft maker), 43

Nakajima C6N Saiun "Myrt" (aircraft), 700

Nakamura, Teruo, 712

Naked City (TV), 624

Naked Truth, The (TV), 624

Nakota (Native Americans), 431

Name of the Game, The (TV), 624

Name That Tune (TV), 624

names, hurricanes and tropical storms, 721

Namibia, Republic of, 116, 223, 399

Nanking, Treaty of (1842), 368

Nanny, The (TV), 624

Nanticoke (Native Americans), 429

Nantucket (steamship), 534

Napoleon I, Emperor (France), 2, 120, 377, 388, 396, 404, 413, 660, 689

Napoleon II, Emperor (France), 377

Napoleon III, Emperor (France), 77, 377, 397

Napoleonic Wars, 377, 401, 689

Nara period (Japan), 389

Narcissus (tugboat), 536

Naronic (ship), 92

Narragansetts (Native Americans), 672

Naruse, Mikio, 240

NASA Launch Operations Center (Cape Canaveral, Florida), 547

Nash (automobile maker), 30, 31

Nash Ambassador (automobile), 31

Nash Healey (automobile), 31

Nash Lafayette (automobile), 31

Nash Rambler (automobile), 31

Nash, Charles, 31

Nash, John, 18

Nash, Ogden, 210

Nash-Kelvinator, 28

Nashville & Chattanooga Railroad Company, 478

Nashville International Airport (Tennessee), 50

Nashville, Chattanooga & St. Louis Railway, 478

Nassar, Gamal Abdel, 129

Nassau Veterans Memorial Coliseum (New York), 574

Nast, Thomas, 67

Nat "King" Cole Show, The (TV), 624

Natchez (lighthouse), 190

Natchez (Native Americans), 429

Natchez (paddle steamer), 535

Nathanael Greene, USS (submarine), 542

Nation's Business (magazine), 222

National Aeronautics and Space Administration (NASA), 44

National African-American Archives Museum (Mobile, Alabama), 547

National Air and Space Museum (Smithsonian Institution, Washington, D.C.), 35, 40, 44, 46, 56

National Air Transit (airline), 47

National Airlines, 47

National Airlines System, 47

National Anthem of the United States, 650

National Assembly (France), 686

National Association for Stock Car Racing (NASCAR), 553

National Association of Base Ball Players, 566

National Association of Professional Base Ball Players, 561

National Association of Securities Dealers Automated Quotations (NASDAQ), 59

National Bank Notes. U.S., 229

National Barn Dance (radio), 465, 473

National Basketball Association (NBA), 576, 577

National Basketball League (NBL), 577

National Beauty Tournament., 147

National Broadcasting Company (NBC), 152, 446, 586

National Cambridge Collectors, 164

National Cash Register, 64

National Cathedral (Washington, D.C.), 15

National Constitution Center (Philadelphia, Pennsylvania), 231

National Convention (France), 686

National Dam Inspection Act, 93

National Deaf-Mute College, 105

National Democratic party (Gold Bugs/Gold Democrats), 442

National Equal Rights party, 442

National Farm and Home Hour (radio), 465

National Football League (NFL), 586

National Glass Company, 164

National Hockey Association, 598

National Hockey League (NHL), 598, 600

National Industrial Recovery Act (NIRA), 636

National Intelligencer (newspaper), 435

National Labor Reform party, 441

National Labor Union (NLU), 181

National League (baseball), 561

National League Park (Philadelphia, Pennsylvania), 565

National Little League Baseball, Inc., 562

National Military Establishment (NME), 639

National Minimum Drinking Age Act, 185

National Museum of Natural History (Washington, D.C.), 14

National Observer (magazine), 222

national origins quota system (immigration), 443

National Park (Washington, D.C.), 559

National Park Airways, 47

National Pike, 492

National Professional Soccer League (NPSL), 608

National Recovery Administration (NRA), 636, 654

National Republican party, 440, 442

National Road, 492

National Security Act (1947)., 639

National Socialist Party (Nazis), 379
National War Labor Board (NWLB), 718
National Weather Service, 722
National Youth Administration (NYA), 637
Nationalist China, 414
Native American scouts, 648
Natwick, Mildred, 270
Nauru, Republic of, 116, 399
Nautilus (brig*)*, 694
Nautilus, USS (submarine), 540, 541
Nauvoo, Illinois, 485
Naval Academy, U.S., 102, 108
Naval Air Station, U.S. (Lakehurst, New Jersey), 51
Naval Postgraduate School, 176
Naval School, 108
Naval Supply Depot (Bayonne, New Jersey), 538
Navarino, Battle of, 521
Navasoto County, Texas, 669
Navin Field (Detroit, Michigan), 556
Navratil, Michael, 100
Navy, Department of the (U.S.), 639
Navy, Secretary of the, 639
Navy, U.S., 35, 37, 39, 40, 42, 79, 93
Nazimova, Alia, 176
NBC Presents: Short Story (radio), 465
NBC Theater (radio), 466
NBC University Theater of the Air, The (radio), 466
NCAA Football Rules Committee, 585
NCR Corporation, 64
Ndimira, Pascal-Firmin, 363
Near East, ancient languages, 11
Nearer My God to Thee (hymn), 100
Nebbs, The (comic strip), 72
Nebraska, 112, 185, 664
Nebraska Territory, 664
Nebraska, USS (battleship), 507
Nebuchadnezzar II, King (Babylon), 118, 134
Neelson, Baby Face, 85
Neewago County, Michigan, 662
Negro American League (NAL) (baseball), 562
Negro League All-Star Game, 563
Negro National League (NNL) (baseball), 562
Neidjie, Bill, 183
Nelson McCoy Pottery Company, 167
Nelson McCoy Sanitary and Stoneware (company), 167
Nelson, Harriet Hilliard, 466
Nelson, Ozzie, 466
Nelson, Rick, 343
Nemaha County, Nebraska, 664
Neolithic, 5
Neosho County, Kansas, 660

Nepal, Kingdom of, 116, 223, 400, 489, 544
Nero Wolfe, The Adventures of (radio), 466
Neruda, Pablo, 210
Nesbitt, Cathleen, 270
Nesbitt, John, 466
Nesser, Al, 587
Netherlands, 10, 11, 116
Netherlands Antilles, 400
Netherlands East Indies, 386
Netherlands Guiana, 412
Netherlands, Kingdom of the, 400
Netherlands, United Provinces of the, 400
Netscape Communications Corporation, 64
networks (radio), 446
Neuilly Bridge (Paris, France), 128
Neuilly, Treaty of, 698
Nevada, 112, 545, 664
Nevada Territory, 664
Nevada, USS (battleship), 507, 713
Nevers Ernie, 591
New Adventure Comics, 73
New Adventures of Michael Shayne (radio), 464
New Adventures of Nero Wolfe, The (radio), 466
New Amsterdam, 642
New Apollo (theater, New York, New York), 150
New Bremen Glass Manufactory, 163
New Brunswick, Canada, 365
New Clinton Hall (New York, New York), 149
New Comics (comic book), 73
New Comiskey Park (Chicago, Illinois), 555
New County, Wisconsin, 670
New Croton Dam, 132
New Deal, 439, 446, 654
New Dick Van Dyke Show, The (TV), 624
New Earl Carroll Theater (New York, New York), 150
New England Confederation, 10
New England Glass Company, 167
New England Glassworks, 167
New England Tea Men (soccer), 610
New England, Dominion of, 8, 641
New English Dictionary on Historical Principles, A, 59
New Fiction Company, 71
New France, 364
New Granada, 9
New Granada, Federated Provinces of, 368
New Granada, Republic of, 403
New Granada, State of, 368, 402
New Granada, United Provinces of, 368

New Granada, United States of, 368, 403
New Granada, Viceroyalty of, 368, 373, 402
New Hampshire, 490, 545, 665
New Hampshire College of Agriculture and Mechanical Arts, 106
New Hampshire, University of, 106
New Hampshire, USS (battleship), 507
New Harmony, Indiana, 484
New Haven Colony, 10
New Haven Municipal Airport (Connecticut), 51
New Haven, Connecticut (trolleys), 635
New Hebrides Condominium, 421
New Jersey, 185, 545, 665
New Jersey Americans (basketball), 578
New Jersey Devils (ice hockey), 601, 602
New Jersey Nets (basketball), 574, 578
New Jersey Reds (basketball), 575
New Jersey State Normal and Model Schools, 104
New Jersey State Normal School in Trenton, 104
New Jersey State Teachers College and State Normal School at Trenton, 104
New Jersey State Teachers College at Glassboro, 107
New Jersey State Teachers College at Trenton, 104
New Jersey Turnpike, 492
New Jersey, USS (battleship), 507
New Lassie, The (TV), 624
New London Bridge (London, England), 125
New Mexico, 75, 665
New Mexico Territory, 655, 664, 665
New Mexico, USS (battleship), 508
New National Gallery (Berlin, Germany), 18
New Netherland, 642
New Opera House (New York, New York), 152
New Orleans Buccaneers (basketball), 578
New Orleans International Airport (Louisiana), 50
New Orleans Jazz (basketball), 579
New Orleans, Battle of, 694
New Orleans, Louisiana, 50, 65
New Penny, The (radio), 458
New River County, Florida, 658
New Scotland Yard, 75
New Sealtest Village Store (radio), 460
New Spain, Viceroyalty of, 397

New Stone Age, 5
New Swan Show (radio), 450
New Sweden, 642
New Territories (China), 368
New WKRP in Cincinnati (TV), 624
New York & Erie Railroad, 477
New York (state), 112, 490, 545, 665
New York Air (airline), 47
New York Airways, 47
New York Americans (ice hockey), 602
New York and Brooklyn Bridge Railway (New York, New York), 632
New York Brickley's Giants (football), 593
New York Building (Queens, New York), 160
New York Bulldogs (football), 594
New York Central Railroad, 478, 483
New York City College of Technology, 106
New York City Community College, 106
New York City Municipal Airport, 49
New York City Technical College, 106
New York Coliseum, 152
New York Cosmos (soccer), 610
New York Curb Exchange, 58
New York Curb Market Association, 59
New York Generals (soccer), 610
New York Giants (baseball), 557, 569
New York Giants (football), 587
New York Gothams (baseball), 569
New York Herald (newspaper), 435
New York Herald-New York Tribune (newspaper), 435
New York Herald-Tribune (newspaper), 435
New York Highlanders (baseball), 557, 571
New York International Airport at Idlewild (Queens, New York), 49
New York Journal-American (newspaper), 435
New York Life Insurance Company, 152
New York Mirror (newspaper), 435
New York Municipal Airport-LaGuardia Field (New York, 49
New York Naval Shipyard, 538
New York Nets (basketball), 576, 579
New York Rangers (ice hockey), 598, 599, 601
New York Roof (theater), 152
New York Shipbuilding (Camden, Neew Jersey), 538
New York Skyliners (soccer), 610

New York State Fair Coliseum (Syracuse, New York), 575
New York State Institute of Applied Arts and Sciences, 106
New York State Pavilion (New York, New York), 161
New York Stock and Exchange Board, 59
New York Stock Exchange, 59
New York Sun (newspaper), 435
New York Telegram (newspaper), 435, 436
New York Telegram and Evening Mail (newspaper), 435
New York Times (newspaper), 67
New York Tribune (newspaper), 435
New York World (newspaper), 436
New York World's Fair (1939-40), 160
New York World's Fair (1964-65), 161
New York World-Journal-Tribune (newspaper), 436
New York World-Telegram & the Sun (newspaper), 436
New York World-Telegram (newspaper), 436
New York Yankees (baseball), 557, 571, 572
New York Yankees (football), 594
New York Yanks (football), 594
New York, British occupation of, 674
New York, Chicago & St. Louis Railroad, 478, 479
New York, Lake Erie and Western Railway, 477
New York, New Haven & Hartford Railroad Company, 478
New York, New York (horsecars), 634
New York, New York (trolleys), 635
New York, New York (U.S. capital), 641
New York, Texas and Mexican Railway, 481
New York, USS (battleship), 508
New York/Brooklyn Americans (ice hockey), 604
New Yorker Hotel (Miami, Florida), 177
New Zealand, 10, 77, 116, 183, 224, 400, 695
New Zealand, Dominion of, 401
Newark Academy (Delaware), 104
Newark and Irvington Street Railway (Newark, New Jersey), 633
Newark College (Delaware), 104
Newark Dodgers (baseball), 563
Newark Evening News (newspaper), 434
Newark International Airport (New Jersey), 50
Newark Liberty International Airport

(New Jersey), 50
Newark Tornadoes (football), 593
Newark, New Jersey, 107
Newell, Marjorie, 100
Newfoundland, Canada, 365, 690
Newgate Prison (London, England), 78
Newhart (TV), 624
Newley, Anthony, 344
Newman, Alfred, 300
Newport County, Rhode Island, 667
Newport, Rhode Island, 667
newspapers, typeface, 12
NewsRadio (TV), 625
Newton Gang, 86
Newton, Charles, 134
Newton, Dock, 86
Newton, Isaac, 496
Newton, Robert, 270
New-York Gazette (newspaper), 435
Nez Percè (Native Americans), 673
Nez Percè War, 673
Niagara Falls Suspension Bridge No. 1 (Niagara Falls, New York), 128
Niagara Falls Suspension Bridge No. 2 (Niagara Falls, New York), 128
Niangua County, Missouri, 663
Niblo's Garden and Theater (New York, New York), 152
Nicaragua, 7, 116, 224
Nicaragua, Republic of, 401
Nicholas Brothers, 138
Nicholas II, Tsar (Russia), 405
Nicholas, Fayard, 138
Nicholas, Harold, 138
Nichols, Ann, 447
Nichols, Maria Longworth, 165, 167
Nichols, Red, 344
Nichols, Terry, 86
Nick Carter, Master Detective (radio), 466
Nickel Plate Road (railroad), 478
Nickerson Field (Boston, Massachusetts), 554
Nicol, Don Pio de Jesus, 656
Nie Rongzhen (Nieh Jung-chen), 367
Niekro, Phil, 569
Nielson, Carl, 300
Niger, 9, 10, 116
Niger, Republic of, 401
Nigeria, 7, 10, 116, 223
Nigeria, Federal Republic of, 401
Nigeria, Northern, 544
Night Beat (radio), 466
Night Court (TV), 625
Night of the Living Duck *(cartoon)*, 67
Nijinsky, Vaslav, 138
Nijo, Nariyuki, 389
Nikolay II, Grand Duke (Finland), 375
Nikonha, 431
Nile, HMS (battleship), 521

Niles' Weekly Register (magazine), 222
Nilsson, Kent, 602
Nimbus (ballet), 139
Niña (Columbus's ship), 155
Nine Lives of Fritz the Cat, The (cartoon), 66
Nine to Five (TV), 625
Ninety-Five Theses, 4
Nippon Maru II (sailing ship), 498
Nirvana, 344
Nissan Motor Company, 29
Niven, David, 270
Nixon, Richard M., 110, 367, 655, 718
Nize Baby (comic strip), 72
Njazidja (island), 369
Nobile, General Umberto, 154
Nobody's Children (radio), 466
Nobska, SS (steamship), 534
Nodaway County, Missouri, 663
Noga (liner), 525
Nolan, Jeanette, 270
Nolan, Lloyd, 270
Nolan, Owen, 605
Nolde, William B., 693
Nomadic (steamship), 538
Nooksack (Native Americans), 429
Noonan, Captain Frederick J., 57
Norfolk & Western No. 611 (locomotive), 475
Norfolk & Western Railway, 478, 479
Norfolk International Airport (Virginia), 50
Norfolk Municipal Airport (Virginia), 50
Norfolk Regional Airport (Virginia), 50
Norfolk Southern Corporation, 478
Norfolk Southern Railway, 479
Normal College (North Carolina), 104
Normal College of the City of New York, 105
Normal School for Colored Students (Alabama), 102
Normal School No. 3 (Bowie State University), 103
Norman kings, 419
Normandie (liner), 530
Norman-Walker, Sir Hugh Selby, 361
Norodom Sihanouk, Prince (Cambodia), 363
Norris, Clarence, 69
Norris, Kathleen, 210
Norris, Paul, 70
North American B-25 Mitchell (aircraft), 43
North American F-100 Super Sabre (aircraft), 43
North American P-51 Mustang

(aircraft), 43
North American Review (magazine), 222
North American SNJ/T-6 Texan (aircraft), 44
North American Soccer League (NASL), 608
North American X-15 (aircraft), 44
North American XB-70 Valkyrie (aircraft), 44
North Atlantic Treaty Organization (NATO), 10, 394
North Borneo (Sabah), 395
North Brother Island (New York, New York), 172
North Carolina, 490, 545, 666, 668
North Carolina Brigade, 681
North Carolina College of Agriculture and Mechanical Arts, 106
North Carolina State University at Raleigh, 106
North Carolina, USS (battleship), 508
North Central Airlines, 47
North Chicago Street Railroad (Chicago, Illinois), 632
North Dakota, 112, 666
North Dakota, USS (battleship), 508
North German Confederation, 379
North Hudson County Railway(Hoboken, New jersey), 632
North Pole, 154, 158
North Union Shaker community, 488
North Vietnam (Democratic Republic of Vietnam), 422, 693
North Yemen, 422
North, Sir Francis, 88
Northampton County, Virginia, 669
Northcott, Baldy, 603
Northeast Airlines, 47
Northern Air Transport (airline), 47
Northern Baseball League, 562
Northern Cross Railroad, 479
Northern Exposure (TV), 625
Northern Ireland, 387, 418
Northern Mariana Islands, Commonwealth of the, 671
Northern Pacific Railroad, 479, 481
Northern Pomo (language), 431
Northern Rhodesia, 8, 423
Northern Territories (Africa), 7
Northrop A-17A (aircraft), 44
Northrop B-2A Spirit "Stealth Bomber" (aircraft), 44
Northrop F-5 (aircraft), 44
Northrop P-61 Black Widow (aircaft), 44
Northrop T-38 Talon (aircraft), 45
Northwest Airlines, 47
Northwest Airways, 48
Northwest Ordinance (1787), 545

Northwest Orient Airlines, 48
Northwest Passage (lighthouse), 190
Northwest Territory, 659, 662, 666, 670
Northwestern League (baseball), 562
Northwestern Pacific Railroad, 481
Norton County, Kansas, 660
Norton Pottery (company), 167
Norton Stoneware Company, 167
Norton Villiers (motorcycle maker), 233
Norton, John, 167
Norvo, Red, 344
Norway, 9, 10, 79, 116, 372, 631
Norway, Kingdom of, 401, 402
Norway, Nevil Shute, 214
Norworth Theater (New York, New York), 152
Notipekago County, Michigan, 662
Notorious B.I.G., 344
Notre Dame University, 576, 583, 585
Nova Scotia, Canada, 365, 690
Novello, Jay, 271
Novograd-Volynski, Ukraine, 715
Nowlan, Philip F., 70, 450
NSU (Neckarsulum Strickmachine Union), 235
NSU K-70 (automobile), 31
Ntare V Ndizeye (Charles Ndizeye), King (Burundi), 363
Nuclear Test Ban Treaty, 721
Nueces Hotel (Corpus Christi, Texas), 177
Numan, Yasin Said, 422
numbers, baseball, 560
nuns (religious attire), 486
Nurakita (island), 417
Nuremberg War Crimes Trials, 78, 720
Nureyev, Rudolf, 138
Nurmi, Paavo, 611
nursing schools, 102
Nuykefetau (island), 417
NV (Nymans-Verkstader) (motorcycle maker), 234
Nyasaland, 8, 394
Nye, James W., 664
Nystul, Captain William Craig, 694
Nzwani (island), 369
O.K. Corral (Tombstone, Arizona), 74
O'Brien, Edmond, 271
O'Brien, George, 271
O'Brien, Pat, 271
O'Casey, Sean, 210
O'Cathasaigh, Sean, 210
O'Connell, Arthur, 271
O'Connor, Sandra Day, 185
O'Connor, Carroll, 271
O'Connor, Donald, 271
O'Connor, Flannery, 210
O'Connor, William Frederick

Travers, 400
O'Grady's *History of Ireland: Heroic Period*, 193
O'Hara, John, 210
O'Keefe, Dennis, 271
O'Leary, Hazel R., 175
O'Malley, J. Pat, 271
O'Neal, Frank, 72
O'Neill, Eugene, 210
O'Neills, The (radio), 466
O'Rourke, James Francis ("Frank"), 554
O'Sullivan Maureen, 271
Oahu Bowl (football), 584
Oakie, Jack, 271
Oakland Ballet (California), 138
Oakland Cable Railway (Oakland, California), 633
Oakland Clippers (soccer), 610
Oakland Invaders (football), 586
Oakland Oaks (basketball), 579
Oakland Raiders (football), 586
Oakland Stompers (soccer), 610
Oakland/California Golden Seals (ice hockey), 604
Oaky Doaks (comic strip), 72
Oates, Warren, 271
Oberlin College, 106
Oberlin Collegiate Institute, 106
Oberon, Merle, 271
Obispeño Chumash (language), 425
Obote, Milton, 417
Obuknov, Anatoly, 138
ocean dumping, 153
Ocean Monarch (liner), 527
Ocean Park Million Dollar Pier (Santa Monica, California), 144
Ocean View Park (Norfolk, Virginia), 144
Ockett, Molly (Mollocket), 430
Octavian, Emperor (Roman Empire), 1, 122
Odd Couple, The (TV), 625
Odeon Theater (New York, New York), 150
Odets, Clifford, 210
Odoacer, 122
Odyssey (poem), 121
Offenbach, Jacques, 301
Official Detective (radio), 466
OGO-6 (orbiting geophysical observatory), 550
Oh! Calcutta! (show), 148
O'Hare, Lieutenant Edward, 49
Ohio, 433, 545
Ohio Agricultural and Mechanical College, 106
Ohio House (Philadelphia, Pennsylvania), 159
Ohio State University, 106
Ohio, USS (battleship), 509
Ohlone (Native Americans), 430
oil, 123

Oil Bowl (football), 584
Ojibwa (Native Americans), 425
Okinawa, 390
Okkuddo County, Michigan, 662
Oklahoma, 75, 112, 185, 666
Oklahoma Territory, 666
Oklahoma! (show), 148
Oklahoma, USS (battleship), 509
Oksner, Bob, 71
Oland, Warner, 271
Old Comiskey Park (Chicago, Illinois), 555
Old Doc Yak (comic strip), 72
Old English Script, 12
Old Gold Hour (radio), 467
Old London Bridge (London, England), 125
Old Persian (language), 11
Old Pretender, 419
Old Sirinek Language (Siberia), 183
Olds, Ransom Eli, 31
Oldsmobile (automobile), 31
'Ōlelo Hawai'I (language), 427
Olentangy Park (Columbus Ohio), 144
oleomargarine, 162
Oligocene Epoch, 3
Oliver, Edna May, 271
Oliver, Gene, 569
Oliver, Joe ("King"), 345
Olivier, (Lord) Laurence, 271
Olmsted, Frederick Law, 19
Olympia (sailing ship), 498
Olympia Stadium (Detroit, Michigan), 574, 599
Olympia Theater Roof Garden (New York, New York), 152
Olympia, USS (cruiser), 692, 698
Olympic (liner), 530
Olympic Stadium (Montreal, Canada), 557
Olympics (1972), 86
Olympics (1996), 87
Omaha, Nebraska, 664
Oman, 223, 544
Oman, Sultanate of, 402
Ommaid (or Omayyud) caliphate, 413
Ommaid dynasty (Syria), 413
Omni (Atlanta, Georgia), 573
Omnibus Railroad and Cable Company (San Francisco, California), 633
Omurano language (Peru), 183
On Your Toes (musical), 136
One Day at a Time (TV), 625
One Day in September (movie), 87
One Man's Family (radio), 466, 474
One World Trade Center (New York, New York), 61, 87
one-cent coin, U.S. ("penny"), 224, 225
Onions, Charles T., 59

Onoda, Hiroo, 712
Onondaga Pottery (company), 167
Onondaga War Memorial Coliseum (Syracuse, New York), 575
Ontario County, Pennsylvania, 667
Ontario, Canada, 365
Oorang Indians (football), 594
Ootah (Inuit), 158
Open Door policy, 654
Operation Barbarossa, 360
Operation Deadlight, 715
Operation Desert Shield, 687
Operation Desert Storm, 687
Operation Dynamo, 702
Operation Frequent Wind, 693
Operation Homecoming, 693
Operation Urgent Fury, 381
Ophüls, Max, 240
opiates, 74
opium, 74
Opper, Frederick B., 70, 71
Oracle Corporation, 64
Oraflex, 173
Orange County, Florida, 658
Orange Free State (South Africa), 411, 678
Orange Tornadoes (football), 594
Orbison, Roy, 345
Orbiting Geophysical Observatory (OGO), 550
Orbiting Solar Observatory (OSO), 550
Order of American Knights, 181
Order of the Sons of Liberty, 181
Ordovician Period, 2
Oregon, 112, 545, 667
Oregon border dispute, 638
Oregon Daily Journal (newspaper), 436
Oregon Journal (newspaper), 436
Oregon Territory, 670
Oregon Trail, 492
Oregon Treaty, 365, 638, 667
Oregon, USS (battleship), 509
Orff, Carl, 301
Organic Act, The, 671
Organization of African Unity, 7, 10
Organization of Eastern Caribbean States, 381
Orient Express, 476
Original Six Era (ice hockey), 598
Oriole Park at Camden Yards (Baltimore, Maryland), 554
Oriskany, USS (carrier), 517
Orlando Air Base (Florida), 50
Orlando Executive Airport (Florida), 50
Orlando Municipal Airport (Florida), 50
Orleans, House of (France), 376
Orleans, Territory of, 660
Ormandy, Eugene, 315
Ornstein, Leo, 301

Orson Welles Radio Almanac (radio), 466

Orson Welles Theater (radio), 464

Orwell, George, 211

Ory, Kid, 345

Osage County, Kansas, 660

Osceola County, Michigan, 662

Osman, 121

OSO-8 (orbiting solar observatory), 550

Ossa (motorcycle maker), 235

Oswald, Lee Harvey, 652

Othello (play), 141

Otoe (Native Americans), 430

Otsego County, Michigan, 662

Ott and Brewer (company), 167

Ottawa (Native Americans), 659

Ottawa Senators (ice hockey), 604, 605

Otto I, Holy Roman Emperor, 398

Ottoman Empire, 121, 356, 361, 362, 371, 373, 381, 387, 390, 402, 405, 416, 545, 690

Ottoman Turks, 118, 685

Oubangui-Chari-Chad, 365

Our American Cousin (play), 652

Our Boarding House (comic strip), 72, 463

Our Gal Sunday (radio), 466

Our Gang comedy, 237

Our Miss Brooks (radio), 466

Our Miss Brooks (TV), 466, 625

Ouray County, Colorado, 657

Ouspenskaya, Maria, 271

Out Our Way (comic strip), 72

Outcault, R.F., 70, 73

Outlaws is Coming, The (movie), 135

Overijssel (Netherlands province), 11

Overland Monthly (magazine), 222

Overland Stage Company, 634

Over-the-Jumps (amusement ride), 145

OW-1 Aerial Coupe (aircraft), 56

Owen, Reginald, 271

Owens, Robert, 484

Owens-Illinois Glass Company, 168

Oxford English Dictionary (OED), 59

Oyler, Andrew ("Andy") Paul, 568

Ozark Air Lines, 48

Ozark County, Missouri, 663

Ozette (Native Americans), 430

Ozu, Yasujiro, 240

Ozzie and Harriet, The Adventures of (radio), 466

Ozzie and Harriet, The Adventures of (TV), 612

P'u-yi, Henry, 366, 390

Pabst Blue Ribbon Show (radio), 454

Pabst Brewing Company, 64

Pacific Air Lines, 48

Pacific Air Transport (airline), 48

Pacific Alaska Airways, 48

Pacific Bell Park (San Francisco, California), 559

Pacific Electric line (trolley), 444

Pacific Northern Airlines, 48

Pacific Northern Airways, 48

Pacific Ocean Park (Santa Monica, California), 144

Pacific Queen (sailing ship), 534

Pacific Railroad of Missouri, 478

Pacific Southwest Airlines, 48

Pacific, War of the, 689

Packard (automobile), 31

Packard, Sammy, 553

packet ship, 531

paddle-wheel, ocean going (steamboat), 535

paddle-wheel, river (steamboat), 535

Paderewski, Ignace Jan, 301

Paganini, Niccolò, 301

Page, Geraldine, 271

Page, Jimmy, 338

Pahlavi dynasty (Iran), 387

Paige, Satchel, 563, 564, 570

Pakenham, Sir Edward, 694

Pakistan, 8, 10, 116, 223

Pakistan, Dominion of, 385

Pakistan, Islamic Republic of, 402

Palace of Fine Art (St. Louis, Missouri), 160

Palace of Fine Arts (Chicago, Illinois), 161

Palace of the Fans (Cincinnati, Ohio), 555

Palau, Republic of, 116, 402

Paleocene Epoch, 3

Paleolithic Age, 5

Paleozoic Era, 2

Palestine, 388, 390

Palestine Liberation Organization (PLO), 392

Paley, William, 630

Palisades Amusement Park (Cliffside Park, New Jersey), 145

Palladio, Andrea, 19

Pallas Athena (liner), 527

Pallette, Eugene, 271

Palm Beach Evening Times (newspaper), 436

Palm Beach Post (newspaper), 436

Palmer Peninsula, 15

Palmer, Alf, 184

Palmer, John M., 442

Palmer, Lilli, 271

Palmer, Nathaniel, 15

Palmeter, Phoebe M., 677

Palmetto Ranch, Battle of, 681

Pamishkimait, Petra, 425

Pamptecough County, North Carolina, 666

Pan American Clipper III (aircraft), 37

Pan American Exposition (Buffalo, New York), 161

Pan American World Airways, 35, 48

Pan, Hermes, 138

Panama, 9, 116, 224, 368

Panama Canal, 131

Panama Limited (train), 483

Panama, Republic of, 402

Panama, State of, 402

Pan-American Grace Airways, 48

Pancho's Hideaway (cartoon), 66

Pangborn, Franklin, 272

Panhard, Adrien, 31

Panhard, Joseph, 31

Panhard, Louis, 31

Panhard-Levassor 24BT (automobile), 31

Pankin, Boris D., 418

Panther Girl of the Kongo (movie), 237

Papal Military Corps, 421

Papal States, 421

Pappas, Milt, 570

Papua and New Guinea, Territory of, 403

Papua New Guinea, 116, 403

Papua, Indonesia, 386

Papua, Territory of, 403

Paradjanov, Sergei, 240

Paraguay, Republic of, 116, 403, 693

Paraguayan War, 693

Paramount (movie studio), 65

Parent, Frederick ("Freddy") Alfred, 572

Paris (liner), 530

Paris Agreements, 705

Paris, France, 10, 378

Paris, Treaty of (1763), 659, 661, 662, 663, 672, 691

Paris, Treaty of (1783), 657, 659, 662, 670, 674, 675

Paris, Treaty of (1814), 396, 407

Paris, Treaty of (1856), 685

Paris, Treaty of (1898), 691

Park Avenue Hotel (New York, New York), 177

Park Theater (New York, New York), 152

Parke, Dr. Thomas, 175

Parker, Bonnie, 84

Parker, Charlie, 345

Parker, Janet, 171

Parker, Quanah (Comanche chief), 426

Parker, Robert B., 197

Parker, Robert LeRoy, 84

Parker, Walter, 697

Parkes, William, 697

Parks Metropolitan Airport (St. Louis, Missouri), 50

Parks, Bert, 147

Parks, Larry, 272

Parnasse contemporain, 193

Parnassians, 193

Parr, Catherine, 419

Parr, Ralph S. (Jr.), 688
Parrish, Maxfield, 25
Parsons, Edwin C., 695
Parsons, Louella, 462
Parthenon (Athens, Greece), 60
Partridge Family, The (TV), 625
Partridge, Frances Marshall, 192
Partridge, Ralph, 192
Pasadena Bowl (football), 584
Pasadena, California (horsecars), 634
Pascagoula River (lighthouse), 190
Paschal, Ben, 564
Pass of Balmaha (sailing ship), 521
Passaic (lighthouse), 190
passenger pigeon, 14
Passing Parade, The (radio), 466
Passing Parade, The (short films), 466
Pasternak, Boris, 211
Pasteur, Louis, 496
Pat Novak, For Hire (radio), 466
patent medicine, 74, 162
Patent Office, U.S., 638, 639
Paterson, Algy, 183
Pathet Lao, 392
Patria (sailing ship), 498
Patrick, Craig, 603
Patrick, Gail, 272
Patrick, Lee, 272
Patrick, Lynn, 601
Patriot for Me, A (play), 142
Patriot, The (movie), 237
Patsayev, Viktor, 549
Patten, Christopher Francis, 368
Patterson, Floyd, 582
Patterson, Louise Thompson, 192
Patton, George S., 716
Patty Duke Show, The (TV), 625
Paul VI, Pope, 486
Paul Whiteman Teen Club (radio), 467
Pause That Refreshes on the Air, The (radio), 467
Pavilion for Japanese Art, Los Angeles County, Museum of Art (California), 17
Pavlecka, Vladimir H., 54
Pavlova, Anna, 138
Pawtuxet (Native Americans), 430
Pax Romana (Roman Peace), 1, 122
Payne, A.B., 72
Payne, John, 272
Payne, Virginia, 463
Payne's Landing, Treaty of, 673
Peace dollar coin, U.S., 226
Peace River Bridge (British Columbia Canada), 128
Peacock (sloop of war), 694
Peale, Charles Willson, 231
Peale's Museum Philadelphia, Pennsylvania), 231
Peanuts (comic strip), 72
Pearce, Alice, 272

Pearcey, Trevor, 117
Pearl Harbor, Hawaii, 699, 713
Pearl, Jack, 460
Pearson, James William, 696
Pearson, John Loughborough, 15
Peary, Hal, 457
Peary, Robert E., 158
Peasants' Revolt (England), 78
Peasants' War, 689
Pease County, Wyoming, 670
Pease, Charlie, 70
Peck, Gregory, 272
Peckinpah, Sam, 240
Peder Skram, HDMS (frigate), 522
Peerce, Jan, 315
Pee-Wee's Playhouse (TV), 625
Peirce, Thomas W., 481
Pelé, 611
Pella Corporation, 64
Pembina County, Minnesota, 662
penal colonies, 77
Penfield, Bob, 145
Penguin, HMS (sloop), 694
Penland, Theodore A., 683
Penn Central Company, 478
Penn Central Corporation, 478
Penn Central Railroad, 478
Penn, John, 667
Penn, William, 186
Penner, Joe, 460
Penners of Park Avenue, The (radio), 460
Pennsylvania, 545, 667
Pennsylvania Assembly, 231
Pennsylvania Canal, 131
Pennsylvania Company for Banking and Trusts (Philadelphia), 58
Pennsylvania Gazette (newspaper), 436
Pennsylvania Gazette, and Weekly Advertiser (newspaper), 436
Pennsylvania Military Academy, 109
Pennsylvania Military College, 109
Pennsylvania Museum & School of Industrial Art, The, 108
Pennsylvania Railroad, 478, 482
Pennsylvania State College, 106
Pennsylvania State House, 231
Pennsylvania Station (New York, New York), 18
Pennsylvania Turnpike, 492
Pennsylvania, University of, 101, 106
Pennsylvania, USS (battleship), 509
Pennsylvania-Central (airline), 48
Pennsylvania-Maryland boundary, 638
Pennsylvanian Period, 2
Penny (magazine), 222
Penny Magazine of the Society for the Diffusion of Useful Knowledge, The, 222
Penny Press (Pittsburgh newspaper), 437

Penny, James, 677
Penobscot (Native Americans), 430
Pensacola, Florida (trolleys), 635
Pension Office (U.S.), 639
Pentagon, 87, 647
Penthouse Party (radio), 467
Pentreath, Dolly, 182
People Are Funny (radio), 467
People Are Funny (TV), 625
People Express (airline), 48
People's Democratic Algerian Republic, 356
People's party (Populists), 442
People's Platform (radio), 473
People's Republic of Croatia within Yugoslavia, 370
People's Temple Commune, 485
Peoples Cable Railway (Kansas City, Missouri), 632
Peoples Railway (Saint Louis, Missouri), 633
Peoria (Native Americans), 428
Peppard, George, 272
Pepper Young's Family (radio), 467
Pepper, Art, 345
Pepper, Claude, 654
Pepsodent Show, The (radio), 449
Pepys, Samuel, 211
Pequaket (Native Americans), 430
Pequot War, 10
Pere Marquette Railroad, 478
Pérez, Alejo (Jr.), 671
Pérez, Alejo (Sr.), 671
Perfect Strangers (TV), 625
Perils of the Wilderness (movie), 237
Perkins, Anthony, 272
Perkins, Carl, 345
Permanent Bridge (Philadelphia, Pennsylvania), 128
Permanent Court of International Justice, 372
Permian Period, 2
Permit, USS (submarine), 540
Perón, Juan, 357
Perry Como Show, The (TV), 625
Perry Mason (radio), 467
Perry Mason (TV), 625
Pershing 1A missile, 721
Pershing, John J., 648
Persia, 359
Persian Empire, 121, 416
Persian Gulf War, 687
personal computers, 117
Peru, 116, 183, 489, 544, 689
Peru, Viceroyalty of, 120, 361, 368, 373, 402, 403
Pescadores, the, 691
Peshkov, Aleksei Maximovich, 203
Pest Pupil (cartoon), 65
Petacci, Clara, 711
Pétain, Henri Philippe, 705
Petco Park (San Diego, California), 559

Pete the Tramp (comic strip), 72
Pete, Shem, 426
Peter Gunn (TV), 625
Peter II, King (Yugoslavia), 408
Peter Stuyvesant (paddle steamer), 534
Peterson, Brent, 601
Pethybridge, Tommy, 57
Petrenko, Vasily, 708
Petrograd, Russia, 406
Petronas Towers II (Kuala Lumpur, Malaysia), 61
Pett, Norman, 71
Petticoat Junction (TV), 625
Pettigrew, Edward, 187
Petty, Richard, 553
Peugeot (manufacturer), 235
Peyton Place (TV), 625
Peyton, Patrick, 454
Pfaltzgraff Pottery (company), 168
Pfeufer, Carl, 71
Pflaum, George A., 73
Pharaoh Museum (Montauk, New York), 429
Pharmacia, 64
Pharos of Alexandria, 134
Phelan, Jim, 591
Phenformin, 173
Phidias, 134
Phil Baker Show, The (radio), 467
Phil Harris-Alice Faye Show (radio), 467
Phil Silvers Show, The (TV), 625
Philadelphia & Reading Railroad, 478
Philadelphia 76ers (basketball), 579
Philadelphia Athletics (baseball), 558, 569
Philadelphia Atoms (soccer), 610
Philadelphia Base Ball Park (Philadelphia, Pennsylvania), 558
Philadelphia Blue Jays (baseball), 572
Philadelphia Bulletin (newspaper), 436
Philadelphia College of Art, 108
Philadelphia College of Pharmacy, 108
Philadelphia College of Pharmacy and Science, 108
Philadelphia College of Textiles and Science, 106
Philadelphia Colleges of the Arts, 108
Philadelphia Flyers (ice hockey), 601
Philadelphia Fury (soccer), 610
Philadelphia Museum College of Art, 108
Philadelphia Museum School of Art, 108
Philadelphia Museum School of Industrial Art, 108
Philadelphia Naval Shipyard

(Pennsylvania), 538
Philadelphia Phillies (baseball), 557, 572
Philadelphia Public Ledger (newspaper), 436
Philadelphia Quakers (baseball), 572
Philadelphia Quakers (ice hockey), 604
Philadelphia Record (newspaper), 437
Philadelphia School of Apothecaries, 108
Philadelphia Spartans (soccer), 610
Philadelphia Textile Institute of the Philadelphia Museum of Art, 106
Philadelphia Textile School of the Pennsylvania Museum of Art, 106
Philadelphia Traction Company (Philadelphia, Pennsylvania), 633
Philadelphia University, 106
Philadelphia USS (sailing ship), 501, 676
Philadelphia Warriors (basketball), 579
Philadelphia, British occupation of, 675
Philadelphia, Pennsylvania (horsecars), 634
Philadelphia, Pennsylvania (U.S. capital), 641
Philadelphia, Pennsylvania, Supreme Court in, 185
Philadelphia, USS (sailing ship), 678
Philadelphia-Pittsburgh Steagles (football), 588
Philae, temple of, 11
Philco Hall of Fame (radio), 467
Philco Radio Time (radio), 449
Philco Television Playhouse (TV), 625
Philip II, King (Spain), 692
Philip III, King (Spain), 121
Philip IV, King (Spain), 692
Philip Marlowe novels, 197
Philip Marlowe, The Adventures of (radio), 467
Philip Morris Playhouse, The (radio), 467
Philip V, King (Spain), 411
Philip VI, King (France), 687
Philippine Sea, USS (carrier), 518
Philippines, 10, 116, 691
Philippines, Battle of the, 703
Philippines, Commonwealth of the, 404
Philippines, Republic of the, 403
Philips Arena (Atlanta, Georgia), 573
Phillip Best Company, 64
Phillips, Holly Gilliam, 339
Phillips, Irna, 472
Phillips, Irving, 72
Phillips, John, 339
Philo Vance, Detective (radio), 467

Phipps, William, 88
Phoenician script, 11
Phoenix 200 race, 552
Phoenix Coyotes (ice hockey), 605
Phoenix, Arizona, 635
Phoenix, River, 272
Phony War, 713
Phyllis (TV), 625
Piaggio (motorcycle maker), 234
Piankashaw (Native Americans), 428
Piast dynasty (Poland), 404
Picasso, Pablo, 25, 692
Pichincha, Battle of, 9, 373
Pichon, Bartellemy, 81
Pickens, Slim, 272
Pickerel, USS (submarine), 540
Pickering County, Mississippi, 663
Pickering, John G., 668
Picket Fences (TV), 625
Pickford, Mary, 272
Pickwick Papers, 78
Pico, Pio, 176
Pidgeon, Walter, 272
Piedmont & Northern Railway, 478
Piedmont (airline), 48
Pierce, Billy, 570
Pierce, Edward Allen, 62
Pierce, Franklin, 443, 653
Pierce-Arrow (automobile maker), 31
Pierce-Arrow VI2 sedan (automobile), 31
Pierotti, Al, 590
pigtail (queque), 367
Pike County, Ohio, 14
Pike, USS (submarine), 539, 540
Pilatus, Rob, 342
Pilgrims, 2, 641
Pillette, Duane, 570
pillory (punishment), 83
Pillsbury House Party (radio), 459
Pillsbury, USS (ship), 714
pilots (aviation), 57
pincers, red-hot (punishment), 83
Pinkerton Detective Agency, 179, 180
Pinta (Columbus's ship), 155
Pinza, Ezio, 315
Pioneer 10 (spacecraft), 551
Pioneer 11 (spacecraft), 551
Pioneer space program, 551
Pioneer Venus I (spacecraft), 551
Pioneer Zephyr (train), 483
Pip, Squeak, and Wilfred (comic strip), 72
pipe organ (Wanamaker), 160
pipeline, oil, 123
Pipes, Jenny, 83
Pippin (show), 148
piracy, 77
Pirandello, Luigi, 211
Pisces, Age of, 1
Piston, Walter, 301
Pitcairn Aviation (airline), 48

Pitre, Marguerite, 80
Pitts, ZaSu, 272
Pittsburgh & Lake Erie Railroad, 478
Pittsburgh & West Virginia, 478
Pittsburgh Alleghenys (baseball), 572
Pittsburgh Aluminum Company, 64
Pittsburgh Catholic College of the
  Holy Ghost, 104
Pittsburgh Innocents (baseball), 572
Pittsburgh Ironmen (basketball), 579
Pittsburgh Penguins (ice hockey),
  601, 602
Pittsburgh Phantoms (soccer), 610
Pittsburgh Pipers/ Condors
  (basketball), 579
Pittsburgh Pirates (baseball), 558,
  572
Pittsburgh Pirates (ice hockey), 604
Pittsburgh Press (newspaper), 437
Pittsburgh Traction Company
  (Pittsburgh, Pennsylvania), 633
Pittsburgh, Pennsylvania (trolleys),
  635
Pius IV, Pope, 4
Pius IX, Pope, 485
Pizarro, Francisco, 120, 361, 403
Planck, Max, 496
Planes of Fame Museum (Chino,
  California), 43
Plant, Robert, 338
Plantagenet kings, 419
Planters Peanut shops, 162
Plastics, Age of, 3
Plath, Sylvia, 211
Players League (baseball), 561
Playhouse Theater (New York, New
  York), 152
Pleasant Hill Shaker community, 488
Pleasant Island, 399
Pleasence, Donald, 272
Pledge of Allegiance, 645
Pleistocene Epoch, 3
Pliny, 134
Pliocene Epoch, 3
Plumley, Frank, 159
Plunger, USS (submarine), 540
plutonium and uranium experiment,
  175
Plymouth Bay, 2
Plymouth Colony, 10, 641
PMC Colleges (Pennsylvania
  Military College and Penn Morton
  College), 109
PNC Park (Pittsburgh, Pennsylvania),
  558
Pocono 500 (automobile race), 552
Poe, Edgar Allan, 211
Poet, SS (ship), 92
Pogo Possum (comic strip), 72
Pogue, William, 549
Pogy, USS (submarine), 538
Point Adams (lighthouse), 190
Point Aux Herbes (lighthouse), 190

Point Pleasant Bridge (Point
  Pleasant, West Virginia), 128
Point San Pablo (Richmond,
  California), 12
Point, Adeline (Musqueam speaker),
  429
Pol Pot, 363
Poland, 11, 116, 631
Poland, Republic of, 404
Polaris project, 542
pole position (Indianapolis 500), 552
Police Woman (TV), 625
poliomyelitis (polio), 171, 174
Polish People's Republic, 404
Polk, James K., 651, 653, 689
Polk, Willis Jefferson, 19
poll tax, 111
Pollock, Jackson, 25
pollution, 153
Polly and Her Pals (comic strip), 72
polo (Olympic event), 606
Polo Grounds (New York, New
  York), 557
Polo, Marco, 119, 158
Polo, Matteo, 158
Polo, Niccolo, 158
Pomo (Native Americans), 431
Pompano, USS (submarine), 540
Pompili, Rudy, 333
Ponape (sailing ship), 498
Ponce de Leon, Juan, 158
Pondicherry, India, 8, 386
Pondimin (fenfluramine), 172
Ponquogue Light, 192
Pons, Lily, 315
Ponselle, Rosa, 315
Pony Express, 444
Poor Richard's Almanack, 59
Poosepatuck (Native Americans),
  431
Pope Villa (Lexington, Kentucky),
  17
Pope, Alexander, 211
Pope, authority of, 484
Pope, John Russell, 19
Pope, Rhonda, 428
Pope, Thomas A., 699
Popov, Leonid Ivanovich, 549
Popovic, Don, 608
Population Registration Act (South
  Africa), 411
population, United States, 444
population, worldwide, 444
Poquelin, Jean Baptiste, 210
Porky Pig (cartoon character), 66
Porpoise, HMS (submarine), 715
Porpoise, USS (submarine), 540
Porsche 1550 Silver Spyder, 27
Porsche, Dr. Ferdinand, 27
Port Royal, Jamaica, 389
Portage Canal, 131
Porter, Katherine Anne, 76, 211
Porter, Thomas, 677

Portia Faces Life (radio), 467
Portland Cable Railway (Portland,
  Oregon), 633
Portland Timbers (soccer), 610
Porto Rico (spelling of name), 671
Portsmouth Treaty, 690
Portugal, 9, 10, 116, 359, 382, 489,
  545, 631
Portugal, and of Brazil, and
  Algarves, United Kingdom of, 362
Portugal/Portuguese Republic, 404
Portuguese Colonies, 544
Portuguese East Africa, 399
Portuguese Guinea (Guinea-Bissau),
  365
Portuguese Timor, 373
Portwey (tugboat), 536
Posey, Thomas, 659
Post Office (Marin County,
  California), 20
Post Office Department, U.S., 445
Post, Emily, 454
Post, George Browne, 19
Post, Wiley, 57
Postage Stamp Currency, U.S., 228
postage, first-class, 445
postal rates (U.S.), 445
Postal Reorganization Act (1970),
  445
Postal Savings System, U.S., 58, 444
Postal Service, U.S., 444, 445, 640
postcards, 445
posteta (Spain), 224
Post-Industrial Age, 3
Post-Romanticism, 5
Pot o' Gold (radio), 467
Potawatoni (Native Americans), 659
Potok, Chaim, 211
Potosi (sailing ship), 497
Potsdam Declaration, 703
Potsdam War Conference
  (Germany), 703
Potteiger, Earl, 592
Potts, John, 696
Pottsville Maroons (football), 588,
  594
Poulenc, Francis, 301, 311
Pound, Ezra, 193
Powder Puff Derby, 51
Powell, Dick, 272
Powell, Eleanor, 272
Powell, Michael, 240
Powell, William, 272
Power, Tyrone, 272
Power, Vic, 569
Powhatan (Native Americans), 431
Practice, The (TV), 626
Praetorian Guards, 122
Prairie College, 106
Pratt, Hawley, 67
Precambrian Time, 2
Precision Optical Research
  Laboratory, The, 64

prehistory, 6
Preminger, Otto, 240
Prendergast, Maurice, 21
Prentice, John, 72
Pre-Raphaelite Brotherhood, 21
Prescott, Canada, 365
Presenting Al Jolson Show (radio), 447
President (theater, New York, New York), 150
President, USS (frigate), 524
Presidential Cup (football), 584
Presidential Medal of Freedom, 180
Presidio and Ferries Railway (San Francisco, California), 633
Presley, Elvis, 273, 346
pressing (punishment), 82
Preston, Robert, 273
Pretty Kitty Kelly (radio), 467
Price Administration, Office of (OPA), 719
Price, George (World War I casualty), 697
Price, Vincent, 273
Priestley, J.B., 211
Priestley, Joseph, 496
Primakov, Yevgeny M., 418
primogeniture (inheritance law), 186, 365
Prince Edward Island, Canada, 365, 690
Prince Valiant, 74
Prince, Mrs. Della Henry (Wiyot speaker), 433
Princess Carla (liner), 527
Princeton University, 101, 107, 584
Princeton, New Jersey (U.S. capital), 641
Princeton, USS (carrier), 518
Principe de Asturias (ship), 98
Principessa Mafalda (ship), 98
Prison Act of 1877 (Great Britain), 78
Prithur Narayan Shan (Gorkha ruler), 400
Private Benjamin (TV), 626
Private Eye (radio), 464
Private Secretary (TV), 626
Private William H. Thomas (ship), 95
privateering, 77
Privy Council (England), 721
Pro Football Hall of Fame, 586
Proctor, Addison G., 652
Proctorsville (lighthouse), 190
Production Code (movies), 236
Professional Bowling Association (PBA), 580
Professional Golf Association (PGA), 597
Progressive Era, 3, 4
Progressive party (Bull Moose), 442
Prohibition, 185
Project Mercury, 548

Prokofiev, Sergei, 302
Promontory Summit, Utah, 479
propeller aircraft, 37
property ownership (apartheid), 411
property, laws on, 186
Protector, The, 12 Wall, 700 (1872), 681
Proterozoic Era, 2
Proust, Marcel, 212
Providence (TV), 626
Providence Cable Tramway (Providence, Rhode Island), 633
Providence Plantations County, Rhode Island, 667
Providence Steam Roller (football), 595
Providence Steam Rollers (basketball), 579
Providence, Rhode Island, 667
Providence, Rhode Island (trolleys), 635
Prudential Family Hour (radio), 467
Prunariu, Dumitru Dorin, 549
Prussia, 380, 544
PT 109 (torpedo boat), 718
Ptolemy I, 1
public dunking (punishment), 83
public execution, 82
Public Ledger & North American (Philadelpia newspaper), 436
Public Works Administration, 654
Puccini, Giacomo, 302
Puch (motorcycle maker), 235
Puch, Johann, 235
Puck (magazine), 222
Pueblo, USS (ship), 650
Puente, Tito, 346
Puerto Rico, 183, 544, 671, 691
Puerto Rico Conservation Trust, 133
Pugh, Alfred, 697
Pugh, Mrs. Yvonne Marichal, 98
Pulaski (ship), 98
Pullins, Albert ("Runt"), 575
Pullman Car Company trolley, #3321, 635
Pullman Palace Car Company (Chicago, llinois), 180
Pullman strike, 161, 180
Pullman, George, 160
Punch & Judy Theater (New York, New York), 152
Punch (magazine), 222
Pungoteague River (lighthouse), 191
pungy (ship), 533
Punic Wars, 690
punishment (execution), 80
punt (Ireland), 224
Punteney, Walt, 85
Purcell, Henry, 302
Pure Food and Drug Act, 162
Purr Chance to Dream (cartoon), 66
Pursuit (radio), 468
Purvis, Robert, 545

Purvis, Will, 82
Pushkin, Aleksandr Sergeyevich, 212
Puss n' Booty (cartoon), 67
Putman's Monthly (magazine), 222
Pyle, Denver, 273
Qaddafi, Muammar al-, 393
Qatar, 223, 544
Qatar, State of, 405
Quackodile Tears (cartoon), 67
Quaker Code of 1682, 186
Quaker Party with Tommy Riggs (radio), 473
Qualcomm Stadium (San Diego, California), 559
Quantum Leap (TV), 626
quarter, U.S., 228
Quartering Act, 676
Quary, Abraham (Nantucket Wampanoag), 432
Quaternary Period, 3
Quayle, Sir Anthony, 273
Quebec (I) War Conference (Canada), 704
Quebec (II) War Conference (Canada), 704
Quebec Bulldogs (ice hockey), 605
Quebec Nordiques (ice hockey), 605
Quebec, Canada, 365
Quebec, New France, 672
Queen, 347
Queen Anne Forecourt, 15
Queen Anne's War, 690
Queen Elizabeth (I) (liner), 98
Queen for a Day (radio), 468
Queen Mary (liner), 530
Queen O' Hearts (play), 139
Queen, HMS (carrier), 715
Queen's College, 107
Queens Museum of Art (Queens, New York), 160
Queenston-Lewiston (steel arch) bridge (Queenston, Canada), 128
Queenston-Lewiston Suspension Bridge No. 1 (Queenston, Canada), 128
Queenston-Lewiston Suspension Bridge No. 2 (Queenston, Canada), 128
Queen—The Illustrated Magazine of Fashion, 222
Quick as a Flash (radio), 468
Quiet, Please (radio), 468
Quinault (language), 431
Quincy, M.E. (TV), 626
Quinn, Anthony, 273
Quinn, Jack, 567
Quinn, William F., 658
Quitter, The (movie), 237
Quiz Kids, The (radio), 468
R 38 (airship), 93
R. Walker & Son (motorcycle maker), 233
R100 (airship), 93

R101 (airship), 93
Ra I (boat), 156
Ra II (boat), 156
Rabinowitz, Solomon Yakov, 194
race, color or previous condition of
    servitude (voting), 112
Rachmaninoff, Sergei, 302
racial segregation (buses), 68
racial segregation (government-
    funded public places), 68
racial segregation (marriage), 69
racial segregation (public schools),
    69
racial segregation (U.S. armed
    forces), 647
Racine Reef (lighthouse), 191
Racine Tornadoes (football), 595
rack (punishment), 83
Racket Squad (TV), 626
racquet (Olympic event), 606
Radama II, King (Madagascar), 394
Radcliffe College, 107
Radcliffe, Ann, 107
Radio City Playhouse (radio), 468
Radio Corporation of America, 64
Radio Flyer, 64
Radio Priest, 446
Radio Reader's Digest (radio), 468
Radio's Town Crier (radio), 473
radioman rating ("Sparks"), 649
Radiophysics Laboratory of the
    Council for Scientific and
    Industrial Research, 117
Radio-Victor Division of Radio
    Corporation of America, 64
Radithor, 173
radium, 173
Radium Dial Company (Ottawa,
    Illinois), 173
radium water, 173
Raffaello (liner), 531
Raffles, Sir Thomas Stamford, 409
Raft, George, 273
Ragged Point (lighthouse), 191
Rahman, Mujibur (sheik), 359
Railroad Hour, The (radio), 468
railroads, 444
rails, not standardized, 475
Railway Post Office (RPO) system,
    444
Rainbow Warrior (ship), 154
Raines, Ella, 273
Rainey, Ma, 347
Rains, Claude, 273
Raisin Bowl (football), 584
Rajagopalachari, Chakravarti, 386
ram schooner, 533
Rama I, King (Thailand), 415
Rama IV, King Mongkut (Thailand),
    415
Rama V, King (Thailand), 415
Rameau, Jean Philippe, 303
Ramos, Pedro, 570

Ramses II (pharoah), 132
Ramsey, Anne, 273
Ranavalona III, Queen (Madagascar),
    394
Rand, Ayn, 212
Randall, Tony, 273
Randolph County, Georgia, 658
Randolph, Lillian, 273, 448
Randolph, Peyton, 641
Randolph, USS (carrier), 518
Ranger 9 (spacecraft), 551
Ranger, USS (carrier), 518
Rankin, Robert, 427
Raphael, 25
Rapp, George, 484
Rappahannock (sailing ship), 537
Ras al-Khaimah (emirate), 418
Rasher, USS (submarine), 541
Rastatt, Treaty of, 692
Rat Pack, 177
Rat Patrol (TV), 626
Rathbone, Basil, 273, 470
rationing, Great Britain (World War
    II), 707
rationing, United States (World War
    II, 717
Ratoff, Gregory, 241
Rauch, Dick, 588, 594
Ravel, Maurice, 303
Ravensbrück (concentration camp),
    704, 710
Rawhide (TV), 626
Rawlings, Marjorie Kinnan, 212
Ray, Aldo, 273
Ray, Jim, 56
Ray, Satyajit, 241
Raye, Martha, 273
Raymond, Alex, 71, 72, 461
RCA Corporation, 64
RCA-Victor, 64
Reading Company, 478
Reading-Hills Station Bridge
    (Muncy, Pennsylvania), 126
Reagan, John Henninger, 680
Reagan, Ronald, 50, 185, 273, 387,
    718
Real McCoys, The (TV), 626
Real People (TV), 626
rear-hinged doors (automobiles), 27
Reason, Age of, 2
Rebecca Shoal (lighthouse), 191
Rebecca T. Ruark (skipjack), 533
Rebellion, War of the, 679
Reconstruction Acts (1867), 682
Reconstruction Finance Corporation
    (RFC), 637
Red Adams (radio), 467
Red Baron, The, 41, 695, 696
Red Buttons Show, The (TV), 626
Red Devil Tools, 64
Red Dye No. 2, 173
Red Guard, Chinese, 367
Red Hannah (whipping post), 84

Red Network, 446
Red Ryder (comic strip), 72
Red Ryder, The Adventures of
    (radio), 468
Red Skelton Show, The (radio), 468
Red Skelton Show, The (TV), 626
Red Thunder Cloud, 424
Redding, Otis, 347
Redfield, William, 273
Redfish Bar (lighthouse), 191
Redgrave, Sir Michael, 273
Redland Field/Crosley Field
    (Cincinnati, Ohio), 555
Redman, Bill, 681
Redux (dexfenfluramine), 172
Reed Experiment, 172
Reed Gold Mine (Concord, North
    Carolina), 170
Reed, Donna, 273
Reed, Oliver, 274
Reed, Walter, 172
Reeve, Christopher, 274
Reeves, George, 274
Reformation, 4
Refugees, Freedmen, and Abandoned
    Lands, Bureau of, 681
Regency (Great Britain), 4, 18
Regina Elena (sailing ship), 498
Regina, Canada, 365
Regulus missile program, 542
Rehi, Tama Horomona, 183
Reid, Kate, 274
Reidy, T.H., 700
Reign of Terror (France), 686
Reinhardt, Django, 347
Relational Software Inc., 64
Reliant Robin, 34
religious habits (clothing), 486
Remarque, Erich Maria, 212
Rembrandt, 25
Remick, Lee, 274
Remington Rand, 64
Remington Steele (TV), 626
Reminiscin' with Singin' Sam (radio),
    470
Renaissance, 1, 4
Renaldo, Duncan, 274
Renault, 28
Rennie, John, 125
Rennie, Michael, 274
Reno Air (airline), 48
Reno, Marcus, 672
Renoir, Jean, 241
Renoir, Pierre Auguste, 25
Rensselaer Institute, 107
Rensselaer Polytechnic Institute, 107
Rensselaer School, 107
Renwick, James (Jr.), 19
Reprisal, USS (carrier), 519
Republic (movie studio), 237
Republic Airlines, 48
Republic F-105 Thunderchief
    (aircraft), 45

Republic F-84
  Thunderstreak/Thunderjet
  (aircraft), 45
Republic P-47 Thunderbolt (aircraft),
  45
Rescued (play), 140
Resettlement Administration, 637
Reshkauko County, Michigan, 662
Resort Air, Inc. (airline), 48
Resphigi, Ottorino, 303
Restigouche, Battle of, 691
Restless Gun, The (TV), 626
Restoration, 5
Retail Credit Company, 64
Réunion, 543, 544
Réunion solitaire, 14
Reuther, Walter, 181
Revenue Cutter Service, 649
Revere, Anne, 274
Revolutionary calendar, 631
Rex (liner), 531
Reza Shah Pahlavi (shah of Iran),
  387
Rhein-Main Air Force Base (West
  Germany), 684
Rhoda (TV), 626
Rhode Island, 112, 185, 186, 545,
  667
Rhode Island College, 103
Rhode Island County, Rhode Island,
  667
Rhode Island, USS (battleship), 509
Rhodes (Greece), 381
Rhodes College, 107
Rhodes Scholars, 102
Rhodes, Cecil, 102, 422
Rhodes, Peyton Nalle, 107
Rhodesia and Nyasaland, Federation
  of, 8, 394, 423
Rhodesian Protectorate, 422
Rialto Theater (New York, New
  York), 153
Rice Institute, 107
Rice University, 107
Rice, Elmer, 212
Rich County, Utah, 669
Rich, Buddy, 347
Rich, Irene, 459
Rich's (store), 63
Richard Diamond, Private Detective
  (radio), 468
Richard II, King (England), 419
Richard III, King (England), 690
Richardson County, Kansas, 660
Richardson, Henry Hobson, 19
Richardson, Sir Ralph, 274
Richardville County, Indiana, 659
Richelieu (play), 141
Richfield Coliseum (Cleveland,
  Ohio), 573
Richland County, Utah, 669
Richmond, Virginia, 669
Richthofen, Baron Manfred von, 41,

695, 696
Rick Husband Amarillo International
  Airport (Texas), 50
Rickmers (sailing ship), 497
Riddle, Nelson, 303
Rider Business College, 107
Rider College, 107
Rider University, 107
Rider-Moore and Steward School of
  Business, 107
Ridgway, Matthew B., 688, 716
Rifleman, The (TV), 626
Riggin, Pat, 602
Riggs, Tommy, 473
Right to Happiness, The (radio), 468
Rigney, Bill, 569
Riley Elf (automobile), 32
Riley Kestrel (automobile), 32
Rilke, Rainer Maria, 212
Rimsky-Korsakov, Nikolai, 303, 311
Rin Tin Tin, 274
Rin Tin Tin (radio), 468
Rin Tin Tin, K-9 Cop (TV), 468
Rinehart, Frank, 85
Rinehart, Mary Roberts, 212
Ringada, Sir Veerasamy, 397
Ringling Brothers and Barnum &
  Bailey Circus, 147
Ringo, John, 74
Rio de Janeiro, Brazil, 362
Rio de la Plata, Viceroyalty of, 357,
  361, 403, 420
Rio Grande Zephyr (train), 483
Rip Kirby (comic strip), 72
Riperton, Minnie, 348
Ripken, Cal (Jr.), 567
Ripley, Robert L., 448
Riptide (TV), 626
Risberg, Charles August ("Swede"),
  571
Risley County, Iowa, 660
Risterucci, Jean, 378
Ritt, Martin, 241
Rittenhouse, John C., 163
Ritter, Thelma, 274
Ritz Brothers, 135
Ritz-Carlton Hotel (New York, New
  York), 177
Riverfront Stadium (Cincinnati,
  Ohio), 555
Riverside Park (Hutchinson, Kansas),
  145
Riverview Beach Amusement Park
  (Pennsville, New Jersey), 145
Riverview Park (Chicago, Illinois),
  145
Rives County, Missouri, 663
RKO Center (New York, New York),
  152
RKO Roxy Theater (New York, New
  York), 152
Roach, John, 537
Road of Life, The (radio), 468

Roanoke (sailing ship), 537
Roanoke College, 107
Roanoke Island's Lost Colony, 642
Robards, Jason (Jr.), 274
Robb, Mrs. Floyd, 100
robbery, 84
Robbins, Frank, 71
Robbins, Jerome, 138
Robert E. Lee (paddle steamer), 535
Robert E. Lee, USS (submarine), 542
Robert F. Kennedy Stadium
  (Washington, D.C.), 559
Robert Montgomery Presents (TV),
  626
Roberts, Ann, 426
Roberts, Dave, 563
Roberts, Robin, 554
Roberts, Rush, 649
Robertson, Alexander, 165
Robertson, Hugh, 165
Robertson, Sherman, 138
Robeson, Paul, 274, 315
Robespierre, Maximilien, 686
Robin Hood, The Adventures of (TV),
  612
Robinson Airlines, 48
Robinson, Bill ("Bojangles"), 274
Robinson, Ed, 595
Robinson, Edward G., 274, 449
Robinson, Edwin Arlington, 212
Robinson, Jackie, 554, 562
Robinson, Sugar Ray, 582
Robinson, Wilbert, 568
Robison Field (Saint Louis,
  Missouri), 559, 560
Robson, Dame Flora, 274
Robson, May, 274
Roche, Des, 604
Roche, Earl, 604
Rochester Jeffersons (football), 595
Rochester Lancers (soccer), 610
Rochester Royals (basketball), 579
Rochester, New York (trolleys), 635
Rock & Roll, 318
Rock Island & LaSalle Rail Road
  Company, 477
Rock Island Independents (football),
  595
Rockaways' Playland (New York),
  145
Rockefeller Center (New York, New
  York), 153
Rockefeller, John D., 62
Rocket, The (roller coaster), 144
Rockford Files, The (TV), 626
Rockingham, Franklin Township,
  New Jersey, 675
Rockland Lake (lighthouse), 191
Rockne, Knute, 583, 585
Rockwell, Norman, 25
Rockwell, Richard, 72
Rocky Fortune (radio), 455, 468
Rodgers, Isaiah, 176

Rodgers, Jimmie, 348
Rodgers, Richard, 303
Rodrigo, Joaquín, 304
Rodriguez solitaire, 14
Rodríguez, Francisco Núñez, 374
Roebling Company, 133
Roebling Wire Rope Machine, 133
Roebling, Charles G., 133
Roebling, John Augustus, 124
Roebling, Washington Augustus, 124
Rogers, Charles ("Buddy"), 274
Rogers, Ginger, 275
Rogers, Isaiah, 177
Rogers, Roy, 275
Rogers, Will, 57, 275
Rogue's Gallery (radio), 468
Rohmer, Sax, 212, 456
Roland, Gilbert, 275
Roland, Jim, 570
Rolle, Esther, 275
roller coasters, 145
Rollercoaster (movie), 144
Rollins, Howard E. (Jr.), 275
Rolls-Royce (automobile maker), 28
Rolscreen Company, 64
Roma (airship), 51, 52, 93
Roman Catholic Relief Act
   (England), 485
Roman Catholicism, 485
Roman Empire, 1, 4, 12, 118, 405,
   413, 418, 690
Roman Literary Cursive Script, 12
Roman Republic, 1, 122
Romance of Helen Trent, The (radio),
   468
Romance of the Seas (clipper ship),
   500
Romania, 11, 116, 405, 489, 631
Romanov dynasty (Russia), 405
Romanov, Grand Duke Mikhail, 405
Romans, Last of the, 19
Romanticism, 1, 5
Romberg, Sigmund, 304
Rome, Italy, 421
Romeo and Juliet (play), 142
Romero, Cesar, 275
Romilly, Colonel Frederick, 101
Rommel, Erwin, 700
Romulus Augustulus, Emperor
   (Roman Empire), 122
Ronald Reagan Washington National
   Airport (Washington, D.C.), 50
Rookies, The (TV), 626
Rookwood Pottery (company), 165,
   167
Room 222 (TV), 626
Roosen, Otto, 696
Roosevelt dime, U.S., 225
Roosevelt Stadium (Jersey City, New
   Jersey), 554
Roosevelt, Franklin D., 132, 170,
   228, 443, 446, 455, 637, 647, 651,
   654, 703, 716

Roosevelt, Theodore, 442, 654, 691
Root, John Wellborn, 19, 61
Rootes Group (automobile maker),
   30, 32
Ropers, The (TV), 626
roque (Olympic event), 606
Rosary College, 104
Rosas, Christi, 86
Roscommon County, Michigan, 662
Rose, Billy, 150, 151
Rose, Della, 85
Rose, Walter ("Tam"), 596
Roseanne (TV), 626
Rosenthal, Joe, 702
Roses and Drums (radio), 468
Roses, War of the, 690
Roseville Pottery Company, 167
Rosie (magazine), 222
Ross, Herbert, 241
Ross, Lee, 563
Ross, Virgil, 67
Rossellini, Roberto, 241
Rossen, Robert, 241
Rossetti, Michael, 21
Rossini, Gioacchino Antonio, 304
Rota, Nino, 304
Rothafel, Samuel Lionel, 468
Rothman International (sports event),
   173
Rotten, Johnny, 348
Rough Riders, 691
Round Island (lighthouse), 191
Roush, Edd J., 561, 572
Rousseau, Jean Jacques, 212
Route 40, 492
Route 66, 492
Route 66 (TV), 626
Routt, John Long, 657
Rove Tunnel (Arles, France), 134
Roventini, Johnny, 460
Rover (automobile maker), 28
Rowan & Martin's Laugh-In (TV),
   627
Rowan College of New Jersey, 107
Rowan University, 107
Rowan, Henry and Betty, 107
rowing (Olympic event), 606
Roxy and His Gang (radio), 468
Roxy Theater (New York, New
   York), 152
Roy Rogers Show, The (radio), 469
Roy Rogers Show, The (TV), 627
Royal Air Force, 34, 37, 41, 45
Royal Albert Bridge (Plymouth,
   England), 123
Royal Anne (oared ship), 525
Royal Ballet (Great Britain), 135
Royal Blue Line (train), 483
Royal Canadian Air Force, 36
Royal Cumberland (company), 168
Royal Enfield (motorcycle maker),
   235
Royal Flying Corps, 696

Royal Welsh Fusiliers, 697
Royal Zoological Gardens (London,
   England), 147
Royall, Kenneth C., 640
Royals Stadium (Kansas City,
   Missouri), 556
Rózsa, Miklós, 304
Ruanda-Urundi, 9, 363, 406
Rubens, Horatio Seymour, 370
Rubens, Peter Paul, 25
Rubinstein, Anton, 304
Rubinstein, Arthur, 315
ruble (USSR), 224
Ruby, Jack, 652
Rudolph, Dick, 567
Rudolph, Eric Robert, 87
Rudy Vallee Show, The (radio), 469
Ruff & Reddy, 66
Ruffin, David, 351
rugby (Olympic event), 606
Ruggles, Charles, 275
Rumania (spelling of name), 405
Rumania, Kingdom of, 405
Rumania, Socialist Republic of, 405
Rumanian People's Republic, 405
Rumann, Sig, 275
Rumsey, Jan, 572
Run For Your Life (TV), 627
Run-DMC, 348
Runge, Paul, 603
Runyon, Damon, 212
Ruppert Stadium (Kansas City,
   Missouri), 556
Rusk County, South Dakota, 668
Rusk County, Wisconsin, 670
Ruskin, John, 213
Russell, Allan, 567
Russell, C.D., 72
Russell, Gail, 275
Russell, Lillian, 142
Russell, Rosalind, 275
Russia, 116, 121, 489, 544, 631, 690,
   695
Russia/Russian Federation, 405
Russian Revolution, 405
Russian Soviet Federated Socialist
   Republic, 390, 406, 417
Russian Turkistan, 416
Russo-Finnish War, 376
Russo-Japanese War, 690
Russo-Turkish Wars, 690
Rusty Riley (comic strip), 72
Rutgers Athletic Center (Piscataway,
   New Jersey), 575
Rutgers College, 107
Rutgers College and the State
   University of New Jersey, 107
Rutgers, the State University of New
   Jersey, 101, 107, 584
Ruth, Babe, 564, 572
Rutherford, Dame Margaret, 275
Rutland Railroad, 481
Rwanda, Republic of (Rwandese

Republic), 9, 116
Ryan Hotel (Saint Paul, Minnesota), 177
Ryan, Irene, 275
Ryan, Leo, 485
Ryan, Robert, 275
Ryan, Ronald, 80
Ryan's Hope (TV), 627
Ryswick, Treaty of, 688
S.S. Kresge Company, 64
SA (Sturm Abteilung), 708
Saarinen, Eero, 19
Sabbathday Lake Shaker community, 488
Sabena Airlines (aircraft), 36
Sabin Point (lighthouse), 191
Sabin vaccine, 171
Sabu, 275
Sacagawea dollar coin, U.S., 227
Sacco, Nicola, 76
Sachs, Lenny, 593
Sadowski, Bob, 569
Safeco Field (Seattle, Washington), 559
Safety at Sea Act (1966), 99
Said bin Taimur, Sultan (Oman), 402
Saier, Vic, 566
Saigon (Vietnam), 422
Sailfish, USS (submarine), 99, 541
Saint Charles Avenue Route (New Orleans, Louisiana), 635
Saint Charles Hotel (Los Angeles, California), 176
Saint Charles Hotel (New Orleans, Louisiana), 177
Saint Christopher (Saint Kitts), 406
Saint Christopher-Nevis-Anguilla, 11
Saint Clara Academy, 104
Saint Croix, 372
Saint Croix River (lighthouse), 191
Saint Domingue, 383, 543
Saint Francis Dam, 94
Saint George Cricket Grounds (New York, New York), 557
Saint Ignatius College, 106
Saint John (island), 372
Saint John County, Kansas, 660
Saint John the Divine, Cathedral of (New York, New York), 23
Saint John's Cathedral (Brisbane, Australia), 15
Saint John's College, 105
Saint Jones County, Delaware, 657
Saint Kitts and Nevis, Federation of, 116, 406
Saint Lawrence Seaway, 129
Saint Louis Academy, 107
Saint Louis All-Stars (football), 595
Saint Louis and San Francisco Railway, 478
Saint Louis Bombers (basketball), 579
Saint Louis Brown Stockings

(baseball), 572
Saint Louis Browns (baseball), 559, 570, 572
Saint Louis Cable and Western Railway (Saint Louis, Missouri), 633
Saint Louis Cardinals (baseball), 572
Saint Louis College, 107
Saint Louis County, Minnesota, 662
Saint Louis Downtown-Parks Airport (Missouri), 50
Saint Louis Eagles (ice hockey), 604, 605
Saint Louis Globe (newspaper), 437
Saint Louis Globe-Democrat (newspaper), 437
Saint Louis Gunners (football), 595
Saint Louis Hawks (basketball), 576, 579
Saint Louis Perfectos (baseball), 572
Saint Louis Railroad (Saint Louis, Missouri), 633
Saint Louis Spirits (basketball), 579
Saint Louis Stars (soccer), 610
Saint Louis Storm (soccer), 608
Saint Louis University, 107
Saint Louis, Missouri (trolleys), 635
Saint Louis-San Francisco Railway, 478
Saint Lucia (nation), 11, 116, 407
Saint Lucie County, Florida, 658
Saint Mary's College of Maryland, 107
Saint Mary's Female Seminary, 107
Saint Mary's Junior College, 107
Saint Mary's Seminary and Junior College, 107
Saint Patrick's Cathedral (New York, New York), 19
Saint Paul City Railway (Saint Paul, Minnesota), 633
Saint Paul Saints (baseball), 562
Saint Paul's Cathedral (London, England), 20, 60
Saint Peter's Basilica (Vatican City, Rome, Italy), 24, 60
Saint Petersburg, Russia, 406
Saint Stephen's College, 103
Saint Thomas (island), 372
Saint Vincent and the Grenadines, 11, 116, 407
Saint Vincent College, 104
Saint, The (radio), 469
Saint, The (TV), 627
Saint-Gaudens double eagle coin, U.S., 227
Saint-Gaudens, Augustus, 25, 227
Saint-Saëns, Camille, 305
Saipan, USS (carrier), 519
Sakai, Tadashige, 389
Sakall, S.Z. ("Cuddles"), 275
Saki, 213
Sakic, Dinko, 711

Salad Bowl (football), 584
Saladin (Salah-el-Din), 120
Salata, Andy, 593
Saleh, Colonel Ali Abdullah, 422
Salem Express (ship), 99
Salem witches, 88
Salk vaccine, 171
Salling, John B., 683
Salmi, Albert, 275
Salmon, USS (submarine), 540, 541
Salt Lake City Municipal Airport (Utah), 51
Salt Lake County, Utah, 669
Salt Lake International Airport (Utah), 51
Salt Lake Trail, 491
Salter, William Dayton, 694
Saluria (lighthouse), 191
Salyut 1 (space laboratory), 549
Salyut 7 (space laboratory), 549
Salyut space station, 549
Sam and Henry (radio), 447
Sam Spade, Detective, The Adventures of (radio), 469
Sam, Jean Vilbrun Guillaume, 383
Samir (ship), 92
Sammy (musical), 138
Sammy Kaye Show, The (radio), 469
Sammy Kaye's Sunday Serenade (radio), 469
Samoa, Independent State of, 116, 407
Sampson, Will, 275
Samuel Hill Pottery (company), 165
San Antonio Spurs (basketball), 578
San Antonio Thunder (soccer), 610
San Diego Cable Railway (San Diego, California), 633
San Diego Clippers (basketball), 579
San Diego Conquistadors (basketball), 576, 579
San Diego East-West Christmas Classic (football), 584
San Diego Jaws (soccer), 610
San Diego Maritime Museum (California), 187
San Diego Padres (baseball), 559
San Diego Rockets (basketball), 579
San Diego Sails (basketball), 579
San Diego Sockers (soccer), 608, 610
San Diego Stadium (San Diego, California), 559
San Diego Toros (soccer), 610
San Diego, California (horsecars), 634
San Francisco 49ers (football), 586
San Francisco Airport (California), 51
San Francisco Chief (train), 483
San Francisco Demons (football), 586
San Francisco Gales (soccer), 610
San Francisco Giants (baseball), 559

San Francisco International Airport (California), 51
San Francisco Naval Shipyard, 539
San Francisco Peace Treaty, 414
San Francisco Solano, Mission, 656
San Francisco Warriors (basketball), 579
San Francisco, California (horsecars), 634
San Ildefonso, Treaty of, 656, 660
San Jacinto, Battle of, 668
San Jacinto, USS (carrier), 519
San Jose Earthquakes (soccer), 610
San Juan Hill, Battle of, 691
San Juan Island (United States), 638
San Marino, Most Serene Republic of, 116, 407
San Miguel County, Colorado, 657
San Stefano, Treaty of, 690
Sanache, Frank, 716
Sanborn, Mabel Young, 485
Sand, George, 213
Sandakan Death March, 703
Sandburg, Carl, 213
Sanders, George, 276
Sanderson, Geoff, 603
Sando Arch (Sando, Sweden), 128
Sandoz Pharmaceuticals, 74
Sands, Bobby, 388
Sands, The (Las Vegas, Nevada), 177
Sandwich Islands, 155
Sanford and Son (TV), 627
Sanford County, Alabama, 655
Sanger, Maria Renata, 88
Sanitary and Ship Canal, 130
Santa Barbara, 191
Santa Cruz County, California, 656
Santa Fe Trail, 493
Santa Isabel, Equatorial Guinea, 374
Santa Maria (Columbus's ship), 155
Santa Maria (liner), 501
Santamaria, Domingo Caycedo y Sanz de, 9
Santee Canal, 131
Santee Sioux (Native Americans), 431
Santo Domingo, 373, 383
Santo Spirito (Florence, Italy), 16
Santos, Lucia dos, 486
São Tomé and Príncipe, Democratic Republic of, 116, 408
Sap, Julius, 100
Sapir, Edward, 432
Saponi (Native Americans), 431
SAR Magazine, The, 677
Saracens, 122
Sarajevo, Bosnia, 695
Saratoga, USS (carrier), 519
Sarawak, 395
Sarber County, Arkansas, 656
Sardinia, Kingdom of, 398
Sargent, Dick, 276
Sargent, John Singer, 26

Sargo, USS (submarine), 540
Sargon II, King (Assyrian Empire), 118
Sarmatians, 122
Sarnia, Ontario (horsecars), 634
Sarnoff, David, 630
Saroyan, William, 213
satellite technology, 611
Satie, Erik, 305
Saturday Evening Post (magazine), 25, 27, 462
Saturday Review of Literature (magazine), 223
Saturday Review/World (magazine), 223
Saturday's Lesson (movie), 237
Saubel, Katherine Silva (Cahuilla speaker), 424
Saud family (Saudi Arabia), 408
Saudi Arabia, Kingdom of, 223, 408, 544, 545
Saugatuck Light (lighthouse), 189
Sauk (Native Americans), 672
Saunders County, Nebraska, 664
Saunders, Alvin, 664
Saury, USS (submarine), 540
Savannah, Georgia, 658
Saved by the Bell (TV), 627
Savings Bonds, U.S., 229, 230
Savings Stamps, U.S., 230
Sawamish County, Washington, 670
Saxe-Coburg monarchs, 420
Sayao, Bidu, 316
Sayers, Dorothy L., 213
Sayre, R.H., 481
scaffold reprieve, 82
scams, schemes and speculations, 64
Scandinavian Star (ship), 99
Scarecrow and Mrs. King (TV), 627
Scarlatti, Alessandro, 305
Scarlatti, Domenico, 305
Scarlet Horsemen, The (movie), 237
Scat Cats (cartoon), 66
Scattergood Baines (radio), 469
Scelbi (Scientific, Electronic and Biological) Computer Consulting Company, 117
Schaffhausen Bridge (Switzerland), 129
Schechter Poultry Corp. v. United States, 636
schemes, scams and speculations, 64
Schildkraut, Joseph, 276
Schiller, Friedrich von, 213
schilling (Austria), 224
Schirra, Walter ("Wally") M., 548
Schmeling, Max, 582
Schmitt, Harrison H. ("Jack"), 548
Schnee, Heinrich, 9
Schoenberg, Arnold, 305
Schoharie Creek Bridge (New York), 129
schools, public, 109

schooner, 531
Schubert, Franz, 305
Schultze, Charles E. ("Bunny"), 71
Schulz, Charles M., 72
Schumann, Robert, 305
Schumann-Heink, Ernestine, 316
Schwagel, Anna Maria, 88
Schwinn (cycle maker), 234
Scientific American (magazine), 634
Scientific Research and Development, Office of (OSRD), 719
Sci–Fi Radio (radio), 469
Scopes, John T., 110
Scorpion, USS (submarine), 99
Scotch Cap (lighthouse), 191
Scotia (paddle steamer), 535
Scotland, 13, 418, 420
Scotland Yard (London, England), 75
Scott (motorcycle maker), 235
Scott Squirrel (motorcycle), 235
Scott, George C., 276
Scott, Isaac H., 683
Scott, John Paul, 79
Scott, Randolph, 276
Scott, Robert Falcon, 158
Scott, Sir Walter, 213
Scott, Winfield, 443, 689
Scott, Zachary, 276
Scottsboro Case, 69
Scovell, Minnie Adams (Tillamook speaker), 432
scow schooner, 533
Scrappy Birthday (cartoon), 65
Screen Actors Guild (SAG), 236
Screen Directors' Playhouse (radio), 469
Screen Guild Theater (radio), 469
Scriabin, Alexander, 306
Scribner, Jimmy, 460
Scribner's Monthly (magazine), 223
Scruggs, Earl, 330
Scythians, 122
Sea Cloud (sailing ship), 498
Sea Cloud of Cayman (sailing ship), 498
Sea Hound, The (radio), 469
Sea Lion, USS (submarine), 540
Sea World, 144
Seaboard Air Line Railroad, 476, 478
Seaboard Coast Line Railroad, 476, 478, 479
Seaboard System Railroad, 476, 479
Seadragon, USS (submarine), 540, 541
Seals Stadium (San Francisco, California), 559
Sealtest Show, The (radio), 469
Sealtest Village Store, The (radio), 460, 469
Searaven, USS (submarine), 541
Searcher, HMS (carrier), 715
Searcy County, Arkansas, 656

Sears Tower (Chicago, Illinois), 61
Sears-Roebuck, 235
seatbelts, 27
Seated Liberty dime, U.S., 225
Seated Liberty dollar coin, U.S., 226
Seated Liberty half dime, U.S., 225
Seated Liberty half dollar, U.S., 226
Seated Liberty quarter, U.S., 226
Seated Liberty twenty-cent coin,
  U.S., 226
Seattle City Railway (Seattle,
  Washington), 633
Seattle Kingdome (Seattle,
  Washington), 559
Seattle Metropolitans (ice hockey),
  598
Seattle Pilots (baseball), 559, 570
Seattle Sounders (soccer), 610
Seattle, Washington (trolleys), 635
Seawolf, USS (submarine), 541
Seberg, Jean, 276
Secession, War of, 679
Second Continental Congress, 643
Second Empire (France), 377
Second Millennium, end of the, 631
Second Mrs. Burton, The (radio), 469
Second Narrows Bridge (Vancouver,
  British Columbia), 129
Second Reich (Germany), 379
Second Republic (France), 376
Second Republic (Spain), 412
Second Squadron, 11th U.S. Cavalry,
  648
Second Street Cable Railway (Los
  Angeles, California), 632
Second Vatican Council (Vatican II),
  486
Secret Agent X-9 (comic strip), 72
Secretariat, 597
securities pricing, 59
Sedgely Porter's Lodge
  (Philadelphia, Pennsylvania), 15
See Ya Later Gladiator (cartoon), 65,
  66
Seeadler (sailing ship), 521
Segovia, Andrès, 316
Segui, Diego, 564
Seinfeld, 627
Selby, James J., 651
Select School (Alfred Univesity), 102
Selective Service System, 647
Selena, 348
Selfridge, Lieutenant Thomas, 56
Seljuk Turks, 121
Sellers, Peter, 276
Seminole Wars, 673
Seminoles (Native Americans), 673
Semper Augustus (tulip bulb), 65
Senator Hotel (Miami Beach,
  Florida), 177
Senegal, 9, 10, 116
Senegal, Republic of, 408
Senegambia, 378, 408

Sennacherib, 134
Senorella and the Glass Huarache
  (cartoon), 67
Seo, Yoshi, 562
Separate Amenities Act (South
  Africa), 411
Sepoy Mutiny (India), 62, 385
September 11, 2001, 87
Sequoia-Kings Canyon National Park
  (California), 13
Sequoyah County, Kansas, 660
Serbia, 695
Serbia and Montenegro, 408
Serbs, Croats and Slovenes,
  Kingdom of, 361, 370, 408, 410
Sergeant Preston of the Canadian
  Mounted Police (radio), 469
serials, movies, 237
Serrano y Uribe, Manuel Fernando,
  368
Service Merchandise (store), 63
Seth Parker (radio), 469
Seth Parker (schooner), 469
Seton Hall College, 107
Seton Hall University, 107
Settles, Mary, 488
Seurat, Georges, 26
Seven Little Foys, 135
Seven Wonders of the Ancient
  World, 133
Seven Years' War, 657, 691
Seventy Seven Sunset Strip (TV), 627
seventy-eight rpm disc phonographs,
  437
Seven-Up Company, 64
Severus, Alexander, Emperor
  (Rome), 123
Severy, Marge, 432
Sevez, Francois, 705
Sevier, John, 668
Sevres, Treaty of, 121
Sewall, Arthur, 537
Seward County, Nebraska, 664
Seward, William H., 655
Seward's Folly, 655
Sex Pistols, The, 348
Seychelles, Republic of, 116, 224,
  409
Seyler, Pierre (World War I
  casualty), 697
Seymour, Samuel J., 653
Shackleton, Ernest, 159
Shackley, Steven, 433
Shadow of Fu Manchu, The (radio),
  456
Shadow, The (radio), 466, 470
Shakers, 487
Shakespeare, William, 213
Shakur, Tupac (2 Pac), 349
Shallow Bay, West Falkland, 14
Shamrock Hotel (Houston, Texas),
  177
Shanawdithit, 423

Shang dynasty (China), 119
Shangri-la (musical), 142
Shangri-La (presidential retreat), 651
Shangri-La, USS (carrier), 519
Shannon, Darrin, 605
Shapp, Milton J., 179
Sharjah (emirate), 418
Shark, USS (submarine), 539
Sharon, Portrait of a Mistress (TV),
  136
Shaw, George Bernard, 213
Shaw, Robert, 276
Shawano County, Michigan, 662
Shawn, Ted, 137
Shawnee (Native Americans), 675
Shawnee Pottery (company), 167
Shay, Madeline Tomer (Penobscot
  speaker), 430
Shays's Rebellion, 661
Shea, First Lieutenant Michael John,
  694
Shearer, Norma, 276
Sheboygan Redskins (basketball),
  579
Shell Chateau (radio), 447
Shell Oil Gas Station (Winston-
  Salem, North Carolina), 60
Shelley, Mary Wollstonecraft, 214
Shelley, Percy Bysshe, 214
Shenandoah (ZR-1) (airship), 93
Shenandoah County, Virginia, 669
Shenandoah CSS (sailing ship), 680,
  682
Shenandoah Valley Railroad, 481
Shepard, Alan B., 548
Sheraton St. Charles (New Orleans,
  Louisiana), 177
Sheridan, Ann, 276
Sheridan, George, 189
Sheridan, Philip H., 681
Sheridan, Richard Brinsley, 214
Sheriff, The (radio), 453, 470
Sherlock Holmes, The Adventures of
  (radio), 470
Sherman, Jane, 137
Sherman, William Tecumseh, 679
Sherwood, Robert Emmet, 194
Shewan, Andrew, 499
Shibe Park (Philadelphia,
  Pennsylvania), 558
Shield five-cent coin, U.S., 225
Shields, Arthur, 276
Shields, C., 481
Shih Huang-ti, 119
Shiloh, Johnny, 683
Shimonoseki, Treaty of, 414, 691
Shine, Ellen Natalia, 100
Shinn, Everett, 21
Shinnecock Bay (lighthouse), 192
shinplasters, 228
Shipley, Dr. William, 427
ship-of-the-line, 522
ships, Morse Code used by, 611

Shirer, William L., 214
Shirley County, Kansas, 660
Shirley Plantation (Charles City, Virginia), 15
Shirley, Anne, 276
Shirley, Massachusetts, Shaker community, 488
Shoalwater Bay (lighthouse), 192
Shocker, Urban, 567
Shoemaker, Willie, 598
shogunates (Japan), 389
Shomo, Frank, 94
shooting (Olympic event), 606
Shore, Dinah, 349
Short Ribs (comic strip), 72
Short, Chris, 557
Short, Luke, 74
Shorter County, Nebraska, 664
Shostakovich, Dmitri, 306
shot clock, 24-second (basketball), 580
Shoup, George L., 659
Show Boat (novel), 536
Show Boat (radio), 470
Show Shop (theater, New York, New York), 150
Showa period (Japan), 389
showboat (steamboat), 535
Shrine Bowl (football), 584
Shriner, Herb, 458
Shurlock, Geoffrey M., 237
Shuster, Joe, 471
Shute, Nevil, 214
shut-outs, consecutive (football), 585
Siam, Kingdom of, 415
Sibelius, Jean, 306
Siberia, 121, 183
Sicilies, Kingdom of the Two, 388
Sick's Stadium (Seattle, Washington), 559
Sicurani, Jean-Charles, 396
side shows, 146
Sideshows by the Seashore (Coney Island, New York), 146
Sidney, George, 241
Sidney, Sylvia, 276
Siebert, Dr. Frank T. (Jr.), 430
Siegel, Jerry, 471
Siegfried Line, 706
Sierra Leone, 7, 10, 116, 544, 545
Sierra Leone, Republic of, 409
Sigismund II (Jagellon ruler), 404
Signal Service, U.S. Army, 722
Sikorsky S-42 Clipper (aircraft), 37
Sikorsky S-61/SH-3 Sea King (Helicopter), 56
silent films, 237
silk-weaving, hand (England), 223
Silly Symphonies (cartoon), 66, 67
Sillywrae Farm (England), 6
Silurian Period, 2
Silver Bridge (Kanauga, Ohio), 128
silver certificates, U.S., 229

silver coins, U.S., 227
silver dollar coins, U.S., 226
Silver Eagle (radio), 470
Silver Meteor (train), 483
Silver Spoons (TV), 627
Silvera, Frank, 276
Silverdome (Pontiac, Michigan), 574
Silverheels, Jay, 276
Silvers, Phil, 276
Sim, Alastair, 276
Simenon, Georges, 214
Simeon II, King (Bulgaria), 363
Simms, Ginny, 456
Simon & Simon (TV), 627
Simon, Joe, 73
Simple Things, The (cartoon), 67
Simplon-Orient Express, 476
Sinai Peninsula, 691
Sinatra, Frank, 276, 349, 468
Sinclair, Upton, 214
Sing Along with Mitch (TV), 627
Singapore, Republic of, 116, 395, 409
Singateh, Sir Farimang Mamadi, 378
Singer (automobile maker), 32
Singer Vogue (automobile), 32
Singin' Sam, The Barbasol Man (radio), 470
Singing Story Lady, The (radio), 470
Single Guy, The (TV), 627
Sinkyone (Native Americans), 431
Sino-Japanese Wars, 414, 691
Siodmak, Robert, 241
Sioux (Native Americans), 431, 662
Sioux City Cable Railway, 633
Sioux Falls, South Dakota (trolleys), 635
Sirk, Douglas, 241
Sisters (TV), 627
Sitting Bull (Sioux chief), 672
Sitting Man, Charles, 673
Siuslaw Alsean (Native Americans), 432
Six Gun Territory (amusement park), 145
Six Million Dollar Man (TV), 627
Six Shooter, The (radio), 470
Six-Day War, 691
Sixty Four Thousand Dollar Question, The (TV), 627
Skate, USS, 540
Skelton, Richard ("Red"), 276
skipjack (ship), 533
Skipjack, USS (submarine), 540
Skippy (comic strip), 72
Skippy Hollywood Theater, The (radio), 470
Sky King (radio), 470
SkyDome (Toronto, Canada), 559, 575
Skylab (space laboratory), 549
skyscrapers, 61
SL 2 (airship), 54

SL 11 (airship), 54
SL 20 (airship), 54
Slaughter County, Iowa, 660
Slaughter County, Washington, 670
Slaughter, Ed, 583
Slaughter, Lenora, 146
Slave Trade Act (1794), 546
slavery, 663
Slayton, Donald K. ("Deke"), 548
Sleuth (movie), 240
Slezak, Walter, 277
slide rule, 497
Sloan, John, 21
Sloan, Richard E., 656
Sloane, Everett, 277
sloop (ship), 534
Slovak National Uprising, 700
Slovak Republic (Slovakia), 371, 409
Slovak Republic within Czechoslovakia, 410
Slovak Socialist Republic, 409
Slovakia, 116
Slovenia, People's Republic of, 410
Slovenia, Republic of, 116, 410
Slovenia, Socialist Republic of, 410
Slovik, Eddie, 81
Sluder, C.L., 43
smack (ship), 534
Small, Elisha, 82
smallpox, 171
Smalls, Biggie, 344
Smetana, Bedrich, 306
Smiley, Rev. Glen, 68
Smilin' Ed and His Buster Brown Gang (radio), 470
Smilin' Ed McConnell Show, The (radio), 470
Smilin' Jack (comic strip), 72
Smith & Heminway Company, 64
Smith, Al, 567
Smith, Alexis, 277
Smith, Apollo M.O., 548
Smith, Barbara, 220
Smith, Bessie, 349
Smith, Clipper, 588
Smith, Donald A., 480
Smith, Hyrum, 485
Smith, Joseph, 485
Smith, Kate, 350, 461
Smith, Latrobe and Company, 126
Smith, Philip E., 367
Smith, Sidney, 71, 72
Smith, Sir C. Aubrey, 277
Smith, Thomas C., 169
Smith, Walter Bedell, 705
Smith, Willie ("The Lion"), 350
Smithsonian Institution (Washington, D.C.), 18, 19
Smitty, 72
Smitty (comic strip), 72
Smokey Joe's Café (show), 148
Smokey Stover (comic strip), 72
smoking, airlines, 173

smoking, bars and restaurants, 174
smoking, workplace, 174
Smothers Brothers Comedy Hour, The (TV), 627
Smyrna River (lighthouse), 188
Smythe, Conn, 605
Smythe, Percy Clinton Sydney (Lord Strangford), 101
Snake, Bessie, 426
Snapper, USS (submarine), 540
Sneland (ship), 714
Snider, Duke, 554
Snow Squall (sailing ship), 498
Snow, Lorenzo, 485
Snowdrop, HMS (ship), 100
Snyder Act, 111
So You Want to Lead a Band (radio), 469
Soap (TV), 627
Sobibor (concentration camp), 710
Socarrás,Carlos Prío, 370
soccer, early leagues, 608
Social Justice (magazine), 446
Social Security, 637, 654
Socialist Federal Republic of Croatia within Yugoslavia, 370
Socialist Unity (Communist) Party (East Germany), 379
Societe Hotchkiss-Delahaye (automobile maker), 29
Society for the Collegiate Instruction of Women, 107
Society of Friends, 70
Society of the Living Dead, The, 173
Soglow, Otto, 71
Soil Conservation Service (U.S.), 6
Sojourner (Mars rover), 550
Solano López, Francisco, 693
Soldier of France, A (play), 140
soldiers, billeting of, 646
Solidarity (labor union), 404
Solitaire (dodo), 14
solitary system (prisons), 78
Solomon Islands, 116, 410
Solomon R. Guggenheim Museum (New York, New York), 20
Solomon, Tommy, 183
Solon, 186
Solti, Sir Georg, 316
Somali Democratic Republic (Somalia), 410
Somalia, 10, 116
Somaliland (Italian colony), 544
Somaliland, Republic of, 410
Somaliland, State of, 410
Somebody Knows (radio), 470
Somers, USS (sailing ship), 82
Somersal, Laura, 433
Sondergaard, Gale, 277
Songhai, Empire of, 121, 122
Songs by Dinah Shore (radio), 453
Songs by Sinatra (radio), 455
Sonny and Cher Comedy Hour, The (TV), 627
Sony, 64
Soo Line (railroad), 476, 479
Soo, Jack, 277
Soong, T.V., 704
Sopwith Camel (aircraft), 45, 695, 696
Sothern, Ann, 277, 463
Sothoron, Allen, 567
Soul Man (TV), 627
Soule, Olan, 277
Sousa, John Philip, 306
South Africa, 116, 183, 224
South Africa, Republic of, 411
South Africa, Union of, 411
South African War, 678
South Arabia, Federation of, 422
South Bend Blue Sox (baseball), 572
South Carolina, 490, 545, 667
South Carolina Military Academy, 103
South Carolina State College, 108
South Carolina State University, 107
South Carolina, USS (battleship), 509
South Dakota, 112, 668
South Dakota State College of Agriculture and Mechanical Arts, 108
South Dakota State University, 108
South Dakota, USS (battleship), 510
South East Asia Treaty Organization (SEATO), 10
South End Grounds (Boston, Massachusetts), 554
South Fork Dam, 94
South Pacific (show), 148
South Pole, 2, 154
South Sea Bubble, 65
South Sea Company, 65
South Side Park (Chicago, Illinois), 555
South Union community, 488
South Vietnam (Republic of Vietnam), 422, 693
South Yemen, 422
Southeast Asia, 8
Southerland, USS (destroyer), 713
Southern Airways, 48
Southern Branch of the University of Idaho, 105
Southern Illinois Normal University, 108
Southern Illinois University, 108
Southern Mississippi, University of, 108
Southern Pacific Railroad, 477, 479, 482
Southern Railroad, 477
Southern Railway, 478, 479
Southern Rhodesia, 8, 423
Southern Yemen, People's Republic of (South Yemen), 422
South-West Africa, 399
Southwest Airlines, 47
Southwest Airways, 48
Southwest Pacific Airlines, 48
Southwest Territory, 668
Southwestern at Memphis, 107
Southwestern Presbyterian University, 107
Southwestern University, 107
Sovereign of the Seas (clipper ship), 499
Sovetsky Sojus (liner), 525
Soyuz 11 (space station), 549
Soyuz 40 (space station), 549
Space Age, 3
Space Patrol (radio), 470
Spain, 8, 116, 120, 224, 544, 545, 631, 691
Spain, Kingdom of, 411
Spandau Prison (Berlin, East Germany), 77
Spanish Armada, 692
Spanish Civil War, 692
Spanish Guinea, 374
Spanish influenza, 171
Spanish Inquisition, 487
Spanish Morocco, 398
Spanish Netherlands, 360
Spanish Succession, War of the, 411, 690, 692
Spanish-American War, 403, 442, 670, 691
Sparks, Bill, 707
Sparks, Ned, 277
Sparling, Jack, 70
SPARS, U.S. Coast Guard Women's Reserve, 649
Sparta, 7
Spearfish, USS (submarine), 540
Spectrum (Philadelphia, Pennsylvania), 574
speculations, schemes and scams, 64
Speedy Gonzalez, 66
Spencer, John C., 82
Spencer, Philip, 82
Spencer, Prince, 138
Spencer-DHB iron lung, 174
Spenser, Edmund, 214
Sperry Corporation, 64
Sperry Rand, 64
Spike & Tyke (cartoon character), 66
Spike Jones Show, The (TV), 628
Spillman Engineering (North Tononwanda, New York), 145
Spinks, Leon, 581
Spirit of St. Louis (aircraft), 57
Spirit, The (comic strip), 72
Spitalny, Phil, 459
spitball, 566
Spokane Cable Railway (Spokane, Washington), 633
Spokane, Portland & Seattle Railway Company, 479

Strauss, Robert S., 418
Stravinsky, Igor, 307
Strayhorn, Billy, 308
streak, consecutive games (baseball), 567
streak, extra point (football), 587
streak, games played (ice hockey), 601
streak, losing (football), 587
streak, scoring (ice hockey), 601
streak, shut-outs (football), 585
streak, winning (basketball), 575, 576
streak, winning (football), 587
streak, winning (golf), 597
streak, winning (Harlem Globetrotters), 575
Streets of San Francisco, The (TV), 628
Strickland, William, 20
Strike it Rich (radio), 471
Strike It Rich (TV), 628
strikes, 180
Strindberg, August, 216
Stripp, Joe, 567
Strode, Woody, 278
Strohl, Alan, 130
Strudwick, Shepperd, 278
Stuart, Gilbert, 26
Stuart, House of, 419
Stuarts (store), 63
Studebaker (automobile), 31, 32
Studebaker Lark (automobile), 32
students, spanking, 79
Studio One (radio), 471
Stuhldreyer, Harry, 583, 585
Stumpff, Hans, 705
Sturgeon, USS (submarine), 540
Sturges, Preston, 241
Stutz (automobile maker), 32
Stutz Bearcat (automobile), 32
Stuyvesant (lighthouse), 192
Stuyvesant, Peter, 642
Suavestre, Stephen, 230
Submarines, U.S. classes, 539
Sucre, Antonio Jose dé, 361
Sucre, Bolivia, 361
Sudan, Democratic Republic of the, 412
Sudan, Republic of the, 412
Sudanese Republic, 395, 408
sudden death, regular-season (football), 587
sudden-death overtime (football), 587
Suddenly Susan (TV), 628
Sudetenland, 371
Suez Canal, 129
Suez Canal Crisis, 374
Suffolk Resolves, 676
Sugar and Spies (cartoon), 66
Sugarfoot (TV), 628
Suhr, Richard ("Gus"), 564
Sui dynasty (China), 119

Sukhothai era (Thailand), 415
Sullavan, Margaret, 278
Sullivan, Arthur S., 308
Sullivan, Ed (cartoonist), 72
Sullivan, Francis L., 278
Sullivan, John L. ("Boston Strong Boy"), 580
Sullivan, Louis H., 20
Sullivan, Mary, 76
Sullivan, Pat, 66
Sumerian (language), 11
Summerville, George ("Slim"), 278
Sumner County, Mississippi, 663
Sumner, Charles, 644, 655
Sumter, Thomas, 675
Sun Shipbuilding & Drydock Company (Pennsylvania), 539
Sun Yaoting, 178
Sunbeam (automobile maker), 32
Sunbeam (manufacturer), 235
Sunbeam (trolley), 635
Sunbeam Corporation, 63
Sunbeam Thirty (automobile), 32
Sunbeam-Talbot (automobile maker), 32
Sundance Kid, The, 84
Sunday Evening at Seth Parker's (radio), 469
Sung dynasty (China), 119
Super Chief (train), 483
Superboy (cartoon), 73
Supercomputer, Father of the, 117
Superior County, Minnesota, 663
Superman, The Adventures of (radio), 471
Supreme Court of the United States, 184, 186, 546
Supreme Executive Council, 667
Supreme Headquarters Allied Powers Europe (SHAPE), 10
Suriname, Republic of (Surinam), 116, 223, 544
Surratt, John, 653
Surveyor 7 (lunar probe), 551
Susan B. Anthony dollar coin, U.S.), 227
Susloparov, Ivan, 705
Suspense (radio), 471
Suspense (TV), 628
Susquehanna (sailing ship), 537
Susquehanna and Tidewater Canal, 131
Sussex County, Delaware, 657
Sutcliffe, Stuart, 321
suttee (sati), 386
Sutter Street Railway (San Francisco, California), 633
Sutter, John (sawmill), 170
Suvac Bay Naval Base (Philippines), 404
Suzuki Loom Works, 64
Suzuki Motor Co., Ltd., 64
Sverdrup Islands, Canada, 365

Swamp Meadow Covered Bridge (Foster, Rhode Island), 124
Swanson, Gloria, 278
Swarthout, Gladys, 316
Swastika, 708
Swaziland, Kingdom of, 116, 412
sweat house, Ohlone, 430
Sweden, 9, 79, 116, 372, 489, 544, 545, 631
Sweden, Kingdom of, 401, 413
Swedish East India Company, 62
Sweeney, Charles W., 717
Sweet Charity (musical), 137
Sweetwater County, Wyoming, 670
Swenson, Karl, 462
Swift, Jonathan, 216
swimming (Olympic event), 607
swine flu, 172
Swinnerton, James, 71
Swiss Guards, 421
Switzer, Carl ("Alfalfa"), 278
Switzerland (Swiss Confederation), 116, 413, 693
Swoose (aircraft), 38
Swordfish, USS (submarine), 541
Sybil, HMS (frigate), 676
Sylvania Electric Products, Inc., 64
Sylvester Pussycat (cartoon character), 66
Synge, John Millington, 216
syphilis, 175
Syracuse China Company, 167
Syracuse Nationals (basketball), 579
Syracuse, New York (horsecars), 634
Syria/Syrian Arab Republic, 7, 10, 116, 413, 691
Szell, George, 316
T.J. Hooker (TV), 628
T'ai-p'ing Rebellion, 692
T'ang dynasty (China), 119, 178
T1, 5546 (steam locomotive), 478
Tabard/Talbot, The (London, England), 491
Tabu (movie), 237
Tachibana, Taneyuki, 389
Tacoma Railway & Motor Company (Tacoma, Washington), 633
Tacoma Stars (soccer), 608
Tacoma, Washington (trolleys), 635
Tacoma-Narrows Bridge ("Galloping Gertie") (Tacoma Narrows, Washington), 129
Tadzikh Autonomous Soviet Socialist Republic, 414
Taft, James, 166
Taft, William Howard, 442, 654
Tagore, Rabindranath, 216
Tailleferre, Germaine, 311
Taisho period (Japan), 389
Taiwan (Republic of China), 414, 691
Tajikistan, Republic of, 116, 414
Take It or Leave It (radio), 454, 467,

471

Third Millennium, 631
Third Reich (Germany), 379, 707
Third Republic (France), 377, 686, 705
Third Rock from the Sun (TV), 628
Thirty Years' War, 4, 9, 692
thirtysomething (TV), 628
thirty-three and 1/3 rpm long-play records, 438
This is Helen Hayes (radio), 458
This is My Best (radio), 466, 472
This Is Nora Drake (radio), 472
This Is Your FBI (radio), 472
This Is Your Life (radio), 472
This is Your Life (TV), 628
Thomas Jefferson, USS (submarine), 542
Thomas W. Lawson (schooner), 532
Thomas, Andrew ("Andy"), 549
Thomas, Dylan, 216
Thomas, Heck, 85
Thompson, David, 672
Thompson, Virginia, 86
Thompson's Amusement Park (Rockaway Beach, New York), 145
Thomson, Tom, 21
Thoreau, Henry David, 217
Thorpe, Elliott Raymond, 716
Thorpe, Jim, 585, 590, 594
Those We Love (radio), 472
Three for the Show (movie), 136
Three M Company, 64
Three Rivers Stadium (Pittsburgh, Pennsylvania), 558
Three Stooges, 135
Three's Company (TV), 628
three-cent coin, U.S., 225
ThreeCom (3Com) Park (San Francisco, California), 559
three-dollar coin, U.S., 227
Thresher, USS (submarine), 99, 541
Throop College of Technology, 103
Throop Polytechnic Institute, 103
Throop University, 103
thumbscrew (punishment), 83
Thunder Alley (TV), 628
Thunder Bay Whiskey Jacks (baseball), 562
Thunder Bay, Canada, 365
Thunderbolt (amusement ride), 146
Thurber, James, 217
Thurmond, Strom, 644
Tibbets, Paul W. (Jr.), 717
Tibbett, Lawrence, 317
Tibet, 119, 121, 368
Ticonderoga, USS (carrier), 520
Tierney, Gene, 279
Tiffany Furnaces (company), 168
Tiffany Glass & Decorating Company, 168
Tiffany Glass Company, 168
Tiffany, Louis Comfort, 168

Tiffin Art Glass Company, 168
Tiffin Crystal (company), 168
Tiffin Glass Company, 168
Tiger Stadium (Detroit, Michigan), 556
Tigris (boat), 157
Tigrone, USS (submarine), 541, 712
Tilden, Samuel J., 111
Tilghman, William ("Bill"), 75
Tillamook (Native Americans), 432
Tillie (amusement park sign), 146
Tillie the Toiler (comic strip), 72
Tiltonsville Pottery Company, 164
Tim Tyler's Luck (comic strip), 72
Timbuktu, 121
Time (magazine), 463
Time to Smile (radio), 454
Tin Goose (aircraft), 36
Tin Lizzie. *See* Ford Model T
Tinker Field (Orlando, Florida), 559
Tinker, Joseph Bert ("Joe"), 566
Tinker-to-Evers-to-Chance trio, 566
tintypes, 439
Tiomkin, Dmitri, 308
Tippett, Sir Michael, 308
Tiru, USS (submarine), 541
Tishomingo (Chickasaw chief), 425
Titanic, RMS (liner), 96, 100
Titian, 21, 26
Titiryn, Peter, 481
Tito, Marshall (Yugoslavia), 408
To Anacreon in Heaven (song), 650
Toast of the Town (TV), 628
Tobacco Road (play*)*, 148
Tobago, HMS (frigate), 676
Tobias, George, 279
Today's Children (radio), 472
Togo, Republic of, 10, 117
Togoland, 415
Toho Cinema (New York, New York), 150
Tojo, Hideki, 720
Tokugawa shogunate, 389
Tokyo Telecommunications Engineering, 64
Tokyo War Crimes Trial, 720
Tokyo, Japan, 43
Toledo Blue Stockings (baseball), 562
Toledo Maroons (football), 596
Toler, Sidney, 279
Tolkien, J.R.R., 193, 217
Tolstoy, Leo, 217
Tom & Jerry (cartoon character), 66
Tom Breneman's Hollywood (radio), 450
Tom Corbett, Space Cadet (radio), 472
Tom Mix Ralston Straightshooters (radio), 472
Tomanawash, Robert (Wanapum tribal elder), 433
Tombaugh, Clyde W., 547

Tommy Riggs and Betty Lou (radio), 473
tomols (Chumash boats), 425
Tonawanda Kardex (football), 596
Tone, Franchot, 279
Tonedagana County, Michigan, 662
Tonga, Kingdom of, 117, 415
Tongass (schooner), 532
Tonight Show Starring Johnny Carson, The (TV), 173, 629
Tonight! with Steve Allen (TV), 629
Tonkin, Gulf of, 693
tonsure, 486
tontine, 88
Tony Wons' Scrapbook (radio), 473
Too Close for Comfort (TV), 629
Toonerville Folks (comic strip), 72
Toots and Casper (comic strip), 72
Topper (TV), 629
Torlonia, Alessandro, 133
Tormé, Mel, 67, 351
Toronto Arenas (ice hockey), 605
Toronto Blizzards (soccer), 608, 610
Toronto Blue Jays (baseball), 559
Toronto City (soccer), 610
Toronto Falcons (soccer), 610
Toronto Huskies (basketball), 579
Toronto Maple Leafs (ice hockey), 598, 600, 602, 605
Toronto Metros (soccer), 610
Toronto Metros-Croatia (soccer), 610
Toronto Saint Patricks (ice hockey), 605
Toronto, Ontario, 365
Toronto, Ontario (trolleys), 635
Torquemada, Tomás de, 487
Torsk, USS (submarine), 715
torture (punishment), 80, 83
Toscanini, Arturo, 317
Touched by an Angel (TV), 629
Toulouse-Lautrec, Henri de, 26
Touré, Samory, 382
Touré, Sekou, 382
Tower of London, 78
Towle Silversmiths, 168
Town Crier, The (radio), 473
Town Hall Tonight (radio), 456
Townes, Harry, 279
Towson State College, 108
Towson State University, 108
Towson University, 108
toys, 163
track and field (Olympic event), 607
Tracy, Lee, 279
Tracy, Spencer, 279
trade dollar coin, U.S., 226
Trafalgar Square (London, England), 18
Trafalgar, Battle of, 689
Trans America (airline), 48
Trans International Airways, 48
Trans States Airlines, Inc, 48
Trans World Airlines, 48

Trans-Alaska Pipeline, 123
Trans-Atlantic Flight, 1919, 57
Trans-Caribbean Airways (airline),
48
Transcaucasian Federation, 357, 358,
379
Transcaucasian Soviet Federated
Socialist Republic, 357, 379
Transcontinental & Western Air
(airline), 48
transistor, 118
Transjordan, 390
Trans-Lux (movie studio), 66
Transportation, Department of (U.S.),
639, 649
Transvaal, South Africa, 411, 678
Transwestern Airlines, 48
Trapper John, M.D. (TV), 629
Traubel, Helen, 317
Travers, Henry, 279
Traymore Hotel (Atlantic City, New
Jersey), 177
Treacher, Arthur, 279
treadwheel, (punishment), 83
Treasure Chest (comic strip), 73
Treasury Bill Certificates, U.S., 230
Treasury Bond Certificates, U.S., 230
Treasury Men in Action (TV), 629
Treasury Note Certificates, U.S., 230
Treasury Notes, U.S., 228, 229
Treaty of San Francisco (1952), 712
Treblinka (concentration camp), 710
Trelawny of the Well (play), 140
Trembles, Mary, 88
Tremont House (Galveston, Texas),
178
Trenholm, George Alfred, 680
Trent, Council of, 486
Trenton Business College, 107
Trenton State College, 104
Trenton, New Jersey (U.S. capital),
641
Trevor, Claire, 279, 449
Triangle Shirtwaist Company, 95
Triassic Period, 3
tribal dance, Ohlone, 430
Tri-City/Tri-Cities Blackhawks
(basketball), 578, 579
tricolor (French symbol), 376
Trinidad and Tobago, Republic of,
11, 117, 223, 415
Trinity College (Connecticut), 108
Trinity College (North Carolina), 104
Triple Alliance, War of the, 693
Tripler Hall (New York, New York),
152
Tripolitan War, 678
Triton, USS (submarine), 541
Triumph (automobile maker), 32
Triumph Acclaim (automobile), 32
Troadec, René, 366
trolleys, 635
Trollope, Anthony, 217

tropical storms, names for, 721
Troy, New York (trolleys), 635
Trucanini (or Truganini), 358
Trucial States, 418
True Detective (magazine), 473
True Detective Mysteries (radio), 473
True Story (magazine), 465
True Whig party (Liberia), 393
Truex, Ernest, 279
Truffaut, François, 241
Trujillo y Molina, Rafael Leonidas,
373
Trujillo, Juan Manuel de Cañas y,
369
Truman, Harry S., 443, 647, 651,
688, 699, 703, 713, 719, 720
Trumbo, Dalton, 217
Trumbull, Jonathan (Sr.), 657
Trump Shuttle (airline), 48
Trumpeter, HMS (carrier), 715
Trust Territory of the Pacific Islands,
396, 397, 402
Truth or Consequences (radio), 473
Tryon County, New York, 665
Tryon, William, 665
tsar, Russian, 405
Tsin (Chin) dynasty (China), 119
Tsushima Strait, Battle of, 690
Tualatin (Native Americans), 432
Tuality County, Oregon, 667
Tuchman, Barbara, 217
Tucker (automobile maker), 32
Tucker and Hemphill (company), 169
Tucker and Hulme (company), 169
Tucker Island (lighthouse), 192
Tucker Porcelain Company, 169
Tucker, Forrest, 279
Tucker, Preston, 32
Tucker, Richard, 317
Tucker, William Ellis, 169
Tudor, Anthony, 139
Tudor, House of, 419
Tufts College, 108
Tufts University, 108, 147
Tufts, Sonny, 279
tugboat (ship), 536
Tugboat Annie (movie), 536
Tulane University, 108
Tulane, Paul, 108
Tulare County, California, 13
Tulip Mania, 65
Tullibee, USS (submarine), 541
Tulsa Roughnecks (soccer), 610
Tuna, USS (submarine), 541
Tunisia, 10, 117
tunnels, 134
Tunney, Gene, 581, 583
Tupac Amaru, 361
Tupac Amaru (Inca leader), 120
Turbot, USS (submarine), 540
Turgenev, Ivan, 217
Turina, Joaquin, 308
Turkey, 8, 117, 184, 489, 690

Turkmen Soviet Socialist Republic,
417
Turkmenistan, Republic of, 117, 416
Turko-Italian War, 393
Turnbull, Sir Richard Gordon, 414
Turner Airlines, 48
Turner Field (Atlanta, Georgia), 554
Turner, Lana, 279
Turner, USS (ship), 99
Turner, William Thomas, 98
Turnesa brothers, 596
Turnpike Stadium (Arlington, texas),
553
Turpin, Ronald, 80
Tuscaloosa Institute, 108
Tuscaloosa, Alabama, 655
Tuscany, Duchy of, 5, 120
Tuscarora Wars, 674
Tuscaroras (Native Americans), 674
Tuskegee Airmen, 700
Tuskegee Study of Untreated
Syphilis in the Negro Male, 175
Tutelo (Native Americans), 431
Tuthill, Harry, 70
Tuttle, Lurene, 279
Tuvalu, 417
Tverdovsky, Oleg, 605
Twain, Mark, 3, 217, 222
Tweed Ring, 440
Tweed, Jack, 51
Tweed, William Marcy ("Boss
Tweed"), 440
Tweed-New Haven Airport
(Connecticut), 51
Tweety & Sylvester (cartoon
character), 66
Twelfth Night (play), 139, 142
Twentieth Century Limited (train),
483
Twentieth-Century Fox (movie
studio), 237
Twenty Eighth Cavalry, U.S. Army,
648
Twenty One Jump Street (TV), 629
Twenty Questions (radio), 473
Twenty Questions (TV), 629
Twenty Thousand Years in Sing Sing
(radio), 473
twenty-cent coin, U.S., 225
twenty-dollar coin, U.S. ("double
eagle"), 227
twenty-five cent, U.S. ("quarter"),
226
Twilight Zone, The (TV), 629
Twilly, Benjamin F., 652
Twin Peaks (TV), 629
Twin Zephyrs (train), 483
Twitty, Conway, 351
Two for the Money (radio), 473
Two Guys (store), 63
Two Guys and a Girl (TV), 629
Two Two Seven (TV), 629
two-and-a-half-dollar ("quarter

eagle") coins, U.S., 227
two-cent coin, U.S., 225
two-dollar bills, U.S., 229
Tyburn Tree, 81
Tyler, John, 695
typhoid fever, 172
Typhoid Mary, 172
Tyringham Shaker community, 488
U-116 (U-boat), 698
U-139 (U-boat), 698
U-2336 (U-boat), 714
U-234 (U-boat), 714
U-2540 (U-boat), 714
U-320 (U-boat), 715
U-3514 (U-boat), 715
U-505 (U-boat), 542, 714
U-534 (U-boat), 715
U-711 (U-boat), 714
U-853 (U-boat), 714
U-881 (U-boat), 714
U-977 (U-boat), 714
U-995 (U-boat), 714
Ubangi-Shari, 8, 365
U-boat (submarine), 542
Ubykh language (Turkey), 184
UCLA Bruins (basketball), 575
Udaina, Tuone, 183
Udina, Antonio, 183
Ueno, Battle at (Japan), 389
Uganda, 7, 117
Uganda, Republic of, 417
Ugly Duckling, The (cartoon), 66
Uhl Pottery (company), 169
Ui (!Ui) languages (South Africa), 183
Ukraine, 117, 417
Ukrainian Autonomous Soviet Socialist Republic, 397
Ukrainian People's Republic, 417
Ukrainian Soviet Socialist Republic, 417
Ulysses (novel), 97
Umm al-Qaiwain (emirate), 418
UN Trust Territories of the Pacific Islands, 671
Unabomber, 87
Un-American Activities, House Committee on, 644
Uncle Don (radio), 473
Uncle Ezra's Radio Station (radio), 473
Uncompahgre County, Colorado, 657
Under Arrest (radio), 473
Undset, Sigrid, 218
UNESCO, 132
unicameral legislature (Nebraska), 664
Unified Scientific Holdings, 27
Uniform Code of Military Justice, 647
Union Association (baseball), 561
Union Cable Railway (Kansas City, Missouri), 632

Union Canal, 131
Union County, South Dakota, 668
Union County, Tennessee, 668
Union Institute, 104
Union Labor party, 441
Union of Soviet Socialist Republics (USSR), 11, 417, 684, 690
Union Pacific Railroad, 477, 479
Union Pacific Railway Company, Southern Branch, 477
Union party, 443
Union Porcelain Company, 169
Union Porcelain Works, 169
Union Square Theater (New York, New York), 153
Union Stock Yards (Chicago, Illinois), 7
Union Trunk Line (Seattle, Washington), 633
Union Village Shaker community, 488
Unisphere, 160
United Air Lines, 35, 46, 47
United Air Lines Flight 175, 87
United Arab Emirates, 223, 418
United Arab Republic, 7, 10, 374, 413
United Artists (movie studio), 237
United Auto Workers, 27, 180
United Center (Chicago, Illinois), 573
United Farm Workers Organizing Committee (AFL-CIO), 180
United Kingdom, 10, 117, 224
United Kingdom of Great Britain, 420
United Kingdom of Great Britain and Ireland, 2, 6, 387, 420
United Kingdom of Great Britain and Northern Ireland, 418, 420
United Libyan Kingdom, 393
United Mexican States, 397
United Nations (UN), 10, 11, 389
United Nations Security Council, 687
United Productions of America (movie studio), 66
United Provinces of the Rio de la Plata, 420
United Rumanian Principalities, 405
United Soccer Association (USA), 608
United Society of Believers in Christ's Second Appearing, 487
United States, 10, 117, 224, 694, 695
United States Capitol (Washington, D.C.), 16, 17, 187
United States Consumer Product Safety Commission, 163
United States Football League (USFL), 586
United States Gazette (newspaper), 437
United States Glass Company, 168

United States Navy Yard (New York), 538
United States Notes, 228, 229
United States Phonograph Company, 437
United States Pottery Company, 169
United States Public Health Service, 175
United States service academies, 102
United States Supreme Court Building (Washington, D.C.), 17
United States v. Jefferson Davis, 679
United States Virgin Islands, 183
United States, USS (frigate), 524
United Telecommunication, 64
Universal Exposition of Saint Louis (Missouri), 160
Universal Instructor in all Arts and Sciences (newspaper), 436
Universal Studios, 65, 66, 237
University Hotel (New York, New York), 176
University of the Arts, 108
University of the Sciences in Philadelphia, 108
unlimited substitutions (football), 587
Until the Final Hour: Hitler's Last Secretary (book), 706
Untouchables, The (TV), 629
Unwattin County, Michigan, 662
Upper Canada, 364
Upper Ferry Bridge (Philadelphia, Pennsylvania), 127
Upper Peru, 361
Upper Senegal, 395
Upper Volta, 9, 10
Upper Volta, Republic of, 363
Urban VIII, Pope, 60
Urga, Mongolia, 398
Ursella, Rube, 587, 595
Uruguay, 117, 544, 693
Uruguay, Eastern Republic of, 420
US Cellular Park (Chicago, Illinois), 555
USAir (airline), 46, 48
USAir Shuttle (airline), 48
USAir/US Airways Arena (Landover, Maryland), 574
Ustinov, Sir Peter, 279
Utah, 112, 185, 669
Utah Jazz (basketball), 579
Utah Stars (basketball), 580
Utah State Agricultural College, 108
Utah State University, 108
Utah State University of Agriculture and Applied Science, 108
Utah Territory, 485, 664, 669
Utah, USS (battleship), 510
Utrecht (Netherlands province), 11
Utrecht, Treaty of, 690, 692
Utrecht, Union of, 11
Uzbek Soviet Socialist Republic, 421

Uzbekistan, Republic of, 117, 420
V-2 rocket, 708
Vaalbooi, Elsie, 183
Väinö I, King (Finland), 376
Vaiont (Vajont) Dam, 94
Valcour Island, Battle of, 676
Valens, Ritchie, 351
Valentine, Jack, 580
Valentino, Rudolph, 279
Valiant Lady (radio), 473
Vallee, Rudy, 469
Valley City Street and Cable Railway
  (Grand Rapids, Michigan), 632
Valley Forge, Pennsylvania, 675
Valley Forge, USS (carrier), 520
Valois, House of (France), 376
ValuJet (airline), 48
Van Bueren Studio, 66
Van Buren County, Missouri, 663
Van Buren, Martin, 440, 441
van Buren, Raeburn, 70
Van Cleef, Lee, 279
Van Dine, S.S., 467
Van Dyck, Anthony, 26
Van Dyke, Woodbridge S., 241
Van Gogh, Vincent, 26
Van Meter, Homer, 85
Van Winkle, Rip, 141
Vancouver Canadians (soccer), 610
Vancouver Canucks (ice hockey),
  603
Vancouver County, Washington, 670
Vancouver Island, Canada, 365
Vancouver Royals (soccer), 610
Vancouver Whitecaps (soccer), 610
Vancouver, Canada, 365
Vandalia, Illinois, 659
Vandals, 122
Vanderbilt Theater (New York, New
  York), 153
Vanguard III (space satellite), 551
Vanguard, HMS (ship), 502
Vanuatu, Republic of, 117, 421
Vanzetti, Bartolomeo, 76
Vardar, Banovina of, 394
Varley, Frederick, 21
Varney Air Lines, 48
Varney, Jim, 279
Vasa (sailing ship), 522
Vasa, House of, 413
Vasconcellos e Sousa, Pedro de, 362
vassals, 119, 179
Vassar College, 108
Vassar Female College, 108
Vaterland (liner), 531
Vatican Belt, 230
Vatican II, 487
Vatican, State of the (Vatican City),
  421
Vatthana, Sri Savang, 392
Vaughan Williams, Ralph, 308
Vaughan, Sarah, 352
Vaughan, Stevie Ray, 352

Vaughn de Leath Show, The (radio),
  473
Vaughn Monroe Show (radio), 450
Vaughn, Norman, 154
Vault of Horror (comic strip), 73
V-E (Victory in Europe) Day, 705
Veeck, Bill, 570
Veidt, Conrad, 279
Velez, Lupe, 280
Velluti, Giovanni, 318
Velocette (motorcycle maker), 236
Veloso, António Elisio Capelo Pires,
  408
Velvet Revolution, 371
Venera 16 (space probe), 551
Venezuela, 9, 117, 182, 184, 544
Venezuela, Republic of, 421
Ventian Period, 2
Venture (store), 63
Vera-Ellen, 280
Verdi, Giuseppe, 309
Vereeniging, Treaty of, 678
Vermont, 545, 669
Vermont, Republic of, 669
Vermont, USS (battleship), 511
Vermont, USS (sailing ship), 523
Verne, Jules, 218
Vernon County, Wisconsin, 670
Vernon Kilns (company), 169
Vernon Potteries, 169
Verrazano Narrows Bridge (New
  York, New York), 125, 126
Versailles, Treaty of, 41, 698, 700
Vespa (motorscooter maker), 233
Veterans Administration, U.S., 639
Veterans Day, 175
Veterans Readjustment Assistance
  Act (1952), 688
Veterans Stadium (Philadelphia,
  Pennsylvania), 558
Veterans' Affairs, U.S. Department
  of, 677
Vic and Sade (radio), 473
Vic Jordan (comic strip), 73
Vichy government (France), 377, 705
Vicious, Sid, 348
Vickers-Supermarine Spitfire
  (aircraft), 45
Victor Borge Show, The (radio), 474
Victor Emmanuel III, King (Italy),
  356, 388
Victor Talking Machine Company,
  63, 64
Victoria (Magellan's ship), 158
Victoria (theater, New York, New
  York), 151
Victoria Luise (liner), 527
Victoria Theater (New York, New
  York), 153
Victoria, Queen (England), 6, 419
Victorian Age, 2, 6
Victory Chimes (schooner), 533
Victory Parade of Spotlight Bands,

The (radio), 470
Victory Pictures (movie studio), 237
Victory ships, 713
Victory, HMS (sailing ship), 522
Vidor, King, 241
Vieira, João Bernardo, 382
Vienna Philharmonic, 318
Viet Cong, 693
Viet Minh, 687
Viet Nam, Empire of, 422
Vietnam, 8, 117, 693
Vietnam War, 693
Vietnam, Socialist Republic of, 421
Viking (sailing ship), 498
Viking 1 (space probe), 551
Viking 2 (space probe), 552
Viking ship (Chicago, Illinois), 161
Villa Borghese (Rome, Italy), 22
Villa Park (Columbus Ohio), 144
Villa Vallee (radio), 469
Villa, Francisco ("Pancho"), 397, 648
Villa-Lobos, Heitor, 309
Vilner, Meir, 388
Vincennes, Indiana, 659
Vincent (motorcycle maker), 236
Vincent, Phillip C., 236
Vine Street Cable Railway
  (Cincinnati, Ohio), 632
Vineland Flint Glass (company), 165
Viper, USS (submarine), 539
Virgin Islands, 671
Virginia, 186, 490, 545, 669
Virginia Agricultural and Mechanical
  College, 108
Virginia Agricultural and Mechanical
  College and Polytechnic Institute,
  108
Virginia and Truckee Railroad, 482
Virginia Central (railroad), 476
Virginia City, Montana, 664
Virginia Collegiate Institute, 107
Virginia Company of London, 641
Virginia Military Institute (VMI),
  102
Virginia Polytechnic and State
  University, 108
Virginia Polytechnic Institute, 109
Virginia Slims (cigarette
  commercial), 173
Virginia Squires (basketball), 580
Virginia, CSS (armor clad ship), 682
Virginia, USS (battleship), 511
Virginian, The (TV), 629
Visigoths, 404
Visit, The (play), 141
Vitagraph (New York, New York),
  151
Vivaldi, Antonio, 309
Vogt, Reidel, 582
Vogue (magazine), 222
Voice of Firestone (radio), 473, 474
Voice of the Turtle, The (play), 148
Voisin (automobile maker), 32

Voisin, Gabriel, 32
Volkov, Vladislav, 549
Volkswagen (automobile maker), 28, 31
Volkswagen Beetle, 34
Volkswagen Rabbit, 34
Volstead Act, 185
Volta, Alessandro, 497
Voltaire, 218
von Rundstedt, Karl, 701
Von Steuben, USS (ship), 529
Voortrekkers, 678
Vorontsov, Yuli M., 418
Voskhod 2 (space flight), 549
Voss, Carl, 605
Vostok 1 (space flight), 550
Vostok 6 (space flight), 550
voting age, 110
Voting Right March (Mongomery, Alabama), 68
Voting Rights Act, 111
Vought F4U Corsair (aircraft), 45, 700
Vought F4U-5 Corsair (aircraft), 37
Vought F-8 Crusader (aircraft), 46
Vox Pop (radio), 474
Voyage of Scarlet Queen, The (radio), 474
Voyager 1 (space probe), 552
Voyager 2 (space probe), 552
W.T. Grant (store), 63
Wabasee County, Michigan, 662
Wabash Cannon Ball (train), 483
Wabash Pittsburgh Terminal Railroad, 478
Wabash Railroad Company, 479
Wabash, St. Louis & Pacific Railway, 479
Wabaunsee County, Kansas, 660
WAC, U.S. Army, 649
Wachovia Center (Philadelphia, Pennsylvania), 574
Waddell, James I., 680
wages, 181
Wages and Hours Act, 179
Wagner, Richard, 309
Wagon Train (TV), 629
Wahkaw County, Iowa, 660
Wailer, Bunny, 340
Wailers, The, 340
Waimarie (paddle steamer), 535
Waka Waka language (Australia), 184
Wake Forest College, 109
Wake Forest Manual Labor Institute, 109
Wake Forest University, 109
Wake Island Avenger (aircraft), 40
Wake Island, Battle of, 703
Walachia (principality), 405
Walburn, Raymond, 280
Walcott, Jersey Joe, 583
Waldo, Daniel, 677

Waldorf Astoria Hotel (New York, New York), 178
Waldorf Theater (New York, New York), 153
Wales, 13, 418, 489
Walesa, Lech, 404
Walker, Barbara Jo, 147
Walker, Mort, 70, 74
Walker, Moses Fleetwood ("Fleet"), 562
Walker, Nancy, 280
Walker, Red, 138
Walker, Robert, 280
Walker, T-Bone, 352
Walker, Welday Wilberforce, 562
Walking Liberty half dollar, U.S., 226
Wall, Lucille, 467
Wallace, George, 69
Wallace, Reginald James, 391
Wallack's (theater, New York, New York), 151
Wallenberg, Raoul, 90
Waller, Thomas ("Fats"), 309
Wallowa (tugboat), 536
Walsh, Annie, 81
Walsh, Chile, 595
Walsh, J.T., 280
Walsh, Jill Paton, 213
Walsh, Raoul, 241
Walston, Ray, 280
Walt Disney (movie studio), 65, 66
Walter Gropius School (Berlin, Germany), 17
Walter Winchell Show, The (radio), 474
Walter, Bruno, 317
Walters, Vernon Anthony, 380
Waltham Abbey (Essex, England), 484
Walton, Sir William, 309
Waltons, The (TV), 629
Waltrip, Michael, 553
Walvis Bay, Namibia, 399
Wambsganss, William Adolph ("Bill"), 571
Wampanoags (Native Americans), 432, 672
wampum beads, 230
wampum belts, 230
Wanamaker, John, 160
Wanapum (Native Americans), 433
Wanarring, Australia, 611
Wanderer (slave ship), 547
Wanted—Dead or Alive (TV), 629
Wapama (schooner), 532
Wappo (Native Americans), 433
War & Pieces (cartoon), 66
War Between the States, 679
War Department, U.S., 640
War Eagle (Sioux chief), 431
War Finance Corporation, 699
War Industries Board, 699

War Information, Office of (OWI), 637, 719
War Manpower Commission (WMC), 637, 719
War Memorial Stadium (Greensboro, North Carolina), 558
War Mobilization and Reconversion, Office of, 719
War of 1812, 187, 694
War of the Rebellion, 681
War Production Board (WPB), 717, 718, 719
War Relief Control Board (WRCB), 720
War Savings Bonds, U.S., 230
War Savings Stamps, U.S., 230
War Time, 631
Waratah (ship), 92
Ward, Jimmy, 603
Waring, Fred, 352
Warner Brothers (movie studio), 65, 66, 67, 237
Warner Theater (Atlantic City, New Jersey), 147
Warner, Charles D., 3
Warren and Wetmore (architects), 177
Warren, Clinton, 177
Warren, Earl, 652
Warren, Francis E., 670
Warren, Harry, 309
Warren, Robert Penn, 218
Warrington, Lewis, 694
Warrosquyoake County, Virginia, 670
Warrungu language (Australia), 184
Warsaw Pact, 11
Warsaw Treaty Organization, 11
Warsaw, Duchy of, 404
Warwick China Company, 169
Wash Tubbs (comic strip), 73
Washburn, William, 176
washers, hand-operated, 223
Washington (state), 112, 670
Washington Academy, 109
Washington and Georgetown Railroad (Washington, D.C.), 634
Washington and Jefferson College, 109
Washington and Lee University, 109
Washington Bullets (basketball), 580
Washington Capitals (ice hockey), 602
Washington Capitols (basketball), 580
Washington Caps (basketball), 580
Washington College, 108, 109
Washington College (Washington and Lee University), 679
Washington County, Iowa, 660
Washington County, New York, 665
Washington County, Oregon, 667
Washington County, Rhode Island,

Notable Last Facts

Western Illinois Normal School, 109
Western Illinois State Teachers College, 109
Western Illinois University, 109
Western Kentucky State College, 109
Western Kentucky State Normal School, 109
Western Kentucky State Normal School and Teachers College, 109
Western Kentucky State Teachers College, 109
Western Kentucky University, 109
Western Michigan College, 109
Western Michigan College of Education, 109
Western Michigan University, 109
Western Pacific Railroad, 482
Western Printing and Lithographing Company, 73
Western Reserve College, 103
Western Samoa, 407
Western State Normal School, 109
Western State Teachers College, 109
Western Union (schooner), 531
Westminster Cinema (New York, New York), 152
Westminster, Abbey of St. Peter, 149
Westmount Arena (Montreal), 603
Weston, Jack, 280
Westover, Russ, 72
Westphalia, Treaty of, 693
Westside Park (Chicago, Illinois), 555
Westward Ho! (clipper ship), 499
wet collodion process (photography), 439
Wexford County, Michigan, 662
Wexler, Payne, 73
Whale Rock (lighthouse), 192
whaler (ship), 536
whales, 12
Wharton, Edith, 219
What a Life! (radio), 447
What's My Line? (TV), 474, 629
What's My Lion? (cartoon), 66
What's My Name? (radio), 474
What's the Name of That Song? (radio), 474
Wheatie one-cent coin, U.S. (Lincoln with wheat back), 225
Wheaton Glass (company), 168
Wheeler-Nicholson, 73
Wheeling Pottery Company, 164
Wheeling, West Virginia, 670
When a Girl Marries (radio), 474
wherry (ship), 536
Whig party, 440, 442, 443, 651
whipping post (punishment), 83
Whirl of Life (movie), 136
Whiskey Rebellion, 695
Whispering Streets (radio), 474
Whistler, The (radio), 474

Whitaker, Steve, 570
White Front (store), 63
White House, 653
White Moth (sailing yacht), 536
White Pass & Yukon Route Railroad, 482
White Sox Park (Chicago, Illinois), 555
White Star Line, 100, 538
White Water Shaker community, 488
White, Al, 44
White, Benjamin F., 664
White, E.B., 219
White, Jesse, 280
White, John, 642
White, Robert T., 693
White, Stanford, 18
Whiteman, Paul, 353, 467
Whitman, Walt, 219
Whitmer, David, 485
Whitney, Caspar, 583
Whitney's Playland-at-the-Beach (San Francisco, California), 145
Whittier, John Greenleaf, 219
Whitty, Dame May, 280
Who, The, 353
Who's the Boss? (TV), 629
whooping crane, 13
Wichita Wings (soccer), 608
Wicker, Ireene, 470
Wickes, Mary, 280
Wickford Harbor (lighthouse), 192
Wickham County, North Carolina, 666
Wickham, Williams C., 480
Widener College, 109
Widener University, 109
wigs, 162
Wilberforce, William, 484
Wilcoxon, Henry, 281
Wild Bill Hickok (radio), 474
Wild Bunch, The, 84
Wild Horse (Wampanoag chief), 432
Wild West Show (Cody), 143
Wild, Wild West (TV), 630
Wilde, Cornel, 281
Wilde, Oscar, 219
Wilder, Laura Ingalls, 219
Wilder, Billy, 242
Wilder, R.A., 481
Wilder, Thornton, 219
Wilding, Michael, 281
Wile E. Coyote & Road Runner (cartoon character), 66
Wiles, Andrew, 497
Wilhelm Bauer (submarine), 714
Wilhelm II, Kaiser (Germany), 379
Wilimette, USS (ship), 96
Wilkins, Roy, 68
Wilkins, William, 720
Will Rogers, USS (submarine), 542
Willapa Bay (lighthouse), 192
Willard Hotel (Washington, D.C.),

178
Willard, Frank, 72
William and Mary University, 101
William Boch and Brothers (company), 169
William Cramp & Sons Ship & Engine Building Company (Pennsylvania), 539
William H. Gratwick House (Buffalo, New York), 19
William L. Douglas (schooner), 533
William Libbey & Son (company), 167
William Marsh Rice University, 107
William the Conqueror, 78, 419
William Young and Company, 170
William, Duke of Gloucester, 419
Williams, Al, 138
Williams, Emlyn, 281
Williams, Hank, 354
Williams, Hubert, 696
Williams, J.R., 72
Williams, John J., 681
Williams, Magdalene, 183
Williams, Mary Lou, 354
Williams, Mrs. Cecil, 173
Williams, Otis, 351
Williams, Paul, 351
Williams, Rhys, 281
Williams, Ted, 566, 570
Williams, Tennessee, 219
Williams, Walter Washington, 683
Williams, William Carlos, 219
Williamsburg Bridge (New York, New York), 125
Williamsburg, Virginia, 669
Williamson, John R., 101
Willington, Delaware, 657
Willow Grove Park (Pennsylvania), 145
Wills, Chill, 281
Willys Motor Company, 33
Willys Motors Ltd., 33
Willys, John North, 33
Willys-Overland (automobile maker), 30, 33
Wilmott, William, 675
Wilson, Jackie, 354
Wilson, Marie, 281, 465
Wilson, Woodrow, 113, 228, 645, 654
Winchell, A. Walter, 702
Winchester Mystery House (San Jose, California), 61
Winding, Kai, 354
Windolph, Charles A., 672
Windows on the World restaurant (New York, New York), 491
Windriver (U.S. Army mule), 648
Windsor (sailing ship), 500
Windsor Theater (New York, New York), 151
Windsor, Marie, 281

Windward Islands colony, 372
Wingate, Paine, 643
Wings (movie), 237
Wings (TV), 630
Winner Take All (radio), 474
Winnie Winkle (comic strip), 73
Winninger, Charles, 281
Winnipeg Jets (ice hockey), 605
Winnipeg, Canada, 365
Winston County, Alabama, 655
Winston Cup (automobile race), 553
Winter Garden Theater (New York, New York), 152
Winter War, 376
Winters, Roland, 281
Winterset (play), 76
Winwood, Estelle, 281
Wirz, Henry, 679
Wisconsin, 545, 670
Wisconsin Center (Milwaukee, Wisconsin), 574
Wisconsin Central (railroad), 477, 479
Wisconsin Central Airlines, 49
Wisconsin State Capitol (Madison), 19
Wisconsin Territory, 659, 662, 670
Wisconsin, USS (battleship), 511
Wise County, Kansas, 660
Wise, John, 55
Wise, Karl, 31
Wistar Glass (company), 170
Wistar, Caspar, 170
Wistarburgh (company), 170
Witch's Tale, The (radio), 474
witchcraft, 88
Witchcraft Act, 88
Witmer, Lightner, 174
Wiyot (Native Americans), 433
Wiz, The (show), 148
WKRP in Cincinnati (TV), 630
Wm. B. Tennison (sailing ship), 498
Wodehouse, P.G., 219, 223
Wogglebug (steam-powered automobile), 553
Wolanin, Craig, 605
Wolf Guts, Clarence, 716
Wolf Island (lighthouse), 192
Wolf, Hugo, 310
Wolfe, Thomas, 219
Wolff, Albert H., 75
Wolseley (automobile maker), 33
Wolseley Princess (automobile), 33
wolves, 13
Woman Citizen (magazine), 223
Woman in My House, The (radio), 474
Woman in White, The (radio), 474
Woman of America (radio), 475
Woman of Courage (radio), 475
Woman's Christian Union (Chicago, Illinois), 19
Woman's College of Baltimore, 105

Woman's College of Baltimore City, 105
Woman's College of Frederick, 105
Woman's Home Companion (magazine), 223
Women Accepted for Voluntary Emergency Service (WAVES), 650
Women's Armed Service Integration Act, 649
Women's Army Auxiliary Corps (WAAC), 649
Women's Army Corps (WAC), 649
Women's Journal, 223
women's rights, 69
women's suffrage (Canada), 112
women's suffrage (United States), 112
women's suffrage (worldwide), 113
Wonder Woman (TV), 630
Wonder Years, The (TV), 630
Wong, Anna May, 281
Wons, Tony, 473
Wood Buffalo National Park, 13
Wood, Bob, 71
Wood, Edward D. (Jr.), 242
Wood, Grant, 27
Wood, John T., 133
Wood, Natalie, 281
Wood, Peggy, 281
Wood, Sam, 242
Wood, Waddy Butler, 20
Wood, Wally, 72
Wood's Museum (New York, New York), 150
Woodbury County, Iowa, 660
Woodbury Program, The (radio), 449
Woodhull, Victoria, 442
Woodley Airways, 49
Woodstock Park (Nashville, Tennessee), 144
Woodward Field (Salt Lake City, Utah), 51
Woodward, John P., 51
Woody Woodpecker (cartoon character), 66, 67
Woolco (store), 63
Woolf, Virginia, 192, 220
Woollcott, Alexander, 473
Woolley, Monty, 281, 463
Woolson, Albert Henry, 683
Woolworth (store), 63
Wordsworth, William, 220
worker's compensation insurance, 182
Working Women (magazine), 223
Workman, Hoge, 590
Works Progress Administration (WPA), 637
Works Projects Administration (WPA), 637, 654
World Federation of Trade Unions, 181

World Football League (WFL), 586
World Health Organization, 171
World Series (baseball), 572
World Theater (New York, New York), 152
World Today (magazine), 221
World War I, 2, 4, 5, 38, 40, 55, 230, 231, 695
World War II, 35, 38, 41, 45, 230, 356, 358, 362, 377, 379, 396, 699
World Wrestling Federation, 586
World's Columbian Exposition (Chicago, Illinois), 161, 180, 681
World's Fair Hop (dance), 136
World's Great Novels (radio), 466
Worth, Irene, 281
Worthington, Henry Clay, 653
Worthington, Henry Gaither, 653
Wotherspoon, Adella, 97
Wounded Knee, Battle of, 674
Wreck of the Edmund Fitzgerald (song), 96
Wren, Sir Christopher, 20, 149
Wright Flyer I ("Kitty Hawk") (aircraft), 55
Wright Flyer II (aircraft), 56
Wright Flyer III (aircraft), 56
Wright, Frank Lloyd, 20, 176
Wright, James, 658
Wright, Orville, 56
Wright, Richard, 220
Wright, Russell, 168
Wright, USS (carrier), 520
Wright, Wilbur, 55
Wright-Patterson Air Force Base, Dayton, Ohio, 361
Wrigley Field (Chicago, Illinois), 555
Wrigley Field (Los Angeles, California), 557
Wrigley, Philip K., 560
Wrigley, William (Jr.), 555, 561
writing systems, 11
Wunderlich, Fritz, 317
Wyandot (Native Americans), 433
Wye, Valentina, 183
Wyler, William, 242
Wynette, Tammy, 354
Wynn, Ed, 454
Wynn, Keenan, 281
Wyoming (schooner), 533
Wyoming (state), 112, 670
Wyoming Massacre, 674
Wyoming Territory, 112, 670
Wyoming, USS (battleship), 512
Wyoming, USS (sailing ship), 683
X Files (TV), 630
X Minus One (radio), 453, 475
Xerxes, 134
Xtreme Football League (XFL), 586
yachting (Olympic event), 607
Yahi (Native Americans), 433
Yale Center for British Art (New

Haven, Connecticut), 17
Yale College, 109
Yale University, 101, 109
Yale, Elihu, 109
Yalta War Conference (Crimea, Ukrainian SSR), 704
Yamaha-engine trail bikes, 233
Yamakura shogunate, 389
Yamasee (Native Americans), 674
Yamasee War, 674
Yanam, India, 8, 386
Yang Chien, 119
Yang Kuang, 119
Yankonan (Native Americans), 432
Yankton Sioux (Native Americans), 431
Yankton, South Dakota, 666, 668
Yao Wenyuan, 367
Yaquina (Native Americans), 432
Yarmouth Castle (ship), 99
Yavitero language (Venezuela), 184
Yayoi period (Japan), 389
Yaztrzemski, Carl, 564
Yeats, William Butler, 220
Yee, Mary (Chumash speaker), 425
Yellow Coach trolley, Model 1208, 635
yellow fever, 172
Yellow Hair (Cheyenne chief), 143
Yellow Kid (comic strip), 73
Yellowstone Park, 12
Yeltsin, Boris, 406, 684
Yemen, 544
Yemen (People's Democratic Republic), 117
Yemen Arab Republic, 117, 422
Yemen Dam, 94
Yemen, People's Democratic Republic of, 422
Yemen, Republic of, 422
Yerington, Henry M., 482
Yi Ch'ok, Emperor (Korea), 391
Yi dynasty (Korea), 391
Yi Pangja, Princess (Korea), 391
Yi Un, Emperor (Korea), 391
Yokel Boy (play), 460
Yokoi, Shoichi, 712
Yom Kippur War, 123
Yoritomo, 389
York County, Virginia, 670
York, Dick, 281
York, House of, 419, 690
York, Pennsylvania (U.S. capital), 640
Yorktown, USS (carrier), 521, 702
Yosemite Sam (cartoon character), 66
You Are There (radio), 475
You Bet Your Life (radio), 475
You Bet Your Life (TV), 630
You Can't Take It With You (play), 142
Young Dr. Malone (radio), 475

Young Pretender, 419
Young Romance (comic strip), 73
Young Widder Brown (radio), 475
Young, Anthony, 567
Young, Brigham, 491
Young, Chic, 449
Young, Doc, 592
Young, Eliza Burgess, 485
Young, Gig, 281
Young, John W., 548
Young, Lester, 355
Young, Loretta, 281
Young, Lyman, 72
Young, Robert, 282, 454
Young, Roland, 282
Young, Sam, 688
Young, Victor, 310
Young, Whitney, 68
Younger, Bob, 86
Younger, Cole, 86
Younger, Jim, 86
Younger, John, 86
Your Hit Parade (radio), 455, 475
Your Hit Parade (TV), 630
Your Show of Shows (TV), 630
Yours Truly, Johnny Dollar (radio), 475
Yüan dynasty, 119
Yugoslavia, 117
Yugoslavia, Socialist Federal Republic of, 394
Yugoslavia, Federal People's Republic of, 410
Yugoslavia, Federal Republic of, 409
Yugoslavia, Kingdom of, 361, 370, 394, 408
Yugoslavia, Socialist Federal Republic of, 408
Zaharias, "Babe" Didrikson, 596
Zaire, Republic of, 369
Zambia, 8, 79, 117, 223, 422
Zanesville Art Pottery, 170
Zanzibar, 7, 9, 414, 545
Zanzibar and Pemba, 544
Zappa, Frank, 355
Zayre (store), 63
Zebu (sailing ship), 498
Zeeland (Netherlands province), 11
Zelaya, Juan Nepomuceno Fernández Con Lindo y, 374
Zeppelin Company, 52
Zeppelins, last raid, 696
Zero Hour, The (radio), 475
Zero, (aircraft), 43
Zeus, Temple of, 134
Zhukov, Georgi, 705
Ziegfeld Follies of the Air (radio), 448, 460, 475
Ziegfeld Theater (New York, New York), 153
Ziegfeld, Florenz, 150, 475
Zimbabwe, 8, 79, 117, 423
Zimbabwe Rhodesia, 423

Zinnemann, Fred, 242
Zinser, Gerard, 718
ZIP +4 system, 445
ZIP, Mr., 445
Zita, Empress (Austria), 358
ZMC-2 (Zeppelin Metal-Clad 2) (airship), 54
Zoarville Station Bridge (Zoarville, Ohio), 126
Zog I, King (Albania), 356
Zola, Emile, 220
Zoning Improvement Plan (ZIP Code), 445
Zoomorphic buildings, 15
Zorro (TV), 630
ZR 2 (airship), 93
ZR 3 (airship), 51
Zuber, William Physick, 668
Zuckert, Eugene M., 647
Zuius, Andrew, 188
Zulu War, 411
Zululand, 411
Zumbrota Bridge (Minnesota), 124
Zundapp (motorcycle maker), 236
Zungul, Steve, 608
Zweirad Union (manufacturer), 233

References (Books)

Abraham, Gerald, *Slavonic and Romantic Music.* New York, NY: St. Martin's Press, Inc., 1968.

Abrams, M.H., *A Glossary of Literary Terms.* New York. NY: Holt, Rinehart and Winston, 1961.

Anderson, John, *Last Survivors in Sail.* London, England: Percival Marshall & Co., 1948.

Andrews, Wayne (editor), Thomas C. Cochran (advisory editor), *Concise Dictionary of American History.* New York, NY: Charles Scribner's Sons, 1962.

Applegate, Ray D., *Trolleys and Streetcars on American Picture Postcards.* New York, NY: Dover Publications, Inc., 1979.

Ashley, Maurice, *England in the Seventeenth Century.* Baltimore, MD: Penguin Books, 1972.

Asimov, Isaac, *Isaac Asimov's Book of Facts.* New York, NY: Bell Publishing Company, 1979.

Attwater, Donald, *A Catholic Dictionary.* New York. NY: The Macmillan Company, 1961.

Avasthi, Smita, *Day by Day: The Nineties* (2 vols.). New York, NY: Facts on File, 2003.

Baker, David, *Flight and Flying–A Chronology.* New York, NY: Facts on File, 1994.

Ballard, Robert D., and Richard Archbold, *Lost Liners: From the Titanic to the Andrea Doria.* New York. NY: Hyperion, 1997.

Ballard, Robert D., with Richard Archbold. Introduction by Ludovic Kennedy, *The Discovery of the Bismarck.* Toronto, Canada: Madison Press Books, 1990.

Beaver, Patrick, *A History of Tunnels,* Secaucus, NJ: Citadel Press, 1973.

Beck, Jerry and Will Friedwald. *Warner Bros. Animation Art: The Characters, the Creators, the Limited Editions.* New York, NY: Hugh Lauten Levin Associates, 1997.

Beckson, Karl, and Arthur Ganz, *Literary Terms, A Dictionary.* New York, NY: The Noonday Press, div. of Farrar, Straus and Giroux, 1989.

Benét, William Rose, *The Reader's Encyclopedia* (2 vols.). New York, NY: Thomas Y. Crowell Company, 1965.

Bergan, Ronald, *The United Artists Story.* New York, NY: Crown Publishers, Inc., 1986.

Berliner, Barbara, with Melinda Corey and George Ochoa, *The Book of Answers: The New York Public Library Telephone Reference Service's Most Unusual and Entertaining Questions.* New York, NY: Fireside/ Simon & Schuster, 1990.

Bickers, Richard Townshend, *The Battle of Britain.* New York, NY: Prentice Hall Press, 1990.

Biographical Directory of the American Congress, 1774-1949, The Continental Congress September 5, 1774, to October 21, 1788, and The Congress of the United States From the First to the Eightieth Congress March 4, 1789, to January 3, 1949, Inclusive. Washington, DC: United States Government Printing Office, 1950.

Black, Henry Campbell, *Black's Law Dictionary.* St. Paul, MN: West Publishing Co., 1979.

Bowen, Catherine Drinker, *Miracle at Philadelphia.* Boston, MA: Little, Brown and Company, 1966.

Boylan, Henry, *A Dictionary of Irish Biography.* Dublin, Ireland: Gill & Macmillan, 1998.

Brewer's Dictionary of Twentieth-Century Phrase and Fable. Boston, MA: Houghton Mifflin Company, 1992.

Bridgwater, William, and Seymour Kurtz, *The Columbia Encyclopedia.* New York. NY: Columbia University Press, 1963.

Britannica Book of the Year Chicago, IL: Encyclopedia Britannica, Inc., 1942–1992.

Brooks, John, *The Fate of the Edsel & Other Business Adventures.* New York, NY: Harper, & Row, Publishers, 1963.

Brooks, Tim, and Earle Marsh, *Complete Dictionary to Prime Time Network and Cable TV*

Shows, 1946-Present. New York, NY: Ballantine Books, 1999.

Brown, David J*., Bridges*, New York, NY: The Macmillan Company, 1993.

Brown, Richard C., *The Human Side of American History.* Boston, MA: Ginn and Company, 1962.

Brown, Roland, *The Encyclopedia of Motorcycles: The Complete Book of Motorcycles and Their Riders.* London, England: Hermes House, 1997.

Brunch, Bryan (editor), *The Science Almanac.* Garden City, NY: Anchor Books, Anchor Press/Doubleday, 1984.

Brunner, Borgna (editor-in-chief), *Time Almanac 2003, with Information Please.* New York, NY: Time Inc. Home Entertainment, 2002.

Burnam, Tom, *The Dictionary of Misinformation.* New York, NY: Harper & Row, Publishers, 1975.

Bulletin Almanacs (Philadelphia). Philadelphia, PA: The Bulletin Company, 1929-1976.

Burrill, Bob, *Who's Who in Boxing,* New Rochelle, NY: Arlington House, 1974.

Byrd, Robert C. (chairman), *A Necessary Fence, The Senate's First Century.* Washington, DC: Government Printing Office, 1989.

California Information Almanac. Garden City, NY: Doubleday Company, Inc., 1966.

Campbell, John P., *Campbell's High School/College Quiz Book.* Columbus, GA: Patrick's Press, 1984.

Canaday, John, *Mainstreams of Modern Art.* New York, NY: Simon and Schuster, Inc., 1959.

Cannon, John, and Ralph Griffiths, *The Oxford Illustrated History of the British Monarchy.* New York, NY: Oxford University Press, 1989.

Carey, John (editor), *Eyewitness to History.* New York, NY: Avon Books, 1990.

Carruth, Gorton, *Encyclopedia of American Facts & Dates.* New York, NY: Harper & Row, Publishers, 1987.

Catholic Encyclopedia Dictionary, The. New York, NY: The Gilmary Society [c1941].

Chronicles of America Series. New Haven, CT: Yale University Press, 1919.

Colin, Jose, *NASL: A Complete Record of The North American Soccer League.* Derby, England: Breedon Books, 1989.

Concise Oxford Dictionary of Linguistics, The. New York, NY: Oxford University Press, 1997.

Connolly, S.J. (editor), *The Oxford Companion to Irish History.* Oxford, England: Oxford University Press, 1998.

Connors, Martin, and Jim Craddock (editors), *Videohound's Golden Movie Book.* Detroit, MI: Visible Ink Press, Div. Gale Research, 1999.

Corey, Melinda, and George Ochoa, *American History: The New York Public Library Book of Answers.* New York, NY: Fireside/Simon & Schuster, 1994.

Cross, Milton, and David Ewen, *Encyclopedia of the Great Composers and Their Music* (2 vols.). Garden City, NY: Doubleday & Company, Inc.,1962.

Crutchfield, James, Bill O'Neal and Dale L. Walker*, Legends of the Wild West,* Lincolnwood, IL: Publications International, Ltd., 1995.

Crystal, David (editor), *Cambridge Factfinder.* Cambridge: Cambridge University Press, 2000.

Current Biography. New York, NY: H.W. Wilson Company, 1940-2003.

Cyclopaedia of American Biography. Detroit, MI: Gale Research Company, 1968.

Dabney, Virginius, *The Last Review: The Confederate Reunion, Richmond 1932.* Chapel Hill, NC: Algonquin Books, 1984.

Daniel, Clifton (editor-in-chief), *20th Century Day by Day.* New York, NY: Dorling Kindersley, 1999.

Davis, Franklin M., Jr., *Came as a Conqueror: U.S. Army's Occupation of Germany, 1945-*

46. New York, NY: The Macmillan Company, 1967.

Delgado, James P., and J. Candace Clifford, *Great American Ships*. Washington, DC: Preservation Press, 1991.

Del Re, Gerard, and Patricia, *History's Last Stand*. New York, NY: Avon Books, 1993.

DeLong, Thomas A., *Radio Stars: An Illustrated Biographical Dictionary of 953 Performers, 1920 through 1960*. Jefferson, NC: McFarland & Company, Inc., Publishers, 1996.

DeLony, Eric, *Landmark American Bridges,* Boston, MA: Bullfinch Press, 1993.

Dictionary of American Biography. New York, NY: Charles Scribner's Sons, 1946-1958, plus supplements.

Donald, David (general editor), *The Encyclopedia of Civil Aircraft*. San Diego, CA: Thunder Bay Press, 1999.

Ditzel, Paul C., *How They Built Our National Monuments*. New York, NY: Bobbs-Merrill, 1976.

Dominic, Zöe, and John Selwyn Gilbert, *Frederick Ashton: A Choreographer and His Ballets*. Chicago, IL: Henry Regnery Company, 1971.

Donald, David (general editor), *The Encyclopedia of Civil Aircraft*. San Diego, CA: Thunder Bay Press, 1999.

Dotz, Warren, *Advertising Character Collectibles: An Identification & Value Guide*. Paducah, KY: Collector Books, 1993.

Dunning, John, *Tune In Yesterday: The Ultimate Encyclopedia of Old-Time Radio 1925-1976*. Englewood Cliffs, NJ: Prentice-Hall, Inc., 1976.

Durant, Will and Ariel, *The Story of Civilization* (10 vols). New York, NY: Simon and Schuster, 1950.

Dupuy, Colonel R. Ernest, and Major General William H. Baumer, *The Little Wars of the United States*. New York, NY: Hawthorn Books, Inc., 1968.

Eco, Umberto, and G. B. Zorzoli, *The Picture History of Invention*. New York, NY: The Macmillan Company, 1963.

Elting, Mary, and Franklin Folsom, *The Answer Book of History*. New York, NY: Grosset & Dunlap Publishers, 1966.

Emerson, Edwin, Jr., *History of the 19th Century, Year by Year* (3 vols.). New York, NY: P. F. Collier and Son 1902.

Encyclopedia Americana (30 vols.). Danbury, CT: Grolier Incorporated, 1985.

Encyclopedia Britannica (11th edition). New York, NY: Encyclopedia Britannica, 1910

Encyclopedia of American Business History and Biography. New York, NY: Facts On File, 1990.

Essoe, Gabe, *The Book of TV Lists*. Westport, CT: Arlington House, 1981.

Ewen, David, *Encyclopedia of Concert Music*. New York, NY: Hill and Wang, 1959.

Ewen, David, *Musicians Since 1900: Performers in Concert and Opera*. New York, NY: H. W. Wilson, 1978,

Facts & Fallacies: Stories of the Strange and Unusual. Pleasantville, NY: The Reader's Digest Association, 1988.

Felton, Bruce, and Mark Fowler, *Felton & Fowler's Famous Americans You Never Knew Existed*. New York, NY: Stein and Day, A Scarborough Book, 1981.

Felton, Bruce, *One of a Kind: A Compendium of Unique People, Places and Things*. New York, NY: William Morrow, 1992.

Fitzgerald, Michael G., *Universal Pictures, A Panoramic History in Words, Pictures, and Filmographies*. New Rochelle, NY: Arlington House Publishers, 1977.

Frelinghhuysen, Alice Cooney, *American Porcelain: 1770-1920*. New York, NY: The Metropolitan Museum of Art, Distributed by Harry N. Abrams, Inc. 1989.

Friedman, Lawrence M., *A History of American Law*. New York, NY: Simon & Schuster, A

Touchstone Book, 1985.

Frost, Lawrence A., *The Custer Album*. Seattle, WA: Superior Publishing Company, 1964.

Fulford, Roger, *Hanover to Windsor*. Glasgow, Great Britain: Fontana/William Collins & Son, Ltd., 1986.

Gall, Timothy L., and Susan B. Gall (editors), *Worldmark Chronology of The Nations* (4 vols.). Detroit, MI: Gale Group, 1999.

Garraty, John A., and Mark C. Carnes (editors), *American National Biography*. New York, NY: Oxford University Press, 1999.

Georgano, Nick (editor), *The Beaulieu Encyclopedia of the Automobile* (3 vols.). Chicago. IL: Fitzroy Dearborn Publishers, 2000.

Gifford, Denis, *American Animated Films: The Silent Era, 1897-1929*. Jefferson, NC: McFarland & Co., c.1990.

Gilbert, Felix, *The End of the European Era, 1890 to the Present*. New York, NY: W.W. Norton & Company, 1979.

Great Adventures: Exploring Land, Sea, Sky with National Geographic. Washington, DC: National Geographic Society, 1963.

Greiff, Constance M. (editor), *Lost America: From the Atlantic to the Mississippi*. Princeton, NJ: The Pyne Press, 1971.

Groner, Alex, & the Editors of American Heritage and Business Week. *The History of American Business & Industry*. New York, NY: American Heritage Publishing Company, 1972.

Gross, Ernie, *This Day in American History*. Jefferson, NC: McFarland & Company, Inc., 2001.

Hake, Ted, *Hake's Guide to Advertising Collectibles: 100 Years of Advertising From 100 Famous Companies* Des Moines, IA: Wallace-Homestead Book Company, Inc., 1992

Hale, John R., *Age of Exploration* (Great Ages and Eras of Man series). New York, NY: Time Inc., 1967.

Hamilton, Edward P., *The French and Indian Wars*. Garden City, NY: Doubleday & Company, Inc. 1962.

Hannings, Bud, *A Portrait of the Stars and Stripes* (2 vols.). Glenside, PA: Seniram Publishing Inc., 1991.

Harder, Kelsie B. (editor), *Illustrated Dictionary of Place Names: United States and Canada*. New York, NY: Facts on File Publications, a Hudson Group Book.

Harper's Encyclopedia of United States History (10 vols.). New York, NY: Harper & Brothers Publishers, 1906.

Harvey, Sir Paul, and J.E. Heseltine, *The Oxford Companion to French Literature*. Oxford, England: The Clarenon Press, 1991.

Hawes, Nigel, *Structures: The Way Things Are Built*. New York, NY: The Macmillan Company, 1990.

Hawke, David Freeman, *Nuts and Bolts of the Past, A History of American Technology, 1776-1860*. New York, NY: Harper & Row, Publishers, 1988.

Heitman, Francis B., *Historical Register of Officers of the Continental Army During the War of the Revolution, April 1775, to December 1783*. Baltimore, MD: Genealogical Publishing Company, 1967.

Henderson, Mary C., *The City and the Theatre*. Clifton, NJ: James T. White & Company, 1973.

Herringshaw, Thomas William, *Encyclopedia of American Biography of the Nineteenth Century*. Chicago, IL: American Publishers Assoc., 1898.

Hillstrom, Kevin, Laurie Hillstrom and Roger Matuz, *The Handy Sports Answer Book*, Detroit, MI: Visible Ink Press, 1999.

Hirsch, E.D., Jr., Joseph F. Kett and James Trefil, *The Dictionary of Cultural Literacy*. Boston, MA: Houghton Mifflin Company, 1988.

Hirschhorn, Clive, *The Universal Story, The Complete History of the Studio and Its 2,641 Films*. New York, NY: Crown Publishers, Inc. 1983.

History Channel (Television Network), *Today in History: A Day by Day Review of World Events*. New York, NY: History Channel/DK Publications, 2003.

Hitchcock, H. Wiley, and Stanley Sadie. *The New Grove Dictionary of American Music*. New York, NY: Grove's Dictionaries of Music, 1986.

Hone, William. *The Every-Day Book; or, Everlasting Calendar of Popular Amusements, Sports, Pastimes, Ceremonies, Manners, Customs and Events* (2 vols.). Detroit, MI: Gale Research Company (reprint of 1827 publication).

Hopkins, H.J., *A Span of Bridges: An Illustrated History*. New York, NY: Praeger, 1970.

Horn, Maurice (editor), *The World Encyclopedia of Comics*. New York, NY: Chelsea House Publishers, 1999.

Hough, Franklin B., *American Biographical Notes: Being Short Notices of Deceased Persons, Chiefly Those Not Included in Allen's or in Drake's Biographical Dictionaries Gathered From Many Sources and Arranged By Franklin B. Hough,* Albany, NY: Joel Munsell, 1875.

Hough, G. L. (editor), *Chambers Dates*. Edinburgh. Scotland: W& R Chambers Ltd., 1989.

Hoxie, Frederick E. (editor), *Encyclopedia of North American Indians*. Boston, MA: Houghton Mifflin Company, 1996.

Hutchins, Robert Maynard (editor-in-chief). *Great Books of the Western World* (54 vols.). Chicago, IL: Encyclopedia Britannica, Inc., 1952.

Hutchinson Encyclopedia of Biography. Oxford, England, Helicon Publishing, 2000.

Information Please Almanacs for the years 1947-1998. Dan Golenpaul Associates, 1947-1976; Information Please Publishing Company, 1977-78; Simon & Schuster, 1979-1981; A&W Publishing Company, 1982; Houghton Mifflin, 1984-94; Inso Corporation, 1995-1996; Information Please LLC, 1997.

Innes, Brian, *The History of Torture,* New York, NY: St. Martin Press, 1998.

Johnson, Michael, *The Native Tribes of North America*. London, England: Compendium Publishing, 1999.

Johnson, Robert Underwood, and Clarence Clough Buel (editors), *Battles and Leaders of the Civil War* (4 vols.). Secaucus. NJ: Castle (reprint of 1887 publication).

Johnson, Rossiter (editor), *Twentieth Century Biographical Dictionary of Notable Americans*. Boston, MA: The Biographical Society, 1904.

Jonas, Susan, and Marilyn Nissenson, *Going, Going, Gone: Vanishing Americana.* San Francisco, CA: Chronicle Books, 1994.

Kane, Joseph Nathan, *The American Counties*. New York, NY: The Scarecrow Press, Inc. 1960.

Kane, Joseph Nathan, *Facts About the Presidents: A Compilation of Biographical and Historical Information*. New York, NY: H.W. Wilson Co., 1981.

Kane, Joseph Nathan, *Famous First Facts: A Record of First Happenings, Discoveries and Inventions in American History*. New York, NY: H.W. Wilson Co., 1997.

Keiser, Albert, *College Names: Their Origin and Significance*. New York, NY: Bookman Associates, Inc., 1952.

Kennedy, Michael, *The Oxford Dictionary of Music*. New York, NY: Oxford University Press, 1985.

Kenyon, J.P., *The Stuarts*. Glasgow, Great Britain: Fontana/William Collins Sons & Co., Ltd., 1986

Kephart, William M., & William W. Zellner, *Extraordinary Groups: An Examination of Un-*

conventional Life-Styles. New York, NY: St. Martin's Press, 1994.

Kernfeld, Barry (editor), *New Grove Dictionary of Jazz.* London, England: Macmillan Press Limited, 1988.

Kipfer, Barbara Ann, *World of Order and Organization: How Things Are Arranged into Hierarchies, Structures and Pecking Orders.* New York, NY: Gramercy Books, 1997.

Kirby, Richard Shelton, Sidney Withington, Arthur Burr Darling and Frederick Gridley Kilgour, *Engineering in History.* New York, NY: Dover Publications, 1990.

Kovel, Ralph and Terry, *Know Your Antiques.* New York, NY: Crown Publishers, Inc., 1990.

Koykka, Arthur S., *Project Remember. A National Index of Gravesites of Notable Americans.* Algonac, MI: Reference Publications, Inc., 1986.

Kronenberger, Louis (editor), *Atlantic Brief Lives: A Biographical Companion to the Arts.* Boston, MA: Little, Brown and Company, An Atlantic Monthly Press Book, 1971.

Kunitz, Stanley, and Howard Haycraft (editors), *American Authors, 1600-1900; a Biographical Dictionary of American Literature.* New York, NY: H.W. Wilson Company, 1938.

Kunitz, Stanley, and Howard Haycraft (editors), *British Authors Before 1800; a Biographical Dictionary.* New York, NY: H.W. Wilson Company, 1952.

Kunitz, Stanley, and Howard Haycraft (editors), *British Authors of the Nineteenth Century.* New York, NY: H.W. Wilson Company, 1936.

Kunitz, Stanley, and Vineta Colby (editors), *European Authors: 1000-1900; a Biographical Dictionary of European Literature.* New York, NY: H.W. Wilson Company, 1967.

Kuttner, Paul, *History's Trickiest Questions.* New York, NY: Owl/Holt, 1992.

Lackman, Ron, *The Encyclopedia of American Radio: An A-Z Guide to Radio from Jack Benny to Howard Stern,* New York, NY: Facts on File, Inc., 2000.

Lambray, Maureen, *The American Film Directors.* New York, NY: Rapoport Press, 1976.

Lane, Hana Umlauf (editor), *The World Almanac Book of Who.* New York, NY: World Almanac Publications, 1980.

Lassiter, William Lawrence, *Shaker Architecture.* New York, NY: Bonanza Books division of Crown Publishers, Inc., 1966.

Lay, M.G., *Ways of the World,* New Brunswick, NJ: Rutgers University Press, 1992.

Leonard, Thomas, *Day by Day: The Seventies* (2 vols.). New York, NY: Facts on File, 1987.

Leonard, Thomas (author), and Richard Burbank and Steven L. Goulden (editors), *Day by Day: The Forties.* New York, NY: Facts on File, 1977.

Lessem, Don, *Dinosaurs to Dodos: An Encyclopedia of Extinct Animals.* New York, NY: Scholastic Reference, 1999.

Levine, Michael L., *African Americans and Civil Rights: From 1619 to the Present.* Phoenix, AZ: Oryx Press, 1996.

Light, Jonathan Fraser, *The Cultural Encyclopedia of Baseball.* Jefferson, NC: McFarland & Company, 1997.

Linberg, Richard C., *White Sox Encyclopedia.* Philadelphia, PA: Temple University Press, 1997.

Longstreet, Stephen, *All Star Cast, An Anecdotal History of Los Angeles.* New York, NY: Thomas Y. Crowell Company, 1977.

Lowry, Philip J., *Green Cathedrals: The Ultimate Celebration of All 271 Major League and Negro League Ballparks Past and Present.* Boston, MA: Addison-Wesley Publishing Company, 1992.

Lurie, Maxine N., and Marc Mappen (editors). *Encyclopedia of New Jersey.* New Brunswick, NJ: Rutgers University Press, 2004.

MacKay, Charles, *Memoirs of Extraordinary Popular Delusions and the Madness of Crowds.* London, England: George Routledge and Sons, 1892.

Madden, W.C., *The All-American Girls Professional Baseball League Record Book: Com-*

prehensive Hitting, Fielding and Pitching Statistics. Jefferson, NC: McFarland & Company, Inc., Publishers, 2000.

Magnusson, Magnus (editor), *Chambers Biographical Dictionary*. Edinburgh, Scotland: W & R Chambers, 1990.

Maguire, Liam, *What's the Score–A One-of-a-Kind Compendium of Hockey Lore Legend History Facts Stats–The Amazing Hockey World of Liam Maguire*. Chicago, IL: Triumph Books, 2001.

Maitland, J.A. Fuller (editor), *Grove's Dictionary of Music and Musicians*, (5 vols.). Philadelphia, PA: Theodore Presser Company, 1925.

Martin, Michael, and Leonard Gelber, *Dictionary of American History*. Totowa, NJ: Littlefield, Adams & Co., 1972.

Matthys, Levy, and Mario Salvadori, *Why Buildings Fall Down*. New York, NY: W.W. Norton & Co., 1992.

McCombs, Don, and Fred L. Worth, *World War II, 4139 Strange and Fascinating Facts.* New York, NY: Wings Books, 1983.

McNeil, Alex, *Total Television: The Comprehensive Guide to Programming from 1948 to the Present.* New York, NY: Penguin Books, 1996.

McShane, Clay, *The Automobile—A Chronology of Its Antecedents, Development, and Impact.* Westport, CT: Greenwood Press, 1997.

Meltzer, Ellen, *Day by Day: The Eighties* (2 vols.). New York, NY: Facts on File, 1995.

Mercer, Derrick and Jerome Burne, *Chronicle of the World*, London, England: Dorling Kindersley, 1996.

Merritt, Jeffrey D. (author) and Steven L. Goulden (editor), *Day by Day: The Fifties*. New York, NY: Facts on File, 1979.

Meyer, Jerome S., *The Book of Amazing Facts*. New York, NY: Lancer Books, 1961.

Mingo, Jack, and Erin Barrett, *Just Curious, Jeeves*. Emeryville, CA: Ask Jeeves, 2000.

Monaco, James, *Who's Who in American Film Now,* Updated Edition, 1975-1986. New York, NY: New York Zoetrope, 1987.

Morgan, Kenneth O. (editor), *The Oxford Illustrated History of Britain*. New York, NY: Oxford University Press.

Morris, Desmond, *The Book of Ages: Who Did What When*. New York, NY: Penguin Books, 1983.

Morris, Robert, *The Truth About the American Flag*. Beach Haven, NJ: Wynnehaven Publishing Co., 1976.

Murphy, Elizabeth Taft, *I Remember, Do You? A Nostalgic Look at Yesterday*. Milwaukee, WI: Ideal Publishing Company, 1973.

Nash, Jay Robert, *Bloodletters and Badmen: A Narrative Encyclopedia of American Criminals from the Pilgrim to the Present*. New York, NY: M. Evans and Company Inc., 1973.

National Party Conventions, 1831-1980. Washington, DC: Congressional Quarterly, Inc., 1983.

Newman, Stanley, and Hal Fittipaldi, *10,000 Answers: The Ultimate Trivia Encyclopedia*. New York, NY: Random House Reference, 2001.

Nisenson, Samuel (illustrator), William A. DeWitt (text). *History's Hundred Greatest Events*. New York: Grosset & Dunlap, Publishers, 1954.

Osmanczyk, Edmund Jan, *Encyclopedia of the United Nations and International Agreements*. New York, NY: Routledge, 2003.

Paine, Lincoln P., *Ships of the World: An Historical Encyclopedia*. Boston, MA: Houghton Mifflin Company, 1997.

Paletta, Lu Ann, and Fred L. Worth, *The World Almanac of Presidential Facts*. New York : World Almanac and Ballantine Books, 1988.

Palmer, Alan, *The Facts on File Dictionary of 20th Century History*. New York, NY: Facts on File, 1979.

Panati, Charles, *Extraordinary Endings of Practically Everything and Everybody,* New York, NY: Harper & Row, 1989.

Parker, Thomas, and Douglas Nelson, *Day by Day: The Sixties* (2 vols.). New York, NY: Facts on File, 1983.

Philadelphia Record Almanacs. Philadelphia, PA: The Philadelphia Record, 1889-1910.

Placzek, Adolf K. (editor), *Macmillan Encyclopedia of Architects*. London, England: The Free Press, 1982.

Plumb, J.H., *England in the Eighteenth Century (1714-1815)*. Baltimore, MD: Penguin Books, 1972.

Plumb, J.H., *The First Four Georges*. Glasgow, Great Britain: Fontana/William Collins & Son, Ltd., 1985.

Postman, Andrew, and Larry Stone, *The Ultimate Book of Sports Lists*. New York, NY: Black Dog and Leventhal Publishers, 2003.

Powell, J.H., *Bring Out Your Dead, The Great Plague of Yellow Fever in Philadelphia in 1793*. New York, NY: Time Incorporated, 1965.

Powicke, Sir F. Maurice, and E. B. Fryde (editors), *Handbook of British Chronology*. London, England: Offices of the Royal Historical Society, 1961.

Purcell, L. Edward, The Shakers. New York, NY: Crescent Books, 1988.

Reference Guide to Famous Engineering Landmarks of the World: Bridges, Tunnels, Dams, Roads and Other Structures. Phoenix, AZ: Oryx Press, 1997.

Riggs, Thomas (editor), *Encyclopedia of Major Marketing Campaigns*, Farmington, MI: The Gale Group, 2000.

Ripley, Robert L., *Ripley's Big Book, Believe It or Not*. New York, NY: Simon & Schuster Publishers, 1934.

Ritter, Lawrence S., *Lost Ballparks: A Celebration of Baseball's Legendary Fields*. New York, NY: Viking Studio Books, 1992.

Robbins, Rossell Hope, *The Encyclopedia of Witchcraft and Demonology*. New York, NY: Crown Publishers Inc., 1959.

Room, Adrian, *Dictionary of Trade Name Origins*. London, England: Routledge & Kegan Paul, 1983.

Roos, Frank J., Jr., *An Illustrated Handbook of Art History*. New York, NY: The Macmillan Company, 1954.

Ruoff, Henry W. (editor), *The Standard Dictionary of Facts*. Buffalo, NY: The Frontier Press Company, 1912.

Rush, George E., *Dictionary of Criminal Justice*. Boston: Allyn & Bacon, Inc., 1978.

Russell, Jeffrey Burton, *Witchcraft in the Middle Ages*. Ithaca, NY: Cornell University Press, 1972.

Sadie, Stanley (editor), *The New Grove Dictionary of Music and Musicians*. London, England: Macmillan Press Ltd., 2001.

Sadie, Stanley (editor), *The New Grove Dictionary of Opera*. New York, NY: Grove's Dictionaries of Music, 1992.

Sandstrom, Gosta E., *Man the Builder*. New York, NY: McGraw-Hill Book Company, 1970.

Schei, V., and Jack Griffin. *Best Book of Trivia*. New York, NY: Gallery Books/W.H. Smith Publishers, Inc., 1985.

Schlesinger, Arthur M., Jr. (general editor), *The Almanac of American History*. New York, NY: G. P. Putnam's Sons, 1983.

Schodek, Daniel I., *Landmarks in American Civil Engineering*. Cambridge, MA: MIT Press, 1987.

Sifakis, Carl, *The Dictionary of Historic Nicknames*. New York, NY: Facts On File Publications, 1984.

Silke, James R., *Here's Looking at You, Kid.* Boston, MA: Little Brown and Company, 1976.

Silver, Nathan, *Lost New York.* New York, NY: American Legacy Press, 1967.

Simon, George T., and Friends, *The Best of the Music Makers.* Garden City, NY: Doubleday & Company, Inc. 1979.

Slee, Christopher, *The Chameleon Book of Lasts.* Huntingdon, England: Chameleon Publishing Limited, 1990.

Slee, Christopher, *The Guinness Book of Lasts.* Enfield, Middlesex, England: Guinness Publishing, 1994.

Smith, Norman, *A History of Dams.* Secaucus, NJ: Citadel Press, 1972.

Spiller, Robert E., Willard Thorp, Thomas J. Johnson, Henry Seidel Canby and Richard M. Ludwig (editors), *Literary History of the United States* (2 vols.). New York, NY: The Macmillan Company, 1974.

Steinman, David B., *Famous Bridges of the World.* New York, NY: Dover Publications, 1961.

Storey, Richard L., and Neville Williams (general editor), *Chronology of the Medieval World: 800-1491.* New York, NY: McKay, 1973.

Stories Behind Everyday Things. Pleasantville, NY: The Reader's Digest Association, 1980.

Strayer, Joseph R., *Dictionary of the Middle Ages* (13 vols. + supplement). New York, NY: Scribner's, 1982, 2004.

Summers Col. Harry G., Jr., *Vietnam War Almanac.* New York, NY: Facts On File Publications, 1985.

Tamarin, Alfred, and Shirley Glubok, *Voyaging to Cathay, Americans in the China Trade.* New York, NY: The Viking Press, Inc., 1976.

Taylor, Michael H. (compiler, editor), *Jane's Encyclopedia of Aviation.* New York, NY: Portland House, 1989.

Thomson, David, *A Biographical Dictionary of Film.* New York, NY: William Morrow and Company, Inc., 1966.

Thomson, David, *England in the Nineteenth Century (1815-1914).* Baltimore, MD: Penguin Books, 1970.

Thorn, John, Pete Palmer, Michael Gershman and David Pietrusza, *Total Baseball.* New York, NY: Total Sports, 1999.

Trent, William Peterfield, John Erskine, Stuart P. Sherman and Carl Van Dorn (editors), *The Cambridge History of American Literature.* New York, NY: The Macmillan Company, 1965.

Turner, Jane (editor), *The Grove Dictionary of Art.* New York, NY: Oxford University Press, 1996.

TV Guide TV Book: 40 Years of the All-time Greatest Television, Facts, Fads, Hits and History. New York, NY: Harper Perennial, Div. of HarperCollins Publishers, 1992.

TV Guide's Television Almanac, 1995 edition. Published by News America Publications.

U.S. Navy, *Dictionary of American Naval Fighting Ships* (8 vols.). Washington, DC: Department of the Navy, Naval History Division, 1960-1981.

Utley, Robert M., and Wilcomb E. Washburn, *The American Heritage History of the Indian Wars.* New York, NY: American Heritage Publishing Company/Bonanza Books, 1977.

Walker, Paul Robert, *Great Figures of the Wild West.* New York, NY: Facts on File, 1992.

Wallace, Irving, David Wallechinsky and Amy Wallace, *Significa.* New York, NY: E.P. Dutton, Inc., 1983.

Wallechinsky, David, *The Complete Book of the Olympics.* London, England: Aurum Press, 2000.

Wallechinsky, David, *The People's Almanac Presents—The Twentieth Century*. New York, NY: Little, Brown and Company, 1995.

Wallechinsky, David and Amy Wallace, *The Book of Lists—The 90's Edition*. New York, NY: Little, Brown and Company, 1993.

Wallechinsky, David and Irving Wallace, *The People's Almanac*. Garden City, NY: Doubleday & Company, Inc., 1975.

Wallechinsky, David and Irving Wallace, *The People's Almanac, #2*. New York, NY: William Morrow and Company, Inc., 1978.

Wallechinsky, David, Irving Wallace and Amy Wallace, *The Book of Lists*. New York, NY: William Morrow and Company, 1977.

Walter, Claire, *The Book of Winners*. New York, NY: Harcourt, 1978.

Webster's Biographical Dictionary. Springfield, MA: G. & C. Merriam Company, Publishers, 1972.

Webster's Guide to American History: A Chronological, Geographical, and Biographical Survey and Compendium. Springfield MA: G. & C. Merriam Company, Publishers, 1971.

Webster's New Geographical Dictionary. Springfield MA: G. & C. Merriam Company, Publishers, 1972.

Wetterau, Bruce, *The New York Public Library Book of Chronologies*. New York, NY: Stonesong Press Book, 1990.

Whitburn, Joel, *The Billboard Book of Top 40 Hits*. New York, NY: Billboard Books, An Imprint of Watson-Guptill Publications, 2000.

White House: An Historic Guide. Washington, DC: White House Historical Association, 1971.

Who Did What, Illustrated Biographical Dictionary. New York, NY: Gallery Books/W.H. Smith Publishers, Inc., 1985.

Williams, Neville (general editor), *Chronology of the Expanding World: 1492-1762*. New York, NY: McKay, 1969.

Wilson, Hugo, *The Encyclopedia of the Motorcycle*. New York, NY: Dorling Kindersley Publishing, Incorporated, 1997.

Wilson, James Grant, and John Fiske (editors), *Appleton's Cylopedia of American Biography*. New York, NY: D. Appleton and Company, 1887-1889.

World Almanac and Book of Facts. New York, NY: World Almanac Books, 1911-2000.

Worth, Fred L., *The Complete Unabridged Super Trivia Encyclopedia*. Los Angeles. CA: Brooke House, 1977.

Worth, Fred L., *Incredible Super Trivia*. New York, NY: Greenwich House, 1984.

Worth, Fred L., *More Super Trivia*. New York, NY: Greenwich House, Dist. by Crown Publisher, Inc., 1981.

Worth, Fred L., *The Trivia Encyclopedia*. Los Angeles, CA: Brooke House, 1974.

Yenne, Bill (general editor), *The History of North American Railroads*. New York, NY: Gallery Books/W.J. Smith Publishers, Inc., 1986.

References—Web Resources

More than 5,000 web sites were explored while verifying facts in *Notable Last Facts*. What follows is a list of web sites that were particularly helpful in that role. The www prefix was omitted for clarity; only the domains are presented. However, some of the sites are accessible only when the www is added to the front of the address.

1812marines.org	(Marine Guard 1812; Billerica, MA)
1911encyclopedia.org	(1911 *Encyclopedia Britannica*, Pagewise, Inc.; Austin TX)
2worldwar2.com	(World War 2 Insightful Essays)
3wheelers.com	(The online A-Z of 3-wheelers; UK)
440.com/twtd	440 Int'l, Those Were the Days, Today in History; Kaneohe, HI)
440int.com/440sat.html	(440 Satisfaction, Where are they now?; Kaneohe, HI)
aaca.org	(Antique Auto Club of America; Hershey, PA)
aagpbl.org	(All-American Girls Professional Baseball League, P.A.V. Studios; Shreveport, LA)
aaregistry.com	(African American Registry; Minneapolis, MN)
abc.net.au./news	(ABC News—Australian Broadcasting Corporation, Australia)
abcnews.go.com	(ABC. Inc.; New York, NY)
about.com	(About, Inc. A PRIMEDIA Company; New York, NY)
aboutfamouspeople.com	(About Famous People, Bookmark, Inc.; Glen Arm, MD)
access.gpo.gov	(U.S. Government Printing Office; Washington, DC)
acepilots.com	(American Aces of WW II; Scarsdale, NY)
aclsal.org	(Atlantic Coast Line & Seaboard Air Line Historical Society; Aurora, OH)
actiontrainvideos.home. att.net	(Action Train Videos; Colorado Springs, CO)
acts2.com/thebibletruth	(Bible Truth Homepage, Bible Baptist Ministries; Clear Creek, IN)
aef.com	(Advertising Educational Foundation; New York, NY)
aeroplanebooks.com	(Aeroplane Books; Williamsburg, VA)
afa.org	(Air Force Association; Arlington VA)
africana.com	(Africana.com, Inc.; Cambridge, MA)
africanpubs.com	(African American Publications, Gale Group, Inc.; Stamford, CT)
agards-bible-timeline.com	(Agards.com; Catheys Valley CA)
airdisaster.com	(Aviation Accident Site; Louisville, KY)
airforcehistory.hq.af.mil	(Air Force History Support Office, Bolling AFB; Washington, DC)
airpac.navy.mil	(Commander, Naval Air Force, Pacific Fleet; San Diego, CA)
airshipsonline.com	(Airship Heritage Trust; Biggleswade, England)
alamhof.org	(Alabama Music Hall of Fame; Tuscumbia, AL)
alaskanative.net	(Alaska Native Heritage Center; Anchorage, AK)
al-bab.com	(Al-Bab—Open Door to the Arab World; London, England)
albemarle-london.com	(Albemarle of London; London, England)
alcan-highway.com	(Alcan Highway—Alaska-Canadian Highway)
alexa.com	(Alexa Internet; San Francisco, CA)
allaboutjazz.com	(All About Jazz, Vision X Software, Inc.; Springfield, PA)

all-baseball.com	(All-Baseball, All the time)
all-moscow.ru	(All-Moscow, IT, LVL Ltd.)
allmovie.com	(All Movie Guide, AEC One Stop Group, Inc.; Ann Arbor, MI)
allmusic.com	(All Music Guide, AEC One Stop Group, Inc.; Ann Arbor, MI)
allvw.com	(All Volkswagen Database; Houston, TX)
alpa.org	(Air Line Pilots Association, Int'l; Washington, DC)
alternatemusicpress.com	(Alternate Music Press—the Multimedia Journal of New Music; Hollywood, CA)
altfrankfurt.com	(AltFrankfurt.com; Louisville, KY)
ama-cycle.org/museum	(Motorcycle Hall of Fame Museum; Pickerington, OH)
amber-sky.com	(Amber Sky Entertainment—Your Show Biz Community)
americanbreweriana.org	(American Breweriana Association)
americancanals.org	(American Canal Society; Freemansburg, PA)
americancatholic.org	(American Catholic, Franciscans/St. Anthony Messenger; Cincinnati, OH)
americancivilwar.info	(American Civil War Portal)
american-classic-motorcycle.com	(American Classic Motorcycle Museum Co.; Asheboro, NC)
americancomposers.org	(American Composers Orchestra; New York NY)
americanheritage.com	(American Heritage Magazine; New York, NY)
americanhistory.si.edu	(Smithsonian National Museum of American History; Washington, DC)
americanpoems.com	(American Poems; Goteborg, Sweden)
americanpresident.org	(American President, University of Virginia; Charlottesville, VA)
americanpresidents.org	(American Presidents—Life Portraits, C-Span; Washington, DC)
americanrhetoric.com	(American Rhetoric, University of Texas at Tyler; Tyler, TX)
americanwest.com	(American West—A Celebration of the Human Spirit, Internet Engineering Services; San Diego, CA)
americaslibrary.gov	(America's Story from America's Library; Library of Congress, Washington, DC)
amistadamerica.org	(Amistad America; New Haven, CT)
amnh.org	(American Museum of Natural History; New York, NY)
amnumsoc.org	(American Numismatic Society; New York, NY)
amonline.com	(Australian Museum Online; Sydney, NSW, Australia)
amphilsoc.org	(American Philosophical Society; Philadelphia, PA)
amtrak.com	(Amtrak; Washington, DC)
amusementresource.com	(AmusementResource.com, Lazer FX; Virginia Beach, VA)
ancestorhunt.com	(Ancestor Hunt)
andreadoria.org	(Andrea Doria – Tragedy and Rescue at Sea; Monroe, NY)
animalpeoplenews.org	(Animal People Online; Clinton, WA)
antiquesandthearts.com	(Antiques and The Arts Online, The Bee Publishing Company; Newton, CT)
anzacs.net/who-killed-the-Red-Baron.htm	(Anzac —Who killed the Red Baron; Blackalls Park, NSW, Australia)
anzacsite.gov.au	(Gallipoli/Anzac Comm. Site, Dept. of Veteran Affairs; Sydney, NSW, Australia)

apacouncil.org	(American Polish Advisory Council)
appalachiantrail.org	(Appalachian Trail Conference; Harper's Ferry, WV)
archiseek.com	(Archiseek; Winnipeg, MB, Canada)
archives.gov	(U.S. National Archives & Records Administration; College Park, MD)
archives.ubalt.edu/steamship/	(Steamship Historical Society of America Collections (SSHSA), University of Baltimore, Baltimore, MD)
areditions.com	(A-R Editions, Inc.; Middleton, WI)
arkansasheritage.com	(Dept. of Arkansas Heritage; Little Rock, AR)
arkivmusic.com	(ArkivMusic, LLC and Muze, Inc.; Bryn Mawr, PA)
arlingtoncemetery.org	(Arlington National Cemetery; Arlington, VA)
army.mil	(US Army; Washington, DC)
army.mod.uk	(British Army, Ministry of Defence; London, England)
arnold.af.mil	(Arnold Engineering Development Center; Arnold AFB, TN)
artandarchitecture.co.uk	(Art & Architecture; London, England)
artcyclopedia.com	(Artcyclopedia; Calgary, AB, Canada)
artfaces.com	(Art Faces—Art Places; Carolina Beach, NC)
arthistory.net	(Arthistory.net; Linda M. Smith, San Mateo, CA)
artic.edu	(Art Institute of Chicago; Chicago, IL)
articons.co.uk	(Art Icons—A Directory of Famous Artists, MagicWebsolutions; UK)
artincontext.com	(Art in Context Center for Communications; New York, NY)
artistdirect.com	(ARTISTdirect, Inc.; Los Angeles, CA)
artnet.com	(ArtNet Corporation; New York, NY)
artsiteguide.com	(Artsiteguide.com; Hemet, CA)
artsworld.com	(Artsworld Channels, Ltd.; Brentford, Middlesex, England)
arttimesjournal.com	(Art Times—A Literary Journal and Resource for All the Arts; Mt. Marion, NY)
asiaweek.com	(Asia Week; now TimeAsia; Quarry Bay, Hong Kong)
asce.org	(American Society of Civil Engineers; Reston, VA)
asme.org	(American Society of Mechanical Engineers; New York, NY)
astronautix.com	(Encyclopedia Astronautica)
athlonsports.com	(Athlon Sports, Inc.—America's Premiere Sports Annuals; Nashville, TN)
atsfrr.net	(Santa Fe Railway Historical & Modeling Society; Midwest City, OK)
au.af.mil/au/afhra/	(Air Force Historical Research Agency; Maxwell AFB, AL)
auschwitz.dk	(Auschwitz; Louis Bülow, Germany)
ausport.gov.au	(Australian Sports Commission; Bruce ACT, Australia)
australia.com	(Australian Tourist Commission; Woolloomooloo, NSW, Australia)
aviation-history.com	(Aviation History On-Line Museum; Whitestone, NY)
aviewoncities.com	(A View on Cities; Van Ermengem Bvba, Antwerp, Belgium)
azrail.org	(Arizona Rail Passenger Association; Scottsdale, AZ)
baberuthmuseum	(Babe Ruth Museum; Baltimore, MD)
badmovieplanet.com	(Bad Movie Planet; Stomp Tokyo, St. Petersburg, FL)
ballparks.com	(Ballparks by Munsey and Suppes, Houston, TX)
ballparksofbaseball.com	(Ballparks of Baseball; Rocky Mount, VA)
ballparkwatch.com	(Ballpark Digest / August Publications; Minnetonka, MN)
bardweb.net	(Shakespeare Resource Center; Glenview, IL)

baroquemusic.org	(Arton Baroque Pages; Michael Sartorius)
bartleby.com	(Bartleby.com—Great Books Online Barleby.com Inc.; New York, NY)
barusa.tripod.com/ghost counties/	(Ghost Counties—Your Guide to America's Dead, Forgotten Counties, Lycos, Inc.; Waltham, MA)
baseball1.com	(Baseball1.com—The Baseball Archive; Rochester, NY)
baseball-almanac.com	(Baseball Almanac; Miami, FL)
baseballhalloffame.org	(National Baseball Hall of Fame and Museum, Inc.; Cooperstown, NY)
baseballhistory.info	(Baseball History Info)
baseballlibrary.com	(Baseball Library, The Idea Logical Company, Inc.; New York, NY)
baseballprimer.com	(Baseball Primer, Baseball Think Factory; Fall River, MA)
baseball-reference.com	(Sports Reference, Inc.; Philadelphia, PA)
basicmusic.net	(Basics4Life.com; Spring Valley, IL)
basketball.com	(Basketball.com, Athomesports Network; Irvine, CA)
basketballreference.com	(Basketballreference.com; Verona, WI)
bassocantante.com	(Bassocantante, Meade Street Productions; South Bend, IN)
battleship.org	(Battleship.org; Iowa Class Preservation Association; Yuba City, CA)
bballsports.com	(Baseball, Basketball, and Hockey Online Statistics Databases)
bbc.co.uk	(British Broadcasting Corporation; London, England)
bcdb.com	(Big Cartoon DataBase; Salt Lake City, UT)
beatles-discography.com	(Beatles-discography.com, Craig Cross; London, England)
bera.org	(Shore Line Trolley Museum; East Haven, CT)
best-of-austria.com	(Best of Austria, NetGrafiX; Vienna, Austria)
biblion.com	(Biblion.com, Biblion, Ltd.; London, England)
bigband-era.com	(Swingin' Down the Lane, Miller Research Group; Little Rock, AR)
biloxi-chitimacha.com	(Biloxi-Chitimacha-Choctaw of Louisiana)
biography.com	(Biography.com, A & E Television Networks; New York, NY)
biography-center.com	(Biography Center, Europeanservers, Ltd; Paris France)
birthplaceofcountrymusic.org	(Birthplace of Country Music Alliance; Bristol, TN)
bismarck-class.dk	(Bismarck & Tirpitz; Germany)
boat-links.com	(John's Nautical, Ace Enterprises; Eugene, OR)
bohemianopera.com	(Bohemian Opera, AGS (KIM))
bonhams.com	(Bonham's Antique Auctions; London, England)
borail.org	(B&O Railroad History Museum; Baltimore, MD)
borhs.org	(Baltimore and Ohio Railroad Historical Society; Baltimore, MD)
born-on-this-day.com	(Born on this Day in History; Franklin C. Baer, Baertracks)
bostonglobe.com	(Boston Globe; Boston, MA)
bowlingmuseum.com	(Int'l Bowling Museum and Hall of Fame; St. Louis, Mo)
brainyencyclopedia.com	(Brainy Encyclopedia, BrainyMedia.com, Xplore, Inc.; Chicago, IL)
brainyhistory.com	(Brainy History—Events by Year, BrainyMedia.com, Xplore, Inc.; Chicago, IL)
brazzil.com	(Brazzil Magazine; Los Angeles, CA)

bridges.civil.rice.edu	(Bridges Project, Dept. of Civil and Environmental Engineering, Rice University, Houston, Texas)
bridges.lib.lehigh.edu	(Digital Bridges, Lehigh Library and Technology Services; Bethlehem, PA)
brightlightsfilm.com	(Bright Lights Film Journal; Portland, OR)
britannia.com	(Britannia.com., LLC; Yorklyn, DE)
britannica.com	(Encyclopedia Britannica, Inc.; Chicago, IL)
britarch.ac.uk	(Council for British Archaeology; York, England)
brooklynjuniorleague.org	(Junior League of Brooklyn; Brooklyn, NY)
brooklynrail.com	(Brooklyn Historic Railway Association; Brooklyn, NY)
burlingtonroute.com	(Burlington Route Historical Society; La Grange, IL)
ca.sports.yahoo.com	(Yahoo Sports Canada, Yahoo!; Sunnyvale, CA)
calendarzone.com	(Calendar Zone; Manchee & McLean, Juneau, AK)
calvin-coolidge.org	(Calvin Coolidge Memorial Foundation, Inc.; Plymouth, VT)
calzephyr.railfan.net	(California Zephyr Virtual Museum)
canadianbaseballnews.com	(Canadian Baseball News; Toronto, ON, Canada)
canalmuseum.org	(D & H Canal Historical Society; High Falls, NY)
canals.org	(National Canal Museum; Easton, PA)
canalsnys.org	(Canal Society of New York State; Manlius, NY)
canalsocietyofnj.org	(Canal Society of New Jersey; Morristown, NJ)
candocanal.org	(C & O Canal Association; Hagerstown, MD)
cantabile-subito.de	(Cantabile-subito —Great singers; Germany)
cartoon.org	(Int'l Museum of Cartoon Art; Boca Raton, FL)
cartoonresearch.com	(Jerry Beck's Cartoon Research; West Hollywood, CA)
caselaw.lp.findlaw.com	(FindLaw, Thompson Business; Stamford, CT)
catholic.net	(Catholic.net; New Haven, CT)
cbc.ca	(CBC/Radio-Canada; Toronto, ON, Canada)
cbcnews.cbc.ca	(CBC Inc.; Ottawa, ON, Canada)
cbmm.org	(Chesapeake Bay Maritime Museum; St. Michael, MD)
cbs.sportsline.com	(SportsLine.com, Ft Lauderdale, FL)
cbsnews.com	(CBS News, CBS, Inc.; New York, NY)
ccel.org	(Christian classic Eternal Library; Grand Rapids, MI)
ccrh.org	(Center for Columbia River History; Vancouver, WA)
cdi.org	(Center for Defense Intelligence; Washington, DC)
celebrityalmanac.com	(Celebrity Almanac; Oak Park, CA)
centennialofflight.gov	(U.S. Centennial of Flight Commission; Washington, DC)
charleston.net	(Post and Gazette; Charleston, SC)
charlestonwv.com	(Charleston Visitor's and Conventions Bureau; Charleston, WV)
chebucto.ns.ca	(Submariners Association; NS, Canada)
cherokee.org	(Cherokee Nation; Tahlequah, OK)
chicagohs.org	(Chicago Historical Society; Chicago, IL)
chicagotribune.com	(Chicago Tribune; Chicago, IL)
chickasaw.net	(Chickasaw Nation, Smokesignals Computer Company; Ada, OK)
childstarlets.com	(Childstarlets.com, David Johnson Dream Factory; Las Vegas, NV)
chin.gc.ca	(Canadian Heritage Information Network; Gastineau, QC, Canada)
chinfo.navy.mil	(U.S. Navy, Office of Information; Washington, DC)

chinookmontana.com	(Chinook Chamber of Commerce; Chinook, MT)
chipublib.org	(Chicago Public Library; Chicago, IL)
chirl.com	(Chronology of Ireland)
choctawnation.com	(Choctaw Nation; Durant, OK)
christianitytoday.com	(Christianity Today Int'l; Carol Stream, IL)
christies.com	(Christies Int'l; New York, NY)
chron.com	(Houston Chronicle, Houston Chronicle Publishing Company; Houston, TX)
chrysler.org	(Chrysler Museum of Art; Norfolk, VA)
chumashlanguage.com	(Language Tutorial; Richard Applegate, PhD and the Santa Ynez Band of Chumash Indians, CA)
ci.cambridge.ma.us	(City of Cambridge; Cambridge, MA)
ci.detroit.mi.us	(City of Detroit; Detroit, MI)
cia.gov/cia/publications /factbook	(Central Intelligence Agency's World Factbook; Washington, DC)
circusweb.com	(Circus Web; Graphics 2000, Las Vegas, NV)
city.windsor.on.ca	(City of Windsor, ON; Windsor, ON, Canada)
citylegacy.com	(City Legacy, New York City Skyline Productions, Inc.; Brooklyn, NY)
cityofnewhaven.com	(City of New Haven, CT; New Haven, CT)
civilwaralbum.com	(Civil War Album; Kingston, OK)
civilwarhome.com	(Shotgun's Home of the American Civil War; Herndon, VA)
civil-war-tribute.com	(A Civil War Tribute —To Remember is to Honor; Monroe Twp., NJ)
classicactresses.com	(Classic Actresses; New York, NY)
classical.net	(Classical.net; CA)
classicalarchives.com	(The Classical Music Archives; Pierre R. Schwob, Palo Alto, CA)
classical-composers.org	(Classical Composers Database)
classicaltheatre.com	(ClassicalTheatre.com—Where the Theater of the Past is Living Today)
classiccarclub.org	(Classic Car Club of America; Des Plaines, IL)
classicimages.com	(Classic Images; Lee Enterprises, Muscatine, IA)
classicmotor.co.uk/museums	(Classic Motor Monthly Museum Listings; Bolton, Lancashire, England)
classicmoviemusicals.com	(Classic Movie Musicals)
classicmovies.com	(ClassicMovies.com, Inc.; Los Angeles, CA)
classicstars.com	(Classicstars.com; RAW Wind Entertainment; Las Vegas, NV)
classicstoday.com	(ClassicsToday.com; David Vernier, Millennium Software Inc., Nashua, NH)
classicthemes.com	(ClassicThemes.com; San Diego, CA)
clatsop-nehalem.com	(Clatsop Nehalem Confederated Tribes; Turner, OR)
clemusart.com	(Cleveland Museum of Art, Plain Dealer Publishing; Cleveland, OH)
clta.on.ca	(Center for Language Training and Assessment, Mississauga, ON, Canada)
cmgww.com	(CMG Worldwide—The Leader in the Intellectual Property Rights Movement; Indianapolis, IN)
cnn.com	(CNN Interactive, Cable News Network; Washington, DC)

cnnsi.com	(CNNSI.com Cable News Network—Sports Illustrated, Atlanta, GA)
cnwhs.org	(Chicago & North Western Historical Society)
coc.ca	(Canadian opera Company; Toronto, ON, Canada)
cohs.org	(Chesapeake and Ohio Historical Society; Clifton Forge, VA)
coinclub.com	(CoinClub.com)
coinfacts.com	(CoinFacts.com; LaJolla, CA)
coinsite.com	(Coin Site; ROKO Design Group, Boca Raton, FL)
collections.ic.gc.ca	(Canada's Digital Collections, Industry Canada Ottawa, ON, Canada)
collectionscanada.ca	(Library and Archives of Canada; Ottawa, ON, Canada)
collegefootball.org	(College Football Hall of Fame and Museum; South Bend, IN)
colophon.com/gallery /Melville	(Melville Press, Colophon Page; New York, NY)
coloradohistory.com	(ColoradoHistory.com, Buena Vista, Co)
commerce.gov	(US Dept. of Commerce; Washington, DC)
concordma.com	(ConcordMa.com; Concord, MA)
coneyislandusa.com	(ConeyIsland.com; Brooklyn, NY)
congressionalcemetery.org	(Association for the Preservation of Historic Congressional Cemetery; Washington, DC)
constellation.com	(USS Constellation Foundation; Baltimore, MD)
content.lib.washington.edu /cities	(Cities and Buildings Database; Allen Library, University of Washington, Seattle, WA)
coolquiz.com	(Cool Quiz!, Intermix Network Property; Jamison, PA)
corsinet.com	(Corsinet.com; Palos Heights, IL)
countrymusichalloffame.org	(Country Music Hall of Fame; Nashville, TN
cprheritage.com	(Canadian Pacific Railway Archives; Montreal, QC, Canada)
cr.nps.gov	(Cultural Resources, National Park Service; Washington, DC)
cr.nps.gov/nr/travel/ civilrights	(NPS—Historic Places of the Civil Rights Movement; Washington, DC)
crimelibrary.com	(Court TV's Crime Library; Court Television Network, LLC; New York, NY)
crisny.org	(Capital Region Information Service of New York; New York, NY)
csamerican.com	(Common Sense Americanism, Charterhouse Systems, Corp.; Clark, NJ)
csl.ca	(Canadian Steamship Group, CSL Group; Montreal, QC, Canada)
csmonitor.com	(Christian Science Monitor; Boston, MA)
cssvirginia.org	(CSS Virginia, Mabry Tyson; Los Altos, CA)
culture.gr	(Hellenic Ministry of Culture; Athens, Greece)
culturekiosque.com	(Culturekiosque: Worldwide, CultureKiosque Publications; New York, NY)
cwc.lsu.edu	(U.S. Civil War Center; Louisiana State University, Baton Rouge, LA)
cyberboxingzone.com	(Cyber Boxing Zone)
cybersleuths.com	(Cyber Sleuths)
dailyalmanacs.com	(Daily Almanacs, United Press Int'l; New York, NY)
dailycatholic.org	(Daily Catholic)
dailycelebrations.com	(Daily Celebrations, Cool Pup)

dallasnews.com	(Dallas Morning News; Dallas, TX)
danube-research.com	(Danube Research—Historic Vessels and Ship Graveyards on the River Danube)
dar.org	(National Society Daughters of the American Revolution; Washington, DC)
data-wales.co.uk	(Data Wales—Edna Hoyt)
dcheritage.org	(Cultural Tourism DC; Washington, DC)
dcmilitary.com	(Comprint Military Publications, Washington, DC)
dcnrhs.org	(Washington, DC, Chapter of the National Railway Historical Society, Inc.; Washington, DC)
dead-or-alive.org	(Dead or Alive?, Kentix Computing)
deathpenaltyinfo.org	(Death Penalty Information Center; Washington, DC)
deepexplorers.com	(Deep Explorers, Inc.; Brielle, NJ)
defenders.org	(Defenders of Wildlife; Washington, DC)
defenselink.mil	(US Dept. of Defense; Washington, DC)
delawaretribeofindians.nsn.us	(Lenni Lenapes; Bartlesvlesville, OK)
denverpost.com	(Denver Post; Denver, CO)
designation-systems.net	(Destination-Systems.net; Andreas Parsch; Germany)
diabetes.org	(American Diabetes Association; Alexandria, VA)
diggerhistory.info	(Digger History—History of Australian & New Zealand Armed Services; Alexandra Hills, Australia)
din-timelines.com	(Din Timelines—World History Timelines, Miller Internet Publishing; PA)
diplomacy.edu	(DiploFoundation; Malta)
disneyshorts.toonzone.net	(Encyclopedia of Disney Animated Shorts, BECorp; Yonkers, NY)
dispatch.com	(The Columbus Dispatch; Columbus, OH)
district.north-van.bc.ca	(North Vancouver Museum & Archives; Vancouver, Canada)
dmwv.org	(Descendants of Mexican War Veterans; Richardson, TX)
doi.gov	(US Dept. of the Interior; Washington, DC)
dorotheum.at	(Dorotheum; Vienna, Austria)
downeastwindjammer.com	(DownEastWindjammer.com; Cherryfield, ME)
dpiwe.tas.gov.au	(Dept. of Primary Industries, Water & Environment; Hobart, Tasmania, Australia)
drgw.org	(Denver & Rio Grand Western —DRGW.net; Colorado Springs, CO)
duhaime.org	(Duhaime Law; Victoria, BC, Canada)
eapoe.org	(Edgar Allan Poe Society of Baltimore; Baltimore, MD)
earlyamerica.com	(Archiving Early America; Tampa Bay, FL)
earlybirds.org	(Early Birds of Aviation—Pioneer Aviation History)
eastlanddisaster.org	(Eastland Disaster Historical Society; Arlington Heights, IL)
ebonyshowcase.org	(Ebony Showcase Theatre & Cultural Arts Center, Inc.; Los Angeles, CA)
eh.net	(Economic History Services; Miami University, Oxford, OH)
ehistory.com	(eHistory; Dept. of History, Ohio State University; Columbus, OH)
einsiders.com	(Entertainment Insiders)
ellisisland.com	(Ellis Island Immigration Museum, National Park Service; Washington, DC)
ellisislandimmigrants.org	(Ellis Island Records)

emergency.com	(Emergency Response and Resource Institute; Chicago, IL)
en.wikipedia.org	(Wikipedia —The Free Encyclopedia, Wikipedia Foundation)
encyclopedia.com	(Encyclopedia.com, Infonautics; King of Prussia, PA)
encyclopedia.mu	(Encyclopedia Mauritiana; Mauritania)
encyclopedia-titanica.org	(Encyclopedia Titanica)
endoftheoregontrail.org	(End of the Oregon Trail Interpretive Center; Oregon City, OR)
english-literature.org	(English Literature; The London School of Journalism; London, England)
enlou.com	(Encyclopedia of Louisiana; David Welch, New Orleans, LA)
enn.com	(Environmental News Network; San Rafael, CA)
entertainment.msn.com	(MSN Entertainment, The Microsoft Corporation; Seattle, WA)
eonline.com	(E! Entertainment Television, Inc.; Los Angeles, CA)
epguides.com	(Episode Guide Pages; Schaumburg, IL)
erha.org	(Electric Railway Historical Association of Southern California; So. Pasadena, CA)
espn.go.com/sportscentury	(Sports Century, ESPN.com; Bristol, CT)
esselen.com	(Esselen Tribe of Monterey County)
esselennation.com	(Ohlone/Costanoan Esselen Nation; Monterey, CA)
essentialsofmusic.com	(Essentials of Music; Sony Music Entertainment Corporation, New York, NY)
ethnologue.com	(Ethnologue, Summer Institute of linguistics; Dallas, TX)
exploratorium.edu	(Exploratorium, Museum of Science, Art and Human Perceptions; San Francisco, CA)
extinctanimal.com	(Extinctanimal.com)
factmonster.com	(FactMonster, Pearson Technology Centre; Old Tappan, NJ)
famousamericans.net	(FamousAmericans.net)
fargo-history.com	(Fargo-History; Fargo, ND)
fas.org	(Federation of American Scientists; Washington, DC)
fashionfinds.com	(Métis Corporation dba Fashionfinds.com; Bridgeport, CT)
fbi.gov	(Federal Bureau of Investigation; Washington, DC)
fda.gov	(Food and Drug Administration; Washington, DC)
federalreserve.gov	(Federal Reserve; Washington, DC)
fiftiesweb.com	(Fifties Web; Fort Lauderdale, FL)
filmsandtv.com	(Filmsandtv.com; Decatur, IL)
filmscoremonthly.com	(Film Score Monthly; Vineyard Haven, LLC; Culver City, CA)
filmsite.org	(Film Site)
findagrave.com	(Find A Grave; Salt Lake City, UT)
firstworldwar.com	(First World War; Birmingham, England)
fjc.gov	(Federal Judicial Center; Washington, DC)
flags.com	(Regal Flags & Poles, Inc.; Westminster, MD)
flagspot.net	(Flags of the World – FOTW; Atlanta, GA)
flight100.org	(American Institute of Aeronautics and Astronautics; Reston, VA)
floridatoday.com	(Florida Today; Melbourne, FL)
flyingyankee.com	(Flying Yankee Restoration Group; Glen, NH)
fnafsoap.com	(Fnafsoap.com; Frankfort, KY)
fobnr.org	(Friends of the Burlington Northern Railroad; West Bend, WI)

foddc.org	(Friends of the Delaware Canal; New Hope, PA)
fodors.com	(Fodor's, Random House; New York, NY)
folger.edu	(Folger Shakespeare Library; Washington, DC)
football.com	(Football.com, Athomesports Network; Irvine, CA)
forbes.com	(Forbes; New York, NY)
forgotten-ny.com	(Forgotten NY; Flushing, NY)
fossick.com	(Fossick; Leong Software Pty Ltd., Ngunnawal, AC, Australia)
founderspatriots.org	(Order of the Founders and Patriots of America; Ridgefield, CT)
foxnews.com	(FNC—Twentieth Century Fox Film Corporation; Los Angeles, CA)
foxtrolley.org	(Fox River Trolley Museum; South Elgin, IL)
frbsf.org	(Federal Reserve Bank of San Francisco; San Francisco, CA)
frick.org/html/collmnf.htm	(Frick Collection; New York, NY)
friendsofpast.org	(Friends of America's Past; Portland, OR)
frommers.com	(Frommer's, Hungry Minds, Inc.; Foster City, CA)
frontiertrails.com	(Frontier Trail.com, Atjeu Publishing LLC; Phoenix, AZ)
funnypaperz.com	(Funny Paperz; Seal Beach, CA)
funtrivia.com	(Trivia Portal; Cambridge, MA)
galafilm.com	(Galafilm Inc.; Montreal, QC, Canada)
galleryofhistory.com	(Gallery of History, Inc.; Las Vegas, NV)
gallipoli-association.org	(Gallipoli Association; Connaught Park Bagshot, Surrey, England)
gazetteonline.com	(Gazette Communications; Cedar Rapids, IA)
gemlimited.com	(Great Entertainment Moments, Ltd., Los Angeles, CA)
getty.org	(J. Paul Getty Trust; Los Angeles, CA)
ghosttowns.com	(Ghost Towns, Atjeu Publishing LLC; Phoenix, AZ)
globaled.org	(American Forum for Global Education; New York, NY)
globalsuzuki.com	(Suzuki Motor Corporation; Hamamatsu-Shi Shizuoka, Japan)
gnrhs.org	(Great Northern Railway Historical Society; Farmington, MN)
goldengate.org	(Golden Gate Bridge; San Rafael, CA)
goldenspike.us	(Golden Spike Railroad Books; Tucson AZ)
goodbyemag.com	(Goodbye! The Journal of Contemporary Obituaries; Brooklyn, NY)
gpo.gov	(U.S. Government Printing Office; Washington, DC)
grahamfoundation.org	(Graham Foundation for Advanced Studies in the Fine Arts; Chicago, IL)
grandi-tenori.com	(Grandi-Tenori, Nordica Invest; Malaga, Spain)
greatbuildings.com	(Great Buildings Collection; Artiface, Eugene, OR)
greatnorthernempire.net	(Great Northern Empire—Then and Now)
greatoceanliners.net	(Great Ocean Liners; Brakne-Hoby, Sweden)
greatships.net	(Great Ships)
greenwichwhs.org.uk	(Maritime Greenwich World Heritage Site; Greenwich, England)
gtwhs.org	(Grand Trunk Western Historical Society; Durand, MI)
guam-online.com	(Guam-online.com; Guam)
guardian.co.uk	(Guardian Newspapers Limited; London, England)
guggenheim.org	(Guggenheim Museum; New York, NY)
hancockshakervillage.org	(Hancock Shaker Village; Pittsfield, MA)

harlemglobetrotters.com	(Harlem Globetrotters Int'l; Phoenix, AZ)
hazegray.org	(Haze Gray & Underway, Naval History and Photography; Bath, ME)
healthopedia.com	(Healthopedia.com)
heanosantiq.com	(Heather's Nostalgic Antiques and Collectibles; Lugoff, SC)
hemmings.com	(Hemming's Motor News; Bennington, VT)
hermetic.ch	(Hermetic Systems; Switzerland)
heroesofhistory.com	(Heroes of History; McPherson, KS)
hfmgv.org	(Henry Ford Museum & Greenfield Village; Dearborn, MI)
hgtv.com	(Home & Garden Television; Knoxville, TN)
hickoksports.com	(Hickok's Sports History; New Bedford, MA)
historicbaseball.com	(Historic Baseball; Greenwood, SC)
historicbridgefoundation.com	(Historic Bridge Foundation; Austin TX)
history.navy.mil	(U.S. Navy—Naval Historical Center Washington Navy Yard; Washington, DC)
historybuff.com	(Newspaper Collectors Society of America; Lansing, MI)
historychannel.com	(A&E Television Networks; Stamford, CT)
historyofcuba.com	(Timetable History of Cuba; San Francisco, CA)
history-of-rock.com	(History of Rock and Roll, Community Graphics of Detroit; Birmingham, MI)
historyorb.com	(HistoryOrb.com; Matua Tauranga, New Zealand)
historyplace.com	(History Place; Quincy, MA)
hmco.com/history	(American History Database, Houghton-Mifflin Company; Boston, MA)
hockeyresearch.com	(Hockey Research Association, Oklahoma City, OK)
hollywood.com	(Hollywood Media Group; Hollywood, CA)
holocaustchronicle.org	(Holocaust Chronicle, Publications Int'l Ltd.; Chicago, IL)
hoophall.com	(Naismith Memorial Basketball Hall of Fame; Springfield, MA)
house.gov	(US House of Representatives; Washington, DC)
hsba.go.jp	(Honshu-Shikoku Bridge Authority – Akashi Kaikyo Bridge; Kobe-City, Japan)
hughespace.com	(Hughes Electronics; Los Angeles, CA)
ibdb.com	(Internet Broadway Database, The League of American Theatres and Producers; New York, NY)
ibhof.com	(Int'l Boxing Hall of Fame and Museum; Canastota, NY)
ibiblio.org	(Ibiblio, University of North Carolina; Chapel Hill, NC)
icecreamusa.com	(Unilever; Greenwich, CT)
ice.org.uk	(Institute of Civil Engineers; London, England)
icomos.org	(Int'l Council of Monuments and Sites; Ottawa, ON, Canada)
icrrhistorical.org	(Illinois Central Historical Society; Paxton, IL)
iht.com	(Int'l Herald Tribune; Paris, France)
Iithe90s.com	(In the 90s)
ils.unc.edu/maritime/	(Maritime History on the Internet, Serials Solutions; Seattle, WA)
imdb.com	(Internet Movie Database, NV Services; Incline Village, NV)
imh.org	(Int'l Museum of the Horse; Lexington, KY)
indiancountry.com	(Indian Country Today, Oneida Indian Nation; Oneida, NY)
indians.org	(American Indian Heritage Foundation; Falls Church, VA)
indigenouspeople.net	(Indigenous Peoples Literature)

infoniagara.com	(Info Niagara; Niagara Falls, ON, Canada)
infoplease.com	(Information Please On-line Directory)
interment.net	(Cemeteries and Cemetery Records, Cemetery Transcription Library)
inthe80s.com	(In the 80s)
ipl.org	(Internet Public Library, School of Info., University of Michigan; Ann Arbor MI)
irm.org	(Illinois Railway Museum; Union, IL)
itn.co.uk	(ITN; London, England)
janm.org	(Japanese American National Museum; Los Angeles, CA)
jazzdisco.org	(Modern Jazz Discography; Jazz Discography Project)
jazzhall.org	(Big Band and Jazz Hall of Fame; San Marcos, CA)
jewishmuseum.org	(Jewish Museum of New York; New York, NY)
jewishpeople.net	(Jewishpeople.net; London, England)
jpl.nasa.gov	(NASA Jet Propulsion Laboratory, California Institute of Technology; Pasadena, CA)
juaneno.com	(Juaneño Band of Mission Indians; San Juan Capistrano, CA)
juneauempire.com	(Juneau [Alaska] Empire—The Online Voice of Alaska, Juneau, AL)
kentuckyexplorer.com	(Kentucky Explorer Magazine; Jackson, KY)
ketupa.net	(Ketupa Project, A Caslon Analytics Media Resource; Canberra, ACT, Australia)
kingfeatures.com	(King Features; New York, NY)
kodak.com	(Eastman Kodak Company; Rochester, NY)
kofc.org	(Knights of Columbus; New Haven, CT)
korean-war.com	(The Korean War Information; Antlers, OK)
krakow-info.com	(Krakow Info; Krakow, Poland)
kultur.gov.tr	(T.C. Kültür ve Turizm Bakanlı_ı; Turkey)
kulturnet.dk	(Royal Danish Navy 1860-1990)
lacma.org	(L.A. County Museum of Art; Los Angeles, CA)
lambiek.net	(Lambiek Comiclopedia; Amsterdam, Netherlands)
lastconfederatewidow.com	(Last Confederate Widow; Shenandoah Valley, VA)
latimes.com	(Los Angeles Times, Tribune Company; Chicago, IL)
lds.org	(Church of Jesus Christ of Latter-day Saints; Kent, WA)
ldsfilm.com	(LDSFilms.com; Provo, UT)
legion.org	(American Legion National Headquarters; Indianapolis, IN)
libertocracy.com	(Libertocracy Association)
lifetimetv.com	(Lifetime Entertainment Services; New York, NY)
lighthousedepot.com	(Lighthouse Depot; Wells, ME)
lihistory.com	(Long Island)
lincolnhighwayassoc.org	(Lincoln Highway Association; Franklin Grove, IL)
lioncrusher.com	(Lioncrusher's Domain, No Business; Manassas, VA)
litencyc.com	(Literary Encyclopedia and Literary Dictionary; London, England)
liveindia.com	(Live India Internet Services; New Delhi, India)
loc.gov	(Library of Congress; Washington, DC)
lonelyplanet.com	(Lonely Planet Publications; Footscray, Victoria, Australia)
lostkingdoms.com	(Australia's Lost Kingdoms; Sydney, NSW, Australia)
lostliners.com	(Lost Liners; Adelphia, MD)
louvre.fr	(Musee du Louvre; Paris, France)

lsjunction.com	(Lone Star Junctions; Fairfax, VA)
luftwaffe-experten.com	(Luftwaffe Experten)
lusitania.net	(Lusitania and Her Last Captain; Leeds, England)
madaboutbeethoven.com	(Mad about Beethoven; London, England)
maestronet.com	(Maestronet; Toronto, ON, Canada)
magazineart.org	(MagazineArt.org, HIDDEN Knowledge; Sand Jose, CA)
maidoftheloch.co.uk	(Maid of the Loch, The Loch Lomond Steamship Co.; Balloch, U.K.)
manataka.org	(Manataka American Indian Council, Hot Springs Reservation, AR)
mariner.org	(Mariner's Museum; Newport News, VA)
maritime.org	(San Francisco Maritime National Park Association; San Francisco, CA)
maritimeheritage.org	(Maritime Heritage Project; Greenwich, England)
maritimematters.com	(Maritime Matters; Los Angeles, CA)
marmus.ca	(Maritime Museum of the Great Lakes; Kingston, ON, Canada)
maryrose.org	(Onboard The Mary Rose, H.M. Naval Base; Portsmouth, England)
masonicworld.com	(Masonic World, JTM eServices; Gaffney, SC)
mayflower.org	(General Society of Mayflower Descendants; Plymouth, MA)
mcmichael.com	(McMichael Canadian Art Collection; Kleinburg, ON, Canada)
mcny.org	(Museum of the City of New York; New York, NY)
meccainc.org	(Miami & Erie Canal Corridor Association; St. Mary's, OH)
medieval.org	(Medieval Music and Arts Foundation)
memorabletv.com	(Memorable TV, Little Acorns Publishing)
memory.loc.gov	(American Memory from the Library of Congress; Washington, DC)
merchantnavyofficers.com	(Merchant Navy Officers, La Ferranderie; Pellevoisin, England)
mercurycenter.com	(Mercury News, Knight Ridder; San Jose, CA)
metmuseum.org	(Metropolitan Museum of Art Association; New York, NY)
metopera.org	(Metropolitan Opera; New York, NY)
miamiindiansofindiana.org	(Miami Indians of Indiana; Peru, IN)
miamination.com	(Miami Tribe of Oklahoma; Miami, OK)
middlesexcanal.org	(Middlesex Canal Association; North Billerica, MA)
militarymuseum.org	(California State Military Museum, California State Military Dept.)
minorleaguenews.com	(Minor League News; Bristol Infotainment; Santa Fe, NM)
missamerica.com	(Miss America Organization; Atlantic City, NJ)
mlb.com	(National League Baseball Properties, Inc.; New York, NY)
mnh.si.edu	(Museum of Natural History; Smithsonian Institute, Washington, DC)
mnhs.org	(Minnesota Historical Society; St. Paul, MN)
moderntimes.vcdh.virginia.edu	(Virginia Center for Digital History, University of Virginia; Charlottesville, VA)
moeyfactory.org	(U.S. Treasury Bureau of Engraving; Washington, DC)
monticello.org	(Thomas Jefferson Foundation, Inc.; Charlottesville, VA)
mopac.org	(Missouri Pacific Historical Society; Ballwin, MO)

moviemaker.com	(MovieMaker Magazine; Portland, ME)
mozartproject.org	(Mozart Project; Hamlin, NY)
mrc.uccb.ns.ca	(Mi'kmaq Resource Centre; UCCB, NS, Canada)
msn.espn.go.com	(MSN—Sports by ESPN; Bristol, CT)
msnbc.com	(MSNBC on the Internet; Redmond, WA)
mta.nyc.ny.us	(Metropolitan Transportation Authority; New York, NY)
mtr.org	(Museum of Television and Radio; New York, NY)
mtv.vo,	(MTV Networks; New York, NY)
mudcat.org	(Mudcat Café; West Chester, PA)
musclecarclub.com	(Muscle Car Club; Redondo Beach, CA)
museum.tv	(Museum of Broadcast Communications; Chicago, IL)
museumofflight.org	(Museum of Flight; Seattle, WA)
museumoftransportation.org	(Museum of Transportation; St. Louis MO)
museumregister.com	(Museumregister.com, Athena World; New York, NY)
musicals101.com	(Musicals 101.com; Jackson Heights, NY)
musicfromthemovies.com	(Music from the Movies, Greyport, Ltd; Taunton, Somerset, England)
musicmoz.org	(Musicmoz; Halifax, NS, Canada)
musicweb.uk.net	(Music Web—Classical Music on the Web; London, England)
myclassiccar.com	(My Classic Car, My Classic Car LLC Abda MCC LLC; Evansville, IN)
mysticseaport.org	(Mystic Seaport Museum, Inc.; Mystic, CT)
nac-cna.ca	(National Arts Centre; Ontario, ON, Canada)
nampows.org	(Nampowa.org; Alexandria, VA)
napha.org	(National Amusement Park Historical Association; Mt. Prospect, IL)
nasa.gov	(National Aeronautics and Space Administration)
nashvillesongwriters foundation.com	(Nashville Songwriters Foundation; Nashville, TN)
nasm.edu	(National Air and Science Museum, Smithsonian Institute; Washington, DC)
national.gallery.ca	(National Gallery of Canada; Ottawa, ON, Canada)
national-army-museum.ac.uk	(National Army Museum; London, England)
nationalaviation.org	(National Aviation Hall of Fame—Honoring America's Air and Space Pioneers)
nationalcenter.org	(National Center for Public Policy Research—Historical Documents)
nationalgallery.org.uk	(The National Gallery; London, England)
nationalgeographic.com	(National Geographic Society; Washington, DC)
nativeamericanmohegans.com	(Native American Mohegans)
native-languages.org	(Native Languages of the Americas; St. Paul, MN)
nativeweb.org	(Native Web—Resources for Indigenous Cultures around the World)
nato.int	(North Atlantic Treaty Organization; Brussels, Belgium)
nba.com	(National Basketball Association; New York, NY)
ncstl.com	(Nashville, Chattanooga & St. Louis Railway—NC&StL Preservation Society; Goodlettsville, TN)
negroleaguebaseball.com	(NegroLeagueBaseball.com; Nashville, TN)
neh.gov	(National Endowment for the Humanities; Washington, DC)
newadvent.org	(Catholic Encyclopedia by K. Knight)

newdeallegacy.org	(National New Deal Preservation Association; Santa Fe, NM)
newigwam.com	(Newigwam.com; New York, NY)
news.bbc.co.uk	(BBC News; Rochester, Kent, England)
newsday.com	(Newsday, Tribune Company; Chicago, IL)
newyorkhistory.info	(Newyorkhistory.info)
newyorktimes.com	(The New York Times Company; New York, NY)
nfl.com	(National Football League; New York, NY)
nga.gov	(National Gallery of Art; Washington, DC)
ngmdb.usgs.gov/Geolex	(National Geographic Map Database—GEOLEX, USGS, U.S. Dept of the Interior; Washington, DC)
niagarafallslive.com	(Niagara Falls Live.com; Niagara Falls, NY)
nhl.com	(National Hockey League; New York, NY)
nhluniforms.com	(NHL Uniforms History)
nhm.ac.uk	(Natural History Museum; London, England)
nhrhta.org	(New Haven Railroad Historical and Technical Association; West Babylon, NY)
nlbm.com	(Negro League Baseball Museum; Kansas City, MO)
nlbpa.com	(Negro League Baseball Players Association; Baltimore, MD)
nmm.ac.uk	(National Maritime Museum; London, England)
nmra.org	(National Model Railroad Association; Chattanooga, TN)
nmwa.org	(National Museum of Women in the Arts; Washington, DC)
noaa.gov	(National Oceanic and Atmospheric Administration, U.S Dept. of Commerce; Washington, DC)
nostalgiacentral.com	(Nostalgia Central; Beckingham, Kent, England)
novaroma.org	(Nova Roma; Wells, ME)
now.org	(National Organization for Women; Washington, DC)
npr.org	(National Public Radio; Washington, DC)
nprha.org	(Northern Pacific Railway Historical Association; Kirkland, WA)
nps.gov	(National Park Service, U.S. Dept of the Interior; Washington, DC)
npwrc.usgs.gov	(Northern Prairie Wildlife Research Center, U.S. Dept of the Interior; Washington, DC)
nrc.gov	(U.S. Nuclear Regulatory Commission; Washington, DC)
nrhs.com	(National Railway Historical Society; Philadelphia, PA)
nrm.org	(National Railway Museum; York, England)
numa.net	(National Underwater and Marine Agency; Austin, TX)
nwhs.org	(Norfolk and Western Historical Society; Roanoke, VA)
nwprrhs.org	(Northwestern Pacific Railroad Historical Society; Santa Rosa, CA)
nycshs.org	(New York Central System Historical Society; Cleveland, OH)
nycsubway.org	(New York City Subway Resources; Jersey City, NJ)
nypost.com	(New York Post, NYP Holdings, Inc.; New York, NY)
nyse.com	(New York Stock Exchange; New York, NY)
nytimes.com	(New York Times Company; New York, NY)
obits.com	(Internet Obituary Network, Liquidarts, LLC; Hartford, CT)
occultopedia.com	(Occultopedia; Gay Marcus, Warren, Mi)
ocean-liners.com	(Monsters of the Sea—The Great Ocean Liners of Time; Plainview, NY)

ohiohistory.org	(Ohio Historical Society; Columbus, OH)
ohiopottery.com	(Ohio Pottery; Twinsburg, OH)
ohwy.com/cardinalbook.com	(Online Highways Guide; Florence, OR)
oldsanteecanalpark.org	(Old Santee Canal Park; Moncks Corner, SC)
old-time.com	(Old Time Radio; Astute Consulting Services; San Antonio, TX)
online-literature.com	(Online-literature.com; Jalic, LLC)
operaitaliana.com	(Opera Italiana; Torino, Italy)
operationdeadlight.co.uk	(Operation Deadlight; Periscope Publishing; Penzance, Cornwall, England)
operaworld.com	(Opera World; Opera Express, Inc.; Comcord, MA)
opioids.com	(Future Opioids; East Sussex, England)
organsociety.org	(Organ Historical Society; Richmond, VA)
oscar.org	(Academy of Motion Picture Arts & Sciences; Beverley Hills, CA)
otrsite.com	(Vintage Radio Place; Whittier, CA)
ourdocuments.gov	(Our Documents; Nat'l Archives and Records Admin., and USA Freedom Corps)
ozcamera.com	(Ozcamera; Laurieton, NSW, Australia)
pa-canal-society.org	(Pennsylvania Canal Society; Easton, PA)
pageantcenter.com	(Pageant Center; Springfield, MA)
panda.org	(WWF Int'l: Wide Fund for Nature; Gland, Switzerland)
panynj.gov	(Port Authority of New York & New Jersey; New York, NY)
parabrisas.com	(Solid—Online Encyclopedia of Lounge, Big Band, Classic Jazz and Space Age Sounds; Parabrisas; Oklahoma, OK)
paris.org	(Paris Pages; San Diego, CA)
paturnpike.com	(PA Turnpike Commission; Highspire, PA)
pbs.org	(Public Broadcasting Service; Alexandria, VA)
pcrrhs.org	(Penn Central Railroad Historical Society; Scotia, NY)
pennies.org	(Americans for Common Cents—The Penny Information Page; Washington, DC)
pianoparadise.com	(Piano Paradise—Composer Biographies)
picturehistory.com	(Picture History; Kunhardt Productions)
pieganinstitute.org	(Piegan Institute—Researching, Promoting and Preserving Native Languages; Browning, MT)
pilgrimhall.com	(Pilgrim Society; Plymouth, MA)
planecrashinfo.com	(Plane Crash Information; Covina, CA)
pmhistsoc.org	(Pere Marquette Historical Society; Grand Haven, MI)
politicalgraveyard.com	(Political Graveyard; Ann Arbor MI)
postalmuseum.si.edu	(Smithsonian National Postal Museum, Smithsonian Institute, Washington, DC)
preserve.org	(Preserve & Protect, Goldfarb & Abrandt; New York, NY)
probertencyclopaedia.com	(Probert Encyclopedia; Southampton, Hampshire, England)
profootballhof.com	(Pro Football Hall of Fame; Canton, OH)
pro-football-reference.com	(Pro-Football-Reference.com)
qmfound.com	(Quartermaster Foundation; Fort Lee, VA)
queenmary.com	(RMS Queen Mary; Long Beach, CA)
queenslandholidays.com.au	(Tourism Queensland; Brisbane, QLD, Australia)
quepo.com	(Quepo Corporation; Brione, BS, Italy)
raf.mod.uk	(Royal Air Force Operations; UK)

railroad.net	(Railfan Internet Services; Rochester, NY)
railroaddata.com	(RailroadData.com—Links to Over 5,000 Railroad Websites; Algona, WA)
railscanada.com	(Rails Canada; Squamish, BC, Canada)
railsusa.com	(Rails USA; Squamish, BC, Canada)
railwaymuseums.org	(Association of Railway Museums; Tujunga, CA)
rcmp-grc.gc.ca	(Royal Canadian Mounted Police; Ottawa, ON, Canada)
readingrailroad.org	(Reading Company Technical & Historical Societies; Reading, PA)
recording-history.org	(Sound Recording Technology History)
recordsinternational.com	(Records Int'l; Tucson, AZ)
recreation.gov	(Recreation.gov, US Army Corps of Engineers)
redhotjazz.com	(Red Hot Jazz Archive; San Francisco, CA)
reelclassics.com	(Reel Classics, L.L.C; Oklahoma City, OK)
refdesk.com	(Refdesk.com)
reference.allrefer.com	(AllRefer.com)
reference.com	(Lexico LLC; Marina del Ray, CA)
religion-online.org	(Religion Online; Escondido, CA)
religiousmovements.lib. virginia.edu	(Religious Movements, University of Virginia; Charlottesville, VA)
remembertheaba.com	(Remember the ABA—American Basketball Association; Boston MA)
retrosheet.org	(Total Sports, Inc.; Newark, DE)
reuters.com	(Reuters Group PLC, Reuters Information Technology; Hauppauge, NY)
revwar.com	(Revolutionary War Reenactment Web Site; Franklin, NC)
rhino.com	(Warner Strategic Marketing; Burbank, CA)
rleggat.com/photohistory	(Robert Legat, A History of Photography; Bedford, England)
rmstitanichistory.com	(RMS Titanic History)
roadtripamerica.com	(Roadtrip America, Flattop Productions; Las Vegas, NV)
rockabillyhall.com	(Rockabilly Hall of Fame, NRS; Appleton, WI)
rockhall.com	(Rock and Roll Hall of Fame and Museum; Cleveland, OH)
royalnavalmuseum.org	(Royal Naval Museum, H.M. Naval Base; Portsmouth, England)
royal-navy.mod.uk	(Royal Navy; UK)
royalopera.org	(Royal Opera House—Covent Gardens; London, England)
rr-fallenflags.org	(Fallen Flags Railroad Photos; Beavercreek, OH)
rrhistorical.com	(Rrhistorical.com, Ribbon Rail Production; Lisle, IL)
rrmuseumpa.org	(Railroad Museum of Pennsylvania; Ribbon Rail Production, Bolingbrook, IL)
rsssf.com	(Rec.Sport.Soccer Statistics Foundation; Salzburg, Austria)
rte.ie/news	(Radio Telefís Éireann (RTÉ) Irish Public Service Broadcasting Organisation)
rusc.com	(RUSC Old Time Radio Show Listings)
russiajournal.com	(Russian Journal Publishing Company; Fredericksburg, VA)
sacredplaces.org	(Partners for Sacred Places; Philadelphia, PA)
sah.org	(Society of Architectural Historians; Chicago, IL)
sar.org	(National Society Sons of the American Revolution; Louisville, KY)
schirmer.com	(G. Schirmer, Inc.; New York, NY)

scholastic.com/library publishing	(Scholastic Library Publishing, Inc.; Danbury, CT)
schoonerman.com	(Schooner and Tall Sailing Ships)
scv.org	(Sons of Confederate Veterans; Columbia, TN)
secondrunning.com	(Second Running—Horse Racing History; Winfield, BC, Canada)
secretservice.gov	(US Secret Service; Washington, DC)
senate.gov	(US Senate; Washington, DC)
sfmuseum.org	(Museum of the City of San Francisco; San Francisco, CA)
shaker.lib.me.us	(United Society of Shakers; New Gloucester, ME)
shakers.org	(Canterbury Shaker Village; Canterbury, NH)
shakervillageky.org	(Shaker Village of Pleasant Hill; Harrodsburg, KY)
shakerworkshops.com	(Sabbathday Lake, Salem Village Craftsmen, Inc.; Auburnham, MA)
shakerwssg.org	(Western Shaker Study Group's web site; Dayton OH)
shakespeare-online	(Shakespeare Online; St. Albert, Alberta, Canada)
shape.nato.int	(Supreme Headquarters Allied Powers Europe)
shgresources.com	(State History Guide Resources., SHG, LLC)
si.edu	(Smithsonian Institute; Washington, DC)
sicilianculture.com	(Sicilian Culture, Cristaldi Communications; Caldwell, NJ)
sitcomsonline.com	(Sitcoms Online; Marietta, Georgia)
slam.canoe.ca	(SLAM—Stanley Cup Winners, CANOE; Toronto, ON, Canada)
smh.com.au	(Sydney Morning Herald; Sydney, NSW, Australia)
smithsonianjazz.org	(Smithsonian Jazz, Smithsonian Institute; Washington, DC)
smithsonianmag.si.edu	(Smithsonian Magazine, Smithsonian Institute; Washington, DC)
sons-of-liberty-sar.org	(Son of Liberty Chapter, Sons of the American Revolution, Home of the Commander in Chief's Guard; Los Angeles, CA)
sooline.org	(Soo Line Historical and Technical Society)
sothebys.com	(Sotheby's; New York, NY)
soulofamerica.com	(Soul of America; Torrance, CA)
soul-patrol.com	(Soul Patrol; East Meadow, NY)
soultracks.com	(Soul Tracks; Ann Arbor, MI)
soulwalking.co.uk	(Soulwalking; Surbiton, Surrey, England)
soundportraits.org	(Sound Portraits Productions; New York, NY)
soundstage.com	(SoundStage; DAS Computers Services Lmt.; Ottawa, ON, Canada)
soundtracks.mainseek.com	(Soundtracks Mainseek.pl; Slask, Poland)
space.com	(Space.com, Imaginova Corp.; New York, NY)
spaceagepop.com	(Space Age Pop; Apo, AE)
spaceline.org	(Space Line; Cape Canaveral, FL)
spaceref.com	(SpaceRef Almanac; ATerra Technologies Corp; BC, Canada)
spaceweekly.com	(Space Weekly)
spanamwar.com	(Spanish American War Centennial Website; Conestoga, PA)
sphts.org	(Southern Pacific Historical & Technical Society; Pasadena, CA)
sportsecyclopedia.com	(Sports E-Cyclopedia)
sportsillustrated.cnn.com	(Sports Illustrated, a CNN Web Site; Atlanta, GA)
sprucegoose.org	(Captain Michael King Smith Evergreen Aviation Educational

	Institute; McMinnville, OR)
spshs.org	(Spokane, Portland & Seattle Railway Historical Society; Vancouver, WA)
ssa.gov	(Social Security Administration; Baltimore, MD)
ssmaritime.com	(SSMaritime; Reuben Goossens; Brisbane Australia)
sss.gov	(Selective Service System, U.S. Armed Forces; Arlington, VA)
steamboats.com	(Steamboats.com; Mesa, AZ)
steamboats.org	(Legend of Steamboatin' The Grand Old South; Munich, Germany)
steamlocomotive.com	(Steamlocomotive.com, Sunshine Software, Inc.; Eagan, MI)
storm.simpson.edu/~RITS	(Rock Island Technical Society; Dexter, IA)
strawberybanke.org	(Lake Champlain Maritime Museum; Portsmouth, NH)
structurae.net	(Structurae; Ratingen, Germany)
submarinesailor.com	(Submarine Sailor, Internetwerks; Renton, WA)
subnet.com	(Subnet; Graphic Enterprises of Marblehead; Marblehead, MA)
subwaywebnews.com	(Subway Web News)
suezcanal.com	(Domain Finance Ltd.; Sharjah, VA)
sunspot.net	(The Baltimore Sun; Baltimore, MD)
suntimes.com	(Chicago Sun-Times; Chicago, IL)
super70s.com	(Super70s.com; Mountainview, CA)
superbeetles.com	(Super Beetles; Toronto, ON, Canada)
supremecourthistory.org	(Supreme Court Historical Society; Washington, DC)
suvcw.org	(Sons of Union Veterans of the Civil War; Pittsburgh, PA)
tapseis.anl.gov	(Trans-Alaska Pipeline System Renewal EIS; Anchorage, AK)
tate.org.uk	(Tate Gallery; London, England)
tbgreats.com	(Thoroughbred Greats)
teachervision.com	(Learning Network; Pearson Technology Centre; Old Tappan, NJ)
techweb.com/encyclopedia	(TechEncyclopedia, CMP Media LLC; Manhasset, NY)
telecomwriting.com	(Private Line; Sacramento, CA)
telephonetribute.com	(Telephone Tribute Home Page; Salome, AZ)
tenorland.com	(Tenorland; Lincoln, NE)
texasindians.com	(Texas Indians; New Braunfels, TX)
thais.it/scultura/	(1200 anni di scultura italiana—1200 Years of Italian Sculpture; Milan, Italy)
thanksforthemusic.com	(Thanks for the Music; Gilbert, AZ)
thbison.com	(Thousand Hills; Colorado)
theaerodrome.com	(The Aerodrome; Oysterville, WA)
theatlantic.com	(The Atlantic Monthly; Boston, MA)
theatrehistory.com	(Theatre History; Valley Village, CA)
thebaseballpage.com	(The Baseball Page; Cooperstown, NY)
thebritishmuseum.ac.uk	(The British Museum; London, England)
themave.com	(Ravin' Maven; Loleta, CA)
thingstodo.com	(Thingstodo.com; Riverton, UT)
thirdreichruins.com	(Third Reich Ruins)
thrillingdetective.com	(Thrilling Detective; Greenfield Park, QC, Canada)
time.com	(Time Inc. Magazine; New York, NY)
timelines.ws	(Timelines of History; Daly City, CA)

timstvshowcase.com	(TimsTVShowcase.com; Mooresville, IN)
titanic.com	(Titanic.com; Rotterdam, Netherlands)
titanic-online.com	(RMS Titanic, Inc.; Clearwater, FL)
titanic-titanic.com	(Titanic! Titanic!; England)
titanic-whitestarships.com	(Titanic and Other White State Line Ships)
tmny.org	(Trolley Museum of New York; Kingston, NY)
toonopedia.com	(Don Markstein's Toonopedia; Phoenix, AZ)
top40-charts.com	(Top 40 Charts; Ricking, NY)
totalbaseball.com	(Totalbaseball.com, Total Sports, Inc.; Raleigh, NC)
trainweb.org	(TrainWeb; Fullerton, CA)
trolleymuseum.org	(Seashore Trolley Museum; Kennebunkport, ME)
tsha.utexas.edu	(Texas State Historical Association; University of Texas at Austin; Austin, TX)
tugboats.com	(Tugboats.com; San Francisco, CA)
tvacres.com	(TV Acres—The Web's Ultimate guide to TV Program Facts)
tvland.classictvhits.com	(TV Land; New York, NY)
tv-now.com	(TV-Now, VisionSoft Corp; Greensboro, NC)
tvtome.com	(TV Tome—John Nestoriak; Rockville, MD)
unep-wcmc.org	(UNEP World Conservation Monitoring Centre; Cambridge, England)
unog.ch	(League of Nations Archives; Geneva, Switzerland)
uphs.org	(Union Pacific Historical Society; Cheyenne, WY)
upi.com	(United Press Int'l; Washington, DC)
uprr.com	(Union Pacific Railroad; Omaha, NE)
usatoday.com	(USA Today, Media West-GSI, Inc.; Reno, NV)
usbr.gov	(U.S. Bureau of Reclamation, U.S. Dept of the Interior; Washington, DC)
uscg.mil	(U.S. Coast Guard Historian's Office; Washington, DC)
usconstitution.net	(US Constitution Online; Williston, VT)
ushistory.org	(USHistory.com, Independence Hall Association; Philadelphia, PA)
ushmm.org	(US Holocaust Memorial Museum; Washington, DC)
usmc.mil	(U.S. Marine Corps Historical Center; Washington Navy Yard, Washington, DC)
usmc-hc.com	(U.S. Marine Corps Historical Company)
usmint.gov	(U.S. Mint, Dept of the Treasury; Washington, DC)
usmm.org	(US Merchant Marines)
usps.com	(US Postal Service)
ussconstitutionmuseum.org	(USS Constitution Museum; Boston, MA)
ustreas.gov	(US Dept. of the Treasury; Washington, DC)
va.gov	(Federal Information Center—Dept of Veterans Affairs; Washington, DC)
vasamuseet.se.	(Vasa Museum –Vasamuseet; Sweden)
vervemusicgroup.com	(Verve Music Group; New York, NY)
vh1.com	(VH1, MTVN Online L.P; New York, NY)
victorianweb.org	(Victorian Web, Macktez Corp.; New York, NY)
victorychimes.com	(Victory Chimes; Port Charlotte, FL)
vintagetrolleys.com	(Portland Vintage Trolleys; Portland, OR)
vitaphone.org	(Vitaphone; San Francisco, CA)
voicechasers.org	(Voice Chasers; Winter Park, FL)

voices.fuzzy.com	(Voice Actor Page; Portland, OR)
wabashanderiecanal.org	(Wabash and Erie Canal Park; Delphi, IN)
wabashcannonballtrail.org	(Wabash Cannonball Trail; Delta, OH)
washington.edu/ark2/	(Cities/Buildings, University of Washington; Seattle, WA)
washingtonpost.com	(Washington Post; Washington, DC)
washingtontimes.com	(Washington Times; Washington, DC)
west-point.org	(WP-Org, Inc.; Floyd, VA)
whalingmuseum.org	(New Bedford Whaling Museum; New Bedford, MA)
what-a-character.com	(What A Character, Illuminagraphic; Leverett, MA)
whha.org	(White House Historical Association; Washington, DC)
whitehouse.gov	(White House; Washington, DC)
who2.com	(Who2—Fine Famous People Fast!)
wire.ap.org	(Associated Press; New York, NY)
wisconsinpottery.org	(Wisconsin Pottery Association; Madison, WI)
wiyot.com	(Wiyot Scared Sites Fund; Loleta, CA)
wmf.org	(World Monument Fund; New York, NY)
worldhistory.com	(WorldHistory.com, InfoBase Ventures; Los Altos, CA)
worldshiptrust.org	(World Ship Trust; London, England)
worldspaceflight.com	(World Space Flight)
worldstatesmen.org	(World Statesmen)
worldwar2database.com	(World War II Multimedia Database, Fordham University; Bronx, NY)
wprrhs.org	(Western Pacific Railroad Historical Society; Portola, CA)
wreckhunter.net	(Hunting New England Wrecks)
wrightstories.com	(Wright Brothers Stories)
wsrhs.org	(Washington State Railroads Historical Society Museum; Pasco, WA)
wwf.org	(World Wildlife Fund Global Network; Washington, DC)
wwnorton.com/nael	(Norton Anthology of English Literature, W.W. Norton, Co; New York, NY)
wyandotte-nation.org	(Wyandotte Nation of Oklahoma; Wyandotte, OK)
ydli.org	(Yinka Déné Language Institute; Vanderhoof, BC, Canada)
yellowairplane.com	(Yellow Airplanes' Home Base)
yendor.com/vanished	(Yendor.com, The Vanished Gallery, Argentina Desaparecidos Project)
yesterdayland.com	(Assoc. of Americans of Indian origin in the New England Area; Andover, MA)
yukoncollege.yk.ca/ynlc	(Yukon Native Language Center, Yukon College; Whitehorse, YT, Canada)
zahzah.com	(Guild GmbH; Colchester, Essex, England)
zoos.50megs.com/extinct.htm	(UK Zoo Directory, About Web Services; Orem, UT)
zpub.com/sf/history	(Zpub.com; San Francisco, CA)

Reference Desk Press, Inc. is committed to preserving ancient forests and natural resources. We elected to print *Notable Last Facts* on 50% post consumer recycled paper, processed chlorine free. As a result, for this printing, we have saved:

23 trees (40' tall and 6-8" diameter)
9,766 gallons of water
3,928 kilowatt hours of electricity
1,077 pounds of solid waste
2,115 pounds of greenhouse gases

Reference Desk Press, Inc. made this paper choice because our printer, Thomson-Shore, Inc., is a member of Green Press Initiative, a nonprofit program dedicated to supporting authors, publishers, and suppliers in their efforts to reduce their use of fiber obtained from endangered forests.

For more information, visit www.greenpressinitiative.org

Colophon

Notable Last Facts was designed and produced by Reference Desk Press, Inc. using Apple® Macintosh-based systems. The dust jacket was created with Adobe Photoshop.™ Page layout, typesetting and page assembly were accomplished with Microsoft Word® and Adobe® Acrobat.™ The dust jacket, cover and title page font is Onyx.® The text pages were set in Times New Roman®, 10 point, black. The text paper is 50 lb. Natures Natural. The end paper is 80 lb. Natures Natural. The dust jacket is 100 lb. Enamel. Binding is Smyth sewn, cased into Arrestox B (Rain Forest Green) with Lustrofoil Gold Foil. Printing and binding were by Thomson-Shore, Inc.